Consumer and Trading Law
Text, Cases and Materials

C. J. MILLER
Professor of English Law, University of Birmingham

BRIAN W. HARVEY
Professor of Law, University of Birmingham

and

DEBORAH L. PARRY
Senior Lecturer in Law, University of Hull

OXFORD UNIVERSITY PRESS · OXFORD
1998

Oxford University Press, Great Clarendon Street, Oxford OX2 6DP
www.oup.co.uk
Oxford New York
Athens Auckland Bangkok Bogotá Buenos Aires Calcutta
Cape Town Chennai Dar es Salaam Delhi Florence Hong Kong Istanbul
Karachi Kuala Lumpur Madrid Melbourne Mexico City Mumbai
Nairobi Paris São Paolo Singapore Taipei Tokyo Toronto Warsaw
and associated companies in
Berlin Ibadan

Oxford is a registered trade mark of Oxford University Press

Published in the United States
by Oxford University Press Inc., New York

British Library Cataloguing in Publication Data
Data available

Library of Congress Cataloging in Publication Data
Miller, C. J. (Christopher J.)
Consumer and trading law: text, cases, and materials / C. J. Miller
Brian W. Harvey, and Deborah L. Parry.
p. cm.
Includes bibliographical references and index.
1. Consumer protection—Law and legislation—Great Britain.
2. Trade regulation—Great Britain. I. Harvey, Brian W.
II. Parry, Deborah L. III. Title.
KD2204.M55 1998 343.4107'1—dc21 98–24210
ISBN 0–19–876479–0
ISBN 0–19–876478–2 (pbk)

1 3 5 7 9 10 8 6 4 2

Typeset by Hope Services (Abingdon) Ltd.
Printed in Great Britain
on acid-free paper by
Bookcraft Ltd., Midsomer Norton, Somerset

Outline table of contents

Contents

Preface

As in the first edition of this book which was published in 1985, our main aim in writing this new edition has been to provide students of consumer law with a wide range of materials on this increasingly important subject. We hope and expect that the text will be of interest and assistance to others, including consumer advisors, legal practitioners dealing with consumer problems and trading standards officers. The materials include extensive extracts from cases and statutes and from Government, Law Commission, Office of Fair Trading and National Consumer Council publications, along with extracts illustrating the approach of other jurisdictions, notably within the Commonwealth, north America and continental Europe. The ever-increasing influence of the European Community is apparent throughout the text. The materials (many of which are not readily accessible elsewhere) are introduced or linked by comments, notes, problems, questions for discussion and suggestions for further reading.

In this new edition we have taken account of such major changes as those introduced by, for example, the Consumer Act 1987, the Sale and Supply of Goods Act 1994, the Package Travel, Package Holidays and Package Tours Regulations 1992, the Unfair Terms in Consumer contracts Regulations 1994 and the General Product Safety Regulations 1994. In addition, there is extensive coverage of materials affecting the enforcement of remedies, for example on small claims procedures, conditional fee agreements and group or class actions.

In preparing the text we have received much help from many sources, including of course, the individuals whose writings feature in it. We hope that all are recognized in the acknowledgments. Laurence Bebbington and his colleagues in the Harding Law Library have assisted greatly in locating material or responding to our requests for information, and our publishers (in particular, Dominic Shryane) have been very helpful in seeing the text through to publication. We are grateful to them and to Mrs Pam Kimmins, secretary to the first two named authors, who has been of great assistance throughout.

We delivered the manuscript to our publishers on 12 January 1998, but have been able to incorporate references to some later developments, including the increases in certain monetary limits in the chapter on consumer credit. Some other developments came too late for inclusion, for example Directive 98/27/EC on injunctions for the protection of consumers interests, and the Amended proposal for a European Parliament and Council Directive on the sale of consumer goods and associated guarantees (COM (98) 217 final, 31 March 1998) as subsequently agreed at the Consumer council on 23 April 1998. The final adoption of this important directive is awaited.

May 1998

C. J. Miller
B. W. Harvey
D. L. Parry

Acknowledgements

Grateful acknowledgment is made to all authors and publishers of extract materials. In particular, the following permissions are noted:

Extracts from the Committee of Advertising Practice (CAP)'s *British Codes of Advertising and Sales Promotion* are reproduced by kind permission of the Advertising Standards Authority (ASA) Limited, 2 Torrington Place, London, WC1E 7HW. The Codes are freely available in their entirety from ASA's website at www.asa.org.uk or by telephoning 0171 580 5555.

Extracts from the 1998 *Restatement (third) of Torts: Product Liability* are reproduced by kind permission of the American Law Institute, 4025 Chestnut Street, Philadelphia, Pa 19104–3099, USA.

Extracts from the Modern Law Review are reproduced by kind permission of Blackwell Publishers, 108 Cowley Road, Oxford, OX4 1JF.

Extracts from British Columbia's Trade Practice Act 1996 (c 457) are reproduced by kind permission of the Province of British Columbia.

Extracts from the All England Law Reports, the New Law Journal and the LEXIS Enggen Library are reproduced by kind permission of Butterworths, Halsbury House, 35 Chancery Lane, London, WC2A 1EL.

Extracts from the Dominion Law Reports are reproduced by kind permission of the Canada Book Inc, 240 Edward Street, Aurora, Ontario, Canada.

Crown copyright material is reproduced with the permission of the Controller of Her Majesty's Stationery Office.

Extracts from the Harvard Law Review are reproduced by kind permission of the editors, Gannett House, 1511 Massachusetts Avenue, Cambridge, Ma 02138, USA.

Extracts from the Law Reports and the Weekly Law Reports are reproduced by kind permission of the Incorporated Council of Law Reporting for England and Wales, 3 Stone Buildings, Lincoln's Inn, London, WC2A 3XN.

Extracts from the *Trading Standards Review* are reproduced by kind permission of the Institute of Trading Standards Administration, 3–5 Hadleigh Business Centre, 351 London Road, Hadleigh, Essex, SS7 2BT.

Extracts from the IOB *Annual Review 1996* are reproduced by kind permission of the Insurance Ombudsman, Walter Merricks, MA, Solicitor.

Extracts from the *European Journal of Marketing* are reproduced by kind permission of MCB University Press Ltd, 60–62 Tolley Lane, Bradford, West Yorkshire, BD8 9BY.

Extracts from National Consumer Council (NCC) publications are reproduced by kind permission of the NCC, 20 Grosvenor Gardens, London, SW1W 0DH.

Extracts from the Annual Reports and other Office of Fair Trading (OFT) publications are reproduced by kind permission of the OFT, Field House, 15–25 Breams Buildings, London, EC4A 1PR.

Extracts from the (1977) 15 Osgoode Hall Law Journal reproduced by kind permission of Osgoode Hall Law School, 4700 Keele Street, North York, Ontario, Canada, M3J 1P3.

Extracts from Baldwin: *Small Claims in the County Courts of England* (1997) are reproduced by kind permission of Oxford University Press, Great Clarendon Street, Oxford, OX2 6DP.

Extracts from the Civil Justice Quarterly (1982), Journal of Business Law (1982), Criminal Appeal Reports 73, Criminal Law Review (1991), Road Traffic Reports, Scots Law Times Reports and the *Supreme Court Practice News* (Issue 5, 17 May 1991) are reproduced by kind permission of Sweet & Maxwell Ltd, Cheriton House, North Way, Andover, Hampshire, SP10 5BE.

Extracts from the *Federal Rules of Civil Procedure, Federal Reporter, Atlantic Reporter, Pacific Reporter,* and *North Eastern Reporter* are reproduced by kind permission of West Publishing, 610 Oppenheim Drive, PO Box 64526, St Paul, Minnesota 55164–0526, USA.

Table of Legislation

Principal references are indicated by bold type

Table of Cases

Principal references are indicated by bold type

CHAPTER 1

The ambit of consumer law

INTRODUCTION

The aims of this introductory chapter are to provide a brief description of the ambit of consumer law and an assessment of its current objectives. It also aims to indicate where a particular topic is examined in more detail in this book and to highlight the ever-increasing importance of the European dimension. In the light of the present abundance of texts and articles on the law of consumer protection it can easily be overlooked, particularly by those studying the subject for the first time, that it is only within the last 20 years that the subject has attained any degree of academic recognition, at least within the United Kingdom. This was in part a reflection of the paucity of relevant case law, and to a great extent, statute law, until the late 1960s.

In retrospect, the publication of the Final Report of the Molony Committee on Consumer Protection (Cmnd 1781, July 1962), which in turn was mainly responsible for the enactment of the Trade Descriptions Act 1968, was a landmark. This Committee also reviewed such central matters as the difficulties faced by consumers in obtaining effective redress through the courts and the unsatisfactory character of manufacturers' guarantees (see paras 403, 415). In terms of reform the Committee favoured evolution, rather than revolution, as paragraph 16 made clear:

16. We received a great weight of criticism of the existing system of consumer protection, accompanied by suggestions for its replacement. Although we observed a measure of justification, as well as unanimity, in the criticisms, we found that some of the suggestions were extravagant in the extreme—extravagant in terms of money cost as well as conception. The consumer, unlike some classes with claims on public bounty, is everybody all the time. The consumer is the taxpayer, and we saw small merit in creating an elaborate new system to assist him in one capacity when he would have to pay for it in the other. In so far as any increased cost fell on industry, recoupment from the consumer would be no less inevitable. Further, in considering bold suggestions for reshaping consumer protection arrangements it was necessary, in our opinion, not merely to balance the money cost, but also the degree of interference with production and distribution methods, against the benefits to the consumer claimed by the proponents of reform. These factors have weighed with us in favouring more stringent legal provisions in aid of the consumer rather than an extensive protective machinery, operating administratively at considerable cost.

Much water has gone under the bridge since that first modern investigation into the unmet needs of the consumer. Politicians see votes in consumer protection and Parliament is keen to be seen to be legislating to strengthen the consumer's position. This tendency has been very greatly enhanced by the impact of the law of the European Union. Whilst originally consumer concerns played a very small part in the development of the European Community and its institutions, within the last decade or so an increasing number of directives has emanated from Europe requiring the UK to bring its law into conformity. The point is considered in more detail below (at pp 12–18).

What, then, can be said to be the key characteristics of modern UK consumer law? Put another way, into what categories can the whole corpus of this law be broken down in policy terms? It is suggested that it is likely that laws properly categorised as involving consumer protection will fall into at least one of the following categories—(a) laws against unsafe products; (b) laws protecting the consumer against goods and services which are not of satisfactory quality; (c) laws imposing criminal liability against fraudulent trading practices; (d) laws requiring producers to give consumers sufficient information about a product to enable the consumer to exercise a prudent buying decision; (e) laws preventing or mitigating economic exploitation of the consumer through lack of competition within the relevant market sector.

CIVIL AND CRIMINAL LAW

A more fundamental division adopted in this book is between protection accorded by the civil and the criminal law. Civil law rights are usually left to the consumer personally to enforce, either through action in the civil courts or through arbitration. Criminal laws, although often technically enforceable by consumers personally, are in practice almost always enforced by Trading Standards Officers employed by local authorities, acting on consumer complaints. But because consumers can obtain the benefit of compensation orders made by the criminal courts in their favour (see below, pp 429–33), the fact that a large part of the enforcement process occurs through the criminal courts does not necessarily mean that the consumer does not obtain personal redress even though the onus of enforcement and its cost falls on the public purse. On the civil side, the improvement of small claims procedures in the county court and the raising of the 'small claims' jurisdiction (presently £3,000) have been an enormous help to the consumer. As has often been pointed out, to confer rights without also providing remedies is a sterile exercise. There is therefore a heavy emphasis in this book on rights of redress: see chs 8 and 9.

INSTITUTIONS PROMOTING CONSUMER PROTECTION

Whilst the present aims and objectives of consumer protection law will be found to fall within the five categories mentioned above, there is another aspect to the picture. It is not enough to leave the development of the law to the cumulative effect of consumer litigation and the plugging of identified gaps by the passing of new criminal laws. Institutions are needed to fight for the interests of the consumer in the corridors of power and to take a strategic view on future development. Of principal importance within the UK is the Office of Fair Trading, established in 1973 along with the passing of the Fair Trading Act 1973. The work of the OFT is often referred to in this book (see eg chs 10 and 11 discussing codes of practice and the duty to trade fairly). Its importance to the development of many aspects of consumer law has been paramount. There are also a number of other institutions. Some, such as the National Consumer Council which was set up in 1975, are to a greater or lesser extent financed by the government. Others are financed primarily by private subscribers—including the Consumers' Association, particularly known for its publication of the magazine *Which?*, designed, by comparative testing, to inform consumers about quality and value for money. At a local level such voluntary organisations as the Citizens' Advice Bureaux (now in receipt of significant public funding) are of major importance in supplying information and advice on a range of matters including consumer protection law. Their position is considered further below (at pp 397–402).

In summary, the total picture of the UK's system of law to protect the consumer involves a number of different elements. Amongst them are the development of the civil law, primarily by statutory reform, providing redress for qualitatively deficient goods and services, and the great increase in the volume and scope of criminal laws designed to punish fraudulent or misleading trading practices or to prohibit the production or circulation of unsafe goods, all in the context of more streamlined administration of consumer redress mechanisms. Much of the reform of statute law in recent years has been on the initiative of one or more of the institutions designed to assist the consumer, such as the Office of Fair Trading or the National Consumer Council. As has been noted (see p 2), the impetus for reform has also been greatly enhanced by relevant activity within the European Union.

Overarching economic laws, particularly relating to the promotion of competition and the prevention of monopolies, are also of the utmost importance and fall within the fifth category of protection mentioned above. However, the law of monopolies, mergers, restrictive practices and competition is of sufficient volume and complexity for it to fall outside the ambit of most consumer law texts, though its primary importance should never be forgotten.

HISTORY

As already indicated, consumer protection law, at least as a subject of study, is of recent vintage. Paradoxically, though, some aspects of it which can be of central importance to the consumer, such as the laws relating to the hallmarking of precious metals, are very ancient in origin. The same applies to laws regulating weights and measures used in trade, the original primary concern of Trading Standards Officers, formally styled Weights and Measures Inspectors. Hallmarking laws currently contained primarily in the Hallmarking Act 1973 can be traced back to 1300. The system's modern functioning depends upon the testing facilities of the Assay Offices established in the late 17th century onwards— in London, Birmingham, Sheffield and Edinburgh. Laws regulating the authorised weights and measures to be used in trade and imposing penalties on traders using false balances can be traced back to Saxon times. A moment's thought will show that unless a buyer can be sure that a metre of cloth is exactly the same length in London as in Birmingham or Paris, and a motorist that a litre of petrol is the same in volume anywhere which sells petrol by the litre, a fundamental condition of fair trading is absent. Although these laws can be classified as consumer protection laws, much of the motivation for that strict enforcement comes from honest traders who resent the unfair competition associated with other traders who are not so scrupulous in guaranteeing uniformity. The title 'Trading Standards Officer' indicates that these officers are concerned with fair trade between traders as well as between trader and consumer. Formerly a number of miscellaneous statutory provisions involving the weight, price and purity of staple items such as bread and coal were enforced by various local authorities (see Harvey and Parry, *The Law of Consumer Protection and Fair Trading* (5th edn, 1996), ch 1).

In terms of legislation, the origins of the Trade Descriptions Act 1968 lie in the Merchandise Marks Acts 1887–1953, whose main defect was that there was no effective enforcement mechanism, and whilst we now look to the Food Safety Act 1990 for the primary guarantees that the food we consume is wholesome, there has been legislation against impure food since 1266. Legislation to redress the imbalance of power as between consumer and supplier by banning or negating certain clauses in standard form contracts is a much more modern idea. Evolution has been primarily due to the political recognition of the individual consumer as an important and under-privileged constituent, lacking resources, whether personal or institutional, to obtain effective redress.

WHO IS THE CONSUMER?

The Molony Committee on Consumer Protection, mentioned above (at p 1) regarded the consumer as one who purchases (or hire-purchases) goods for private use or consumption (para 2). The private consumer of services is equally a 'consumer', as the Molony Committee admitted, but for reasons of practicability this aspect of consumerism was not investigated. It was also subsequently realised that the definition of a 'consumer' should be extended to include anyone who consumes goods or services at the end of the chain of production, thus catching the otherwise excluded plaintiff in *Donoghue v Stevenson* [1932] AC 562.

Legislative attempts to define a 'consumer' conform to the above principles. Thus, for example, the Unfair Contract Terms Act 1977 states that a party to a contract 'deals as consumer' in relation to another party if—'(a) he neither makes the contract in the course of a business nor holds himself out as doing so; and (b) the other party does make the contract in the course of a business'; (s 12). The EC derived Unfair Terms in Consumer Contracts Regulations 1994 defines 'consumer' as meaning 'a natural person who, in making a contract to which these Regulations apply, is acting for purposes which are outside his business' (reg 2). Along the same lines, 'consumer goods' are defined in the Consumer Protection Act 1987, Part II (relating to consumer safety), as 'any goods which are ordinarily intended for private use or consumption' (s 10(7)).

Based on these ideas, a consumer is a private person acquiring goods or services for his or her private use or consumption. This standard definition does not prevent difficult problems arising in the classification of both consumers and traders. Is a doctor buying a car (on which he will claim some tax relief) indulging in a consumer or a commercial transaction? If this is a consumer transaction, when the doctor sells that car is he trading, i.e. acting in the course of a business? (The courts have taken the view that normally business transactions imply some degree of regularity: see eg, *R & B Customs Brokers Co Ltd v United Dominions Trust Ltd* [1988] 1 All ER 847, below, pp 357–8). Nevertheless, for practical purposes the position is clear enough and in broad economic terms the consumer is a person on the end of perhaps a long line of production and supply directed primarily at private buyers. It is also implicit in this scenario that the consumer's resources are likely to be less than those of the supplier. The inequality of bargaining power thus revealed provides one of the key political motives behind the promotion of legislation, whether at the EU or national level. A primary objective of such legislation is to mitigate the effects of this inequality of bargaining power. Judges, particularly Lord Denning, deserve much credit for bringing this point graphically to public attention in some of the cases preceding the remedial legislation. (See, for instance, the long line of cases on exemption clauses and the evolution of the doctrine of 'fundamental breach', dealt with in works on the law of contract and mentioned in ch 7).

Some institutions and writers construe 'consumer law' more widely as also embracing the interests of, for instance, a private investor. If by that is meant the private investors in unit trusts, investment trusts, stocks and shares and the like, the definition of 'consumer' would need to be substantially widened. In truth, the private investor is not operating as a 'consumer' as normally understood. Producers of goods and services need capital and the provision of capital by, amongst others, private investors is part of the apparatus of the producer. The need to protect the investor in these circumstances is uncontroversial. The

Financial Services Act 1986 is a comprehensive attempt to do so, owing its birth to Professor LCB Gower's review of investor protection (see Cmnd 9125, 1984). Investor protection should be regarded as separate and distinct from consumer protection law, although in many cases the need for protection arises from the same fundamental consideration, namely inequality of bargaining power. (Some financial services, such as insurance, may involve both elements of saving and investment—eg life policies—and also elements of consumer services—eg motor and house insurance—see ch 4, pp 182–98). Other situations where there are bipartite transactions involving, broadly, a producer and a consumer, may be part of an existing corpus of law with its own principles and rules. A prime example is the law of landlord and tenant. The tenant is a consumer of the landlord's services, but the subject has developed its own complex statutory codes and for reasons of convenience, if not logic, this corpus of law is excluded from consumer law textbooks.

CONSUMER AFFAIRS STRATEGY

An interesting paper on the development of a consumer affairs strategy was produced by the Consumer Affairs Division of the Office of Fair Trading in 1996. The paper supplies a cogent framework within which ideas for enhancing measures to protect consumers could be developed. It was published as a consultation exercise. The need for consumer affairs work in the light of an analysis of complaints is expressed as follows:

Consumer Affairs Strategy—A Consultation Paper, June 1996

2.1. The need for measures to protect consumers has long been recognised, and over the years a substantial statutory framework has been developed to address that need. There is abundant evidence that consumers remain in need of the protection provided by the legislation. The Office's most recent Consumer Dissatisfaction Survey suggested that, in the year to November 1994, consumers had cause for complaint about the purchase of goods or services on nearly 90 million occasions. Almost half of those surveyed reported that they had cause for complaint on at least one occasion. Although the proportion of complaints resolved to the consumer's satisfaction was higher than in previous similar surveys, for services it was still only 56%. In the year to September 1995, the number of complaints reported to the Office by Trading Standards Departments, Citizens Advice Bureaux and other organisations was just over 800,000—an increase per return submitted of 42.5% over the year to September 1990.

2.2. Notwithstanding these figures, it is open to question whether, in general terms, the problems encountered by consumers are increasing. On the one hand, the safety and reliability of many goods appear to have improved in recent years. But, on the other hand, the prevalence of trading malpractices such as the clocking of second-hand cars, and the sale of counterfeit goods, remains at a high level. The level of consumer spending has almost trebled since 1950, so that there are more transactions in which problems can occur. The proportion of households with a telephone or central heating has more than doubled since 1972. Broader trends—such as the level of consumer debt, the difficult trading environment for many businesses, and the development of new and more complex goods and services—also have an impact on consumers.

2.3. Whatever the actual trends in consumer detriment, the increase in the level of dissatisfaction and in the number of complaints indicates that the public's expectations of those working in the consumer affairs field is growing. This pressure is compounded by the growth in the body of consumer legislation, particularly in response to EU initiatives. By contrast, resources devoted to consumer affairs have not risen.

The OFT describes its present role as follows:

4.1. The Office's role in consumer affairs work is derived essentially from the statutory powers and duties of the Director General under the following pieces of legislation:
Fair Trading Act 1973;
Consumer Credit Act 1974;
Estate Agents Act 1979;
Control of Misleading Advertisements Regulations 1988;
Unfair Terms in Consumer Contracts Regulations 1994.

4.2. The legislation provides for the Office to promote and safeguard the interests of consumers in a variety of ways:

it **regulates the conduct of business,** by administering a licensing system for consumer credit traders (and, in effect, a negative licensing system for estate agents) and taking action, where necessary, against problem traders under Part III of the Fair Trading Act . . . ; and by taking action to prevent misleading advertisements . . . and unfair terms in consumer contract . . .

it **promotes good practice** by traders, in particular by encouraging the adoption of industry codes of practice . . . ;

it **publishes information** designed to help consumers avoid problems, and to advise them what to do when things go wrong. It also publishes guidance for traders on their obligations under the legislation which it administers . . . ;

it **conducts research** into issues of concern to consumers . . . ;

it **advises the Government** on issues of concern to consumers. This may include recommending changes to consumer legislation, or representing the consumer interest in commenting on proposed changes to other legislation . . . ;

The Office has no significant direct involvement in either the enforcement of quality standards . . . or the provision of means of securing redress . . .

The discussion paper then goes on to discuss the aim of consumer affairs work. In fact three aims are specified, namely (1) empowering consumers through information and redress; (2) protecting them by preventing abuse; (3) promoting competitive and responsible supply. The paper explains these three points in greater detail as follows:

5.2. Some explanation of some of the points in this statement may be helpful. It is important to work in the **longer term** interests of consumers. The aim is to improve the overall position of consumers in a sustainable way—this may well not be achieved if, for example, intervention has a seriously adverse effect on suppliers, perhaps causing them to withdraw from the market, or significantly increasing their costs.

5.3. So far as the interests of **vulnerable consumers** are concerned, the first principle is that any action which is taken should be likely to promote the interests of consumers in aggregate, while taking care that no particular group is unacceptably disadvantaged. In certain cases, action may be justified which is specifically targeted at protecting the interests of vulnerable consumers—for example the young, the elderly, people with disabilities, people of limited education, those on low incomes, and ethnic minorities (particularly those for whom English is not their first language). This might take the form of information aimed specifically at the needs of such groups, or more direct action against a consumer problem whose effect is felt disproportionately by a particular group. There may even be cases where action to protect vulnerable consumers is justified even if consumer welfare in aggregate is slightly reduced, for example because of the increased costs involved.

5.4. The promotion of **competitive and responsible supply** is a task which is shared between those working in the consumer affairs field, and those—including the Office of Fair Trading's Competition Policy Division—whose job it is to enforce competition legislation. While we believe that the existence of market structures capable of providing choice is a fundamental element in the promotion of consumers' interests, we recognise that competition policy alone is not sufficient to ensure that such interests are adequately protected.

The paper then attempts to state the guiding principles which should govern the OFT's work.

6.1. . . . We believe that the interests of consumers are best served by a marketplace in which they are able to exercise genuine choice. It is essential, therefore, that our work should promote consumers' confidence, and thus their ability to spend effectively and efficiently. This will not only help consumers to help themselves, but should in its turn lead to more effective and efficient production, and growth in the economy as a whole. Consumers are, generally, the best judges of their own interests, and it is therefore for them to make their own choices based on those interests and according to their own values. While direct intervention may be necessary when things go wrong, the main emphasis of consumer affairs work should be to empower consumers to look after themselves.

One of the key features of the economic model of a 'perfect market' is the assumption that in order to make prudent spending decisions the consumer must have information. The OFT comments:

6.2. This is a difficult area. It is rarely clear how much or which information a consumer needs and can use. Many consumers are soon sated with details of electrical goods or financial services products. However, markets may not, in themselves, lead to the availability of all the information which consumers need to make good choices. Some producers may seek to distinguish their wares artificially by stressing comparatively minor features. Some sellers may be unwilling to reveal their interest (eg commissions) in the sales of particular products. An essential part of our work is therefore to promote the availability of useful and accurate information, either by encouraging suppliers or third parties to provide it, or—where the market fails to meet the need—by publishing it ourselves. We may also need to use our powers to intervene to ensure the integrity of information given to consumers by suppliers.

6.3. In the long term, and given the availability of sufficient information, competition should ensure that dishonest traders, and others who fail to meet acceptable standards, do not thrive. But we recognise that markets are imperfect. Consequently, in order for consumers to be adequately protected from the worst and most dangerous choices, and to have the confidence necessary to play an effective part in the operation of the marketplace, regulation may be necessary to ensure that bad practice can be avoided or dealt with promptly. In extreme cases, traders failing to reach acceptable standards may even have to be excluded from the market altogether. The intervention of regulatory authorities can play an important part in helping to redress the imbalance which almost invariably exists between consumers and suppliers of goods and services . . .

Applying the guiding principles mentioned, how in the future could the OFT's role be developed? Because institutional consumer protection in the UK has developed in a higgledy-piggledy manner and with a measure of duplication between institutions, it is not surprising to read that a number of correspondents commented to the OFT that there was a need for greater coordination of consumer affairs work in the UK. To take quality standards, for example, the paper states:

7.6. At present the Office has no direct involvement in the setting or monitoring of quality standards, which are generally imposed by legislation administered by other bodies (such as Trading Standards Departments) or voluntarily by bodies such as the British Standards Institution or trade associations. We do, however, have an indirect involvement, in that poor quality of goods sold or of services provided may be grounds for action on our part under Part III of the Fair Trading Act, and in so far as the codes of practice which we support may contain provisions relating to quality.

7.7. Our present lack of direct involvement in this activity reflects not only our limited statutory power to engage in this type of work, but also—largely as a consequence of that lack of power—the fact that we have not found it necessary to acquire expertise in it. (This is not to say, however, that we could not acquire such expertise, either by learning it ourselves or by working together with those, whether in industry or elsewhere, who already possess it.) On the other hand, the present system appears to work well, drawing as it does on the expertise of those with detailed knowledge of specific product areas in the development of standards, and the experience in areas such as product testing of those responsible for monitoring compliance with the standards.

On the vital question of the availability of information about products which is accurate and useful, prudent consumer choices both benefit consumers personally and contribute to the efficient operation of the market. But the cost to the producer/supplier in supplying information should be measured against the benefit to the consumer of having that information, and 'information overload' is a possibility which needs to be avoided.

It is pointed out that the enforcement of regulatory legislation is primarily in the hands of local authorities (with the potential for variations in the intensity of enforcement between one area and another), and that the role of the OFT is essentially one of monitoring. Acknowledging the good work of LACOTS (Local Authorities Coordinating Body On Trading Standards) the paper nevertheless questions (see para 7.11) whether the OFT should not take a more active role in promoting consistency of enforcement.

On the control of traders, the Paper points out that consumers should be able to have confidence in the fitness of the businesses with which they deal. The OFT does have a significant statutory role in the control of traders, particularly via the control mechanism supplied by the Consumer Credit Act 1974. A consumer credit licence can be withdrawn even where evidence of unfitness to hold a licence arises from trading activities unrelated to the provision of credit (see para 7.14 and below, pp 283–93). There is also the 'negative' licensing system applicable to estate agents where the Director General can issue warning and prohibition orders (see below, pp 293–4). Further, the Director General has powers under Part III of the Fair Trading Act 1973 to seek assurances from traders about their future conduct or to bring proceedings for Court Orders. These latter powers are nevertheless regarded as weak and the OFT has long argued for reform: (see para 7.15 and below, pp 547–65). The important development of the control of unfair terms in standard form contracts is achieved by use of the powers given to the Director General under the Unfair Terms in Consumer Contracts Regulations 1994 (see below, pp 379–82), though it is still too early to assess the effectiveness of the Office's operations in this area.

The availability of effective and accessible redress mechanisms is recognised as an important feature of consumer protection. The OFT plays virtually no direct part in this activity. The Paper points out that though the work of the small claims court is central to the provision of redress: 'It is, nevertheless, generally recognised that the courts cannot be the sole recourse for consumers seeking redress and that there is, therefore, a significant role to be played by other mechanisms such as the ombudsman schemes.' The OFT's role is seen to be a coordinating one. (see paras 7.28–7.29, and below, pp 425–8).

Finally, the OFT continues to place great importance on the provision of information, education and advice to consumers. All this must be targeted effectively at those people who need it. Here the OFT acknowledges the value of the work of Citizens Advice Bureaux and other local advice centres, Trading Standards Departments, Ombudsmen and other similar organisations (para 7.33). However, a lack of systematic liaison with other potential providers of information is diagnosed so that both gaps and overlaps in coverage may occur (para 7.34). The results of comparative product testing are promulgated appropriately by bodies independent of government, particularly the Consumers' Association. It is noted, however, that in Sweden a National Consumer Authority operates a laboratory where goods are tested (para 7.34). The Paper includes a brief assessment of the present system as follows:

7.40. We consider that our strengths and weaknesses in this activity are in many ways similar to those referred to in the discussion of our information work. We have considerable experience in carrying out investigations into areas of concern to consumers, in identifying the core issues, and in proposing remedies which have, in many cases, subsequently been implemented in the form of either new legislation or changes in industry practice. Our influence and reputation as a central Government department have undoubtedly helped us both to obtain the necessary information from industry, and to follow through our recommendations. We recognise, however, that there is a lack of coordination of the resources available both to us and to the numerous other organisations who engage from time to time in this type of work, so that gaps and overlaps in coverage may arise. We recognise also that—while we do select issues for investigation on the basis of a number of defined criteria—there is scope for us to adopt a more systematic approach towards identifying those areas where the use of our resources can be of greatest benefit to consumers.

7.41. We intend to address the problem of coordinating the resources devoted to this type of work by proposing more active liaison between the bodies involved, with a view to discussing areas of mutual interest, and in particular forward work programmes. Regular meetings of this type should go some way towards ensuring that those issues which need to be addressed are dealt with, and dealt with by the most appropriate body. We recognise, however, that the bodies concerned, despite their common overall objective of promoting the interests of consumers, each have their own priorities, and that how they allocate their resources is ultimately a matter for them . . .

7.42. We will also consider the scope for more active liaison with those engaged in academic research into issues of concern to consumers. Such research, sponsored and promoted in some cases by the Office, may be the most appropriate means of addressing some of the more theoretical issues arising in the field of consumer affairs, while the Office concentrates in its own work on more practical issues of potential direct benefit to consumers.

7.43. We intend also to build on work which is already under way to devise guidelines to assist in the identification of areas where detriment to consumers is likely to occur and where remedies may be available. We aim to continue to attempt to understand how consumers may best be helped in a complex and changing marketplace, including by analysing the operations in different sectors of retailers, of commercial providers of advice, and of others whom consumers might expect to act to simplify their choices.

CIVIL AND CRIMINAL ASPECTS OF PROTECTION

In assessing the effectiveness of consumer protection in the UK, it is a good exercise to imagine what advice might be given to another country—perhaps eager to enter into an association with the European Union—which has no consumer protection system to speak of. The luxury of a plethora of institutions, all sharing some responsibilities but involving some duplication of effort but without eliminating all gaps, (the picture of the UK's position suggested by the OFT's discussion paper above) would not be an economic or attractive solution. If we were to start again, one might propose the establishment of a much more powerful Office of Fair Trading fully in charge of all aspects of enforcement and monitoring of the law and the provision of advice for citizens. Agencies could be established locally to maintain an important feature of the UK's system of enforcement and advice on the spot where the problem arises.

There is, though, a limit in any civilised system to how much central government institutions could and should do at public expense to protect the consumer. Where there is no question of the supply of dangerous goods or fraudulent behaviour by the producer/supplier, it is inevitable and natural that the consumer should look to the civil law for redress. In other words, the problem moves from one of public law into the domain of private law. The enforcement of such civil rights will be at the consumer's own expense, so it is important that our putative country's legal system should have an efficient and inexpensive small claims provision (see ch 8, pp 409–22).

Civil law will, however, be inadequate to protect against dangerous products and fraudulent or misleading trading behaviour. Here, the criminal law must be used and the route the UK has generally adopted is to impose strict criminal liability on the producer/supplier but subject to a central defence involving the concept of due diligence (see ch 15, pp 709–24). There appears to be no viable alternative to this dual system of law, though much thinking has taken place on whether there should be a degree of de-criminalisation, a 'middle system' of law. Honest traders object to being treated as criminals where technical breaches of the law involve them in the criminal process. In the UK considerable importance has been attached to the development, often with the support of the OFT, of Codes of Practice. If these work, they will improve standards in the trading sector involved, though unless given statutory form (as is the case with price indications), they will bind only those who decide to join relevant trade associations. Rogue traders are unlikely to be members (see ch 10).

In September 1997 the Director General of Fair Trading presented proposals to the Parliamentary Under Secretary of State for Competition and Consumer Affairs to 'plug the holes' in the current law. The proposals, which would include 'stop' orders requiring a trader to end an unfair course of conduct, 'banning' orders, fines or prison sentences for those who do not comply, and joint enforcement powers of both the OFT and local trading standards departments, would involve legislative amendments to Part III of the Fair Trading Act 1974 (see ch 11).

THE IMPACT OF EUROPE

FUNDAMENTAL PRINCIPLES

It is now obvious to any student of United Kingdom consumer protection law that an increasing amount of the relevant legislation has its genesis in initiatives taken by the European Community (EC). Accordingly, a brief introduction is required to assist those who may be relatively unfamiliar with the mechanisms and policies involved at the European level. More detailed consideration is contained in Harvey and Parry, op cit, ch 2; Weatherill, *EC Consumer Law and Policy* (1997) Lonbay (ed) *Enhancing the Legal Position of the European Consumer* (1996); and Reich, 'Protection of Consumers' Economic Interests by the EC' (1992) 14 Sydney LR 23.

A study of the impact of EC law on the consumer reflects the extent to which it has influenced UK domestic law in general. One of the founding principles of the European Community was the establishment of a common market in which trade between member states was not affected by tariff or non-tariff barriers. An obstacle to the achievement of that objective was the differing laws of member states. This in turn necessitated legislation, enforced through the European Commission and the European Court of Justice (ECJ), to harmonise a wide range of national measures that affect production and marketing. A fundamental principle is that regulatory factors affecting business competitiveness, for example, the cost of compliance with safety laws or of giving non-excludable consumer guarantees, should be as far as possible uniform throughout the member states—the well known concept of the level playing field. In the resulting single market, the consumer should in principle be able to shop anywhere in the Union, making 'prudent shopping decisions' based on the highest quality at the cheapest price, and provided he or she buys duty paid goods for private consumption, bring them back without restrictions. Indeed, the present shopping traffic between Dover and the French supermarkets in Calais, for example, bears testament to the working of this concept, though there are still many ways in which the arrangement falls short of a true single market. The existence of border controls is one, and the problems of enforcing a British consumer's rights, if the goods are defective, in the French courts, with their different procedures and underlying substantive law, is another.

EC LEGISLATION

Authority for European Community legislation was originally derived from Article 100 of the EC Treaty (the so-called harmonisation article). This permits the Council, acting unanimously on a proposal from the Commission and after consulting the European Parliament and the Economic and Social Committee, to issue directives for the approximation of such laws, regulations or administrative provisions of the member states as directly affect the establishment or functioning of the common market. This article provided the basis for the directive on liability for defective products (85/374/EEC). The Single European Act of 1986 permitted harmonisation to be advanced through a qualified majority procedure under Articles 100a and 189b. The increasing importance of consumer protection and the use of the new procedure are to be seen in the Treaty on European Union of 1993, which added a new Title XI to the EC Treaty. Further minor amendments will be introduced when the Amsterdam Treaty of 1997 comes into force and this Treaty will also renumber the articles contained in the EC Treaty. At the time of writing Article 129a provides:

1. The Community shall contribute to the attainment of a high level of consumer protection through:

  (a) measures adopted pursuant to Article 100a in the context of the completion of the internal market;
  (b) specific action which supports and supplements the policy pursued by the Member States to protect the health, safety and economic interests of consumers and to provide adequate information to consumers.

2. The Council, acting in accordance with the procedure referred to in Article 189b and after consulting the Economic and Social Committee, shall adopt the specific action referred to in paragraph 1(b).

3. Action adopted pursuant to paragraph 2 shall not prevent any Member State from maintaining or introducing more stringent protective measures. Such measures must be compatible with this Treaty. The Commission shall be notified of them.

Article 189 of the EC Treaty sets out the various ways in which the EC may legislate. It provides:

In order to carry out their task and in accordance with the provisions of this Treaty, the European Parliament acting jointly with the Council, the Council and the Commission shall make regulations, issue directives, take decisions, make recommendations or deliver opinions.

A regulation shall have general application. It shall be binding in its entirety and directly applicable in all Member States.

A directive shall be binding, as to the result to be achieved, upon each Member State to which it is addressed, but shall leave to the national authorities the choice of form and methods.

A decision shall be binding in its entirety upon those to whom it is addressed.

Recommendations and opinions shall have no binding force.

Directives are by far the most important form of legislation for present purposes and usually they are transposed or incorporated into United Kingdom law by regulations made under s 2(2) of the European Communities Act 1972. Occasionally, as in the case of the product liability directive, implementation may be by primary legislation, that is by an Act of Parliament.

Sometimes, it may be argued that a member state has not transposed a directive correctly (or indeed at all) by the stipulated date. In such circumstances the Commission may proceed under Article 169 of the EC Treaty or another member state may initiate proceedings under Article 170. Alternatively, a national court may refer questions on the interpretation or effect of Community provisions to the ECJ for a preliminary ruling under Article 177. Of itself, this may be of limited value to consumers who claim to be prejudiced by the failure. The question then arises as to whether they may rely on the alleged non-implementation and have their rights determined as they would have been if the directive had been implemented. This was considered by the ECJ in *Faccini Dori v Recreb srl*, Case C–91/92 [1995] All ER (EC) 1, where the relevant directive (85/577/EEC) concerned cancellation rights in contracts with consumers which have been negotiated away from business premises. The contract was for an English language correspondence course and it had been entered into near a railway station in Milan. In essence, the ECJ concluded on a reference for a preliminary ruling from the Italian courts (at 22) that:

In the absence of measures transposing Directive 85/577 within the prescribed time limit, consumers cannot derive from the directive itself a right of cancellation as against traders with whom they have concluded a contract or enforce such a right in a national court. However, when applying provisions of national law, whether adopted before or after the directive, the national court must interpret them as far as possible in the light of the wording and purpose of the directive.

This lack of what is usually (if somewhat inelegantly) called 'horizontal direct effect' is to be seen also in such cases as *Marshall v Southampton and South-West Hants Area Health Authority*, Case 152/84, [1986] ECR 723 (where the context was sex discrimination) and *El Corte Inglés SA v Christina Blázquez Rivero* Case C–192/94 (where a consumer was held unable to rely on Directive 87/102/EEC on consumer credit which had not been implemented in Spain). A similar limit does not apply where a sufficiently precise obligation is imposed by a regulation (which is directly applicable in all member states) or by a Treaty provision.

Although such a failure to transpose a directive will not confer rights against typical business suppliers of goods or services, the ECJ has held that it may none the less confer some limited rights. These may be described briefly under three headings. First, the failure to transpose a directive by the prescribed date cannot operate to the advantage of an 'organ of the state' which, broadly speaking, encompasses public authorities. This principle of 'vertical direct effect' is to be seen in *Foster v British Gas plc* Case C–188/89, [1990] ECR I–3313. Secondly, the ECJ has developed the '*Marleasing* doctrine', which sets out the requirement for interpretation noted in *Faccini Dori* (above) and which applies to all national legislation which covers the same ground as a directive, even if it is not specifically enacted to implement it. In the context of consumer law the third development is more important. It is usually known as the principle of State liability and it enables an individual to claim damages from a member state in tort where loss has been suffered through non-implementation within the prescribed period. The operation of the principle, and the response given by the ECJ to a submission that the state had had insufficient time, is to be seen in extracts from the following leading case.

Dillenkofer v Federal Republic of Germany Cases C–178/94, 179/94, 188/94, 189/94 and 190/94

Council Directive 90/314/EEC on package travel was to be transposed into the laws of member states by 31 December 1992, but was not transposed into German law until 1 July 1994. The directive contains important safeguards against the insolvency of operators. The plaintiffs had purchased package travel holidays and suffered loss following the insolvency of two operators in 1993. They sought compensation from the Federal Republic of Germany on the basis that they would have been protected against such insolvency if the directive had been implemented by the prescribed date. The German court referred a number of questions to the ECJ for a preliminary ruling under Article 177 of the EC Treaty. The judgment of the Court was delivered on 8 October 1996. Having set out the questions to be addressed and referred to leading cases in point (including *Francovich v Italy*, Cases C–6/90 and C–9/90, [1991] ECR I–5357 and *Brasserie du Pêcheur and Factortame*, Cases C–46/93 and C–48/93 [1996] All ER (EC) 301), the judgment continued:

21. In *Brasserie du Pêcheur and Factortame*, at paragraphs 50 and 51, . . . the Court, having regard to the circumstances of the case, held that individuals who have suffered damage have a right to reparation where three conditions are met: the rule of law infringed must have been intended to confer rights on individuals; the breach must be sufficiently serious; and there must be a direct causal link between the breach of the obligation resting on the State and the damage sustained by the injured parties.

22. Moreover, it is clear from the *Francovich* case which, like these cases, concerned nontransposition of a directive within the prescribed period, that the full effectiveness of the third paragraph of Article 189 of the Treaty requires that there should be a right to reparation where the result prescribed by the directive entails the grant of rights to individuals, the content of

those rights is identifiable on the basis of the provisions of the directive and a causal link exists between the breach of the State's obligation and the loss and damage suffered by the injured parties.

. . .

25. On the one hand, a breach of Community law is sufficiently serious if a Community institution or a Member State, in the exercise of its rule-making powers, manifestly and gravely disregards the limits on those powers (see Joined Cases 83/76, 94/76, 4/77, 15/77 and 40/77 *HNL and Others v Council and Commission* [1978] ECR 1209, paragraph 6; *Brasserie du Pêcheur and Factortame*, paragraph 55 . . .) On the other hand, if, at the time when it committed the infringement, the Member State in question was not called upon to make any legislative choices and had only considerably reduced, or even no, discretion, the mere infringement of Community law may be sufficient to establish the existence of a sufficiently serious breach. . . .

26. So where, as in *Francovich*, a Member State fails, in breach of the third paragraph of Article 189 of the Treaty, to take any of the measures necessary to achieve the result prescribed by a directive within the period it lays down, that Member State manifestly and gravely disregards the limits on its discretion.

27. Consequently, such a breach gives rise to a right to reparation on the part of individuals if the result prescribed by the directive entails the grant of rights to them, the content of those rights is identifiable on the basis of the provisions of the directive and a causal link exists between the breach of the State's obligation and the loss and damage suffered by the injured parties: no other conditions need be taken into consideration.

28. In particular, reparation of that loss and damage cannot depend on a prior finding by the Court of an infringement of Community law attributable to the State (see *Brasserie du Pêcheur*, paragraphs 94 to 96), nor on the existence of intentional fault or negligence on the part of the organ of the State to which the infringement is attributable (see paragraphs 75 to 80 of the same judgment).

The ECJ went on to conclude (para 46) that the directive did entail the grant to package travellers of rights guaranteeing a refund of money paid over and their repatriation in the event of the organiser's insolvency and that the content of those rights was sufficiently identifiable. It then went on to address an argument based on insufficiency of time and held:

52. According to the order for reference, the German Government claimed that the period prescribed for transposition of the Directive was too short, in particular because of the considerable difficulties which introduction of a system of security conforming with the Directive would create in Germany for the economic sector concerned. In that connection, the German Government pointed out that the Directive could not be implemented simply by enacting legislative amendments: it had to rely on the collaboration of third parties (travel organizers, insurers and credit institutions).

53. That kind of circumstance cannot justify a failure to transpose a directive within the prescribed period. It is settled case-law that a Member State may not rely on provisions, practices or situations prevailing in its own internal legal system to justify its failure to observe the obligations and time-limits laid down by a directive (see, for instance, Case 283/86 *Commission v Belgium* [1988] ECR 3271, paragraph 7).

54. If the period allowed for the implementation of a directive does, indeed, prove to be too short, the only step compatible with Community law available to the Member State concerned is to take the appropriate initiatives within the Community in order to have the competent

Community institution grant the necessary extension of the period (see Case 52/75 *Commission v Italy* [1976] ECR 277, paragraph 12).

The overall conclusion was in part that:

1. Failure to take any measure to transpose a directive in order to achieve the result it prescribes within the period laid down for that purpose constitutes *per se* a serious breach of Community law and consequently gives rise to a right of reparation for individuals suffering injury if the result prescribed by the directive entails the grant to individuals of rights whose content is identifiable and a causal link exists between the breach of the State's obligation and the loss and damage suffered.

2. The result prescribed by Article 7 of Council Directive 90/314/EEC of 13 June 1990 on package travel, package holidays and package tours entails the grant to package travellers of rights guaranteeing a refund of money paid over and their repatriation in the event of the organizer's insolvency; the content of those rights is sufficiently identifiable.

3. In order to comply with Article 9 of Directive 90/314, the Member State should have adopted, within the period prescribed, all the measures necessary to ensure that, as from 1 January 1993, individuals would have effective protection against the risk of the insolvency of the organizer and/or retailer party to the contract.

As is apparent from Article 129a of the EC Treaty (see above, p 13), the Community is seeking to attain a high level of consumer protection. Reference has already been made to the directive on package travel (see above, pp 15–17) and there are also directives on a wide range of other matters including consumer credit (see below, p 281), 'doorstep contracts', advertising (see below, pp 528–9) product liability (see below, pp 223–9), unfair contract terms (see below, p 332) and general product safety, (see below, p 599). In a related area the Office of Fair Trading plays an important role in assisting the European Commission in monitoring the application of the Community competition rules (particularly Articles 85 and 86 of the EC Treaty). It participates in meetings of the Community's Advisory Committee on Restrictive Practices and Monopolies and also participates in the competition work of the OECD. Some of the earlier directives have been castigated by Sir Gordon (now Lord) Borrie, then Director General of Fair Trading, as being irrelevant, retrograde and damaging to national interests: see Borrie, *The Development of Consumer Law and Policy* (1984), p 106.

Of the directives in this area awaiting implementation, the Distance Contracts Directive (Directive 97/7) is of particular interest (see S. Singleton, 'The Distance Contracts Directive' (1997) 16 Trading Law, 311). Its aim is to harmonise the regulation of mail order and other distance selling devices, designed to lead to a contract. To be caught the scheme must be an organised one (ie, part of a systematic scheme of selling) and used exclusively to effect the contract (so a home visit by a salesman would put the transaction outside the scope of the directive). Junk mail, catalogues, cold telephone calling, newspaper mail orders and unsolicited faxes and electronic mail messages appear to be all caught. Financial transactions, payphone and automatic vending machine contracts are excluded. Where the directive applies the consumer must be given certain basic information before the contract is formed—for example, the identity of the supplier, full prices involved, arrangements for delivery and payment, and how long any offer is open for. There is then a right of withdrawal within seven working days of receipt without any payment other than the cost of returning the goods. Any money paid to the supplier must be repaid to the consumer within thirty days. This directive is required to be implemented by 4 June 2000.

CHAPTER 2

The framework of remedies: representations, warranties and promotional claims

INTRODUCTION

The first part of this book is concerned with the content, scope and effectiveness of the private law remedies available to consumers where damage or loss is caused by some fault in the provision of goods or services.

Whether a consumer will have a remedy in respect of any given complaint will be affected by a variety of factors. One is the relationship, if any, between the parties and in particular whether it is contractual. Another is whether the defendant is a trader or a private individual, a consumer's rights being more extensive in the former case. Again, the position may depend on the nature of the damage or loss suffered, and on whether physical injury or property damage is involved. Other things being equal, a remedy will be available more readily in such cases than in cases where, for example, the complaint is that the goods are shoddy or that a service has not had the promised effect.

STATEMENTS OF OPINION, FACT AND CONTRACTUAL PROMISE

If B makes a statement to A about the condition or quality of goods or about services to be provided, or if such a statement is contained in a written contract, it may fall into any one of three broad categories. Some such statements are mere puffs of the 'whiter than white' variety and of no legal effect. They are controlled, if at all, through such voluntary measures as Codes of Practice (see below, ch 10). Similarly, the statement may be no more than an honest expression of opinion or an estimate and as such it will again not normally ground liability in damages if it proves to be ill-informed. (Cf, however, the position under the Trade Descriptions Act 1968, s 3(3) especially and *Holloway v Cross* [1981] 1 All ER 1012 (QBD), below, p 630). The second broad category encompasses statements of fact or 'mere representations' which may induce a person (A) to enter a contract in reliance on the statement being true, but which do not form part of the contract. Nowadays there will be a remedy in damages in such cases if the statement is false provided at least that the person making the statement (B) did not have reasonable grounds for believing it to be true (see generally the Misrepresentation Act 1967, s 2). Also, it may be open to A to rescind or set aside the contract. Thirdly, the statement may constitute a contractual term or promise in the sense that B has 'warranted', for example, that goods have certain attributes or has 'guaranteed' that services will conform to a particular description or produce a particular result. A will then have a remedy for damages for breach of contract if the goods or services are not as warranted or if the promise is not fulfilled and may also, depending on the nature of the term broken (whether a condition or a warranty) or perhaps on the consequences of the breach (innominate term) be entitled to treat the contract as having been repudiated. Such express terms are commonplace in a wide range of everyday consumer transactions including the sale of goods (especially when they are second-hand), home improvements, car servicing and the provision of holidays.

The above matters are dealt with fully in the standard texts on the law of contract and sale of goods: see eg Treitel, *The Law of Contract* (9th edn, 1995), ch 9; Cheshire Fifoot and Furmston, *Law of Contract* (13th edn, 1996), pp 125–35, 273–306; Atiyah, *The Sale of Goods* (9th edn, 1995), ch 6; and *Benjamin's Sale of Goods* (5th edn, 1997), ch 10.

The following cases illustrate the distinction between statements of opinion, fact and promise.

Dick Bentley Productions Ltd v Harold Smith (Motors) Ltd [1965] 2 All ER 65, [1965] 1 WLR 623, Court of Appeal

Lord Denning MR: The second plaintiff, Mr Charles Walter Bentley, sometimes known as Dick Bentley, brings an action against Harold Smith (Motors) Ltd for damages for breach of warranty on the sale of a car. Mr Bentley had been dealing with Mr Smith (to whom I shall refer in the stead of the defendant company) for a couple of years and told Mr Smith he was on the lookout for a well vetted Bentley car. In January, 1960, Mr Smith found one and bought it for £1,500 from a firm in Leicester. He wrote to Mr Bentley and said: 'I have just purchased a Park Ward power operated hood convertible. It is one of the nicest cars we have had in for quite a long time.' Mr Smith had told Mr Bentley earlier that he was in a position to find out the history of cars. It appears that with a car of this quality the makers do keep a complete biography of it.

Mr Bentley went to see the car. Mr Smith told him that a German baron had had this car. He said that it had been fitted at one time with a replacement engine and gearbox, and had done twenty thousand miles only since it had been so fitted. The speedometer on the car showed only twenty thousand miles. Mr Smith said the price was £1,850, and he would guarantee the car for twelve months, including parts and labour. That was on the morning of Jan 23, 1960. In the afternoon Mr Bentley took his wife over to see the car. Mr Bentley repeated to his wife in Mr Smith's presence what Mr Smith had told him in the morning. In particular that Mr Smith said it had done only twenty thousand miles since it had been refitted with a replacement engine and gearbox. Mr Bentley took it for a short run. He bought the car for £1,850, gave his cheque and the sale was concluded. The car was a considerable disappointment to him. He took it back to Mr Smith from time to time. [His Lordship referred briefly to some work done on the car and continued:] Eventually he brought this action for breach of warranty. The county court judge found that there was a warranty, that it was broken, and that the damages were more than £400, but as the claim was limited to £400, he gave judgment for the plaintiffs for that amount.

The first point is whether this representation, namely that the car had done twenty thousand miles only since it had been fitted with a replacement engine and gearbox, was an innocent misrepresentation (which does not give rise to damages), or whether it was a warranty. It was said by Holt, CJ,[1] and repeated in *Heilbut, Symons & Co v Buckleton*.[2]

'An affirmation at the time of the sale is a warranty, provided it appear on evidence to be so intended.'

But that word 'intended' has given rise to difficulties. I endeavoured to explain in *Oscar Chess Ltd v Williams*[3] that the question whether a warranty was intended depends on the conduct of the parties, on their words and behaviour, rather than on their thoughts. If an intelligent bystander would reasonably infer that a warranty was intended, that will suffice. What conduct, then? What words and behaviour, lead to the inference of a warranty?

Looking at the cases once more, as we have done so often, it seems to me that if a representation is made in the course of dealings for a contract for the very purpose of inducing the other party to act on it, and it actually induces him to act on it by entering into the contract, that is prima facie ground for inferring that the representation was intended as a warranty. It is not necessary to speak of it as being collateral. Suffice it that the representation was intended to be acted on and was in fact acted on. But the maker of the representation can rebut this inference if he can show that it really was an innocent misrepresentation, in that he was in fact innocent of fault in making it, and that it would not be reasonable in the circumstances for him to be bound by it. In the *Oscar Chess* case[4] the inference was rebutted. There a man had bought a second-hand car and received it with a log-book, which stated the year of the car, 1948. He afterwards resold the car. When he resold it he simply repeated what was in the log-book and passed it on to the buyer. He honestly believed on reasonable grounds that it was true. He was completely innocent of any fault. There was no warranty by him but only an innocent misrepresentation. Whereas in the present case it is very different. The inference is not rebutted. Here we have a dealer Mr Smith, who was in a position to know, or at least to find out, the history of the car. He could get it by writing to the makers. He did not do so. Indeed it was done later. When the history of this car was examined, his statement turned out to be quite wrong. He ought to have known better. There was no reasonable foundation for it.

[His Lordship summarised the history of the car, and continued:] The county court judge found that the representations were not dishonest. Mr Smith was not guilty of fraud. But he made the statement as to twenty thousand miles without any foundation. And the judge was well justified in finding that there was a warranty. He said:

'I have no hesitation that as a matter of law the statement was a warranty. Mr Smith stated a fact that should be within own his knowledge. He had jumped to a conclusion and stated it as a fact. A fact that a buyer would act on.'

That is ample foundation for the inference of a warranty. So much for this point.

I hold that the appeal fails and should be dismissed.

Danckwerts LJ: I agree with the judgment of Lord Denning MR.

Salmon LJ: I agree. I have no doubt at all that the learned county court judge reached a correct conclusion when he decided that Mr Smith gave a warranty to the second plaintiff, Mr Bentley, and that that warranty was broken. Was what Mr Smith said intended and understood as a legally binding promise? If so, it was a warranty and as such may be part of the contract of sale or collateral to it. In effect, Mr Smith said: 'If you will enter into a contract to buy this motor car from me for £1,850, I undertake that you will be getting a motor car which has done no more than twenty thousand miles since it was fitted with a new engine and a new gearbox.'

I have no doubt at all that what was said by Mr Smith was so understood and was intended to be so understood by Mr Bentley.

I accordingly agree that the appeal should be dismissed.

Appeal dismissed.

[1] In *Crosse v Gardner* (1688) Carth 90 and *Medina v Stoughton* (1700) 1 Salk 210.

[2] [1911–13] All ER Rep 83 at 92; [1913] AC 30 at 49. The words quoted were ascribed by Lord Moulton to Holt CJ. They appear in the judgment of Buller J, in *Pasley v Freeman* ((1789) 3 Term Rep 51 at 57, 100 ER 450 at 453) where he said '. . . it was rightly held by Holt CJ, [in *Crosse v Gardner* (1688) Carth 90, 90 ER 656 and *Medina v Stoughton* (1700) 1 Salk 210, 91 ER 188], and has been uniformly adopted ever since, that an affirmation at the time of sale is a warranty, provided it appear on evidence to have been so intended'.

[3] [1957] 1 All ER 325 at pp 328, 329.

[4] [1957] 1 All ER 325.

NOTES

It is generally agreed that Lord Denning's emphasis on the question of fault is somewhat misplaced. If B warrants to A that an article has certain characteristics it is not in point that B was honestly and reasonably mistaken in believing this to be so. Indeed this is the essence of a guarantee properly so-called. (Cf the position under the Misrepresentation Act 1967, s 2.) Nonetheless, presumably an intelligent bystander will infer a warranty much more readily where a person is in a position to know the truth and often such a person will be at fault in failing to discover it. As between a dealer and a consumer obviously it is generally the former who will fill this role. In the *Oscar Chess* case to which Lord Denning referred the seller was a private individual.

Similar difficulties of distinction arose in cases decided under the Sale of Goods Act 1979, s 13 (implied condition as to correspondence with description: see *Beale v Taylor* [1967] 3 All ER 253, [1967] 1 WLR 1193 (below, p 91) and cf *Harlingdon & Leinster Enterprises Ltd v Christopher Hull Fine Art Ltd* [1990] 1 All ER 737, [1991] 1 QB 564 (below, p 88).

For a case involving the breach of an express warranty that a Rolls Royce car was 'in excellent condition' see *Peter Symmons & Co v Cook* (1981) 131 NLJ 758 (R Rougier, QC: QBD); see also below, pp 357 and 358 for further references.

Esso Petroleum Co Ltd v Mardon [1976] 2 All ER 5, [1976] QB 801, Court of Appeal

The plaintiffs 'Esso' had acquired a site on a busy main street for development as a petrol filling station. Their original calculations showed an estimated annual throughput of some 200,000 gallons from the third year of operation. However the conditions on which planning permission was subsequently granted were such that this estimate should have been revised to a much lower figure. This was not done. During negotiations with the defendant for the tenancy of the site Esso's experienced local manager told him of this estimate and in April 1963 an agreement for three years was concluded. An annual throughput of some 60,000–70,000 gallons was all that could be expected realistically and the agreement was a financial disaster for the tenant. In July 1964 he tendered notice to quit but he was granted rather a new tenancy to run from September 1964 and at a reduced rent. Matters did not improve and Esso claimed possession of the station and moneys due. The defendant, Mardon, counter-claimed for damages in respect of the manager's representation. The trial judge, Lawson J, rejected his claim for breach of warranty but held that Esso were liable in tort for breach of their own duty of care when advising him of the estimated throughput. However he limited damages to the loss suffered up to September 1964. The defendant, Mardon, appealed.

Lord Denning MR, having stated the facts, continued: Such being the facts, I turn to consider the law. It is founded on the representation that the estimated throughput of the service station was 200,000 gallons. No claim can be brought under the Misrepresentation Act 1967 because that Act did not come into force until 22nd April 1967, whereas this representation was made in April 1963. So the claim is put in two ways: first, that the representation was a collateral warranty; second, that it was a negligent misrepresentation. I will take them in order.

Collateral warranty
Ever since *Heilbut, Symons & Co v Buckleton*[1] we have had to contend with the law as laid down by the House of Lords that an innocent misrepresentation gives no right to damages. In order to escape from that rule, the pleader used to allege—I often did it myself—that the misrepresentation was fraudulent, or alternatively a collateral warranty. At the trial we nearly always succeeded on collateral warranty. We had to reckon, of course, with the dictum of Lord Moulton[2] that 'such collateral contracts must from their very nature be rare'. But more often than not the court elevated the innocent misrepresentation into a collateral warranty; and thereby did justice—in advance of the Misrepresentation Act 1967. I remember scores of cases of that kind, especially on the sale of a business. A representation as to the profits that had been made in the past was invariably held to be a warranty. Besides that experience, there have been many cases since I have sat in this court where we have readily held a representation—which induces a person to enter into a contract—to be a warranty sounding in damages. I summarised them in *Dick Bentley Productions v Harold Smith (Motors) Ltd*[3] . . .

Counsel for Esso retaliated, however, by citing *Bisset v Wilkinson*[4] where the Privy Council said that a statement by a New Zealand farmer that an area of land 'would carry 2,000 sheep' was only an expression of opinion. He submitted that the forecast here of 200,000 gallons was an expression of opinion and not a statement of fact; and that it could not be interpreted as a warranty or promise.

Now, I would quite agree with counsel for Esso that it was not a warranty—in this sense— that it did not *guarantee* that the throughput *would* be 200,000 gallons. But, nevertheless, it was a forecast made by a party, Esso, who had special knowledge and skill. It was the yardstick (the 'e a c') by which they measured the worth of a filling station. They knew the facts. They knew the traffic in the town. They knew the throughput of comparable stations. They had much experience and expertise at their disposal. They were in a much better position than Mr Mardon to make a forecast. It seems to me that if such a person makes a forecast—intending that the other should act on it and he does act on it—it can well be interpreted as a warranty that the forecast is sound and reliable in this sense that they made it with reasonable care and skill. It is just as if Esso said to Mr Mardon: 'Our forecast of throughput is 200,000 gallons. You can rely on it as being a sound forecast of what the service station should do. The rent is calculated on that footing.' If the forecast turned out to be an unsound forecast, such as no person of skill or experience should have made, there is a breach of warranty. Just as there is a breach of warranty when a forecast is made 'expected to load' by a certain date if the maker has no reasonable grounds for it: see *Samuel Sanday & Co v Keighley, Maxted & Co*;[5] or bunkers 'expected 600/700 tons': see *The Pantanassa*[6] by Diplock J. It is very different from the New Zealand case[7] where the land had never been used as a sheep farm and both parties were equally able to form an opinion as to its carrying capacity.

In the present case it seems to me that there was a warranty that the forecast was sound, that is that Esso had made it with reasonable care and skill. That warranty was broken. Most negligently Esso made a 'fatal error' in the forecast they stated to Mr Mardon, and on which he took the tenancy. For this they are liable in damages. The judge, however, declined to find a warranty.[8] So I must go further.

Negligent misrepresentation

Assuming that there was no warranty, the question arises whether Esso are liable for negligent mis-statement under the doctrine of *Hedley Byrne & Co Ltd v Heller & Partners Ltd*.[9] It has been suggested that *Hedley Byrne*[9] cannot be used so as to impose liability for negligent pre-contractual statements; and that, in a pre-contract situation, the remedy (at any rate before the 1967 Act) was only in warranty or nothing . . .

. . . [I] cannot accept counsel for Esso's proposition. It seems to me that *Hedley Byrne*,[9] properly understood, covers this particular proposition: if a man, who has or professes to have special knowledge or skill, makes a representation by virtue thereof to another—be it advice, information or opinion—with the intention of inducing him to enter into a contract with him, he is under a duty to use reasonable care to see that the representation is correct, and that the advice, information or opinion is reliable. If he negligently gives unsound advice or misleading information or expresses an erroneous opinion, and thereby induces the other side into a contract with him, he is liable in damages. This proposition is in line with what I said in *Candler v Crane Christmas & Co*,[10] which was approved by the majority of the Privy Council in *Mutual Life and Citizens' Assurance Ltd v Evatt*.[11] And the judges of the Commonwealth have shown themselves quite ready to apply *Hedley Byrne*[9] between contracting parties: see, in Canada, *Sealand of the Pacific Ltd v Ocean Cement Ltd*[12] and, in New Zealand, *Capital Motors Ltd v Beecham*.[13]

Applying this principle, it is plain that Esso professed to have—and did in fact have—special knowledge or skill in estimating the throughput of a filling station. They made the representation—they forecast a throughput of 200,000 gallons—intending to induce Mr Mardon to enter into a tenancy on the faith of it. They made it negligently. It was a 'fatal error'. And thereby induced Mr Mardon to enter into a contract of tenancy that was disastrous to him. For this misrepresentation they are liable in damages.

Damages

Now for the measure of damages. Mr Mardon is not to be compensated here for 'loss of a bargain'. He was given no bargain that the throughput *would* amount to 200,000 gallons a year. He is only to be compensated for having been induced to enter into a contract which turned out to be disastrous for him. Whether it be called breach of warranty or negligent misrepresentation, its effect was *not* to warrant the throughput, but only to induce him to enter into the contract. So the damages in either case are to be measured by the loss he suffered. Just as in the case of *Doyle v Olby (Ironmongers) Ltd*,[14] he can say: 'I would not have entered into this contract at all but for your representation. Owing to it, I have lost all the capital I put into it. I also incurred a large overdraft. I have spent four years of my life in wasted endeavour without reward; and it will take me some time to re-establish myself.'

For all such loss he is entitled to recover damages. It is to be measured in a similar way as the loss due to a personal injury. You should look into the future so as to forecast what would have been likely to happen if he had never entered into this contract; and contrast it with his position as it is now as a result of entering into it. The future is necessarily problematical and can only be a rough-and-ready estimate. But it must be done in assessing the loss.

Now for the new agreement of 1st September 1964. The judge limited the loss to the period from April 1963 to September 1964, when the new agreement was made. He said that from 1st September 1964 Mr Mardon was carrying on the business 'on an entirely fresh basis, of which the negligent mis-statement formed no part'.

I am afraid I take a different view. It seems to me that from 1st September 1964, Mr Mardon acted most reasonably. He was doing what he could to retrieve the position, not only in his own interest, but also in the interest of Esso. It was Esso who were anxious for him to stay on. They had no other suitable tenant to replace him. They needed him to keep the station as a going concern and sell their petrol. It is true that by this time the truth was known, that the throughput was very short of 200,000 gallons, but nevertheless, the effect of the original mis-statement was still there. It laid a heavy hand on all that followed. The new agreement was an attempt to mitigate the effect. It was not a fresh cause which eliminated the past. It seems to me that the losses after 1st September 1964 can be attributed to the original mis-statement, just as those before . . .

Ormrod and Shaw LJJ agreed that the appeal should be allowed.

Appeal allowed; cross-appeal dismissed.
Subsequently the court approved the terms of a settlement between the parties as to the damages to be paid to Mr Mardon which was indorsed on counsels' briefs but not made public.

1 [1913] AC 30, [1911–13] All ER Rep 83.
2 [1913] AC 30 at 47, [1911–13] All ER Rep 83 at 90.
3 [1965] 2 All ER 65 at 67, [1965] 1 WLR 623 at 627 [above, p 20].
4 [1927] AC 177, [1926] All ER Rep 343.
5 (1922) 27 Com Cas 296.
6 [1958] 2 Lloyd's Rep 449 at 455–7.
7 See particularly [1927] AC at 183, 184, [1926] All ER Rep at 346, 347.
8 [1975] 1 All ER at 215, 216, [1975] QB at 825, 826.
9 [1963] 2 All ER 575, [1964] AC 465.
10 [1951] 1 All ER 426 at 433, 434, [1951] 2 KB 164 at 179, 180.
11 [1971] 1 All ER 150, [1971] AC 793.
12 (1973) 33 DLR (3d) 625.
13 [1975] 1 NZLR 576.
14 [1969] 2 All ER 119, [1969] 2 QB 158.

Note. Some assistance on the quantification of damages where a projected earnings forecast was not made with reasonable care is to be derived from *Lion Nathan Ltd v CC Bottlers Ltd* [1996] 1 WLR 1438 (PC).

As the above cases and *Lambert v Lewis* [1980] 1 All ER 978, CA, below, pp 62–3, indicate there is a wide range of options available in the classification of statements made in a contractual context. The English approach, requiring that contractual warranties be dependent on promissory intent (see *Heilbut, Symons & Co v Buckleton* [1913] AC 30, HL), has not always found favour in other common law jurisdictions. For example, in the United States Uniform Commercial Code Art 2–313 the test is whether the relevant affirmation of fact or promise is 'part of the basis of the bargain'. An alternative approach is to place emphasis on the question of 'reliance'. This is the approach preferred by the Ontario Law Reform

Commission in its 'Report on Sale of Goods' (1979) (see ch 6, pp 135–45). The accompanying draft Bill contains the following provision.

Report on Sale of Goods 1979 (Ontario Law Reform Commission)

5.10. Express warranties by seller, etc

(1) A representation or promise in any form relating to goods that are the subject of a contract of sale made by the seller, manufacturer or distributor of the goods is an express warranty and binding upon the person making it,

    (a) if the natural tendency of such representation or promise is to induce the buyer, or buyers generally if the representation or promise is made to the public, to rely thereon; and

    (b) if, in the case of a representation or promise not made to the public, the buyer acts in reliance upon the representation or promise.

Irrelevant factors

(2) Subsection 1 applies to a representation or promise made before or at the time the contract was made and whether or not,

    (a) it was made fraudulently or negligently;

    (b) there is privity of contract between the person making the representation or promise and the buyer;

    (c) it was made with a contractual intention; or

    (d) any consideration was given in respect of it.

Express warranties by buyer

(3) This section applies *mutatis mutandis* to a representation or promise made by the buyer.

(For further reference to manufacturers' express warranties see below, p 57 et seq.)

In English law the importance of distinguishing between contractual terms and 'mere representations' has been considerably reduced by two developments referred to in *Esso Petroleum Co Ltd v Mardon* [1976] 2 All ER 5, [1976] 2 WLR 583, above, p 22. The first is the decision in *Hedley Byrne & Co Ltd v Heller & Partners Ltd* [1964] AC 465, [1963] 2 All ER 575, HL, and the second is the Misrepresentation Act 1967. Both now provide a remedy in damages for negligent misrepresentations. The *Hedley Byrne* decision is discussed in detail in the standard texts on the law of tort: see, for example, Markesinis & Deakin, *Tort Law* (3rd edn, 1994), pp 86–99; *Winfield & Jolowicz on Tort* (14th edn, 1994), pp 290–305; *Street on Torts* (9th edn, 1993), pp 206–12. For discussion of the Misrepresentation Act 1967 see Treitel, op cit, at p 324 et seq; Cheshire, Fifoot and Furmston, op cit, at p 288 et seq; Atiyah and Treitel (1967) 30 MLR 369.

By s 2(1) of the 1967 Act it is the person making the statement who has the onus of proving a reasonable ground for believing it to be true. In this the Act has an advantage over the *Hedley Byrne* principle where it is the plaintiff representee who must establish negligence. The Act may have an advantage also where the representation is made innocently and without fault since by s 2(2) damages may be awarded in lieu of the traditional remedy of rescission.

It is in relation to the approach to quantifying damages that it is most likely that the distinction between representations and warranties will remain important. In very general terms damages for breach of contract are awarded to place the plaintiff in the position he would have enjoyed if the contract had been performed and the promise fulfilled whereas in tort damages are awarded to compensate for losses incurred through reliance on the representation. There are differences also in the rules governing remoteness of damage where the 'reasonable foreseeability' test in tort is perhaps somewhat less restrictive than the equivalent 'reasonable contemplation of the parties' test in contract. For more detailed discussion of damages in contract and tort respectively see Cheshire, Fifoot and Furmston, op cit, at pp 607–24; Treitel, op cit, at pp 838–912; Street, op cit, at pp 249–64; Winfield and Jolowicz , op cit, at pp 147–88, 632–75.

It is clear that it is the tort-based approach which applies where the claim is based on the *Hedley Byrne* principle. Similarly, the better view is that the same approach is applicable to actions based on the Misrepresentation Act 1967, s 2: see *Andre & Cie SA v Ets Michel Blanc & Fils* [1977] 2 Lloyds Rep 166 at 181 (Ackner J); *F & H Entertainments Ltd v Leisure Enterprises Ltd* (1976) 120 Sol Jo 331 (Walton J); *Naughton v O'Callaghan* [1990] 3 All ER 191 at 196 (Waller J); Cheshire, Fifoot and Furmston, op cit, at p 304; Treitel, op cit, at p 334, but contrast *Jarvis v Swan's Tours Ltd* [1973] QB 233, [1973] 1 All ER 71, CA; *Watts v Spence* [1976] ch 165, [1975] 2 All ER 528. More controversially, it has also been held that damages under s 2(1) of the 1967 Act should be calculated on the basis of the same principles as apply to the tort of deceit: see *Royscot Trust Ltd v Rogerson* [1991] 2 QB 297, [1991] 3 All ER 294. These principles are more favourable than the standard rules applicable to the law of negligence: see *Smith New Court Securities Ltd v Scrimgeour Vickers (Asset) Management Ltd* [1996] 3 WLR 1051.

Finally it is important to note that the *Hedley Byrne* principle applies even though there is no apparent contract between the parties. Indeed this is its principal sphere of application. Conversely it has been held that the 1967 Act applies only where there is a contractual relationship between the parties and not, for example, when the defendant is merely acting as an agent for a third party: see *Resolute Maritime Inc v Nippon Kaiji Kyokai, The Skopas* [1983] 2 All ER 1, [1983] 1 WLR 857. The point may be of some importance when consumers deal with travel agents, estate agents and other agents.

PROBLEMS

In the light of the above materials consider the following cases:
1. Boswell owns an art gallery in which he displays an unsigned painting. Jonson, a private collector, shows an interest in the work and asks Boswell who painted it. Boswell replies, 'It is almost certainly an early Picasso'. Jonson then agrees to buy the painting for £50,000. In fact, and unbeknown to Boswell, it is by another artist and worth only £500. As an early Picasso it would have been worth £500,000. Twelve months later Jonson discovers the true facts.

   Advise Jonson. Would your advice be different if Boswell had been a private collector selling off part of his collection?
2. Ada is approached by Bert, a seller of double-glazing systems. Bert asks her

what her annual heating bill is and Ada replies, '£600'. Bert says, 'We estimate that in an average year you would save a good £150 with our system'. Ada has the system installed at a cost of £3,000. In the following year (when the weather is 'normal') Ada's savings are only £50. She expects to continue to live in the house for another thirty or so years.

Advise Ada. How, if at all, would it affect the position if Bert had added, 'At the very least we can guarantee savings of £100'?

3. Chisel, a private collector of objets d'art, approaches Hammer, an auctioneer, and asks him to sell a vase on his behalf. Chisel describes it as 'early Ming' and this description is printed in Hammer's catalogue. Chisel knows that the description is entirely erroneous but Hammer believes it to be correct. The vase is bought by Sickle, a private collector. Six months later Sickle discovers the truth.

Advise Sickle as to any remedy which he may have against (i) Chisel and (ii) Hammer, assuming there are no relevant conditions of sale. (See, in an analogous context, *Harlingdon & Leinster Enterprises Ltd v Christopher Hull Fine Art Ltd* [1990] 1 All ER 737, [1991] 1 QB 564, below, p 88.)

4. TV World, advertising in the local Leamington Spa press, states 'We will beat any TV HiFi and Video price by £50 on the spot'. A similar notice is displayed outside its high street shop. Peter sees a television set on sale in a high street shop for £199 and he seeks to buy one from TV World for £149. TV World refuses to sell it to him at that price.

Advise Peter. (See *Warwickshire County Council v Johnson* [1993] 1 All ER 299, HL, ch 14, pp 675–9.)

THE CLASSIFICATION OF CONTRACTUAL TERMS

Traditionally, English law has classified contractual terms as either conditions or warranties, the classification being important to the consequences of breach. Prima facie breach of a condition will give 'innocent' parties the right to treat the contract as having been repudiated and also free them from an obligation to perform their own contractual undertakings, whereas breach of a warranty will give rise only to an entitlement to damages. In many consumer transactions there are important implied terms as to quality etc which by statute are designated 'conditions' (see, for example, the Supply of Goods (Implied Terms) Act 1973, ss 9 and 10, below pp 81, the Sale of Goods Act 1979, ss 13 and 14, below pp 80 and the Supply of Goods and Services Act 1982, ss 3, 4, 8 and 9, below, pp 83 and 84). In other contracts the parties themselves may choose to describe a stipulation as a condition, as where an insurance contract provides that the answers to certain questions shall form the 'basis of the contract' (see below, p 187 et seq). The result is to be seen in such cases as *Barber v NWS Bank plc* [1996] 1 All ER 906, (express condition that finance company was owner of the vehicle in a conditional sale). Alternatively, an attempt may be made to stipulate the contrary, as where a contract to install fitted cupboards or double-glazing provides that 'time shall not be of the essence of the contract'. The use by the parties of the word 'condition' will not necessarily be taken as a conclusive indication that they intended that any breach, no matter how trivial, would give rise to an entitlement to treat the contract as having been repudiated: see *Schuler AG v Wickman Machine Tool Sales Ltd* [1974] AC 235, [1973] 2 All ER 39, HL.

Many consumer contracts will contain express terms of varying degrees of importance, for example contracts for the provision of services such as home removals, dry-cleaning, car servicing (where the terms may be incorporated by reference to the manufacturer's handbook) and holidays. In holiday contracts it is obvious that some terms will be more important than others. This suggests that there are benefits in a flexible approach to such matters.

The Law Commission Working Paper No 85 on the Sale and Supply of Goods (1983) contains a helpful discussion of the notion of an innominate or intermmediate term.

Sale and Supply of Goods (1983) (Law Commission Working Paper No 85) pp 26–34

I. SALE OF GOODS

2.24. The first question which we consider is the extent to which the buyer's remedies for breach of one of the statutory implied terms depend on whether the term is classified as a condition or warranty. The position is different in English and Scots law but in both jurisdictions the existing law on this point is, in our view, open to criticism.

The buyer's remedies: conditions and warranties

(i) *English law*
2.25. *The statutory distinction between conditions and warranties.* The word 'condition' is not specifically defined in the Sale of Goods Act, though section 11(3) of the 1979 Act defines it by inference when it states that:

Whether a stipulation in a contract of sale is a condition, the breach of which may give rise to a right to treat the contract as repudiated, or a warranty, the breach of which may give rise to a claim for damages but not a right to reject the goods and treat the contract as repudiated, depends in each case on the construction of the contract . . .

In addition to being defined by inference in this provision, 'warranty' is also defined expressly in section 61(1) of the 1979 Act as:

an agreement with reference to goods which are the subject of a contract of sale, but collateral to the main purpose of such contract, the breach of which gives rise to a claim for damages, but not to a right to reject the goods and treat the contract as repudiated.

The statutory implied terms as to title, description, quality, fitness for purpose and correspondence with sample are all classified as conditions in the Act. The statutory implied terms as to freedom from encumbrances and quiet possession are classified as warranties.

2.26. *Effect of the statutory distinction.* It will be seen that whether a statutory implied term is a condition or a warranty has a profound effect on the buyer's remedies for breach. If the term is a condition, the buyer (provided that he has not waived the condition,[1] or elected to treat its breach as a mere breach of warranty[2] or accepted the goods within the meaning of the Act[3]) can reject the goods,[4] treat the contract as repudiated and recover the price if it has already been paid.[5] If the term is a warranty the buyer is confined to a claim for damages.[6]

2.27. *Developments in the common law.* It was at one time thought[7] that in English law the distinction between conditions and warranties was the main criterion for determining the effects of breach of contract in general. However, this supposition was rejected in *Hongkong Fir Shipping Co Ltd v Kawasaki Kisen Kaisha Ltd*[8] where the stipulation as to seaworthiness in a charterparty was held to be neither a condition nor a warranty but an intermediate or innominate term. It was held that because such a term could be broken in many different ways, ranging from the most trivial to the most serious, the innocent party's right to treat the contract as at an end depended on the nature and effect of the breach in question. The right of the innocent party to treat the contract as at an end depended on whether he had been deprived 'of substantially the whole benefit which it was intended he should obtain from the contract.'[9] This test which is the same as that for frustration makes it extremely difficult for the innocent party to reject. It was extended into the law of sale in *Cehave v Bremer*[10] where an express term that the goods were to be shipped in good condition was breached but it was held that the circumstances were not sufficiently serious to justify rejection. The court relied on section 61(2) of the Sale of Goods Act 1893 in holding that the common law rules preserved by that subsection prevented an exclusive distinction between condition and warranty and allowed the court, where appropriate, to regard a particular express term as innominate.

2.28. This important development has been approved by the House of Lords in more recent cases[11] and it is clear that the statutory classification of terms in the Sale of Goods Act as conditions or warranties is not to be treated as an indication that the law knows no terms other than conditions and warranties.[12] Whether a term is a condition or a warranty or an innominate term depends on the intention of the parties, as ascertained from the construction of the contract. Even if the parties do not expressly classify a term as a condition it may nevertheless be construed as a condition if it is clear what the parties intended. This is more likely if certainty is very important in the context, if the term is one the breach of which is likely to be clearly established one way or the other, or if compliance with the term is necessary to enable the other party to perform another term. In *Bunge Corpn v Tradax*, for example, a stipulation as to time in an f.o.b. contract was held to be a condition: the stipulation regulated a series of acts to be done one after another by parties to a string of contracts.[13] The House of Lords in that case specifically drew attention to the distinction between such a term and a term with a flexible content such as the seaworthiness clause in the *Hongkong Fir*[14] case. The seaworthiness clause can be 'broken by the presence of trivial defects easily and rapidly remediable as well as by defects which must inevitably result in a total loss of the vessel'.[15] Where the same term can be broken both by slight and unimportant departures from the contract and by important and serious defects, it is unlikely, in the absence of some express indication to the contrary, to be the intention of the parties that the innocent party can terminate for every breach (ie the term is a condition) or for no breach (ie the term is a warranty).

2.29. *Assessment of the statutory distinction.* It is, in our view, necessary to assess the statutory classification of implied terms in contracts for the sale or supply of goods in the light of these common law developments. The first point to be made is that it is an essential feature of the implied term as to quality in a sale of goods contract that a breach may vary from the trivial to one which renders the goods wholly useless. Some matters can be easily and rapidly repaired; some defective or unsuitable goods can, and in most cases in practice normally will, be replaced at once. For example, in *Jackson v Rotax Motor and Cycle Co*[16] a large proportion of motor horns delivered under a contract of sale were dented and badly polished but could easily have been made merchantable at a trifling cost. Other departures from the contract, however, cannot be promptly and simply repaired, and either replacement is impracticable or to substitute goods will amount to a new contract. There are many cases in which seriously defective goods have been delivered which could not be replaced or rapidly repaired. Replacement within the terms of the contract may, moreover, be impossible.

2.30. In our view, if the Sale of Goods Act did not classify the implied terms as to quality and fitness as conditions of the contract, a court today would not so classify them in the absence of a clear indication that this was what the parties to the particular contract intended. The present classification of these terms is inconsistent with the developed common law.

2.31. Another, and perhaps more serious, criticism of the classification of most of the implied terms in the Sale of Goods Act as conditions is that it leads to inflexibility and to a danger that the obligation of the seller to supply goods of the appropriate quality will be watered down. If a defect is a minor one the court may be reluctant to allow rejection and so, under the present law, may be tempted to hold that there is no breach at all of the implied term as to quality. This is illustrated by two recent cases to which we have already referred. In *Millars of Falkirk Ltd v Turpie*[17] it was held that it was not a breach of contract to deliver a car in a condition which was admittedly defective and required repair; while in *Cehave v Bremer* Lord Denning MR said[18] that the implied condition was only broken if the defect was so serious that a commercial man would have thought that the buyer should be able to reject the goods. These cases illustrate the difficulties to which the rigid classification gives rise, and lower courts are bound by the precedents thus created. There has, moreover, been express criticism[19] of the inflexibility of the present law as to compliance with description. In several earlier cases[20] the court, in deciding whether the buyer should be entitled to terminate the contract, concentrated entirely on whether there had been a breach of the implied term as to description and not at all on the effect that such a breach had had on the contract as a whole. In one of these cases[21] it was expressly found that the goods were commercially within the specification. Some of these decisions were recently said in the House of Lords to be 'excessively technical'.[22]

2.32. There has also been criticism[23] of the concept of the implied warranty for the breach of which the buyer is only entitled to damages. This criticism has been highlighted by a recent development in the common law relating to remedies for breach of express terms. Although the present state of the law is unclear on the point,[24] recent judicial dicta[25] and some academic opinion[26] have suggested that there may well be circumstances in the law of sale where a deliberate breach of a minor express term or an accumulation of breaches of such a minor term would entitle the injured party to treat the contract as at an end. In other words, the argument runs, there should not be a category of express terms or warranties for the breach of which rejection is never available.

(ii) *Scots Law*

. . .

(iii) *Conclusion for both jurisdictions*
2.37. The conclusion we reach is that in both English and Scots law the classification of the statutory implied terms as conditions or warranties is inappropriate and liable to produce unreasonable results.

---

[1] Section 11(2).
[2] Ibid.
[3] Section 11(4). See paras 2.48 to 2.60, below.
[4] We discuss later whether the seller has the right to require the buyer to accept repair or replacement of rejected goods. See para 2.38, below.
[5] The right to recover the price would appear to be a right in restitution and to be preserved by s 54 of the 1979 Act; see *Chitty on Contracts*, 25th edn (1983), Vol 1, para 4376; *Benjamin's Sale of Goods*, 2nd edn (1981), para 929 and Treitel, *The Law of Contract*, 5th edn (1979), at p 774.

6 See also s 53.
7 *Benjamin's Sale of Goods*, 2nd edn (1981), para 757.
8 [1962] 2 QB 26.
9 Ibid, per Diplock LJ at 70.
10 [1976] QB 44.
11 *Reardon Smith Line Ltd v Hansen-Tangen* [1976] 1 WLR 989 at 998, per Lord Wilberforce;
   Bunge Corpn v Tradax SA [1981] 1 WLR 711.
12 *Bunge Corpn v Tradax SA* (above) per Lord Scarman at 718.
13 Whether a clause laying down the time by which an act must be done is or is not a condition
   still depends, however, on the true construction of the particular clause in question: *Bremer
   Handelsgesellschaft mbH v Vanden Avenne-Izegem PVBA* [1978] 2 Lloyd's Rep 109. Where
   earlier authorities (eg *Bowes v Shand* (1877) 2 App Cas 455, HL and *Behn v Burness* (1863)
   3 B & S 751) have held a clause to be a condition, it is likely that later parties using a similar clause will also be assumed to intend their term to be a condition.
14 [1962] 2 QB 26; see also *The Ymnos* [1982] 2 Lloyd's Rep 574 at 583 per Goff J.
15 Ibid at 71 per Diplock LJ; see also *Toepfer v Lenersan-Poortman NV* [1978] 2 Lloyd's Rep
   555.
16 [1910] 2 KB 937, CA.
17 1976 SLT (Notes) 66.
18 [1976] QB 44 at 62.
19 *Reardon Smith Line Ltd v Hansen-Tangen* [1976] 1 WLR 989 per Lord Wilberforce at 998.
20 See eg *Arcos Ltd v Ronaasen* [1933] AC 470, HL and *Re Moore & Co Ltd & Landauer & Co*
   [1921] 2 KB 519, CA.
21 *Arcos Ltd v Ronaasen* (above).
22 *Reardon Smith Line Ltd v Hansen-Tangen* [1976] 1 WLR 989 per Lord Wilberforce at 998.
   The seller may in some circumstances have the right to replace the goods: for the difficulties and uncertainties that surround this right see para 2.38, below.
23 *Benjamin's Sale of Goods*, 2nd edn (1981), para 758.
24 Ibid.
25 *Cehave v Bremer* [1976] QB 44 per Lord Denning MR at 60, per Ormrod LJ at 82 to 84.
26 Treitel *The Law of Contract*, 5th edn (1979) at pp 608–10.

The above conclusion was not adopted in the final report (whether for consumer or non-consumer transactions) so that (with the exception of Scotland) the
relevant implied terms are still designated 'conditions': see 'Sale and Supply of
Goods' (Law Com No 160, Scot Law Com No 104, Cmnd 137, 1987), at paras
4.15 and 4.21. Elsewhere the Ontario Law Reform Commission has recommended the abandonment of the distinction between conditions and warranties in
contracts for the sale of goods: see the 'Report on Consumer Warranties and
Guarantees in the Sale of Goods' (1972), at p 31 and the 'Report on the Sale of
Goods' (1979) at p 151.

PROBLEMS

The above discussion is concerned with contracts for the supply of goods where
there are sound arguments for adopting the 'wait and see' approach of the
Hongkong Fir Shipping case. However, such an approach may be difficult to apply
in practice in other consumer contracts.
    Consider the following case.

A brochure advertising an 'Ideal 3 day Christmas break' at the Belleview Hotel states that; 'Baby sitting facilities are always available to ensure a complete rest.' On arrival at the hotel on Christmas eve clients are informed that these facilities have been withdrawn. Benjamin and Chitty both wish to cancel their holiday. Benjamin has eight young children. Chitty has no children but he fears that the lack of such facilities will mean that dinners will be far less peaceful than he had expected.

Advise Benjamin and Chitty.

ADOPTING A MANUFACTURER'S REPRESENTATIONS

Later in this chapter we consider the extent to which manufacturers of goods may be held liable for failure to meet their general advertising or promotional claims (see below, at pp 57–70 and for discussion of manufacturers' guarantees, see below, at pp 274–8). Here we raise a related and similarly basic issue on which there seems to be a curious dearth of English authority or discussion in point.

Cochran v McDonald. 161 Pacific Reporter, 2d series 305 (1945), Supreme Court of Washington

The facts are stated in the judgment of Grady J.

Grady Justice: This action was originally brought by O. K. Cochran against Winterine Manufacturing Company, a corporation, to recover damages for breach of warranty. In an amended complaint H. D. McDonald, doing business as McDonald & Company, was joined as a defendant. The plaintiff was unable to secure legal service of process upon Winterine Manufacturing Company, and the case proceeded to trial against McDonald & Company as the sole defendant. At the close of the evidence submitted by the plaintiff its sufficiency was challenged by the defendant, which challenge was sustained by the court and a judgment was entered dismissing the action. The motion of the plaintiff for a new trial was denied and this appeal followed.

The factual situation as disclosed by the record is as follows: Winterine Manufacturing Company manufactured a product known as Antarctic Antifreeze to be used in motor vehicles to prevent freezing in cold weather. The company assigned to respondent the western part of Washington for the distribution of its product and he purchased from it a large quantity of the antifreeze. The antifreeze was put up in sealed gallon jugs and to each jug the manufacturer affixed a label upon which was printed the following:

'Antarctic Antifreeze. The Manufacturer's Guarantee on Antarctic Antifreeze is Insured by an Old Line Casualty Company. Manufactured by Winterine Manufacturing Company, Denver, Colorado.

'Guarantee. The Manufacturer of this Antifreeze Guarantees: 1. If used according to directions, in a normal cooling system, Antarctic Antifreeze will protect the cooling system from freezing for a full winter season. 2. It will not cause rust or deteriorate the hose, radiator or engine of your car. 3. It will not cause damage to the finish of your car. 4. It will not evaporate. 5. It will not leak out of a cooling system tight enough to hold water.

'Directions for Use. Do not mix with any other antifreeze. Drain cooling system, make certain it is clean and leakproof. Put in proper amount of Antarctic to afford the required freezing protection. (See your dealer's "Protective Chart.") Add water. Fill to within about 2 inches of top of radiator.'

The respondent sold a quantity of the antifreeze to Huletz Auto Electric Co and it resold to a Texaco service station. The appellant purchased a gallon jug of the antifreeze from the service station. Before making the purchase appellant read what was on the label. He testified that this induced him to buy the antifreeze and that he relied upon the representations printed thereon. Appellant put the antifreeze in the radiator of his automobile. Damage was done to the radiator and motor of appellant's automobile. An analysis of the antifreeze showed that it contained highly corrosive elements and was unfit for the purpose designed. The inherently dangerous character of the article was not known to respondent and there was nothing about it as handled by him indicating anything out of the ordinary. It was only upon use of the antifreeze that its character became known.

The appellant presents three grounds of liability of respondent to him:

(1) Upon the express warranty printed upon the label affixed to the article by the manufacturer.

(2) Upon an implied warranty of fitness for the purpose intended when the article resold is noxious and dangerous to property.

(3) Upon an implied warranty of fitness for the purpose intended under the Uniform Sales Act.

We shall discuss the foregoing in the order set forth.

(1) The question presented is whether a wholesaler, who purchases goods from the manufacturer of them who has affixed a written warranty of quality or fitness for the purpose intended by reselling the goods to a vendee is liable upon the warranty to an ultimate purchaser who relies upon the warranty in making his purchase, puts the goods to use and suffers damage to his property by reason of a breach of the warranty.

In our discussion of this branch of the case we shall refer only to express warranties as the subject of implied warranty is treated later in this opinion.

[1] We have not found in our research many cases dealing with the precise question we are now considering, but the courts passing upon the question, and the text writers, seem to agree that the applicable principle of law is that a dealer is not liable upon an express warranty of a manufacturer which is put out with or attached to the goods manufactured unless he, in some way, adopts the warranty and makes it his own when selling the goods to others, and that by merely selling the goods he does not adopt the warranty of the manufacturer as his own. *Pemberton v Dean* 88 Minn 60, 92 NW 478, 60 LRA 311, 97 Am St Rep 503; *Cool v Fighter* 239 Mich 42, 214 NE 162; *Wallace et al v McCampbell* 178 Tenn 224, 156 SW2d 442, 55 CJ Sales, 684, § 687.

In 55 CJ, supra, the author states:

'A purchaser of personal property with warranty, who in reselling it to another adopts, by his conduct at the resale, the warranty of his seller, thereby assumes a warranty of the same character as that which was expressly accorded to him. The fact of resale does not of itself constitute an adoption of prior warranties so as to render the seller liable for failure of the goods to comply with such warranties; and this is true even though the words of warranty are physically affixed to the goods.'

The *Pemberton* case, supra, although not citing any supporting authority, is a leading case on the subject and is the basis for the text pronouncing the foregoing rule in 24 RCL Sales, 158, § 430, and 46 Am Jur Sales, 495, § 313 . . . We think, under the foregoing authorities, that the correct rule of law is that a vendor of goods is not liable upon the express warranty of the manufacturer unless in making a sale he adopts the warranty as his own, or such warranty is specifically assigned to his vendee.

[2] The respondent in this case did not sell the antifreeze to appellant, and having had no transaction with him did not either adopt the warranty as to him or assign the warranty to him. It must follow, therefore, that the respondent is not liable to appellant upon the express warranty of the manufacturer . . .

The court then considered and dismissed the alternate theories on which it was sought to ground liability and concluded:

The judgment is affirmed.

Beals C J and **Simpson** and **Jeffers JJ**, concur.

Steiner J, concurs in the result.

NOTES

1. In the *Cochran* case the respondent was a wholesale rather than a retail dealer but there is no reason to suppose that the court would have adopted a different approach to the express warranty issue if the plaintiff had sued the Texaco garage which sold the antifreeze to him. The *Pemberton* case cited in the judgment involved a retailer (emery wheel warranted as able to operate at 1,800 revolutions per minute).
2. The Ontario Law Reform Commission (OLRC) commented on the decision as follows in its 'Report on Consumer Warranties and Guarantees in the Sale of Goods' (1972) at p 35:

> Taken to its logical conclusion it would absolve the typical retailer of responsibility for the accuracy of the labelling of most of the goods displayed on his shelves, since it is evident that he does not affix them himself. The common assumption of commercial lawyers, and indeed the assumption implicit in many Anglo-Canadian decisions, has been that a retailer does adopt as his own at least the descriptive parts of such labels by the mere act of displaying the goods. If this assumption is correct, the distinction would appear to lie between such descriptive materials and express undertakings by the manufacturer guaranteeing satisfaction and promising some form of redress if the goods are found defective.
>
> The distinction is a difficult one to apply and may give rise to anomalous results. There is some evidence in the *Uniform Commercial Code*[1] that the draftsmen may have intended to hold the seller responsible for all the contents of the labels on his goods. In our opinion, this is a sound approach. The Commission therefore recommends that, in the proposed Act, the rule in section 14 be changed in order to provide that, in a consumer sale, promises or affirmations or fact made on the label or container or otherwise accompanying the goods shall be deemed to be part of the description of the goods, or otherwise an express warranty by the seller, whether the labels or containers originated from the seller or not. It is appreciated that this will impose a heavy onus on the seller, but it appears to us in quality to be no different from the strict liability that is imposed on him under the existing law for breach of the implied warranties and conditions.

> [1] UCC 2–314

(For the implied condition of correspondence with description see generally below, at pp 87–95.)
3. The European Commission has issued a Proposal for a European Parliament and Council Directive on 'The Sale of Consumer Goods and Associated Guarantees' (COM 95), 520, final). Under it conformity of the goods with the contract of sale would require one to take into account 'public statements made about them by the seller, the producer or his representative': Art 2.2(d). See

also Art 3.2 and Art 5 (Guarantees). The proposed directive is printed below, at pp 119–22.

4. The following provision of a Canadian statute provides a possible model for dealing with the point.

Saskatchewan Consumer Protection Act 1996

Express warranties in labels or packages, in advertising, deemed part of description

47(1) A retail seller is a party to express warranties contained on labels or packages accompanying or attached to a consumer product sold by the retail seller to a consumer unless the retail seller has made it clear to the consumer prior to the sale that the retail seller does not adopt the express warranties.

(2) Subject to subsection (3), no retail seller is a party to any express warranties contained in any advertisement originating from or carried out by a manufacturer unless the retail seller expressly or impliedly adopts those warranties.

(3) Notwithstanding that a retail seller does not adopt the express warranties mentioned in subsections (1) and (2), any descriptive statements that appear on the label or container or otherwise accompany the consumer product, for the purposes of clause 48(c), are deemed to be part of the description of the product.

Section 39 of this Act contains the following definitions of 'consumer' and 'consumer product':

(d) 'consumer' means a person who buys a consumer product from a retail seller and includes a non-profit organization, whether incorporated or not, that has objects of a benevolent, charitable, educational, cultural or recreational nature and that acquires a consumer product from a retail seller, but no person who:

   (i) acquires a consumer product for the purpose of resale shall be a consumer respecting that product;

   (ii) intends to use a consumer product in a business or who intends to use the product predominantly for business purposes but also for personal, family or household purposes is a consumer respecting that product, except that where goods are consumer products within the meaning of subclause (e)(ii) the individual or the corporation is a consumer for the purposes of this Part;

(e) 'consumer product':

   (i) means any goods ordinarily used for personal, family or household purposes and, without restricting the generality of the foregoing, includes any goods ordinarily used for personal, family or household purposes that are designed to be attached to or installed in any real or personal property, whether or not they are so attached or installed; and

   (ii) includes any goods bought for agricultural or fishing purposes by an individual or by a family farming corporation but does not include any implement the sale of which is governed by the provisions of *The Agricultural Implements Act*;

The reference in s 47(3) to clause 48(c) is to a warranty that 'where the sale of the product is a sale by description . . . the product corresponds with the description.' By s 53 of the Act, the retail seller is presumed (unless the contrary is clearly indicated) to adopt any 'additional written warranty' which accompanies or is attached to a consumer product—for example, by the manufacturer. In general terms such a warranty is a written undertaking to repair, replace, or make a refund etc in respect of, the consumer product if it breaks down etc (s 39(b)).

5. Another way of approaching the question is via the implied condition of satisfactory (previously merchantable) quality (see generally below, p 95 et seq). The Uniform Commercial Code contains the following provision:

2–314.(2) Goods to be merchantable must be at least such as ... (f) conform to the promises or affirmations of fact made on the container or label if any.

In a later report on Sale of Goods (1979) the OLRC commends this provision (at p 205) as striking 'a reasonable balance between providing no guidance as to what types of representations the merchant-seller is deemed to adopt as his own, and holding him responsible for everything the manufacturer may say . . .'

6. It seems clear that some representations will not be impliedly adopted if only because buyers will not assume that retailers are in any way associated with them. For example, a manufacturer may invite consumers to return goods directly 'if not fully satisfied' (the goods being entirely satisfactory and fit for their purpose). At the other extreme it cannot be doubted that a retailer will be liable (under s 13 of the Sale of Goods Act 1979, below, pp 80, 87–95) if a manufacturer makes incorrect statements (for example on labels or elsewhere) forming part of the goods' description. In between these two extremes there is room for doubt.

PROBLEMS

Consider the civil liability of a retail seller B to a consumer buyer A when B sells to A goods manufactured by D in the following cases:

(i) A buys a garment with a label sewn in reading 'Guaranteed Shrinkproof'. The garment is not shrinkproof.

(ii) A buys a fertiliser on the packet of which is a statement, 'Guaranteed to Double your Yield'. A's yield is not doubled. Would it affect the position if D had made the statement in its general television advertising rather than on the packet and B was (a) aware, (b) unaware of it?

(iii) A buys a cosmetic marked, 'Absolutely safe for all skins'. The cosmetic is neither unsatisfactory in terms of quality (see below, p 95 et seq) nor otherwise defective (see below, p 240 et seq) but A suffers an unpleasant allergic reaction. (The position of D may be considered in the light of the materials printed below, at pp 57–70, 274–8.)

PRIVITY OF CONTRACT

In English law the privity of contract doctrine assumes considerable importance in relation to everyday consumer transactions. Briefly it produces the following consequences for the scope of liability for breach of the implied conditions as to quality etc in a contract for the sale of consumer goods.

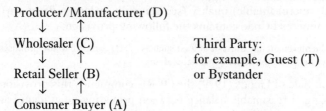

Producer/Manufacturer (D)

Wholesaler (C)　　　　　　　　　Third Party:
　　　　　　　　　　　　　　　　for example, Guest (T)
Retail Seller (B)　　　　　　　　or Bystander

Consumer Buyer (A)

(The arrows indicate respectively goods which are sold 'down' the chain (↓), and a buyer (A) suing (B) who sues (C) and so on (↑)).

In terms of the above diagram the consumer buyer, A, may sue only the retail seller, B, who will then sue the wholesaler, C, and so on up to the manufacturers, D. The corresponding implied conditions will run down the chain from D–C–B–A. If B is insolvent or cannot be traced A cannot seek to sue C or D directly, basing the claim on the implied conditions. Nor for that matter may B sue D directly if B cannot trace C: see *Lambert v Lewis* [1980] 1 All ER 978, CA (revsd in part [1982] AC 225, HL), below, pp 62–3. Of course this is without prejudice to any claims which the parties may formulate on some other basis, typically in tort. This limitation is now widely referred to as the 'vertical' privity barrier. The other barrier of 'horizontal' privity effectively prevents third parties, T, from availing themselves of the benefits of the implied conditions of a contract. Such third parties are not parties to the contract and in a formal sense it is easy enough to understand that they may not benefit from its terms. However, as the following case illustrates, the results may be indefensible in practice. The case is helpful also as illustrating the inter-relation of contract (sale) and tort in this area. When reading it, it should be noted that the Consumer Protection Act 1987 (below, pp 229–55) now imposes strict liability in tort on the manufacturer (D), whether it is A or T who is suing.

Daniels and Daniels v R White and Sons Ltd and Tarbard [1938] 4 All ER 258, King's Bench Division

The facts appear in the judgment.

Lewis J: The first plaintiff, Mr Daniels, is a street trader. He hawks and trades in secondhand clothing and secondhand furniture. Mr Daniels claims damages for negligence against R. White & Sons, Ltd, who are manufacturers and bottlers of, amongst other things, lemonade. The second plaintiff, his wife, also claims damages for negligence against R. White & Sons, Ltd. The negligence alleged is that the defendants, in breach of the duty which they owed to the plain-tiffs, supplied a bottle of lemonade which in fact contained carbolic acid. The bottle of lemon-ade was in fact obtained by the male plaintiff from a Mrs Tarbard, the licensee of a public-house known as the Falcon Arms, Falcon Terrace, Battersea, in the county of London. Both plaintiffs allege as against the first defendants, who are, as I say, manufacturers and bottlers, that they did not exercise reasonable care as manufacturers to prevent injury being done to the consumers or purchasers of their wares. The male plaintiff also sues Mrs Tarbard, from whom the bottle of lemonade was actually obtained, alleging, first of all, that, under the Sale of Goods Act, in the circumstances there was an implied warranty that the lemonade was reasonably fit for the pur-pose of drinking, that it contained no deleterious and noxious matter, and/or that it was of mer-chantable quality, relying, as I read that plea, upon the Sale of Goods Act 1893, s 14(1), (2).

On July 23, the male plaintiff, who was a customer of the Falcon Arms, went into the Falcon Arms at about 7 pm with a jug, in order to purchase a jug of beer, and, as he said, a bottle of R. White's lemonade, which is the lemonade made and bottled by the first defendants . . .

Having obtained his jug of beer and his bottle of lemonade, he then proceeded quite a short distance to his own home. It was a very hot day. On arriving home, the first thing he did was to take out the stopper of the lemonade bottle, having first of all torn away the paper label which was stuck over the top of the bottle, which paper label I find was intact when it was sold to him. Having opened the bottle, he then poured a little lemonade into the jug of beer . . . Both hus-band and wife drank almost simultaneously, and they both immediately realised that there was something burning in the liquid which they had taken, and they at once thought they had been poisoned. I need not go into the details, but in fact it was estimated, on an analysis of what remained in the bottle, that that bottle of lemonade contained 38 grains of carbolic acid, and that would amount to half-a-teaspoonful . . .

That was the case for the plaintiffs, and at the end of the plaintiffs' case a submission that there was no case to answer was made to me by counsel for the first defendants. The position was this. After a certain discussion for the purpose of the submission, it was said that they had to assume and accept that here was a bottle which, when purchased, quite properly had its stop-per in, and also had the label pasted over the top, but which, on the evidence called by the plain-tiffs at that stage, contained carbolic acid, and that, as a result of drinking the contents of the bottle, the two plaintiffs had suffered damage. That, said counsel for the first defendants—and he said it quite accurately—is the only evidence in the case. He prayed in aid a statement which is to be found at the end of the opinion of Lord Macmillan in *M'Alister (or Donoghue) v Stevenson*,[1] in which, said counsel, Lord Macmillan was saying that those facts are not sufficient to establish a *prima facie* case. Lord Macmillan said, at p 622:

The burden of proof must always be upon the injured party to establish that the defect which caused the injury was present in the article when it left the hands of the party whom he sues, that the defect was occasioned by the carelessness of that party, and that the circumstances are such as to cast upon the defender a duty to take care not to injure the pursuer. There is no presumption of negligence in such a case as the present, nor is there any justification for applying the maxim, *res ipsa loquitur*. Negligence must be both averred and proved. The appellant accepts this burden of proof, and in my opinion she is entitled to have an opportunity of discharging it if she can . . .

His Lordship considered the evidence against the manufacturer and continued:

Even if the true view be that there was here a case for the defendants to answer, I am quite satisfied that they have answered it, and that the plaintiffs, as a result, have entirely failed to prove to my satisfaction that the defendant company were guilty of a breach of their duty toward the plaintiffs—namely, a duty to take reasonable care to see that there should be no defect which might injure the plaintiffs. For that reason, I think that the plaintiffs' claim against the first defendants fails . . .

With regard to the other defendant, I confess that there is one consideration which ought really perhaps to be taken into account, and that is this. She was, of course, entirely innocent and blameless in the matter. She had received the bottle three days before from the first defendants, and she sold it over the counter to the husband, and the husband, of course, is the only one who has any rights in contract and breach of warranty against her. There is no issue of fact between the husband and Mrs Tarbard. They entirely agree as to what happened—namely, that Mr Daniels came into the public-house, the licensed premises, and said, 'I want a bottle of R. White's lemonade,' and R. White's lemonade was what she gave him. The question which arises is, on those facts, the bottle in fact containing carbolic acid, and, the lemonade, therefore, not being of merchantable quality, whether or not the second defendant is liable.

. . . If it is a case of goods sold by description by a seller who deals in goods of that description, there is an implied condition that the goods shall be of merchantable quality. Unfortunately for Mrs Tarbard, through no fault of hers, the goods were not of merchantable quality. It was suggested by Mr Block that there was an opportunity of examination so as to bring the matter within the proviso to s 14(2) of the Act, and he cited an authority to me, but I do not think that the authority takes him the length which he would wish it to do. I therefore find that this was a sale by description, and therefore hold—with some regret, because it is rather hard on Mrs Tarbard, who is a perfectly innocent person in the matter—that she is liable for the injury sustained by Mr Daniels through drinking this bottle of lemonade. However, that, as I understand it, is the law and therefore I think that there must be judgment for Mr Daniels, who is the only person who can recover against Mrs Tarbard.

Judgment for the male plaintiff against the second defendant for £21 15s, and judgment for the first defendants against both plaintiffs. Costs on the High Court scale.

[1] [1932] AC 562.

Some of the points which emerge from this case are discussed in later chapters, for example the fact that Mrs Tarbard was liable in contract although she was 'perfectly innocent' (see below, pp 118–19) and the standard of care demanded of manufacturers at common law (see below, p 204 et seq). As to the latter it may be said that negligence would be inferred much more readily nowadays.

One limited way of escaping from the constraints of horizontal privity is suggested by the following case.

Lockett v A & M Charles Ltd [1938] 4 All ER 170, King's Bench Division

The plaintiffs, who were husband and wife, stopped for lunch at a hotel at Bray owned by the defendant company. The meal included whitebait, and the female plaintiff, having swallowed a mouthful, refused to eat the remainder. Subsequently she was taken ill. The plaintiffs claimed that the food was unfit for human consumption and that there was a breach of an implied term of the contract under which the meal was supplied.

Tucker J, having stated that he was satisfied that the plaintiff's food poisoning had been caused by the whitebait, continued: With regard to the female plaintiff's position in respect of breach of warranty, every proprietor of a restaurant is under a duty to take reasonable care to see that the food which he supplies to his guests is fit for for human consumption. If he does not take such reasonable steps, and if he is negligent, a person who buys the food which he supplies can recover damages from him based on his negligence. As, however, there is no allegation of such negligence in this case, it must be assumed that the proprietor of the hotel and his servants could not be at fault in any way, and either plaintiff can recover only if he or she establishes that there was a contract between him or her and the proprietor of the hotel.

Counsel for the defendants submitted that, where a man and a woman, be they husband and wife or not, go into a restaurant and the man orders dinner, *prima facie* the only inference is that the man alone makes himself liable in contract to the proprietor of the hotel. He agreed that every case must depend on its own circumstances, and that there might very easily be circumstances in which that inference could not be drawn, and that there might be a case where it was quite apparent that the woman was going to pay, and that in fact, to use counsel's expression, she was in charge of the proceedings. Counsel also agreed that, where somebody orders a private room at a hotel, entertains a large party, and makes arrangements beforehand, there is no question but that he is the only person who is contracting with the hotel, and that his guests who attend have no contractual relationship with the proprietor of the hotel. Counsel, however, argues that, in the ordinary case where a man and a woman go into a hotel, it is naturally assumed that the man is going to pay for the meal, and that he is the one making the contract, unless there is evidence to the contrary.

In this particular case, there is very little evidence to show precisely what happened in the hotel in that respect . . . It is what may be described as completely neutral evidence, and simply a case where a man and a woman sat down at a table and ordered their food, and I think that I am entitled to assume that the man asked the woman what she would have, and that she accordingly ordered her meal. There was no specific evidence as to who actually paid for the lunch, but everybody is agreed in fact that the husband did.

Counsel for the plaintiffs is, in my opinion, right when he submits that, when persons go into a restaurant and order food, they are making a contract of sale in exactly the same way as they are making a contract of sale when they go into a shop and order any other goods. I think that the inference is that the person who orders the food in a hotel or restaurant *prima facie* makes himself or herself liable to pay for it, and when two people—whether or not they happen to be husband and wife—go into a hotel and each orders and is supplied with food, then, as between those persons and the proprietor of the hotel, each of them is making himself liable for the food which he orders, whatever may be the arrangement between the two persons who are eating at the hotel. On the facts in this case, it is, in my opinion, right to hold that there was a contract implied by the conduct of the parties between the plaintiff, Mrs Lockett, and the defendants when she ordered and was supplied with the whitebait at the Hotel de Paris.

. . . [Where] there is no evidence to indicate to the proprietor of the hotel what the relationship between the parties is, and where there is no evidence that one or the other is in charge of the proceedings, and yet one or the other takes on himself the position of a host entertaining his guests, the proper inference of law is that the person who orders and consumes the food is liable to pay for it as between himself and the proprietor of the restaurant. If that is so, it follows beyond all doubt that there is an implied warranty that the food supplied is reasonably fit for human consumption. I hold that the whitebait delivered in this case were not reasonably fit for human consumption, and that there was a breach of warranty. Accordingly I give judgment for the male plaintiff for the agreed sum of £99 8s, and for Mrs Lockett for £100.

NOTE

The case was decided well before the rise of the feminist movement and some may find it surprising that Tucker J made the assumption on which the plaintiff's success depended. For other cases see *Daly v General Steam Navigation Co Ltd, The Dragon* [1980] 3 All ER 696, [1981] 1 WLR, 120 (boat tickets) and *Benjamin's Sale of Goods* (5th edn, 1997), para 13–016. Of course in a different context a similar

42   The framework of remedies

assumption may lead to less welcome results. By s 3 of the Theft Act 1978 a person commits an offence if he or she 'makes off' without paying, knowing that payment on the spot for a service is 'required or expected' from him or her.

QUESTIONS

Would the result have been different if the evidence was that the husband had
ordered for both himself and his wife? Suppose that they had been accompanied
by a child and that he had been poisoned. Would the child have recovered in contract?

Perhaps predictably it was Lord Denning, MR, who sought in the following
case to make a somewhat more substantial inroad into the privity limitation.

**Jackson v. Horizon Holidays Ltd [1975] 3 All ER 92, [1975] 1 WLR 1468,
Court of Appeal**

The plaintiff, a successful young businessman, had contracted with the defendants for a family holiday in Ceylon for himself, his wife and two young children.
The total cost was £1,200. The holiday was a disaster. The defendants admitted
liability and disputed only the amount of damages payable. The trial court judge
had awarded £1,100, having taken into account the mental distress and inconvenience suffered (see also below, p 165 et seq), but had not itemised the award.

Lord Denning MR, having stated the facts of the case, continued: Counsel for Horizon
Holidays suggests that the judge gave £100 for diminution in value and £1,000 for the mental
distress. But counsel for Mr Jackson suggested that the judge gave £600 for the diminution in
value and £500 for the mental distress. If I were inclined myself to speculate, I think the suggestion of counsel for Mr Jackson may well be right. The judge took the cost of the holidays at
£1,200. The family only had about half the value of it. Divide it by two and you get £600. Then
add £500 for the mental distress.

On this question a point of law arises. The judge said that he could only consider the mental distress to Mr Jackson himself, and that he could not consider the distress to his wife and
children. He said:

' . . . the damages are the Plaintiff's; that I can consider the effect upon his mind of his wife's
discomfort, vexation and the like, although I cannot award a sum which represents her vexation.'

Counsel for Mr Jackson disputes that proposition. He submits that damages can be given not
only for the leader of the party, in this case, Mr Jackson's own distress, discomfort and vexation, but also for that of the rest of the party.

We have had an interesting discussion as to the legal position when one person makes a contract for the benefit of a party. In this case it was a husband making a contract for the benefit of
himself, his wife and children. Other cases readily come to mind. A host makes a contract with
a restaurant for a dinner for himself and his friends. The vicar makes a contract for a coach trip
for the choir. In all these cases there is only one person who makes the contract. It is the husband, the host or the vicar, as the case may be. Sometimes he pays the whole price himself.

Occasionally he may get a contribution from the others. But in any case it is he who makes the contract. It would be a fiction to say that the contract was made by all the family, or all the guests, or all the choir, and that he was only an agent for them. Take this very case. It would be absurd to say that the twins of three years old were parties to the contract or that the father was making the contract on their behalf as if they were principals. It would equally be a mistake to say that in any of these instances there was a trust. The transaction bears no resemblance to a trust. There was no trust fund and no trust property. No, the real truth is that in each instance, the father, the host or the vicar, was making a contract himself for the benefit of the whole party. In short, a contract by one for the benefit of third persons.

What is the position when such a contract is broken? At present the law says that the only one who can sue is the one who made the contract. None of the rest of the party can sue, even though the contract was made for their benefit. But when that one does sue, what damages can he recover? Is he limited to his own loss? Or can he recover for the others? Suppose the holiday firm puts the family into a hotel which is only half built and the visitors have to sleep on the floor? Or suppose the restaurant is fully booked and the guests have to go away, hungry and angry, having spent so much on fares to get there? Or suppose the coach leaves the choir stranded half-way and they have to hire cars to get home? None of them individually can sue. Only the father, the host or the vicar can sue. He can, of course, recover his own damages. But can he not recover for the others? I think he can. The case comes within the principle stated by Lush LJ in *Lloyd's v Harper*:[1]

'... I consider it to be an established rule of law that where a contract is made with *A* for the benefit of *B*, *A* can sue on the contract for the benefit of *B*, and recover all that *B* could have recovered if the contract had been made with *B* himself.'

It has been suggested that Lush LJ was thinking of a contract in which A was trustee for B. But I do not think so. He was a common lawyer speaking of the common law. His words were quoted with considerable approval by Lord Pearce in *Beswick v Beswick*.[2] I have myself often quoted them. I think they should be accepted as correct, at any rate so long as the law forbids the third persons themselves to sue for damages. It is the only way in which a just result can be achieved. Take the instance I have put. The guests ought to recover from the restaurant their wasted fares. The choir ought to recover the cost of hiring the taxis home. There is no one to recover for them except the one who made the contract for their benefit. He should be able to recover the expense to which they have been put, and pay it over to them. Once recovered, it will be money had and received to their use. (They might even, if desired, be joined as plaintiffs.) If he can recover for the expense, he should also be able to recover for the discomfort, vexation and upset which the whole party have suffered by reason of the breach of contract, recompensing them accordingly out of what he recovers.

Applying the principles to this case, I think that the figure of £1,100 was about right. It would, I think, have been excessive if it had been awarded only for the damage suffered by Mr Jackson himself. But when extended to his wife and children, I do not think it is excessive. People look forward to a holiday. They expect the promises to be fulfilled. When it fails, they are greatly disappointed and upset. It is difficult to assess in terms of money; but it is the task of the judges to do the best they can. I see no reason to interfere with the total award of £1,100.

I would therefore dismiss this appeal.

Orr LJ. I agree.

James LJ. In this case Mr Jackson, as found by the judge on the evidence, was in need of a holiday at the end of 1970. He was able to afford a holiday for himself and his family. According to the form which he completed, which was the form of Horizon Holidays Ltd, he booked what was a family holiday. The wording of that form might in certain circumstances give rise to a contract in which the person signing the form is acting as his own principal and as agent for others. In the circumstances of this case, as indicated by Lord Denning MR, it would be wholly unrealistic to regard this contract as other than one made by Mr Jackson for a family holiday. The judge found that he did not get a family holiday. The costs were some £1,200. When he came back he felt no benefit. His evidence was to the effect that, without any exaggeration, he felt terrible. He said: 'The only thing, I was pleased to be back, very pleased, but I had nothing at all from that holiday.' For my part, on the issue of damages in this matter, I am quite content to way that £1,100 awarded was the right and proper figure in those circumstances. I would dismiss the appeal.

Appeal dismissed. Leave to appeal to the House of Lords refused.

1 (1880) 16 Ch D 290 at 321, CA.
2 [1967] 2 All ER 1197 at 1212, [1968] AC 58 at 88.

Although the result of *Jackson's* case is sensible and probably correct, Lord Denning's reasoning has since been disapproved in the House of Lords in *Woodar Investment Development Ltd v Wimpey Construction UK Ltd* [1980] 1 All ER 571, [1980] 1 WLR 277, HL. In a case in which A had contracted with B to pay a sum of money to T Lord Wilberforce said (at pp 576–7):

1. The majority of the Court of Appeal followed, in the case of Goff LJ with expressed reluctance, its previous decision in *Jackson v Horizon Holidays Ltd.*[1] I am not prepared to dissent from the actual decision in that case. It may be supported either as a broad decision on the measure of damages (per James LJ) or possibly as an example of a type of contract, examples of which are persons contracting for family holidays, ordering meals in restaurants for a party, hiring a taxi for a group, calling for special treatment. As I suggested in *New Zealand Shipping Co Ltd v A M Satterthwaite & Co Ltd,*[2] there are many situations of daily life which do not fit neatly into conceptual analysis, but which require some flexibility in the law of contract. *Jackson's* case[1] may well be one.

I cannot agree with the basis on which Lord Denning MR put his decision in that case. The extract on which he relied from the judgment of Lush LJ in *Lloyd's v Harper*[3] was part of a passage in which Lush LJ was stating as an 'established rule of law' that an agent (sc an insurance broker) may sue on a contract made by him on behalf of the principal (sc the assured) if the contract gives him such a right, and is no authority for the proposition required in *Jackson's* case,[1] still less for the proposition, required here, that, if Woodar made a contract for a sum of money to be paid to Transworld, Woodar can, without showing that it has itself suffered loss or that Woodar was agent or trustee for Transworld, sue for damages for non-payment of that sum. That would certainly not be an established rule of law, nor was it quoted as such authority by Lord Pearce in *Beswick v Beswick.*[4]

1 [1975] 3 All ER 92, [1975] 1 WLR 1468.
2 [1974] 1 All ER 1015 at 1020, [1975] AC 154 at 167.
3 (1880) 16 Ch D 290 at 321.
4 [1967] 2 All ER 1197, [1968] AC 58.

A similar view was expressed by Lord Russell (ibid at p 585). Whether the disapproval will make any difference in practice to the quantum of damages awarded in family holiday cases is unclear. A sympathetic judge might choose to place more emphasis on the distress of the contracting party in witnessing the family suffering.

Both the above cases mention agency as a qualification to the privity rule and there is no doubt that this doctrine may have a part to play. Where A contracts with B as an agent for a third party, T, T will have a contract with B and benefit from its terms. However, as Lord Denning noted in *Jackson's* case, above, p 42, agency doctrines usually cannot be applied realistically in everyday consumer transactions, although it seems that they were invoked more recently in *Wilson v Best Travel Ltd* [1993] 1 All ER 353 (Phillips J). Also they can work in reverse since where A contracts only as an agent for T he will acquire no personal rights under the contract.

PROBLEM

Claude asks his son Al, aged five, to go to the local corner shop owned by Bert to buy a tin of corned beef. Al does so, saying to Bert, 'Dad says will you put it on his account please.' Al eats the corned beef for his supper and suffers food poisoning.

Advise Al. See *Heil v Hedges* [1951] 1 TLR 512.

A further implication of privity is that usually a third party is not entitled to benefit from any protection purportedly conferred on him in a contract between A and B. So in the well-known case of *Adler v Dickson* [1955] 1 QB 158, [1954] 3 All ER 397, CA, the master and boatswain of the P and O ship *Himalaya* were not protected by a general exclusion clause in a contract between an injured passenger and the P and O company. The same conclusion was reached on very different facts involving a contract for the carriage of goods by sea in the leading case of *Scruttons Ltd v Midland Silicones Ltd* [1962] AC 446, [1962] 1 All ER 1, HL (stevedores denied protection under bill of lading). However, in this latter case Lord Reid noted a number of ways (including agency) in which such third parties as stevedores might be accorded contractual protection. Not unnaturally those responsible for drafting commercial contracts have since sought—and with some success—so to re-word their contracts as to produce the desired result: see *New Zealand Shipping Co Ltd v A M. Satterthwaite & Co Ltd* [1975] AC 154, [1974] 1 All ER 1015, PC; *Port Jackson Stevedoring Pty Ltd v Salmond and Spraggon (Australia) Pty Ltd, The New York Star* [1980] 3 All ER 257, [1981] 1 WLR 138, PC; cf *The Mahkutai* [1996] 3 WLR 1 (PC) where the extension was held to be inapplicable to an exclusive jurisdiction clause. For comment on these cases see the Law Commission Report on 'Privity of Contract: Contracts For The Benefit of Third Parties' (Law Com No 242, 1996), paras 2.19–2.35.

The recent cases have a distinctly commercial flavour and the precise route to protection (whether agency or the offer of a unilateral contract to the third party) is not always clear. However, the important point is that the higher courts now seem willing to extend protection to third parties on appropriate facts. This may have implications for consumer contracts. The position is discussed further in ch 7, at pp 369–70.

In spite of the opportunities afforded by agency and similar doctrines English law is still committed to the essentials of the privity of contract requirement in both its horizontal and vertical form. Recently, the Law Commission has considered reform of the privity of contract requirement and has made a number of recommendations which, if implemented, would have a limited effect. The following extracts indicate the extent of the proposed changes.

Privity of Contract: Contracts for the Benefit of Third Parties (Law Commission Report No 242, 1996).

Section C Central Reform Issues

Part VII The Test of Enforceability

1. Consultation and Our Recommendation

7.1. In the Consultation Paper the test of enforceability was identified as the central issue involved in reform of the third party rule.[1] The test of enforceability provides the answer to the question, 'When (ie in what circumstances) does a third party have the right to enforce a contract or contractual provision to which he/she is not a party?' The Consultation Paper set out six possible tests. These were as follows:

(i)   a third party may enforce a contract which expressly in its terms purports to confer a benefit directly on him;[2]

(ii) a third party may enforce a contract in which the parties intend that he should receive the benefit of the promised performance, regardless of whether they intend him to have an enforceable right of action or not;

(iii) a third party may enforce a contract in which the parties intend that he should receive the benefit of the promised performance and also intend to create a legal obligation enforceable by him (the 'dual intention' test);

(iv) a third party may enforce a contract where to do so would effectuate the intentions of the parties and either the performance of the promise satisfies a monetary obligation of the promisee to him or it is the intention of the promisee to confer a gift on him;

(v)   a third party may enforce a contract on which he justifiably and reasonably relies, regardless of the intentions of the parties;

(vi) a third party may enforce a contract which actually confers a benefit on him, regardless of the purpose of the contract or the intention of the parties.

. . .

Having considered the responses to the Consultation Paper the Commission's preference was for a modified version of test (iii), the 'dual intention' test.

7.6. We therefore recommend that:

(8) the test of enforceability should be as follows:

(a) a third party shall have the right to enforce a contractual provision where that right is given to him—and he may be identified by name, class or description—by an express term of the contract (the 'first limb');

(b) a third party shall also have the right to enforce a contractual provision[6] where that provision purports to confer a benefit on the third party, who is expressly identified as a beneficiary of that provision, by name, class or description (the 'second limb'); but there shall be no right of enforceability under the second limb where on the proper construction of the contract it appears that the contracting parties did not intend the third party to have that right (the 'proviso').

(Draft Bill, clause 1(1) and 1(3) (the first and second limbs), clause 1(2) (the proviso) and clause 7(1) and 7(2)(a)).

. . .

2. The First Limb of the Test of Enforceability

7.10. This limb is largely self-explanatory. It is satisfied where the contract contains words such as 'and C shall have the right to enforce the contract' or 'C shall have the right to sue'. In our view, it would also cover an exclusion (or limitation) clause designating third parties (eg 'C shall be excluded from all liability to A for damage caused in unloading the goods') because an exclusion clause, as a legal concept, has no meaning unless it is intended to affect legal rights and, where the third party is expressly designated as a person whose liability is excluded, the plain meaning of the exclusion clause is that the third party is to have the benefit of it without having to rely on enforcement by the promisee.[9] We also tend to think that a clause such as 'and the obligation to build to a safe standard shall enure for the benefit of subsequent owners and tenants for a period of ten years' falls within this first limb so as to be enforceable by subsequent owners and tenants. Of course, even express words sometimes give rise to questions of interpretation (as the last example shows) but the great merit of this limb of the test is that it should give rise to very few disputes.

. . .

3. The Second Limb of The Test of Enforceability

(1) General Aspects of the Second Limb

7.17. This limb is concerned to cover those situations where the parties do not expressly contract to confer a legal right on the third party. *In general terms it establishes a rebuttable presumption in favour of there being a third party right where a contractual provision purports to confer a benefit on an expressly designated third party. But that presumption is rebutted where on the proper construction of the contract the parties did not intend to confer a right of enforceability on the third party.* In our view, this second limb achieves a satisfactory compromise between the aims of effecting the intentions of the contracting parties while not producing an unacceptable degree of uncertainty in the law. It is very similar to (and would seem to reach the same results as) the sole test of enforceability in the New Zealand Contracts (Privity) Act 1982. It may also be said to come close to the Law Revision Committee's proposals that the contract must expressly purport to confer a benefit directly on a third party.

7.18. Three features of this second limb are noteworthy:

(i) Express designation by name, class or description is a necessary *but not a sufficient condition* for raising the rebuttable presumption. Although rare, a third party could be designated in the contractual provision that is sought to be enforced even though no benefit is to be conferred on that third party. For example, an employer may take out an insurance policy to cover loss that *it suffers* where a key employee is injured or ill. Although the employee may be mentioned in the relevant contractual obligation of the insurer to pay the employer ('we promise to indemnify [the employer] against loss suffered through the illness of [the employee]') that contractual obligation does not purport to benefit the third party. Again, if A contracts with B to pay him £1000 on C's death or when C attains the age of 21, it is clear that no benefit is to be conferred on C even though C is expressly designated by name.

(ii) The contracting parties must intend the third party to be benefited by the particular contractual provision (that is, the contractual provision sought to be enforced) and not some other contractual provision. Say, for example, a building contractor enters into a design and build contract. The fact that the 'build obligations' expressly purport to benefit subsequent owners does not mean to suggest that the subsequent owners are intended to be beneficiaries of the 'design obligations'.

(iii) The presumption of enforceability is rebutted where the proper objective construction of
the contract is that the parties did not intend the third party to have the right of enforceability. The onus of proof will be on the contracting parties (usually in practice the
promisor), so that doubts as to the parties' intentions will be resolved in the third party's
favour. A promisor who wishes to put the position beyond doubt can exclude any liability
to the third party that he might otherwise have had. But to allay the fears of the construction industry we should clarify that, even if there is no express contracting out of our proposed reform, we do not see our second limb as cutting across the chain of sub-contracts
that have traditionally been a feature of that industry. For example, we do not think that
in normal circumstances an owner would be able to sue a sub-contractor for breach of the
latter's contract with the head-contractor. This is because, even if the sub-contractor has
promised to confer a benefit on the expressly designated owner, the parties have deliberately set up a chain of contracts which are well understood in the construction industry as
ensuring that a party's remedies lie against the other contracting party only. In other
words, for breach of the promisor's obligation, the owners' remedies lie against the head-
contractor who in turn has the right to sue the sub-contractor. On the assumption that that
deliberately created chain of liability continues to thrive subsequent to our reform, our
reform would not cut across it because on a proper construction of the contract—construed
in the light of the surrounding circumstances (that is, the existence of the connected head-
contract and the background practice and understanding of the construction industry)—
the contracting parties (for example, the sub-contractor and the head-contractor) did not
intend the third party to have the right of enforceability.[12] Rather the third party's rights
of enforcement in relation to the promised benefit were intended to lie against the head-
contractor only and not against the promisor. For similar reasons we consider that the second limb of our test would not normally give a purchaser of goods from a retailer a right
to sue the manufacturer (rather than the retailer) for breach of contract as regards the quality of the goods.

. . .

(3) The Application of the Second Limb of the Test to Various Hypothetical Situations

. . .

7.39. 12. B engages A to build a conservatory onto his daughter C's house as a birthday present. Through A's failure to use proper care in constructing the conservatory, C's house suffers structural damage and her valuable collection of orchids is ruined. If A has promised to
confer the benefit (the building of a conservatory using reasonable care) on C, who has been
expressly identified, C will have the right to sue A for breach of that contractual provision (subject to rebuttal by A under the proviso to the second limb).

7.40. 13. Mr B books two rooms in a luxury hotel owned by A Ltd in the Lake District for a
two week holiday for himself and his wife and children. On arrival, the hotel has double booked
and cannot offer alternative accommodation. Mr B's party are forced to stay in a hotel a long
distance away, which, though more expensive, has less celebrated cuisine and few facilities. Mr
B's wife and children, who will have been expressly identified, will have a right to sue A Ltd
(subject to rebuttal by A Ltd under the proviso to the second limb) for any additional expenses
incurred as a result of the hotel's breach of contract, and for the loss of enjoyment resulting
from the double booking.[29]

7.41. 14. On Mr and Mrs C's marriage, their wealthy relative B buys an expensive 3 piece suite
as a wedding gift from A Ltd, a well known Central London department store with a reputation for quality. She makes it clear when purchasing the 3 piece suite that it is a gift for friends
and indeed the delivery slip and instructions show that it is to be sent to Mr and Mrs C's home
and should be left with the housekeeper as it is a gift. After 2 weeks of wear the fabric on the

suite wears thin and frays, and after 3 weeks, two castors collapse. Subject to rebuttal by A Ltd under the proviso to the second limb, Mr and Mrs C can sue A Ltd for breach of an implied term in the contract that the goods be of a satisfactory quality.[30] A Ltd have promised to confer a benefit (the suite of satisfactory quality) on Mr and Mrs C,[31] who have been expressly identified by name.

7.42. 15. Again, the above example, save that A Ltd are entirely unaware that the suite is a gift for anyone, and is delivered to B's home. Mr and Mrs C could not sue A Ltd, since the contract between B and A Ltd does not purport to confer a benefit on Mr and Mrs C, who have not been expressly identified.

7.43. 16. B & Co's standard form of building contract contains an exclusion clause which seeks to exclude the liability to its clients of 'all agents, servants, employees and subcontractors' engaged by B & Co in the performance of the contract works for any loss and damage occasioned other than through wilful misconduct. A & Co, a developer using B & Co's services in constructing nuclear power plants, discovers that one of these is built on dangerously unstable ground, and will have to be decommissioned. The surveyor engaged by B & Co to carry out the site survey, Mr C, has clearly been negligent. Mr C has extensive professional indemnity cover. Mr C seeks to claim the benefit of the exclusion clause in A & Co's contract with B & Co to prevent A & Co from recovering against him in tort for negligence. Mr C would succeed under the first limb of our test or, on the basis that the exclusion clause is a promise to confer a benefit (the exclusion of liability) on Mr C, who is expressly identified by class, under the second limb.

. . .

5. A Special Test of Enforceability for Consumers?
7.54. Some consultees argued that a test of enforceability based on effecting parties' intentions would not go far enough in protecting consumers. Rather they urged us to go beyond effecting the contracting parties' intentions and to *impose* a measure of consumer protection. In effect, their suggestion was that, where the third party is a consumer, reform should be based on options (v) and (vi). Clearly third party consumers stand to gain from our proposals. For example, under our proposals a manufacturer and retailer could expressly confer legal rights on the purchaser to enforce the contract as regards the quality of the goods purchased, thereby affording the purchaser a remedy if the retailer became insolvent.[44] Again a retailer and a purchaser could in their contract expressly confer a right of enforceability on a third party for whom the goods are being bought. Indeed where a contractual provision in the contract of sale purports to confer a benefit on a third party, who is expressly identified, the third party will have a right of enforceability subject to the retailer establishing that, on the proper construction of the contract, the retailer and purchaser did not intend to confer that right.[45] Similarly where a lead holiday-maker makes a booking for a holiday for a number of persons on terms set out in a booking form, the other members of the party will be able to sue in the event of a breach of contract (subject to the proper construction of the contract being that the parties did not intend to confer that legal right).[46] Again in a construction contract between a head-contractor and the owner a subsequent owner or tenant who is expressly given legal rights to enforce the contract will be able to do so: as, subject to rebuttal, will the subsequent owner or tenant on whom the contract purports to confer a benefit and who has been expressly identified.[47]

7.55. However, while our proposals will therefore mean that consumer third parties will have rights that they do not at present have, our proposals do not automatically give consumers such rights. We consider that the automatic conferring of contractual rights on third parties who are consumers rests on policy considerations that need to be tackled in relation to specific areas. We do not think that they can properly be addressed through the kind of general reform with which we are here concerned. Indeed we think that it would be dangerous—in terms of producing a potential conflict of reform proposals—for us here to embark on specific measures of consumer protection when there are other reform initiatives under discussion in specific areas, based on protecting consumers. We have in mind particularly consumer guarantees[48] and the rights of subsequent purchasers or tenants to sue for defective construction work.[49] Rather our strategy is to reform the general law of contract, based on effecting contracting parties' intentions, which then leaves the way free for more radical consumer protection measures in future in specific areas.

7.56. We therefore recommend that:

(9) there should be no special test of enforceability for consumers in our proposed legislation.

[1] See Consultation Paper No 121, para 5.8.
[2] This was the test advocated by the Law Revision Committee's Sixth Interim Report (1937), para 48. The Committee did not analyse its proposed test in detail so that it did not clarify whether the contracting parties must have intended to confer a legal right of enforceability: on the face of it there is no such requirement (so that the test is a wide one) but some of our consultees construed the test as laying down that the parties must expressly confer a legal right of enforceability (so that the test is a narrow one).
[6] The contractual provision could be implied, albeit that the third party must be expressly identified: see examples 11 and 14 in paras 7.38 and 7.41 below.
[9] This means that our reform provides a solution to the enforcement of 'Himalaya' clauses by third parties that does not involve any of the complexity or artificiality that the courts have been forced into in order to render such clauses enforceable: see paras 2.24–2.35 above.
[12] In a classic statement of the law on the proper construction of a contract in *Reardon Smith Line Ltd v Yngvar Hansen-Tangen* [1976] 1 WLR 989, 995–996 Lord Wilberforce said, 'No contracts are made in a vacuum; there is always a setting in which they have to be placed. The nature of what it is legitimate to have regard to is usually described as "the surrounding circumstances" but this phrase is imprecise: it can be illustrated but hardly defined. In a commercial contract it is certainly right that the court should know the commercial purpose of the contract and this in turn presupposes knowledge of the genesis of the transaction, the background, the context, the market in which the parties are operating'.
[29] This is not a package holiday within the Package Travel, Package Holidays and Package Tours Regulations 1992 (SI 1992/3288): see para 2.62 above.
[30] Our understanding is that, although delivery is to be made to a third party, the contract will qualify as a contract for the sale of goods to the promisee for the purposes of the Sale of Goods Act 1979 so that the relevant term will be implied by reason of ss 13–14 of the 1979 Act. But it should be noted that to qualify as a contract for the sale of goods within the definition in s 2(1) of the Sale of Goods Act 1979 ('A contract of sale of goods is a contract by which the seller transfers or agrees to transfer the property in goods to the buyer for a money consideration, called the price') one must assume that, although delivery is to be made to the third party, there is a moment in time at which property first passes to the promisee. Although not directly on the point, we have found the following cases of assistance: *E & S Ruben Ltd v Faire Brothers & Co Ltd* [1949] 1 KB 254; *Jarvis v Williams* [1955] 1 WLR 71. Even if we are wrong on this, one can readily assume that, irrespective of the statute, the courts would normally imply a term that the goods be of satisfactory quality.
[31] If there is to be no delivery to a third party it will normally be difficult to argue that a contract of sale purports to confer a benefit on a third party.
[44] Without such an express term, the purchaser would normally have no such right because even if expressly identified as a beneficiary of the manufacturer's contract with the retailer, the chain of contracts giving the purchaser a remedy against the retailer for the manufacturer's breach means that on a proper construction of the contract, construed in the light of

the surrounding circumstances, the manufacturer and retailer do not intend to confer a legal right of enforceability on the third party.

45 See example 14 in para 7.41 above. Contrast example 15.

46 See example 13 in para 7.40 above.

47 See example 10 in para 7.37 above.

48 See European Commission, *Green Paper on Guarantees for Consumer Goods and After-Sales Services*, COM (93) 509 final, 1993. See also *Consumer Guarantees*, a Consultation Document issued by the Department of Trade and Industry, February 1992.

49 See, eg, *Latent Defects Liability and 'Build' Insurance*, a Consultation Paper issued by the Department of the Environment, April 1995, paras 33–39.

NOTE

As the above extracts indicate, these proposals would have a limited effect on everyday consumer transactions. The requirement of 'express identification' would rarely be satisfied and hence the 'horizontal' privity limitation would remain largely intact (contrast examples 12 and 14 with example 15 in the extract printed above). Similarly, there would be few inroads into the limitations of 'vertical' privity and it would be unusual for a consumer to have a contractual remedy against the manufacturer (see para 7.18 (iii) and note 44 to para 7.54, above). For helpful discussion of the report, see Adams, Beyleveld and Brownsword, 'Privity of Contract—the Benefits and Burdens of Law Reform' (1997) 60 MLR 238.

In some other jurisdictions privity of contract plays a much less significant role. In considering some of the approaches noted below, readers should pay particular attention to whether they breach 'horizontal' or 'vertical' privity or both. A complete picture can be obtained only after considering a manufacturer's liability in tort for economic loss: see below, ch 5, pp 215–22.

The following is a provision of the American Uniform Commercial Code (individual States being free to adopt any—or indeed none—of the three alternatives).

Uniform Commercial Code

§ 2–318 THIRD PARTY BENEFICIARIES OF WARRANTIES EXPRESS OR IMPLIED

Alternative A

A seller's warranty whether express or implied extends to any natural person who is in the family or household of his buyer or who is a guest in his home if it is reasonable to expect that such person may use, consume or be affected by the goods and who is injured in person by breach of the warranty. A seller may not exclude or limit the operation of this section.

Alternative B

A seller's warranty whether express or implied extends to any natural person who may reasonably be expected to use, consume or be affected by the goods and who is injured in person by breach of the warranty. A seller may not exclude or limit the operation of this section.

Alternative C

A seller's warranty whether express or implied extends to any person who may reasonably be expected to use, consume or be affected by the goods and who is injured by breach of the warranty. A seller may not exclude or limit the operation of this section with respect to injury to the person of an individual to whom the warranty extends . . .

A more limited provision is contained in the New Zealand Consumer Guarantees Act 1993, s 24, which provides:

24. *Rights of donees*–Where a consumer acquires goods from a supplier and gives them to another person as a gift, that person may, subject to any defence which would be available to the supplier against the consumer, exercise any rights or remedies under this Part of this Act which would be available to that person if he or she had acquired the goods from the supplier, and any reference in this Part of this Act to a consumer shall include a reference to that person accordingly.

PROBLEM

Jo, a pensioner, buys two tins of salmon from his local supermarket. The salmon is served to Jo and to two guests as part of their afternoon tea. Owing to a defect in the canning process which took place in Canada the salmon is contaminated and the parties become seriously ill. The foreign manufacturer is highly reputable, the supermarket is innocent of all fault and the importer is insolvent.

Advise Jo and his guests on the basis of (i) English law, (ii) UCC Art 2–318, (iii) the New Zealand Consumer Guarantees Act and (iv) the Law Commission proposals.

The following American case is of general interest as a landmark decision even if the theory of liability which it espouses has since been overtaken by a widespread acceptance of an alternative theory of strict liability in tort (see below, ch 5, pp 255–72).

Henningsen v Bloomfield Motors, Inc. 161 A.2d 69 (1960), Supreme Court of New Jersey

The plaintiffs had acquired a new Plymouth sedan car manufactured by the Chrysler Corporation and sold through an authorised dealer. The car had been purchased by a husband as a gift for his wife and the wife was injured when faulty steering caused it to go out of control as she was driving it. There was no evidence of negligence to go to the jury and the case proceeded solely on the issues of the implied warranty of merchantability. The manufacturer's attempted disclaimer contained in a limited warranty or guarantee (described as 'a sad commentary upon the automobile manufacturers' marketing practices') was held to be void as being inimical to the public good. The husband's claim against the dealer (Bloomfield Motors) was straightforward but the remaining claims were more difficult to establish. The court dealt first with the husband's claim against Chrysler.

Francis J . . . Chrysler points out that an implied warranty of merchantability is an incident of a contract of sale. It concedes, of course, the making of the original sale to Bloomfield Motors, Inc, but maintains that this transaction marked the terminal point of its contractual connection with the car. Then Chrysler urges that since it was not a party to the sale by the dealer to Henningsen, there is no privity of contract between it and the plaintiffs, and the absence of this privity eliminates any such implied warranty.

There is no doubt that under early common-law concepts of contractual liability only those persons who were parties to the bargain could sue for a breach of it. In more recent times a noticeable disposition has appeared in a number of jurisdictions to break through the narrow barrier of privity when dealing with sales of goods in order to give realistic recognition to a universally accepted fact. The fact is that the dealer and the ordinary buyer do not, and are not expected to, buy goods, whether they be foodstuffs, or automobiles, exclusively for their own consumption or use . . .

Although only a minority of jurisdictions have thus far departed from the requirement of privity, the movement in that direction is most certainly gathering momentum. Liability to the ultimate consumer in the absence of direct contractual connection has been predicated upon a variety of theories. Some courts hold that the warranty runs with the article like a covenant running with land; others recognize a third-party beneficiary thesis; still others rest their decision on the ground that public policy requires recognition of a warranty made directly to the consumer . . .

Under modern conditions the ordinary layman, on responding to the importuning of colorful advertising, has neither the opportunity nor the capacity to inspect or to determine the fitness of an automobile for use; he must rely on the manufacturer who has control of its construction, and to some degree on the dealer who, to the limited extent called for by the manufacturer's instructions, inspects and services it before delivery. In such a marketing milieu his remedies and those of persons who properly claim through him should not depend 'upon the intricacies of the law of sales'. The obligation of the manufacturer should not be based alone on privity of contract. It should rest, as was once said, upon 'the demands of social justice.' *Mazetti v Armour & Co*, 75 Wash 622, 135 P 633, 635, 48 LRANS, 213 (Sup Ct 1913) . . .

Accordingly, we hold that under modern marketing conditions, when a manufacturer puts a new automobile in the stream of trade and promotes its purchase by the public, an implied warranty that it is reasonably suitable for use as such accompanies it into the hands of the ultimate purchaser. Absence of agency between the manufacturer and the dealer who makes the ultimate sale is immaterial . . .

THE DEFENCE OF LACK OF PRIVITY AGAINST MRS HENNINGSEN

Both defendants contend that since there was no privity of contract between them and Mrs Henningsen, she cannot recover for breach of any warranty made by either of them. On the facts, as they were developed, we agree that she was not a party to the purchase agreement. *Faber v Creswick* 31 NJ 234, 156 A2d 252 (1959). Her right to maintain the action, therefore, depends upon whether she occupies such legal status thereunder as to permit her to take advantage of a breach of defendants' implied warranties.

[26] For the most part the cases that have been considered dealt with the right of the buyer or consumer to maintain an action against the manufacturer where the contract of sale was with a dealer and the buyer had no contractual relationship with the manufacturer. In the present matter, the basic contractual relationship is between Claus Henningsen, Chrysler, and Bloomfield Motors, Inc. The precise issue presented is whether Mrs Henningsen, who is not a party to their respective warranties, may claim under them. In our judgment, the principles of those cases and the supporting texts are just as proximately applicable to her situation. We are convinced that the cause of justice in this area of the law can be served only by recognizing that she is such a person who, in the reasonable contemplation of the parties to the warranty, might be expected to become a user of the automobile . . .

[28] It is important to express the right of Mrs Henningsen to maintain her action in terms of a general principle. To what extent may lack of privity be disregarded in suits on such warranties? . . . It is our opinion that an implied warranty of merchantability chargeable to either an automobile manufacturer or a dealer extends to the purchaser of the car, members of his family, and to other persons occupying or using it with his consent. It would be wholly opposed

to reality to say that use by such persons is not within the anticipation of parties to such a warranty of reasonable suitability of an automobile for ordinary highway operation. Those persons must be considered within the distributive chain . . .

It is not necessary in this case to establish the outside limits of the warranty protection. For present purposes, with respect to automobiles, it suffices to promulgate the principle set forth above . . .

Under all of the circumstances outlined above, the judgments in favor of the plaintiffs and against the defendants are affirmed.

NOTES

1. The approach of the New Jersey Supreme Court may be compared with the traditional approach of Lewis J, in *Daniels and Daniels v R White & Sons Ltd and Tarbard* [1938] 4 All ER 258, above, p 38.
2. For an interesting case decided under the civil law system of Quebec see *General Motors Products of Canada Ltd v Kravitz* (1979) 93 DLR (3d) 481 (Can, SC). The respondent, Kravitz, had purchased a new 1968 General Motors (GM) Oldsmobile car from an authorised dealer, Plamondon. The car had serious latent defects which rendered it unfit for use and on the basis of which the respondent brought an action both against Plamondon and GM. It was held that Kravitz was entitled to succeed against GM by suing on the legal warranty against defects in the contract between GM and Plamondon. Moreover an exemption clause did not defeat the claim.

The reasoning in this case may seem strange to common lawyers but it has implications which should not be overlooked. The inability of Plamondon to rely on an exemption clause as against Kravitz is paralleled by our own provisions in the Unfair Contract Terms Act 1977, s 6 (see below, pp 356–60). However, the same section enables such clauses to operate within the distributive chain (for example between manufacturer and dealer) provided that they satisfy a requirement of reasonableness. If the equivalent of the French 'action directe' were to be adopted in English law presumably it would be necessary to ensure that such protection was not effectively by-passed, so depriving the manufacturer of the protection he would otherwise enjoy. The Law Commission adopted a different approach to third party rights, but recognised a similar danger and concluded that it would not be appropriate to extend the full benefits of the Unfair Contract Terms Act 1977 to third parties (Law Com No 242, paras 13.9–13.13). See further ch 7, p 370 and, for the manufacturer's liability in tort for economic loss, see also below ch 5, pp 215–22.

A statute of a Canadian province contains the following provisions.

Saskatchewan Consumer Protection Act 1996

Subsequent owners

41(1) Subject to subsection (2), persons who derive their property or interest in a product from or through the consumer, whether by purchase, gift, operation of law or otherwise, are, regardless of their place in the sequence of dealings respecting the product, deemed:

(a) to be given by the retail seller or manufacturer the same statutory warranties that the consumer was deemed to have been given pursuant to sections 48 and 50;

(b) to receive from the warrantor the same additional written warranties that the consumer received and, for the purposes of any provision of this Part, unless otherwise provided in this Part:

(i) have rights and remedies against the retail seller, manufacturer or warrantor equal to but not greater than the rights and remedies the consumer has pursuant to this Part; and

(ii) are subject to any defences or rights of set-off that could be raised against the consumer pursuant to this Part.

(2) No retail seller who acquires a product from or through a consumer for the purposes of resale or for use predominantly in a business has any rights pursuant to subsection (1) respecting that product.

Manufacturers deemed to give statutory warranties

50 . . .

(2) Subject to subsection (3), the manufacturer of consumer products is deemed to give consumers of those products the same statutory warranties respecting those products as the retail seller is deemed to have given pursuant to clauses 48(b) to (h).

(3) A manufacturer of consumer products is liable only for the manufacturer's own breach of the statutory warranties or of any express or additional written warranties that the manufacturer has given to consumers and, without limiting the generality of the foregoing, the application of subsection (2) is subject to the following:

(a) no provision of clause 48(b) applies respecting any security interest that is not created by the manufacturer or any lien, charge or encumbrance not arising as the result of any act or default on the manufacturer's part;

(b) no manufacturer is bound by any description applied by the retail seller to the consumer products without the authority or consent of the manufacturer;

(c) for the purpose of clause 48(d), the consumer is deemed to have notice of a defect if disclosure of the defect was made directly or indirectly to the retail seller and was intended by the manufacturer to reach the consumer and in the normal course of events could reasonably be expected by the manufacturer to reach the consumer.

(d) no provision of clause 48(e) applies where, without the consent of the manufacturer, any consumer product:

(i) is sold by a retail seller to a consumer as being fit for a purpose that is not the ordinary purpose of the product; or

(ii) at the time of sale, is in such a state, age or condition that it is unreasonable for the consumer to conclude that it is fit for the purpose for which it is commonly supplied.

No privity of contract required

55. In any action brought pursuant to this Part against a manufacturer, retail seller or warrantor for breach of a statutory, express or additional written warranty, lack of privity of contract between the person bringing the action and the retail seller, manufacturer or warrantor is not a defence, and the retail seller, manufacturer or warrantor is conclusively presumed to have received consideration.

Section 48(b)–(f) is broadly equivalent to the United Kingdom Sale of Goods Act 1979, ss 12–15, below, p 80. For s 48(g) and (h), see below, p 117. For the definition of 'consumer' and 'consumer product', see above, p 36.

Similarly, and as further evidence of what now seems to be a widespread trend against insistence on privity of contract requirements, Australia has adopted the following provision.

Australian Trade Practices Act 1974

74D Action in respect of goods of unmerchantable quality

(1) Where

    (a) a corporation, in trade or commerce, supplies goods manufactured by the corporation to another person who acquires the goods for re-supply;

    (b) a person (whether or not the person who acquired the goods from the corporation) supplies the goods (otherwise than by way of sale by auction) to a consumer;

    (c) the goods are not of merchantable quality; and

    (d) the consumer or a person who acquires the goods from, or derives title to the goods through or under, the consumer suffers loss or damage by reason that the goods are not of merchantable quality;

the corporation is liable to compensate the consumer or that other person for the loss or damage and the consumer or that other person may recover the amount of the compensation by action against the corporation in a court of competent jurisdiction.

(2) Subsection (1) does not apply:

    (a) if the goods are not of merchantable quality by reason of:

        (i) an act or default of any person (not being the corporation or a servant or agent of the corporation); or

        (ii) a cause independent of human control;

occurring after the goods have left the control of the corporation;

    (b) as regards defects specifically drawn to the consumer's attention before the making of the contract for the supply of the goods to the consumer; or

    (c) if the consumer examines the goods before that contract is made, as regards defects that the examination ought to reveal.

(3) Goods of any kind are of merchantable quality within the meaning of this section if they are as fit for the purpose or purposes for which goods of that kind are commonly bought as it is reasonable to expect having regard to:

    (a) any description applied to the goods by the corporation;

    (b) the price received by the corporation for the goods (if relevant); and

    (c) all the other relevant circumstances.

A similar provision is contained in the New Zealand Consumer Guarantees Act 1993, ss 25 and 26.

Within the United Kingdom the Department of Trade and Industry has issued a consultation document on 'Consumer Guarantees' (February, 1992). The document sought views on whether manufacturers or, in the case of imported goods, importers, should be jointly and severally liable with the seller for the satisfactory quality of the goods under the Sale of Goods Act. Similar ideas were mooted in the European Commission Green Paper on 'Guarantees for Consumer Goods and After-Sales Services' (Com (93) 509), 15 November 1993). These ideas were not proceeded with.

MANUFACTURERS' EXPRESS WARRANTIES AND PROMOTIONAL CLAIMS

INTRODUCTION

An earlier section raised the question of the extent to which retailers may be said impliedly to adopt the unsubstantiated claims and misdescriptions of manufacturers whose goods they are selling: see above, pp 33–7. This section is concerned with the liability of manufacturers themselves (other than under a straightforward contract of sale) for express warranties and general advertising or promotional claims. The related question of liability under a manufacturer's guarantee is considered in a later chapter: see below, ch 5, pp 274–8.

EXPRESS WARRANTIES AND PROMOTIONAL CLAIMS

When manufacturers or producers give a personal assurance to a consumer who later acquires the goods through a third party or takes some equivalent step there should be no difficulty in holding them liable under a collateral contract. There are several well-known English cases in point, including *Wells (Merstham) Ltd v Buckland Sand and Silica Co Ltd* [1965] 2 QB 170, [1964] 1 All ER 41 and *Shanklin Pier Ltd v Detel Products Ltd* [1951] 2 KB 854, [1951] 2 All ER 471. In addition such cases as *Brown v Sheen and Richmond Car Sales Ltd* ([1950] 1 All ER 1102), *Andrews v Hopkinson* ([1957] 1 QB 229, [1956] 3 All ER 422) and *Yeoman Credit Ltd v Odgers* ([1962] 1 All ER 789, [1962] 1 WLR 215) were all concerned with the common situation in which assurances are given by a motor dealer with the consumer entering a credit transaction with a finance company thereafter. (For the liability of the finance company on such facts see now s 56 of the Consumer Credit Act 1974, p 299, below).

It is possible to use a similar approach to hold manufacturers civilly liable to consumers where the claims or assurances are not given directly and personally but are contained rather in leaflets and general advertising material. So in *Carlill v Carbolic Smoke Ball Co* [1893] 1 QB 256, CA, the plaintiff was held to be contractually entitled to the £100 reward which the defendants had advertised in the *Pall Mall Gazette* as being payable to anyone who contracted influenza after using the carbolic smoke ball in the prescribed manner. The following case is noted in Borrie and Diamond *The Consumer, Society and the Law* (4th edn, 1981) at pp 108–9.

Wood v Letrik Ltd (1932) Times, 12 January, King's Bench Division

AN ELECTRIC COMB: £500 AWARDED ON A GUARANTEE

Before Mr Justice Rowlatt

His Lordship gave judgment for the plaintiff for the amount claimed in this action, in which Mr Francis Arthur Wood, of Bronwen, Newlands-Avenue, Radlett, Herts, sought to recover from Letrik, Limited, of 70, Milton-Street, EC, vendors of the 'Letrik' electric comb, £500, which he said the defendants guaranteed in an advertisement that they would pay if the comb failed to cure grey hair after 10 days' use.

The case for the plaintiff was that, having read in a periodical an advertisement of the defendants which began: 'New hair in 72 hours. Letrik Electric Comb. Great news for hair sufferers. What is *your* trouble?

Is it grey hair? In 10 days not a grey hair left. £500 guarantee.'

He bought one of the combs and used it as directed, the only result being that, instead of restoring the original colour of his hair, which was prematurely turning grey, it scratched his head and made him feel uncomfortable.

The defendants denied that they guaranteed to pay £500 in such circumstances. That sum, they said, was intended to cover only the return of the price of the combs.

Mr T Eastham KC and Mr Rober Fortune appeared for the plaintiff; Mr F S Laskey for the defendants.

Mr Eastham, addressing his Lordship, said that the plaintiff bought and used the comb on the terms of the offer which he accepted by performing the conditions. The words were a pledge or undertaking to pay £500 in the event of a grey hair being left on the plaintiff's head at the end of 10 days' use of the comb. If an intelligent meaning could be given to the words it could not be said that the phrase meant nothing and was illusory. The point that performance was impossible was a bad one because the advertisement itself stated that the comb actually did what was promised. No coupon qualifying the defendants' guarantee was inserted: they did not alter the advertisement or withdraw the offer, and until they did so it was effective.

JUDGMENT

His Lordship in giving judgment, said that the plaintiff sought to recover £500 under a contract to be found in an advertisement which, according to the construction for which he contended, offered him that sum if he used the comb and it did not cure his grey hair. He said that he had used the comb, that it did not cure his grey hair, and that he wanted the £500.

Claims of that nature had been before the Courts for many years since *Carlill v Carbolic Smoke Ball Company* (9 *The Times* LR 124; [1893] 1 QB 256) and it was quite clear that there was no reason in law why one person should not say to another: 'You use this comb, or this article of mine, and I guarantee to you that it will have certain effects; and I contract with you that if it does not have those effects I will pay you a certain sum.' That was a perfectly good contract. If the conditions were complied with by the user of the article it was simply a question of the meaning of the advertisement and proof of compliance with its terms.

In the advertisement before him it was not specifically stated to whom it was addressed—whether to the purchaser or the user. The present plaintiff was both purchaser and user, but it seemed to him (his Lordship) that the advertisement was clearly addressed, and must be addressed, to the user; and the act of using would certainly be sufficient compliance with the advertisement and a sufficient consideration for the promise.

What did the advertisement mean? In the first place, was it intended as a contract at all or as a mere puff—meaningless but attractive words? The word 'guarantee' was about as emphatic a word in the contract as one could well imagine. He had construed the advertisement according to the plain meaning which ordinary sensible people would attach to it. When people read the word 'guarantee' they understood that the person using it was offering to bind himself to be responsible for the happening, continuance, or existence of a certain state of facts.

As regarded the £500, he was asked to say that that was a mere flourish. He had inquired of Mr Atkinson [director of the defendant company] whether it was, and he replied, 'Yes'. He (his Lordship) did not think that the £500 guarantee could be treated as a mere flourish. It might be a question of what it meant, but it must be treated as a serious statement.

There was another question. It was suggested that the defendants were not really bound by that advertisement at all; that it was not there by their authority. It appeared that the advertisement was inserted through the instrumentality of an advertising agency. The agency might have been contractors, but on behalf of the defendants they put in that advertisement and had sent in their bill including it. It had never been repudiated, nor had any complaint been made about it. He could not take a view other than that the defendants were bound by it.

THE QUESTION OF THE COUPON

In another case the defendants had inserted a coupon which very much limited the meaning of the words '£500 guarantee'. It explained that they only guaranteed £500 as fortifying the repayment of 3s 6d spent on the comb. That was perfectly futile and merely misleading, but the defendants had not put the coupon into the advertisement in the present case, and they were bound by the advertisement as it appeared.

With regard to the impossibility of performance, it was said that to enable the plaintiff to recover he would have to show that the promise was that the hair, already grey, and he (his Lordship) supposed dead, would be rejuvenated, and the actual cells turned to their original colour by the use of the comb; and that, as that was an obvious impossibility, the contract was void, and there was no reality in the consideration.

If a man contracted to do a thing which was obviously impossible it was merely nonsense. If a man contracted to go to the moon he was talking nonsense, and the law recognized no contract of that kind. If a man 100 years ago had contracted that his voice would be audible many miles away it would have been held to be impossible, but he did not see why anybody should think that it was impossible for living grey hair to resume its original hue.

The defendants put in their advertisement the picture of a man whose hair was said to have been thin and going grey, that he looked about 45 and was only 35, and that on the tenth day the greyness had gone entirely, 'the comb having done the trick.' The defendants had also stated in the advertisement that 'not one has failed to do everything we claim for it.'

Then it was said that after all there was no real proof that the advertisement had ever been complied with or the money really earned. One did not regard an action of that kind with favour, but it was not his business to regard it with favour or disfavour. It was rather a windfall for the plaintiff, but he (his Lordship) did not see why Mr Wood should not say: 'Here is a man who says that my hair will be turned to the colour of my boyhood and if it is not I shall get £500. I will try it. I shall be pleased to have my hair dark again.' There was no reason why a man should not take that attitude in all seriousness.

It was contended that the plaintiff did not properly try the comb. The advertisement stated: 'You simply use it in place of your ordinary comb and in the same way.' In the box supplied there was a little blue paper which said: 'To get the full benefit you should use it for five minutes.' The plaintiff said that he combed his hair for several minutes in the morning when he got up and in the evening and that he also took the comb to his office and had a comb now and again when he felt inclined to spare a few moments in going on with the cure. (Laughter.) That was the most natural thing in the world to do.

Then it was said that on the true construction the advertisement could only mean that the comb made the hair grow again through the roots, and that it did not appear that the plaintiff's hair was not growing again from the roots. He (his Lordship) was not impressed by that. If that comb had ever made anybody's hair grow again from the roots he would have listened to evidence on that point with great pleasure, because it would have been very material. Possibly there were numerous persons who could have come and said that the comb had made their hair grow brown again from the roots, though the plaintiff had said that it had not done that for him. The defendants might have called the man at Forest-hill, whose picture appeared in the advertisement and whose hair was said to have been very thin and going grey. If they had called him and he said that the comb had done what was stated he (his Lordship) might have doubted whether the plaintiff had gripped at the roots with his comb.

So soon as the claim was made it was open to the defendants to say to the plaintiff: 'Make an appointment so that somebody may inspect your hair and report on its condition.' That was often done in cases in those Courts, but no such step was taken. He could not doubt that the comb failed in its operation. It was a comb which had a battery in it and if all went well there was probably a circuit set up between the teeth of the comb so that electricity passed to the scalp.

He thought the plaintiff was entitled to recover, that he had complied with the advertisement which amounted to a contract, and that there was no answer to the action.

Judgment for the plaintiff was accordingly entered for the £500 claimed.

A stay of execution for 14 days was granted on the terms that the money was paid into Court.

QUESTIONS

To what extent should it affect the issue if the suggested contract is to do something which is apparently impossible (like going to the moon in 1932)? Was the plaintiff gullible or credulous? Should this matter? (see further below, pp 63–4.) What would you estimate to be the equivalent value today of £500 in 1932?

A similar approach was adopted in the following more recent (if less colourful) case.

Bowerman v ABTA Ltd (1995) 145 New Law Journal, p 1815, Court of Appeal

The notice describing ABTA's scheme of protection against the financial failure of ABTA members which is displayed in offices of tour operators that are members of the scheme would be regarded by an ordinary member of the public as intended to create legal relations with customers of ABTA members and is therefore contractually binding on ABTA in respect of the promises made in the notice.

The plaintiff, a 15-year-old schoolgirl, booked a skiing trip organised by the second plaintiff, a teacher at her school. The tour operator through which the trip was organised was a member of the Association of British Travel Agents (ABTA) protection scheme and prominently displayed a notice as required by ABTA rules 'describing ABTA's scheme of protection against the financial failure of ABTA members'. The notice stated, inter alia, that 'ABTA seeks to arrange for you to continue with the booked arrangement as far as possible'. 'ABTA ensures that you will be able to return to the United Kingdom', 'The scheme is for your benefit' and 'ABTA still protects you'. The trip was later cancelled when the tour operator ceased to trade. A refund of all payments, except a holiday insurance premium of £10, was made to the plaintiff and assigned to another tour operator which took over the arrangements for the trip. The plaintiff claimed that ABTA should reimburse the holiday insurance premium which she had had to pay to the new tour operator. Mitchell J dismissed the claim and the plaintiff appealed.

Waite LJ: [It] is common ground that the question of whether or not ABTA is liable to reimburse the £10 insurance is not to be determined by reference to the specific knowledge or belief of either plaintiff. It rests upon the view that would be taken of ABTA's published statements by a hypothetical figure, namely the ordinary member of the public. For the purposes of this appeal there has only been one such statement to consider from that perspective. It is the [ABTA] notice . . .

The central issue in this appeal is whether the ordinary member of the public, reading the notice as a whole, would regard it as intended to create legal relations between ABTA and those who buy tours or holidays through its members. In searching for the answer to that question, there is little assistance to be gained, in my view, from precedent. *Carlill v Carbolic Smoke Ball Co* [1893] 1 QB 256 is, of course, celebrated authority for the test to be applied in such cases (the impact made by an offer or representation on the mind of the ordinary member of the public), but that is undisputed. Its particular facts are, however, too remote from this case to provide any guidance on the basis of similarity; for what was there under consideration was a brief advertisement announcing unequivocally that the reward would be paid to anyone who contracted influenza after making the required use of the ball for a stipulated period, whereas the issue in this case arises from the equivocation resulting from the introduction of words capable of bearing a promissory or representational meaning into a varied textual context in which words of obligation appear side by side with words of lesser commitment . . .

In the end the case depends, as with so many questions involving construction of a document, upon impression—in this instance an impression gained by the court at one remove through the eyes of the hypothetical member of the public . . . My own view is that the notice—notwithstanding the bewildering miscellany it contains of information, promise, disclaimer and reassurance—would be understood by the ordinary member of the public as importing an intention to create legal relations with customers of ABTA members. The words that are crucial to the present case, 'Where holidays or other travel arrangements have not yet commenced at the time of failure, ABTA arranges for you to be reimbursed the money you have paid in respect of your holiday arrangements', would in my judgment be understood by the ordinary reader as words of clear promise which do not lose their significance or their promissory character through being associated in the same context with words connoting a lesser degree of commitment . . .

I would allow the appeal . . .

Hobhouse LJ: In the present case we have listened to arguments advanced on behalf of the defendants (ABTA) which echo in almost every respect those rejected by the Court of Appeal [in *Carlill v Carbolic Smoke Ball Co* [1893] 1 QB 256] more than a century ago. The main question in the present case is whether those arguments have a greater validity in relation to the differently worded document which ABTA caused to be published and which the second plaintiff, read and relied on . . .

ABTA . . . have made it a corner-stone of the promotion of their members to publish how ABTA protects the travelling and holiday making public from these risks . . . Whether [the notice] contains an offer, whether it is sufficiently clear to be legally enforceable, and whether it discloses an intention to enter into legal relations, all depend upon the evaluation of what is said in this written document . . . The relevant consideration is what, if anything, the document says or offers as between ABTA and the member of the public who reads it and then books with an ABTA member . . . Turning to the document itself, it is accepted that the words of Bowen LJ [in *Carlill*] are apt: 'It was intended to be issued to the public and to be read by the public. How would an ordinary person reading this document construe it?' [The question is] whether the document is simply telling the public about a scheme which ABTA has for its own members or whether it goes further than this and contains an offer which a member of the public can take up and hold ABTA to should the ABTA member with whom the member of the public is dealing fail financially. I prefer the latter view . . . the document has to be read as a whole. It is clearly intended to have an effect on the reader and to lead him to believe that he is getting something of value. The scheme is an ABTA scheme in relation to its members but it is a scheme of protection of the customers of ABTA members. It emphasises that it is 'to protect you their customers' and is 'for your benefit' . . . It is an inevitable inference that what ABTA is saying is that it, ABTA, will do something for the customer if the member should fail financially . . .

In my judgment this document is intended to be read and would reasonably be read by a member of the public as containing an offer of a promise which the customer is entitled to accept by choosing to do business with an ABTA member. A member of the public would not analyse his situation in legal terms but he would clearly understand that this notice would only apply to him if he should choose to do business with an ABTA member and he would also understand that if he did so he would be entitled to hold ABTA to what he understood ABTA to be promising in this document. In my judgment it satisfies the criteria for a unilateral contract and contains promises which are sufficiently clear to be capable of legal enforcement. The principles established in *Carlill* apply. The plaintiffs are entitled to enforce the right of reimbursement given to them. This conclusion also covers the question of intent to create legal relations. The document as reasonably read by a member of the public would be taken to be an offer of a legally enforceable promise . . .

I would allow the appeal.

Hirst LJ dissented.

NOTES

1. In *Carlill v Carbolic Smoke Ball Co* and the above cases the successful claims were in respect of stated or readily ascertainable sums. It is likely that the same will be true of many situations in which manufacturers invite consumers to contact them directly, perhaps through 'flash offers' on the goods themselves or vouchers distributed at the point of sale.

2. A modern example of the dangers associated with advertising when the consequences are not thought through carefully is to be seen in the Hoover 'free flights' campaign in 1992–3. Any person entering into a contract with a retailer to purchase any Hoover product costing £100 or more was promised two free return airline tickets from the UK to the US or various destinations in Europe. It seems that numerous successful claims were brought on failure to honour this promise: see [1995] Current Law, para 1570; *Daily Telegraph*, 9 December 1994 and *The Times*, 28 February 1997.

3. In principle liability might be extended to include claims for unliquidated damages based on a manufacturer's general advertising. In *Lambert v Lewis* [1980] 1 All ER 978, CA the manufacturers of a dangerously designed coupling or towing hitch (Dixon-Bate) claimed in their advertising that it was 'foolproof' and that the pin 'locked absolutely'. However, one such coupling allowed a trailer to become unhitched from a Land Rover, which in turn, led to an accident involving death and personal injury to the plaintiffs. The Court of Appeal proceeded on the basis that the retail seller of the coupling

(Lexmead) was liable to compensate the end-purchaser (the owner of the Land Rover) under s 14 of the Sale of Goods Act in respect of the damages which it had been required to pay to the plaintiffs. Lexmead, being unable to identify its own intermediate supplier (and so having no claim under a contract of sale), sought to recover the relevant amount from Dixon-Bate directly, pointing to the statements in the latter's advertising material. The Court held that the claim failed both under the *Carlill* approach and under the *Hedley Byrne* principle (see above, pp 26–7). As to the former, the relevant statements were not intended to be contractual promises and were not acted on as such. Similarly, the *Hedley Byrne* principle did not apply since the necessary 'special relationship' between manufacturer and distributor was not present. On further appeal to the House of Lords (see [1981] 1 All ER 1185) these conclusions proved to have no practical importance. The House agreed with the trial court judge (Stocker J) that Lexmead was not liable to the owner and end-purchaser who had been negligent in using the coupling over a prolonged period when it was clearly damaged and dangerous. It was this negligence, rather than Lexmead's breach of contract, which had caused the end-purchaser's financial loss. This being so, there was no loss for Lexmead to pass on to Dixon-Bate. In spite of this conclusion, the general approach of the Court of Appeal remains important. It is an open question whether the Court would have adopted a different approach had the proceedings involved a claim by an injured consumer, rather than a dealer. For a comment on the case, see Hervey, 'Winner Takes All' (1981) 44 MLR 575.

4. In a different context it is relevant also to note that where it is claimed that goods have characteristics (for example being 'waterproof' or 'shrinkproof ') which they do not possess there will be potential criminal liability under the Trade Descriptions Act 1968 (see below, ch 13) and the possibility of a compensation order in favour of consumers who are affected thereby: see below, pp 429–33.

5. If English law is to develop in this area there will need to be a compromise between two competing considerations. One is that it is arguable that manufacturers should not feel aggrieved if unsubstantiated advertising claims form a basis for civil liability. Indeed one may have some sympathy with the view of Professor Trebilcock when he writes (in 'Private Law Remedies for Misleading Advertising' (1972) 22 Univ Toronto LJ 1, 4):

It should never lie in the mouth of an advertiser to argue that a claim was a mere puff and ought not to have been paid attention to. He ought irrebuttably to be presumed to have made the claim for a purpose and if somebody, as intended, acts on the claim, no matter how irrationally, the seller should be obliged to live with it.

The competing consideration is a concern not to introduce an open-ended liability—more especially where such liability may both be strict and encompass economic losses.

6. If a somewhat more wide-ranging liability were to be imposed in respect of manufacturers' advertising claims a key issue would be the degree of

intelligence or scepticism to be attributed to the typical consumer to whom the words are addressed. Some assistance may be gained from the case law on fair comparative advertising. In _Vodaphone Group plc v Orange Personal Communication Services Ltd_ [1997] FSR 34 (a case involving the Trade Marks Act 1994, s 10(6)) Jacob J stated (at pp 38–9) that: 'The public are used to the ways of advertisers and expect a certain amount of hyperbole . . . The test is whether a reasonable man would take the claim being made as one made seriously.' See also _Compaq Computer Corp v Dell Computer Corp_ [1992] FSR 93 and _Chanel v Triton_ [1993] RPC 32 (CA). The Control of Misleading Advertisement Regulations 1988, SI 1988/915 (see below, pp 529–32) are also relevant, as is the Code of Advertising and Sales Promotion (below, p 514).

7. In the USA in Federal Trade Commission cases the public has been regarded as 'that vast multitude which includes the ignorant, the unthinking and the credulous' (see, eg _Charles of the Ritz Distributors Corp v Federal Trade Com'n_ (1944) 143 F 2d 676). For references to other FTC cases under 15 USC § 45 (Unfair Methods of Competition) see the annotations to the section in the United States Code Annotated (USC). They contain a wealth of references to advertising techniques which are familiar on both sides of the Atlantic. For a case noting that there are limits to the 'ignorant, unthinking and credulous' test see _Standard Oil Co of California v FTC_ 577 F 2d 653 (1978) (CA, 9th Circ) where Kennedy J said (at 657), 'We do not think that any television viewer would have a level of credulity so primitive that he could expect to breath fresh air if he stuck his head into a bag inflated by exhaust, no matter how clean it looked.' (A television advertisement for a petrol additive had shown a balloon attached to the exhaust of a car being inflated with transparent vapour.)

8. Recently a European Commission Proposal for a European Parliament and Council Directive on 'The Sale of Goods and Associated Guarantees' (COM (95), final 520) has envisaged liability for guarantees and associated advertising: see Art 5. The proposed directive is printed below, at pp 119–22.

In the US and in parts of the Commonwealth there has been much less reluctance to extend the scope of civil liability to cover unsubstantiated advertising claims. The following is a leading American case.

Randy Knitwear Inc v American Cyanamid Co 11 NY 2d 5, 181 NE 2d 399 (1962), Court of Appeals of New York

The facts appear in the judgment of Judge Fuld. (Footnotes omitted.)

Fuld J: 'The assault upon the citadel of privity', Chief Judge Cardozo wrote in 1931, 'is proceeding in these days apace.' (_Ultramares Corp v Touche_ 255 NY 170, 180, 174 NE 441, 445, 74 ALR 1139.) In these days, too, for the present appeal, here by leave of the Appellate Division on a certified question, calls upon us to decide whether, under the facts disclosed, privity of contract is essential to maintenance of an action against a manufacturer for breach of express warranty.

American Cyanamid Company is the manufacturer of chemical resins, marketed under the registered trade-mark 'Cyana', which are used by textile manufacturers and finishers to process fabrics in order to prevent them from shrinking. Apex Knitted Fabrics and Fairtex Mills are manufacturers of fabrics who were licensed or otherwise authorised by Cyanamid to treat their goods with 'Cyana' and to sell such goods under the 'Cyana' label and, with the guaranty that they were 'Cyana' finished. Randy Knitwear, a manufacturer of children's knitted sportswear and play clothes, purchased large quantities of these 'Cyana' treated fabrics from Apex and Fairtex. After most of such fabrics had been made up into garments and sold by Randy to customers, it was claimed that ordinary washing caused them to shrink and to lose their shape. This action for breach of express warranty followed, each of the 3 parties being made the subject of a separate count. After serving its answer, Cyanamid, urging lack of privity of contract, moved for summary judgment dismissing the cause of action asserted against it, and it is solely with this cause of action that we are concerned.

Insofar as relevant, the complaint alleges that Cyanamid 'represented' and 'warranted' that the 'Cyana' finished fabrics sold by Fairtex and Apex to the plaintiff would not shrink or lose their shape when washed and that the plaintiff purchased the fabrics and agreed to pay the additional charge for the cost involved in rendering them shrink-proof 'in reliance upon' Cyanamid's representations. However, the complaint continues, the fabrics were not as represented since, when manufactured into garments and subjected to ordinary washing, they shrank and failed to hold their shape. The damages suffered are alleged to be over $208,000.

According to the complaint and the affidavits submitted in opposition to Cyanamid's motion, the representations relied upon by the plaintiff took the form of written statements expressed not only in numerous advertisements appearing in trade journals and in direct mail pieces to clothing manufacturers, but also in labels or garment tags furnished by Cyanamid. These labels bore the legend,

'A
Cyana
Finish
This Fabric Treated for
Shrinkage
Control
Will Not Shrink or
Stretch Out of Fit
Cyanamid',

and were issued to fabric manufacturers using the 'Cyana Finish' only after Cyanamid had tested samples of the fabrics and approved them. Cyanamid delivered a large number of these labels to Fairtex and Apex and they, with Cyanamid's knowledge and approval, passed them on to garment manufacturers, including the plaintiff, so that they might attach them to the clothing which they manufactured from the fabrics purchased.

As noted, Cyanamid moved for summary judgment dismissing the complaint against it on the ground that there was no privity of contract to support the plaintiff's action. The court at Special Term denied the motion and the Appellate Division unanimously affirmed the resulting order . . .

It was in this precise type of case, where express representations were made by a manufacturer to induce reliance by remote purchasers, that 'the citadel of privity' was successfully breached in the State of Washington in 1932. (See *Baxter v Ford Motor Co*, 168 Wash 456, 12 P2d 409, 15 P2d 1118, 88 ALR 521; same case after new trial, 179 Wash 123, 35 Pd2 1090.) It was the holding in the *Baxter* case that the manufacturer was liable for breach of express warranty to one who purchased an automobile from a retailer since such purchaser had a right to rely on representations made by the manufacturer in its sales literature, even though there was no privity of contract between them. And in the 30 years which have passed since that decision, not only have the courts throughout the country shown a marked, and almost uniform, tendency to discard the privity limitation and hold the manufacturer strictly accountable for the truthfulness of representations made to the public and relied upon by the plaintiff making his purchase, but the vast majority of the authoritative commentators have applauded the trend and approved the result.

The rationale underlying the decisions rejecting the privity requirement is easily understood in the light of present-day commercial practices. It may once have been true that the warranty which really induced the sale was normally an actual term of the contract of sale. Today, however, the significant warranty, the one which effectively induces the purchase, is frequently that given by the manufacturer through mass advertising and labeling to ultimate business users or to consumers with whom he had no direct contractual relationship.

The world of merchandising is, in brief, no longer a world of direct contract; it is, rather, a world of advertising and, when representations expressed and disseminated in the mass communications media and on labels (attached to the goods themselves) prove false and the user or consumer is damaged by reason of his reliance on those representations, it is difficult to justify the manufacturer's denial of liability on the sole ground of the absence of technical privity. Manufacturers make extensive use of newspapers, periodicals and other media to call attention, in glowing terms, to the qualities and virtues of their products, and this advertising is directed at the ultimate consumer or at some manufacturer or supplier who is not in privity with them. Equally sanguine representations on packages and labels frequently accompany the article throughout its journey to the ultimate consumer and, as intended, are relied upon by remote purchasers. Under these circumstances, it is highly unrealistic to limit a purchaser's protection to warranties made directly to him by his immediate seller. The protection he really needs is against the manufacturer whose published representations caused him to make the purchase.

The policy of protecting the public from injury, physical or pecuniary, resulting from misrepresentations outweighs allegiance to an old and out-moded technical rule of law which, if observed, might be productive of great injustice. The manufacturer places his product upon the market and, by advertising and labeling it, represents its quality to the public in such a way as to induce reliance upon his representations. He unquestionably intends and expects that the product will be purchased and used in reliance upon his express assurance of its quality and, in fact, it is so purchased and used. Having invited and solicited the use, the manufacturer should not be permitted to avoid responsibility, when the expected use leads to injury and loss, by claiming that he made no contract directly with the user.

It is true that in many cases the manufacturer will ultimately be held accountable for the falsity of his representations, but only after an unduly wasteful process of litigation. Thus, if the consumer or ultimate business user sues and recovers, for breach of warranty, from his immediate seller and if the latter in turn, sues and recovers against his supplier in recoupment of his damages and costs, eventually, after several separate actions by those in the chain of distribution, the manufacturer may finally be obliged 'to shoulder the responsibility which should have been his in the first instance.' (*Hamon v Digliani* 148 Conn 710, 717, 174 A. 2d 294, 297; see *Kasler & Cohen v Slavouski* [1928] 1 KB 78, where there was a series of 5 recoveries, the manufacturer ultimately paying the consumer's damages, plus a much larger sum covering the costs of the entire litigation.) As is manifest, and as Dean Prosser observes this circuity of action is 'an expensive, time-consuming and wasteful process, and it may be interrupted by insolvency, lack of jurisdiction, disclaimers, or the statute of limitations'. (Prosser, 'The Assault upon the Citadel Strict Liability to the Consumer', 69 Yale LJ 1099, 1124.)

Indeed, and it points up the injustice of the rule, insistence upon the privity requirement may well leave the aggrieved party, whether he be ultimate business user or consumer, without a remedy in a number of situations. For instance, he would be remediless either where his immediate seller's representations as to quality were less extravagant or enthusiastic than those of the manufacturer or where—as is asserted by Fairtex in this very case . . . there has been an effective disclaimer of any and all warranties by the plaintiff's immediate seller. Turning to the case before us, even if the representations respecting 'Cyana' treated fabric were false, the plaintiff would be foreclosed of all remedy against Fairtex, if it were to succeed on its defense of disclaimer, and against Cyanamid because of lack of privity . . . Although we believe that it has already been made clear, it is to be particularly remarked that in the present case the plaintiff's reliance is not on newspaper advertisements alone. It places heavy emphasis on the fact that the defendant not only made representations (as to the nonshrinkable character of 'Cyana Finish' fabrics) in newspapers and periodicals, but also repeated them on its own labels and tags which accompanied the fabrics purchased by the plaintiff from Fairtex and Apex. There is little in reason or logic to support Cyanamid's submission that it should not be held liable to the plaintiff even though the representations prove false in fact and it is ultimately found that the plaintiff relied to its harm upon such representations in making its purchases.

We perceive no warrant for holding—as the appellant urges—that strict liability should not here be imposed because the defect involved, fabric shrinkage, is not likely to cause personal harm or injury. Although there is language in some of the opinions which appears to support Cyanamid's contention [References omitted.], most of the courts which have dispensed with the requirements of privity in this sort of case have not limited their decisions in this manner. [References omitted.] And this makes sense. Since the basis of liability turns not upon the character of the product but upon the representation, there is no justification for a distinction on the basis of the type of injury suffered or the type of article or goods involved . . .

In concluding that the old court-made rule should be modified to dispense with the requirement of privity, we are doing nothing more or less than carrying out an historic and necessary function of the court to bring the law into harmony 'with modern-day needs and with concepts of justice and fair dealing.' [References omitted.]

The order appealed from should be affirmed, with costs, and the question certified answered in the negative.

Froessel J (concurring): We concur in result only. We agree with Judge Fuld that defendant, American Cyanamid Company, may be held liable for its express representations (as to the non-shrinkable character of 'Cyana Finish' fabrics) in newspapers and periodicals where they have been repeated on its own labels and tags delivered by Cyanamid to fabric manufacturers such as Fairtex and Apex, to be passed on to garment manufacturers such as plaintiff, so that they might attach them to the clothing cut from the fabrics purchased, all allegedly with Cyanamid's knowledge and authorization.

We do not agree that the so-called 'old court-made rule' should be modified to dispense with the requirement of privity without limitation. We decide cases as they arise, and would affirm in this case under the facts here disclosed.

Desmond CJ, and **Burke** and **Foster JJ**, concur with **Fuld J**.

Froessel J, concurs in result only in a separate opinion in which **Dye** and **Van Voorhis JJ**, concur.

Order affirmed, etc.

In the *Baxter* case decided in the Washington Supreme Court in 1932 and referred to by Judge Fuld the Ford Motor Company had made the following claims in its catalogues and printed matter:

> Triplex Shatter-Proof Glass Windshield. All of the new Ford cars have a Triplex shatter-proof glass windshield—so made that it will not fly or shatter under the hardest impact. This is an important safety factor because it eliminates the dangers of flying glass—the cause of most of the injuries in automobile accidents. In these days of crowded, heavy traffic, the use of this Triplex glass is an absolute necessity. Its extra margin of safety is something that every motorist should look for in the purchase of a car—especially where there are women and children.

The plaintiff who had purchased a Ford sedan car from a dealer was partially blinded when a pebble from a passing car struck and broke his windscreen.

Denying that the absence of a contract of sale between Ford and the plaintiff was a sufficient reason to preclude recovery, Herman J said in a much-cited passage (see 88 ALR 521, 525–6):

> Since the rule of caveat emptor was first formulated, vast changes have taken place in the economic structures of the English speaking peoples. Methods of doing business have undergone a great transition. Radio, bill-boards, and the products of the printing press have become the means of creating a large part of the demand that causes goods to depart from factories to the ultimate consumer. It would be unjust to recognize a rule that would permit manufacturers of goods to create a demand for their products by representing that they possess qualities which they, in fact, do not possess, and then, because there is no privity of contract existing between the consumer and the manufacturer, deny the consumer the right to recover if damages result from the absence of those qualities, when such absence is not readily noticeable.

Frequently it will be possible in such cases to view the product and the statement as one and so conclude that the product itself was 'defective'. For example, a statement may be attached to or otherwise accompany a product, as by being included on a label, package or instruction leaflet; and a product may be defective specifically because it is accompanied by unwarranted representations of safety or inadequate warnings or directions for safe use. If physical injury or property damage is suffered liability may then be imposed under the principles of *Donoghue v Stevenson* ([1932] AC 562, HL, below, pp 204–15) or the strict liability provisions of the Consumer Protection Act 1987 (below, pp 229–55). The definition of a 'defect' in the 1987 Act refers specifically to the need to have regard to 'the manner in which, and purposes for which, the product has been marketed': see s 3(2)(a). However, there will be cases in which it may not be a natural use of language to describe the product as 'defective' and where separate provision should be made for false statements themselves. The Ontario Law Reform Commission illustrated the point in its 'Report on Products Liability' (1979), pp 28–9, with the following example:

> Damage may be caused, not by a defect in the product itself, but by something said about the product. For example, a wire cable perfectly capable of lifting a one-half ton weight may become very dangerous if it is inaccurately described as capable of supporting two tons. If the cable is accompanied by the misleading description, it would be possible to classify the cable and its descriptive material, taken as a whole, as a 'defective' product. The misleading statement and the product may, however, come from separate sources. For example, the product may come from a retailer and the descriptive material may come from a manufacturer. In this kind of situation, it is difficult to describe the product as 'defective'. The real complaint is that the statement is misleading.

For a Canadian case arising out of an alleged breach of an express warranty, see *Naken v General Motors of Canada Ltd* (1979) 92 DLR (3d) 100 (Ont CA), below, p 463.

An interesting provision is contained in the Australian Trade Practices Act 1974, as amended:

Australian Trade Practices Act 1974

74G Actions in respect of non-compliance with express warranty

(1) Where:

    (a) a corporation, in trade or commerce, supplies goods (otherwise than by way of sale by auction) manufactured by the corporation to a consumer; or

    (b) a corporation, in trade or commerce, supplies goods manufactured by the corporation to another person who acquires the goods for re-supply and a person (whether or not the person who acquired the goods from the corporation) supplies the goods (otherwise than by way of sale by auction) to a consumer;

and

    (c) the corporation fails to comply with an express warranty given or made by the corporation in relation to the goods; and

    (d) the consumer or a person who acquires the goods from, or derives title to the goods through or under, the consumer suffers loss or damage by reason of the failure;

the corporation is liable to compensate the consumer or that other person for the loss or damage and the consumer or that other person may recover the amount of the compensation by action against the corporation in a court of competent jurisdiction.

(2) For the purposes of any action instituted by a person against a corporation under this section, where:

    (a) an undertaking, assertion or representation was given or made in connection with the supply of goods or in connection with the promotion by any means of the supply or use of goods; and

    (b) the undertaking, assertion or representation would, if it had been given or made by the corporation or a person acting on its behalf, have constituted an express warranty in relation to the goods;

it shall be presumed that the undertaking, assertion or representation was given or made by the corporation or a person acting on its behalf unless the corporation proves that it did not give or make, and did not cause or permit the giving or making of, the undertaking, assertion or representation.

By section 74A(1):

In this Division—

'express warranty', in relation to goods, means an undertaking, assertion or representation in relation to:

    (a) the quality, performance or characteristics of the goods;

    (b) the provision of services that are or may at any time be required in respect of the goods;

    (c) the supply of parts that are or may at any time be required for the goods; or

    (d) the future availability of identical goods, or of goods constituting or forming part of a set of which the goods in relation to which the undertaking, assertion or representation is given or made form part;

given or made in connection with the supply of the goods or in connection with the promotion by any means of the supply or use of the goods, the natural tendency of which is to induce persons to acquire the goods;

'manufactured' includes grown, extracted, produced, processed and assembled.

Consider the following cases on the basis of the position in (i) English civil law; (ii) the *Randy Knitwear* case; (iii) the Australian Trade Practices Act; and (iv) the European Commission proposals. (Compare also the potential liability in English law under the provisions of the Trade Descriptions Act 1968 imposing criminal liability, below, ch 13.)

1. The Carbolic Smoke Ball Company advertises as follows: 'Use our Smoke Ball according to instructions and you will be free from Influenza this winter. Results guaranteed'. Alfredo buys a Smoke Ball from his local chemist shop, uses it according to instructions and contracts influenza. He is off work for two weeks with an agreed loss of income of £500.

   Advise Alfredo.

2. Frogman publishes an advertisement in the Sunday press which portrays a swimmer emerging from a pool with a watch on his wrist. The advertisement reads, 'You need never be without a Frogman's watch'. Pamina purchases a Frogman's watch and on diving into a pool finds that it is not waterproof. The retailer who sold the watch to her is insolvent.

   Advise Pamina. Suppose further that Pamina had given the watch to a friend, Tamino, as a present and that Tamino, having read the advertisement, dives into a pool with the same result.

3. Giles, a farmer, attends a local Town and Country Fair where he visits a trade stand and explains to a representative of the XY Tractor Company that he is looking for a new harvester. The representative hands him a brochure containing details of XY's Greenfield Harvester and a list of approved dealers. The brochure claims: 'You'll harvest over 65 tons per hour with ease'. Giles buys a Greenfield Harvester from his local dealer and finds that it is quite incapable of harvesting at the rate claimed. However, it is well able to harvest at the average rate for a harvester of this size and power. The dealer is now insolvent.

   Advise Giles. (See *Murray v Sperry Rand Corpn* (1979) 96 DLR (3d) 113 (Ont) and cf *International Harvester Co of Australia Pty Ltd v Carrigan's Hazeldene Pastoral Co* (1958) 100 CLR 644 (Aust HC).

   Would it affect your advice if it had been the local dealer who had given XY's brochure to Giles? Suppose further that the dealer is insolvent and that Giles wishes to rescind the contract or reject the harvester. Against whom should be proceed? To whom should he seek to return it? (Consider also in this context the position of the manufacturer of the various products in the cases (i)–(iii) above, p 37.

   Related issues concerning manufacturers' guarantees are discussed below, ch 5, at pp 274–8.

CHAPTER 3

Contracts for the supply of goods

INTRODUCTION

The statistics published in the Annual Reports of the Director General of Fair Trading indicate the range of consumer complaints related to goods and services, grouping them according to the type of goods and services and the trading practice called into question. As might be expected, such items as secondhand cars, car repairs and servicing, radio, television and other electrical goods, clothing and clothing fabrics, and home maintenance, repairs and improvements all feature prominently. Usually the most consistent complaint is of defective goods or substandard service. The Office of Fair Trading also publishes information relating to problems in particular sectors. Further general information is published by such bodies as the National Consumer Council and the Consumers' Association.

The following extract is of interest as indicating the range of complaints.

'Consumer Guarantees', House of Lords Select Committee on the European Communities (Session 1996–97, 10th Report, HL 57), pp 42–3

Supplementary Memorandum by the Director-General of Fair Trading

CONSUMER COMPLAINTS RELATING TO DEFECTIVE GOODS AND GUARANTEES

This memorandum sets out the principal information available to the Office of Fair Trading on consumer complaints which may be relevant to the Sub-Committee's consideration of the draft Directive on sale of goods and associated guarantees. The information comes from various sources, and comparisons between data from different sources should be made only with care.

1994 CONSUMER DISSATISFACTION SURVEY

This is the most recent in a series of such surveys commissioned by the Office. Its overall purpose is to establish the number of causes for complaint about different categories of goods and services, the likelihood of affected consumers taking action, and what happened after they had complained.

The main relevant conclusions of the survey *in so far as they relate to goods* were as follows:
— for the United Kingdom as a whole, the survey suggests that there were 37.3 million causes for complaint during the year to November 1994;
— among respondents who had been exposed during the preceding 12 months to the goods categories in question, at least one in 10 had experienced cause for complaint about: new cars; large white goods; and TV, satellite, VCRs and camcorders;
— on average, consumers with cause for complaint actually made a complaint on 66 per cent of occasions;
— more than 60 per cent of causes for complaint about goods were the result of the products being defective, either when first used or subsequently;
— overwhelmingly, complaints were raised first with the seller of the goods giving cause for complaint;
— after a first complaint action had been taken, 82 per cent of causes for complaint about goods were resolved to respondents' satisfaction. Satisfaction rates after complaining have risen consistently over the past four OFT surveys into consumer dissatisfaction;
— complaints about goods were most likely to have been satisfied by a replacement. The second most likely satisfactory outcome was a successful repair, and the third a full refund;
— just under two-fifths of unsatisfactory outcomes to a complaint action were pursued further.

The results of the survey have been published and can therefore be made available on request. They do not, however, identify cross-border complaints specifically.

CONSUMER COMPLAINTS REPORTED BY TRADING STANDARDS DEPARTMENTS, ETC

The OFT collects from Trading Standards Departments, and some Citizens Advice Bureaux, quarterly statistics on the complaints which they have received. These statistics are published quarterly, and a summary appears in my Annual Report. The data are limited in both coverage and the detail of classification. With these limitations, some relevant figures are as follows:
— 811,186 complaints about goods and services were recorded in the year ending March 1996;
— of specified goods sectors, the three to attract most complaints in the first quarter of 1996 were second-hand cars; radio, TV and other electrical goods; and clothing and clothing fabrics;
— analysing complaints about goods and services by trading practice, 48 per cent were about sub-standard quality and 7 per cent about difficulty in obtaining redress.

More detailed published analyses are available on request. Again, cross-border complaints are not specifically identified.

COMPLAINTS ABOUT CROSS-BORDER TRANSACTIONS

From November 1995 to November 1996, the OFT received 163 complaints from people overseas—not confined to the EU—about consumer problems they had encountered in the United Kingdom. Of these, only 11 were about defective goods purchased in the UK. No central record is kept of complaints by UK consumers about problems they have encountered when shopping abroad.

The Office's Belgian counterpart has provided some figures for complaints about cross-border transactions in goods. The total for 1995 was 847, and for the first six months of 1996 it was 401. They broke down by sector as follows:

	1995	January to June 1996
Cars	297	170
Furniture	320	144
Electrical goods	93	28
Other	140	48
Total	850	390

These figures, which we have now received in writing, differ marginally from those quoted to the Sub-Committee, which had been received by telephone. Distance selling complaints were separately identified and were respectively 170 and 121 for the periods in question. The figures appear to cover cross-border complaints in both directions, and we cannot be sure that they are comprehensive. They should therefore be regarded as indicating the types of cross-border transaction that give rise to complaint in a part of Europe with several land frontiers, rather than absolute numbers.

1993 GUARANTEES SURVEY

This OFT survey was designed to ascertain how many consumers had experienced problems with guarantees over the previous three years, and the nature of those problems. It covered both ordinary guarantees provided with the product at no extra charge to the consumer, and extended warranties provided against an additional payment, and embraced both goods and services. The main findings were that:

— 74 per cent of UK consumers recalled acquiring goods or services carrying some form of guarantee during the specified time period;
— about 27 per cent of these consumers had made one or more claims—a figure equivalent to approximately 20 per cent of all adults;
— of the claims made, approximately 76 per cent had been against ordinary guarantees;
— 98 per cent of claims under ordinary guarantees were in respect of goods, with the largest number being in relation to hi-fi, TVs, computers and similar products (31 per cent), white goods (22 per cent) and cars (10 per cent);
— 22 per cent of claims under ordinary guarantees gave rise to problems. There were on average 1.5 problem areas cited per problem claim. Problems were essentially about performance under the guarantee—such as delays, recurrence of faults after repair, attitude of the supplier, refusal to replace goods, and poor workmanship—rather than denial of liability by manufacturer or retailer;
— the survey suggested that just under 5 per cent of the adult population had experienced problems in claiming under a guarantee of any type. Since about three-quarters of problem claims were against ordinary guarantees, it seems likely that somewhat less than 4 per cent of the adult population as a whole had experienced problems in claiming under an ordinary guarantee;
— 56 per cent of problems encountered in claiming under ordinary guarantees were resolved to the claimant's satisfaction. Just under 40 per cent were not resolved. This suggests that less than 2 per cent of the adult population as a whole had an unresolved problem in claiming under an ordinary guarantee.

The full results of this survey have not been published, though the figures quoted above are in the public domain.

For a reference to the 1994 Survey, see the Annual Report of the Director General of Fair Trading 1996, p 21; also Consumer Dissatisfaction: OFT Research Paper 9 (OFT, 176, November, 1996).

Where consumers have such complaints relating to faulty goods the remedies for breach of express contractual terms or following a misrepresentation (see above, p 19 et seq) have long been supplemented by an important range of implied terms as to quality and related matters. These terms which are styled 'conditions' (see above, p 28 et seq and below, p 79 et seq) generally apply only where goods are supplied 'in the course of a business'. Moreover they cannot be excluded as against one who 'deals as consumer': see the Unfair Contract Terms Act 1977, ss 6(2) and 7(2), below, pp 356–60. This chapter is concerned with their content and scope.

SALES AND RELATED TRANSACTIONS

Until the 1980s it was important to distinguish between the various types of legal transaction under which the property in or the possession of goods might pass from a supplier to a consumer. If the contract was of sale, terms were implied by the Sale of Goods Act 1979 (see ss 13–14 especially, below, p 80). Statutory terms were implied also in hire-purchase transactions (see the Supply of Goods (Implied Terms) Act 1973, ss 9–10, below, p 81) and on the redemption of trading stamps for goods (see the Trading Stamps Act 1964, s 4). These provisions remain in force. However, there are many everyday consumer transactions which do not fall into the above legal categories. For example, consumers may hire such goods as television sets and do-it-yourself equipment or acquire goods by way of barter or a contract for work and materials. This last and perhaps arcane expression covers such important and expensive transactions as the installation of central heating, double glazing, cavity insulation and the repair of cars, all of which involve the supply of both goods and services in one contract. For many years there were no statutory implied terms in such transactions although frequently a court was willing to imply terms as to quality etc under the guise of giving effect to the parties' intentions.

THE DISTINCTION BETWEEN SALE
AND ANALOGOUS TRANSACTIONS

The distinction between a contract of sale which envisages a transfer of property in goods 'for a money consideration, called the price' (see s 2(1) of the 1979 Act) and a contract of hire where possession only is transferred creates few problems. However, the distinction between contracts of sale and contracts of barter and for work and materials is far less clear-cut. In a Working Paper which led eventually to statutory reform the Law Commission referred to a number of commonplace consumer transactions which might have been classified as barter rather than sale. Having discussed the position in the case of a trade-in or part-exchange, the Commission continued:

Implied Terms in Contracts for the Supply of Goods (Law Commission Working Paper No 71) (1977)

Barter

. . .

20. Another kind of transaction that may be outside the provisions of the Sale of Goods Act involves the supply of goods in return for stamps, coupons, wrappers or labels. Sometimes goods are offered in return for such things without requiring the payment of money; more often the acceptance of the offer requires the payment of a sum in cash as well. The supply of goods on the redemption of trading stamps was recognised as being outside the ambit of the Sale of Goods Act 1893, so special provision was made for it.[1] However there remain other transactions for which no provision has yet been made, transactions involving the supply of goods in return for things other than stamps, with or without the payment of money in addition. For example, in *Chappell & Co Ltd v Nestlé Co Ltd*[2] the defendants advertised a gramophone record for supply to members of the public for a sum of money together with three of their chocolate wrappers. The essential nature of the transaction was not put in issue in the case but one of the Law Lords was disposed to think that it was not, strictly speaking, a sale.[3] Such transactions are a regular feature of ordinary retail trade. The promotion of particular products often involves the distribution of coupons, vouchers and the like; the customer may trade these in as part of the consideration for the supply of the goods in order to get a reduction in the price that would otherwise be payable. There is, as yet, no clear authority on the status of such a transaction; either it is a sale and subject to the provisions of the Sale of Goods Act 1893 or it is barter and subject only to the rules established at common law.

. . .

35. Another difficulty could arise on facts such as occurred in *Chappell & Co Ltd v Nestlé Co Ltd* to which we referred earlier.[4] What if the record supplied by the chocolate manufacturers had been unfit to play or of unmerchantable quality? It might be argued that since the suppliers were not 'dealers' in records and it was not in the course of their business to supply records, no terms relevant to the quality of the record should be implied. Such an argument might be sustainable on an analogy with the original wording of section 14 of the Sale of Goods Act 1893.[5] This section has been amended since and, in the case of a sale, terms as to quality are now implied wherever the goods are supplied in the course of a business, whether or not the seller deals in the goods in question or sells them as a regular feature of his business.[6] The position on sale has thus been put on a slightly different footing by the Supply of Goods (Implied Terms) Act 1973, but of course that Act does not apply to contracts of barter. The common law position remains unclear.

36. There seems to be a need for greater clarity in relation to contracts for work and materials as well . . .

[1] Trading Stamps Act 1964, s 4, now amended by Supply of Goods (Implied Terms) Act 1973, s 16.
[2] [1960] AC 87.
[3] Ibid, at p 109, per Lord Reid.
[4] [1960] AC 87; see para 20, above.
[5] See, however, the Canadian case of *Buckley v Lever Bros Ltd* [1953] 4 DLR 16 in which it was assumed on similar facts that the Sale of Goods Act *did* apply and the argument just put was rejected.
[6] Sale of Goods Act 1893, ss 14(2) and 14(3) . . . These sections were put in their present form by Supply of Goods (Implied Terms) Act 1973, s 3.

NOTE

For further discussion of the distinction between sale and related transactions see *Benjamin's Sale of Goods* (5th edn, 1997) paras 1–030–077); Atiyah, *Sale of Goods* (9th edn, 1995), pp 5–27; the Law Commission Report, 'Implied Terms in Contracts for the Supply of Goods' (Law Com No 95 1979) para 27 et seq and materials there cited.

Fortunately, so far as the implying of terms is concerned, the question whether such transactions are to be classified as sale or barter is no longer of practical importance since the coming into force on 4 January 1983 of the Supply of Goods and Services Act 1982. This Act (see ss 3–4 and 8–9, below, pp 83–5) applies to any such contract, and to contracts for work and materials and of hire, equivalent obligations as to correspondence with description, quality and fitness for purpose as are implied in a contract of sale: see Palmer (1983) 46 MLR 619. However, it is still important to determine whether goods have been supplied contractually, rather than gratuitously, and it may be important also to determine when or where any such contract was formed.

CONTRACTS AND THEIR FORMATION

The general principles of the law of contract which assist in determining whether goods have been supplied pursuant to a contract are discussed in the standard texts on the law of contract: see, for example, Treitel, *The Law of Contract* (9th edn, 1995), at pp 8–16; Cheshire Fifoot and Furmston, *Law of Contract* (15th edn, 1996), at pp 28–37. Their importance in the present context is that they may affect such issues as a consumer's entitlement both to complain if goods are faulty and to recover damages if they are dangerous and cause injury. As was seen in *Daniels and Daniels v R White & Sons Ltd and Tarbard* [1938] 4 All ER 258 (above, p 38) a retail seller is strictly liable where goods which are not of satisfactory (previously merchantable) quality cause physical injury, but usually such liability will arise only when a contract can be established. Of course the rules governing the formation of a contract will determine also when a consumer is contractually bound to buy or otherwise acquire goods. The following extract from a Law Commission report indicates an area where the distinction between contracts and gifts may not be entirely clear.

Implied Terms in Contracts for the Supply of Goods (Law Com No 95) (1979)

The contract of supply

30. In our working paper we explained that we would not be concerned with non-contractual transactions such as gift where there was no *contract* to supply the goods in question.[1] However, the borderlines separating (a) gift from sale and (b) gift and sale from contracts analogous to sale are not always clear, a point which is well illustrated by *Esso Petroleum Co Ltd v*

Commissioners of Customs and Excise.[2] Esso had devised a petrol sales promotion scheme which involved the distribution of coins to petrol stations. Each coin was stamped with the likeness of one of the English footballers selected for the 1970 World Cup Competition, and the object of the scheme was that the petrol station proprietor should offer to give away a coin for every four gallons of Esso petrol which motorists bought. The coins were of little intrinsic value but it was hoped that motorists would wish to build up a full set of 30. The coins were advertised as 'Going free, at your Esso Action Station now'. The question to be decided was whether the coins were being 'sold' and were accordingly chargeable to purchase tax. Pennycuick V-C held that the coins were being sold; the Court of Appeal, reversing his decision, held that the coins were not being sold but were being distributed as gifts and that no tax was due. In the House of Lords, opinions were divided. Lord Fraser's opinion was that there was a sale; Viscount Dilhorne and Lord Russell thought that the Court of Appeal were right in holding that the coins were being distributed as gifts. Lord Simon and Lord Wilberforce both concluded that the supply of the coins to the motorists was contractual but without there being a sale; the consideration for the transfer of the coin or coins was not a money payment but the undertaking by the motorist to enter into a collateral contract to purchase the appropriate quantity of Esso petrol: accordingly it was not a gift, but it was not a sale either.

31. The result of the *Esso* case was that the House of Lords decided, Lord Fraser dissenting, that the coins had not been 'sold' and that they were therefore exempt from purchase tax. For our purposes the significance of the case is on a more general point. It shows that the distinctions between gifts and sales and contracts analogous to sale are not always easy to draw and that the consequences of the distinction can be important.

32. Under the existing law a person who receives a gift has no right of redress against the donor merely because the gift is of unmerchantable quality or does not correspond with the donor's description of it. The person receiving the gift may have a remedy in tort if the gift causes injury or damage which is attributable to negligence on the donor's part. But that is another matter: he has no remedy in contract against the donor for the simple reason that there is no contract between them. To the extent that the offer of worthless goods, without charge, as part of a sales promotion, is against the public interest it is primarily the concern of the Office of Fair Trading. We therefore do not intend to examine the law of gift in this report.

---

[1] Working Paper No 71, para 11.
[2] [1976] 1 WLR 1.

In the case of sales in supermarkets it is well known that the basic rule is that a contract is not concluded by a consumer buyer taking goods off a shelf and putting them into a trolley or basket. Usually it is concluded only at the check-out point: see generally *Pharmaceutical Society of Great Britain v Boots Cash Chemists Southern Ltd* [1953] 1 QB 401, [1953] 1 All ER 482, CA; and *Fisher v Bell* [1961] 1 QB 394, [1960] 3 All ER 731. The position has been discussed in some detail in relation to the law of theft where the following case is of interest and importance. However, it should be noted that in a prosecution for theft the emphasis is on when property in and possession of the goods (as opposed to mere custody) passes to the consumer and this may occur after the parties have agreed to buy and sell the goods in question.

Davies v Leighton (1978) Times, 29 June, (1978) 68 Cr App Rep 4, [1978] Crim LR 575, Queen's Bench Division

The prosecutor was appealing on a case stated by Clwyd Justices who had dismissed an information against the defendant, Myra Leighton, alleging theft of one bag of apples and one of tomatoes, contrary to ss 1 and 7 of the Theft Act 1968.

Mr Justice Ackner said that the defendant was alleged to have stolen the apples and tomatoes, valued at 13p and 20p respectively, at a store in Wrexham, in May, 1976. The store had a self-service area for the purchase of foodstuffs. Within that area there was a counter for the sale of fruit and vegetables manned by an assistant, who weighed the quantity required by a customer, and bagged and priced it. The bag was handed to the customer, who was expected to pay the cashier at the exit.

On the day in question the defendant was observed by a store detective to acquire the bags of apples and tomatoes from the assistant and to carry them in her hand to an off-licence section of the store. There she bought some wine, which she paid for and placed in her own shopping trolley. She also placed the apples and tomatoes in the trolley and, after joining a queue at the exit, left the store without paying for the apples and tomatoes.

She was stopped outside by the detective, and when she returned to the store she claimed that she had paid for the goods although she could not produce a receipt.

At the conclusion of the prosecution case before the justices, a submission was made on behalf of the defendant that ownership of the goods in question passed to the defendant when she received them from the assistant and, therefore, unless there was prima facie evidence that she had not intended to pay for them before they were handed to her, the justices could not convict because the Theft Act required that there should be a dishonest appropriation of property belonging to another. The contention was that when she took the goods through the checkout, the property had already passed to her.

. . .

The law was well settled in relation to purchases in a supermarket. In *Lacis v Cashmart* ([1969] 2 QB 400, [at] 407) Lord Parker, Lord Chief Justice, said: 'The fundamental question . . . is: what is the intention of the parties . . . In my judgment when one is dealing with a case such as this, particularly a shop of the supermarket variety . . . the intention of the parties quite clearly as it seems to me is that the property shall not pass until the price is paid. That as it seems to me is in accordance with the reality and in accordance with commercial practice.'

. . .

In *Martin v Puttick* [1968] 2 QB 82 Mr Justice Winn said that 'the limit of the authority of the meat counter assistant is clearly merely to hand over and wrap up the meat and not to deal in any way with any transfer of property from the owner of the shop to the customer'. That statement seemed applicable to the present case, where the customer asked the assistant for the quantity required.

There was no reference to the assistant being in a managerial or other special category, when a different situation might arise. The justices had come to the wrong conclusion, namely, that the property had passed when the defendant received the goods. In fact and in law, the property never passed because she never paid for the goods.

Mr Justice Talbot and the **Lord Chief Justice** agreed.

The appeal was allowed, and the case was ordered to be sent back for the hearing to continue.

NOTES

1. The leading case on theft in supermarkets is now *R v Morris, Anderton v Burnside* [1984] AC 320, [1983] 3 All ER 288. See generally J C Smith, *The Law of Theft* (8th edn, 1997), paras 2–06 and 2–38. See also *Warwickshire County Council v Johnson* [1993] 1 All ER 299 (HL) on misleading price claims.

2. For a reference to some of the problems of determining when a contract is completed in more modern methods of selling through the medium of television see the Office of Fair Trading paper, 'Micro-electronics and Retailing' (September 1982), para 3.56 et seq, and on the Internet, see Fair Trading, Summer 1997, pp 13–16.

QUESTION

For what reasons may consumers sometimes have difficulty in establishing that defective goods were purchased from a particular shop or other source?

PROBLEMS

1. The Pennymede Courier publishes the following advertisement which has been inserted by Pinetree Kitchens, 'Free Double Oven Worth £800 when you buy a Pinetree Luxury Fitted Kitchen'. Andrea has such a kitchen installed by Pinetree and finds that the oven is defective and does not work.
   Advise Andrea.
2. Supersave operates a supermarket in Littletown. It has a section which deals in cheese and paté and a separate counter which sells wines and spirits. One Saturday evening when the shop is about to close Amantha asks the assistant for a pound of duck paté and half of a fine Stilton cheese. The paté is cut out of a bowl and the Stilton cut in two. Both are then placed in polythene bags and the price is marked on the bags to be paid at the check-out point. Bill goes to the wines and spirits counter and pays for two bottles of sparkling wine. Amantha decides that she does not wish to buy the paté and cheese but the shop assistant refuses to take them back. As Bill is waiting in the check-out queue to pay for other goods one of his bottles explodes, causing him facial injury.
   Advise Amantha and Bill.
3. Multistores is a company with a head office in London and some one hundred retail shops in the United Kingdom. Meg buys a cassette recorder from Multistores when on holiday in Plymouth and on returning home to Newcastle she discovers that it is defective. The Newcastle branch agrees that it is defective but declines to deal with the matter.
   Advise Meg.

STATUTORY IMPLIED TERMS AS TO QUALITY AND RELATED MATTERS

As has been noted above (p 74), statutory terms as to the quality of goods and materials supplied are now implied in most important consumer transactions including contracts of sale, hire-purchase, work and materials and hire. Although the terms are virtually identical, it is convenient to set out the statutory text of the various provisions before examining their main requirements and implications.

The text is printed as amended by the Sale and Supply of Goods Act 1994, and, in the case of the Supply of Goods (Implied Terms) Act 1973, by the Consumer Credit Act 1974, with the amendments being printed in square brackets.

Sale of Goods Act 1979

13. Sale by description
(1) Where there is a contract for the sale of goods by description, there is an implied [term] that the goods will correspond with the description.

[(1A) As regards England and Wales and Northern Ireland, the term implied by subsection (1) above is a condition.]

(2) If the sale is by sample as well as by description it is not sufficient that the bulk of the goods corresponds with the sample if the goods do not also correspond with the description.

(3) A sale of goods is not prevented from being a sale by description by reason only that, being exposed for sale or hire, they are selected by the buyer.

(4) Paragraph 4 of Schedule 1 below applies in relation to a contract made before 18th May 1973.

14. Implied terms about quality or fitness
(1) Except as provided by this section and section 15 below and subject to any other enactment, there is no implied [term] about the quality or fitness for any particular purpose of goods supplied under a contract of sale.

[(2) Where the seller sells goods in the course of a business, there is an implied term that the goods supplied under the contract are of satisfactory quality.

(2A) For the purposes of this Act, goods are of satisfactory quality if they meet the standard that a reasonable person would regard as satisfactory, taking account of any description of the goods, the price (if relevant) and all the other relevant circumstances.

(2B) For the purposes of this Act, the quality of goods includes their state and condition and the following (among others) are in appropriate cases aspects of the quality of goods—
  (a) fitness for all the purposes for which goods of the kind in question are commonly supplied,
  (b) appearance and finish,
  (c) freedom from minor defects,
  (d) safety, and
  (e) durability.

(2C) The term implied by subsection (2) above does not extend to any matter making the quality of goods unsatisfactory—
  (a) which is specifically drawn to the buyer's attention before the contract is made,
  (b) where the buyer examines the goods before the contract is made, which that examination ought to reveal, or
  (c) in the case of a contract for sale by sample, which would have been apparent on a reasonable examination of the sample.]

(3) Where the seller sells goods in the course of a business and the buyer, expressly or by implication, makes known—
  (a) to the seller, or
  (b) where the purchase price or part of it is payable by instalments and the goods were previously sold by a credit-broker to the seller, to that credit-broker,
any particular purpose for which the goods are being bought, there is an implied [term] that the goods supplied under the contract are reasonably fit for that purpose, whether or not that is a purpose for which such goods are commonly supplied, except where the circumstances show

that the buyer does not rely, or that it is unreasonable for him to rely, on the skill or judgment of the seller or credit-broker.

(4) An implied [term] about quality or fitness for a particular purpose may be annexed to a contract of sale by usage.

(5) The preceding provisions of this section apply to a sale by a person who in the course of a business is acting as agent for another as they apply to a sale by a principal in the course of business, except where that other is not selling in the course of a business and either the buyer knows that fact or reasonable steps are taken to bring it to the notice of the buyer before the contract is made.

[(6) As regard England and Wales and Northern Ireland, the terms implied by subsections (2) and (3) above are conditions.]
. . .

Supply of Goods (Implied Terms) Act 1973

9. Bailing or hiring by description

(1) Where under a hire-purchase agreement goods are bailed or (in Scotland) hired by description, there is an implied [term] that the goods will correspond with the description, and if under the agreement the goods are bailed or hired by reference to a sample as well as a description, it is not sufficient that the bulk of the goods corresponds with the sample if the goods do not also correspond with the description.

[(1A) As regards England and Wales and Northern Ireland, the term implied by subsection (1) above is a condition.]

(2) Goods shall not be prevented from being bailed or hired by description by reason only that, being exposed for sale, bailment or hire, they are selected by the person to whom they are bailed or hired.]

10. Implied undertakings as to quality or fitness

(1) Except as provided by this section and section 11 below and subject to the provisions of any other enactment, including any enactment of the Parliament of Northern Ireland, or the Northern Ireland Assembly there is no implied [term] as to the quality or fitness for any particular purpose of goods bailed or (in Scotland) hired under a hire-purchase agreement.

[(2) Where the creditor bails or hires goods under a hire purchase agreement in the course of a business, there is an implied term that the goods supplied under the agreement are of satisfactory quality.

(2A) For the purposes of this Act, goods are of satisfactory quality if they meet the standard that a reasonable person would regard as satisfactory, taking account of any description of the goods, the price (if relevant) and all the other relevant circumstances.

(2B) For the purposes of this Act, the quality of the goods includes their state and condition and the following (among others) are in appropriate cases aspects of the quality of goods—

(a) fitness for all the purposes for which goods of the kind in question are commonly supplied,

(b) appearance and finish,

(c) freedom from minor defects,

(d) safety, and

(e) durability.

(2C) The term implied by subsection (2) above does not extend to any matter making the quality of goods unsatisfactory—

(a) which is specifically drawn to the attention of the person to whom the goods are bailed or hired before the agreement is made, (*b*) where that person examines the goods before the agreement is made, which that examination ought to reveal, or

(*c*) where the goods are bailed or hired by reference to a sample, which would have been apparent on a reasonable examination of the sample.]

(3) Where the creditor bails or hires goods under a hire-purchase agreement in the course of a business and the person to whom the goods are bailed or hired expressly or by implication, makes known—

(*a*) to the creditor in the course of negotiations conducted by the creditor in relation to the making of the hire-purchase agreement, or

(*b*) to a credit-broker in the course of negotiations conducted by that broker in relation to goods sold by him to the creditor before forming the subject matter of the hire-purchase agreement,

any particular purpose for which the goods are being bailed or hired, there is an implied [term] that the goods supplied under this agreement are reasonably fit for that purpose, whether or not that this is a purpose for which such goods are commonly supplied, except where the circumstances show that the person to whom the goods are bailed or hired does not rely, or that it is unreasonable for him to rely, on the skill or judgment of the creditor or credit-broker.

(4) An implied [term] as to quality or fitness for a particular purpose may be annexed to a hire-purchase agreement by usage.

(5) The preceding provisions of this section apply to a hire-purchase agreement made by a person who in the course of a business is acting as agent for the creditor as they apply to any agreement made by the creditor in the course of a business, except where the creditor is not bailing or hiring in the course of a business and either the person to whom the goods are bailed or hired knows that fact or reasonable steps are taken to bring it to the notice of that person before the agreement is made.

(6) In subsection (3) above and this subsection—

(*a*) 'credit-broker' means a person acting in the course of a business of credit brokerage.

(*b*) 'credit brokerage' means the effecting of introductions of individuals desiring to obtain credit—

(i) to persons carrying on any business so far as it relates to the provision of credit, or

(ii) to other persons engaged in credit brokerage.]

[(7) As regards England and Wales and Northern Ireland, the terms implied by subsections (2) and (3) above are conditions.]

Supply of Goods and Services Act 1982, Part I (Supply of Goods)

CONTRACTS FOR THE TRANSFER OF PROPERTY IN GOODS

1. The contracts concerned

(1) In this Act [in its application to England and Wales and Northern Ireland] a 'contract for the transfer of goods' means a contract under which one person transfers or agrees to transfer to another the property in goods, other than an excepted contract.

(2) For the purposes of this section an excepted contract means any of the following—

(a) a contract of sale of goods;

(b) a hire-purchase agreement;

(c) a contract under which the property in goods is (or is to be) transferred in exchange for trading stamps on their redemption;

(d) a transfer or agreement to transfer which is made by deed and for which there is no consideration other than the presumed consideration imported by the deed;

(e) a contract intended to operate by way of mortgage, pledge, charge or other security.

(3) For the purposes of this Act [in its application to England and Wales and Northern Ireland] a contract is a contract for the transfer of goods whether or not services are also provided or to be provided under the contract, and (subject to subsection (2) above) whatever is the nature of the consideration for the transfer or agreement to transfer.

. . .

3. Implied terms where transfer is by description

(1) This section applies where, under a contract for the transfer of goods, the transferor transfers or agrees to transfer the property in the goods by description.

(2) In such a case there is an implied condition that the goods will correspond with the description.

(3) If the transferor transfers or agrees to transfer the property in the goods by sample as well as by description it is not sufficient that the bulk of the goods corresponds with the sample if the goods do not also correspond with the description.

(4) A contract is not prevented from falling within subsection (1) above by reason only that, being exposed for supply, the goods are selected by the transferee.

4. Implied terms about quality or fitness

(1) Except as provided by this section and section 5 below and subject to the provision of any other enactment, there is no implied condition or warranty about the quality or fitness for any particular purpose of goods supplied under a contract for the transfer of goods.

[(2) Where, under such a contract, the transferor transfers the property in goods in the course of a business, there is an implied condition that the goods supplied under the contract are of satisfactory quality.

(2A) For the purposes of this section and section 5 below, goods are of satisfactory quality if they meet the standard that a reasonable person would regard as satisfactory, taking account of any description of the goods, the price (if relevant) and all the other relevant circumstances.

(3) The condition implied by subsection (2) above does not extend to any matter making the quality of goods unsatisfactory—

    (a) which is specifically drawn to the transferee's attention before the contract is made,

    (b) where the transferee examines the goods before the contract is made, which that examination ought to reveal, or

    (c) where the property in the goods is transferred by reference to a sample, which would have been apparent on a reasonable examination of the sample.]

(4) Subsection (5) below applies where, under a contract for the transfer of goods, the transferor transfers the property in goods in the course of a business and the transferee, expressly or by implication, makes known—

    (a) to the transferor, or

    (b) where the consideration or part of the consideration for the transfer is a sum payable by instalments and the goods were previously sold by a credit-broker to the transferor, to that credit-broker,

any particular purpose for which the goods are being acquired.

(5) In that case there is (subject to subsection (6) below) an implied condition that the goods supplied under the contract are reasonably fit for that purpose, whether or not that is a purpose for which such goods are commonly supplied.

(6) Subsection (5) above does not apply where the circumstances show that the transferee does not rely, or that it is unreasonable for him to rely, on the skill or judgment of the transferor or credit-broker.

(7) An implied condition or warranty about quality or fitness for a particular purpose may be annexed by usage to a contract for the transfer of goods.

(8) The preceding provisions of this section apply to a transfer by a person who in the course of a business is acting as agent for another as they apply to a transfer by a principal in the course

of a business, except where that other is not transferring in the course of a business and either
the transferee knows that fact or reasonable steps are taken to bring it to the transferee's notice
before the contract concerned is made.

. . .

CONTRACTS FOR THE HIRE OF GOODS

6. The contracts concerned

(1) In this Act [in its application to England and Wales and Northern Ireland] a 'contract for
the hire of goods' means a contract under which one person bails or agrees to bail goods to
another by way of hire, other than an excepted contract.

(2) For the purposes of this section an excepted contract means any of the following—

    (a) a hire-purchase agreement;

    (b) a contract under which goods are (or are to be) bailed in exchange for trading stamps
       on their redemption.

(3) For the purposes of this Act [in its application to England and Wales and Northern
Ireland] a contract is a contract for the hire of goods whether or not services are also provided
or to be provided under the contract, and (subject to subsection (2) above) whatever is the
nature of the consideration for the bailment or agreement to bail by way of hire.

. . .

8. Implied terms where hire is by description

(1) This section applies where, under a contract for the hire of goods, the bailor bails or
agrees to bail the goods by description.

(2) In such a case there is an implied condition that the goods will correspond with the
description.

(3) If under the contract the bailor bails or agrees to bail the goods by reference to a sample
as well as a description it is not sufficient that the bulk of the goods corresponds with the sample if the goods do not also correspond with the description.

(4) A contract is not prevented from falling within subsection (1) above by reason only that,
being exposed for supply, the goods are selected by the bailee.

9. Implied terms about quality or fitness

(1) Except as provided by this section and section 10 below and subject to the provisions of
any other enactment, there is no implied condition or warranty about the quality or fitness for
any particular purpose of goods bailed under a contract for the hire of goods.

[(2) Where, under such a contract, the bailor bails goods in the course of a business, there
is an implied condition that the goods supplied under the contract are of satisfactory quality.

(2A) For the purposes of this section and section 10 below, goods are of satisfactory quality
if they meet the standard that a reasonable person would regard as satisfactory, taking account
of any description of the goods, the consideration for the bailment (if relevant) and all the other
relevant circumstances.

(3) The condition implied by subsection (2) above does not extend to any matter making the
quality of goods unsatisfactory—

    (a) which is specifically drawn to the bailee's attention before the contract is made,

    (b) where the bailee examines the goods before the contract is made, which that examina-
       tion ought to reveal, or

    (c) where the goods are bailed by reference to a sample, which would have been apparent
       on a reasonable examination of the sample.]

(4) Subsection (5) below applies where, under a contract for the hire of goods, the bailor bails
goods in the course of a business and the bailee, expressly or by implication, makes known—

    (a) to the bailor in the course of negotiations conducted by him in relation to the making
      of the contract, or

(b) to a credit-broker in the course of negotiations conducted by that broker in relation to goods sold by him to the bailor before forming the subject matter of the contract, any particular purpose for which the goods are being bailed.

(5) In that case there is (subject to subsection (6) below) an implied condition that the goods supplied under the contract are reasonably fit for that purpose, whether or not that is a purpose for which such goods are commonly supplied.

(6) Subsection (5) above does not apply where the circumstances show that the bailee does not rely, or that it is unreasonable for him to rely, on the skill or judgment of the bailor or credit-broker.

(7) An implied condition or warranty about quality or fitness for a particular purpose may be annexed by usage to a contract for the hire of goods.

(8) The preceding provisions of this section apply to a bailment by a person who in the course of a business is acting as agent for another as they apply to a bailment by a principal in the course of a business, except where that other is not bailing in the course of a business and either the bailee knows that fact or reasonable steps are taken to bring it to the bailee's notice before the contract concerned is made.

(9) . . .

THE SCOPE OF PART I OF THE SUPPLY OF GOODS AND SERVICES ACT 1982

Although Part I of the above Act imposes obligations as to the quality of the goods supplied in the most important types of consumer contracts which are neither contracts for the sale of goods nor hire-purchase agreements, the precise scope of its coverage is not wholly clear. Part II which imposes an obligation of reasonable care in the provision of services (see s 13) is noted below, p 152. Professor Palmer has discussed some areas of doubt and omissions within Part I as follows:

'The Supply of Goods and Services Act 1982' (1983) 46 MLR 619, 621–2

The Act may also apply to goods which are, according to usual practice, supplied as an adjunct to services and abandoned when those services are completed: for example, the provision for tea chests by a removal company.[1] But its application to other title-transferring transactions may not have been so clearly envisaged and may occasion surprise to trading organisations. Some, it is true, may be an acceptable subject-matter for sections 1 to 5: for example, the award of prizes in competitions; the supply of products to agents or canvassers in return for (or for use in) services which they perform for the supplier; the provision of 'free' meals to employees as part of their contract of employment; the use by a hotel guest or perhaps by a tenant of consumable goods supplied on the premises, for which no independent consideration is required; the supply of a replacement chattel by a trader to a customer who is dissatisfied with the goods already supplied to him (where the buyer's consideration is presumably, at least in part, his forbearance from taking legal action under the original, compromised contract); and the collateral contract between the dealer and the debtor under a hire-purchase agreement, where the debtor's consideration is his entry into the hire-purchase agreement with a distinct party, the finance house.[2] The prospect of exposing other transactions to sections 1 to 5 is more alarming: for example, the transfer by an employer-corporation of its property in a company car to an employee as part of a dismissal or redundancy settlement . . .

This apparent elasticity is the more curious in view of the fact that certain aspects of the supply of goods do not appear to enjoy the benefit of sections 2 to 5 because the contract involves no passing of property. An example is the use of materials which are consumed in the course of their application by the supplier, such as dyes, lotions, solvents and shampoos. It seems that the consumer cannot be a transferee within section 1(1) because there can be no property in goods which are dissipated.[3] Although terms similar to those in section 4 of the 1982 Act seem impliable in such a case at common law,[4] the lack of statutory treatment is regrettable, especially since there is no statutory formulation of the implied terms governing quality of services beyond the anaemic obligation of reasonable care and skill in section 13. The silence of the statute on these points shows the peril of segregating provisions upon the quality of goods and services[5] and consigns contracts like that in *Ingham v Emes*[6] to the very state of uncertainty and inferiority which, in comparable areas, the Act is concerned to relieve . . .

[1] *Sed quaere*: must there be a contractual *right* to the transfer in the transferee? Possibly the question may be answered by holding that the abandonment of property is not a transfer *to him*.

[2] Tentatively recognised by McNair J in *Andrews v Hopkinson* [1957] 1 QB 229 as capable of generating similar implied terms to those in the Sale of Goods Act. The application of the 1982 Act to such a contract, whereby property is transferred to the transferee via a third (and independently-contracting) party, seems probable but somewhat problematic.

[3] Cf *Borden (UK) Ltd v Scottish Timber Products Ltd* [1979] 3 All ER 961.

[4] *Ingham v Emes* [1955] 2 QB 366.

[5] Cf Law Com No 95 (1979), paras 61–3.

[6] [1955] 2 QB 366; see also *Parker v Oloxo Ltd* [1937] 3 All ER 524, (1980) 43 MLR 193, 197.

NOTE

It has been held that the relationship between a public electricity supplier and a tariff customer is not a contractual one: see *Norweb plc v Dixon* [1995] 3 All ER 952 (QBD).

QUESTIONS

1. Art and Ben have each received a National Health prescription from their doctor. Blacks, the chemists, dispenses the prescribed drug from a batch which is contaminated and both Art and Ben become seriously ill. Art has a certificate which exempts him from payment and Ben has paid the standard prescription charge.

   Is either transaction subject to (i) the Sale of Goods Act 1979 or (ii) the Supply of Goods and Services Act 1982? See generally *Appelby v Sleep* [1968] 2 All ER 265 at 269 per Lord Parker, CJ, *Pfizer v Ministry of Health* [1965] AC 512, [1965] 1 All ER 450, HL. (For the definition of a contract for the sale of goods see above, p 74).

2. Is a dentist subject to the implied terms of Part I of the 1982 Act as to the quality of the materials 'supplied' to a private fee-paying patient when she (i) fills a cavity, (ii) injects a pain-killing substance into his gums and (iii) uses gas as an anaesthetic before extracting a tooth?

3. Claude and Dick own adjoining terrace houses both of which have been attacked by dry rot. They call in the services of Pestakill, a specialist contrac-

tor, who carries out the standard form of treatment by painting replacement timber with a fungicide which is also pumped under pressure into holes drilled into the walls. Owing to an error by the manufacturer and unknown to all concerned the fungicide is fifty times its normal concentration. Standard precautions which have been taken are insufficient to ensure safety. Claude is burned when he touches a window and some fluid comes into contact with his hand. Two days later when the fungicide has dried out Dick returns home and becomes ill when breathing in the resultant fumes.

Advise Claude and Dick as to whether they benefit from the implied terms of Part I of the 1982 Act.

CORRESPONDENCE WITH DESCRIPTION

The implied condition of correspondence with description may be important in a substantial number of consumer transactions. This is especially true of cases where a consumer has not seen the goods and is ordering them in response to an advertisement or by reference to a catalogue. Mail order transactions provide a notable example. The leading cases on the scope and implications of s 13 of the Sale of Goods Act 1979 have a strongly commercial flavour: see in particular *Ashington Piggeries Ltd v Christopher Hill Ltd* [1972] AC 441, [1971] 1 All ER 847, HL; *Arcos Ltd v E A Ronaasen & Son* [1933] AC 470, HL and *Re Moore & Co Ltd and Landauer & Co* [1921] 2 KB 519, CA. They establish that the section is concerned only with matters which touch on the identity or essential characteristics of the goods and not with matters which affect quality alone: see the *Ashington Piggeries* case where toxic herring meal was still within the contract description although it was lethal to mink. However, if the matter does affect the goods' description it seems that precise compliance is required if breach of s 13 is to be avoided. At least this is true of such matters as measurements and quantity: see *Arcos Ltd v E A Ronaasen & Son*, above, where in a well-known passage Lord Atkin said (ibid at p 479):

If the written contract specifies conditions of weight, measurement and the like, those conditions must be complied with. A ton does not mean about a ton, or a yard about a yard. Still less when you descend to minute measurements does ½ inch mean about ½ inch. If the seller wants a margin he must and in my experience does stipulate for it.

Moreover, the implied term as to correspondence with description being designated an implied condition, its breach will prima facie entitle the other party to reject the goods. As Professor Diamond has said, with due allowance for de minimis deviations, 'If the term broken is a condition, the buyer can reject however little harm has been done. There is no such thing as a "slight breach of condition"': see Diamond, 'Commerce, Customers and Contracts' (1978) 11 Melbourne University Law Review 563, 567. See also Coote, 'Correspondence with Description in the Law of Sale of Goods' (1976) 50 ALJ 17; Stoljar, 'Conditions, Warranties and Descriptions of Quality in Sale of Goods II' (1953)

16 MLR 174. Where the breach is 'slight' this remedy may not be available in 'non-consumer' cases, but it remains intact for consumers: see s 15A of the Sale of Goods Act 1979.

The requirement that the sale be 'by description' gave rise to difficulty in the following case.

Harlingdon & Leinster Enterprises Ltd v Christopher Hull Fine Art Ltd [1990] 1 All ER 737, Court of Appeal

The defendant art dealers carried on business from a London gallery and they were owned and controlled by Hull. In 1984 Hull was asked to sell two oil paintings which had been described in a 1980 auction catalogue as being by Gabriele Münter, an artist of the German expressionist school. Hull had no expertise in this area. He took the paintings to Christie's who expressed interest and he also telephoned the plaintiffs, who carried on business as art dealers at a London gallery specialising in the German expressionist school. He told the plaintiffs that he had two paintings by Münter for sale and an employee of the plaintiffs (Runkell) visited the defendants' gallery to view them. Hull made it clear that he did not know much about the paintings and that he was not an expert in them. Runkell agreed to buy one of the paintings for £6,000 without asking any questions about their provenance or making any further inquiries. The invoice for the painting described it as being by Gabriele Münter. The painting was later discovered to be a forgery and the plaintiffs, having reimbursed their own customer to whom the painting had been sold on, sued to recover the contract price. They based their claim in part on s 13 of the 1979 Act. Judge Oddie held that s 13 was inapplicable in the absence of reliance by the plaintiffs on the defendants and he dismissed the claim. The plaintiffs then appealed to the Court of Appeal.

Nourse LJ, having stated the facts and considered earlier authorities, continued:

. . . In theory it is no doubt possible for a description of goods which is not relied on by the buyer to become an essential term of a contract for their sale. But in practice it is very difficult, and perhaps impossible, to think of facts where that would be so. The description must have a sufficient influence in the sale to become an essential term of the contract and the correlative of influence is reliance. Indeed, reliance by the buyer is the natural index of a sale by description. It is true that the question must, as always, be judged objectively and it may be said that previous judicial references have been to subjective or actual reliance. But each of those decisions, including that of Judge Oddie in the present case, can be justified on an objective basis. For all practical purposes, I would say that there cannot be a contract for the sale of goods by description where it is not within the reasonable contemplation of the parties that the buyer is relying on the description. For those purposes, I think that the law is correctly summarised in these words of *Benjamin* p 641, which should be understood to lay down an objective test:

'Specific goods may be sold as such . . . where, though the goods are described, the description is not relied upon, as where the buyer buys the goods such as they are.'

In giving his decision on this question Judge Oddie said:

'There can clearly be a sale by description where the buyer has inspected the goods if the description relates to something not apparent on inspection. Every item in a description which constitutes a substantial ingredient in the identity of the thing sold is a condition.'

Later, having said that he had not been referred to any similar case where a sale in reliance on a statement that a painting was by a particular artist had been held to be a sale by description, the judge continued:

'In my judgment such a statement could amount to a description and a sale in reliance on it to a sale by description within the meaning of the 1979 Act. However, on the facts of this case I am satisfied that the description by Mr Hull before the agreement was not relied on by Mr Runkel in making his offer to purchase which was accepted by Mr Hull. I conclude that he bought the painting as it was. In these circumstances there was not in my judgment a sale by description.'

I agree. On a view of their words and deeds as a whole the parties could not reasonably have contemplated that the defendants were relying on the plaintiffs' statement that the painting was by Gabriele Münter. On the facts which he found the judge could not, by a correct application of the law, have come to any other decision.

Stuart-Smith LJ,dissenting, having cited part of Judge Oddie's judgment, continued:

[The] nub of his conclusion is that Mr Runkel did not rely on the description but on his own judgment as to the authorship of the painting. For my part I have great difficulty in understanding how the concept of reliance fits into a sale by description. If it is a term of the contract that the painting is by Münter the purchaser does not have to prove that he entered into the contract in reliance on this statement. This distinguishes a contractual term or condition from a mere representation which induces a purchaser to enter into a contract. In the latter case the person to whom the representation is made must prove that he relied on it as a matter of fact.

. . .

In my judgment the matter can be tested in this way. If following the telephone conversation Mr Runkel had arrived at the defendants' gallery, seen the painting, bargained about the price and agreed to buy it, it seems to me beyond argument that it would have been a sale by description. And indeed counsel for the defendants was at one time disposed to concede as much. Had the invoice been a contractual document, as it frequently is, again it seems to me clear that the sale would have been a sale by description. In fact the invoice was written out subsequently to the oral contract; but the judge held, rightly as it seems to me, that it gave effect to what had been agreed. It was cogent evidence of the oral contract.

How does it come about that what would otherwise be a sale by description in some way ceased to be one? It can only be as a result of the conversation between Mr Hull and Mr Runkel before the bargain was actually struck. If Mr Hull had told Mr Runkel that he did not know one way or the other whether the painting was by Münter in spite of the fact that he had so described it or that he could only say that the painting was attributed to Münter, and that Mr Runkel must make up his mind for himself on this point, I can well see that the effect of what had previously been said about the identity of the painter might have been cancelled or withdrawn and was no longer effective at the time of the contract. But Mr Hull did not say that, as the judge found. And I cannot see that this is the effect of what was said. Merely to say that he knew nothing of the painter and did not like her paintings does not in any way to my mind necessarily mean that he was cancelling or withdrawing what he had previously said, based as it was on the auction catalogue. Nor does the fact that it was recognised that the plaintiffs were more expert in German expressionist art than Mr Hull advance the matter. It would, in my judgment, be a serious defect in the law if the effect of a condition implied by statute could be excluded by the vendor's saying that he was not an expert in what was being sold or that the purchaser was more expert than the vendor. That is not the law; it has long been held that conditions implied by statute can only be excluded by clear words. There is nothing of that kind in this case . . .

Slade LJ agreed that the appeal should be dismissed, saying:

. . . There is no statutory definition of the phrase 'a contract for the sale of goods by description'. One has to look to the ordinary meaning of words and the decided cases for guidance as to its meaning. I think that the guidance to be derived from the cases cited to us, which have been referred to by Nourse and Stuart-Smith LJJ, is surprisingly limited. There may be little difficulty in applying the phrase in the case of a sale of unascertained or future goods, since there can be no contract for the sale of goods of these categories, except by reference to a description of some sort. The greater difficulty is likely to arise in cases such as the present where the sale is of 'specific goods' within the meaning of s 61 of the 1979 Act, that is to say, 'goods identified and agreed on at the time a contract of sale is made' . . .

While some judicial dicta seem to support the view that there can be no sale by description unless there is actual reliance on the description by the purchaser, I am not sure that this is strictly correct in principle. If a party to a contract wishes to claim relief in respect of a misrepresentation as to a matter which did not constitute a term of the contract, his claim will fail unless he is able to show that he relied on this representation in entering into the contract; in general, however, if a party wishes to claim relief in respect of a breach of *a term* of the contract (whether it be a condition or warranty) he need prove no actual reliance.

Nevertheless, where a question arises whether a sale of goods was one by description, the presence or absence of reliance on the description may be very relevant in so far as it throws light on the intentions of the parties at the time of the contract. If there was no such reliance by the purchaser, this may be powerful evidence that the parties did not contemplate that the authenticity of the description should constitute a term of the contract, in other words, that they contemplated that the purchaser would be buying the goods *as they were*. If, on the other hand, there was such reliance (as in *Varley v Whipp* [1900] 1 QB 513, where the purchaser had never seen the goods) this may be equally powerful evidence that it was contemplated by both parties that the correctness of the description would be a term of the contract (so as to bring it within s 13(1)).

So far as it concerns s 13(1), the issue for the court in the present case was and is, in my judgment, this: on an objective assessment of what the parties said and did at and before the meeting at Motcomb Street, and of all the circumstances of the case, is it right to impute to them the common intention that the authenticity of the attribution to Gabriele Münter should be a term of the contract of sale? The proper inferences to be drawn from the evidence and the findings of primary fact by the judge are matters on which different minds can take different views, as the cogent judgments of Nourse and Stuart-Smith LJJ have shown. However, I for my part feel no doubt that the answer to the crucial issue is, No . . .

The form of the invoice subsequently made out in favour of the plaintiffs does not, in my judgment, assist the plaintiffs' case. By that time the contract had already been concluded. While the reference to Gabriele Münter in the invoice is quite consistent with the parties having made the origin of the picture a term of the contract, it can equally well be read as merely a convenient mode of reference to a particular picture which both parties knew to have been attributed to Gabriele Münter (and indeed both still thought to be her work).

For these reasons, I agree with the conclusions of Nourse LJ and the judge that this was not a sale falling within s 13(1) of the 1979 Act. In my view, one cannot impute to the parties a common intention that it should be a term of the contract that the artist was Gabriele Münter
. . .

Appeal dismissed.

NOTE

It will be seen that the implied condition as to correspondence with description cannot be excluded as against a person who 'deals as consumer' and otherwise can be excluded only to the extent that the 'requirement of reasonableness' is satisfied: see the Unfair Contract Terms Act 1977, s 6(2)(a) and (3), below, pp 356–60. In this case the terms was not 'excluded'. Rather, it was held that it did not apply since the contract was not one of a sale 'by description'.

QUESTION

Would the result of the case have been different if the buyer had been a private collector, rather than a dealer with a specialist interest in the German expressionist school of painting?

A further feature of this implied condition is that, unlike the implied conditions as to quality and fitness for purpose below, it applies to private transactions no less than to occasions where goods are supplied 'in the course of a business'. The importance of this point and the borderline between matters of description and quality are illustrated in the following cases.

Beale v Taylor [1967] 3 All ER 253, [1967] 1 WLR 1193, Court of Appeal

The facts are set out in the judgment.

Sellers LJ: . . . The defendant seller, Mr Taylor, had a car which he believed to be a Herald convertible, 1961, 1200 twin-carburettor car. He apparently had driven it for some time and done a considerable mileage with it and wished to dispose of it. I think that it had been in an accident, and certainly it was not in very good condition. The seller inserted an advertisement in about April, 1966, in a well-known paper for the sale of secondhand cars. That was in these terms: 'Herald convertible, white, 1961, twin carbs., £190. Telephone Welwyn Garden', and it gives a telephone number, 'after 6.0 p.m.'. The plaintiff buyer, who was born in 1946 and has been driving cars for some little time, or his mother, or both, saw that advertisement, got in touch with the seller, and went along to his home to see the car. They saw it and had a run in it. The buyer did not drive because there was no insurance for him. I do not know whether his mother went in the car too. After that run and some discussion the buyer made an offer, or his mother made an offer, to buy the car for £160, which the seller accepted. There was a little delay while the balance of the purchase price was paid, and then the buyer drove it away. From the outset apparently the buyer found that the steering was pulling to the left-hand side, so much so that he said that, in his journey from Welwyn Garden City to St Albans, his arms ached; and he eventually after a short time put it in a garage to be checked over. Then it was found by the garage people that, instead of being a car of that description—that being a 1961 1200 Triumph Herald convertible—it was in fact a car which was made up of two cars. The back portion apparently was of that description but the front portion, which had been welded on about half-way, somewhere under the driver's seat, and which contained the engine, was an older, earlier model, the 948 cc model, and these two parts had been made into this one structure. Having regard to the nature of the welding of the two chassis together, as described by the expert who was called, it is not surprising that the car was not running properly. It had also apparently had an accident, as I have said, and it was condemned as being unsafe to take on the road.

The question then arose what was to happen with regard to the purchase price which the buyer had paid to the seller. Instead of the matter being settled amicably, which might have been the wisest thing to do in order to save the money which has been involved in costs, the matter went to court. The buyer relied on the fact that there had been a description of this vehicle as a

Triumph Herald 1200 motor car with the registration number 400 RDH and that the vehicle which was delivered did not correspond with that description. The seller, who conducted his own defence and apparently put in his written defence as well, denied that it was a sale by description and said that, on the contrary, it was

'the sale of a particular car as seen, tried and approved, the [buyer] having an abundant opportunity to inspect and test the car.'

He denied that the buyer had in the circumstances suffered any loss or damage. Of course a person may purchase a commodity relying entirely on his own judgment in the matter, and there may be no representation at all. Perhaps one hundred years ago more credence might have been given to the seller's defence than is given now, but, since the Sale of Goods Act 1893, the rule caveat emptor has been very much modified. Section 13 of the Sale of Goods Act, 1893, provides that

'Where there is a contract for the sale of goods by description, there is an implied condition that the goods shall correspond with that description; . . .'

and certainly there is good authority for saying that, if the buyer has not seen the goods, then in the ordinary way the contract would be one where the buyer relied on the description alone. Sale of goods by description may, however, apply where the buyer has seen the goods if the deviation of the goods from the description is not apparent; but even then (and I am quoting now from a well-known text book, *Chalmers' Sale of Goods* (15th edn), when the parties are really agreed on the thing sold a misdescription of it in the contract may be immaterial.

The question in this case is whether this was a sale by description or whether, as the seller contends, this was a sale of a particular thing seen by the buyer and bought by him purely on his own assessment of the value of the thing to him. We were referred to a passage in the speech of Lord Wright in *Grant v Australian Knitting Mills Ltd*,[1] which I think is apt as far as this case is concerned. Lord Wright said:

'It may also be pointed out that there is a sale by description even though the buyer is buying something displayed before him on the counter; a thing is sold by description, though it is specific, so long as it is sold not merely as the specific thing but as a thing corresponding to a description, eg, woollen under-garments, a hot water bottle, a secondhand reaping machine, to select a few obvious illustrations'

—and, I might add, a secondhand motor car. I think that, on the facts of this case, the buyer, when he came along to see this car, was coming alone to see a car as advertised, that is, a car described as a 'Herald convertible, white, 1961'. When he came along he saw what ostensibly was a Herald convertible, white, 1961, because the evidence shows that the '1200' which was exhibited on the rear of this motor car is the first model of the '1200' which came out in 1961; it was on that basis that he was making the offer and in the belief that the seller was advancing his car as that which his advertisement indicated. Apart from that, the selling of a car of that make, I would on the fact of it rather agree with the submission of the seller that he was making no warranties at all and making no contractual terms; but fundamentally he was selling a car of that description. The facts as revealed very shortly afterwards show that that description was false. It was unfortunately not false to the knowledge of the owner who was selling nor of the buyer, because no one could see from looking at the car in the ordinary sort of examination which would be made that it was anything other than that which it purported to be. It was only afterwards that, on examination, it was found to be in two parts. I think that that is a sufficient ground on which to decide this case in favour of the buyer . . .

Danckwerts LJ: I agree.

Baker J: I agree.

Appeal allowed. No order as to costs of the appeal.

[1] [1935] All ER Rep 209 at 215, [1936] AC 85 at 100.

Smith v Lazarus (1981) (unreported) 23 June, (Lexis transcript) Court of Appeal

Lawton LJ: This is an appeal by a Mr Lazarus, who was the defendant at the trial, against a judgment given against him by His Honour Judge Taylor in the Southend County Court on 29 July 1980 whereby the learned judge gave judgment for the plaintiff, Mr George Smith, in the sum of £351, including interest of £49, together with the costs of the claim.

Mr Lazarus is a gentleman who did not see fit to go into the witness box in the county court. It may be he was very wise to keep out of the witness box. Apparently one of the things he does is to advertise motor cars for sale. He has certainly done so on two occasions. Unfortunately we have not before us the form of the advertisement which led to the series of untoward events with which we are concerned. It suffices to say, however, that early in December 1978 he advertised a motor car for sale in the *Evening Echo*, which circulates in the Southend area. The probabilities are that, in the course of describing the motor car in the advertisement, he put something like this in it: 'Full MOT'. The plaintiff saw the advertisement, went round to Mr Lazarus's house to have a look at the car. It was dark when he arrived. He only examined it cursorily. He then decided to buy it. Mr Lazarus then drove him to his house and the car was left outside.

The next morning Mr Smith had a better look at what he had bought and was appalled, as well he might have been, at what Mr Lazarus had sold him. It seemed to Mr Smith—and he was right in the assumptions which he made—that the motor car was not roadworthy. This being December there was some delay before the Automobile Association could make an inspection. They did make an inspection on 2 January 1979 and they came to the conclusion, as the learned judge found, that the vehicle was unfit for use on the road because its structure was so badly corroded that it would be unsafe to drive it; and anyway, the engine had frozen up during the time it was standing outside Mr Smith's house, and the consequence of so freezing was to cause a good deal of damage to the mechanics of the motor car.

If Mr Lazarus had been an upright man one would have expected him, when these defects were brought to his attention, to take the car back and return the price; but that, apparently, is not Mr Lazarus' way of dealing. He took his stand on caveat emptor: Mr Smith had bought a pig in a poke and had to put up with the pig, having got it. Was Mr Lazarus entitled in law to refuse to return the price?

Mr Smith and his advisers suspected that Mr Lazarus was in trade as a motor dealer, selling his motor cars, as is well-known some dishonest motor dealers do, by pretending to be a private individual and inserting advertisements in local newspapers. The reason they suspected that that is what he was up to was that it came to their notice that there had been an earlier advertisement in the *Evening Echo* in respect of another motor car. On the basis of their suspicions they put their claim in this way: firstly, that there had been a breach by Mr Lazarus of implied warranties of fitness under the provisions of section 14 of the Sale of Goods Act 1979 as amended. Secondly—and this was by a late amendment—that as there had been a reference, in the course of the negotiations for the sale, to a recent MOT certificate having been obtained in respect of the car, as one had been obtained about a fortnight before the sale it followed, so it was submitted, that Mr Lazarus was impliedly warranting that the motor car was structurally safe for use on the road. And thirdly the suggestion was made that what had been sold by Mr Lazarus to Mr Smith was not a motor car at all but a piece of useless machinery; and it was said to be a piece of useless machinery because the AA report suggested that the defects were so grave that it would be a waste of money to try and put them right.

As I have already said, Mr Lazarus prudently kept out of the witness box, and the result was that all the learned judge had was evidence of advertising two vehicles for sale over a short period in the *Evening Echo*. He came to the conclusion that that was not enough to prove that Mr Lazarus was selling in the course of business. That finding cannot, in my judgment, be challenged . . .

The learned county court judge, however, clearly sympathised with Mr Smith, as I do, and seems to have been anxious to have found some way of compensating him for what, clearly, was a shady trading practice by Mr Lazarus. The conclusion he came to, according to the note of his judgment which was taken by Mr Matthews, was this—and I read from the note—

'Mr Smith paid Lazarus £310 for a car. He did not get a car. A car is something you can use and drive. The vehicle was unroadworthy. He paid for a car. What he got was almost valueless piece of machinery. Having regard to contents of report the consideration fails'.

Mr Matthews, on behalf of Mr Lazarus, has challenged the judgment on that point. He has pointed out that this is a classic case of caveat emptor: Mr Smith bought what he was shown by Mr Lazarus. Because of the circumstances, and perhaps because of Mr Smith's lack of knowledge about motor cars, he did not make a thorough examination of the motor car, and in the ordinary way, unless warranties can be implied, or express warranties are given, a purchaser has to take what he is shown, with all its faults. It is up to him to discover what the faults are.

There was no evidence here that there was any misrepresentation which would bring into operation the Misrepresentation Act. There was not enough evidence to show that Mr Lazarus was selling the car in the course of business. It follows that the ordinary common law principles of caveat emptor did apply. And if Mr Smith did get a motor car which was a useless motor car, unfortunately he has to bear the resulting loss. The problem is: Did he get a motor car?

The learned judge may have had in mind, when giving his judgment, the case of *Karsales (Harrow) Ltd v Wallis* [1956] 2 All ER 866, [1956] 1 WLR 936. In the course of his judgment in that case Lord Justice Denning (as he then was) said this:

'When the defendant inspected the car prior to signing the application form, the car was in excellent condition and would go, whereas the car which was subsequently delivered to him was no doubt the same car but it was in a deplorable state and would not go. That breach went to the root of the contract and disentitles the lender from relying on the exempting clause'.

No question of an exempting clause arises in this case, and in any event the case of *Karsales (Harrow) Ltd v Wallis* is distinguishable on its facts, because in the passage in the judgment to which I have referred, Lord Justice Denning was saying that what the purchaser was shown was not what he got; whereas in this case what Mr Smith was shown was what he got. It follows, therefore, that it is impossible to say that there was any change in the identity of the subject matter of the sale.

For my part, with very great regret, I find I am unable to accept the learned judge's finding that what was delivered to Mr Smith was not a motor car: it was a motor car, but one of very poor quality indeed. Mr Smith's mistake as to the quality of what he was buying is not a reason why he should not pay for what he was buying.

I would allow the appeal.

Shaw LJ: I agree.

Fortunately for Mr Lazarus we have to decide this appeal on the legalities and not the moralities of this matter. In all but the strict sense of the law Mr Lazarus cheated Mr Smith out of £310. I find it a matter of great regret that this court can do nothing to enable Mr Smith to recover his money.

I would allow this appeal.

Sir Stanley Rees: I agree with both judgments.

Appeal allowed, with costs; defendant to have no costs in the court below; order of County Court judge set aside.

NOTES

1. For the offence which is committed when it can be proved that a person is disguising the fact that a sale is 'in the course of a business' see the Business Advertisements (Disclosure) Order 1977, SI 1977/1918 and below, p 540 et seq.
2. For discussion of the extent to which retailers impliedly adopt descriptions and promotional claims of the manufacturers whose goods they are selling see above, p 33 et seq.

QUESTIONS

1. In the following advertisement, which words form part of the contract description: '1992 Mini Metro K Registration 27,000 miles. One careful lady owner'?
2. In the example in Lord Wright's speech in *Grant v Australian Knitting Mills* [1936] AC 85 at 100, cited above, p 92 would there have been a 'sale by description' if the hot water bottle had not been marked or otherwise labelled as such? Suppose that it had been so labelled and that it had burst the first time it was used, being quite incapable of holding hot water: would there then have been a breach of s 13?

SATISFACTORY QUALITY AND FITNESS FOR PURPOSE

The implied terms of, for example, s 14 of the Sale of Goods Act 1979, above, p 80, constitute the cornerstone of consumers' rights in relation to the quality and fitness for purpose of goods and materials supplied. Subject to a provision for sales through agents (see s 14(5) of the 1979 Act) the terms are implied only where goods are supplied 'in the course of business'. In *Boyter v Thompson* [1995] 3 All ER 135, [1995] 2 AC 628, where the subject matter of the sale was an unseaworthy cabin cruiser, the House of Lords confirmed that the effect of s 14(5) (above, p 81) is to render a private undisclosed principal potentially liable.

In the course of a business

The delimitation according to whether an act is done 'in the course of business' appears in a variety of contexts. The expression is considered further when discussing a similar limitation in the Trade Descriptions Act 1968, s 1, below, pp 609–14, and the Business Advertisements (Disclosure) Order 1977, below, p 547. (See in particular the contrasting cases of *Davies v Sumner* [1984] 1 WLR 405; affd [1984] 3 All ER 831, HL below, p 609, and *Blakemore v Bellamy* [1983] RTR 303, below, p 544). It is also relevant to the definition of the expression 'deals as consumer' and hence to the extent of the protection afforded by the Unfair Contract Terms Act 1977, s 12 (below, p 328). (See *R & B Customs Brokers Co Ltd v United Dominions Trust Ltd* [1988] 1 All ER 847, [1988] 1 WLR 321, below, p 357.) An approach which requires 'some degree of regularity' in selling the relevant goods restricts criminal liability in the one context and expands consumer protection in the other. However, in the present context a similar approach may restrict the application of s 14. The origins of the expression 'in the course of a business' as applied to s 14 may be seen in the following extract.

Exemption Clauses in Contracts—Law Commission's First Report: Amendments to the Sale of Goods Act 1893 (1969) (Law Com No 24)

Subsection (1) of section 14

. . .

Recommendations for amending the subsection

31. The Molony Committee recommended two amendments to subsection (1). The first of these concerned the requirement that, in order to give rise to the implied condition of fitness, the goods must be 'of a description which it is in the course of the seller's business to supply'. The Molony Committee took the view that if a retailer sells an article in the course of business, he should be answerable for both its merchantability and its fitness for purpose whether or not he has traded in the same line previously. 'The test should be whether he sells by way of trade to the particular purchaser and not whether he makes a habit of trading in similar goods, which is a circumstance not necessarily known to the purchaser.'[1] We associate ourselves with these arguments and recommend that the condition of fitness for purpose should be implied into all sales other than those in which the seller sells in a private capacity. In other words, the condition should be implied whenever the seller is acting in the course of a business[2] even though he may not be a dealer in goods of the relevant description.[3]

. . .

[1] Final Report, paragraph 443; the arguments there advanced with reference to merchantable quality were adopted in paragraph 447 with reference to fitness for purpose.
[2] The Molony Committee, in the text quoted from paragraph 443 of their Final Report, suggested that the test should be whether the seller sells 'by way of trade'. We prefer the formula 'in the course of business' which, unlike the phrase 'by way of trade', does not lend itself to a restrictive interpretation tending in the direction of making the seller's particular trade the applicable test. Such a restrictive interpretation would defeat our main purpose which is to ensure that the conditions implied by section 14 are imposed on every trade seller, no matter whether he is or is not habitually dealing in goods of the type sold.
[3] Thus, for example, where a coal merchant whose business it is to supply coal sells one of his delivery vehicles the condition of fitness should be implied; for the sale is part of the seller's business activities, even though he is not a dealer in vehicles.

NOTES

1. Section 14(1) of the Sale of Goods Act 1893 has since been re-numbered s 14(3), and is now in the 1979 Act.
2. The word 'business' is defined by the Sale of Goods Act 1979, s 61(1) to include 'a profession and the activities of any government department . . . or local or public authority'. See also the Supply of Goods and Services Act 1982, s 18(1). In this area, as in others, there will be difficulty in deciding whether a

given activity is a 'business' as opposed to a pastime or some other non-trading pursuit: see *Benjamin's Sale of Goods* (5th edn, 1997), para 11–046.

The following Scottish case is of some assistance in indicating the scope of the expression 'in the course of a business' as used in the present context.

Buchanan-Jardine v Hamilink 1981 SLT (Notes) 60, Outer House

A contract for the sale of a farm and estate provided that the purchasers would take over the livestock at a valuation. Thereafter two cows reacted positively to tests for tuberculosis. The purchasers retained part of the purchase price and counter-claimed for damages in respect of their losses.

Lord Dunpark, having stated the facts of the case, is reported as adding: The legal basis of the purchasers' claim was stated thus: 'Prior to the sale the seller had carried on business as a farmer on said land and estate and had acquired the stock in the course of that business. The sale of the stock to the purchasers was made in the course of the seller's said business. It was accordingly a term of the contract of sale that the stock should be of merchantable quality. The two cows which were discovered to be tuberculosis reactors were such reactors when the contract of sale was concluded on 21 December 1977 and therefore at that date they were not of merchantable quality.'

The case came in procedure roll before Lord Dunpark sitting in the Outer House. In indicating that a proof would be appropriate provided that the purchasers gave more specification of their losses the Lord Ordinary dealt with several preliminary arguments on behalf of the seller. In considering and rejecting a submission that s 14(2) of the Sale of Goods Act did not apply to the sale of the livestock his Lordship said:

'Counsel's second ground of irrelevancy was that s 14(2) did not apply to the sale of this livestock in respect that this was not a sale "in the course of a business", notwithstanding the defenders' averment that it was. His short point was that this was a private sale of a whole enterprise and that such a sale, which terminated the business, was not a sale "in the course of a business". He did not suggest that farming was not a business or that the pursuer had not been carrying on such a business when he sold his farm, with stock and implements to the defenders . . . In my opinion anyone who sells any part of his business equipment must sell that part "in the course of his business". It can make no difference whether he sells only one item or the whole of the goods used by him for the purpose of a business. Moreover, it is significant, although not relevant to this case, that since 1973 the warranty of merchantable quality has applied to all goods sold "in the course of a business", whether or not the seller "deals" in the goods sold. I have no doubt that this sale of livestock was made by the pursuer "in the course of a business".'

QUESTIONS

1. If the farmer had sold off his combine harvester rather than his cattle would such a sale have attracted the implied terms of s 14 of the Act?
   Would it be desirable in principle that it should have done so?
2. If a university bookshop sells new books, or a student body purchases and re-sells secondhand books, is this done in the course of a 'business'?

Satisfactory quality

The statutory definitions of 'satisfactory quality' now contained in the Sale of Goods Act 1979, s 14 (above, p 80) and related provisions were introduced by the Sale and Supply of Goods Act 1994. This superseded the requirement of 'merchantable quality' which was formerly defined by s 14(6) of the 1979 Act as follows:

'Goods of any kind are of merchantable quality within the meaning of subsection (2) above if they are as fit for the purpose or purposes for which goods of that kind are commonly bought as it is reasonable to expect having regard to any description applied to them, the price (if relevant) and all other relevant circumstances.'

This definition originated in a Law Commission Report entitled 'Exemption Clauses in Contracts: First Report: Amendments to the Sale of Goods Act 1893 (Law Com No 24, 1969). Previously the Act contained no definition of 'merchantable quality', leaving the test to be supplied by the developing common law. The central test adopted was based on the deceptively simple notion of 'fitness for purpose'. Thereafter doubts were expressed as to whether the new statutory definition adequately covered both cosmetic defects which did not affect the functioning of the goods and cases where defects were individually minor and yet cumulatively serious. In 1978 the Consumers' Association became involved in such a case based on the sale of a new Reliant Scimitar car which had many defects of varying degrees of importance. Counsel had advised that the buyer was not entitled to reject the car as being unmerchantable and this led to the Association organising a seminar in which academics and practitioners presented papers. An edited version of the proceedings was published under the title *Merchantable Quality: What Does it Mean?* (CA, 1979, editor Professor J Macleod). After the seminar Mr Donald Stewart MP, was persuaded to introduce a private member's bill to reform the law. The Bill was withdrawn on the matter being referred by the Lord Chancellor to the Law Commission which was asked to consider:

(a) whether the undertakings as to quality and fitness of goods implied under the law relating to the sale of goods, hire-purchase and other contracts for the supply of goods require amendment;
(b) the circumstances in which a person to whom goods are supplied under a contract of sale, hire-purchase or other contract for the supply of goods is entitled, where there has been a breach by the supplier of a term implied by statute, to:
    (i) reject the goods and treat the contract as repudiated;
    (ii) claim against the supplier a diminution or extinction of the price;
    (iii) claim damages against the supplier;
(c) the circumstances in which, by reason of the Sale of Goods Act 1893,[1] a buyer loses the right to reject the goods; and to make recommendations.

[1] The various enactments relating to the sale of goods are now consolidated in the Sale of Goods Act 1979.

The Law Commission duly published a Working Paper entitled 'Sale and Supply of Goods' (Law Commission Working Paper No 85, 1983) which, in turn, led to the publication of a Report, 'Sale and Supply of Goods' (Law Com No 160, 1987). The recommendations and accompanying draft Bill contained in the Report were largely adopted in the Sale and Supply of Goods Act 1994, except that the Act expresses the standard in terms of 'satisfactory' as opposed to 'acceptable' quality. Having discussed the basic test of quality now contained in s 14(2A) of the Act whereby goods must meet 'the standard that a reasonable person would regard as satisfactory [acceptable], taking account of any description of the goods, the price (if relevant) and all the other relevant circumstances', the Report continues as follows:

Sale and Supply of Goods (Law Com No 160, 1987)

. . .

(ii) The second element: the list of aspects of quality
3.28. What we have been describing so far has been the basic test of quality, phrased in general terms, and stating a principle only. The second element that we envisage in the new definition of quality is a list of various specific aspects of quality. Any or all of the listed matters could be taken into account in a particular case in order to decide whether the goods were up to the required quality or not. Other matters, not listed, might of course also be relevant, but in our view it would be helpful to buyers and sellers alike to have their attention drawn specifically to a number of the more commonly important matters that help to make up the quality of goods. Not all of these would be relevant in every case.

3.29. The reason for our proposing such a list of aspects of quality is that one of the defects of the present definition is its heavy emphasis on fitness for purpose as the only criterion of quality. Although 'fitness for purpose' does extend beyond mere functional fitness,[23] and is, of course, almost always relevant, it is only one among many aspects of quality. Specific mention of fitness for purpose but not of the other aspects may obscure the relevance of those other aspects. We recommend a wider list, in which no one element would have priority, in which not all the elements would always be relevant, and which would leave room for other, unlisted, matters to be taken into account. This reference to more than one factor has been the approach used or proposed in other countries.[24]

3.30. In the Consultative Document we suggested a number of matters which might be included in a list of aspects of quality. Our views on some of them have changed but we discuss them all below.

Fitness for purpose
3.31. Fitness or purpose or 'usability' is almost always a very important aspect of quality. The criticism of the present definition is not that fitness for purpose is stressed, but that it is stressed to the exclusion of everything else. We said in the Consultative Document that fitness for purpose should certainly feature as an aspect of quality but only as one among others. That remains our view. This 'demotion' of the requirement of fitness for purpose is intended to show that the required quality of goods does not depend only on their 'usability' or their functional fitness for purpose. Thus, for example, a new car should not only be capable of being driven safely and effectively on the road, but should also do so 'with the appropriate degree of comfort, ease of handling and reliability and . . . of pride in the vehicle's outward and interior appearance'.[25]

3.32. We mentioned in the Consultative Document[26] that goods of a particular description and price have been held to be of merchantable quality so long as they were saleable or usable for *some* purpose consistent with the description and price, even if the buyer privately had in mind a different but still common purpose.[27] The cases in which this was decided were before the definition of merchantable quality was introduced in 1973; but although the use of pre-1973 cases has been disapproved,[28] in this instance it does not appear that the 1973 definition was intended to alter the law on the point.[29] We said in the Consultative Document[30] that in our opinion the better view of the 1973 definition was that the matter was to be decided in the context of the whole definition, so that the goods need not necessarily be fit for *all* their normal purposes;[31] and this view has now been confirmed by the Court of Appeal in *M/S Aswan Engineering Establishment Co v Lupdine Ltd*[32] . . .

3.36. Although not without doubt on the part of some of us, we have reached the conclusion . . . that goods of a particular description and price should be fit for *all* their common purposes unless there is an indication to the contrary. If the buyer has a particular uncommon purpose in mind it is always open to him to make this known to the seller, and rely on section 14(3) of the 1979 Act. If, on the other hand, the seller knows that his goods are not fit for one or more of the purposes for which goods of that kind are commonly supplied, he may ensure that the description of the goods excludes any common purpose for which they are unfit, or otherwise indicates that the goods are not fit for all their common purposes. If he does not do so, and it is not clear from the other circumstances, then the seller may be in breach of the implied quality term if he sells goods which are commonly supplied for two purposes but which are fit for only one.

State or condition

3.37. The state or condition of goods is included in 'quality' under the present law.[34] We suggested no change in the Consultative Document and we suggest none here, except that the reference to 'state or condition' should in our view be brought forward and included in the implied term as to quality, instead of being found only at the end of the Act in the definition section.[35]

Appearance, finish, and freedom from minor defects

3.38. We suggested in the Consultative Document that the new definition of quality should specifically refer to appearance, finish, and freedom from minor defects as an aspect of quality. On consultation this proposal was generally supported, particularly as regards minor defects, and we therefore recommend that such a reference should be included in the new definition.[36]

3.39. On consideration, however, we now propose that 'appearance and finish' be separated from 'freedom from minor defects', and that these two matters be referred to separately instead of together in the new definition. This will avoid any possible implication that a 'minor defect' must be a defect in appearance or finish. Minor defects may, of course, relate to appearance or finish, but they may also be (for example) minor malfunctions in the operation of a machine and have nothing to do with appearance or finish.

3.40. Both of these proposed references may be relevant more to new goods than to second-hand goods, and perhaps more to consumer purchases than to business purchases. One of the criticisms of the present law is that the extent to which minor imperfections in appearance, finish, or functioning are a breach of contract is no longer clear.[37] These references to appearance and finish and to freedom from minor defects as aspects of quality are intended to show that in appropriate cases the buyer (in particular, the buyer of new goods) is entitled to expect that the goods will be free from even small imperfections. Thus dents, scratches, minor blemishes and discolourations, and small malfunctions will in appropriate cases be breaches of the implied term as to quality, provided they are not so trifling as to fall within the principle that matters which are quite negligible are not breaches of contract at all.[38] Whether or not any particular defect or blemish is a breach of contract will depend on the facts of the case. For example, second-hand goods might be expected to have some marks or minor defects: these may not be breaches of contract, and the price of the goods may reflect this. Another example which was put to us on consultation was articles made of earthenware or pottery, or natural products in general. These will always contain what some might argue to be slight inconsistencies or imperfections, but we do not intend these necessarily to be breaches of contract. Where it is in the nature of the goods in question that small differences or inconsistencies will occur from place to place in the body of the material used or from article to article, such differences or inconsistencies may not be defects or imperfections at all.

3.41. Further, it will not always be appropriate to judge quality by reference to appearance and finish or to the existence of minor defects. For example, appearance and finish and the existence of minor defects are plainly irrelevant in the case of a car sold for scrap, or of the purchase of a hundredweight of manure. The references to appearance and finish and to freedom from minor defects will, on the other hand, be particularly relevant in the case of new consumer goods such as cars, 'white goods' and clothes . . .

3.43. The references which we propose to minor defects and to appearance and finish should make it easier for a court faced with the facts of (for example) *Millars of Falkirk Ltd v Turpie*[40] to reach a different conclusion from that which was reached in that case on the existing wording of section 14(6), although . . . this cannot be absolutely guaranteed. In that case the buyer was left with no remedy at all for a leak in the power-assisted steering system of his new car. We do not think that in such a case the buyer should have to put up even with minor defects without a remedy (apart, of course, from those defects of which he should have been aware at the time of sale, or which were specifically drawn to his attention). In our view the references to appearance and finish and (in particular) to minor defects should help to emphasise that the requirement of quality does not depend entirely on fitness for purpose.

Safety
3.44. In the Consultative Document we pointed out that it was clearly an important element in the implied term that goods should be reasonably safe when used for any of their normal purposes. We did not propose any alteration in the law here, but asked whether a specific provision on safety should be incorporated in the statute.

3.45. On consultation there was general support for such a provision . . .

3.46. Our view is, therefore, that safety should be included in the list of aspects of quality which we propose as part of the new definition.[41] Although this may result in some overlap with Parts I and II of the Consumer Protection Bill (if enacted in its original form), that Bill would perform an essentially different function, and we therefore do not think that a reference to safety should after all be omitted from the Sale of Goods Act.

Durability . . .

[23] *Rogers v Parish (Scarborough) Ltd* [1987] 2 WLR 353.
[24] For example: US Uniform Commercial Code, s 2–314; and the proposed Canadian Uniform Sale of Goods Act, s 5.13(1), adopted by the Uniform Law Conference of Canada (1981).
[25] *Rogers v Parish (Scarborough) Ltd* [1987] 2 WLR 353, 359, *per* Mustill LJ. It would therefore not usually be sufficient that a car (even a second-hand car) was 'in a usable condition' or 'in a roadworthy condition, fit to be driven along the road in safety' (*Bartlett v Sidney Marcus Ltd* [1965] 1 WLR 1013, 1016 and 1017, *per* Lord Denning MR). Equally, the car in *Millars of Falkirk Ltd v Turpie* 1976 SLT (Notes) 66 would also fail the test of quality on our proposed definition.
[26] At para 2.3.
[27] *Kendall v Lillico* [1969] 2 AC 31; *B S Brown & Son Ltd v Craiks Ltd* 1970 SC (HL) 51, [1970] 1 WLR 752.
[28] *Rogers v Parish (Scarborough) Ltd* [1987] 2 WLR 353.

[29] Exemption Clauses in Contracts First Report: Amendments to the Sale of Goods Act 1893 (1969), Law Com No 24; Scot Law Com No 12; paras 40 ff.

[30] At para 4.13.

[31] P S Atiyah, *The Sale of Goods* 7th edn (1985), pp 121–8; *Benjamin's Sale of Goods* 2nd edn (1981), para 808; cf Aubrey L Diamond, 'The Law Commissions' First Report on Exemption Clauses' (1970), 33 MLR 77; R M Goode, *Commercial Law* (1982), p 261.

[32] [1987] 1 WLR 1.

[34] 1979 Act, s 61(1).

[35] See the proposed s 14(2B) in cl 1(1) of the draft Bill annexed to this Report.

[36] Ibid.

[37] The recent case of *Bernstein v Pamsons Motors (Golders Green) Ltd*, *The Times*, 25 October 1986, has not dispelled these doubts, and indeed certain obiter remarks of Rougier J in that case appear to imply that some types of defect common in new cars are not breaches of contract. This case should however be contrasted with *Rogers v Parish (Scarborough) Ltd* [1987] 2 WLR 353.

[38] Commonly expressed as 'de minimis non curat lex'. This is to be contrasted with the restriction which we propose below (in Part 4) on the non-consumer's right to terminate the contract and reject the goods. In the latter case there will still be a breach of contract, but the buyer will be deprived of one of the available remedies and will be confined to his remedy in damages.

[40] 1976 SLT (Notes) 66: see para 2.12 above.

[41] See the proposed s 14(2B) contained in cl 1(1) of the draft Bill annexed to this Report.

For extracts from the Report relating to durability, see below, pp 114–16. For a proposal for a European Parliament and Council Directive on the Sale of Consumer Goods and Associated Guarantees (COM (95) 520, final), Art 2, see below, p 120.

Although the following case to which reference was made in the Law Commission Report predates the new statutory test of 'satisfaction quality', it remains of general interest and importance.

Rogers v Parish (Scarborough) Ltd [1987] 2 All ER 232, [1987] QB 933, Court of Appeal

In November 1991 the plaintiff, a Yorkshire businessman, bought from the defendants a new Range Rover car. The contract price was around £16,000 and thus considerably in excess of the price level of an ordinary family car. The Range Rover was sold with a manufacturers' warranty which provided that, for 12 months after delivery, parts requiring replacement or repair because of a manufacturing or material defect would be replaced or repaired free of charge. The warranty stated, as did the contract for the sale of the Range Rover itself, that nothing contained therein was to affect the statutory rights of the purchaser. After a few weeks' use, the Range Rover proved unsatisfactory and was replaced with another. The parties were content to have their relationship governed by the terms of the original contract and warranty. The replacement Range Rover was no more satisfactory. Although driveable, it had faulty oil seals and defects in the engine, gearbox and bodywork. After several attempts at repair, problems with the engine and gearbox persisted. In particular, the engine misfired at all speeds and the gearbox was excessively noisy. In May 1992, after the Range Rover had been driven for about 5,500 miles, the plaintiffs rejected it on the grounds that it was not of merchantable quality within s 14(6) of the Sale of Goods Act 1979 and that the defendants were therefore in breach of s 14(2) of that Act. The judge found that the defects were capable of being repaired and not such as to render the car unroadworthy, unusable or unfit for any of the normal purposes for which a Range Rover might be used. He further held that the plaintiffs had failed to establish that the Range Rover was not of merchantable quality and unfit for the purposes for which it was required. The plaintiffs appealed.

Mustill LJ, having stated the facts of the case and quoted from the first instance judgment continued:

There are two respects in which the judge in my opinion applied a test which was not that of s 14(6). [He] gave much weight to the fact that the defects were capable of repair and that the defendants had in some measure been able to repair them. Yet the fact that a defect is reparable does not prevent it from making the res venditur unmerchantable if it is of a sufficient degree (see *Lee v York Coach and Marine* [1977] RTR 35). The fact, if it was a fact, that the defect had been repaired at the instance of the purchaser, which in the present case does not appear to be so, might well have had an important bearing on whether the purchaser had by his conduct lost his right to reject, but it cannot in my view be material to the question of merchantability, which falls to be judged at the moment of delivery. Furthermore, the judge applied the test of whether the defects had destroyed the workable character of the car. No doubt this echoed an argument similar to the one developed before us that, if a vehicle is capable of starting and being driven in safety from one point to the next on public roads and on whatever other surfaces the car is supposed to be able to negotiate, it must necessarily be merchantable. I can only say that this proposition appears to have no relation to the broad test propounded by s 14(6) even if, in certain particular circumstances, the correct inference would be that no more could be expected of the goods sold.

This being so, I think it legitimate to look at the whole issue afresh with direct reference to the words of s 14(6). Starting with the purpose for which 'goods of that kind' are commonly bought, one would include in respect of any passenger vehicle not merely the buyer's purpose of driving the car from one place to another but of doing so with the appropriate degree of comfort, ease of handling and reliability and, one may add, of pride in the vehicle's outward and interior appearance. What is the appropriate degree and what relative weight is to be attached to one characteristic of the car rather than another will depend on the market at which the car is aimed.

To identify the relevant expectation one must look at the factors listed in the subsection. First, the description applied to the goods. In the present case the vehicle was sold as new. Deficiencies which might be acceptable in a secondhand vehicle were not to be expected in one purchased as new. Next, the description 'Range Rover' would conjure up a particular set of expectations, not the same as those relating to an ordinary saloon car, as to the balance between performance, handling, comfort and resilience. The factor of price was also significant. At more than £16,000 this vehicle was, if not at the top end of the scale, well above the level of the ordinary family saloon. The buyer was entitled to value for his money.

With these factors in mind, can it be said that the Range Rover as delivered was as fit for the purpose as the buyer could reasonably expect? The point does not admit of elaborate discussion. I can only say that to my mind the defects in engine, gearbox and bodywork, the existence of which is no longer in dispute, clearly demand a negative answer.

It is, however, also necessary to deal with an argument based on the fact that the vehicle was sold with the benefit of a manufacturers' warranty, a fact which was relied on to show that the buyer was required to take in his stride to a certain degree at least the type of defects which would otherwise have amounted to a breach of contract. Speaking for myself, I am far from satisfied that this argument is open to the defendants at all, having regard to the express disclaimer in the contract of sale, and also in the warranty, of any intention to vary the buyer's rights at common law and also having regard to s 6 of the Unfair Contract Terms Act 1977. Nor am I convinced that this objection can satisfactorily be answered by saying that the argument founded on the warranty operates not to deprive the buyer of his common law rights but rather as a relevant circumstances for the purposes of s 14(6) operating simply to diminish the reasonable expectations of the buyer.

Moreover, I am not clear about the logic underlying the argument. Assume that on an accurate balancing of all the relevant circumstances it could be said that the buyer of a new Range Rover could reasonably expect it to have certain qualities and that accordingly he has a contractual right to receive a vehicle possessing those qualities and to recover damages, including damages for any consequential loss, if it does not possess them. Can it really be right to say that the reasonable buyer would expect less of his new Range Rover with a warranty than without one? Surely the warranty is an addition to the buyer's rights, not a subtraction from them, and, it may be noted, only a circumscribed addition since it lasts for a limited period and does not compensate the buyer for consequential loss and inconvenience. If the defendants are right the buyer would be well advised to leave his guarantee behind in the showroom. This cannot be what the manufacturers and dealers intend or what their customers reasonably understand . . .

Finally I should mention that the defendants sought to contend, on the argument of the appeal, that even if there had been a breach of s 14 the first plaintiff had, by his conduct, precluded himself from rejecting the car. This point was not pleaded by either defendant, nor was it mentioned in the judgment in the court below or in either defendant's respondent's notice. Since the argument could not in any event have been explored by this court in the absence of findings about the entire course of dealings between the parties between the dates of delivery and rejection we considered it inappropriate to allow this matter to be raised before us.

In the result I would allow the appeal . . .

Woolf LJ and **Sir Edward Eveleigh** agreed that the appeal should be allowed.

Appeal allowed.

The following is another important case involving problems associated with a new car.

Bernstein v Pamson Motors (Golders Green) Ltd [1987] 2 All ER 220, Queens Bench Division

On 7 December 1984 the plaintiff took delivery of a new Nissan Laurel motor car from the defendants, the contract price being around £8,000. On 3 January 1985, when the car had done about 140 miles, it broke down on the M3 motorway. The cause of the problem was that a piece of sealant had entered the lubrication system during assembly and cut off the oil supply to the camshaft, which then seized up. Happily, the plaintiff had managed to pull in to the hard shoulder, thus avoiding what would otherwise have been a highly dangerous situation. The car had to be collected by the emergency services and towed to a local garage on the following day. The plaintiff purported to reject it as not being of merchantable quality, but the defendant refused to take it back. Later the same month the car was repaired under the manufacturers' warranty at no cost to the plaintiff at which point it was effectively 'as good as new'. The total repair time was some 20 hours.

Rougier J, having noted the facts of the case, went on to consider some of the issues which were relevant when determining whether a car was of 'merchantable' quality within the meaning of s 14(6) of the 1979 Act.

...

First and foremost it is perhaps self-evident that the court must look not only at the nature of the defect itself, considered in isolation, but also its likely effect on the performance of the car. In *Bartlett v Sidney Marcus Ltd* [1965] 2 All ER 753, [1965] 1 WLR 1013 the Court of Appeal decided that the two basic requirements of any car, certainly a secondhand car, was, first, that it should be capable of being driven and, second, that it should be capable of being driven in safety, and that statement I respectfully adopt. A car that will not move is useless; a car that will move as intended but is a death trap to its occupants is worse than useless. In my judgment it would be only in the most exceptional case (of which I cannot for the moment imagine an example) that a new car which on delivery was incapable of being driven in safety could ever be classed as being of merchantable quality.

At this stage it is necessary to discuss the question of whether the fact that the defect under review is easily discoverable is relevant to the question of merchantability. It was argued that if a defect existed which prevented the car being driven in safety, but which was perfectly obvious, for example the absence of a wheel, that would not render the car unmerchantable. On reflection, however, I do not think that the question of discoverability by itself affects the issue; in other words, the question of whether the defect is latent or patent is immaterial. . . .

To take an . . . extreme example, a car with a battery lead missing is immobile. Strictly speaking it is probably true that it is not of merchantable quality, nor fit for its purpose, until the missing lead is fitted. In practice the question does not arise simply because the omission is repaired before the buyer accepts delivery. A car with a loosely fitted lead, which subsequently comes adrift, could hardly be described as unmerchantable in view of the various other factors which I am about to consider, especially that concerning the speed and ease with which the matter can be put right.

In *Bartlett v Sidney Marcus Ltd* it was decided that the two attributes of, to use an ugly word, driveability and safety were the only ones which the buyer of a secondhand motor car was entitled to expect. Undoubtedly, however, the buyer of a new car is entitled to something more, how much more depending on the various considerations of description, price and all other relevant circumstances.

I turn, therefore, to additional considerations which are likely to be material, though not necessarily in their order of importance.

First, there is the ease or otherwise with which the defect may be remedied, or, to put the matter another way, the intractability of the defect. Some faults in a car prove particularly difficult to trace and rectify, but keep manifesting themselves in some way or another . . .

Similarly, the time which is taken and the expense of rectification, evidencing as it does the seriousness of the defect, are relevant considerations. The work of a moment such as would be comprised in attaching a battery lead in the example already quoted would hardly, if ever, justify rescission. Many days spent off the road in the repair shop might have a different effect. In relation to the above consideration, it was argued on behalf of the defendants that the fact that any work of rectification is carried out under a manufacturer's warranty, or similar term of guarantee, is a material circumstance. In my judgment, this is not so; if one looks, as the 1979 Act suggests, at the nature and effect of the defect itself, I do not believe that the question of who pays for the repair can be relevant. If, for any reason, it was the buyer who had to foot the bill, and the defect was not of such a nature that he was justified in rescinding the contract, he could be adequately compensated in damages.

Which brings me on to the next relevant factor, namely whether the defect is of such a kind that it is in fact *capable* of being satisfactorily repaired so as to produce a result as good as new. This in all cases will be a question of fact, but in general terms I would give as my opinion that if the defect is so serious, or of such fundamental a kind that no amount of repair, however well performed, will ever bring the car properly to its pristine state, then it will be almost impossible to see how a car so handicapped could pass the test of merchantability. . . .

There is also the cumulative effect of a series of relatively minor defects to consider, 'a congeries of defects' as was stated in one case. Here again it is a question of degree, but clearly there could come a stage when an army of minor, unconnected defects would be evidence of such bad workmanship in the manufacture, or on the assembly line generally, as to amount in toto to a breach of the condition of merchantability.

So far I have dealt only with mechanical matters, but it may well be that in appropriate cases cosmetic factors will also apply depending on the description and price applied to any individual car. No buyer of a brand new Rolls-Royce Corniche would tolerate the slightest blemish on its exterior paintwork; the purchaser of a motor car very much at the humbler end of the range might be less fastidious.

It remains to apply the principles outlined above to the facts of the present case . . .

On delivery there was, in strict physical terms, a tiny blemish, a blob of sealant that could and did have a dramatic effect when it caused the camshaft to seize and the car to grind to a halt. The defect was repairable and was in fact repaired. After which the car was as good as new. Now is this the sort of thing that a new car buyer must accept as being part of the inevitable teething troubles, or is it a defect which goes beyond any such description and renders the car either not reasonably fit for its purpose or not as fit for its purpose as it is reasonable to expect in all the circumstances so as to render it unmerchantable?

In my judgment a defect of this kind, leading to this result, even though repairable, goes far beyond that which a buyer must accept. I think that a car in such condition falls well on the other side of the line. In so saying I wish to make it quite clear that in my opinion the facts of the case do not disclose the slightest ground for criticism of Nissan methods of production and assembly in general, nor should their reputation suffer thereby. This indeed was one chance in many thousand and had it been material I should have firmly held that the facts of this case do not begin to disclose any want of due care on the part of the manufacturers either in their assembly or their quality control.

The two facts which have most influenced me in coming to my decision are first the safety consideration: I do not think it was by any means fanciful to suggest that when the camshaft began to seize up a situation of considerable potential danger had arisen. Second, I have been influenced by the extent and the area of the *potential damage* and consequently the risk that such damage might still exist. While I cannot go so far as Mr Atkins in describing this breakdown as a catastrophic one, nevertheless it was, in my opinion, a major breakdown. Reverting to the language of the section, it is not reasonable for the buyer of a new car of this type and price to expect to sustain a major breakdown in the first 150 miles. Consequently I find that, at the time of the delivery of this car to the plaintiff, it was not of merchantable quality, still less was it fit for its purpose . . .

His Lordship then went on to conclude that the plaintiff had 'accepted' the car and so was confined to a remedy in damages. This aspect of the case is considered further, below, pp 130–1.

NOTES

1. For a further and more extreme example involving a used car (a Fiat X19) which had been resold after having been submerged in water and written off

by an insurance company, see *Shine v General Guarantee Corp Ltd* [1988] 1 All ER 911, CA.

2. For general discussion of satisfactory quality and fitness for purpose, see *Benjamin's Sale of Goods* (5th edn, 1997), para 11–049 et seq; Atiyah, *The Sale of Goods* (9th edn, 1995) pp 128–77.

3. *Cehave NV v Bremer Handelsgellschaft mbH (The Hansa Nord)* [1975] 3 All ER 739, [1976] QB 44, CA, is an extreme example of goods being held to be of merchantable quality under the old law. The citrus pulp pellets could still be used as a base for cattle feed in spite of their being damaged through overheating. Indeed the buyers had repurchased them at a price which was well below the contract price (£32,000 as against some £100,000) and used them in accordance with their original intentions. The facts of the case are so peculiar that it is unlikely that they can be regarded as being of general application.

4. For examples of cases holding goods to be unmerchantable although the defects were relatively minor, see *International Business Machines Co v Shcherban* [1925] 1 DLR 864 (Sask CA) (computing scale with broken glass dial costing 30 cents to replace); *Winsley Bros v Woodfield Importing Co* [1929] NZLR 480 (planing machine with a defect which could be remedied at a cost of approximately one per cent of the purchase price).

5. In two important cases decided before there was a statutory definition of 'merchantable quality' the House of Lords held that goods were merchantable when fit for one of the purposes for which they might be used although unfit (and indeed in one case lethal) when used for another purpose: see *Henry Kendall & Sons v William Lillico & Sons Ltd* [1969] 2 AC 31, [1968] 2 All ER 444 (groundnut extractions unfit for poultry but safe for use as cattle food) and *BS Brown & Son Ltd v Craiks Ltd* [1970] 1 All ER 823, [1970] 1 WLR 752, HL (cloth unfit for use as dress material but suitable for industrial purposes). In the former case the buyers were able to invoke what is now s 14(3) of the Act since their 'particular purpose' (compounding into feed for animals and poultry *generally*) had been made known to the sellers. Section 14 (2B)(a) now refers to 'fitness for *all* the purposes for which goods of the kind in question are commonly supplied': see para 3.36 of the Law Commission Report noted above at pp 99–100.

6. An alternative approach to defining the appropriate standard is contained in the following American provision.

Uniform Commercial Code

§2–314. IMPLIED WARRANTY: MERCHANTABILITY; USAGE OF TRADE
(1) Unless excluded or modified (Section 2–316), a warranty that the goods shall be merchantable is implied in a contract for their sale if the seller is a merchant with respect to goods of that kind. Under this section the serving for value of food or drink to be consumed either on the premises or elsewhere is a sale.
(2) Goods to be merchantable must be at least such as
  (a) pass without objection in the trade under the contract description; and

(b) in the case of fungible goods, are of fair average quality within the description; and

(c) are fit for the ordinary purposes for which such goods are used; and

(d) run, within the variations permitted by the agreement, of even kind, quality and quantity within each unit and among all units involved; and

(e) are adequately contained, packaged, and labelled as the agreement may require; and

(f) conform to the promises or affirmations of fact made on the container or label if any.

(3) Unless excluded or modified (Section 2–316) other implied warranties may arise from course of dealing or usage of trade.

For a reference to Art 2–314(2)(f) see above, p 37.

QUESTIONS

1. Should a new dishwasher be regarded as lacking in satisfactory quality when delivered if it (i) has an unsightly scratch across the front panel but washes dishes to perfection; (ii) does not work at all but the problem can be rectified by a small amount of rewiring; (iii) is electrically dangerous but again the fault can be rectified easily; (iv) lacks baskets to hold the cutlery there being a three week delay in obtaining them from the manufacturers?

2. If, in a given sector of industry, the typical standard of quality is at best unreliable and often poor (notwithstanding that goods are sold at a relatively high price) should this lower the standard that 'a reasonable person would regard as satisfactory'?

Qualifications to liability

The qualifications to the scope of the implied condition of satisfactory quality now contained in s 14(2C)(a) and (b) (see above, p 80) were previously to be found in s 14(2)(a) and (b). (Section 14 (2C)(c) also contains qualifications to liability which may occasionally be relevant when a consumer buys goods by sample). In principle, it is right that liability should not extend to defects specifically drawn to the buyer's attention before the contract is made. However, the disapplying of s 14(2) may constitute a trap for a buyer who learns of a problem before the contract is concluded but reasonably assumes that it will be rectified: see *R & B Customs Brokers Co Ltd v United Dominions Trust Ltd* [1988] 1 All ER 847.

Fitness for purpose

The implied condition of reasonable fitness for purpose of, for example, s 14(3) of the Sale of Goods Act 1979 overlaps considerably with the implied condition of satisfactory quality now contained in s 14(2). Indeed in many cases the implied conditions are argued in the alternative without any clear distinction being taken between the two. However, there are cases in which the position of the buyer will vary according to which sub-section is being considered. For example, in *Baldry v Marshall* [1925] 1 KB 260, CA the specified particular purpose was a comfortable car suitable for touring and this was not satisfied by the supply of an eight-cylinder Bugatti. Similarly, the House of Lords showed itself willing to define the relevant purpose very broadly in both *Henry Kendall & Sons v William Lillico & Sons Ltd* [1969] 2 AC 31, [1968] 2 All ER 444 (compounding groundnut extraction into feed for animals and poultry generally) and the *Ashington Piggeries* case [1972] AC 441, [1971] 1 All ER 847 (compounding herring-meal into animal feeding-stuffs), so facilitating recovery under what is now s 14(3) of the Act. The cases which follow were argued in terms of the same provision (formerly s 14(1) of the Act) but they introduce also additional points of general interest.

Griffiths v Peter Conway Ltd [1939] 1 All ER 685, Court of Appeal

The facts are set out in the judgment

Sir Wilfred Green, MR: This is an appeal by the plaintiff in the action, Mrs Griffiths, against the judgment of the judge who dismissed her action. The defendants are retail tailors, and in June, 1937, the plaintiff bought from them a Harris tweed coat, which was specially made for her. Shortly after she began to wear the coat, she developed dermatitis, and suffered from a very severe and prolonged attack of that disease. She brought the present action to recover damages against the defendants on the ground of breach of warranty, and the only breach of warranty relied upon before us is that dealt with by the Sale of Goods Act 1893, s 14(1) . . .

The judge found, and his finding of fact is not challenged in this court, as follows:

' . . . the real cause of the trouble was not in the cloth alone, because there was nothing in the cloth that would have affected a normal person's skin. The trouble was that, because Mrs Griffiths' skin was not normal, it had what Dr O'Donovan has called an idiosyncratic effect, so that what the plaintiff got was idiosyncratic contact dermatitis, a thing which no purveyor of cloth or wearing apparel could really guard against to any further extent than purveyors of this cloth have guarded against there being anything harmful in its texture.'

That finding is, of course, that no normal skin would have been affected by this cloth. There was nothing in it which would affect a normal skin, but the plaintiff unfortunately had an idiosyncrasy, and that was the real reason why she contracted this disease.

On the basis of that finding, which is not challenged, Mr Morris says: 'Take the language of the section, and the present case falls within it.' He says that the buyer, Mrs Griffiths, expressly made known to the defendants the particular purpose for which the coat was required—that is to say, for the purpose of being worn by her, Mrs Griffiths, when it was made. Once that state of affairs is shown to exist, Mr Morris says that the language of the section relentlessly and without any escape imposes upon the seller the obligation which the section imports.

It seems to me that there is one quite sufficient answer to that argument. Before the condition as to reasonable fitness is implied, it is necessary that the buyer should make known, expressly or by implication, first of all the particular purpose for which the goods are required. The particular purpose for which the goods were required was the purpose of being worn by a woman suffering from an abnormality. It seems to me that, if a person suffering from such an abnormality requires an article of clothing for his or her use, and desires to obtain the benefit of the implied condition, he or she does not make known to the seller the particular purpose merely by saying: 'The article of clothing is for my own wear.' The essential matter for the seller to know in such cases with regard to the purposes for which the article is required consists in the particular abnormality or idiosyncrasy from which the buyer suffers. It is only when he has that knowledge that he is in a position to exercise his skill or judgment, because how can he decide and exercise skill or judgment in relation to the suitability of the goods that he is selling for the use of the particular individual who is buying from him unless he knows the essential characteristics of that individual? The fact that those essential characteristics are not known, as in the present case they were not known, to the buyer does not seem to me to affect the question. When I speak of 'essential characteristics,' I am not, of course, referring to any variations which take place and exist within the class of normal people. No two normal people are precisely alike, and, in the matter of sensitiveness of skin, among people who would be described as normal their sensitiveness must vary in degree.

This does not mean that there is a line which it is the function of the court, or of a medical witness, to draw with precision, so as to define all cases where normality ceases and abnormality begins. The impossibility of drawing such a line by reference to some scientific formula or something of that kind does not mean that, for the present purpose, the difference between normality and abnormality is a thing that must be disregarded, or cannot be ascertained. It is a question that no judge and no jury would have any real difficulty in deciding on the evidence in any particular case. In this particular case, the judge has found the existence of abnormality, and, that being so, it seems to me impossible to say that the seller here had the particular purpose pointed out to him so as to show that the buyer relied on his skill or judgment. After all, the object of that is to enable the seller to make up his mind whether or not he will accept the burden of the implied condition, and the effect of the argument addressed to us would be to impose that implied condition upon the seller without his having the opportunity of knowing the vital matter which would affect his mind.

. . .

MacKinnon, LJ: I agree. If Mr Morris had not so abundantly proved to the contrary, I should have thought that this appeal was unarguable.

Goddard, LJ: I agree with both judgments.

Appeal dismissed, with costs.

NOTES

This decision was approved by the House of Lords in *Slater v Finning Ltd* [1996] 3 All ER 398. A claim under s 14(3) failed when excessive wear on a new camshaft arose from the tendency of the purchaser's vessel to produce excessive torsional resonance. This abnormal feature was not made known to the seller and was indeed unknown to both buyer and seller.

The following case, although decided against a commercial background, raised issues which are of general importance in a consumer context.

Wormell v RHM Agriculture (East) Ltd [1986] 1 All ER 769, [1986] 1 WLR 36, Queen's Bench Division

In the spring of 1983 the plaintiff farmer was prevented by wet and cold weather from getting onto his land until much later than usual to spray his crops to kill wild oats. He accordingly asked the defendants, who sold agricultural chemicals and herbicides, to recommend a wild oat killer that could be used later than usual. The defendants recommended a particular herbicide manufactured by Shell ('Commando') and the plaintiff purchased some £6,438 worth of that herbicide from them. The instructions on each can of herbicide stated that it ought not to be applied beyond a recommended stage of crop growth. The plaintiff understood this to mean that the danger was one of damage to the crop, which was a risk he was prepared to run. In fact, the problem was that the herbicide was simply ineffective beyond a certain stage of growth. Hence the plaintiff lost the cost of the herbicide and of the labour involved in applying it. He sought to recover compensation under s 14 of the Sale of Goods Act.

Piers Ashworth QC, having set out the facts of the case, continued: On the evidence called I have no hesitation in saying that Commando is certainly an effective wild oat killer provided it is applied at specified times. I am satisfied that there was nothing wrong with the particular batch that the plaintiff bought. Subject to one caveat, I would have no difficulty in saying that the Commando was of merchantable quality. The caveat refers to the word 'goods'. It is a Sale of *Goods* Act, and the implied condition of 'merchantable quality', as indeed the condition to which I come [ie s 14(3)] relates to the *goods* supplied. What I shall have to consider is what is meant by 'goods' in this context. If it simply means the Commando herbicide itself, then clearly it is merchantable. I do not propose to develop that when considering the question of merchantable quality because both parties are agreed that if the plaintiff cannot succeed on the next implied condition, he will not succeed on the condition of merchantable quality . . .

Were these instructions terms of the contract? In my view they were not. Furthermore, they were not representations as such made either by the defendants or by Shell. They were certainly not terms of the contract because they were introduced much too late. If they were not terms of the contract, what is their relevance? It is clear that I have to consider what is meant by the word 'goods' in the 1979 Act. One could construe 'goods' in a case such as this to mean simply the herbicide Commando itself, or one could construe it to mean the herbicide Commando in its container with its packing and its instructions.

A moment's thought seems to me to point forcefully to the latter construction. No one would sell, for example, a jugful of this chemical or any other. No one would sell it without detailed instructions for its use. Indeed, if a chemical such as this were to be sold with no instructions, unless it is something which can be scattered round any time like talcum powder, I would regard it as totally unmerchantable. A user must know how he is to use it and when he is to use it. In my view, if one gives a narrow meaning to the word 'goods', ie simply the chemical itself, then it inevitably follows that any such sale must be of goods which are not of merchantable quality and not reasonably fit for use, because one simply does not know how they are to be used. I have therefore come to the conclusion that one can only give a sensible meaning to the word 'goods' in a case such as the present if one takes 'goods' to mean the package of the chemical with its instructions. All of those, it seems to me, are part of the goods. One must look at all of them as a whole to see if they are of merchantable quality, and in particular whether they are reasonably fit for the purpose for which they are sold.

When one looks at it like that, then, although in a sense it can be said that the user is relying on the instructions supplied by the manufacturer, nevertheless by selling goods with such instructions the seller is warranting that the chemical, when used in accordance with those instructions, will be reasonably fit for its purpose. If, for example, a chemical, eg a weedkiller was sold with the instructions, 'This can be used at any time; this can be applied at any time to growing crops; it will kill the weeds and will not harm the crops' (that is not the present case, but let us take it as an example), and if in fact the position was that if it was applied in January or February it would be useless, if it was applied in March or April it would kill the weeds but not harm the crops, and if it was applied in May or June it would kill both weeds and crop, then it seems to me that it would be artificial to say that that was reasonably fit for its purpose because at one stage (March to April in that example) it would do precisely what it was meant to. That is an extreme example where there is a statement on the instructions, 'This can be applied at any time'. However, equally, it seems to me, if there is no such instruction as to when it can be applied exactly the same would apply. It could not reasonably be said to be reasonably fit for its purpose if it is fit for its purpose only at certain unspecified times . . .

My view is that the instructions here were misleading. I appreciate that they are approved by the Advisory Council and by the schemes run within the industry. I appreciate that they cannot be changed without permission. Nevertheless, the onus must be firstly on the manufacturer to ensure that his instructions are clear. These in my view were not clear, indeed I think they were positively misleading.

If a retailer then sells the goods (that is the chemical together with its container and instructions) and those instructions make the goods not reasonably fit for their purpose, in my view there is a breach of s 14(3) of the 1979 Act. Furthermore, it is a breach by the retailer, ie the seller, even though the seller himself may not have sufficient technical knowledge to know whether or not these instructions are accurate. He of course would have his remedy against the manufacturer, and in this case it has been made clear to me that Shell are standing behind the retailer.

Accordingly, I find that there was a breach and that this breach caused, not damage to the plaintiff's crops, but caused him to waste his money, and in particular to waste his Commando. He had already bought it, but no one has suggested that it could not have been kept and used if need be the following year. Furthermore, he has wasted the money involved in spraying the Commando. There is no claim that because the Commando failed his weed infestation of wild oats is worse. Clearly there could be no such claim, because in fact in the climatic conditions of 1983 no wild oat killer could have been applied. So far as the condition of his ground is concerned, it is certainly no worse than if he had not sprayed. . . .

Judgment for the plaintiff.

NOTE

The Court of Appeal allowed the appeal on the ground that the instructions were not misleading (see [1987] 1 WLR 1091), but did not throw any doubts on the proposition that the container and the instructions formed part of the 'goods' supplied under the contract. See also *Geddling v Marsh* [1920] 1 KB 668 (defective bottle) and *Wilson v Rickett, Cockerell & Co Ltd* [1951] 1 QB 598 (explosive material in Coalite).

QUESTIONS

1. In such cases as *Griffith v Peter Conway Ltd* (above, p 109) should it be irrelevant that the buyer did not know of her abnormality and so could not communicate it? Does this decision in any way qualify the strict nature of the liability (see below, pp 118–19) usually associated with s 14 of the Act?

2. It has been observed that: 'The vast majority of modern appliances (washing machines, tumble dryers, video recorders, home computers, etc) are accompanied by detailed instructions for use and it is hard to believe that they would be considered fit for their purpose without them. Shops which sell imported goods (for example, cameras) accompanied by instructions written in an incomprehensible translation from the original Japanese may find themselves subject to a wider range of liability than they had envisaged.': see Miller, *All ER Rev 1986*, p 77. In what circumstances is such a potential liability likely to assume practical importance?

3. In what circumstances is it realistic in an age of national brand-name advertising to conclude that there has been reliance on the skill and judgment of the
   seller? See *Junior Books Ltd v Veitchi Co Ltd* [1982] 3 All ER 201 at 214 per
   Lord Roskill.
4. Greenfingers has a large overgrown garden. He sees a newspaper advertisement in a Sunday magazine which shows a Greenbelt Mower cutting through
   long wet grass in an overgrown orchard. Since this corresponds closely with
   his requirements he buys such a mower from his local garden centre. In fact
   the mower is incapable of cutting grass in the manner indicated.

   Consider the garden centre's liability under s 14(3) of the 1979 Act. Would
   it affect the position if the garden centre had displayed a large placard featuring the same advertisement?

   (See also above, pp 37 and 70.)

Durability, spare parts and servicing facilities

There is no doubt that a major source of consumer dissatisfaction and complaint
is that goods are insufficiently durable and are liable to break down or wear out in
an unreasonably short period of time. This is particularly true of such goods as
washing machines and tumble dryers ('white goods') and stereo systems ('brown
goods'). There has been some difficulty in determining the extent to which any
requirement of durability is recognised in English Law. The following case is of
interest in this context.

Crowther v Shannon Motor Co (a firm) [1975] 1 All ER 139, [1975] 1 WLR 30, Court of Appeal

The facts are set out in the judgment of Lord Denning MR

Lord Denning MR. The plaintiff, Mr Crowther, is a young man interested in art. In 1972 he
bought a secondhand motor car from the defendants who were reputable dealers in
Southampton. It was a 1964 Jaguar. He bought it on 17th July 1972 for the sum of £390. The
dealers commended it. They said that 'it would be difficult to find a 1964 Jaguar of this quality
inside and out'. They added that for a Jaguar 'it is hardly run in'. Mr Crowther looked carefully at it. He took it for a trial run. The next day it was tested by the Ministry of Transport
officials. The report of the test was satisfactory. So Mr Crowther bought the Jaguar. He did not
take the words of puff seriously. But he relied on the sellers' skill and judgment. There was
clearly an implied condition under s 14(1) of the Sale of Goods Act 1893 that the car was reasonably fit for the purpose for which he required it and which he made known to the sellers.

That was 17th July 1972. The mileage as stated on the mileometer at that time was 82,165
miles. Mr Crowther took the car. He drove it on some long journeys. He went up to the north
of England and back. He went round Hampshire. He went over 2,000 miles in it. He found that
it used a great deal of oil. But he managed to drive it for three weeks. Then on 8th August 1982,
when he was driving up the M3 motorway, it came to a full stop. The engine seized up. The
car was towed into a garage. The engine was found to be in an extremely bad condition. So
much so that it had to be scrapped and replaced by a reconditioned engine. The car was out of
use for a couple of months or so.

Mr Crowther brought an action in the county court for damages from the dealers. He called as a witness a previous owner of the car, a Mr Hall. He gave evidence that he had bought it from these selfsame dealers about eight months before. He had paid them about £400 for it. He had used it for those eight months and then sold it back in July 1972 to these very dealers. When he resold it to them he knew the engine was in a very bad state, but he did not disclose it to them. He left them to find out for themselves. He was himself an engineer. He gave a trenchant description of the engine:

'At the time of resale I thought the engine was clapped out. I do not think this engine was fit to be used on a road, not really, it needed a rebore.'

The judge accepted the evidence of Mr Hall. He held that there was a breach of s 14(1) of the 1893 Act. He awarded Mr Crowther damages in the sum of £460.37 with costs. Now there is an appeal to this court by the dealers. They say there was no justification for the finding that this car was not reasonably fit for the purpose. The mileage when they sold it was 82,165 miles. The mileage when it 'clapped out' was 84,519 miles. So that in the three weeks it had gone 2,354 miles.

Counsel for the dealers, who put the case very cogently before us, submitted that a car which had covered 2,354 miles must have been reasonably fit for the purpose of driving along the road. He drew attention to a case some years ago in this court, *Bartlett v Sidney Marcus Ltd*.[1] We emphasised then that a buyer, when he buys a secondhand car, should realise that defects may appear sooner or later. In that particular case a defect did appear in the clutch. It was more expensive to repair than had been anticipated. It was held by this court that the fact that the defect was more expensive than had been anticipated did not mean that there had been any breach of the implied condition. But that case seems to me to be entirely distinguishable from the present case. In that case it was a minor repair costing £45 after 300 miles. Here we have a very different case. On the dealers' own evidence, a buyer could reasonably expect to get 100,000 miles life out of a Jaguar engine. Here the Jaguar had only done 80,000 miles. Yet it was in such a bad condition that it was 'clapped out' and after some 2,300 miles it failed altogether. That is very different from a minor repair. The dealers themselves said that if they had known that the engine would blow up after 2,000 miles, they would not have sold it. The reason obviously was because it would not have been reasonably fit for the purpose.

Some criticism was made of a phrase used by the judge. He said: 'What does "fit for the purpose" mean?' He answered: 'To go as a car for a reasonable time.' I am not quite sure that that is entirely accurate. The relevant time is the time of sale. But there is no doubt what the judge meant. If the car does not go for a reasonable time but the engine breaks up within a short time, that is evidence which goes to show it was not reasonably fit for the purpose at the time it was sold. On the evidence in this case, the engine was liable to go at any time. It was 'nearing the point of failure', said the expert, Mr Wise. The time interval was merely 'staving off the inevitable'. That shows that at the time of the sale it was not reasonably fit for the purpose of being driven on the road. I think the judge on the evidence was quite entitled to find there was a breach of s 14(1) of the 1893 Act and I would therefore dismiss the appeal.

Orr and **Browne LLJ** agreed with Lord Denning.

Appeal dismissed.

[1] [1965] 2 All ER 753, [1965] 1 WLR 1013.

The Law Commission considered the issue of durability in some detail and reached the following conclusions:

Sale and Supply of Goods (Law Com No 160, 1987)

Durability

. . .

3.48. There are three issues, in particular, which must be resolved in connection with an implied requirement about how long goods should last:

(i) Should the requirement be that the goods should last for a *reasonable* time, or should it lay down a *specific* length of time for which goods should last?

(ii) Should the requirement be broken at the time of supply or at the later time when the goods are shown not to have lasted as long as they should?

(iii) Should the requirement be part of the implied term as to quality or should it be a separate implied term?

We discuss these questions in turn.

3.49. *Duration or durability requirement?* We do not think it would be possible to provide a definite indication of how long goods should last or in what condition. First, how long goods last will generally depend very much on the treatment they get. It would be unreasonable to insist that goods which are treated badly should last as long as the same goods treated well. Although this may make it hard for a court to say whether the requirement of durability has been broken, especially if a long time has passed since the sale, we think this is unavoidable. Secondly, different types of goods have different life expectancies; and different grades of the same type of goods also (and quite properly) have different life expectancies. Thirdly, the length of time for which complex goods should last will often depend on what component is in question. Clearly the buyer should not be entitled to complain about a watch if its battery runs down after its normal life expectancy—though he should be able to do so if it runs down sooner. If it is not the battery but part of the mechanism of the watch that wears out, the buyer will be entitled to complain after a much longer period.

. . .

3.51. Our conclusion, therefore, is that a requirement of *durability* should be such that the goods would be required to last for a *reasonable* time. This would make it possible to apply the requirement to all types of goods, and to take into account whether the goods had been well or badly treated.

3.52. It should be noted that what we proposed is not the same as saying that the goods should remain of 'acceptable quality', or any other definite or objectively ascertainable quality, for a reasonable time. As we have said above,[46] we do not think it practicable to provide any definite indication of how long goods should last or in what condition. To require that goods should remain for a reasonable time at the *same* level of quality as they were when supplied is too stringent: it takes no account of use or proper natural deterioration . . . Equally, it is too narrow to require that the goods should (when supplied) be such that they are capable of remaining fit for their purpose for a reasonable length of time. A car which still runs as a car, but whose paintwork deteriorates sooner than it should, is not sufficiently durable.

3.53. *When should the requirement bite?* The next question is a somewhat technical one: should a requirement of durability apply at the same time as the implied term about quality (ie, generally, at the time of supply), so that goods should *at the time of supply* be such that they will prove to be reasonably durable in normal use; or should it apply later, so that it would be broken only when the goods break down or otherwise prove not to be durable? In other words, should a defect or want of quality which manifests itself later be *evidence* that the goods were not of the correct quality at the moment of supply, or should it be in itself a separate breach of contract?

. . .

3.56. In our view . . . a requirement of durability should apply at the time of supply, not later. It is at that time that the goods need to satisfy the requirement of durability. Of course it will often not be until later that the lack of durability will be discovered; but this will simply show that, at the time of supply, the goods were not sufficiently durable.[47] We see nothing inconsistent, illogical or difficult about this 'must have been' approach. It is possible that this concept may have been obscured by discussion of the question whether the implied term as to quality or fitness for purpose is a 'continuing warranty'.[48] This phrase might be taken to mean that the 'warranty' of durability is one which is broken after, and not at, the time of supply. We do not think this is what users of the phrase intend. The question whether or not the implied term as to fitness for purpose or merchantability is a 'continuing warranty' concerns, not the time when the promise of durability is broken, but the content of the initial promise—namely, the length of time to which the initial promise extends . . .

3.57. *Should the durability requirement be a separate term?* In the Consultative Document we suggested that durability should be included as one of the relevant matters in considering whether the goods were of the quality required by the contract. On consultation many agreed with this proposal. It was, however, also suggested to us that durability should be the subject of a new and separate implied term. We have considered this latter suggestion but have decided not to recommend it. The main reason is that there is no purpose in having a separate implied term unless it says something more than could be said by simply including durability as an aspect of quality in the implied term about quality. Our view is that listing durability in this way will achieve what we seek to achieve.

46 Para 3.49.
47 This was the approach of Lord Denning MR in *Crowther v Shannon Motor Co* [1975] 1 WLR 30 (CA).
48 This phrase was used by Lord Diplock in *Lambert v Lewis* [1982] AC 225, 276, where he said: 'The implied warranty of fitness for a particular purpose relates to the goods at the time of delivery under the contract of sale in the state in which they were delivered. I do not doubt that it is a continuing warranty that the goods will continue to be fit for that purpose for a reasonable time after delivery, so long as they remain in the same apparent state as that in which they were delivered, apart from normal wear and tear.' See, generally, for example, W. C. H. Ervine, 'Durability, Consumers and the Sale of Goods Act', 1984 JR 147.

This recommendation was incorporated as s 14(2B)(e) of the 1979 Act so that durability is now an aspect of the quality of goods.

A further important issue is whether there should be any legal obligation to ensure that spare parts and servicing facilities remain available over a reasonable or even a specified period. The issue is closely related to such matters as the existence and legal status of manufacturers' express warranties and guarantees (see above, pp 57–70 and below, pp 274–8) and the extent of their liability for economic loss (see below, pp 215–22). In principle it seems clear that there would be benefits to consumers in recognising such an obligation since the unavailability of even a cheap spare part may render an expensive consumer durable quite unusable. Moreover, the modern tendency to replace and discard is not apt to encourage the craftsman whose repairing skills might make good the deficiency. However, there are serious practical problems involved and the Law Commission does not favour the imposition of additional legal obligations of this kind. The Commission's reasoning appears in the following extract.

Sale and Supply of Goods (Law Com No 160, 1987)

Spare parts and servicing facilities
3.66. When goods break down or are damaged they may become useless unless they can be repaired and unless spare parts are available. However, there appears to be no legal obligation on the seller or supplier to maintain stocks or to provide servicing facilities.[53] The question

arises whether such obligation should be created. This matter was considered by the Law Commission in its Report on Implied Terms in Contracts for the Supply of Goods[54] and it was concluded that it would be wrong to create any such obligation. Hardly any support for this idea was received on consultation and it was thought that if such an obligation applied to all kinds of contracts involving all kinds of goods it could, in many cases, impose hardship on the retailer, particularly the small shopkeeper. It was feared the cost of providing such extra stocks and facilities, which might be considerable, would have to be passed on to the consumer. Further problems arose. Should the obligation continue even if the manufacturer went out of business? Should periods be laid down, product by product, for the time over which spares should be maintained? Should the obligation apply equally to custom-made goods and second-hand goods? Should there be a distinction between 'functional' parts and 'non-functional' parts? It was thought that if these problems were avoided by an obligation on the retailer couched in general terms it would be so imprecise as to be of no real value to the customer. It seems to us that such a conclusion remains valid. The existence of a manufacturer's code of practice settled under the auspices of the Office of Fair Trading, and making special reference to the provision of spare parts and servicing facilities, is much more likely to benefit the consumer.

[53] It appears that this is so from *L Gent & Sons v Eastman Machine Co Ltd* (CA, 7 February 1985, unreported).

[54] (1979) Law Com No 95, para 115.

NOTES

1. The possibility of imposing such an obligation on manufacturers, as opposed to retail sellers, was considered in the Law Commission Report on 'Implied Terms in Contracts for the Supply of Goods' (Law Com No 95, 1979) at paras 123–7. However, no such recommendation was made. Any such obligation would need to be considered alongside a manufacturer's liability for what is essentially economic loss (see below, pp 215–22).

2. For the relevance of codes of practice see below ch 10, at pp 499–511 especially.

3. In some other jurisdictions a different approach has been adopted. The following example is taken from the Saskatchewan Consumer Protection Act 1996.

STATUTORY WARRANTIES

Statutory warranties
48. Where a consumer product is sold by a retail seller, the following warranties are deemed to be given by the retail seller to the consumer: . . .
(g) that the product and all its components are to be durable for a reasonable period, having regard to all the relevant circumstances of the sale, including:
  (i) the description and nature of the product;
  (ii) the purchase price;
  (iii) the express warranties of the retail seller or manufacturer; and
  (iv) the necessary maintenance the product normally requires and the manner in which it has been used;
(h) where the product normally requires repairs, that spare parts and repair facilities will be reasonably available for a reasonable period after the date of sale of the product.

Section 50(2) of the Act provides in part that 'the manufacturer of consumer products is deemed to give to consumers of those products the same statutory warranties respecting those products as the retail seller is deemed to give pursuant to ss 48(b) to (h). Accordingly, obligations as to durability, spare parts and repair facilities are imposed on manufacturers directly. See also above, p 55. For the definition of a 'consumer product' see above, p 36.

The New Zealand Consumer Guarantees Act 1993, s. 12, similarly provides:

12. **Guarantee as to repairs and spare parts**—(1) Subject to sections 41 and 42 of this Act, where goods are first supplied to a consumer in New Zealand (whether or not that supply is the first-ever supply of the goods), there is a guarantee that the manufacturer will take reasonable action to ensure that facilities for repair of the goods and supply of parts for the goods are reasonably available for a reasonable period after the goods are so supplied.

(2) Part III of this Act gives the consumer a right of redress against the manufacturer where the goods fail to comply with the guarantee in this section.

The main exception in s 42 provides:

42. **Exception in respect of repairs and parts**—(1) Section 12 of this Act does not apply where reasonable action is taken to notify the consumer who first acquires the goods from a supplier in New Zealand, at or before the time the goods are supplied, that the manufacturer does not undertake that repair facilities and parts will be available for those goods.

(2) Where reasonable action is taken to notify the consumer who first acquires the goods from a supplier in New Zealand, at or before the time the goods are supplied, that the manufacturer does not undertake that repair facilities and parts will be available for those goods after the expiration of a specified period, section 12 of this Act shall not apply in relation to those goods after the expiration of that period.

Strict contractual liability

Contractual liability in respect of goods which are not of satisfactory quality or unfit for their purpose is not dependent on proof that the seller had failed to exercise reasonable care: see *Daniels and Daniels v R White & Sons Ltd and Tarbard* [1938] 4 All ER 258, above, p 38. The point has been confirmed in modern decisions of the House of Lords. Thus in *Henry Kendall & Sons v William Lillico & Sons* Lord Reid said that s 14(1) (now 14(3)) covers 'defects which are latent in the sense that even the utmost skill and judgment on the part of the seller would not have detected them' ([1969] 2 AC 31, 84). Similarly, liability was imposed in the *Ashington Piggeries* case even though, in the words of Lord Diplock, 'in the then state of knowledge, scientific and commercial, no deliberate exercise of human skill or judgment could have prevented the meal from having its toxic effect upon mink. It was sheer bad luck' ([1972] AC 441, 498).

An equivalent strict liability is imposed in hire-purchase transactions (see the Supply of Goods (Implied Terms) Act 1973, ss 9 and 10, above, p 81) and the Supply of Goods and Services Act 1982 has removed doubts as to the strictness of the obligation where the property in goods is transferred under a contract which falls within the scope of that Act, notably contracts for work and materials and contracts of hire.

In the context of consumer transactions the supplier may accordingly be liable when, for example, goods are supplied in a container or pre-packed and even though the defect is discoverable only by a minute chemical analysis: see, for example, *Jackson v Watson & Sons* [1909] 2 KB 193, CA (tinned salmon); *Frost v Aylesbury Dairy Co* [1905] 1 KB 608, CA (milk containing typhoid germs); *Grant v Australian Knitting Mills Ltd* [1936] AC 85 at 100, PC (excess of free sulphites in underpants); *Wren v Holt* [1903] 1 KB 610 (arsenic in beer). The point is frequently overlooked by those who argue against the imposition of strict liability on manufacturers or producers of defective products: see below ch 5, at pp 222–55.

PROBLEM

For many years Smith has run a corner shop in Bridgtown where he sells a range of commodities including cigarettes and fruit. Jones, one of his most faithful and long-standing customers, always makes a point of buying his cigarettes from Smith's. Jones, who smokes some thirty cigarettes a day, has now contracted lung cancer and it is accepted that this has been caused by his smoking. Thomas buys six oranges from Smith's shop and on eating them becomes seriously ill. Chemical analysis establishes that they were part of a consignment which had been injected with a poison in furtherance of a political campaign.

    Advise Jones and Thomas.

A European initiative

As in many other areas of consumer law it is possible that English law will be affected by a proposal emanating from the European Commission.

Proposal for a European Parliament and Council Directive on the Sale of Consumer Goods and Associated Guarantees

(96/C 307/09)

(Text with EEA relevance)

COM (95) 520 final—96/0161 (COD)

(Submitted by the Commission on 23 August 1996)

Article 1

Scope and definitions

1. The purpose of this Directive is the approximation of the laws, regulations and administrative provisions of the Member States on the sale of consumer goods and associated guarantees in order to ensure a uniform minimum level of consumer protection in the context of the internal market.

2. For the purposes of this Directive,

(a) *Consumer* means any natural person who, in the contracts covered by this Directive, is acting for purposes which are not directly related to his trade, business or profession;

(b) *Consumer goods* means any goods, excluding buildings, normally intended for final use or consumption;

(c) *Seller* means any natural or legal person who sells consumer goods in the course of his trade, business or profession;

(d) *Guarantee* means any additional undertaking given by a seller or producer, over and above the legal rules governing the sale of consumer goods, to reimburse the price paid, to exchange, repair or handle a product in any way, in the case of non-conformity of the product with the contract.

Article 2
Conformity with the contract

1. Consumer goods must be in conformity with the contract of sale.

2. Goods shall be deemed to be in conformity with the contract if, at the moment of delivery to the consumer:

(a) they comply with the description given by the seller and possess the qualities of the goods which the seller has held out to the consumer as a sample or model;

(b) they are fit for the purposes for which goods of the same type are normally used;

(c) they are fit for any particular purpose for which the consumer requires them and which he had made known to the seller at the time of conclusion of the contract, except where the circumstances show that the buyer did not rely on the seller's explanations;

(d) their quality and performance are satisfactory given the nature of the goods and the price paid and taking into account the public statements made about them by the seller, the producer or his representative.

3. Any lack of conformity resulting from incorrect installation of the goods shall be considered to be equivalent to lack of conformity of the goods with the contract, if the goods were installed by the seller or under his responsibility.

Article 3
Obligations of the seller

1. The seller shall be liable to the consumer for any lack of conformity which exists when the goods are delivered to the consumer and which becomes manifest within a period of two years unless, at the moment of conclusion of the contract of sale, the consumer knew or could not be unaware of the lack of conformity.

2. When the goods are not in conformity with the public statements made by the producer or his representative, the seller shall not be liable if:

— the seller shows that he did not know and could not reasonably know the statement in question,

— the seller shows that at the time of sale he corrected the statement, or

— the seller shows that the decision to buy the goods could not have been influenced by the statement.

3. Until proof of the contrary any lack of conformity which becomes manifest within six months of delivery shall be presumed to have existed at the time of delivery, unless this presumption is incompatible with the nature of the goods or the nature of the lack of conformity.

4. When a lack of conformity is notified to the seller, pursuant to Article 4, the consumer shall be entitled to ask the seller either to repair the goods free of charge within a reasonable period, or to replace the goods, when this is possible, or to demand an appropriate price reduction or

rescission of the contract. Exercise of the right of rescission or replacement of the good is limited to one year.

Member States may provide that the scope of the rights referred to in the first subparagraph be limited in the case of a minor lack of conformity.

5. When the final seller is liable to the consumer because of a lack of conformity resulting from an act of commission or omission by the producer, a previous seller in the same chain of contracts or any other intermediary, the final seller shall be entitled to pursue remedies against the responsible person, under the conditions laid down by national law.

Article 4
Obligations of the consumer

1. In order to benefit from the rights referred to in Article 3(4) the consumer must notify the seller of any lack of conformity within a period of one month from the date on which he detected the lack of conformity or ought normally to have detected it.

2. Notifications made pursuant to paragraph 1 shall interrupt the limitation period provided for in Article 3(4).

Article 5
Guarantees

1. Any guarantee offered by a seller or producer shall legally bind the offerer under the conditions laid down in the guarantee document and the associated advertising and must place the beneficiary in a more advantageous position than that resulting from the rules governing the sale of consumer goods set out in the national provisions applicable.

2. The guarantee must feature in a written document which must be freely available for consultation before purchase and must clearly set out the essential particulars necessary for making claims under the guarantee, notably the duration and territorial scope of the guarantee, as well as the name and address of the guarantor.

Article 6
Binding nature of the provisions

1. Any contractual terms or agreements concluded with the seller before notification of the lack of conformity which waive or restrict the rights resulting from this Directive shall not be binding on the consumer.

2. Member States shall take the necessary measures to ensure that, irrespective of the law applicable to the contract, and when the contract has a close connection with the territory of the Member States, consumers are not deprived of the protection afforded by this Directive.

Article 7
National law and minimum protection

1. The rights resulting from this Directive shall be exercised without prejudice to other rights which the consumer may rely on under the national rules governing contractual or non-contractual liability.

2. Member States may adopt or maintain in force more stringent provisions, compatible with the Treaty, in the field covered by this Directive, to ensure a higher level of consumer protection.

Article 8
Transposition

1. Member States shall bring into force the laws, regulations and administrative provisions necessary to comply with this Directive not later than . . . (*). They shall immediately inform the Commission thereof.

When Member States adopt these provisions, these shall contain a reference to this Directive, or shall be accompanied by such reference at the time of their official publication. The procedure for such reference shall be adopted by Member States.

2. Member States shall communicate to the Commission the provisions of national law which they adopt in the field covered by this Directive.

Article 9
Entry into force

This Directive shall enter into force on the 20th day following that of its publication in the *Official Journal of the European Communities.*

Article 10
Addressees

This Directive is addressed to the Member States.

* Two years after its publication in the *Official Journal of the European Communities.*

NOTES

1. This proposal was printed in the Official Journal of the European Communities on 16.10.1996: see OJ No C307, p 8. For some of the issues raised by it see the Consultation Documents issued by the Department of Trade and Industry (18 September 1996, and 21 July 1997). There is much valuable discussion and comment in the Report of the House of Lords Select Committee on the European Communities on 'Consumer Guarantees' (10th Report, 1996–97) (HL 57).
2. In addition to the scope of the implied terms noted above, the proposal is relevant also to the issue of remedies (see the text which follows), to the broader question of manufacturers' guarantees (see below, pp 274–8) and to a retailer's liability for a manufacturer's promotional claims (see above, pp 33–7).

QUESTIONS

1. Article 2.2 of the proposed Directive refers to the relevant time as being 'the moment of delivery to the consumer'. Is this the same point of time as in English law?
2. Would Article 3.1 impose a more extensive requirement of durability than the one now contained in s 14(2B)(e) of the 1979 Act?

REMEDIES FOR BREACH OF THE IMPLIED TERMS

In illustrating the remedies available for breach of the implied terms as to quality and related matters noted above an initial distinction must be taken between contracts for the sale of goods and other contracts of supply. The former are covered by statutory provisions whereas the latter are subject only to the common law and general contractual principles. The area is one in which there is considerable uncertainty even as to matters which are of everyday concern.

Contracts for the sale of goods

The following are the principal provisions which govern the remedies available to the buyer on breach of the implied conditions of sections 13 and 14 of the Sale of Goods Act 1979: see above, pp 80–1. The relevant provisions are printed as amended by the Sale and Supply of Goods Act 1994, the amendments being printed in square brackets.

Sale of Goods Act 1979

11. When condition to be treated as warranty

[(1) This section does not apply to Scotland.]

(2) Where a contract of sale is subject to a condition to be fulfilled by the seller, the buyer may waive the condition, or may elect to treat the breach of the condition as a breach of warranty and not as a ground for treating the contract as repudiated.

(3) Whether a stipulation in a contract of sale is a condition, the breach of which may give rise to a right to treat the contract as repudiated, or a warranty, the breach of which may give rise to a claim for damages but not to a right to reject the goods and treat the contract as repudiated, depends in each case on the construction of the contract; and a stipulation may be a condition, though called a warranty in the contract.

(4) [Subject to section 35A below] where a contract of sale is not severable and the buyer has accepted the goods or part of them, the breach of a condition to be fulfilled by the seller can only be treated as a breach of warranty, and not as a ground for rejecting the goods and treating the contract as repudiated, unless there is an express or implied term of the contract to that effect.

(5) . . .

(6) Nothing in this section affects a condition or warranty whose fulfilment is excused by law by reason of impossibility or otherwise.

(7) Paragraph 2 of Schedule 1 below applies in relation to a contract made before 22 April 1967 or (in the application of this Act to Northern Ireland) 28 July 1967.

34. Buyer's right of examining the goods

. . .

Unless otherwise agreed, when the seller tenders delivery of goods to the buyer, he is bound on request to afford the buyer a reasonable opportunity of examining the goods for the purpose of ascertaining whether they are in conformity with the contract [and, in the case of a contract for sale by sample, of comparing the bulk with the sample.]

35. Acceptance

(1) The buyer is deemed to have accepted the goods [subject to subsection (2) below—
    (a) when he intimates to the seller that he has accepted them, or

(b) when the goods have been delivered to him and he does any act in relation to them which is inconsistent with the ownership of the seller.

(2) Where goods are delivered to the buyer, and he has not previously examined them, he is not deemed to have accepted them under subsection (1) above until he has had a reasonable opportunity of examining them for the purpose—

(a) of ascertaining whether they are in conformity with the contract, and

(b) in the case of a contract for sale by sample, of comparing the bulk with the sample.

(3) Where the buyer deals as consumer or (in Scotland) the contract of sale is a consumer contract, the buyer cannot lose his right to rely on subsection (2) above by agreement, waiver or otherwise.

(4) The buyer is also deemed to have accepted the goods when after the lapse of a reasonable time he retains the goods without intimating to the seller that he has rejected them.

(5) The questions that are material in determining for the purposes of subsection (4) above whether a reasonable time has elapsed include whether the buyer has had a reasonable opportunity of examining the goods for the purpose mentioned in subsection (2) above.

(6) The buyer is not by virtue of this section deemed to have accepted the goods merely because—

(a) he asks for, or agrees to, their repair by or under an arrangement with the seller, or

(b) the goods are delivered to another under a sub-sale or other disposition.

(7) Where the contract is for the sale of goods making one or more commercial units, a buyer accepting any goods included in a unit is deemed to have accepted all the goods making the unit; and in this subsection 'commercial unit' means a unit division of which would materially impair the value of the goods or the character of the unit.

(8) Paragraph 10 of Schedule 1 below applies in relation to a contract made before 22nd April 1967 or (in the application of this Act to Northern Ireland) 28th July 1967.

[35A. Right of partial rejection

(1) If the buyer—

(a) has the right to reject the goods by reason of a breach on the part of the seller that affects some or all of them, but

(b) accepts some of the goods, including, where there are any goods unaffected by the breach, all such goods,

he does not by accepting them lose his right to reject the rest.

(2) In the case of a buyer having the right to reject an instalment of goods, subsection (1) above applies as if references to the goods were references to the goods comprised in the instalment.

(3) For the purposes of subsection (1) above, goods are affected by a breach if by reason of the breach they are not in conformity with the contract.

(4) This section applies unless a contrary intention appears in, or is to be implied from, the contract.]

36. Buyer not bound to return rejected goods

Unless otherwise agreed, where goods are delivered to the buyer, and he refuses to accept them, having the right to do so, he is not bound to return them to the seller, but it is sufficient if he intimates to the seller that he refuses to accept them.

53. Remedy for breach of warranty

(1) Where there is a breach of warranty by the seller, or where the buyer elects (or is compelled) to treat any breach of a condition on the part of the seller as a breach of warranty, the buyer is not by reason only of such breach of warranty entitled to reject the goods; but he may—

(a) set up against the seller the breach of warranty in diminution or extinction of the price, or

(b) maintain an action against the seller for damages for the breach of warranty.

(2) The measure of damages for breach of warranty is the estimated loss directly and naturally resulting, in the ordinary course of events, from the breach of warranty.

(3) In the case of breach of warranty of quality such loss is prima facie the difference between the value of the goods at the time of delivery to the buyer and the value they would have had if they had fulfilled the warranty.

(4) The fact that the buyer has set up the breach of warranty in diminution or extinction of the price does not prevent him from maintaining an action for the same breach of warranty if he has suffered further damage.

[(5) This section does not apply to Scotland.]

Rejection

The terminology of s 11(3) and (4) of the 1979 Act suggests that a breach of condition, for example, as to correspondence with description or satisfactory quality, will give rise to a right to reject the goods and treat the contract as repudiated. In addition, the buyer may claim damages for breach of contract, and these may include compensation for personal injury and property damage. A breach of warranty will give rise to a right to damages only. However, the precise implications of the entitlement to reject are less clear and in a leading text it has been said that: 'The right to reject is separate from the right to repudiate the contract, and circumstances giving rise to a right of rejection do not, even if the right is exercised, necessarily put an end to the contract. The seller can usually, until the time for performance has expired, therefore, tender a conforming delivery.': see Atiyah, *The Sale of Goods* (9th edn, 1995) at p 449; also *Benjamin's Sale of Goods* (5th edn, 1997) at paras 12–028 to 12–031 where it is concluded that 'the right at common law to "cure" defects by retender is limited.'

Consider the following cases:

1. On 1 June Butter and Worth both agree to buy new 'Washcleen 1000' dishwashers from their local department store. The store does not have any machines in stock but it assures both Butter and Worth that it will obtain one from the manufacturer for delivery within ten days. Butter pays cash in advance and Worth agrees to pay cash on delivery. On 6 June the store delivers to Butter a 'Washcleen 800' dishwasher. Butter telephones to point out that this is the wrong model and the store apologises, stating that it will deliver the correct model from stock the following day. Butter who has discovered that he can buy the machine much more cheaply elsewhere demands the return of his money and declines the suggested arrangement. On 7 June the store delivers to Worth a 'Washcleen 1000'. The machine is defective and floods the kitchen floor without causing any damage. Worth telephones to complain, the store apologises and promises to send a service-man around immediately. The service-man explains that the defect can be remedied by changing a faulty part and that he has the necessary part in his van. Worth insists that the machine be removed, adding that he would rather buy another machine elsewhere. Advise the store.

2. Ada goes to her local delicatessen shop where she buys a Snorter pork pie. When she cuts it at home she finds that it is mouldy and unwholesome. She

returns to the shop to complain and demands her money back but the shop offers rather a replacement pie which Ada declines to accept.

Advise Ada.

NOTE

Article 2–508 of the United States Uniform Commercial Code contains the following provision:

Cure by seller of improper tender or delivery: replacement

(1) Where any tender or delivery by the seller is rejected because non-conforming and the time for performance has not yet expired, the seller may seasonably notify the buyer of his intention to cure and may then within the contract time make a conforming delivery.

(2) Where the buyer rejects a non-conforming tender which the seller had reasonable grounds to believe would be acceptable with or without money allowance the seller may if he seasonably notifies the buyer have a further reasonable time to substitute a conforming tender.

In its Working Paper No 85 (1983), at paras 4.43–4.47, the Law Commission proposed a relatively complex scheme whereby a seller would be able to insist on having the opportunity to cure defects (by repair or replacement) where the nature and consequences of the breach were slight. However, the idea was abandoned in its Report for reasons which were explained as follows:

Sale and Supply of Goods (Law Com No 160, 1987)

4.13. On consultation there was much support for our suggested scheme of 'cure'. However, two principal, and formidable, lines of objection emerged. First, it was suggested that the scheme was generally too adverse to consumers' interests because it gave the supplier a ground upon which he could argue that the buyer was not entitled to return defective goods and claim the price back. Secondly, we had recognised in the Consultative Document that the scheme left many questions unanswered. We said that if the scheme were to try to answer in advance all the many questions which would arise, it would become so complicated as to be unacceptable. However, because consumer sale transactions almost always fell into a recognised pattern, we felt justified in putting such a simple scheme forward for consultation. On consultation and in our reconsideration of this subject many of the unanswered questions were raised. For example, did the seller have to redeliver the 'cured' goods to the buyer or did the buyer have to collect them? What if by this time the buyer had moved far away? How promptly should the cure be effected? At whose risk were the goods while the cure was in progress? At whose risk were they to be while being redelivered to the buyer? These were but a few of the many practical problems which, it was pointed out, would be likely to arise under this entirely new scheme of remedies, which would probably have to apply to a very great many transactions. It was suggested that although the scheme sounded superficially attractive, when it was exposed to the merciless test of being put into practice, it was likely to prove a breeding ground for dispute and uncertainty, ultimately leading to a more unsatisfactory situation than exists at present and almost certainly being to the detriment of consumers.

4.14. We have decided not to recommend a 'cure' scheme for consumer transactions, although not all of us are without regret on the matter. We are, in short, not sufficiently confident that such a scheme would be more beneficial to buyers and sellers generally than is the present law. The number of instances of consumers who at present unreasonably seek to reject goods is, we believe, very small. . . . In legal theory the consumer has the absolute right to reject for any defect. True, he may seldom exercise that right, almost always being prepared to accept repair or replacement. However, if the seller is unreasonable it is against that legal background that the discussion takes place. Any legal ground upon which rejection might arguably be resisted, however weak such ground might be on the facts, gives the seller a potential weapon with which to undermine the position of the ordinary consumer. Sometimes, moreover, what the law is believed to be is more important than what it is. There should be no ambiguity or misunderstanding about the rights of the consumer buyer.

The following is a modern statutory provision containing detailed coverage of the same ground as the Law Commission.

Saskatchewan Consumer Protection Act 1996

Remedies for breach of statutory or express warranties
57(1) Where there is a breach by a manufacturer or retail seller of a statutory warranty mentioned in section 48 or of an express warranty mentioned in section 45:
  (a) and where the breach is remediable and not of a substantial character:
      (i) the party in breach shall, within a reasonable period, make good the breach free of charge to the consumer but, where the breach has not been remedied within a reasonable period, the consumer shall be entitled to have the breach remedied elsewhere and to recover from the party in breach all reasonable costs incurred in having the breach remedied; and
      (ii) the consumer is entitled to recover damages for losses that he or she has suffered and that were reasonably foreseeable as liable to result from the breach regardless of whether the breach is remedied;
  (b) and where the breach is of a substantial character or is not remediable, the consumer, at his or her option, may exercise the remedies pursuant to clause (a) or, subject to subsections (2) and (3), the consumer may:
      (i) reject the consumer product; and
      (ii) if he or she exercises his or her right to reject, he or she is entitled to recover the purchase price from the party in breach and to recover damages for any other losses that he or she has suffered and that were reasonably foreseeable as liable to result from the breach.
(2) The consumer shall exercise his or her right to reject the consumer product pursuant to clause (1) (b) within a reasonable period pursuant to subsection (3), except where the consumer delays the exercise of his or her right to reject because he or she has relied on assurances made by the party in breach or the party's agent that the breach would be remedied and the breach was not remedied.
(3) For the purposes of subsection (2), regardless of whether the right to reject is being exercised by the consumer or a person mentioned in subsection 41(1), a reasonable period:
  (a) runs from the time of delivery of the product to the consumer; and
  (b) consists of a period sufficient to permit any testing, trial or examination of the consumer product that may be normally required by consumers of that product and as may be appropriate considering the nature of the product, for the purpose of determining the conformity of the product to the obligations imposed pursuant to this Part on the party in breach.
. . .

Where party in breach must repair product
59(1) Where the provisions of subsection 57(1) apply so that the party in breach is required to repair the consumer product, the consumer shall return the product to the place of business of, or to any repair facility or service outlet operated by:

(a) the retail seller, where the retail seller is the party in breach;
(b) the manufacturer, where the manufacturer is the party in breach; or
(c) either of them, where both are in breach.

(2) No consumer is obliged to return the consumer product pursuant to subsection (1) to the party in breach if, by reason of the nature of the breach or the size, weight or method of attachment or installation of the product, it cannot be removed or transported without significant cost to the consumer.

(3) In the circumstances mentioned in subsection (2) the party in breach shall collect and arrange for the transportation and return of the product at his or her own expense or shall cause the repair to be made at the site where the product is located.

(4) For the purposes of subclause 57(1)(a)(i), the reasonable period runs from the time when the party in breach receives the consumer product but, where subsection (2) applies, the reasonable period runs from the time when the consumer advises the party in breach of the defect in the consumer product.

The loss of the right to reject

Assuming that the circumstances are such that a consumer buyer has the right to reject goods, two further issues may then arise. One is whether the goods have been effectively rejected. The other is whether the right to reject has been lost through acceptance of the goods within s 11(4) and ss 34 and 35 of the 1979 Act. The first issue arose in the following case.

Lee v York Coach and Marine [1977] RTR 35, Court of Appeal

On 7 March 1974 the defendant garage sold to the plaintiff a 1967 Morris 1100 car at a purchase price of £355. The car had a number of defects affecting its safety and the plaintiff gave the defendants several opportunities to rectify them. She then took it to another garage, Dutton-Forshaw, which declined to issue a test certificate. The plaintiff's claim for the return of the purchase price was dismissed by Judge Merrilees who held that the defendants were not in breach of s 14 of the Sale of Goods Act. The plaintiff then appealed to the Court of Appeal.

Cairns LJ, having outlined the facts of the case continued: The plaintiff took the car to the defendants again, but they were still unwilling to do any further work on it, and so she took it home and stood it in her drive and there is has stood ever since. Nobody has had any use of it since April 1974.

On the 26 April 1974 the plaintiff's solicitors, whom in the meanwhile she had consulted, wrote a letter to the defendants complaining of numerous defects in the car, and saying: 'We must ask you please to remedy all these defects without delay or to refund £355 to Mrs Lee'. Clearly up to this stage there had been no actual rejection of the car by the plaintiff, and the highest that it can be put in relation to this letter from her solicitors would be that there was a conditional rejection, in the sense that she would reject if the defendants were not willing to do the necessary repairs. The defendants replied to that letter on 29 April saying that they had done certain work on the car after delivery, and continuing:

'This work was carried out some three weeks ago without you taking this vehicle back for MOT to Forshaws, as we did agree to bleed brakes and fit extra brake pipes if required by Forshaws, also repair horn and speedo. This we will do in order that MOT standard is attained for Forshaws'.

It appears from that that the defendants were offering to do some work, but not everything that had been asked for by the plaintiff's solicitors in their letter.

The next step that was taken on behalf of the plaintiff was to have the vehicle examined by a Mr Stone, who is a Department of the Environment vehicle examiner. He made his examination on 8 May and he listed six defects:

'(1) Severe corrosion of brake pipings at off side front near to hose union, and at near side front hose union. (2) Corrosion of rear brake pipings. (3) Play in near side steering swivels bottom. (4) Horn button broken and horn not working. (5) Off side drive shaft inner flange loose. (6) Rear subframe weakened by extensive corrosion.'

On the strength of that report the plaintiff's solicitors wrote to the defendants again on 10 May further complaining of the defects, and saying in the course of the letter:

'Mrs Lee would have been justified in rescinding the contract on that basis'—that is on the basis that the car was unroadworthy—'In our opinion she may still be entitled to do so'.

Again I observe that that was not absolute rejection on the part of the solicitors as agents for the plaintiff. Indeed, if the earlier letter could have been considered to be a conditional rejection, they were in this letter in effect saying merely as a matter of opinion that she would have been entitled to rescind in the past, and she might still be entitled to do so, without saying that she did so.

In reply to that letter the defendants wrote on the 16 May offering to do certain further work to the car, but saying that they would require a signed satisfaction note from Mrs Lee that the work had been carried out to her satisfaction before the vehicle left their premises. She was unwilling, having regard to the previous history, to sign any satisfaction note without further opportunity of having the car tested, and accordingly she did not take the car back to them for any further attempt to put it in order, and, indeed, did nothing more about it until the 19 September, when she started the county court proceedings.

In her particulars of claim allegations were made that the car was not of merchantable quality and was not fit for the purpose of being driven safely on the road, in breach of the conditions in the Sale of Goods Act 1893, as amended by the Supply of Goods (Implied Terms) Act 1973. It was then stated: 'In the premises the plaintiff is entitled to and does reject the said car' and she claimed repayment of purchase price of £355 and, in the alternative damages. The defendants' defence we have not seen, but we understand that it was a comprehensive denial of the allegations in the particulars of claim.

. . .

I reach the clear conclusion that there was a breach of both implied statutory conditions here, and that in those circumstances the plaintiff would have been entitled to reject. But I do not think she ever did reject. I have indicated what in my view is the effect of the two letters written on her behalf by her solicitors, which are the high water mark of any case for rejection before the action was started. She purported to reject in her particulars of claim. That will not do; it is too late. I, therefore, consider that she is entitled not to the return of the purchase money, but to damages, and as no issue has been raised as to the correctness of the amount of damages, I would allow the appeal and award her £100 damages.

Stephenson LJ I agree. This second hand car was not, in my opinion of the evidence which the judge accepted, of merchantable quality within section 14(2) and section 62(1A) of the Act of 1893, or reasonably fit for the particular purpose for which it was bought by Mrs Lee within section 14(3) . . . But I also agree that Mrs Lee did not, for the reasons given by Cairns LJ, reject the car or treat the contract of sale as repudiated, at least until she brought this action in September 1974. She must, therefore, be taken to have accepted the car and compelled by section 11(1)(c) of the Act of 1893 [see now s 11(4)] to treat the sellers' breaches of condition as breaches of warranty. She is not entitled to reject the car, but she is entitled to damages by section 53 of the Act of 1893. She must keep what is left of the car and be content with the now agreed damages of £100 which the judge would have awarded her.

I agree to that extent the appeal should be allowed.

Bridge LJ I agree . . .

Appeal allowed. Plaintiff awarded £100 damages. Order below for defendant's costs set aside and an order substituted for plaintiff's costs below on the scale appropriate to £100 damages. No order for costs in the Court of Appeal.

If the requirement of an unequivocal rejection is satisfied it will be effective only if the goods have not been accepted. The rules as to what constitutes acceptance are printed above: see ss 34 and 35 of the 1979 Act. They have been modified quite considerably by the provisions of the Sale and Supply of Goods Act 1994, s 2, which give effect to further recommendations in the Law Commission Report on 'Sale and Supply of Goods' (Law Com No 160, 1987). In practice, usually the most difficult issue is whether the buyer is to be deemed to have accepted the goods within s 35(4). This will be so when, after the lapse of 'a reasonable time', he 'retains the goods without intimating to the seller that he has rejected them'. The point was discussed in the following case, the facts of which are printed above at p 104. It should be noted that the case was decided before the amendments introduced by the 1994 Act.

Bernstein v Pamson Motors (Golders Green) Ltd [1987] 2 All ER 220, Queen's Bench Division

Rougier J, having concluded that the plaintiff's new Nissan Laurel motor car was not of merchantable (now satisfactory) quality, continued:

This in turn prompts the inquiry: what is a reasonable time in the circumstances? And here the 1979 Act ceases to be helpful. By s 59 'a reasonable time' is defined as a question of fact, no more, as if it could be anything else.

The submission made on behalf of the defendants is that in the context of the sale of new motor car a reasonable time must entail a reasonable time to inspect and try out the car *generally* rather than with an eye to any specific defect, and that to project the period further would be artificial and contrary to the general legal proposition that there should, whenever possible, be finality in commercial transactions. At first I regret to say this proposition got a hostile reception on the ground that a mere 140-odd miles, and some three weeks, part of which were occupied by illness, were not nearly enough to afford the plaintiff any opportunity of discovering this wholly latent defect.

However, it was pointed out, and in my view rightly, that the whole concept of discovery of any *particular* defect and subsequent affirmation of the contract was only material in contracts of hire purchase and that there was nothing in the Sale of Goods Act 1979 to justify any analogous approach. This distinction was clearly stated by Webster J in the recent case of *Laurelgates Ltd v Lombard North Central Ltd* (1983) 133 NLJ 720.

In effect, it was argued, the wording of s 35 of the 1979 Act creates its own implied affirmation, as it were, by stating merely that once a buyer has had the goods for a reasonable time, *not,* be it noted, related to the opportunity to discover any particular defect, he is deemed to have accepted them. I think that this submission is correct.

In my judgment, the nature of the particular defect, discovered ex post facto, and the speed with which it might have been discovered, are irrelevant to the concept of reasonable time in s 35 as drafted. That section seems to me to be directed solely to what is a reasonable practical interval in commercial terms between a buyer receiving the goods and his ability to send them back, taking into consideration from his point of view the nature of the goods and their function, and from the point of view of the seller the commercial desirability of being able to close his ledger reasonably soon after the transaction is complete. The complexity of the intended function of the goods is clearly of prime consideration here. What is a reasonable time in relation to a bicycle would hardly suffice for a nuclear submarine.

Turning to the facts of the present case one asks whether some three weeks and 140-odd miles constitute a reasonable time after taking delivery of a new motor car? I am bound to say that I think the answer is Yes. Adopting, as I do, the suggestion of counsel for the defendants that a reasonable time means reasonable time to examine and try out the goods in general terms, the evidence persuades me that such a time had elapsed by 3 January 1985. I discount the period when the plaintiff was ill because reasonable seems to me to be referable to the individual buyer's situation as well as to that of the seller. But the plaintiff after recovering, had taken two or three short trips in his car for the express purpose of trying it out, and had opportunity to make more trips had he wished to do so. In the circumstances I consider he must be deemed to have accepted the goods within the meaning of s 35 so that he is compelled to treat his claim under s 14 as a claim for breach of warranty and thereby to limit his remedy to damages rather than to rescission of the entire contract.

What then is the proper measure of his damages? Clearly, in my judgment, he is entitled to the cost of making his way back home on the day of the breakdown, plus the loss of his full tank of petrol, as pleaded, in the sum of £32.90 between them. Additionally, I think he is entitled to be compensated for a totally spoilt day, comprising nothing but vexation, and for this I would award the sum of £150.

He was without his car for a lengthy period, but in my judgment only five days' loss of use can properly be awarded, taking us to 8 January when he declined the defendants' offer of a substitute and for those five days I would award £50.

In appropriate circumstances, by virtue of s 53(3) of the 1979 Act, the purchaser who has been compelled to treat a breach of condition as to quality as a breach of warranty would be entitled to the difference between the value of the goods at the time of delivery to him and the value they would have had if they had fulfilled the warranty. Unhappily for the plaintiff in this case, there is no evidence before me to suggest that the two value figures are different. Therefore no loss or diminution of value has been proved under this heading. His damages therefore remain limited to the total of the sums I have outlined.

Judgment for the plaintiff accordingly.

NOTES

1. In *Rogers v Parish Scarborough Ltd* [1987] 2 All ER 232, [1987] QB 933, above, p 102, the defendants left it too late to argue that the Range Rover could not, in any event, be rejected. The Court of Appeal did not allow submission on the point.

2. For a case in which a buyer of a new and defective Chrysler car was successful in claiming damages, but too late to reject, see *Jackson v Chrysler Acceptances Ltd* [1978] RTR 474, CA.

3. For an attempt to specify more precise time limits, see the Proposal for a European Parliament and Council Directive on the Sale of Consumer Goods and Associated Guarantees (above, pp 119–22), Arts 3.4 and 4.1. It is unclear whether the buyer has the right to stipulate which of the four alternatives specified in Art 3.4 the seller must comply with. However, on a literal reading it seems that, provided that the one month requirement of Art 4.1 is complied with, the buyer would still have the right to reject the goods for a lack of conformity (which was more than 'minor') after (say) eleven months, no matter how much they had deteriorated in the meantime. This seems unrealistically generous.

Long v Lloyd [1958] 2 All ER 402, [1958] 1 WLR 753, Court of Appeal

The following case, involving a contract for the sale of a secondhand lorry, is concerned with the loss of the right to rescind for misrepresentation rather than the loss of the right to reject for breach of condition. However, it is clear that the two situations have features in common.

Pearce LJ, having set out the facts of the case in some detail, continued:

We should next refer to the facts of *Leaf's* case and the observations made by the members of the court on those facts. The contract was a contract for the sale of a picture which the sellers innocently misrepresented to have been painted by Constable. The buyer took delivery of the picture and kept it for a matter of five years. He was then informed on attempting to sell the picture that it was not a Constable. Thereupon he brought his action for rescission on the ground that the sellers had misrepresented, albeit innocently, the identity of the artist. He could have claimed damages for breach of warranty but refrained from doing so. On these facts Denning, LJ, after referring to s 11(1)(c) and s 35 of the Sale of Goods Act, 1893, said this ([1950] 1 All ER at p 695):

'In this case this buyer took the picture into his house, and five years passed before he intimated any rejection. That, I need hardly say, is much more than a reasonable time. It is far too late for him at the end of five years to reject this picture for breach of any condition. His remedy after that length of time is for damages only, a claim which he has not brought before the court . . . although rescission may in some cases be a proper remedy, nevertheless it is to be remembered that an innocent misrepresentation is much less potent than a breach of condition. A condition is a term of the contract of a most material character, and, if a claim to reject for breach of condition is barred, it seems to me a fortiori that a claim to rescission on the ground of innocent misrepresentation is also barred. So, assuming that a contract for the sale of goods may be rescinded in a proper case for innocent misrepresentation, nevertheless, once the buyer has accepted, or is deemed to have accepted, the goods, the claim is barred. In this case the buyer must clearly be deemed to have accepted the picture. He had ample opportunity to examine it in the first few days after he bought it. Then was the time to see if the condition or representation was fulfilled, yet he has kept it all this time and five years have elapsed without any notice of rejection. In my judgment, he cannot now claim to rescind . . . '

Jenkins LJ, founded himself on the five years' delay as being far in excess of the reasonable time within which the right to claim rescission, if it ever existed, should have been exercised; and while expressing no dissent from, did not advert to, Denning LJ's view to the effect that the buyer's acceptance of the picture in itself barred any right there might otherwise have been to claim rescission. Sir Raymond Evershed MR, said (ibid, at p 696):

'I also agree that this appeal should be dismissed, for the reasons which have already been given. On the facts of this case it seems to me that the buyer ought not now to be allowed to rescind this contract . . . [ibid, at p 697] If a man elects to buy a work of art or any other chattel on the faith of some representation, innocently made, and delivery of the article is accepted, then it seems to me that there is much to be said for the view that on acceptance there is an end of that particular transaction, and that, if it were otherwise, business dealings in these things would become hazardous, difficult, and uncertain.'

As to the facts of the present case, counsel for the plaintiff contrasts the period of only a few days between the delivery of the lorry to the plaintiff and his purported rescission of the contract with the period of five years in *Leaf's* case. He says the plaintiff was entitled to a reasonable time within which to ascertain the true condition of the lorry and to exercise (if so advised) the right of rescission which for the present purpose he must be assumed to have had. It is of course obvious that so far as time is concerned this case bears no resemblance to *Leaf's* case. Nevertheless, a strict application to the facts of the present case of Denning LJ's view to the effect that the right (if any) to rescind after completion on the ground of innocent misrepresentation is barred by acceptance of the goods must necessarily prove fatal to the plaintiff's case. Apart from special circumstances, the place of delivery is the proper place for examination and for acceptance. It was open to the plaintiff to have the lorry examined by an expert before driving it away but he chose not to do so. It is true, however, that the truth of certain of the representations, for example, that the lorry would do eleven miles to the gallon could not be ascertained except by use and therefore the plaintiff should have a reasonable time to test it. Until he had had such an opportunity it might well be said that he had not accepted the lorry, always assuming, of course, that he did nothing inconsistent with the ownership of the seller. An examination of the facts, however, shows that on any view he must have accepted the lorry before he purported to reject it.

Thus, to recapitulate the facts, after the trial run the plaintiff drove the lorry home from Hampton Court to Sevenoaks, a not inconsiderable distance. After that experience he took it into use in his business by driving it on the following day to Rochester and back to Sevenoaks with a load. By the time he returned from Rochester he knew that the dynamo was not charging, that there was an oil seal leaking, that he had used eight gallons of fuel for a journey of forty miles and that a wheel was cracked. He must also, as we think, have known by this time that the vehicle was not capable of forty miles per hour. As to oil consumption, we should have thought that, if it was so excessive that the sump was practically dry after three hundred miles, the plaintiff could have reasonably been expected to discover that the rate of consumption was unduly high by the time he had made the journey from Hampton Court to Sevenoaks and thence to Rochester and back. On his return from Rochester the plaintiff telephoned to the defendant and complained about the dynamo, the excessive fuel consumption, the leaking oil seal and the cracked wheel. The defendant then offered to pay half the cost of the reconstructed dynamo which the plaintiff had been advised to fit, and the plaintiff accepted the defendant's offer. We find this difficult to reconcile with the continuance of any right of rescission which the plaintiff might have had down to that time.

The matter does not rest there. On the following day the plaintiff, knowing all that he did about the condition and performance of the lorry, despatched it, driven by his brother, on a business trip to Middlesbrough. That step, at all events, appears to us to have amounted, in all the circumstances of the case, to a final acceptance of the lorry by the plaintiff for better or for worse, and to have conclusively extinguished any right of rescission remaining to the plaintiff after completion of the sale.

. . .

Appeal dismissed. Leave to appeal to the House of Lords granted.

QUESTIONS

1. Was Denning LJ correct in saying in *Leaf's* case (cited above, p 132) that 'if a claim to reject for breach of condition is barred it seems to me a fortiori that a claim to rescission on the ground of innocent misrepresentation is also barred'?

   Might not a buyer 'accept' goods without knowing their true condition and yet not be barred from rescission for misrepresentation on ascertaining the truth soon thereafter? For a reference to the principles of affirmation see below pp 135–8. Note, however, that the Misrepresentation Act 1967, s 2(2) gives a court the power to declare a contract subsisting and to award damages in lieu of rescission.

2. In *Long v Lloyd* it was suggested that the plaintiff's acceptance of the defendant's offer to pay half the cost of the reconstructed dynamo was 'difficult to reconcile with the continuance of any right of rescission'. As to the effect on acceptance, see s 35(6)(a) of the 1979 Act (above, p 124). When an ineffective repair is being carried out (eg under a manufacturer's guarantee) is the clock stopped for the purpose of the 'reasonable time' for rejection within s 35(4)?

3. To the extent that the implied condition of satisfactory quality recognises durability as an aspect of the quality of goods (see s 14(2B)(e) of the 1979 Act, above, pp 80, 113–17) will this be vindicated by a remedy in damages only?

PROBLEMS

1. Wedgwood buys an expensive twelve-cover set of china from his local antique shop. It is delivered by the store's van and he signs a delivery note which reads 'I confirm that these goods have been received in good condition'. On opening the box containing the china two days later Wedgwood discovers that several items have been badly chipped during package or transit. He wishes to reject the china.

   Advise Wedgwood.

2. Hermitage orders two cases of a 1995 Rhone as part of an opening offer from a specialist vintner, Gerard. He expects to drink the wine from 2010 onwards. He wishes to know how the provisions as to acceptance may affect him should the wine prove to be unsatisfactory in terms of quality.

   Advise Hermitage. How, if at all, would the position be affected if the proposed Directive on the Sale of Consumer Goods and Associated Guarantees were implemented in English Law?: cf Articles 3.1, 3.3, 3.4 and 4.1, above, pp 120–1.

3. On 1 January 1997 Beatle buys a new stereo set from his local dealer Fastbuck, paying £500 cash. When he opens the package at home he finds that the set has a guarantee provided by the manufacturer, Ginushi, which reads as follows: 'We guarantee this stereo set for three months from the date of purchase. Any necessary replacement part will be provided free of charge within this period'. The set works quite satisfactorily for two weeks and then stops working on 15 January. On the same day Beatle takes it back to Fastbuck, who returns it to

Ginushi. The set is ready for collection on 1 February and is collected by Beatle from Fastbuck on that day. It works satisfactorily until 15 March and then breaks down again. Beatle takes it back to Fastbuck saying, 'Look I am getting fed up with this. Make sure it is fixed properly this time or I shall be wanting my money back'. The set is returned to Ginushi for repair and is collected by Beatle from Fastbuck on 30 March. It works well until 15 April and then breaks down again.

Advise Beatle as to what remedies, if any, he may have against (i) Fastbuck and (ii) Ginushi. For the position of Ginushi see also above, pp. 57–70, below, pp 274–8.

Other contracts for the supply of goods

The position where goods are supplied other than under a contract of sale has been summarised conveniently in the following extract from a Law Commission Working Paper.

Sale and Supply of Goods (1983) Law Commission Working Paper No 85

English law: affirmation
2.61. In this section we are concerned not only with contracts of hire, hire-purchase, barter and for work and materials but also with consumer conditional sale agreements, which are equated with hire-purchase agreements for the purpose of 'acceptance'[1] and are subject to the same common law principle of affirmation.

2.62. Unlike a buyer, the customer in any of the other contracts for the supply of goods does not lose his right to bring the contract to an end by virtue of provisions similar to those contained in the Sale of Goods Act, but by virtue of the common law doctrine of affirmation. If he is held to have affirmed the contract he can thereafter only sue for damages. The following principles have emerged in the general law of contract and appear to be of general application:

  (i)   on discovering the breach, an innocent party must elect between his available remedies;[2]
  (ii) it seems that as a general[3] rule an innocent party cannot be held to have affirmed the contract, unless he had knowledge of the breach;
  (iii) affirmation may be express if the innocent party expressly refuses to accept the other party's repudiation of the contract;[4]
  (iv) affirmation may be implied if the innocent party does some act such as pressing for the performance of the contract from which it may be inferred that he recognises the continued existence of the contract;[5]
  (v)   mere inactivity by the innocent party after discovering the breach will not of itself constitute affirmation, unless (a) the other party would be prejudiced by the delay in treating the contract as repudiated or (b) the delay is of such length as to constitute evidence of a decision to affirm the contract;[6]
  (vi) affirmation must be total in the sense that the innocent party cannot affirm part of the contract and disaffirm the rest.[7]

2.63. In applying the doctrine of affirmation to hire-purchase agreements the tendency of the courts has been wherever possible to protect the right of the hirer to reject defective goods. However, authority in this area of the law is scanty.[8] There are no reported cases in which the doctrine of affirmation has been applied to contracts of barter or for work and materials, but there is no reason to suppose that it would not be applicable. The doctrine appears to have been applied in a contract of hire.[9]

[1] Supply of Goods (Implied Terms) Act 1973, s 14.
[2] *Kammins Ballrooms Co Ltd v Zenith Investments (Torquay) Ltd* [1971] AC 850 per Lord Diplock at p 853.
[3] See however *Panchaud Freres SA v Etablissements General Grain Co* [1970] 1 Lloyd's Rep 53, where the Court of Appeal, stressing the need for finality in commercial transactions, created a limited exception of uncertain ambit to the general rule. It held that a buyer who rejected shipping documents on an inadmissible ground could not subsequently justify this on grounds which he could have detected, but did not detect at the time and which he only discovered three years later.
[4] *White and Carter (Councils) Ltd v McGregor* [1962] AC 413.
[5] *Suisse Atlantique Société d'Armement Maritime SA v Rotterdamsche Kolen Centrale NV* [1967] 1 AC 361.
[6] *Allen v Robles* [1969] 1 WLR 1193.
[7] *Suisse Atlantique* case (above).
[8] See *Yeoman Credit Ltd v Apps* [1962] 2 QB 508; *Farnworth Finance Ltd v Attryde* [1970] 1 WLR 1053.
[9] *Guarantee Trust of Jersey Ltd v Gardner* (1973) 117 Sol Jo 564.

In its Report on 'Sale and Supply of Goods' (Law Com No 160, 1987) the Law Commission did not recommend that the Sale of Goods Act rules on loss of the right to terminate the contract should be extended to other contracts of supply: see paras 5.43–5.49.

The following case is perhaps the single most important example discussing the notion of affirmation in relation to a consumer hire-purchase transaction.

Farnworth Finance Facilities Ltd v Attryde [1970] 2 All ER 774, [1970] 1 WLR 1053, Court of Appeal

Lord Denning MR. The first defendant is a civil servant employed by the Ministry of Aviation at Aberporth in Cardiganshire. In 1964, when he was aged 23, he wanted a new motor cycle. He read an advertisement issued by the Enfield Cycle Co Ltd and decided to get a Royal Enfield Interceptor. He went to dealers, the second defendants, King's Motors (Oxford) Ltd of Wolverhampton. They got a machine from the makers and supplied it to him on hire-purchase terms. The finance company was Farnworth Finance Facilities Ltd of Cardiff, the plaintiffs. The second defendants had the forms in their office at Wolverhampton. The first defendant signed them and took delivery of the machine. The cash price was £427 5s 10d. The finance charges were £89 16s. Add £1 option to purchase. Thus making a total hire-purchase price of £518 1s 10d. The first defendant paid £155 5s 10d down, with instalments payable over the next three years at £10 1s a month.

The first defendant took delivery of the machine on 11 July 1964. But he had a lot of trouble with it. He took it back to the second defendants. They tried to correct the faults, but did not succeed. So he took it back to the makers, the Enfield Cycle Co Ltd at Redditch. They had it for nine days—from 21 to 31 July 1964. They remedied some defects, but they did not succeed in remedying all the faults. On 13 August, the first defendant took it back again to the Enfield Cycle Co Ltd. They had it this time for some weeks. He did not get it back until 15 October 1964. They had remedied some defects, but not all. He used it for five weeks, from 15 October to 23 November. But he found that there were still serious faults. The last straw was on Saturday, 21 November 1964. As he was turning out from a drive, the rear chain broke. The broken chain knocked a hole in the crank case and caused considerable damage. It would be a very expensive repair. He decided that he would not go on with it any further. He wrote on Monday, 23 November 1964:

'I am not making any further effort to get Enfields or things to put things right. I have tried hard enough and got nowhere. Obviously I will not continue to pay hire charges for a machine I cannot use and which has been a troublesome burden ever since I've had it. Please come and repossess the bike you will find it at the address given at the start of this letter.'

That was his address in Cardiganshire. So being utterly disappointed, he rejected the machine.

It was a big loss to him: for he had paid £155 10s down. He had paid four instalments of £10 1s. So he had paid £195 14s. The plaintiffs, or someone on their behalf, came and took possession of the machine. They sold it for £142 5s. They then sued the first defendant for a further £149 1s. He no longer had the motor cycle, and he was now being sued for a further £149 1s. He resisted the claim on the ground that the plaintiffs had been guilty of a fundamental breach of their obligations under the contract. He put in a counterclaim for his own loss. The plaintiffs said that, if they were in breach, they could claim indemnity from the second defendants. So they joined them as defendants.

The action was tried by his Honour Judge Temple-Morris QC at Cardiff. He accepted the first defendant's evidence in its entirety . . .

His Lordship then discussed the position of the second defendants and referred to the doctrine of fundamental breach (see below, p 321) and continued:

As between the plaintiffs and the first defendant, there was no express term about the condition of the machine. But there were implied terms. It has been established by a series of cases in this court that, in a hire-purchase agreement of a motor vehicle there are a number of implied terms which are of fundamental importance. These cases are: *Yeoman Credit Ltd v Apps*,[1] *Astley Industrial Trust Ltd v Grimley*[2] and *Charterhouse Credit Co Ltd v Tolly*.[3] These cases show that it is an implied condition that the machine should correspond with the description and that it should be reasonably fit for the purpose for which it was hired; which means, of course, that it should be roadworthy. In addition, the machine in this case was expressly described as 'new', which adds emphasis to the implied terms. A new motor cycle should at any rate be a workman-like motor cycle which is safe to be used on the roads.

There were clearly breaches of those implied terms . . .

The next question is whether the first defendant affirmed the contract. Counsel for the second defendants points out that the first defendant had ridden this bicycle for 4,000 miles. Even after he got it back from the makers on 15 October he had used it for five or six weeks till 23 November and had ridden 3,000 miles on it. Counsel said that by using it all that time the first defendant had affirmed the contract and it was too late for him to repudiate it. But as the argument proceeded, I think that counsel for the first defendant gave the right answer. He pointed out that affirmation is a matter of election. A man only affirms a contract when he knows of the defects and by his conduct elects to go on with the contract despite them. In this case the first defendant complained from the beginning of the defects and sent the machine back for them to be remedied. He did not elect to accept it unless they were remedied. But the defects were never satisfactorily remedied. When the rear chain broke, it was the last straw. It showed that the machine could not be relied on. This knowledge was not brought home to him until this last final incident. The first defendant was entitled to say then: 'I am not going on with this machine any longer. I have tried it long enough.' After all, it was a contract of hiring. The machine was not his until the three years had been completed—and the price paid. Owing to the defects, the first defendant was entitled to throw up the hiring; to say he would have no more to do with it; and to claim damages. The judge found that the first defendant did not affirm the contract and I agree with him.

. . .

There is one other point, and that is on damages. Counsel for the second defendants said that the first defendant ought to give credit for the use which he had of the motor cycle for 4,000 miles. He relied on *Charterhouse Credit Co Ltd v Tolly*[3] when such a credit was allowed. But it seems to me that the value of any use had by the first defendant is offset by the great amount of trouble he had. So no credit need be given for the use. I see no reason for interfering with the award of the judge on damages.

So the plaintiffs are liable to the first defendant. But they are entitled to claim over against the second defendants on the express promise that the machine was in a roadworthy condition. They can recover against them the full amount of £149 1s, and for the £195 9s 10d that they have to pay the first defendant. The judge so ordered. I find that there is no fault to be found with the judgment of the judge in this case, and I would dismiss the appeal.

Fenton Atkinson and Megaw LLJ agreed with Lord Denning's judgment.

Appeal dismissed.

[1] [1961] 2 All ER 281, [1962] 2 QB 508.
[2] [1963] 2 All ER 33, [1963] 1 WLR 584.
[3] [1963] 2 All ER 432, [1963] 2 QB 683.

NOTES

1. The entitlement of a consumer to recover all the money paid out by way of a deposit or instalments will depend on establishing a total failure of consideration. In the above case the use 'enjoyed' by the hirer was offset by the trouble which he had suffered. In *Charterhouse Credit Co Ltd v Tolly* [1963] 2 QB 683, [1963] 2 All ER 432, CA, where it was conceded that some element of benefit had been received, Donovan LJ explained the method of calculating damages as follows (at p 439):

> The point seems to be free from direct authority, but an application of basic principle does, I think, yield the true and just solution. The general rule in cases of breach of contract is that a plaintiff is entitled to be placed, so far as money can do it, in the same position as he would have been in had the contract been performed (per Parke B in *Robinson v Harman*[1]). This involves considering what would have been the hirer's position had there been no continuing breach of the contract by the finance company. He would then have had a suitable car delivered to him on hire-purchase terms. He would have been liable for the initial payment plus three monthly instalments. These payments would have been much higher than payments for mere hire alone, on account of the eventual option to purchase for the purely nominal sum of £1. The hirer has, in fact, paid the initial payment of £90, and under this judgment must pay the three instalments amounting to £47 4s. For this outlay, however, he has received nothing, owing to the finance company's breach of contract, except the two rides to Greenwich. What is required to put him, so far as money can, in the same position as if the contract had been performed? To my mind it is a sum equal to the cost of hiring a similar car on similar terms as to the eventual option to purchase for £1. There is no reason why one should not adopt as the figure of that cost what the hirer actually has to pay to the finance company for the like hiring in the present case, to wit, £90 and £47 4s. less a small sum for the two journeys he made in the car, which I would put at £5. The net figure thus becomes £132 4s.
>
> I reject counsel for the finance company's argument that all to which the hirer is entitled is the cost of hiring another similar car. That would not of itself be restitutio in integrum, for the contract here was not one of simple hire but of hire-purchase.

[1] (1848) 1 Exch 850 at 855.

In contracts of hire-purchase, hire, barter and conditional sales usually it will be possible for the defective goods to be made available for collection by the supplier. Sometimes this will be true of contracts of work and materials. For example if a contract to supply and fit a carpet is so classified it may not be unduly difficult for the supplier to take up any that has been laid. However, there will be many situations in which at best this would create serious practical problems. The following case provides an interesting example of the position of the contractor and customer in such a situation.

Bolton v Mahadeva [1972] 2 All ER 1322, [1972] 1 WLR 1009, Court of Appeal

The plaintiff agreed with the defendant to install central heating in the defendant's house. The contract price for the central heating installation was a lump sum of £560. On completion of the work the defendant complained that the work was defective and refused to pay. At the trial the county court judge found that because of a defective flue, fumes affected the condition of the air in the living rooms. Moreover the house was on average ten per cent less warm than it should have been with such a system, but the deficiency varied from room to room and in some rooms it was much greater. In each case the expenditure necessary to cure these defects was £40. The judge held that because of those and other deficiencies the defendant was entitled to set off £174.50 against the contract price. He gave judgment for the plaintiff for the balance accordingly. The defendant appealed.

Cairns LJ, having outlined the facts of the case, continued: The main question in the case is whether the defects in workmanship found by the judge to be such as to cost £174 to repair— ie between one-third and one-quarter of the contract price—were of such a character and amount that the plaintiff could not be said to have substantially performed his contract. That is, in my view, clearly the legal principle which has to be applied to cases of this kind.

The rule which was laid down many years ago in *Cutter v Powell*[1] in relation to lump sum contracts was that, unless the contracting party had performed the whole of his contract, he was not entitled to recover anything. That strong rule must now be read in the light of certain more recent cases to which I shall briefly refer. The first of those cases is *H Dakin & Co Ltd v Lee*[2] a decision of the Court of Appeal, in which it was held that, where the amount of work which had not been carried out under a lump sum contract was very minor in relation to the contract as a whole, the contractor was entitled to be paid the lump sum, subject to such deduction as might be proper in respect of the uncompleted work. It is necessary to observe that the headnote of *H Dakin & Co Ltd v Lee*[2] was based, not on the judgments in the Court of Appeal, but on the judgments that had been delivered in the Divisional Court; and, as was pointed out in *Vigers v Cook*[3] that headnote does not properly represent the grounds of the decision of the Court of Appeal in that case. The basis on which the Court of Appeal did decide *H Dakin & Co Ltd v Lee*[2] is to be found in a passage of the judgment of Lord Cozens-Hardy MR.[4] I do not think it is necessary to read it in full, but I read this short passage:[5]

'But to say that a builder cannot recover from a building owner merely because some item of the work has been done negligently or inefficiently or improperly is a proposition which I should not listen to unless compelled by a decision of the House of Lords. Take a contract for a lump sum to decorate a house; the contract provides that there shall be three coats of oil paint, but in one of the rooms only two coats of paint are put on. Can anybody say that under these circumstances the building owner could go and occupy the house and take the benefit of all the decorations which had been done in the other rooms without paying a penny for all the work done by the builder, just because only two coats of paint had been put on in one room where they ought to have been three?'

. . .

Perhaps the most helpful case is the most recent one of *Hoenig v Isaacs*.[6] That was a case where the plaintiff was an interior decorator and designer of furniture who had entered into a contract to decorate and furnish the defendant's flat for a sum of £750; and, as appears from the statement of facts, the Official Referee who tried the case at first instance found that the door of a wardrobe required replacing, that a bookshelf which was too short would have to be remade, which would require alterations being made to a bookcase, and that the cost of remedying the defects was £55 18s 2d. That is on a £750 contract. The ground on which the Court of Appeal in that case held that the plaintiff was entitled to succeed, notwithstanding that there was not complete performance of the contract, was that there was substantial performance of the contract and that the defects in the work which there existed were not sufficient to amount to a substantial degree of non-performance.

In considering whether there was substantial performance I am of opinion that it is relevant to take into account both the nature of the defects and the proportion between the cost of rectifying them and the contract price. It would be wrong to say that the contractor is only entitled to payment if the defects are so trifling as to be covered by the de minimis rule.

. . .

Now, certainly it appears to me that the nature and amount of the defects in this case were far different from those which the court had to consider in *H Dakin & Co Ltd v Lee*[2] and *Hoenig v Isaacs*.[6] For my part, I find it impossible to say that the judge was right in reaching the conclusion that in those circumstances the contract had been substantially performed. The contract was a contract to install a central heating system. If a central heating system when installed is such that it does not heat the house adequately and is such, further, that fumes are given out, so as to make living rooms uncomfortable, and if the putting right of those defects is not something which can be done by some slight amendment of the system, then I think that the contract is not substantially performed.

The actual amounts of expenditure which the judge assessed as being necessary to cure those particular defects were £40 in each case. Taking those matters into account and the other matters making up the total of £174, I have reached the conclusion that the judge was wrong in saying that this contract had been substantially completed; and, on my view of the law, it follows that the plaintiff was not entitled to recover under that contract.

. . .

So far as the defendant's claim in respect of fees for the report which he obtained from his expert is concerned, it seems to me clear that that report was obtained in view of a dispute which had arisen and with a view to being used in evidence if proceedings did become necessary, and in the hope that it would assist in the settlement of the dispute without proceedings being started. In those circumstances, I think that the judge was right in reaching the conclusion that that report was something the fees for which, if recoverable at all, would be recoverable only under an order for costs.

So far as concerns the damages in respect of the inconvenience to which the defendant was put, the judge, as I have said, assessed that inconvenience at £15. I must say that, on the evidence, it seems to me to be a low figure; but obviously it is a figure which is incapable of any exact assessment, and I am not prepared to say that the judge was wrong in assessing that sum.

. . .

It appears to me that the result should be this, that the appeal should be allowed and the judgment in favour of the plaintiff should be set aside. It is not, I think, contested that there is in respect of the extras a sum of £61 which was due to the plaintiff at the commencement of the action; that, of course, is far less than the £400 which had been paid into court. If Sachs and Buckley LJ agree with the judgment which I have delivered, it will be for consideration then as to the exact form of the order that this court should make.

Buckley LJ I agree and do not wish to add anything.

Sachs LJ I agree that this appeal should be allowed, for the reasons given by Cairns LJ.

. . .

When, however, one looks at the aggregate of the number of defects that he held to have been established, at the importance of some of those defects, and at the way in which some of them prevented the installation being one that did what was intended, I find myself, like Cairns LJ, quite unable to agree that there was a substantial performance by the plaintiff of this lump sum contract. It is not merely that so very much of the work was shoddy, but it is the general ineffectiveness of it for its primary purpose that leads me to that conclusion.

So far as the law is concerned, I would merely add that it seems to me to be compactly and accurately stated in Cheshire and Fifoot[7] in the following terms:

'. . . the present rule is that "so long as there is substantial performance the contractor is entitled to the stipulated price, subject only to a cross-action or counter-claim for the omissions or defects in execution"'[8]

and, to 'cross-action or counter-claim', I would of course add 'set-off'. The converse, however, is equally correct—if there is not a substantial performance, the contractor cannot recover. It is on the application of that converse rule that the plaintiff's case here fails. This rule does not work hardly on a contractor if only he is prepared to remedy the defects before seeking to resort to litigation to recover the lump sum. It is entirely the fault of the plaintiff contractor in this instant case that he has placed himself in a difficulty by his refusal on 4 December 1969 to remedy the defects of which complaint was being made.

. . .

Appeal allowed; judgment set aside, there being substituted therefore judgment for the plaintiff for £46; plaintiff to repay the balance of £354 within 14 days.

[1] (1795) 6 Term Rep 320, [1775–1802] All ER Rep 159.
[2] [1916] 1 KB 566.
[3] [1919] 2 KB 475 at 483.
[4] [1916] 1 KB at 578 at 579.
[5] [1916] 1 KB at 579.
[6] [1952] 2 All ER 176.
[7] The Law of Contract (7th edn, 1969), p 492.
[8] 2 Smith's Leading Cases (13th edn), p 19.

For discussion of the doctrine of substantial performance see Cheshire, Fifoot and Furmston, *Law of Contract* (13th edn, 1996), at pp 545–6. See also the Law Commission Report, 'Pecuniary Restitution on Breach of Contract' (Law Com No 121, 1983).

QUESTIONS

1. Would the result of this case have been the same if the contractor had wished to remedy the defects but the defendant had denied him the opportunity, fearing that his apparent incompetence might only make things worse? Is there a risk that a consumer will be taken to have affirmed the contract if he allows a contractor an opportunity to rectify gross defects? How should contractors protect themselves, particularly where the sum involved is substantial—as is the case of contracts to construct a conservatory?

2. Suppose that in the above case the householder had paid the full cost of the installation in advance. Would he have recovered his prepayment in full or only some lesser sum? Is the overall position satisfactory?

NOTE

A further difficulty may arise when, objectively, the contractor's breach does not lead to any readily identifiable loss and may even confer a financial benefit. Consider the following.

PROBLEM

Marjoram, a rich young pop star, decides to have her kitchen extensively rebuilt. The contract is awarded to Bodgit and the price of £80,000 includes fitted cupboards, replumbing and new appliances. She stipulates that the floor be tiled with bright pink Roman mosaic tiles, this being her favourite colour. She is away on tour when the work is done. Bodgit, being unable to locate tiles of the right colour, or contact Marjoram, substitutes exactly the same make and quality of tiles, but in a tasteful light green. Marjoram returns from her tour and demands that the tiles be ripped up and replaced with pink ones. The evidence of an expert valuer is that the value of the house is considerably higher with the tiles used by Bodgit, than with the bright pink ones.

Discuss on the assumption that the total cost of replacing the tiles is (1) £40,000 (since much of the kitchen has to be removed and rebuilt); or (ii) £7,000 (£5,000 for the tiles and £2,000 for associated labour).

(See, generally, *Ruxley Electronics and Construction v Forsyth* [1995] 3 All ER 268, HL—swimming pool not complying with contractual specifications—and Coot, 'Contract Damages, *Ruxley* and the Performance Interest' [1997] CLJ 537.

CANCELLATION OF CONTRACTS

Usually, it is not open to a consumer to cancel a contract, for example on the ground that the purchase is now seen as a regrettable impulse buy or because the goods can be acquired more cheaply elsewhere. For many years there has been an exception in the case of regulated consumer credit agreements signed by the debtor off trade premises: see the Consumer Credit Act 1974, ss 67–73. In 1985 the Council of the EEC adopted a Directive on contracts concluded away from business premises (Council Directive 85/577/EEC: the 'Doorstep Selling' Directive). This was implemented in English Law through the following provisions. In the case of timeshares, both cash and credit transactions are covered by the Timeshares Act 1992.

The Consumer Protection (Cancellation of Contracts Concluded away from Business Premises) Regulations 1987

(SI 1987/2117, as amended by SI 1988/958)

Citation and commencement

1. These Regulations may be cited as the Consumer Protection (Cancellation of Contracts Concluded away from Business Premises) Regulations 1987 and shall come into force on 1st July 1988.

Interpretation

2.—(1) In these Regulations—

'business' includes a trade or profession;

'consumer' means a person, other than a body corporate, who, in making a contract to which these Regulations apply, is acting for purposes which can be regarded as outside his business;

'goods' has the meaning given by section 61(1) of the Sale of Goods Act 1979;

'land mortgage' includes any security charged on land and in relation to Scotland includes any heritable security;

'notice of cancellation' has the meaning given by regulation 4(5) below;

'security' in relation to a contract means a mortgage, charge, pledge, bond, debenture, indemnity, guarantee, bill, note or other right provided by the consumer, or at his request (express or implied), to secure the carrying out of his obligations under the contract;

'signed' has the same meaning as in the Consumer Credit Act 1974; and

'trader' means a person who, in making a contract to which these Regulations apply, is acting for the purposes of his business, and anyone acting in the name or on behalf of such a person.

(2) In Scotland any provision in these Regulations requiring a document to be signed shall be complied with by a body corporate if the document is properly executed in accordance with the law of Scotland.

Contracts to which the Regulations apply

3.–(1) These Regulations apply to a contract, other than an excepted contract, for the supply by a trader of goods or services to a consumer which is made—

(a) during an unsolicited visit by a trader—
  (i) to the consumer's home or to the home of another person; or
  (ii) to the consumer's place of work;

(b) during a visit by a trader as mentioned in paragraph (a)(i) or (ii) above at the express request of the consumer where the goods or services to which the contract relates are other than those concerning which the consumer requested the visit of the trader, provided that when the visit was requested the consumer did not know, or could not reasonably have known, that the supply of those other goods or services formed part of the trader's business activities;

(c) after an offer was made by the consumer in respect of the supply by a trader of the goods or services in the circumstances mentioned in paragraph (a) or (b) above or (d) below; or

(d) during an excursion organised by the trader away from premises on which he is carrying on any business (whether on a permanent or temporary basis).

(2) For the purposes of this regulation an excepted contract means

(a) any contract—
  (i) for the sale or other disposition of land, or for a lease or land mortgage;
  (ii) to finance the purchase of land;
  (iii) for a bridging loan in connection with the purchase of land; or
  (iv) for the construction or extension of a building or other erection on land: Provided that these Regulations shall apply to a contract for the supply of goods and their incorporation in any land or a contract for the repair or improvement of a building or other erection on land, where the contract is not financed by a loan secured by a land mortgage;

(b) any contract for the supply of food, drink or other goods intended for current consumption by use in the household and supplied by regular roundsmen;

(c) any contract for the supply of goods or services which satisfies all the following conditions, namely—
  (i) terms of the contract are contained in a trader's catalogue which is readily available to the consumer to read in the absence of the trader or his representative before the conclusion of the contract;
  (ii) the parties to the contract intend that there shall be maintained continuity of contact between the trader or his representative and the consumer in relation to the transaction in question or any subsequent transaction; and
  (iii) both the catalogue and the contract contain or are accompanied by a prominent notice indicating that the consumer has a right to return to the trader or his representative goods supplied to him within the period of not less than 7 days from the day on which the goods are received by the consumer and otherwise to cancel the contract within that period without the consumer incurring any liability, other than any liability which may arise from the failure of the consumer to take reasonable care of the goods while they are in his possession;

(d) contracts of insurance to which the Insurance Companies Act 1982 applies;

(e) investment agreements within the meaning of the Financial Services Act 1986 and agreements for the making of deposits within the meaning of the Banking Act 1987 in respect of which Regulations have been made for regulating the making of unsolicited calls under section 34 of that Act;

(f) any contract not falling within sub-paragraph (g) below under which the total payments to be made by the consumer do not exceed £35; and

(g) any contract under which credit within the meaning of the Consumer Credit Act 1974 is provided not exceeding £35 other than a hire-purchase or conditional sale agreement.

(3) In this regulation 'unsolicited visit' means a visit by a trader, whether or not he is the trader who supplies the goods or services, which does not take place at the express request of the consumer and includes a visit which takes place after a trader telephones the consumer (otherwise than at his express request) indicating expressly or by implication that he is willing to visit the consumer.

Cancellation of Contract

4.—(1) No contract to which these Regulations apply shall be enforceable against the consumer unless the trader has delivered to the consumer notice in writing in accordance with paragraphs (3) and (4) below indicating the right of the consumer to cancel the contract within the period of 7 days mentioned in paragraph (5) below containing both the information set out in Part I of the Schedule to these Regulations and a Cancellation Form in the form set out in Part II of the Schedule and completed in accordance with the footnotes.

(2) Paragraph (1) above does not apply to a cancellable agreement within the meaning of the Consumer Credit Act 1974 or to an agreement which may be cancelled by the consumer in accordance with terms of the agreement conferring upon him similar rights as if the agreement were such a cancellable agreement.

(3) The information to be contained in the notice under paragraph (1) above shall be easily legible and if incorporated in the contract or other document shall be afforded no less prominence than that given to any other information in the document apart from the heading to the document and the names of the parties to the contract and any information inserted in handwriting.

(4) The notice shall be dated and delivered to the consumer—

    (a) in the cases mentioned in regulation 3(1)(a), (b) and (d) above, at the time of the making of the contract, and

    (b) in the case mentioned in regulation 3(1)(c) above, at the time of the making of the offer by the consumer.

(5) If within the period of 7 days following the making of the contract the consumer serves a notice in writing (a 'notice of cancellation') on the trader or any other person specified in a notice referred to in paragraph (1) above as a person to whom notice of cancellation may be given which, however expressed and whether or not conforming to the cancellation form set out in Part II of the Schedule to these Regulations, indicates the intention of the consumer to cancel the contract, the notice of cancellation shall operate to cancel the contract.

(6) Except as otherwise provided under these Regulations, a contract cancelled under paragraph (5) above shall be treated as if it had never been entered into by the consumer.

(7) Notwithstanding anything in section 7 of the Interpretation Act 1978, a notice of cancellation sent by post by a consumer shall be deemed to have been served at the time of posting, whether or not it is actually received.

Recovery of money paid by consumer

5.—(1) Subject to regulation 7(2) below, on the cancellation of a contract under regulation 4 above, any sum paid by or on behalf of the consumer under or in contemplation of the contract shall become repayable.

(2) If under the terms of the cancelled contract the consumer or any person on his behalf is in possession of any goods, he shall have a lien on them for any sum repayable to him under paragraph (1) above.

(3) Where any security has been provided in relation to the cancelled contract, the security, so far as it is so provided, shall be treated as never having had effect and any property lodged with the trader solely for the purposes of the security as so provided shall be returned by him forthwith.

Repayment of credit

6.—(1) Notwithstanding the cancellation of a contract under regulation 4 above under which credit is provided, the contract shall continue in force so far as it relates to repayment of credit and payment of interest.

(2) If, following the cancellation of the contract, the consumer repays the whole or a portion of the credit—
   (a) before the expiry of one month following service of the notice of cancellation, or
   (b) in the case of a credit repayable by instalments, before the date on which the first instalment is due,
no interest shall be payable on the amount repaid.

(3) If the whole of a credit repayable by instalments is not repaid on or before the date specified in paragraph (2)(b) above, the consumer shall not be liable to repay any of the credit except on receipt of a request in writing signed by the trader stating the amounts of the remaining instalments (recalculated by the trader as nearly as may be in accordance with the contract and without extending the repayment period), but excluding any sum other than principal and interest.

(4) Repayment of a credit, or payment of interest, under a cancelled contract shall be treated as duly made if it is made to any person on whom, under regulation 4(5) above, a notice of cancellation could have been served.

(5) Where any security has been provided in relation to the contract, the duty imposed on the consumer by this regulation shall not be enforceable before the trader has discharged any duty imposed on him by regulation 5(3) above.

[(6) In this regulation, the following expressions have the meanings hereby assigned to them:—
'cash' includes money in any form;
'credit' means a cash loan and any facility enabling the customer to overdraw on a current account;
'current account' means an account under which the customer may, by means of cheques or similar orders payable to himself or to any other person, obtain or have the use of money held or made available by the person with whom the account is kept and which records alterations in the financial relationship between the said person and the customer and;
'repayment', in relation to credit, means the repayment of money—
   (a) paid to a consumer before the cancellation of the contract; or
   (b) to the extent that he has overdrawn on his current account before the cancellation.]

Return of goods by consumer after cancellation

7.—(1) Subject to paragraph (2) below, a consumer who has before cancelling a contract under regulation 4 above acquired possession of any goods by virtue of the contract shall be under a duty, subject to any lien, on the cancellation to restore the goods to the trader in accordance with this regulation, and meanwhile to retain possession of the goods and take reasonable care of them.

(2) The consumer shall not be under a duty to restore—
   (i) perishable goods;
   (ii) goods which by their nature are consumed by use and which, before the cancellation, were so consumed;
   (iii) goods supplied to meet an emergency; or
   (iv) goods which, before the cancellation, had become incorporated in any land or thing not comprised in the cancelled contract,

but he shall be under a duty to pay in accordance with the cancelled contract for the supply of the goods and for the provision of any services in connection with the supply of the goods before the cancellation.

(3) The consumer shall not be under any duty to deliver the goods except at his own premises and in pursuance of a request in writing signed by the trader and served on the consumer either before, or at the time when, the goods are collected from those premises.

(4) If the consumer—
  (i) delivers the goods (whether at his own premises or elsewhere) to any person on whom, under regulation 4(5) above, a notice of cancellation could have been served; or
  (ii) sends the goods at his own expense to such a person,
he shall be discharged from any duty to retain possession of the goods or restore them to the trader.

(5) Where the consumer delivers the goods as mentioned in paragraph (4)(i) above, his obligation to take care of the goods shall cease; and if he send the goods as mentioned in paragraph (4)(ii) above, he shall be under a duty to take reasonable care to see that they are received by the trader and not damaged in transit, but in other respects his duty to take care of the goods shall cease.

(6) Where, at any time during the period of 21 days following the cancellation, the consumer receives such a request as is mentioned in paragraph (3) above and unreasonably refuses or unreasonably fails to comply with it, his duty to retain possession and take reasonable care of the goods shall continue until he delivers or sends the goods as mentioned in paragraph (4) above, but if within that period he does not receive such a request his duty to take reasonable care of the goods shall cease at the end of that period.

(7) Where any security has been provided in relation to the cancelled contract, the duty imposed on the consumer to restore goods by this regulation shall not be enforceable before the trader has discharged any duty imposed on him by regulation 5(3) above.

(8) Breach of a duty imposed by this regulation on a consumer is actionable as a breach of statutory duty.

Goods given in part-exchange

8.—(1) This regulation applies on the cancellation of a contract under regulation 4 above where the trader agreed to take goods in part-exchange (the 'part-exchange goods') and those goods have been delivered to him.

(2) Unless, before the end of the period of ten days beginning with the date of cancellation, the part-exchange goods are returned to the consumer in a condition substantially as good as when they were delivered to the trader, the consumer shall be entitled to recover from the trader a sum equal to the part-exchange allowance.

(3) During the period of ten days beginning with the date of cancellation, the consumer, if he is in possession of goods to which the cancelled contract relates, shall have a lien on them for—
  (a) delivery of the part-exchange goods in a condition substantially as good as when they were delivered to the trader; or
  (b) a sum equal to the part-exchange allowance;
and if the lien continues to the end of that period it shall thereafter subsist only as a lien for a sum equal to the part-exchange allowance.

(4) In this regulation the part-exchange allowance means the sum agreed as such in the cancelled contract, or if no such sum was agreed, such sum as it would have been reasonable to allow in respect of the part-exchange goods if no notice of cancellation had been served.

. . .

No contracting-out

10.—(1) A term contained in a contract to which these Regulations apply is void if, and to the extent that, it is inconsistent with a provision for the protection of the consumer contained in these Regulations.

(2) Where a provision of these Regulations specifies the duty or liability of the consumer in certain circumstances a term contained in a contract to which these Regulations apply is inconsistent with that provision if it purports to impose, directly or indirectly, an additional duty or liability on him in those circumstances.

Service of documents

11.—(1) A document to be served under these Regulations on a person may be so served—
   (a) by delivering it to him, or by sending it by post to him, or by leaving it with him, at his proper address addressed to him by name;
   (b) if the person is a body corporate, by serving it in accordance with paragraph (a) above on the secretary or clerk of that body; or
   (c) if the person is a partnership, by serving it in accordance with paragraph (a) above on a partner or on a person having the control or management of the partnership business.

(2) For the purposes of these Regulations, a document sent by post to, or left at, the address last known to the server of the document as the address of a person shall be treated as sent by post to, or left at, his proper address.

Regulation 4(1)

SCHEDULE

PART I

Information to be Contained in Notice of Cancellation Rights.

1. The name of the trader.

2. The trader's reference number, code or other details to enable the contract or offer to be identified.

3. A statement that the consumer has a right to cancel the contract if he wishes and that this right can be exercised by sending or taking a written notice of cancellation to the person mentioned in paragraph 4 within the period of 7 days following the making of the contract.

4. The name and address of a person to whom notice of cancellation may be given.

5. A statement that the consumer can use the cancellation form provided if he wishes.

PART II

Cancellation Form to be Included in Notice of Cancellation Rights

(Complete, detach and return this form ONLY IF YOU WISH TO CANCEL THE CONTRACT.)
To: [1]
I/We* hereby give notice that I/we* wish to cancel my/our* contract [2]
Signed
Date
*Delete as appropriate

NOTES

1. Trader to insert name and address of person to whom notice may be given.

2. Trader to insert reference number, code or other details to enable the contract or offer to be identified. He may also insert the name and address of the consumer.

For further EC initiatives in this area, see the Commission Recommendations of 7 April 1992 on distance selling (92/295/EEC) (OJ No L 156, 10.6.1992, p 21) and Directive 97/7/EC of the European Parliament and Council on the protection of consumers in respect of distance contracts (OJ No L 144, 4.6.1997, p 19). For helpful discussion of distance selling in the European context, see Howells in Lonbay (ed), *Enhancing The Legal Position of the European Consumer* (1996), Ch 8. For an important decision of the Court of Justice of the European Communities concerning Directive 86/877/EEC, see *Faccini Dori v Recreb Srl*, Case C–91/92 [1995] 1 All ER (EC) 1, above, p 14.

CHAPTER 4

Contracts for the supply of services

INTRODUCTION

Examples of consumer complaints involving the provision of services are noted in the Annual Reports of the Director General of Fair Trading and in such other sources as 'Consumer Dissatisfaction: A Report on Surveys Undertaken for the Office of Fair Trading' (February, 1986). Such contracts for the supply of services fall into two broad categories: (i) those including provision of goods or materials and (ii) those not including such provision. Frequently any given sector (for example home repairs and improvements or repairs and servicing to motor vehicles) will include both types of complaint. For instance, a plumber may contract for the supply of work and materials, as when he installs a central heating system, or he may provide a service simpliciter, as when he unblocks a drain. Other contracts will fall predominantly or exclusively into what may be termed the 'pure services' category, notably those for the provision of holidays or entertainment, cleaning or film processing or a service of a professional nature.

In the last chapter reference was made to Part I of the Supply of Goods and Services Act 1982 and its statutory implied terms as to the quality of materials supplied: see above, p 83. Part II of the 1982 Act also is important as introducing other implied terms into contracts for the supply of services. It originates in a National Consumer Council paper, 'Service Please' (1981) and was intended to be only an interim measure in as much as the Law Commission was asked to consider, in the light of Part II of the 1982 Act:

(a) what reforms, if any, should be made to the terms to be implied by law in a contract for the supply of a service; (b) whether, as against a consumer, the exclusion or restriction of the supplier's liability for breach of any such implied terms should be prohibited; (c) the consequences of breach by a supplier of any such terms.

The Commission published a Report 'Implied Terms in Contracts for the Supply of Services' (Law Com No 156, 1986) which contains much useful discussion, but did not recommend any changes in the law.

The relevant terms of Part II of the 1982 Act provide as follows:

Supply of Goods and Services Act 1982

PART II (SUPPLY OF SERVICES)

12. The contracts concerned

(1) In this Act a 'contract for the supply of a service' means, subject to subsection (2) below, a contract under which a person ('the supplier') agrees to carry out a service.

(2) For the purposes of this Act, a contract of service or apprenticeship is not a contract for the supply of a service.

(3) Subject to subsection (2) above, a contract is a contract for the supply of a service for the purposes of this Act whether or not the goods are also—

 (a) transferred or to be transferred, or

 (b) bailed or to be bailed by way of hire,

under the contract, and whatever is the nature of the consideration for which the service is to be carried out.

(4) The Secretary of State may by order provide that one or more of sections 13 to 15 below shall not apply to services of a description specified in the order, and such an order may make different provision for different circumstances.

(5) The power to make an order under subsection (4) above shall be exercisable by statutory instrument subject to annulment in pursuance of a resolution of either House of Parliament.

13. Implied terms about care and skill

In a contract for the supply of a service where the supplier is acting in the course of a business, there is an implied term that the supplier will carry out the service with reasonable care and skill.

14. Implied term about time for performance

(1) Where, under a contract for the supply of a service by a supplier acting in the course of a business, the time for the service to be carried out is not fixed by the contract, left to be fixed in a manner agreed by the contract or determined by the course of dealing between the parties, there is an implied term that the supplier will carry out the service within a reasonable time.

(2) What is a reasonable time is a question of fact.

15. Implied term about consideration

(1) Where, under a contract for the supply of a service, the consideration for the service is not determined by the contract, left to be determined in a manner agreed by the contract or determined by the course of dealing between the parties, there is an implied term that the party contracting with the supplier will pay a reasonable charge.

(2) What is a reasonable charge is a question of fact.

16. Exclusion of implied terms, etc

(1) Where a right, duty or liability would arise under a contract for the supply of a service by virtue of this Part of this Act, it may (subject to subsection (2) below and the 1977 Act) be negatived or varied by express agreement, or by the course of dealing between the parties, or by such usage as binds both parties to the contract.

(2) An express term does not negative a term implied by this Part of this Act unless inconsistent with it.

(3) Nothing in this Part of this Act prejudices—

 (a) any rule of law which imposes on the supplier a duty stricter than that imposed by section 13 or 14 above; or

 (b) subject to paragraph (a) above, any rule of law whereby any term not inconsistent with this Part of this Act is to be implied in a contract for the supply of a service.

(4) This Part of this Act has effect subject to any other enactment which defines or restricts the rights, duties or liabilities arising in connection with a service of any description.

Several orders have been made under s 12(4): see the Supply of Services (Exclusion of Implied Terms) Order 1982, SI 1982/1771; the Supply of Services (Exclusion of Implied Terms) Order 1983, SI 1983/902; and the Supply of Services (Exclusion of Implied Terms) Order 1995, SI 1995/1. To the extent specified they exclude such services as those provided by, eg, advocates, company and building society directors, and arbitrators.

The remainder of this chapter is divided into two parts. The first covers some points of general interest or application especially in relation to the 1982 Act. The second covers some particular sectors such as holidays and insurance which are of concern to consumers. Inevitably this second section is highly selective and many important sectors are not covered. For example, professional services are touched on only briefly and we have not sought to cover such areas as the services provided by the nationalised and formerly nationalised industries. Further discussion may be found in both general and specialist works: see for example Harvey and Parry, *The Law of Consumer Protection and Fair Trading* (5th edn, 1996, ch 7); Dugdale, Stanton and Parkinson, *Professional Negligence* (3rd edn, 1997); Palmer, *Bailment* (2nd edn, 1991); 'Home Improvements: A Report by the Director General of Fair Trading' (1983) and the subsequent survey 'Home Improvements' (1993); 'Estate Agency' (Office of Fair Trading, 1990); and 'Car Servicing and Repairs: A Report by the Director General of Fair Trading' (1985).

SOME GENERAL CONSIDERATIONS

As s 12(3) of the 1982 Act makes clear, a contract for the provision of a service is within the scope of the Act whether or not it is accompanied by the transfer of property in or possession of goods. The reverse is true also, so that by s 1(3) of the Act, above, p 83, 'a contract is a contract for the transfer of goods whether or not services are also provided'. So the service or 'work' element in a contract for work and materials is subject to the terms of sections 13–15, above. The same provisions may apply to contracts of hire which may have a servicing element also, notably in the case of television rentals and similar long-term arrangements. As in the case of Part I of the Act the various obligations apply only where the service is supplied by way of contract and 'in the course of a business': see above, pp 76–9 and 95–7. For comment and discussion see Murdoch, 'Contracts for the Supply of Services under the 1982 Act' (1983) Lloyd's Maritime and Commercial Law 652; Palmer (1983) 46 MLR 619, 627 et seq. See also the National Consumer Council report 'Service Please' (1981) on which Part II of the Act was based; Woodroffe, *Goods and Services—The New Law* (1982); Lawson, *The Supply of Goods and Services Act 1982* (1982).

FAULTY WORK

The following case serves to illustrate some of the distinctions which may result from treating obligations relating to work and materials as falling into separate categories.

Stewart v Reavell's Garage [1952] 1 All ER 1191, [1952] 2 QB 545, Queen's Bench Division

The plaintiff was a motorist with no technical knowledge who owned a 1929 Bentley speed model with powerful brakes. He took the car to the defendants, an experienced firm of car repairers, to have the brake-drums and brake-shoes re-lined. The re-lining of brake-drums was work of a specialist nature which the defendants did not undertake. The plaintiff preferred to have brake-drums made from an unwelded circle of metal and he suggested a particular firm. However, the price they quoted was too high. A quotation was obtained from another firm, Re-Lined Brake-Drums, whom the defendants recommended and who duly did the work as sub-contractors of the defendants. Unknown to the plaintiff, their method involved welding. The re-lined brake-drums were fitted and tested by the defendants. Soon after the plaintiff had taken delivery of the car he applied the brakes. There was a loud noise and vibration and the car swung to the right and hit a tree. The accident was caused by the lining on a front brake-drum coming away from the drum. It seems that such strip metal lining was unsatisfactory for brake-drums and moreover that the sub-contractors had not fitted it properly. There was no negligence on the defendants' part, whether in their choice of sub-contractors or in their fitting or testing of the drums.

Sellers J, having referred to the facts of the case, continued: The somewhat difficult question of the liability of the defendants depends on the terms, expressed or implied, of the contract, and must be determined on their true effect. This was not a contract for the sale of goods to which s 14 of the Sale of Goods Act, 1893, could be applied. It was a contract for work done and materials supplied. Into that type of contract there may also be implied an absolute warranty of fitness for the intended purpose, if the circumstances show that the particular purpose is made known to the repairer and that the work of repair is of the type which the repairer holds himself out to perform either by himself or others as his sub-contractors, and, no less important, if the circumstances show that the purpose was made known so as to show that the customer relied on the repairer's skill and judgment in the matter.

I would adapt to this kind of contract some words of Lord Wright which state the standard of proof in a case of the sale of goods in *Cammell Laird & Co Ltd v Manganese Bronze & Brass Co Ltd* ([1934] AC 423). The standard of proof is equally applicable to the present case. Such a reliance must be affirmatively shown. The customer must bring home to the mind of the repairer that he is relying on him in such a way that the repairer can be taken to have contracted on that footing. The reliance is to be the basis of a contractual obligation. There is a passage in the judgment of Du Parcq J, in *G H Myers & Co v Brent Cross Service Co*, which provides a concise statement of the law applicable ([1934] 1 KB 55):

' . . . I think that the true view is that a person contracting to do work and supply materials warrants that the materials which he uses will be of good quality and reasonably fit for the purpose for which he is using them, unless the circumstances of the contract are such as to exclude any such warranty. There may be circumstances which would clearly exclude it. A man goes to a repairer and says: "Repair my car; get the parts from the makers of the car and fit them". In such a case it is made plain that the person ordering the repairs is not relying upon any warranty except that the parts used will be parts ordered and obtained from the makers. On the other hand, if he says "Do this work, fit any necessary parts", then he is in no way limiting the person doing the repair work, and the person doing the repair work is, in my view, liable if there is any defect in the materials supplied, even if it was one which reasonable care could not have discovered.'

The present case does not fall precisely under either of the classes the learned judge enumerated. If the plaintiff's first suggestion had been accepted and those sub-contractors had done the work, I think it would have been very much the same as saying: 'Get the parts from the makers of the car' and the facts would have negatived any reliance by the plaintiff on the defendants' skill and judgment in respect of the lining to the brake-drums. The particular purpose of the work which the plaintiff contracted to have done was obvious. It was the very object of the arrangement, namely, to be provided with an efficient braking system for his Bentley car, which was a car specially designed for speed, and, therefore, required a braking system adequate for such speeds as were in contemplation. The size and type of the drums themselves indicated a powerful braking system. The question arises whether this purpose, made known, as it was, to the defendants, was made known to them so as to show that the plaintiff relied on their skill and judgment. I find that the effect of what was said and done when the parties entered into the contract was that the plaintiff did rely on the defendants as experienced repairers to repair the brakes in a suitable and efficient manner, and it was left to them to obtain suitable sub-contractors to do the lining of the drums and to arrange for a suitable type of drum lining to be fitted. The plaintiff's original request for a cast-iron sleeve—that is a sleeve without a weld— was not carried out. The defendants and not the plaintiff substituted for that a strip-metal sleeve with a weld and, although some mention of the Re-Lined Brake Drums, Ltd's quotation was made known to the plaintiff, more particularly as to price, he was not informed that this sleeve involved a weld. Once the defendants departed from the plaintiff's suggestion of a cast-iron sleeve, the type of lining was a matter within their province as repairers. It was their duty, in the circumstances, to provide good workmanship, materials of good quality, and a braking system reasonably fit for its purpose, and they failed to do so by reason of the faulty off-side front brake-drum lining. In fact, though unwittingly, the defendants handed over to the plaintiff a highly dangerous vehicle. The faulty lining caused the accident and the damage to the plaintiff's car, and the plaintiff is, therefore, entitled to recover damages in this action . . .

Judgment for plaintiff for £283 2s 4d damages, less an amount set off in respect of work done. Counterclaim dismissed.

NOTES

1. The relevant term as to reasonable fitness for purpose is now imposed by the Supply of Goods and Services Act 1982, s 4(5).
2. It seems that in *Stewart v Reavell's Garage* the source of the problem with the brake was two-fold: (i) the choice of an unsatisfactory material as a lining and (ii) the fact that the fitting was done incorrectly.

    For further discussion of other services see Harvey and Parry, op cit, at pp 173–6.

QUESTIONS

1. In such cases precisely what are the respective spheres of application of ss 4 (above, p 83) and 13 of the 1982 Act?
2. Will 'goods supplied under the contract' be 'reasonably fit for that purpose' within s 4(5) of the Act or of satisfactory quality within s 4(2) if they are sound and in no way defective but fitted incorrectly?
3. Suppose that Bodgit Plumbers have contracted with Greenpeace to service and maintain her central heating system and that the contract provides for an annual visit, with Greenpeace paying the cost of any replacement parts which may be needed. What is the source and nature of Bodgit's obligations under the 1982 Act when it causes damage to Greenpeace's property by (i) fitting a faulty replacement part correctly; (ii) fitting a non-faulty replacement part incorrectly; (iii) making an incorrect adjustment to an existing part?

DELAYS

Delays in carrying out servicing, repairs and building work (including double-glazing) are discussed in 'Simple Justice', pp 13–17 especially, from which it appears that problems are widespread and a major source of dissatisfaction. The National Consumer Council refers to two aspects of the problem at p 13 of the above paper:

Work started late or performed slowly can cause as many problems as work done badly. Complaints about the time element in a service fall into two categories. There are those cases where a date for the commencement or completion of the work has been agreed between both parties and subsequently ignored by the contractor. And there are others—more common in our experience—where no time limit is agreed but the consumer thinks the contractor has taken unreasonably long to perform the service.

Section 14 of the 1982 Act, above, p 152, restates the common law applicable to the latter situation. The following case provides an example of a delay which the Court of Appeal agreed was unreasonable in the circumstances. It also raises a further point of general interest and application.

Charnock v Liverpool Corpn [1968] 3 All ER 473, [1968] 1 WLR 1498, Court of Appeal

The plaintiff owned a car which was involved in a collision caused by negligence on the part of the driver of the other vehicle. He took it to the defendant repairers where he met his insurers' assessor and an estimate was agreed. A reasonable time for carrying out the repairs was at most five weeks. The repairers took eight weeks to complete the work, having given priority to warranty repairs on cars made by the Rootes Group. The plaintiff, who had not been warned of the delay, claimed as damages the cost of hiring a replacement car over this additional three-week period. The Presiding Judge of the Court of Passage at Liverpool awarded the plaintiff £53 damages and the defendant repairers now appealed to the Court of Appeal.

Salmon LJ. . . . I have no doubt at all, on the facts of the present case, that the judge's finding that there were in fact two contracts is unassailable. In my view there was a clear contract to be inferred from the facts between the repairers and the plaintiff car owner that in consideration of the plaintiff leaving his car with the repairers for repair the repairers would carry out the repairs with reasonable expedition and care, and that they would be paid by the insurance company. No doubt on the documents here the repairers took the precaution of entering into another contract with the insurers that the insurers would pay; and if they had not paid the insurers could have been sued; but this does not relieve the repairers from their obligations to the car owner. So much for the first point.

The second point is even shorter. The judge found that the repairers broke their contract with the plaintiff in that they failed to repair the car within a reasonable time. There was ample evidence before him that a reasonable time for carrying out these repairs should not have exceeded five weeks. Since the repairers in fact took eight weeks, they were in breach of their contract. Counsel for the repairers has argued vigorously that the finding that the work was not done within a reasonable time is not supportable; but I confess that I am quite unable to detect any real substance in the argument. The reason why the repairers were unable to do their work within a reasonable time, namely five weeks, was that when they took on the work their labour force was very much under strength. Moreover the holiday period was approaching; and, further, and perhaps most importantly, they had an arrangement (which no doubt was commercially of great value to them) with the Rootes Group that any warranty work should be given precedence. Warranty work, as the phrase was used in this case, related to cases in which cars which had been sold developed some fault in breach of the warranty given to the car owner: the car was then brought in and repaired so that it should comply with the warranty. As this arrangement with the Rootes Group was of great commercial value to these garage owners, they gave precedence to any warranty work and let any work such as the work for the present plaintiff wait. I cannot see for myself how the fact that they chose to take on the work knowing of the three factors to which I have referred can possibly entitle them to say 'Well, we could have done it within five weeks' (which is generally recognised in the trade as a reasonable time in which to perform the work) 'but for these three factors which prevented us from doing so'. . . . I agree that the appeal should be dismissed.

Winn and **Harman LJJ** agreed.

Appeal dismissed.

QUESTIONS

1. If an insurance company has contracted with a repairer to pay the full cost of repair, what consideration does the car owner furnish to support the repairer's contractual obligations to do the work in a reasonable time etc? Presumably the question does not arise if, as is usually the case, the car owner's insurance policy is subject to an excess which is paid to the repairer directly.

2. If a consumer has contracted with a specialist firm for the supply and installation of, for example, bedroom cupboards of a standard size, what would be a reasonable time for the completion of the work:
   (i) ten days, (ii) three weeks, (iii) two months or (iv) some longer period?

Is this a matter which is governed by the delay which is typical in the trade or by the expectations of a reasonable consumer? At what point should one feel confident in advising a consumer to cancel such a contract and engage another supplier? What are the risks of purporting to cancel before 'a reasonable time' has passed?

PROBLEMS OF COST

Some of the problems associated with the cost of services are discussed in the following extract:

Services and the Law: A Consumer View (National Consumer Council, 1981) (p 17 et seq)

When shoppers make a purchase they nearly always know the price in advance. If they are unhappy about the price being asked they do not buy the goods. The same is true of some types of service. Dry cleaners, shoe repairers, furniture removers and hairdressers usually indicate their prices for the job they are asked to do, enabling consumers to shop around until they find a price which suits them.

However, with some jobs the contractor may be reluctant to give a firm quotation because he has little idea until he starts work of what the job will entail. This is true of car and electrical repairs, for example. A consumer who has been given no idea of what the price will be is clearly in a very vulnerable position. And those who need work carried out in an emergency are especially at risk, as the Price Commission pointed out in its 1977 report on call-out charges. With reference to 24-hour emergency plumbers it stated: 'In the worst cases, particularly in an emergency where for example leaking water is harming furnishings and decorations, the total bill may be as high as an irresponsible plumber thinks he can get away with.' The Commission found examples of householders who had been charged £26 for a replacement tap washer and £120 for fitting twenty feet of copper pipe in four hours—and these, it should be remembered, were 1974–76 prices.

. . .

Even if the consumer suspects that the charge is exorbitant, it takes courage to refuse to pay for work already done. Once the job is completed he is likely to pay the bill either because he wants his goods back (as in the case of cars and small electrical repairs) or because he fears retaliatory action by the contractor, in the form of a county court summons or worse.

. . .

The OFT [the Office of Fair Trading] encourages members of trade associations to offer customers an estimate of the likely cost of work wherever possible so that they can shop around before choosing a contractor. But when an estimate is only a rough guide, the contractor who discovers that the job is more complicated that he originally thought can charge more. Some have been known to take advantage of this fact.

Mr W was given a verbal estimate of £200 by an emergency plumbing service to unblock a drain. When the work was completed five hours later the firm demanded £426.75. Mr W paid but alleged that the price was unreasonable, took the firm to court and won back £200. (*Which?* Personal Service)

. . .

Mr C, an ex-policeman, authorised a repair to his car which, he was told, would cost in the region of £300. On collecting the vehicle he was handed a bill for £678. He refused to pay and was sued by the garage. The court ordered him to pay £375 for the work. (*Which? Personal Service*)

. . .

So far we have considered cases where a charge for the work was not fixed in advance. But what of consumers who do agree a price with a contractor, only to discover later that this was extortionate? This might apply where it is impractical for consumers to collect comparison quotations in advance. Most domestic appliance repairers, for example, levy a call-out charge simply for giving an estimate. A consumer who has already paid £12 or more for a diagnosis is likely to accept the engineer's quotation, however high.

. . .

Garages handling breakdown and serious crash repairs are also in a strong position because they know customers may be unable to compare prices. The July 1980 issue of the AA magazine *Drive* contained evidence of extortionate prices charged by some garages for crash repairs. The magazine took a crashed Ford Fiesta to twenty garages and asked for estimates for repair. These ranged from £276 plus parts to £2,225 (the true cost was estimated by the Motor Insurance Research Centre at around £800). Even among members of the Vehicle Builders and Repairers Association—which has negotiated a code of practice with the OFT—there was up to 100 per cent difference in labour charges. 'The vehicle accident repair trade is full of inconsistencies, incompetence and irregularities,' the report concluded.

NOTES

1. Where a service is supplied under circumstances which fall within section 15 of the 1982 Act, above, p 152, the consumer is obliged to pay only a 'reasonable charge'.
2. It is generally agreed that a 'quotation' indicates a fixed price which cannot be exceeded even when unexpected difficulties are encountered whereas the use of the word 'estimate' allows for a margin.

QUESTIONS

1. What are the factors which may fairly be taken into account in deciding the extent, if any, to which an account may exceed an estimate?
2. Is it possible to say that there is a maximum percentage increase (if only in theory) which should never be exceeded or does it depend also on the sums of money involved? Other things being equal, which is likely to be the more acceptable in a consumer contract (i) a bill for £4.00 compared with an estimate of £2.50 or (ii) a bill for £1,500 compared with an estimate of £1,000? Is a consumer entitled to insist on paying a sum which is *less* than the estimate if the work proves to be easier or quicker than expected?
3. Protection against extortionate credit bargains is now provided by the Consumer Credit Act 1974, ss 137–40, below, pp 306–13. Is there any reason of principle or insuperable practical difficulty to prevent a similar measure of protection being extended to persons who pay extortionate cash prices? Is it

not likely that some of the most vulnerable members of society, notably the elderly, will save money and pay cash rather than buy on credit? See generally p 37 et seq for discussion of protection against unjust or unfair contract terms.

4. Consider the following case.

Vulnerable lives in a cottage which is in need of some modernisation. She returns home one evening to find that an unlagged pipe has burst, causing water to pour down from the attic. She contacts Shark, a plumber, who comes over immediately, turns off the water at the mains and fixes the burst joint. There has been no discussion of the price for the work which takes about half an hour including travelling time. He has now presented a bill for £200.

The burst pipe necessitates extensive redecoration of the main rooms of the cottage and Vulnerable accepts a quotation of £2,500 from Renoir, a decorator. Renoir has now explained that he has miscalculated the cost of the materials involved. He has presented a bill for £3,200.

Vulnerable's septic tank is in need of renewal. She obtains an estimate of £3,200 from Drainaway for fitting a new tank and associated piping. Of this £1,700 is the cost of the tank itself. When he begins the work Drainaway discovers that Vulnerable's garden is built on rock. Instead of the work taking him two days as he had calculated it takes him four. Moreover he has to hire specialist excavating machinery at an additional cost of £200. He wishes to know what price he may legitimately charge.

Advise Vulnerable and Drainaway.

STRICTER CONTRACTUAL OBLIGATIONS

As s 16(3)(a) of the 1982 Act makes clear the implied obligations of s 13 of the Act operate without prejudice to any stricter obligations which have been undertaken. The following commercial case provides a good example of a situation in which such an obligation was held to have arisen.

Greaves & Co (Contractors) Ltd v Baynham Meikle & Partners [1975] 3 All ER 99, [1975] 1 WLR 1095, Court of Appeal

Lord Denning, MR. This case arises out of a new kind of building contract called a 'package deal'. The building owners were Alexander Duckham & Co Ltd. They wanted a new factory, warehouse and offices to be constructed at Aldridge in Staffordshire. The warehouse was needed as a store in which barrels of oil could be kept until they were needed and despatched, and in which they could be moved safely from one point to another. The 'package deal' meant that the building owners did not employ their own architects or engineers. They employed one firm of contractors, the plaintiffs, to do everything for them. It was the task of the contractors not only to provide the labour and materials in the usual way but also to employ the architects and engineers as sub-contractors. The contractors were to do everything as a 'package deal' for the owners.

Now, as between the owners and the contractors, it is plain that the owners made known to the contractors the purpose for which the building was required, so as to show that they relied on the contractors' skill and judgment. It was therefore the duty of the contractors to see that the finished work was reasonably fit for the purpose for which they knew it was required. It was not merely an obligation to use reasonable care. The contractors were obliged to ensure that the finished work was reasonably fit for the purpose. That appears from the recent cases in which a man employs a contractor to build a house: *Miller v Cannon Hill Estates Ltd*;[1] *Hancock v B W. Brazier (Anerley) Ltd*.[2] It is a term implied by law that the builder will do his work in a good and workmanlike manner; that he will supply good and proper materials; and it will be reasonably fit for human habitation. Similarly in this case the contractors undertook an obligation towards the owners that the warehouse should be reasonably fit for the purpose for which, they knew it was required, that is as a store in which to keep and move barrels of oil. In order to get the warehouse built, the contractors found they needed expert skilled assistance, particularly in regard to the structural steel work. The warehouse was to be built according to a new system which was just coming into use. It was a composite construction system in structural steel and concrete. First there would be a steel frame erected to carry the walls and floors. Next they would get planks made of pre-cast concrete and bring them on to the site. They would place these planks in position along the floors, etc. Then, in order to bind those planks firmly together, they would pour ready-mixed concrete in and above the planks, thus forming a solid floor. This method of construction had recently been introduced into use in England. It is governed by the British Standard Code of Practice 1965, CP 117.

The contractors employed a firm of experts, the defendants, Messrs Baynham Meikle and Partners, structural engineers, to design the structure of the building and, in particular, the first floor of it. There were discussions with them about it. It was made known to them—and this is important—that the floors had to take the weight of stacker trucks—sometimes called fork-lift trucks. These were to run to and fro over the floors carrying the drums of oil. The structural engineers, Baynham Meikle, were given the task of designing the floors for that purpose.

Mr Baynham made his designs: the warehouse was built and put into use. It was used for the transport of these oil drums with the stacker trucks. But, after a little time, there was a lot of trouble. The floors began to crack. The men took strong objection to working there. They thought it was dangerous. The cracks seemed to be getting worse. So much so that the experts were called in. Attempts were made to cure the trouble, but without success. The position now is that the warehouse is of very limited use. It is anticipated that remedial works will have to take place at great expense. The damages are said to come to £100,000.

What was the cause of this cracking of the floors? The structural engineers said that it was due to the shrinkage of the concrete for which they were not responsible. There was nothing wrong, they said, with the design which they produced. But the judge did not accept that view. He found[3] that the majority of the cracks were caused by vibration and not by shrinkage. He held[4] that the floors were not designed with sufficient strength to withstand the vibration which was produced by the stacker trucks.

On those findings the first question is: what was the duty of the structural engineers towards the contractors? The judge found[4] that there was an implied term that the design should be fit for the use of loaded stacker trucks; and that it was broken. Alternatively, that the structural engineers owed a duty of care in their design, which was a higher duty than the law in general imposes on a professional man; and that there was a breach of that duty.

To resolve this question, it is necessary to distinguish between a term which is implied by law and a term which is implied in fact. A term implied by law is said to rest on the *presumed* intention of both parties; whereas, a term implied in fact rests on their *actual* intention.

It has often been stated that the law will only imply a term when it is reasonable and necessary to do so in order to give business efficacy to the transaction; and, indeed, so obvious that both parties must have intended it. But those statements must be taken with considerable qualification. In the great majority of cases it is no use looking for the intention of both parties. If you asked the parties what they intended, they would say that they never gave it a thought; or, if they did, the one would say that he intended something different from the other. So the courts imply—or, as I would say, impose—a term such as is just and reasonable in the circumstances. Take some of the most familiar of implied terms in the authorities cited to us. Such as the implied condition of fitness on a sale of goods at first implied by the common law and afterwards embodied in the Sale of Goods Act 1893. Or the implied warranty of fitness on a contract for work and materials: *Young & Marten Ltd v McManus Childs Ltd.*[5] Or the implied warranty that a house should be reasonably fit for human habitation: see *Hancock v B W Brazier.*[2] And dozens of other implied terms. If you should read the discussions in the cases, you will find that the judges are not looking for the intention of both parties; nor are they considering what the parties would answer to an officious bystander. They are only seeking to do what is 'in all the circumstances reasonable'. That is how Lord Reid put it in *Young & Marten Ltd v McManus Childs Ltd*;[6] and Lord Upjohn[7] said quite clearly that the implied warranty is 'imposed by law'.

Apply this to the employment of a professional man. The law does not usually imply a warranty that he will achieve the desired result, but only a term that he will use reasonable care and skill. The surgeon does not warrant that he will cure the patient. Nor does the solicitor warrant that he will win the case. But, when a dentist agrees to make a set of false teeth for a patient, there is an implied warranty that they will fit his gums: see *Samuels v Davis.*[8]

What then is the position when an architect or an engineer is employed to design a house or a bridge? Is he under an implied warranty that, if the work is carried out to his design, it will be reasonably fit for the purpose? Or is he only under a duty to use reasonable care and skill? This question may require to be answered some day as a matter of law. But in the present case I do not think we need answer it. For the evidence shows that both parties were of one mind on the matter. Their common intention was that the engineer should design a warehouse which would be fit for the purpose for which it was required. That common intention gives rise to a term implied *in fact . . .*

In the light of that evidence it seems to me that there was implied in fact a term that, if the work was completed in accordance with the design, it would be reasonably fit for the use of loaded stacker trucks. The engineers failed to make such a design and are, therefore, liable.

If there was, however, no such absolute warranty of fitness, but only an obligation to use reasonable care and skill, the question arises: what is the degree of care required? The judge said:[4]

'In the special circumstances of this case, by his knowledge of the requirement and the warning about vibration, it can be said that there was a higher duty imposed on him than the law in general imposes on a medical or other professional man.'

I do not think that was quite accurate. It seems to me that in the ordinary employment of a professional man, whether it is a medical man, a lawyer, or an accountant, an architect or an engineer, his duty is to use reasonable care and skill in the course of his employment. The extent of this duty was described by McNair J in *Bolam v Friern Hospital Management Committee*,[9] approved by the Privy Council in *Chin Keow v Government of Malaysia*:[10]

' . . . where you get a situation which involves the use of some special skill or competence, then the test whether there has been negligence or not is not the test of the man on the top of a Clapham omnibus, because he has not got this special skill. The test is the standard of the ordinary skilled man exercising and professing to have that special skill . . . It is well-established law that it is sufficient if he exercises the ordinary skill of an ordinary competent man exercising that particular art.'

In applying that test, it must be remembered that the measures to be taken by a professional man depend on the circumstances of the case. Although the judge talked about a 'higher duty',[4] I feel sure that what he meant was that in the circumstances of this case special steps were necessary in order to fulfil the duty of care: see *Readhead v Midland Rly Co.*[11] In this case a new mode of construction was to be employed. The Council of British Standards Institution had issued a circular which contained this note:

'The designer should satisfy himself that no undesirable vibrations can be caused by the imposed loading. Serious vibrations may result when dynamic forces are applied at a frequency near to one of the natural frequencies of the members.'

Mr Baynham was aware of that note but he read it as a warning against resonances, ie rhythmic impulses, and not as a warning against vibrations in general. So he did not take measures to deal with the random impulses of stacker trucks. There was evidence, too, that other competent designers might have done the same as Mr Baynham. On that ground the judge seems to have thought that Mr Baynham had not failed in the ordinary duty of care. But that does not excuse him. Other designers might have fallen short too. It is for the judge to set the standard of what a competent designer would do. And the judge, in the next breath, used words which seem to me to be a finding that Mr Baynham did fail. It is a key passage;[3]

'I do, however, find that he knew, or ought to have known, that the purpose of the floor was safely to carry heavily laden trucks and that he was warned about the dangers of vibration and did not take these matters sufficiently into account. The design was inadequate for the purpose.'

It seems to me that that means that Mr Baynham did not take the matters sufficiently into account which he ought to have done. That amounts to a finding of breach of the duty to use reasonable care and skill. On each of the grounds, therefore, I think the contractors are entitled to succeed. They are entitled to a declaration of liability and indemnity. I would, accordingly, dismiss the appeal.

Browne and **Geoffrey Lane LJJ** agreed.

Appeal dismissed.

[1] [1931] 2 KB 113, [1931] All ER Rep 93.
[2] [1966] 2 All ER 901, [1966] 1 WLR 1317.
[3] [1974] 3 All ER 666 at 672, [1974] 1 WLR 1261 at 1268.
[4] [1974] 3 All ER at 672, [1974] 1 WLR at 1269.
[5] [1968] 2 All ER 1169, [1969] 1 AC 454.
[6] [1968] 2 All ER at 1171, 1172, [1969] 1 AC at 465, 466.
[7] [1968] 2 All ER at 1175, [1969] 1 AC at 471.
[8] [1943] 2 All ER 3, [1943] 1 KB 526.
[9] [1957] 2 All ER 118 at 121, [1957] 1 WLR 582 at 586.
[10] [1967] 1 WLR 813.
[11] (1869) LR 4 QB 379 at 393, [1861–73] All ER Rep 30 at 39.

NOTES

1. For a further case involving an obligation stricter than the exercising of reasonable care see *G K Serigraphics (a firm) v Dispro Ltd* (1980) CA (available on Lexis) cited by Palmer (1983) 46 MLR 619.
2. The Australian Trade Practices Act 1974, s 74, contains the following provision which is of general application:

Warranties in relation to the supply of services

74 (1) In every contract for the supply by a corporation in the course of a business of ser-

vices to a consumer there is an implied warranty that the services will be rendered with due care and skill and that any materials supplied in connexion with those services will be reasonably fit for the purpose for which they are supplied.

(2) Where a corporation supplies services (other than services of a professional nature provided by a qualified architect or engineer) to a consumer in the course of a business and the consumer, expressly or by implication, makes known to the corporation any particular purpose for which the services are required or the result that he or she desires the services to achieve, there is an implied warranty that the services supplied under the contract for the supply of the services and any materials supplied in connexion with those services will be reasonably fit for that purpose or are of such a nature and quality that they might reasonably be expected to achieve that result, except where the circumstances show that the consumer does not rely, or that it is unreasonable for him or her to rely, on the corporation's skill or judgment.

(3) A reference in this section to services does not include a reference to services that are, or are to be, provided, granted or conferred under:

(a) a contract for or in relation to the transportation or storage of goods for the purposes of a business, trade, profession or occupation carried on or engaged in by the person for whom the goods are transported or stored; or

(b) a contract of insurance.

3. The EEC Commission suggested a somewhat different approach in its 'Proposal for a Council Directive on the Liability of Suppliers of Services' (Com (90) 482 final) submitted on 9 November 1990. The basic principle would have been as follows:

Article 1
Principle
1. The supplier of a service shall be liable for damage to the health and physical integrity of persons or the physical integrity of movable or immovable property, including the persons or property which were the objects of the service, caused by a fault committed by him in the performance of the service.
2. The burden of proving the absence of fault shall fall upon the supplier of the service.
3. In assessing the fault, account shall be taken of the behaviour of the supplier of the service who, in normal and reasonably foreseeable conditions, shall ensure the safety which may reasonably be expected.
4. Whereas the mere fact that a better service existed or might have existed at the moment of performance or subsequently shall not constitute a fault.

. . .

This proposal with its reverse-onus approach was not adopted.

4. For the potential criminal liability which may be incurred in respect of false statements concerning services (although not a simple failure to keep a contractual promise) see the Trade Descriptions Act 1968, s 14, below, p 642 et seq.

SOME PARTICULAR EXAMPLES

HOLIDAYS

Contracts for the provision of holidays are a good example of an area in which consumers may suffer extreme inconvenience and disappointment through failure to provide an agreed service. Here some protection is afforded through the Association of British Travel Agents' (ABTA) codes of practice. See generally as to codes ch 10 below. The following case establishes a point of general significance.

Jarvis v Swans Tours Ltd [1973] 1 All ER 71, [1973] QB 233, Court of Appeal

Lord Denning MR. The plaintiff, Mr Jarvis, is a solicitor employed by a local authority at Barking. In 1969 he was minded to go for Christmas to Switzerland. He was looking forward to a skiing holiday. It is his one fortnight's holiday in the year. He prefers it in the winter rather than in the summer.

Mr Jarvis read a brochure issued by Swans Tours Ltd. He was much attracted by the description of Mörlialp, Giswil, Central Switzerland. I will not read the whole of it, but just pick out some of the principal attractions:

'HOUSE PARTY CENTRE with special resident host . . . Mörlialp is a most wonderful little resort on a sunny plateau . . . Up there you will find yourself in the midst of beautiful alpine scenery, which in winter becomes a wonderland of sun, snow and ice, with a wide variety of fine ski-runs, a skating-rink and an exhilarating toboggan run . . . Why did we choose the Hotel Krone . . . mainly and most of all, because of the "Gemutlichkeit" and friendly welcome you will receive from Herr and Frau Weibel . . . The Hotel Krone has its own Alphütte Bar which will be open several evenings a week . . . No doubt you will be in for a great time, when you book this houseparty holiday . . . Mr. Weibel, the charming owner, speaks English.'

On the same page, in a special yellow box, it was said:

'SWANS HOUSEPARTY IN MORLIALP. *All these Houseparty arrangements are included in the price of your holiday.* Welcome party on arrival. Afternoon tea and cake for 7 days. Swiss Dinner by candlelight. Fondue-party. Yodler evening. Chali farewell party in the "Alphutte Bar". Service of representative.'

Alongside on the same page there was a special note about ski-packs: 'Hire of Skis, Sticks and Boots . . . 12 days £11.10.'

In August 1969, on the faith of that brochure, Mr Jarvis booked a 15 day holiday, with ski-pack. The total charge was £63.45, including Christmas supplement. He was to fly from Gatwick to Zurich on 20 December 1969 and return on 3 January 1970.

The plaintiff went on the holiday, but he was very disappointed. He was a man of about 35 and he expected to be one of a houseparty of some 30 or so people. Instead, he found there were only 13 during the first week. In the second week there was no houseparty at all. He was the only person there. Mr Weibel could not speak English. So there was Mr Jarvis, in the second week, in this hotel with no houseparty at all, and no one could speak English, except himself. He was very disappointed, too, with the skiing. It was some distance away at Giswil. There were no ordinary length skis. There were only mini-skis, about 3 ft long. So he did not get his skiing as he wanted to. In the second week he did get some longer skis for a couple of days but then, because of the boots, his feet got rubbed and he could not continue even with the long skis. So his skiing holiday, from his point of view, was pretty well ruined.

There were many other matters, too. They appear trivial when they are set down in writing, but I have no doubt they loomed large in Mr Jarvis's mind, when coupled with the other disappointments . . .

What is the legal position? I think that the statements in the brochure were representations or warranties. The breaches of them give Mr Jarvis a right to damages. It is not necessary to decide whether they were representations or warranties; because, since the Misrepresentation Act 1967, there is a remedy in damages for misrepresentation as well as for breach of warranty.

The one question in the case is: what is the amount of damages? The judge seems to have taken the difference in value between what he paid for and what he got. He said that he intended to give 'the difference between the two values and no other damages' under any other head. He thought that Mr Jarvis had got half of what he paid for. So the judge gave him half the amount which he had paid, namely, £31.72. Mr Jarvis appeals to this court. He says that the damages ought to have been much more . . .

What is the right way of assessing damages? It has often been said that on a breach of contract damages cannot be given for mental distress. Thus in *Hamlin v Great Northern Rly Co*[2] Pollock CB said that damages cannot be given 'for the disappointment of mind occasioned by the breach of contract'. And in *Hobbs v London South Western Rly Co*[3] Mellor J said that—

'. . . for the mere inconvenience, such as annoyance and loss of temper, or vexation, or for being disappointed in a particular thing which you have set your mind upon, without real physical inconvenience resulting, you cannot recover damages.'

The courts in those days only allowed the plaintiff to recover damages if he suffered physical inconvenience, such as, having to walk five miles home, as in *Hobb's case*;[4] or to live in an overcrowded house: see *Bailey v Bullock*.[5]

I think that those limitations are out of date. In a proper case damages for mental distress can be recovered in contract, just as damages for shock can be recovered in tort. One such case is a contract for a holiday, or any other contract to provide entertainment and enjoyment. If the contracting party breaks his contract, damages can be given for the disappointment, the distress, the upset and frustration caused by the breach. I know that it is difficult to assess in terms of money, but it is no more difficult than the assessment which the courts have to make every day in personal injury cases for loss of amenities. Take the present case. Mr Jarvis has only a fortnight's holiday in the year. He books it far ahead, and looks forward to it all that time. He ought to be compensated for the loss of it.

A good illustration was given by Edmund Davies LJ in the course of the argument. He put the case of a man who has taken a ticket for Glyndebourne. It is the only night on which he can get there. He hires a car to take him. The car does not turn up. His damages are not limited to the mere cost of the ticket. He is entitled to general damages for the disappointment he has suffered and the loss of the entertainment which he should have had. Here, Mr Jarvis's fortnight's winter holiday has been a grave disappointment. It is true that he was conveyed to Switzerland and back and had meals and bed in the hotel. But that is not what he went for. He went to enjoy himself with all the facilities which the defendants said he would have. He is entitled to damages for the lack of those facilities, and for his loss of enjoyment.

A similar case occurred in 1951. It was *Stedman v Swan's Tours*.[6] A holiday-maker was awarded damages because he did not get the bedroom and the accommodation which he was promised. The county court judge awarded him £13 15s. This court increased it to £50.

I think the judge was in error in taking the sum paid for the holiday, £63.45, and halving it. The right measure of damages is to compensate him for the loss of entertainment and enjoyment which he was promised, and which he did not get. Looking at the matter quite broadly,

I think the damages in this case should be the sum of £125. I would allow the appeal accordingly.

Edmund Davies LJ. . . . When a man has paid for and properly expects an invigorating and amusing holiday and, through no fault of his, returns home dejected because his expectations have been largely unfulfilled, in my judgment it would be quite wrong to say that his disappointment must find no reflection in the damages to be awarded. . . . Instead of 'a great time', the plaintiff's reasonable and proper hopes were largely and lamentably unfulfilled. To arrive at a proper compensation for the defendants' failure is no easy matter. But in my judgment we should not be compensating the plaintiff excessively were we to award him the £125 damages proposed by Lord Denning MR. I therefore concur in allowing this appeal.

Stephenson LJ agreed.

Appeal allowed; damages of £125 awarded.

2 (1856) 1 H & N 408 at 411.
3 (1875) LR 10 QB 111 at 122, [1874–80] All ER Rep 458 at 463.
4 (1875) LR 10 QB 111, [1874–80] All ER Rep 458.
5 [1950] 2 All ER 1167.
6 (1951) 95 Sol Jo 727.

NOTES

1. For further cases involving the award of damages to disappointed holiday-makers see, for example, *Jackson v Horizon Holidays Ltd* [1975] 3 All ER 92, [1975] 1 WLR 1468, CA, above, p 42, *Adcock v Blue Sky Holidays Ltd* (CA, 13 May 1980, unreported but available on Lexis) and *Williams v Travel Promotions Ltd (trading as Voyages Jules Verne)*, The Times, 9 March 1998. See also *Which?*, March 1997; *Holiday Which?*, Summer 1997, Autumn 1997. In the *Adcock* case where the Court of Appeal increased the damages awarded to £500, a figure which was broadly equivalent to the cost of the holiday, Cumming-Bruce LJ is reported as having described the position as follows:

   Contracts for holidays vary on their facts very greatly. The facilities offered by the tour company vary enormously from case to case. It would be a grave mistake to look at the facts in, for example, the *Jackson* case or the *Jarvis* case and compare those facts with the facts in another case as a means of establishing the measure of damages. In the present case, which was a contract for the provision of facilities for a ski-ing holiday in the first week of January . . . the representation that the accommodation would be warm and friendly and that the bedrooms would have the amenities of central heating, hot baths or showers and hot water, were of the greatest importance . . . On the facts found by the Judge, those facilities were so markedly absent that the holiday provided was such that the enjoyment of all the members of the party was very substantially reduced; and they are entitled to compensation not only for their physical sufferings, but also for the distress that they experienced instead of obtaining enjoyment for their expenditure.

2. For examples of holiday cases involving a potential liability under the Trade Descriptions Act 1968, s 14, see *R v Sunair Holidays Ltd* [1973] 2 All ER 1233, [1973] 1 WLR 1105, CA below, p 646, and *Wings Ltd v Ellis* [1984] 3 All ER 577, [1984] 3 WLR 965, below, p 662.

An interesting example of the application of s 13 of the Supply of Goods and Services Act 1982 is contained in the following case.

Wilson v Best Travel Ltd [1993] 1 All ER 353, Queen's Bench Division

Mrs Cheryl Bromley had made a booking with the defendants on behalf of a party of five for a holiday at the Vanninarchis Beach Hotel on the Greek island of Kos. The party included the plaintiff, who was the fiancé of her elder daughter. Regrettably, the holiday got off to a very bad start when he tripped and fell through a glass patio door which shattered, causing multiple injuries. The door complied with relevant Greek regulations, including those of the Greek tourist organisation, EOT. However, it was at least arguable that, if the plaintiff's accident had occurred in England, the hotelier would be held to be in breach of the common duty of care imposed by s 2(2) of the Occupiers Liability Act 1957. The question was whether the defendants were to be judged against higher English safety standards.

Phillips J, having set out the facts of the case and cited s 13 of the 1982 Act, continued:

The nature of the services provided by a travel agent when arranging a holiday can vary enormously, depending on the nature of the holiday. I am satisfied, having read their brochure, that the service provided by the defendants included the inspection of the properties offered in their brochure.

. . .

In my judgment, one of the characteristics of accommodation that the defendants owed a duty to consider when inspecting properties included in their brochure was safety. The defendants owe their customers, including the plaintiff, a duty to exercise reasonable care to exclude from the accommodation offered any hotel whose characteristics were such that guests could not spend a holiday there in reasonable safety. I believe that this case is about the standard to be applied in assessing reasonable safety. It is necessary at this stage to turn to the evidence in relation to the glass fitted in the doors of the Vanninarchis Beach Hotel.

. . .

What is the duty of a tour operator in a situation such as this? Must he refrain from sending holidaymakers to any hotel whose characteristics, in so far as safety is concerned, fail to satisfy the standards which apply in this country? I do not believe that his obligations in respect of the safety of his clients can extend this far. Save where uniform international regulations apply, there are bound to be differences in the safety standards applied in respect of the many hazards of modern life between one country and another. All civilised countries attempt to cater for these hazards by imposing mandatory regulations. The duty of care of a tour operator is likely to extend to checking that local safety regulations are complied with. Provided that they are, I do not consider that the tour operator owes a duty to boycott a hotel because of the absence of some safety feature which would be found in an English hotel unless the absence of such a feature might lead a reasonable holidaymaker to decline to take a holiday at the hotel in question. On the facts of this case I do not consider that the degree of danger posed by the absence of safety glass in the doors of the Vanninarchis Beach Hotel called for any action on the part of the defendants pursuant to their duty to exercise reasonable care to ensure the safety of their clients.

It is perhaps significant that Mr Norris [counsel for the plaintiff] did not expand on what action the defendants should have taken. It was not suggested that they had a duty to warn clients of this characteristic or that such a warning would have prevented the accident in this case. What was, I think, implicit in the plaintiff's case was that the defendants should not have permitted the Vanninarchis Beach Hotel to feature in their brochure. If that contention were valid, it would, on the evidence of Mr Vanninarchis, apply to many, if not the majority, of the other hotels, pensions and villas featured in the defendants' brochure and no doubt the brochures of the other tour operators who send their clients to Greece. . . .

Judgment for the defendants.

QUESTION

Since the contract was concluded by Mrs Bromley, rather than the plaintiff, on what basis did the plaintiff have a contractual claim? (see above, pp 42–5.)

It is a feature of many holidays, and in particular holidays which are taken abroad, that services are performed by persons who are not directly employed by the tour organiser. These may range from hoteliers to coach operators and local guides. The following case is of interest as indicating some of the factors affecting the tour organiser's liability.

Wong Mee Wan v Kwan Kin Travel Services Ltd [1995] 4 All ER 745, Privy Council

The first defendant was a Hong Kong travel company from whom the plaintiff's daughter, a resident of Hong Kong, had bought a package tour of part of mainland China. The tour was for an 'all-in' price and on terms specified in the tour brochure which was headed 'Kwan Kin Travel Tours—everything more comprehensively and thoughtfully worked out'. At the border with China the group was joined by Mr Ho, a tour guide employed by the second defendant, a travel company carrying on business in China. The group progressed to Pak Tang Lake, which was the focal point of the tour, but arrived too late to catch the ferry. There was then no practical alternative to taking a speedboat across the lake and this involved three separate trips to carry the entire group of 24 persons. On the third trip the speedboat, which was driven by an employee of the third defendant, went excessively fast, hitting a fishing junk. The plaintiff's daughter was thrown into the water and drowned. In subsequent proceedings the Court of Appeal of Hong Kong held that Mr Ho and the driver of the speedboat had both been negligent but that the first defendant, the tour company, was not in breach of any duty of care owed to the deceased and hence not liable to her. The plaintiff appealed to the Privy Council.

Lord Slynn, having set out the facts of the case, continued:
The issue is . . . whether in this particular contract the first defendant undertook no more than that it would arrange for services to be provided by others as its agents (where the law would imply a term into the contract that it would use reasonable care and skill in selecting those other persons) or whether it itself undertook to supply the services when, subject to any exemption clause, there would be implied into the contract a term that it would as supplier

carry out the services with reasonable care and skill (see *Curtis v Chemical Cleaning and Dyeing Co Ltd* [1951] 1 All ER 631, [1951] 1 KB 805).

There are of course many contracts under which a person agrees to supply services when he may arrange for his obligations to be performed by others, and where it is indeed contemplated that he will do so. . . .

The fact that the supplier of services may under the contract arrange for some or all of them to be performed by others does not absolve the supplier from his contractual obligation. He may be liable if the service is performed without the exercise of due care and skill on the part of the sub-contractor just as he would be liable if the sub-contractor failed to provide the service or failed to provide it in accordance with the terms of the contract. The obligation undertaken is thus, if the person undertaking to supply the services performs them himself, that he will do so with reasonable skill and care, and that if, where the contract permits him to do so, he arranges for others to supply the services, that they will be supplied with reasonable skill and care (see *Chitty on Contracts* (27th edn, 1994) pp 987–8, paras 19–046 and 19–047).

The distinction between the two categories of case—where the party agrees merely as agent to arrange for services to be provided and where he undertakes to supply the services—is drawn in *Craven v Strand Holidays (Canada) Ltd* (1982) 40 OR (2d) 186, 142 DLR (3d) 31.
. . .

The heading of the brochure 'Kwan Kin Travel Tours—everything more comprehensively and thoughtfully worked out' gives some indication that it is the first defendant who has undertaken the task of supplying the package tours. Throughout the detailed itinerary it is always 'we' who will do things—board the bus, go for lunch, live in the hotel. Their Lordships do not think that 'we' is to be read simply as referring to the customers—ie in an attempt to lay the foundation for a friendly atmosphere on the tours. 'We' includes the company offering the tour and integrates the company into each stage of the tour. . . .

Taking the contract as a whole their Lordships consider that the first defendant here undertook to provide and not merely to arrange all the services included in the programme, even if some activities were to be carried out by others. The first defendant's obligation under the contract that the services would be provided with reasonable skill and care remains even if some of the services were to be rendered by others, and even if tortious liability may exist on the part of those others. It has not been suggested that Miss Ho Shui Yee was in contractual relations with the others.

In their Lordships' view it was an implied term of the contract that those services would be carried out with reasonable skill and care. That term does not mean, to use the words of Hodgson J in *Wall v Silver Wing Surface Arrangements Ltd*, that the first defendant undertook an obligation to ensure 'the safety of all the components of the package'. The plaintiff's claim does not amount to an implied term that her daughter would be reasonably safe. It is a term simply that reasonable skill and care would be used in rendering the services to be provided under the contract. The trip across the lake was clearly not carried out with reasonable skill and care in that no steps were taken to see that the driver of the speedboat was of reasonable competence and experience and the first defendant is liable for such breach of contract as found by the trial judge.

Their Lordships of course appreciate the desire of the Court of Appeal to avoid imposing a burden which is 'intolerable' on package tour operators. It must, however, be borne in mind that the tour operator has the opportunity to seek to protect himself against claims made against him in respect of services performed by others by negotiating suitable contractual terms with those who are to perform those services. He may also provide for insurance cover. He may include an appropriate exemption clause in his contract with the traveller. It also has to be borne in mind, in considering what is 'tolerable' or reasonable between the parties, that a traveller in the position of Miss Ho Shui Yee could have no influence on the terms negotiated by the tour operator with third parties, and if injured by their lack of care would, if having no right against the package tour operator, be obliged to pursue a claim in a foreign country. The difficulty involved in doing so does not need to be elaborated. . . .

Accordingly their Lordships will humbly advise her Majesty that the appeal should be allowed . . .

Appeal allowed.

NOTES

1. For an unreported case reaching the opposite conclusion on its own particular facts, see *Wall v Silver Wing Surface Arrangements Ltd* (Hodgson J, 18 November 1981, above, p 170) (plaintiff injured on having to jump from hotel bedroom window when usual means of escape locked). See also Nelson Jones and Stewart, 'Tour Operators—For Services Rendered' (1983) Law Society Gazette 2047.

2. Within Europe the overall position has been affected by Council Directive 90/314/EEC on Package Travel, Package Holidays and Package Tours (OJ No L158, 30.6.1990, p 59). This has now been implemented in English Law by the following provisions.

The Package Travel, Package Holidays and Package Tours Regulations 1992 SI 1992/3288

Citation and commencement

1. These Regulations may be cited as the Package Travel, Package Holidays and Package Tours Regulations 1992 and shall come into force on the day after the day on which they are made.

Interpretation

2.—(1) In these Regulations—
'brochure' means any brochure in which packages are offered for sale;
'contract' means the agreement linking the consumer to the organiser or to the retailer, or to both, as the case may be;
'the Directive' means Council Directive 90/314/EEC on package travel, package holidays and package tours;
'offer' includes an invitation to treat whether by means of advertising or otherwise, and cognate expressions shall be construed accordingly;
'organiser' means the person who, otherwise than occasionally, organises packages and sells or offers them for sale, whether directly or through a retailer;
'the other party to the contract' means the party, other than the consumer, to the contract, that is, the organiser or the retailer, or both, as the case may be;
'package' means the pre-arranged combination of at least two of the following components when sold or offered for sale at an inclusive price and when the service covers a period of more than twenty-four hours or includes overnight accommodation:—
    (a) transport;
    (b) accommodation;
    (c) other tourist services not ancillary to transport or accommodation and accounting for a significant proportion of the package,
    and
    (i) the submission of separate accounts for different components shall not cause the arrangements to be other than a package.
    (ii) the fact that a combination is arranged at the request of the consumer and in accordance with his specific instructions (whether modified or not) shall not of itself cause it to be treated as other than pre-arranged;
and
'retailer' means the person who sells or offers for sale the package put together by the organiser.

(2) In the definition of 'contract' in paragraph (1) above, 'consumer' means the person who takes or agrees to take the package ('the principal contractor') and elsewhere in these Regulations 'consumer' means, as the context requires, the principal contractor, any person on whose behalf the principal contractor agrees to purchase the package ('the other beneficiaries') or any person to whom the principal contractor or any of the other beneficiaries transfers the package ('the transferee').

Application of Regulations

3.—(1) These Regulations apply to packages sold or offered for sale in the territory of the United Kingdom.

(2) Regulations 4 to 15 apply to packages so sold or offered for sale on or after 31st December 1992.

(3) Regulations 16 to 22 apply to contracts which, in whole or part, remain to be performed on 31st December 1992.

Descriptive matter relating to packages must not be misleading

4.—(1) No organiser or retailer shall supply to a consumer any descriptive matter concerning a package, the price of a package or any other conditions applying to the contract which contains any misleading information.

(2) If an organiser or retailer is in breach of paragraph (1) he shall be liable to compensate the consumer for any loss which the consumer suffers in consequence.

Requirements as to brochures

5.—(1) Subject to paragraph (4) below, no organiser shall make available a brochure to a possible consumer unless it indicates in a legible, comprehensible and accurate manner the price and adequate information about the matters specified in Schedule 1 to these Regulations in respect of the packages offered for sale in the brochure to the extent that those matters are relevant to the packages so offered.

(2) Subject to paragraph (4) below, no retailer shall make available to a possible consumer a brochure which he knows or has reasonable to cause to believe does not comply with the requirements of paragraph (1).

(3) An organiser who contravenes paragraph (1) of this regulation and a retailer who contravenes paragraph (2) thereof shall be guilty of an offence and liable:—
  (a) on summary conviction, to a fine not exceeding level 5 on the standard scale; and
  (b) on conviction on indictment, to a fine.

(4) Where a brochure was first made available to consumers generally before 31st December 1992 no liability shall arise under this regulation in respect of an identical brochure being made available to a consumer at any time.

Circumstances in which particulars in brochure are to be binding

6.—(1) Subject to paragraphs (2) and (3) of this regulation, the particulars in the brochure (whether or not they are required by regulation 5(1) above to be included in the brochure) shall constitute implied warranties (or, as regards Scotland, implied terms) for the purposes of any contract to which the particulars relate.

(2) Paragraph (1) of this regulation does not apply—
  (a) in relation to information required to be included by virtue of paragraph 9 of Schedule 1 to these Regulations; or
  (b) where the brochure contains an express statement that changes may be made in the

particulars contained in it before a contract is concluded and changes in the particulars so contained are clearly communicated to the consumer before a contract is concluded.

(3) Paragraph (1) of this regulation does not apply when the consumer and the other party to the contract agree after the contract has been made that the particulars in the brochure, or some of those particulars, should not form part of the contract.

Information to be provided before contract is concluded

7.—(1) Before a contract is concluded, the other party to the contract shall provide the intending consumer with the information specified in paragraph (2) below in writing or in some other appropriate form.

(2) The information referred to in paragraph (1) is:—
    (a) general information about passport and visa requirements which apply to British Citizens who purchase the package in question, including information about the length of time it is likely to take to obtain the appropriate passports and visas;
    (b) information about health formalities required for the journey and the stay; and
    (c) the arrangements for security for the money paid over and (where applicable) for the repatriation of the consumer in the event of insolvency.

(3) If the intending consumer is not provided with the information required by paragraph (1) in accordance with that paragraph the other party to the contract shall be guilty of an offence and liable:—
    (a) on summary conviction, to a fine not exceeding level 5 on the standard scale; and
    (b) on conviction on indictment, to a fine.

Information to be provided in good time

8.—(1) The other party to the contract shall in good time before the start of the journey provide the consumer with the information specified in paragraph (2) below in writing or in some other appropriate form.

(2) The information referred to in paragraph (1) is the following:—
    (a) the times and places of intermediate stops and transport connections and particulars of the place to be occupied by the traveller (for example, cabin or berth on ship, sleeper compartment on train);
    (b) the name, address and telephone number—
        (i) of the representative of the other party to the contract in the locality where the consumer is to stay,
    or, if there is no such representative
        (ii) of an agency in that locality on whose assistance a consumer in difficulty would be able to call,
    or, if there is no such representative or agency, a telephone number or other information which will enable the consumer to contact the other party to the contract during the stay; and
    (c) in the case of a journey or stay abroad by a child under the age of 16 on the day when the journey or stay is due to start, information enabling direct contact to be made with the child or the person responsible at the place where he is to stay; and
    (d) except where the consumer is required as a term of the contract to take out an insurance policy in order to cover the cost of cancellation by the consumer or the cost of assistance, including repatriation, in the event of accident or illness, information about an insurance policy which the consumer may, if he wishes, take out in respect of the risk of those costs being incurred.

(3) If the consumer is not provided with the information required by paragraph (1) in accordance with that paragraph the other party to the contract shall be guilty of an offence and liable:—

(a) on summary conviction, to a fine not exceeding level 5 on the standard scale; and

(b) on conviction on indictment, to a fine.

Contents and form of contract

9.—(1) The other party to the contract shall ensure that:

(a) depending on the nature of the package being purchased, the contract contains at least the elements specified in Schedule 2 to these Regulations;

(b) subject to paragraph (2) below, all the terms of the contract are set out in writing or such other form as is comprehensible and accessible to the consumer and are communicated to the consumer before the contract is made; and

(c) a written copy of these terms is supplied to the consumer.

(2) Paragraph (1)(b) above does not apply when the interval between the time when the consumer approaches the other party to the contract with a view to entering into a contract and the time of departure under the proposed contract is so short that it is impracticable to comply with the sub-paragraph.

(3) It is an implied condition (or, as regards Scotland, an implied term) of the contract that the other party to the contract complies with the provisions of paragraph (1).

(4) In Scotland, any breach of the condition implied by paragraph (3) above shall be deemed to be a material breach justifying rescission of the contract.

Transfer of bookings

10.—(1) In every contract there is an implied term that where the consumer is prevented from proceeding with the package the consumer may transfer his booking to a person who satisfies all the conditions applicable to the package, provided that the consumer gives reasonable notice to the other party to the contract of his intention to transfer before the date when departure is due to take place.

(2) Where a transfer is made in accordance with the implied term set out in paragraph (1) above, the transferor and the transferee shall be jointly and severally liable to the other party to the contract for payment of the price of the package (or, if part of the price has been paid, for payment of the balance) and for any additional costs arising from such transfer.

Price revision

11.—(1) Any term in a contract to the effect that the prices laid down in the contract may be revised shall be void and of no effect unless the contract provides for the possibility of upward or downward revision and satisfies the conditions laid down in paragraph (2) below.

(2) The conditions mentioned in paragraph (1) are that—

(a) the contract states precisely how the revised price is to be calculated;

(b) the contract provides that price revisions are to be made solely to allow for variations in:—

(i) transportation costs, including the cost of fuel;

(ii) dues, taxes or fees chargeable for services such as landing taxes or embarkation or disembarkation fees at ports and airports, or

(iii) the exchange rates applied to the particular package; and

(3) Notwithstanding any terms of a contract,

(i) no price increase may be made in a specified period which may not be less than 30 days before the departure date stipulated; and

(ii) as against an individual consumer liable under the contract, no price increase may be made in respect of variations which would produce an increase of less than 2%, or such greater percentage as the contract may specify, ('non-eligible variations') and that the non-eligible variations shall be left out of account in the calculation.

Significant alterations to essential terms

12. In every contract there are implied terms to the effect that—
    (a) where the organiser is constrained before the departure to alter significantly an essential term of the contract, such as the price (so far as regulation 11 permits him to do so), he will notify the consumer as quickly as possible in order to enable him to take appropriate decisions and in particular to withdraw from the contract without penalty or to accept a rider to the contract specifying the alterations made and their impact on the price; and
    (b) the consumer will inform the organiser or the retailer of his decision as soon as possible.

Withdrawal by consumer pursuant to regulation 12 and cancellation by organiser

13.—(1) The terms set out in paragraphs (2) and (3) below are implied in every contract and apply where the consumer withdraws from the contract pursuant to the term in it implied by virtue of regulation 12(a), or where the organiser, for any reason other than the fault of the consumer, cancels the package before the agreed date of departure.

(2) The consumer is entitled—
    (a) to take a substitute package of equivalent or superior quality if the other party to the contract is able to offer him such a substitute; or
    (b) to take a substitute package of lower quality if the other party to the contract is able to offer him one and to recover from the organiser the difference in price between the price of the package purchased and that of the substitute package; or
    (c) to have repaid to him as soon as possible all the monies paid by him under the contract.

(3) The consumer is entitled, if appropriate, to be compensated by the organiser for non-performance of the contract except where—
    (a) the package is cancelled because the number of persons who agree to take it is less than the minimum number required and the consumer is informed of the cancellation, in writing, within the period indicated in the description of the package; or
    (b) the package is cancelled by reason of unusual and unforeseeable circumstances beyond the control of the party by whom this exception is pleaded, the consequences of which could not have been avoided even if all due care had been exercised.

(4) Overbooking shall not be regarded as a circumstance falling within the provisions of sub-paragraph (b) of paragraph (3) above

Significant proportion of services not provided

14.—(1) The terms set out in paragraphs (2) and (3) below are implied in every contract and apply where, after departure, a significant proportion of the services contracted for is not provided or the organiser becomes aware that he will be unable to procure a significant proportion of the services to be provided.

(2) The organiser will make suitable alternative arrangements, at no extra cost to the consumer, for the continuation of the package and will, where appropriate, compensate the consumer for the difference between the services to be supplied under the contract and those supplied.

(3) If it is impossible to make arrangements as described in paragraph (2), or these are not accepted by the consumer for good reasons, the organiser will, where appropriate, provide the consumer with equivalent transport back to the place of departure or to another place to which the consumer has agreed and will, where appropriate, compensate the consumer.

Liability of other party to the contract for proper performance of obligations under contract

15.—(1) The other party to the contract is liable to the consumer for the proper performance of the obligations under the contract, irrespective of whether such obligations are to be performed by that other party or by other suppliers of services but this shall not affect any remedy or right of action which that other party may have against those other suppliers of services.

(2) The other party to the contract is liable to the consumer for any damage caused to him by the failure to perform the contract or the improper performance of the contract unless the failure or the improper performance is due neither to any fault of that other party nor to that of another supplier of services, because—

    (a) the failures which occur in the performance of the contract are attributable to the consumer;

    (b) such failures are attributable to a third party unconnected with the provision of the services contracted for, and are unforeseeable or unavoidable; or

    (c) such failures are due to—

        (i) unusual and unforeseeable circumstances beyond the control of the party by whom this exception is pleaded, the consequences of which could not have been avoided even if all due care had been exercised; or

        (ii) an event which the other party to the contract or the supplier of services, even with all due care, could not foresee or forestall.

(3) In the case of damage arising from the non-performance or improper performance of the services involved in the package, the contract may provide for compensation to be limited in accordance with the international conventions which govern such services.

(4) In the case of damage other than personal injury resulting from the non-performance or improper performance of the services involved in the package, the contract may include a term limiting the amount of compensation which will be paid to the consumer, provided that the limitation is not unreasonable.

(5) Without prejudice to paragraph (3) and paragraph (4) above, liability under paragraphs (1) and (2) above cannot be excluded by any contractual term.

(6) The terms set out in paragraphs (7) and (8) below are implied in every contract.

(7) In the circumstances described in paragraph (2)(b) and (c) of this regulation, the other party to the contract will give prompt assistance to a consumer in difficulty.

(8) If the consumer complains about a defect in the performance of the contract, the other party to the contract, or his local representative, if there is one, will make prompt efforts to find appropriate solutions.

(9) The contract must clearly and explicitly oblige the consumer to communicate at the earliest opportunity, in writing or any other appropriate form, to the supplier of the services concerned and to the other party to the contract any failure which he perceives at the place where the services concerned are supplied.

. . .

Regulation 5

SCHEDULE 1

Information to be included (in addition to the price) in brochures where relevant to packages offered

1. The destination and the means, characteristics and categories of transport used.

2. The type of accommodation, its location, category or degree of comfort and its main features and, where the accommodation is to be provided in a member State, its approval or tourist classification under the rules of that member State.

3. The meals which are included in the package.

4. The itinerary.

5. General information about passports and visa requirements which apply for British citizens and health formalities required for the journey and the stay.

6. Either the monetary amount or the percentage of the price which is to be paid on account and the timetable for payment of the balance.

7. Whether a minimum number of persons is required for the package to take place and, if so, the deadline for informing the consumer in the event of cancellation.

8. The arrangements (if any) which apply if consumers are delayed at the outward or homeward points of departure.

9. The arrangements for security for money paid over and for the repatriation of the consumer in the event of insolvency.

Regulation 9

SCHEDULE 2

Elements to be included in the contract if relevant to the particular package

1. The travel destination(s) and, where periods of stay are involved, the relevant periods, with dates.

2. The means, characteristics and categories of transport to be used and the dates, times and points of departure and return.

3. Where the package includes accommodation, its location, its tourist category or degree of comfort, its main features and, where the accommodation is to be provided in a member State, its compliance with the rules of that member State.

4. The means which are included in the package.

5. Whether a minimum number of persons is required for the package to take place and, if so, the deadline for informing the consumer in the event of cancellation.

6. The itinerary.

7. Visits, excursions or other services which are included in the total price agreed for the package.

8. The name and address of the organiser, the retailer and, where appropriate, the insurer.

9. The price of the package, if the price may be revised in accordance with the term which may be included in the contract under regulation 11, an indication of the possibility of such price revisions, and an indication of any dues, taxes or fees chargeable for certain services

(landing, embarkation or disembarkation fees at ports and airports and tourist taxes) where such costs are not included in the package.

10. The payment schedule and method of payment.

11. Special requirements which the consumer has communicated to the organiser or retailer when making the booking and which both have accepted.

12. The periods within which the consumer must make any complaint about the failure to perform or the inadequate performance of the contract.

. . .

NOTES

1. The Regulations were made on 22 December 1992 and came into force on the following day. Other aspects of the Regulations cover such points as bonding and insurance, offences and enforcement: see below, pp 446–51. See, generally, Rinkes in Lonbay (ed), *Enhancing the Legal Position of the European Consumer* (1996), ch 12.
2. For an important decision of the Court of Justice of the European Communities concerning the liability of Member States for non-transposition of the Package Travel Directive see *Dillenkofer v Federal Republic of Germany* (C–178/94, 8.10.1996), above, pp. 15–17.

PROBLEMS

1. Artemus enters the Spa Town travel agency in Leamington. He books a fully-inclusive winter package holiday with Walhalla Tours for a fifteen-day holiday in the Hotel Espana in Westpool. He pays Spa Town in advance. Walhalla has dealt with the Hotel Espana over many years and always found it to be entirely reliable. During the fifteen days when Artemus is at the hotel the central heating breaks down, the food is well below standard and there are many other disappointments.

   Advise Artemus as to the potential liability, if any, of (i) Spa Town, (ii) Walhalla and (iii) the Hotel Espana, noting the provisions of the Package Travel, Package Holidays and Package Tours Regulations 1992, SI 1992/3288. (As to the position of agents under the Misrepresentation Act 1967 see *Resolute Maritime Inc v Nippon Kaiji Kyokai, The Skopas* [1983] 2 All ER 1, [1983] 1 WLR 857.)

2. On 1 June Bertram enters the Castle travel agency to enquire about a coach service operated by Motorway Travel. He buys a ticket for Motorway's service from Warwick to Heathrow Airport for 10 June explaining to the girl on the desk that this is the last date on which his transatlantic airline ticket is valid. Because it has been maintained badly Motorway's coach breaks down and Bertram misses his flight. Advise Bertram.

   If Motorway Travel had become insolvent and ceased trading on 5 June what advice would you give the Castle travel agency from whom Bertram is reclaiming the £15 which he has paid for his ticket?

BAILMENT

Contracts of bailment cover a wide range of transactions in which a consumer's goods are handed over into the possession of a business. For example, a car may be sent to a garage for repair, a coat to the cleaners, a film for processing or household goods may be transported or stored. Frequently in such cases the issue will be the effectiveness of an exemption or limitation clause. This matter is discussed in the extracts in chapter 7 below. See, for example, *Woodman v Photo Trade Processing Ltd* (His Honour Judge Clarke, May 1981), below, p 343; *Waldron-Kelly v British Railways Board* (His Honour Judge Brown, March 1981), and *McCutcheon v David MacBrayne Ltd* [1964] 1 All ER 430, [1964] 1 WLR 125, HL. The following case involved a limitation clause and the doctrine of fundamental breach of contract, but it is important also as illustrating a further point of some practical importance.

Levison v Patent Steam Carpet Cleaning Co Ltd [1977] 3 All ER 498, [1978] QB 69, Court of Appeal

The plaintiffs, Mr and Mrs Levison, owned a Chinese carpet which was worth £900. They arranged to have it cleaned by the defendant company. When it was collected by the defendants' van driver Mr Levison signed a form of which clause 2(a) stated that the maximum value of the carpet, based on its area, was deemed to be £40. By clause 5 it was further provided that, 'All merchandise is expressly accepted at the owner's risk'. The defendants recommended that owners should insure their goods. The carpet was never returned—presumably because it had been stolen—and the plaintiffs (or effectively their insurers) sued to recover its full value. Judgment was given for this amount, that is £900, and the defendants appealed to the Court of Appeal. On the issue of the burden of proof the following points were made:

Lord Denning MR. . . . I am clearly of opinion that, in a contract of bailment, when a bailee seeks to escape liability on the ground that he was not negligent or that he was excused by an exception or limitation clause, then he must show what happened to the goods. He must prove all the circumstances known to him in which the loss or damage occurred. If it appears that the goods were lost or damaged without any negligence on his part, then, of course, he is not liable. If it appears that they were lost or damaged by a slight breach, not going to the root of the contract, he may be protected by the exemption or limitation clause. But, if he leaves the cause of loss or damage undiscovered and unexplained, then I think he is liable: because it is then quite likely that the goods were stolen by one of his servants; or delivered by a servant to the wrong address; or damaged by reckless or wilful misconduct; all of which the offending servant will conceal and not make known to his employer. Such conduct would be a fundamental breach against which the exemption or limitation clause will not protect him.

The cleaning company in this case did not show what had happened to the carpet. They did not prove how it was lost. They gave all sorts of excuses for non-delivery and eventually said it had been stolen. Then I would ask: by whom was it stolen? Was it by one of their own servants? or with his connivance? Alternatively, was it delivered by one of their servants to the wrong address? In the absence of any explanation, I would infer that it was one of these causes. In none of them would the cleaning company be protected by the exemption or limitation clause.

Conclusion. I think the judge was quite right in holding that the burden or proof was on the cleaning company to exclude fundamental breach. As they did not exclude it, they cannot rely on the exemption or limitation clauses. I would, therefore, dismiss this appeal.

Sir David Cairns . . . In *J Spurling Ltd v Bradshaw*[1] Denning LJ said:

'A bailor, by pleading and presenting his case properly, can always put the burden of proof on the bailee. In the case of non-delivery, for instance, all he need plead is the contract and a failure to deliver on demand. That puts on the bailee the burden of proving either loss without his fault (which would be a complete answer at common law) or, if the loss was due to his fault, that it was a fault from which he is excluded by the exempting clause: see *Cunard SS Co v Buerger*[2] and *Woolmer v Delmer Price Ltd.*[3] I do not think the Court of Appeal in *Alderslade v Hendon Laundry Ltd*[4] had the burden of proof in mind at all.'

I respectfully agree with that passage. Parker LJ[5] expressly refrained from considering whether *Woolmer v Delmer Price Ltd*[3] was wrongly decided. It is in my judgment open to this court either to approve or to overrule McNair J's decision[6] and for my part I would approve it because, however difficult it may sometimes be for a bailee to prove a negative, he is at least in a better position than the bailor to know what happened to the goods while in his possession.

The considerations applicable to bills of lading and to policies of marine insurance (see *The Glendarroch*;[7] *Munro, Brice & Co v War Risks Association Ltd*[8]) are not in my judgment applicable to cases such as the present.

Accordingly I would hold that the onus was on the defendants, that they did not discharge it and that the appeal should be dismissed.

Orr LJ agreed.

Appeal dismissed.

[1] [1956] 2 All ER 121 at 125, [1956] 1 WLR 461 at 466.
[2] [1927] AC 1, [1926] All ER Rep 103.
[3] [1955] 1 All ER 377, [1955] 1 QB 291.
[4] [1945] 1 All ER 244, [1945] KB 189.
[5] [1956] 2 All ER 121 at 128, [1956] 1 WLR 461 at 470.
[6] [1955] 1 All ER 377, [1955] 1 QB 291.
[7] [1894] P 226, [1891–4] All ER Rep 484.
[8] [1918] 2 KB 78, [1916–17] All ER Rep 981.

NOTE

The above case is important as indicating the incidence of the onus of proof where goods have been lost. However, it may be necessary to establish initially that there is an obligation to exercise reasonable care in relation to the safeguarding of a customer's property. The point is discussed in detail in Palmer *Bailment* (2nd edn, 1991: see ch V especially). It arose in the following case.

Ashby v Tolhurst [1937] 2 All ER 837, [1937] 2 KB 242, Court of Appeal

The plaintiff drove his motor car onto a piece of ground belonging to the defendants, paid 1s, and was handed a ticket marked 'Sea Way Car Park. Car Park Ticket'. The ticket contained an exemption clause stating that:

The proprietors do not take any responsibility for the safe custody of any cars or articles there, nor for any damage to the cars or articles however caused, nor for any injuries to any persons, all cars being left in all respects entirely at their owners' risk. Owners are requested to show ticket when required.

When the plaintiff returned to the car park he found that the car was no longer there whereupon the attendant explained that it had been removed by the plaintiff's 'friend' who wanted it to ride to Thorpe Bay. The plaintiff who did not have any such friend in the area brought an action which succeeded at first instance. The defendants now appealed to the Court of Appeal.

Sir Wilfred Greene, MR, having stated the facts of the case, continued: It seems to me that reading the document as a whole, including its own description of itself, namely, 'car park ticket,' it really means no more than this: the holder of this ticket is entitled to park his car in the Sea Way Car Park, but reading it quite shortly, this does not mean that the proprietors are going to be responsible for it. If that be the true construction of the document, and I think it is, the argument that the presence of these exempting conditions points to the view that they are inserted in order to remove a contractual liability which would otherwise be there disappears and, in my opinion, the argument, when applied to a document of this kind, is not one of any real weight. If that be the true view, the relationship was a relationship of licensor and licensee alone, and that relationship in itself would carry no obligations of the licensor towards the licensee in relation to the chattel left there, no obligation to provide anybody to look after it, no liability for any negligent act of any person in the employment of the licensor who happened to be there.

There is one other way, I think, of usefully testing the position, and that is to consider in whom possession of this car was at the relevant time. In doing that, of course, one has to be careful to see that one is not unconsciously begging the whole question; but it would be a surprising result, I think, if the effect of the relationship between these parties was that when the car was left on this piece of ground possession of the car in the legal sense became vested in the owners of the park. It would involve the consequence that the owners of the park could maintain an action of trespass, they could maintain an action of conversion if their special property in the car was interfered with. As I say, that argument must not be used in such a way as to beg the question, but it would be rather a surprising result if, when a man left his car on land like this and paid 1s for the privilege of doing so, the possession passed in a way in which it certainly would not pass if he left it in a public park in a square in London and paid the attendant 6d for the ticket, or whatever he has to pay. In such a case possession, it seems to me, clearly would not pass; I quite fail to see why possession should pass in a case such as this. That, as I say, is merely a way of looking at the matter and is not, of course, a conclusive argument.

. . .

Romer LJ: I agree. . . . [In] order that there shall be a bailment there must be a delivery by the bailor, that is to say, he must part with his possession of the chattel in question. In the present case there is no evidence whatever of any delivery in fact of the motor car to the attendant on behalf of the defendants. All I can see is that the plaintiff left his car on the car park, paying the sum of 1s for the privilege of doing so. It is true that, if the car had been left there for any particular purpose that required that the defendant should have possession of the car, a delivery would rightly be inferred, and, if the car had been left at the car park for the purposes of being sold or by way of pledge or for the purposes of being driven away to some other place or indeed for the purposes of safe custody, delivery of the car, although not actually made, would readily be inferred. It is perfectly plain in this case that the car was not delivered to the defendants for safe custody. You cannot infer a contract by A to perform a certain act out of circumstances in which A had made it perfectly plain that he declines to be under any contractual liability to perform that act. The defendants made it as clear as writing can make it in the ticket which was delivered to the plaintiff that they would not take any responsibility for the safe custody of any car. One cannot infer, therefore, in those circumstances that the car was left in the car park for the purpose of being in the custody of the defendants. It is perfectly plain that the car was not left there for any other purpose. That being so, it is impossible, it seems to me, to find that the car was delivered to the defendants or that there was any contract of bailment.

. . .

Scott LJ agreed.

Appeal allowed.

Consider the following cases:
1. Groucho takes his car to the Downtown garage for repair. When he returns to collect it two days later the garage owner explains that it has been extensively damaged by a burglar who has broken into the premises to steal car radios. He adds that his burglar alarm system which is usually reliable failed to operate on the night in question.
    Advise Groucho.
2. Eva dines at the Goodfood restaurant, leaving her valuable fur jacket on a peg close to her table. The jacket is stolen by a sneak-thief whose general appearance should have alerted the waiters to the fact that he was not an ordinary diner. The restaurant has not taken any precautions to safeguard its customers' property.
    Advise Eva. Would the position be different if the jacket had been stolen from the ladies' cloakroom where Eva had left it with an attendant?

CONTRACTS OF INSURANCE

Contracts of insurance provide a further example of an area which is of considerable importance to consumers and in which, it may be argued, reform is long overdue. In this section reference is made to some of the more central issues of this complex and specialist subject. For further discussion, see Birds *Modern Insurance Law* (3rd edn, 1993), Clarke, *The Law of Insurance Contracts* (2nd edn, 1994), the Law Commission Report on Non-Disclosure and Breach of Warranty (Law Com No 104, Cmnd 8064, 1980) *Which?* March 1991, p 133, and the Annual Reports of the Insurance Ombudsman Bureau.

Duty of disclosure

The general rule of English law is that a person must refrain from making positive misrepresentations and yet is not obliged to volunteer information as such. However, as may be seen from the following case, the position is different where contracts of insurance are concerned.

Woolcott v Sun Alliance and London Insurance Ltd [1978] 1 All ER 1253, [1978] 1 WLR 493, Queen's Bench Division

In 1961 the defendant insurers issued a block insurance policy against fire and other risks. The policy was in favour of the Bristol and West Building Society, as mortgagees, and the several mortgagors recorded in its annex from time to time. In 1972 the plaintiff applied to the society for an advance of £12,000 to enable him to purchase certain property. In the standard application form he was asked to state the amount for which he wished the Society to insure the property, but there was no question which related to his moral character. Neither was he asked to complete a separate proposal form for insurance. He did not disclose the fact that he had several convictions including one for robbery, for which he had been sentenced to twelve years' imprisonment. Some two years after the purchase of the property it was destroyed by fire. The defendants indemnified the society to the extent of its security but, having learnt of the plaintiff's convictions, repudiated his claim for the excess. In subsequent proceedings it was held that the policy of insurance was not a joint insurance but rather an insurance by two persons, that is the mortgagee and the mortgagor, for their respective interests.

Caulfield J, having stated the facts of the case and reached the above conclusion on the first issue, continued: On the second issue in this action I refer to s 17 and 18 of the Marine Insurance Act 1906. By s 17: 'A contract of marine insurance is a contract based upon the utmost good faith and if the utmost good faith be not observed by either party the contract may be avoided by the other party', and s 18:

'(1) Subject to the provisions of this section, the assured must disclose to the insurer, before the contract is concluded, every material circumstance which is known to the assured, and the assured is deemed to know every circumstance which in the ordinary course of business ought to be known by him. If the assured fails to make such disclosure, the insurer may avoid the contract.

'(2) Every circumstance is material which would influence the judgment of a prudent insurer in fixing the premium or determining whether he will take the risk.'

I refer now to the judgment of MacKenna J in *Lambert v Co-operative Insurance Society*.[1] This judgment I have found most comprehensive and most helpful, and I have followed the principles which are fully explained in the judgment of MacKenna J (who was giving the first judgment of the Court of Appeal):[2]

'Everyone agrees that the assured is under a duty of disclosure and that the duty is the same when he is applying for a renewal as it is when he is applying for the original policy. The extent of that duty is the matter in controversy. There are, at least in theory, four possible rules or tests which I shall state: (1) The duty is to disclose such facts only as the particular assured believes to be material; (2) It is to disclose such facts as a reasonable man would believe to be material; (3) It is to disclose such facts as the particular insurer would regard as material; (4) It is to disclose such facts as a reasonable or prudent insurer might have treated as material.'

Ultimately, in a most comprehensive judgment, the learned judge then went on to conclude that the proper test was the fourth test, and the principles which he has explained in that case I have followed in reaching my judgment on this particular issue.

The duty, in my judgment, rested on the plaintiff, when he completed his application form for a loan, to disclose his criminal record for, by that application, he was accepting that the society would effect insurance of his property on his behalf as well as their own behalf. I do no think the absence of a proposal form for insurance modifies in any degree the duty of disclosure on the plaintiff. The plaintiff knew the society would be effecting a policy of insurance on their own behalf and on his behalf, and accordingly, in my judgment, there was a duty on the plaintiff to disclose such facts as a reasonable or prudent insurer might have treated as material.

On the third issue I have accepted the evidence of the underwriters who have given evidence. I accept that the criminal record of an assured can affect the moral hazard which insurers have to assess; indeed this is almost self-evident. I therefore hold that on the particular facts of this case the non-disclosure of a serious criminal offence like robbery by the plaintiff was a material non-disclosure.

For these reasons the defendants, in my judgment, are entitled to avoid the policy insofar as that policy affects the plaintiff's separate interest. There will be judgment accordingly.

Judgment for the defendants.

[1] [1975] 2 Lloyd's Rep 485.
[2] [1975] 2 Lloyd's Rep 485 at 487.

NOTE

In the *Lambert* case to which Caulfield J referred it was held that the defendants were entitled to avoid liability under an 'all risks' policy covering jewellery when the insured did not disclose her husband's convictions for theft. Characteristically Mackenna J added, 'The defendant company would act decently if, having established the point of principle, they were to pay her.': [1975] 2 Lloyd's Rep 485 at 491. For a critical comment on this case see Merkin (1976) 39 MLR 478. For a contrasting case, see *Hair v Prudential Assurance Co Ltd* [1983] 2 Lloyd's Rep 667, and for detailed discussion of the test of materiality of disclosure in a commercial context, see *Pan Atlantic Insurance Co Ltd v Pine Top Insurance Co Ltd* [1994] 3 All ER 581 (HL). In this latter case a majority of the House of Lords held that under s 18(2) of the 1906 Act (see above), which reflected the common law, the 'influence' on the judgment of an insurer would not have to be 'decisive'. It is sufficient that the relevant fact was one which would be taken into account. However, non-disclosure would lead to an entitlement to avoid the contract only if it induced the particular insurer to make the policy on the relevant terms.

Although there is general agreement that a broadly-based duty of disclosure is inappropriate for consumer contracts, there is no overall consensus as to how precisely the law should be reformed. The differing views expressed by the Law Commission and the National Consumer Council (NCC) may be seen in the following extracts from the NCC response to the Law Commission's report. Having argued in favour of a separate régime for consumer insurance contracts the NCC continues:

Insurance Law—Non Disclosure and Breach of Warranty (National Consumer Council) (1981)

THE DUTY OF DISCLOSURE

. . .

4.6.1. The Law Commission has stuck to the approach of its working-paper that changes should be limited to reform, but not abolition, of the duty of disclosure. The precise reforms now proposed, however, are not as favourable to policyholders as those of the working-paper. The reforms cover:—

(i) The extent of the duty where there is no proposal form
(ii) The extend of the duty where there is a proposal form
(iii) Renewals.

Where there is no proposal form

4.6.2. Most consumer insurance is taken out on the basis of a completed proposal form, but there are exceptions such as:—

* temporary cover (eg motor insurance) pending completion of proposal form;
* some holiday insurance (tick in brochure);
* slot machine insurance (eg at airports).

The Law Commission rejected the abolition of the duty of disclosure and, where there is no proposal form, they recommended instead that the duty of disclosure should be reduced so that it should extend to a fact which is:—

(i) material to the risk
(ii) known to the applicant or within his assumed knowledge
and
(iii) one which a reasonable man in the position of the applicant would disclose to his insurers.

4.6.3. The test of 'materiality' would remain largely the same as the present law, which is that a fact is material if it would influence a prudent insurer. The restriction of the duty to facts within the insured person's knowledge is a clear improvement on the present law which enables insurers to seek disclosures of facts not known to the insured. The Commission spells out that a person should be assumed to know a material fact if it would have been ascertainable by reasonable enquiry and if a reasonable man applying for the insurance in question would have ascertained it. In other words, the insured person cannot say that he did not know facts which were obviously relevant and which he could easily find out, but he is not expected to engage in an elaborate investigation into all possible facts.

4.6.4. The third element in the above formulation introduces the objectivity which the present law lacks. A reasonable man would not disclose facts which apparently had no bearing on the risks to be insured. The wording proposed ignores personal idiosyncrasies, but effectively puts the reasonable man into the shoes of the person actually taking out insurance. Thus, more would be expected of a large business than an individual.

4.6.5. The Law Commission claims that the above formulation would remove one of the major mischiefs in the present law and would be in accordance with common sense and fair to both parties. It is undeniable that the proposals outlined are a considerable improvement on the present law. The problem remains, however, that there is no proposal form to be completed by the consumer and he is given no specific opportunity to consider the duty of disclosure, let alone actually to disclose material facts. It is suggested that it is simply not realistic ever to expect consumers either to know that they have to make 'voluntary' disclosures or to have any sensible idea as to what sort of information has to be disclosed . . .

4.6.7. If the insurers want information they should ask for it, rather than expect the law to require consumers to do the impossible. *NCC considers that where there is no proposal form the duty of disclosure on consumers should (apart from deliberate concealment) be abolished.* It is accepted that the insurer should have the right to repudiate the policy later on full investigation, but that he should be on risk with regard to claims occurring in any interim period of investigation.

Where there is a proposal form

4.6.8. Nearly all consumer insurance is initiated by the completion of a proposal form. The Law Commission do not foresee any difficulty in separately identifying these and propose that applications for insurance made in connection with applications for mortgages should be treated as proposal forms. The major criticism of the present law is that the insured may well be unaware that he is under a residual duty to disclose material facts *after* answering a series of questions in the proposal form. This is, the Law Commission say, 'a trap for the insured . . . which requires reform for the protection of the insured'.

4.6.9. The *provisional* recommendations made by the Law Commission in 1979 were welcomed by NCC. Subject to deliberate concealment, the suggestion then made was that there should be *no* duty beyond accurate answers to specific questions and that no general questions (eg 'Is there anything else . . . ') should be permitted. The effect would be to abolish the residual duty.

4.6.10. The final recommendation is different. The insurance industry has persuaded the Commission that, despite the superficial attractions of the provisional solution, proposal forms can only elicit information of a standard nature and that the provisional solution would result in lengthy, detailed and complex proposal forms. It is said that proposers might be aware of facts which any reasonable person would realise should be disclosed, but about which insurers could not reasonably be expected to ask questions. The examples quoted relate to business insurance (eg a business man who knows that his quality control system is inadequate). Accordingly, the Law Commission have now recommended:–

   (i)   A duty to volunteer information in addition to answering all questions should be retained.
   (ii) The duty should be reduced to the same level as for cases where there is no proposal form (see above).
   (iii) All proposal forms should have clear and explicit warnings about the existence and the extent of the duty to volunteer information and of the consequences of failure.
   (iv) A copy of the completed proposal form should be supplied to the insured persons.

4.6.11. The new recommendations are clearly less satisfactory for consumers and perhaps illustrate most vividly the need for separate treatment of consumer insurance. Whilst there may be unlimited factors affecting business insurance, consumer insurance is reasonably standardised. There must be a limit to the types of factors relevant to, say, household or motor insurance . . .

4.6.12. Relevant questions usually appear on proposal forms already. If they do not, and the insurer considers the type of information to be relevant, then specific questions should be devised and included . . . If the type of information sought can be described, there should be a question. *If it cannot be described, consumers should not be expected to think of it for themselves.*

4.6.13. *NCC is therefore firmly of the view that for consumer insurance where proposal forms are used:—*

   (i)   Insurance should be confined to specific questions in all cases.
   (ii) Any residual duty of disclosure should be abolished.
   (iii) General questions should be outlawed (or only permitted with the approval of the Director-General of Fair Trading).
   (iv) Insurers should supply a copy of completed proposal forms.
   (v)   *Prescribed* warnings should be prominently displayed with regard to whatever duties are finally imposed upon people taking out insurance.

Renewals

4.8.1. The vast majority of insurance contracts are made by way of renewal which creates a new contract. The present law imposes a fresh duty to disclose all facts which are material at the date of renewal. The extent of the duty is the same as on the original application. This usually means, assuming original compliance, that the duty extends to material changes in circumstances. In practice, if people do not know of the duty when they take out the original insurance, they are even less likely to be aware of its existence on renewal. Moreover, even if the duty is known about, the insured person is usually unable to refer to documents which record information which he previously supplied.

4.8.2. The Law Commission solutions are conditioned by their previous proposals. They recommended:—

    (i)   The duty of disclosure on renewal should be retained and the same standard of duty should apply as for the original application (ignoring, of course, information previously disclosed).

    (ii) Specific questions should be answered to the best of the person's knowledge and belief.

    (iii) Renewal notices should contain warnings about the duty of disclosure.

    (iv) Insurers should supply copies of renewal notices containing relevant information.

4.8.3. The last three points are completely acceptable, but the primary recommendation is defective for the same reasons as outlined in connection with the original policy. *NCC believes that for consumer insurances:–*

    (i)   Where there was previously a proposal form, the renewal notice should specifically ask about material changes in the disclosed information.

    (ii) Otherwise, if there was no proposal form, there should be no duty of disclosure on renewal. If specific types of information are wanted, appropriate questions should be asked on renewal.

Misstatements, warranties and 'basis of the contract' clauses

In principle it may be thought that consumers seeking assurance or insurance will be less deserving of sympathy if they give an incorrect answer when filling in a proposal form, rather than merely omit to volunteer information the relevance of which they may not appreciate. However, there may be unfairness also in making an entitlement to claim under a policy dependent on answering all questions correctly. The following case provides an example of the importance of giving complete and truthful answers.

Kumar v Life Insurance Corpn of India [1974] 1 Lloyd's Rep 147, Queen's Bench Division

Mr Justice Kerr: This action arises out of a claim by Mr Kumar as administrator of the estate of his wife. It is a claim for £1500, the sum insured under a life policy issued by the defendants. Mrs Kumar unfortunately died on June 10, 1968 and this is how this claim arises. The defendants contend that the policy is void under its terms or that it has been avoided because of incorrect answers given in the personal statement which accompanied the proposal form. Alternatively, they claim the same result because of a non-disclosure of material facts. The facts said not to have been disclosed are the same as those which in their submission falsified the answers which were given in the personal statement. In the alternative to his main claim the plaintiff claims the return of the premium which has been paid under the policy.

    Mr Kumar is of Indian nationality and his wife was also Indian. He came to this country in 1960 and she came in 1965. He is a dentist by profession. She worked as dentist's receptionist. They were both well educated, and Mrs Kumar was described by one witness as an intelligent, agreeable and educated woman.

On Feb 4, 1966, at the Central Middlesex Hospital, Mrs Kumar then being 23, gave birth to a child by a Caesarean operation; to be precise, by a lower segment Caesarean incision. It is necessary shortly to describe this well-known procedure. It takes place under the administration of a general anaesthetic and consists of surgically opening the abdominal wall, entering the peritoneal cavity, and then making a surgical division of the lower section of the uterus and delivering the baby through these openings, which are then stitched. In this case it was a so-called elective Caesarean in that it was planned in advance due to an inadequate pelvis and a breech presentation.

Having successfully had her baby in this way, Mrs Kumar . . . then consulted Dr Gregory at her local Family Planning Centre. She asked whether she could be put on the 'pill', ie to be prescribed oral contraceptives to avoid another pregnancy because of the advice she had been given in relation to her Caesarean.

Dr Gregory was called for the plaintiff and I fully accept her evidence. It is of some significance how Mrs Kumar informed Dr Gregory of her past medical history. Having been asked if she had had an operation, she said 'No', and Dr Gregory wrote down this answer. She was then asked about the history of her pregnancy and mentioned the Caesarean. Dr Gregory said in evidence that she did not make the correction, and commented that she is often amused by the fact that ladies from the East do not consider a Caesarean to be an operation. Since this is a crucial issue it is right to expand it shortly at this stage.

Dr Gregory, and indeed all the doctors who were called on both sides, had no hesitation in considering that a Caesarean was an operation. One doctor described it as a major operation. I have no doubt whatever it is properly to be described as an operation, both as a matter of ordinary English and as a matter of medical terminology. It is unnecessary and undesirable to define or to circumscribe the limits of the word 'operation' for present purposes. Many examples were given in argument, such as the extraction of a tooth under anaesthetic, dealing with an ingrown toe nail, piercing somebody's ears under a local anaesthetic, or an operative delivery of a baby with forceps. . . .

In October, 1966, Mrs Kumar took out a policy out of which this action arises. There is considerable conflict of evidence about the circumstances in which this happened, and I must deal with these in a moment. Before doing so it is convenient to go to the end of this unhappy story. She remained on the 'pill' until about January, 1968. She then wanted to have another baby and became pregnant. She unfortunately died on June 10, 1968, following an operation for a ruptured ectopic gestation. This was due to the fact that the foetus became implanted in the fallopian tubes instead of in the uterus. It is common ground that Mrs Kumar's death, although in the course of pregnancy, had no causal connection whatever with her Caesarean operation. But it is also common ground that this is not directly relevant and that it does not affect the issues which I have to decide.

. . .

I then come finally to the forms which had to be completed by any would-be insured. The forms are in three parts which are bound together as seven numbered pages. Pages 1 and 2 consist of a proposal and declaration; pp 2 to 5 consist of a personal statement, the contents of which are 'to be obtained from the life to be assured by the Medical Examiner and a Declaration by the proposer'. Then finally on pp 6 and 7 there is the confidential report of the medical examiner which is to be signed by him together with his qualifications, and he is instructed 'to satisfy himself completely about the identity of the life to be insured'. It is necessary for me to read certain parts of the two declarations. At the end of the proposal form the proposer declares as follows:

'I, the person whose life is hereinbefore proposed to be assured do hereby declare that the foregoing statements and answers are true in every particular and agree and declare that those statements and this declaration along with the further statements made or to be made before the Medical Examiner and the declaration relative thereto shall be the basis of the contract of insurance between me and the Life Insurance Corporation of India and that if any untrue averment be contained therein, the said contract shall be absolutely null and void and all monies which shall have been paid in respect thereof shall stand forfeited to the Corporation.'

Then at the end of the personal statement the proposer declares:

'I do hereby declare that the foregoing answers have been given by me after fully understanding the questions and the same are true in every particular and that I have not withheld any information and I do hereby agree that this declaration together with the proposal for assurance shall be the basis of the contract made between me and the Life Insurance Corporation of India.'

Then he had to sign this, and it also had to be signed by the medical examiner.

The effect of these declarations was incorporated in the insurance policy which was subsequently issued to Mrs Kumar so that no question about the contractual effectiveness of these declarations arises.

His Lordship then considered the conflict of evidence as to whether Mr or Mrs Kumar had discussed the Caesarean delivery in the presence of Mr Koley, the defendants' agent who had completed the form. He continued:

I must read what are now the crucial questions and answers in the personal statement of Mrs Kumar.

'Question 4(d):] Have you consulted a medical practitioner within the last five years, if so give details. [Answer:] No.'

The defendants contend that this answer was incorrect or untrue because she had consulted Dr Gregory in the way in which I have described.

'[Question 8(a):] Did you ever have any operation, accident or injury, if so give details. [Answer:] No.'

and the defendants contend that that is incorrect because of her Caesarean.

'[Question 9(b):] Have you ever been in any hospital, asylum or sanatorium for a check-up, observation, treatment or an operation, if so give details. [Answer:] No (only delivery).

The defendants say that that is inaccurate because the words 'only delivery' suggest normal delivery and not delivery by means of a Caesarean.

. . .

I then turn to the main issue whether the Caesarean was ever mentioned to Mr Koley. . . . I do not think that it ever crossed her or Mr Kumar's mind at that time or at any other time that the Caesarean should have been disclosed. I accept Mr Koley's evidence that, having written down the answers first at their place and then in relation to the personal statement at his place, Mr and Mrs Kumar read through these answers perhaps fairly quickly, but were content with them and then signed these forms.

It follows from what I have said that the answer to question 8(a), whether Mrs Kumar had ever had an operation, was incorrect and that Mr Koley did not know that it was incorrect. The answer to question 4(d) is more difficult. The question was whether or not Mrs Kumar had ever consulted a medical practitioner within the last five years. It is obvious that every visit to a doctor is not a consultation for the purposes of that question. I think that it must be shown that the visit was for a purpose material to a life assurance policy and not merely of such negligible potential materiality that it should be ignored. . . .

She had been advised not to have a baby for two years, and she went to see Dr Gregory to ask whether in these circumstances and in the light of this advice she could and should go on the 'pill'. I think on balance that this was a consultation within question 4(d), but I am thankful not to have to decide this case on that issue alone, as I should have been unhappy to do so. I would, however, have been forced to decide this case against Mr Kumar even on the basis of that question, as I see it. However, the clearly incorrect answer to question 8(a) in relation to the operation relieves me from the necessity of deciding this case solely on that point. For the sake of completeness I should add that I regard the answer to question 9(b), 'No (only delivery)' as not being accurate. The question, in effect for present purposes, is whether Mrs Kumar had ever been in any hospital for, among other things, an operation. The answer, 'No (only delivery)' was in my view sufficiently accurate not to be a false answer. I reject the suggestion that 'only delivery' excludes the possibility of a Caesarean since the question contains a reference to an operation.

. . .

That only leaves one issue. As I mentioned, Mr Kumar alternatively claims the return of the premium paid, which amounts to a little over £100 in relation to Mrs Kumar's policy. He says that he is entitled to recover this because the defendants have claimed to avoid the policy ab initio and have succeeded in doing so. The defendants resist this by virtue of the words which would make the premium forfeited in the event of incorrect answers being given. It is right to say that they had already offered to return the premium ex gratia in full settlement, but that this was refused. They have also undertaken through their Counsel to repay this premium in any event ex gratia, whatever the result of this case, but they want to have the point decided.

I had some doubts, without looking at the books, whether in the absence of any fraud (and there was clearly no fraud in this case), such a term might not be unenforceable as being a penalty. But these doubts have been set at rest by a long and clear line of authority to which I have been referred. I need only mention the names of three cases: *Duckett v Williams* (1834) 2 Cromp & M 348; *Thomson v Weems* in the House of Lords per Lord Blackburn, (1884) 9 App Cas 671, and *Sparenborg v Edinburgh Life Assurance Company*, [1912] 1 KB 195. These cases clearly show that it is settled law that if the provision is clear and explicit and provides for the forfeiture of a premium in the event of a proposal form or similar document being incorrectly answered, such a provision can be enforced by the insurance company even in the absence of fraud. It follows that the claim for return of premium fails and that this action must be dismissed.

Judgment for the defendants.

QUESTIONS

1. Would you have described a Caesarean delivery as an 'operation'?
2. Would the plaintiff have been entitled to recover the premiums if the 'basis of the contract' clause had not contained a provision for forfeiture of the premiums?

NOTE

The leading case most directly in point is the decision of the House of Lords in *Dawsons Ltd v Bonnin* [1922] 2 AC 413. A firm of contractors in Glasgow had insured a motor vehicle against damage by fire and third party risks. A term of the contract provided that 'material misstatement or concealment of any circumstance by the insured material to assessing the premium herein, or in connection with any claim, shall render the policy void.'

In reply to a question in the proposal form, 'State full address at which the vehicle will usually be garaged,' the answer given was 'Above Address,' meaning the firm's ordinary place of business in Glasgow. This was not true, as the lorry was usually garaged at a farm on the outskirts of Glasgow. The inaccurate answer in the proposal was given by inadvertence. The lorry having been destroyed by fire at the garage, the insured claimed payment under the policy. The House of Lords held that, although the misstatement was not material, the recital in the policy that the proposal should be the basis of the contract made the truth of the statements a condition of the insurer's liability. Hence the claim failed. Viscount Haldane added (at p 424):

It is clear that the answer was textually inaccurate. I think that the words employed in the body of the policy can only be properly construed as having made its accuracy a condition. The result may be technical and harsh, but if the parties have so stipulated we have no alternative, sitting as a Court of justice, but to give effect to the words agreed on. Hard cases must not be allowed to make bad law.

The views of the National Consumer Council and the recommendations of the Law Commission may be seen in the following additional extracts from the paper referred to above:

Insurance Law—Non Disclosure and Breach of Warranty (National Consumer Council) (1981)

5. WARRANTIES

5.1. A warranty is an assurance or promise made by the insured person as part of the contract of insurance. It may be a stipulation about the existence or continuation of a state of affairs or about the performance or non performance of an act by the insured. The following are examples:—
* that a car is, and will remain, roadworthy
* that a house has, and will continue to have, two fire extinguishers
* that the insured person will notify the insurer of any increase in the risk or of any possible claim.

5.2. Warranties can be (and are) created in a number of ways and can be classified as relating to past, present or future fact or behaviour. Strict compliance is required and any breach, however trivial, entitles the insurer to repudiate the policy. This is the case regardless of the materiality of the term, the insured person's state of mind or any connection between breach and loss. This means, to take the above examples, that a claim could be *rejected*:—
* for theft of the car which had faulty steering
* for flood damage caused to the house with only one fire extinguisher
* for a holiday cancelled due to a broken leg where the insured person did not notify additional business commitments which might have (but did not) cause the holiday to be cancelled.

5.3. The Law Commission identified three major defects in the present law:–
  1. It is quite wrong that the insurer should be entitled to repudiate a policy for breach of a warranty which *is not material to the risk*.

2. It is unjust that rejection should be available for *any breach* of a warranty which is material, no matter how irrelevant the breach may be to the loss.
3. Material warranties should be ascertainable from a written document which is available to the consumer.

5.4. The Law Commission concluded that there is a formidable case for reform and that again, it is not sufficient to rely upon the self regulating statements of practice. The reforms proposed by the Law Commission are largely consistent with NCC's evidence. It is therefore proposed only to set out the main elements, which are as follows:—

(i)   A contractual term should only be treated as a warranty if it is material to the risk.
(ii) There should be a presumption that a contractual provision is a warranty, but this should be rebuttable if the insured person can show that it relates to a matter which is not material to the risk.
(iii) To be effective, a warranty must be contained in a written document furnished to the insured person.
(iv) Breach of warranty should not entitle the insurer to reject claims where the insured person can show:—
    (a) the loss is of a different *type* from the particular type of loss which the broken warranty was intended to safeguard against; or
    (b) even if the loss is of the same type, the breach could not have increased the risk that the loss would occur in the way in which it did in fact occur.
(v)   Insurers should still be able to repudiate a policy for the future on account of breach of warranty, but there should be no retrospective effect.

. . .

6. 'BASIS OF THE CONTRACT' CLAUSES

6.1. Insurers often pre-empt the issue as to whether a particular fact is 'material' by including in the proposal form a declaration whereby the insured person warrants the accuracy of all answers to questions, usually declaring that all answers are to form the basis of the contract. The legal effect is to make all answers into warranties so as to entitle repudiation for any breach of warranty regardless of materiality to the risk. This double security for insurance companies compounds the law's unfairness and has been widely criticised.

6.2. The Law Commission agreed with the criticism and concluded that any basis of the contract clause should be ineffective to the extent that it converts statements about past or present facts into warranties. The result would be, for example, that a statement that a house is constructed of brick and slate would not constitute a warranty. The situation is different with regard to future (promissory) warranties because they are necessary, from the insurers' point of view, to minimise the risk and the insured person will be protected by the measures which are proposed for warranties generally.

6.3. *NCC agrees with the Law Commission's proposals for dealing with 'basis of the contract' clauses.* The Department of Trade's contrary conclusions are not thought to be convincing.

The conclusion in the following case was distinctly more favourable to the insured consumer.

Economides v Commercial Union Assurance Co plc [1997] 3 All ER 636, Court of Appeal

The plaintiff, a student, had had an index-linked household contents insurance policy with the defendant insurers since January 1988. By the time for renewal in 1991 the sum insured would have stood at some £12,800. However, in 1990 his parents had come to live with him, bringing with them a substantial amount of jewellery and other valuables. At the suggestion of his father (a retired senior police officer) the sum insured was increased by some £3,000 to £16,000. In fact this was a considerable underestimate since the contents were now worth some £40,000 of which nearly £30,000 was represented by valuables. It was a term of the policy that the maximum recoverable for any valuables was one third of the total sum insured and that the plaintiff was under a duty to disclose all known facts. The policy also contained the following declaration: 'I/We declare that the statements and particulars given above and overleaf are to the best of my/our knowledge and belief, true and complete, that the sums insured under this Plan will be maintained on an up-to-date basis and that this proposal shall form the basis of the contract between me/us and the insurers.'

In addition the renewal notice had stated that the insured should 'advise us . . . of any circumstances which may have changed since the proposal was made, so that the insurer can reassess the risk if necessary'. It added that failure to do so may mean that the policy may not operate fully or even at all.

In October 1991 the plaintiff's new flat was burgled and property worth some £31,000 was stolen. When he claimed on the policy the defendants repudiated liability, alleging both misrepresentation and non-disclosure of material facts. They contended that since at the time of the burglary the contents were valued at £40,000, the plaintiff had misrepresented both the total sum insured as £16,000 and the total value of the valuables when renewing the policy. Further or alternatively, the plaintiff had not disclosed the full cost of replacing the contents or that the valuables were worth considerably more than one-third of the actual total value. The recorder upheld those contentions. The plaintiff appealed. It was agreed that if the policy were effective the sum recoverable would be some £7,815.

Simon Brown LJ, having set out the facts of the case, continued:

Misrepresentation

. . .

What then was meant by the appellant's representation that, as at January 1991, he believed that the full contents value was £16,000? The judge below considered three possible meanings: (i) that £16,000 was in fact the full value; (ii) that the appellant honestly believed that £16,000 was the full value and had reasonable grounds for his belief; (iii) that he honestly believed that £16,000 was the full value.

The judge understood Ms Kinsler, for the respondent, to be contending for both (i) and (ii) and found in her favour on both, ie on (i), alternatively (if that went too far), on (ii). He rejected the appellant's argument in favour of (iii). Ms Kinsler told us that she never in fact put the case as high as (i) and certainly does not contend for that now. In the result, the issue on appeal is between (ii) and (iii): when making a representation such as this, is the assured stating merely that he honestly believes the accuracy of his valuation or is he going further and impliedly stating too that he has reasonable grounds for that belief? . . .

His Lordship then considered a number of authorities noted in Peter Gibson LJ's judgment (below) and continued:

Mr Bartlett submits that the approach adopted by the judge below and urged afresh by Ms Kinsler on appeal is fundamentally flawed. His starting point is s 20 of the Marine Insurance

Act 1906—one of a group of sections which it is now established apply equally to non-marine as to marine insurance (see *PCW Syndicates v PCW Reinsurers* [1996] 1 All ER 774, [1996] 1 WLR 1136). The relevant subsections of s 20 are:

'(3) A representation may be either a representation as to a matter of fact, or as to a matter of expectation or belief.

(4) A representation as to a matter of fact is true, if it be substantially correct, that is to say, if the difference between what is represented and what is actually correct would not be considered material by a prudent insurer.

(5) A representation as to a matter of expectation or belief is true if it be made in good faith
. . .'

Mr Bartlett relies in particular on sub-s (5) . . . He accepts, as inevitably he must, that the appellant had to have some basis for his statement of belief in this valuation; he could not simply make a blind guess: one cannot believe to be true that which one has not the least idea about. But, he submits, and this is the heart of the argument, the basis of belief does not have to be an objectively reasonable one. What the appellant's father told him here was a sufficient basis for his representation: he was under a duty of honesty, not a duty of care.

In my judgment, these submissions are well-founded. . . .

I would hold, therefore, that the sole obligation on the appellant when he represented to the respondent on renewal that he believed the full contents value to be £16,000 was that of honesty. That obligation the judge apparently found him to have satisfied. Certainly, given that the appellant was at the time aged 21, given that the figure for the increase in cover was put forward by his father, and given that father was a retired senior police officer, inevitably better able than the appellant himself to put a valuation on the additional contents, there would seem to me every reason to accept the appellant's honesty. . . .

Non-disclosure

The appellant formally admitted for the purpose of these proceedings below:

'1. The following were material facts: (a) The full cost of replacing all the contents of the plaintiff's premises as new ("the sum insured"); (b) whether the total value of . . . "valuables" exceeded one-third of the sum insured. 2. Those facts induced the defendant to enter into the contract on the terms agreed.'

During argument before us, however, it became apparent that what is really being said here is that the appellant was bound to disclose: (i) that the full cost of replacing the contents was substantially more than £16,000; and (ii) that the valuables were worth very considerably more than £5,333 (or, indeed, very substantially more than one-third of the actual total value of the contents).

. . .

It seems to me that the governing principle is that to be found in s 18(1) of the 1906 Act:

'Subject to the provisions of this section, the assured must disclose to the insurer, before the contract is concluded, every material circumstance which is known to the assured, and the assured is deemed to know every circumstance which, in the ordinary course of business, ought to be known by him. If the assured fails to make such disclosure, the insurer may avoid the contract.'

It is clearly established that an assured such as this appellant, effecting insurance cover as a private individual and not 'in the ordinary course of business', must disclose only material facts known to him; he is not to have ascribed to him any form of deemed or constructive knowledge.

. . .

And as was said by Fletcher Moulton LJ in *Joel v Law Union and Crown Insurance Co* [1908] 2 KB 863 at 884:

'The duty is a duty to disclose, and you cannot disclose what you do not know. The obligation to disclose, therefore, necessarily depends on the knowledge you possess.'

In short, I have not the least doubt that the sole obligation on an assured in the position of this appellant is one of honesty. Honesty, of course, requires, as Lord Mcnaghten said in the *Blackburn Low* case, that the assured does not wilfully shut his eyes to the truth. But that, sometimes called Nelsonian blindness—the deliberate putting of the telescope to the blind eye—is equivalent to knowledge, a very different thing from imputing knowledge of a fact to someone who is in truth ignorant of it.

The test, accordingly, for non-disclosure was, in my judgment, precisely the same as that for misrepresentation, that of honesty. And by the same token that the appellant was under no obligation to make further inquiries to establish reasonable grounds for his belief in the accuracy of his valuations, so too he was not required to inquire further into the facts so as to discharge his obligation to disclose all material facts known to him. Indeed, the appellant's case on non-disclosure seems to me a fortiori to his case on misrepresentation. *The Association of British Insurers' Statement of General Insurance Practice* states with regard to proposal forms: '(d) Those matters which insurers have found generally to be material will be the subject of clear questions in proposal forms.' Where, as here, material facts duly are dealt with by specific questions in the proposal form and no sustainable case of misrepresentation arises, it would be remarkable indeed if the policy could then be avoided on grounds of non-disclosure. . . .

Peter Gibson LJ . . .

The recorder never addressed the question whether the statements made by the plaintiff were true to the best of the plaintiff's knowledge and belief. Instead he considered whether the plaintiff had impliedly misrepresented that he had reasonable grounds for his belief. The recorder dismissed the submission of Mr Bartlett, for the plaintiff, that there was no representation by the plaintiff that he had reasonable grounds for his belief as 'inconsistent with commercial reality and common sense'. For the reasons given by Simon Brown LJ, all the cases relied on by the recorder and Ms Kinsler are distinguishable. It is, in my opinion, important to keep in mind in considering these cases by whom and in what circumstances the representation in question was made. For example, in *Brown v Raphael* [1958] 2 All ER 79, [1958] Ch 636 the statement of belief came from reputable solicitors in respect of a matter (the aggregable estate of the annuitant) which they would be expected to know and on which they had advised the vendor. Again in *Highlands Insurance Co v Continental Insurance Co* [1987] 1 Lloyd's Rep 109 the relevant representation was made by a professional underwriter. With such cases can be contrasted a case such as the present where the statement is made by a layman with no relevant skills. Like Simon Brown LJ, I regard s 20(5) of the Marine Insurance Act 1906 as providing the conclusive answer to this point. On its face, it applies to all representations as to matters of expectation or belief. It is with considerable diffidence and unease that I differ from Steyn J's view, albeit expressed obiter, in the *Highlands* case on this point in a field in which he has such great expertise. But the statutory test, consistent with the common law which s 20 enacted (see eg *Anderson v Pacific Fire and Marine Insurance Co* (1872) LR 7 CP 65 at 69), is one of good faith which is necessarily subjective and I find it impossible to see how consistently with s 20(5) an objective test of reasonableness can be imported by way of an implied representation. Once statute deems an honest representation as to a matter of belief to be true, I cannot see that there is scope for inquiry as to whether there were objectively reasonable grounds for that belief. Of course the absence of reasonable grounds for belief may point to the absence of good faith for that belief. But in a case such as the present where the bad faith of the plaintiff is not alleged, I can see no basis for the implication of a representation of reasonable grounds for belief.

I would add that even if I am wrong on this point and the plaintiff must be taken to have impliedly represented that he had reasonable grounds for his belief, I would hold that the representation was accurate. In my judgment, a 21-year-old student could reasonably adopt the valuation estimate of his parents who owned the chattels the subject of the estimate, particularly when his father was a senior policeman. . . .

I come next to the question of non-disclosure. The issue before the recorder turned on the extent of knowledge which must be established in order to give rise to actionable non-disclosure. The recorder found assistance from Spencer Bower Turner and Sutton *Actionable Non-Disclosure* (2nd edn, 1990) pp 56 and 75, dealing with presumptive knowledge (commonly called constructive knowledge). But the author was not considering what knowledge was necessary for the purposes of non-disclosure in an insurance contract. The recorder found that the plaintiff wilfully shut his eyes to the reality of the situation. If there was such Nelsonian blindness on the plaintiff's part, then that would be equivalent to actual knowledge and would not be constructive knowledge. But that would be tantamount to dishonesty on the part of the plaintiff in failing to disclose what he would have seen, if only he had chosen to open his eyes. The recorder does not go so far and the evidence of the plaintiff was that he genuinely considered what he said to the insurers to be true. The recorder simply says that the plaintiff failed to make inquiries. Ms Kinsler does not suggest that this was a finding of wilful and reckless failure to make inquiries. It is a finding of constructive knowledge. But here again the answer lies in the 1906 Act. As s 18(1) has been interpreted, in my view correctly, there is no need for a private individual to disclose what he does not actually know. Constructive knowledge is not relevant (see *Deutsche Ruckversicherung AG v Walbrook Insurance Co Ltd, Group Josi Re (formerly known as Group Josi Reassurance SA) v Walbrook Insurance Co Ltd* [1996] 1 All ER 791 at 807–808, [1996] 1 WLR 1152 at 1168–1169). Accordingly, in my judgment, the recorder erred in relation to non-disclosure also: there was no failure to disclose material circumstances known to the plaintiff.

For these, as well as the reasons given by Simon Brown LJ, and in acceptance of Mr Bartlett's helpful submissions, I too would allow this appeal.

Sir Iain Glidewell agreed that the appeal should be allowed.

Appeal allowed.

QUESTION

1. The form of the declaration was that the statements etc were 'to the best of my knowledge and belief, true and complete'. Would the result have been the same if the declaration had been that the statements *were* true and this was the basis of the contract?

NOTES

1. On the issue of disclosure, this decision should be compared with the reference to 'assumed knowledge' in the extract from the Law Commission Report (para 4.6.3) cited above, p 185.
2. The recommendations of the Law Commission and the views of the National Consumer Council did not lead to specific statutory reforms. However, the potential harshness of the earlier and formal legal position as it affects consumers has been mitigated in practice by a number of developments, including, of course, the *Commercial Union* case. First, statements of practice dating

back to 1977 have been strengthened through the re-issue in 1986 of revised statements of General Insurance Practice and Long Term Insurance Practice (see Forte, 'The Revised Statements of Insurance Practice' (1986) 49 MLR 754). Although these provisions do not have legal effect, they provide considerable protection in practice. For example, the problems associated with 'basis of the contract' clauses are alleviated by the following provision:

Proposal Forms

1.(a) The declaration at the foot of the proposal form should be restricted to completion according to the proposer's knowledge and belief.

(b) Neither the proposal form nor the policy shall contain any provision converting the statements as to past or present fact in the proposal form into warranties. But insurers may require specific warranties about matters which are material to the risk.

. . .

Similarly, the effect of non-disclosure and misrepresentation is mitigated by the following:

Claims

2 (a) Under the conditions regarding notification of a claim, the policyholder shall not be asked to do more than report a claim and subsequent developments as soon as reasonably possible except in the case of legal processes and claims which a third party requires the policyholder to notify within a fixed time where immediate advice may be required.

(b) An insurer will not repudiate liability to indemnify a policyholder:—

(i) on grounds of non-disclosure of a material fact which a policyholder could not reasonably be expected to have disclosed;

(ii) on grounds of misrepresentation unless it is a deliberate or negligent misrepresentation of a material fact;

(iii) on ground of a breach of warranty or condition where the circumstances of the loss are unconnected with the breach unless fraud is involved.

Paragraph 2(b) above does not apply to Marine and Aviation policies.

(c) Liability under the policy having been established and the amount payable by the insurer agreed, payment will be made without avoidable delay.

(For discussion of the above, see Hodgin in Lonbay (ed) *Enhancing the Legal Position of the European Consumer* (1996), ch 6, at pp 108–22.)

3. The second main development was the launching in March 1981 of an Insurance Ombudsman Bureau with a remit to deal with complaints by consumers as to the handling of claims. The Ombudsman must have regard, *inter alia* to general principles of good insurance practice and he has power to make awards up to £100,000 binding on members. Annual reports are issued. In *Pan Atlantic Insurance Co Ltd v Pine Top Insurance Co* [1993] 1 Lloyd's Rep 496, at p 508, Sir Donald Nicholls, VC, noted that English law is committed to an 'all or nothing' approach, and that more satisfactory results might be achieved through adopting a principle of proportionality. It is arguable that this might also be true of the not untypical situation of under-insurance as in the *Commercial Union* case. The Insurance Ombudsman is able to apply this

principle in consumer complaints. See further below, pp 425–8 and *Consumer Redress Mechanisms* (Office of Fair Trading, November 1991), paras 4.73–4.74 and Appendix 2, Table 2.
4. The third development was the establishing of the Personal Insurance Arbitration Service with a remit to resolve complaints (with the consent of the member insurance company) through arbitration.
5. Finally, the potential effect of the Unfair Terms in Consumer Contracts Regulations 1994, SI 1994/3159 is noted below, at p 388.

QUESTIONS

1. On the facts of *Dawsons Ltd v Bonnin* [1922] 2 AC 413, above, pp 190–1, would the insurer be justified in repudiating liability under para 2(b)(ii) of the Statement of General Insurance Practice if the insured had been a private individual?
2. Does para 2(b)(i) add to the protection provided through the *Commercial Union* case? If so, in what respect?

SURVEYORS, VALUERS AND OTHER PROFESSIONALS

In recent years there have been notable developments in the range of liability for professional negligence some of which may benefit consumers in the wide sense of the word. One such development is illustrated by the following case. For a text on the subject see Dugdale, Stanton and Parkinson, *Professional Negligence* (3rd edn, 1997).

Yianni v Edwin Evans & Sons (a firm) [1981] 3 All ER 592, [1982] QB 438, Queen's Bench Division

In October 1974 the then owners of an end-of-terrace house, 1 Seymour Road in North London, discovered serious defects in its foundations. Without remedying the defects they sold it to P in about April 1975. P carried out extensive, but essentially cosmetic repairs and redecoration, and then offered to resell the house to the plaintiffs for £15,000. The plaintiffs approached the Halifax Building Society for a loan of £12,000 and paid the society a survey fee of £33 for the valuation which the society was required by s 25 of the Building Societies Act 1962 to arrange to have carried out. The society instructed the defendants, a well-established firm of valuers and surveyors, to inspect and value the house. They named the plaintiffs as the purchasers, the purchase price and the loan required. The defendants inspected the house and reported to the society that it was adequate security for a loan of £12,000. The offer of an advance was duly made and the plaintiffs received a copy of the society's booklet which stated that it did not accept responsibility for the condition of the property offered as security. Borrowers were advised that the valuer's report was confidential to the society and that if they required a survey for their own information they should instruct an independent surveyor. The society also sent to the plaintiffs a notice under s 30 of the 1962 Act stating that the making of an advance would not imply that it was warranting that the purchase price was reasonable. The plaintiffs, in common with 90 per cent of applicants for mortgages to purchase lower-priced houses, accepted the society's offer without having the house surveyed independently. In January 1976 they completed the purchase and soon thereafter discovered cracks in the foundations which, it was estimated, would cost some £18,000 to repair. In subsequent proceedings the defendants admitted negligence in inspecting the house and reporting that it was adequate security for a loan of £12,000 but denied that they owed the plaintiffs a duty of care.

Park J, having stated the facts of the case and referred to the judgment of Denning LJ in *Candler v Crane, Christmas & Co* [1951] 2 KB 164, [1951] 1 All ER 426 at 433–436, CA and the decisions of the House of Lords in such cases as *Hedley Byrne & Co Ltd v Heller & Partners Ltd* [1964] AC 465, [1963] 2 All ER 575, HL and *Anns v Merton London Borough Council* [1978] AC 728, [1977] 2 All ER 492, HL continued: Accordingly, guided by the passages in the judgment of Denning LJ in *Candler's* case and by the speeches in the House of Lords cases, I conclude that, in this case, the duty of care would arise if, on the evidence, I am satisfied that the defendants knew that their valuation of 1 Seymour Road, in so far as it stated that the property provided adequate security for an advance of £12,000, would be passed on to the plaintiffs who, notwithstanding the building society's literature and the service of the notice under s 30 of the 1962 Act, in the defendants' reasonable contemplation would place reliance on its correctness in making their decision to buy the house and mortgage it to the building society. What therefore does the evidence establish?

These defendants are surveyors and valuers. It is their profession and occupation to survey and make valuations of houses and other property. They make reports about the condition of property they have surveyed. Their duty is not merely to use care in their reports, they also have a duty to use care in their work which results in their reports. On the instructions of the building society, the defendants sent a representative to 1 Seymour Road to make a survey and valuation of that property. He knew that the object of the survey was to enable the defendants, his employers, to submit a report to the building society for the use of the directors in discharging their duty under s 25 of the Act. The report, therefore, had to be directed to the value of the property and to any matter likely to affect its value. The defendants knew, therefore, that the director or other officer in the building society who considered their report would use it for the purpose of assessing the adequacy of 1 Seymour Road as security for an advance. There is no evidence that the building society had access to any other reports or information for this purpose or that the defendants believed or assumed that the building society would have any information beyond that contained in their report. Accordingly, the defendants knew that the director or other officer of the building society who dealt with the plaintiffs' application would rely on the correctness of this report in making on behalf of the Society the offer of a loan on the security of 1 Seymour Road. The defendants therefore knew that the plaintiffs would receive from the building society an offer to lend £12,000, which sum, as the defendants also knew, the plaintiffs desired to borrow. It was argued that, as the information contained in the defendants' report was confidential to the directors, the defendants could not have foreseen that the contents of their report would be passed on to the plaintiffs. But the contents of the report never were passed on. This case is not about the contents of the entire report, it is about that part of the report which said that 1 Seymour Road was suitable as security for a loan of £12,000. The defendants knew that that part would have to be passed on to the plaintiffs, since the reason for the plaintiffs' application was to obtain a loan of £12,000. Accordingly, the building society's offer of £12,000, when passed on to the plaintiffs, confirmed to them that 1 Seymour Road was sufficiently valuable to cause the building society to advance on its security 80% of the purchase price. Since that was also the building society's view the plaintiffs' belief was not unreasonable.

It was argued that there was no reasonable likelihood that the plaintiffs would rely on the fact that the defendants had made a valuation report to the building society or, alternatively, that the defendants could not reasonably have foreseen or contemplated first, that the plaintiffs would rely on the valuation in the report or, second, that they would act unreasonably in failing to obtain an independent surveyor's report for their own guidance. These submissions were founded on the fact that the defendants would know that the plaintiffs would have been provided with the building society's literature and that the building society, for its own protection, would have served with their offer the statutory notice pursuant to s 30 of the 1962 Act. Now these defendants, plainly, are in a substantial way of business in London as surveyors and valuers. The documents show that they have an address at Down Street, Mayfair, and another in Lavender Hill, London SW11. They must have on their staff some members of the Royal Institute of Chartered Surveyors. The terms of the building society's request to them to value 1 Seymour Road indicated that they had regularly carried out valuations for the Halifax, and no doubt for other building societies. Mr Hunter's evidence is that for some six years over 90% of applicants for a building society mortgage have relied on the building society's valuation, as represented by the building society's offer of an advance, as a statement that the house in question is worth at least that sum. These applicants, and in particular applicants seeking to buy houses at the lower end of the property market, do not read building society literature, or, if they do, they ignore the advice to have an independent survey and also the terms of the statutory notice. Mr Hunter's evidence was unchallenged. No witness was called to suggest that he had in any way misrepresented the beliefs, conduct and practice of the typical applicant. I think that Mr Hunter was telling me what was common knowledge in the professional world of building societies and of surveyors and valuers employed or instructed by them. I am satisfied that the defendants were fully aware of all these matters.

The defendants' representative who surveyed and valued 1 Seymour Road noted the type of dwelling house it was, its age, its price and the locality in which it was situated. It was plainly a house at the lower end of the property market. The applicant for a loan would therefore almost certainly be a person of modest means who, for one reason or another, would not be expected to obtain an independent valuation, and who would be certain to rely, as the plaintiffs in fact did, on the defendants' valuation as communicated to him in the building society's offer. I am sure that the defendants knew that their valuation would be passed on to the plaintiffs and that the defendants knew that the plaintiffs would rely on it when they decided to accept the building society's offer.

For these reasons I have come to the conclusion that the defendants owed a duty of care to the plaintiffs because, to use the words of Lord Wilberforce in *Anns v London Borough of Merton*, there was a sufficient relationship of proximity such that in the reasonable contemplation of the defendants carelessness on their part might be likely to cause damage to the plaintiffs.

I turn now to consider whether there are any considerations which ought to negative or to reduce or limit the scope of the duty or the class of person to whom it is owed. Counsel for the defendants submitted that for a number of reasons of policy the plaintiffs should have no remedy against the defendants. First he said a decision in favour of the plaintiffs would encourage applicants for a mortgage to have no independent survey of the house they wished to buy. I can see nothing objectionable in a practice which would result in a house being surveyed once by one surveyor. In my view, the Abbey National, since September 1980, have adopted a sensible procedure for dealing with the survey problem, if it is a problem. Mr Hunter said that as a matter of courtesy the Abbey National now disclose their valuation report to applicants. He also said: 'We felt that we had information which had been obtained by qualified and experienced people and it was of benefit to give that information to the applicant.' In addition, the Abbey National are about to introduce a report on condition and valuation so that, as Mr Hunter put it, the applicant has the choice of either the standard building society mortgage valuation report or the report on condition and valuation which covers the popular conception of structural survey, market valuation and mortgage valuation.

Counsel also submitted that if the defendants were held liable to the plaintiffs no professional man would be able to limit his liability to a third party, even if he could do so to his own client. He would be at the mercy of a client who might pass on his report to a third party and, as defects in the property he had surveyed might not manifest themselves for many years, he would be likely to remain under a liability for those defects he ought to have detected for a very long period, and at the end of the period, for an unlimited amount by way of damages. In my view, the only person to whom the surveyor is liable is the party named in the building society's 'Instructions to Valuer' addressed to him. That party, as well as the building society, has to be regarded as his client. That does not seem to me to be unreasonable, since, to his knowledge, his fee for the valuation is paid by that party to the building society which hands it over to him. On this submission, it can also be said that the surveyor's report is concerned with the valuation of a dwelling house, the condition of which is important only in so far as it affects its value at that time. It is common knowledge that in the ordinary way, the market value of a dwelling house is not static. Consequently, a valuation made at one time for the purpose of assessing its suitability as security for a loan would be of limited use. . . .

. . . Finally counsel said that the plaintiffs should be held guilty of contributory negligence because they failed to have an independent survey, made no inquiries with the object of discovering what had been done to the house before they decided to buy it, failed to read the literature provided by the building society and generally took no steps to discover the true condition of the house. It is true that the plaintiffs failed in all these respects, but that failure was due to the fact that they relied on the defendants to make a competent valuation of the house. I have been given no reason why they were unwise to do so. I have earlier read the paragraph under the heading 'Valuation' in the building society's handbook which Mr Yianni did not read. No doubt if the paragraph had been in stronger terms, and had included a warning that it would be dangerous to rely on the valuer's report, then I think that the plaintiffs might well have been held to be negligent. But, in my judgment, on the evidence the allegation of contributory negligence fails.

In my judgment for these reasons the defendants are liable to pay damages to the plaintiffs for the grievous loss they have suffered by the defendants' negligence.

Judgment for the plaintiffs.

NOTES

1. This decision was approved by the House of Lords in *Smith v Eric S Bush* and *Harris v Wyre Forest District Council* [1990] 1 AC 831, [1989] 2 All ER 514. Lord Griffiths added a caveat which was generally concurred in by other members of the House, saying (at pp 859–860 and 532, respectively):

> It must, however, be remembered that this is a decision in respect of a dwelling house of modest value in which it is widely recognised by surveyors that purchasers are in fact relying on their care and skill. It will obviously be of general application in broadly similar circumstances. But I expressly reserve my position in respect of valuations of quite different types of property for mortgage purposes, such as industrial property, large blocks of flats or very expensive houses. In such cases it may well be that the general expectation of the behaviour of the purchaser is quite different. With very large sums of money at stake

prudence would seem to demand that the purchaser obtain his own structural survey to guide him in his purchase and, in such circumstances with very much larger sums of money at stake, it may be reasonable for the surveyors valuing on behalf of those who are providing the finance either to exclude or limit their liability to the purchaser.

The issue of excluding or limiting liability is noted further in ch 7, at pp 348–9, especially.

2. For the position with respect to limitation periods where the defect becomes apparent only after a length delay, see the Limitation Act 1980, s 14A, as inserted by the Latent Damage Act 1986, s 1. Note the over-riding 15 year 'long-stop' provision running from the date of the negligent conduct which caused the damage.

3. For a case involving liability following treatment for dry rot, see *Ackerman v Protim Services* [1988] 2 EGLR 259 (CA).

QUESTIONS

1. If failure to discover the need for re-building and under-pinning the plaintiffs' house had caused damage to the adjoining terrace house should the plaintiffs' neighbour have been entitled to recover against the defendant surveyors?

2. Should one's attitude to the result of such cases differ according to whether the hapless occupier has an operative first-party property insurance covering the results of subsidence?

CHAPTER 5
Product liability

INTRODUCTION

Strict contractual liability for breach of the implied terms as to quality in contracts for the sale of goods has long been a feature of English law. So in *Daniels and Daniels v R White & Sons Ltd and Tarbard* [1938] All ER 258, above, p 38, the retail vendor of a bottle of lemonade contaminated by carbolic acid during its bottling process was liable although she was 'perfectly innocent'; see also above, pp 118–19. However, such strict liability extends only to contracting parties (like Mr Daniels in the above case), the privity of contract limitation preventing third parties (like Mrs Daniels) from benefiting from the implied terms: see above, p 38 et seq. For many years this strict contractual liability was paralleled by a supposed rule of non-liability in tort: see *Winterbottom v Wright* (1842) 10 M & W 109. It was only in 1932 in the leading case of *Donoghue v Stevenson* [1932] AC 562, HL that it was established authoritatively in the House of Lords that a manufacturer is prima facie liable on proof of negligence when a defect in his goods causes personal injury or property damage to a consumer. The background of the case was of shock and severe gastro-enteritis allegedly suffered as a result of drinking a bottle of ginger beer contaminated by the remnants of a decomposed snail and Lord Atkin said at p 599:

> My Lords, if your Lordships accept the view that this pleading discloses a relevant cause of action you will be affirming the proposition that by Scots and English law alike a manufacturer of products, which he sells in such a form as to show that he intends them to reach the ultimate consumer in the form in which they left him with no reasonable possibility of intermediate examination, and with the knowledge that the absence of reasonable care in the preparation or putting up of the products will result in an injury to the consumer's life or property, owes a duty to the consumer to take that reasonable care.
>
> It is a proposition which I venture to say no one in Scotland or England who was not a lawyer would for one moment doubt. It will be an advantage to make it clear that the law in this matter, as in most others, is in accordance with sound common sense.

In fact two fellow-members of the House of Lords *did* doubt the 'proposition' and the duty of care was established on the basis of a bare three to two majority. In recent years discussion has centred on a move from a system which requires proof of negligence to a system of strict liability now to be found in Part I of the

Consumer Protection Act 1987. However, there are circumstances in which the law of negligence remains important even in the case of claims by consumers. The point is discussed below, at pp 204–15. The following cases are of interest as indicating the scope of liability under a negligence-based system. In reading them it is helpful to consider (i) the various respects in which it was alleged that the product was defective and (ii) the standard of care required.

LIABILITY IN NEGLIGENCE

Hill v James Crowe (Cases) Ltd [1978] 1 All ER 812, Queen's Bench Division

The facts are set out in the judgment:

Mackenna J read the following judgment. On 25 January 1973 the plaintiff, Mr Hill, was working as a lorry driver employed by A A Kent Ltd. His work took him that day to a warehouse owned by Newbold Shipping Services at Silvertown in the East End of London, where he had to load on to his lorry a number of packed wooden cases and also cartons containing television sets. A fork-lift truck, operated by one of Newbold's men, lifted the cases on to the floor of the lorry, where Mr Hill moved them into a suitable position. The cases covered the floor of the lorry, which was then ready to receive the cartons which would also be brought to him by the truck. He was standing on one of the cases waiting for the first load of cartons when he fell to the ground, injuring his ankle and, more seriously, his right hand.

He brings this action against James Crowe (Cases) Ltd, whom I shall call 'Crowe', claiming that his accident was caused by their negligence. Crowe are in business as packers of goods for shipment overseas, and in the course of this business they manufacture wooden cases. They had made at least one of the cases which had been loaded on to Mr Hill's lorry to carry a quantity of household goods from London to Lagos in West Africa for delivery to a Miss Ronke Allison. Mr Hill alleges that just before he fell he had been standing on the end of this case when some of the boards stove in, causing him to lose his balance and fall. He says that the case was badly nailed. The fact of his accident, he argues, by itself proves bad manufacture, and if it does not he says that he has proved by the testimony of a credible witness that not enough nails were used to fasten the boards. Crowe, he says, owed a duty to those who were likely to come in contact with the case in transit to make it strong enough to withstand the foreseeable hazards of its journey; and one of these was the likelihood of persons standing on it in the course of loading who might be injured if the boards caved in. They had neglected this duty, and their negligence was the cause of this accident for which they are liable in damages.

On liability there are four issues (1) Did Mr Hill fall because the boards of the packing case he was standing on caved in? If so, (2) was the packing case badly made? If so, (3) ought the maker to have foreseen that if it were badly made persons in Mr Hill's position might suffer injury in some such way as Mr Hill was injured and to have taken care to make it properly, so that their failure to do so was in law negligence? If so, (4) had the case on which Mr Hill was standing been made by Crowe? I have no hesitation in answering all these questions in Mr Hill's favour.

. . .

In spite of Mr Crowe's evidence, I find that the accident happened while the plaintiff was standing on the packing case which Crowe had made; that it was caused by the end caving in;

and that it caved in because it had been very badly nailed. If the case can be brought within the rule in *Donoghue v Stevenson*[1] liability is established.

. . .

Counsel for Crowe relied on *Daniels and Daniels v R White & Sons Ltd and Tarbard*.[2] The plaintiff in that case had bought at a public house a sealed bottle of lemonade made by the defendant manufacturers and sold by them to the public house. The bottle contained, in addition to the lemonade, a quantity of carbolic acid which it was contended had caused injury to the plaintiff, who sued the manufacturers. His action failed. The manufacturers satisfied Lewis J, the trial judge, that they had a good system of work in their factory and provided adequate supervision. He said:[3]

'I am quite satisfied, however, on the evidence before me, that the work of this factory is carried on under proper supervision, and, therefore, that there has been no failure of duty owed by the defendant company to the plaintiffs.'

With respect, I do not think that this was a sufficient reason for dismissing the claim. The manufacturer's liability in negligence did not depend on proof that he had either a bad system of work or that his supervision was inadequate. He might also be vicariously liable for the negligence of his workmen in the course of their employment. If the plaintiff's injuries were a reasonably foreseeable consequence of such negligence, the manufacturer's liability would be established under *Donoghue v Stevenson*.[1] *Daniels and Daniels v R White & Sons Ltd and Tarbard*[2] has been criticised, I think justly, in *Charlesworth on Negligence*[4] and I do not propose to follow it.

I hold Crowe liable in negligence. I find that there was no contributory negligence on Mr Hill's part, and I turn to the question of damages.

[His Lordship then considered the extent of the plaintiff's injuries and the medical evidence relating thereto and assessed total damages in the sum of £8,298.81.]

Judgment for the plaintiff.

[1] [1932] AC 562, [1932] All ER Rep 1.
[2] [1938] 4 All ER 258.
[3] [1938] 4 All ER 258 at 263.
[4] 5th edn (1971), p 398.

QUESTIONS

Obviously wooden packing cases, unlike ladders, are not built for people to stand on. Would the decision have been different if the case had been nailed together correctly but was still insufficiently strong to carry the lorry driver's weight?

Suppose it had been marked 'Danger. Do not stand on this case'. Would the plaintiff have recovered then?

It is clear from this decision that negligence may be found in the fault of an individual employee as well as in the manufacturer's quality control system. The Privy Council had made the same point in *Grant v Australian Knitting Mill Ltd* [1936] AC 85 where the plaintiff had contracted dermatitis as a result, it was alleged, of wearing the defendants' undergarments. Distinguishing between the position of the retail seller and the manufacturers Lord Wright said at pp 100–1:

The retailers, accordingly, in their Lordships' judgment are liable in contract: so far as they are concerned, no question of negligence is relevant to the liability in contract. But when the position of the manufacturers is considered, different questions arise: there is no privity of contract between the appellant and the manufacturers: between them the liability, if any, must be in tort, and the gist of the cause of action is negligence. The facts set out in the foregoing show, in their Lordships' judgment, negligence in manufacture. According to the evidence, the method of manufacture was correct: the danger of excess sulphites being left was recognised and was guarded against: the process was intended to be fool proof. If excess sulphites were left in the garment, that could only be because some one was at fault. The appellant is not required to lay his finger on the exact person in all the chain who was responsible, or to specify what he did wrong. Negligence is found as a matter of inference from the existence of the defects taken in connection with all the known circumstances: even if the manufacturers could by apt evidence have rebutted that inference they have not done so.

NOTE

For an application of this principle, see *Carroll v Fearon*, *The Times*, 26 January 1998 (Dunlop liable for death and injury when radial tyre disintegrated in use).

QUESTION

If circumstances are such that the defects must have been present from the time the product left the manufacturer's control are there any advantages in establishing the excellence of a quality control system?

NOTE

Hill v James Crowe (Cases) Ltd involved a relatively simple product. There may be more difficulty in establishing liability in negligence where more complex products are concerned: see, eg, *Evans v Triplex Safety Glass Co Ltd* [1936] 1 All ER 283 (Porter J), where the claim against the defendant windscreen manufacturer failed. It seems that English law does not hold manufacturers of finished or end products liable for negligence on the part of manufacturers of components incorporated into their products: see, by way of analogy, *Taylor v Rover Co Ltd* [1966] 2 All ER 181, [1966] 1 WLR 1491, and Miller and Lovell, *Product Liability* (1977), at pp 199–207.

Vacwell Engineering Co Ltd v B.D.H. Chemicals Ltd (formerly British Drug Houses Ltd) [1969] 3 All ER 1681, [1971] 1 QB 88, Queen's Bench Division

The defendants manufactured a chemical, boron tribromide, which they marketed for industrial use in glass ampoules bearing a warning label 'harmful vapour'. Following discussion with the defendants, the plaintiffs used the chemical in their business of manufacturing transistor materials. In order to prepare the chemical the labels were washed off the ampoules in sinks containing water and a detergent. In April 1966 a visiting Russian physicist was engaged in this task when there was a violent explosion resulting in his death and in extensive damage to the plaintiffs' premises. In all probability one of the ampoules had been dropped into the sink where it had shattered, releasing the chemical into the water. The ensuing reaction had broken the glass of the other ampoules, causing a major explosion. At the time the explosive properties of boron tribromide on contact with water were unknown to the defendants; neither were they referred to in a standard work on the industrial hazards of chemicals, nor in three other modern works which the defendants had apparently consulted. Nonetheless the dangers had been detailed in scientific literature dating from 1878. The present proceedings were based on both contract and tort.

Rees J, having held that the defendants, B.D.H., were liable in contract for breach of an implied condition of fitness for purpose (above, p 95 et seq) continued: The duty which Vacwell allege rested on B.D.H. was to take reasonable care to ascertain major industrial hazards of chemicals marketed by them and to give warning of such hazards to their customers. It was not argued before me that there was an absolute duty on B.D.H. to give warning of industrial hazards of dangerous chemicals, whether they could have discovered them by the exercise of reasonable care or not. I find that the duty to take reasonable care as stated above is the duty which rested on B.D.H. in the circumstances of this case. I have already reviewed the evidence in relation to this aspect of the matter and I need not repeat it. I am satisfied that B.D.H. failed to comply with their duty in two respects: first, they failed to provide and maintain a system for carrying out an adequate research into scientific literature to ascertain known hazards; secondly, by Mr Hill and Dr Muir they failed to carry out an adequate research into the scientific literature available to them in order to discover the industrial hazards of a new, or little-known, chemical. If that duty had been complied with, I have no doubt that the explosion hazard noted by Gautier and others would have come to light and a suitable warning been given, which would have prevented Vacwell dealing with the ampoules of boron tribromide as they did. The greater part of the observations which I have made earlier in this judgment in relation to causation and remoteness of damage apply in the present context also. But in tort, foreseeability of damage is the paramount test.

. . .

Here, it was a foreseeable consequence of the supply of boron tribromide without warning—and a fortiori with an irrelevant warning about harmful vapour—that, in the ordinary course of industrial user, it could come into contact with water and cause a violent reaction and possibly an explosion. It would also be foreseeable that some damage to property would, or might, result. In my judgment, the explosion and the type of damage being foreseeable, it matters not in the law that the magnitude of the former and the extent of the latter were not.

Finally, I turn to the question of the contributory negligence of Vacwell. The conduct of Vacwell must be looked at in the context that they knew of the risks arising from the harmful fumes caused on contact between boron tribromide and air or water. They also knew that there was some reaction between boron tribromide and water. Consequently, they dealt with the chemical on the footing that some minor harm might arise from inhaling the vapour or from the splashing of the chemical; they did not know, and it is not now alleged that they ought to have known, of the uniquely dangerous explosion hazard. Further, one must also take into account that the positive warning given to them by B.D.H. itself supported a reasonable inference that there was no other major hazard likely to arise in the ordinary course of industrial process. It is alleged against Vacwell that, even if it were justifiable to immerse one or a few ampoules of boron tribromide in water, it was obviously dangerous to immerse between 40 and 100 ampoules in each of two adjacent sinks. It is further alleged that there was carelessness on the part of the Russian scientist in using detergent which made the ampoules slippery and in allowing one or more of the ampoules to fall from his hand into the sink. I have considered these allegations with great care.

Having regard to all the circumstances and to the evidence which I accept, I do not find it negligent on the part of Vacwell to have decided to place 200 ampoules in water in two adjacent sinks. The evidence does not justify a finding that they ought to have known that there was a risk by so doing that the breaking of one or two ampoules would cause anything but the minimum harm for which they had adequate protection available in the form of gas-masks; nor that the breaking of one or two ampoules could cause the remainder to disintegrate. I have hesitated whether a finding of negligence should be made against the Russian scientist on the footing that, if he dropped an ampoule, it necessarily means that he was careless. There is no evidence as to precisely what happened, and in all the circumstances I am not prepared to hold that he was negligent. Even if such a finding had been justified by the evidence, in the context of this case the blame to be apportioned in respect of this negligence is so minimal as perhaps to fall into that category of which the law would refuse to take account.

Judgment for Vacwell.

NOTE

Subsequently the Court of Appeal approved the terms of a settlement on the basis that Rees J had been correct in adopting this approach to the question of remoteness of damage in tort. However, a reduction of 20% in the damages to be assessed by an Official Referee was agreed to take account of the possibility of contributory negligence: see [1971] 1 QB 88, pp 111–12.

On the general question of failure to give adequate warnings and directions for use see Miller and Lovell, op cit, ch 12; Macleod, 'Instructions as to the Use of Consumer Goods' (1981) 97 LQR 550. For the position under the Consumer Protection Act 1987, see below, pp 240–4.

QUESTION

What are the principal factors of which account should be taken in deciding whether warnings or directions for use are (i) necessary, (ii) sufficient?

Walton and Walton v British Leyland UK Ltd (1978) (unreported), Judgment of 12 July, Queen's Bench Division

The Honourable Mr Justice Willis. The facts and tragic results of the accident which gave rise to this claim are not in dispute and can be shortly stated. Mr and Mrs Victor Walton, the Plaintiffs, were on holiday in this country from Australia. During the evening of 22 April 1976 they were travelling northwards on the M1 motorway as passengers in an Austin Allegro motor car, owned and driven by the first Plaintiff's brother, Mr Albert Walton. At a point near Newport Pagnell when the car was travelling at 50–60 mph the *rear nearside wheel* came off, the driver lost control and the vehicle collided with the central crash barrier. Both plaintiffs are elderly, in their sixties. Miraculously the first plaintiff, who is a handicapped person, escaped with minor injuries; his wife was thrown from the car; she suffered catastrophic injuries which it is not necessary to detail, and has been left a quadriplegic.

Although both the first and second defendants saw fit in their pleadings to allege negligence on the part of the driver, Albert Walton, those allegations were properly withdrawn by Counsel on the first day of the trial: during the course of the case by the first defendant an agreement inter partes was announced that both plaintiffs are entitled to recover their damages in full—

the sums to be assessed later—subject to a reservation immaterial to these proceedings, for the negligence of one or more or all the defendants. From that point my sole task has been to decide whether one of the three defendants is solely to blame or, if more than one, to apportion the degrees of negligence. The Allegro, as a new range to replace the Austin 1300, had been introduced in May 1973. The car in question was manufactured by Leylands and left their works in February 1974. Its intermediate history is unrecorded by the evidence, save that it must be assumed to have remained in the possession and under the control of a franchise holder or authorised Leyland dealer until it was sold as a new car by Duttons to Mr Walton, its first owner, on 1 November 1974.

It is now necessary to go back somewhat in the history of the Allegro. A significant alteration in its design compared with eg the Maxi and 1300 range was the introduction of tapered roller bearings in the rear hub assembly which had to be adjusted in a different way from earlier models fitted with roller bearings. The Marina was designed in a similar way. This was a bearing designed by the well-known firm of Timken, and it is fitted to a great many makes of car world wide; it is a tried method and no criticism is sought to be made of Leylands for using it in the Marina and Allegro. Its proper adjustment involves what is technically described as 'end float', to produce a certain amount of play in the wheel which is apparent upon its rotation and rocking after it has been properly adjusted.

According to the documents I have seen, the first rumblings that all was not well with the rear hub assembly of the Allegro had been heard by Leylands by at least October 1973, and probably earlier. On the 17th of that month Leylands circulated a 'Product Bulletin' to the Service Managers of (inter alios) all their accredited dealers, with a request to bring the information therein to all workshop personnel. This drew attention to the change in the method of adjusting the new rear hub bearing and emphasised the importance of correct 'end float; and the risk of bearings seizing up if enough 'end float' was not provided.

The information contained in this Bulletin, as in certain later ones was, according to a note on the document, to be treated as confidential by the recipients. It seems to have been a very ineffective method of averting the gathering storm.

It does not appear that any similar Bulletins on this topic were issued until 9 August 1974, when a diagrammatic illustration of the importance of the difference between torque tightening (for ball bearings) and end float (for roller bearings) was issued, with a similar distribution. This was followed by a Bulletin of 25 September 1974 to all dealers (and some others whom it is immaterial to try to identify) in which the recipients were told that all cars produced since a certain chassis number (in fact about 16 September 1974) incorporated a larger retaining washer in the rear hub assembly 'to improve bearing security', and urging the importance of fitting such washers 'when servicing the rear hub bearings or brakes of earlier vehicles'. I shall have to return to this document together with a letter from Leylands, dated 24 October, which followed it addressed to 'All distributors and Retail Dealers (Cars) UK for the attention of their Managing Directors and Service Managers'. In the background Leylands realised they had a very serious problem on their hands with, and in the context of the problem, only with the Allegro. Speaking with the experience of an engineer with Leylands and its various predecessors since 1940, Mr de Lassalle, the only Company witness, could recall nothing similar in scope and seriousness. By the 12 December 1973 some diagnosis of the problem had been made, and on that day a 'major' modification to the Allegro was authorised, namely a new special washer 'to provide an additional bearing retention safety feature'.

The alarming story of what was happening to Allegros in this country and abroad can be gleaned in part from Leyland's 'Product Problem Progress Card'. The 'problem' was identified as 'Rear wheel bearing failure—Wheel Adrift'; it runs from an entry on 17 December 1973, with many entries month by month through 1974 as the evidence accumulated until its conclusion in early March 1975.

I only propose to select entries to illustrate the scale of the problem as it was presented to Leylands.

In the month to 22 August not less than 10 cases of bearing failures, some with wheels adrift, had been reported from the continent.

By 5 September a total of 50 cases of failure had been reported to Leylands.

By 26 October no less than '100 cases of wheel adrift to date' are recorded as having been reported, ie 50 more in seven weeks.

In January 1975, three further failures were reported 'thought to be due to corrosion'. A further case from this cause is entered on 7 February.

Leylands were naturally anxious to identify, if they could, the cause of so many bearing failures, many involving wheels coming off, or 'adrift', if there is any sensible difference. It could discover none. Lives were plainly at risk, but so were sales, and a solution or at least a palliative had to be found urgently. It is clear from the documents and the evidence of Mr de Lassalle that early on in Leyland's investigation the expert consensus was to put the blame for the bearing failure on mechanics, careless or unfamiliar with the new technique of 'end float' adjustment, and so producing overtightening. This in turn would lead to overheating, then to bearing collapse, and in the worst cases to wheels coming off. The design was satisfactory, there was little evidence of corrosion being the cause, proper adjustment and greasing of the bearing was accepted as having been correctly done at the factory, and so the conclusion was reached that the fault lay with mechanics when working on the brakes or other parts of the rear hub assembly, and particularly at 12,000 miles service when the brakes had to be attended to. This conclusion appears to leave quite unexplained why similar problems did not appear to affect Marinas which had made their debut a little earlier, and were fitted with similar roller bearings. Mr Barber, the Deputy Chairman, at least, was writing urgently on 10 September 1974 about a serious Allegro accident in Italy a letter addressed to senior officials saying (inter alia) 'I am still not satisfied with the solution to the loss of rear wheels on the Allegro. The larger washer will certainly stop the wheels coming off in some cases but there has been at least one example of the hub itself fracturing and the larger washer obviously cannot help when that happens. To my untutored eye it looks as if the bearing is not up to the job. Will you please have this investigated.'

The reference to the larger washer is explained by the tests which had been carried out during the summer. These assumed the cause of failure basically to be due to negligent mechanics, and involved the simulation of such negligence by deliberately overtightening and testing to failure. The tests were not designed, therefore, to diagnose the cause of bearing failure but to try to find a palliative to avert the worse results should bearing failure occur. The proposal finally adopted to remedy the assumed basic cause was a limited education programme directed to mechanics working in distributors' garages.

Meantime the tests had satisfied most of Leyland's experts (but not Mr de Lassalle) that the worst potential and possibly fatal consequences of roller bearing failure could be mitigated by incorporating a larger diameter washer. With the above exception, all the experts before me agreed that the larger washer, while not preventing hub bearing failure, would prevent the wheel coming off and give a driver sufficient warning to enable him with luck to control or regain control of his car and so avoid the sort of disaster which befell the Plaintiffs. This was the Test conclusion expressed on 2 October 1974. 'The (larger) washer is effective in preventing the wheel from coming adrift when bearing failure occurs.' The decision to incorporate the larger washer had been effective on Allegros since 16 September: the Princess model was modified to provide this ab inito, and the Allegro dealers had been alerted.

It is, however, necessary to advert to the letter of 16 September 1974 from Mr Griffin, the Chief Engineer, advising Mr Perry and Mr King how to reply to Mr Barber's memorandum referred to above:

'Re Hubs and Bearings

The design was introduced to satisfy performance demands at lower cost, and it is true to state that provided design requirements are adhered to no problem would be experienced. Unfortunately the design is not idiot proof and will therefore continuously involve risk. The risk becomes greater as vehicles become older and evermore carelessly maintained. *Had we incorporated the large washer from the commencement the risk would have been tolerable . . .* Engineering have considered the possibility of recall action but do not favour it owing to the fact that it would *damage the product*, and historically the response is too low to guarantee fixing the problem and thereby remove our liability.'

'Damage the product' is agreed to be a euphemism for 'be bad for sales'

The extent to which the public at large was given any inkling of the true state of affairs was a television programme on 14 October 1974 having reference to a single case of a wheel 'becoming detached', and a Press release next day which read

'We have had a small number of rear wheel bearing failures reported and the evidence shows that failure can be brought about by corrosion arising from water ingress and/or maladjustment during vehicle servicing. Action has already been taken to correct any irregularities in new vehicle production and any cases arising in service are being dealt with as necessary.'

This form of commercial camouflage of the true state of affairs was no doubt thought to be justified in the circumstances.

Meantime on 17 October 1974 'Engineering and Service' were recommending that a recall campaign at a cost of £300,000 was not justified, that an intensive education campaign to 'franchise outlets' should be mounted and that authority should be given for fitting the larger washer when attention was being given to the rear hub or rear brake servicing. 'This should protect the customer against subsequent malpractice.'

I have thought it right to set out as briefly as I can, from such documents as I have seen, which are plainly incomplete, what information was available to Leylands about the appalling record of 'wheels adrift' on the Allegro, the problem as they saw it and the steps they took to try to remedy or palliate it, and considerations which seem to have influenced the course they took. I have done so because all these events occurred prior to 1 November 1974 when Mr Walton bought his car. I now return to that car. It had not been fitted with the recommended washers before sale.

Mr Walton is a meticulous owner: he was, up to the purchase of the Allegro in question a loyal customer of Leyland products. That he is no longer need occasion no surprise. He had owned a succession of Austin and other Leyland models. Apart from the dealer services, his cars have been serviced over the past 30 years, to his complete satisfaction, by the Third Defendants—Blue House—and still are. The drivers' handbook was in the car at all material times. The Allegro he bought was a thoroughly bad car: it was in and out of Duttons throughout 1975 for various defects to be remedied and parts replaced under warranty: by way of example only, the clutch had to be replaced on no less than four occasions. Mr Walton was so dissatisfied with it that he tried in effect to get the year's warranty extended beyond 1975; Leylands authorised an examination by Duttons who reported only minor defects on 24 November 1975. The first trouble connected with the ultimate disaster occurred in January 1975 when Mr Walton noticed a noise in the *rear offside wheel* and took the car to Duttons. I am asked to infer and Duttons admit that on that occasion they fitted the larger washer when they replaced the bearing on the rear offside wheel only. The case against them proceeds on that basis. The mileage was 1,614.

The 6,000 miles service was carried out by Blue House on 6 June 1975 at a mileage of 5,014, and the 12,000 mile service on 9 March 1976 at a mileage of 11,906. At that service the brakes were attended to, the bearings adjusted on each side, and the wheels replaced. When the accident occurred without any warning on 22 April 1976 the mileage was 13,335, so that a distance of some 1,400 miles had been covered since the service, this includes five runs of about 150 miles each. I pass over for the moment the condition of the rear assembly when it was examined after the accident, in order to complete the sorry history of this car. It was repaired at a Bedford Garage of a Leyland agent on a special Allegro jig and was collected by Mr Walton in July 1976 and driven back to Washington, a distance of about 200 miles. The next day he heard a grinding noise in the *rear offside wheel*. He was taking no chances and sent for a low loader from Blue House. On examination the outer bearing was found to have collapsed but the larger washer was there and the wheel had not come off.

The car was examined by an experienced police vehicle examiner about an hour after the accident. The outer bearing had collapsed and the inner cone had been welded by excessive heat onto the stub axle. His view was that the basic cause of the bearing collapse was overtightening of the retaining nut exacerbated by lack of grease, although the destruction was such that there was nothing to point one way or another to overtightening or lack of grease by looking at the parts themselves. He agreed with other experts that there are other, though less likely, explanations of bearing collapse. He found nothing to indicate that the rear offside wheel, which was undamaged, had been overtightened.

The case against Duttons now is that they should have fitted the larger diameter washer to both hubs when the car was brought to them in January 1975 to attend to Mr Walton's complaint about the noise in the rear offside wheel . . .

His Lordship considered the evidence on this point and concluded that 'Duttons were blameless in this matter'. He then considered the suggestion that Blue House Garage had overtightened the retaining nut, so causing the bearing to collapse, and continued:

It is no more than speculation in favour of one theory where other possibilities cannot be excluded, and I decline to hold that it was overtightening which caused the bearing to collapse.

What then of Leyland's responsibility in the matter? In my judgment it is total. It is not being wise after the event to state that had the larger washer been fitted to Mr Walton's car the accident would, in all probability, not have happened. Over a period of about a year, until October 1974, Leylands were faced with mounting and horrifying evidence of Allegro wheels coming adrift. Any of the cases reported to them could have had fatal results for the occupants of the cars concerned and other road users. They assumed, rightly or wrongly, that apart from isolated cases of corrosion, human error on the part of the mechanics was the cause of the bearing failures. The Deputy Chairman was gravely disturbed; the view of the Chief Engineer by 16 September 1974 was that the design, not being 'idiot proof', would continuously involve risk, a risk which he thought would have been tolerable had the larger washer been fitted from the start.

From that date, therefore, if not before, the Engineering Section considered the risk to those who were driving Allegros which had not been fitted with the larger washers on both rear hub assemblies of their wheels coming adrift to be 'intolerable'. What, in such circumstances, is the standard of care towards users of their products to be expected of a manufacturer in the position of Leylands? They were entirely satisfied that the large washer provided a safety factor which could confidently be expected, following stringent tests, to prevent a wheel coming adrift if the bearing failed. All cars manufactured after 16 September 1974 were fitted with the approved safety device. Some steps, in my view totally inadequate, were taken to give instructions on the lines of what Dutton Forshaw were recommended to do but only to dealers. Outside this limited safety net were left, in ignorance of the risk to which Leylands knew they were subject, a very large number of Allegro owners, including Mr Walton and his passengers. In my view, the duty of care owed by Leylands to the public was to make a clean breast of the problem and recall all cars which they could in order that the safety washers could be fitted. I accept, of course, that manufacturers have to steer a course between alarming the public unnecessarily and so damaging the reputation of their products, and observing their duty of care towards those whom they are in a position to protect from dangers of which they and they alone are aware. The duty seems to me to be the higher when they can palliate the worst effects of a failure which, if Leyland's view is right, they could never decisively guard against. They knew the full facts; they saw to it that no-one else did. They seriously considered recall and made an estimate of the cost at a figure which seems to me to have been in no way out of proportion to the risks involved. It was decided not to follow this course for commercial reasons. I think this involved a failure to observe their duty to care for the safety of the many who were bound to remain at risk, irrespective of the recommendations made to Leyland dealers and to them alone.

If I am wrong in equating the duty to take reasonable care in the circumstances of this case with the obligation to have recalled cars for fitting of safety washers, and so have put it too high, it was in my view at least their duty to ensure that all cars still in stock and unsold by the time the washer palliative was proven were fitted with this safety feature before sale. It is sufficient for Mr Walton's purposes that the duty is put no higher than that. This would have saved Mr Walton and his passengers and, in my judgment, Leylands were negligent in having failed to do so.

NOTE

For further references to the question of product recall and liability for economic loss, see below, pp 215–22.

QUESTION

If manufacturers are to be subject to the potentially onerous requirement of recalling dangerously defective products would it be in point to enquire whether they had been negligent in failing to discover the dangers when marketing the products?

THE POSITION OF RETAILERS

In most cases the liability of retailers will be in contract and for breach of implied terms as to quality and fitness for purpose of the Sale of Goods Act, 1979: see above, pp 95–113. Occasionally, there may be liability also under the strict liability provisions of the Consumer Protection Act, 1987: see below, pp 229–55. The following case is concerned with a retailer's potential liability in negligence.

Fisher v Harrods Ltd [1966] Lloyd's Rep 500, Queen's Bench Division

The defendants, the renowned London store, had sold a jewellery cleaning fluid, Couronne, which contained isopropyl alcohol and ammonium oleate and which was purchased by a third party for the use of the plaintiff. The fluid was supplied in a plastic bottle with a plastic bung and a screw top. As the plaintiff was squeezing the bottle the bung shot out and some fluid splashed into and damaged her eye. Couronne has been manufactured by a company which had few assets and which was uninsured. The action was brought in negligence.

McNair J, having referred to the facts of the case and the plaintiff's evidence, continued: In addition to the evidence of the plaintiff herself as to the ejection of the fluid from the container in the quantity she described, I had the evidence of a number of ladies who had had similar but not identical experiences. Lady Carrington purchased a bottle of Couronne from the defendants in the first half of September, 1963, but had no occasion to use it until November, 1963, when she was minded to clean her jewellery. It had no sticky label on it, but, after unscrewing the red cap, she assumed that there must be a hole in the plug though it was invisible to the eye. She held it over a small bowl, and as nothing came out she shook it twice slowly over the bowl, then gave it a gentle pressure and, as soon as she did this, the bung flew out and all the liquid came out over a polished table; the French polish on the table was quite burnt away. The bung was found quite a distance away and the bottle was destroyed.

. . .

I now turn to the question of the defendants' liability. First as to the facts in relation to the putting of Couronne on the market. The defendants first came into contact with Couronne when, in May, 1962, Mr Nash, the experienced buyer for the jewellery department, was approached by Mr Meyer (whom he had never met before) with a proposal that the defendants might market for him his Couronne Jewellery Cleaner . . . According to Mr Nash it was not the practice of the defendants, even when an unknown salesman approached a buyer with a new product from an unknown manufacturer, to make any inquiries as to the status of the manufacturer . . . Though Mr Meyer told him that he had just started to manufacture, he made no inquiries as to his previous experience, or whether he had any qualifications, or had had the proposed compound tested by a chemist. The defendants have an analytical department but it did not occur to Mr Nash to send it to them (though now he thinks it would have been wise to have done so); but if told by the analytical department that it contained 50 per cent alcohol this would not have conveyed to him that it was more dangerous than any other cleaner.

. . .

Though the question of duty to make inquiries must depend on the facts of each particular case, since in the end the question must always be whether the party charged has exercised reasonable care in all the circumstances, I was referred to a number of authorities in which questions very similar to those in the present case have arisen. Perhaps the nearest is the decision of Mr Justice Stable in *Watson v Buckley, Osborne, Garrett & Co Ltd and Wyrovoys Products Ltd* [1940] 1 All ER 174, in which the learned Judge found the distributors of hair dye were liable for failure to make proper inquiries and tests when purchasing a hair dye from a stranger. At p 181, the learned Judge says this:

' . . . Ogee Ltd [—the distributors—] were not dealing with an old-established manufacturer who had been supplying them for years. They were, in essence, dealing with a gentleman who had emerged quite unexpectedly from Spain . . . They never saw where it was manufactured. They took no steps to ascertain under what sort of supervision the manufacture was carried on. When deliveries were made, no test of any sort, kind or description was made . . . '

The learned judge is emphasizing, as I think rightly, the standard of care to be exercised by a distributor when dealing with an unknown supplier.

. . .

Without attempting to lay down any rule of law of general application I have reached the conclusion, on the facts of this case, that the defendants did not measure up to the standard of care which should have been exercised in their acceptance of Mr Meyer's request that they should market Couronne. If they had made any inquiries they would have found out that Mr Meyer was a man of no qualifications for, or experience in, the manufacture of a cleaning product and no qualifications for making a proper choice of its constituent.

...

Mr Moir, an experienced industrial chemist called on behalf of the plaintiff, expressed the view that he would not expect a substance of this kind to be put on the market without some warning, this view being based on his experience of substances which are accompanied by a warning when put on the market . . .

In my judgment this Couronne should not have been put on the market even with a pierced plug without instructions as to the manner in which the liquid was to be got out of the container and without a warning as to the danger if it came into contact with the eyes; *a fortiori* it should not have been put on the market with a blind plug without a similar or more stringent warning—such as was used later—namely, 'Keep away from the eyes.'

It may be said, however, that the defendants, though initially at fault for putting it on the market in July, 1962, were not at fault in September, 1963, when the particular bottle which caused the plaintiff's injuries was sold, in view of the lack of complaints to them of any untoward occurrences in the intervening months. There is some force in this point, though it has to be borne in mind that several of the ladies who gave evidence as to their mishaps with the Couronne did not report to the defendants.

...

In my judgment the defendants' initial fault in putting this commodity on the market without making proper inquiries, and without seeing that an adequate warning of danger was affixed to the bottles, was and remained the effective cause of the plaintiff's injuries.

...

There will accordingly be judgment for the plaintiff for £1995 18s and that judgment carries costs.

NOTE

On appropriate facts liability in negligence may also be imposed on wholesalers, on those who hire out products, on repairers, installers and many other categories of potential defendants. See also *Devilez v Boots Pure Drug Co Ltd* (1962) 106 Sol Jo 552.

DAMAGE TO PROPERTY AND ECONOMIC LOSS

Liability in negligence under the *Donoghue v Stevenson* principle extends to straightforward cases of damage to property, no less than to physical injury. The decision of the House of Lords in *Junior Books Ltd v Veitchi Co Ltd* [1982] 3 All ER 201, [1983] 1 AC 520, holding that a factory owner was entitled to recover against a nominated sub-contractor for the cost of repairing a defective concrete floor, appeared to have opened up the possibility of liability for pure economic loss. The decision was based in part on *Anns v Merton London Borough* [1977] 2 All ER 492, [1978] AC 728. However, in two subsequent decisions the House of Lords declined to follow the same path. Both cases also involved defective buildings, rather than defective products, but clearly there is a very close analogy between the two situations. In the first decision, *D & F Estates Ltd v Church Commissioners for England* [1988] 2 All ER 992, [1989] AC 177, the House held that the lessees of a flat could not recover in tort against a builder whose sub-contractor had carried out plastering work negligently with a consequent need for remedial work. The second decision contains a wide-ranging discussion of the potential limits to liability in such cases.

Murphy v Brentwood District Council [1990] 2 All ER 908, [1991] AC 398, House of Lords

In 1970 the plaintiff purchased, from a construction company, a semi-detached house newly constructed on an in-filled site on a concrete raft foundation to prevent damage from settlement. The plans for the raft foundation were submitted to the defendant council for building regulation approval prior to the construction of the houses. The council referred the plans and calculations to consulting engineers and on their recommendation approved the design under the building regulations and byelaws. In 1981 the plaintiff noticed serious cracks in his house and discovered that the raft foundation was defective and that differential settlement beneath it had caused it to distort. The plaintiff was unable to carry out the necessary repairs to the foundation, which would have cost £45,000, and in 1986 the plaintiff sold the house subject to the defects for £35,000 less than its market value in sound condition. He brought an action against the council claiming that it was liable for the consulting engineers' negligence in recommending approval of the plans and alleging that he and his family had suffered an imminent risk to health and safety because gas and soil pipes had broken and there was a risk of further breaks. The judge, who found as a fact that the plaintiff had been exposed to an imminent risk to health and safety, held the council liable for the consulting engineers' negligence and awarded the plaintiff damages of £38,777, being the loss on the sale of the house and expenses. The council appealed to the Court of Appeal, which dismissed the appeal. The council then appealed to the House of Lords which unanimously allowed the appeal, overruling its earlier decision in *Anns*.

The following extracts from the speech of Lord Bridge point to the current position so far as defective products are concerned.

Lord Bridge . . .

Dangerous defects and defects of quality

If a manufacturer negligently puts into circulation a chattel containing a latent defect which renders it dangerous to persons or property, the manufacturer, on the well-known principles established by *Donoghue v Stevenson* [1932] AC 562, [1932] All ER Rep 1, will be liable in tort for injury to persons or damage to property which the chattel causes. But if a manufacturer produces and sells a chattel which is merely defective in quality, even to the extent that it is valueless for the purpose for which it is intended, the manufacturer's liability at common law arises only under and by reference to the terms of any contract to which he is a party in relation to the chattel; the common law does not impose on him any liability in tort to persons to whom he owes no duty in contract but who, having acquired the chattel, suffer economic loss because the chattel is defective in quality. If a dangerous defect in a chattel is discovered before it causes any personal injury or damage to property, because the danger is now known and the chattel cannot be safely used unless the defect is repaired, the defect becomes merely a defect in quality. The chattel is either capable of repair at economic cost or it is worthless and must be scrapped. In either case the loss sustained by the owner or hirer of the chattel is purely economic. It is recoverable against any party who owes the loser a relevant contractual duty. But it is not recoverable in tort in the absence of a special relationship of proximity imposing on the tortfeasor a duty of care to safeguard the plaintiff from economic loss. There is no such special relationship between the manufacturer of a chattel and a remote owner or hirer.

I believe that these principles are equally applicable to buildings. If a builder erects a structure containing a latent defect which renders it dangerous to persons or property, he will be liable in tort for injury to persons or damage to property resulting from that dangerous defect. But, if the defect becomes apparent before any injury or damage has been caused, the loss sustained by the building owner is purely economic. If the defect can be repaired at economic cost, that is the measure of the loss. If the building cannot be repaired, it may have to be abandoned as unfit for occupation and therefore valueless. These economic losses are recoverable if they flow from breach of a relevant contractual duty, but, here again, in the absence of a special relationship of proximity they are not recoverable in tort. The only qualification I would make to this is that, if a building stands so close to the boundary of the building owner's land that after discovery of the dangerous defect is remains a potential source of injury to persons or property on neighbouring land or on the highway, the building owner ought, in principle, to be entitled to recover in tort from the negligent builder the cost of obviating the danger, whether by repair or by demolition, so far as that cost is necessarily incurred in order to protect himself from potential liability to third parties. . . .

The complex structure theory

In my speech in the *D & F Estates* case [1988] 2 All ER 992 at 1006–1007, [1989] AC 177 at 206–207 I mooted the possibility that in complex structures or complex chattels one part of a structure or chattel might, when it caused damage to another part of the same structure or chattel, be regarded in the law of tort as having caused damage to 'other property' for the purpose of the application of *Donoghue v Stevenson* principles. I expressed no opinion as to the validity of this theory, but put it forward for consideration as a possible ground on which the facts considered in *Anns* might be distinguishable from the facts which had to be considered in *D & F Estates* itself. I shall call this for convenience 'the complex structure theory' and it is, so far as I can see, only if and to the extent that this theory can be affirmed and applied that there can be any escape from the conclusions I have indicated above under the rubric 'Dangerous defects and defects of quality'.

The complex structure theory has, so far as I know, never been subjected to express and detailed examination in any English authority. I shall not attempt a review of the numerous authorities which bear on it in the different state jurisdictions in the United States of America. However, some significant landmarks must be mentioned. In *Quackenbush v Ford Motor Co* (1915) 167 App Div 433, a decision of the Appellate Division of the Supreme Court of New York, the plaintiff recovered damages in tort from the manufacturer for damage to her Ford motor car caused by an accident attributable to faulty manufacture of the brakes. It is at least highly doubtful if the reasoning of this decision can now be supported consistently with the unanimous opinion of the United States Supreme Court in *East River Steamship Corp v Transamerica Delaval Inc* (1986) 476 US 858 that a manufacturer incurs no liability in tort for damage occasioned by a defect in a product which injures itself. Blackmun J, delivering the opinion of the court, said (476 US 858 at 870):

'We realize that the damage may be qualitative, occurring through gradual deterioration or internal breakage. Or it may be calamitous . . . But either way, since by definition no person or other property is damaged, the resulting loss is purely economic. Even when the harm to the product itself occurs through an abrupt, accident-like event, the resulting loss due to repair costs, decreased value, and lost profits is essentially the failure of the purchaser to receive the benefit of its bargain—traditionally the core concern of contract law.'

Quackenbush is, in any event, no authority for the proposition that, once a defect in a complex chattel is discovered, there is a remedy in tort against the manufacturer on the ground that the cost of repairing the defect was necessarily incurred in order to prevent further damage to other parts of the chattel. A striking illustration of this is *Trans World Airline Inc v Curtiss-Wright Corp* (1955) 1 Misc 2d 477, in which the airline, having discovered defects in the engines fitted to some of their planes, fortunately before any accident occurred, chose not to sue the plane manufacturer in contract, but sued the engine manufacturers in tort. The manufacturer was held not liable. This and other relevant American authorities are extensively reviewed in the illuminating judgment of the British Columbia Court of Appeal delivered by Tysoe JA in *Rivtow Marine Ltd v Washington Iron Works* [1972] 3 WWR 735. The court held that the manufacturers were not liable in tort to the hirers of a crane for the cost of repair rendered necessary when the crane was found to be dangerously defective in use. This decision was affirmed by the Supreme Court of Canada by a majority of seven to two (see [1974] SCR 1189). Since Lord Wilberforce in *Anns* [1977] 2 All ER 492 at 505, [1978] AC 728 at 760 referred with approval to the dissenting judgment of Laskin J in that case, which he described as 'of strong persuasive force', I have read and reread that judgment with the closest attention. I have to say, with all respect, that I find it wholly unconvincing. It depends on the same fallacy as that which vitiates the judgments of Lord Denning MR and Sachs LJ in *Dutton*. In particular, in equating the damage sustained in repairing the chattel to make it safe with the damage which would have been suffered if the latent defect had never been discovered and the chattel had injured somebody in use, the judgment ignores the circumstance that once a chattel is known to be dangerous it is simply unusable. If I buy a secondhand car and find it to be faulty, it can make no difference to the manufacturer's liability in tort whether the fault is in the brakes or in the engine, ie whether the car will not stop or will not start. In either case the car is useless until repaired. The manufacturer is no more liable in tort for the cost of the repairs in the one case than in the other.

. . .

A critical distinction must be drawn here between some part of a complex structure which is said to be a 'danger' only because it does not perform its proper function in sustaining the other parts and some distinct item incorporated in the structure which positively malfunctions so as to inflict positive damage on the structure in which it is incorporated. Thus, if a defective central heating boiler explodes and damages a house or a defective electrical installation malfunctions and sets the house on fire, I see no reason to doubt that the owner of the house, if he can prove that the damage was due to the negligence of the boiler manufacturer in the one case or the electrical contractor in the other, can recover damages in tort on *Donoghue v Stevenson* principles. But the position in law is entirely different where, by reason of the inadequacy of the foundations of the building to support the weight of the superstructure, differential settlement and consequent cracking occurs. Here, once the first cracks appear, the structure as a whole is seen to be defective and the nature of the defect is known. Even if, contrary to my view, the initial damage could be regarded as damage to other property caused by a latent defect, once the defect is known the situation of the building owner is analogous to that of the car owner who discovers that the car has faulty brakes. He may have a house which, until repairs are effected, is unfit for habitation, but, subject to the reservation I have expressed with respect to ruinous buildings at or near the boundary of the owner's property, the building no longer represents a source of danger and as it deteriorates will only damage itself.

For these reasons the complex structure theory offers no escape from the conclusion that damage to a house itself which is attributable to a defect in the structure of the house is not recoverable in tort on *Donoghue v Stevenson* principles, but represents purely economic loss which is only recoverable in contract or in tort by reason of some special relationship of proximity which imposes on the tortfeasor a duty of care to protect against economic loss.

Lord Mackay, Lord Keith, Lord Brandon, Lord Ackner, Lord Oliver and **Lord Jauncey** all agreed that the appeal should be allowed.

Appeal allowed.

QUESTION

In *Walton v British Leyland (UK) Ltd* (1978), above, pp 208–13, Willis J suggested that Leyland was under a duty to 'recall all cars which they could in order that the safety washers could be fitted.' Is this still arguable in the light of the above decision?

NOTES

1. There are several persuasive, if less than overwhelming, arguments for not countenancing a broadly-based entitlement to recover against a manufacturer in tort where goods are shoddy, or even dangerous, without having caused any personal injury or property damage. For example, a manufacturer might thereby be deprived of the benefit of an otherwise enforceable exemption or limitation clause in the contract between himself and the retailer. Similarly, there may be difficulty in ascertaining the qualitative standard by reference to which the goods are to be judged. However, this is less likely to be a practical problem in everyday consumer transactions and some jurisdictions are less constrained by 'vertical' privity requirements: see, eg, the Australian Trade Practices Act 1974, s 74(D), above, p 56.

2. The decisions in *D & F Estates Ltd v Church Commissioners for England* and *Murphy v Brentwood DC* have not found favour in other Commonwealth jurisdictions: see, eg, *Bryan v Maloney* (1995) 128 ALR 163 (High Court of Australia); *Winnipeg Condominium Corporation No 36 v Bird Construction Co Ltd* (1995) 121 DLR (4th) 193 (Supreme Court of Canada); *Invercargill City Council v Hamlin* [1994] 3 NZLR 513 (New Zealand Court of Appeal) and on appeal [1996] 1 All ER 756 (Privy Council). For general discussion of *Murphy*, see Hayes, 'After Murphy: Building on the Consumer Protection Principle' (1992) 12 OJLS 112, and for discussion of the above Commonwealth decisions, see Martin, 'Defective Premises—the Empire Strikes Back' (1996) 59 MLR 116. For an earlier, but still valuable, discussion of the general issues, see Cane, 'Physical Loss, Economic Loss and Products Liability', (1979) 95 LQR 117. For a subsequent English case holding damage within the defective product to amount to irrecoverable economic loss, see *Nitrigin Eireann Teoranta v Inco Alloys Ltd* [1992] 1 All ER 854 (cracking within alloy pipe).

3. Although the 'complex structure theory' to which Lord Bridge refers (see

above, p 217), is hardly a satisfactory explanation for the decision in *Anns*, it should have a limited application to cases involving defective products. In *Murphy* Lord Keith took the following example involving a building (see pp 922 and 470 respectively):

> In *D & F Estates Ltd v Church Cmrs for England* [1988] 2 All ER 992, [1989] AC 177 both Lord Bridge and Lord Oliver expressed themselves as having difficulty in reconciling the decision in *Anns* with pre-existing principle and as being uncertain as to the nature and scope of such new principle as it introduced. Lord Bridge suggested that in the case of a complex structure such as a building one element of the structure might be regarded for *Donoghue v Stevenson* purposes as distinct from another element, so that damage to one part of the structure caused by a hidden defect in another part might qualify to be treated as damage to 'other property' (see [1988] 2 All ER 992 at 1006, [1989] AC 177 at 206). I think that it would be unrealistic to take this view as regards a building the whole of which had been erected and equipped by the same contractor. In that situation the whole package provided by the contractor would, in my opinion, fall to be regarded as one unit rendered unsound as such by a defect in the particular part. On the other hand, where, for example, the electric wiring had been installed by a sub-contractor and due to a defect caused by lack of care a fire occurred which destroyed the building, it might not be stretching ordinary principles too far to hold the electrical sub-contractor liable for the damage. If in the *East River* case the defective turbine had caused the loss of the ship the manufacturer of it could consistently with normal principles, I would think, properly have been held liable for that loss.

4. For further discussion and problems involving the provisions of the Consumer Protection Act 1987, see below, at pp 244–5.

In the extract from Lord Bridge's speech in the *Murphy* case cited above (at p 218) reference was made to the following decision of the Supreme Court of Canada. It is of interest as indicating an alternative basis on which liability may be grounded.

Rivtow Marine Ltd v Washington Iron Works (1973) 40 DLR (3d) 530, Supreme Court of Canada

The plaintiff was the charterer of a log barge, the Rivtow Carrier, which was equipped with two pintle-type cranes designed and manufactured by the first defendants, Washington. In September 1966, some eighteen months after the commencement of the charter and at a time when the coastal logging business was at its height, the charterers learned that a crane which was virtually identical to their own and which had also been designed and manufactured by Washington had collapsed, killing its operator. As a precautionary measure, they ordered the Rivtow Carrier to return to Vancouver for inspection. This revealed that both cranes had serious structural defects in the legs of the pintle masts, necessitating extensive dismantling, modification, repair and reassembly lasting some thirty days. The plaintiff claimed compensation for the cost of repair and for loss of profits during the period in which the barge was inoperative. Washington admitted that the cracking in the legs of the crane was caused by defects in design attributable to the carelessness of their engineers; that by February 1966 they were aware that other cranes of this type had developed similar structural defects in operation; and that thirty days was a reasonable period in which to carry out the necessary modifications. They denied, however, that they had any liability to compensate in respect of the loss suffered. This view was accepted by the British Columbia Court of Appeal. The charterers then appealed to the Supreme Court of Canada. The court was unanimous in allowing the appeal and in awarding damages, but divided about the basis on which damages were to be assessed. The majority view was expressed in the following extract.

Ritchie J. . . . . As I have indicated, the judgment of the Court of Appeal in this case appears to me to proceed on the assumption that Walkem and Washington owed a duty of care to the appellant as being a person ' . . . so closely and directly affected' by the faulty design of the cranes that they ought reasonably to have had it in contemplation as being so affected in directing their mind to the known defects which are here called in question.

Proceeding on this assumption, I take it that the Court of Appeal would have treated the respondents as being liable for damages attributable to personal injury or damage to property resulting from defects in the cranes, but Mr Justice Tysoe, in concluding his reasons for judgment at p 579 said:

In my opinion the law of British Columbia as it exists today is that neither a manufacturer of a potentially dangerous or defective article nor other person who is within the proximity of relationship contemplated in *Donoghue v Stevenson* is liable in tort, as distinct from contract, to an ultimate consumer or user for damage arising in the article itself, or for economic loss resulting from the defect in the article, but only for personal injury and damage to other property caused by the article or its use. It is my view that to give effect to the claims of Rivtow it would be necessary to extend the rule of liability laid down in *Donoghue's* case beyond what it now is. I do not feel this Court would be justified in extending it so that it covers the character of damage suffered by Rivtow. I think that, if that is to be done, it must be left to a higher Court to do it.

Mr Justice Tysoe's conclusion was based in large measure on a series of American cases, and particularly *Trans World Airlines Inc v Curtiss-Wright Corpn et al* (1955) 148 NYS 2d 284, where it is pointed out that the liability for the cost of repairing damage to the defective article itself and for the economic loss flowing directly from the negligence, is akin to liability under the terms of an express or implied warranty of fitness and as it is contractual in origin cannot be enforced against the manufacturer by a stranger to the contract. It was, I think, on this basis that the learned trial Judge disallowed the appellant's claim for repairs and for such economic loss as it would, in any event, have sustained even if the proper warning had been given. I agree with this conclusion for the same reasons; but while this finding excludes recovery for damage to the article and economic loss directly flowing from Washington's negligence and faulty design, it does not exclude the additional damage occasioned by breach of the duty to warn of the danger.

In the present case, both Washington as manufacturer and Walkem as its representative, knew that the appellant relied on them for advice concerning the operation of the pintle cranes, and in my opinion a clear duty lay upon them both to warn the appellant of the necessity for repairs as soon as they had become aware of the defects and the potential danger attendant thereon.

. . .

That liability for this damage does not flow from negligence in design and manufacture is illustrated by the fact that Walkem, which was not a party to such negligence, is equally liable with Washington for failing to warn the appellant. The difference between the two types of liability and consequent damage is that one may arise without the manufacturer having any knowledge of the defect, whereas the other stems from his awareness of the danger to which the defect gives rise.

. . .

[In quantifying damages the court agreed with the approach of the trial court judge whose figures of $90,000 (earnings in the high season) less $30,000 (average monthly earnings), leaving $60,000, were accepted.]

Laskin J (dissenting in part) . . . I agree with the award of damages so far as it goes, but I would enlarge it to include as well the cost of repairs. . . .

Appeal allowed; trial judgment restored.

NOTES

1. In *Dow Corning Corp v Hollis* (1996) 129 DLR (4th) 609 the Supreme Court of Canada confirmed that a manufacturer had a duty to warn the medical profession of potential dangers involving the rupturing of a silicone breast implant, including those coming to its notice after manufacture and distribution of the product. The plaintiff was entitled to succeed on proof that she would probably not have accepted the product if proper warning had been given.
2. For an English case which may have recognised a duty to warn of subsequently discovered dangers see *Wright v Dunlop Rubber Co Ltd* (1972) 13 KIR 255, CA (carcinogenic properties of anti oxidant).

THE INTRODUCTION OF STRICT LIABILITY

Since the early 1970s there has been widespread debate in the United Kingdom and the rest of Europe over the desirability of introducing a wider measure of strict liability for defective products. Within the United Kingdom the principal studies have been carried out by the Law Commissions and the Royal Commission on Civil Liability and Compensation for Personal Injury (the Pearson Commission): see respectively the Law Commissions' joint report, 'Liability for Defective Products' (Law Com No 82, Scot Law Com No 45, Cmnd 6831, 1977) and the Pearson Commission report (Cmnd 7054, 1978) ch 22. Both reports recommend that strict liability be imposed on producers of defective products which cause death or personal injury. At European level a similar proposal is to be found in the Council of Europe (Strasbourg) Convention on Products Liability in regard to Personal Injury and Death: see Miller *Product Liability and Safety Encyclopaedia*, Div V, para [173] et seq.

The above initiatives were overtaken by activity within the EEC which led eventually to a Council Directive on the approximation of the laws, regulations and administrative provisions of the member States concerning liability for defective products (85/374/EEC). With the benefit of hindsight one can see that it is regrettable that reform should have been concentrated on this particular European initiative which Sir Gordon Borrie has described as 'a well-intentioned directive but one damaging to national initiatives': see *The Development of Consumer Law and Policy—Bold Spirits and Timorous Souls* (1984), p 116. The reason for the suggested damage is the inevitable delay which was associated with seeking a consensus among countries whose legal systems had no common basis of liability. For example, French law was associated with a wide measure of strict liability (see generally Mazeaud, *La Responsabilité des Fabricants et Distributeurs* (Economica, 1975) and the Quebec case *General Motors Products of Canada Ltd v Kravitz* (1979) 93 DLR (3d) 481 (Supreme Court of Canada, above, p 54) whereas in West Germany negligence or fault was required but the onus of proof was on the defendant manufacturer: see the decision of the 6th Civil Senate of 26 November 1968 (BGHZ 51.91) in the 'fowl-pest' or defective chicken vaccine case, extracted with helpful comments in Markesinis, *The German Law of Obligations, Vol II, The Law of Torts: A Comparative Perspective* (3rd edn, 1997), p 493 et seq.

In the result, it did not prove possible to achieve complete consensus and the Directive contains a number of optional provisions: see Articles 15 and 16, printed below. The following is the text of the Directive as agreed on 25 July 1985.

COUNCIL DIRECTIVE

of 25 July 1985

on the approximation of the laws, regulations and administrative provisions of the Member States concerning liability for defective products

(85/374/EEC)

THE COUNCIL OF THE EUROPEAN COMMUNITIES

Having regard to the Treaty establishing the European Economic Community, and in particular Article 100 thereof,

Having regard to the proposal from the Commission,[1]

Having regard to the opinion of the European Parliament,[2]

Having regard to the opinion of the Economic and Social Committee,[3]

Whereas approximation of the laws of the Member States concerning the liability of the producer for damage caused by the defectiveness of his products is necessary because the existing divergences may distort competition and affect the movement of goods within the common market and entail a differing degree of protection of the consumer against damage caused by a defective product to his health or property;

Whereas liability without fault on the part of the producer is the sole means of adequately solving the problem, peculiar to our age of increasing technicality, of a fair apportionment of the risks inherent in modern technological production;

Whereas liability without fault should apply only to movables which have been industrially produced; whereas, as a result, it is appropriate to exclude liability for agricultural products and game, except where they have undergone a processing of an industrial nature which could cause a defect in these products; whereas the liability provided for in this Directive should also apply to movables which are used in the construction of immovables or are installed in immovables;

Whereas protection of the consumer requires that all producers involved in the production process should be made liable, in so far as their finished product, component part or any raw material supplied by them was defective; whereas, for the same reason, liability should extend to importers of products into the Community and to persons who present themselves as producers by affixing their name, trade mark or other distinguishing feature or who supply a product the producer of which cannot be identified;

Whereas, in situations where several persons are liable for the same damage, the protection of the consumer requires that the injured person should be able to claim full compensation for the damage from any one of them;

Whereas, to protect the physical well-being and property of the consumer, the defectiveness of the product should be determined by reference not to its fitness for use but to the lack of the safety which the public at large is entitled to expect; whereas the safety is assessed by excluding any misuse of the product not reasonable under the circumstances;

Whereas a fair apportionment of risk between the injured person and the producer implies that the producer should be able to free himself from liability if he furnishes proof as to the existence of certain exonerating circumstances;

Whereas the protection of the consumer requires that the liability of the producer remains unaffected by acts or omissions of other persons having contributed to cause the damage; whereas, however, the contributory negligence of the injured person may be taken into account to reduce or disallow such liability;

Whereas the protection of the consumer requires compensation for death and personal injury as well as compensation for damage to property; whereas the latter should nevertheless be limited to goods for private use or consumption and be subject to a deduction of a lower threshold of a fixed amount in order to avoid litigation in an excessive number of cases; whereas this Directive should not prejudice compensation for pain and suffering and other non-material damages payable, where appropriate, under the law applicable to the case;

Whereas a uniform period of limitation for the bringing of action for compensation is in the interests both of the injured person and of the producer;

Whereas products age in the course of time, higher safety standards are developed and the state of science and technology progresses; whereas, therefore, it would not be reasonable to make the producer liable for an unlimited period for the defectiveness of his product; whereas, therefore, liability should expire after a reasonable length of time, without prejudice to claims pending at law;

Whereas, to achieve effective protection of consumers, no contractual derogation should be permitted as regards the liability of the producer in relation to the injured person;

Whereas under the legal systems of the Member States an injured party may have a claim for damages based on grounds of contractual liability or on grounds of non-contractual liability other than that provided for in this Directive; in so far as these provisions also serve to attain the objective of effective protection of consumers, they should remain unaffected by this Directive; whereas, in so far as effective protection of consumers in the sector of pharmaceutical products is already also attained in a Member State under a special liability system, claims based on this system should similarly remain possible;

Whereas, to the extent that liability for nuclear injury or damage is already covered in all Member States by adequate special rules, it has been possible to exclude damage of this type from the scope of this Directive;

Whereas, since the exclusion of primary agricultural products and game from the scope of this Directive may be felt, in certain Member States, in view of what is expected for the protection of consumers, to restrict unduly such protection, it should be possible for a Member State to extend liability to such products;

Whereas, for similar reasons, the possibility offered to a producer to free himself from liability if he proves that the state of scientific and technical knowledge at the time when he put the product into circulation was not such as to enable the existence of a defect to be discovered may be felt in certain Member States to restrict unduly the protection of the consumer; whereas it should therefore be possible for a Member State to maintain in its legislation or to provide by new legislation that this exonerating circumstance is not admitted; whereas, in the case of new legislation, making use of this derogation should, however, be subject to a Community stand-still procedure, in order to raise, if possible, the level of protection in a uniform manner throughout the Community;

Whereas, taking into account the legal traditions in most of the Member States, it is inappropriate to set any financial ceiling on the producer's liability without fault; whereas, in so far as there are, however, differing traditions, it seems possible to admit that a Member State may derogate from the principle of unlimited liability by providing a limit for the total liability of the producer for damage resulting from a death or personal injury and caused by identical items with the same defect, provided that this limit is established at a level sufficiently high to guarantee adequate protection of the consumer and the correct functioning of the common market;

Whereas the harmonization resulting from this cannot be total at the present stage, but opens the way towards greater harmonization; whereas it is therefore necessary that the Council receive at regular intervals, reports from the Commission on the application of this Directive, accompanied, as the case may be, by appropriate proposals;

Whereas it is particularly important in this respect that a re-examination be carried out of those parts of the Directive relating to the derogations open to the Member States, at the expiry of a period of sufficient length to gather practical experience on the effects of these derogations on the protection of consumers and on the functioning of the common market,

HAS ADOPTED THIS DIRECTIVE:

Article 1

The producer shall be liable for damage caused by a defect in his product.

Article 2

For the purpose of this Directive 'product' means all movables, with the exception of primary agricultural products and game, even though incorporated into another movable or into an immovable. 'Primary agricultural products' means the products of the soil, of stock-farming and of fisheries, excluding products which have undergone initial processing. 'Product' includes electricity.

Article 3

1. 'Producer' means the manufacturer of a finished product, the producer of any raw material or the manufacturer of a component part and any person who, by putting his name, trade mark or other distinguishing feature on the product presents himself as its producer.

2. Without prejudice to the liability of the producer, any person who imports into the Community a product for sale, hire, leasing or any form of distribution in the course of his business shall be deemed to be a producer within the meaning of this Directive and shall be responsible as a producer.

3. Where the producer of the product cannot be identified, each supplier of the product shall be treated as its producer unless he informs the injured person, within a reasonable time, of the identity of the producer or of the person who supplied him with the product. The same shall apply in the case of an imported product, if this product does not indicate the identity of the importer referred to in paragraph 2, even if the name of the producer is indicated.

Article 4

The injured person shall be required to prove the damage, the defect and the causal relationship between defect and damage.

Article 5

Where, as a result of the provisions of this Directive, two or more persons are liable for the same damage, they shall be liable jointly and severally, without prejudice to the provisions of national law concerning the rights of contribution or recourse.

Article 6

1. A product is defective when it does not provide the safety which a person is entitled to expect, taking all circumstances into account, including:
(a) the presentation of the product;
(b) the use to which it could reasonably be expected that the product would be put;
(c) the time when the product was put into circulation.

2. A product shall not be considered defective for the sole reason that a better product is subsequently put into circulation.

Article 7

The producer shall not be liable as a result of this Directive if he proves:
(a) that he did not put the product into circulation; or
(b) that, having regard to the circumstances, it is probable that the defect which caused the damage did not exist at the time when the product was put into circulation by him or that this defect came into being afterwards; or
(c) that the product was neither manufactured by him for sale or any form of distribution for economic purpose nor manufactured or distributed by him in the course of his business; or
(d) that the defect is due to compliance of the product with mandatory regulations issued by the public authorities; or
(e) that the state of scientific and technical knowledge at the time when he put the product into circulation was not such as to enable the existence of the defect to be discovered; or
(f) in the case of a manufacturer of a component, that the defect is attributable to the design of the product in which the component has been fitted or to the instructions given by the manufacturer of the product.

Article 8

1. Without prejudice to the provisions of national law concerning the right of contribution or recourse, the liability of the producer shall not be reduced when the damage is caused both by a defect in the product and by the act or omission of a third party.

2. The liability of the producer may be reduced or disallowed when, having regard to all the circumstances, the damage is caused both by a defect in the product and by the fault of the injured person or any person for whom the injured person is responsible.

Article 9

For the purpose of Article 1, 'damage' means:
(a) damage caused by death or by personal injuries;
(b) damage to, or destruction of, any item of property other than the defective product itself, with a lower threshold of 500 ECU, provided that the item of property:
  (i) is of a type ordinarily intended for private use or consumption, and
  (ii) was used by the injured person mainly for his own private use or consumption.

This Article should be without prejudice to national provisions relating to non-material damage.

Article 10

1. Member States shall provide in their legislation that a limitation period of three years shall apply to proceedings for the recovery of damages as provided for in this Directive. The limitation period shall begin to run from the day on which the plaintiff became aware, or should reasonably have become aware, of the damage, the defect and the identity of the producer.

2. The laws of Member States regulating suspension or interruption of the limitation period shall not be affected by this Directive.

Article 11

Member States shall provide in their legislation that the rights conferred upon the injured person pursuant to this Directive shall be extinguished upon the expiry of a period of 10 years from the date on which the producer put into circulation the actual product which caused the damage, unless the injured person has in the meantime instituted proceedings against the producer.

Article 12

The liability of the producer arising from this Directive may not, in relation to the injured person, be limited or excluded by a provision limiting his liability or exempting him from liability.

Article 13

This Directive shall not affect any rights which an injured person may have according to the rules of the law of contractual or non-contractual liability or a special liability system existing at the moment when this Directive is notified.

Article 14

This Directive shall not apply to injury or damage arising from nuclear accidents and covered by international conventions ratified by the Member States.

Article 15

1. Each Member State may
(a) by way of derogation from Article 2, provide in its legislation that within the meaning of Article 1 of this Directive 'product' also means primary agricultural products and game;
(b) by way of derogation from Article 7(e), maintain or, subject to the procedure set out in paragraph 2 of this Article, provide in this legislation that the producer shall be liable even if he proves that the state of scientific and technical knowledge at the time when he put the product into circulation was not such as to enable to existence of a defect to be discovered.

2. A Member State wishing to introduce the measure specified in paragraph 1(b) shall communicate the text of the proposed measure to the Commission. The Commission shall inform the other Member States thereof.

The Member State concerned shall hold the proposed measure in abeyance for nine months after the Commission is informed and provided that in the meantime the Commission has not submitted to the Council a proposal amending this Directive on the relevant matter. However, if within three months of receiving the said information, the Commission does not advise the Member State concerned that it intends submitting such a proposal to the Council, the Member State may take the proposed measure immediately.

If the Commission does submit to the Council such a proposal amending this Directive within the aforementioned nine months, the Member State concerned shall hold the proposed measure in abeyance for a further period of 18 months from the date on which the proposal is submitted.

3. Ten years after the date of notification of this Directive, the Commission shall submit to the Council a report on the effect that rulings by the courts as to the application of Article 7(e) and of paragraph 1(b) of this Article have on consumer protection and the functioning of the common market. In the light of this report the Council, acting on a proposal from the Commission and pursuant to the terms of Article 100 of the Treaty, shall decide whether to repeal Article 7(e).

Article 16

1. Any Member State may provide that a producer's total liability for damage resulting from a death or personal injury and caused by identical items with the same defect shall be limited to an amount which may not be less than 70 million ECU.

2. Ten years after the date of notification of this Directive, the Commission shall submit to the Council a report on the effect on consumer protection and the functioning of the common market of the implementation of the financial limit on liability by those Member States which have used the option provided for in paragraph 1. In the light of this report the Council, acting on a proposal from the Commission and pursuant to the terms of Article 100 of the Treaty, shall decide whether to repeal paragraph 1.

Article 17

This Directive shall not apply to products put into circulation before the date on which the provisions referred to in Article 19 enter into force.

Article 18

1. For the purposes of this Directive, the ECU shall be that defined by Regulation (EEC) No 3180/78,[4] as amended by Regulation (EEC) No 2626/84.[5] The equivalent in national currency shall initially be calculated at the rate obtaining on the date of adoption of this Directive.

2. Every five years the Council, acting on a proposal from the Commission, shall examine and, if need be, revise the amounts in this Directive, in the light of economic and monetary trends in the Community.

Article 19

1. Member States shall bring into force, not later than three years from the date of notification of this Directive, the laws, regulations and administrative provisions necessary to comply with this Directive. They shall forthwith inform the Commission thereof.[6]

2. The procedure set out in Article 15(2) shall apply from the date of notification of this Directive.

Article 20

Member States shall communicate to the Commission the texts of the main provisions of national law which they subsequently adopt in the field governed by this Directive.

Article 21

Every five years the Commission shall present a report to the Council on the application of this Directive and, if necessary, shall submit appropriate proposals to it.

Article 22

This Directive is addressed to the Member States.

Done at Brussels, 25 July 1985.

[1] OJ No C 241, 14.10.1976, p 9 and OJ No C 271, 26.10.1979, p 3.
[2] OJ No C 127, 21.5.1979, p 61.
[3] OJ No C 114, 7.5.1979, p 15.
[4] OJ No L 379, 30.12.1978, p 1.
[5] OJ No L 247, 16.9.1984, p 1.
[6] This Directive was notified to the Member States on 30 July 1985.

NOTES

1. In the result, the legislation of member states implementing the Directive has been substantially similar in most respects so far as the optional provisions covering the 'development risks' defence, primary agricultural products and the financial ceiling are concerned: see Kelly & Attree (eds), *European Product Liabilities* (2nd edn, 1996).
2. The Commission of the European Communities reported on 13.12.1995 that it did not consider it necessary at that stage to submit any proposals for amendment to the Directive, although the position was still being monitored: see COM (95) 617 final.
3. The Directive was implemented in English law by the following provision, Part I of which came into force on 1 March 1988: see the Consumer Protection Act 1987 (Commencement No 1) Order 1987, SI 1987/1680.

CONSUMER PROTECTION ACT 1987

PART I: PRODUCT LIABILITY

Purpose and construction of Part I

1.—(1) This Part shall have effect for the purpose of making such provision as is necessary in order to comply with the product liability Directive and shall be construed accordingly.

(2) In this Part, except in so far as the context otherwise requires:

'agricultural produce' means any produce of the soil, of stock-farming or of fisheries;

'dependent' and 'relative' have the same meaning as they have in, respectively, the Fatal Accidents Act 1976 and the Damages (Scotland) Act 1976;

'producer', in relation to a product, means—

(a) the person who manufactured it;

(b) in the case of a substance which has not been manufactured but has been won or abstracted, the person who won or abstracted it;

(c) in the case of a product which has not been manufactured, won or abstracted but essential characteristics of which are attributable to an industrial or other process having been carried out (for example, in relation to agricultural produce), the person who carried out that process;

'product' means any goods or electricity and (subject to subsection (3) below) includes a
product which is comprised in another product, whether by virtue of being a component part or raw material or otherwise; and

'the product liability Directive' means the Directive of the Council of the European
Communities, dated 25th July 1985, (No 85/374/EEC) on the approximation of the
laws, regulations and administrative provisions of the member States concerning liability for defective products.

(3) For the purposes of this Part a person who supplies any product in which products are comprised, whether by virtue of being component parts or raw materials or otherwise, shall not be
treated by reason only of his supply of that product as supplying any of the products so comprised.

Liability for defective products

2.—(1) Subject to the following provisions of this Part, where any damage is caused wholly
or partly by a defect in a product, every person to whom subsection (2) below applies shall be
liable for the damage.

(2) This subsection applies to—
  (a) the producer of the product;
  (b) any person who, by putting his name on the product or using a trade mark or other
      distinguishing mark in relation to the product, has held himself out to be the producer
      of the product;
  (c) any person who has imported the product into a member State from a place outside the
      member States in order, in the course of any business of his, to supply it to another.

(3) Subject as aforesaid, where any damage is caused wholly or partly by a defect in a product, any person who supplied the product (whether to the person who suffered the damage, to
the producer of any product in which the product in question is comprised or to any other person) shall be liable for the damage if—
  (a) the person who suffered the damage requests the supplier to identify one or more of
      the persons (whether still in existence or not) to whom subsection (2) above applies in
      relation to the product;
  (b) that request is made within a reasonable period after the damage occurs and at a time
      when it is not reasonably practicable for the person making the request to identify all
      those persons; and
  (c) the supplier fails, within a reasonable period after receiving the request, either to com-
      ply with the request or to identify the person who supplied the product to him.

(4) Neither subsection (2) nor subsection (3) above shall apply to a person in respect of any
defect in any game or agricultural produce if the only supply of the game or produce by that
person to another was at a time when it had not undergone an industrial process.

(5) Where two or more persons are liable by virtue of this Part for the same damage, their
liability shall be joint and several.

(6) This section shall be without prejudice to any liability arising otherwise than by virtue
of this Part.

Meaning of 'defect'

3.—(1) Subject to the following provisions of this section, there is a defect in a product for
the purposes of this Part if the safety of the product is not such as persons generally are entitled to expect; and for those purposes 'safety', in relation to a product, shall include safety with
respect to products comprised in that product and safety in the context of risks of damage to
property, as well as in the context of risks of death or personal injury.

(2) In determining for the purposes of subsection (1) above what persons generally are entitled
to expect in relation to a product all the circumstances shall be taken into account, including—
  (a) the manner in which, and purposes for which, the product has been marketed, its get-up,
      the use of any mark in relation to the product and any instructions for, or warnings with
      respect to, doing or refraining from doing anything with or in relation to the product;

(b) what might reasonably be expected to be done with or in relation to the product; and

(c) the time when the product was supplied by its producer to another;

and nothing in this section shall require a defect to be inferred from the fact alone that the safety of a product which is supplied after that time is greater than the safety of the product in question.

Defences

4.—(1) In any civil proceedings by virtue of this Part against any person ('the person proceeded against') in respect of a defect in a product it shall be a defence for him to show—

(a) that the defect is attributable to compliance with any requirement imposed by or under any enactment or with any Community obligation; or

(b) that the person proceeded against did not at any time supply the product to another; or

(c) that the following conditions are satisfied, that is to say—

(i) that the only supply of the product to another by the person proceeded against was otherwise than in the course of a business of that person's; and

(ii) that section 2(2) above does not apply to that person or applies to him by virtue only of things done otherwise than with a view to profit; or

(d) that the defect did not exist in the product at the relevant time; or

(e) that the state of scientific and technical knowledge at the relevant time was not such that a producer of products of the same description as the product in question might be expected to have discovered the defect if it had existed in his products while they were under his control; or

(f) that the defect—

(i) constituted a defect in a product ('the subsequent product') in which the product in question had been comprised; and

(ii) was wholly attributable to the design of the subsequent product or to compliance by the producer of the product in question with instructions given by the producer of the subsequent product.

(2) In this section 'the relevant time', in relation to electricity, means the time at which it was generated, being a time before it was transmitted or distributed, and in relation to any other product, means—

(a) if the person proceeded against is a person to whom subsection (2) of section 2 above applies in relation to the product, the time when he supplied the product to another;

(b) if that subsection does not apply to that person in relation to the product, the time when the product was last supplied by a person to whom that subsection does apply in relation to the product.

Damage giving rise to liability

5.—(1) Subject to the following provisions of this section, in this Part 'damage' means death or personal injury or any loss of or damage to any property (including land).

(2) A person shall not be liable under section 2 above in respect of any defect in a product for the loss of or any damage to the product itself or for the loss of or any damage to the whole or any part of any product which has been supplied with the product in question comprised in it.

(3) A person shall not be liable under section 2 above for any loss of or damage to any property which, at the time it is lost or damaged, is not—

(a) of a description of property ordinarily intended for private use, occupation or consumption; and

(b) intended by the person suffering the loss or damage mainly for his own private use, occupation or consumption.

(4) No damages shall be awarded to any person by virtue of this Part in respect of any loss of or damage to any property if the amount which would fall to be so awarded to that person, apart from this subsection and any liability for interest, does not exceed £275.

(5) In determining for the purposes of this Part who has suffered any loss of or damage to property and when any such loss or damage occurred, the loss or damage shall be regarded as

having occurred at the earliest time at which a person with an interest in the property had knowledge of the material facts about the loss or damage.

(6) For the purposes of subsection (5) above the material facts about any loss of or damage to any property are such facts about the loss or damage as would lead a reasonable person with an interest in the property to consider the loss or damage sufficiently serious to justify his instituting proceedings for damages against a defendant who did not dispute liability and was able to satisfy a judgment.

(7) For the purposes of subsection (5) above a person's knowledge includes knowledge which he might reasonably have been expected to acquire—

(a) from facts observable or ascertainable by him; or

(b) from facts ascertainable by him with the help of appropriate expert advice which it is reasonable for him to seek;

but a person shall not be taken by virtue of this subsection to have knowledge of a fact ascertainable by him only with the help of expert advice unless he has failed to take all reasonable steps to obtain (and, where appropriate, to act on) that advice.

(8) Subsections (5) to (7) above shall not extend to Scotland.

Application of certain enactments etc

6.—(1) Any damage for which a person is liable under section 2 above shall be deemed to have been caused—

(a) for the purposes of the Fatal Accidents Act 1976, by that person's wrongful act, neglect or default;

(b) for the purposes of section 3 of the Law Reform (Miscellaneous Provisions) (Scotland) Act 1940 (contribution among joint wrongdoers), by that person's wrongful act or negligent act or omission;

(c) for the purposes of section 1 of the Damages (Scotland) Act 1976 (rights of relatives of a deceased), by that person's act or omission; and

(d) for the purposes of Part II of the Administration of Justice Act 1982 (damages for personal injuries, etc.—Scotland), by an act or omission giving rise to liability in that person to pay damages.

(2) Where—

(a) a person's death is caused wholly or partly by a defect in a product, or a person dies after suffering damage which has been so caused;

(b) a request such as mentioned in paragraph (a) of subsection (3) of section 2 above is made to a supplier of the product by that person's personal representatives or, in the case of a person whose death is caused wholly or partly by the defect, by any dependant or relative of that person; and

(c) the conditions specified in paragraphs (b) and (c) of that subsection are satisfied in relation to that request,

this Part shall have effect for the purposes of the Law Reform (Miscellaneous Provisions) Act 1934, the Fatal Accidents Act 1976 and the Damages (Scotland) Act 1976 as if liability of the supplier to that person under that subsection did not depend on that person having requested the supplier to identify certain persons or on the said conditions having been satisfied in relation to a request made by that person.

(3) Section 1 of the Congenital Disabilities (Civil Liability) Act 1976 shall have effect for the purposes of this Part as if—

(a) a person were answerable to a child in respect of an occurrence caused wholly or partly by a defect in a product if he is or has been liable under section 2 above in respect of any effect of the occurrence on a parent of the child, or would be so liable if the occurrence caused a parent of the child to suffer damage;

(b) the provisions of this Part relating to liability under section 2 above applied in relation to liability by virtue of paragraph (a) above under the said section 1; and

(c) subsection (6) of the said section 1 (exclusion of liability) were omitted.

(4) Where any damage is caused partly by a defect in a product and partly by the fault of the person suffering the damage, the Law Reform (Contributory Negligence) Act 1945 and section 5 of the Fatal Accidents Act 1976 (contributory negligence) shall have effect as if the defect were the fault of every person liable by virtue of this Part for the damage caused by the defect.

(5) In subsection (4) above 'fault' has the same meaning as in the said Act of 1945.

(6) Schedule 1 to this Act shall have effect for the purpose of amending the Limitation Act 1980 and the Prescription and Limitation (Scotland) Act 1973 in their application in relation to the bringing of actions by virtue of this Part.

(7) It is hereby declared that liability by virtue of this Part is to be treated as liability in tort for the purposes of any enactment conferring jurisdiction on any court with respect to any matter.

(8) Nothing in this Part shall prejudice the operation of section 12 of the Nuclear Installations Act 1965 (rights to compensation for certain breaches of duties confined to rights under that Act).

Prohibition on exclusions from liability

7. The liability of a person by virtue of this Part to a person who has suffered damage caused wholly or partly by a defect in a product, or to a dependant or relative of such a person, shall not be limited or excluded by any contract term, by any notice or by any other provision.

Power to modify Part I

8.—(1) Her Majesty may by Order in Council make such modifications of this Part and of any other enactment (including an enactment contained in the following Parts of this Act, or in an Act passed after this Act) as appear to Her Majesty in Council to be necessary or expedient in consequence of any modification of the product liability Directive which is made at any time after the passing of this Act.

(2) An Order in Council under subsection (1) above shall not be submitted to Her Majesty in Council unless a draft of the Order has been laid before, and approved by a resolution of, each House of Parliament.

Application of Part I to Crown

9.—(1) Subject to subsection (2) below, this Part shall bind the Crown.

(2) The Crown shall not, as regards the Crown's liability by virtue of this Part, be bound by this Part further than the Crown is made liable in tort or in reparation under the Crown Proceedings Act 1947, as that Act has effect from time to time.

. . .

Interpretation

45.—(1) In this Act, except in so far as the context otherwise requires— . . .

'business' includes a trade or profession and the activities of a professional or trade association or of a local authority or other public authority; . . .

'goods' includes substances, growing crops and things comprised in land by virtue of being attached to it and any ship, aircraft or vehicle; . . .

'personal injury' includes any disease and any other impairment of a person's physical or mental condition; . . .

'substance' means any natural or artificial substance, whether in solid, liquid or gaseous form or in the form of a vapour, and includes substances that are comprised in or mixed with other goods; . . .

Meaning of 'supply'

46.—(1) Subject to the following provisions of this section, references in this Act to supplying goods shall be construed as references to doing any of the following, whether as principal or agent, that is to say—

(a) selling, hiring out or lending the goods;
(b) entering into a hire-purchase agreement to furnish the goods;
(c) the performance of any contract for work and materials to furnish the goods;
(d) providing the goods in exchange for any consideration (including trading stamps) other than money;
(e) providing the goods in or in connection with the performance of any statutory function; or
(f) giving the goods as a prize or otherwise making a gift of the goods;

and, in relation to gas or water, those references shall be construed as including references to providing the service by which the gas or water is made available for use.

(2) For the purposes of any reference in this Act to supplying goods, where a person ('the ostensible supplier') supplies goods to another person ('the customer') under a hire-purchase agreement, conditional sale agreement or credit-sale agreement or under an agreement for the hiring of goods (other than a hire-purchase agreement) and the ostensible supplier—

(a) carries on the business of financing the provision of goods for others by means of such agreements; and
(b) in the course of that business acquired his interest in the goods supplied to the customer as a means of financing the provision of them for the customer by a further person ('the effective supplier'),

the effective supplier and not the ostensible supplier shall be treated as supplying the goods to the customer.

(3) Subject to subsection (4) below, the performance of any contract by the erection of any building or structure on any land or by the carrying out of any other building works shall be treated for the purposes of this Act as a supply of goods in so far as, but only in so far as, it involves the provision of any goods to any person by means of their incorporation into the building, structure or works.

(4) Except for the purposes of, and in relation to, notices to warn or any provision made by or under Part III of this Act, references in this Act to supplying goods shall not include references to supplying goods comprised in land where the supply is effected by the creation or disposal of an interest in the land.

(5) Except in Part I of this Act references in this Act to a person's supplying goods shall be confined to references to that person's supplying goods in the course of a business of his, but for the purposes of this subsection it shall be immaterial whether the business is a business of dealing in the goods.

(6) For the purposes of subsection (5) above goods shall not be treated as supplied in the course of a business if they are supplied, in pursuance of an obligation arising under or in connection with the insurance of the goods, to the person with whom they were insured.

(7) Except for the purposes of, and in relation to, prohibition notices or suspension notices, references in Parts II to IV of this Act to supplying goods shall not include—

(a) references to supplying goods where the person supplied carries on a business of buying goods of the same description as those goods and repairing or reconditioning them;
(b) references to supplying goods by a sale of articles as scrap (that is to say, for the value of materials included in the articles rather than for the value of the articles themselves).

(8) Where any goods have at any time been supplied by being hired out or lent to any person, neither a continuation or renewal of the hire or loan (whether on the same or different terms) nor any transaction for the transfer after that time of any interest in the goods to the person to whom they were hired or lent shall be treated for the purposes of this Act as a further supply of the goods to that person.

(9) A ship, aircraft or motor vehicle shall not be treated for the purposes of this Act as supplied to any person by reason only that services consisting in the carriage of goods or passengers in that ship, aircraft or vehicle, or in its use for any other purpose, are provided to that person in pursuance of an agreement relating to the use of the ship, aircraft or vehicle for a particular period or for particular voyages, flights or journeys.

. . .

Short title, commencement and transitional provision

50.—(1) This Act may be cited as the Consumer Protection Act 1987.

(2) This Act shall come into force on such day as the Secretary of State may by order made by statutory instrument appoint, and different days may be so appointed for different provisions or for different purposes.

. . .

(7) Nothing in this Act or in any order under subsection (2) above shall make any person liable by virtue of Part I of this Act for any damage caused wholly or partly by a defect in a product which was supplied to any person by its producer before the coming into force of Part I of this Act.

(8) Expressions used in subsection (7) above and in Part I of this Act have the same meanings in that subsection as in that Part.

SCHEDULE 1

LIMITATION OF ACTIONS UNDER PART I

PART I:

ENGLAND AND WALES

1. After section 11 of the Limitation Act 1980 (actions in respect of personal injuries) there shall be inserted the following section—

'11A.—(1) This section shall apply to an action for damages by virtue of any provision of Part I of the Consumer Protection Act 1987.

(2) None of the time limits given in the preceding provisions of this Act shall apply to an action to which this section applies.

(3) An action to which this section applies shall not be brought after the expiration of the period of ten years from the relevant time, within the meaning of section 4 of the said Act of 1987; and this subsection shall operate to extinguish a right of action and shall do so whether or not that right of action had accrued, or time under the following provisions of this Act had begun to run, at the end of the said period of ten years.

(4) Subject to subsection (5) below, an action to which this section applies in which the damages claimed by the plaintiff consist of or include damages in respect of personal injuries to the plaintiff or any other person or loss of or damage to any property, shall not be brought after the expiration of the period of three years from whichever is the later of—

(a) the date on which the cause of action accrued; and

(b) the date of knowledge of the injured person or, in the case of loss of or damage to property, the date of knowledge of the plaintiff or (if earlier) of any person in whom his cause of action was previously vested.

(5) If in a case where the damages claimed by the plaintiff consist of or include damages in respect of personal injuries to the plaintiff or any other person the injured person died before the expiration of the period mentioned in subsection (4) above, that subsection shall have effect as respects the cause of action surviving for the benefit of his estate by virtue of section 1 of the Law Reform (Miscellaneous Provisions) Act 1934 as if for the reference to that period there were substituted a reference to the period of three years from whichever is the later of—

(a) the date of death; and

(b) the date of the personal representative's knowledge.

(6) For the purposes of this section 'personal representative' includes any person who is or has been a personal representative of the deceased, including an executor who has not

proved the will (whether or not he has renounced probate) but not anyone appointed only as a special personal representative in relation to settled land; and regard shall be had to any knowledge acquired by any such person while a personal representative or previously.

(7) If there is more than one personal representative and their dates of knowledge are different, subsection (5)(b) above shall be read as referring to the earliest of those dates.

(8) Expressions used in this section or section 14 of this Act and in Part I of the Consumer Protection Act 1987 have the same meanings in this section or that section as in that Part; and section 1(1) of that Act (Part I to be construed as enacted for the purpose of complying with the product liability Directive) shall apply for the purpose of construing this section and the following provisions of this Act so far as they relate to an action by virtue of any provision of that Part as it applies for the purpose of construing that Part.'

NOTE

As s 1(1) of the 1987 Act makes clear, the purpose of Part I is to secure compliance with the product liability Directive and it must be construed accordingly. This explicit link may be important since there are a number of respects in which the wording of the Act differs significantly from that of the Directive. Section 2(6) is similarly important in that it makes it clear that the remedies provided by the Act are additional to those available under the existing law. Hence where the damage is of a type which falls outside the Act recovery may be pursued on some other basis, for example, in negligence or contract. Examples include damage to property where the sum involved is less than £275 (see s 5(4)) and personal injury outside the ten year cut off provision (see s 11A(3) of the Limitation Act, 1980). Indeed, it is likely that in many cases claims will be argued in the alternative. For detailed discussion of Part I of the 1987 Act, see Miller, *Product Liability and Safety Encyclopaedia*, Div III; see also Stapleton, *Product Liability* (1994); Clark, *Product Liability* (1989).

At the time of writing there has been a singular lack of reported cases decided under the 1987 Act. Some of the possible reasons for this are discussed in the National Consumer Council Report 'Unsafe Products' (November, 1995). Further reference is made to this below: see pp 254–5. In view of the absence of reported cases some of the more important and contentious issues may be addressed by raising questions and posing problems under a number of headings. The solutions will require detailed reference to the relevant sections of the Act and the corresponding provisions of the Directive.

Persons subject to liability

Section 2 of the Act, as amplified in particular by s 1(2) and (3), sets out the range of defendants who may be subject to potential liability under the strict liability provisions of Part I of the Act.

Consider the following cases:

1. Nikko a highly reputable manufacturer of children's toys based in Japan, exports several dangerously defective toys which are imported into the United

Kingdom by Olaf and sold on to Pricewars, a supermarket chain. Pricewars, by agreement with Nikko, has arranged for the toys to be packaged in boxes which carry the label 'Toys by Pricewars: Made in Japan'. One such toy is sold to Rose and when used by her daughter, Sally, it fractures, causing Sally serious facial injury. Advise Rose and Sally.

2. Adam is a maintenance engineer, who is employed by Reliability Ltd to service lifts. When servicing a lift in the University of Midshire be replaces a component in a part which is critical to safety. The component was manufactured some five years previously by a company which is no longer in business. The component is defective, causing the lift to fall when a student, Blackstone, is using it. Blackstone suffers serious injury. It is accepted that both Adam and Reliability Ltd have exercised all possible care. Advise Blackstone.

Products within the scope of the Act

The definition of 'product' in s 1(2) of the Act (see also s 45(1) for the definition of 'goods') is relatively broad and the only further limitation (see s 2(4)) concerns 'agricultural produce' (as defined in s 1(2)) and game. None the less it is clear that very considerable difficulties may arise in the application of the Act to certain types of product, including agricultural produce, computers and other sources of information, and medical devices.

Agricultural produce

In considering the scope of liability for such produce the limitation in terms of not having 'undergone an industrial process' (s 2(4)) needs to be linked to the definition of 'producer' in s 1(2) and compared with both Article 2 of and the preamble to the Directive. What reasons, if any, might justify the limited liability under the Act in respect of agricultural produce?

Consider the following cases:

1. Besthens owns a large-scale chicken farm on which it breeds chickens both for egg production and for distribution to supermarkets. Eggs are graded and boxed and sold on to the retail trade. One batch is found to contain salmonella and Ada suffers severe food poisoning when she uses a fresh egg to make mayonnaise. Chickens are prepared and frozen by Besthens and again sold on to the retail trade. Barbara also suffers food poisoning when she prepares and eats a slightly under-cooked chicken which is similarly found to contain salmonella.

   Advise Ada and Barbara as to the liability of Besthens. How, if at all, might the position of Ada differ if the mayonnaise had been produced and sold in jars by a third party?

2. Apple grows fruit on a commercial basis. He sprays his pears with a chemical preservative manufactured by Orange and sells them on to the retail trade in boxes. A tin of the preservative was manufactured to the wrong strength and hence defective and Carol becomes ill through eating several of Apple's pears

which have been treated with it. Apple also grows vegetables which he sells on to market traders. One particular crop of carrots causes food poisoning to Diane because, prior to planting, the soil had been treated with a defective fertiliser which had again been manufactured by Orange. Orange is no longer in business.

Advise Carol and Diane. How, if at all, might the position of Diane differ if the carrots had been treated with a defective insecticide (i) when growing in the soil or (ii) when growing hydrophonically, that is, in water?

NOTE

The European Commission has proposed that the exception for primary agricultural products and game should be removed: see COM (97) 478 final (OJ C 337, 7.11.97, p 54).

Computers and information

Nowadays, there will be many occasions on which injury or damage may be caused by defects within a computer system, for example when it is being used in such a way as might affect the operation of an aeroplane, hospital or factory. For example, a computer software failure in a guidance system is reported as having led to the loss of the Ariane 501 rocket: see *The Times*, 24 July 1996, p 7. Similar dangers may arise through other means of storing and transmitting information. For discussion, see Whittaker, 'European Product Liability and Intellectual Products' (1989) 105 LQR 125; Stapleton in Cane and Stapleton (eds), *Essays for Patrick Atiyah* (1991), at pp 269–70. Some assistance as to the potential application of the 1987 Act may be found by way of analogy in the following case:

St Albans City and District Council v International Computers Ltd [1996] 4 All ER 481, Court of Appeal

The plaintiff authority had suffered financial loss through defects in a computer system used in administering its collection of the community charge. The initial question was the application of the implied terms as to quality and fitness for purpose of the Sale of Goods Act 1979 and the Supply of Goods and Services Act 1982 (see generally, above, pp 95–113).

Sir Iain Glidewell made the following observations: In both the Sale of Goods Act 1979, s 61, and the Supply of Goods and Services Act 1982, s 18, the definition of goods includes 'all personal chattels other than things in action and money'. Clearly, a disk is within this definition. Equally clearly, a program, of itself, is not.

If a disk carrying a program is transferred, by way of sale or hire, and the program is in some way defective, so that it will not instruct or enable the computer to achieve the intended purpose, is this a defect in the disk? Put more precisely, would the seller or hirer of the disk be in breach of the terms as to quality and fitness for purpose implied by s 14 of the 1979 Act and s 9 of the 1982 Act? Mr Dehn QC, for ICL, argues that they would not. He submits that the defective program in my example would be distinct from the tangible disk, and thus that the 'goods'—the disk—would not be defective.

There is no English authority on this question, and indeed we have been referred to none from any common law jurisdiction. The only reference I have found is an article published in 1994 by Dr Jane Stapleton. This is to a decision in *Advent Systems Ltd v Unisys Corp* (1991) 925 F 2d 670 that software is a 'good'; Dr Stapleton notes the decision as being reached 'on the basis of policy arguments'. We were referred, as was Scott Baker J, to a decision of Rogers J in the Supreme Court of New South Wales, *Toby Constructions Products Pty Ltd v Computa Bar (Sales) Pty Ltd* [1983] 2 NSWLR 48. The decision in that case was that the sale of a whole computer system, including both hardware and software, was a sale of 'goods' within the New South Wales legislation, which defines goods in similar terms to those in the English statute. That decision was in my respectful view clearly correct, but it does not answer the present question. Indeed, Rogers J specifically did not answer it. In expressing an opinion I am therefore venturing where others have, no doubt wisely, not trodden.

Suppose I buy an instruction manual on the maintenance and repair of a particular make of car. The instructions are wrong in an important respect. Anybody who follows them is likely to cause serious damage to the engine of his car. In my view, the instructions are an integral part of the manual. The manual including the instructions, whether in a book or a video cassette, would in my opinion be 'goods' within the meaning of the 1979 Act, and the defective instructions would result in a breach of the implied terms in s 14.

If this is correct, I can see no logical reason why it should not also be correct in relation to a computer disk onto which a program designed and intended to instruct or enable a computer to achieve particular functions has been encoded. If the disk is sold or hired by the computer manufacturer, but the program is defective, in my opinion there would prima facie be a breach of the terms as to quality and fitness for purpose implied by the 1979 Act or the 1982 Act.

However, in the present case, it is clear that the defective program 2020 was not sold, and it seems probable that it was not hired. The evidence is that, in relation to many of the program releases, an employee of ICL went to St Albans' premises where the computer was installed taking with him a disk on which the new program was encoded, and himself performed the exercise of transferring the program into the computer.

As I have already said, the program itself is not 'goods' within the statutory definition. Thus a transfer of the program in the way I have described does not, in my view, constitute a transfer of goods. It follows that in such circumstances there is no statutory implication of terms as to quality or fitness for purpose.

Would the contract then contain no such implied term? The answer must be sought in the common law. The terms implied by the 1979 Act and the 1982 Act were originally evolved by the courts of common law and have since by analogy been implied by the courts into other types of contract. Should such a term be implied in a contract of the kind I am now considering, for the transfer of a computer program into the computer without any transfer of a disk or any other tangible thing on which the program is encoded? . . .

In my judgment a contract for the transfer into a computer of a program intended by both parties to instruct or enable the computer to achieve specified functions is one to which Lord Pearson's words apply. In the absence of any express term as to quality or fitness for purpose, or of any term to the contrary, such a contract is subject to an implied term that the program will be reasonably fit for, ie reasonably capable of achieving the intended purpose.

. . .

Appeal allowed in part.

NOTES
1. For an equivalent limitation in the 1987 Act, see s 4(1)(b) and the definition of 'supply' in s 46.
2. Dr Stapleton in *Essays for Patrick Atiyah* (above) writes (at p 269): 'Suppose that the designer (A) of a navigational software program incorrectly enters the height of a mountain, causing a plane to crash. If the software package is to be a "product" for the purposes of the Directive, is a map incorrectly drawn by B, which carries identically incorrect information to the pilot, also to be a product?' In answer to this question, if both the program and the map are 'supplied' by A and B respectively, are they potentially subject to strict liability?

PROBLEM

Carservice Ltd publishes a car maintenance manual which is written by one of its employees, James. The manual contains dangerously inaccurate information and it is purchased from a retailer by Ron, who uses it to service his car. This results in extensive damage to the engine of the car and to its bodywork when the car runs into a concrete wall. Ron's passenger, Sally, is injured.

Advise Carservice and James at to their potential liability. Consider also the potential liability of the printer of the manual.

Medical devices

The application of the Act to medical devices (eg those which are used in hospitals to carry out operations) is often straightforward once it can be shown that the device was defective and caused injury. It is arguable that more difficult issues are raised when the very purpose of the operation is to insert the relevant part into the body— as in an operation to insert a pacemaker or a valve, or attach an artificial leg.

PROBLEM

Harry is operated on for a routine hip replacement and it is agreed that the hospital and the entire medical team have exercised all possible care. He claims that he is continuing to suffer severe pain and that the artificial replacement hip was 'defective', causing hip dislocations.

Advise Harry as to whether the artificial hip is a 'product' for the purposes of the 1987 Act: see *The Times*, 19 and 21 February 1998 (allegedly faulty Capital 3M hip replacements).

The definition of a defect

A central feature of the 1987 Act is the definition of a 'defect' contained in s 3. This is couched in terms of the level of safety which persons generally are entitled to expect. In determining the relevant standard all the circumstances have to be taken into account, including certain specified circumstances. In essence, this is an objective test, based on the expectations of a hypothetical (reasonable) consumer. Where the product has not been manufactured in accordance with specifications (as in *Daniels v R White & Sons Ltd and Tarbard*, above, p 38) it should be easy enough to apply. Consumers are entitled to expect that lemonade will not contain carbolic acid. The more difficult cases are alleged defects of design or composition or where the complaint is of inadequate warning or instructions for safe use. In such cases it is inevitable that the standard should be a qualified one. No one suggests that petrol is defective simply because it has explosive qualities or that otherwise wholesome butter is defective because it may increase levels of cholesterol and the risk of a heart attack. In other cases, and notably those involving pharmaceutical products, the decision may turn on a very careful balancing of the risks and benefits involved, these being relevant residual circumstances within s 3(2): see, generally, Ferguson, *Drug Injuries and the Pursuit of Compensation* (1996), ch 8. Frequently, much will depend on the nature of the warning which has been given. Sometimes a warning will not be practicable, or would simply be inadequate, so that an adverse judgment will carry the implication that the product needs to be re-designed. For detailed consideration of the requirement of a 'defect', see Stapleton, *Product Liability* (1994), ch 10, and 'Products Liability Reform—Real or Illusory?' (1986) 6 OJLS 392.

The following Canadian case, although decided under a negligence-based system, is of general interest on the question of warnings.

Buchan v Ortho Pharmaceutical (Canada) Ltd (1986) 25 DLR (4th) 658, Ontario Court of Appeal

The plaintiff, aged 23 and a non-smoker, suffered a stroke in September 1971, which left her partially paralysed, shortly after she started taking oral contraceptives manufactured and distributed by the defendants. The contraceptives had been prescribed for her by her doctor. Previously she had been in excellent health. The evidence established that the stroke was caused by the oral contraceptives and that the defendant was aware of the risk of a stroke. In an action for damages the trial judge gave judgment for the plaintiff and the defendant appealed. The reasons for dismissing the appeal are stated fully in the Dominion Law Report as follows:

> The defendant failed to warn of the danger of stroke inherent in the use of the oral contraceptive and the failure caused or materially contributed to her injuries. There was no question of any defect or impropriety in the manufacture of the oral contraceptive, nor of its efficacy when taken as prescribed. A manufacturer of a product has a duty to warn consumers of dangers inherent in the use of its product of which it knows or has reason to know. The warning must be adequate. It should be communicated clearly and understandably in a manner calculated to inform the user of the nature of the risk and the extent of the danger; it should be in terms commensurate with the gravity of the potential hazard, and it should not be neutralized or negated by collateral efforts on the part of the manufacturer. The nature and extent of any given warning will depend on what is reasonable having regard to all the facts and

circumstances relevant to the product in question. The duty is a continuous one requiring that the manufacturer warn, not only of dangers known at the time of sale, but also of dangers discovered after the product has been sold and delivered. Ordinarily, the warning must be addressed directly to the person likely to be injured. It is not, however, necessary that that be done in every case. Where, for example, the product is a highly technical one that is intended or expected to be used only under the supervision of experts, a warning to the experts will suffice. Similarly, a warning to the ultimate user may not be necessary where intermediate examination is anticipated or the intervention of a learned intermediary is understood.

In the case of prescription drugs, the duty of manufacturers to warn consumers is discharged if the manufacturer provides prescribing physicians with adequate warning of the potential danger. The prescribing physician is in a position to take into account the propensities of the drug and the susceptibilities of the patient. He has the duty of informing himself of the benefits and potential dangers of any medication he prescribes, and of exercising his independent judgment as a medical expert based on his knowledge of the patient and the product. In taking the drug, the patient is expected to, and it can be presumed does, place primary reliance on his doctor's judgement. Very recently several state courts in the US have concluded that oral contraceptives bear characteristics which render them vastly different from other prescription drugs and which demand that manufacturers be required to warn users directly of risks associated with their use. For the purpose of deciding this case it will be assumed that the learned intermediary rule applies. Liability must be determined within a 1971 framework; changes which have since occurred in either the state of medical knowledge or the form of warnings provided consumers or physicians are not relevant.

Like other drug manufacturers, the defendant uses a number of methods of communicating information to doctors about its birth control products including pamphlets, package inserts, advertisements, letters and oral information by sales representatives. However, none of the defendant's information intended for doctors contained any warning or made any mention of the risk of stroke associated with the use of oral contraceptives. The warnings to physicians in the United States made by the defendant's sister company showed that the defendant was aware or should have been aware of the association between oral contraceptive use and stroke. Moreover, the expert testimony and the exhibits disclosed an abundance of published information in medical and scientific journals prior to and at the time the plaintiff was prescribed the oral contraceptive which linked the use of oral contraceptives with stroke.

Notwithstanding that in December, 1970, the Minister of Health circulated a report to all physicians in Canada which provided the same information about oral contraceptives and strokes as that provided by the defendant's sister company to physicians in the United States, the defendant was not relieved of its duty to warn the medical profession. A drug manufacturer who seeks to rely on the intervention of prescribing physicians under the learned intermediary doctrine to except itself from the general common law duty to warn consumers directly must actually warn prescribing physicians.

The conduct of a prescribing doctor may exonerate the manufacturer from liability where the evidence establishes that, as a result of what the doctor knew, adequate warnings would have had no effect on whether or not he would have prescribed the drug. Once the breach of duty to warn prescribing physicians has been established, it is fair and reasonable to presume that the inadequacy of the warning was a contributing cause of the ingestion of the drug. It ought not to be incumbent on a plaintiff to prove as part of her case what her doctor might or might not have done had he been adequately warned. One can assume that a doctor would not ignore a proper warning or fail to disclose a material risk or otherwise act negligently. Even if the evidence were to indicate that the doctor was negligent, the manufacturer would not be shielded from liability if such negligence were a foreseeable consequence of the breach of duty to warn. The presumption may, of course, be rebutted if the defendant comes forth with evidence that, despite the inadequacy of the warning, the doctor's conduct toward his patient would have been the same whether or not the manufacturer was in breach of the duty. However, the defendant's inadequate warnings coupled with its promotional sales tactics over a protracted period of time played a role in the formulation of the doctor's opinion as to the safety of oral contraceptives and the necessity to inform patients of the attendant risks. It is not unreasonable to conclude that the doctor's failure to disclose the risk of stroke to the plaintiff was contributed to by the inadequacy of the defendant's warnings and the promotional tactics of its pharmaceutical sales-man. The doctor's intervention cannot operate to exonerate the defendant from liability for its breach of duty.

When a manufacturer's breach of the duty to warn is found to have influenced a physician's opinion as to the safety of a drug thereby contributing to the physician's non-disclosure of a material risk and the consumer's ingestion of the drug, the manufacturer is not entitled to require the injured consumer to prove that a reasonable consumer in her position would not have taken the drug if properly warned. Whether the particular consumer would have taken the drug even with a proper warning is a matter to be decided by the trier of fact on all the relevant evidence. It was open to the trial judge, viewing the evidence as he did, to credit the plaintiff's testimony that she would not have taken the pill had she been told of the danger of stroke, and to determine the causation issue accordingly. Whether a so-called reasonable woman in the plaintiff's position would have done likewise is beside the point. The selection of a method of preventing unwanted pregnancy in the case of a healthy woman is a matter, not of medical treatment, but of personal choice, and it is not unreasonable that notice of a serious potential hazard to users of oral contraceptives could influence her selection of another method of birth control. So long as the court is satisfied that the plaintiff herself would not have used the drug if properly informed of the risks, the causation issue should be concluded in her favour regardless of what other women might have done.

NOTE

See also *Dow Corning Corp v Hollis* (1996) 129 DLR (4th) 609 (Canadian Supreme Court).

QUESTIONS

1. In considering whether a product is defective in design, or because of inadequate warnings, is there any material distinction to be taken between a strict liability system and one which is based on proof of negligence? Does strict liability imply that the product should be safer?

2. Where a particular type of product (e.g. cosmetics) is subject to detailed and regularly updated legislative requirements should a court be able to hold that it is defective notwithstanding complete compliance with such requirements? Would this amount to a constitutional anomaly?: see *Alberry & Budden v BP Oil and Shell UK Ltd* (1980) 124 Sol Jo 376, CA (lead content of petrol complying with regulations made under the Control of Pollution Act).

3. A newspaper report recounted how a three year old child had suffocated and died after climbing into a tumble dryer in his parents' kitchen (see *The Times*, 3 September 1997, p 11). What arguments might be employed in support of a contention that the tumble dryer was (or was not) defective?

4. Medical evidence has now clearly established that cigarettes cause serious illness to those who smoke them regularly and packets carry warnings to this

effect. Outline the main issues which might be raised in support of (or against) a contention that cigarettes are 'defective'.

5. In the case of many products (eg motor cars and such domestic appliances as fridges) safety features have increased very significantly over the years. If a given product was designed in 1982, manufactured in 1989 (and then kept in stock), supplied by the manufacturer in 1992, and caused an accident and resultant injury in 1995, what is the year against which the relevant standard of safety is to be judged?

Damage and loss covered

Section 5 of the 1987 Act specifies the types of damage and loss which are within the scope of Part I of the Act. The equivalent provision in Article 9 of the Directive differs in its wording in a number of respects. It should be considered when answering the questions and problems set out below. Where the Act is inapplicable there remains the possibility of recovering either in negligence (see above, pp 204–13) or, on appropriate facts, in contract—for example, under the Sale of Goods Act 1979, s 14 (see above, p 95 et seq).

QUESTIONS

1. Does the reference to 'loss of . . . property' in s 5(1) imply that manufacturers of such products as burglar and car alarms, and locks may be liable under the Act when property (eg a car or house contents) is stolen, although not damaged? Would the manufacturer of a defective carrier bag be liable when it is supplied by a jewellery shop to a customer and a fragile and expensive piece of jewellery falls out and is (i) damaged or (ii) lost?: see *Aswan Engineering Establishment Co v Lupdine Ltd* [1987] 1 All ER 135, at p 159 per Nicholls LJ.
2. Is there 'damage' within s 5(1) when a defective product causes the following: (i) the contamination of land and consequent need to cleanse the soil; (ii) dust to settle in large quantities with a consequent need to have a house cleaned and expensive stereo equipment repaired?: cf *Losinjska Plovidba v Transco Overseas Ltd* [1995] 2 Lloyds LR 395; *Blue Circle Industries plc v Ministry of Defence, The Times*, 11 December 1996 and *Hunter v Canary Wharf Ltd* [1996] 1 All ER 482, CA, and on appeal [1997] 2 All ER 426, HL.

PROBLEMS

Consider the following cases, both under the 1987 Act and under any alternative ground of liability including negligence.

1. Richard, who lives in a luxury block of flats, has recently purchased a washing machine manufactured in the United Kingdom by Saul plc. The machine is defective and leaks soon after it is installed, causing damage to flats below, which are owned by Tom and Ulrich. Tom has to have his lounge replastered and repainted and a carpet cleaned. Ulrich, a solicitor, who frequently works

from home complains of damage to his law reports and to his top of the range computer, which he uses both for professional and private purposes. It is accepted that Richard has exercised all possible care. Advise Tom and Ulrich.

2. Gerryhatrick has recently purchased a new television set costing £600 from a retailer who is now insolvent. A defective valve implodes, causing the set to shatter beyond repair, but no personal injury or damage to any other item of property follows. The set was manufactured by Blowout and the valve had been supplied by Component Ltd, a specialist producer. Gerryhatrick cannot afford to buy a new set.

Advise Gerryhatrick as to the liability, if any, of (i) Blowout and (ii) Component Ltd. Would Component Ltd's liability be different according to whether the valve had been (a) part of the original set or (b) a replacement part?

2. Danegeld is a manufacturer of coffee pots all of which have been sold to consumers through an independent mail order company which is now insolvent. Altogether some 10,000 such pots have been sold. It is now apparent that all the pots are dangerously defective owing to a defect in the glue which has been used to stick on the handles. The glue was supplied by an independent company which is also insolvent. Amanda has been scalded when her coffee pot broke. Ben, knowing of her injuries, feels that it is not safe to use his pot any further. Claude owns a coffee pot but is unaware of the danger. Both Amanda and Ben wish to claim compensation from Danegeld.

Advise Amanda and Bert. Consider also whether Danegeld is legally obliged at common law to take steps to warn owners of the pots once it knows of the dangers. Would it affect the position if the pots had been sold through numerous retailers, rather than the one mail order company? (Note also the provisions of s 13 of the Act—'notices to warn', below, p 588.)

Defences and qualifications to liability

Section 4 of the 1987 Act sets out a number of important defences, and further qualifications to liability are contained elsewhere, for example contributory negligence (s 6(4)) and the ten year cut off point inserted into the Limitation Act 1980, s 11A(3). By far the most controversial defence is that contained in s 4(1)(e) which corresponds to Article 7(e) of the Directive. This is usually known as the 'development risks' or alternatively the 'state of the art' defence. There is no doubt that the defence considerably dilutes the strict liability usually associated with the Act. For general discussion, see Newdick, 'The Development Risk Defence of the Consumer Protection Act 1987' (1988) 47 CLJ 455; 'Risk, Uncertainty and Knowledge in the Development Risks Defence' (1991) 20 Anglo-Am LR 309; Clark, *Product Liability* (1989), ch 6.

In *Beshada v Johns-Manville Products Corp*, 447 A2d 539 (1982) the New Jersey Supreme Court rejected the availability of a similar defence in a case involving asbestos-related illness. Some of the practical difficulties associated with any such defence were noted as follows:

The 'state-of-the-art' at a given time is partly determined by how much industry invests in safety research. By imposing on manufacturers the costs of failure to discover hazards, we create an incentive for them to invest more actively in safety research . . . The vast confusion that is virtually certain to arise from any attempt to deal in a trial setting with the concept of scientific knowability constitutes a strong reason for avoiding the concept altogether by striking the state-of-the-art defense.

Scientific knowability, as we understand it, refers not to what in fact was known at the time, but to what could have been known at the time. In other words, even if no scientist had actually formed the belief that asbestos was dangerous, the hazards would be deemed 'knowable' if a scientist could have formed that belief by applying research or performing tests that were available at the time. Proof of what could have been known will inevitably be complicated, costly, confusing and time consuming. Each side will have to produce experts in the history of science and technology to speculate as to what knowledge was feasible in a given year. We doubt that juries will be capable of even understanding the concept of scientific knowability, much less be able to resolve such a complex issue. Moreover, we should resist legal rules that will so greatly add to the cost both sides incur in trying a case.

The concept of knowability is complicated further by the fact, noted above, that the level of investment in safety research by manufacturers is one determinant of the state-of-the-art at any given time. Fairness suggests that manufacturers not be excused from liability because their prior inadequate investment in safety rendered the hazards of their product unknowable. Thus, a judgment will have to be made as to whether defendants' investment in safety research in the years preceding distribution of the product was adequate. If not, the experts in the history of technology will have to testify as to what would have been knowable at the time of distribution if manufacturers had spent the proper amount on safety in prior years. To state the issue is to fully understand the great difficulties it would engender in a courtroom.

The same court later confined this decision to cases involving asbestos: see *Feldman v Lederle Laboratories*, 479 A 2d 374 (1984).

Many commentators believed that the wording of s 4(1)(e) was significantly more favourable to manufacturers than the equivalent provision in Article 7(e) of the Directive. On this basis the Directive would not have been correctly transposed. The European Commission sought a declaration to this effect and the case was heard in May 1997.

Commission of the European Communities v United Kingdom of Great Britain and Northern Ireland. Court of Justice of the European Communities, Case C–300/95

JUDGEMENT OF THE COURT (Fifth Chamber) 29 May 1997

APPLICATION for a declaration that, by failing to take all the measures necessary to implement Council Directive 85/374/EEC of 25 July 1985 on the approximation of the laws, regulations and administrative provisions of the Member States concerning liability for defective products (OJ 1985 L 210, p 29), in particular Article 7(e) thereof, the United Kingdom has failed to fulfil its obligations under that directive and under the EC Treaty.

Judgment

1. By application lodged at the Court Registry on 20 September 1995, the Commission of the European Communities brought an action under Article 169 of the EC Treaty for a declaration that, by failing to take all the measures necessary to implement Council Directive 85/374/EEC

of 25 July 1985 on the approximation of the laws, regulations and administrative provisions of the Member States concerning liability for defective products (OJ 1985 L 210, p 29; 'the Directive'), in particular Article 7(e) thereof, the United Kingdom has failed to fulfil its obligations under that directive and under the EC Treaty.

2. The object of the Directive is to bring about approximation of the laws of the Member States concerning liability for defective products, divergences in which may 'distort competition and affect the movement of goods within the common market and entail a differing degree of protection of the consumer against damage caused by a defective product to his health or property' (first recital in the preamble).

3. According to Article 1 of the Directive, the producer shall be liable for damage caused by a defect in his product.

4. Article 4 provides that the injured person shall be required to prove the damage, the defect and the causal relationship between defect and damage.

5. However, Article 7 sets out a number of defences enabling the producer to avoid liability. The seventh recital in the preamble to the Directive states in this connection that 'a fair apportionment of risk between the injured person and the producer implies that the producer should be able to free himself from liability if he furnishes proof as to the existence of certain exonerating circumstances'.

6. Accordingly,

'The producer shall not be liable as a result of this Directive if he proves:

. . .

(e) that the state of scientific and technical knowledge at the time when he put the product into circulation was not such as to enable the existence of the defect to be discovered;

. . .

7. Under Article 19 of the Directive, Member States were required to take the measures necessary to comply with it by no later than 30 July 1988. The United Kingdom implemented the Directive by means of Part I of the Consumer Protection Act 1987 ('the Act'), which came into force on 1 March 1988.

8. Section 1(1) of the Act is worded as follows:

'This Part shall have effect for the purpose of making such provision as is necessary to comply with the product liability Directive and shall be construed accordingly.'

9. Section 4(1)(e), which purports to implement Article 7(e) of the Directive, provides as follows:

'In any civil proceedings by virtue of this Part against any person . . . in respect of a defect in a product it shall be a defence for him to show

. . .

(e) that the state of scientific and technical knowledge at the relevant time was not such that a producer of products of the same description as the product in question might be expected to have discovered the defect if it had existed in his products while they were under his control'.

10. The Commission took the view that the Act did not properly transpose the Directive and, on 26 April 1989, sent the United Kingdom Government a letter of formal notice in accordance with the procedure laid down by Article 169 of the Treaty, requesting it to submit its observations on six complaints listed therein within a period of two months.

11. By letter dated 19 July 1989, the United Kingdom denied the Commission's allegations. Although it accepted that the wording of the Act was different from that of the Directive, it argued that under Article 189 of the EEC Treaty Member States were entitled to choose appropriate wording when implementing a directive, provided that the intended result of the directive was achieved.

12. On 2 July 1990, the Commission addressed a reasoned opinion to the United Kingdom pursuant to Article 169 of the Treaty. It accepted the right of a Member State to choose its own wording to implement a directive, provided that the national rules achieved the intended result. Nevertheless, it maintained its position with respect to all but one of the six complaints set out in its letter of formal notice.

13. By letter of 4 October 1990, the United Kingdom reiterated its view that the Directive was correctly implemented by the Act.

14. The United Kingdom's arguments persuaded the Commission that four of its remaining complaints should be abandoned, particularly in view of the rule in section 1(1) of the Act under which the relevant provisions were to be construed in conformity with the Directive.

15. However, considering that the wording of section 4(1)(e) was unambiguous and would have to be interpreted *contra legem* by the courts in the United Kingdom in order to conform to the Directive, the Commission decided to seek a ruling from the Court on the compatibility of section 4(1)(e) of the Act with Article 7(e) of the Directive.

16. In its application, the Commission argues that the United Kingdom legislature has broadened the defence under Article 7(e) of the Directive to a considerable degree and converted the strict liability imposed by Article 1 of the Directive into mere liability for negligence.

17. The Commission submits that the test in Article 7(e) of the Directive is objective in that it refers to a state of knowledge, and not to the capacity of the producer of the product in question, or to that of another producer of a product of the same description, to discover the defect. However, by its use of the words 'a producer of products of the same description as the product in question [who] might be expected to have discovered the defect', section 4(1)(e) of the Act presupposes a subjective assessment based on the behaviour of a reasonable producer. It is easier for the producer of a defective product to demonstrate, under section 4(1)(e), that neither he nor a producer of similar products could have identified the defect at the material time, provided that the standard precautions in the particular industry were taken and there was no negligence, than to show, under Article 7(e), that the state of scientific and technical knowledge was such that no-one would have been able to discover the defect.

18. The Commission adds that, whilst section 1(1) of the Act constitutes a most helpful indication to British courts, it cannot suffice to render lawful language which clearly on its face runs counter to the wording of the Directive and could be construed consistently with the Directive only by interpretation *contra legem*.

19. The United Kingdom Government does not challenge the Commission's interpretation of Article 7(e) of the Directive as setting out an 'objective' and not a 'subjective' test. It considers, however, that section 4(1)(e) of the Act sets out the same test as Article 7(e) of the Directive and does not provide for liability founded on negligence.

20. The Government submits that, in so far as Article 7(e) can be interpreted in the abstract in a factual vacuum, it lays down an 'objective' test in the sense that the 'state of scientific and technical knowledge' mentioned therein does not refer to what the producer in question actually knows or does not know, but to the state of knowledge which producers of the class of the producer in question, understood in a generic sense, may objectively be expected to have. This is precisely the meaning of section 4(1)(e) of the Act.

21. The United Kingdom Government points out that, in any event, courts in the United Kingdom are required to interpret section 4(1)(e) consistently with Article 7(e) by virtue of section 1(1) of the Act or of the general principle that legislation implementing Community law should be construed so as to accord therewith.

22. It argues that, in view of section 1(1) of the Act and the absence of any decision of a national court on the meaning of section 4(1)(e), the Commission is not in a position to say that the latter section is incompatible with Article 7(e). It could succeed in its argument only if it could show conclusively that section 4(1)(e) is completely incapable of bearing the same legal meaning as Article 7(e).

23. In order to determine whether the national implementing provision at issue is clearly con-

trary to Article 7(e) as the Commission argues, the scope of the Community provision which it purports to implement must first be considered.

24. In order for a producer to incur liability for defective products under Article 4 of the Directive, the victim must prove the damage, the defect and the causal relationship between defect and damage, but not that the producer was at fault. However, in accordance with the principle of fair apportionment of risk between the injured person and the producer set forth in the seventh recital in the preamble to the Directive, Article 7 provides that the producer has a defence if he can prove certain facts exonerating him from liability, including 'that the state of scientific and technical knowledge at the time when he put the product into circulation was not such as to enable the existence of the defect to be discovered' (Article 7(e)).

25. Certain general observations can be made as to the wording of Article 7(e) of the Directive.

26. First, as the Advocate General rightly observes in paragraph 20 of his Opinion, since that provision refers to 'scientific and technical knowledge at the time when [the producer] put the product into circulation', Article 7(e) is not specifically directed at the practices and safety standards in use in the industrial sector in which the producer is operating, but, unreservedly, at the state of scientific and technical knowledge, including the most advanced level of such knowledge, at the time when the product in question was put into circulation.

27. Second, the clause providing for the defence in question does not contemplate the state of knowledge of which the producer in question actually or subjectively was or could have been apprised, but the objective state of scientific and technical knowledge of which the producer is presumed to have been informed.

28. However, it is implicit in the wording of Article 7(e) that the relevant scientific and technical knowledge must have been accessible at the time when the product in question was put into circulation.

29. It follows that, in order to have a defence under Article 7(e) of the Directive, the producer of a defective product must prove that the objective state of scientific and technical knowledge, including the most advanced level of such knowledge, at the time when the product in question was put into circulation was not such as to enable the existence of the defect to be discovered. Further, in order for the relevant scientific and technical knowledge to be successfully pleaded against the producer, that knowledge must have been accessible at the time when the product in question was put into circulation. On this last point, contrary to what the Commission seems to consider, Article 7(e) of the Directive raises difficulties of interpretation which, in the event of litigation, the national courts will have to resolve having recourse, if necessary, to Article 177 of the EC Treaty.

30. For the present, it is the heads of claim raised by the Commission in support of its application that have to be considered.

31. In proceedings brought under Article 169 of the Treaty the Commission is required to prove the alleged infringement. The Commission must provide the Court with the material necessary for it to determine whether the infringement is made out and may not rely on any presumption (see, in particular, Case C–62/89 *Commission v France* [1990] ECR I–925, para 37).

32. The Commission takes the view that inasmuch as section 4(1)(e) of the Act refers to what may be expected of a producer of products of the same description as the product in question its wording clearly conflicts with Article 7(e) of the Directive in that it permits account to be taken of the subjective knowledge of a producer taking reasonable care, having regard to the standard precautions taken in the industrial sector in question.

33. That argument must be rejected in so far as it selectively stresses particular terms used in section 4(1)(e) without demonstrating that the general legal context of the provision at issue fails effectively to secure full application of the Directive. Taking that context into account, the Commission has failed to make out its claim that the result intended by Article 7(e) of the Directive would clearly not be achieved in the domestic legal order.

34. First, section 4(1)(e) of the Act places the burden of proof on the producer wishing to rely on the defence, as Article 7 of the Directive requires.

35. Second, section 4(1)(e) places no restriction on the state and degree of scientific and technical knowledge at the material time which is to be taken into account.

36. Third, its wording as such does not suggest, as the Commission alleges, that the availability of the defence depends on the subjective knowledge of a producer taking reasonable care in the light of the standard precautions taken in the industrial sector in question.

37. Fourth, the Court has consistently held that the scope of national laws, regulations or administrative provisions must be assessed in the light of the interpretation given to them by national courts (see, in particular, Case C–382/92 *Commission v United Kingdom* [1994] ECR I–2435, para 36). Yet in this case the Commission has not referred in support of its application to any national judicial decision which, in its view, interprets the domestic provision at issue inconsistently with the Directive.

38. Lastly, there is nothing in the material produced to the Court to suggest that the courts in the United Kingdom, if called upon to interpret section 4(1)(e), would not do so in the light of the wording and the purpose of the Directive so as to achieve the result which it has in view and thereby comply with the third paragraph of Article 189 of the Treaty (see, in particular, Case C–91/92 *Faccini Dori v Recreb* [1994] ECR I–3325, para 26). Moreover, section 1(1) of the Act expressly imposes such an obligation on the national courts.

39. It follows that the Commission has failed to make out its allegation that, having regard to its general legal context and especially section 1(1) of the Act, section 4(1)(e) clearly conflicts with Article 7(e) of the Directive. As a result, the application must be dismissed.

(A report of the case which includes the Opinion of Advocate-General Tesauro is also printed in the All England Law Reports [1997] EC 481.)

NOTES

1. Neither the Pearson Commission nor the Law Commission would have allowed a 'development risk' defence: see, respectively, Cmnd 7054, 1978, para 1259 and Law Com No 82, 1977, para 105. As the Pearson Commission noted: 'To exclude development risks from a regime of strict liability would be to leave a gap in the compensation cover, through which, for example, the victim of another thalidomide disaster might easily slip.'

2. In contractual claims under the Sale of Goods Act 1979, s 14, no equivalent defence exists: see above, pp 118–19.

QUESTIONS

1. Is there now any material distinction (other than the reversal of the burden of proof) between liability based on negligence and the test of s 4(1)(e)? In such cases as *Beshada v Johns-Manville Products Corp*, above, pp 245–6, is it sensible to impose an apparent duty to warn of a 'scientifically unknowable risk'?

2. If the 'person proceeded against' is an importer, rather than a producer, how is the s 4(1)(e) defence to be applied?

3. Consider the potential application of s 4(1)(e) to the following cases:

(i) a tyre manufacturer who claims that in the ordinary process of production it is technically impossible to achieve a higher safety standard than 99.9999 per cent and that the production of the occasional defective tyre is inevitable;

(ii) a drug manufacturer who agrees that his product carries a risk which is statistically predictable in general terms, but scientifically impossible to predict in any specific case;

(iii) a manufacturer of a tumble dryer in the example noted above (see p 243), who claims that before the death through suffocation of the young child the risk had quite simply never been contemplated;

(iv) a manufacturer of meat products who is uncertain as to the possible future effects of BSE even if he scrupulously follows all the current regulations and 'official' guidance.

Causation and remoteness of damage

The 1987 Act does not ease the burden of proving that the allegedly defective product actually caused the damage of which the plaintiff complains. Particularly in cases involving vaccines or pharmaceutical products this may be a major hurdle. The following case provides a good example of some of the difficulties involved. Although decided under a system requiring proof of negligence, the same problems arise where liability is strict.

Loveday v Renton, *The Times*, 31 March 1988, Queen's Bench Division

Lord Justice Stuart-Smith said the issue to be tried was whether pertussis vaccine could cause permanent brain damage in young children.

If the answer was 'yes' the plaintiff's counsel had invited his Lordship to define in what circumstances it was so proved, so as to limit the scope of the issues of specific causation.

If the plaintiff failed to discharge the burden of proof in the present case it seemed improbable that the other 200 or so other cases, presently stayed, would proceed to trial.

Wellcome Foundation were not known to be the vaccine manufacturers but they applied, pursuant to Order 15, rule 6(2)(b) of the Rules of the Supreme Court, to be joined as defendants. Although no allegation of negligence was made against them, they had an important interest as the only manufacturer still making pertussis vaccine in the UK.

The case of *Bolam v Friern Hospital Management Committee* ([1957] 1 WLR 582) made it clear that it was for the court to decide as a question of fact whether the vaccine could cause permanent brain damage in young children and the onus of doing so was on the plaintiff on the balance of probabilities.

His Lordship found that Mr Brodie had correctly accepted that for the plaintiff to succeed he had to show the person administering the vaccine did so in disregard of one or more of the contra-indications. Strictly speaking, the question did not arise since his Lordship was concerned with causation.

So far as the plaintiff sought to rely on the contra-indications as evidence of the opinions of experts not called as witnesses that the vaccine could cause brain damage, that evidence was inadmissible in law. It was not known who held the opinions or the basis for them and was hearsay.

It was, however, part of the medical evidence in the case and the experts were entitled to and had commented on it.

The allegation made in the reamended statement of claim was that 'Pertussis vaccine . . . liberates pyrogens . . . causing fever; fever in young children can cause convulsions, convulsions can cause hypoxia and anoxia which in turn can cause brain damage'.

Medical and expert opinion was deeply divided on the issue. The question had to be determined on all the evidence in the case, which was primarily the oral evidence of the witnesses, tested in cross-examination.

The court could not simply accept the opinion or belief of witness, however eminent, that such was or was not the case. The basis for the opinion had to be examined and tested against other evidence for consistency and logic and the validity of the reasoning.

The question was not answered by showing that there was a respectable and responsible body of medical opinion that the vaccine could, albeit rarely, cause permanent brain damage, or that that view might be more likely than the contrary.

The opinion of others not called to give evidence was not admissible to prove the truth of the opinion. That was also the case with the advice contained in the contra-indications against the vaccine published from time to time by the DHSS and similar bodies in other countries.

The plaintiff put forward four suggested biological mechanisms: febrile convulsions, anaphylactic shock, neurotoxic effect and adjuvant effect.

In his Lordship's judgment all four were improbable. However, the least improbable was that a prolonged febrile convulsion might cause permanent brain damage. It was theoretically possible that if pertussis vaccine could cause permanent brain damage, there were other unknown mechanisms. But if that postulate was established, then one of those four mechanisms was the most likely explanation, and in his Lordship's view, it was pointless to speculate about other mechanisms.

By far the most important epidemiological evidence was derived from the National Childhood Encephalopathy Study, the report of which was published in 1981. It was unique because it was the only case control study which attempted to answer the question before the court.

Although the evidence in the study supported the conclusion that the diphtheria tetanus pertussis (DTP) vaccine sometimes caused febrile convulsions, it did not provide evidence that such convulsions following the vaccine caused permanent brain damage. The results of the study did not support the plaintiff's case.

His Lordship was conscious of the force of the argument on close temporal association, notwithstanding that the reports took no account of background incidence and the force of the question 'Surely it cannot all be coincidence?'

In his Lordship's judgment there were probably several factors that explained the close temporal assertion:

(a) The coincidental manifestation of a hitherto covert condition.

(b) The coincidental occurrence of deterioration in a child not previously neurologically normal in whom such an occurrence was more likely to occur. Vaccination might have had a triggering effect, but the event was bound to occur.

(c) The coincidental effect of a virus disease.

(d) The provocation of febrile convulsions in a child with a low convulsion threshold.

(e) The provocation of febrile convulsions in a child with an underlying pathology or epilepsy. In such a case the underlying pathology or epilepsy was responsible for the ultimate malign outcome and not the rise in temperature attributable to the vaccine.

(f) Biased reporting, manifested both by a natural tendency to abbreviate time between the onset of symptoms and an event such as vaccination and to attribute the cause to the vaccine, especially when it had acquired a poor reputation.

(g) A tendency to watch children more closely after vaccination and observe sooner or more readily the onset of insidious symptoms and relate them to the vaccine.

His Lordship was conscious that it was the plaintiff's case that it was only children who were in some way vulnerable who were affected. The vulnerabilities referred to in groups (a) to (e) above might explain why such events occasionally occurred in close temporal association with this vaccination and indeed other vaccinations as well, but it did not show that any brain damage or epilepsy which resulted was due to the vaccine as opposed to the underlying pathology.

The plaintiff had failed to show on the balance of probabilities that pertussis vaccine could cause permanent brain damage in young children. It was possible that it did; the contrary could not be proved. But in the result the plaintiff's claim failed.

Even if his Lordship had found in favour of the plaintiff on this preliminary issue, in his Lordship's view any plaintiff would face insuperable difficulties in establishing negligence on the part of the doctor or nurse who administered the vaccine.

Such a claim would have to be based on the ground that the vaccination had been given in spite of the presence of certain contra-indications.

(A fuller report is contained in [1990] 1 Med LR 117.)

NOTES

1. For discussion of this and other cases, see Ferguson, *Drug Injuries and the Pursuit of Compensation* (1996), ch 9; Goldberg 'Vaccine Damage and Causation—Social and Legal Implications' (1996), 3 JSSL 100; 'Causation and Medicinal Products—A Legal and Probability Analysis' [1996] Consum LJ 57. In Ireland the Supreme Court has been satisfied as to the establishment of the causal link in another case involving the pertussis vaccine: see *Best v Wellcome Foundation* [1994] 5 Med LR 81.

QUESTIONS

1. If the pertussis or some similar vaccine were to be proved to have caused brain damage in an individual case (without, as in *Best v Wellcome Foundation*, any production defect being alleged within a batch) will liability follow under the 1987 Act? Is such a product necessarily to be judged 'defective' (see, above, pp 240–4)? Are oral contraceptives 'defective' if associated risks (eg thrombosis and hypertension) are warned against in accompanying information leaflets?: see Ferguson, 'An Ill for every Pill' (1995) 145 NLJ 846.
2. What test of remoteness of damage should be applied under a strict liability system? As to remoteness generally, see Markesinis and Deakin, *Tort Law* (3rd edn, 1994) at pp 181–92. Is assistance to be derived from the decision of the House of Lords in *Cambridge Water Co Ltd v Eastern Counties Leather plc* [1994] 1 All ER 53 (nuisance and liability under the *Rylands v Fletcher* doctrine)?

Possible reasons for lack of case law

As was noted above (see p 236) there has been a singular lack of reported case law decided under Part I of the 1987 Act, even though the Act has been in force since 1 March 1988. The National Consumer Council conducted a survey of solicitors and others, but was not able to reach any firm conclusions to explain the apparent lack of activity. The following extract contains some useful general information.

Unsafe Products: National Consumer Council, November 1995

3. Why is the Act not being used? our theories

We have thought about the possible reasons why the Consumer Protection Act appears to be so little used. The reasons we considered were: problems funding cases, for example lack of legal aid; lack of awareness of the Act among consumers; lack of awareness of the Act among solicitors; cases still coming through; settlements being made but not generally reported—insurance companies might be making secrecy a condition of settlement; the problems of the 'development risk defence' and primary agricultural product exemption.

What we have found in considering the evidence for this report confirms that all of these factors may be playing a part. Because it has been so difficult to get examples of cases where the Act has been used, we do not feel that it is possible to ascribe reasons. But it has become clear that court action is not the easiest or most appropriate route to compensation for any but individual high-value claims.

4. Our evidence for this report

When we started to look at the effect of the product liability provisions of the Consumer Protection Act we were faced with a complete lack of evidence. We took . . . steps to gather information.

. . .

Although we were disappointed at the number of responses we received, nevertheless we have found that there are a number of solicitors who are using or considering using the Act. For interest we list some of the products involved. Claims have not succeeded in all cases, but the list gives an idea of the breadth of use the Act could be put to. Some of these cases are discussed in more detail below.

Claims have been made as a result of damage caused by: food poisoning—from chicken curry, lemon meringue pie, sandwiches and a wedding banquet, exploding bottles, surgical scissors, inadequate wing mirrors on a truck, lap seat belts, a heart pacemaker, a fan belt, a glass panel in a caravan, the aircraft involved in the M1 air crash, fireworks, a hair steamer, luggage clips, an electrical circuit breaker, faulty studs on football boots, a dressing gown which caught fire, an anorak with a hood cord, supermarket trolleys, sports lockers, a folding aluminium ladder, bicycle wheels where the materials used could not stand up to the stress forces placed on them when ridden over rough ground, a glass storage jar which shattered, an outdoor working platform which blew over, defective bolts on a climbing frame, the starting handle of a cement mixer which broke the user's nose, and numerous kitchen appliances.

Claims for damage caused by pharmaceutical products and infected blood products have also cited the Act. The case of people infected with hepatitis C from blood transfusions gives an indication of why it may be too early to say whether the Act will prove effective in medical cases. People given blood transfusions in surgery following accidents have difficulty claiming against the health authority if the transfusion was given to save life. A claim under the Act against the manufacturers of the blood could prove successful, since there appears to be evidence that blood donations were collected from groups with a high risk of infection with diseases including hepatitis C. There are some cases in the pipeline. But since a claim can only be made if the transfusion took place after the Act came into force on 1 March 1988, they have not progressed far enough for anyone to say whether they will be successful. In drugs cases too, it is necessary to prove that the product was supplied on or after 1 March 1988.

Another possible use of the Act that has been suggested to us is for claims for injury caused by cars fitted with 'bull bars'. These bars originated in Australia, where they are called 'roo bars' and give protection for those driving in the outback if the vehicle comes into contact with kangaroos. Not surprisingly, in the United Kingdom, the main function they serve is cosmetic.

Evidence appears to show that injuries caused by cars fitted with these bars are very often much more severe than injuries caused by an equivalent accident caused by a car which is not fitted with the bars. Since the bars are merely cosmetic, a claim might be made on the grounds that the manufacturers have not made the cars as safe as people generally are entitled to expect.

So far as we know this has not been tested by legal action, but it raises an interesting issue about the raising of safety standards. The cars to which these bars are fitted may not be unsafe for those who drive in them—although there is some evidence that where airbags are fitted the bull bars may adversely affect the mechanism of the airbags. They do, however, appear to be more dangerous for those outside the car. This raises the question of the definition of 'defect'. Could a pedestrian argue that car manufacturers should design cars which minimise dangers to them? Cars could be made like fortified tanks to make them more safe for the drivers and passengers, with considerable increased danger for pedestrians and other drivers. How will the courts achieve a balance of interests?

SOME AMERICAN DEVELOPMENTS

The historical insistence within the United Kingdom on proof of negligence has long since ceased to be a feature of the law of some other jurisdictions, especially the United States of America. The theories of liability based on breach of express and implied warranties have been noted already: see respectively *Randy Knitwear Inc v American Cyanamid Co* 181 NE 2d 399, above, p 64, and *Henningsen v Bloomfield Motors Inc* (1960) 161 A 2d 69, above, p 52. This section contains material illustrating some of the principal developments through a theory which was freed from the intricacies of the law of sales and based squarely on the law of tort. The following case is seen generally as the most important in establishing the theory of strict liability in tort.

STRICT LIABILITY IN TORT

Greenman v Yuba Power Products Inc 377 P 2d 897 (1962) Supreme Court of California

Traynor Justice. Plaintiff brought this action for damages against the retailer and the manufacturer of a Shopsmith, a combination power tool that could be used as a saw, drill, and wood lathe. He saw a Shopsmith demonstrated by the retailer and studied a brochure prepared by the manufacturer. He decided he wanted a Shopsmith for his home workshop, and his wife bought and gave him one for Christmas in 1955. In 1957 he bought the necessary attachments to use the Shopsmith as a lathe for turning a large piece of wood he wished to make into a chalice. After he had worked on the piece of wood several times without difficulty, it suddenly flew out of the machine and struck him on the forehead, inflicting serious injuries. About ten and a half months later, he gave the retailer and the manufacturer written notice of claimed breaches of warranties and filed a complaint against them alleging such breaches and negligence.

After a trial before a jury, the court ruled that there was no evidence that the retailer was negligent or had breached any express warranty and that the manufacturer was not liable for the breach of any implied warranty. Accordingly, it submitted to the jury only the cause of action alleging breach of implied warranties against the retailer and the causes of action alleging negligence and breach of express warranties against the manufacturer. The jury returned a verdict for the retailer against plaintiff and for plaintiff against the manufacturer in the amount of $65,000. The trial court denied the manufacturer's motion for a new trial and entered judgment on the verdict. The manufacturer and plaintiff appeal. Plaintiff seeks a reversal of the part of the judgment in favor of the retailer, however, only in the event that the part of the judgment against the manufacturer is reversed.

Plaintiff introduced substantial evidence that his injuries were caused by defective design and construction of the Shopsmith . . . The jury could therefore reasonably have concluded that the manufacturer negligently constructed the Shopsmith. The jury could also reasonably have concluded that statements in the manufacturer's brochure were untrue, that they constituted express warranties,[1] and that plaintiff's injuries were caused by their breach.

[1] The manufacturer contends, however, that plaintiff did not give it notice of breach of warranty within a reasonable time and that therefore his cause of action for breach of warranty is barred by section 1769 of the Civil Code. Since it cannot be determined whether the verdict against it was based on the negligence or warranty cause of action or both, the manufacturer concludes that the error in presenting the warranty cause of action to the jury was prejudicial.

. . .

The notice requirement of section 1769, however, is not an appropriate one for the court to adopt in actions by injured consumers against manufacturers with whom they have not dealt. (*La Hue v Coca-Cola Bottling* 50 Wash 2d 645, 314 P 2d 421 at 422; *Chapman v Brown* DC 198 F Supp 78, 85; affd *Brown v Chapman* 9 Cir, 304 F 2d 149.) 'As between the immediate parties to the sale [the notice requirement] is a sound commercial rule, designed to protect the seller against unduly delayed claims for damages. As applied to personal injuries, and notice to a remote seller, it becomes a booby-trap for the unwary. The injured consumer is seldom "steeped in the business practice which justified the rule," [James, Product Liability, 34 Texas L Rev 44, 192 197] and at least until he has had legal advice it will not occur to him to give notice to one with whom he has had no dealings.' (Prosser, Strict Liability to the Consumer, 69 Yale LJ 1099, 1130, footnotes omitted.) . . . We conclude, therefore, that even if plaintiff did not give timely notice of breach of warranty to the manufacturer, his cause of action based on the representations contained in the brochure was not barred.

[2] Moreover, to impose strict liability on the manufacturer under the circumstances of this case, it was not necessary for plaintiff to establish an express warranty as defined in section 1732 of the Civil Code.[2] A manufacturer is strictly liable in tort when an article he places on the market, knowing that it is to be used without inspection for defects, proves to have a defect that causes injury to a human being. Recognized first in the case of unwholesome food products, such liability has now been extended to a variety of other products that create as great or greater hazards if defective. [Citations omitted.] . . .

[3] Although in these cases strict liability has usually been based on the theory of an express or implied warranty running from the manufacturer to the plaintiff, the abandonment of the requirement of a contract between them, the recognition that the liability is not assumed by agreement but imposed by law [Citation omitted] and the refusal to permit the manufacturer to define the scope of its own responsibility for defective products [citations omitted] make clear that the liability is not one governed by the law of contract warranties but by the law of strict liability in tort. Accordingly, rules defining and governing warranties that were developed to meet the needs of commercial transactions cannot properly be invoked to govern the manufacturer's liability to those injured by their defective products unless those rules also serve the purposes for which such liability is imposed.

[4] We need not recanvass the reasons for imposing strict liability on the manufacturer. They have been fully articulated in the cases cited above. (See also 2 Harper and James, Torts,

§§ 28.15–28.16, pp 1569–1574; Prosser, Strict Liability to the Consumer, 69 Yale LJ 1099; *Escola v Coca-Cola Bottling Co* 24 Cal 2d 453 at 461, 150 P 2d 436, concurring opinion.) The purpose of such liability is to insure that the costs of injuries resulting from defective products are borne by the manufacturers that put such products on the market rather than by the injured persons who are powerless to protect themselves. Sales warranties serve this purpose fitfully at best. (See Prosser, Strict Liability to the Consumer, 69 Yale LJ 1099, 1124–1134.) In the present case, for example, plaintiff was able to plead and prove an express warranty only because he read and relied on the representations of the Shopsmith's ruggedness contained in the manufacturer's brochure. Implicit in the machine's presence on the market, however, was a representation that it would safely do the jobs for which it was built. Under these circumstances, it should not be controlling whether plaintiff selected the machine because of the statements in the brochure, or because of the machine's own appearance of excellence that belied the defect lurking beneath the surface, or because he merely assumed that it would safely do the jobs it was built to do. It should not be controlling whether the details of the sale from manufacturer to retailer and from retailer to plaintiff's wife were such that one or more of the implied warranties of the sales act arose. (Civ Code, § 1735.) 'The remedies of injured consumers ought not to be made to depend upon the intricacies of the law of sales.' (*Ketterer v Armour & Co* DC 200 F 322 at 323; *Klein v Duchess Sandwich Co* 14 Cal 2d 272, 282, 93 P 2d 799.) To establish the manufacturer's liability it was sufficient that plaintiff proved that he was injured while using the Shopsmith in a way it was intended to be used as a result of a defect in design and manufacture of which plaintiff was not aware that made the Shopsmith unsafe for its intended use.

[5] The manufacturer contends that the trial court erred in refusing to give three instructions requested by it. It appears from the record, however, that the substance of two of the requested instructions was adequately covered by the instructions given and that the third instruction was not supported by the evidence.

The judgment is affirmed.

Gibson CJ, and **Schauer, McComb, Peters, Tobriner** and **Peek JJ**, concur.

1. In this respect the trial court limited the jury to a consideration of two statements in the manufacturer's brochure.
(1) 'WHEN SHOPSMITH IS IN HORIZONTAL POSITION—Rugged construction of frame provides rigid support from end to end. Heavy centerless-ground steel tubing insures perfect alignment of components.' (2) 'SHOPSMITH maintains its accuracy because every component has positive locks that hold adjustments through rough or precision work.'
2. 'Any affirmation of fact or any promise by the seller relating to the goods is an express warranty if the natural tendency of such affirmation or promise is to induce the buyer to purchase the goods, and if the buyer purchases the goods relying thereon. No affirmation of the value of the goods, nor any statement purporting to be a statement of the seller's opinion only shall be construed as a warranty.'

One of the more remarkable features of this case was the relative brevity of the judgment through which a proposition of such far-reaching importance was propounded. Thereafter general acceptance of the theory was assisted (if not assured) by its being adopted by the influential American Law Institute whose provision and some of whose comments are printed below:

Restatement (second) of Torts (1965)

§402A. Special Liability of Seller of Product for Physical Harm to User or Consumer
(1) One who sells any product in a defective condition unreasonably dangerous to the user or consumer or to his property is subject to liability for physical harm thereby caused to the ultimate user or consumer, or to his property, if
    (a) the seller is engaged in the business of selling such a product, and
    (b) it is expected to and does reach the user or consumer without substantial change in the condition in which it is sold.
(2) The rule stated in subsection (1) applies although
    (a) the seller has exercised all possible care in the preparation and sale of his product, and
    (b) the user or consumer has not bought the product from or entered into any contractual relation with the seller.

Caveat:
The Institute expresses no opinion as to whether the rules stated in this section may not apply
    (1) to harm to persons other than users or consumers;
    (2) to the seller of a product expected to be processed or otherwise substantially changed before it reaches the user or consumer; or
    (3) to the seller of a component part of a product to be assembled.

Comment:
    a. This section states a special rule applicable to sellers of products. The rule is one of strict liability, making the seller subject to liability to the user or consumer even though he has exercised all possible care in the preparation and sale of the product.

. . .

    f. Business of selling. The rule stated in this Section applies to any person engaged in the business of selling products for use or consumption. It therefore applies to any manufacturer of such a product, to any wholesale or retail dealer or distributor, and to the operator of a restaurant. It is not necessary that the seller be engaged solely in the business of selling such products. Thus the rule applies to the owner of a motion picture theatre who sells popcorn or ice cream, either for consumption on the premises or in packages to be taken home.
    The rule does not, however, apply to the occasional seller of food or other such products who is not engaged in that activity as a part of his business . . .
    g. Defective condition. The rule stated in this Section applies only where the product is, at the time it leaves the seller's hands, in a condition not contemplated by the ultimate consumer, which will be unreasonably dangerous to him. The seller is not liable when he delivers the product in a safe condition, and subsequent mishandling or other causes make it harmful by the time it is consumed. The burden of proof that the product was in a defective condition at the time that it left the hands of the particular seller is upon the injured plaintiff; and unless evidence can be produced which will support the conclusion that it was then defective, the burden is not sustained.
    Safe condition at the time of delivery by the seller will, however, include proper packaging, necessary sterilisation, and other precautions required to permit the product to remain safe for a normal length of time when handled in a normal manner.
    h. A product is not in a defective condition when it is safe for normal handling and consumption. If the injury result from abnormal handling, as where a bottled beverage is knocked against a radiator to remove the cap, or from abnormal preparation for use, as where too much salt is added to food, or from abnormal consumption, as where a child eats too much candy and is made ill, the seller is not liable. Where, however, he has reason to anticipate that danger may result from a particular use, as where a drug is sold which is safe only in limited doses, he may

be required to give adequate warning of the danger (see Comment *j*), and a product sold without such warning is in a defective condition.

The defective condition may arise not only from harmful ingredients, not characteristic of the product itself either as to presence or quantity, but also from foreign objects contained in the product, from decay or deterioration before sale, or from the way in which the product is prepared or packed . . .

i. Unreasonably dangerous. The rule stated in this Section applies only where the defective condition of the product makes it unreasonably dangerous to the user or consumer. Many products cannot possibly be made entirely safe for all consumption, and any food or drug necessarily involves some risk of harm, if only from over-consumption. Ordinary sugar is a deadly poison to diabetics, and castor oil found use under Mussolini as an instrument of torture. That is not what is meant by 'unreasonably dangerous' in this section. The article sold must be dangerous to an extent beyond that which would be contemplated by the ordinary consumer who purchases it, with the ordinary knowledge common to the community as to its characteristics. Good whisky is not unreasonably dangerous merely because it will make some people drunk, and is especially dangerous to alcoholics; but bad whisky, containing a dangerous amount of fusel oil, is unreasonably dangerous . . .

j. Directions or warning. In order to prevent the product from being unreasonably dangerous, the seller may be required to give directions or warning, on the container, as to its use. The seller may reasonably assume that those with common allergies, as for example to eggs or strawberries, will be aware of them, and he is not required to warn against them. Where, however, the product contains an ingredient to which a substantial number of the population are allergic, and the ingredient is one whose danger is not generally known, or if known is one which the consumer would reasonably not expect to find in the product, the seller is required to give warning against it, if he has knowledge, or by the application of reasonable, developed human skill and foresight should have knowledge, of the presence of the ingredient and the danger. Likewise in the case of poisonous drugs, or those unduly dangerous for other reasons, warning as to use may be required . . .

k. Unavoidably unsafe products. There are some products which, in the present state of human knowledge, are quite incapable of being made safe for their intended and ordinary use. These are especially common in the field of drugs. An outstanding example is the vaccine for the Pasteur treatment of rabies, which not uncommonly leads to very serious and damaging consequences when it is injected. Since the disease itself invariably leads to a dreadful death, both the marketing and the use of the vaccine are fully justified, notwithstanding the unavoidable high degree of risk which they involve. Such a product, properly prepared, and accompanied by proper directions and warning, is not defective, nor is it *unreasonably* dangerous. The same is true of many other drugs, vaccines, and the like, many of which for this very reason cannot legally be sold except to physicians, or under the prescription of a physician. It is also true in particular of many new or experimental drugs as to which, because of lack of time and opportunity for sufficient medical experience, there can be no assurance of safety, or perhaps even of purity of ingredients, but such experience as there is justifies the marketing and use of the drug notwithstanding a medically recognizable risk. The seller of such products, again with the qualification that they are properly prepared and marketed, and proper warning is given, where the situation calls for it, is not to be held to strict liability for unfortunate consequences attending their use, merely because he has undertaken to supply the public with an apparently useful and desirable product, attended with a known but apparently reasonable risk.

l. User or consumer. In order for the rule stated in this Section to apply, it is not necessary that the ultimate user or consumer have acquired the product directly from the seller, although the rule applies equally if he does so. He may have acquired it through one or more intermediate dealers. It is not even necessary that the consumer have purchased the product at all. He may be a member of the family of the final purchaser, or his employee, or a guest at his table, or a mere donee from the purchaser. The liability stated is one in tort, and does not require any contractual relation, or privity of contract, between the plaintiff and the defendant . . .

NOTES

1. As comment *f* makes clear, strict liability is regarded as being applicable to all who are engaged in the business of 'selling' products. It does not apply only to manufacturers or producers. The same view has been adopted by the courts: see, for example, *Vandermark v Ford Motor Co* 391 P 2d 168 (1964) (Supreme Court of California) (seller of car) and in general Frumer and Friedman *Products Liability*, Vol 2A. Some decisions have gone further to include business suppliers generally, for example those who hire out a defective product: see *Citrone v Hertz Truck Leasing and Rental Service* 212 A 2d 769 (New Jersey, 1965) (motor vehicle).

2. Another question which attracted substantial comment and differences of opinion is whether American courts should follow the *Restatement* formula and require that the product be shown to be both 'in a defective condition' and 'unreasonably dangerous'. One view is that the 'unreasonably dangerous' requirement is apt to introduce an element of negligence or fault into a strict liability system. *Cronin v JBE Olson Corpn* 104 Cal Rptr 433 (1972) is an early and leading decision of the Californian Supreme Court. The plaintiff was driving a bread delivery van which collided with another vehicle when the force of the collision broke an aluminium safety hasp, releasing bread trays which, in turn, propelled him through the windscreen. There was evidence that the safety hasp was porous and defective with a low tolerance to force, but the defendants contended that they had been prejudiced by the lack of a finding that it was unreasonably dangerous. Dismissing the objection the court said (at 443):

> We believe the *Greenman* formulation is consonant with the rationale and development of products liability law in California because it provides a clear and simple test for determining whether the injured plaintiff is entitled to recovery. We are not persuaded to the contrary by the formulation of s 402A which inserts the factor of an 'unreasonably dangerous' condition into the equation.

Predictably the courts of some other States have disagreed and stressed the importance of establishing that the product is 'unreasonably dangerous'. A collection of cases is to be found in Frumer and Friedman, op cit, Vol 2A. Two early leading articles which continue to be influential are Keeton, 'Products Liability: liability without fault and the requirement of a defect', 41 Texas LR 855 (1963); Traynor, 'The Ways and Meanings of Defective Products and Strict Liability', 32 Tenn LR 363 (1965).

The *Restatement* formula is usually characterised as embodying a test of 'defectiveness' which is based on consumer expectations. In this it is similar to the EEC Directive (Art 6) and the Consumer Protection Act 1987 (s 3(1)). As with the Directive and the Act, it does not distinguish explicitly between the various types of defect, for example between defects of production and design. Although the formula was influential over many years, the American Law Institute decided in 1991 that the matter needed to be looked at afresh and two leading commentators, Professors Henderson and Twerski, were charged with drafting a new formula. The result was a considerable expanded statement covering a wide field.

Restatement (Third) of Torts: Products Liability, American Law Institute (1997)

CHAPTER 1

LIABILITY OF COMMERCIAL PRODUCT SELLERS BASED ON PRODUCT DEFECTS AT TIME OF SALE

TOPIC 1

LIABILITY RULES APPLICABLE TO PRODUCTS GENERALLY.

§ 1. Liability of Commercial Seller or Distributor for Harm Caused by Defective Products

One engaged in the business of selling or distributing products who sells or distributes a defective product is subject to liability for harm to persons or property caused by the defect.

§ 2. Categories of Product Defect

A product is defective when, at the time of sale or distribution, it contains a manufacturing defect, is defective in design, or is defective because of inadequate instructions or warnings. A product:

(a) contains a manufacturing defect when the product departs from its intended design even though all possible care was exercised in the preparation and marketing of the product;

(b) is defective in design when the foreseeable risks of harm posed by the product could have been reduced or avoided by the adoption of a reasonable alternative design by the seller or other distributor, or a predecessor in the commercial chain of distribution, and the omission of the alternative design renders the product not reasonably safe;

(c) is defective because of inadequate instructions or warnings when the foreseeable risks of harm posed by the product could have been reduced or avoided by the provision of reasonable instructions or warnings by the seller or other distributor, or a predecessor in the commercial chain of distribution, and the omission of the instructions or warnings renders the product not reasonably safe.

§ 3. Circumstantial Evidence Supporting Inference of Product Defect

It may be inferred that the harm sustained by the plaintiff was caused by a product defect existing at the time of sale or distribution, without proof of a specific defect, when the incident that harmed the plaintiff:

(a) was of a kind that ordinarily occurs as a result of product defect; and

(b) was not, in the particular case, solely the result of causes other than product defect existing at the time of sale or distribution.

§ 4. Noncompliance and Compliance with Product Safety Statutes or Regulations

In connection with liability for defective design or inadequate instructions or warnings:

(a) a product's noncompliance with an applicable product safety statute or administrative regulation renders the product defective with respect to the risks sought to be reduced by the statute or regulation; and

(b) a product's compliance with an applicable product safety statute or administrative regulation is properly considered in determining whether the product is defective with respect to the risks sought to be reduced by the statute or regulation, but such compliance does not preclude as a matter of law a finding of product defect.

TOPIC 2

LIABILITY RULES APPLICABLE TO SPECIAL PRODUCTS OR PRODUCT MARKETS

§ 5. Liability of Commercial Seller or Distributor of Product Components for Harm Caused by Products Into Which Components Are Integrated

One engaged in the business of selling or otherwise distributing product components who sells or distributes a component is subject to liability for harm to persons or property caused by a product into which the component is integrated if:

(a) the component is defective in itself, as defined in this Chapter, and the defect causes the harm; or

(b) (1) the seller or distributor of the component substantially participates in the integration of the component into the design of the product; and

(2) the integration of the component causes the product to be defective as defined in this Chapter; and

(3) the defect in the product causes the harm.

§ 6. Liability of Seller or Other Distributor for Harm Caused by Defective Prescription Drugs and Medical Devices

(a) A manufacturer of a prescription drug or medical device who sells or otherwise distributes a defective drug or medical device is subject to liability for harm to persons caused by the defect. A prescription drug or medical device is one that may be legally sold or otherwise distributed only pursuant to a health care provider's prescription.

(b) For purposes of liability under Subsection (a), a prescription drug or medical device is defective if at the time of sale or other distribution the drug or medical device:

(1) contains a manufacturing defect as defined in § 2(a); or

(2) is not reasonably safe due to defective design as defined in Subsection (c); or

(3) is not reasonably safe due to inadequate instructions or warnings as defined in Subsection (d).

(c) A prescription drug or medical device is not reasonably safe due to defective design if the foreseeable risks of harm posed by the drug or medical device are sufficiently great in relation to its foreseeable therapeutic benefits that reasonable health care providers, knowing of such foreseeable risks and therapeutic benefits, would not prescribe the drug or medical device for any class of patients.

(d) A prescription drug or medical device is not reasonably safe because of inadequate instructions or warnings if reasonable instructions or warnings regarding foreseeable risks of harm are not provided to:

(1) prescribing and other health care providers who are in a position to reduce the risks of harm in accordance with the instructions or warnings; or

(2) the patient when the manufacturer knows or has reason to know that health care providers will not be in a position to reduce the risks of harm in accordance with the instructions or warnings.

(e) A retail seller or other distributor of a prescription drug or medical device is subject to liability for harm caused by the drug or device if:

(1) at the time of sale or other distribution the drug or medical device contains a manufacturing defect as defined in § 2(a); or

(2) at or before the time of sale or other distribution of the drug or medical device the retail seller or other distributor fails to exercise reasonable care and such failure causes harm to persons.

§ 7. Liability of Commercial Seller or Distributor for Harm Caused by Defective Food Products

One engaged in the business of selling or otherwise distributing food products who sells or distributes a defective food product under § 2, § 3, or § 4 is subject to liability for harm to persons or property caused by the defect. Under § 2(a) a harm-causing ingredient of the food product constitutes a defect if a reasonable consumer would not expect the food product to contain that ingredient.

§ 8. Liability of Commercial Seller or Distributor of Defective Used Products

One engaged in the business of selling or otherwise distributing used products who sells or distributes a defective used product is subject to liability for harm to persons or property caused by the defect if the defect:

(a) results from the seller's failure to exercise reasonable care; or

(b) is a manufacturing defect under § 2(a) or a defect that may be inferred under § 3 and the seller's marketing of the product would cause a reasonable person in the position of the buyer to expect the used product to present no greater risk of defect than if the product were new; or

(c) is a defect under § 2 or § 3 in a used product remanufactured by the seller or a predecessor in the commercial chain of distribution of the used product; or

(d) arises from a used product's noncompliance under § 4 with a product safety statute or regulation applicable to the used product.

A used product is a product that, prior to the time of sale or other distribution referred to in this Section, is commercially sold or otherwise distributed to a buyer not in the commercial chain of distribution and used for some period of time.

CHAPTER 2

LIABILITY OF COMMERCIAL PRODUCT SELLERS NOT BASED ON PRODUCT DEFECTS AT TIME OF SALE

§ 9. Liability of Commercial Product Seller or Distributor for Harm Caused by Misrepresentation

One engaged in the business of selling or otherwise distributing products who, in connection with the sale of a product, makes a fraudulent, negligent, or innocent misrepresentation of material fact concerning the product is subject to liability for harm to persons or property caused by the misrepresentation.

§ 10. Liability of Commercial Product Seller or Distributor for Harm Caused by Post-Sale Failure to Warn

(a) One engaged in the business of selling or otherwise distributing products is subject to liability for harm to persons or property caused by the seller's failure to provide a warning after the time of sale or distribution of a product if a reasonable person in the seller's position would provide such a warning.

(b) A reasonable person in the seller's position would provide a warning after the time of sale if:

(1) the seller knows or reasonably should know that the product poses a substantial risk of harm to persons or property; and

(2) those to whom a warning might be provided can be identified and may reasonably be assumed to be unaware of the risk of harm; and

(3) a warning can be effectively communicated to and acted on by those to whom a warning might be provided; and

(4) the risk of harm is sufficiently great to justify the burden of providing a warning.

§ 11. Liability of Commercial Product Seller or Distributor for Harm Caused by Post-Sale Failure to Recall Product

One engaged in the business of selling or otherwise distributing products is subject to liability for harm to persons or property caused by the seller's failure to recall a product after the time of sale or distribution if:

(a) (1) a governmental directive issued pursuant to a statute or administrative regulation specifically requires the seller or distributor to recall the product; or

(2) the seller or distributor, in the absence of a recall requirement under Subsection (1), undertakes to recall the product; and

(b) the seller or distributor fails to act as a reasonable person in recalling the product.

CHAPTER 3

LIABILITY OF SUCCESSORS AND APPARENT MANUFACTURERS

§ 12. Liability of Successor for Harm Caused by Defective Products Sold Commercially by Predecessor

A successor corporation or other business entity that acquires assets of a predecessor corporation or other business entity is subject to liability for harm to persons or property caused by a defective product sold or otherwise distributed commercially by the predecessor if the acquisition:

(a) is accompanied by an agreement for the successor to assume such liability; or

(b) results from a fraudulent conveyance to escape liability for the debts or liabilities of the predecessor; or

(c) constitutes a consolidation or merger with the predecessor; or

(d) results in the successor becoming a continuation of the predecessor.

§ 13. Liability of Successor for Harm Caused by Successor's Own Post-Sale Failure to Warn

(a) A successor corporation or other business entity that acquires assets of a predecessor corporation or other business entity, whether or not liable under the rule stated in § 12, is subject to liability for harm to persons or property caused by the successor's failure to warn of a risk created by a product sold or distributed by the predecessor if:

(1) the successor undertakes or agrees to provide services for maintenance or repair of the product or enters into a similar relationship with purchasers of the predecessor's products giving rise to actual or potential economic advantage to the successor, and

(2) a reasonable person in the position of the successor would provide a warning.

(b) A reasonable person in the position of the successor would provide a warning if:

(1) the successor knows or reasonably should know that the product poses a substantial risk of harm to persons or property; and

(2) those to whom a warning might be provided can be identified and can reasonably be assumed to be unaware of the risk of harm; and

(3) a warning can be effectively communicated to and acted upon by those to whom a warning might be provided; and

(4) the risk of harm is sufficiently great to justify the burden of providing a warning.

§ 14. Selling or Otherwise Distributing as One's Own a Product Manufactured by Another

One engaged in the business of selling or otherwise distributing products who sells or distributes as its own a product manufactured by another is subject to the same liability as though the seller or distributor were the product's manufacturer.

CHAPTER 4

PROVISIONS OF GENERAL APPLICABILITY

TOPIC 1

CAUSATION

§ 15. General Rule Governing Causal Connection Between Product Defect and Harm

Whether a product defect caused harm to persons or property is determined by the prevailing rules and principles governing causation in tort.

§ 16. Increased Harm Due to Product Defect

(a) When a product is defective at the time of sale and the defect is a substantial factor in increasing the plaintiff's harm beyond that which would have resulted from other causes, the product seller is subject to liability for the increased harm.

(b) If proof supports a determination of the harm that would have resulted from other causes in the absence of the product defect, the product seller's liability is limited to the increased harm attributable solely to the product defect.

(c) If proof does not support a determination under Subsection (b) of the harm that would have resulted in the absence of the product defect, the product seller is liable for all of the plaintiff's harm attributable to the defect and other causes.

(d) A seller of a defective product who is held liable for part of the harm suffered by the plaintiff under Subsection (b), or all of the harm suffered by the plaintiff under Subsection (c), is jointly and severally liable with other parties who bear legal responsibility for causing the harm, determined by applicable rules of joint and several liability.

§ 17. Apportionment of Responsibility Between or Among Plaintiff, Sellers and Distributors of Defective Products, and Others

(a) A plaintiff's recovery of damages for harm caused by a product defect may be reduced if the conduct of the plaintiff combines with the product defect to cause the harm and the plaintiff's conduct fails to conform to generally applicable rules establishing appropriate standards of care.

(b) The manner and extent of the reduction under Subsection (a) and the apportionment of plaintiff's recovery among multiple defendants are governed by generally applicable rules apportioning responsibility.

§ 18. Disclaimers, Limitations, Waivers, and Other Contractual Exculpations as Defenses to Products Liability Claims for Harm to Persons

Disclaimers and limitations of remedies by product sellers or other distributors, waivers by product purchasers, and other similar contractual exculpations, oral or written, do not bar or reduce otherwise valid products liability claims against sellers or other distributors of new products for harm to persons.

§ 19. Definition of 'Product'

For purposes of this Restatement:

(a) A product is tangible personal property distributed commercially for use or consumption. Other items, such as real property and electricity, are products when the context of their distribution and use is sufficiently analogous to the distribution and use of tangible personal property that it is appropriate to apply the rules stated in this Restatement.

(b) Services, even when provided commercially, are not products.

(c) Human blood and human tissue, even when provided commercially, are not subject to the rules of this Restatement.

§ 20. Definition of 'One Who Sells or Otherwise Distributes'

For purposes of this Restatement:

(a) One sells a product when, in a commercial context, one transfers ownership thereto either for use or consumption or for resale leading to ultimate use or consumption. Commercial product sellers include, but are not limited to, manufacturers, wholesalers, and retailers.

(b) One otherwise distributes a product when, in a commercial transaction other than a sale, one provides the product to another either for use or consumption or as a preliminary step leading to ultimate use or consumption. Commercial nonsale product distributors include, but are not limited to, lessors, bailors, and those who provide products to others as a means of promoting either the use or consumption of such products or some other commercial activity.

(c) One also sells or otherwise distributes a product when, in a commercial transaction, one provides a combination of products and services and either the transaction taken as a whole, or the product component thereof, satisfies the criteria in Subsection (a) or (b).

§ 21. Definition of 'Harm to Persons or Property': Recovery for Economic Loss

For purposes of this Restatement, harm to persons or property includes economic loss if caused by harm to:

(a) the plaintiff's person;

(b) the person of another when harm to the other interferes with an interest of the plaintiff protected by tort law; or

(c) the plaintiff's property other than the defective product itself.

NOTES

1. For helpful comments on the background to the new *Restatement*, see Owen, 'Defectiveness Restated: Exploding the "Strict" Products Liability Myth' (1996) University of Illinois LR, p 743.
2. The above provision, although potentially highly influential, does not, of course, have direct legislative effect. Neither did the Department of Commerce Model Uniform Product Liability Act, 1979 which was issued for voluntary adoption by individual states. In fact many states now have their own statutes.

QUESTIONS

1. Is it a sensible use of language to characterise liability for defects of design and inadequate warning under the new *Restatement* formula as being 'strict'? If a 'reasonable alternative design' (see § 2(b)) is simply not available does this mean that the product is not 'defective', no matter how great the danger?
2. Is the distinction taken in the *Restatement* between construction and design defects sufficiently clear-cut to enable a different basis of liability to be applied to the two types of defect?

   Into which category should one place *Cronin v JBE Olsen Corpn*, 104 Cal Rptr 433 (1972), the facts of which were outlined above, p 260?

   What are the main reasons which might suggest that courts should be less willing to impose liability in cases of allegedly defective design?
3. In cases where a defective component causes damage to the finished product in which it has been incorporated (eg an electrical part leading to the destruction of a car by fire) is the component manufacturer subject to liability under the *Restatement* formula? Compare the EC Directive, Art 9(b), above, p 227, and the Consumer Protection Act 1987, s 5(2), above, p 231.

The following case is a good example of the innovatory approach which some American courts have been prepared to adopt when dealing with complex product liability claims.

Judith Sindell v Abbott Laboratories, Maureen Rogers v Rexall Drug Company 607 P 2d 924 (1980) Supreme Court of California

(Footnotes omitted unless otherwise indicated)

Mosk Justice. This case involves a complex problem both timely and significant: may a plaintiff, injured as the result of a drug administered to her mother during pregnancy, who knows the type of drug involved but cannot identify the manufacturer of the precise product, hold liable for her injuries a maker of a drug produced from an identical formula?

Plaintiff Judith Sindell brought an action against eleven drug companies . . . on behalf of herself and other women similarly situated. The complaint alleges as follows:

Between 1941 and 1971, defendants were engaged in the business of manufacturing, promoting, and marketing diethylstilbestrol (DES), a drug which is a synthetic compound of the female hormone estrogen. The drug was administered to plaintiff's mother and the mothers of the class she represents,[1] for the purpose of preventing miscarriage. In 1947, the Food and Drug Administration authorised the marketing of DES as a miscarriage preventative, but only on an experimental basis, with a requirement that the drug contain a warning label to that effect.

DES may cause cancerous vaginal and cervical growths in the daughters exposed to it before birth, because their mothers took the drug during pregnancy. The form of cancer from which these daughters suffer is known as adenocarcinoma, and it manifests itself after a minimum latent period of 10 or 12 years. It is a fast-spreading and deadly disease, and radical surgery is required to prevent it from spreading. DES also causes adenosis, precancerous vaginal and cervical growths which may spread to other areas of the body. The treatment for adenosis is cauterization, surgery, or cryosurgery. Women who suffer from this condition must be monitored by biopsy or colposcopic examination twice a year, a painful and expensive procedure. Thousands of women whose mothers received DES during pregnancy are unaware of the effect of the drug.

In 1971, the Food and Drug Administration ordered defendants to cease marketing and promoting DES for the purpose of preventing miscarriages, and to warm physicians and the public that the drug should not be used by pregnant women because of the danger to their unborn children.

. . .

As a result of the DES ingested by her mother, plaintiff developed a malignant bladder tumor which was removed by surgery. She suffers from adenosis and must constantly be monitored by biopsy or colposcopy to insure early warning of further malignancy.

The first cause of action alleges that defendants were jointly and individually negligent in that they manufactured, marketed and promoted DES as a safe and efficacious drug to prevent miscarriage, without adequate testing or warning, and without monitoring or reporting its effects.

A separate cause of action alleges that defendants are jointly liable regardless of which particular brand of DES was ingested by plaintiff's mother because defendants collaborated in marketing, promoting and testing the drug, relied upon each other's tests, and adhered to an industry-wide safety standard. DES was produced from a common and mutually agreed upon formula known as a fungible drug interchangeable with other brands of the same product; defendants knew or should have known that it was customary for doctors to prescribe the drug by its generic rather than its brand name and that pharmacists filled prescriptions from whatever brand of the drug happened to be in stock.

Other causes of action are based upon theories of strict liability, violation of express and implied warranties, false and fraudulent representations, misbranding of drugs in violation of federal law, conspiracy and 'lack of consent.'

Each cause of action alleges that defendants are jointly liable because they acted in concert, on the basis of express and implied agreements, and in reliance upon and ratification and exploitation of each other's testing and marketing methods.

Plaintiff seeks compensatory damages of $1 million and punitive damages of $10 million for herself. For the members of her class, she prays for equitable relief in the form of an order that defendants warn physicians and others of the danger of DES and the necessity of performing certain tests to determine the presence of disease caused by the drug, and that they establish free clinics in California to perform such tests.

Defendants demurred to the complaint. While the complaint did not expressly allege that plaintiff could not identify the manufacturer of the precise drug ingested by her mother, she stated in her points and authorities in opposition to the demurrers filed by some of the defendants that she was unable to make the identification, and the trial court sustained the demurrers of these defendants without leave to amend on the ground that the plaintiff did not and stated she could not identify which defendant had manufactured the drug responsible for her injuries. Thereupon, the court dismissed the action. This appeal involves only five of ten defendants named in the complaint. . . .

This case is but one of a number filed throughout the country seeking to hold drug manufacturers liable for injuries allegedly resulting from DES prescribed to the plaintiffs' mothers since 1947.[2] According to a note in the Fordham Law Review, estimates of the number of women who took the drug during pregnancy range from 1½ million to 3 million. Hundreds, perhaps thousands, of the daughters of these women suffer from adenocarcinoma, and the incidence of vaginal adenosis among them is 30 to 90 percent. (Comment, *DES and a Proposed Theory of Enterprise Liability* (1978) 46 Fordham L Rev 963, 964–967 [hereafter Fordham Comment].) Most of the cases are still pending. With two exceptions,[3] those that have been decided resulted in judgments in favour of the drug company defendants because of the failure of the plaintiffs to identify the manufacturer of the DES prescribed to their mothers.[4] The same result was reached in a recent California case. (*McCreery v Eli Lilly & Co* (1978) 87 Cal App 3d 77 [at] 82–84, 150 Cal Rptr 730.) The present action is another attempt to overcome this obstacle to recovery.

[1] We begin with the proposition that, as a general rule, the imposition of liability depends upon a showing by the plaintiff that his or her injuries were caused by the act of the defendant or by an instrumentality under the defendant's control . . .

There are, however, exceptions to this rule. Plaintiff's complaint suggests several bases upon which defendants may be held liable for her injuries even though she cannot demonstrate the name of the manufacturer which produced the DES actually taken by her mother. The first of these theories, classically illustrated by *Summers v Tice* (1948) 33 Cal 2d 80, 199 P 2d 1, places the burden of proof of causation upon tortious defendants in certain circumstances. The second basis of liability emerging from the complaint is that defendants acted in concert to cause injury to the plaintiff. There is a third and novel approach to the problem, sometimes called the theory of 'enterprise liability,' but which we prefer to designate by the more accurate term of 'industry-wide' liability, which might obviate the necessity for identifying the manufacturer of the injury-causing drug. We shall conclude that these doctrines, as previously interpreted, may not be applied to hold defendants liable under the allegations of this complaint. However, we shall propose and adopt a fourth basis for permitting the action to be tried, grounded upon an extension of the *Summers* doctrine.

. . .

Should we require that plaintiff identify the manufacturer which supplied the DES used by her mother or that all DES manufacturers be joined in the action, she would effectively be precluded from any recovery. As defendants candidly admit, there is little likelihood that all the manufacturers who made DES at the time in question are still in business or that they are subject to the jurisdiction of the California courts. There are, however, forceful arguments in favour of holding that plaintiff has a cause of action.

In our contemporary complex industrialized society, advances in science and technology create fungible goods which may harm consumers and which cannot be traced to any specific producer. The response of the courts can be either to adhere rigidly to prior doctrine, denying recovery to those injured by such products, or to fashion remedies to meet these changing needs. Just as Justice Traynor in his landmark concurring opinion in *Escola v Coca Cola Bottling Co* (1944) 24 Cal 2d 453 [at] 467–468, 150 P 2d 436, recognized that in an era of mass production and complex marketing methods the traditional standard of negligence was insufficient to govern the obligations of manufacturer to consumer, so should we acknowledge that some adaptation of the rules of causation and liability may be appropriate in these recurring circumstances.

. . .

[5] Where, as here, all defendants produced a drug from an identical formula and the manufacturer of the DES which caused plaintiff's injuries cannot be identified through no fault of plaintiff, a modification of the rule of *Summers* is warranted. As we have seen, an undiluted *Summers* rationale is inappropriate to shift the burden of proof of causation to defendants because if we measure the chance that any particular manufacturer supplied the injury-causing product by the number of producers of DES, there is a possibility that none of the five defendants in this case produced the offending substance and that the responsible manufacturer, not named in the action, will escape liability.

But we approach the issue of causation from a different perspective: we hold it to be reasonable in the present context to measure the likelihood that any of the defendants supplied the product which allegedly injured plaintiff by the percentage which the DES sold by each of them for the purpose of preventing miscarriage bears to the entire production of the drug sold by all for that purpose. Plaintiff asserts in her briefs that Eli Lilly and Company and 5 or 6 other companies produced 90 percent of the DES marketed. If at trial this is established to be the fact, then there is a corresponding likelihood that this comparative handful of producers manufactured the DES which caused plaintiff's injuries, and only a 10 percent likelihood that the offending producer would escape liability.

If plaintiff joins in the action the manufacturers of a substantial share of the DES which her mother might have taken, the injustice of shifting the burden of proof to defendants to demonstrate that they could not have made the substance which injured plaintiff is significantly diminished. While 75 to 80 percent of the market is suggested as the requirement by the Fordham Comment (at p 996), we hold only that a substantial percentage is required.

The presence in the action of a substantial share of the appropriate market also provides a ready means to apportion damages among the defendants. Each defendant will be held liable for the proportion of the judgment represented by its share of that market unless it demonstrates that it could not have made the product which caused plaintiff's injuries. In the present case, as we have seen, one DES manufacturer was dismissed from the action upon filing a declaration that it had not manufactured DES until after plaintiff was born. Once plaintiff has met her burden of joining the required defendants, they in turn may cross-complaint against other DES manufacturers, not joined in the action, which they can allege might have supplied the injury-causing product.

Under this approach, each manufacturer's liability would approximate its responsibility for the injuries caused by its own products. Some minor discrepancy in the correlation between market share and liability is inevitable; therefore, a defendant may be held liable for a somewhat different percentage of the damage than its share of the appropriate market would justify. It is probably impossible, with the passage of time, to determine market share with mathematical exactitude. But just as a jury cannot be expected to determine the precise relationship between fault and liability in applying the doctrine of comparative fault . . . the difficulty of apportioning damages among the defendant producers in exact relation to their market share does not seriously militate against the rule we adopt. As we said in *Summers* with regard to the liability of independent tortfeasors, where a correct division of liability cannot be made 'the trier of fact may make it the best it can.' (33 Cal 2d at p 88, 199 P 2d at 5.)

We are not unmindful of the practical problems involved in defining the market and determining market share, but these are largely matters of proof which properly cannot be determined at the pleading stage of these proceedings. Defendants urge that it would be both unfair and contrary to public policy to hold them liable for plaintiff's injuries in the absence of proof that one of them supplied the drug responsible for the damage. Most of their arguments, however, are based upon the assumption that one manufacturer would be held responsible for the products of another or for those of all other manufacturers if plaintiff ultimately prevails. But under the rule we adopt, each manufacturer's liability for an injury would be approximately equivalent to the damages caused by the DES it manufactured.

The judgments are reversed.

Bird CJ, and **Newman** and **White JJ** concur.
Richardson Justice, dissenting.

I respectfully dissent. In these consolidated cases the majority adopts a wholly new theory which contains these ingredients: The plaintiffs were not alive at the time of the commission of the tortious acts. They sue a generation later. They are permitted to receive substantial damages from multiple defendants without any proof that any defendant caused or even probably caused plaintiffs' injuries.

Although the majority purports to change only the required burden of proof by shifting it from plaintiffs to defendants, the effect of its holding is to guarantee that plaintiffs will prevail on the causation issue because defendants are no more capable of disproving factual causation than plaintiffs are of proving it. 'Market share' liability thus represents a new high water mark in tort law. The ramifications seem almost limitless, a fact which prompted one recent commentator, in criticizing a substantially identical theory, to conclude that 'Elimination of the burden of proof as to identification [of the manufacturer whose drug injured plaintiff] would impose a liability which would exceed absolute liability.' (Coggins *Industry-Wide Liability* (1979) 13 Suffolk L Rev 980, 988, fn omitted; see also, pp 1000–1001.) In my view, the majority's departure from traditional tort doctrine is unwise.

. . .

I would affirm the judgments of dismissal.
Clark and **Manuel JJ**, concur.
Rehearing denied; **Clark, Richardson** and **Manuel JJ**, dissenting.

[1] The plaintiff class alleged consists of 'girls and women who are residents of California and who have been exposed to DES before birth and who may or may not know that fact or the dangers' to which they were exposed. Defendants are also sued as representatives of a class of drug manufacturers which sold DES after 1941.

[2] DES was marketed under many different trade names.

[3] In a recent New York case a jury found in the plaintiff's favor in spite of her inability to identify a specific manufacturer of DES. An appeal is pending. (*Bichler v Eli Lilly & Co* (Sup Ct NY 1979).) A Michigan appellate court recently held that plaintiffs had stated a cause of action against several manufacturers of DES even though identification could not be made. (*Abel v Eli Lilly & Co* (decided Dec 5, 1979) Docket No 60497.) That decision is on appeal to the Supreme Court of Michigan.

[4] Eg *Gray v United States* (SD Tex 1978) 445 F Supp. 337. In their briefs, defendants refer to a number of other cases in which trial courts have dismissed actions in DES cases on the ground stated above.

NOTES

1. It is obvious that such cases raise issues of great complexity for the common law, but the factual situation on which *Sindell* was based is by no means unique or even unusual. For example, the dangers of asbestos are by now well known and it would be surprising if the passage of time did not reveal the carcinogenic properties of many other products. For comment on the case see Teff, 'Market Share Liability—A Novel Approach to Causation' (1982) 31 ICLQ 840; Kors, 'Refining Market Share Liability' 33 Stanford LR 937 (1981); Goldberg, 'Causation and Drugs: The Legacy of Diethylstilbestrol' (1996) 25 Anglo-American Law Review 286. For further discussion of class actions see below, ch 8, pp 458–81.
2. The approach of *Sindell* has generally not been adopted outside DES cases: see eg, *Shackil v Lederle Laboratories*, 561 A 2d 511, 528 (1989) (New Jersey Supreme Court); Goldberg, op cit, p 287, note 5.

QUESTIONS

1. How would English law deal with the following aspects of the *Sindell* case: (i) the fact that the injuries were pre-natal; (ii) the time-lapse associated with the minimum latent period of ten or twelve years before the manifestation of cancer; (iii) the inability to identify any particular manufacturer as being responsible for a given plaintiff's condition?
2. If an English court were to accept that petrol with its present permitted lead content was 'defective' because of its well-established effect on the brains of young children and others would the problems of causation be (i) essentially the same as those of the *Sindell* case or (ii) significantly different? How should they be resolved? For an attempt to raise the issue see *Budden v BP Oil Ltd* (1980) 124 Sol Jo 376.

SOME COMMONWEALTH EXAMPLES

There are many other examples of statutory provisions in Commonwealth jurisdictions and indeed elsewhere (see eg the Japanese Product Liability Act 1994). The Australian Trade Practices Act, 1974, Part VA, is based closely on the Consumer Protection Act, 1987. An exhaustive study was earlier produced by the Law Reform Commissions of Australia and Victoria: see 'Product Liability', ALRC No 51, VLRC, No 27. For comment on the Act, see Travers, 'Australia's New Product Liability Law' (1993) 67 ALJ 516.

The statutes of some Canadian provinces also have introduced a wide measure of liability for damage or loss caused by defective products. In some cases an entitlement to recover is dependent on there being a breach of contract (for example of the implied term as to quality) although there is no requirement that there be privity of contract between the parties. In others liability is based on tort and hence is not dependent on showing a breach of contract. Some provisions are confined to 'consumer products' whereas other proposals for reform are not so limited—no doubt in recognition of the fact that other products are capable of injuring consumers who come into contact with them. The following extract illustrates one such approach.

The Saskatchewan Consumer Protection Act 1996

39. Interpretation
In this Part:

. . .

(l) 'retail seller' means a person who sells consumer products to consumers in the ordinary course of his or her business but, subject to subsection 50(1), does not include a trustee in bankruptcy, receiver, liquidator, sheriff, auctioneer or person acting under an order of a court;

(m) 'sale' means a transaction in which the retail seller transfers or agrees to transfer the general property in a consumer product to a consumer for a valuable consideration and includes but is not restricted to:

(i)   a conditional sale;

(ii)   a contract of lease or hire;

(iii) a transaction under which a consumer product is supplied to a consumer along with services;

and any reference in this Part to 'buy', 'buying', 'bought', 'sell', 'sold' or 'selling' is to be construed accordingly;

User may recover damages
64. A person who may reasonably be expected to use, consume or be affected by a consumer product and who suffers personal injury as a result of a breach, by a retail seller or manufacturer, of a statutory warranty mentioned in clauses 48(c) to (f) is entitled, as against the retail seller or manufacturer, to recover damages arising from personal injuries that he or she has suffered and that were reasonably foreseeable as liable to result from the breach.

NOTES

1. This Act is partly a re-enactment of a 1977 Act which was based on the Report of the Ontario Law Reform Commission on Consumer Warranties and Guarantees in the Sale of Goods (1972). For comment see also the Commission's 'Report on Products liability' (1979), pp 39–41.

2. The non-excludable statutory warranties of s 48(c) to (f) relate respectively to description, acceptable quality, fitness for a particular purpose and sales by sample. All apply only where 'a consumer product is sold by a retail seller'. For the definition of 'consumer' and 'consumer product' see s 39(d) and (e) of the Act, above, p 36. By s 41(1), above, p **55**, subsequent consumer owners (for

example by way of purchase or gift) are deemed to be given the same statutory warranties as the original consumer. By s 50(2):

> the manufacturer of consumer products is deemed to give to consumers of those products the same statutory warranties respecting those products as the retail seller is deemed to have given . . .

Both provisions are subject to qualifications but the general effect is to confer on consumer buyers and those who derive title through them additional rights going beyond those conferred in the case of personal injury by s 64.

QUESTIONS

1. Which, if any, of the following are consumer products within the meaning of s 39(e) (see above, p 36): (i) a coin-operated washing machine used for example in a university launderette, (ii) an anti-nauseant medicine sold by chemists to combat morning sickness during pregnancy, (iii) a defective seat being one of a row of joined seats in a public cinema; (iv) a bus; and (v) a lorry?
2. It is said that section 64 of the Saskatchewan Act provides a remedy based on strict liability. Is it clear that it does? Do the words 'reasonably foreseeable' import an element of fault or do they affect only the question of remoteness of damage? Is there a distinction between these two possibilities?

MANUFACTURERS' GUARANTEES

Manufacturers' guarantees may take a variety of form. Some may be little more than expressions of general company policy, for example an assurance of 'aiming to give complete satisfaction'. Others may provide consumers with benefits going well beyond the demands imposed by the general law, as when a manufacturer of cassettes promises, 'Every recording as good as the first or we will give you a new tape'. Yet others may be positively detrimental or misleading, as by seeking to substitute strictly limited rights for those which would otherwise be conferred by statute or the common law. So far English law has been primarily concerned with this last category of so-called guarantees, rather than with seeking, for example, to prescribe minimum contents for such guarantees. For example, it will be seen later that s 5 of the Unfair Contract Terms Act 1977 invalidates 'guarantees' of consumer goods which seek to exclude or restrict liability under a contract to supply the goods in question: see below, at p 326 and p 356, and for a comment on the Scottish equivalent of this section see Cusine, 'Manufacturers' Guarantees and Unfair Contract Terms Act' [1980] Juridical Review 185.

For valuable (if somewhat dated) surveys of guarantees, see Trebilcock, 'Manufacturers' Guarantees' (1972) 18 McGill LJ 1; Vickers, 'Warranties Guaranteed' [1979] JBL 406. Some of the economic implications of guarantees are discussed in perceptive articles by Priest, 'A Theory of the Consumer Product

Warranty' (1981) 90 Yale LJ 1297 and Whitford, 'Comment on A Theory of the Consumer Product Warranty' (1982) 91 Yale LJ 1371.

Another approach has been to create a criminal offence under Part II of the Fair Trading Act 1973 (below, p 538) in the following circumstances.

The Consumer Transactions (Restrictions on Statements) Order 1976 (SI 1976/1813, as amended by SI 1978/127)

Article 5

(1) This Article applies to goods which are supplied in the course of a business by one person ('the supplier') to another where, at the time of the supply, the goods were intended by the supplier to be, or might reasonably be expected by him to be, the subject of a subsequent consumer transaction.

(2) A supplier shall not—

    (a) supply goods to which this Article applies if the goods bear, or are in a container bearing, a statement which sets out or describes or limits obligations (whether legally enforceable or not) accepted or to be accepted by him in relation to the goods; or

    (b) furnish a document in relation to the goods which contains such a statement,

unless there is in close proximity to any such statement another statement which is clear and conspicuous and to the effect that the first mentioned statement does not or will not affect the statutory rights of a consumer.

(3) A person does not contravene paragraph (2) above—

    (i) in a case to which sub-paragraph (a) of that paragraph applies, unless the goods have become the subject of a consumer transaction;

    (ii) in a case to which sub-paragraph (b) applies, unless the document has been furnished to a consumer in relation to goods which were the subject of a consumer transaction, or to a person likely to become a consumer pursuant to such a transaction; or

    (iii) by virtue of any statement if before the date on which this Article comes into operation the document containing, or the goods or container bearing, the statement has ceased to be in his possession.

NOTE

For Article 3 of this Order see below, p 384 et seq and for the offence arising from non-compliance with the Order, see s 23 of the Fair Trading Act 1973, below, p 540.

The general mischief at which this provision is aimed is easy to understand. Consumers should not be misled into believing that a guarantee represents the totality of their rights in the event of the goods proving to be defective. This is particularly important now that it is clear beyond argument that a manufacturer's guarantee operates as an addition to such rights, and not in diminution of them: see *Rogers v Parish (Scarborough) Ltd* [1987] QB 933, [1987] 2 All ER 232, CA, above, p 102.

More recently, there have been attempts to provide additional protection. In September 1989 the National Consumer Council issued a wide-ranging report entitled 'The Consumer Guarantee', the essence of which was to require manufacturers of listed products to state whether they were covered by a consumer guarantee. Any such guarantee would have to have a minimum content and it was envisaged that the statement 'No Consumer Guarantee' was unlikely to be an attractive proposition in a competitive market. A Consumer Guarantees Bill was introduced by Mr Martyn Jones, MP, but did not make any significant progress. Subsequently, in 1992, the Department of Trade and Industry issued a Consultation Document with an altogether more limited proposal, namely that: 'The manufacturer should be civilly liable under statute for the performance of his guarantee to the consumer. In cases where the manufacturer is outside the UK, the manufacturer's guarantee would be enforceable against the importer.' The Department explained why it did not favour the National Consumer Council's approach as follows.

Consumer Guarantees: A Consultation Document (DTI, February 1992)

Background to the Proposals
7. The National Consumer Council (NCC) in their April 1989 Report 'Competing in Quality', and the subsequent Consumer Guarantees Bill (a private Member's Bill presented in 1989/90 which did not reach the statute book) favoured legislation defining different categories of guarantee and prescribing minimum provisions for each of them. Such an approach would, in the Government's view, be unnecessarily bureaucratic and run the risk of creating loopholes that could be exploited by manufacturers seeking to avoid taking responsibility for the quality of their products. A better approach would be to legislate by focusing on the substance of the manufacturer's promise, whether it is called a guarantee or warranty, given in relation to the goods in question. This was the approach taken in the Unfair Contract Terms Act 1977 (section 5(2)(b)).
8. Whilst the proposals acknowledge that certain legal underpinning may be desirable, the Government does not consider it appropriate to lay down in legislation the detailed provisions that should be contained in guarantees, or to prescribe the periods they should cover. Such matters are best left to market forces operating in a free competitive environment. Legislation requiring manufacturers to give guarantees is also not favoured, for similar reasons. Nor does the Government believe that the present proposals should be restricted to particular identified goods or classes of goods. The proposals are intended to be of general application and contemplate no special cases.

NOTE

See also 'Consumer Guarantees: A Discussion Paper' (OFT, August 1984); 'Consumer Guarantees: A Report by the Director General of Fair Trading' (OFT, June 1986).

More recently the focus has shifted to the Commission of the European Communities which in November 1993 issued a Green Paper on 'Guarantees for Consumer Goods and After Sales Service' (COM (93) 509). This contains much useful information on the position in individual member States. This in turn has led to a proposal dated 23 August 1996 for a European Parliament and Council Directive on the Sale of Consumer Goods and Associated Guarantees (COM (95) 520). This is printed above, at pp 119–22. The most directly relevant provision known as the 'Commercial Guarantee' is reprinted here for ease of reference. It states:

Article 5

Guarantees

1. Any guarantee offered by a seller or producer shall legally bind the offerer under the conditions laid down in the guarantee document and the associated advertising and must place the beneficiary in a more advantageous position than that resulting from the rules governing the sale of consumer goods set out in the national provisions applicable.

2. The guarantee must feature in a written document which must be freely available for consultation before purchase and must clearly set out the essential particulars necessary for making claims under the guarantee, notably the duration and territorial scope of the guarantee, as well as the name and address of the guarantor.

The word 'guarantee' is defined in Article 1.2(d) to mean: 'any additional undertaking given by a seller or producer, over and above the legal rules governing the sale of consumer goods, to reimburse the price paid, to exchange, repair or handle a product in any way, in the case of non-conformity of the product with the contract.'

In the accompanying Explanatory Memorandum the Commission justifies this provision as follows:

Article 5

Paragraph 1

This paragraph establishes the principle, which seems self-evident, that any guarantee legally binds the guarantor in accordance with the conditions laid down in the guarantee document. This does not imply any legal qualification in respect of the guarantee (contract, unilateral promise, etc), which could also vary depending on the person of the guarantor and national legal traditions. This paragraph, however, also gives guarantee references in advertising the same status as actual guarantee conditions. In reality, consumers never have access to guarantee documents prior to purchase. Hence, the only contact the consumer has with guarantees is through advertising. It is on the basis of advertising pertaining to guarantees that the consumer's confidence and expectations are built up. Thus, advertising statements must be looked on as an integral part of the guarantee conditions. A similar principle was also established at Community level in the context of Directive 90/314/EEC of 13 June 1990 on package travel, package holidays and package tours, Article 3(2) of which prescribes that '[t]he particulars contained in the brochure are binding on the organiser or retailer . . . '.

This paragraph thus establishes the principle that guarantees must put the consumer in a more advantageous position than that resulting from the arrangements established by the national rules applicable. It is not necessary that all features of the commercial guarantee offered should go beyond the national rules applicable; it is enough that the consumer's position should be improved in some respect.

Paragraph 2

To ensure transparency and adequate information of consumers, all guarantees must be in writing and contain certain minimum particulars. However, when a guarantee infringes the rules, just as when it infringes Article 5(1), this should not in any way affect the guarantee's validity: the consumer may still rely on the guarantee and require that it be honoured. But Member States must take effective measures to prevent such guarantees from being offered, to ensure that the objectives are achieved and to reduce sources of potential disputes.

In order to ensure absolute transparency, this paragraph also establishes the right that consumers who wish to do so shall be free to consult the guarantee documents before purchasing goods.

QUESTIONS

1. What legal impediments might exist under current English law if a consumer seeks to establish that a manufacturer's guarantee is legally binding?
2. What does the expression 'more advantageous position' imply when it is the producer who offers the guarantee? Does the United Kingdom producer currently have any obligations to a remote consumer as to the quality (as opposed to the safety) of the goods? Must the position be 'more advantageous' overall (including rights under the contract of sale) or only vis-à-vis the producer?
3. The word 'producer' is not defined in the context of the above proposal and hence presumably is synonymous with 'manufacturer'. The proposal is promoted in the interest of facilitating cross-border shopping within the European Community and yet it envisages that the guarantee may define its territorial scope. Is it likely that it will have any practical effect where goods are manufactured in another EU country (let alone in the Far East or elsewhere) and imported into the United Kingdom?
4. What is the effect of the reference to 'associated advertising' in Article 5.1? Would this introduce a significantly wider liability in respect of promotional claims than is currently the case in English law?: see above, pp 57–70.

NOTE

The above proposal does not touch directly on the issue of extended warranties or long-term guarantees some of which are often similar to insurance policies. Frequently, these are either very expensive and used as a means of counterbalancing an apparent price reduction, or of little value when issued by a company with a short life-expectancy. The British Retail Consortium has issued a 'Code of Practice on Extended Warranties of Electrical Goods', the operation of which is monitored by the Office of Fair Trading. See generally 'Extended Warranties on Electrical Goods' (OFT, December 1994); 'Price Transparency in the Sale of Extended Warranties by Electrical Retailers' (OFT, January 1996); and *Which?*, February 1998, pp 12–13.

CHAPTER 6

Aspects of consumer credit

THE BACKGROUND

The 1960s saw a dramatic increase in consumer awareness and, parallel with this development, a widespread dissatisfaction with the complexities of the law governing consumer credit. In 1968 the Secretary of State for Trade and Industry appointed the Crowther Committee with the following terms of reference:

(i) to enquire into the present law and practice governing the provision of credit to individuals for financing purchases of goods and services for personal consumption;

(ii) to consider the advantages and disadvantages of existing and possible alternative arrangements for providing such credit, having regard to the interests of consumers, traders and suppliers of credit including depositors;

(iii) to consider in particular whether any amendment of the Moneylenders Acts is desirable; and

(iv) to make recommendations.

The Crowther Committee reported in March 1971 (Cmnd 4596) and their two volume Report made far-reaching criticisms of the then law and extensive proposals for reform. Their diagnosis of the situation was expressed in the Committee's Report (para 4.2.1) as follows:

The defects in the present law fall broadly into seven groups:

(i) Regulation of transactions according to their form instead of according to their substance and function.

(ii) The failure to distinguish consumer from commercial transactions.

(iii) The artificial separation of the law relating to lending from the law relating to security for loans.

(iv) The absence of any rational policy in relation to third party rights.

(v) Excessive technicality.

(vi) Lack of consistent policy in relation to sanctions for breach of statutory provisions.

(vii) Overall, the irrelevance of credit law to present day requirements, and the resultant failure to provide just solutions to common problems.

A coherent economic policy for dealing with the problem of consumer debt, as well as the more technical matter of rationalising the law, was an essential precondition for proposing radical legislation. In the field of consumer credit there had been steadily increasing legislative regulation since the first Hire-Purchase Act in 1938. This not only controlled the form and contents of credit agreements together with the rights and duties of the parties. It extended the controls so as to give the Secretary of State power to impose restrictions on the disposal, acquisition or possession of articles of any description under hire-purchase agreements etc, and this power was used since 1943 to restrict excessive credit, primarily by governing the minimum amount of any deposit. Although the Crowther Committee stated that 'terms control should find no place among the weapons of economic policy' (para 8.2.24), these powers have in fact been used at times since 1971 as a way of restraining demand and combating inflation. Contraventions of any such Orders made under the Act constitute criminal offences.

As indicated above, this policy was not in accordance with the Crowther Committee's view of economic policy, which it expressed thus:

Chapter 3.9 Guidelines for Social Policy

3.9.1. Given the principles of economic policy which we have advocated, our general view is that the state should interfere as little as possible with the consumer's freedom to use his knowledge of the consumer credit market to the best of his ability and according to his judgment of what constitutes his best interests. While it is understandable and proper for the state to be concerned about the things on which people spend their money and even to use persuasion to influence the scale of values implied by their expenditure patterns, it remains a basic tenet of a free society that people themselves must be the judge of what contributes to their material welfare.

3.9.2. Our examination of the social effects of consumer credit has not uncovered any strong social reasons for departing significantly from this view. Since the vast majority of consumers use credit wisely and derive considerable benefit from it, the right policy is not to restrict their freedom of access by administrative and legal measures but to help the minority who innocently get into trouble to manage their financial affairs more successfully—without, however, also making conditions easier for the fraudulent borrower. The basic principle of social policy must, therefore, be to reduce the number of defaulting debtors. This is in everybody's interest.

The Crowther Committee proposed two separate new statutes. One was designed to regulate, in particular, security interests in any goods by recording and safeguarding them. The other was designed to confer substantial consumer protection along uniform lines for all forms of credit and to regulate credit advertising. Only one statute was passed—the Consumer Credit Act 1974—though it incorporated a few aspects of the proposed Lending and Security Act.

The Report was followed by a White Paper, 'The Reform of the Law on Consumer Credit' (1972–3, Cmnd 5427) which commented:

The recommendations of the Crowther Committee were generally welcomed by all. Passage of the Bill outlined in this White Paper will mean the start of a new era in consumer credit. The industry will be freed from outdated restrictions and, for the first time, the consumer will have comprehensive protection and that truth in lending which is so necessary if he is to choose rationally. There will also be sufficient flexibility to allow for the development of new types of credit business. Thus a framework will have been established for further development of the industry which will be fair both to the provider of credit and to the consumer.

It was not until 1985 that the Consumer Credit Act 1974 was fully implemented, different aspects of it being introduced in stages. The late 1980s saw concerns over the ease with which credit could be obtained, with the associated risks of consumers borrowing more than they could afford. At the same time there was a desire by the Conservative Government to reduce the burdens on business and to remove or simplify the controls over certain credit activities. The White Paper *Releasing Enterprise* (1988, Cm 512) recommended the removal of all business lending and hiring from the scope of the Act, sought simplification of certain aspects of the Act and its Regulations, and a considerable reduction in the types of business requiring a consumer credit licence (see below). Consultations over these proposals followed and in 1994, as part of the Deregulation Initiative, the Department of Trade and Industry published *Deregulation Task Force's Proposals for Reform* which included a number of recommendations regarding credit laws. Meanwhile the Director General of Fair Trading, who is charged with the central enforcement of the Act, conducted his own investigations into deregulation proposals, producing the following reports, inter alia: *Consumer Credit Deregulation* (OFT, June 1994), *The Working and Enforcement of the Consumer Credit Act 1974* (OFT, August 1994), and *The Treatment of Business Consumers under the Consumer Credit Act 1974* (OFT, September 1994). This was followed, in 1995, by a DTI consultation paper specifically on credit issues: *Deregulation of United Kingdom Consumer Credit Legislation*. Some small changes regarding quotations regulations were then enacted. The change of government in 1997 has meant that no further deregulation steps have been taken to date.

EUROPEAN DEVELOPMENTS

Meanwhile the European Community was considering the regulation of consumer credit throughout the Community. At the end of 1986 the EC Directive on Consumer Credit (87/102/EEC, OJ No L 42/48, 12.2.87) was introduced. Much of it is based on the provisions of the Consumer Credit Act 1974, although it is not as extensive. It requires disclosure of annual percentage rates of interest (APRs) in advertisements, controls the form and content of agreements, provision of certain information, the regulation of credit grantors by licensing or other methods, and measures to cover connected lender liability, early settlements, and repossessions. An amending Directive (90/88/EEC, OJ No L 61, 10.3.90) was passed, introducing a common method for calculating annual percentage rates of charge for credit. Few changes to United Kingdom law had to be made to incorporate the original Directive and changes necessary for the amended version were postponed during the transitional period. In 1996 a further modification was proposed (COM(96)79 of 12.4.96) to use a single Community mathematical formula for calculating APRs (some countries having been permitted to continue to use a different method) and to introduce a Community logo. To date this has not been adopted.

CONSIDERATION OF THE 1974 ACT

The Act has 193 sections, five Schedules and numerous regulations made under it. Discussion will focus on a selection of these provisions where case law or other developments have occurred. (A number of areas have either not generated any case law to date or, if cases have arisen, these are concerned with detailed technical provisions of regulations or turn on specific facts.) For detailed information on the Act reference should be made to such loose-leaf works as Goode, *Consumer Credit Legislation*; Guest & Lloyd, *Encyclopaedia of Consumer Credit Law*, and *Butterworths Trading and Consumer Law*, Division 4.

REGULATED AGREEMENTS

Most of the provisions of the Act operate only when there is a 'regulated agreement', defined by s 189 to mean 'a consumer credit agreement, or consumer hire agreement, other than an exempt agreement'. Exempt agreements are those described in s 16 of the Act or in regulations made thereunder. Broadly speaking these comprise agreements with local authorities, building societies, insurance companies and other specified institutions, connected with the purchase of land, and for certain short-term credit, low cost credit, and credit to finance foreign trade. The definitions of a 'consumer credit agreement' and a 'consumer hire agreement' are to be found in ss 8 and 15 respectively:

8. Consumer credit agreements

(1) A personal credit agreement is an agreement between an individual ('the debtor') and any other person ('the creditor') by which the creditor provides the debtor with credit of any amount.

(2) A consumer credit agreement is a personal credit agreement by which the creditor provides the debtor with credit not exceeding [£25,000].

(3) A consumer credit agreement is a regulated agreement within the meaning of this Act if it is not an agreement (an 'exempt agreement') specified in or under section 16.

15. Consumer hire agreements

(1) A consumer hire agreement is an agreement made by a person with an individual (the 'hirer') for the bailment or (in Scotland) the hiring of goods to the hirer, being an agreement which—

(a) is not a hire-purchase agreement, and
(b) is capable of subsisting for more than three months, and
(c) does not require the hirer to make payments exceeding [£25,000].

(2) A consumer hire agreement is a regulated agreement if it is not an exempt agreement.

An 'individual' is currently given a wide meaning under the Act and includes (by s 189(1)) 'a partnership or other unincorporated body of persons not consisting entirely of bodies corporate'. There are proposals to remove lending and hiring to businesses from the scope of the Act, see *Consumer Credit Deregulation*, OFT,

June 1994, Chapter 4, and *Deregulation of United Kingdom Consumer Credit Legislation, A Consultation Document*, DTI, August 1995.

There has been some litigation concerning calculating the £15,000 limit (the financial limit until 1 May 1998) for agreements, for example *Huntpast Ltd v Leadbeater* [1993] CCLR 15, CA and *Humberclyde Finance Ltd v A G Thompson & EM Thompson (t/a A G Thompson, a firm)* (1996) 16 Tr. L 242, CA. The decisions turn on the detailed wording of the Consumer Credit (Total Charge for Credit) Regulations 1980 (SI 1980/51).

THE LICENSING SYSTEM

CREDIT AND HIRING BUSINESSES

The Act produced a potentially powerful regulatory weapon by requiring all proprietors of consumer credit, consumer hire or ancillary credit businesses to be licensed by the Director. The licensing provisions are to be found in Part III of the Act:

23. Businesses needing a licence

(1) Subject to this section, a licence is required to carry on a consumer credit business or consumer hire business.
(2) A local authority does not need a licence to carry on a business.

39. Offences against Part III

(1) A person who engages in any activities for which a licence is required when he is not a licensee under a licence covering those activities commits an offence.
(2) A licensee under a standard licence who carries on business under a name not specified in the licence commits an offence.

. . .

40. Enforcement of agreements made by an unlicensed trader

(1) A regulated agreement, other than a non-commercial agreement, if made when the creditor or owner was unlicensed, is enforceable against the debtor or hirer only where the Director has made an order under this section which applies to the agreement.
(2) Where during any period an unlicensed person ('the trader') was carrying on a consumer credit business or consumer hire business, he or his successor in title may apply to the Director for an order that regulated agreements made by the trader during that period are to be treated as if he had been licensed.

. . .

NOTES

1. Similar provisions apply to ancillary credit businesses, for example, debt-collectors, under ss 147 and 149.
2. Section 189(2) indicates that 'A person is not to be treated as carrying on a

particular type of business merely because occasionally he enters into transactions belonging to a business of that type'.

3. If the creditor only makes non-regulated agreements, for example all loans are over £25,000, there is no requirement to be licensed.

Two cases illustrate the issues considered by the courts in determining whether or not a licence is required:

Wills v Wood (1984) 128 Sol Jo 222, Court of Appeal

Fox LJ: The plaintiff, Mr Wills, is now about 73 years of age. He was a hotelier, but in 1967 he retired because of ill health. He sold his hotel and received a net sum of £26,000. So he had some capital to invest. The judge found that he sought and received advice from solicitors, Messrs Hubbards, as to the best way of 'investing' that capital so as to provide him with an income. On the solicitors' advice he used part of the £26,000 to buy stocks and shares. Subsequently, and again on the solicitors' advice, he lent money on security of mortgages. This latter type of 'investment', said the judge, was thereafter repeated, in each case to clients of the solicitors who in each case effected the arrangements and drew the deeds. Mr Wills never met any of the borrowers personally. Over the period 1972–6 (inclusive) loans on mortgage were made to some 13 different borrowers. Loans were at the rate of about 9%–12% It is not suggested that such rates were unreasonable. As a result, Mr Wills drew a modest income from the mortgage interest. In 1972–3 it was £1,292; in 1973–4 it was £771; in 1974–5 it was £743, and in 1975–6 it was £1,143.

In June 1973, at the instigation of his solicitors, Mr Wills lent £2,000 to Miss Wood on mortgage of her house at 12%. In October 1973 and August 1974 Mr Wills advanced to Miss Wood two further sums of £500 upon the same security and at the same rate of interest.

In the present proceedings Mr Wills seeks to recover the amount of the loan which (apart from the defences raised by Miss Wood to which I will refer) is due and owing to him. The judge, however, dismissed the claim and ordered repayment to Miss Wood of some £2,392 in respect of interest which she has paid to Mr Wills in respect of the loans since they were made. Miss Wood, under this decision, thus relieves Mr Wills of some £5,300 at no cost to herself.

This result is said to be justified by defences raised on Miss Wood's behalf and accepted by the judge.

The first is that Mr Wills was an unlicensed moneylender. The judge held that Mr Wills was 'a person whose business is that of moneylending' within section 6 of the Moneylenders Act 1900.

In my opinion the only thing that Mr Wills had in common with persons whose business is that of moneylending is that from time to time he lent money at interest. But you do not carry on the business of moneylending simply by lending money at interest. You do not necessarily carry on any business at all by doing that. You may be simply an investor. In her narrative of the facts, the judge used the words 'invest' and 'investment' in relation to Mr Wills' disposition of his £26,000 and the lending on mortgage. She was quite right to do so. 'Investment' is exactly what Mr Wills was engaged in. But there is a fundamental difference between investment and carrying on a business. That can be seen, for example, in income tax law where a mere investor is not taxable as a trader. In the present case, in my view, the indications are strongly against any conclusion other than that this was a man engaged on quite ordinary investment. I refer, in particular, to the following circumstances. He lent only to clients of the solicitors whom they put forward; he lent only on mortgage and not on personal security; the rates of interest were in line with ordinary institutional rates and there were lengthy periods when he lent nothing at all.

In my view the argument that Mr Wills was carrying on business as a moneylender is quite without substance and must be rejected.

R v Roy Marshall (1990) 90 Cr App R 73, Court of Appeal

Taylor LJ. On February 15, 1988, at Beverley Crown Court this appellant was convicted of engaging in the activity of a credit broker, for which a licence is required under the Consumer Credit Act 1974 when not a licensee under that Act, contrary to section 39(1) of the Consumer Credit Act 1974. He was conditionally discharged for three years and ordered to pay £500 costs. . . . He now appeals on a point of law against his conviction.

Having examined the evidence as to six transactions in which the appellant had been involved as a double glazing salesman the court considered the submissions made during the trial regarding s 189(2).

The learned judge took the view that the word 'merely' in section 189(2) was of specific meaning. He decided that this was a complicated matter, not a simple matter at all, and the proper way to deal with it in regard to the jury was to write out his direction for them so that they could take it with them into the jury room and have it to consult as they deliberated about their verdict. . . . What the learned judge said was this:

'The Prosecution must prove that the defendant made at least two such introductions and must prove that he made those introductions as a deliberate part of his business to induce customers to acquire his goods or to use his services. If he only made one introduction he did not break the law. If all he did was that occasionally he made introductions not as part of his way of selling his goods or services but because he was assisting customers who wanted that help then again he did not break the law. But if he made more than one introduction as a deliberate part of the conduct of his business to induce potential customers to acquire his goods or use his services it is open to you to conclude that he did conduct an ancillary credit business and he was not entitled to do that unless he had a licence.'

There are two aspects of that as to which criticism has been made. Clearly the learned judge excluded the possibility of the jury considering only one introduction, because section 189(2) refers to the word 'transactions' in the plural. It is submitted that the unfortunate way in which the direction was framed may have given the impression to the jury that once more than one transaction had been made and was proved, then the word 'occasionally' had been exceeded. The use of the phrase 'made at least two such introductions and must prove that he made those introductions as a deliberate part of his business' rather suggests that. At the very end of his summing-up, having given the jury this written document, the learned judge came back to his direction and said this . . . :

' . . . if on the balance that defence is made out and you are sure that he did on at least two transactions make credit introductions as part of his business in the sense I have explained to you, if he did that for some part of the period of sixteen months that is drafted in the indictment, then, unhappily, it would be your duty to find him guilty.'

That passage is capable of being understood, and may have been understood by the jury as implying that once more than two transactions were made out that was an end of the matter so far as section 189(2) was concerned. Of course it was not an end of the matter; it was a matter for the jury to decide what the word 'occasionally' meant and whether it had been exceeded in this case. That is one aspect of the direction; but the more fundamental aspect of the direction as to which there is criticism is the way in which the learned judge drew a distinction between that which the appellant may have done as part of his way of selling his goods or services on the one hand, and what he may have done to assist a customer who specifically sought his help on the other. He was directing the jury that if the appellant, even on two or three occasions, was offering credit facilities as part of his package to a customer, then section 189(2) could have no application. It only applied to permit occasional transactions, said the judge, if the occasional transactions were such as came by way of initiative from the customer who wanted assistance and all the appellant was doing was providing assistance in response to such a request. [Counsel for the appellant] says there is no way in which that distinction can be spelt out from the wording of section 189(2).

. . . [W]e agree that the learned judge drew a distinction there which the section simply does not permit to be drawn, The subsection clearly contemplates within its terms that there could be transactions entered into occasionally which belonged to a business of the type in question, namely, an ancillary credit business which would not fall foul of the Act. The crucial matter would be whether it was done occasionally or more than occasionally. There is no provision in the section for drawing a distinction between transactions initiated by the seller as opposed to those initiated by the customer . . . Our construction of section 189(2) is supported by a passage in *Consumer Credit Legislation* by Professor Goode. At paragraph 693, the learned editor says:

'Hence regularity of activity is necessary before that activity can be regarded as a business activity so as to attract the licensing provisions. Thus a person making occasional bridging loans for his clients or customers would not on that account alone be carrying on a consumer credit business.'

Appeal allowed, conviction quashed.

The following decision illustrates an unsuccessful attempt to evade the licensing requirement imposed on persons engaged in credit brokerage within s 145 of the Act.

Hicks v Walker (1984) 148 JP 636, Queen's Bench Division

Watkins LJ. On the 6 May, 1982, the Appellant preferred a number of informations against the Respondents who are Graham Walker, Frank Reynolds, the company Frank Reynolds Ltd and Kenneth Purchase . . .

The informations were directed to contraventions of the Consumer Credit Act 1974, in particular section 39(1) which provides: 'A person who engages in any activities for which a licence is required when he is not a licensee under a licence covering those activities commits an offence.' In the informations it was alleged . . . that Walker on or about 1 June, 1980, unlawfully engaged in the activity of credit brokerage without a licence on behalf of a customer named John Charles Broadmeadow. Arising out of that transaction it was further alleged that Frank Reynolds Ltd and Kenneth Purchase aided, abetted, counselled or procured the commission by Walker of the offence.

. . .

Walker is a motor car dealer. He had applied for and failed to obtain a licence under Part III of the Act, entitling him to carry on credit and hire business. He had-made application under section 25 of the Act. His application failed because the Director was not satisfied that Walker was a fit person to hold such a licence. Nevertheless, he leased premises at Failings Park Service Station, Cannock Road, Wolverhampton. He was the proprietor there of a firm called 'All Quality Cars'. He was acquainted with the Respondent Frank Reynolds who was a director of Frank Reynolds Ltd. Walker sub-let a part of the premises which he had rented to the company which had a Consumer Credit Act licence.

The Respondent Kenneth Purchase was employed upon the premises sub-let by Frank Reynolds Ltd. He was described in the course of evidence as a salesman. So far as one can tell from the evidence Frank Reynolds Ltd at no time had cars to sell at the sub-let premises. The only cars which were available for sale at the Service Station were the property of Walker. It was the practice of Purchase to act not only in the capacity of a servant of the company, but also so as to assist Walker in his dealings with persons who came to the premises to buy motor cars.

So if a person came to the premises and purchased a car and paid outright for it with cash or by cheque the transaction was exclusively between Walker and that customer, although Purchase may have played a part by acting as agent for Walker in that transaction. If a customer came to the premises who was unable to pay outright for a motor car which he wished to purchase, that person was informed either by Walker or by Purchase that credit facilities could be arranged. If the customer was agreeable to such an arrangement being made it was customary for Purchase to inform his employers that a customer of Walker's was anxious to obtain hire purchase facilities. Thereupon the company got in touch with the United Dominions Trust or some other hire purchase company and made the necessary arrangements. The car in question was sold by Walker to the company and therefore the company was able to give a good title of that motor car to the hire purchase company.

From time to time a customer came to the premises who wished to put his own car in in part exchange. In that event the company took over the car as part of the hire purchase transaction and sold it to Walker thus enabling him, if he wished, to offer that car for sale.

Evidence was provided of the understanding of the hire purchase companies as to who it was they were dealing with in the numerous transactions which went on by the combination of Walker, Purchase, the company and the hire purchase companies. The hire purchase companies thought that they were dealing exclusively with the company. They had no idea that they were dealing with Walker. Had they been so informed they would have enquired whether Walker was licensed under Part III of the Act.

The understanding of Broadmeadow, Swadkins and Hyden was that they were dealing with either Walker or Purchase or Purchase on behalf of Walker. In entering into the hire purchase agreements into which they all three entered they were assisted primarily by Purchase, but upon at least one occasion by Purchase with the assistance of Walker.

At the close of the case for the prosecution it was contended on behalf of the Respondents that there was insufficient evidence to show that Walker had at any time been responsible for effecting an introduction either to Purchase or directly to the company of a customer so that that customer could be the recipient of hire purchase arrangements in respect of a car offered for sale by Walker. He had, so it was submitted, merely been an errand boy by collecting on occasions the necessary forms for the hire purchase arrangements to be made.

Mr Parker, who appeared for the Appellants in the court below, submitted that the evidence established, first, that Walker had no licence; secondly, that the initiation of the transactions took place upon his premises; thirdly, that Purchase was on occasions although a servant of the company, an agent for him; and fourthly, he was well aware that the object of Purchase being upon the premises in those dual capacities was so as to facilitate the granting of hire purchase facilities to Walker's customers.

The opinion of the stipendiary magistrate was that the Appellant had failed to make out a prima facie case of unlawfully engaging in the activity of credit brokerage as defined in section 145 of the Consumer Credit Act 1974. She was of the view that Walker's title to the cars in question was insufficient for that purpose. She asks this question: 'The question for the opinion of the High Court is whether the Appellant had produced sufficient evidence to establish a prima facie case that the Respondent Walker had effected introductions to persons within the meaning of section 145(2)(a)(i) or section 145(2)(c) of the Consumer Credit Act 1974.'

The provisions, so far as they need to be read, of section 145 are these: '(1) An ancillary credit business is any business so far as it comprises or relates to—(a) credit brokerage . . . (2) Subject to section 146(5), credit brokerage is the effecting of introductions—(a) of individuals desiring to obtain credit—(i) to persons carrying on businesses to which this sub-paragraph applies' and '(c) of individuals desiring to obtain credit, or to obtain goods on hire, to other credit-brokers.' The allegation of the Appellant was that Walker introduced credit brokerage business to a credit broker, that the evidence was sufficient to create at least a prima facie case that Walker had done that and that the others had counselled or procured him to do it.

I am left in no doubt whatsoever that the deputy stipendiary magistrate was in error in coming to the conclusion that there was no prima facie case of contravention by Walker and the others of the provisions of the Act, section 145 especially. One has only to examine the activities of Purchase to see that what he did was consistent with an unlawful arrangement come to by Walker on the one hand and Reynolds and his company on the other. Purchase in his two guises moved from one role to the other as circumstances demanded. At one moment he was merely assisting Walker in the straightforward business of selling motor cars either for cash or other outright payment, and at another moment he was introducing to his employers a customer of Walker who could not pay for a motor car and therefore needed credit facilities. From that time onwards the company took over the transaction and obtained credit facilities from the hire purchase company of its selection.

It seems to me to be an inescapable inference from the way in which Purchase was said to have acted that when he was informing his employers that hire purchase facilities were needed he was acting as an agent for Walker and on his behalf effecting an introduction of credit brokerage facilities to a credit broker.

For the reasons I have outlined there was in my opinion a prima facie case and the deputy stipendiary magistrate was wrong to find to the contrary. Seeing that we are not asked to remit this case to the court below for the hearing to be resumed I would merely allow this appeal.

Forbes J agreed.

Appeal allowed; no order as to costs.

The following extracts explain the background to the licensing system and how the system operates.

'Licensing Practice under the Consumer Credit Act' by Gordon Borrie, then Director General of Fair Trading (1982) JBL 91 (Footnotes omitted)

The objectives of licensing

First, let us recall the objectives of licensing. The Report of the Committee on Consumer Credit, chaired by the late Lord Crowther, considered that:

'the more unscrupulous type of credit grantor may well take the view that the occasional check on his malpractices . . . in an isolated transaction is not a serious deterrent. and is outweighed by the financial advantages he may derive from evading the law;'

and, later, came to the conclusion that:

'many of the difficulties, anomalies and confusions that now exist have arisen from past attempts to regulate part of a field where functions are constantly overlapping. . . . Our basic approach is that . . . the law should treat all who grant consumer credit . . . as far as possible in the same way . . . It follows that in respect of licensing, everyone should likewise be treated in the same way . . . we do not think it would be right simply to abolish these [the then existing licensing] provisions without putting anything else in their place.' [see paras 6.3.3 and 7.2.1].

Professor Goode, a leading member of the Crowther Committee, expands on this in his Consumer Credit Legislation Manual: 'No consumer legislation, however sophisticated, is likely to have more than a marginal impact if not under-pinned by effective enforcement machinery.' [para 324]. I entirely agree.

...

Validity of applications

The terms of section 25(1) of the Act make it clear that, provided a person satisfies me as to his fitness and that the names under which he wishes to trade are not misleading, I must, on application, grant him a licence. There is, however, a first step. An application must be made, and this must be in valid form, because section 6 of the Act provides that an improperly made application is 'of no effect.'

...

The 'right' to a licence

Once I have a valid application, section 25(1) of the Act gives an apparent 'right' to a licence. This right, is, however, blurred by the fact that I have to be satisfied as to the trading name or names of the applicant and as to his fitness. In considering fitness I am obliged under section 25(2) to take into account not only 'any circumstances appearing to [me] to be relevant' but also specific matters relating to the applicant, his employees or associates. The 'right' to a licence is, therefore, more akin to a limited administrative decision—limited because I can only refuse a licence if there has been a failure to satisfy me on one of the grounds set out in section 25(2).

Further, while section 25(1) of the Act appears to put the formal burden of proof on an applicant to show that he is a fit person to hold (or continue to hold) a licence, that onus is also blurred because that section has to be read in conjunction with section 27(1) under which I have a statutory obligation not only to give the applicant written notice that I am 'minded to' refuse his application or to grant it in different terms and give him an opportunity to make representations to me but—more important—I am also obliged to give *reasons* why I am minded to take such action. These reasons must obviously be put in such a way that they identify the matters I am concerned about, so that appropriate representations may be made by the applicant. If in any individual case I were unable to quote adequate reasons for refusal, etc, backed up by the relevant evidence, I would be bound to grant the application.

The 'minded to refuse' notice

If I consider that I have material to warrant refusal of a licence application, I have to follow a precise procedure laid down in the Act and regulations. (The procedure for granting a licence in different terms, or for revocation, suspension or variation of a licence is much the same and my comments below can be read as generally applying equally to these other forms of action as to refusal of an application.)

The first step I have to take is to issue a *minded to refuse notice* ('an MTR') . . .

In section 25(2) I am required, in considering fitness, to have regard to any relevant evidence about the applicant, his employees, agents or associates but in particular to whether any such person has:

(a) committed any offence involving fraud or other dishonesty, or violence,
(b) contravened any provision made by or under the Act, or by or under any other enactment regulating the provision of credit to individuals or other transactions with individuals,
(c) practised discrimination on grounds of sex, colour, race or ethnic or national origins in, or in connection with, the carrying on of any business, or
(d) engaged in business practices appearing to me to be deceitful or oppressive, or otherwise unfair or improper (whether unlawful or not).

In general, therefore, an MTR will contain any material coming within section 25(2) that raises serious and reasonably reliable doubts and reservations as to fitness. The policy of the Office of

Fair Trading has been to regard the standard of fitness imposed by the Consumer Credit Act as a high one; I have a statutory duty to be satisfied that an applicant is a fit person to hold a licence and I cannot possibly be fully satisfied in this respect if doubts and reservations are raised and not answered.

In assembling an MTR the relevance of evidence to the licence category applied for is borne in mind. Any applicant for any category of licence who has been convicted of a serious criminal offence which is not spent or very old must expect to go through the full scrutiny of licensing procedure. Even here, however, there is a degree of 'weighting' for different categories of licence. A conviction for violence is always a serious matter, but vitally crucial to an application for a debt-collecting licence. Similarly, convictions for fraud and dishonesty are serious, but very serious indeed in respect of a debt-adjuster or for a person who is constantly dealing with other people's money. More generally, conviction for VAT and income tax evasion indicates an individual's lack of integrity which could easily spill over into relations with consumers should financial problems arise.

The least easily refuted evidence likely to be cited in an MTR consists of details of convictions and convictions which are not spent. They figure very highly in the material cited in MTRs. Generally speaking, we would not expect an isolated unspent conviction many years ago—other than for a very serious offence—to figure in an MTR. By contrast, however, such a conviction would take on much greater relevance if it were repeated or if it were one of a long series of similar convictions for serious offences continuing over many years.

The most difficult kind of MTR, however, is where a case has been constructed solely of complaints sent in by Trading Standards Officers or members of the public. It is in the nature of complaints, even where these take the form of formal witness statements, that they comprise only one side of the story and are in a form where the applicant or his legal representatives are often unable to test their veracity and accuracy during the course of representations. It is also in the nature of complaints that, whilst the complainant considers that he remembers very clearly the transaction he is complaining about—because to him it is a special transaction—to the trader that transaction may be just one of very many and he may not be able to recollect it at all. It follows that counterstatements designed to show that the complaint is misconceived may raise sufficient questions about the validity of the complaint that we are unable to make a finding of fact on the issues raised. In short, it is very difficult for me to arrive at a decision which is not favourable to the applicant in those cases which are comprised solely of complaints. Such cases are, however, very rare indeed, for we would try to obtain other supportive evidence to lend weight to the proposed case . . .

Some, if not the greater part, of the material used in an MTR is not likely to be contemporaneous. As a basic rule we would use the most up to date evidence we can. However, section 25(2)(d) of the Act refers to a trader who '*has committed offences*' '*has engaged* in business practices,' not '*is committing*' offences or '*is engaging*' in business practices. Therefore the material which my Office has to use in an MTR is evidence that shows the applicant has—in the past committed offences or engaged in a business practice, which must mean that, in this latter context, the practice has been carried out over a period of time. Of course I accept that the relevant time for deciding fitness is the moment when the licensing decision is made.

A great deal of the evidence that is likely to be cited in an MTR comes within section 25(2)(d) of the Act which requires me, *inter alia*, to take into account in considering an application whether the applicant has engaged in business practices appearing to me to be 'deceitful or oppressive, or otherwise unfair or improper (whether unlawful or not).' The inclusion of this phrase specifically in this section, wherein I am already required to have regard to any relevant circumstances, is a clear indication that I can object to certain trading practices and use the licensing system either to compel a course of conduct which the applicant or licensee may not be legally obliged to adopt at present or to require him to refrain from activities which he is at present legally entitled to pursue . . .

Representations

In general I think it right that I should set a high standard of fitness; that I should use the licensing powers to improve trading standards; that if there is material questioning fitness it should be tested by being put to the applicant. But in doing this I am conscious that, especially as far as the smaller trader is concerned, my Office must bend over backwards to help him with what will seem a difficult procedure. Nowhere is this policy more apparent than in our procedures for representations.

. . .

(Details of the procedures currently followed can be found below.)

Results of licensing

. . . Results can often be obtained without going to the extreme of refusing, revoking or suspending a licence, including the drawing up of fairer agreements and the provision of compensation to members of the public who have been overcharged and unfairly treated. Another unmeasurable benefit of licensing consists of those businesses which have declined, after consideration, to carry on or launch a particular scheme because they think it might endanger their licences; or those businesses which, in order to safeguard their licence, are now issuing firm instructions to employees on their behaviour; or those businesses which have tightened up their own procedures and redrafted their agreements and publicity material to the same end.

Annual Report of the Director General of Fair Trading 1993, pp 14–15

The work of an adjudicating officer

The Director General's powers to refuse or revoke consumer credit licences and to prohibit persons from carrying on estate agency work [see below, p 293] are exercised by Adjudicating Officers—senior members of his staff specially authorized for the purpose.

The OFT's adjudication procedures were designed to ensure fairness, and were approved by the Council on Tribunals. Their primary principle is separation within the OFT of the responsibility for investigation and the responsibility for adjudication. An officer appointed to adjudicate on a particular case sees only the notice it is intended to issue and the supporting evidence. This material will be sent to the trader concerned only if the Adjudicating Officer is satisfied that the evidence raises serious and reliable doubts and reservations about the trader's fitness. The notice indicates that the Adjudicating Officer is 'minded to' revoke or refuse a licence or prohibit someone from engaging in estate agency work and sets out the basis for that view. Such notices are prepared by teams of investigators, who will have had legal advice: any allegations that cannot be substantiated are kept on a separate file to which the Adjudicating Officer has no access.

An Adjudicating Officer must be, and is, shielded from the opinions of others, including those of OFT colleagues, trading standards officers and the media. Nevertheless, if an officer has seen or heard any press, television, or radio reports about a case, it is right and proper that they are cited in the supporting material so that the trader has the chance to counter any possible bias in the reporting.

When a notice is issued, the Adjudicating Officer's preliminary view is based only on the case against the trader. The legislation requires that recipients of notices must have an opportunity to submit, through written and/or oral representations, their side of the story. Oral hearings are held in private and are as informal as possible. No one is sworn or cross-examined, and questioning is restricted to what is necessary to clarify the facts and to exclude irrelevant material. If new matters come up, the hearing can, if the trader wishes, be adjourned and reasonable notice given of any fresh matters which the Adjudicating Officer may propose to take into account.

The Adjudicating Officer's preliminary view may be changed by a trader's representations: while the facts may be correct, there may be circumstances which soften their significance; or past offences may be isolated and uncharacteristic, perhaps committed at a time of great pressure or under serious provocation. In some cases, those responsible for misconduct may have left the trader's business altogether, or the Adjudicating Officer may be satisfied that an individual has learnt from the experience of conviction and is unlikely to reoffend.

It is the Adjudicating Officer's duty to weigh and balance all the evidence and to arrive at a view about fitness. The objective, under the law, is not to punish past misdeeds, but to judge impartially the current fitness of those concerned in relation to their activities, and to decide whether there is an ongoing risk of detriment to consumers. In one early appeal case, the appeal tribunal held that a system of licensing is effective not only when a licence is revoked, but when remediable defects are brought to light, and are remedied. An Adjudicating Officer will of course, weigh very carefully any claims that a trader with a record of malpractice has reformed. If, however, he considers that such claims are well founded (for example if a company has passed into new hands) then the right decision within the law will be to determine in favour of the trader.

If an Adjudicating Officer does decide against a trader, there is a formal written determination which explains the reasons for the decision. The reasoning and the decision itself are however open to challenge through an appeal to the Secretary of State for Trade and Industry, and thereafter on a point of law to the High Court.

Over the years, about half of all cases have been determined adversely, and one-third favourably (often with undertakings as to future conduct). The rest have been resolved by withdrawal of the application or surrender of the licence. The proportion of favourable determinations has tended to fall in recent years. Procedures and the conduct of hearings are regularly monitored by the Council on Tribunals—to date, without adverse criticism.

The Annual Report of the Director General of Fair Trading for 1996 (HMSO, 1997) indicates the progress of licensing applications. There were 17,202 new licence applications in 1996, 16,504 licences being issued. Applications to vary were 6,331, 5,912 being issued. 7,548 renewal applications were received, 6,415 renewals were issued. A total of 21,595 licences lapsed. From 1976 to 1996 a total of 421,474 licence applications have been received and 403,642 licences have been issued. The following extract discusses 'minded to revoke' and 'minded to refuse' notices to the end of 1996.

In 1996, 136 notices were served on applicants and licensees about their fitness to be granted, or to retain, a licence. . . . Local authority enforcement officers play an essential role in this field, both by providing information about applicants and licensees, and by assisting in subsequent investigations. The 136 notices issued during 1996 were made up as follows:

'Minded to revoke' an existing licence	83
'Minded to refuse' an application for a licence	53
'Minded to grant the application but in terms different from those applied for'	0
'Minded to refuse the application to vary an existing licence'	0
'Minded to vary compulsorily an existing licence'	0
Total	136

Anyone who receives such a notice has the opportunity to make written or oral representations, or both, against the proposed course of action. By comparison with the out-turn for 1995, a greater number (and a higher proportion) of applicants and licensees exercised this right in 1996: traders made representations in 82 of the 120 cases determined (68%)—compared with 77 of the 138 cases determined (56%) the year before—while 76% of those who elected to do so also asked for a personal hearing. During the course of the year, 145 cases were cleared, broken down as follows:

Determined favourably	49
Applications refused	23
Licence revoked	48
Application granted but in terms different from those applied for	0
Applications withdrawn	6
Licences surrendered	11
Notices withdrawn	8
Total	145

Two appeals to the Secretary of State were dismissed with one appellant lodging an appeal in the Court of Session in Scotland. Ten appeals were upheld, of which nine involved companies within the same group. Four appeals remained outstanding at the end of the year.

. . .

Looking at different trading sectors, the motor trade attracted the largest number of notices issued. Motor traders also accounted for the largest numbers of licences revoked and applications refused, followed by traders in the financial services sector.

The 'positive licensing' system has attracted criticism on the ground of its administrative cost both to the Office of Fair Trading and to prospective licensees. Proponents of this system argue that there are commensurate benefits to the public by the positive control which can be exercised over a wide sector of the retail market. In 1988 the Government proposed moving ancillary credit and hire traders to a system of negative licensing. This did not meet with support from successive Directors; see, for example, *Review of Consumer Credit Licensing: Comments from the Director General of Fair Trading on the Proposals of the Department of Trade and Industry*, OFT, December 1988 and *Consumer Credit Deregulation*, OFT, June 1994, ch 9, where alternative measures were suggested.

ESTATE AGENCY

An interesting contrast to the 1974 Act in terms of licensing policy is provided by the Estate Agents Act 1979. The overall supervision and enforcement of the 1979 Act is also the responsibility of the Director General of Fair Trading. However, no positive system of licensing or registration is imposed. Subject to ss 22 and 23 (dealing respectively with standards of competence to be provided by Regulation and prohibition of bankrupts) any person may practise as an estate agent until such time as he is shown unfit to do so. The question of an agent's fitness or unfitness is a matter for the Director who may, if the requirements of the Act are satisfied, either make a warning order under s 4 or make an order prohibiting the unfit estate agent from doing estate agency work under s 3. For a prohibition order to be made the person in question must either have been convicted of one of the offences listed in the Act (particularly one involving fraud or other dishonesty or violence), committed discrimination, failed to comply with an obligation imposed under the Act or have been engaged in a practice which, in relation to estate agency work, has been declared undesirable by an Order made by the Secretary of State. From the case of *Antonelli v Secretary of State for Trade and Industry* [1998] 1 All ER 997, CA, it can be seen that offences committed abroad, prior to the commencement of the 1979 Act may be taken into consideration in making a s 3 order.

It must also be borne in mind that many other professions are regulated by their own professional body. Solicitors, for example, are subject to the disciplinary regulations of the Law Society under statutory powers which now emanate from the Solicitors Act 1974. (See also *Pickles v Insurance Brokers Registration Council* [1984] 1 All ER 1073, [1984] 1 WLR 748 for a decision on the exercise by the IBRC of the power to refuse registration of a firm of insurance brokers under the Insurance Brokers (Registration) Act 1977).

QUESTIONS

Assess the advantages and disadvantages of the positive licensing system which operates under the Consumer Credit Act 1974. Do you think that the administrative complications and expense that are involved justify the results? Can you identify sectors of the market for goods or services whose operations are likely to fall outside the ambit of the licensing control under the 1974 Act and, if so, identify what other statutory regulation may be available to control undesirable activities?

CREDIT TOKENS

The volume of credit transactions initiated through, for instance, Mastercard or Visa credit cards is such that it is necessary to regulate both the issue of credit tokens and the agreement between the debtor and the credit card company. There are estimated to be over 30 million credit cards. Problems inevitably arise if such cards get lost and misused particularly where they were unsolicited in the first place.

Sections 14 and 51 of the 1974 Act are of particular interest in this connection. They state as follows:

14. Credit-token agreements

(1) A credit-token is a card, check, voucher, coupon, stamp, form, booklet or other document or thing given to an individual by a person carrying on a consumer credit business who undertakes—

　(a) that on the production of it (whether or not some other action is also required) he will supply cash, goods and services (or any of them) on credit, or

(b) that where, on the production of it to a third party (whether or not any other action is also required), the third party supplies cash, goods and services (or any of them), he will pay the third party for them (whether or not deducting any discount or commission), in return for payment to him by the individual.

(2) A credit-token agreement is a regulated agreement for the provision of credit in connection with the use of a credit-token.

(3) Without prejudice to the generality of section 9(1), the person who gives to an individual an undertaking falling within subsection (1)(b) shall be taken to provide him with credit drawn on whenever a third party supplies him with cash, goods or services,

(4) For the purposes of subsection (1), use of an object to operate a machine provided by the person giving the object or a third party shall be treated as the production of the object to him.

. . .

51. Prohibition of unsolicited credit-tokens

(1) It is an offence to give a person a credit-token if he has not asked for it.

(2) To comply with subsection (1) a request must be contained in a document signed by the person making the request, unless the credit-token agreement is a small debtor-creditor-supplier agreement.

(3) Subsection (1) does not apply to the giving of a credit-token to a person—

    (a) for use under a credit-token agreement already made, or

    (b) in renewal or replacement of a credit-token previously accepted by him under a credit-token agreement which continues in force, whether or not varied.

NOTE

The definition of 'credit-token' in s 14(1) covers such examples as credit cards issued by individual stores, such credit cards as Mastercard and Barclaycard, cheques and vouchers, and cash cards used to obtain cash from banks' computerised cash machines (but not cheque cards guaranteeing cheques up to a stated amount). Section 9(1), referred to in s 14(3), states that 'In this Act "credit" includes a cash loan, and any other form of financial accommodation.'

In the following case the Director instigated the first prosecution under this section, which has been in force since 1 July 1977.

Elliott v Director General of Fair Trading [1980] 1 WLR 977, [1980] ICR 629, Queen's Bench Division

Lord Lane CJ. This is an appeal by way of case stated from Surrey justices sitting at Kingston and arises under the provisions of the Consumer Credit Act 1974. The facts are scarcely in dispute and they are these. The defendant company deals in footwear and the first defendant, Mr Elliott, is a director of the company. There is no dispute that the guilt or innocence of the director depends upon the guilt or innocence of the company.

The company devised an idea to increase its sale of footwear to the public. The method adopted which has come under the scrutiny of the Director General of Fair Trading was as follows. There was sent to selected members of the public an envelope containing certain materials. The envelope itself was, so to speak, an advertising ploy because it contained, when opened out and cut away, first of all an illustrated advertisement for the Elliott Caterpillar shoe and then the only other material part was an insert in the centre of the piece of paper which represented the envelope saying:

'Your Elliott credit account card valid for immediate use. With your card in your hand, walk into any Elliott shop: give us your signature, show us simple identification, such as a cheque card and walk out of the shop with your purchase *and all the credit you need.* Please remember to sign your card as soon as you receive it. It is perfectly secure; it cannot be used by anyone until we have their signature in the shop.'

At the head of that page where it is cut away, it says, with two arrows, 'Cut away front of envelope to see offer inside.' Inside there were a number of other documents. . . .

The other item which was contained in the envelope is the central feature of the case. It is a piece of paper measuring about two inches by three or thereabouts, the size and shape of the ordinary credit card. It may not be plastic, but it is plasticised and gives the appearance at any rate of being a plastic card, again like the ordinary bank credit card. On the face of it it contains this lettering: 'The Elliott Account T Elliott & Sons Ltd London valid September 1, 1977–August 30, 1978,' and below that are a series of what I may describe as computer figures or figures which are intended to look like computer figures again as, for example, on an American Express card, but nothing, be it noted, embossed.

On the reverse side appears this: first of all, the word 'signature' and then a box again such as you get on a credit card designed obviously for the signature to be placed in it, and then these words:

'1. This credit card is valid for immediate use. 2. The sole requirement is your signature and means of identification. 3. Credit is immediately available if you have a bank account. Sign the card as soon as you receive it; it is perfectly secure because it can only be used when a signature has been accepted at an Elliott shop. T ELLIOTT & SONS.'

In those circumstances the Director General of Fair Trading preferred four informations against the first defendant and four informations against the company, each based upon an allegation that those documents, including that card, had been sent to specified individuals in contravention of section 51(1) of the Consumer Credit Act 1974, which reads: 'It is an offence to give a person a credit-token if he has not asked for it.'

There is no dispute that these documents were sent to the persons alleged. There is no doubt that the persons alleged had not asked for them. The only question is: was this a credit-token within the meaning of the Act. In order to discover the definition of 'credit-token,' one turns to section 14(1) of the same statute and that reads:

His Lordship recited s 14(1) above and continued:

To narrow the problem down still further, the real contest in this case is whether the word 'undertakes' in that definition has been fulfilled by the defendants to these summonses.

The defendant's case, argued as always by Mr Beloff with great skill and persuasion and charm, is this. Mr Beloff submits that the word 'undertakes' means 'makes an offer which is capable of being accepted by the customer so as to impose upon the trader a legally binding obligation to supply to the customer goods on credit.' He goes on to submit that, since the production of the card here did not entitle the customer to the supply of goods on credit but only enabled him to apply for a credit card which would be given when he had signed a certain form of mandate to which I will come in a minute and also other documents, on that basis what the justices found to be a credit card, namely, this little bit of board which I have described before, was not in fact a credit card at all. In fact, despite the wording on this card which I have already read, the credit card was not valid for immediate use. The sole requirement was not the customer's signature and means of identification. Credit was not immediately available if the customer had a bank account. Thus, one reaches the interesting, if somewhat unattractive, proposition that, because those statements on the back of the card are not true, therefore this document, which prima facie appears to be a credit-token, is not in fact one at all. The fact of the matter was that when the customer arrived at the shop, before any credit was in fact extended to the customer, he or she would have to fill in a direct debiting mandate to the bank, and would have to sign other documents.

The submission made by Mr Beloff is that, since all those other matters had to be carried out before credit could be extended, therefore this card cannot constitute a credit-token agreement within the Act.

In my judgment, that argument fails at the outset. The word is 'undertakes', and there is no necessity for any contractual agreement or possibility of contractual agreement to exist. One looks at the card and one asks oneself whether, on the face or on the back of that card, the defendant company is undertaking that on the production of the card cash, goods and services (or any of them) will be supplied on credit. The answer is yes. The card says 'This credit card is valid for immediate use. The sole requirement is your signature . . . Credit is immediately available if you have a bank account.' The fact that none of those statements is true does not absolve the card from being what it purports to be, namely, a credit-token card.

The argument of Mr Beloff that it is so obvious to anybody who stops to think for a moment that this card cannot do what it says without further agreements being entered into strikes me as being irrelevant. The card on the face of it and the back of it is a credit-token card, and that is all that is required. On that basis alone I would dismiss this appeal.

But there is a further basis on which I would found my judgment. Assume for the purposes of argument that the first half of Mr Beloff's argument is correct and that this cannot amount to the necessary undertaking. One then turns to inquire what about the rest of the agreements and so on which have to be signed before credit in truth can be obtained by the customer.

I repeat the words of section 14(1):

'A credit-token is a card, check, voucher, coupon, stamp, form, booklet or other document or thing given to an individual by a person carrying on a consumer credit business, who undertakes a) that on the production of it (whether or not some other action is also required) he will supply cash, goods and services . . . on credit . . . '

The other matters which had to be filled in, in my judgment, plainly fall within the words '(whether or not some other action is also required).' Even if the card cannot be looked at on its own, as I believe it can, nevertheless the further matters which have to be completed before credit is extended fall clearly within the words and parenthesis which I have read. On that basis too the justices were right in coming to the conclusion that they did. For those reasons I would dismiss this appeal.

Woolf J. I agree.

Appeal dismissed with costs.

NOTE

Section 84 limits the debtor's liability arising out of accidental loss of a credit token to £50, though there is no such limit if the misuse is by a person acquiring possession with the debtor's consent. Liability for subsequent misuse ceases altogether after giving notice of loss to the creditor. Agreements for the issue of credit tokens are subject to Part V of the Act, relating to entry into, withdrawal from and formalities governing regulated agreements, and s 85 requires the creditor to give the debtor a copy of any executed agreement.

ADVERTISING CREDIT

The advertising of credit is regulated, by means of criminal sanctions, under Part IV of the Act, in particular ss 43–7, 151–2, and associated regulations. Any advertisement where the advertiser indicates a willingness to provide credit or to enter into an agreement for the bailment or hiring of goods may be regulated, subject to certain exemptions (s 43 and the Consumer Credit (Exempt Advertisements) Order 1985, SI 1985/621). It is to be noted that it is not just the advertising of regulated agreements which is affected. For example, the advertising of mortgages from banks and building societies, which often are exempt agreements, are frequently the subject of prosecutions under the Act, (eg *Scarborough Building Society v Humberside Trading Standards Department* [1997] CCLR 47, Queen's Bench Division).

The form and content of advertisements are regulated by s 44 and the regulations made thereunder; the current ones being the Consumer Credit (Advertisements) Regulations 1989, SI 1989/1125. There are three categories of advertisement: 'simple', 'intermediate' and 'full' and the Regulations specify the permitted and required information for each category. Thus a 'simple' advertisement only permits name, logo, address, telephone number, occupation, and additional information, providing this does not indicate that the person is willing to provide credit and no prices of goods, services, land, etc., are mentioned. A 'full' advertisement must, inter alia, contain details of deposits, variable payments, warnings about the risk of loss of a home where used as security, and the annual percentage rate (APR). An offence is committed for failure to comply with the Regulations: s 47(1). The advertising of goods or services on credit, where the advertiser is not prepared to provide them for cash, is prohibited by s 45 and any advertisement which 'conveys information which in a material respect is false or misleading' is also an offence (s 46).

Case law on advertising often involves detailed consideration of the wording of the Regulations and their applications to specific facts. Of more general interest the following are worth noting.

In *Jenkins v Lombard North Central plc* [1984] 1 All ER 828, [1984] 1 WLR 307, Queen's Bench Divisional Court, it was held that price stickers supplied to a garage, bearing a finance company's logo, were not 'indicating a willingness to provide credit' and thus were not regulated under Part IV. At most they suggested the finance company could provide credit.

A misleading claim that 0% credit was provided can been seen in *Metsoja v H Norman Pitt & Co Ltd* [1989] 153 JP 485, Queen's Bench Divisional Court, (where a credit buyer, in fact, received a smaller part-exchange allowance than a cash buyer). In contrast in *Ford Credit plc v Normand* 1994 SLT 318 the expression '0 per cent finance or 10 per cent discount' was found not to be misleading under s 46, but was, however, in breach of s 44 and the Consumer Credit (Advertisements) Regulations 1989.

The advertising of mortgages, in particular where a low fixed rate applies for a year or two, followed by the 'normal' rate of the bank or building society has caused difficulties. In one case: *National Westminster Bank v Devon County Council, Devon County Council v Abbey National PLC* (1993) 158 JP 156, Queen's Bench Divisional Court, it was permissible to calculate the APR for the whole life of the mortgage using the low starter rate, whereas in *Scarborough Building Society v Humberside Trading Standards Department* [1997] CCLR 47, Queen's Bench Division, this approach was rejected and an offence, under s 46, confirmed.

IMPLIED TERMS AS TO QUALITY

In consumer credit transactions the legal supplier of goods is subject to standard obligations as to correspondence with description, quality and fitness for purpose. In the case of a credit sale these obligations are to be found in the Sale of Goods Act 1979, ss 13–14, above, pp 80–1. In the case of a hire-purchase agreement equivalent obligations are set out in the Supply of Goods (Implied Terms) Act 1973 ss 9 and 10, as amended, above, pp 81–2. The general content of these obligations, including the remedies available on breach, are discussed in ch 3, at p 79 et seq. especially. Control over attempts to exclude or restrict liability as against one who 'deals as consumer' within s 12 of the Unfair Contract Terms Act 1977, below, p 328, is discussed in ch 7 at pp 356–60, as is the effect of the Unfair Terms in Consumer Contracts Regulations 1994, at pp 332–42, especially.

ANTECEDENT NEGOTIATIONS

Section 56 of the Consumer Credit Act 1974 deals with 'antecedent negotiations', that is negotiations with the debtor or hirer by the creditor, owner or a credit-broker, in relation to the making of any regulated agreement (see above, p 282). In the case of a typical hire-purchase agreement, a dealer will negotiate with a 'customer' with a view to the formation of an agreement whereunder a finance company buys the goods from the dealer and then as creditor lets them on hire (with an option to purchase) to the debtor. Section 56(2) states that in the case of any debtor-creditor-supplier agreement, negotiations with the debtor shall be deemed to be conducted by the negotiator in the capacity of agent of the creditor as well as in his actual capacity. The practical effect of s 56 (read with s 189(1)) is that any statements, representations, express terms or undertakings, oral or written, made by the credit-broker to the debtor confer upon the debtor the right to sue the creditor if there is a breach of any of these matters. This liability is not excludable (s 56(3)). Section 56 states as follows:

56. Antecedent negotiations

(1) In this Act 'antecedent negotiations' means any negotiations with the debtor or hirer—

(a) conducted by the creditor or owner in relation to the making of any regulated agreement, or

(b) conducted by a credit-broker in relation to goods sold or proposed to be sold by the credit-broker to the creditor before forming the subject-matter of a debtor-creditor-supplier agreement within section 12(a), or

(c) conducted by the supplier in relation to a transaction financed or proposed to be financed by a debtor-creditor-supplier agreement within section 12(b) or (c),

and 'negotiator' means the person by whom negotiations are so conducted with the debtor or hirer.

(2) Negotiations with the debtor in a case falling within subsection (1)(b) or (c) shall be deemed to be conducted by the negotiator in the capacity of agent of the creditor as well as in his actual capacity.

(3) An agreement is void if, and to the extent that, it purports in relation to an actual or prospective regulated agreement—

(a) to provide that a person acting as, or on behalf of, a negotiator is to be treated as the agent of the debtor or hirer, or

(b) to relieve a person from liability for acts or omissions of any person acting as, or on behalf of, a negotiator.

(4) For the purposes of this Act, antecedent negotiations shall be taken to begin when the negotiator and the debtor or hirer first enter into communication (including communication by advertisement), and to include any representations made by the negotiator to the debtor or hirer and any other dealings between them.

An example of liability being imposed on a finance company under this section can be seen in *Forthright Finance Ltd v Ingate, Ingate v Carlyle Finance Ltd* [1997] 4 All ER 99, CA. Here a garage failed to keep its promise to discharge an existing credit agreement on a car traded in, in part-exchange, for another car. The finance company involved in the new purchase was held liable for the garage's representations when the garage ceased trading and had to indemnify the customer for her loss.

CREDITOR'S LIABILITY FOR THE ACTS OF THE SUPPLIER

In many transactions the creditor and the legal supplier will be one and the same person. For example this is true of hire-purchase agreements where, as has been noted above, the supplier's obligations as to quality are governed by the Supply of Goods (Implied Terms) Act 1973, ss 9 and 10, as amended. However the 1974 Act goes further than this and affects other types of 'debtor-creditor-supplier agreements'.

Section 75 contains the, at first sight, startling principle that in certain circumstances the creditor who makes possible the supply by a third party of goods (the 'connected lender') should be jointly and severally liable with the supplier in respect of a relevant misrepresentation or breach of contract. The Crowther Committee, commenting on the relationship between a lender who makes advances to borrowers pursuant to a regular business relationship between the lender and supplier, pointed out that to a considerable extent the financier and the dealer are engaged in a joint venture. This joint venture has many features. Suppliers who advertise credit card facilities, such as Mastercard or Visa, do so because they believe (normally correctly) that this increases the volume of business. A commission of various sizes is paid to the credit card company on each sale. The Office of Fair Trading, in a review of the operation of s 75, made the following comments on its effect and the reasoning behind its creation:

Connected Lender Liability, a Review by the Director General of Fair Trading of section 75 of the Consumer Credit Act 1974, OFT, March 1994 (footnotes omitted)

2.4. Although section 75 is concerned with breach of contract or misrepresentations by a supplier, it does not itself provide any legal remedies. An aggrieved consumer would have to take action under other laws, such as the Misrepresentation Act 1967 or the Sale of Goods Act 1979, in order to invoke liability under section 75. But because of section 75 the consumer is free to decide whether to sue either the supplier or the provider of credit, or both for the full amount of his claim.

. . .

2.6. Section 75 in fact reflects an important distinction made in the 1971 Crowther report, which paved the way for the Act, between connected and unconnected loans. A connected loan arose where purchases were made from a supplier with credit advanced to the consumer by a lender who was connected with the supplier in the sense of there being a pre-existing arrangement or contemplated arrangement between them. An unconnected loan arose where purchases were made for cash provided to a consumer by an independent lender who had no connection with the supplier. The Crowther Committee took the view that there was no reason to regard a sale in which a consumer utilised an unconnected loan as any different, for consumer protection purposes, from a normal cash sale or to treat the loan as other than a normal loan. But where a connected loan was involved, it regarded the sale and loan aspects of the transaction as linked. It was argued by the Committee that, to an extent, the creditor and supplier were engaged in a joint venture to their mutual advantage and that their respective roles could not therefore be treated in isolation.

2.7. The Committee concluded that where a transaction involved a connected loan (now defined as a debtor-creditor-supplier agreement under section 12(b) or (c) of the Act), the connected lender as well as the supplier ought to bear some responsibility for the quality of the goods or services supplied. One circumstance justifying this was where a connected lender put pressure upon, or offered inducements to, a supplier to promote business to that lender's benefit. Where misrepresentation or breach of contract then arose, it would be unfair and insufficient for the consumer as debtor to have a remedy only against the supplier, his obligation to continue repaying the lender remaining unaffected. The Crowther Committee therefore recommended that a connected lender should be answerable in damages to a debtor for misrepresentations or breach of contract on the part of the supplier. This was enacted by section 75.

Section 75 states as follows:

75. Liability of creditor for breaches by supplier
(1) If the debtor under a debtor-creditor-supplier agreement falling within section 12(b) or (c) has, in relation to a transaction financed by the agreement, any claim against the supplier in respect of a misrepresentation or breach of contract, he shall have a like claim against the

creditor, who, with the supplier, shall accordingly be jointly and severally liable to the debtor.

(2) Subject to any agreement between them, the creditor shall be entitled to be indemnified by the supplier for loss suffered by the creditor in satisfying his liability under subsection (1), including costs reasonably incurred by him in defending proceedings instituted by the debtor.

(3) Subsection (1) does not apply to a claim—

(a) under a non-commercial agreement, or

(b) so far as the claim relates to any single item to which the supplier has attached a cash price not exceeding [£100] or more than [£30,000].

(4) This section applies notwithstanding that the debtor, in entering into the transaction, exceeded the credit limit or otherwise contravened any term of the agreement.

(5) In an action brought against the creditor under subsection (1) he shall be entitled, in accordance with rules of court, to have a supplier made a party to the proceedings.

The essence of s 75(1) is that connected-lender liability applies to debtor-creditor-supplier agreements in which the creditor and the supplier are not one and the same person. Accordingly s 75 does not apply to hire-purchase agreements, conditional sale agreements or credit sale agreements. Thus where the debtor buys goods by using his Mastercard or Visa card the creditor is jointly and severally liable with the seller to the debtor for damages in respect of any misrepresentation or breach of contract. It should be noted that this liability does not attach to such credit card agreements as Diners Club and American Express where the entire debt must be discharged monthly, since these are exempt debtor-creditor-supplier agreements under s 16(5) of the Act.

The effect of s 75 was considered in the following case:

United Dominions Trust v Taylor [1980] SLT (Sh Ct) 28

The facts are set out in the judgment of the Sheriff Principal.

The Sheriff Principal (R. Reid QC). The pursuers made a loan to the defender for the purchase of a motor car from a supplier, who is not a party to the action. The defender avers that the car was represented to him as being in good condition, roadworthy and fit for use on public roads and that it was none of these things. He has intimated the alleged misrepresentation and breach of contract to the supplier and the pursuers and has refused to pay the monthly instalments of loan repayment as they fall due. In the present action the pursuers sue for the balance of the loan and interest. The defender has pleaded the supplier's misrepresentation and breach of contract as a defence to the action and contends that he is entitled to do so under the terms of s 75(1) of the Consumer Credit Act 1974 . . . The pursuers admit that the agreement with them is covered by the Consumer Credit Act 1974 and the parties' agents were agreed that the whole transaction was a debtor-creditor-supplier agreement in terms of ss 11(1)(b) and 12(b) of the Act.

In opening the appeal the defender argued that he had relevantly averred that the contract had been rescinded on the ground of the supplier's misrepresentation and breach of contract and that, by virtue of s 75(1), the rescission affected both the contract of sale with the supplier and the contract of loan with the pursuers. The question, according to the appellant, was whether the words 'any claim against the supplier' included a claim of rescission of the contract with the supplier and the answer he proposed was that, as a matter of ordinary English usage, they plainly did. The pursuers' reply to this argument was that there were two contracts and that the grounds of rescission of the contract with the supplier, namely, misrepresentation and breach of contract, could only apply to that contract. These grounds could not constitute 'a like claim against the creditor' because there was no question of the contract of loan having been induced by misrepresentation or of there being a breach of contract in relation to it. The pursuers' agent also presented the wider argument that s 75(1) was intended to enable the debtor to exercise claims against the creditor, such as claims for restitution or damages, but not to plead a right as a defence to an action by a creditor because the claims referred to in the subsection were limited to those whose enforcement would make the creditor jointly and severally liable with the supplier to the pursuer. The pursuers' agent accepted that there would be anomalous results if these limited rights were exercised while the loan contract remained operative but he contended that these difficulties arose from the wording of the subsection.

I do not agree with the pursuers' argument. The subject-matter of the section is 'any claim against the supplier in respect of a misrepresentation or breach of contract'. The claims which leap to mind as being open in these circumstances are claims to rescind the contract, to claim restitution of any sums paid to the supplier and to claim any damage which the debtor has sustained. It would be odd, to say the least, if the right to rescind was not available against the creditor and the right to restitution, which depends on rescission, was available. The section goes on to provide that, where such claims against the supplier exist, the debtor shall have 'a like claim against the creditor'. The section does not require that the claim against the creditor shall be justifiable on like grounds to the claim against the supplier, merely that it shall be the same sort of claim. The words 'a like claim' are thus wide enough to include a claim for rescission although the creditor has given no grounds for rescission of the loan contract.

This view of the subsection has been confirmed by a consideration of other provisions of the Act, particularly as they relate to debtor-creditor-supplier agreements. The long title of the Act narrates inter alia that the Act establishes a new system of licensing and other control of traders concerned with the provision of credit and their transactions. A reading of the Act discloses that it has created a completely new system of classifications and remedies to take effect whenever consumer credit is associated with the contracts of sale and hire. These statutory remedies have been superimposed on existing contractual remedies. One of the innovations of the Act is to treat two or more contracts which are economically part of one credit transaction as transactions which are legally linked. Where these linked transactions contain two contracts the fate of each contract depends on the other, even where the parties to the contracts are different. This approach leaves no room for the idea of privity of contract which is fundamental to the common law of contract. It is for that reason that I am unable to agree with the learned sheriff's use of the principle of privity of contract to throw light on the meaning of the subsection.

The present contract between the parties is agreed to be a debtor-creditor-supplier agreement under the Act, ie a consumer credit agreement regulated by the Act of the type in which credit is given for a restricted purpose or use in a transaction between a debtor and the supplier (who is not also the creditor) and made by the creditor under pre-existing arrangements between himself and the supplier (ss 11(1)(b) and 12(b)). In such circumstances the contract of sale between the debtor and the supplier is a transaction linked to the credit agreement (s 19(1)(b)). Withdrawal from the credit agreement operates as withdrawal from the contract of sale and cancellation of the credit agreement as a similar effect on the contract of sale (ss 57(1), 69(1)); and there are other circumstances in which a credit agreement and the transaction linked to it stand or fall together (see Goode on *Consumer Credit Act 1974*, para 19.9). All these are instances of cases in which events affecting the credit agreement operate also in the transaction linked to it. In precisely the same way s 75(1) ensures that rescission of the contract of sale shall operate as rescission of a credit agreement linked to it where both form part of a debtor-creditor-supplier agreement.

[The sheriff principal then considered the defender's averments and decided to allow a proof before answer.]

The pursuers appealed to the Court of Session but subsequently abandoned the appeal. It is understood that the decision was set aside on the facts.

NOTES

1. The decision in *United Dominions Trust Ltd v Taylor* has been criticised (see eg Goode, *Consumer Credit* (para 681) and Davidson, (1980) 96 LQR 343). The question is whether if a debtor has a claim to rescind the contract of sale for, for example, misrepresentation, he will by virtue of s 75 then have a 'like claim' to rescind the credit agreement. The more obvious meaning and effect of s 75(1) is that the creditor is required to accept liability as an additional or alternative defendant where the debtor has a claim against the legal supplier for breach of contract or misrepresentation etc. On appropriate facts this may extend to recovery of the contract price and an indemnity against liability to pay interest etc under the credit agreement: see Diamond, *Commercial and Consumer Credit* (1982), pp 268–9. However, it seems that there is no right to rescind the credit agreement as such, since this agreement is distinct from the contract of supply to which it is linked. Admittedly the position may be different if a credit-broker (dealer) makes a false statement about the *credit* agreement itself. By s 56, above, such a statement would be regarded as having been made by the 'negotiator' (dealer) as an agent for the creditor, so giving rise to a possible entitlement to rescind the credit agreement.
2. The Court of Appeal has ruled that an English court has jurisdiction to hear claims under s 75 with regard to purchases of foreign timeshare properties using a credit card or loan from British banks: see *Jarrett v Barclays Bank plc; Jones v First National Bank plc; Peacock v First National Bank plc* [1997] 2 All ER 484.
3. The Director General proposed reform of s 75 to (i) limit the liability of credit-card issuers to the amount charged to the credit card, rather than the full purchase price, (ii) change the monetary upper limit to £25,000, and (iii) allow card issuers the same right as card-holders against insurers or bond administrators where operative to protect customers payments: see *Connected Lender Liability, a second report*, OFT May 1995. The DTI consulted on these proposals in *Connected Lender Liability in the United Kingdom*, December 1995 and in October 1996 announced no changes in the law were proposed. (DTI Press Notice P/96/803).

QUESTIONS

Consider the possible civil liability (if any) of the parties in the following cases with particular reference to the statutory or common law sources of any such liability:

(i) Jake, the sole proprietor of Bombsite Garages, tells Richard, a would-be purchaser of a Mini that it has had 'one careful lady owner'. Richard acquires the

Mini on hire-purchase from Sharkville Finance Company. Later he learns that the car had previously been owned by a hire company and moreover that it is not of satisfactory quality.

(ii) Rupert decides to have his house double-glazed and he employs Samuel to do the work. Samuel arranges finance through Lendit Finances which advances a loan of £3,000 to Rupert. The loan is repayable over twelve months. The work is done very badly and Samuel is now insolvent. Would it affect the position if Rupert had borrowed the money from his bank?

(iii) Xavier buys an electric carving knife and a dishwasher from his local department store. The knife costs £35 and the dishwasher £280 and Xavier uses his Mastercard to pay for both. Two days later the dishwasher floods his kitchen causing extensive damage to the basement below, and Xavier is electrocuted when using the knife. Both the dishwasher and the knife are defective. How, if at all, might it affect the position if the shop assistant had assured him that the knife was 'absolutely safe'?

TIME ORDERS

The court has a number of powers when hearing cases concerning enforcement of agreements. In particular, under s 129:

129. Time orders
(1) [Subject to subsection (3) below] if it appears to the court just to do so—
  (a) on an application for an enforcement order; or
  (b) on an application made by a debtor or hirer under this paragraph after service on him of—
    (i) a default notice, or
    (ii) a notice under section 76(1) or 98(1); or
  (c) in an action brought by a creditor or owner to enforce a regulated agreement or any security, or recover possession of any goods or land to which a regulated agreement relates,
the court may make an order under this section (a 'time order').
(2) A time order shall provide for one or both of the following, as the court considers just—
  (a) the payment by the debtor or hirer or any surety of any sum owed under a regulated agreement or a security by such instalments, payable at such times, as the court, having regard to the means of the debtor or hirer and any surety, considers reasonable;
  (b) the remedying by the debtor or hirer of any breach of a regulated agreement (other than non-payment of money) within such period as the court may specify.
(3) Where in Scotland a time to pay direction or a time to pay order has been made in relation to a debt, it shall not thereafter be competent to make a time order in relation to the same debt.

Section 136 goes on to state:

136. Power to vary agreements and securities
The court may in an order made by it under this Act include such provision as it considers just for amending any agreement or security in consequence of a term of the order.

In the Court of Appeal Leggatt LJ laid down certain principles to be applied in making time orders in the following case:

Southern and District Finance plc v Barnes; J and J Securities Ltd v Ewart; Equity Home Loans Ltd v Lewis [1996] 1 FCR 679 Court of Appeal

The cases concerned credit agreements secured on property where possession orders were being sought and the home owners applied for time orders.

Leggatt LJ:

Judicial control

(1) When a time order is applied for, or a possession order sought of land to which a regulated agreement applies, the court must first consider whether it is just to make a time order. That will involve consideration of all the circumstances of the case, and of the position of the creditor as well as the debtor.

(2) When a time order is made, it should normally be made for a stipulated period on account of temporary financial difficulty. If, despite the giving of time, the debtor is unlikely to be able to resume repayment of the total indebtedness by at least the amount of the contractual instalments, no time order should be made. In such circumstances it will be more equitable to allow the regulated agreement to be enforced.

(3) When a time order is made relating to the non-payment of money:
  (a) the 'sum owed' means every sum which is due and owing under the agreement but where possession proceedings have been brought by the creditor that will normally comprise the total indebtedness; and
  (b) the court must consider what instalments would be reasonable both as to amount and timing, having regard to the debtor's means.

(4) The court may include in a time order any amendment of the agreement, which it considers just to both parties, and which is a consequence of a term of the order. If the rate of interest is amended, it is relevant that smaller instalments will result both in a liability to pay interest on accumulated arrears and, on the other hand, in an extended period of repayment. But to some extent the high rate of interest usually payable under regulated agreements already takes account of the risk that difficulties in repayment may occur.

(5) If a time order is made when the sum owed is the whole of the outstanding balance due under the loan, there will inevitably be consequences for the term of the loan or for the rate of interest or both.

(6) If justice requires the making of a time order, the court should suspend any possession order that it also makes, so long as the terms of the time order are complied with.

EXTORTIONATE CREDIT BARGAINS

Under the Moneylenders Act 1900 courts were given the power to reopen money-lending transactions and set aside agreements if satisfied that the interest was excessive and that the transaction was harsh and unconscionable. The Moneylenders Act 1927 laid down that there was a rebuttable presumption that an interest rate in excess of 48% per annum was excessive and the transaction harsh and unconscionable. The 1974 Act greatly expanded these principles. Sections 137–40 enable the court to reopen credit agreements *whatever the amount of the credit*. The only limitation is that the debtor must be an individual as defined in the Act (see p 282). It will be seen that the way these sections operate is not with reference to a stated rate of interest which must not be exceeded but rather to a number of criteria which the court is directed to consider.

137. Extortionate credit bargains
(1) If the court finds a credit bargain extortionate it may re-open the credit agreement so as to do justice between the parties.

(2) In this section and sections 138 to 140—
(a) 'credit agreement' means any agreement between an individual (the 'debtor') and any other person (the 'creditor') by which the creditor provides the debtor with credit of any amount, and
(b) 'credit bargain'—
   (i) where no transaction other than the credit agreement is to be taken into account in computing the total charge for credit, means the credit agreement, or
   (ii) where one or more other transactions are to be so taken into account, means the credit agreement and those other transactions, taken together.

138. When bargains are extortionate
(1) A credit bargain is extortionate if it—
(a) requires the debtor or a relative of his to make payments (whether unconditionally, or on certain contingencies) which are grossly exorbitant, or
(b) otherwise grossly contravenes ordinary principles of fair dealing.

(2) In determining whether a credit bargain is extortionate, regard shall be had to such evidence as is adduced concerning—
(a) interest rates prevailing at the time it was made,
(b) the factors mentioned in subsections (3) to (5), and
(c) any other relevant considerations.

(3) Factors applicable under subsection (2) in relation to the debtor include—
(a) his age, experience, business capacity and state of health; and
(b) the degree to which, at the time of making the credit bargain, he was under financial pressure, and the nature of that pressure.

(4) Factors applicable under subsection (2) in relation to the creditor include—
(a) the degree of risk accepted by him, having regard to the value of any security provided;
(b) his relationship to the debtor; and
(c) whether or not a colourable cash price was quoted for any goods or services included in the credit bargain.

(5) Factors applicable under subsection (2) in relation to a linked transaction include the question how far the transaction was reasonably required for the protection of debtor or creditor, or was in the interest of the debtor.

139. Reopening of extortionate agreements
(1) A credit agreement may, if the court thinks just, be reopened on the ground that the credit bargain is extortionate—
(a) on an application for the purpose made by the debtor or any surety to the High Court, county court or sheriff court; or
(b) at the instance of the debtor or a surety in any proceedings to which the debtor and creditor are parties, being proceedings to enforce the credit agreement, any security relating to it, or any linked transaction; or
(c) at the instance of the debtor or a surety in other proceedings in any court where the amount paid or payable under the credit agreement is relevant.

(2) In reopening the agreement, the court may, for the purpose of relieving the debtor or a surety from payment of any sum in excess of that fairly due and reasonable, by order—
(a) direct accounts to be taken, or (in Scotland) an accounting to be made, between any persons,

(b) set aside the whole or part of any obligation imposed on the debtor or a surety by the credit bargain or any related agreement,

(c) require the creditor to repay the whole or part of any sum paid under the credit bargain or any related agreement by the debtor or a surety, whether paid to the creditor or any other person,

(d) direct the return to the surety of any property provided for the purposes of the security, or

(e) alter the terms of the credit agreement or any security instrument.

(3) An order may be made under subsection (2) notwithstanding that its effect is to place a burden on the creditor in respect of an advantage unfairly enjoyed by another person who is a party to a linked transaction.

(4) An order under subsection (2) shall not alter the effect of any judgment.

(5) In England and Wales an application under subsection (l)(a) shall be brought only in the county court in the case of—

(a) a regulated agreement, or

(b) an agreement (not being a regulated agreement) under which the creditor provides the debtor with fixed-sum credit . . . or running-account credit . . .

. . .

140. Interpretation of sections 137 to 139

Where the credit agreement is not a regulated agreement, expressions used in sections 137 to 139 which, apart from this section, apply only to regulated agreements, shall be construed as nearly as may be as if the credit agreement were a regulated agreement.

These provisions were considered in the following cases.

Ketley v Scott [1981] ICR 241, Chancery Division

The defendant, Mr Scott, had contracted to buy a flat at a favourable price and then paid a deposit of £2,250. Mr Scott was unable to complete (because of lack of funds) on the final day allowed for completion. He therefore applied for and obtained a loan from the plaintiffs of £20,500 secured (inter alia) by a legal charge, to enable him and his wife to complete. The interest was expressed as being 12% over 3 months, this being equal to 48% per annum. He did not declare to the plaintiffs that he had given a legal charge on the property to his bank to cover an overdraft and was liable under certain further guarantees to third parties.

The plaintiffs sued for payment due and possession and obtained judgment, but an enquiry was ordered into the question of whether the interest was 'extortionate'.

Foster J. . . . In my judgment the rate of interest charged was not extortionate within the meaning of section 138 in all the circumstances of the case. But even if I am wrong in this conclusion, the court can reopen the bargain under section 139—and I quote—'if the court thinks just.' In this case I do not think that the court should do so, for the following reasons: (a) Mr Scott failed, on the application form, to disclose his overdraft with the bank. (b) He never disclosed the guarantee up to £5,000 which he had given to some of his companies. (c) He failed to disclose that he had given a legal charge to his bank to secure his overdraft which, if registered first, would have given it priority. (d) He failed to disclose the valuation of £24,000 given to him in August 1978. It was a professional valuation but he put in the application form a value of £30,000. In view of these four deceitful acts I would not be prepared to reopen the transaction.

In the answer to the enquiry I shall declare that the interest payable under the said legal charge should remain.

Declaration accordingly.

The Court of Appeal in *Wills v Wood* (1984) 128 Sol Jo 222, took a similar hardheaded policy decision, as is indicated in the concurring judgment of Fox LJ:

Wills v Wood (1984) 128 Sol Jo 222, Court of Appeal

For the facts of this case, see above, p 284.

Fox LJ. The second contention advanced on behalf of Miss Wood is that each of the loans was an 'extortionate credit bargain' within section 138(1) of the Consumer Credit Act 1974. The judge accepted that; she held that the bargain, in each case, 'grossly contravenes the principles of fair dealing' within section 138(1)(b).

It is not suggested that the terms of the loans were oppressive or in any way objectionable. They were, in fact, quite ordinary mortgage transactions at reasonable rates of interest. What Miss Wood is really complaining of is that she should have been lent money at all. Her financial position, it is said, was such that borrowing could only be harmful. The judge said: 'Had the defendant received independent advice I am satisfied that she would have been strongly advised against borrowing more money.' But if Miss Wood acted to her detriment in borrowing these sums, that may be because she was not properly advised by her solicitors or because she chose to act on her own judgment. It was not, however, because of any unfairness of dealing as between herself and Mr Wills. She was of full age and capacity; she wanted loans on reasonable terms and that is what she got. Mr Wills had no contact with her and had no knowledge of her private circumstances. Nobody acting on his behalf misled her or induced her to grant the mortgages. It is quite true that his solicitors were also Miss Wood's solicitors. But in their capacity as Mr Wills' solicitors they did nothing wrong or unfair. Let me suppose that they failed to advise Miss Wood properly. That was in their capacity as her solicitors and is a matter between her and them. In relation to the establishment of a gross contravention of the ordinary principles of fair dealing, I do not see on what basis Mr Wills can in any way be responsible for such failure or its consequences or be fixed with knowledge of it.

In my opinion the case is altogether outside the provisions of section 138(1) of the Consumer Credit Act, and there was no contravention of any principle of fair dealing.

For the above reasons . . . I would allow the appeal.

Sir John Donaldson, MR delivered a concurring judgment and **Stephen Brown LJ** agreed.

Appeal allowed.

A final example of the issues which are under consideration in deciding whether or not an agreement is extortionate arises in:

Davies v Directloans Ltd [1986] 2 All ER 783, Chancery Division

The case concerned a couple (the plaintiffs) who, in seeking to purchase a property, had been unable to obtain a mortgage and who, instead, agreed to pay the defendants £17,450 (the balance of the purchase price) at 21.6% interest, by 120 equal monthly instalments. Having got into arrears and a possession order being sought, the plaintiffs sold the property and paid off the debt. The plaintiffs then sought to reopen the credit agreement on the grounds that it was an extortionate credit bargain within s 138. Much of the case concerned a detailed consideration of the circumstances in which the loan was made, but the judge, **Edward Nugee QC**, laid down a number of guidelines to assist in deciding whether an agreement ought to be reopened. On s 138(1) in general he stated:

Section 138(1) contains a comprehensive definition of 'extortionate' for the purposes of the 1974 Act, and it is neither necessary nor permissible to look outside the Act at earlier authorities in order to ascertain its meaning.

. . .

Under the 1974 Act the test is not whether the creditor has acted in a morally reprehensible manner, but whether one or other of the conditions of s 138(1) is fulfilled, and although it may be thought that if either condition is fulfilled there is likely to be something morally reprehensible about the creditor's conduct, the starting and ending point in determining whether a credit bargain is extortionate must be the words of section 138(1).

Regarding s 138(3)(b) and consideration of financial pressure he indicated:

Nearly every purchaser who borrows money in order to complete his purchase is under some degree of financial pressure. It is only if the lender takes advantage of the pressure that this factor is in my judgment relevant in considering whether the loan is extortionate.

To determine the rate of interest charged the judge referred to the Consumer Credit Tables, published by HMSO, and used to calculate the annual percentage rate of charge (APR):

I am told by counsel that no case has decided that it is right to take the APR into account for the purposes of s 138 of the 1974 Act. Section 138(2)(a) requires the court to have regard to interest rates prevailing at the time the credit bargain was made; and, now that HMSO, with the aid of computer technology, has made it comparatively simple to determine the true rate of interest, it would in my judgment be wrong to use any other rate, without at all events recognising that other ways of stating the rate of interest may be misleading.

In referring to 'grossly exorbitant' he said:

These words are not defined by the Act and must be given their ordinary meaning. 'Exorbitant' is defined by the *Shorter Oxford English Dictionary* as 'Exceeding ordinary or proper bounds; excessive; outrageously large'; 'grossly' is defined as 'excessively; flagrantly'.
    Lord Cranworth (then Rolfe B) said, in a well-known passage in *Wilson v Brett* (1843) 11 M & W 113 at 115–116, 152 ER 737 at 739, that he—

'could see no difference between negligence and gross negligence—that it was the same thing, with the addition of a vituperative epithet . . . '

Given the already strong signification of the word 'exorbitant', I am tempted to echo this sentiment, since it is difficult to conceive of a credit bargain which required the debtor to make payments which were exorbitant but which the creditor could satisfy the court was not extortionate.

On the facts of the case, having looked at all the circumstances in which the loan was made, the court found that it was not an extortionate credit bargain.

Reform

The Director General conducted a detailed examination of the operation of ss 137–40 in 1991 at the request of the Government. His report was published by the OFT and the following extracts demonstrate the findings of the investigation and the conclusions reached:

Unjust Credit Transactions, A Report by the Director General of Fair Trading on the provisions of sections 137–140 of the Consumer Credit Act 1974

Assessment of the current position

4.3. The Office can, therefore, conclude with some confidence that the extortionate credit provisions of the Act have not been widely used. Moreover, analysis of the decided cases indicates that the courts have only been willing to reopen agreements in very clear cut cases where the risk has been low and the statutory factors very clearly and heavily weighed in the borrower's favour. In reviewing the various judgments it seems clear that, although they have taken other matters into account, the courts appear to be primarily influenced by rates of interest. The concept of 'the ordinary principles of fair dealing' has received little or no attention.

At the time of the report the OFT knew of 23 court cases, in 15 of which the issue of whether or not a credit bargain was extortionate was decided. The debtor was successful in establishing an extortionate credit bargain in only 4 cases.

4.9. As indicated, above the courts have to date largely focused on credit costs (APRs and interest rates) as indicators of extortionate credit. The Office is clear, however, that the cost of credit alone, in particular the level of APR, is only a limited indicator of an unjust credit transaction except where rates are so outrageous as to be manifestly out of line with rates prevailing in that sector of the market. The courts have, however, largely failed to consider whether practices engaged in by lenders (or brokers) have 'grossly contravened the ordinary principles of fair dealing'. The Office is aware of various practices in the credit market which, it has concluded, would point towards an unjust credit transaction. Such practices may 'grossly contravene the ordinary principles of fair dealing', but the absence of any positive judicial guidance has added to other factors which discourage more cases being taken to and tested in the courts. The practices may also merit adverse licensing action by the Director General and this has been taken where appropriate. But the Office usually receives complaints on a fragmented basis without sufficient depth or width of evidence against a particular licensee—and without any court judgments—so that the draconian step of licence revocation may not be readily available.

. . .

4.18. [T]he Office does not believe that the extortionate credit provisions in sections 137–140 of the Act have effectively addressed the problem perceived by the Crowther Committee as the legislators intended. They have failed to deter, or to provide redress for debtors where so-called 'bargains' are so oppressive as to be socially harmful.

4.19. The Office believes that there are three principle reasons why these provisions have failed:

(i) The statutory wording in section 138, defining the concept of extortionate credit, is unsatisfactory. It is unnecessarily restrictive—or has been so interpreted—with undue emphasis on credit charges and it fails to offer a clear indication either to the courts or to debtors, as to whether a particular credit transaction is extortionate. Furthermore, there have been considerable changes in the credit market since the Act was passed. New forms of lending have emerged where—whether from deception or exploitation by the lender or because of the borrower's ignorance or desperate situation—credit is taken on terms (which may not necessarily include high interest rates) which no sensible person, with independent advice, would find acceptable.

(ii) The current wording is also unfamiliar. It is not certain whether the power to reopen a credit bargain extends to all transactions involving various abuses which are to be found on the margins of the market. In all cases of doubt or exclusion, the debtor will be without relief, remaining bound by the contractual commitment.

(iii) Consumers have been unwilling or unable themselves to take cases to court. The Office's view, supported by respondents to its consultation letter, is that there are several reasons for this. The first is simply that they are unaware that they have the statutory right. The Office's own research has shown that 83% of consumers were unaware that they could seek court action if they were being charged an extortionate amount on a loan. Secondly, consumers may fear that if they went to court they may jeopardise their future access to credit. This would be particularly relevant in the case of low income borrowers who have limited choice in their sources of credit, perhaps having to rely upon one particular lender.

4.20. More generally, there is a series of financial, cultural and practical obstacles which severely inhibit access to the courts for this purpose.

Recommendations

1. The Government should introduce legislation to reform and develop sections 137–140 of the Consumer Credit Act, re-casting them with a view to making them work as originally intended. The concept of an 'unjust credit transaction' should replace that of an 'extortionate credit bargain'. In such cases the court would, as now, have the power to reopen an agreement, on application by the debtor (or surety), so as to do justice between the parties.

2. A finding that a transaction involves excessive—not grossly exorbitant—payments should be a factor in determining whether the transaction was unjust.

3. A new test of whether the transaction involved business activity which was deceitful or oppressive or otherwise unfair or improper (whether unlawful or not)—using the same statutory wording as is used to asses the fitness of a trader to hold a credit licence—should be a further factor in determining whether a transaction was unjust.

4. The other factors to be taken into account should remain as they are, but with one addition—'the lender's care and responsibility in making the loan, including steps taken to find out and check the borrower's credit-worthiness and ability to meet the full terms of the agreement'.

5. The court should be empowered to re-open a credit transaction of its own motion. It should also be stated explicitly that this would apply to defended and undefended cases.

6. The court should be required to notify the Director General of each case where a credit transaction has been found to be unjust.

7. The Director General and local authority trading standards departments should be empowered to initiate proceedings for a declaration that a particular credit transaction or any particular aspect of it shall be deemed unjust. Such power should be exercisable only in the public interest.

8. Tougher penalties should be introduced for the unlicensed (ie illegal) provision of credit.

NOTES

1. To date no statutory amendments of the extortionate credit provisions have been forthcoming.

2. For further discussion of the provisions see Bentley and Howells, 'Judicial Treatment of Extortionate Credit Bargains', [1989] Conv 164 and 'Loansharks and Extortionate Credit Bargains—2', [1989] Conv 234.
3. For discussion of other potentially 'unfair' or 'unjust' contract terms, see below, ch 7, at pp 371–5, especially.

CHAPTER 7

Exemption clauses and unfair contract terms

INTRODUCTION

For many years the obligations concerning contracts for the supply of goods and services (referred to in chs 3 and 4 respectively) could be excluded or limited by a suitably-worded exemption or limitation clause. Indeed such clauses were commonplace and prima facie binding on consumers and others even though they were neither understood nor read. This was but a reflection of the classical freedom of contract theory, but the effect on individuals was described by Lord Denning MR as 'a bleak winter for our law of contract' (see *George Mitchell (Chesterhall) Ltd v Finney Lock Seeds Ltd* [1983] QB 284, [1983] 1 All ER 108, below, p 319). Of course the problem was exacerbated by the growth in the use of standard form contracts or contracts of adhesion. Professor Slawson has noted the prevalence and typical nature of such contracts in an influential article.

'Standard Form Contracts and Democratic Control of Lawmaking Power' by Slawson (1971) 84 Harvard LR 529, at pp 529–31:

Standard form contracts probably account for more than ninety-nine percent of all the contracts now made . . . The contracting still imagined by courts and law teachers as typical, in which both parties participate in choosing the language of their entire agreement, is no longer of much more than historical importance . . . The predominance of standard forms is the best evidence of their necessity. They are characteristic of a mass production society and an integral part of it . . . But the overwhelming proportion of standard forms are not democratic because they are not, under any reasonable test, the agreement of the consumer or business recipient to whom they are delivered. Indeed, in the usual case, the consumer never even reads the forms, or reads it only after he has become bound by its terms. Even the fastidious few who take the time to read the standard form may be helpless to vary it. The form may be part of an offer which the consumer has no reasonable alternative but to accept.

. . .

Forms standardised to achieve economies of mass production and mass merchandising will also, under the present system, almost certainly be unfair, because if they were not, their issuers would probably lose money. An unfair form will not deter sales because the seller can easily arrange his sales so that few if any buyers will read his forms, whatever their terms, and he risks nothing because the law will treat his forms as contracts anyway. The user of an unfair form does not even stand to lose any significant number of future sales because the contingencies against which his forms provide him protection are normally of a kind which only infrequently occur (although when they do, the buyer may lose a great deal). When such a contingency arises the buyer will not usually be in a position to compare the form he bought with others he might have bought instead. Most buyers probably believe (correctly) that the forms they could have bought from a competing seller would have been just as bad anyway. An unfair form thus normally constitutes a costless benefit which a seller refuses at his peril . . .

In most Western legal systems such considerations have led to statutory control of exemption clauses and in some jurisdictions of unfair contract terms generally. Sometimes the controls apply to standard form contracts specifically. Other controls are of more general application, although they may also have particular provisions applicable to such contracts. In the United Kingdom the Unfair Terms in Consumer Contracts Regulations 1994 apply to terms which have not been individually negotiated (including standard form contracts) whereas the Unfair Contract Terms Act 1977 is of more general application.

INCORPORATION AND PRINCIPLES OF CONSTRUCTION

Even before the advent of statutory control the full rigours of the common law were often mitigated in practice by the court's insistence that an exemption clause be incorporated in the contract and apt to cover the plaintiff's claim. Such matters are no longer important where the clause is in any event void by virtue of the Unfair Contract Terms Act 1977. However, there are many consumer transactions where exemption clauses are not void but are subject rather to the 'test of reasonableness' under the 1977 Act. For example, a consumer's goods may have been lost or damaged in a house removal or when being cleaned or processed or a holiday may have gone disastrously wrong. Alternatively, a contract term may be subject to a requirement that it must not be 'unfair'. In any such case it is possible for a court to conclude that an exemption clause is both 'reasonable' (or some other term is 'fair') and yet ineffective, for example because it has not been incorporated into the contract. For this reason the common law rules of incorporation and construction cannot be ignored and are indeed the logical starting point for any inquiry.

The basic requirement for incorporation is that there be either a signed contractual document (as in *L'Estrange v Graucob Ltd* [1934] 2 KB 394) or that reasonable notice of the exempting provision be given before the contract is concluded. Precisely what constitutes 'reasonable notice' is often unclear (see *Woodman v Photo Trade Processing Ltd*, below, p 343).

The following leading case is relevant to the issue.

Interfoto Picture Library Ltd v Stiletto Visual Programmes Ltd [1988] 1 All ER 348; [1989] QB 433, Court of Appeal.

The defendant advertising agency required photographs of the 1950s for a presentation for a client. On 5 March 1984 they telephoned the plaintiffs, who ran a library of photographic transparencies, inquiring whether the plaintiffs had any photographs of that period which might be suitable for the presentation. On the same day the plaintiffs despatched to the defendants 47 transparencies packed in a Jiffy bag with a delivery note which clearly specified that the transparencies were to be returned by 19 March and which under the heading 'Conditions' printed prominently in capitals, set out nine printed conditions in four columns. Condition 2 stated that all transparencies were to be returned within 14 days from the date of delivery and that 'A holding fee of £5.00 plus VAT per day will be charged for each transparency which is retained by you longer than the said period of 14 days'. The defendants telephoned to acknowledge receipt of the transparencies, but it was unlikely that they read any of the conditions. In the result, they did not use them but put them to one side and forgot about them. The transparencies were not returned to the plaintiffs until 2 April. The plaintiffs sent the defendants an invoice for £3,783.50, being the holding charge calculated at £5 per transparency per day from 19 March to 2 April. The defendants refused to pay and the plaintiffs brought an action against them claiming the amount of the invoice. The trial judge gave judgment for the plaintiffs and the defendants appealed.

Dillon LJ, having stated the facts of the case, continued: The question is therefore whether condition 2 was sufficiently brought to the defendants' attention to make it a term of the contract which was only concluded after the defendants had received, and must have known that they had received the transparencies *and* the delivery note.

This sort of question was posed, in relation to printed conditions, in the ticket cases, such as *Parker v South Eastern Rly Co* (1877) 2 CPD 416, [1874–80] All ER Rep 166, in the last century. At that stage the printed conditions were looked at as a whole and the question considered by the courts was whether the printed conditions as a whole had been sufficiently drawn to a customer's attention to make the whole set of conditions part of the contract; if so the customer was bound by the printed conditions even though he never read them.

More recently the question has been discussed whether it is enough to look at a set of printed conditions as a whole. When for instance one condition in a set is particularly onerous does something special need to be done to draw customers' attention to that particular condition? In an obiter dictum in *J Spurling Ltd v Bradshaw* [1956] 2 All ER 121 at 125, [1956] 1 WLR 461 at 466 (cited in *Chitty on Contracts* (25th edn, 1983) vol 1, para 742, p 408) Denning LJ stated:

'Some clauses which I have seen would need to be printed in red ink on the face of the document with a red hand pointing to it before the notice could be held to be sufficient.'

Then in *Thornton v Shoe Lane Parking Ltd* [1971] 1 All ER 686, [1971] 2 QB 163 both Lord Denning MR and Megaw LJ held as one of their grounds of decision, as I read their judgments, that where a condition is particularly onerous or unusual the party seeking to enforce it must show that that condition, or an unusual condition of that particular nature, was fairly brought to the notice of the other party. Lord Denning restated and applied what he had said in the *Spurling* case, and held that the court should not hold any man bound by such a condition unless it was drawn to his attention in the most explicit way (see [1971] 1 All ER 686 at 689–690, [1971] 2 QB 163 at 169–170).

. . .

Condition 2 of these plaintiffs' conditions is in my judgment a very onerous clause. The defendants could not conceivably have known, if their attention was not drawn to the clause, that the plaintiffs were proposing to charge a 'holding fee' for the retention of the transparencies at such a very high and exorbitant rate.

At the time of the ticket cases in the last century it was notorious that people hardly ever troubled to read printed conditions on a ticket or delivery note or similar document. That remains the case now. In the intervening years the printed conditions have tended to become more and more complicated and more and more one-sided in favour of the party who is imposing them, but the other parties, if they notice that there are printed conditions at all, generally still tend to assume that such conditions are only concerned with ancillary matters of form and are not of importance. In the ticket cases the courts held that the common law required that reasonable steps be taken to draw the other parties' attention to the printed conditions or they would not be part of the contract. It is in my judgment a logical development of the common law into modern conditions that it should be held, at it was in *Thornton v Shoe Lane Parking Ltd*, that, if one condition in a set of printed conditions is particularly onerous or unusual, the party seeking to enforce it must show that that particular condition was fairly brought to the attention of the other party.

In the present case, nothing whatever was done by the plaintiffs to draw the defendants' attention particularly to condition 2; it was merely one of four columns' width of conditions printed across the foot of the delivery note. Consequently condition 2 never, in my judgment became part of the contract between the parties.

I would therefore allow this appeal and reduce the amount of the judgment which the judge awarded against the defendants to the amount which he would have awarded on a quantum meruit on his alternative findings, ie the reasonable charge of £3.50 per transparency per week for the retention of the transparencies beyond a reasonable period, which he fixed at 14 days from the date of their receipt by the defendants.

Bingham LJ. In many civil law systems, and perhaps in most legal systems outside the common law world, the law of obligations recognises and enforces an overriding principle that in making and carry out contracts parties should act in good faith. This does not simply mean that they should not deceive each other, a principle which any legal system must recognise; its effect is perhaps most aptly conveyed by such metaphorical colloquialisms as 'playing fair', 'coming clean' or 'putting one's cards face upwards on the table'. It is in essence a principle of fair and open dealing. In such a forum it might, I think, be held on the facts of this case that the plaintiffs were under a duty in all fairness to draw the defendants' attention specifically to the high price payable if the transparencies were not returned in time and, when the 14 days had expired, to point out to the defendants the high cost of continued failure to return them.

English law has, characteristically, committed itself to no such overriding principle but has developed piecemeal solutions in response to demonstrated problems of unfairness. Many examples could be given. Thus equity has intervened to strike down unconscionable bargains. Parliament has stepped in to regulate the imposition of exemption clauses and the form of certain hire-purchase agreements. The common law also has made its contribution, by holding that certain classes of contract require the utmost good faith, by treating as irrecoverable what purport to be agreed estimates of damage but are in truth a disguised penalty for breach, and in many other ways.

The well-known cases on sufficiency of notice are in my view properly to be read in this context. At one level they are concerned with a question of pure contractual analysis, whether one party has done enough to give the other notice of the incorporation of a term in the contract.

At another level they are concerned with a somewhat different question, whether it would in all the circumstances be fair (or reasonable) to hold a party bound by any conditions or by a particular condition of an unusual and stringent nature.

. . .

The crucial question in the case is whether the plaintiffs can be said fairly and reasonably to have brought condition 2 to the notice of the defendants. The judge made no finding on the point, but I think that it is open to this court to draw an inference from the primary findings which he did make. In my opinion the plaintiffs did not do so. They delivered 47 transparencies, which was a number the defendants had not specifically asked for. Condition 2 contained a daily rate per transparency after the initial period of 14 days many times greater than was usual or (so far as the evidence shows) heard of. For these 47 transparencies there was to be a charge for each day of delay of £235 plus value added tax. The result would be that a venial period of delay, as here, would lead to an inordinate liability. The defendants are not to be relieved of that liability because they did not read the condition, although doubtless they did not; but in my judgment they are to be relieved because the plaintiffs did not do what was necessary to draw this unreasonable and extortionate clause fairly to their attention. I would accordingly allow the defendants' appeal and substitute for the judge's award the sum which he assessed on the alternative basis of quantum meruit.

In reaching the conclusion I have expressed I would not wish to be taken as deciding that condition 2 was not challengeable as a disguised penalty clause. This point was not argued before the judge nor raised in the notice of appeal. It was accordingly not argued before us. I have accordingly felt bound to assume, somewhat reluctantly, that condition 2 would be enforceable if fully and fairly brought to the defendants' attention.

Appeal allowed.

In addition to the cases cited in the above extracts, see *McCutcheon v David MacBrayne Ltd* [1964] 1 All ER 430, [1964] 1 WLR 125, HL; *Hollier v Rambler Motors (AMC) Ltd* [1972] 2 QB 71, [1972] 1 All ER 399, CA; also Treitel, *The Law of Contract* (9th edn), pp 197–201. For penalty clauses, see Treitel, op cit, pp 899–902.

The operation of the principles of construction and the general development of common law and statutory controls have been traced by Lord Denning MR in a commercial case which, as Lord Diplock was to remark ([1983] 2 All ER 737, 739), was probably also the last in which the House of Lords would have the opportunity of enjoying Lord Denning's 'eminently readable style'. Its valedictory nature provides a further reason for these extracts.

George Mitchell (Chesterhall) Ltd v Finney Lock Seeds Ltd [1983] 1 All ER 108, [1983] QB 284, Court of Appeal

Lord Denning MR

In outline

Many of you know Lewis Carroll's *Through the Looking Glass*. In it there are these words (ch 4):

' "The time has come," the Walrus said,
  "To talk of many things:

Of shoes—and ships—and sealing wax—
  Of cabbages—and kings . . . "'

Today it is not 'of cabbages and kings', but of cabbages and whatnots. Some farmers, called George Mitchell (Chesterhall) Ltd, ordered 30 lb of cabbage seed. It was supplied. It looked just like cabbage seed. No one could say it was not. The farmers planted it over 63 acres. Six months later there appeared out of the ground a lot of loose green leaves. They looked like cabbage leaves but they never turned in. They had no hearts. They were not 'cabbages' in our common parlance because they had no hearts. The crop was useless for human consumption. Sheep or cattle might eat it if hungry enough. It was commercially useless. The price of the seed was £192. The loss to the farmers was over £61,000. They claimed damages from the seed merchants, Finney Lock Seeds Ltd. The judge awarded them that sum with interest. The total comes to nearly £100,000.

The seed merchants appeal to this court. They say that they supplied the seed on a printed clause by which their liability was limited to the cost of the seed, that is £192. They rely much on two recent cases in the House of Lords: *Photo Production Ltd v Securicor Transport Ltd* [1980] 1 All ER 556, [1980] AC 827 and *Ailsa Craig Fishing Co Ltd v Malvern Fishing Co Ltd* [1983] 1 All ER 101 (the two *Securicor* cases) . . .

Are the conditions part of the contract?

The farmers were aware that the sale was subject to some conditions of sale. All seed merchants have conditions of sale. They were on the back of the catalogue. They were also on the back of the invoice each year. So it would seem that the farmers were bound at common law by the terms of them. The inference from the course of dealing would be that the farmers had accepted the conditions as printed, even though they had never read them and did not realise that they contained a limitation on liability. . . .

The natural meaning

There was much discussion before us as to the construction of that condition. I am much impressed by the words I have emphasised. Taking the clause in its natural plain meaning, I think it is effective to limit the liability of the seed merchants to a return of the money or replacement of the seeds. The explanation they give seems fair enough. They say that it is so as to keep the price low, and that if they were to undertake any greater liability the price would be much greater.

After all, the seed merchants did supply seeds. True, they were the wrong kind altogether. But they were seeds. On the natural interpretation, I think the condition is sufficient to limit the seed merchants to a refund of the price paid or replacement of the seeds.

The hostile meaning

Before the decisions of the House of Lords in the two *Securicor* cases, I would have been inclined to decide the case as the judge did. I would have been 'hostile' to the clause. I would have said that the goods supplied here were different *in kind* from those that were ordered, and that the seed merchants could not avail themselves of the limitation clause. But in the light of the House of Lords cases, I think that that approach is not available. . . .

To my mind these two cases have revolutionised our approach to exemption clauses. In order to explain their importance, I propose to take you through the story.

The heyday of freedom of contract

None of you nowadays will remember the trouble we had, when I was called to the Bar, with exemption clauses. They were printed in small print on the back of tickets and order forms and invoices. They were contained in catalogues or timetables. They were held to be binding on any person who took them without objection. No one ever did object. He never read them or knew what was in them. No matter how unreasonable they were, he was bound. All this was done in the name of 'freedom of contract'. But the freedom was all on the side of the big concern which had the use of the printing press. No freedom for the little man who took the ticket or order form or invoice. The big concern said, 'Take it or leave it.' The little man had no option but to take it. The big concern could and did exempt itself from liability in its own interest without regard to the little man. It got away with it time after time. When the courts said to the big concern, 'You must put it in clear words,' the big concern had no hesitation in doing so. It knew well that the little man would never read the exemption clauses or understand them.

It was a bleak winter for our law of contract. It is illustrated by two cases, *Thompson v London Midland and Scottish Rly Co* [1930] 1 KB 41, [1929] All ER Rep 474 (in which there was exemption from liability, not on the ticket, but only in small print at the back of the timetable, and the company were held not liable) and *L'Estrange v F Graucob Ltd* [1934] 2 KB 394, [1934] All ER Rep 16 (in which there was complete exemption in small print at the bottom of the order form, and the company were held not liable).

The secret weapon

Faced with this abuse of power, by the strong against the weak, by the use of the small print of the conditions, the judges did what they could to put a curb on it. They still had before them the idol, 'freedom of contract'. They still knelt down and worshipped it, but they concealed under their cloaks a secret weapon. They used it to stab the idol in the back. This weapon was called 'the true construction of the contract'. They used it with great skill and ingenuity. They used it so as to depart from the natural meaning of the words of the exemption clause and to put on them a strained and unnatural construction. In case after case, they said that the words were not strong enough to give the big concern exemption from liability, or that in the circumstances the big concern was not entitled to rely on the exemption clause. If a ship deviated from the contractual voyage, the owner could not rely on the exemption clause. If a warehouseman stored the goods in the wrong warehouse, he could not pray in aid the limitation clause. If the seller supplied goods different in kind from those contracted for, he could not rely on any exemption from liability. If a shipowner delivered goods to a person without production of the bill of lading, he would not escape responsibility by reference to an exemption clause. In short, whenever the wide words, in their natural meaning, would give rise to an unreasonable result, the judges either rejected them as repugnant to the main purpose of the contract or else cut them down to size in order to produce a reasonable result.

. . .

Fundamental breach

No doubt had ever been cast thus far by anyone. But doubts arose when in this court, in a case called *Karsales (Harrow) Ltd v Wallis* [1956] 2 All ER 866, [1956] 1 WLR 936, we ventured to suggest that if the big concern was guilty of a breach which went to the 'very root' of the contract, sometimes called a 'fundamental breach', or at other times a 'total failure' of its obligations, then it could not rely on the printed clause to exempt itself from liability. This way of putting it had been used by some of the most distinguished names in the law . . . But we did make a mistake, in the eyes of some, in elevating it, by inference, into a 'rule of law'. That was too rude an interference with the idol of 'freedom of contract.' We ought to have used the secret weapon. We ought to have said that in each case, on the 'true construction of the contract' in that case, the exemption clause did not avail the party where he was guilty of a fundamental breach or a breach going to the root. That is the lesson to be learnt from the 'indigestible' speeches in *Suisse Atlantique Société d'Armement Maritime SA v Rotterdamsche Kolen Centrale NV* [1966] 2 All ER 61, [1967] 1 AC 361. They were all obiter dicta. The House were dealing with an agreed damages clause and not an exemption clause and the point had never been argued in the courts below at all. It is noteworthy that the House did not overrule a single decision of the Court of Appeal. Lord Wilberforce appears to have approved them (see [1966] 2 All

ER 61 at 92–93, [1967] 1 AC 361 at 433). At any rate, he cast no doubt on the actual decision in any case.

The change in climate

In 1969 there was a change in climate. Out of winter into spring. It came with the first report of the Law Commission on Exemption Clauses in Contracts (Law Com no 24) which was implemented in the Supply of Goods (Implied Terms) Act 1973. In 1975 there was a further change. Out of spring into summer. It came with their second report on Exemption Clauses (Law Com no 69) which was implemented by the Unfair Contract Terms Act 1977. No longer was the big concern able to impose whatever terms and conditions it liked in a printed form, no matter how unreasonable they might be. These reports showed most convincingly that the courts could and should only enforce them if they were fair and reasonable in themselves and it was fair and reasonable to allow the big concern to rely on them. So the idol of 'freedom of contract' was shattered. In cases of personal injury or death, it was not permissible to exclude or restrict liability at all. In consumer contracts any exemption clause was subject to the test of reasonableness.

These reports and statutes have influenced much the thinking of the judges. At any rate, they influenced me as you will see if you read *Gillespie Bros & Co Ltd v Roy Bowles Transport Ltd* [1973] 1 All ER 193 at 200, [1973] QB 400 at 416 and *Photo Production Ltd v Securicor Transport Ltd* [1978] 3 All ER 146 at 153, [1978] 1 WLR 856 at 865:

'Thus we reach, after long years, the principle which lies behind all our striving: the court will not allow a party to rely on an exemption or limitation clause in circumstances in which it would not be fair or reasonable to allow reliance on it; and, in considering whether it is fair and reasonable, the court will consider whether it was in a standard form, whether there was equality of bargaining power, the nature of the breach, and so forth.'

The effect of the changes

What is the result of all this? To my mind it heralds a revolution in our approach to exemption clauses; not only where they exclude liability altogether and also where they limit liability; not only in the specific categories in the Unfair Contract Terms Act 1977, but in other contracts too. Just as in other fields of law we have done away with the multitude of cases on 'common employment', 'last opportunity', 'invitees' and 'licensees' and so forth, so also in this field we should do away with the multitude of cases on exemption clauses. We should no longer have to go through all kinds of gymnastic contortions to get round them. We should no longer have to harass our students with the study of them. We should set about meeting a new challenge. It is presented by the test of reasonableness . . .

Applying the test of reasonableness then imposed by the Supply of Goods (Implied Terms) Act 1973, s 4, his Lordship concluded that it would not be fair or reasonable to allow the seed merchants to rely on the clause to limit their liability. Oliver and Kerr LLJ concurred in dismissing the appeal but held that the clause did not as a matter of construction limit the defendant's liability.

Appeal dismissed. [On further appeal the House of Lords dismissed the appeal on grounds which reflected the reasoning of Lord Denning (see [1983] 2 All ER 737 and below, p 365).]

NOTE

On the question of construction, see also the Unfair Terms in Consumer Contracts Regulations 1994, reg 6 (below, p 334).

THE INTRODUCTION OF STATUTORY CONTROL

As was noted in Lord Denning's judgment in *George Mitchell (Chesterhall) Ltd v Finney Lock Seeds Ltd* [1983] QB 284, [1983] 1 All ER 108, CA, above, statutory control over exemption clauses was introduced into English law following two reports by the Law Commission. The first (Law Com No 24) was concerned with the implied terms of ss 13–15 of the Sale of Goods Act and exemption clauses in relation to such terms. The following extracts from para 65 et seq of the report indicate the background to the introduction of statutory control over exemption clauses in consumer sales.

Exemption Clauses in Contracts First Report: Amendments to the Sale of Goods Act 1893 (Law Commission) (Law Com No 24) (1969)

65. During the past few decades the habit of ousting the implied terms by express contractual provisions has become a widely practised technique of the law of sale at all levels of commerce; it has received a steadily growing impetus from the ubiquitous appearance of standard contracts on the economic scene. By the time the Molony Committee published their Final Report, they were firmly of opinion that the main criticism that could be levelled at the law of sale of goods concerned

'the ease and frequency with which vendors and manufacturers of goods exclude the operation of the statutory conditions and warranties by provisions in guarantee cards or other contractual documents'.

. . .

67. The Molony Committee collected a great deal of evidence on the question whether the practice of contracting out was widespread in consumer sales. The results were stated in the following terms:

'The answer is that it [ie the practice of contracting out] is universal in the motor vehicle trade, and general in respect of electrical and mechanical appliances. In all these cases it is associated with guarantees or 'warranties' as the motor car manufacturers term them; and is inspired, no doubt, by the fact that the goods are complex and mass produced. These classes of goods are comparatively expensive. The practice also appears in many other types of business conducted by means of catalogues or requiring an order form to be completed by the purchaser. In these no guarantee is given in return. Our conclusion is that it would be unwise to regard the contracting out practice as the prerogative of particular trades or to assume that it may not spread beyond its present limits.'[1]

68. On the strength of the evidence which they had collected, the Molony Committee declared themselves compelled to view the practice of contracting out as a general threat to consumer interest, in the sense that 'heavy and irrecoverable loss may fall upon the consumer who is unlucky enough to get a defective article.'[2] . . .

After reviewing and rejecting a certain number of objections to a prohibition of 'contracting out' (into the merits of which we need not go apart from stating our broad agreement with the Molony Committee's reasoning)[3] they found an overriding argument in favour of prohibiting 'contracting out'. The mischief was that this practice enabled well-organised commerce 'consistently to impose unfair terms on the consumer and to deny him what the law means him to have.'[4] On the whole, the consumer did not even know how he was being treated; but where he was alive to the position, he found it difficult and sometimes impossible to avoid submitting to the terms of business universally adopted, because he had no bargaining power of sufficient weight. This being the essence of the case for intervention in support of the consuming public, the Molony Committee endorsed the soundness of the case and accepted the need to ban 'contracting out'. They took the view that in order to be effective the prohibition must extend to the efforts of any person to relieve the retailer of liability, whether made before, at or after the moment of sale. The sanction was to be a denial of legal effect to any provisions relieving the retailer of his statutory liabilities.

. . .

76. The proposal that in sales to private consumers any purported exclusion of statutory conditions and warranties should be made ineffective by statute has received substantial support; but the support was by no means unanimous. As was to be expected, all the consumer organisations were wholeheartedly in favour of an unqualified ban; broad support came also from various representative organisations of commerce, including the retail trade; and outright opposition was confined to The Law Society, a distinguished firm of auctioneers and an individual contributor. But in between these two extreme positions there were a fair number of critical comments and alternative proposals. The suggestions included the restriction of the ban to selected fields where there was positive evidence of abuse; the provisions of facilities for the validation of exemption clauses by some such body as the Restrictive Practices Court; the mitigation of the ban by the introduction of a reasonableness test; exceptional treatment for second-hand or imperfect goods; preservation of the seller's right to exclude any reliance on his skill and judgment; and various points of detail.

. . .

79. . . . [It] is clear to us that there is widespread public misunderstanding and uncertainty about the purchaser's legal rights against the retailer where the manufacturer's 'guarantee' is offered and accepted. It is our view that legislation, in addition to providing a remedy against effective and oppressive contracting out, can perform the important function of clarifying the legal position of the private consumer. Whatever rights a buyer may have against the manufacturer, and they may be valuable rights, it may be the local retailer rather than the distant (possibly overseas) manufacturer with whom the buyer can most conveniently discuss a complaint and perhaps come to terms, or, in the last resort, litigate his claim. In our view the rights of the private consumer against his seller under the statutory conditions and warranties should be expressly and clearly maintained and safeguarded by the law.

80. Accordingly we unanimously recommend that the statutory conditions and warranties implied by sections 13–15 of the Sale of Goods Act should apply to a sale to private consumers notwithstanding any term of the contract express or implied to the contrary . . .

[1] Final Report, paragraph 427.
[2] Final Report, paragraph 431.
[3] ibid, paragraphs 432–4.
[4] ibid, paragraph 435.

This recommendation was implemented in relation to contracts for the sale of goods and also to hire-purchase agreements and agreements for the redemption of trading stamps by the Supply of Goods (Implied Terms) Act 1973. Following the Law Commission's Second Report on Exemption Clauses (Law Com No 69, 1975) much more extensive controls were introduced by the Unfair Contract Terms Act 1977.

THE UNFAIR CONTRACT TERMS ACT 1977

This Act, the main provisions of which are printed below, gives effect, with modifications, to recommendations made by the Law Commissions in their Second Report on Exemption Clauses (Law Com No 69; Scot Law Com No 39, August 1975). Apart from s 8 which is concerned with the avoidance of liability for misrepresentations, and s 6(4) which is concerned with sale and hire purchase, the controls introduced or restated by Part I of the Act generally apply only to 'business liability' (see s 1(3) and s 14). The scheme of the Act is to render certain exemption clauses or notices void and certain others ineffective except insofar as they satisfy the requirement of reasonableness of s 11 of the Act.

The Unfair Contract Terms Act 1977 (as amended by the Sale of Goods Act 1979, the Supply of Goods and Services Act 1982 and the Occupiers' Liability Act 1984)

PART I AMENDMENT OF LAW FOR ENGLAND AND WALES
AND NORTHERN IRELAND

Introductory

1. Scope of Part I
(1) For the purposes of this Part of this Act, 'negligence' means the breach—
  (a) of any obligation, arising from the express or implied terms of a contract, to take reasonable care or exercise reasonable skill in the performance of the contract;
  (b) of any common law duty to take reasonable care or exercise reasonable skill (but not any stricter duty);
  (c) of the common duty of care imposed by the Occupiers' Liability Act 1957 or the Occupiers' Liability Act (Northern Ireland) 1957.
(2) This Part of this Act is subject to Part III; and in relation to contracts, the operation of sections 2 to 4 and 7 is subject to the exceptions made by Schedule 1.
(3) In the case of both contract and tort, sections 2 to 7 apply (except where the contrary is stated in section 6(4)) only to business liability, that is liability for breach of obligations or duties arising—
  (a) from things done or to be done by a person in the course of a business (whether his own business or another's); or
  (b) from the occupation of premises used for business purposes of the occupier;
and references to liability are to be read accordingly but liability of an occupier of premises for breach of an obligation or duty towards a person obtaining access to the premises for recreational or educational purposes, being liability for loss or damage suffered by reason of the dangerous state of the premises, is not a business liability of the occupier unless granting that person such access for the purposes concerned falls within the business purposes of the occupier.
(4) In relation to any breach of duty or obligation, it is immaterial for any purpose of this Part of this Act whether the breach was inadvertent or intentional, or whether liability for it arises directly or vicariously.

Avoidance of liability for negligence, breach of contract, etc

2. Negligence liability

(1) A person cannot by reference to any contract term or to a notice given to persons generally or to particular persons exclude or restrict his liability for death or personal injury resulting from negligence.

(2) In the case of other loss or damage, a person cannot so exclude or restrict his liability for negligence except in so far as the term or notice satisfies the requirement of reasonableness.

(3) Where a contract term or notice purports to exclude or restrict liability for negligence a person's agreement to or awareness of it is not of itself to be taken as indicating his voluntary acceptance of any risk.

3. Liability arising in contract

(1) This section applies as between contracting parties where one of them deals as consumer or on the other's written standard terms of business.

(2) As against that party, the other cannot by reference to any contract term—
  (a) when himself in breach of contract, exclude or restrict any liability of his in respect of the breach; or
  (b) claim to be entitled:
    (i) to render a contractual performance substantially different from that which was reasonably expected of him, or
    (ii) in respect of the whole or any part of his contractual obligation, to render no performance at all,

except in so far as (in any of the cases mentioned above in this subsection) the contract term satisfies the requirement of reasonableness.

4. Unreasonable indemnity clauses

(1) A person dealing as consumer cannot by reference to any contract term be made to indemnify another person (whether a party to the contract or not) in respect of liability that may be incurred by the other for negligence or breach of contract, except in so far as the contract term satisfies the requirement of reasonableness.

(2) This section applies whether the liability in question—
  (a) is directly that of the person to be indemnified or is incurred by him vicariously;
  (b) is to the person dealing as consumer or to someone else.

Liability arising from sale or supply of goods

5. 'Guarantee' of consumer goods

(1) In the case of goods of a type ordinarily supplied for private use or consumption, where loss or damage—
  (a) arises from the goods proving defective while in consumer use; and
  (b) results from the negligence of a person concerned in the manufacture or distribution of the goods,

liability for the loss or damage cannot be excluded or restricted by reference to any contract term or notice contained in or operating by reference to a guarantee of the goods.

(2) For these purposes—
  (a) goods are to be regarded as 'in consumer use' when a person is using them, or has them in his possession for use, otherwise than exclusively for the purposes of a business; and
  (b) anything in writing is a guarantee if it contains or purports to contain some promise or assurance (however worded or presented) that defects will be made good by complete or partial replacement, or by repair, monetary compensation or otherwise.

(3) This section does not apply as between the parties of a contract under or in pursuance of which possession or ownership of the goods passed.

6. Sale and hire-purchase

(1) Liability for breach of the obligations arising from—

    (a) [section 12 of the Sale of Goods Act 1979] (seller's implied undertakings as to title, etc);

    (b) section 8 of the Supply of Goods (Implied Terms) Act 1973 (the corresponding thing in relation to hire-purchase).

cannot be excluded or restricted by reference to any contract term.

(2) As against a person dealing as consumer, liability for breach of the obligations arising from—

    (a) [section 13, 14 or 15 of the 1979 Act] (seller's implied undertakings as to conformity of goods with description or sample, or as to their quality or fitness for a particular purpose);

    (b) section 9, 10 or 11 of the 1973 Act (the corresponding thing in relation to hire-purchase),

cannot be excluded or restricted by reference to any contract term.

(3) As against a person dealing otherwise than as consumer, the liability specified in subsection (2) above can be excluded or restricted by reference to a contract term, but only in so far as the term satisfies the requirements of reasonableness.

(4) The liabilities referred to in this section are not only the business liabilities defined by section 1(3), but include those arising under any contract of sale of goods or hire-purchase agreement.

7. Miscellaneous contracts under which goods pass

(1) Where the possession or ownership of goods passes under or in pursuance of a contract not governed by the law of sale of goods or hire-purchase, subsections (2) to (4) below apply as regards the effect (if any) to be given to contract terms excluding or restricting liability for breach of obligation arising by the implication of law from the nature of the contract.

(2) As against a person dealing as consumer, liability in respect of the goods' correspondence with description or sample, or their quality or fitness for any particular purpose, cannot be excluded or restricted by reference to any such term.

(3) As against a person dealing otherwise than as consumer, that liability can be excluded or restricted by reference to such a term, but only in so far as the term satisfies the requirement of reasonableness.

[(3A) Liability for breach of the obligations arising under section 2 of the Supply of Goods and Services Act 1982 (implied terms about title etc. in certain contracts for the transfer of the property in goods) cannot be excluded or restricted by reference to any such term.]

(4) Liability in respect of—

    (a) the right to transfer ownership of the goods, or give possession; or

    (b) the assurance of quiet possession to a person taking goods in pursuance of the contract,

cannot [in a case to which subsection (3A) does not apply] be excluded or restricted by reference to any such term except in so far as the term satisfies the requirement of reasonableness.

(5) This section does not apply in the case of goods passing on a redemption of trading stamps within the Trading Stamps Act 1964 or the Trading Stamps Act (Northern Ireland) 1965.

Other provisions about contracts

8. Misrepresentation

(1) In the Misrepresentation Act 1967, the following is substituted for section 3—

'3. Avoidance of provision excluding liability for misrepresentation

If a contract contains a term which would exclude or restrict—

    (a) any liability to which a party to a contract may be subject by reason of any misrepresentation made by him before the contract was made; or

    (b) any remedy available to another party to the contract by reason of such a misrepresentation,

that term shall be of no effect except in so far as it satisfies the requirement of reasonableness as stated in section 11(1) of the Unfair Contract Terms Act 1977; and it is for those claiming that the term satisfies the requirement to show that it does.'
(2) The same section is substituted for section 3 of the Misrepresentation Act (Northern Ireland) 1967.

9. Effect of breach
(1) Where for reliance upon it a contract term has to satisfy the requirement of reasonableness, it may be found to do so and be given effect accordingly notwithstanding that the contract has been terminated either by breach or by a party electing to treat it as repudiated.
(2) Where on a breach the contract is nevertheless affirmed by a party entitled to treat it as repudiated, this does not of itself exclude the requirement of reasonableness in relation to any contract term.

10. Evasion by means of secondary contract
A person is not bound by any contract term prejudicing or taking away rights of his which arise under, or in connection with the performance of, another contract, so far as those rights extend to the enforcement of another's liability which this Part of this Act prevents that other from excluding or restricting.

Explanatory provisions

11. The 'reasonableness' test
(1) In relation to a contract term the requirement of reasonableness for the purposes of this Part of this Act, section 3 of the Misrepresentation Act 1967 and section 3 of the Misrepresentation Act (Northern Ireland) 1967 is that the term shall have been a fair and reasonable one to be included having regard to the circumstances which were, or ought reasonably to have been, known to or in the contemplation of the parties when the contract was made.
(2) In determining for the purposes of section 6 or 7 above whether a contract term satisfies the requirement of reasonableness, regard shall be had in particular to the matters specified in Schedule 2 to this Act; but this subsection does not prevent the court or arbitrator from holding, in accordance with any rule of law, that a term which purports to exclude or restrict any relevant liability is not a term of the contract.
(3) In relation to a notice (not being a notice having contractual effect), the requirement of reasonableness under this Act is that it should be fair and reasonable to allow reliance on it, having regard to all the circumstances obtaining when the liability arose or (but for the notice) would have arisen.
(4) Where by reference to a contract term or notice a person seeks to restrict liability to a specified sum of money, and the question arises (under this or any other Act) whether the term or notice satisfies the requirement of reasonableness, regard shall be had in particular (but without prejudice to subsection (2) above in the case of contract terms) to—
   (a) the resources which he could expect to be available to him for the purpose of meeting the liability should it arise; and
   (b) how far it was open to him to cover himself by insurance.
(5) It is for those claiming that a contract term or notice satisfies the requirement of reasonableness to show that it does.

12. 'Dealing as consumer'
(1) A party to a contract 'deals as consumer' in relation to another party if—
   (a) he neither makes the contract in the course of a business nor holds himself out as doing so; and
   (b) the other party does make the contract in the course of a business; and

(c) in the case of a contract governed by the law of sale of goods or hire-purchase, or by section 7 of this Act, the goods passing under or in pursuance of the contract are of a type ordinarily supplied for private use or consumption.

(2) But on a sale by auction or by competitive tender the buyer is not in any circumstances to be regarded as dealing as consumer.

(3) Subject to this, it is for those claiming that a party does not deal as consumer to show that he does not.

13. Varieties of exemption clause

(1) To the extent that this Part of this Act prevents the exclusion or restriction of any liability it also prevents—

    (a) making the liability or its enforcement subject to restrictive or onerous conditions;

    (b) excluding or restricting any right or remedy in respect of the liability, or subjecting a person to any prejudice in consequence of his pursuing any such right or remedy;

    (c) excluding or restricting rules of evidence or procedure;

and (to that extent) sections 2 and 5 to 7 also prevent excluding or restricting liability by reference to terms and notices which exclude or restrict the relevant obligation or duty.

(2) But an agreement in writing to submit present or future differences to arbitration is not to be treated under this Part of this Act as excluding or restricting any liability.

14. Interpretation of Part I

In this Part of this Act—

'business' includes a profession and the activities of any government department or local or public authority;

'goods' has the same meaning as in the [Sale of Goods Act 1979];

'hire-purchase agreement' has the same meaning as in the Consumer Credit Act 1974;

'negligence' has the meaning given by section 1(1);

'notice' includes an announcement, whether or not in writing, and any other communication or pretended communication; and

'personal injury' includes any disease and any impairment of physical or mental condition.

[Part II which applies only to Scotland is omitted.]

PART III—PROVISIONS APPLYING TO WHOLE OF UNITED KINGDOM

Miscellaneous

26. International supply contracts

(1) The limits imposed by this Act on the extent to which a person may exclude or restrict liability by reference to a contract term do not apply to liability arising under such a contract as is described in subsection (3) below.

(2) The terms of such a contract are not subject to any requirement of reasonableness under section 3 or 4: and nothing in Part II of this Act shall require the incorporation of the terms of such a contract to be fair and reasonable for them to have effect.

(3) Subject to subsection (4), that description of contract is one whose characteristics are the following—

    (a) either it is a contract of sale of goods or it is one under or in pursuance of which the possession or ownership of goods passes; and

    (b) it is made by parties whose places of business (or, if they have none, habitual residences) are in the territories of different States (the Channel Islands and the Isle of Man being treated for this purpose as different States from the United Kingdom).

(4) A contract falls within subsection (3) above only if either—

    (a) the goods in question are, at the time of the conclusion of the contract, in the course of carriage, or will be carried, from the territory of one State to the territory of another; or

(b) the acts constituting the offer and acceptance have been done in the territories of different States; or
(c) the contract provides for the goods to be delivered to the territory of a State other than that within whose territory those acts were done.

27. Choice of law clauses

(1) Where the proper law of a contract is the law of any part of the United Kingdom only by choice of the parties (and apart from that choice would be the law of some country outside the United Kingdom) sections 2 to 7 and 16 to 21 of this Act do not operate as part of the proper law.

(2) This Act has effect notwithstanding any contract term which applies or purports to apply the law of some country outside the United Kingdom, where (either or both)—

(a) the term appears to the court, or arbitrator or arbiter to have been imposed wholly or mainly for the purpose of enabling the party imposing it to evade the operation of this Act; or
(b) in the making of the contract one of the parties dealt as consumer, and he was then habitually resident in the United Kingdom, and the essential steps necessary for the making of the contract were taken there, whether by him or by others on his behalf.

(3) [applies to Scotland].

28. Temporary provision for sea carriage of passengers

(1) This section applies to a contract for carriage by sea of a passenger or of a passenger and his luggage where the provisions of the Athens Convention (with or without modification) do not have, in relation to the contract, the force of law in the United Kingdom.

(2) In a case where—

(a) the contract is not made in the United Kingdom, and
(b) neither the place of departure nor the place of destination under it is in the United Kingdom,

a person is not precluded by this Act from excluding or restricting liability for loss or damage, being loss or damage for which the provisions of the Convention would, if they had the force of law in relation to the contract, impose liability on him.

(3) In any other case, a person is not precluded by this Act from excluding or restricting liability for that loss or damage—

(a) in so far as the exclusion or restriction would have been effective in that case had the provisions of the Convention had the force of law in relation to the contract; or
(b) in such circumstances and to such extent as may be prescribed, by reference to a prescribed term of the contract.

(4) For the purpose of subsection (3)(a), the values which shall be taken to be the official values in the United Kingdom of the amounts (expressed in gold francs) by reference to which liability under the provisions of the Convention is limited shall be such amounts in sterling as the Secretary of State may from time to time by order made by statutory instrument specify.

(5) In this section,—

(a) the references to excluding or restricting liability include doing any of those things in relation to the liability which are mentioned in section 13 or section 25(3) and (5); and
(b) 'the Athens Convention' means the Athens Convention relating to the Carriage of Passengers and their Luggage by Sea, 1974; and
(c) 'prescribed' means prescribed by the Secretary of State by regulations made by statutory instrument;

and a statutory instrument containing the regulations shall be subject to annulment in pursuance of a resolution of either House of Parliament.

29. Saving for other relevant legislation

(1) Nothing in this Act removes or restricts the effect of, or prevents reliance upon any contractual provision which—

(a) is authorised or required by the express terms or necessary implication of an enactment; or

(b) being made with a view to compliance with an international agreement to which the United Kingdom is a party, does not operate more restrictively than is contemplated by the agreement.

(2) A contract term is to be taken—

(a) for the purposes of Part I of this Act, as satisfying the requirement of reasonableness; and

(b) [applies to Scotland]

if it is incorporated or approved by, or incorporated pursuant to a decision or ruling of, a competent authority acting in the exercise of any statutory jurisdiction or function and is not a term in a contract to which the competent authority is itself a party.

(3) In this section—

'competent authority' means any court, arbitrator or arbiter, government department or public authority;

'enactment' means any legislation (including subordinate legislation) of the United Kingdom or Northern Ireland and any instrument having effect by virtue of such legislation; and

'statutory' means conferred by an enactment.

. . .

General

31. Commencement; amendments; repeals

(1) This Act comes into force on 1 February 1978.

(2) Nothing in this Act applies to contracts made before the date on which it comes into force; but subject to this, it applies to liability for any loss or damage which is suffered on or after that date.

(3) The enactments specified in Schedule 3 to this Act are amended as there shown.

(4) The enactments specified in Schedule 4 to this Act are repealed to the extent specified in column 3 of that Schedule.

32. Citation and extent

(1) This Act may be cited as the Unfair Contract Terms Act 1977.

(2) Part I of this Act extends to England and Wales and to Northern Ireland; but it does not extend to Scotland.

(3) [applies to Scotland].

(4) This Part of this Act extends to the whole of the United Kingdom.

SCHEDULE I SCOPE OF SECTIONS 2 TO 4 AND 7

Section 1(2)

1. Sections 2 to 4 of this Act do not extend to—

(a) any contract of insurance (including a contract to pay an annuity on human life);

. . .

2. Section 2(1) extends to—

(a) any contract of marine salvage or towage;

(b) any charterparty of a ship or hovercraft; and

(c) any contract for the carriage of goods by ship or hovercraft;

but subject to this sections 2 to 4 and 7 do not extend to any such contract except in favour of a person dealing as consumer.

3. Where goods are carried by ship or hovercraft in pursuance of a contract which either—
   (a) specifies that as the means of carriage over part of the journey to be covered, or
   (b) makes no provision as to the means of carriage and does not exclude that means,
then sections 2(2), 3 and 4 do not, except in favour of a person dealing as a consumer, extend to the contract as it operates for and in relation to the carriage of the goods by that means.
. . .

SCHEDULE 2—'GUIDELINES' FOR APPLICATION OF REASONABLENESS TEST

Sections 11(2) and 24(2)
The matters to which regard is to be had in particular for the purposes of sections 6(3), 7(3) and (4), 20 and 21 are any of the following which appear to be relevant—
   (a) the strength of the bargaining positions of the parties relative to each other, taking into account (among other things) alternative means by which the customer's requirements could have been met;
   (b) whether the customer received an inducement to agree to the term, or in accepting it had an opportunity of entering into a similar contract with other persons, but without having to accept a similar term;
   (c) whether the customer knew or ought reasonably to have known of the existence and extent of the term (having regard, among other things, to any custom of the trade and any previous course of dealing between the parties);
   (d) where the term excludes or restricts any relevant liability if some condition is not complied with, whether it was reasonable at the time of the contract to expect that compliance with that condition would be practicable;
   (e) whether the goods were manufactured, processed or adapted to the special order of the customer.
[Schedules 3 (Amendment of Enactments) and 4 (Repeals) are omitted.]

THE UNFAIR TERMS
IN CONSUMER CONTRACTS REGULATIONS 1994

Although the 1977 Act provided much needed statutory protection, it is relatively narrow in scope. Further controls have been introduced as a result of a European initiative which led to the Council Directive (No 93/13/EEC) on unfair terms in consumer contracts. The following regulations are expressed as implementing the Directive.

The Unfair Terms in Consumer Contracts Regulations 1994, SI 1994/3159

Citation and commencement

1. These Regulations may be cited as the Unfair Terms in Consumer Contracts Regulations 1994 and shall come into force on 1st July 1995.

Interpretation

2.—(1) In these Regulations—
   'business' includes a trade or profession and the activities of any government department or local or public authority;
   'the Community' means the European Economic Community and the other States in the European Economic Area;

'consumer' means a natural person who, in making a contract to which these Regulations apply, is acting for purposes which are outside his business;

'court' in relation to England and Wales and Northern Ireland means the High Court, and in relation to Scotland, the Court of Session;

'Director' means the Director General of Fair Trading;

'EEA Agreement' means the Agreement on the European Economic Area signed at Oporto on 2 May 1992 as adjusted by the protocol signed at Brussels on 17 March 1993;

'member State' shall mean a State which is a contracting party to the EEA Agreement but until the EEA Agreement comes into force in relation to Liechtenstein does not include the State of Liechtenstein;

'seller' means a person who sells goods and who, in making a contract to which these Regulations apply, is acting for purposes relating to his business; and

'supplier' means a person who supplies goods or services and who, in making a contract to which these Regulations apply, is acting for purposes relating to his business.

(2) In the application of these Regulations to Scotland for references to an 'injunction' or an 'interlocutory injunction' there shall be substituted references to an 'interdict' or 'interim interdict' respectively.

Terms to which these Regulations apply

3.—(1) Subject to the provisions of Schedule 1, these Regulations apply to any term in a contract concluded between a seller or supplier and a consumer where the said term has not been individually negotiated.

(2) In so far as it is in plain, intelligible language, no assessment shall be made of the fairness of any term which—

    (a) defines the main subject matter of the contract, or

    (b) concerns the adequacy of the price or remuneration, as against the goods or services sold or supplied.

(3) For the purposes of these Regulations, a term shall always be regarded as not having been individually negotiated where it has been drafted in advance and the consumer has not been able to influence the substance of the term.

(4) Notwithstanding that a specific term or certain aspects of it in a contract has been individually negotiated, these Regulations shall apply to the rest of a contract if an overall assessment of the contract indicates that it is a pre-formulated standard contract.

(5) It shall be for any seller or supplier who claims that a term was individually negotiated to show that it was.

Unfair terms

4.—(1) In these Regulations, subject to paragraphs (2) and (3) below, 'unfair term' means any term which contrary to the requirement of good faith causes a significant imbalance in the parties' rights and obligations under the contract to the detriment of the consumer.

(2) An assessment of the unfair nature of a term shall be made taking into account the nature of the goods or services for which the contract was concluded and referring, as at the time of the conclusion of the contract, to all circumstances attending the conclusion of the contract and to all the other terms of the contract or of another contract on which it is dependent.

(3) In determining whether a term satisfies the requirement of good faith, regard shall be had in particular to the matters specified in Schedule 2 to these Regulations.

(4) Schedule 3 to these Regulations contains an indicative and non-exhaustive list of the terms which may be regarded as unfair.

Consequence of inclusion of unfair terms in contracts

5.—(1) An unfair term in a contract concluded with a consumer by a seller or supplier shall not be binding on the consumer.

(2) The contract shall continue to bind the parties if it is capable of continuing in existence without the unfair term.

Construction of written contracts

6. A seller or supplier shall ensure that any written term of a contract is expressed in plain, intelligible language, and if there is doubt about the meaning of a written term, the interpretation most favourable to the consumer shall prevail.

Choice of law clauses

7. These Regulations shall apply notwithstanding any contract term which applies or purports to apply the law of a non member State, if the contract has a close connection with the territory of the member States.

Prevention of continued use of unfair terms

8.—(1) It shall be the duty of the Director to consider any complaint made to him that any contract term drawn up for general use is unfair, unless the complaint appears to the Director to be frivolous or vexatious.

(2) If having considered a complaint about any contract term pursuant to paragraph (1) above the Director considers that the contract term is unfair he may, if he considers it appropriate to do so, bring proceedings for an injunction (in which proceedings he may also apply for an interlocutory injunction) against any person appearing to him to be using or recommending use of such a term in contracts concluded with consumers.

(3) The Director may, if he considers it appropriate to do so, have regard to any undertakings given to him by or on behalf of any person as to the continued use of such a term in contracts concluded with consumers.

(4) The Director shall give reasons for his decision to apply or not to apply, as the case may be, for an injunction in relation to any complaint which these Regulations require him to consider.

(5) The court on an application by the Director may grant an injunction on such terms as it thinks fit.

(6) An injunction may relate not only to use of a particular contract term drawn up for general use but to any similar term, or a term having like effect, used or recommended for use by any party to the proceedings.

(7) The Director may arrange for the dissemination in such form and manner as he considers appropriate of such information and advice concerning the operation of these Regulations as may appear to him to be expedient to give to the public and to all persons likely to be affected by these Regulations.

SCHEDULE I, Regulation 3(1)

CONTRACTS AND PARTICULAR TERMS EXCLUDED FROM THE SCOPE OF THESE REGULATIONS

These Regulations do not apply to—
  (a) any contract relating to employment;
  (b) any contract relating to succession rights;

(c) any contract relating to rights under family law;

(d) any contract relating to the incorporation and organisation of companies or partnerships; and

(e) any term incorporated in order to comply with or which reflects—

   (i) statutory or regulatory provisions of the United Kingdom; or

   (ii) the provisions or principles of international conventions to which the member States or the Community are party.

SCHEDULE 2, Regulation 4(3)

ASSESSMENT OF GOOD FAITH

In making an assessment of good faith, regard shall be had in particular to—

(a) the strength of the bargaining positions of the parties;

(b) whether the consumer had an inducement to agree to the term;

(c) whether the goods or services were sold or supplied to the special order of the consumer, and

(d) the extent to which the seller or supplier has dealt fairly and equitably with the consumer.

SCHEDULE 3, Regulation 4(4)

INDICATIVE AND ILLUSTRATIVE LIST OF TERMS WHICH MAY BE
REGARDED AS UNFAIR

1. Terms which have the object or effect of—

(a) excluding or limiting the legal liability of a seller or supplier in the event of the death of a consumer or personal injury to the latter resulting from an act or omission of that seller or supplier;

(b) inappropriately excluding or limiting the legal rights of the consumer vis-à-vis the seller or supplier or another party in the event of total or partial non-performance or inadequate performance by the seller or supplier of any of the contractual obligations, including the option of offsetting a debt owed to the seller or supplier against any claim which the consumer may have against him;

(c) making an agreement binding on the consumer whereas provision of services by the seller or supplier is subject to a condition whose realisation depends on his own will alone;

(d) permitting the seller or supplier to retain sums paid by the consumer where the latter decides not to conclude or perform the contract, without providing for the consumer to receive compensation of an equivalent amount from the seller or supplier where the latter is the party cancelling the contract;

(e) requiring any consumer who fails to fulfil his obligation to pay a disproportionately high sum in compensation;

(f) authorising the seller or supplier to dissolve the contract on a discretionary basis where the same facility is not granted to the consumer, or permitting the seller or supplier to retain the sums paid for services not yet supplied by him where it is seller or supplier himself who dissolves the contract;

(g) enabling the seller or supplier to terminate a contract of indeterminate duration without reasonable notice except where there are serious grounds for doing so;

(h) automatically extending a contract of fixed duration where the consumer does not indicate otherwise, when the deadline fixed for the consumer to express this desire not to extend the contract is unreasonably early;

(i) irrevocably binding the consumer to terms with which he had no real opportunity of becoming acquainted before the conclusion of the contract;

(j) enabling the seller or supplier to alter the terms of the contract unilaterally without a valid reason which is specified in the contract;

(k) enabling the seller or supplier to alter unilaterally without a valid reason any characteristics of the product or service to be provided;

(l) providing for the price of goods to be determined at the time of delivery or allowing a
seller of goods or supplier of services to increase their price without in both cases giving
the consumer the corresponding right to cancel the contract if the final price is too high
in relation to the price agreed when the contract was concluded;

(m) giving the seller or supplier the right to determine whether the goods or services supplied are in conformity with the contract, or giving him the exclusive right to interpret
any term of the contract;

(n) limiting the seller's or supplier's obligation to respect commitments undertaken by his
agents or making his commitments subject to compliance with a particular formality;

(o) obliging the consumer to fulfil all his obligations where the seller or supplier does not
perform his;

(p) giving the seller or supplier the possibility of transferring his rights and obligations under
the contract, where this may serve to reduce the guarantees for the consumer, without
the latter's agreement;

(q) excluding or hindering the consumer's right to take legal action or exercise any other
legal remedy, particularly by requiring the consumer to take disputes exclusively to arbitration not covered by legal provisions, unduly restricting the evidence available to him
or imposing on him a burden of proof which, according to the applicable law, should lie
with another party to the contract.

2. Scope of subparagraphs 1(g), (j) and (l)

(a) Subparagraph 1(g) is without hindrance to terms by which a supplier of financial services
reserves the right to terminate unilaterally a contract of indeterminate duration without
notice where there is a valid reason, provided that the supplier is required to inform the
other contracting party or parties thereof immediately.

(b) Subparagraph 1(j) is without hindrance to terms under which a supplier of financial services reserves the right to alter the rate of interest payable by the consumer or due to the
latter, or the amount of other charges for financial services without notice where there is
a valid reason, provided that the supplier is required to inform the other contracting
party or parties thereof at the earliest opportunity and that the latter are free to dissolve
the contract immediately.

Subparagraph 1(j) is also without hindrance to terms under which a seller or supplier
reserves the right to alter unilaterally the conditions of a contract of indeterminate duration, provided that he is required to inform the consumer with reasonable notice and that
the consumer is free to dissolve the contract.

(c) Subparagraphs 1(g), (j) and (l) do not apply to:
— transactions in transferable securities, financial instruments and other products or
services where the market price is linked to fluctuations in a stock exchange quotation or index or a financial market rate that the seller or supplier does not control;
— contracts for the purchase or sale of foreign currency, traveller's cheques or international money orders denominated in foreign currency;

(d) Subparagraph 1(l) is without hindrance to price indexation clauses, where lawful, provided that the method by which prices vary is explicitly described.

GENERAL NOTE

The relationship between the 1977 Act and the 1994 Regulations is complex and
it may be thought regrettable that these two sources of control were not combined
(see Reynolds (1994) 110 LQR 1). The Department of Trade and Industry con-

sidered the matter but concluded that this was not possible: see 'Implementation of the EC Directive on Unfair Terms in Consumer Contracts (93/13/EEC)' (September, 1994). In the result, we now have two separate and overlapping régimes dealing with unfair terms in consumer contracts. In areas of potential overlap the consumer will seek to rely on the provision which gives the greatest protection. If a term is void and ineffective under the Act there is no point is arguing whether it is 'unfair' under the Regulations. Other terms which are subject only to the 'requirement of reasonableness' under the Act will also often need to be judged against the standard of fairness of the Regulations. The two standards are similar, but not necessarily identical. In other cases the term may be of a type which is not within the scope of the Act and yet is within the Regulations. Such a term may (but need not necessarily) be subject to a further alternative source of control—for example, if it is a penalty clause. There are further complications. Some types of contract are excluded from the scope of the Act (see s 26 and Sch 1) and some from that of the Regulations (see Sch 1), but the lists are not identical. The Regulations define the word 'consumer' (in reg 2(1)) and the Act states the circumstances in which a person 'deals as consumer' (in s 12), but the tests are not the same. The Regulations do not apply to terms which have been individually negotiated, but there is no equivalent overriding limitation in the Act.

The following general points may be noted.

2(i) Commencement date and scope. An initial difficulty concerns the commencement date. The Regulations came into force on July 1, 1995 whereas the corresponding Directive states (in art 10) that its provisions must be complied with no later than December 31, 1994 and 'shall be applicable to all contracts concluded after 31 December 1994'. In the case of contracts concluded between these two dates, the doctrine of 'direct effect' may provide relief for an individual affected, but only against a body which is an 'organ of the state': see, *Foster v British Gas plc* Case C–188/89 [1990] ECR I–3313, 3348–49. Further, it is arguable that a claim in tort for damages may lie against the United Kingdom government at the suit of a 'consumer' who has incurred loss as a result of the failure to transpose the Directive within the prescribed period: see *Francovich and Bonifaci v Italian Republic* Cases 6, 9/90 [1991] ECR I–5357; *Dillenkofer v Federal Republic of Germany* Case C–178/94, above, pp 14–17.

Subject to this, the Regulations apply to any term in a contract concluded between a 'seller' or 'supplier' and a 'consumer' (see reg 2(1)), 'where the said term has not been individually negotiated'. Regulation 3(3), (4) and (5) elaborates on the notion of individual negotiation.

(ii) Definition of subject matter and adequacy of consideration. Regulation 3(2) contains provisions governing both of these heads where the seller or supplier uses 'plain, intelligible language'. A further reference to such language is contained in reg 6, the second limb of which embodies the *contra preferentum* principle.

(iii) **The test and effect of unfairness**. The basic definition of an 'unfair term' in reg 4(1) contains several elements, namely that 'contrary to the requirement of good faith' the term must cause a significant imbalance in the rights and obligations under the contract and do so to the detriment of the consumer. These matters are elaborated in reg 4(2), (3) and (4), and Schedule 3 contains an indicative (and non-exhaustive) list (the 'grey list') of terms which may be regarded as unfair. The effect of including an unfair term in a contract is as stated in reg 5 and is essentially similar to the position under the Unfair Contract Terms Act 1977.

The main types of clause which are potentially subject to control under the Regulations are discussed in Bulletins issued by the Office of Fair Trading: see 'Unfair Contract Terms' (Issue No 1, May 1996, Issue No 2, September 1996, Issue No 3, March 1997 and Issue No 4, December 1997). Further reference is made to these Bulletins later in this chapter. Undoubtedly, the aspect of the Regulations and Directive which is least familiar in the United Kingdom is the notion of 'good faith'. Professor Beale has discussed this in the following terms.

Beale in Beatson and Friedmann (eds) *Good Faith and Fault in Contract Law* (1995), ch 9

Legislative Control of Fairness: The Directive on Unfair Terms in Consumer Contracts

. . .

The test of unfairness

When we turn to the test of when a term in a consumer contract is to be treated as unfair we come to one of the conceptual problems. The test laid down in the Directive is not immediately applicable to the problems which I identified earlier. It is to be regarded as unfair

. . . if, contrary to the requirement of good faith, it causes a significant imbalance in the parties' rights and obligations arising under the contract, to the detriment of the consumer.[70]

The word 'imbalance' has connotations of exploitation of the old-fashioned kind. If the arguments used earlier are correct, this would open to the seller or supplier the defence that the harsh clause resulted in a cheaper deal for the consumer, with the result that there was no overall imbalance. It was on just this ground that the French legislature rejected this test when considering what was to become the *Loi Scrivener* of 1978.[71] In addition, it seems, the Directive restricts relief to cases where there has not been good faith. To English lawyers this may have connotations of conscious misleading, or at least a reckless attitude as to whether the other party has been misled by the standard form. It does not seem to apply readily to a case where the consumer has simply not read the standard form, although the form is not misleading, still less to cases where the supplier simply indicates that it is not willing to alter the form in the consumer's favour.

In this respect, earlier drafts of the Directive again seemed more satisfactory: in the 1990 version,[72] for instance, significant imbalance and incompatibility with good faith were alternatives, rather than cumulative. There were also two other grounds for unfairness: that the term caused performance of the contract to be unduly detrimental to the consumer, or that it caused the performance to be significantly different to what the consumer could legitimately expect. The Economic and Social Committee wanted to add a further criterion, the 'non-transparency of a contract term'.[73] The House of Lords Select Committee on the European Communities favoured adding the test of reasonableness, although noting that this term has a different meaning in civil law jurisdictions.[74] In contrast, in the first debate of the proposal in the European Parliament, a Spanish member protested against all the grounds except good faith as being too much the British solution; only good faith was in accord with the civil law tradition. His argument was turned down so sharply by the Commission representative that it is a little surprising to see that this voice of reaction appears to have come close to winning the day.

However, it seems probable that concerns over the tests of imbalance and absence of good faith appropriate may be premised on interpretations of those phrases which are too narrow. First, we should think of imbalance not just in a narrow 'deviation from market price' sense, but in terms of balancing overall interests. Thus there may be imbalance if, by using a term, the supplier reduces the price slightly, and thereby gains a few extra sales, but at the price of placing a very large potential loss on the small number of consumers for whom the risk will materialize.[75] It has been noted that the test adopted by the Directive is close in its wording to the German Act on Standard Contract terms of 1976.[76] The so-called 'General Clause' of that Act refers to 'undue advantage to such an extent as to be incompatible with good faith'.[77] It seems that this has been interpreted as requiring the courts to look at the overall balance of advantage in the general run of cases.[78] Witz notes that the courts have frequently rejected the argument that a harsh clause is acceptable because it leads to a lower price being charged to the consumer.[79]

Secondly, it is clear that in several civilian systems 'good faith' has been developed very much beyond what we might immediately think of. As Bingham LJ said in the *Interfoto* case.

In many civil law systems . . . [t]his does not simply mean that they should not deceive each other, a principle which any legal system must recognize; its effect is perhaps most aptly conveyed by such metaphorical colloquialisms as 'playing fair', 'coming clean' or 'putting one's cards face upwards on the table.' It is in essence a principle of fair and open dealing.[80]

French law has used the concept of good faith in performance to avoid onerous conditions.[81] Other legal systems seem to have gone beyond the kind of disclosure requirement that Bingham LJ's words suggest. The Dutch Hoge Raad, admittedly in a case of mistake, laid down as early as 1957 a very broad requirement: the parties must let their conduct be guided by the legitimate interests of the other party.[82] This kind of approach can clearly be used to hold either a failure to draw the other's attention to a harsh clause or a refusal to negotiate to be not consistent with good faith. (The new Netherlands Civil Code, Article 6.233, uses the test of whether the contract is unreasonably onerous.) Germany also uses the good faith test extensively, both under the Law of Standard Contracts and under BGB § 242. The test does not seem to be purely a procedural one. Although the 'transparency' of the clause is a very important factor,[83] commentators have noted that the German courts tend to judge the clause by whether there was any real choice open to the customer[84] and have discussed the balance of interests in general terms, rather than in relation to the particular position of the individual consumer.[85] It seems that conceptual tools have been rewrought to meet new tasks, just as the notion of unconscionability in Anglo-American law was re-worked in *Williams v Walker-Thomas Furniture Co*[86] to mean terms which are unreasonably favourable to one party and an absence of meaningful choice for the other.

Certainly the Preamble to the Directive suggests a broad interpretation of the imbalance and good faith tests.[87] The sixteenth paragraph refers specifically to the strength of the bargaining position of the parties, whether the consumer had an inducement to agree to the term and whether the goods or services were sold or supplied to the special order of the consumer— words apparently taken directly from the guidelines on reasonableness in UCTA Schedule 2— and whether the party has taken the other's legitimate interests into account. Dean notes that when the Common Position was agreed, it was made clear that reasonableness should form part of the test of unfairness.[88] The Consultation Paper suggested that the tests of unfairness and reasonableness are likely to produce similar results in most cases, but that there is no guarantee that this will always be the case.[89]

I suspect that good faith has a double operation. First, it has a procedural aspect. It will require the supplier to consider the consumer's interests.[90] However, a clause which might be unfair if it came as a surprise may be upheld if the business took steps to bring it to the consumer's attention and to explain it. Secondly, it has a substantive content: some clauses may cause such an imbalance that they should always be treated as being contrary to good faith and therefore unfair.[91] A clause excluding liability for death or personal injury caused by negligence might be an example.

Probably, as Professor Diamond said in his evidence to the House of Lords Select Committee, imprecision is inevitable.[92] In effect a great deal of discretion is left to the court or other decision maker.[93]

Advantages of a grey list

This element of discretion gives cause for concern simply because of the uncertainty involved for business. In the United Kingdom we have blacklisted clauses only after very careful consideration, but in some ways it may be easier for business to know that a particular clause is always invalid than to know that it may or may not be invalid according to the circumstances and, dare one say it, the whim of the decision maker.[94] If the clause is absolutely banned the business knows what risks it must bear or insure against, even if they are hard to quantify; whereas with a general 'fairness' or 'reasonableness' test there will always be the fear that the clause may be struck down while a competitor's clause, perhaps worded in a slightly different way or presented to the consumer in a slightly different manner, may be upheld.

Even a grey list may go some way towards reducing uncertainty, and it is good that the Regulations incorporate one. Grey lists should be as full as possible. When any type of term is subject to review under the new unfairness test, a grey list may be much more useful as guidance to business than a set of guidelines like UCTA, Schedule 2. Section 68A of the Australian Trade Practices Act[95] is interesting: a clause limiting the liability of a supplier of goods to a non-consumer may limit the supplier's liability to replacement of the goods, repair of the goods, or payment of the cost of replacement or of repair unless reliance on the clause is shown not to be fair and reasonable. The substance of this provision, with the burden of proof on the buyer, may be thought too weak even to protect non-consumers, but the style of the section does seem to give fuller guidance than the equivalent sections of UCTA. Could a similar approach be used in grey lists?

Schedule 3 of the Regulations incorporates just the grey list in the Annex to the Directive. I would like to have seen a much fuller list. I would also be happier if the grey-listed terms were presumptively invalid, whereas the Regulations leave the burden of proving unfairness on the consumer.[96]

[70] Article 3(1); r 4. The term is to be judged by the circumstances at the time the contract was concluded, Article 4(1). Section 11(1) of UCTA is the same on this point.

[71] J Ghestin, *Le contrat: formation* (2nd edn, 1988), para 602.

[72] COM(90) 322 fin—SYN 285 (OJ C 243, 28.9.1990, p 2).

[73] Opinion on the proposal for a Council Directive on unfair terms in consumer contracts (91/C159/13) (OJ C 159, 17.6.1991, p 34), para 2.5.3.

[74] House of Lords, 6th Report (1991–92) HL 28, para 74.

[75] It may be interpreted as requiring that the consumer have certain rights irrespective of the price: H Collins, 'Good Faith in European Contract Law' (1994) 14 Ox JLS 229.

[76] eg K G Weil and F Puis, 'Le droit allemand des conditions générales d'affaires revu et corrigé par la directive communautaire relative aux clauses abusives' (1994) Rev int droit comparé 125. It should be noted that the German Act contains separate provisions on surprising clauses (§ 2) and prohibiting certain clauses altogether (§ 11) but the absence of

parallels from the Directive does not necessarily mean that Art 3 of the Directive must be interpreted more narrowly.

[77] Standard Contracts Law (AGB-Gesetz) of 1976, § 9.1.

[78] Witz, *Droit Privé Allemand* (1992), § 457.

[79] Ibid, § 459.

[80] *Interfoto Picture Library Ltd v Stilletto Visual Programmes Ltd* [1989] QB 433, at 439.

[81] N S Wilson, 'Freedom of Contract and Adhesion Contracts' (1965) 14 ICLQ 172; and see J Ghestin, *Le Contrat: Formation* (2nd edn, 1988), para 608–2.

[82] HR 15-11-1957. See M E Storme, *La bonne foi dans la formation des contracts en droit neerlandais*, Report to the Capitant Association (1992).

[83] See Reich, 'Le Principe de la transparence des clauses limitatives relatives au contenu des prestations dans le droit allemand des conditions générales des contrats' in J Ghestin (ed), *Les clauses limitatives ou exonératoires de responsabilité en Europe* (1990), 77–93.

[84] H W Micklitz, 'La loi allemande relative au régime juridique des conditions générales des contrats du 9 decembre 1976' (1989) 41 Rev int droit comparé 101, 109; J P Dawson, 'Unconscionable Coercion: The German Version' (1976) 89 Harvard L Rev 1041, 1114. Dawson states that before the Standard Contracts Law the courts were concerned with preventing unfair surprise but also with preventing one-sided contracts and ensuring 'elementary contractual justice' (pp 1110 et seq). See also Schmidt-Salzer, 'Droit allemand' in J Ghestin (ed), *Les clauses limitatives ou exoneratoires de responsabilité en Europe* (1990), at p 57: 'en matière de conditions générales ce qui est inattendu est aussi déraisonable: ce qui n'est pas raisonable, est légalement inattendu'.

[85] Witz, *Droit Privé Allemand* (1992) § 457.

[86] 121 US App DC 315, 350 F 2d 445 (1965).

[87] On use of the preambles to interpret directives see Case C–106/89 *Marleasing SA v La Comercial Internacional de Alimentación SA* [1990] ECR I–4135, [1992] 1 CMLR 305 and P Duffy, 'Unfair contract terms and the draft EC directive' [1993] JBL 67.

[88] M Dean, 'Unfair Contract Terms: The European Approach' (1993) 56 MLR 581, 585, referring to the Consumer Council of 29 June 1992.

[89] *A Further Consultation Document* (. . .), Comment on Art 3(1).

[90] Thus the requirement of good faith does more than exclude certain types of unacceptable conduct: cf R Brownsword, 'Two Concepts of Good Faith' (forthcoming, JCL). I have benefited greatly from extensive discussion of good faith with Professor Brownsword. The views expressed here are not necessarily his.

[91] Article 3 does not require that the significant imbalance be caused by the absence of good faith. See also H Collins, 'Good Faith in European Contract Law' (1994) 14 Ox JLS 229, 250. On this point I have to disagree with the provisional views of Brownsword, Howells and Wilhelmsson, 'Between Market and Welfare: Some Reflections on Article 3 of the EC Directive on Unfair Terms in Consumer Contracts' (forthcoming), although their paper is a very interesting discussion of the various interpretations of the good faith requirement. I am very grateful to my colleague Chris Willett for useful discussions on Art 3 and for letting me see his forthcoming paper 'The Directive on Unfair Terms in Consumer Contracts'.

[92] See House of Lords, 6th Report (1991–92) HL 28, para 74.

[93] J Ghestin and Marchessaux, 'Les téchniques d'élimination des clauses abusives en Europe', in J Ghestin (ed), *Les clauses abusives dans les contrats-types en France et en Europe* (1991), p 57.

[94] Kessler thought that one of the reasons for standard contract forms was to guard against judicial irrationality: F Kessler, 'Contracts of Adhesion—Some Thoughts About Freedom of Contract' (1993) 43 Colum L Rev 629, 631–2.

[95] Inserted by Trade Practices Amendment Act (No 2) 1977.

[96] *A Further Consultation Document* (. . .), comment to Art 3(3).

For further discussion of the problems of defining 'unfairness', see Beale, 'Inequality of Bargaining Power' (1986) 6 OJLS 123; 'Unfair Contract Terms in Britain and Europe' [1989] CLP 197; Smith, 'In Defence of Substantive Fairness' (1996) 112 LQR 138; Willett (ed), *Aspects of Fairness in Contract* (1996); Harrison, *Good Faith in Sales* (1997), ch 19 especially.

THE SCOPE OF PROTECTION

The scope of protection may be conveniently considered under a number of headings, both in terms of the 1977 Act and the 1994 Regulations.

NEGLIGENCE LIABILITY

Section 2 of the 1977 Act is based on the recommendations in Part III of the Law Commission's Second Report on Exemption Clauses. The outright 'ban' in s 2(1) of the Act on terms or notices which purport to exclude or restrict liability for death or personal injury resulting from negligence goes beyond the Law Commission's recommendations. The Commission favoured a more selective and sectoral approach which would have covered for example the liability of carriers, car park occupiers and those who operate such mechanical devices as 'Big Dippers' or lifts. The categories might be extended by statutory instrument following a recommendation by the Director General of Fair Trading (see paras 95–7 of the report).

Schedule 3, para 1(a), to the Regulations also makes provision for cases of death and personal injury, but this does not appear to add to the scope of the protection accorded by s 2(1).

So far as other types of loss or damage are concerned, the 'requirement of reasonableness' imposed by s 2(2) of the Act covers a wide range of everyday consumer transactions. Examples include the carriage, warehousing and storage of goods, laundering, dry cleaning, film processing and damage to vehicles and other property in car parks and car washes. In such cases a consumer will be protected normally by s 3 of the Act also. This covers attempts to exclude liability by reference to contract terms (although not notices). Nothing will turn on which section the case is argued under.

The Regulations may also be relevant in such cases (see Sch 3, para 1(b), in particular) and there is considerable overlap between the matters taken into account when applying the test of reasonableness and when assessing good faith (see, respectively s 11 of the Act and reg 4 of and Sch 2 to the Regulations). Note also the guidelines of Sch 2 to the Act which do not, strictly speaking, apply directly to the examples given above.

The following case is of general interest as indicating a broadly favourable approach to a consumer plaintiff in one such everyday transaction.

Woodman v Photo Trade Processing Ltd (1981) (unreported), Judgment of 7 May, Exeter County Court

His Honour Judge Clarke. In this arbitration pursuant to Order 19 of the County Court Rules, Photo Trade Processing Ltd ('PTP') now seek to set aside the award of Mr Registrar Lewis dated 26 June 1980. They also ask for a new trial.

By that award the Learned Registrar had upheld the claim of the Plaintiff, Mr Woodman, in which he alleged that PTP had lost certain photographic films which in June 1979 he had entrusted to a shop in Exeter named Dixons for developing and printing. Dixons at all times were agents for PTP. The loss of Mr Woodman's films was undisputed, but by way of Defence PTP sought to rely upon a clause in their contract with the Plaintiff limiting their liability to the replacement of the lost films with new ones.

In the course of the arbitration the Plaintiff submitted that the alleged clause was of no effect because it did not satisfy the requirement of reasonableness laid down by the Unfair Contract Terms Act 1977 ('The Act'). In upholding that submission the Learned Registrar in his judgment specifically considered and applied the various tests of 'reasonableness' set out in Section 11 and Schedule 2 of the Act, those matters having been drawn to his attention in the course of argument. Before me, however, Mr Meeke for PTP submitted that the terms of Sections 6 & 7 of the Act make Schedule 2 inapplicable to the type of contract in issue in this case. Hence, he argued, there was an error of law on the face of the arbitration award, thereby opening the discretion to set aside the award (*Meyer v Leanse* [1958] 3 All ER 213). Mr Tench appearing for Mr Woodman (or, to be more accurate, for his personal representatives in view of Mr Woodman's death since the arbitration) agreed with that proposition.

I accept that Schedule 2 does not apply. The only relevant provision is Section 11; Subsection (1) of which requires that the clause should be 'a fair and reasonable one to be included having regard to the circumstances which were, or ought reasonably to have been, known to or in the contemplation of the parties when the contract was made.' There is a specific consideration to which I will refer later in Section 11(4), but otherwise the question of what is 'fair and reasonable' is at large and undefined in the Act.

In considering that wide question of what is 'fair and reasonable' the 'guidelines' set out in Schedule 2 for other types of contract would be among the matters necessarily needing consideration in this case. But Mr Meeke submitted, and Mr Tench accepted that the Learned Registrar, by treating Section 11(1) and 11(4) and Schedule 2 of the Act as if they were exhaustive of the matters to be considered, might have construed the question of reasonableness too narrowly. Accordingly I exercised my discretion to set aside the award and proceeded to a re-hearing. It is right to say, however, now that I have heard full argument, that I do not think that the Registrar did omit any relevant consideration.

For the purpose of the re-hearing both parties agreed to accept the facts as set out in the Learned Registrar's award without calling any further evidence. I will not repeat those facts except to the extent that I find it necessary to refer to them for the purpose of my decision.

The missing items are alleged to be 23 out of a reel of 36 exposures on 35 mm film which Mr Woodman had, by arrangement, taken of a friend's wedding, intending to give them to those friends as a wedding present. He did not, however, reveal the subject matter of the photographs when he handed them in to Dixons, nor did he give any special instructions. All he got back were 13 of the negatives with prints therefrom. This suggests that the 23 negatives somehow became separated and lost during the processing rather than in Dixons shop, but in any event it would (unless explained) constitute a breach of the inevitable implied term that PTP would exercise reasonable care. By Section 1(1) of the Act such a breach is classified as 'negligence.' No explanation was offered as to how these films could have become lost without fault.

The clause relied upon by PTP, and held by the Learned Registrar to have become incorporated in the contract between the parties, was printed on a card measuring 4½ inches square, exhibited on the front of the Dixons shop counter. This card was not produced in evidence, but

in view of the number of words which the Registrar held to have been printed upon it, I conclude that the lettering must have been fairly small. I regard myself as bound by the Registrar's
finding of fact that the notice was 'adequately displayed' to Mr Woodman; but having regard
to the quantity of advertising material usually displayed in photographers' shops I am not surprised that Mr Woodman says he did not see it. I would not wish this judgment to be regarded
as any indication that a card of this size would constitute adequate notice except in exceptional
circumstances.

The important part of the notice read as follows:—

'All photographic materials are accepted on the basis that their value does not exceed the cost
of the material itself. Responsibility is limited to the replacement of films. No liability will be
accepted, consequential or otherwise, however caused.'

I accept that such a clause, if upheld under the Unfair Contract Terms Act, would be sufficient
to exclude liability for any loss including loss by negligence on the part of PTP. It is therefore
a 'contract term or notice' within the meaning of Section 2(2) of the Act which raises the
requirement of reasonableness.

Evidence was given before the Registrar that similar exclusion clauses were 'standard practice throughout the trade.' In their Defence PTP plead that it is 'the custom among photographic processors.' In the course of argument Mr Meeke submitted that firms did exist who
would, at a cost, carry out film processing and accept liability for their work, but there was no
evidence before the Registrar of any such alternative. Specialist firms may exist, but I am bound
to conclude on the evidence that Mr Woodman had no realistic alternative.

Any analysis of the clause in question in this case shows that it preserves liability for what
may be called the 'tangible loss', namely the value of the film itself, but it excludes liability for
the intangible value of the picture itself. That intangible value would vary enormously. A few,
such as an owner's photograph of his house or garden, could be re-photographed without difficulty. Most would be in the nature of holiday photographs the loss of which would cause at
least disappointment. In some cases, such as the wedding photographs in the present case where
no other photographer attended, real distress would be caused by their loss. A few photographs,
such as a picture of a loved-one shortly before death, would be almost priceless to grief stricken
relatives. In the circumstances of the present case I conclude that virtually all the photographs
handed in at Dixons would be of a personal nature rather than for any commercial or industrial
use, so the consequences of loss are emotional rather than economic.

The consequences of loss to Mr Woodman consisted of his disappointment in having failed
his friend's expectations, rather than the disappointment of being unable to see the photographs
themselves, but such consequences are all of the same nature. They are all losses of expected
enjoyment. On the evidence I conclude that it was foreseeable to PTP that Mr Woodman would
suffer some loss of enjoyment if they lost his films.

. . .

I now turn to consider the 'requirement of reasonableness' in relation to the clause in question.
I was asked, particularly by Mr Meeke and to some extent by Mr Tench, if I found this particular clause to be unreasonable, to go further and suggest what type of clause would
be reasonable. To some extent I must consider the reasonableness of alternatives in order to throw
light upon the reasonableness of the clause in question. But I must stress that it is no part of my
function to lay down what type of clause PTP should use. That must be for them to decide.

PTP argue that the clause they use is reasonable, and for the benefit of the public and themselves, because it enables them to operate a cheap mass-production technique. No evidence was
adduced as to the extent of their cost savings as a result of the absence of claims and the absence
of checking mechanisms to prevent loss, but I suspect that it amounts to more than the 'few
pence' on every film suggested by Mr Tench. In these cost-conscious days I accept that a cheap

mass-production service is desirable, and it is probably good enough for the vast majority of ordinary photographers who could well complain if they have to pay more in order to protect the interests of a minority whose pictures are of greater value.

The Act, however, does not require me to consider only what is reasonable for the majority of the public. I have to consider whether the term in this particular contract is fair and reasonable 'having regard to the circumstances which were, or ought reasonably to have been, known to or in the contemplation of the parties when the contract was made.' Dixons did not know what I would call the 'picture value' of Mr Woodman's photographs, but I conclude that it ought reasonably have been within their contemplation that:—

(1) His photographs might have a high 'picture value', and
(2) He might be entrusting the film to them because he had no alternative.

I was told that there are, as yet, no reported authorities on the Unfair Contract Terms Act itself; but I was referred to three cases which provide some guidance.

Firstly there is *Peek v North Staffordshire Rly Co* (1863) 10 HL Cas 493, a decision on Section 7 of Railway and Canal Traffic Act 1854 which permitted transport undertakings to impose conditions limiting their liability if adjudged by a Court to be just and reasonable. The clause under scrutiny in that case excluded all liability for loss or injury to various categories of fragile goods 'unless declared and insured according to their value.' It is a clause less onerous to the customer than that in the present case to the extent that PTP excluded liability without any option of declaring and insuring a special risk. And yet the House of Lords found the North Staffordshire Railway clause to be unreasonable.

Three main reasons emerge for the decision in *Peek*'s case:—

1 because it excluded liability for the consequences of negligence as well as mere accident,
2 because the railway was in a monopoly situation which realistically forced the customer to agree to their terms of business, and
3 because the only alternatives offered to the customer were either total exclusion of liability or insurance at a fixed rate which the Court regarded as so exorbitant as to compel customers to accept exclusion of liability.

Peek's case is complicated by the obligation laid upon common carriers to carry for reasonable remuneration; but it has strong bearing upon the present case because PTP, by adopting the same terms as the rest of the trade, also offers its customers no choice.

The present case is also similar because of the exclusion of liability for negligence as well as accident, but I do not regard this feature with the same degree of horror as did the House of Lords in *Peek*'s case. The mischief is the same in that the trader is enabled to drop his standards with impunity, but the pressure of public opinion upon traders to maintain standards are stronger than they were in 1863. Furthermore it must be less objectionable to exclude liability for negligence where the items are comparatively small in value. A common carrier may handle cargoes of immensely greater value than any photograph.

The exclusion clause in the present case is marginally more reasonable than that in *Peek*'s case because it at least preserves liability for the 'tangible value' of the films. But it is less reasonable in that it offers no insurance facility whatever. Insurance is a matter that I am specifically required to consider by Section 11(4) of the Act. No doubt PTP could insure, but in the circumstances of this particular trade where no claims are likely to be really heavy, it would be more reasonable to satisfy claims out of their resources boosted by increased charges to their customers.

If there is to be insurance, it would have to be remembered that only the customer knows the 'intangible value' of his films. A system could be devised whereby a customer discloses the insurance value of his films when he hands them in for processing, but I do not regard insurance as a requirement of reasonableness in the film processing trade. The customer cannot buy a replacement photograph with his insurance moneys. What he really wants in some assurance that the processor will take extra care not to lose his more precious pictures.

Next I was referred to *Levison v Patent Steam Carpet Cleaning Co Ltd* [1977] 3 All ER 498, where Lord Denning, MR, anticipating the introduction of the Unfair Contract Terms Act, held that a limitation of liability clause was unreasonable because the cleaning company had not specifically drawn it to the attention of the customer and advised him to insure. Comparing that with the present case, Mr Woodman's attention was not specifically drawn to the exclusion clause, nor was he advised to procure his own insurance (not that insurance would be readily available to him in such circumstances).

Thirdly I was referred to *A Schroeder Music Publishing Co Ltd v Macaulay* [1974] 1 WLR 1308 where Lord Diplock, dealing with a contract alleged to be an unreasonable restraint of trade, posed as a test of fairness the question of 'whether the restrictions are both reasonably necessary for the protection of the legitimate interests of the promisee and commensurate with the benefits secured to the promisor under the contract.'

Applying that test to the present case, I think that PTP do have a legitimate interest in keeping their costs down in order to remain competitive in the trade. But it cannot be regarded as reasonably necessary to protect that interest by compelling everybody, including the few who have high value photographs, to take their chance with the PTP mass-production system. For the majority of customers the lower prices resulting from excluded liability may be a commensurate benefit, but even then the balance is uncertain because he does not know the extent of the risk he runs to get those lower prices.

No evidence was offered as to the frequency with which films are lost during the PTP process. However, on this particular contract with Mr Woodman the balance must be to his disadvantage because of the importance of his particular photographs.

I conclude therefore that the clause in question is unreasonable having regard to almost all the criteria mentioned in the three authorities I have referred to. I have also considered the criteria set out in Schedule 2 of the Act, but in the circumstances of this case they seem to add nothing new, except that only to the extent that account should be taken of 'alternative means by which the customers' requirements could have been met.' It is the feasibility of those alternatives which I must now consider.

Mr Tench suggested three possible alternatives, one of which was that PTP should accept all liability for negligence but exclude it for 'mishap.' This would certainly be reasonable from the customer's point of view, provided that the burden of proving 'mishap' falls upon PTP once the customer has proved the loss of films entrusted to them. But there would be few such 'mishaps' and in practice it would be virtually equivalent to the acceptance of full liability. As such I think it leans unreasonably against PTP.

A further suggestion by Mr Tench was that there should be some standardised level of compensation for the loss of 'picture-value' in every case. For example, 10 times the film cost or processing cost. I was referred to the 'Code of Practice for the Photographic Industry,' and paragraph 47 of that code states 'The Consumer may be informed of the reasonable compensation offered in the event of a film being lost or damaged by the processor or retailer.' This appears to envisage some sort of pre-arranged formula for compensation (another example of which is paragraph 76 which suggests a 'refund' as appropriate where developing and printing work is considered unsatisfactory because of an irreparable defect). However, I do not think that such a system, by itself, can be fair and reasonable in this trade because of the degree of uniformity in film costs and processing charges. In some industries servicing charges vary widely according to the delicacy or amount of work needing to be done, and in those instances compensation calculated as a multiple of servicing charges would achieve a sort of rough justice. But photographic film is reasonably uniform in price, and the developing and printing process is more or less uniform in cost. Compensation as a multiple of either figure would therefore also fall within a narrow range, and what is fair to the bulk of customers would be less than fair to a minority.

The Code of Practice appears to recognise this difficulty in that paragraph 49 adds a further recommendation for the benefit of that minority. This paragraph reads:—

'The Retailer will advise the laboratory if an order being placed for processing is of exceptional value or importance, before the order is accepted, provided he has been informed by the consumer. There may be a special service combined with a higher price.'

The authors of the Code therefore do envisage the need for additional care in some cases, and it is that element that is totally lacking in the PTP terms of business. The so-called 'Special Service' was Mr Tench's third suggestion. He called it a 'two-tier System' of a normal service with total exclusion of liability and a special service at a higher charge with full acceptance of liability.

Even if such a special service were to provide for a standardised level of compensation at an appropriately high level to suit the needs of the minority, such a system has all the benefits to the customer of giving him a choice. It presents him with an alternative where he can reasonably expect more than normal care to be taken of his photographs.

But it is not necessarily the case that PTP should have to set up such a special service for themselves. If Mr Meeke is right and specialised laboratories do exist who accept liability and who are accessible to the general public, then PTP only have to refer their customers who want it to that laboratory. Such a system would certainly require that the choice be brought to the attention of all customers. Furthermore the Special Service option would have to be identified (ie name and address) and made convenient so that the customer is not indirectly compelled to accept the normal service.

Not many customers would opt for such a special service at a higher price (although Mr Woodman might well have been among that few if he had had the option) and I conclude that it would still leave ample scope for PTP to continue its low-cost mass-production technique for ordinary holiday photography.

In the light of the Code of Practice I reach the conclusion that some such form of two-tier system is not only reasonable but practicable. Accordingly PTP (on whom the burden lies under Section 11(5) of the Act) have failed to persuade me that the clause which they applied to Mr Woodman's contract satisfies the statutory test of reasonableness.

It remains for me to consider the question of damages. It seems to me that the disappointment and distress suffered by Mr Woodman was quite exceptional and yet well within the range of what was foreseeable to PTP. I would not differ from the view of the Learned Registrar that the sum of £75 is appropriate.

In accordance with an arrangement with Counsel I will not state what order as to costs I consider appropriate in the absence of argument on the point. My proposal on the matter will only become an order if neither party has, within 21 days, given notice of an intention to argue it.

I appreciate that the Defendants succeeded in persuading me that the arbitration award should be set aside, but in the event I conclude that the error of law did not invalidate either the outcome of the litigation or the processes by which the Learned Registrar reached his decision. Costs should follow the event. The Plaintiff should have his costs on Scale 3.

It was a case involving difficult questions of law where the assistance of Solicitor and Counsel was invaluable, and I am indebted to them both. The Registrar will have his discretion on taxation.

NOTE

The facts of *Levison v Patent Steam Carpet Cleaning Co Ltd* [1978] QB 69, [1977] 3 All ER 498, CA, are set out above, p 179.

The decision of the House of Lords in the following case is important in its conclusion on another issue on which views had been divided. It is helpful also in providing guidance on the test of reasonableness. The latter aspect is noted below, at pp 366–7.

Smith v Eric S Bush and Harris v Wyre Forest District Council [1989] 2 All ER 514, [1990] 1 AC 831, House of Lords

The issue in these cases was whether a surveyor instructed by a mortgagee to value a house owed the prospective private purchasers a duty in tort to carry out the valuation with reasonable skill and care and whether a prominent disclaimer by or on behalf of the surveyor was effective to prevent liability in negligence from arising. In the *Smith* case the report had indicated that no essential repairs were required, whereas chimneys were in a dangerous state and later collapsed causing considerable damage.

Lord Griffiths, having stated the facts of the case, continued: Counsel for the surveyors conceded that on the facts of this case the surveyors owed a duty of care to Mrs Smith unless they were protected by the disclaimer of liability. He made this concession, he said, because the surveyors knew that their report was going to be shown to Mrs Smith and that Mrs Smith would, in all probability, rely on it, which two factors would create the necessary proximity to found the duty of care. He submitted, however, that, if the surveyor did not know that his report would be shown to the purchaser, no duty of care would arise and that the decision in *Yianni v Edwin Evans & Sons (a firm)* [1981] 3 All ER 592, [1982] QB 438 was wrongly decided. I shall defer consideration of this question to the second appeal, for it does not arise on the facts of the present case. Suffice it to say, for the moment, that on the facts of the present case it is my view that the concession made by counsel is correct.

At common law, whether the duty to exercise reasonable care and skill is founded in contract or tort, a party is as a general rule free, by the use of appropriate wording, to exclude liability for negligence in discharge of the duty. The disclaimer of liability in the present case is prominent and clearly worded and, on the authority of *Hedley Byrne & Co Ltd v Heller & Partners Ltd* [1963] 2 All ER 575, [1964] AC 465, in so far as the common law is concerned effective to exclude the surveyors' liability for negligence. The question then is whether the Unfair Contract Terms Act 1977 bites on such a disclaimer. In my view it does.

The Court of Appeal, however, accepted an argument based on the definition of negligence contained in s 1(1) of the 1977 Act, . . .
It held that, as the disclaimer of liability would at common law have prevented any duty to take reasonable care arising between the parties, the Act had no application. In my view this construction fails to give due weight to the provisions of two further sections of the Act. . . .

Lord Griffiths quoted ss 11(3) and 13(1) and continued: I read these provisions as introducing a 'but for' test in relation to the notice excluding liability. They indicate that the existence of the common law duty to take reasonable care, referred to in s 1(1)(*b*), is to be judged by considering whether it would exist 'but for' the notice excluding liability. The result of taking the notice into account when assessing the existence of a duty of care would result in removing all liability for negligent misstatements from the protection of the Act. It is permissible to have regard to the second report of the Law Commission on *Exemption Clauses* (Law Com no 69), which is the genesis of the Unfair Contract Terms Act 1977, as an aid to the construction of the Act. Paragraph 127 of that report reads:

'Our recommendations on this Part of the report are intended to apply to exclusions of liability for negligence where the liability is incurred in the course of a person's business. We consider that they should apply even in cases where the person seeking to rely on the exemption clause was under no legal obligation (such as a contractual obligation) to carry out the activity. This means that, for example, conditions attached to a licence to enter on to land, and disclaimers of liability made where information or advice is given, should be subject to control . . . '

I have no reason to think that Parliament did not intend to follow this advice and the wording of the Act is, in my opinion, apt to give effect to that intention. This view of the construction of the Act is also supported by the judgment of Slade LJ in *Phillips Products Ltd v Hyland* [1987] 2 All ER 620, [1987] 1 WLR 659, when he rejected a similar argument in relation to the construction of a contractual term excluding negligence.

His Lordship and the other members of the House of Lords concluded that the disclaimer did not satisfy the 'requirement of reasonableness' and that the surveyor was liable.

NOTES

1. For a further reference to this case, see above, pp 201–2.
2. The situation in this case and in *Phillips Products Ltd v Hyland* [1987] 2 All ER 620 should be contrasted with one in which a contracting party seeks an indemnity against the financial consequences of liability from another: see *Thompson v T Lohan Plant Hire Ltd* [1987] 2 All ER 631, CA.
3. For a case holding that conveyancing solicitors were not entitled to summary judgment when seeking to rely on a standard disclaimer as to the accuracy of information furnished on inquiry, see *First National Commercial Bank plc v Loxleys, The Times*, 14 November 1996.

QUESTIONS

1. In *Woodman v Photo Trade Processing Ltd* (above), should the printed card have been regarded as giving adequate notice of the relevant provisions?
2. What would be the effect of applying the 1994 Regulations (see, in particular, reg 4, and Schedules 2 and 3, para 1(b)) to the facts of (i) *Woodman v Photo Trade Processing Ltd* and (ii) *Smith v Eric S Bush*?
3. Consider the following cases both in the light of the 1977 Act and the 1994 Regulations.

    (1) Al takes his cashmere coat for which he has recently paid £500 to the Topclass Cleaners for cleaning. He is handed a ticket which states that 'All clothes are accepted for cleaning subject to our standard conditions'. He does not ask what these standard conditions are. When he comes to collect the coat he is informed that owing to a fault in the cleaning process it has been irreparably damaged. The 'standard conditions' limit liability to £50 in the case of any one item.

    Advise Al whether the conditions form part of his contract with Topclass. Consider also the position if the standard conditions had been displayed (at some length) behind the counter but Al had not delayed the Saturday morning queue by stopping to read them.

    (2) Fastprint Films advertises its film processing service as follows: 'Send Fastprint Films your pictures and you need never have the bother of buying another film again . . . That's because for each film you send us, we'll give you a free film back . . . with your developed prints'. This statement is contained

on the envelopes used by customers to send their films to Fastprint. The envelopes also contain the following statement in somewhat smaller print:

IMPORTANT: We seek to take every care of photographic material in our possession but if it should be lost or damaged our liability is limited to the cost of the unexposed film plus the refund of the processing charge and postage. Except as above all liability for any loss or damage, including consequential loss, however caused (even if it is our fault) is excluded. If you consider your film is of exceptional value, please arrange your own insurance.

Cannon sends six films to Fastprint for processing. The work is done satisfactorily and he receives six free films along with his developed prints. Cannon then leaves for his holiday of a lifetime, touring the USA. He uses the six films to take pictures of his wife against a background of the Grand Canyon and other unforgettable sights. On returning to England he posts the films to Fastprint for developing, using Fastprint's envelopes. Owing to Fastprint's carelessness the films are damaged when being developed. Cannon has not arranged his own insurance and Fastprint is relying on its limitation clause. Cannon seeks your advice as to (i) the terms of his contract with Fastprint and (ii) whether the limitation clause in binding on him.

Advise Cannon.

Consider also the position if the cause of the unsatisfactory results lay in a fault in the films which had been supplied.

(3) The Downtown Garage displays the following notice in a prominent position in front of the car wash on its premises: 'No liability whatsoever can be accepted for any damage to cars using this facility whether such damage is caused by a malfunction of the equipment or otherwise. All aerials must be fully retracted'. Art forgets to retract his radio aerial and it is damaged beyond repair. Bert's back windscreen is broken when a malfunction in the equipment causes it to go out of control.

Advise Art and Bert.

LIABILITY ARISING IN CONTRACT

Section 3 of the 1977 Act is potentially of considerable importance in consumer transactions, especially in relation to the holiday trade. The section, which applies inter alia where one party 'deals as consumer' is based on recommendations in the Law Commission's Second Report on Exemption Clauses (Law Com No 69, 1975) paras 143–6 especially. Although s 3(2)(a) presupposes a breach of contract by the other contracting party, s 3(2)(b) does not. Rather it is concerned with a contracting party who so defines his obligations as to leave himself considerable latitude in the manner of performing them. Here there is a difficult distinction to be drawn between acceptable precision in defining a limited obligation and a clause which prima facie falls within the control of the subsection. The Law

Commission provides the following example for the former type of case in para 143 of its report:

If a decorator agrees to paint the outside woodwork of a house except the garage doors, no-one can seriously regard the words of exception as anything but a convenient way of defining the obligation; it would surely make no difference if the promise were to paint the outside wood-work with a clear proviso that the contractor was not obliged to paint the garage doors, or if there were a definition clause brought to the promisee's attention saying that 'outside wood-work' did not include the garage doors. Such provisions do not . . . deprive the promisee of a right of a kind which social policy requires that he should enjoy, nor do they, like the provisions excluding liability for breach of contractual obligations . . . give the promisor the advantage of appearing to promise more than he is in fact promising.

A probable example of the latter situation is to be found in a case decided well before the coming into force of the 1977 Act but which is still helpful as indicating a situation where s 3(2)(b) might now be applicable. Although the plaintiffs were travel agents, they might just as easily have been disappointed holiday-makers.

For further discussion of the distinction between clauses which define obligations and those which provide defences see generally Coote *Exception Clauses* (1964) chs 1 and 8 especially, and compare the speeches of Lord Wilberforce and Lord Diplock in *Photo Production Ltd v Securicor Transport Ltd* [1980] AC 827, [1980] 1 All ER 556, HL.

Anglo-Continental Holidays Ltd v Typaldos Lines (London) Ltd [1967] 2 Lloyd's Rep 61, Court of Appeal

This was an appeal by the defendants, Typaldos Lines (London) Ltd, from a decision of his Honour Judge Herbert at Westminster County Court ordering them to pay £447 10s damages to the plaintiffs, Anglo-Continental Holidays Ltd for breach of contract in connection with a holiday cruise in August, 1965. The facts appear in the judgment of Lord Denning MR.

Lord Denning MR. The plaintiffs are a firm of travel agents. The defendants are shipowners who run cruises in the Mediterranean. In November, 1964, the travel agents made a booking with the shipowners. They booked 10 cabins on a ship called the *Atlantica* for a round trip start-ing on Aug 12, 1965. The *Atlantica* was a large ship of 22,000 tons built in 1931. She was to start from Venice and go to various places in Greece and on to Israel. In particular, she was to go to Haifa and stay there two days. On one of those days there was to be an excursion to Jerusalem and on the next day a full-day excursion to Galilee. The ship was to get back to Venice after a 14 days' cruise.

The travel agents have a considerable connection with the Jewish community. They arranged for a party of young Jewish boys and girls, with two leaders—in all 28 people—to go on this trip in the Mediterranean for their holidays in August, 1965. But there was trouble because the defendants did not issue the tickets. The plaintiffs made several inquiries and the defendants said for some time it would be all right. But then came a bombshell. About a week before the holiday was to begin, the shipowners told the travel agents there had been an error in the book-ings. They were sorry but they could not take this group on the *Atlantica*. Instead they were ready to give them good cabins on another ship called the *Angelika*. The *Angelika* was to leave on the same day and was to do the same itinerary, but she was going to omit two short calls at Split and Izmir.

The travel agents were very upset. They did not know what to do. At first they wrote letters to the young people suggesting that they might accept this new proposal. But on the very next day they had second thoughts. Some of the group had begun to complain. The travel agents then decided that it would not be right to accept the new proposal at all. So they cancelled the arrangement altogether: and they claimed damages against the shipowners.

It appears that the proffered ship, the *Angelika*, was much inferior to the *Atlantica*. She was a very old ship built in 1910, and was only 9000 tons, much smaller than the *Atlantica* and she had not got the swimming pools or accommodation such as the *Atlantica* had. Most important of all, the *Angelika* did not go to Haifa for two whole days. She was only there for some eight hours. That was only time enough to go for a short trip to Tiberias. There would not be time to go to Tel-Aviv and Jerusalem.

In answer to the claim the shipowners relied on a clause in the handbook which they issued to travel agents. It said:

Steamers, Sailing Dates, Rates and Itineraries
are subject to change without prior notice.

The scope of this clause is of some importance: because we are told it is the first time it has been considered by the Courts in relation to passengers.

Let me say at once that I have some doubt whether this clause formed part of the contract. It is printed on the back of a handbook which gives an account of all the voyages which were going to take place in the coming year. It is mixed up with clauses which are plainly not contractual, such as:

'All passengers are required to possess valid passports . . . '

These clauses may be said to be only notes for the information of those about to travel: and not contractual conditions at all.

We were shown, however, specimen passenger tickets issued by the steamship line. These tickets contain (in small print, of course), equally wide conditions which purport to enable the shipowners to change the ship or the sailing dates, or to omit itinerary ports, and the like. (But not, it appears, the rates chargeable.) The travel agents must have seen these tickets, and in the circumstances I am prepared to assume that the clause did have contractual force.

In my opinion a steamship company cannot rely on a clause of this kind so as to alter the substance of the transaction. For instance, they could not say: 'We will change you from this fine modern ship to an old tramp'. Nor could they say: 'We are putting the sailing dates back a week'. Nor could they say: 'We are taking you to the Piraeus instead of to Haifa'. The law on the subject is settled by the cases starting with *Glynn v Margetson & Co* [1893] AC 351, and finishing with *Sze Hai Tong Bak Ltd v Rambler Cycle Co Ltd* [1959] AC 576, [1959] 2 Lloyd's Rep 114 [see also [1959] 3 All ER 182]. No matter how wide the terms of the clause, the Courts will limit it and modify it to the extent necessary to enable effect to be given to the main object and intent of the contract.

Applied to this case, we have to ask ourselves: Was the proposed trip by the *Angelika* in substance a performance of the contract or was it a serious departure from it? To my mind there is only one answer. It was a radical departure. The change over from the 22,000-ton *Atlantica* (with two swimming pools and lots of accommodation) to this small old 'crate' (as one of the witnesses called the *Angelika*) was itself a substantial departure. But most important of all was the shortened time at Haifa. The climax of the trip for these Jewish boys and girls was two days at Haifa, whereas they only were to have eight hours. The defendants cannot excuse it by reliance on the clause.

I am quite satisfied that the steamship company were guilty of a breach of their contract. They had, we we now know, heavily over-booked. They had too many people for the *Atlantica* and they tried to switch their group over to the *Angelika*. They had no right to do this. The travel agents were entitled to cancel the booking and are entitled to damages.

It was suggested that, in mitigation of damages, the travel agents ought to have accepted the proffered cabins on the *Angelika*, but I do not think that it would be reasonable to expect them to do so.

The remaining question is: How much damages? The travel agents are entitled to damages for the loss of profit of £377 10s and £20 for calls and postage. They also claim damages for loss of custom or goodwill. The Judge put it as reputation. He awarded a sum of £50 on this head. The steamship company challenge this award of £50.

It is most unusual in a case of breach of contract for damages to be given for loss of goodwill. But in principle I see no reason why it should not be given if it is a loss such as might be reasonably foreseen to be a consequence of the breach. In this case I think it was reasonably foreseeable. A cancellation at the last moment would affect the goodwill and standing of the travel agents. The only difficulty is proof of loss. There was some proof of general loss of business but that was all. The Judge said this:

'I think that this is too vague to prove special damage. But some loss of the plaintiffs' reputation can, I think, be assumed to have flowed in the ordinary course from the defendants' breach . . . '

He awarded £50 as a reasonable sum. I do not think it is necessary in cases of this kind to prove any specific loss of business. If the breach is such as to be calculated to cause loss of goodwill, the Judge can assign a reasonable sum as damages without requiring positive proof of loss. I think the sum of £50 was justifiable in the circumstances of this case.

In my view the appeal should be dismissed.

Lord Justice Davies. I agree in every respect with my Lord's judgment and do not wish to add anything.

Lord Justice Russell. I assume (though I am not sure on the point) that the reference to the 'Steamers, Sailing Dates, Rates and Itineraries' on the back of the brochure did form part of the contract between the parties. Nevertheless a reasonable construction must be put upon such a term, and as a matter of construction the defendants were not enabled thereby to alter the substance of the arrangement. Whether they attempted to do so must be, in a sort of package deal like this, a question of degree and perhaps to some extent of general impression. But in my view a combination of all the matters which were in fact involved in the substitution of the *Angelika* for the *Atlantica* together did constitute an alteration of the substance of the arrangement . . .

[His Lordship then considered the question of damages for loss of goodwill, agreeing with the County Court Judge, and continued]:

I would only add this. The case below went really mainly on the assumption that the so-called special condition, that the

Steamers, Sailing Dates, Rates and Itineraries

are subject to change without prior notice was an exemption clause, and the learned County Court Judge treated it as an exemption clause. Then it was sought to find out if there had been a breach of a fundamental term. With deference, I think the learned County Court Judge was wrongly led into that approach. It is not an exemption clause, as is pointed out. It is a clause under which the actual contractual liability may be defined, and not one which will excuse from the actual contractual liability. In the end of the day the approach as to the scope of the clause may not be substantially different. As I have said, I prefer to state it as being a matter of construction of a general clause, and the propounder of that clause cannot be enabled thereby to alter the substance of the arrangement.

I agree that the appeal fails.

The appeal was accordingly dismissed, with costs.

QUESTIONS

Did Lord Denning MR and Russell LJ approach the 'subject to change without prior notice' clause in the same way? If not which approach is correct?

NOTES

1. An individual consumer clearly 'deals as a consumer' within the first limb of s 3(1), and hence it will not usually be in point to ask whether the second limb ('deals . . . on the other's written standard terms of business') will also be satisfied. Consider, however, the potential application of the 1994 Regulations in such cases as *Anglo-Continental Holidays Ltd v Typaldos Lines (London) Ltd* (assuming that it is a disappointed holiday-maker, rather than the travel agent, who is suing). Which of the terms in the indicative or 'grey' list of Schedule 3 appear to be particularly relevant? What is the effect of reg 3(2)(a) if the relevant term (i) is or (ii) is not drafted in 'plain, intelligible language'?
2. For further materials involving holidays including extracts from the Package Travel, Package Holidays and Package Tours Regulations 1992, SI 1992/3288, see above, pp 165–78.
3. For references to a decision in which the Unfair Terms in Consumer Contracts Regulations 1994 were used to strike down a clause imposing a redemption penalty on a mortgage, see *The Times* 7 February 1998.
4. Suppose that the following term is included in the conditions of a shipping company here called XYZ which contracts directly with consumers after placing advertisements in the national press.

Alteration of the contract
(1) Every reasonable effort will be made to adhere to the advertised route and timetable but any route or port may be altered or omitted or times or dates changed for any cause which XYZ and/or the Master of the Ship in their absolute discretion shall consider to be just and reasonable.
(2) XYZ has the right to charge the fare in force on the date of sailing. In the case of a return booking, the fare payable shall be that in force on the date of sailing of the return voyage. Where such a fare is more than that shown on the ticket the difference must be paid before the Passenger embarks. For the purposes of these Conditions the word 'fare' shall include any surcharge imposed by XYZ up to the date of sailing.
(3) XYZ and/or the Master of the Ship may at any time, if in their absolute discretion they consider it necessary to do so, transfer the Passenger from one berth to another adjusting the fare accordingly . . .

QUESTIONS

1. Is it likely that the above conditions would be effective to enable the company to (i) omit a port which was a major attraction or (ii) transfer a passenger from first-class to 'steerage'? How would the Package Travel etc Regulations apply to the above terms?
2. What is the effect of the following: (i) a notice outside a cricket ground, 'Play Cannot be Guaranteed: No Refunds', (ii) a statement in an opera company's booking conditions, 'The Management Reserves the Right to Make Changes in the Cast Without Notice', (iii) a label sewn into a blouse stating: 'Dry Clean Only' and (iv) a notice in a china chop: 'Breakages must be Paid For'? (See also s 13 of the Unfair Contract Terms Act, above, pp 329 and 348.)

PROBLEM

In the light of ss 2, 3 and 4 of the 1977 Act and the extract from the Law Reform (Frustrated Contracts) Act 1943 printed below, consider the following:

The standard form booking conditions of the Moneypenny Company which operates its own hotels on an accommodation only basis provide in part as follows:

Although Moneypenny Company (hereinafter Moneypenny) always uses its best endeavours to provide its valued customers with a peaceful and enjoyable holiday, all bookings are expressly subject to the following conditions:
(i) Moneypenny cannot accept liability for death, personal injury or inconvenience caused to or suffered by its customers, howsoever caused;
(ii) in the event of loss of or damage to customers' luggage Moneypenny's liability is limited to £20 per suitcase or similar container. All other liability for damage to customers' property is hereby expressly excluded;
(iii) in booking with Moneypenny, customers hereby undertake to indemnify the company in the event of injury or damage being caused by Moneypenny's employees or agents when dealing with customers' property;
(iv) although Moneypenny expressly endeavours to accommodate clients in hotels which they have specified it reserves the right to use other hotels at its absolute discretion;
(v) in the event of Moneypenny being obliged to cancel the arrangements for a holiday by virtue of events wholly outside its control it is regretted that no refunds can be made and no compensation paid.

Advise Moneypenny as to the enforceability of these provisions under (i) the 1977 Act and (ii) the 1994 Regulations, noting the precise source of the relevant provisions.

(The Law Reform Frustrated Contracts Act 1943 provides in part as follows:

1. Adjustment of rights and liabilities of parties to frustrated contracts
(1) Where a contract governed by English law has become impossible of performance or been otherwise frustrated, and the parties thereto have for that reason been discharged from the further performance of the contract, the following provisions of this section shall, subject to the provisions of section two of this Act, have effect in relation thereto.
(2) All sums paid or payable to any party in pursuance of the contract before the time when the parties were so discharged (in this Act referred to as 'the time of discharge') shall, in the case

of sums so paid, be recoverable from him as money received by him for the use of the party by whom the sums were paid, and, in the case of sums so payable, cease to be so payable:

Provided that, if the party to whom the sums were so paid or payable incurred expenses before the time of discharge in, or for the purpose of, the performance of the contract, the court may, if it considers it just to do so having regard to all the circumstances of the case, allow him to retain or, as the case may be, recover the whole or any part of the sums so paid or payable, not being an amount in excess of the expenses so incurred.

...

(4) In estimating, for the purposes of the foregoing provisions of this section, the amount of any expenses incurred by any party to the contract, the court may, without prejudice to the generality of the said provisions, include such sum as appears to be reasonable in respect of overhead expenses and in respect of any work or services performed personally by the said party.

GUARANTEES OF GOODS

General concern about the misleading nature of some guarantees was apparent from the extracts from the Law Commission's First Report on Exemption Clauses in Contracts (Law Com No 24) printed above, pp 323–4. The problems were recognised also in the Molony Committee report of 1962 (Cmnd 1781, paras 474–78 especially) which said with particular reference to the so-called guarantees then current in the motor trade that:

In return for discretionary, limited and unenforceable promises of attention to defects of manu - facture, the consumer is induced unknowingly to forfeit the only right he might be able to maintain against the manufacturer; as well as apparently conceding his Sale of Goods Acts rights against the retailer.

Of course there are problems of a more general nature associated with 'guarantees' and reference is made to these elsewhere (see above, pp 274–8).

Section 5 of the 1977 Act nullifies in the circumstances specified any effect which 'guarantees' of consumer goods might otherwise have had as exclusion clauses in the relationship between manufacturers and the consumers of their goods.

QUESTION

It has been suggested by some commentators that this may sometimes coincidentally render unenforceable any additional obligations which a manufacturer would otherwise have been regarded as undertaking vis-à-vis consumers.

Consider why s 5 might have this effect.

SALE AND RELATED TRANSACTIONS: DEALING AS CONSUMER

Many consumer transactions will fall within ss 6 and 7 of the 1977 Act, thereby giving complete protection against exemption clauses to anyone who 'deals as consumer' (see s 12 of the Act). Such transactions include contracts of sale and hire-purchase (s 6) and a wide range of other contracts whereby the property or possession in goods is transferred to consumers (s 7). This latter category includes contracts for work and materials and contracts of hire. Where the transferee does not 'deal as consumer' any such exemption clause must satisfy the 'reasonableness' test (s 11). The notion of dealing as consumer was considered in the following case.

R & B Customs Brokers Co Ltd v United Dominions Trust Ltd [1988] 1 All ER 847, [1988] 1 WLR 321, Court of Appeal

The plaintiffs, a private company with two directors and shareholders, had purchased a Colt Shogun car from the defendants. The conditional sale agreement purported to exclude any implied conditions as to quality etc. The roof of the car leaked and in subsequent proceedings the first instance judge found that the plaintiff had dealt as consumer for the purposes of s 12 of the Act and hence that the exclusion clause was wholly ineffective. The defendant appealed to the Court of Appeal.

Dillon LJ, having set out the facts of the case and the relevant statutory provisions, continued: It is accepted that the conditions in paras (*b*) and (*c*) in s 12 (1) are satisfied. This issue turns on the condition in para (*a*). Did the company neither make the contract with the defendants in the course of a business nor hold itself out as doing so?

In the present case there was no holding out beyond the mere facts that the contract and the finance application were made in the company's corporate name and in the finance application the section headed 'Business Details' was filled in to the extent of giving the nature of the company's business as that of shipping brokers, giving the number of years trading and the number of employees, and giving the names and addresses of the directors. What is important is whether the contract was made in the course of a business.

In a certain sense, however, from the very nature of a corporate entity, where a company which carried on a business makes a contract it makes that contract in the course of its business; otherwise the contract would be ultra vires and illegal. Thus, where a company which runs a grocer's shop buys a new delivery van, it buys it in the course of its business. Where a merchant bank buys a car as a 'company car' as a perquisite for a senior executive, it buys it in the course of its business. Where a farming company buys a Landrover for the personal and company use of a farm manager, it again does so in the course of its business. Possible variations are numerous. In each case it would not be legal for the purchasing company to buy the vehicle in question otherwise than in the course of its business. Section 12 does not require that the business in the course of which the one party, referred to in the condition in para (*a*), makes the contract must be of the same nature as the business in the course of which the other party, referred to in the condition in para (*b*), makes the contract, eg that they should both be motor dealers.

We have been referred to one decision at first instance under the 1977 Act, *Peter Symmons & Co v Cook* (1981) 131 NLJ 758, but the note of the judgment is too brief to be of real assistance. More helpfully, we have been referred to decisions under the Trade Descriptions Act 1968, and in particular to the decision of the House of Lords in *Davies v Sumner* [1984] 3 All ER 831, [1984] 1 WLR 1301. . . .

His Lordship then considered the speech of Lord Keith in *Davies v Sumner*, a case concerned with the expression 'in the course of a . . . business' in the Trade Descriptions Act 1968. Relevant extracts are printed below, at pp 611–12. He then continued:

Lord Keith emphasised the need for some degree of regularity, and he found pointers to this in the primary purpose and long title of the 1968 Act. I find pointers to a similar need for regularity under the 1977 Act, where matters merely incidental to the carrying on of a business are concerned, both in the words which I would emphasise, 'in the course of' in the phrase 'in the course of a business' and in the concept, or legislative purpose, which must underlie the dichotomy under the 1977 Act between those who deal as consumers and those who deal otherwise than as consumers.

This reasoning leads to the conclusion that, in the 1977 Act also, the words 'in the course of business' are not used in what Lord Keith called 'the broadest sense'. I also find helpful the phrase used by Lord Parker CJ and quoted by Lord Keith, 'an integral part of the business carried on'. The reconciliation between that phrase and the need for some degree of regularity is, as I see it, as follows: there are some transactions which are clearly integral parts of the businesses concerned, and these should be held to have been carried out in the course of those businesses; this would cover, apart from much else, the instance of a one-off adventure in the nature of trade where the transaction itself would constitute a trade or business. There are other transactions, however, such as the purchase of the car in the present case, which are at the highest only incidental to the carrying on of the relevant business; here a high degree of regularity is required before it can be said that they are an integral part of the business carried on and so entered into in the course of that business.

Applying the test thus indicated to the facts of the present case, I have no doubt that the requisite degree of regularity is not made out on the facts. Mr Bell's evidence that the car was the second or third vehicle acquired on credit terms was in my judgment and in the context of this case not enough. Accordingly, I agree with the judge that, in entering into the conditional sale agreement with the defendants, the company was 'dealing as consumer'. The defendants' cl 2(a) is thus inapplicable and the defendants are not absolved from liability under s 14(3).

There is a different approach which I would wish to leave open for a future case since it was not argued before us. If the company had never been incorporated and Mr Bell had bought the car personally for personal (or domestic) and business use it would, I apprehend, have been difficult to argue that he had not been dealing as a consumer in buying the car. On facts such as those of the present case it would seem anomalous and in some measure disquieting if a different result were reached if the car was bought by a company for the personal and business use of its two directors. It occurs to me that in such circumstances it could well be appropriate to pierce the corporate veil and look at the realities of the situation as in *DHN Food Distributors Ltd v Tower Hamlets London Borough* [1976] 3 All ER 462 esp at 467–468, [1976] 1 WLR 852 esp at 860–861 per Lord Denning MR and Goff LJ.

It follows that it is unnecessary to decide whether, if the company had been dealing otherwise than as a consumer, the defendants' cl 2(a) excluding all liability under, inter alia, s 14(3) satisfied the requirement of reasonableness. . . .

Neill LJ agreed.

Appeal dismissed.

NOTES

1. For a similar conclusion, see *Rasbora Ltd v JCL Marine Ltd* [1977] 1 Lloyd's Rep 645 and, it seems, *Peter Symmons & Co v Cook* (1981) 131 NLJ 758.

2. The issue was discussed in the following terms by the Law Commission in its First Report on Exemption Clauses (Law Com No 24, 1969).

> 83. We have considered in the light of the evidence some of the types of case in which it might be appropriate to extend the proposed protection to purchasers buying otherwise than for private use or consumption. Obvious cases are motor cars, typewriters and electric heaters sold to doctors or members of other professions; here, as a matter of justice and common sense, the sale may, in all material respects, be indistinguishable from a sale to a private purchaser.
>
> . . .
>
> 84. It is our conclusion that provision should be made to extend protection from exemption clauses to purchasers in the types of case illustrated in paragraph 83. There are two ways in which this could be achieved. One way would be to extend the definition of 'consumer sale' so as to cover cases of this kind. Alternatively, if in accordance with the proposals favoured by some of us protection from exemption clauses were to be afforded to business sales generally by a test of reasonableness applied by the courts, purchasers in the above-mentioned type of case would have the benefit of that protection.

QUESTIONS

1. In the result the statutory reform which followed opted for the 'alternative' approach of applying a test of reasonableness to business sales.

   This suggests that the reasoning in the above case was not in accordance with the Law Commission's assumptions. Is it none the less desirable that a small private company should benefit from the full statutory protection of ss 6(2) and 7(2)?

2. What are the main points of similarity and contrast between the protection afforded by the 1977 Act (ss 6(2), 7(2) and 12) and the 1994 Regulations? Would the plaintiffs in the above case have benefited from the 1994 Regulations?

   Consider the following cases under both potential sources of protection.

3. Grabit and Run are solicitors in partnership in Midtown. They acquire the following goods on the partnership account: (i) a powerful computer to run a legal database; (ii) a coffee-making machine for use of the secretarial staff; (iii) a secondhand Jaguar car at auction. All three items fail to meet a standard of satisfactory quality.

4. Jerrybuilder is a builder and plumber whose standard form contract contains the following provisions: 'Whilst Jerrybuilder always endeavours to carry out work with the maximum speed in no case will time be of the essence of the contract. Completion dates are approximations only. Jerrybuilder reserves the right to increase the contract price to reflect increases in manufacturers' prices and regrets that he cannot accept liability for defects in materials bought in from third party suppliers or for negligence on his own part howsoever arising. It is a condition of this contract that the customer must pay a one-third deposit before work can be commenced, this sum to be forfeited if the customer decides not to proceed with the contract work.'

Gullible, a private customer, seeks your advice as to whether the above conditions are enforceable. Advise Gullible.

MISREPRESENTATIONS

Perhaps predictably most of the reported cases concerning exemption clauses in relation to misrepresentations have been about the sale of real property (see eg *Overbrooke Estates Ltd v Glencombe Properties Ltd* [1974] 3 All ER 511, [1974] 1 WLR 1335; *Collins v Howell-Jones* (1980) 259 Estates Gazette 331, CA; *South Western General Property Co Ltd v Marton* (1982) 263 Estates Gazette 1090; *Walker v Boyle* [1982] 1 All ER 634, [1982] 1 WLR 495; *McGrath v Shah* (1987) 57 P & CR 452; *Thomas Witter Ltd v TBP Industries Ltd* (1995) 14 Tr LR145 and see *Howard Marine and Dredging Co Ltd v A Ogden & Sons (Excavations) Ltd* [1978] QB 574, [1978] 2 All ER 1134, CA (hire of barges).

The following case is about property but the approach of the Court of Appeal is potentially helpful in the context of consumer transactions and it makes a distinction of general importance.

Cremdean Properties Ltd v Nash (1977) 244 Estates Gazette 547, Court of Appeal

This was an appeal by the first defendant against a decision of Fox J (1977) 241 Estates Gazette 837 on a preliminary issue arising in proceedings brought by the plaintiffs in respect of the sale to them of a block of properties. The plaintiffs were seeking rescission of the contracts of sale and in the alternative damages on the ground of alleged misrepresentation in the invitation to tender as to the amount of available office space. The preliminary issue to be tried was whether certain clauses contained in a footnote to the conditions of sale were effective to exclude liability for inaccuracy of the information. Fox J had ordered that the action should proceed to trial.

Bridge LJ. Mr Newsom's able argument on behalf of the defendant can really be summarised very shortly. In effect what he says is this. The terms of the footnote are not simply, if contractual at all, a contractual exclusion either of any liability to which the defendant would otherwise be subject for any misrepresentation in the document, or of any remedy otherwise available on that ground to the plaintiff. The footnote is effective, so the argument runs, to nullify any representation in the document altogether; it is effective, so it is said, to bring about a situation in law as if no representation at all had ever been made. For my part, I am quite unable to accept that argument. I reject it primarily on the simple basis that on no reading of the language of the footnote could it have the remarkable effect contended for. One may usefully analyse the footnote by dividing it into three parts. The first part is embodied in the words: 'These particulars are prepared for the convenience of an intending purchaser or tenant and although they are believed to be correct their accuracy is not guaranteed . . . ' That is something quite different from saying 'any representation in this document shall be deemed not to be a representation.' On the contrary, this part of the footnote is clearly intended to exclude contractual liability for the accuracy of any representation; so far from saying that there has been no representation, it is reinforcing the fact that there have been representations by indicating that they are believed to be correct.

The second part of the footnote is embodied in the words: ' . . . any error, omission or misdescription shall not annul the sale or be grounds on which compensation may be claimed'—that, I think Mr Newsom concedes, is nothing more or less than a purported exclusion of liability which would otherwise accrue on the ground of any misrepresentation in the statements to be found elsewhere in the document.

Finally, the third part of the footnote is embodied in the words: 'Any intending purchaser or tenant must satisfy himself by inspection or otherwise as to the correctness of each of the statements contained in these particulars.' That part of the footnote may have considerable importance when this action comes to trial, as bearing upon the question of fact that will arise at the trial, as to whether the plaintiffs relied upon any misrepresentation. But for present purposes we, of course, have to assume the truth of what is pleaded, namely, that the representation as to office space was false and that the plaintiffs relied upon the alleged misrepresentation. Clearly the third part of this footnote, again on any reading of its language, does not amount even to a purported annulment of the very existence of any representation embodied in the earlier parts of this document.

In support of his argument Mr Newsom relied upon a decision of Brightman J in a case called *Overbrooke Estates Ltd v Glencombe Properties Ltd* reported in [1974] 1 WLR 1335 [also (1974) 232 Estates Gazette 829]. That was a case where the plaintiff vendors were seeking to enforce a contract of sale made through auctioneers and where the defendant purchasers sought to rely upon an alleged misrepresentation by the auctioneers to avoid their liability under the contract. It was a case in which the auction particulars included a sentence in the following terms: 'The vendors do not make or give, and neither the auctioneers nor any person in the employment of the auctioneers has any authority to make or give any representation or warranty in relation to these properties.' It was alleged that, that clause notwithstanding, subsequently the auctioneers, before the defendants contracted to purchase the property, had made certain oral and inaccurate representations about some of its attributes, and it was argued on behalf of the defendants that the clause in the auction particulars purporting to limit the auctioneers' authority to make any representations on the vendors' behalf was a clause excluding, or purporting to exclude, or limit, liability, which could only take effect subject to the provisions of section 3 of the Misrepresentation Act 1967.

Brightman J deals with that argument . . . [as follows]

'In my judgment section 3 of the Act will not bear the load which Mr Irvine seeks to place upon it. In my view the section only applies to a provision which would exclude or restrict liability for a misrepresentation made by a party or his duly authorised agent, including of course an agent with ostensible authority. The section does not, in my judgment, in any way qualify the right of a principal publicly to limit the otherwise ostensible authority of his agent. The defendants' second argument fails.'

I respectfully agree entirely with the whole of that reasoning. With respect to Mr Newsom's argument I am unable to see that it has any application at all to the facts of the present case, because there never was any question here but that the agents acting for the first defendant and the other defendants, when they published the document on which the plaintiffs rely as embodying the relevant misrepresentation, had the full authority of their principals to say what they did say in the document. It is one thing to say that section 3 does not inhibit a principal from publicly giving notice limiting the ostensible authority of his agents; it is quite another thing to say that a principal can circumvent the plainly intended effect of section 3 by a clause excluding his own liability for a representation which he has undoubtedly made.

I am quite content to found my judgment in this case on the proposition that the language of the footnote relied upon by Mr Newsom simply does not, on its true interpretation, have the effect contended for. But I would go further and say that if the ingenuity of a draftsman could devise language which would have that effect, I am extremely doubtful whether the court would allow it to operate so as to defeat section 3. Supposing the vendor included a clause which the purchaser was required to, and did, agree to in some such terms as 'notwithstanding any statement of fact included in these particulars the vendor shall be conclusively deemed to have made no representation within the meaning of the Misrepresentation Act 1967,' I should have thought that that was only a form of words the intended and actual effect of which was to exclude or restrict liability, and I should not have thought that the courts would have been ready to allow such ingenuity in forms of language to defeat the plain purpose at which section 3 is aimed . . .

Agreeing, **Scarman LJ** said: I agree in particular with the observations that my Lord made about the submissions put to the court by Mr Maurice, following his leader. Nevertheless, the case for the appellant does have an audacity and a simple logic which I confess I find attractive. It runs thus: a statement is not a representation unless it is also a statement that what is stated is true. If in context a statement contains no assertion, express or implied, that its content is accurate, there is no representation. *Ergo*, there can be no misrepresentation; *ergo*, the Misrepresentation Act 1967 cannot apply to it. Humpty Dumpty would have fallen for this argument. If we were to fall for it, the Misrepresentation Act would be dashed to pieces which not all the King's lawyers could put together again . . .

Buckley LJ agreed with both judgments and did not wish to add anything.

The appeal was dismissed with costs, to be taxed and paid forthwith.

NOTES

1. For a contrasting case in which an estate agent's disclaimer was held to be effective as against a 'sophisticated' member of the public buying a house at the top end of the market, see *McCullagh v Lane Fox & Partners, The Times*, 22 December 1995, CA. The disclaimer provided, *inter alia*, that: 'None of the statements contained in these particulars as to this property are (sic) to be relied on as statements or representations of fact. Any intending purchaser must satisfy themselves by inspection or otherwise as to the correctness of each of the statements contained in these particulars.'

2. The Office of Fair Trading has discussed 'entire agreement' clauses in the context of the 1994 Regulations in the following extract.

Unfair Contract Terms: Issue No 1, May 1996

What are 'entire agreement' clauses?

2.1. Paragraph 1(n) of Schedule 3 to the Regulations, the 'indicative and illustrative list of terms which may be regarded as unfair' (the 'grey list'), indicates that clauses are unfair if they have the object or effect of:

(n) limiting the seller's or supplier's obligation to respect commitments undertaken by his agents or making his commitments subject to compliance with a particular formality.

2.2. We are concerned here with the first part, which has the effect of placing standard form 'entire agreement clauses' under particular suspicion of unfairness. It also disposes of the argument advanced by some suppliers that an entire agreement clause is a core term, and thus exempt from the fairness test in regulation 3(2). A fairly typical example, in this case drawn from a double-glazing contract, is as follows:

The placing of an order with the company will be deemed to bind the customer to the following terms and conditions and no oral representations shall bind the company. Any variation or alteration in the following terms and conditions shall only be binding upon the company if made in writing and signed by a director of the company.

2.3. A standard entire agreement clause is aimed at enabling a business to escape liability for:

> promises that conflict with or add to the commitments in the standard written contract—for instance an agreement to a deadline by which goods will be supplied; and

> 'misrepresentations'—statements which do not amount to promises, but which have the effect of encouraging the consumer to enter into a contract—for instance the claim that an item has sold in large quantities and that this is the last one in stock.

2.4. The following fairly typical examples of unfair terms drawn from a mobile phone airtime contract and a 'cashback' promotion company, aim to exclude liability under both headings:

You agree that this Agreement is the complete and exclusive statement between us which supersedes all understandings or prior agreements oral or written, and all representations or other communications between us relating to the subject matter of the Agreement.

The Holder admits that having entered into this agreement and becoming bound by its terms and conditions he has not relied on any written or oral representations made by the Authorised Supplier or its agents or servants and this Agreement and its terms and conditions contains the whole of the terms agreed and binding on the parties.

2.5. Such clauses are singled out for attention in the grey list because there is an obvious temptation to traders to encourage or allow employees to win sales by making false promises and misrepresentations. Since entire agreement clauses are often buried in small print, which the consumer does not get to read until too late, and may not understand in any case, the unrestricted use of such clauses would permit such conduct to occur with impunity. It would also permit a trader to disregard a reasonable promise made on his behalf in good faith, such as a delivery date, when it becomes inconvenient.

2.6. We recognise that entire agreement clauses are often aimed at protecting a legitimate interest, and not at cheating consumers. The fact that such clauses are so common supports such a view. They are not used only by rogues. But it is the potential *effect* of the clauses, not the intention, that matters. In assessing the unfairness of such clauses, we cannot be swayed by the argument that a business does not intend to use clauses in an abusive way. Protection for the consumer cannot rely on a trader's good intentions.

Can entire agreement clauses ever be fair?

2.7. Of course, Schedule 3 is only a 'grey', not a 'black', list. Entire agreement clauses are not therefore invariably unfair. In theory, such a clause, like every other kind of potentially unfair term, may be made fair or less unfair in one or more of various ways, for example by being:

> narrowly drafted, so that it does no more than protect the legitimate interest of the business, without imposing any burden on the consumer or giving the business any unfair advantage;

> balanced by another clause putting an equal and opposite burden on the business or giving an unequal advantage to the consumer;

used according to procedures which ensure it is specifically drawn to the attention of, and explained to, consumers before the conclusion of contracts, so that they are realistically able to accept or reject any disadvantage or burden that it imposes.

For further references to the work of the Office of Fair Trading in relation to potentially unfair contract terms, see below, at pp 379–82.

Consider the following case.

Angus wishes to sell his Victorian house and he puts it in the hands of Messrs Locke and Key, estate agents. Their particulars refer to the house as having been 'recently rewired throughout'. In fact this is untrue since only the lighting has been recently rewired whilst the power circuit is old and seriously defective. Bert has bought the house having read these particulars which also contain the following statements:

These particulars do not constitute or form part of any contract. Whilst Messrs Locke and Key take every care in the preparation of these particulars they hereby state both on behalf of themselves and the Vendor that no intending purchaser should rely on any of the statements herein as statements or representations of fact and the intending purchaser should make his own inspection and enquiries in order to satisfy himself of their authenticity and no responsibility is accepted for any error or omission herein.

Some two months after completion Bert discovers the state of the wiring and seeks your advice as to whether he has a remedy against (i) Angus; (ii) Locke and Key. Advise Bert.

NOTE

As to an agent's personal position under s 2(1) of the Misrepresentation Act 1967 see *Resolute Maritime Inc v Nippon Kaiji Kyokai, The Skopas* [1983] 2 All ER 1, [1983] 1 WLR 857.

QUESTION

If a consumer is in dispute with a contractor, and an agreement is reached to settle the dispute on payment of (say) two-thirds of the outstanding amount claimed, is the agreement subject to either the 1977 Act or the 1994 Regulations?: see ss 2 and 10 of the Act and *Tudor Grange Holdings Ltd v Citibank NA* [1991] 4 All ER 1.

THE TEST OF REASONABLENESS

In many consumer transactions exemption clauses will not be void but rather will be subject to the test of reasonableness of s 11 of the Act. Schedule 2 to the Act lists a number of guidelines to be considered specifically in relation to ss 6 and 7. Although Sch 2 will not affect consumers directly, since a relevant clause would be void in their case, the guidelines may be thought to be no more than expressions of common sense matters to which the courts would wish to have regard more generally. The case of *Woodman v Photo Trade Processing Ltd* (above, p 343) is helpful as discussing the requirement of reasonableness in the context of a consumer transaction. In the following case the House of Lords considered it in the context of a commercial transaction but made a number of points of general interest and application. (For another commercial case see *R W Green Ltd v Cade Bros Farms* [1978] 1 Lloyd's Rep 602.)

George Mitchell (Chesterhall) Ltd v Finney Lock Seeds Ltd [1983] 2 All ER 737, [1983] 2 AC 803, House of Lords

The facts of this case are as stated in Lord Denning's judgment in the Court of Appeal (above, p 319) from which the sellers of the cabbage seed were now appealing. (Section 55(5) of the Sale of Goods Act 1979 to which Lord Bridge refers is the equivalent of Sch 2 to the 1977 Act.)

Lord Bridge of Harwich . . . This is the first time your Lordships' House has had to consider a modern statutory provision giving the court power to override contractual terms excluding or restricting liability, which depends on the court's view of what is 'fair and reasonable'. The particular provision of the modified s 55 of the 1979 Act which applies in the instant case is of limited and diminishing importance. But the several provisions of the Unfair Contract Terms Act 1977 which depend on 'the requirement of reasonableness', defined in s 11 by reference to what is 'fair and reasonable', albeit in a different context, are likely to come before the courts with increasing frequency. It may, therefore, be appropriate to consider how an original decision what is 'fair and reasonable' made in the application of any of these provisions should be approached by an appellate court. It would not be accurate to describe such a decision as an exercise of discretion. But a decision under any of the provisions referred to will have this in common with the exercise of a discretion, that, in having regard to the various matters to which the modified s 55(5) of the 1979 Act, or s 11 of the 1977 Act direct attention, the court must entertain a whole range of considerations, put them in the scales on one side or the other and decide at the end of the day on which side the balance comes down. There will sometimes be room for a legitimate difference of judicial opinion as to what the answer should be, where it will be impossible to say that one view is demonstrably wrong and the other demonstrably right. It must follow, in my view, that, when asked to review such a decision on appeal, the appellate court should treat the original decision with the utmost respect and refrain from interference with it unless satisfied that it proceeded on some erroneous principle or was plainly and obviously wrong . . .

The only other question of construction debated in the course of the argument was the meaning to be attached to the words 'to the extent that' in sub-s (4) and, in particular, whether they permit the court to hold that it would be fair and reasonable to allow partial reliance on a limitation clause and, for example, to decide in the instant case that the respondents should recover, say, half their consequential damage. I incline to the view that, in their context, the words are equivalent to 'in so far as' or 'in circumstances in which' and do not permit the kind of judgment of Solomon illustrated by the example.

But for the purpose of deciding this appeal I find it unnecessary to express a concluded view on this question.

My Lords, at long last I turn to the application of the statutory language to the circumstances of the case. Of the particular matters to which attention is directed by paras (a) to (e) of s 55(5), only those in paras (a) to (c) are relevant. As to para (c), the respondents admittedly knew of the relevant condition (they had dealt with the appellants for many years) and, if they had read it, particularly cl 2, they would, I think, as laymen rather than lawyers, have had no difficulty in understanding what it said. This and the magnitude of the damages claimed in proportion to the price of the seeds sold are factors which weigh in the scales in the appellants' favour.

The question of relative bargaining strength under para (a) and of the opportunity to buy seeds without a limitation of the seedsman's liability under para (b) were interrelated. The evidence was that a similar limitation of liability was universally embodied in the terms of trade between seedsmen and farmers and had been so for very many years. The limitation had never been negotiated between representative bodies but, on the other hand, had not been the subject of any protest by the National Farmers' Union. These factors, if considered in isolation, might have been equivocal. The decisive factor, however, appears from the evidence of four witnesses called for the appellants, two independent seedsmen, the chairman of the appellant company, and a director of a sister company (both being wholly-owned subsidiaries of the same parent). They said that it had always been their practice, unsuccessfully attempted in the instant case, to negotiate settlements of farmers' claims for damages in excess of the price of the seeds, if they thought that the claims were 'genuine' and 'justified'. This evidence indicated a clear recognition by seedsmen in general, and the appellants in particular, that reliance on the limitation of liability imposed by the relevant condition would not be fair or reasonable.

Two further factors, if more were needed, weigh the scales in favour of the respondents. The supply of autumn, instead of winter, cabbage seed was due to the negligence of the appellants' sister company. Irrespective of its quality, the autumn variety supplied could not, according to the appellants' own evidence, be grown commercially in East Lothian. Finally, as the trial judge found, seedsmen could insure against the risk of crop failure caused by supply of the wrong variety of seeds without materially increasing the price of seeds.

My Lords, even if I felt doubts about the statutory issue, I should not, for the reasons explained earlier, think it right to interfere with the unanimous original decision of that issue by the Court of Appeal. As it is, I feel no such doubts. If I were making the original decision, I should conclude without hesitation that it would not be fair or reasonable to allow the appellants to rely on the contractual limitation of their liability.

I would dismiss the appeal.

Lords Diplock, Scarman, Roskill and **Brightman** concurred in dismissing the appeal for the reasons given by Lord Bridge.

Appeal dismissed.

Further guidance was given by Lord Griffiths in another decision which came before the House of Lords.

Smith v Eric S Bush and Harris v Wyre Forest District Council [1989] 2 All ER 514, [1990] 1 AC 831, House of Lords

For the facts of this case, see above, p 348.

Lord Griffiths, having quoted s 11 of the 1977 Act (above, p 328), continued: It is clear, then, that the burden is on the surveyor to establish that in all the circumstances it is fair and reasonable that he should be allowed to rely on his disclaimer of liability.

I believe that it is impossible to draw up an exhaustive list of the factors that must be taken into account when a judge is faced with this very difficult decision. Nevertheless, the following matters should, in my view, always be considered.

(1) Were the parties of equal bargaining power? If the court is dealing with a one-off situation between parties of equal bargaining power the requirement of reasonableness would be more easily discharged than in a case such as the present where the disclaimer is imposed on the purchaser who has no effective power to object.

(2) In the case of advice, would it have been reasonably practicable to obtain the advice from an alternative source taking into account considerations of costs and time? In the present case it is urged on behalf of the surveyor that it would have been easy for the purchaser to have obtained his own report on the condition of the house, to which the purchaser replies that he would then be required to pay twice for the same advice and that people buying at the bottom end of the market, many of whom will be young first-time buyers, are likely to be under considerable financial pressure without the money to go paying twice for the same service.

(3) How difficult is the task being undertaken for which liability is being excluded? When a very difficult or dangerous undertaking is involved there may be a high risk of failure which would certainly be a pointer towards the reasonableness of excluding liability as a condition of doing the work. A valuation, on the other hand, should present no difficulty if the work is undertaken with reasonable skill and care. It is only defects which are observable by a careful visual examination that have to be taken into account and I cannot see that it places any unreasonable burden on the valuer to require him to accept responsibility for the fairly elementary degree of skill and care involved in observing, following up and reporting on such defects. Surely it is work at the lower end of the surveyor's field of professional expertise.

(4) What are the practical consequences of the decision on the question of reasonableness? This must involve the sums of money potentially at stake and the ability of the parties to bear the loss involved, which, in its turn, raises the question of insurance. There was once a time when it was considered improper even to mention the possible existence of insurance cover in a lawsuit. But those days are long past. Everyone knows that all prudent, professional men carry insurance, and the availability and cost of insurance must be a relevant factor when considering which of two parties should be required to bear the risk of a loss. We are dealing in this case with a loss which will be limited to the value of a modest house and against which it can be expected that the surveyor will be insured. Bearing the loss will be unlikely to cause significant hardship if it has to be borne by the surveyor but it is, on the other hand, quite possible that it will be a financial catastrophe for the purchaser who may be left with a valueless house and no money to buy another. If the law in these circumstances denies the surveyor the right to exclude his liability, it may result in a few more claims but I do not think so poorly of the surveyors' profession as to believe that the floodgates will be opened. There may be some increase in surveyors' insurance premiums which will be passed on to the public, but I cannot think that it will be anything approaching the figures involved in the difference between the Abbey National's offer of a valuation without liability and a valuation with liability discussed in the speech of my noble and learned friend Lord Templeman. The result of denying a surveyor, in the circumstances of this case, the right to exclude liability will result in distributing the risk of his negligence among all house purchasers through an increase in his fees to cover insurance, rather than allowing the whole of the risk to fall on the one unfortunate purchaser.

I would not, however, wish it to be thought that I would consider it unreasonable for professional men in all circumstances to seek to exclude or limit their liability for negligence. Sometimes breathtaking sums of money may turn on professional advice against which it would be impossible for the adviser to obtain adequate insurance cover and which would ruin him if he were to be held personally liable. In these circumstances it may indeed be reasonable to give the advice on a basis of no liability or possibly of liability limited to the extent of the adviser's insurance cover. . . .

NOTE

It has been held that a plaintiff wishing to challenge the reasonableness of standard conditions in a contract does not have to raise the issue in the pleadings: see *Sheffield v Pickfords Ltd*, *The Times*, 17 March 1997, CA.

ARBITRATION AGREEMENTS

It is not uncommon for consumer contracts to make provision for disputes to be settled by arbitration. The Consumer Arbitration Agreements Act 1988 provided a measure of control, but this has now been repealed and replaced by the following provisions.

Arbitration Act 1996

Consumer arbitration agreements

Application of unfair terms regulations to consumer arbitration agreements
89.—(1) The following sections extend the application of the Unfair Terms in Consumer Contracts Regulations 1994 in relation to a term which constitutes an arbitration agreement.

For this purpose 'arbitration agreement' means an agreement to submit to arbitration present or future disputes or differences (whether or not contractual).

(2) In those sections 'the Regulations' means those regulations and includes any regulations amending or replacing those regulations.

(3) Those sections apply whatever the law applicable to the arbitration agreement.

Regulations apply where consumer is a legal person
90. The Regulations apply where the consumer is a legal person as they apply where the consumer is a natural person.

Arbitration agreement unfair where modest amount sought
91.—(1) A term which constitutes an arbitration agreement is unfair for the purposes of the Regulations so far as it relates to a claim for a pecuniary remedy which does not exceed the amount specified by order for the purposes of this section.

(2) Orders under this section may make different provision for different cases and for different purposes.

(3) The power to make orders under this section is exercisable—
(a) for England and Wales, by the Secretary of State with the concurrence of the Lord Chancellor,
(b) for Scotland, by the Secretary of State with the concurrence of the Lord Advocate, and
(c) for Northern Ireland, by the Department of Economic Development for Northern Ireland with the concurrence of the Lord Chancellor.

(4) Any such order for England and Wales or Scotland shall be made by statutory instrument which shall be subject to annulment in pursuance of a resolution of either House of Parliament.

(5) Any such order for Northern Ireland shall be a statutory rule for the purposes of the Statutory Rules (Northern Ireland) Order 1979 and shall be subject to negative resolution, within the meaning of section 41(6) of the Interpretation Act (Northern Ireland) 1954.

Small claims arbitration in the county court

Exclusion of Part I in relation to small claims arbitration in the county court

92. Nothing in Part I of this Act applies to arbitration under section 64 of the County Courts Act 1984.

NOTES AND QUESTIONS

1. The amount specified in s 91 has been fixed at £3,000: see the Unfair Arbitration Agreements (Specified Amount) Order 1996, SI 1996/3211, art 2. The most relevant provision of the 1994 Regulations is reg 4(4), Sch 3, para 1(q), but it seems that the effect of s 91(1) is to make any such term requiring arbitration automatically 'unfair' so that it is, in effect, on a 'black' list.
2. Many codes of practice contain provisions for conciliation and arbitration (see, generally, below, ch 8, at pp 423–5 and ch 10). If a consumer enters into such an arbitration agreement voluntarily, and the arbitrator finds in favour of the trader, does s 91 entitle the consumer to ignore the decision and sue in the county court in the hope of obtaining a more favourable outcome? What arguments might be advanced on behalf of the trader if the consumer seeks to do so?

PROTECTING THIRD PARTIES

In an earlier section on privity of contract (see p 45) it was noted that usually a third party (C) (eg an employee) is not entitled to benefit from any protection purportedly conferred on him in a contract between A and B. However, various routes to protection have been constructed whereby C becomes, in effect, a party to a separate contract. Although the main cases are commercial, they are capable of applying in a consumer context. The following hypothetical example based on a standard form contract of a cross-channel operator illustrates the point.

Passenger/Accompanied Vehicle Tickets Terms and Conditions for Carriage of Passengers and Accompanied Vehicles and Property

. . .

7. (A) The purpose of this Clause is to confer on the servants and agents of the Carrier, and on independent contractors engaged from time to time by the Carrier or its servants or agents ('Protected Persons'), the benefit of protection from liability for claims which may be made by the Passenger.

(B) By accepting this Ticket the Passenger shall be deemed to offer to the Carrier as agent for each of the Protected Persons (and the Carrier so accepts such offer) to confer on them the following protections:—

(1) Where acceptance of the offer constitutes a contract of which English law is the proper law, the benefit of every limitation of or exemption from liability, and of every defence

or immunity from claims, provided for the benefit of the Carrier under this Ticket; or

(2) In any other case, complete and total exemption from all liability and immunity from all claims howsoever arising and whether or not involving any negligence or fault on the part of the Protected Person.

(C) The consideration for such offer and for any contract made pursuant thereto shall be the provision or prospective provision by any of the Protected Persons of any services for the benefit, whether direct or indirect, of the Passenger or in connection with the performance by the Carrier of its obligations under this Ticket.

(D) Acceptance by the Carrier of such offer shall be deemed to be ratified severally by the Protected Persons (whether or not any of them has actual knowledge of the terms of the offer) upon their providing any such service as aforesaid whether or not the Passenger has notice thereof.

QUESTIONS

1. Ignoring the provisions of the Athens Convention (see below, p 388) is this clause effective in achieving its objective? Is it realistic to regard individual employees, who, for example, may deal with customers' cars, as principals of the Carrier? Is it desirable that they should enjoy such protection as the law permits to the contracting Carrier?
2. Assume that an employee has damaged a passenger's car. Would such a provision, if effective to create a contract between the employee and passenger, be subject to control under (i) the Unfair Contract Terms 1977, s 2(2), or (ii) the Unfair Terms in Consumer Contracts Regulations 1994? Note that s 2(2) will apply only to a 'business liability' (see s 1(3)) and note also the definition of 'supplier' of services in reg 2(1) of the 1994 Regulations.

NOTE

In its Report on 'Privity of Contract: Contracts for the Benefit of Third Parties' (Law Com No 242, July 1996) the Law Commission recommended modifications to the privity of contract rule which would have only a limited effect in consumer transactions: see above, pp 46–51. In such cases, the third party (C) would not be a contracting party, but would be allowed to enforce a contract made for his benefit between A and B. However, the Commission recommends (see para 10.23) that C's rights be circumscribed so that:

Where the third party seeks to rely on the test of enforceability to enforce an exclusion or limitation clause (or conceivably an analogous type of clause) he may do so only to the extent that he could have done so had he been a party to the contract (where the phrase 'had he been a party to the contract' means to refer to matters that affect the validity of the clause as between the contracting parties as well as matters affecting validity or enforceability that relate only to the third party).

There are also provisions for defences, set offs and counterclaims.

UNJUST OR UNCONSCIONABLE CONTRACTS

With the coming into force of the Unfair Terms in Consumer Contracts Regulations 1994 (see above, pp 332–6) it is less important to determine the extent to which English law grants relief against 'unjust' or 'unconscionable' bargains. Certainly, there are well-recognised areas where relief may be granted, for example under the common law of duress or the equitable rules of undue influence. These are discussed in the standard texts on the law of contract: see eg Treitel, *The Law of Contract* (9th edn, 1995), Ch 10, and Cheshire, Fifoot and Furmston, *Law of Contract* (13th edn, 1996), pp 317–33. Relief is also granted in the case of contracts which are in unreasonable restraint of trade (including contracts for exclusive services): see *A Schroeder Music Publishing Co Ltd v Macaulay* [1974] 3 All ER 616, [1974] 1 WLR 1308, HL, and Treitel, op cit, at pp 411–32. In addition, there are more specific statutory provisions the general purpose of which is to control contracts which might otherwise be unfair. Prominent examples include the Consumer Credit Act 1974, ss 137–9 (above, pp 306–13) dealing with extortionate credit bargains, and ss 67–73 which concern the cancellation of agreements concluded off business premises. In *Lloyd's Bank Ltd v Bundy* [1975] QB 326, [1974] 3 All ER 757, Lord Denning, MR sought to draw a number of categories together under the broad principle of inequality of bargaining power. However, although this may often be a relevant feature in cases of undue influence (and is an important guide on the issue of 'reasonableness' and 'fairness' in the 1977 Act and 1994 Regulations), it now seems that it is not sufficient as a free-standing principle in its own right: see, eg, *National Westminster Bank Ltd v Morgan* [1985] AC 686, [1985] 1 All ER 821. At least one other Commonwealth jurisdiction has developed a broader approach to setting contracts aside where there has been 'unconscionable' conduct: see, eg, the decision of the High Court of Australia in *Commercial Bank of Australia Ltd v Amadio* (1983) 151 CLR 447. A persuasive argument for the recognition of a general principle is to be found in Waddams, 'Unconscionability in Contracts' (1976) 39 MLR 369. Similar ideas are to be found in proposals for a general duty to trade 'fairly' (see below, ch 11, at pp 553–68).

In another example the West German Civil Code (BGB) has both a duty of good faith (para 242) (which has fed through into our Unfair Terms in Consumer Contracts Regulations 1994, reg 4(1)), and the following provision (para 138) (translation from Peden *The Law of Unjust Contracts* (1982)):

1. A legal transaction which is contrary to public policy is void.
2. A legal transaction is also void whereby a person exploiting the need, carelessness or inexperience of another, causes to be promised or granted to himself or to a third party in exchange for a performance, pecuniary advantages which exceed the value of the performance to such an extent that, under the circumstances, the pecuniary advantages are in obvious disproportion to the performance.

In addition, the Law of Standard Contract Terms of 1976 contains both a list of clauses which are invalid per se (§ 11) or unless requirements of reasonableness are satisfied (§ 10) and a further and more general provision (§ 9) (translation by Nina Galston 26 AJCL 568):

§ 9 General clauses
(1) Stipulations in standard contract terms are invalid if the contracting partner prejudices unreasonably the command of good faith.
(2) In case of doubt, an unreasonable prejudice is presumed if a stipulation
    (a) cannot be reconciled with the fundamental idea underlying the legal rule from which it deviates, or
    (b) so limits essential rights or duties inherent in the nature of the contract that attainment of the purpose of the contract is jeopardized.

For discussion of BGB paras 138 and 142 see Angelo and Ellinger, 'Unconscionable Contracts—A Comparative Study' (1979) 4 Otago LR 300 and Peden *The Law of Unjust Contracts* (1982) p 5 et seq. For discussion of the Standard Contract Terms Act 1976 see Von Marshall, 'The New German Law on Standard Contract Terms' (1979) Lloyd's MCLQ 278 and Sandrock, 'The Standard Terms Act 1976 of West Germany' (1978) 26 AJCL 551. See also below, p 494 for further extracts from the 1976 Act.

In common law jurisdictions the leading example of a broadly-based provision controlling unconscionable conduct reads as follows.

Uniform Commercial Code

Part 3. General Obligation and Construction of Contract

. . .

§ 2–302. Unconscionable Contract or Clause

(1) If the court as a matter of law finds the contract or any clause of the contract to have been unconscionable at the time it was made the court may refuse to enforce the contract, or it may enforce the remainder of the contract without the unconscionable clause, or it may so limit the application of any unconscionable clause as to avoid any unconscionable result.

(2) When it is claimed or appears to the court that the contract or any clause thereof may be unconscionable the parties shall be afforded a reasonable opportunity to present evidence as to its commercial setting, purpose and effect to aid the court in making the determination.

Official Comment

Prior Uniform Statutory Provision: None.

Purposes:
1. This section is intended to make it possible for the courts to police explicitly against the contracts or clauses which they find to be unconscionable. In the past such policing has been accomplished by adverse construction of language, by manipulation of the rules of offer and acceptance or by determinations that the clause is contrary to public policy or to the dominant purpose of the contract. This section is intended to allow the court to pass directly on the unconscionability of the contract or particular clause therein and to make a conclusion of law as to its unconscionability. The basic test is whether, in the light of the general commercial background and the commercial needs of the particular trade or case, the clauses involved are so one-sided as to be unconscionable under the circumstances existing at the time of the making of the contract. Subsection (2) makes it clear that it is proper for the court to hear evidence

upon these questions. The principle is one of the prevention of oppression and unfair surprise (cf *Campbell Soup Co v Wentz*, 172 F 2d 80, 3d Cir 1948) and not of disturbance of allocation of risks because of superior bargaining power.

. . .

NOTES

Some leading American scholars have argued that, having regard to the Official Comment to the Code, § 2–302 is concerned to protect against procedural, rather than substantive, unconscionability: see Leff, 'Unconscionability and the Code: The Emperor's New Clause' (1967) 115 U Pa LR 485. On this basis the mere existence of a harsh clause or contract, would be insufficient without exploitation of the weakness or gullibility of the other party or unfair surprise. For more recent comments, see Goldsmith, 'Enforcing the Unconscionability Doctrine' (1996) 11 Journal of Contract Law 26; Farnsworth, *Contracts* (1990), p 323 et seq and cases there cited. The following examples of the distinction between procedural and substantive unconscionability are provided by Peden in *The Law of Unjust Contracts* (1982) at p 36:

Any of the following elements may constitute procedural unconscionability: absence of meaningful choice, superiority of bargaining power, the contract being an adhesion contract, unfair surprise, sharp practices and deception. Examples of substantive unconscionability include overall imbalance, unfair price, and individual clauses which disclaim implied warranties, exclude or limit remedies, accelerate payments and give a right to enter premises, repossess or terminate without notice.

While elements of procedural unconscionability can be enumerated and discussed in the abstract, they may not make the contract unconscionable if the overall result is fair. Conversely, the courts have tended to baulk at relieving a party from a contract which has produced an unfair result unless there was present some element of procedural unconscionability.

QUESTION

In the light of the above comments are the Unfair Contract Terms Act 1977 and the Unfair Terms in Consumer Contracts Regulations 1994 concerned with (i) Procedural matters, (ii) substantive matters or (iii) both?

In spite of its open-textured wording, § 2–302 is restricted as to the remedies which may be granted. The court may (i) refuse to enforce the contract, (ii) enforce the remainder of the contract without the unconscionable clause, or (iii) so limit the application of the unconscionable clause as to avoid any unconscionable results. An example of a somewhat wider provision is contained in the New South Wales Contracts Review Act 1980 which enables a court to provide wide-ranging relief against oppressive, unconscionable or unjust contracts. (The term 'unjust' is defined by s 4(1) to include that which is 'unconscionable, harsh or oppressive' and detailed guidelines are provided by s 9.)

New South Wales Contract Review Act 1980

7. Principal relief.

(1) Where the Court finds a contract or a provision of a contract to have been unjust in the circumstances relating to the contract at the time it was made, the Court may, if it considers it just to do so, and for the purpose of avoiding as far as practicable an unjust consequence or result, do any one or more of the following:—

    (a) it may decide to refuse to enforce any or all of the provisions of the contract;

    (b) it may make an order declaring the contract void, in whole or in part;

    (c) it may make an order varying, in whole or in part, any provision of the contract;

. . .

(2) Where the Court makes an order under subsection (1)(b) or (c), the declaration or variation shall have the effect as from the time when the contract was made or (as to the whole or any part or parts of the contract) from some other time or times as specified in the order.

. . .

8. Ancillary relief.

Schedule 1 has effect with respect to the ancillary relief that may be granted by the Court in relation to an application for relief under this Act.

Ancillary relief

1. Where the Court makes a decision or order under section 7, it may also make such orders as may be just in the circumstances for or with respect to any consequential or related matter, including orders for or with respect to—

    (a) the making of any disposition of property;

    (b) the payment of money (whether or not by way of compensation) to a party to the contract;

    (c) the compensation of a person who is not a party to the contract and whose interests might otherwise be prejudiced by a decision or order under this Act;

    (d) the supply or repair of goods;

    (e) the supply of services;

    (f) the sale or other realisation of property;

    (g) the disposal of the proceeds of sale or other realisation of property;

    (h) the creation of a charge on property in favour of any person;

    (i) the enforcement of a charge so created;

    (j) the appointment and regulation of the proceedings of a receiver of property; and

    (k) the recission or variation of any order of the Court under this clause,

and such orders in connection with the proceedings as may be just in the circumstances.

2. The Court may make orders under this Schedule on such terms and conditions (if any) as the Court thinks fit.

PROBLEM

Gullible takes her old Ford car to the Downtown garage for repair saying that the engine is working badly. She asks Downtown to 'fix it'. Downtown does so at a cost of £400 which it is agreed is the going rate for the labour and materials involved. Before starting the work Downtown noticed that the car's chassis was corroded so badly that the car was fit only for scrap. However, he was glad of the work and did not say anything to Gullible until she had paid her bill. Is Downtown's conduct to be regarded as 'unconscionable'? Would it be subject to control (i) in English law, (ii) under the provisions of the New South Wales Act?

CONTROLLING THE USE OF EXEMPTION CLAUSES AND UNFAIR CONTRACT TERMS

INTRODUCTION

Although the Unfair Contract Terms Act 1977 and the Unfair Terms in Consumer Contracts Regulations 1994 are of great importance, their true effect will depend largely on the extent to which their provisions are observed in practice. If exemption, limitation or other potentially 'unfair' clauses continue to be used by businesses it is probable that most consumers will not realise that they are legally ineffective. It is clear beyond argument that many businesses (including highly reputable ones) have continued to use terms which are either void (eg attempts to exclude liability for death or personal injury resulting from negligence) or singularly unlikely to meet a requirement of 'reasonableness' or 'fairness'.

SOME TECHNIQUES OF CONTROL

A variety of techniques is available to control the use of unfair contract terms including (i) encouraging the inclusion of fairer contract terms, for example through codes of practice, (ii) subjecting standard-form contracts to a system of prior validation, (iii) seeking assurance that particular terms will not be used, and if they are not forthcoming injunctive relief, and (iv) creating criminal offences based on the use of such terms. In this and in other areas discussed in chs 9 and 11 it is likely that there will be a role for public agencies and perhaps consumer organisations. Francis Reynolds has discussed some of the above techniques and their possible application in English law when commenting on a paper presented by Professor Hellner at an Anglo-Swedish seminar in 1979. Both papers are perceptive and informative and now appear in *Law and the Weaker Party* Vol 1, editor Alan Neal (Professional Books 1981). In reading the extract it should be noted that the law has moved on somewhat, most notably in the powers accorded to the Director General of Fair Trading by the Unfair Terms in Consumer Contracts Regulations 1994, reg 8 (see above, p 334, and below, p 483). Professor Reynolds comments at p 100 et seq in relation to the Swedish Consumer Ombudsman and Market Court:

Law and the Weaker Party, Vol 1

The second line of reflection . . . concerns the Consumer Ombudsman and the Market Court. It again arises from the limited nature of the United Kingdom Unfair Contract Terms Act; for not only is that Act confined to exemption and indemnity clauses, its effect on the use of such clauses is limited to empowering courts to ignore in whole or (perhaps) in part such a clause in particular litigation. There is no power to prevent even the particular proponent from using and relying on such a clause again and again. Again, there are more extensive powers in Sweden (and Germany).

It is perhaps the central point of Professor Hellner's paper that statutory control of unfair contract terms tends to move from the objective of 'weeding out' unfair terms into that of promoting suitable contract relations: 'The policy of counteracting unfair contract terms recedes behind a policy of providing suitable contract rules.' But this leads to legislation which is either too detailed; or refers to vague and shifting standards such as 'reasonableness'; or in the effort to provide rules for every type of a particular contract adopts a compromise which is appropriate only to some cases, and may be too strong or weak for others. The only solution, he suggests, is the adoption of a two-stage system, with a first-level official or body (in Sweden the Consumer Ombudsman) who is able to refer at a secondary level to some form of administrative, legal or quasi-legal body with coercive powers (the Market Court). It should be noted that the Swedish system does not involve prior validation of terms (an experiment tried in Israel and normally reported as not successful[1]), but rather a mechanism for prior (or subsequent) invalidation. In Sweden the first level negotiations are conducted by a Governmental official and the second level powers exercised by a body which is at least quasi-legal: this may be contrasted with the system under the German *AGB-Gesetz* where the first level is in a sense entrusted to private consumer and commercial organizations and the second to the ordinary courts. The orders made under the German Law seem however to have a more general effect than the injunctions issued by the Market Court, and this is strengthened by provisions for the official registration of judgments against particular clauses.[2]

There is of course no system of either type in the United Kingdom: but what is worth noting and is indeed striking is that most of the ingredients of the Swedish system exist here somewhere, if differently arranged. There is a Governmental official who exercises some measure of first-level control over contracts, the Director-General of Fair Trading (who also of course has functions in relation to uncompetitive trade practices); and he is reinforced in some cases at least by a special court, the Restrictive Practices Court (and it should be noted that the Swedish Market Court was originally created to deal with Restrictive Practices, its consumer functions being a later addition). These powers are not, of course, confined to exemption clauses. Although the Director-General has no power officially to approve contract terms, he is specifically required by the Fair Trading Act 1973[3] to encourage the adoption of codes of practice safeguarding the interests of consumers; and several have in fact been produced. It is true that there are limits on this. The Codes are only voluntary. Disapproval by the Director-General can only remove the privilege of stating that the Code was prepared in consultation with the Office of Fair Trading. The Director-General also has power to bring persons and bodies before the Restrictive Practices Court,[4] but only in the case of persistent breaches of the criminal or civil law detrimental to consumers, as the undertakings secured, printed in his Annual Report, show. There is no power, for example, to require a trader not to use contract terms which are plainly contrary to the Unfair Contract Terms Act, or have been held unreasonable by a court. In such and related cases there are only indirect powers—perhaps reluctance to issue a licence under the Consumer Credit Act 1974 to a trader whose terms of business are unsatisfactory; where the terms used fall within the definition of a restrictive trade practice, to secure their alteration as a prerequisite to reporting to the Secretary of State that they are not of such significance as to call for investigation by the Court.[5] On the other hand there is one power which is perhaps novel: it has been termed 'acceleration of the legislative machinery'.[6] The

Director-General has power to make recommendations for the prohibition of specific practices by delegated legislation. . . . But the Fair Trading Act 1973 itself creates a special procedure for the creation of delegated legislation by way of a referral to a special body, the Consumer Protection Advisory Committee. It does however appear from the outside as if the procedure is cumbersome: and the statutory Orders which have emerged make illegal particular practices very specifically defined in the tight style of English Parliamentary draftsmen.[7] Nevertheless, once a practice has been made illegal by this method, the Director-General can take those who continue in it to the Restrictive Practices Court.

So the ingredients are there, but disordered.

[1] See Hondius, (1978) 26 Am J Comp L 525, 529–32; Berg, (1979) 28 ICLQ 560.
[2] See in general von Marschall, [1979] Lloyd's Maritime and Commercial Law Quarterly 278.
[3] s 124(3).
[4] s 35.
[5] Under the Restrictive Trade Practices Act 1976, s 21(2).
[6] Hondius, (1978) 26 Am J Comp L 525, 547.
[7] They are the Mail Order Transactions (Information) Order 1976 (SI 1976 No 1812) which requires disclosure of advertisers' addresses; the Consumer Protection (Restrictions on Statements) Order 1976 (SI 1976 No 1813, amended by SI 1978 No 127), which prohibits certain wrong or misleading statements by sellers as to consumer rights; and the Business Advertisements (Disclosure) Order 1977 (SI 1977 No 1918), which prohibits business advertisements so presented as to appear private advertisements.

Of course none of the techniques mentioned by Professor Reynolds is without its difficulties.

Promoting fair contract terms

Many of the codes of practice associated with the Office of Fair Trading contain provisions which are intended to promote the use of fair contract terms. The following are examples:

Code of Practice for domestic laundry and cleaning services

Exclusion Clauses
15. Any clause which is intended unreasonably to exclude, limit or restrict the launderer's/cleaner's legal liability is contrary to the Code and will be in certain cases unenforceable at law. Members of the Association will therefore not attempt to restrict either their liability for certain types of damage caused by their negligence, or the amount of fair compensation which they will pay. They may however wish to ask the customer, at the time the article is accepted, for an indication of the value which the customer places on the article; this may be done when the article is clearly of exceptional value or of unusual manufacture (see para 20).

Owner's Risk Clauses
16. These clauses are only inconsistent with the Code if their effect may be to exclude, limit or restrict legal liability; in such cases they may also be unenforceable at law. There may be certain articles however, such as curtains, where the Member can foresee that some damage may be an inevitable consequence of the application of the laundering, drycleaning or dyeing process even though that process will be expertly applied. In such cases therefore the Member may ask the customer to acknowledge (in writing) his acceptance of the risk of such damage occurring.

Acceptance of this risk by the customer will not relieve the Member from liability if he is negligent and so this procedure is in complete accordance with the Code.

Code of Practice: Vehicle Body Repairs

Guarantee

5.5(a) The repairer shall provide a written guarantee in respect of workmanship and materials (which will not detract from a customer's rights under the Supply of Goods and Services Act 1982 and at Common Law) to exchange or repair any defective parts which need replacement or repair by reason of defective material or workmanship during repair.

5.5(b) (i) The guarantee in respect of workmanship shall be for a period of not less than twenty-four months or 24,000 miles use whichever occurs first from the date on which the repairs were executed. Any exclusion should be drawn to the customer's attention.

(ii) The guarantee in respect of materials shall be for a period of either:—

Twenty-four months or 24,000 miles use, whichever occurs first from the date on which the repairs were executed; or in respect of repairs undertaken using materials which are subject to a manufacturer's guarantee for the period of such guarantee; whichever of the two periods occurs first from the date on which the repairs were executed.

Any exclusion should be drawn to the customer's attention

5.5(c) This period shall be extended to compensate for any prolonged period that a vehicle is off the road for rectification of faults or further work which is required as a result of previous workmanship being defective. This should also apply in the case of repetition outside the guarantee of a fault which had previously been the subject of rectification work during the guarantee period.

5.5(d) The repairer should permit the transfer of the unexpired portion of any valid guarantee to subsequent owners. This would apply only to the work actually carried out by the repairer and which was detailed in the original specification for repair. No claim will be met under this guarantee if the vehicle has been:

5.6(a) Used for competitions, racing or record attempts or otherwise than for private or commercial use of the owner, or other users with his permission;

5.6(b) damaged by wear and tear, neglect, corrosion (other than that covered by the manufacturer's warranties at 5.8), improper use or failure to maintain in accordance with the manufacturer's recommendations, or abused in any way;

5.6(c) damaged in any subsequent accident.

Codes of practice are discussed below ch 10.

Prior validation

This technique was discussed in some detail by the Law Commission in its Second Report on Exemption Clauses (Law Com No 69 paras 290–314) and rejected. The Commission felt that the advantages of such a system, including the fostering of certainty, were outweighed by the disadvantages. There are indeed practical and theoretical problems in any attempt to apply a test of reasonableness in the abstract. As the Law Commission noted (para 311), the circumstances which are relevant, for example the relative strength of the bargaining positions of the contracting parties, are much easier to apply in 'the particular circumstances of a particular contract between particular parties' than in a vacuum. This is true but it is easy to overstate the difficulties. In particular it is probable that most consumers entering standard-form contracts do so against a background of broadly similar strength (or weakness) when compared with the supplier of the goods or services in question. Nevertheless most commentators seem to agree that the most frequently cited example of a system of prior validation, the Israeli Standard Contracts Law (ISCL) 1964, has been something of a failure. For comments on this provision, see Deutsch, *Unfair Contracts* (1977), at pp 246–7; Berg, 'The Israeli Standard Contracts Law 1964' (1979) 28 ICLQ 560. Interestingly, Sir Gordon (now Lord) Borrie commented when Director General of Fair Trading that: 'It is perhaps unfortunate that this idea [that is, prior validation] was not pursued': see Borrie, 'Standard Form Contracts in England' [1978] JBL 317 at p 323.

Injunctive Relief

An alternative technique is to seek assurances from, and if necessary injunctive relief against, individual traders who use unenforceable contract terms.

As has been noted (see above, p 375), the Unfair Terms in Consumer Contracts Regulations 1994, reg 8, contain important provisions to prevent the continued use of unfair terms. The text is set out above: see p 334. In a recent bulletin the Office of Fair Trading has described the Director-General's role as follows:

Unfair Contract Terms (Issue No 1, May 1996) (Office of Fair Trading)

The role of the Director General of Fair Trading

1.1. The Unfair Terms in Consumer Contracts Regulations are a major addition to the United Kingdom's consumer protection legislation, giving the Director General of Fair Trading important new responsibilities. Essentially, the new Regulations give him the role of preventing business suppliers of goods and services from continuing to use unfair terms in their standard-form contracts with consumers. They implemented the 1993 European Community Directive on Unfair Contract Terms. In the Regulations themselves the building blocks that make up his powers and duties are set out in Regulation 8, as follows: *a duty to consider complaints and to consider whether standard form contract terms are unfair; a right to go to court to prevent the continued use, and recommendation for use of any unfair terms; a right to have regard to undertakings by the parties in deciding whether to take legal action; an obligation to give reasons for his decisions whether or not to apply for a court order; widely-drawn powers to give out information and advice about the operation of the Regulations.*

1.2. The Director General can act, however, only if he receives complaints, and he has a duty to take up every one—although those that are merely frivolous and vexatious can be filtered out. While complaints from consumers generally provide some first-hand evidence of *actual* detriment, that is not necessary to trigger action under the Regulations. It is enough simply to show that standard contract terms used by traders have the *potential* to be unfair. To date, apart from consumers themselves, local authority Trading Standards Departments have been the main source of the complaints that have been received.

1.3. In practice, the Director General's responsibilities are handled on a day-to-day basis by a specialist group set up within the Office of Fair Trading (OFT), and known as the Unfair Contract Terms Unit (the Unit).

. . .

When do we resort to legal proceedings?

1.7. The Director General's sanction against unfair terms is to apply to the courts for an injunction or an interdict to stop them being used in the future. This is the last resort, but where it does prove necessary to warn suppliers that proceedings will be started, that warning will invariably be followed through. An injunction can be sought against anyone (such as a trade association) recommending the use of the unfair terms.

1.8. The Director General may 'have regard' to undertakings about the use of unfair terms. But this does not mean that a supplier with unfair contract terms faces the stark choice between formal undertakings or legal proceedings. We seek voluntary change. While we aim to be robust in applying the Regulations we are not inflexible in our dealings with suppliers. We pursue a fair administrative process of negotiation. We open a dialogue with the business involved and only when this proves unsuccessful and unconstructive will we move on to the formal legal process. . . .

1.9. When we identify unfair terms in consumer contracts we invite the supplier to modify or drop them. We may ask for more information before making a decision about unfairness. Where the supplier belongs to a trade association, we may find it appropriate to approach that body as well. It is to the credit of suppliers that most, to date, have been willing to co-operate with us to improve their standard terms and conditions. While we have no authority to draft terms for individual suppliers (a task for which, in any event, we do not have the resources), we assist as much as we can by pointing them in the right direction.

1.10. The process of negotiation produces change by voluntary agreement that is hidden from view. This Bulletin has been designed to draw attention to some of the more noteworthy cases that we have dealt with, so opening up the assessment process to a wider audience for information and discussion.

1.11. One of the key mechanisms of effective enforcement is publicity—the more widely that people are aware of the right to fairness and equity in standard contract terms, the more effective the Regulations are likely to be in promoting change. Accordingly, one of our main objectives, particularly before they came into force on 1 July 1995, was to draw attention to the Regulations and to encourage businesses to review their standard-form consumer contracts in the light of the new law. After 1 July, the balance of the Unit's activities shifted to enforcement, in response to a steady flow of complaints.

. . .

Which suppliers use unfair contract terms?

1.19. In the main it is smaller suppliers who have shown least awareness of the Regulations, although a number of firms with household names continue to make use of unfair terms. In our experience, most instances of unfair terms appear to be as much the result of excessive caution on the part of suppliers as of a deliberate wish to deny consumers a fair deal. In many cases, suppliers have told us that they would not normally rely on an unfair term in practice, but they retain it 'just in case'. They have generally proved willing to co-operate in bringing their terms and conditions in line with the Regulations when we point out the potential for unfairness. We have not, so far, had to initiate any legal proceedings. (One company has agreed to give undertakings as an alternative to our taking legal action. At the time of writing, the precise terms of the undertakings were still being finalised. The case will be reported in the next Bulletin.)

1.20. We are resolute in our aim of persuading business to discontinue the use of unfair contract terms. As Part 3 of this Bulletin shows, we have already had success in improving standard contract terms in a wide range of businesses including supermarket car washes, caravans, holiday caravan sites, travel, motor car retailing, furniture and carpets, and double glazing.

Relationship with government and other regulators

1.21. The Regulations do not apply to any term incorporated in order to comply with, or which reflects, statutory or regulatory provisions of the United Kingdom. However, the preamble to the EC Directive requires that Member States ensure that unfair terms are not included in such national provisions, 'particularly because this Directive also applies to trades, businesses or professions of a public nature'. The Director General will therefore advise government departments and regulators about the application of the Regulations to standard terms in consumer contracts which may escape assessment for unfairness under the Regulations because of the application of statute or regulatory authority. The OFT maintains regular contact with other regulatory bodies and ombudsmen, and with consumer bodies, including the Consumers' Association and the National Consumer Council.

. . .

More recently the following extract contains more information about the objectives and contents of the bulletins.

Annual Report of the Director-General of Fair Trading 1996, p 32

The Unfair Contract Terms Bulletin

The decisions made under the Unfair Terms in Consumer Contracts Regulations 1994 can have widespread repercussions, and are of interest to both suppliers and consumer advisers. During the course of 1996 the OFT published the first two issues of *Unfair Contract Terms*, a periodical bulletin about its work under this important new piece of legislation.

One of the bulletin's primary functions is to record the details of those contracts that have been improved to bring them into line with the requirements of the regulations. Without such a record, effective monitoring and enforcement on a nationwide basis would be much more difficult. There have, for example, been instances where local trading standards departments have drawn the OFT's attention to the continued use of unfair terms—despite earlier pledges that they would be dropped. In some cases, these lapses have proved to have been wilful, in others the firms concerned have blamed communication problems with branches or subsidiaries.

Another of the bulletin's objectives is to provide reference material about the kind of unfair terms that are pursued under the legislation, and to show by example how they can be modified to remove their potential to work to the detriment of consumers. The underlying intention here is to help businesses understand the thrust of the regulations, and to provide suppliers and consumer advisers with signposts to the meaning of 'unfairness' in this context. A third aim is to promote a greater public awareness of the regulations and to give notice to suppliers that unfair contract terms will be pursued. The regulations will be more effective in promoting change if consumers are conscious of the right to fairness in standard contract terms. The bulletin also promotes well-informed discussion about a new area of law.

Case reports in the bulletin show that unfair terms are widely used and that they are particularly prevalent in market sectors which are historically prone to give rise to consumer dissatisfaction—such as double glazing and kitchen installation, bathroom installation and plumbing, home furnishings, and travel. Other clusters of complaints—such as those about wedding arrangements, including contracts for banqueting, wedding dresses, and car hire—are more surprising. Liability exclusion notices are also in common use.

Issues Nos 1 and 2 of the bulletin each included articles on particular aspects of the regulations. The first discusses the common use of 'entire agreement' clauses which purport to limit a supplier's obligation to respect commitments made by its agents. Such clauses may encourage a trader to allow its employees to win sales by making false promises and representations, and so enable it to disregard a reasonable promise made in good faith—such as a delivery date—when it becomes inconvenient. The article points out that most entire agreement clauses seen by the OFT have the potential for unfairness under the regulations. Bulletin No 2 includes an article on the requirement that contracts should be in plain and intelligible language. It discusses the OFT's approach to enforcement, the use of specialist jargon, style, structure and the use of small print, and the importance of plain language in the context of ensuring that consumers have the opportunity to examine contract terms before they are contractually committed. It concludes that the use of obscure language and small print (so often found in tandem) is futile, if not counter-productive, and should be jettisoned.

The bulletins also give details of a total of 62 contracts where, at the request of the OFT, all unfair terms had been dropped or suitably amended to bring them into line with the requirements of the regulations. By the end of 1996 action had been completed on a further 39 cases (details of which are given in bulletin No 3, published in March 1997). In 1996, in lieu of legal proceedings, a total of nine undertakings, affecting five businesses, were also given to the Director General. These are reproduced in full in the bulletins, but brief details are given in Appendix B.1.

NOTES

1. Although the bulk of the work of the Unfair Contract Terms Unit appears to concern 'small suppliers', there have also been examples of legitimate complaints about firms with national reputations (eg retail stores, an oil company and local authorities). The bulletins issued by the OFT contain much valuable (if disturbing) information, grouping the specimen terms under headings which correspond to the paragraphs in Schedule 3 to the Regulations (the 'grey' list), with further examples of terms which are not in plain and intelligible language. The bulletins also contain guidance on standard terms with potential for unfairness in particular sectors (eg double glazing and home improvements) and the text of undertakings given to the Director-General under reg 8(3).

2. The Director-General of Fair Trading is the only person upon whom a power is conferred by reg 8(2). The question whether this is consistent with the corresponding Directive is raised in a later chapter (at pp 483–4), as is the possibility of extending the power to consumer organizations.

A further example of a somewhat different approach is to be found in the following provision in Swedish law:

Swedish Consumer Contract Terms Act (1994)

General provisions

Section 1

This Act applies to contract terms used by businessmen when they offer goods, services or other utilities to consumers.

The Act also applies to contract terms used by businessmen when they convey such offers from a businessman or someone else.

Section 2

In this Act:

consumer: means any natural person mainly acting for purposes falling outside business activity,

businessman: means any natural or legal person acting for purposes related to his or its business activity, irrespective of whether it is public or private.

Market law rules

Section 3

If a contract term referred to in Section 1 is unfair towards the consumer, having regard to price and other circumstances, the Market Court may prohibit the businessman from using the same or substantially the same terms in the future in similar cases, provided the prohibition is called for in the public interest or is otherwise in the interest of consumers or competitors.

A prohibition may also be issued to employees of the businessman and to others acting on behalf of the businessman.

An association of businessmen using or recommending the use of an unfair contract term may be prohibited from using or recommending the term in the future.

A prohibition shall be made subject to a default fine unless this is, for special reasons, unnecessary.

Section 4

An issue concerning prohibition is dealt with by the Market Court upon the application of the Consumer Ombudsman. If the Consumer Ombudsman in a particular case decides not to make any application, an application may be made by an association of businessmen, consumers or wage- or salary-earners.

Section 5

A decision on an issue concerning prohibition does not prevent the same issue being reconsidered provided it is justified by changed circumstances or some other special reason.

Section 6

If there is a special reason, a prohibition may also be issued for the period pending a final decision being taken.

Section 7

An issue concerning prohibition may, in cases which are not of major importance, be determined by the Consumer Ombudsman by issuing to a person who may be assumed to have used an unfair contract term a prohibition order for approval immediately or within a certain period (prohibition order).

If a prohibition order is approved, it applies as if it were a prohibition of the Market Court. However, approval after the time prescribed by the order is not valid.

More detailed provisions concerning prohibition orders are issued by the Government.

. . .

Professor Hellner has commented as follows on an earlier version of this provision: see *Law and the Weaker Party* (Vol 1, editor Alan Neal), pp 89–90.

The Act to Prohibit Improper Contract Terms

The Act to Prohibit Improper Contract Terms, which dates from 1971, has been mentioned already.[1] At present it constitutes the most important weapon in Sweden for combating unfair contract terms. Under this Act, a special Court, the Market Court (which has other tasks as well), can issue injunctions against the future use of terms which are considered improper. Such an injunction may only be issued against a merchant, and the power of the Market Court is limited to contracts where the other party is a consumer. The injunction must be directed against a particular merchant (or an employee of a merchant), and it will prohibit him from using the term found improper, or anything which constitutes essentially that same term, in the future. If the merchant does not comply with the injunction, he will be liable to pay a monetary penalty, the amount of which is set in association with the issuing of the injunction.

An injunction has effect only in relation to the merchant against whom it is directed. It does not invalidate the term found improper, even if the merchant uses it after the injunction has been issued. Any other merchant, against whom no injunction has been issued, may also use the same term, and he can do so without risk of any penalty until he himself is made the subject of an injunction. However, it is possible that in such a case a court will set the term aside, under § 36 of the Contracts Act.

. . .

The Act does not apply only to standard terms, since individual terms, too, may be made subject to injunctions. However, in practice, the terms to which the Act is applied are standard terms; it is not worth taking up individual terms for consideration. A term can be made the subject of an injunction even if it does not yet form part of a contract; it is sufficient that it is included when the merchant presents an offer for a contract . . .

[1] Lag om förbud mot oskäliga avtalsvillkor (SFS 1971: 112). The following survey is based on the author's report 'Non-judicial control of standard terms' for the 8th Colloquy of European Law, Neuchatel, 6–8 June 1978, arranged by the Council of Europe. Parts of the report are reproduced verbatim.

The criminal law

The final technique to be noted here is the creation of criminal offences based on the use of void or unenforceable terms. In principle it may be argued that any such power should be used sparingly and only in relation to terms which are unambiguously void. The demands of certainty in the criminal law must preclude any question of creating offences based on the use of terms which are unenforceable only if they fail to satisfy a test of reasonableness (for example under ss 2(2) or 3 of the Unfair Contract Terms Act, above). In English law Part II of the Fair Trading Act 1973 (below, p 538) confers a power to create offences where it can be established that a practice operates to the economic detriment of consumers but this has been used only infrequently. The scope and interpretation of one such offence based on the use of void terms is to be seen in the following case.

Hughes v Gillian Hall, Hughes v Owen Hall [1981] RTR 430, Queen's Bench Division

Donaldson LJ. These are two appeals by case stated from the decisions of Staffordshire Justices who were confronted with charges against the two defendants alleging offences under article 3(*d*) of the Consumer Transactions (Restrictions on Statements) Order 1976, as amended, and section 23 of the Fair Trading Act 1973.

The facts which gave rise to these offences were that both defendants were involved in a second-hand car business, and they sold cars in circumstances in which the purchasers were given documents which included the magic phrase 'sold as seen and inspected'.

It was argued before the justices that the giving of such a document did not offend against the Order of 1976 and the justices came to the conclusion that that submission was well founded.

In order that the justices' conclusion and my view may be understood, it is necessary to refer first of all to the Order of 1976. The relevant paragraph is in the article 3, which provides:

'A person shall not, in the course of business . . . (*d*) furnish to a consumer in connection with the carrying out of a consumer transaction or to a person likely, as a consumer, to enter into such a transaction, a document which includes a statement which is a term of that transaction and is void or inconsistent as aforesaid, or, if it were a term of that transaction or were to become a term of a prospective transaction, would be so void or inconsistent.'

The reference to the document being 'void . . . as aforesaid' is a reference to an earlier part of article 3 namely, paragraph (*c*) as amended consequent on section 6 of the Unfair Contract Terms Act 1977. The other thing which is to be said before leaving article 3(*d*) is that it is important to notice that it applies to a document furnished not only in connection with or as part of a transaction, but to a document including a term which *might* have been included in the contract and, if so included, would have been void under section 6 of the Act of 1977. The use of the word 'void' perhaps is not as happy as it might have been, because the effect of section 6 of the Act of 1977 is perhaps not to avoid the term but to prevent the term having the effect contemplated by the section.

Section 6(2) of the Unfair Contract Terms Act 1977 provides:

'As against a person dealing as consumer, liability for breach of the obligations arising from—(a) section 13, 14 or 15 of the "—Sale of Goods Act 1893—" . . . (b) section 9, 10 or 11 of the "—Supply of Goods (Implied Terms) Act 1973—" . . . cannot be excluded or restricted by reference to any contract term'.

The justices stated:

'We were of the opinion that the defendant would be guilty if he had furnished a statement which was void by virtue of section 6(2) of the Unfair Contract Terms Act 1977.'

That conclusion thus far is accepted by both parties. They go on to state:

'The statement "sold as seen and inspected" would be void if its effect was to exclude the consumer's legal rights.'

I think that perhaps, subject to adding 'under the Sale of Goods Act', that too would be accepted by both parties. Then the justices . . . continue:

'The consumer's legal rights would not be avoided because the term used is too vague, it does not express clearly what its intention is, and if construed strictly, against the defendant's interests, and without extrinsic evidence, it would not enable the defendant to avoid civil liability. The term would not, therefore, be void by virtue of the above Act, and accordingly we upheld the submissions of no case to answer and dismissed the two informations.'

It is that last conclusion which lies at the heart of this appeal. It is said by counsel for the defendants that the justices are not only right in saying that the term is too vague, but that it would have no effect anyway. If the car was sold by description, it would make no difference to the purchaser's right, that the implied warranty of description was negatived. He could rely upon the express terms of the contract. He says again that, if the buyer in fact examines the goods before the contract is made, then there is no warranty as to merchantability as regards defects which that examination ought to have revealed. Similarly he says in relation to section 14(3) of the Act of 1893 that there is no implied warranty of fitness for a particular purpose, unless the buyer expressly or by implication had made known to the seller the particular purpose for which the goods are bought. If the purchaser did make the purpose known, then this clause will not affect the matter one way or another.

I do not accept these submissions. I think that, if a clause was included in the contract saying 'sold as seen and inspected', prima facie and subject always to what else might be expressly said in the contract, that would negative a sale by description. It would be a sale of a specific object as seen and inspected. That would exclude the implied warranty under section 13 of the Sale of Goods Act 1893 and whether or not or how much it left in the way of an express obligation would depend upon the rest of the contract. For example, it would still be open to the purchaser to complain that he got a different car from the one he had seen and inspected. But in my judgment he would lose some of his rights, even if he might still have other rights. This to my mind is quite sufficient to create an offence under this Act, because anything which has that effect would be voided by section 6(2) of the Unfair Contract Terms Act 1977.

For these reasons I think that the justices were incorrect.

I have not expressly referred to their suggestion that it was too vague. It must be implicit in what I have said that it is not too vague. The clause has to be considered in the context of people who buy and sell secondhand cars, and not in the context of marine insurance brokers. In the context in which it is used, I have no doubt as to what it should be understood as meaning.

I would allow the appeal.

Bingham J. I agree.

Appeal allowed with costs. Case remitted to the justices with a direction to continue the hearing.

NOTES

1. In *Cavendish-Woodhouse Ltd v Manley* (1984) 148 JP 299, 82 LGR 376, QBD, it was held that the words 'bought as seen' on a cash sale invoice for furniture did not contravene the above provision. In the judgment of the court the words merely confirmed that the purchaser had seen the goods that he had bought. They did not purport to exclude implied terms as to fitness or quality in respect of defects which had not been seen. At best this distinction is a very fine one.

2. In addition to the offence indicated by the above case, article 3 of the Order applies also to a person who displays on business premises a notice containing a statement purporting to apply a term which would be void by virtue of s 6 of the 1977 Act. There are similar provisions for void terms in advertisements or on the goods themselves or their containers. (For article 5 of the Order which is concerned with manufacturers' guarantees see above, p 275).

Consider the following cases in terms of any potential liability arising by virtue of article 3 of the 1976 Order and the Fair Trading Act:

1. Angus runs a corner shop where he has a prominent notice reading: 'Goods Cannot be Exchanged: Examine your Change: Mistakes Cannot be Rectified'.
2. Art, a car dealer, agrees to sell and Bert, a private purchaser, to buy a second-hand car standing on Art's forecourt. Its mileometer reading is 25,000 miles but Art has placed a sticker above it stating: 'Mileage Not Guaranteed'. The terms of the written contract provide that 'The Buyer shall inspect the goods and buy in Reliance on his Own Judgment. No Liability can be accepted for Defects which are Discoverable on Inspection'.

   Would it affect the position if the car (a) had done 55,000 miles or (b) was badly corroded as should have been obvious on inspection?
3. Pancho runs a car-hire business. The terms of his standard-form contract provide inter alia that 'No Liability can be Accepted for any Damage Loss and Inconvenience resulting from the use of vehicles However Caused'.
4. Montagu runs a safari park a main feature of which is a pride of lions. At the entrance to the park is a large notice stating: 'DANGER. Visitors Enter the Park at their Own Risk. No Liability can be accepted for Personal Injury However Caused.'

SOME EXEMPTED CONTRACTS

Not all contracts are within the scope of the Unfair Contract Terms Act 1977 or the Unfair Terms in Consumer Contracts Regulations 1994 and indeed some of the exempted contracts are of particular importance to consumers. In this section a brief reference is made to contracts of insurance, and contracts for the carriage of passengers and their luggage by sea and air.

CONTRACTS OF INSURANCE

By para 1(a) of Sch 1 to the 1977 Act, ss 2 to 4 of the Act do not extend to 'any contract of insurance'. Sir Gordon (now Lord) Borrie has described this exemption as 'amazing': see *The Development of Consumer Law and Policy—Bold Spirits and Timorous Souls* (1984), at p 110. It was defended by Mr John Fraser during the Committee stage of the then Avoidance of Liability (England and Wales) Bill as follows:

Insurance is excluded because, generally speaking, exemption clauses used in insurance contracts define the risk, rather than constitute real exemption clauses. Secondly, contracts of insurance involving international trade are beneficial to this country. It might put our insurance industry at a considerable disadvantage if it had to comply with the provisions of the Bill. Therefore for practical reasons Schedule 1 leaves out insurance contracts from the scope of the Bill.

(See HC Official Report, SC C, 9 March 1977, col 44.)

Contracts of insurance are not specifically exempted from the scope of the 1994 Regulations, although they may benefit in particular from reg 3(2)(a) whereby: 'In so far as it is in plain, intelligible language, no assessment shall be made of the fairness of any term which—(a) defines the main subject matter of the contract'. On the face of it, this leaves open the possibility of challenging such terms which are not in 'plain intelligible language'. This seems to be consistent with the preamble to the Directive on which the Regulations are based (which envisages that 'terms which *clearly* define or circumscribe the insured risk') shall not be open to challenge (emphasis supplied): see Council Directive 93/13/EEC.

As has been noted above (see pp 196–8), the overall position of consumer insurance contracts has been improved in relatively recent years, both through the developing case law and through the adoption of statements of practice and the work of the Insurance Ombudsman Bureau.

CARRIAGE BY SEA

The United Kingdom is a party to the Athens Convention Relating to the Carriage of Passengers and their Luggage by Sea. By s 183(1) of the Merchant Shipping Act 1995, 'The provisions of [this] Convention . . . as set out in Part I of Schedule 6 . . . shall have the force of law in the United Kingdom.' Article 7 of the Convention contains limitations to liability for death or personal injury and Article 8 for loss of or damage to luggage. These are outwith the controls both of the 1977 Act (see s 29(1)(b)) and the 1994 Regulations (see reg 3(1) and Sch 1, para (e)(ii)).

As may be expected, major shipping companies avail themselves of the benefits of these limitations. The extract which follows is taken from the conditions of such a company.

Package Contract and Booking Information

Your holiday contract with Cunard

Please note:

All the information in this brochure forms part of your Contract with Cunard for your holiday.
. . .

V Carrier's rights and obligations

Article 8
CUNARD'S OBLIGATIONS
Cunard agrees to provide the Services either itself or by sub-contracting its obligations under the Package Contract.

Article 9
LIMITATION OF LIABILITY: CUNARD AND PERFORMING CONTRACTORS
In these Conditions, Cunard excludes or limits its liability for the provision of the Services. In relation to any Performing Contractor the Passenger agrees that:

9.1. the Performing Contractor is entitled to benefit in the same way as Cunard from all exclusions and limitations of liability to which Cunard is entitled in these Conditions; and

9.2. no Performing Contractor or its employees or agents will in any circumstances have any liability to the Passenger which exceeds the liability of Cunard for any loss, death, injury or damage arising directly or indirectly from any act or default on the part of the Performing Contractor or its employees or agents during or in connection with its performance of any part of the Package Contract.

Article 10

10.1. Cunard's liability for death, injury or loss of or damage to any property of the Passenger is limited to the amounts set out in the relevant International Convention.

10.2. If the Stage of the Package during which the loss, death, injury or damage occurred is known Cunard's liability in respect of such loss, death, injury or damage will be determined by the provisions of any applicable International Convention, as amended or supplemented by the relevant national law. In such circumstances, the relevant Stage of the Package will be treated as if the Passenger had made separate and direct contract with Cunard or the Performing Contractor in respect of that particular Stage and as if the Passenger had received as evidence of that separate and direct contract any particular document which must be issued in order to make such International Convention or national law applicable.

10.3. If the Stage of the Package during which the loss, death, injury or damage occurred is not known or if no International Conventional or national law would apply, Cunard's liability for such loss, death, injury or damage will be determined by the provisions of the Athens Convention.

. . .

CARRIAGE BY AIR

Similar limitations apply to the carriage of passengers and their luggage by air. The following short extracts are concerned with loss of luggage and injury to passengers respectively.

Collins v British Airways Board [1982] 1 All ER 302, [1982] QB 734, Court of Appeal

The facts are set out in the judgment of Lord Denning MR.

Lord Denning MR. When you travel by air to a foreign country and your baggage is lost or damaged, what compensation can you recover from the airlines? Usually you can only recover a limited amount under the Warsaw Convention. Many people are aware of this limitation. So they insure so as to cover the full value. It is only a small premium. But suppose you do not insure and are relegated to the Warsaw Convention, what damages can you get? It depends on the terms of the ticket. Most of us know the procedure, but for those who do not, I will tell you what happens when you go on international carriage. You have your ticket beforehand. It is described as a 'Passenger ticket and baggage check'. It has tear-off strips for the stages of the journey. You go to the reception desk with your baggage. You keep your hand luggage to take with you on the aircraft. You put the heavier baggage onto the weighing machine. The young lady fastens the baggage tags onto the pieces and clips the corresponding tags onto your ticket. They go off down the conveyor belt. (You do not see your baggage again until you retrieve it, if you are lucky, at your destination.) The young lady hands you back your ticket with the tags clipped on it. Off you go to wait for the time when your flight is called. She may, or may not, have written anything onto your ticket, but you do not read it at that time. You probably do not read it at all, unless you do so on the aircraft for want of anything better to do.

Now suppose your luggage is lost and you sue the airline for damages. What amount of damages can you recover? According to the judge in this case, it depends on what the young lady has written on your ticket. There is a little tiny space in which she can insert the number of pieces and the weight of your baggage. If she has written something there (it is probably quite undecipherable), you can recover only a limited amount. The limit is that stated in the Warsaw Convention. But, if she has written nothing, you can recover the full value of your baggage, regardless of the Warsaw Convention. So says the judge in this case. This does seem a strange state of the law. We have to see whether it is right or not.

The facts

To come to the facts of this case. On 8 November 1977 British Airways issued two tickets to Mr and Mrs Collins for a round trip from Manchester to Los Angeles and back, with stops at London on the way out and New York on the way back. The tickets were marked plainly 'Passenger ticket and baggage check'. On the outward journey the young lady at the desk at Manchester filled in the little space for 'baggage check' with the figures '2/46', meaning two pieces weighing 46 kg.

On arrival at Los Angeles, Mr and Mrs Collins collected their two pieces quite safely. They did some shopping in Los Angeles and came back with three pieces. They arrived, however, late at the airport. There was no time to check in their baggage and put it on their plane. So they went aboard the aircraft with their tickets and no entry whatever in the little space for 'Baggage checked'. There was no time for it. They were told that the baggage would be forwarded on to Manchester by the next British Airways flight. That was done. But, owing to the delay, some thieves were able to ransack the three pieces. They stole the contents and forwarded the three pieces to Manchester. They arrived 24 hours later. When Mr and Mrs Collins took delivery of the three pieces, they were nearly empty. Thereupon Mr and Mrs Collins claimed the value of the contents, £2,000. British airways said that the limit under the Warsaw Convention was £580.20, and paid that sum into court.

It is obvious that the airline had no opportunity at all of filling in the little space on the baggage check. Nevertheless because nothing was written there, Mr and Mrs Collins claim full damages. This does seem strange to me. But it all turns on the true interpretation of the Warsaw Convention which has the force of law by s 1 of the Carriage by Air Act 1961.

[His Lordship then held that the omission to fill in the baggage check at Los Angeles was merely an 'irregularity' which did not bar the airline from claiming the benefit of the limited liability under the Convention. Hence the appeal should be allowed. **Eveleigh LJ** agreed that the appeal should be allowed. **Kerr LJ** dissented.]

Appeal allowed.

Goldman v Thai Airways International Ltd [1983] 3 All ER 693, [1983] 1 WLR 1186, Court of Appeal

The facts as stated in the headnote to the report were as follows:

The plaintiff was a passenger on a flight from London to Bangkok aboard an aircraft owned and operated by the defendant airline. During the flight the pilot failed to illuminate the seat belt sign when the aircraft entered an area for which moderate clear air turbulence had been forecast and when severe turbulence was encountered in that area the plaintiff, whose seat belt was not fastened, was thrown from his seat and sustained severe injuries. The plaintiff brought an action for damages against the defendants under the Warsaw Convention, as amended at The Hague in 1955 and as set out in Sch 1 to the Carriage by Air Act 1961. Article 22(1) of the convention limited the amount of damages recoverable to approximately £11,800, but art 25 provided that the limitation on the amount recoverable did not apply if it was shown that 'the damage resulted from an act or omission of the carrier [which was] done with intent to cause damage or recklessly and with knowledge that damage would probably result'.

The trial court judge found that the pilot's conduct fell within the provisions of Art 25 and he awarded damages of some £41,000. The defendants appealed.

O'Connor LJ. . . . A passenger injured during a flight governed by the Warsaw Convention as amended at The Hague in 1955 can recover damages up to a limited sum without proof of fault (arts 17 and 22). Article 20 allows the airline to avoid even the limited payment in certain circumstances. Article 25 allows the passenger to escape the limitation of art 22 if he proves—

'that the damage resulted from an act or omission of the carrier, his servants or agents, done with intent to cause damage or recklessly and with knowledge that damage would probably result . . .'

It must be remembered that art 22 imposes limits not only for personal injury, but also for loss of or damage to goods, so that 'the damage' referred to in art 25 may be personal injury or damage to goods. This makes the provisions of an act 'done with intent to cause damage' more readily intelligible. This provision shows that the limited recompense is to be the normal liability, and that only exceptional wrongdoing is to avoid the limit. It is in this context that the provision 'recklessly and with knowledge that damage would probably result' has to be construed.

In the present case the plaintiff had to prove that his injury resulted from an act or omission of Captain Swang, done recklessly with knowledge that damage would probably result.

The judge has found that Captain Swang flew the aircraft into an area where CAT was forecast without illuminating the seat belt sign in breach of the requirements of the airline's manual of instructions, and that in so doing he acted recklessly. This finding was based on the judge's acceptance of the evidence of the plaintiff's expert witnesses, in preference to those of the defendants, and on his assessment of Captain Swang as a witness. Having read the whole of the evidence, I would not have come to the same conclusion, but I am conscious that in this court we must be slow to differ from the findings of the trial judge which depend on his assessment of the witnesses. There was evidence that it was good practice to belt up before entering an area where moderate CAT was forecast. Equally there was evidence that careful pilots exercised a discretion and waited for tell-tale signs of light turbulence before pinning the passengers to their seats. There is not, and indeed there could not have been, a finding that that evidence was deliberately dishonest. It follows that even if I accept the judge's finding that Captain Swang's omission to light the seat belt sign was reckless, I do not think that there was any evidence from which the judge could conclude that Captain Swang had knowledge that damage would result from his omission.

I cannot construe art 25 by such considerations as wine glasses falling off trays. The damage must be connected with the act or omission, and there was no evidence that Captain Swang knew that injury to passengers would probably result from this omission. The judge seems to have thought that any sort of damage was enough. I think he fell into error in so doing. I do not think that the plaintiff came anywhere near proving that Captain Swang knew that damage would probably result, and accordingly the plaintiff cannot invoke the relief given by art 25 of the convention.

Eveleigh and **Purchas LLJ** agreed that the appeal should be allowed.

Appeal allowed. Judgment for plaintiff for £11,700. Leave to appeal refused.

NOTE

In *Sidhu v British Airways plc* [1997] 1 All ER 193 the plaintiffs had been passengers on a scheduled BA flight which was stranded at Kuwait airport following the Iraqi invasion in August 1990. The House of Lords held that the Warsaw Convention provides the sole basis for a remedy in cases falling within its scope. Accordingly, an action outside the two year time limit (see Article 29) failed.

CHAPTER 8

The enforcement of private law remedies I: some problems of individual redress

INTRODUCTION

The notable changes in substantive laws recorded in previous chapters have been intended (at least in part) to benefit consumers. But such changes, however desirable, are insufficient without genuine access to justice for those whom the laws are intended to serve. Here the record is patchy. The New Law Journal commented in September 1979:

If legislation specifically enacted for the protection of ordinary consumers is not to be seen as a mere 'paper tiger', changes in procedural law are likely to be required in aid of its enforcement. Without such changes, substantive law reform may well prove a pointless exercise. It is a measure of the failure of existing procedures that recourse to the courts is not universally available to wronged individuals. In that situation, it is manifestly a fraudulent claim that equality of access to justice is one of the hallmarks of our legal system.

The barriers to effective redress take many forms and it would be unrealistic to believe that all can be removed or even diminished significantly. The individual consumer must both perceive that he or she has a legitimate grievance and be prepared to do something about it. This will depend in part on the general level of consumer education and on access to information and advice. Many will fall at the first hurdle. Redress may depend on there being an accessible procedure for dealing with 'small claims', whether through the courts or through conciliation or arbitration facilities. This in turn may be affected by the availability of legal aid. However, even the most accessible court will be a disappointment if the debtor is insolvent or if a successful plaintiff runs up against problems in enforcing a judgment debt. These and other issues of individual redress are illustrated by the materials and cases in this chapter. In the following chapter we begin with material on conditional fees which some see as an alternative to civil legal aid. Attention is then focused on some aspects of what Professor Mauro Cappelletti has termed the 'second wave of the access to justice approach', namely the problems of providing legal representation to diffuse and collective interests (see Cappelletti and Garth, 'Access to Justice: The Newest Wave in the Worldwide Movement to Make Rights Effective' (1978) 27 Buffalo LR 181, 197). Here concern is with such matters as representative and 'class' or group actions which some have found increasingly attractive as a means of dealing with collective grievances. This leads to discussion of a possible role for both consumer organisations and public agencies in taking on public interest litigation. Accordingly the ground covered by the two chapters is very extensive although it all falls within the one broad connecting theme.

There is a wealth of comparative information on these topics in the Florence 'Access to Justice' series (1978–79): see Vol 1 *Access to Justice: A World Survey* (eds M Cappelletti and B Garth); Vol 2, *Access to Justice: Promising Institutions* (eds M Cappelletti and J Weisner); Vol 3, *Access to Justice: Emerging Issues and Perspectives* (eds M Cappelletti and B Garth); Vol 4, *Access to Justice: Anthropological Perspective* (ed K F Koch). For other general surveys see I Ramsay, 'Consumer Redress Mechanisms for Poor-Quality and Defective Products' (1981) 31 Univ Toronto LJ 117; C J Miller, 'Some Problems of Individual and Collective Consumer Redress in English Law' in S D Anderman (ed), *Law and the Weaker Party* Vol II (1982) p 121; 'Barriers to Justice' (National Association of Citizens Advice Bureaux, 1995); Paterson and Goriely, *A Reader on Resourcing Civil Justice* (1996); Smith, *Justice: Redressing the Balance* (1997). Further European material is to be found in the European Commission's Green Paper, 'Access of Consumers to Justice and the Settlement of Consumer Disputes in the Single Market' (COM (93) 576 final) of 16 November 1993; see also the subsequent Commission Communication 'Action Plan on Consumer Access to Justice and the Settlement of Consumer Disputes in the Internal Market' (COM (96) 13 final) of 14 February 1996.

PROBLEMS AND COMPLAINTS

The Annual Reports of the Director General of Fair Trading provide information about the range and quantity of complaints in any given year. The relevant tables are derived from information supplied by local authority trading standards and environmental health departments and other local advisory agencies. Although such figures are helpful, there is no doubt that they represent only the tip of the iceberg. Faced with such problems, many consumers will simply do nothing. Others will take a conscious decision to transfer their custom elsewhere ('exit' as it is sometimes known) and others will voice their complaint only to their supplier. None of these will appear in the returns from which the Office of Fair Trading figures are derived. The point is recognised and elaborated on in the following extract.

Consumer Redress Mechanisms (Office of Fair Trading, November 1991)

. . .

2.3. The use of . . . redress mechanisms is more the last resort than the first step for consumers pursuing a complaint. The first action of most consumers will generally be to take up their complaint with their supplier. If they fail to gain immediate satisfaction they may press their case again with the supplier, or even the manufacturer, and possibly seek the support or advice of a Trading Standards Department, a Citizens Advice Bureau or a consumer organisation specific to the sector. If they still remain dissatisfied, they may then resort to the appropriate redress mechanisms.

2.4. OFT surveys had brought out some very relevant findings:—

(a) *many consumers have complaints*
   The OFT's surveys have consistently indicated that over 40% of the adult population had cause for complaint about goods or services supplied in any twelve month period.

(b) *high proportions take actions with suppliers*
   Of those with cause for complaints, about three in every four take their complaint up with their suppliers, and the same proportion applies overall to both the goods sectors and the services sectors. Across the individual goods sectors in particular, the percentages taking action are higher in those sectors where the price of the goods supplied is higher.

(c) *the success rates of such actions vary with sectors*
   Across the goods sectors as a whole, over two-thirds of those taking action with suppliers do achieve satisfaction. The success rates tend to be greater in the food and drink, footwear, clothing and toys and games sectors than in the household appliance, furniture and motor vehicles sectors, where the average costs of the goods supplied tends to be higher.

   For the services sectors as a whole, the average success rate is much lower, with less than one-third of consumer actions with suppliers being successful. The success rates are particularly low in the building, holidays and professional services sectors.

(d) *relatively small numbers of consumers use the redress mechanisms*
   Despite the high levels of consumer dissatisfaction remaining after actions with suppliers, only small numbers of consumers do resort to the redress mechanisms. OFT survey work indicates that fewer than one in a thousand of all consumers, or under ¼% of those with complaints, use the redress mechanisms.

   Statistics of consumer use of particular mechanisms are not comprehensive and may be open to different interpretations. Those available suggest that the consumer redress mechanisms are used by the minority, and often by a very small proportion, of dissatisfied consumers in particular sectors. For example, it has been estimated that some 12,500 consumer disputes are handled each year by the small claims procedure in England and Wales.[2] The Insurance Ombudsman handled some 1,900 complaints last year, and the conciliation machinery of the Retail Motor Industry Federation handled some 1,500 complaints with arbitration resulting in some 40 cases. Such numbers are small compared with the probable numbers of dissatisfied consumers, and the actual use of redress mechanisms appears well below the potential demand.

2.5. It can be rightly argued that in the longer-term competition between suppliers should lead to lower consumer dissatisfaction, and indeed OFT work on consumer loyalty confirms that many dissatisfied consumers will switch to alternative suppliers. Yet the forces of competition may work slowly, particularly in those sectors where competition is less intense or where monopolies exist. Moreover, they provide no present help to those consumers who have paid for shoddy goods or work or who have been the victims of malpractice.

2.6. The OFT regards the redress mechanisms as a key element in consumer protection. Not only do they enable consumers to press a complaint until its proper conclusion, but they also provide an important influence over the consumer/supplier relationship generally. Indeed the more effective a redress mechanism is the more it should be used by consumers. Paradoxically, the introduction or improvement of redress mechanisms should put pressure on suppliers to be more ready to make settlements with dissatisfied consumers, and even to improve the quality of their goods or services so that the need for such settlements is reduced.

2.7. In recent years there have been encouraging developments in redress mechanisms. More use has been made of the small claims procedures, more ombudsmen have been appointed for particular activities, more sectoral codes of practice have been introduced or improved, and new regulatory bodies have been set up in the services and utility sectors. Yet it remains a matter of some concern that more consumers do not make use of these mechanisms both to resolve their complaints and, by so doing, to influence the behaviour of suppliers and traders.

2.8. Clearly there are still many consumers who do not take up their complaints or do not follow them through. OFT research suggests some 'can't be bothered' or 'don't think it would do any good'. But underlying this is the finding that awareness amongst consumers of their rights, and in particular of the redress mechanisms available, is limited. . . .

[2] National Consumer Council, *Ordinary Justice*, HMSO 1989.

When consumers do complain there are obvious advantages in having the matter resolved without invoking the assistance of an independent third party. Indeed, an effective complaints procedure can be of considerable benefit to the company concerned. However, this can often mask the danger that the complaint is not settled on terms which are objectively satisfactory. An example is noted by Alan Milner in 'Settling Disputes: The Changing Face of English Law', (1974) 20 McGill LJ 522, 523:

One technique of dispute settlement which I shall mention but briefly is that of *settlement by inertia*. By this I mean that when a dispute arises, one party to it, although recognising the existence of the dispute, accepts a situation unfavourable to himself and does little or nothing about it. This is in all probability the most common way in which disputes are 'settled' . . . For example, I was recently told with obvious cynicism by a public relations officer in a large commercial concern that customer inertia always operated in favour of the company. More often than not, dissatisfied customers did not complain; if they did, and received no reply for some considerable time, the chances were better than 50% that they would take no further action. The company then treated the complaint as 'settled'.

A slightly more optimistic picture is suggested by another American study by Ross and Littlefield ('Complaints as a Problem-Solving Mechanism' (1978) 12 Law and Society Review 199).

It may be assumed that usually the potential consumer litigant will be at an inherent disadvantage. Some of the reasons for this which have been outlined by for example Professors Cappelletti and Garth (see (1978) 27 Buffalo LR 181, at p 186 et seq) include the greater financial resources of organisations, their ability to withstand the delays of litigation and their competence to recognise and pursue a claim of defence. Having discussed these points, the authors note a further advantage (at p 191; footnotes omitted):

Professor Galanter has developed the distinction between what he calls 'one-shot' and 'repeat-player' litigants, based primarily on the frequency of encounters with the judicial system.[1] He has suggested that this distinction corresponds to a large extent to that between individuals, who typically have isolated and infrequent contacts with the judicial system, and ongoing organizations, with a long-term judicial experience. The advantages of the repeat player, according to Galanter, are numerous: (1) experience with the law enables better planning for litigation; (2) the repeat player has economies of scale because he has more cases; (3) the repeat player has opportunities to develop informal relations with members of the decision-making institution; (4) he may spread the risk of litigation over more cases; and (5) he can utilize strategies with particular cases to secure a more favorable posture for future cases. It appears that because of these advantages, organizational litigants are indeed more effective than individuals. There are clearly fewer problems in mobilizing organizations to take advantage of their rights, often against just those ordinary people who in their posture as consumers, for example, are most reluctant to seek the benefits of the legal system.

   This gap in access can be most effectively attacked, according to Galanter, if individuals find ways of aggregating their claims and developing long-term strategies to counteract the advantages of the organizations they must often face . . .

[1] See Galanter, 'Why the "Haves" Come out Ahead: Speculations on the Limits of Legal Change' (1974) 9 Law and Society Review 95; Afterword: Explaining Litigation (1975) 9 Law and Society Review 347.

Similar points have been made by, for example, Professor Ison (see 'Small Claims' (1972) 35 MLR 18). This points to the role of group or class actions (see below, pp 458–81).

CONSUMER ADVICE AND LEGAL AID

The availability of advice and, where appropriate, of legal aid is of major importance to the effective enforcement of consumers' rights. For convenience the materials in this section are divided into two parts covering first, the role of such voluntary organisations as the Citizens' Advice Bureaux (CABx) and second professional legal advice and the civil legal aid scheme. Further very important sources of advice include the government sponsored National Consumer Council, the Consumers' Association, the National Federation of Consumer Groups and, of course, the Office of Fair Trading. The OFT publication 'Consumers' Information Needs' (February, 1991) contains useful information on the sources of and need for advice. More detailed information is contained in Harvey and Parry, *The Law of Consumer Protection and Fair Trading* (5th edn, 1996), at pp 48–54. See also the Report of the Royal Commission on Legal Services (the Benson Commission) Cmnd 7648, 1979, chs 7 and 8 especially.

CITIZENS ADVICE BUREAUX AND SIMILAR SOURCES OF ADVICE

Within the United Kingdom the principal source of local and non-specialist consumer information and advice is the Citizens Advice Bureau (CAB) service. Begun at the outbreak of war in 1939 and built on the work of existing voluntary organisations the service traditionally covers a wide field. In 1984 it was the subject of a report by Sir Douglas Lovelock and his committee who had been appointed by the Secretary of State with the following terms of reference: 'To review the functioning of the National Association of Citizens Advice Bureaux and to make recommendations, with a view to ensuring that the Association offers the best possible service and support to local citizens advice bureaux; and that the monies available to the Association are spent in the most effective way'. (See the Review of the National Association of Citizens Advice Bureaux, Cmnd 9139, 1984.) The review had been announced by Dr Gerard Vaughan, then Minister for Consumer Affairs, against a background of increased government funding to the central body of the service (NACAB). Dr Vaughan had stated earlier that he 'felt it proper to inquire if the money was being used effectively' (see Hansard 40 HC Official Report (6th series), col 676, 12 April 1983). The other aspect of concern to the Minister was 'allegations of changing attitudes within some CABs and the taking up of campaigns that some people have seen as going outside the generally accepted scope of the service' (ibid). (As to this latter point the Lovelock Committee found 'relatively few and relatively minor instances to justify this concern' (para 1.9)). The report itself contains much helpful information on the growth, work, aims and funding of the service.

After discussing the establishment of the service and a period of contraction in the years 1945–60 followed by one of resurgence and growth (including a substantial Development Grant in 1974) the report continues as follows:

Review of the National Association of Citizens Advice Bureaux, Cmnd 9139, 1984

. . .

4.16. The then Department of Trade and Industry's prime objective in offering the Development Grant to the CAB Service was to improve the availability and quality of advice on consumer matters. In accepting the grant, however, the National CAB Council made it clear that the CAB'x provided a generalist advice service and that there was therefore no question of earmarking the money for consumer matters: it would instead be used to improve the quality and coverage of the CAB Service as a whole. In this aim the National CAB Council was generally successful. It was now in a position to offer short-term funding to set up bureaux in partnership with local authorities or to pay for the improvement of existing bureaux by capital improvements, increased staff or special experimental projects. Inevitably the distribution of finance between the bureaux was somewhat uneven, since it was usually carried out on the basis of immediate need, and some areas of the country remained underprovided with advice services. But the number of bureaux and extensions in the United Kingdom as a whole increased by 33 per cent from 615 in 1973–74 to 818 in 1978–79. More significantly, demand for the CABx' services increased: enquiries went up from 1.9 million to 3.3 million, an increase of 74 per cent.

. . .

4.18. In 1979 the Minister of Consumer Affairs, Mrs Oppenheim, decided to end the scheme of Government grants to Consumer Advice Centres (CACs) from 1980. In announcing the end of the scheme Mrs Oppenheim said 'I recognise that this may lead to the closure of some centres and so increase the workload of other advisory services . . . In particular, the Citizens Advice Bureaux may well have a good part to play in the future . . . I am anxious to encourage the CAB because it is a voluntary service which is both cost effective and economical'. In

November 1979 she announced that the Department of Trade's grant to NACAB would be doubled from £1.85 million in 1979–80 to £4 million in 1980–81.

4.19. NACAB took the view that the new money should be used partly to develop support services to bureaux from Area Offices and Central Office, and partly to help those bureaux most affected by closure of CACs. It was not used, as the Development Grant had been, specifically to increase the number of bureaux, though the number did increase steadily each year. (The number rose from 859 in the United Kingdom as a whole in 1979–80 to 936 in 1982–83 (9 per cent).) Because the CACs had been concentrated in inner city areas, on Merseyside, and in the Manchester, Yorkshire and Humberside, West Midlands, South Wales and Greater London Areas, the great bulk (68 per cent) of the grants in 1980–81 went to bureaux in these Areas. Bureaux elsewhere found themselves little better off.

. . .

4.23. The Service was expanding anyway in response to the pressures of demand. During the period from 1973–74 to 1982–83 demand for advice and information increased dramatically, with enquiries going up from 1.9 million to 5 million. The type of enquiry also changed in response to changing economic and social conditions. Consumer enquiries, including debt problems, for instance, increased steadily throughout, reflecting the effect of inflation on people's income and spending patterns. In the late 1970s and early 1980s, as the recession began to bite, the fastest growing category of enquiry related to social security. A feature of these categories of enquiry was that many of the cases involved were increasingly complicated and difficult to deal with. Another feature of the development of the Service's workload during this period was an increasing involvement in representing clients at tribunals.

4.24. Under NACAB's prompting, the Service adapted to this larger and more complex workload by adopting increasingly rigorous and professional standards of performance at the bureau level and by developing a limited degree of specialization. Standards were raised by the laying down of more demanding training requirements, an increase in the minimum number of hours expected of bureau workers, the introduction of a compulsory retirement age and the encouragement of the appointment of paid Organisers in bureaux to ensure continuity and consistency of service. As far as specialization was concerned, the most notable development was the setting up of Tribunal Representation Units (TRUs) to provide technical back-up for bureau workers representing clients at tribunals. The first TRU was set up by a bureau in Newcastle in 1976 and NACAB set up another with assistance from the EEC Anti-Poverty Programme in Wolverhampton in 1976. A dozen more were set up in the next few years. The units were generally staffed by between two and five specialist workers with clerical support. Within the limitations of their catchment areas the units were successful in persuading bureaux to take on tribunal representation work (roughly half of all bureaux now do so) and, on the basis of a good track record, in encouraging claimants to bring cases to bureaux. There was also a modest degree of specialization in the field of legal services, following a NACAB Council decision in the late 1970s to encourage bureaux in the major centres to hire in-house community lawyers.

. . .

Later in the report the Lovelock Committee notes the main principles which govern the conduct of the CAB service, namely that it is impartial, confidential, free of charge, independent and generalist. It discusses its aims and what is involved in the process of giving advice as follows:

5.1. **The Aims**

The CAB Service defines its aims as being:

(a) To ensure that individuals do not suffer through ignorance of their rights and responsibilities or of the services available; or through an inability to express their needs effectively.

(b) To exercise a responsible influence on the development of social policies and services, both locally and nationally.

5.2. These aims, which are known respectively as the First and Second Aims, were approved by the Council of the National Association of Citizens Advice Bureaux (NACAB) in April 1977 after an extensive process of consultation lasting two years with Area Offices and other interested parties . . .

5.7. The First Aim

There has been a wide consensus since the Second World War that the provision of an advice service is a necessary and useful function in modern society. The need for such a service has been recognised in a series of major reports over the last 40 years. Sir William Beveridge's report on Social Insurance and Allied Services in 1942,[1] for instance, recommended that there should be an advice bureau in every local security office which could be able to tell every person in doubt or difficulty 'not only about the official provision for social security but about all the other organs—official, semi-official and voluntary, central or local—which may be able to help him in his difficulty'. The Rushcliffe Report on Legal Aid and Legal Advice[2] recommended in 1945 that the CAB Service continue to offer first level advice and help after the war. We have already referred to the recommendations in the same vein by the Younghusband, Ingleby and Molony Committees (paragraphs 4.12 and 4.13). Most recently, the Benson Commission on Legal Services[3] concluded in 1979 that a 'competent, accessible, independent national network of generalist advice agencies is needed' and that CAB's should be the 'basic generalist advice service'. It has even been asserted by the National Consumer Council in its pamphlet *The Fourth Right of Citizenship*[4] and by NACAB in representations to us that access to information and advice is a right. We accept that a citizen has a right to information on matters such as legislation which affects his life and livelihood, though such a right would be hard to define and expensive to finance. We are not convinced that the right to information implies a right to advice. However, there is no need to go so far. The operations of both the welfare state and the market economy have become bewilderingly complex and, like our predecessors in this field, we see a clear need for a generalist advice and information service.

5.8. It is sometimes assumed that a generalist advice and information service simply provides information to enquirers in the manner of, say, a tourist office. NACAB has been at some pains to explain to us that 'advice work is more than the simple activity of looking up answers to questions and telling the client what the advice worker would do if he or she were in the client's shoes'. It has been suggested that the following breakdown gives a better picture of the process of advice-giving.

(a) *Diagnosis.* This is in some ways the most important stage. The diagnosis of the problem is often straightforward, in which case the advice worker may move directly to the next stage of the process. But in a proportion of cases the client's questions do not reveal his or her real concerns and, where this is so, these concerns must be uncovered before proceeding further;

(b) *Information-giving.* The presentation of relevant facts in a way which can be understood by the client;

(c) *Advice-giving.* The presentation of the options open to the client and their implications;

(d) *Referral.* There will be some enquiries which the bureau cannot answer or which can be more appropriately answered elsewhere, in which case it should refer to a specialist agency such as a solicitor, Law Centre, Money Advice Centre, Housing Advice Centre, etc, or to the appropriate Government Department, local authority department or statutory body;

(e) *Action/Advocacy.* The worker may become involved in a direct attempt to resolve the client's problem. This may mean writing a letter or contacting an agency by telephone on behalf of the client; or just representing a client's case, for example at a tribunal hearing. These are the activities justified by the last clause of the First Aim . . .

1. Special Insurance and Allied Services, HMSO, 1942, para 397.
2. Report of the Committee on Legal Aid and Legal Advice in England and Wales, HMSO 1945, para 185.
3. The Royal Commission on Legal Services: Final Report, HMSO, 1979, para 44.5.
4. Fourth Right of Citizenship, National Consumer Council, July 1977.

Since the publication of the Lovelock Committee report in 1984 the CAB service has continued to develop through periods of financial stringency. The Annual Report of the National Association of Citizens' Advice Bureaux for 1996/97 indicates that the service handled nearly 6.5 million enquiries in that year and received 5.4 million visits by clients. A significant proportion of the enquiries (some 405,000) related to consumer issues, although the figure for social security was much higher (almost 2 million). The service now operates 720 main bureaux with a further 1026 linked outlets and it is staffed by some 28,000 people, 90 per cent of whom are volunteers. A small number of CABx employ a solicitor and around 60 per cent of main bureaux have a volunteer solicitor rota. Some CABx operate a service within county courts. So far as funding is concerned, some comes from central government (to fund the National Association) and from private sources. However, the bulk (over 80 per cent) comes from local authorities (£44.56 million in 1996–7), increasingly through contracts for local service level agreements. The Lovelock Committee found that the advantages of dual funding outweighed the disadvantages.

In a section on Litigants in Person Lord Woolf has commented as follows on the role of advice agencies in duty advice schemes:

Access to Justice: Interim Report to the Lord Chancellor on the Civil Justice System in England and Wales, June 1995, Chap 17

33. More work is required to ensure that people facing legal proceedings obtain advice before the day of the hearing. For those who fail to obtain advice beforehand, the court-based duty advice schemes provide a final opportunity for help, albeit at the last minute. Over the last decade a number of duty advice schemes have been established in the county courts, mainly as offshoots of advice agencies and law centres. In 1992, the National Consumer Council in *Court without Advice* found just over 30 such schemes, mainly in urban areas, at a time when there were 267 county courts. The schemes vary in their operation: some provide advice alone, others representation in court or help in negotiating with an opponent. Some only offer advice on the day while others will provide continuing assistance on the case. Some schemes operate on housing possession days, others extend beyond this to debt matters.

. . .

34. As the Civil Justice Review recognised, the success of duty advice schemes depends partly on court support. The Review recommended that courts provide accommodation for duty advice services (Recommendation 52(iii)). Some courts now do this, either allocating an interview room for the day or, more satisfactorily from the point of view of the schemes, a permanent place as well where files and books can be left. Courts also routinely provide a telephone and photocopying facilities. . . .

35. The Civil Justice Review recommended appointment of court officers as a link with advice agencies. Liaison on duty advice schemes should clearly be one of their important functions. Involving advice agencies in court users' committees can also help. I have received strong support from judges and court staff for duty advice schemes. They appreciate the additional help given to defendants, the impact this has on judicial decision making, and the ability to list more cases which the scheme makes possible. . . .

36. Support for duty advice schemes should be a duty of the court and of the judiciary, both in terms of providing accommodation and other resources and encouraging litigants to use them. Part-time judges should be made aware of the schemes by courts and of the need to support them through Judicial Studies Board training. The National Consumer Council identified the key role of ushers, bailiffs and other more junior court staff in channelling people to duty advice schemes. It also noted the variable quality of information and publicity about the schemes, and published detailed good practice guidelines covering the organisation and in-court operation of duty advice schemes, publicity, recruitment and training.

37. Proper funding is basic to the success of duty advice schemes. The Civil Justice Review recommended that advice agencies should be encouraged to run duty advice schemes, and if they did should be eligible for legal aid funding (Recommendation 52). The Legal Aid Board commissioned some detailed research on how many county courts had a level of business justifying a duty advice service and its potential cost. The research found that housing and debt work was concentrated in a limited number of courts (some 65 for housing and 82 for debt). Estimating the number of persons who might use the service, and the average time which might be demanded for each case, it calculated that the cost of a duty advice scheme in those courts on Green Form rates to be from £800,000 to £1.7 million. Despite these very modest amounts the resources have not been made available. I recommend that there should be a duty advice scheme funded by legal aid at each of the courts identified as handling housing and debt work. I also recommend the exploration of ways of providing more general assistance, by the provision of a Citizens Advice Bureau or similar facility at those court centres where the workload would justify it and that the possibility of legal aid funding for such a service should be considered.

(For the 'Civil Justice Review', see the *Report of the Review Body on Civil Justice* (Cm 394, 1988).

Apart from CABx and other national organisations noted above (at p 397), much advice is also given through the news media. The National Consumer Council Report on 'Information and Advice Services in the United Kingdom' (1983) contains the following general description of the scope and role of information and advice services through the 'media' (at p 32):

(e) The Media
There are numerous information—and sometimes advice—services provided by the media; for example, straightforward information items in the press; phone-ins on local radio; readers' advice columns in the national, provincial and local press; readers' advice columns in a multitude of magazines; information slots on national and regional television; information slots on national and local radio; and public service announcements. The number of people asking for information and/or advice either as a direct result of a broadcast or following media requests for people to send in their problems, shows the major role played by the media in this connection.

There is no reason to suppose that the role of the media has diminished since 1983, although the particular programmes have changed.

LEGAL AID AND ADVICE

However valuable the work of such agencies as Citizens Advice Bureaux, it must be desirable in principle that consumers should have access to specifically legal and professional advice. This is so even if one accepts that there is an element of truth in Stewart Macaulay's observation that lawyers rarely go beyond an essentially conciliatory and therapeutic role when dealing with consumers as clients (see Macaulay, 'Lawyers and Consumer Protection Laws' (1979) 14 Law and Society Review 115). In England and Wales the main source of legal advice is the legal aid scheme. This falls into four parts, namely (i) the legal advice and assistance or Green Form scheme, (ii) the civil legal aid scheme, (iii) the criminal legal aid scheme, and (iv) the scheme for 'assistance by way of representation' (or ABWOR), which allows representation in domestic and certain child care proceedings in magistrates' courts and in specified tribunals. This section is concerned with only the first two parts. More detailed discussion of the problems associated with legal aid and advice, including proposals for reform, is to be found in such sources as the Report of the Royal Commission on Legal Services (the Benson Commission), Cmnd 7648, 1979, chs 5 and 10–13 especially; the Annual Reports of the Legal Aid Board (most recently for 1996–7); the Green Paper issued by the Lord Chancellor's Department, 'Legal Aid—Targeting Need' (Cm 2854, May, 1995) and the subsequent White Paper 'Striking the Balance: The Future of Legal Aid in England and Wales' (Cm 3305, 1996); Goriely, 'The Government's Legal Aid Reforms' in Zuckerman & Cranston (eds), *Reform of Civil Procedure* (1995), ch 18; Sir Peter Middleton, 'Review of Civil Justice and Legal Aid: Report to the Lord Chancellor' (1997).

Legal advice and assistance

The Legal Aid Act 1988, Part III, enables applicants to obtain legal advice under the so-called Green Form scheme. Unless the Legal Aid Board agrees to more, legal representatives, including participating solicitors, can give up to two hours advice at a fixed hourly rate on any aspect of law (except conveyancing and wills) and three hours in the case of applications for divorce or judicial separation. This is subject to financial limits, both as to 'disposable' (that is, after disregarded sums) capital and 'disposable' income. The relevant qualifying figures are updated annually, the detailed rules for assessment being given in the Legal Advice and Assistance Regulations 1989, SI 1989/340, as amended. As from 6 April 1998 the limit for eligibility in the case of disposable capital for a person without dependants was £1,000. In the case of income, such a person who is in receipt of income support and certain other passported benefits, or who has a weekly disposable income of not more than £80, will be eligible (subject to satisfying the requirements as to capital). The relevant figures are set out in, for example, the New Law Journal, 20 March 1998, p 404.

Although the Green Form scheme is of considerable benefit to people of modest means, expenditure on consumer problems is relatively small when compared with certain other heads. The Annual Report of the Legal Aid Board for 1996–97 indicates (see p 101) that 34,261 bills were paid under this head in 1996–7 at a total cost of £2.791 million, with a further 86,730 at a cost of £6.818 million under the head hire-purchase and debt. The corresponding figures for welfare benefits were 165,416 bills at a cost of over £13 million and for advice on housing matters 114,775 bills at a cost of some £12 million.

Civil legal aid

The Green Form scheme does not extend to court work (other than the limited scheme for assistance by way of representation to which reference was made above). However, provision is made by the related scheme for civil legal aid. The financial qualifications are again dependent on the applicant's disposable capital and income being within the current financial limits. These limits differ from those which apply to the Green Form scheme which, as the Benson Commission noted (at para 12.34), 'assumes the provision of a smaller range of services at lower cost.' The detailed rules for assessment are set out in the Civil Legal Aid (Assessment of Resources) Regulations 1989, SI 1989/339, as amended. As at 6 April 1998 the lower capital limit was £3,000 and the upper limit generally £6,750 (£8,560 for personal injury). The corresponding figures for disposable annual income were £2,625 and £7,777 (£8,571 for personal injury). In between these limits applicants pay an assessed contribution unless they are on income support or certain other passported benefits, which carry an automatic eligibility to free legal aid.

In addition to meeting financial criteria the applicant must also satisfy a 'merits' test which has a dual element, namely that (i) there are legal reasons for giving assistance and (ii) it is reasonable in all the circumstances to give legal aid. The test is applied by the Legal Aid Board which is also taking over responsibility from specialists in the Benefits Agency for determining financial eligibility. The Royal Commission on Legal Service (1979) (the Benson Commission) outlined the non-financial requirements as follows:

The tests to be applied
13.24. An applicant for civil legal aid is required to show that he has reasonable grounds for taking, defending or being a party to proceedings. In addition, he may be refused legal aid if it appears unreasonable that he should receive it in the particular circumstances of the case. Under the first part of this test an applicant has to show that he has a good case in law and in fact. In our view, this test should be retained unchanged.
13.25. The second part of the test is concerned with the merits of the case generally and the extent to which there would be real advantage in pursuing it. This involves wider considerations going beyond the legal merits. The time honoured method used by legal aid committees in applying this test is, as the Law Society have told us in evidence, to ask:—

'What advice would be given to the applicant if he were a private client with means which were not over-abundant but which were adequate to meet the probable costs of the case without involving him in hardship?'

. . .

13.26. The matter was considered in 1956 by the Select Committee on Estimates of the House of Commons which took the view that it is wrong to adopt the actions of the man of adequate but not over-abundant means as the test of whether legal aid should be granted. We agree with the Select Committee and, while we believe that it is important that legal aid committees should continue to apply strict criteria in sifting the applications for legal aid which come before them, we think that they should take into account any factors peculiar to the applicant or his case which might justify the grant of legal aid. For the reasons given by the Select Committee, the factors to be considered should include such matters as injury to an applicant's reputation, status, civil rights or personal dignity; in such cases, we think that a certificate will often be justified though the sums of money involved may be small. We agree with the change in the criteria which enables legal aid to be granted where a case is of such a nature that success by an applicant would benefit a large number of other people in similar situations. This might include claims by consumers and social security or employment cases of potentially wide application though involving relatively small claims.

When payments are made usually it will be to solicitors, although there is a significant increase in the number and value of payments to the 'not for profit' sector (including CABx and Law Centres) from 1990–91 onwards. Relevant figures are contained in the Annual Report of the Legal Aid Board 1996–97, at p 121. It should also be noted that where a recipient of legal aid is successful the legal aid fund will recoup its costs from the costs awarded and where there is a deficiency will have a statutory charge over money recovered by or preserved for the assisted party: see the Legal Aid Act 1988, s 16(5) and (6). This is particularly important where the non-assisted party does not meet the costs in full.

Some points of criticism

Over the years the operation of the Green Form scheme and the civil legal aid system have attracted criticism. For example, it was argued that the fee limit for disposable capital (particularly in the case of legal advice and assistance) was unrealistically low and that the eligibility limits for civil legal aid could operate unfairly in relation to people who were moderately well off. This led the Benson Commission to recommend (see para 12.32 of its report) that the eligibility limits for both capital and income should be abolished. The recommendation was not accepted: see 'The Government Response to the Report of the Royal Commission on Legal Services', Cmnd 9077, 1983, pp 10–11.

More recently, the main emphasis has shifted towards seeking to control the escalating costs of publically funded legal advice and aid, which doubled over the five year period leading up to 1995–6 and was forecast to continue to rise by over £100 million per year thereafter. The following brief extracts indicate the thinking of the then Conservative Government:

Striking the Balance: The Future of Legal Aid in England and Wales, Cm 3305, June 1996

THE CASE FOR REFORM

The need to control costs

1.6. The doubling in five years in the cost of legal aid, despite continuing efforts to contain it, demonstrates that the current controls are insufficient. The only means of control available are reducing the types of case the scheme covers, tightening the financial eligibility limits, or putting downward pressure on the fees paid to lawyers. It is not possible to control the number of cases coming into the system.

1.7. Limiting the types of case covered and reducing financial eligibility are crude ways to control cost. Whole classes of case, or people whose finances are above a fixed level, are cut out. But no account is taken of how important a particular case may be to the person concerned, or whether that person can really afford or find some other way to fund appropriate legal services.

1.8. However, the Government would be better able to balance the interests of taxpayers and those who may need legal help, if we could decide how much should be spent on legal aid.

Ensuring efficiency and quality

1.9. Controlling costs by limiting lawyers' fees has not proved particularly effective in the past. In fact, in some ways the current scheme gives the highest rewards to lawyers who do more work than is necessary. But if too much pressure is put on fees, there is a risk that providers of legal help will let quality suffer rather than become more efficient. It is therefore important not only that legal aid is paid for in a way that encourages efficiency, but also that robust mechanisms are applied to ensure that quality is maintained.

1.10. We do not believe that the current system allows the Government, through the Legal Aid Board, to get the best possible balance of quality and efficiency when it buys legal services. This is because the scheme is open to any lawyer, whether or not they are competent in the type of case concerned, but generally not to other types of provider.

1.11. Nor do we believe that the current arrangements are ideal for the providers of legal services themselves. They do not know how much legally-aided work they will get or, because most fees are decided and paid after the event, how much they will be paid and when. This makes it difficult for providers to run their businesses efficiently and effectively.

Better addressing need

1.12. The current legal aid scheme is largely restricted to meeting the costs of going to court and other lawyers' expenses. Little or no money reaches those who provide other services that might be more appropriate and cost-effective, such as advice agencies, mediation and other forms of alternative dispute resolution. And there is no way of ensuring that services address priorities and reach those in greatest need.

1.13. The Legal Aid Board has to rely heavily on the advice of clients' lawyers in deciding whether to grant legal aid. However, a number of respondents to the consultation process made the point to us that too many weak or trivial cases are pursued under legal aid. But it cannot be an adverse criticism that lawyers, who are rightly concerned to do the best for their clients, advise them to pursue such cases. This is because most legally-aided clients have everything to win and little to lose, even if their cases are unsuccessful.

The need to ensure fairness

1.14. There is also widespread public concern that the availability of legal aid can create unfairness towards unassisted litigants, who may themselves be only just outside the eligibility limits. While legally-aided parties' liability to contribute to their own and their opponents' costs is very limited, their unassisted opponents often have no prospect of recovering their costs even if they win. Legally-aided parties have little incentive to keep down costs and may drive up their opponents' costs unnecessarily. Faced with this, unassisted parties can be under pressure to settle cases in their opponents' favour, even when their opponents were given legal aid for relatively weak cases. Such situations create injustice and waste. It is vital to the future of legal aid that it enjoys the support of the public. So we need to restore confidence that the scheme is fair and excludes weak or trivial cases.

1.15. Similarly, in the criminal sphere, there is nothing to discourage the defence from unnecessarily delaying the trial process simply to 'put off the evil day' or in the hope that this will obstruct a fair trial. This can undermine the fair treatment that victims and witnesses are entitled to expect, the chances of achieving just results and, by wasting resources, the interests of other defendants waiting to be tried and of the taxpayer.

Conclusion

1.16. For these reasons, the Government has concluded that radical change is needed:
- to provide effective means of controlling overall costs;
- to encourage efficiency, while maintaining quality;
- to target the available resources on the most appropriate and cost-effective services and the most deserving cases; and
- to promote fair treatment for all concerned, and discourage irresponsible behaviour such as driving up an opponent's costs.

Reform

1.17. The Government intends to meet these objectives by making five main changes. These are:
- replacing the present open-ended approach to resources with pre-determined budgets that can be allocated to meet local demand within national priorities;
- extending the scheme to new types of providers and services;
- introducing contracts between providers of services and the Legal Aid Board for specified services of defined quality at an agreed price;
- a new test for deciding whether civil cases should be given legal aid. This will target available resources on the most deserving cases; and
- changing the rules governing financial conditions to increase the potential liability of assisted persons to contribute to their own and, in civil cases, their opponents' costs.

1.18. The Legal Aid Board will have the major responsibility for making the reforms happen, by making contracts with providers of legal services.

1.19. The Government intends to widen the reach of legal aid to provide a broader and more flexible range of services. Solicitors and barristers in private practice will continue to play the largest role. But advice agencies, salaried lawyers, mediators and others will also be included. As a result, legal aid will, in principle, be capable of providing any help that can either:
- prevent court proceedings or questions that would demand a legal solution from arising, or
- promote their settlement or other disposal, in accordance with the law and in a way that will produce an enforceable result.

The form of that help will range from information about available services and initial advice and assistance, to various kinds of more substantial service, including mediation and help preparing and presenting court cases.

The Lord Chancellor would have the power to make regulations setting out the criteria to determine whether aid should be granted and the Legal Aid Board would be responsible for ensuring that they were applied consistently across the country (see paras 2.16–2.18). It was envisaged that implementation would be progressive and require legislation (see paras 6.1–6.21) and begin with advice and assistance in civil law and family matters. Pilot schemes were started.

NOTES

1. For detailed comments on the Green Paper which preceded these conclusions, see Goriely, 'The Government's Legal Aid Reforms' in Zuckerman & Cranston (eds), *Reform of Civil Procedure* (1995), ch 18.

2. With the election of the Labour Government in May 1997 the future of the above proposals was placed in some doubt. However, the Annual Report of the Legal Aid Board for 1996–97 contains the following statements in the Chairman's Introduction:

> During the year the Board worked on initiatives associated with legal aid reform. The new Lord Chancellor has endorsed the objectives of better control of costs, better targeting of resources and value for money. He has established a review secretariat to advise him on whether the previous Government's policies were the best means of meeting these objectives. In the meantime, he has instructed that existing plans, including pilot schemes, should go ahead. We are progressing the not-for-profit contracting pilot which began with 42 agencies. We expect to achieve significant expansion this year. At the end of 1996 work began to construct a contracting pilot involving solicitors in private practice. This will cover all civil advice and assistance normally delivered under green form, except matrimonial/family. Criminal advice and assistance will not be included in the pilot. Over 840 franchised solicitors' offices responded to an invitation to express interest in taking part in the pilot which will run in our London, Nottingham, Leeds and Liverpool areas. A total of 146 solicitors' offices, representing 119 firms, were selected to take part. In the summer of 1996 the Board began work aimed at piloting family mediation services. We selected 37 suppliers in 13 geographical locations to enter the pilot from June 1997. All these initiatives involve research projects which will be co-ordinated by our own Legal Aid Board Research Unit.

3. The new Lord Chancellor, Lord Irvine of Lairg, asked Sir Peter Middleton to report to him on the proposals and his report was published in September 1997: see 'Review of Civil Justice and Legal Aid' and the comments of Master R L Turner (1997) 147 NLJ 1727. The outcome will probably be a considerable reduction in the availability of civil legal aid, although perhaps not to the extent originally anticipated. In the residue of cases it is likely that the 'merits test' will be tightened. It is envisaged that conditional fee agreements will have a much greater role to play in filling the gap: see *The Times*, 4 October 1997, p 1, 18 October 1997, p 22, 13 February 1998, 5 March 1998, p 12, 17 March 1998, p 39, 24 March 1998, pp 6 and 41; also 'Legal Action', November 1997, p 4. No doubt, legal expenses insurance will become increasingly important. For

further discussion of the issues, see the Consultation Paper issued by the Lord Chancellor's Department, 'Access to Justice with Conditional Fees' (March, 1998) and the critical comments of Mears, 'Gamma minus' (1998) 148 NLJ 486.

4. Finally, it should be noted that civil legal aid (as opposed to advice and assistance) will, in any event, have only a very modest role to play in everyday consumer transactions. This is particularly true now that small claims for sums not exceeding £3,000 (possibly rising to £5,000 in the future) are usually referred to arbitration and that following such a reference only very limited legal costs are awarded. This is discussed further in the materials which follow.

OBTAINING COMPENSATION: SMALL CLAIMS AND OTHER PROCEDURES

INTRODUCTION

A consumer who seeks to obtain compensation in respect of faulty or misdescribed goods or services will, depending on the circumstances, have a number of possible avenues of redress. The first and most important is a civil action. In principle, this may be either in the High Court or in the county court. The division of business between the two is now largely governed by the High Court and County Courts Jurisdiction Order 1991, SI 1991/724 made under the Courts and Legal Services Act 1990, s 1. This builds on the recommendations in the 'Report of the Review Body on Civil Justice' (Cm 394, 1988). In general terms cases involving amounts below £25,000 are tried in the county court and those involving a sum in excess of £50,000 in the High Court. In between these limits allocation will depend on such matters as the complexity and importance of the case. Much of civil justice is now under review. The outcome may be the introduction of new 'fast-track' and 'multi-track' procedures. For details of what is proposed, see the Working Paper issued by the Lord Chancellor's Department, 'Access to Justice: Judicial Case Management, The Fast Track and Multi-Track', July 1997. Within the county court system there is a special arbitration procedure for dealing with 'small claims' where the amount involved does not exceed £3,000. This is considered in more detail below. (For a brief discussion of procedure in other county court claims, see Harvey and Parry, *The Law of Consumer Protection and Fair Trading* (5th edn, 1996), pp 208–11). The second possibility is that the dispute will be resolved through the conciliation and arbitration procedures established under a trade association code of practice negotiated under the auspices of the Office of Fair Trading. Thirdly, there will be cases where matters are referred to an ombudsman under schemes established in the financial sector and elsewhere. Finally, there will be cases in which compensation may be provided under the Powers of Criminal Courts Act 1973, as amended. For example, the defendant may be convicted of an offence under the Trade Descriptions Act 1968 and a compensation order might then be made in favour of an aggrieved consumer.

Some of the general issues which arise when considering the above avenues of redress are indicated in the cases and materials which follow. For a helpful, if now somewhat dated survey, see 'Consumer Redress Mechanisms: A Report by the Director General of Fair Trading into Systems for Resolving Consumer Complaints' (OFT, November 1991).

COUNTY COURTS AND 'SMALL CLAIMS'

The problems associated with 'small claims' have generated a voluminous amount of literature. Some of the earlier surveys include the Consumer Council study, 'Justice Out of Reach: A Case for Small Claims Courts' (HMSO, 1970); Applebey, 'Small Claims in England and Wales' in *Access to Justice* (eds Cappelletti and Weisner) Vol II, Book II (1979) p 685); 'Simple Justice: A Consumer View of Small Claims Procedures in England and Wales' (National Consumer Council, 1979), ch 11, especially; and, for a description of the position as it had developed in 1981, Thomas, 'Small Claims—The New Arrangements' (1981) 131 NLJ 429. A somewhat more recent description, including later developments, is to be found in the judgment of Beldam, LJ in *Afzal v Ford Motor Co Ltd* [1994] 4 All ER 720, at pp 726–31. His Lordship concluded his summary by saying (at p 731)

> Over a period of 20 years, therefore, Parliament has provided and the County Court Rules Committee, in the light of experience, has developed a scheme for court-based automatic arbitration for claims in which the amount involved does not exceed £1,000. The present rules contain a code of practice and procedure applicable to such claims. Parliament's object was described by Lord Diplock in *Hobbs v Marlowe* [1977] 2 All ER 24 at 256, [1978] AC 16 at 40–41. He said:
>
> 'Parliament and the rule committee in introducing the small claims scheme and amending the rules as to costs recoverable from the other party, gave effect to a public policy that as a general rule a person seeking to enforce a claim for less than £100 should act as his own lawyer with such assistance as is available to him at the office of the county court, the local citizens' advice bureau or consumer advice centre or, if he chooses to instruct a lawyer, should do so at his own expense and not at the expense of the person against whom the claim is made. I say as a general rule, because under CCR Ord 47, r 13, the county court judge retains a discretion to award costs on such scale as he thinks fit if he certifies that a difficult question of law or a question of fact of exceptional complexity is involved.'

More recently, Sir Thomas Bingham, MR, has said that 'the small claims arbitration procedure is no more, and no less, than a procedure for resolving low value claims, almost always by the district judge, with a minimum of formality and expense.': see *Joyce v Liverpool City Council* [1995] 3 All ER 110, 119. Since then the main development has been a substantial increase in the small claims limit to £3,000 (£1,000 in the case of personal injury) as recommended by Lord Woolf, in his Interim Report on 'Access to Justice' (June, 1995), ch 16. There are proposals to raise the limit still further to £5,000: see the Consultation Paper issued by the Lord Chancellor's Department, 'Access to Justice The Small Claims Procedure', November 1997.

The main regulations which govern references to arbitration in the case of small claims are as follows:

COUNTY COURT RULES

ORDER 19

REFERENCE TO ARBITRATION OR FOR INQUIRY AND REPORT OR TO EUROPEAN COURT

PART I—COUNTY COURT ARBITRATION

Interpretation and application

1. In this Part of this Order, unless the context otherwise requires—
    'lay representative' means a person exercising a right of audience by virtue of an order made under section 11 of the Courts and Legal Services Act 1990 (representation in county courts),
    'reference' means the reference of proceedings to arbitration under section 64 of the Act,
    'order' means an order referring proceedings to arbitration under that section, and
    'outside arbitrator' means an arbitrator other than the judge or district judge.

2.—In this Part of this Order—
    (a) Rules 3 and 4 apply only to small claims automatically referred to arbitration under rule 3, and
    (b) Rules 5 to 10 apply to all arbitrations.

Automatic reference of small claims

3.—(1) Any proceedings, except those mentioned in paragraph (1A), in which the sum claimed or amount involved does not exceed £3,000 (leaving out of account the sum claimed or amount involved in any counterclaim) shall stand referred for arbitration by the district judge upon the receipt by the court of a defence to the claim.

(1A) Paragraph (1) shall not apply to proceedings which include—
    (a) a claim for possession of land;
    (b) a claim for damages for personal injuries which exceeds £1,000.

(2) Where any proceedings are referred for arbitration by the district judge under paragraph (1), he may, after considering the defence and whether on the application of any party or of his own motion, order trial in court if he is satisfied—
    (a) that a difficult question of law or a question of fact of complexity is involved; or
    (b) that fraud is alleged against a party; or
    (c) that the parties are agreed that the dispute should be tried in court; or
    (d) that it would be unreasonable for the claim to proceed to arbitration having regard to its subject matter, the size of any counterclaim, the circumstances of the parties or the interests of any other person likely to be affected by the award.

(3) Where the district judge is minded to order trial in court of his own motion—
    (a) the proper officer shall notify the parties in writing specifying on which of the grounds mentioned in paragraph (2) the district judge is minded to order trial in court;
    (b) within 14 days after service of the proper officer's notice on him, a party may give written notice stating his reasons for objecting to the making of the order;
    (c) if in any notice under sub-paragraph (b) a party so requests, the proper officer shall fix a day for a hearing at which the district judge—
        (i) shall decide whether to order trial in court, and
        (ii) may give directions regarding the steps to be taken before or at any subsequent hearing as if he were conducting a preliminary appointment or, as the case may be, a pre-trial review;

and, in the absence of any request under sub-paragraph (c), the district judge may, in the absence of the parties, order trial in court.

(4) For the purposes of paragraph (1), 'a defence to the claim' includes a document admitting liability for the claim but disputing or not admitting the amount claimed.

Restriction on allowance of costs in small claims
4.—(1) In this rule 'costs' means—
    (a) solicitors' charges,
    (b) sums allowed to a litigant in person pursuant to Order 38, rule 17,
    (c) a fee or reward charged by a lay representative for acting on behalf of a party in the proceedings.

(2) No costs shall be allowed as between party and party in respect of any proceedings referred to arbitration under rule 3, except—
    (a) the costs which were stated on the summons or which would have been stated on the summons if the claim had been for a liquidated sum;
    (aa) in proceedings which include a claim for an injunction or for an order for specific performance or similar relief, a sum not exceeding £260 in respect of the cost of legal advice obtained for the purpose of bringing or defending that claim;
    (b) the costs of enforcing the award, and
    (c) such further costs as the district judge may direct where there has been unreasonable conduct on the part of the opposite party in relation to the proceedings or the claim therein.

(3) Nothing in paragraph (2) shall be taken as precluding the award of the following allowances—
    (a) any expenses which have been reasonably incurred by a party or a witness in travelling to and from the hearing or in staying away from home;
    (b) a sum not exceeding £50 in respect of a party's or a witness's loss of earnings when attending a hearing;
    (c) a sum not exceeding £200 in respect of the fees of an expert.

(4) Where trial in court is ordered, paragraph (2) shall not apply to costs incurred after the date of the order.

(5) Where costs are directed under paragraph (2)(c), those costs shall not be taxed and the amount to be allowed shall be specified by the arbitrator or the district judge.

The arbitrator
5.—(1) Unless the court otherwise orders, the district judge shall be the arbitrator.

(2) An order shall not be made referring proceedings to the Circuit judge except by or with the leave of the judge.

(3) An order shall not be made referring proceedings to an outside arbitrator except with the consent of the parties.

(4) Where proceedings are referred to an outside arbitrator, the order shall be served on the arbitrator as well as on the parties, but it shall not, unless the court directs, be served on anyone until each party has paid into court such sum as the district judge may determine in respect of the arbitrator's remuneration.

. . .

Conduct of hearing
7.—(1) Any proceedings referred to arbitration shall be dealt with in accordance with the following paragraphs of this rule unless the arbitrator otherwise orders.

(2) The hearing may be held at the court house, at the court office or at any other place convenient to the parties.

(3) The hearing shall be informal and the strict rules of evidence shall not apply; unless the

arbitrator orders otherwise, the hearing shall be held in private and evidence shall not be taken on oath.

(4) At the hearing the arbitrator may adopt any method of procedure which he may consider to be fair and which gives to each party an equal opportunity to have his case presented; having considered the circumstances of the parties and whether (or to what extent) they are represented, the arbitrator—

    (a) may assist a party by putting questions to the witnesses and the other party; and

    (b) should explain any legal terms or expressions which are used.

(5) If any party does not appear at the arbitration, the arbitrator may, after taking into account any pleadings or other documents filed, make an award on hearing any other party to the proceedings who may be present.

(6) With the consent of the parties and at any time before giving his decision, the district judge may consult any expert or call for an expert report on any matter in dispute or invite an expert to attend the hearing as assessor.

(7) The arbitrator may require the production of any document or thing and may inspect any property or thing concerning which any question may arise.

(8) The arbitrator shall inform the parties of his award and give his reasons for it to any party who may be present at the hearing.

Setting awards aside

8.—(1) Where proceedings are referred to arbitration, the award of the arbitrator shall be final and may only be set aside pursuant to paragraph (2) or on the ground that there has been misconduct by the arbitrator or that the arbitrator made an error of law.

(2) Where an award has been given in the absence of a party, the court shall have power, on that party's application, to set the award aside and to order a fresh hearing, as if the award were a judgment and the application were made pursuant to Order 37, rule 2.

(3) An application by a party to set aside an award made by a district judge or an outside arbitrator on the ground mentioned in paragraph (1) shall be made on notice and the notice shall be served within 14 days after the day on which the award was entered as the judgment of the court.

(4) An application under paragraph (3) shall, giving sufficient particulars, set out the misconduct or error of law relied upon.

(5) Order 37, rule 1 (rehearing of proceedings tried without a jury) shall not apply to proceedings referred to arbitration.

Mode of voluntary reference

9.—(1) Except as provided by rule 3, a reference shall be made only on the application of a party to the proceedings sought to be referred.

(2) Unless the court otherwise directs, an application by a party to any proceedings for a reference may be made—

    (a) in the case of a plaintiff, by request incorporated in his particulars of claim;

    (b) in the case of a defendant, by request incorporated in any defence or counterclaim of his;

    (c) in any case, on notice under Order 13, rule 1.

(3) Where an application for a reference is made under paragraph (1) and the proceedings are not referred to arbitration under rule 3, the following provisions shall apply:—

    (a) Subject to rule 5(2) and sub-paragraphs (b) and (c) below, an order may be made by the district judge.

    (b) If the court is satisfied that an allegation of fraud against a party is in issue in the proceedings, an order shall not be made except with the consent of that party.

    (c) Where the district judge is minded to grant an application under paragraph (1), the proper officer shall notify the parties in writing accordingly and within 14 days after service of the proper officer's notice on him, a party may give written notice stating his reasons for objecting to the reference; if in any such notice a party so requests, the proper officer shall fix a day for a hearing at which the district judge shall decide whether to grant the application and, in the absence of any such request, the district judge may consider the application in the absence of the parties.

Costs
10. Subject to rule 4, the costs of the action up to and including the entry of judgment shall be in the discretion of the arbitrator to be exercised in the same manner as the discretion of the court under the provisions of the County Court Rules.

NOTES

1. For helpful notes on Order 19, see *The County Court Practice 1997* (The Green Book), Part 5; and for more general discussion, see Applebey, *A Practical Guide to the Small Claims Court* (1994); Baldwin, *Small Claims Courts in England and Wales* (1997) and 'Raising the Small Claims Limit' in Zuckerman & Cranston (eds), *Reform of Civil Procedure* (1995); Lord Woolf's Interim Report on 'Access to Justice' (June 1995), ch 16; The National Audit Office Report, 'Handling Small Claims in the County Courts' (1996).
2. According to *The County Court Practice 1997*, p 2057, in 1995 88,170 county court cases were disposed of by arbitration as compared with 24,477 by trial. It is to be expected that the predominance of arbitration will be increased now that the limit has been raised to £3,000. In addition to the procedure for automatic reference to arbitration, there is also a procedure for voluntary reference in r 9, although the 'no-costs' rule will not apply (see r 2(a)).
3. There are some important general issues in the application of Order 19, including the following:

(i) Rescinding the Reference to Arbitration

Order 19, r 3(2) indicates the circumstances which may lead to the proceedings being heard in court, rather than by arbitration. Previously r 3(2)(a) used the expression 'exceptional complexity', but following the recommendation in Lord Woolf's Interim Report on 'Access to Justice', ch 16, paras 10 and 66, the word 'exceptional' was removed to leave a greater measure of discretion. However, it is clear that r 3(2) should still be applied restrictively.

In *Afzal v Ford Motor Co Ltd* [1994] 4 All ER 720 (at p 734) Beldam, LJ said of r 3(2)(d) that:

'Subject matter' refers to the nature of a claim generally but in the context of the other provisions of r 3(2) we take it to refer to some quality of the subject matter of the claim of sufficient importance to the parties or to one of them to justify trial in court; for example, a claim for damages for trespass which could have far-reaching consequences for the rights of the parties or a claim involving ownership of a family heirloom. Cases which may be regarded as 'test' cases could be catered for under r 3(2)(d) as cases in which the interests of other persons are likely to be affected by the award.

The matter was considered further in another decision of the Court of Appeal, which also settled an important issue arising out of claims under s 11 of the Landlord and Tenant Act 1985 to enforce a landlord's repairing covenant.

Joyce v Liverpool City Council [1995] 3 All ER 110, [1996] QB 252, Court of Appeal

Sir Thomas Bingham MR. These appeals raise an important and disputed question. The question is: in proceedings by a domestic tenant alleging a breach by his landlord of a repairing covenant, may a district judge sitting as small claims arbitrator grant relief by way of specific performance or injunction?

The question is important to the tenant because the answer determines whether a tenant's claim in which such relief is sought may be referred to small claims arbitration. That in turn determines whether, if successful, the tenant may recover his legal costs and thus, in practice, whether he will be granted legal aid and have the benefit of legal representation. The landlord will often have the benefit of representation either by lawyers or employees experienced in resisting such claims, so the tenant (if unrepresented) may be at an obvious disadvantage in preparing and presenting his claim.

The question is of importance to landlords. Where the tenant is legally represented, the cost to the landlord of resolving a claim within the financial limit of the small claims arbitration procedure is likely to exceed, by a significant factor, the financial value of the claim. Many defendant landlords (such as that in these cases) are local authorities, some of them burdened with an ageing housing stock and under constant pressure to make ends meet. The cost to them of meeting tenants' legal costs, added to the cost of making good defects, is not inconsiderable.

The importance of this question is not limited to claims for breach of repairing covenants, for if the district judge's small claims arbitration procedure is precluded in any proceeding in which equitable relief by way of specific performance is sought various claims otherwise apparently suitable for the more informal and summary procedure would have to go to trial: for example very petty disputes between neighbours based on allegations of trespass or assault or nuisance, or perhaps claims for the return of goods of small value.

. . .

His Lordship then set out the facts of the cases, considered the powers of judges and district judges of the county court, and concluded:

Rescission of automatic reference
If, contrary to his primary argument, a district judge had power to order specific performance under the small claims arbitration procedure and so to entertain under that procedure an action in which such relief was claimed, counsel for the tenants submitted that the judges below had misapplied *Afzal v Ford Motor Co Ltd* [1994] 4 All ER 720 by wrongly treating that authority as requiring s 11 claims, where the cost of repairs plus the likely general damages would not exceed £1,000, to be automatically subject to the small claims arbitration procedure. This argument on analysis involved three contentions: first, as to the effect of *Afzal*; secondly, as to the differences between accidents at work and claims under s 11; and, thirdly, as to the unfairness of expecting an unrepresented tenant to prepare and present a case against a well-armed and represented landlord.

In *Afzal* this court undoubtedly discountenanced the view that claims against employers arising out of accidents at work were necessarily unsuitable for determination under the small claims arbitration procedure (at 733). The court pointed out that the grounds for revocation of an automatic reference specified in Ord 19, r 3(2)(a) referred not merely to the existence of a question of law but to a difficult question of law and not merely to the existence of a question of fact but to a question of fact of exceptional complexity (at 734). The court also pointed out that the claimant's lack of representation could not of itself provide a ground for ordering a trial in court where the defendant was represented, since Ord 19 r 7(4) expressly recognised that one party might be represented and the other not (at 734). While holding that the judge's rescission of the reference to arbitration in 16 cases could not be supported, however, the court did not substitute its own decision that the cases should be referred to arbitration, but instead remitted them for individual consideration by the district judge (at 735). This shows that while in the ordinary way low value claims will be determined under the small claims arbitration procedure the final decision must rest with the district judge who is charged with the task of doing substantial justice in the particular case. It is for him to decide, making a judgment in accordance with the rules, whether—

'it would be unreasonable for the claim to proceed to arbitration having regard to its subject matter . . . the circumstances of the parties or the interests of any other person likely to be affected by the award.' (See Ord 19, r 3(2)(d).)

He, as the final decision-maker, is likely to be the best judge whether that test is met in any given case or whether it is not. Great respect should be paid to his decision, not only because of his experience of dealing with individual cases but also because of the knowledge he will have of the local situation.

It is of course true that an accident at work is, in fact and in law, very different from a landlord's breach of a repairing covenant. But that is in itself of little or no significance. In either field, difficult questions of fact and law may arise in borderline cases. But in either, the solution is likely to be fairly obvious in the ordinary run of cases. It may be that expert evidence will be more important in s 11 claims than in many claims against employers, but armed with an expert's report (which will have been obtained, usually with legal assistance, before proceedings are issued) the burden on the tenant of preparing and presenting his case is proportionately reduced. It must also be borne in mind that the common defects likely to fall within the financial scope of the small claims arbitration procedure—immovable or ill-fitting windows, minor leaks in the roof, over-flowing drains, defective boilers—are not things which the average tenant (or the tenant's spouse) will find it hard to understand or describe.

In *Pepper v Healey* [1982] RTR 411 the plaintiff claimed damages arising out of a motor collision which the defendant said had never occurred. The plaintiff had no insurance against legal costs and so was obliged to conduct the case herself. The defendant was insured and legally represented. In that situation the registrar thought it unreasonable to send the case to arbitration. On appeal the judge and the Court of Appeal supported his decision. This authority was relied on as establishing a general rule. In our view it did not. It represented an exercise of judgment in a particular case at a time when the small claims arbitration procedure was, perhaps, a good deal less well established than it now is.

We have seen a helpful and well-prepared leaflet entitled 'An arbitration hearing–how do I prepare?'. It might also be helpful (unless they already do this) if citizens' advice bureaux or the county court itself were to make available written guidance specifically directed to s 11 claims. The district judge conducting a small claims arbitration is under a clear duty to ensure that the case of the claimant does not go by default: see Ord 19, r 7. If the defendant's conduct puts the claimant to unreasonable expense the claimant can be compensated: see Ord 19, r 4(2)(c). Despite all these safeguards cases will arise in which, despite the smallness of the sums involved, justice cannot be done to an unrepresented claimant under the arbitration procedure. Trial may then be ordered. But for the great mass of small and relatively simple claims the arbitration procedure must be the norm. Section 11 claims cannot form any general exception. Reasonable housing conditions are without doubt a condition of ordinary human happiness,.

But the evidence before us does suggest that court trial of minor s 11 claims yields a benefit to the legal profession out of all proportion to that gained by the tenant and diverts the funds of local authority landlords from purposes more germane to their public function.

. . .

Appeal dismissed.

(Since the decision in *Afzal*, the test is now one of complexity, rather than 'exceptional' complexity: see above, pp 411 and 414.)

(ii) Inflated and Artificially Low Claims

It is now clear that the procedure for automatic reference to arbitration cannot be avoided by inflating the claim to an artificially high figure. This will be an abuse of process, which will justify restricting costs to the limited amounts recoverable under the small claims procedure. The test is based on what the plaintiff could reasonably expect to be awarded: see *Afzal v Ford Motor Co Ltd* [1994] 4 All ER 720, at pp 736–7. Presumably, it is open to the district judge to order a trial of the action under r 3(2) and of his own motion if of the opinion that the amount claimed is artificially low.

(iii) The No-Costs Rule

The no-costs rule is perhaps the single most important feature of the county court arbitration procedure. It is intended to benefit consumer litigants who can thus (so the theory goes) afford to litigate without the spectre of a general liability for an opponent's legal costs to act as a disincentive. None the less, some may feel that there is no reason in principle why such litigants should be put in a position of *having* to forego legal costs no matter how strong their case. Do-it-yourself litigation may have its attractions for some, but others may prefer to engage a 'professional'—perhaps because they are inarticulate or simply have better or different things to do with their time. Be that as it may, the limits to the scope of recoverable costs and allowances are as stated in r 4, although costs may be awarded also on an application to set aside an award under r 8.

The main flexibility within the no-costs rule lies in the provision for 'unreasonable conduct' contained in r 4(2)(c). In *Newland v Boardwell* [1983] 3 All ER 179, [1983] 1 WLR 1453, the Court of Appeal held that insurance companies had demonstrated unreasonable conduct by admitting negligence but not admitting injuries, loss, and damage when the only real dispute was as to quantum. (However, the plaintiffs had not incurred costs *through*, or in consequence of, such conduct as was then required.) Rule 3(4) makes it clear that the automatic reference procedure is activated by admitting liability whilst disputing quantum. Unreasonable conduct may be demonstrated by defending proceedings where there is no arguable defence (see *Bloomfield v Roberts* [1988] CLY 2948) or raising a speculative or unsupportable defence (see the judgment of Beldam, LJ in *Afzal v Ford Motor Co Ltd* [1994] 4 All ER 720, at p 747).

(iv) Lay and Legal Representation

Consumers may represent themselves as 'litigants in person' (see further below, pp 433–4) and lay representatives are now accorded a right of audience where their client attends a small claims hearing: see the Lay Representatives (Rights of Audience) Order 1992, SI 1992/1966 and the corresponding Practice Direction. The right extends to addressing the judge and, subject to the procedure adopted by the judge, to calling and examining witnesses.

The question whether legal representation should be allowed at small claims hearings has also been debated. The National Consumer Council commented as follows in 'Simple Justice' (1979), pp 95–6:

Legal representation

. . .

24. In all our discussions on this issue—with advice agencies, registrars, consumer organisations, the legal profession and so on—there was unanimous agreement that lawyers should not be necessary in the arbitration procedure. But there is no consensus on whether this aim should be achieved by improving the system gradually so that the need for representation diminishes, and its use disappears; or whether the issue should be tackled by an outright ban on legal representation. Many of the arguments for and against such a ban are contained in Chapter 9. Essentially these arguments are, on the one hand, that arbitration will never be a simple, informal and cheap means of redress that enables consumers to claim their rights if lawyers are present at hearings. On the other hand, there is the feeling that restricting one's right to obtain the services of a lawyer is a restriction of individual freedom and choice and may limit the chances of getting justice. It is also argued that lawyers and legal argument can be necessary in certain cases involving small amounts of money; and that some individuals are not confident enough to bring their case without some form of legal or lay representation. These opposing views are difficult to reconcile.

25. As we saw in Chapter 9, the old Consumer Council recommended that legal representation should not be allowed in small claims arbitration, although not without searching consideration. As the Council said, 'the principle that a man should be entitled to have a lawyer speaking for him at a judicial hearing is one deserving of great respect'. However, as the Council pointed out, this was a principle and not practice, and the majority of individuals would not have lawyers even if they were permitted to do so.

26. *On balance we conclude that arbitration as a procedure for the effective disposal of small claims cannot work satisfactorily, in the majority of cases, if representation as such is permitted. We therefore call for a ban on representation in the vast majority of cases heard by arbitration.* The only exceptions, to answer some of the arguments against such a ban would be:
   - where the registrar certifies that the claim involved a difficult decision of law, or questions of fact of exceptional complexity (which cases, as we have already argued, would be referred to trial);
   - where the registrar certifies that the interests of justice require that legal or lay representation should be permitted;
   - where both parties agree to the use of representation.

27. Even where representation at an arbitration is permitted in accordance with the last two exceptions, no legal costs would be allowed . . .

This recommendation was discussed in February 1980 by the County Court Rule Committee which concluded that 'no restriction should be placed by the Rules of Court on the litigant's right to be represented in county court arbitrations.' For a more recent survey of the role of lawyers at small claims hearings, see Baldwin, *Small Claims in the County Courts in England and Wales* (1997), at pp 77–88. As Professor Baldwin notes with examples (see p 78, n 41): 'Legal representation is not permitted in all countries.'

(v) The Conduct of the Hearing

The essential feature of a small claims hearing as stated in CCR Ord 19, r 7(2), is that it is 'informal' and 'the strict rules of evidence shall not apply.' The arbitrator is given a wide measure of discretion as to the procedure to be adopted so as to give each party an equal opportunity to present their case. However, the rules of natural justice must be observed. The following case provides an example of a procedure which was held not to meet the requirements of natural justice.

Chilton v Saga Holidays plc [1986] 1 All ER 841, Court of Appeal

The plaintiff, who was representing himself, had sued the defendant company in respect of a holiday which did not match up to his expectations. The company was represented by a solicitor, who applied to the registrar to cross-examine the plaintiff and Mrs Chilton. The registrar refused, saying: 'In cases where one side is unrepresented, I do not allow cross-examination. All questions to the other side will be put through me.' On application to set aside the award, the county court judge upheld the approach of the registrar. Saga Holidays appealed to the Court of Appeal.

Sir John Donaldson MR. . . .

I regret to say that I find myself in total disagreement with the county court judge and, of course, with the registrar. It is quite right that the small claims procedure is intended to be informal. It is intended that no one shall be disadvantaged by not being represented by counsel. But that is quite different from saying that the procedure adopted must be such as to deprive anybody of the services of solicitors or counsel if they wish to have them. It would have been open to the rule-making body, subject to any question of vires, to have provided by rules that in small claims arbitrations neither party should be represented by lawyers.

. . .

However, no such rule has been made, and it must follow that Saga Holidays were entitled to be represented. It would seem from what the registrar has said that, if Mr Chilton had been represented, he would have had no objection to cross-examination. What he seems to have overlooked is that both courts and arbitrators in this country operate on an adversarial system of achieving justice. It is a system which can be modified by rules of court; it is a system which can be modified by contract between the parties; but, in the absence of one or the other, it is basically an adversarial system, and it is fundamental to that that each party shall be entitled to tender their own evidence and that the other party shall be entitled to ask questions designed to probe the accuracy or otherwise, or the completeness or otherwise, of the evidence which has been given.

. . .

Mr Chilton has argued his case in this appeal with great moderation, great enthusiasm and great skill. What he says is that, where there is unequal expertise available to the two sides, the party with the greater expertise must be disadvantaged to the point at which they have the same expertise effectively as the other party. That seems to me to be a perversion of what the rule requires, which is 'a fair and equal opportunity to each party to present his case'.

The problem which arises where you have one represented party and one unrepresented party is very well known to all judges and in particular to judges who deal with small claims in the county court. It becomes the duty of the judge so far as he can, without entering the arena to a point where he is no longer able to act judicially, to make good any deficiencies in the advantages available to the unrepresented party. We have all done it; we all know that it can be done and that it can be done effectively. That is the proper course to be adopted. The informality which is stressed by the rule and the requirement that the arbitrator may adopt any method of procedure which he considers to be convenient (it would have been better perhaps if it had said 'just and convenient') covers the situation where, as so often happens, a litigant in person is quite incapable of cross-examining but is perfectly capable in the time available for cross-examination of putting his own case. The judge or the registrar then picks up the unrepresented party's complaints and puts them to the other side.

. . .

I think that the registrar and the county court judge were plainly wrong in this case in refusing to allow Saga Holidays to ask questions of Mr Chilton, and I would therefore set the award aside.

Slade LJ and **Lloyd LJ** agreed.

Appeal allowed. No order as to costs.

Although the current wording of r 7(4) differs slightly from the corresponding provision under consideration in the above case, there is no reason to doubt that the entitlement to cross-examine remains. However, it seems that district judges adopt differing approaches in conducting hearings. Professor Baldwin identified four such approaches in his book, *Small Claims in the County Courts in England and Wales* (1997), at pp 58–66: (i) 'going for the jugular' (or identifying the central issues at an early stage and sticking to them); (ii) 'hearing the parties' (or allowing the parties greater latitude to develop their arguments in their own way); (iii) 'passive' (or talking to each of the parties like a solicitor interviewing clients); and (iv) 'mediatory' (or encouraging the parties to agree their own solution). His research also reached the following conclusion (op cit at pp 71–2):

> In the interviews the author conducted with district judges, he was surprised to discover that it was only a minority who took the view that it was their unequivocal duty strictly to apply legal principles in reaching decisions in dealing with small claims. In other words, a majority felt that they could disregard the law in making decisions if in their view the law would produce an unjust outcome. Rightly or wrongly, many judges felt that, when they were dealing with small claims, it was more appropriate to seek solutions that would provide a standard of justice that would be understood and accepted as fair by the parties, even if this meant disregarding the laws.

In his Interim Report on 'Access to Justice' (June 1995), Lord Woolf regarded the variations in practice and approach as 'the greatest weakness of the system at present' and concluded that all district judges and deputy district judges should be trained in handling small claims, to ensure a more consistent approach (see ch 16, paras 34–5 and Recommendation (6)).

(vi) Businesses as Plaintiffs

Over many years there has been discussion as to the extent to which small claims procedures have been 'colonised' by large commercial organisations so as to operate primarily as a convenient debt collection agency for them. This has led to suggestions that businesses should not be allowed to institute proceedings: see, eg Ison, (1972) 35 MLR 18, at p 24 et seq; Cranston, 'Access to Justice for Consumers' (1979) Journal of Consumer Policy 291. Some examples of Australian legislation which confine the ability to sue to 'consumers' or those who acquire goods or services otherwise than in a business context, are noted by Yin and Cranston, 'Small Claims Tribunals in Australia' in Whelan (ed), *Small Claims Courts* (1990), ch 4. However, the National Consumer Council in its report 'Simple Justice' (1979) did not favour this limitation (see p 94).

A more recent English survey by Professor Baldwin contains the following information.

Small Claims in the County Courts in England and Wales (1997), at pp 25–7 (footnotes omitted)

Who makes use of the small claims procedure and for what purposes?

It is important at the outset to determine who is involved in small claims and what kind of issues arise in these disputes. As discussed in Chapter 1, there has been a great deal of discussion in the academic literature about whether the small claims procedure has been hijacked by commercial and business interests from the individual consumers for whom it was originally devised. It has become fashionable in this literature to depict the small claims arena as one in which business organizations can pursue small debts cheaply, and American writers often refer to small claims courts as being 'colonized' by business interests. Table 1 shows the kinds of plaintiffs and defendants involved in the small claims hearings included in the 1,800 files examined. These results highlight the very important point about the small claims arena that it is extensively used by small firms, traders, and individuals.

Table 2.1. *Who sues whom in small claims*

Plaintiffs	Defendants		
			%
Large firm/org. *v* other large firm/org.		5	0.3
Large firm/org. *v* small firm/trader		70	3.9
Large firm/org. *v* individual		188	10.4
Small firm/trader *v* large firm/org.		10	0.6
Small firm/trader *v* other small firm/trader		429	23.8
Small firm/trader *v* individual		440	24.4
Individual *v* large firm/org.		48	2.7
Individual *v* small firm/trader		238	13.2
Individual *v* other individuals		362	20.1
Other types of party		10	0.6
		1800	100.0

Table 1 shows that small firms featured as plaintiffs or defendants (or both) in about two thirds of all hearings in this sample. Indeed, in almost a quarter, small firms appeared against other small firms. Public organizations (like local authority departments, hospitals, and universities) and large commercial or business concerns (like banks and building societies) appeared much less commonly, whether as plaintiffs or defendants. But individuals featured in over 70 per cent of all hearings, albeit almost as often as defendants as plaintiffs. The small claims procedure is not, therefore, monopolized, as some writers have argued, by big business or, indeed, by other large and powerful organizations: it is used mainly by small business concerns and by private individuals.

It is worth considering carefully the role of individuals in this picture because the small claims procedure in England was, after all, primarily created to serve their interests. Have private individuals become the victims of the procedure rather than the beneficiaries? While it is true that they were more likely to be involved in actions as defendants than as plaintiffs, private individuals still activated the procedure in a considerable proportion of all claims. The fact that well over a third of plaintiffs were individuals rather than business organizations clearly indicates that considerable use is still being made of small claims procedures in England by those for whom it was originally intended. Again, the figures presented in Table 1 scarcely support the common portrayal of the small claims procedure as subjugated to the requirements of large business users.

The matter was also discussed by Lord Woolf in his Interim Report on 'Access to Justice' (June 1995). He reached the following conclusions (see ch 16):

. . .

Should businesses be prevented from using this scheme

17. It is a standard criticism that small claims courts, wherever they exist, are dominated by business litigants, especially those collecting debts. However, research in other jurisdictions has generally concluded that there are no significant disadvantages in allowing businesses to use the small claims procedure and that this may in fact facilitate a defence by a lay person without the need to instruct a lawyer, provided that the possibility is sufficiently advertised. Although larger businesses may have professional representation, the role of the district judge in 'holding the ring' is designed to ensure fairness of treatment. The growing number of small businesses and self-employed people makes it desirable to provide a low cost accessible forum for the resolution of disputes arising from the businesses they are engaged in. I therefore see no need to make any change which would exclude businesses from using the scheme.

. . .

QUESTIONS

1. In the light of the above materials do you consider that it is desirable to exclude or admit (i) legal representation and (ii) businesses as plaintiffs?
2. What reasons might be advanced for the lower limit of £1,000 (as opposed to £3,000) in the case of 'a claim for damages for personal injuries'? In calculating this limit are medical expenses and loss of earnings etc, to be taken into account, as well as pain and suffering etc?

Venue

Another issue of considerable practical importance is where the proceedings are to be commenced. The relevant provision is contained in the County Court Rules 1981, Ord 4, r 3 which provides in part as follows:

General provisions as to actions
2(1) An action may be commenced—
    (a) in the court for the district in which the defendant or one of the defendants resides or carries on business,
    (b) in the court for the district in which the cause of action wholly or in part arose, or
    (c) in the case of a default action, in any county court.
(2) Where the plaintiff sues as assignee, the action shall be commenced only in a court in which the assignor might have commenced the action but for the assignment.

If proceedings are commenced in the wrong court then by Ord 16, r 2

Proceedings commenced in wrong court
. . . the judge or [district judge] may, subject to rule 3,—
    (a) transfer the proceedings to the court in which they ought to have been commenced, or
    (b) order the proceedings to continue in the court in which they have been commenced, or
    (c) order the proceedings to be struck out.

QUESTIONS

In the light of the above it is important to select the right county court. Consider the following cases—
1. The Angus Mail Order Co which has its place of business in Westshire advertises as follows in the *Sunday Excess*: 'Thousands of Bargain Offers for Sale. Quickcount Minicomputers only £150, plus post and package. Send your money now.' Bert who lives 500 miles away in Eastshire sends his cheque for the full amount and a Quickcount Computer is duly despatched to him. It arrives safely but soon develops serious faults. The opinion of a local expert whom Bert has consulted is that the faults will never be remedied satisfactorily. Angus Mail Order refuses to refund the purchase price or to provide a replacement. Hotel accommodation in Westshire is expensive. Bert wishes to institute proceedings in the county court and seeks your advice as to whether he may sue in Eastshire. Advise Bert.
2. Pamela, who is on holiday in Northshire, takes her expensive leather coat to the Upmarket Cleaners for dry-cleaning. When she collects it the lining is badly shrunk. Upmarket claims that the shrinkage has been caused by a defect in the material and they refuse to offer any compensation. Pamela has now returned home to Southshire where an independent expert has reported that the fabric is not defective and that the fault lies in the cleaning. She seeks your advice as to where she should sue. Advise Pamela.

CONCILIATION, ARBITRATION AND CODES OF PRACTICE

Conciliation and arbitration procedures intended to resolve disputes without invoking the traditional courts have been developed within several areas of English law. These include labour relations (eg Advisory Conciliation and

Arbitration Service and race relations (the Commission for Racial Equality). The same has been true of consumer disputes where there has been something of a proliferation of codes of practice containing provisions for conciliation, arbitration and independent testing.

The general advantages and limitations of such codes are discussed in ch 10, below. In the present context it may be said that there is general agreement that such procedures may offer sensible alternatives to litigation, particularly where the sum involved is low. (As has been noted (see pp 368–9), compulsory arbitration clauses where the sum involved does not exceed £3,000 are controlled by the Arbitration Act 1996, s 91 and the Unfair Terms in Consumer Contracts Regulations 1994.) The following extracts from a Report by the Director General of Fair Trading into systems for resolving consumer complaints point to some of the issues raised by conciliation and arbitration schemes.

Consumer Redress Mechanisms (November, 1991)

Conciliation and arbitration schemes

. . .

4.39. Most consumer arbitrations take place as a result of arbitration schemes contained in codes of practice drawn up by trade associations in consultation with the OFT. Under section 124(3) of the Fair Trading Act 1973 the Director General of Fair Trading has a duty 'to encourage relevant trade associations to prepare, and to disseminate to their members, codes of practice for guidance in safeguarding and promoting the interests of consumers'. The OFT provides general advice to trade associations on 'best practice' but has focused its limited resources on encouraging codes of practice in those sectors where there has been a high level of consumer dissatisfaction. An important feature of almost all these codes is the provision of conciliation and arbitration facilities. Since 1974, 29 such codes have been drawn up in consultation with the OFT, covering such diverse sectors as credit, footwear, photography, package holidays and funerals. . . . There are also a number of arbitration schemes in the financial services sector. . . .

4.40. The OFT has taken the view that independent arbitration has an important role to play in that it can provide the consumer with the option of a relatively quick, simple and inexpensive method of seeking redress in a dispute with a trader who subscribes to a code of practice. The arbitration system should however be seen as complementary to, and not as replacing, court procedures.

4.41. The OFT has established a model procedure for complaints handling to which most schemes conform. This makes clear that complaints should be taken up with the trader concerned who should make every effort to resolve the problem at that stage. If it does not prove possible to resolve the problem at this stage the trader should advise the consumer of the availability of assistance from CABx and Trading Standards Departments, and of the conciliation services of the trade association. The only exceptions to this procedure are the Post Office Codes, where the Post Office Users' National Council (POUNC) becomes involved at this stage; and the Footwear Code, where disputes relating to the quality of shoes may be resolved by use of a footwear testing scheme.

4.42. If conciliation by the trade association does not achieve a satisfactory settlement and the consumer wishes to pursue the matter further, most of the codes give the consumer, as an alternative to taking the case to the county court or the sheriff court, the option of referring the dispute to independent arbitration. The decision of the arbitrator is binding on both parties and conducted on a documents only basis, that is to say, the parties put their cases in writing to the arbitrator, and there is usually no opportunity for an oral hearing. To this the Glass and Glazing Federation's scheme is an exception, site visits being relatively common.

4.43. In order to use an arbitration scheme the consumer must pay a registration fee which is usually less than £40. A further considerable advantage of these arbitration schemes for consumers lies in the fact that even should they lose they are not liable for more than another sum equivalent to the original registration fee. Should they win the registration fee is refunded. The fee charged does not cover the cost of arbitration which is heavily subsidised by the trade association and, in effect, by arbitrators who agree to act in these schemes for fees which do not usually exceed £100, which is considerably less than they would charge in other arbitrations. An arbitrator's fee may be more than this where a site visit is involved. . . .

4.44. Most arbitration schemes approved by the OFT are administered by the Chartered Institute of Arbitrators, though the motor trade schemes make separate arrangements and use an independent panel of arbitrators. The Institute maintains a register of its members who are qualified arbitrators and they will be appointed by the Institute when a dispute is referred to arbitration. Arbitrators have a variety of backgrounds, for example law, engineering, accountancy and medicine.

. . .

NOTES

1. The Report later identifies (see ch 6) the main strengths and weaknesses of such schemes. The strengths are said to include procedural flexibility, low cost, the possibility of speedy resolution through a documents-only procedure (as opposed to an oral hearing) a convenient timetable, a specialist adjudicator, legally binding awards and private adjudications. The weaknesses include different perceptions of these apparent strengths—for example, lengthy delays after unsuccessful attempts at conciliation, the absence of an opportunity to amplify the case orally, and the fact that privacy contributed to a lack of knowledge about the schemes. Thus, although some schemes (notably that of the Association of British Travel Agents or ABTA) were well known and quite heavily used, others were rarely, if ever, used. Conciliation is also sometimes seen as being biased towards the trader.
2. For further discussion, see 'Redress Procedures Under Codes of Practice' (Office of Fair Trading, 1981); 'Out of Court' (National Consumer Council, 1991); 'Settling Consumer Disputes' (National Consumer Council, 1993).
3. Further information on conciliation and arbitration is to be found in the Annual Reports of the relevant trade associations.

OMBUDSMAN SCHEMES

A further means of obtaining compensation is indicated in the following extract.

Developments in Consumer Redress (Office of Fair Trading, June 1996)

. . .

3.5. Another alternative to the courts is an ombudsman procedure. The function of the ombudsman was originally established in the United Kingdom to act within the public sector in 1967.[3] It was only in the 1980s that the ombudsman in the administrative sector was joined by his namesakes in the private sector. The financial services sector in particular was interested in this kind of complaints handling. The first scheme in this sector came into existence in 1981; the Insurance Ombudsman Bureau. It was established by three major insurance companies,[4] whose actions may have become more industrious by the thought of an ombudsman being forced upon them.[5] The financial services sector was subsequently swamped by the creation of other ombudsmen modelled on their progenitor. In 1986, the Banking Ombudsman Bureau was set up and in 1987 the Building Societies Ombudsman scheme came into existence which was quickly followed by the founding of the Investment Ombudsman,[1] the Pensions Ombudsman and, most recently, the Personal Investment Authority Ombudsman scheme.

3.6. The ombudsmen in the financial services sector are an attractive alternative to the courts for consumers. They provide a speedy and informal procedure which is free of charge for the complainant. Moreover the complainant can still take the case to court if he is not satisfied with the result of the ombudsman procedure.[2] Moreover the award of the ombudsmen is usually binding on the member company. Most schemes appear to be quite successful, especially the well established ones like the Insurance and Banking Ombudsman schemes.

[3] The Parliamentary Commissioner for Administration was created by the Parliamentary Commissioners Act 1967.

[4] General Accident Insurance, Guardian Royal Exchange and the Royal. See R W Hodgin, 'Ombudsmen and Other Complaints Procedures in the Financial Services Sector in the United Kingdom', *Anglo-American Law Review*, 1992.

[5] See J Birds and C Graham, 'Complaints Mechanisms in the Financial Services Industry', *Civil Justice Quarterly*, 1988, pp 313–328.

[1] Until May 1992 the Investment Ombudsman was known as the Investment Referee.

[2] Provided that the complainant did not accept the Ombudsman's decision in final settlement. An exception to this is the Pensions Ombudsman scheme, the outcome of which is always binding on both parties. If necessary it can be enforced through the County Courts.

NOTES

The above extract is from the text of a paper presented to a symposium by Ms Wendala Jacobs from the University of Utrecht. Ms Jacobs cites several sources which discuss either general issues or specific schemes: see, eg 'Ombudsman Services: Consumer Views of the Office of the Building Societies Ombudsman and the Insurance Ombudsman Bureau' (National Consumer Council, June 1993). For further descriptions and evaluations of such schemes, see 'Consumer Redress Mechanisms' (Office of Fair Trading, November 1991), pp 37–43 and 55–60 and a detailed report by the Consumers' Association, 'Ombudsmen' (1997). This latter report points to the fact that public awareness of ombudsmen schemes is low, with even the best-known schemes, the Banking Ombudsman and the Insurance Ombudsman, being recognised by only 42 per cent of people surveyed.

The following extract illustrates the jurisdiction, functions and duties of the Insurance Ombudsman.

The Insurance Ombudsman Bureau Annual Review 1996

Terms of Reference

A. Jurisdiction

The Ombudsman has jurisdiction:

To consider any complaint (including a dispute or claim) referred to him in connection with or arising out of a policy (or proposed policy) of insurance but subject to these conditions:

(i)   The policy must be:

   (a) with a Member of the Bureau (including a member of Lloyd's); and

   (b) taken out by or on behalf of or for an individual; and

   (c) underwritten within the United Kingdom, Isle of Man or Channel Islands; and

   (d) governed by the law of England and Wales, Scotland, Northern Ireland, the Isle of Man or any of the Channel Islands.

(ii) The complaint must:

   (a) concern a claim under the policy or the marketing or administration, but not the underwriting, of the policy; and

   (b) have been considered by a senior officer of the Member and his offer or observations not accepted by the complainant; and

   (c) be referred to the Ombudsman within six months after such offer or observations (or later if the Member agrees); and

   (d) be referred by the original policyholder (or a successor in title otherwise than for value) who must be ordinarily resident in the United Kingdom, Isle of Man or Channel Islands (or a member of HM armed forces) or have been when the policy was effected; and

   (e) not concern any third party's entitlement to the policy money; and

   (f) not concern the actuarial standards, tables and principles which the Member applies to its long term insurance business (including the method of calculation of surrender values and paid up policy values and the bonus system and bonus rate applicable to the policy in question) but may concern the application of LAUTRO rules; and

   (g) not be the subject of proceedings in or decision of any court of law (or arbitration); and

   (h) not have been previously referred to the Ombudsman, unless new evidence is available.

(iii) The complaint may concern

   (a) equity release schemes marketed under the generic name of Home Income Plans;

   (b) unit trust investments (and 'policy' and 'policyholder' should be construed accordingly except in para 2(a)).

(iv) The complaint may not concern:

   (a) aspects of a policy which relate to a business or trade carried on by the complainant, unless the Member agrees;

   (b) policies which provide an indemnity or guarantee for the repayment of a mortgage or loan secured on property, unless the complainant is specifically named as the person insured.

(v)   The Ombudsman may investigate any complaint to see whether it is within his jurisdiction.

B. Functions

The Ombudsman's functions are:

(i)   To act as a counsellor or conciliator in order to facilitate the satisfaction, settlement or withdrawal of the complaint.

(ii) To act as an investigator and adjudicator in order to determine the complaint by upholding or rejecting it wholly or in part.

(iii) Where the complaint is upheld, wholly or partially, to make a monetary award against the Member binding up to £100,000 (or £20,000 a year for permanent health insurance) and being a recommendation only as to any excess.
(iv) To make such other recommendations or such representations as he thinks fit to the complainant, to the Member or to Council. However, neither the complainant nor Council shall be informed of any recommendation or representation under this paragraph as to any payment (ex gratia or otherwise) being made by a Member unless the Member agrees.

C. Duties

The Ombudsman's duties are:
(i)   To have regard to and act in conformity with—
      (a) the terms of any contract;
      (b) any applicable rule of law, judicial authority or statutory provision; and
      (c) the general principles of good insurance, investment or marketing practice, the ABI's Statements and Codes of Insurance Practice, and the LAUTRO and IMRO rules; but with (c) prevailing over (b) in favour of the complainant.
(ii) To have regard to (without being bound by) any previous decision of any Ombudsman.
(iii) To have regard to (without being bound by) any guidance of a general nature given by Council.
(iv) In the light of (1) (2) and (3), to assess what solution would be fair and reasonable in all the circumstances.
(v)   To attend as required any meeting (or part) of Council to provide reports, information and assistance.
(vi) To provide an Annual Report to Council for publication and for the Members.
(vii) Not to disclose any confidential information (except to persons properly entitled to such disclosure).

NOTES

1. In the above report the Ombudsman comments as follows on the scope of the scheme (see p 6):

   Scope of the scheme
   3.3. An important feature of the scheme has always been that no fee is charged to applicants, as opposed to the now substantial fees charged by civil courts. Lord Woolf's enquiry into civil justice has highlighted the overall cost of going to law and has commended greater use of Ombudsman schemes. In this context it must be a matter of serious concern that our scheme is unable to respond to over 50% of those who contact the Bureau each year—over 34,000 enquirers—because their complaints fall outside the scope of the scheme—either because their cases concern non-member companies, brokers or intermediaries, a third party issue, underwriting issues, or because the policyholder is not an individual but a small commercial concern. These are serious defects in the scheme, and I shall devote some of this report to a review of these aspects.

2. In 1996 nearly 5,000 new cases were referred to the Ombudsman, with awards ranging from £1 million to £5. A high proportion of the cases (77% in 1996) is dealt with by mediation rather than formal decision. In 1996 the insurer's decision was revised in favour of the policyholder in some 35% of the cases.

3. For a further reference to the Insurance Ombudsman, see above, p 197.

COMPENSATION ORDERS

A further method of obtaining redress is through the making of a compensation order following a conviction under the Powers of Criminal Courts Act 1973, s 35(1), as amended. Section 35 provides:

35. Compensation orders against convicted persons

[(1) Subject to the provisions of this Part of this Act and to section 40 of the Magistrates' Courts Act 1980 (which imposes a monetary limit on the powers of a magistrates' court under this section), a court by or before which a person is convicted of an offence, instead of or in addition to dealing with him in any other way, may, on application or otherwise, make an order (in this Act referred to as 'a compensation order') requiring him to pay compensation for any personal injury, loss or damage resulting from that offence or any other offence which is taken into consideration by the court in determining sentence [or to make payments for funeral expenses or bereavement in respect of a death resulting from any such offence, other than a death due to an accident arising out of the presence of a motor vehicle on a road; and a court shall give reasons, on passing sentence, if it does not make such an order in a case where this section empowers it to do so].

(1A) Compensation under subsection (1) above shall be of such amount as the court considers appropriate, having regard to any evidence and to any representations that are made by or on behalf of the accused or the prosecutor.]

(2) In the case of an offence under the Theft Act 1968, where the property in question is recovered, any damage to the property occurring while it was out of the owner's possession shall be treated for the purposes of subsection (1) above as having resulted from the offence, however and by whomsoever the damage was caused.

[(3) A compensation order may only be made in respect of injury, loss or damage (other than loss suffered by a person's dependants in consequence of his death) which was due to an accident arising out of the presence of a motor vehicle on a road, if—
  (a) it is in respect of damage which is treated by subsection (2) above as resulting from an offence under the Theft Act 1968; or
  (b) it is in respect of injury, loss or damage as respects which—
    (i) the offender is uninsured in relation to the use of the vehicle; and
    (ii) compensation is not payable under any arrangements to which the Secretary of State is a party;
and where a compensation order is made in respect of injury, loss or damage due to such an accident, the amount to be paid may include an amount representing the whole or part of any loss of or reduction in preferential rates of insurance attributable to the accident.

(3A) A vehicle the use of which is exempted from insurance by section 144 of the Road Traffic Act 1972 is not uninsured for the purposes of subsection (3) above.

(3B) A compensation order in respect of funeral expenses may be made for the benefit of anyone who incurred the expenses.

(3C) A compensation order in respect of bereavement may only be made for the benefit of a person for whose benefit a claim for damages for bereavement could be made under section 1A of the Fatal Accidents Act 1976.

(3D) The amount of compensation in respect of bereavement shall not exceed the amount for the time being specified in section 1A(3) of the Fatal Accidents Act 1976.]

(4) In determining whether to make a compensation order against any person, and in determining the amount to be paid by any person under such an order, the court shall have regard to his means so far as they appear or are known to the court.

[(4A) Where the court considers
(a) that it would be appropriate both to impose a fine and to make a compensation order; but
(b) that the offender has insufficient means to pay both an appropriate fine and appropriate compensation,
the court shall give preference to compensation (though it may impose a fine as well).]

(5) ...

NOTES

1. The following subsection is substituted for sub-s (4) above by the Criminal Justice Act 1988, s 170(1), Sch 15, paras 38, 40, as from a day to be appointed under s 171(1)—

   '(4) In determining whether to make a compensation order against any person, and in determining the amount to be paid by any person under such an order, it shall be the duty of the court—
   (a) to have regard to his means so far as they appear or are known to the court; and
   (b) in a case where it is proposed to make against him both a compensation order and a confiscation order under Part VI of the Criminal Justice Act 1988, also to have regard to its duty under section 72(7) of that Act (duty where the court considers that the offender's means are insufficient to satisfy both orders in full to order the payment out of sums recovered under the confiscation order of sums due under the compensation order).'

2. The monetary limit in the case of magistrates courts is now £5,000 in respect of each offence: see the Criminal Justice Act 1991, s 17(3) and sch 4. Provisions for enforcement and appeals, review, and the effect of compensation orders on a subsequent award of damages in civil proceedings are contained in ss 36–38 of the 1973 Act.

   According to Table 7.21 of the *Criminal Statistics England and Wales 1996* (Cm 3764, November 1997), at p 187, some 89,000 offenders were ordered to pay compensation by magistrates' courts in 1996, the average compensation being £158. The figures for the Crown Court were around 5,700 and £1,014, respectively. (Compensation orders were used as the sole or main penalty only in a small proportion of the cases.) Theft, handling and offences involving violence against the person featured prominently. Although there is no separate entry for consumer protection statutes, one may infer that relatively few orders are made. The Tables in the *Annual Report of the Director General for Fair Trading 1996* (see pp 77–82) suggest that convictions under the Trade Descriptions Act 1968 are more likely to lead to compensation orders (a total amount of a modest £183,000 in 1996) than are convictions under other consumer protection statutes. The apparent reluctance to use compensation orders may reflect the fact that the report on which the power to make compensation orders was based (see the Report of the Advisory Council on the Penal System,

'Reparation by the Offender', HMSO 1970) positively discouraged the making of orders in respect of 'regulatory offences', saying (at para 61):

> Our general approach to this matter is that compensation should be available in criminal pro-ceedings in respect of what might be termed 'common law' offences and not regulatory offences. We recognise that it may not be possible to legislate to give effect to this intention; and if no satisfactory provision can be drafted, it will be necessary to leave the matter to the discretion of the courts and to rely on their good sense to resort to their powers to order com-pensation only in cases where this is justified by the character of the offence.

However, a preference for a compensation order, rather than a fine was expressed by Lord Hailsham LC in a leading case under the Trade Descriptions Act 1968: see *Wings v Ellis* [1984] 3 All ER 577, at 583, [1984] 3 WLR 965, at 973 below, pp 667–8, and this is now reflected in s 35(4A) of the 1973 Act. Also, Sir Gordon (now Lord) Borrie has called for 'a little more boldness to be encouraged': see *The Development of Consumer Law and Policy* (1984), p 69.

The facts of the following case are far removed from the context of consumer protection legislation. However, it is helpful as raising a number of issues.

Bond v Chief Constable of Kent [1983] 1 All ER 456, [1983] 1 WLR 40, Queen's Bench Division

Griffiths LJ. This is an appeal by way of case stated from an order of the magistrates sitting in the petty sessional division of Gravesham who, on 15 January 1982, after the appellant had pleaded guilty to a charge of causing damage to property contrary to s 1(1) of the Criminal Damage Act 1971, made an order that he pay the sum of £25 as compensation to the occupier of the house that he had damaged because of the distress and anxiety suffered by the occupier as a result of the appellant's behaviour.

The facts of the case are briefly these. In the early hours of 30 August 1981 the occupiers of the house were aroused by noises coming from their front garden, and became aware of the presence of a man behaving strangely and stumbling about. They telephoned the police but before the police arrived a stone was thrown through the window of the house. The occupier of the house was terrified, fearing that there would be a sustained attack and felt compelled to gather his wife and children into one room for safety. The police, on arrival, found the appel-lant to be in a drunken state. He was then arrested and taken to Gravesend police station.

The magistrates were asked by the prosecutor to consider awarding £25 compensation which was the cost of replacing the damaged window, but of their own motion they also considered whether or not they should not award some modest sum to compensate the occupier of the house for what must undoubtedly have been a most terrifying and frightening experience.

They considered the terms of s 35(1) of the Powers of Criminal Courts Act 1973, which pro-vides that 'on application or otherwise' they may make 'an order . . . requiring [the appellant] to pay compensation for any personal injury, loss or damage resulting from that offence . . .' The magistrates rightly considered that there was a sufficient nexus between the behaviour and the terror caused to the occupier. Indeed, it was the only cause of the occupier's terror.

In those circumstances it appears to me that the only question for consideration by this court is whether the fright and distress suffered can be fairly covered by either the words 'personal injury' or 'damage' contained in s 35.

We have been referred to three authorities by counsel for the appellant but the first two, in my view, carry the matter that we have to decide nowhere.

. . .

The next case was *R v Vivian* [1979] 1 All ER 48, [1979] 1 WLR 291. In that case the defendant had been convicted of taking and driving away a motor car, and driving it recklessly. In the course of that he collided with and damaged another car, the estimate of repairs being £209. The judge in that case ordered him to pay compensation in the sum of £100. However, the estimate was fiercely contested by the defendant as being grossly excessive, and this court held that a compensation order should not be made unless the sum claimed by the victim as compensation for damage resulting from the offence was either agreed or had been proved. That case is clearly limited to what I will call 'quantifiable physical damage'. It has no application to small sums of money awarded for personal injury or for the results of behaviour with which we are concerned in this case.

The final case was *R v Thomson Holidays Ltd* [1974] 1 All ER 823, [1974] QB 592. In that case, Thomson Holidays Ltd had sold a package holiday and they were convicted of an offence under the Trade Descriptions Act 1968, the nature of which was that they had recklessly made a false representation in the course of their trade or business as to the amenity or accommodation provided by their hotel, contrary to s 14(1)(*b*) of that Act. The facts revealed that the hotel fell very, very far short of the legitimate expectations of anyone reading the brochure and, as a result, the customers had been very gravely disappointed in their holiday. They were awarded the modest sum of £50 by way of compensation for that disappointment.

. . .

If the disappointment and inconvenience of a ruined holiday falls within the word 'damage' in s 35 of the Powers of Criminal Courts Act 1973, I for my part have no doubt that the terror directly occasioned by this attack on the occupier's house falls either within 'personal injury' or alternatively within the word 'damage' in s 35 of the 1973 Act, and the magistrates were fully entitled to award the modest sum of £25. I would dismiss this appeal.

McCullough J. I agree. In *R v Thomson Holidays Ltd* [1974] 1 All ER 823 at 829, [1974] QB 592 at 599 Lawton LJ said:

'Parliament, we are sure, never intended to introduce into the criminal law the concepts of causation which apply to the assessment of damages under the law of contract and tort.'

In my judgment, the sense of that observation is this: that in assessing whether compensation should be awarded under s 35 of the Powers of Criminal Courts Act 1973 the court should approach the matter in a broad commonsense way and should not allow itself to become enmeshed in the refined questions of causation which can sometimes arise in claims for damages under the law of contract or tort. The court simply has to ask itself whether the loss or damage can fairly be said to have resulted from the offence. The court plainly did that.

Appeal dismissed.

QUESTIONS

Is there a necessary equivalence between the disappointed customers in the *Thomson Holidays* case and the claimant in the above case? What would the position have been if the claimant had been neither (i) the occupier of the property on which the damage occurred nor (ii) the victim, it seems, of an assault?

NOTES

1. For further discussion of compensation orders generally, see H Street, 'Compensation Orders and the Trade Descriptions Act' [1974] Crim LR 345; R Tarling and P Softley, 'Compensation Orders in the Crown Court' [1976] Crim LR 422; P S Atiyah, 'Compensation Orders and Civil Liability' [1979] Crim LR 504; J Vennard, 'Magistrates' Assessments of Compensation for Injury' [1979] Crim LR 510 and T Newburn, *The Use and Enforcement of Compensation Orders in Magistrates' Courts* (Home Office Report No 102, 1988).
2. In *R v Chappel* [1984] Crim LR 574 the court refused to accept a contention that the existence of a potential civil liability to compensate was a precondition for the making of a valid compensation order. The case concerned an order to compensate the Customs and Excise in respect of a loss arising out of failure to make VAT returns.
3. In *R v Maynard* [1983] Crim LR 821 the court was concerned with a case in which a compensation order for £3,236 had been made following six convictions for obtaining money by deception by altering car mileages. Reducing this sum it was held that compensation orders could take account of only the actual loss suffered by the victim. They could not be used as a punitive measure to remove the profit from the crime.
4. In *R v Crutchley and Tonks* (1994) 15 Cr App R (S) the Court of Appeal held that a compensation order could not be made in respect of loss or damage arising from admitted offences which had not been charged nor taken into consideration. The case was one in which the accused was charged on the basis of specimen counts only. See also *R v Hose* (1995) 16 Cr App R (S) 682, CA.

LITIGANTS IN PERSON

In his article 'The Growth of Litigants in Person in English Civil Proceedings' (1997) 16 CJQ 127 George Applebey comments:

Everyone has an almost unrestricted right to represent themselves without a solicitor or barrister and in one area, the small claims procedure, litigants in person are positively encouraged. The practice of litigating in person is a particularly English one. Few other countries, common law as well as civilian, show any inclination towards it. In many other jurisdictions it is either not allowed, or irrelevant because of other legal provisions (such as legal expenses insurance). The increase in litigants in person in England is therefore an interesting development.

Do-it-yourself litigation may have an appeal for some (although by no means all) consumer litigants. It was in recognition of this fact that the Litigants in Person (Costs and Expenses) Act 1975 made provision for the recovery of costs and expenses by litigants in person in civil proceedings. In the case of actions in the High Court the detailed provisions are contained in RSC Ord 62, r 18. Equivalent provisions for the county courts are contained in CCR 1981, Ord 38, r 17, which provides as follows:

Litigant in person

17.—(1) Where in any proceedings any costs of a litigant in person are ordered to be paid by any other party or in any other way, then, subject to the following paragraphs of this rule, there may be allowed to the litigant in person such costs as would have been allowed if the work and disbursements to which the costs relate had been done or made by a solicitor on his behalf together with any payments reasonably made by him for legal advice relating to the conduct of or the issues raised by the proceedings, and the provisions of these rules shall apply with the necessary modifications to the costs of a litigant in person as they apply to solicitors' charges and disbursements.

(2) Nothing in rule 18 or Appendix B shall apply where the plaintiff is a litigant in person.

(3) In relation to the costs of a litigant in person, rule 19(1) shall have effect as if for the words 'and the solicitor for the party to whom they are payable so desires' there were substituted the words 'and the court does not otherwise order'.

(4) Where the costs of a litigant in person are taxed or assessed without taxation—

    (a) he shall not be allowed more than such sum as would be allowed in the High Court in respect of the time reasonably spent by him in doing any work to which the costs relate if in the opinion of the court he has not suffered any pecuniary loss in doing the work, and

    (b) the amount allowed in respect of any work done by the litigant in person shall not in any case exceed two-thirds of the sum which in the opinion of the court would have been allowed in respect of that work if the litigant had been represented by a solicitor.

(5) Where the costs of a litigant in person are assessed under Appendix C, or where on the taxation of the costs of a litigant in person he is allowed a charge for attending court to conduct his own case, then, notwithstanding anything in rule 13, he shall not be entitled to a witness allowance for himself in addition.

(6) For the purposes of this rule a litigant in person does not include a litigant who is a practising solicitor.

NOTES

1. For a detailed discussion of the implications of what is now RSC Ord 62, r 18, see *Hart v Aga Khan Foundation (UK)* [1984] 2 All ER 439, [1984] 1 WLR 994, CA. The current hourly rate for the purposes of r 17(4)(a) is £9.25.

2. With the increase in the small claims limit to £3,000 (see above, p 410) it is particularly important to note that for the purposes of the 'no-costs' rule 'costs' includes 'sums allowed to a litigant in person pursuant to Order 38, rule 17'. Accordingly, the litigant in person is restricted to the costs and allowances for which Ord 19, r 4(2) and (3) makes provision (see above, p 412).

3. For discussion of the performance of Litigants in Person in the Royal Courts of Justice, see Applebey, op cit, pp 133–6, who summarises the views of Lord Justice Otton's committee.

THE ENFORCEMENT OF JUDGMENT DEBTS IN THE COUNTY COURT

INTRODUCTION

Consumers who have succeeded in obtaining a county court judgment might be forgiven for assuming that enforcement would follow as a matter of course. However this is far from the case. The onus of enforcement is placed rather on the successful litigant and the process can be expensive, time-consuming and ultimately frustrating—especially where the debtor proves to be a man of straw. Such factors have led to continual demands for the reform of enforcement procedures. In 'Simple Justice', the National Consumer Council report on Small Claims Procedures (1979), the difficulties with enforcement were said (at p 44) to 'undermine the whole system of redress for civil claims'. Drawing on the results of surveys of both consumers and advice agencies in England and Wales, the NCC concluded that:

It is pointless trying to make it easier to bring a small consumer claim in the courts if, at the end of the day, the claimant is left with a hollow victory. We consider that this brings the law and the courts into disrepute. We therefore conclude that the improvement of enforcement procedures must become a priority for the Lord Chancellor.

Unfortunately, it seems that matters have not improved significantly since 1979 and indeed Professor Baldwin has recently commented as follows in *Small Claims in the County Courts in England and Wales* (1997), at p 128:

Many plaintiffs have such bad experiences at this stage that it causes them to re-appraise the value of pursuing small claims in the first place. Indeed, a number become so jaundiced and disillusioned as a result of their failure to enforce the court's judgment that they say that they would not contemplate using the small claims procedure again in the future. These attitudes stand in such sharp contrast to the largely positive views of litigants discussed in the previous chapter that it is clearly important to ascertain what is going wrong to produce this change of heart.

This section is concerned with the methods available for the enforcement of judgment debts in the county court and the problems associated with them. In addition to the Simple Justice report reference may be made to the following: the 'Report of the Committee on the Enforcement of Judgment Debts' (Cmnd 3909, February 1969) (the Payne Report), the Report of the Review Committee on Insolvency Law and Practice (Cmnd 8558, 1982), ch 5 (the Cork Committee), Applebey, *A Practical Guide to the Small Claims Court* (1994), ch 13, Baldwin, *Small Claims in the County Courts in England and Wales* (1997), ch 5, *The County Court Practice 1997* (the 'Green Book').

METHODS OF ENFORCEMENT

Several methods of enforcement are available to a judgment creditor. The two principal methods are a warrant of execution against goods (see the County Courts Act 1984, s 86, and CCR Ord 26) and an attachment of earnings order (see the Attachment of Earnings Act 1971 and CCR Ord 27). Other methods include garnishee proceedings (see CCR Ord 30), a charging order (see the Charging Orders Act 1979 and CCR Ord 31), and the appointment of a receiver (see CCR Ord 32). A fee is payable in respect of each method of enforcement, but the costs are recoverable, being outwith the 'no costs' rule (see CCR Ord 19 r 4(3)(b), above, p 412).

Before seeking to enforce judgment the creditor ought initially to determine whether the debtor has the means to pay. This may be facilitated by an oral examination before the district judge or a senior appointee, who has the power to require the debtor to produce relevant books and documents (see CCR Ord 25, r 3). Refusal to attend the court or to answer questions will be a contempt of court.

Although the warrant of execution against goods is an appropriate method to use against a trade debtor with business assets, this is often not the case with a private debtor. With the exception of motor vehicles (which in any event will often be the property of a finance company) secondhand consumer goods have little value, especially when sold by auction. (See in the different context of repossession by finance companies, the Report of the Crowther Committee on Consumer Credit, Cmnd 4596, 1971, para 6.646).

Some of the main problems associated with enforcing judgments through an attachment of earnings order and the limits to which the process is subject are noted in the following paragraphs from the Cork Committee report:

254. This procedure attracts substantial criticism. It was introduced for judgment debts in 1971 as a result of the Payne Committee's recommendations,[1] and has met with limited success. Debtors who frequently change jobs or who are unemployed or self-employed are able to avoid this type of enforcement. The Payne Committee also recommended the endorsement of the Employee's P45 Income Tax Form (which is issued on termination of employment) with a note or code reference indicating the existence of an Attachment of Earnings Order. The new employer would be aware of this and would be obliged to take action to comply with the order or to notify the debtor's local County Court that he had commenced employment. This proposal has not been implemented and several of those who have given evidence to us have argued that it should be. We consider that further consideration should be given to this or some other solution to the problem of the debtor in respect of whom an Attachment of Earnings Order is in force and who frequently changes his job.

. . .

257. We recommend that the definition of 'earnings' be amended so as to bring within the scope of Orders for the Attachment of Earnings those self-employed persons who work regularly for one employer at an hourly or piece rate, or on commission. We have received representations that the procedure for obtaining Orders for Attachment of Earnings is too slow and involves unnecessary paperwork. We believe that a careful review of the procedure is likely to show that the elimination of some steps is feasible without reducing the overall effectiveness of the procedure and that this will result in a saving of the time of clerical staff and bailiffs.

[1] See the Report of the Committee on the Enforcement of Judgment Debts (the Payne Committee), Cmnd 3909, 1969 para 580 et seq.

NOTE

The Attachment of Earnings Act 1971, s 24 (1)(a), defines earnings as sums payable 'under a contract of services', so the self-employed are still not subject to such orders. Although debtors and their employers are obliged to notify changes of employment (see s 15 of the 1971 Act and Form N338), it seems that the above problems remain largely unresolved. For a wide ranging survey, see Wilson and Ford, 'Recovering Debt: the Effectiveness of Attachment of Earnings' (1992) 11 CJQ 363.

BUT FIRST FIND YOUR DEFENDANT

A successful civil action must of necessity depend on the plaintiff being able to trace an appropriate defendant. Sometimes this will be impossible, as when a receipt is lost or a product is unlabelled. There is another aspect of the problem which may prove just as intractable when it comes to issuing a summons or enforcing a judgment. This can be done only if the correct name and address of the defendant can be established.

The Companies Act 1985 contains provisions whereby the company name must appear outside its place of business (s 348) and in its correspondence and order forms (ss 349 and 351), which must also contain the address of its registered office. The Business Names Act 1985 contains disclosure requirements as to names and addresses for the service of documents (s 4) in the case of persons, who are subject to the Act. Broadly speaking, individuals or partnerships are not so subject (s 1) if they use a business name which comprises only of their surnames with limited additions (forenames or initials). A breach of an obligation as to disclosure is not only an offence (s 7), but it may also prevent the person or company from suing on the contract (s 5). However, since the abolition of the Registry of Business Names in 1982 there is no central register of business names. This may make it more difficult to discover the identity and location of proprietors of small businesses.

Some of the main arguments for retaining the register were put by Mr Donald Anderson MP when speaking in the Second Reading debate on the Companies (No 2) Bill (see 5 HC Official Report (6th series) col 690 (1981)). He summarised the case put by the National Consumer Council as follows:

The council says, in short, that the abolition of the registry could

'produce a paradise for shady traders, who would find it much easier to conceal their true identity, from customers, trading standards officers and investigative journalists and broadcasters trying to track them down.'

The council concludes that the Government should retain the Registry of Business Names in a new, revitalised and self-financing form. If the Government are so concerned about the hard cash of this matter, it is not difficult to increase the registration fee.

In points of detail, the council states that consumers will need to be able to trace the correct name and address of the trader whom they wish to sue, which is essential if they are to pursue a court judgment to enforcement.

. . .

As to particular flaws in the Bill relating to consumers seeking to enforce their rights, the Minister will know that the NCC has mentioned that the new system will be of no use to consumers where a business has ceased trading, and therefore the information that is available within the premises or on the business stationery will be of no assistance. It will be impossible to trace the owners, even though those owners of a business may have personal assets upon which creditors might be entitled to claim in seeking to enforce their judgments.

Similar problems could arise where a business does not have premises which are open to customers or may move its address frequently. The NCC has asked:

'How will the new requirements be enforceable against mobile-van traders, itinerant "hotel sale" traders or market stall holders? It won't be easy for a mail-order customer in Nottingham to find out, who owns a defaulting business in Exeter.'

PREPAYMENTS AND INSOLVENCY

INTRODUCTION

Over the years much attention has been focused on the problems faced by consumers who have made payments in advance for goods or services. The practice of requiring prepayments is widespread both in mail order and other transactions and the associated problems have been reviewed on several occasions, notably by the Office of Fair Trading. The following extract from an Office of Fair Trading Consultative Paper is helpful as indicating the variety of goods and services involved.

Pre-payment in Non-Mail Order Transactions—A Consultative Paper on a Proposed Reference to the Consumer Protection Advisory Committee (Office of Fair Trading, January 1979)

1. This paper reviews the problems faced by consumers who make pre-payments and seeks views upon a proposed reference by the Director General of Fair Trading (DGFT) to the Consumer Protection Advisory Committee (CPAC) recommending that traders (other than mail order traders) who accept pre-payment from consumers should be required to give standard written statements about despatch times and about the consumer's entitlement to a refund if goods and/or services are not supplied within a specified or reasonable time.

The problem
2. Consumers who have paid in advance frequently complain of delays in the delivery of goods or the performance of services. About 24,000 such complaints are reported to the OFT by

Trading Standards Officers each year, about half of which concern full or partial pre-payments made to shops or to suppliers of services. . . . Although the precise nature of the problem varies with each kind of transaction—made to measure or specially ordered goods, standard goods stocked elsewhere, services which may be subject to the availability of materials—the essential weakness is that many consumers do not have a clear idea of their rights or how to secure them. As a consequence delivery or completion dates are often not stated or are uncertain and this weakens the ability of consumers to pursue complaints effectively. The economic effects of the delay upon the consumer may consist in the impaired utility of goods needed by a particular date, vulnerability to price increases, loss of interest on the pre-payment and, where insolvency on the part of the trader intervenes, complete loss of money.

NOTES

1. The immediate result of this consultative process was that the Office of Fair Trading concluded that 'legislation was not practicable and that the improvements which are needed should instead be sought through self-regulation': see *Beeline*, No 21, December 1980, p 5. However, the problem has been further discussed, both within particular sectors and more generally. The main sources include: The Office of Fair Trading Discussion Paper and subsequent Report on 'The Protection of Consumer Prepayments' (October 1984 and March 1986, respectively); Ogus and Rowley, 'Prepayments and Insolvency' (Office of Fair Trading, October 1984); the Office of Fair Trading Discussion Paper and subsequent Report on 'Home Improvements' (March 1982 and June 1983, respectively), 'Mail Order Protection Schemes: a Review by the Office of Fair Trading' (March 1986); and, more recently, 'Pre-Paid Funeral Plans' (Office of Fair Trading, May 1995). In the report on Funeral Plans the OFT called for statutory regulation to safeguard the substantial long-term pre-payments which are often involved. It seems that a total of around £130 million is in issue.

2. An earlier reference to the Consumer Protection Advisory Committee had led to the Mail Order Transactions (Information) Order 1976, SI 1976/1812, requiring that mail order companies include their name and address in advertisements. See 'Prepayment for Goods, A Report on Practices Relating to Prepayment in Mail Order Transactions and in Shops', (HC 285 Session 1975/76) and the Supporting Dossier (17/2) prepared by the Director General of Fair Trading. For more general discussion of Part II of the Fair Trading Act 1973 under which the order was made see below, pp 538–47.

SOME APPROACHES TO THE PROBLEM

Several approaches to the problems associated with consumer prepayments have been suggested over the years. Some of these are summarised in the following extract which outlines the conclusions of an Office of Fair Trading Report on The Protection of Pre-payments in 1986:

Annual Report of the Director General of Fair Trading 1986, pp 14–15

The protection of consumer prepayments

A report, published in March, showed that nearly a third of consumers had made some kind of prepayment in 1982 and 1983. Almost half of these had done so more than once. Six per cent of those interviewed who had made a prepayment in the two-year survey period said that they had not received the goods or services ordered; in over half of these cases no refund, or only a partial refund, had been obtained. It was estimated that some £18 million had been lost in each year. Individual losses could be substantial, although most were small.

About 25 per cent of the transactions in which people lost money had been made in response to newspaper or magazine advertisements by post or telephone. A further 25 per cent had been completed at a trader's premises, 15 per cent in the customer's own home, and 13 per cent by ordering from catalogues or brochures by post or telephone.

Three main approaches to giving consumers extra protection were considered: changes in the law; voluntary measures by traders; and steps consumers could take to help themselves. The Office took the view that further voluntary measures were the best way forward, and that there was scope for improvements in the existing voluntary protection schemes. More legislation was not justified. The report noted, however, that the Office would continue to monitor the position.

Both the quality and the coverage of the existing protection schemes could be improved, and more publicity was needed for them. There was also scope to establish new schemes. The Office was always willing to discuss this with traders and trade associations that operated in markets with a substantial prepayment element.

A number of the report's recommendations were directed at consumers themselves. They included warnings to think twice before making any kind of prepayment, and against handing over money in advance to unknown traders—particularly when buying by post. Practical steps that consumers could take to protect their money were also spelled out. These points will be given wider circulation in a new Office advisory booklet due to be published early in 1987.

The Office of Fair Trading discussed the problems of prepayments within the construction industry in its 'Home Improvements' Discussion Paper (March 1982) and in a resultant Report (June 1983).

Home Improvements: A Discussion Paper (Office of Fair Trading, 1982)

Payment in Advance

3.21. A requirement for a pre- or staged payment, ie paying for goods and services in advance or making interim payments to a contractor as the job advances, is a common feature in the home improvement sector and the building trade. This is often because a substantial proportion of the cost of the job relates to materials which the supplier has to purchase in advance, and many tradesmen are reluctant or unable to wait until all of the work is completed before obtaining some payment. Builders merchants usually give a month's credit. If a contractor asks for payment in advance it may indicate that he is not considered credit-worthy by local merchants. If householders have been asked to pay in full or to pay a substantial deposit, they may in fact have paid out a considerable sum of money before they know whether they will be satisfied with the job when it is completed. Advance payment may also affect the chances of the consumer obtaining effective redress if he has a dispute with the supplier.

3.22. Moreover, payment in advance for work to be undertaken can be followed by the disappearance of the supplier before the work is started or completed or the trader may become insolvent and go into liquidation before the work is completed. Householders should recognise the possible risks of making payments in advance, before satisfactory completion of the work, which may not be related to any actual costs incurred. They should always approach requests for payment in advance with healthy scepticism and, before agreeing to payment, should satisfy themselves, first that the trader concerned has an established business, secondly, that the advance payment is reasonably related to the costs which the trader may be expected to have incurred, and thirdly, that there is every likelihood of the contract being completed.

3.23. It has also to be said that there are major shortcomings in the protection available to consumers in the event of the insolvency of the supplier. Some progress has, however, been made on the basis of voluntary action by certain trade interests. A useful measure of protection for householders who pay deposits for double glazing work is provided by the Deposit Indemnity Fund operated by the Glass and Glazing Federation.

. . .

3.24. Valuable, however, as such schemes such as that operated by the Glass and Glazing Federation may be, the experience of recent years suggests that the protection available to householders in the event of the insolvency of the supplier requires strengthening. . . .

As the above paper notes, codes of practice certainly have a part to play in protecting prepayments, whether through a bonding scheme or simply through seeking to ensure reasonable delivery dates. Codes of practice are considered in more detail in ch 10 below.

The preliminary conclusions of the Office of Fair Trading as expressed in its resultant Home Improvements report (1983) para 5.10 were that: 'the most extreme remedy of a ban on pre-payments is not an acceptable or desirable solution: more feasible would be a requirement that pre-payments should be placed in a separate trust account and used only when the trader has fulfilled the terms of the contract.' The same approach is to be seen in the Customers' Prepayments (Protection) Bill which was introduced by Mr Robin Squire MP under the Ten Minute rule. Although the Bill did not make any further progress, it succeeded in attracting some publicity for the problems which it sought to tackle. Having noted that an exercise carried out by the National Federation of Consumer Groups based on mail order complaints had shown that 'of 2,641 such complaints between July 1977 and March 1982, 26 per cent involved the liquidation of a company or the cessation of trading', he continued 22 HC Official Report (6th Series) cols 847–9, 28 April 1982:

My Bill will require that every advance payment, prepayment or deposit, however described, paid by a consumer to a company will be placed in a separate account to be known as a 'customers' prepayment account'. At all times that sum will be held in trust on behalf of the consumer and would not be available as capital, for loan, guarantee or other business purposes for the supplying company. Title in that money should remain in the customer's hands at all times. After, not before, the performance of the contract—the delivery of goods or the supply of services—the firm, individual or company concerned may then withdraw from the customer's account the amount paid by the consumer for that purpose.

In the event of any insolvency or bankruptcy, the sums held by the company shall not only remain the property of the consumer but shall be repaid to him or her one month after the declaration of liquidation or bankruptcy. Any failure to observe that would, as in the case of failure under any other aspect of company law, lead to fine or a prison sentence or both and the disqualification of the directors for the appropriate period.

No new principle is involved here. For many years solicitors have been required to maintain separate client accounts. More recently, the same requirement has been imposed upon estate agents under the Estate Agents Act 1979. Many other trading undertakings today voluntarily follow similar procedures.

. . .

Many business men insist on a ROMALPA clause in their contracts which has the effect of reserving title to them in goods sold and delivered unless and until payment is received, thus protecting them should the buyer become insolvent. I submit that what is legitimate business practice in selling to consumers should equally apply to consumers attempting to purchase.

NOTE

This idea is developed in a National Federation of Consumer Groups paper, 'Prepayments: Protecting Consumers' Deposits' (1984).

QUESTIONS

It is practicable to require that 'every advance payment' be placed in a separate trust fund? If not, which, if any, of the following might be subjected to such a requirement—(i) the payment of a train fare for travel the following day; (ii) an annual subscription to the Automobile Association or a London club; (iii) the payment of an annual premium to an insurance company, or (iv) an advance payment to a vehicle repairer undertaking work on a car?

Another approach to the problem is indicated in the following passages from the Home Improvements Discussion Paper.

Home Improvements: A Discussion Paper (Office of Fair Trading, 1982)

5.5. The ease with which the directors of a company which has failed can set up a new company and often do so, trading in the same line of business is worrying. In extreme cases, traders can be prosecuted for fraud or theft but there are many cases in which hard evidence of offences is difficult to find, but consumers suffer persistently whether as a result of fraudulence or incompetence on the part of a trader. Although the Insolvency Act 1976 (recently amended by the Companies Act 1981) provides for the disqualification of directors of failed companies in certain circumstances, this has proved in practice to be a rarely used power . . .
5.6. Against this background the Office suggested in evidence in 1979 to the Committee appointed by the Department of Trade to investigate changes necessary in insolvency law, chaired by Sir Kenneth Cork, that consumers' claims should be given preferential status or at least equal status with preferential claims. It is understood that the Cork Committee is to report shortly, and the Office hope that the Committee will, in their report, support this change in the law. Such a change would provide substantial benefit to householders with claims against traders in the home improvement sector.

NOTE

In *R v Hall* [1972] 2 All ER 1009, [1973] QB 126, travel agents were convicted on seven counts of theft in respect of deposits and payments for air trips to America.

None of the trips materialised and no refund was made. The money, the defendants claimed, had been paid into the firm's general trading account. The Court of Appeal quashed the convictions. However, Edmund Davies, LJ agreed (at pp 1011–12) that cases could 'conceivably arise where by some special arrangement . . . the client could impose on the travel agent an obligation' to retain and deal with the property or its proceeds in a particular way (see the Theft Act 1968, s 5(3)). On appropriate facts a trader may also be guilty of obtaining property (which term includes money) by deception contrary to s 15 of the 1968 Act. The bonding requirements in the Package Travel, Package Holidays and Package Tours Regulations 1992, SI 1992/3288 (below, pp 446–50) now provide considerable protection in this area.

The Cork Committee duly reported as follows:

Review Committee on Insolvency Law and Practice, Cmnd 8558 (1982)

Payments in advance for goods and services

1048. We have received many complaints that members of the public who pay in advance for goods and services have no remedy except as unsecured creditors in the event of the insolvency of the trader. They do not see themselves treated as ordinary providers of unsecured credit, though this is how they find themselves, except in those cases where special schemes have been established for their protection. Payments of this kind are made, for example, to mail order houses, to travel and entertainment promoters and, frequently, to building and repair contractors for house repairs and improvement.

1049. Programmes on television and radio, and articles in the press and other media have expressed concern that the present law is thought to be unjust to members of the public paying in advance for goods and services. The Committee has heard evidence to the effect that a considerable number of companies, dealing direct with the public, which become insolvent, have accepted or required payment prior to the delivery of the goods or services. In many cases they have started business with a totally inadequate capital, often a minimal £2. We have been urged to recommend that legislation should require all such money to be paid into special accounts having trust status, from which it could not be withdrawn by the trader for use as part of his general funds.

1050. We understand the sense of grievance felt by those who have lost money in such circumstances, but we are satisfied that the proposal is impracticable. In many cases, advance payments are an essential part of the trader's working capital. For example, a mail order company often has to purchase and pay for the goods which have been ordered by the customer, or for materials from which to manufacture them, before delivery; a tour operator often needs to use the deposits received from his clients in paying a deposit to the foreign hotel. In any case it would not be within our terms of reference to make a recommendation of this nature, unrelated to insolvency or possible insolvency.

1051. The trader's right to mix the money with his own and use it as part of his general funds is fatal to the existence of a trust. Some of those who have given evidence to us, recognising that it is not practical to require a separate account to be maintained, have urged that nevertheless payments in advance for goods or services should be repaid in full in the event of the trader's insolvency. In effect, this is to call for the creation of a new class of preferential claim.

1052. In our view, this attitude is misguided. The customer who pays in advance for goods or services to be supplied later extends credit just as surely as the trader who supplies in advance goods or services to be paid for later. There is no essential difference. Each gives credit; and if the credit is misplaced, each should bear the loss rateably.

. . .

1054. Of course, any trader is free, by taking the appropriate steps, to create a trust which will prevail in the event of his insolvency. In *Re Kayford Ltd* [1975] 1 WLR 279, the Court had to deal with a company whose chief suppliers got into financial difficulties and could not meet the company's orders; from that stage on, the company opened a special account for the receipt of moneys from customers for goods not yet delivered to them and from which withdrawals would only be made if the goods were later delivered; this account was held to have been validly constituted as a 'trust account'.

QUESTIONS

Do you agree with the Cork Committee (para 1052) that there is 'no essential difference' between the customer who makes prepayments for goods or services and the trader who supplies goods or services on credit? Ought customers to see themselves as 'ordinary providers of unsecured credit'?

NOTES

As may be seen from the above extracts, the Cork Committee did not favour either the preferential status or the compulsory trust account approach. Rather it sought to improve the position of unsecured creditors generally, for example by reducing or eliminating various types of preferential debts (see ch 32 of the Report). The details of the proposals for subjecting directors to civil liability for 'wrongful trading' are to be found in ch 44 of the Report. In essence there would be wrongful trading where liabilities, including the receipt of prepayments, were incurred 'with no reasonable prospect of meeting them' (para 1783) and where a director ought to have known that this was so—an objective test, unlike the subjective test for fraudulent trading of the then Companies Act 1948, s 332. This proposal has been broadly implemented and is now to be found in s 214 of the Insolvency Act 1986. By s 214(1), past and present directors of a company in insolvent liquidation may, on the application of the liquidator, 'be liable to make such contribution (if any) to the company's assets as the court thinks proper.' (See further Gower's *Principles of Modern Company Law* (6th edn, 1997), pp 153-5.) By s 10 of the Company Directors Disqualification Act 1986, participation in such wrongful trading is also a ground for making an order disqualifying a person from acting as a director for up to 15 years.

In 1982 the Cork Committee was concerned to end the mischief reflected in what it termed the 'widespread dissatisfaction at the ease with which a person trading through the medium of one or more companies with limited liability can allow such a company to become insolvent, form a new company, and then carry on trading much as before leaving behind him a trail of unpaid creditors, and often repeating the process several times' (para 1813)—a phenomenon sometimes known as the 'Phoenix Syndrome'. It is to be hoped that in the intervening years this phenomenon has become less prevalent.

QUESTIONS

1. Trader enters a contract with Householder whereby he agrees to supply and fit double-glazing in Householder's London flat. He asks for and receives £1,000 cash, saying, 'I need it to buy materials for the job'. Trader pays the money into his business account at the Dogger Bank. The following week he withdraws £1,000 in cash from this account, spending £500 in buying materials for another customer, Ivan, and the remaining £500 at the races. Trader then becomes insolvent. Discuss Trader's criminal liability under the Theft Act, s 5(3). Would it affect the position if the money had been spent directly without it passing through his bank account?

2. In February 1997 Oenophile receives a catalogue from Vintner advertising 1995 Rhones at 'opening prices'. He immediately orders ten cases of Hermitage at £280 per case. The wine is to be bottled in France later that year and delivered in 1998 when shipping, duty and VAT charges will be invoiced separately. In March 1997 Oenophile's cheque for £2,800 is cashed by Vintner and in April 1997 Oenophile is informed that Vintner is in liquidation. Advise Oenophile.

3. Carpetbaggers Ltd places a notice in the window of its shop reading, 'Thousands of Rolls of Top Quality Carpet. Only £10 per square metre. Order Now'. On 1 June Partridge orders 50 square metres of carpet from the shop, paying £500 in advance. On 3 June the carpet is cut according to Partridge's measurements and placed in a corner of Carpetbaggers' warehouse for delivery at the end of the month. The following day Carpetbaggers goes into liquidation.

   Advise Partridge who is claiming to be entitled to the carpet as against the liquidator. [See generally the Sale of Goods Act 1979, ss 17 and 18; Atiyah, *Sale of Goods* (9th edn, 1995), ch 17.

BONDING ARRANGEMENTS

In a number of areas there are bonding arrangements which operate to the benefit of consumers. Examples are to be found in such areas as holiday travel and mail order.

HOLIDAY TRAVEL

Holiday travel is an area in which very substantial prepayments are often made many months in advance. This has given rise to considerable difficulty over the years with the collapse of such major operators as Court Line and Laker. The Air

Travel Reserve Fund Agency was established in 1975. In an Adjournment debate on 10 February 1984 Mr Dick Douglas, MP, explained that:

> The fund's concept was to make payments to or for the customers of air travel organisers in respect of losses or liabilities incurred by them. In support of that concept is the licence administered by the Civil Aviation Authority, given to air travel organisers after having been assessed as being financially able to meet their commitments. Part of the licence assessment relates to the ability to meet a bond laid down by the CAA. There is also another bond for members of the Association of British Travel Agents.

(See 53 HC Official Report (6th series) col 1118. The operation of the fund was reviewed, although no fundamental changes were considered necessary: see 'Review of Arrangements for Protecting the Clients of Air Travel Organisers' (Sir Peter Lane, 1984.)

Nowadays the most important source of protection is through the following provisions:

The Package Travel, Package Holidays and Package Tours Regulations 1992, SI 1992/3288

. . .

Security in the event of insolvency—requirements and offences

16.—(1) The other party to the contract shall at all times be able to provide sufficient evidence of security for the refund of money paid over and for the repatriation of the consumer in the event of insolvency.

(2) Without prejudice to paragraph (1) above, and subject to paragraph (4) below, save to the extent that—

  (a) the package is covered by measures adopted or retained by the member State where he is established for the purpose of implementing Article 7 of the Directive; or

  (b) the package is one in respect of which he is required to hold a licence under the Civil Aviation (Air Travel Organisers' Licensing) Regulations 1972 (SI 1972/223) or the package is one that is covered by the arrangements he has entered into for the purposes of those Regulations,

the other party to the contract shall at least ensure that there are in force arrangements as described in regulations 17, 18, 19 or 20 or, if that party is acting otherwise than in the course of business, as described in any of those regulations or in regulation 21.

(3) Any person who contravenes paragraph (1) or (2) of this regulation shall be guilty of an offence and liable:—

  (a) on summary conviction to a fine not exceeding level 5 on the standard scale; and

  (b) on conviction on indictment, to a fine.

(4) A person shall not be guilty of an offence under paragraph (3) above by reason only of the fact that arrangements such as are mentioned in paragraph (2) above are not in force in respect of any period before 1 April 1993 unless money paid over is not refunded when it is due or the consumer is not repatriated in the event of insolvency.

(5) For the purposes of regulations 17 to 21 below a contract shall be treated as having been fully performed if the package or, as the case may be, the part of the package has been completed irrespective of whether the obligations under the contract have been properly performed for the purposes of regulation 15.

Bonding

17.—(1) The other party to the contract shall ensure that a bond is entered into by an authorised institution under which the institution binds itself to pay to an approved body of which that other party is a member a sum calculated in accordance with paragraph (3) below in the event of the insolvency of that other party.

(2) Any bond entered into pursuant to paragraph (1) above shall not be expressed to be in force for a period exceeding eighteen months.

(3) The sum referred to in paragraph (1) above shall be such sum as may reasonably be expected to enable all monies paid over by consumers under or in contemplation of contracts for relevant packages which have not been fully performed to be repaid and shall not in any event be a sum which is less than the minimum sum calculated in accordance with paragraph (4) below.

(4) The minimum sum for the purposes of paragraph (3) above shall be a sum which represents:—
- (a) not less than 25% of all the payments which the other party to the contract estimates that he will receive under or in contemplation of contracts for relevant packages in the twelve month period from the date of entry into force of the bond referred to in paragraph (1) above; or
- (b) the maximum amount of all the payments which the other party to the contract expects to hold at any one time, in respect of contracts which have not been fully performed,

whichever sum is the smaller.

(5) Before a bond is entered into pursuant to paragraph (1) above, the other party to the contract shall inform the approved body of which he is a member of the minimum sum which he proposes for the purposes of paragraphs (3) and (4) above and it shall be the duty of the approved body to consider whether such sum is sufficient for the purpose mentioned in paragraph (3) and, if it does not consider that this is the case, it shall be the duty of the approved body so to inform the other party to the contract and to inform him of the sum which, in the opinion of the approved body, is sufficient for that purpose.

(6) Where an approved body has informed the other party to the contract of a sum pursuant to paragraph (5) above, the minimum sum for the purposes of paragraphs (3) and (4) above shall be that sum.

(7) In this regulation—
'approved body' means a body which is for the time being approved by the Secretary of State for the purposes of this regulation;
'authorised institution' means a person authorised under the law of a member State [of the Channel Islands or of the Isle of Man] to carry on the business of entering into bonds of the kind required by this regulation.

Bonding where approved body has reserve fund or insurance

18.—(1) The other party to the contract shall ensure that a bond is entered into by an authorised institution, under which the institution agrees to pay to an approved body of which that other party is a member a sum calculated in accordance with paragraph (3) below in the event of the insolvency of that other party.

(2) Any bond entered into pursuant to paragraph (1) above shall not be expressed to be in force for a period exceeding eighteen months.

(3) The sum referred to in paragraph (1) above shall be such sum as may be specified by the approved body as representing the lesser of—

(a) the maximum amount of all the payments which the other party to the contract expects to hold at any one time in respect of contracts which have not been fully performed; or

(b) the minimum sum calculated in accordance with paragraph (4) below.

(4) The minimum sum for the purposes of paragraph (3) above shall be a sum which represents not less than 10% of all the payments which the other party to the contract estimates that he will receive under or in contemplation of contracts for relevant packages in the twelve month period from the date of entry referred to in paragraph (1) above.

(5) In this regulation 'approved body' means a body which is for the time being approved by the Secretary of State for the purposes of this regulation and no such approval shall be given unless the conditions mentioned in paragraph (6) below are satisfied in relation to it.

(6) A body may not be approved for the purposes of this regulation unless—

(a) it has a reserve fund or insurance cover with an insurer authorised in respect of such business in a member State [the Channel Islands or the Isle of Man] of an amount in each case which is designed to enable all monies paid over to a member of the body of consumers under or in contemplation of contracts for relevant packages which have not been fully performed to be repaid to those consumers in the event of the insolvency of the member; and

(b) where it has a reserve fund, it agrees that the fund will be held by persons and in a manner approved by the Secretary of State.

(7) In this regulation, authorised institution has the meaning given to that expression by paragraph (7) of regulation 17.

Insurance

19.—(1) The other party to the contract shall have insurance under one or more appropriate policies with an insurer authorised in respect of such business in a member State under which the insurer agrees to indemnify consumers, who shall be insured persons under the policy, against the loss of money paid over by them under or in contemplation of contracts for packages in the event of the insolvency of the contractor.

(2) The other party to the contract shall ensure that it is a term of every contract with a consumer that the consumer acquires the benefit of a policy of a kind mentioned in paragraph (1) above in the event of the insolvency of the other party to the contract.

(3) In this regulation:

'appropriate policy' means one which does not contain a condition which provides (in whatever terms) that no liability shall arise under the policy, or that any liability so arising shall cease:—

(i) in the event of some specified thing being done or omitted to be done after the happening of the event giving rise to a claim under the policy;

(ii) in the event of the policy holder not making payments under or in connection with other policies; or

(iii) unless the policy holder keeps specified records or provides the insurer with or makes available to him information therefrom.

Monies in trust

20.—(1) The other party to the contract shall ensure that all monies paid over by a consumer under or in contemplation of a contract for a relevant package are held in the United Kingdom by a person as trustee for the consumer until the contract has been fully performed or any sum of money paid by the consumer in respect of the contract has been repaid to him or has been forfeited on cancellation by the consumer.

(2) The costs of administering the trust mentioned in paragraph (1) above shall be paid for by the other party to the contract.

(3) Any interest which is earned on the monies held by the trustee pursuant to paragraph (1) shall be held for the other party to the contract and shall be payable to him on demand.

(4) Where there is produced to the trustee a statement signed by the other party to the contract to the effect that—

(a) a contract for a package the price of which is specified in that statement has been fully performed;

(b) the other party to the contract has repaid to the consumer a sum of money specified in that statement which the consumer had paid in respect of a contract for a package; or

(c) the consumer has on cancellation forfeited a sum of money specified in that statement which he had paid in respect of a contract for a relevant package,

the trustee shall (subject to paragraph (5) below) release to the other party to the contract the sum specified in the statement.

(5) Where the trustee considers it appropriate to do so, he may require the other party to the contract to provide further information or evidence of the matters mentioned in sub-paragraph (a), (b) or (c) of paragraph (4) above before he releases any sum to that other party pursuant to that paragraph.

(6) Subject to paragraph (7) below, in the event of the insolvency of the other party to the contract the monies held in trust by the trustee pursuant to paragraph (1) of this regulation shall be applied to meet the claims of consumers who are creditors of that other party in respect of contracts for packages in respect of which the arrangements were established and which have not been fully performed and, if there is a surplus after those claims have been met, it shall form part of the estate of that insolvent other party for the purposes of insolvency law.

(7) If the monies held in trust by the trustee pursuant to paragraph (1) of this regulation are insufficient to meet the claims of consumers as described in paragraph (6), payments to those consumers shall be made by the trustee on a pari passu basis.

Monies in trust where other party to contract is acting otherwise than in the course of business

21.—(1) The other party to the contract shall ensure that all monies paid over by a consumer under or in contemplation of a contract for a relevant package are held in the United Kingdom by a person as trustee for the consumer for the purpose of paying for the consumer's package.

(2) The costs of administering the trust mentioned in paragraph (1) shall be paid for out of the monies held in trust and the interest earned on those monies.

(3) Where there is produced to the trustee a statement signed by the other party to the contract to the effect that—

(a) the consumer has previously paid over a sum of money specified in that statement in respect of a contract for a package and that sum is required for the purpose of paying for a component (or part of a component) of the package;

(b) the consumer has previously paid over a sum of money specified in that statement in respect of a contract for a package and the other party to the contract has paid that sum in respect of a component (or part of a component) of the package;

(c) the consumer requires the repayment to him of a sum of money specified in that statement which was previously paid over by the consumer in respect of a contract for a package; or

(d) the consumer has on cancellation forfeited a sum of money specified in that statement which he had paid in respect of a contract for a package,

the trustee shall (subject to paragraph (4) below) release to the other party to the contract the sum specified in the statement.

(4) Where the trustee considers it appropriate to do so, he may require the other party to the contract to provide further information or evidence of the matters mentioned in sub-paragraph (a), (b), (c) or (d) of paragraph (3) above before he releases to that other party any sum from the monies held in trust for the consumer.

(5) Subject to paragraph (6) below, in the event of the insolvency of the other party to the contract and of contracts for packages not being fully performed (whether before or after the insolvency) the monies held in trust by the trustee pursuant to paragraph (1) of this regulation shall be applied to meet the claims of consumers who are creditors of that other party in respect of amounts paid over by them and remaining in the trust fund after deductions have been made in respect of amounts released to that other party pursuant to paragraph (3) and, if there is a surplus after those claims have been met, it shall be divided amongst those consumers pro rata.

(6) If the monies held in trust by the trustee pursuant to paragraph (1) of this regulation are insufficient to meet the claims of consumers as described in paragraph (5) above, payments to those consumers shall be made by the trustee on a pari passu basis.

(7) Any sums remaining after all the packages in respect of which the arrangements were established have been fully performed shall be dealt with as provided in the arrangements or, in default of such provision, may be paid to the other party to the contract.

Offences arising from breach of regulations 20 and 21

22.—(1) If the other party to the contract makes a false statement under paragraph (4) of regulation 20 or paragraph (3) of regulation 21 he shall be guilty of an offence.

(2) If the other party to the contract applies monies released to him on the basis of a statement made by him under regulation 21(3)(a) or (c) for a purpose other than that mentioned in the statement he shall be guilty of an offence.

(3) If the other party to the contract is guilty of an offence under paragraph (1) or (2) of this regulation he shall be liable—

(a) on summary conviction to a fine not exceeding level 5 of the standard scale; and

(b) on conviction on indictment, to a fine.

. . .

Later sections include provisions for enforcement and defences etc.

NOTES

1. The relevant definitions are contained in reg 2, which is printed above, at pp 171–2. The expression 'the other party to the contract' means the organiser of the package and the retailer who sells it.
2. The required bonding arrangement depends on whether there is an approved body with a reserve fund or insurance (reg 18) or not (reg 17).

3. For general discussion, see Rinkes, 'Air Travel and Package Holidays' in Lonbay (ed), *Enhancing the Legal Position of the European Consumer* (1996), ch 12.
4. Particularly where the situation falls outside the scope of the Regulations (eg because accommodation only is provided) consumers may well be advised to pay by credit card and so avail themselves of the potential benefit of the Consumer Credit Act 1974, s 75, above, pp 300–304.

MAIL ORDER

Mail order protection schemes run by the newspaper and periodical publishers' trade associations date from April 1975. The main National Newspaper Mail Order Protection Scheme (MOPS) contains provisions for safeguarding readers' money, sometimes through the use of a Stakeholder or Readers' Account which operates when an advertiser ceases to trade. The Scheme also states that forward trading, that is receiving readers' money and then purchasing goods to fulfil orders, is not permitted. The advertiser is expected to hold and wholly own adequate stocks to meet reasonable responses. The operation of the several schemes was last reviewed by the Office of Fair Trading in 1986: see 'Mail Order Protection Schemes' (March, 1986). The review concluded that: 'while the schemes provided a generally effective and helpful protection for cash-with-order shoppers within their own terms, additional protection was needed. Research had indicated that the existing schemes protected only seven per cent of all cash-with-order advertisements placed and just over ten per cent of the losses suffered by consumers, which ran to over £4 million a year. The Office is following up the recommendations of the report with the various bodies concerned about ways of widening coverage and making consumers more aware of the protection afforded': see the *Annual Report of the Director General of Fair Trading 1986*, p 15. In the Annual Report for 1987 the Director General indicated (at p 19) that steps were to be taken to strengthen the safeguards available under the main schemes and to give them more publicity. The terms of the scheme are printed in *Butterworths Trading and Consumer Law*, Vol 2, Div 5, para 762 et seq.

CHAPTER 9

The enforcement of private law remedies II: conditional fees and collective redress

INTRODUCTION

The main concern of this chapter is with collective as opposed to individual redress, principally through representative and class or group actions and the work of public agencies and consumer organisations. However, we first discuss the following relatively recent development.

CONDITIONAL FEE AGREEMENTS

The background to CFAs is described by Professor Ian Scott as follows:

Supreme Court Practice News: Issue 5, May 17, 1991

Conditional Fee Agreements

Contingency fee agreements between lawyer and client are not enforceable in English law. In the *Report of the Review Body on Civil Justice* (Cm 394, 1988) it was noted that, under a contingency fee system, the plaintiff's lawyer takes an agreed percentage of the damages recovered if he wins but makes no charge if he loses. Thus the plaintiff need have no fear about having to meet his own costs in litigation. There is in Scotland a long tradition of a lawyer acting on a 'speculative' basis. The arrangement there is that the lawyer will be paid his normal fee if the case is successful, and if the case is lost he will be paid nothing. The Review Body was not able to make a full study of this matter. However, it recommended that, if other issues relating to the financing of litigation or to competition policy should be found to impinge on the ban on contingency fees and other incentive schemes, that ban should be open to re-examination. The matter was re-opened in the *Green Paper on Contingency Fees* (Cm 571, 1989) where various contingency fee systems were discussed and firm proposals for a limited scheme were put forward in the *White Paper on Legal Services*. As a result, the matter was dealt with in the Courts and Legal Services Act 1990, s 58.

Courts and Legal Services Act 1990, s 58

Conditional fee agreements

58.—(1) In this section 'a conditional fee agreement' means an agreement in writing between a person providing advocacy or litigation services and his client which—

(a) does not relate to proceedings of a kind mentioned in subsection (10);

(b) provides for that person's fees and expenses, or any part of them, to be payable only in specified circumstances;

(c) complies with such requirements (if any) as may be prescribed by the Lord Chancellor; and

(d) is not a contentious business agreement (as defined by section 59 of the Solicitors Act 1974).

(2) Where a conditional fee agreement provides for the amount of any fees to which it applies to be increased, in specified circumstances, above the amount which would be payable if it were not a conditional fee agreement, it shall specify the percentage by which that amount is to be increased.

(3) Subject to subsection (6), a conditional fee agreement which relates to specified proceedings shall not be unenforceable by reason only of its being a conditional fee agreement.

(4) In this section 'specified' proceedings' means proceedings of a description specified by order made by the Lord Chancellor for the purposes of subsection (3).

(5) Any such order shall prescribe the maximum permitted percentage for each description of specified proceedings.

(6) An agreement which falls within subsection (2) shall be unenforceable if, at the time when it is entered into, the percentage specified in the agreement exceeds the prescribed maximum permitted percentage for the description of proceedings to which it relates.

(7) Before making any order under this section the Lord Chancellor shall consult the designated judges, the General Council of the Bar, the Law Society and such other authorised bodies (if any) as he considers appropriate.

(8) Where a party to any proceedings has entered into a conditional fee agreement and a costs order is made in those proceedings in his favour, the costs payable to him shall not include any element which takes account of any percentage increase payable under the agreement.

(9) Rules of court may make provision with respect to the taxing of any costs which include fees payable under a conditional fee agreement.

(10) The proceedings mentioned in subsection (1)(a) are any criminal proceedings and any proceedings under—

(a) the Matrimonial Causes Act 1973;

(b) the Domestic Violence and Matrimonial Proceedings Act 1976;

(c) the Adoption Act 1976;

(d) the Domestic Proceedings and Magistrates' Courts Act 1978;

(e) sections 1 and 9 of the Matrimonial Homes Act 1983;

(f) Part III of the Matrimonial and Family Proceedings Act 1984;

(g) Parts I, II or IV of the Children Act 1989; or

(h) the inherent jurisdiction of the High Court in relation to children.

The two provisions which follow contain further important details.

The Conditional Fee Agreements Order 1995, SI 1995/1674

Citation and commencement

1. This Order may be cited as the Conditional Fee Agreements Order 1995 and shall come into force on the day after the day on which it was made.

Specified proceedings

2.—(1) The proceedings specified for the purpose of section 58(4) of the Courts and Legal Services Act 1990 (conditional fee agreements in respect of specified proceedings not to be unenforceable) are the following:—

(a) proceedings in which there is a claim for damages in respect of personal injuries or in respect of a person's death, and 'personal injuries' includes any disease and any impairment of a person's physical or mental condition;

(b) proceedings in England and Wales by a company which is being wound up in England and Wales or Scotland;

(c) proceedings by a company in respect of which an administration order made under Part II of the Insolvency Act 1986 is in force;

(d) proceedings in England and Wales by a person acting in the capacity of—

    (i) liquidator of a company which is being wound up in England and Wales or Scotland; or

    (ii) trustee of a bankrupt's estate;

(e) proceedings by a person acting in the capacity of an administrator appointed pursuant to the provisions of Part II of the Insolvency Act 1986;

(f) proceedings before the European Commission of Human Rights and the European Court of Human Rights established under article 19 of the Convention for the Protection of Human Rights and Fundamental Freedoms opened for signature at Rome on 4th November 1950, ratified by the United Kingdom on 8th March 1951, which came into force on 3rd August 1953,

provided that the client does not have legal aid in respect of the proceedings.

(2) Proceedings specified in paragraph (1) shall be specified proceedings, notwithstanding that they are concluded without the commencement of court proceedings.

(3) In paragraphs (1)(b) and (1)(d) 'company' means a company within the meaning of section 735(1) of the Companies Act 1985 or a company which may be wound up under Part V of the Insolvency Act 1986.

(4) Where legal aid in respect of the proceedings to which a conditional fee agreement relates is granted after that agreement is entered into the proceedings shall cease to be specified from the date of the grant.

(5) In this article, 'legal aid' means representation under Part IV of the Legal Aid Act 1988.

Maximum permitted percentage increase on fees

3. For the purpose of section 58(5) of the Courts and Legal Services Act 1990 the maximum permitted percentage by which fees may be increased in respect of each description of proceedings specified in article 2 is 100%.

The Conditional Fee Agreements Regulations 1995, SI 1995/1675

Citation commencement and interpretation

1.—(1) These Regulations may be cited as the Conditional Fee Agreements Regulations 1995 and shall come into force on the day after the day on which they are made.

(2) In these Regulations—

'agreement', in relation to an agreement between a legal representative and an additional legal representative, includes a retainer;

'legal aid' means representation under Part IV of the Legal Aid Act 1988;

'legal representative' means a person providing advocacy or litigation services.

Agreements to comply with prescribed requirements

2. An agreement shall not be a conditional fee agreement unless it complies with the requirements of the following regulations.

Requirements of an agreement

3. An agreement shall state—

(a) the particular proceedings or parts of them to which it relates (including whether it relates to any counterclaim, appeal or proceedings to enforce a judgment or order);

    (b) the circumstances in which the legal representative's fees and expenses or part of them are payable;

    (c) what, if any, payment is due—

        (i)   upon partial failure of the specified circumstances to occur;

        (ii) irrespective of the specified circumstances occurring; and

        (iii) upon termination of the agreement for any reason;

    (d) the amount payable in accordance with sub-paragraphs (b) or (c) above or the method to be used to calculate the amount payable; and in particular whether or not the amount payable is limited by reference to the amount of any damages which may be recovered on behalf of the client.

Additional requirements

4.—(1) The agreement shall also state that, immediately before it was entered into, the legal representative drew the client's attention to the matters specified in paragraph (2).

(2) The matters are—

    (a) whether the client might be entitled to legal aid in respect of the proceedings to which the agreement relates, the conditions upon which legal aid is available and the application of those conditions to the client in respect of the proceedings;

    (b) the circumstances in which the client may be liable to pay the fees and expenses of the legal representative in accordance with the agreement;

    (c) the circumstances in which the client may be liable to pay the costs of any other party to the proceedings; and

    (d) the circumstances in which the client may seek taxation of the fees and expenses of the legal representative and the procedure for so doing.

Application of regulation 4

5. Regulation 4 shall not apply to an agreement between a legal representative and an additional legal representative.

Form of agreement

6. An agreement shall be in writing and, except in the case of an agreement between a legal representative and an additional legal representative, shall be signed by the client and the legal representative.

Amendment of agreement

7. Where it is proposed to extend the agreement to cover further proceedings or parts of them regulations 3 to 6 shall apply to the agreement as extended.

NOTES

1. Both the above provisions came into force on 5 July 1995. Since then, the perception of what is and is not lawful in relation to contingent fees has been affected by the decision in *Thai Trading Co v Taylor* (1998), *The Times*, 6 March, CA This permits agreements whereby a solicitor is paid ordinary costs if the case is won, but not if it is lost. See also *Bevan Ashford v Geoff Yeandle (Contractors) Ltd* (1998), *The Times*, 23 April.

2. As was noted above (see p 408), the Lord Chancellor has announced proposals for a very considerable increase in the scope of the conditional fee or 'no win, no fee' system and a reduction in civil legal aid. Such proposals are supported on the ground that they open up access to justice for those who are moderately well off, but they are also opposed to the extent that they would operate at the expense of legal aid for those who are currently entitled to it.

3. A survey by Stella Yarrow (see *The Price of Success*, Policy Studies Institute, 1997) indicates that nearly all agreements observe the Law Society's suggested ceiling of a success fee of 25 per cent of damages awarded and only a small proportion approach the permitted 100 per cent uplift. However, further difficulties are associated with the risk of losing a case with a consequent need to meet the opponent's costs. 'No win, no fee' does not provide protection against this (although the small claims procedure does: (see above, p 417), and hence the prudent litigant must take out insurance cover. The Law Society's Accident Line Protect insurance scheme has been prominent in arranging such cover. For general discussion, see Zander, 'Two cheers for conditional fees—maybe' (1997) 147 NLJ 1438; and a selection of articles and comments in *The Times*, 25 May 1993, p 29 (Michael Cook), 11 July 1995, p 33 (Michael Napier), 29 October 1996, p 37 (Frances Gibb), 4 October 1997, p 1 (Frances Gibb and Nicholas Wood), 14 October 1997, p 41 (Philip Sycamore), 16 October 1997, p 8 (Frances Gibb), 21 October 1997, p 41, 28 October 1997, p 20 (Adrian Zuckerman).

QUESTIONS AND NOTES

1. Under a 'no win, no fee' system there is an obvious incentive for solicitors to take on cases in which the chances of success are very high—as when carbolic acid is found in lemonade or a surgical instrument is left in a stomach. What considerations will be important in cases where the outcome is less clear-cut?
2. Robert Owen, QC, as Chairman of the Bar, is reported as saying 'To pursue a claim . . . litigants will have to take out an insurance premium in case they lose and have to pay the other side's costs. The minimum of such a premium would be £100 which people now on legal aid could not afford . . . In a medical negligence case I am appearing in at present, the client has had to pay £15,000 in insurance for £100,000 worth of cover for legal costs': see *The Times*, 16 October 1997, p 8. If such figures are at all typical what, if anything, might be done to remove or reduce the disincentive? The difficulties associated with removing medical negligence claims from the legal aid scheme have been recognised in the Consultation Paper 'Access to Justice with Conditional Fees' (March 1998), paras 3.15–3.21. It is now envisaged that, at least in the short term, legal aid will remain available in such cases, but only through approved providers.
3. Another critical issue is whether lawyers acting for an unsuccessful plaintiff under a conditional fee agreement may be liable in respect of the defendant's costs. In *Hodgson v Imperial Tobacco Ltd*, *The Times*, 13 February 1998, the Court of Appeal held in the context of litigation against tobacco companies that the very limited risk of being held liable (eg following a wasted costs order under under s 51(6) of the Supreme Court Act 1981) was no different from under other fee arrangements.
4. The conditional fee system will not be available to a defendant, who must pay legal fees unconditionally to the extent that they are not covered by legal aid. Does this place defendants in an unfair situation?

REPRESENTATIVE AND CLASS OR GROUP ACTIONS

INTRODUCTION

There will be many cases in which consumers suffer what may be termed a 'common wrong'. Such cases fall into two broad categories. First, there are those in which injury, damage or inconvenience is caused in a single incident, for example an aeroplane or coach crash, a mass poisoning or a disastrous holiday package. Second, there are cases in which consumers have a common or broadly similar complaint, perhaps because they have been injured individually by a drug (for example, Thalidomide or Opren) or bought a product with a common design defect or relied on the self-same advertisement. For consumers generally, there are advantages in a system which permits the amalgamation or joint treatment of such claims. It is likely that an individual's bargaining strength will be increased through not standing alone and society as a whole has an interest in avoiding a proliferation of actions based on substantially similar facts. Moreover, as Richard Tur has noted when discussing the attractions of a class action procedure (see 'Litigation and the Consumer Interest: the Class Action and Beyond' (1982) 2 Legal Studies 135, 153):

> [It] meets one of the most obvious restraints upon litigation by pooling the interests and possibly the resources of many plaintiffs, each of whom may have suffered modest loss. If A defrauds B of £5,000,000 the law provides a remedy; if A has the wit to defraud one million individuals of £5 each, absent any class action procedure, he runs little risk of civil action on the motion of any one of them: 'By the simple device of committing numerous small wrongs, law breakers might escape the arm of justice as long as they stay clear of criminal sanctions and the reach of repressive administrative action' [citing Homburger (1971) 71 Columbia LR 609, 641].

The literature in this area is now voluminous and it includes the following: Jolowicz, 'Protection of Diffuse, Fragmented and Collective Interests in Civil Litigation: English Law' (1983) 42 CLJ 222; 'General Ideas and the Reform of Civil Procedure' (1983) 3 Legal Studies 295; Arthur Miller, 'Of Frankenstein Monsters and Shining Knights: Myth, Reality and the "Class Action Problem"' (1979) 92 Harvard LR 664; Fisch, 'European Analogues to the Class Action: Group Actions in France and Germany' (1979) 27 AJCL 51; 'Report on Class Actions' (Ontario Law Reform Commission, 1982); Lindblom & Watson, 'Complex Litigation—A Comparative Perspective' (1993) 12 CLJ 33; Mildred in Miller, *Product Liability and Safety Encyclopaedia* (1998), Div III A; Cramton, 'Individualized Justice, Mass Torts and Settlement Class Actions' (1995) 80 Cornell LR 811 and other articles in the same issue.

JOINDER AND CONSOLIDATION

In English law there has long been provision for the joinder of parties and the consolidation of actions involving common questions of law or fact (see respectively

RSC, Ord 15, r 4 and Ord 4, r 9). The essential difference between joinder and consolidation is that in the former case the parties bring their action by means of the same writ.

Joinder may be appropriate if P1, P2 and P3 have all been injured in the same accident and the only live issue is whether the defendant (D) was negligent. However, if P1 sues D separately and succeeds in his action the traditional view is that it remains open to D to deny negligence (or, as the case may be, that his product is defective or of unsatisfactory quality etc) in any subsequent action brought by P2. As between D and P1 the matter is res judicata but as between D and P2 (with whom P1 is not 'privy') issue estoppel will not prevent D from disputing even central findings of fact in the earlier action: see generally *Cross and Tapper on Evidence* (8th edn, 1995), pp 83–91.

TEST CASES AND LEAD ACTIONS

It is unlikely that joinder and consolidation will of themselves be a practical proposition where a multiplicity of potential plaintiffs is involved. In any event the approach may not help where individual claims are too small to warrant litigation. As an alternative it may be agreed to single out a particular action and treat it as a test case. In practice this may prove to be perfectly adequate as a means of vindicating multiple claims, especially where public authorities are involved. This seems to have been true of *Congreve v Home Office* ([1976] QB 629, [1976] 1 All ER 697, CA) where some 17,000 colour television licence holders were involved, Mr Congreve being 'their leader'.

The Supreme Court Procedure Committee has commented as follows on test cases or lead actions.

Guide for Use in Group Actions (May, 1991)

Having referred to RSC Order 4, rule 9, which enables a court to order 'causes or matters to be consolidated on such terms as it thinks just or order them to be tried at the same time or one immediately after another or . . . any of them to be stayed until after the determination of any of them', the Guide continues:

The powers under RSC Order 4 rule 9 may be used by the judge in charge of the litigation to select certain lead actions and stay others so that certain typical situations can be the subject of judicial decision for the benefit of other litigants in other cases within the Group.

A decision of fact in a lead action is in strict law not binding on other parties in other actions unless they have agreed in advance that the decision is to bind them, or unless there is an order of the court to that effect. However, in appropriate circumstances, the court will strike out as an abuse of the process a claim or defence which seeks, in the absence of some special reason, to relitigate a point determined in the lead action. One such circumstance justifying an order to strike out would be the situation where the litigant whose claim or defence is put in question had previously been given full opportunity to be heard on the selection of lead cases and had not objected to the choice made.[14] To avoid later disputes as to the binding nature of findings in the lead actions, consideration should be given to applications for express orders in advance of the trial of the lead actions that parties to all other actions in the Group should be bound by the findings of fact in the lead actions. Once a party has been involved in the selection of lead cases to determine specific issues, that party should pursue to judgment, and not seek, without very good reason, to abandon or 'buy-off' any specific lead case designed to test that issue.

This procedure of lead actions can be useful if there is co-operation on both sides, with perhaps some prodding from the judge in charge of the case. A substantial defendant may, for reasons of commerce or expediency, prefer to have a host of actions dealt with expeditiously and comparatively cheaply. Certainly, over several years past, employers and trades unions have co-operated in selecting plaintiffs in trades union financed litigation concerning industrial injuries to obtain judicial decisions on the appropriate damages over a range of cases to help legal advisers on both sides reach settlements of other cases.

It is important that a sufficient number of lead cases should be chosen to obtain decisions on all the points required for the disposal of as many of the cases in the group as possible. Equally, to achieve the greatest saving in interlocutory costs, the selection of lead cases should be made as soon as possible. On the other hand, some issues may not become apparent until fairly late in the preparations for trial. A measure of flexibility will usually be appropriate in Group litigation. It may be that at an early stage it may be appropriate to select a few lead actions, staying other actions for some but not all purposes: it might be appropriate to order that the pleadings should be completed in all or most actions and that discovery should in the first instance be limited to the lead actions and to some other actions which might later, as a result of discovery, be added as additional lead actions. The greatest cost benefit from selection of lead cases is likely to be obtained by early selection, but sometimes selection has to be delayed until after some expensive investigations have been made in some if not all of the cases.

At one time it was thought that by selecting a legally aided plaintiff with a nil contribution as plaintiff in a lead action, the device of the lead action might be used so as to ensure that expensive litigation was disposed of on the plaintiffs' side wholly at the expense of the Legal Aid Fund. However, Hirst J in *Davies (Joseph Owen) v Eli Lilley & Co and ors*, upheld by the Court of Appeal,[15] ordered on 8 May 1987 that as from 1 June 1987, unless otherwise ordered, in respect of any action within certain co-ordinated arrangements for the trial or disposal of the actions any costs which were ordered to be borne by or fell to be borne by the plaintiff should be borne proportionately by all plaintiffs within the arrangements. The Court of Appeal held that the order was within the judge's jurisdiction under RSC Order 62 rule 3(3) and said that Hirst J was 'to be congratulated on producing a very fair and workable order in a novel and highly complex situation'. Fairness as between legally aided plaintiffs and other plaintiffs, and justice to the defendants required that order.

[14] *Ashmore v British Coal Corporation* [1990] 2 WLR 1437. See also *Arnold v National Westminster Bank* [1990] 2 WLR 304 and *NW Water Authority v Binnie and Partners* [1990] 3 All ER 547.

[15] [1987] 1 WLR 1136.

In relatively recent years judges have dealt with group actions or multi-party litigation along the lines indicated above. A leading example is *AB v John Wyeth and Brother Ltd*, [1993] 4 Med LR 1, *The Times*, 20 October 1992 (the Benzodiazepine or Halcion and Valium litigation), where Ian Kennedy J had set a cut-off date related to applications for legal aid. As the Court of Appeal noted in upholding this decision, the effect was to place a time limit on entitlement to join the existing group litigation and not to prevent would-be claimants from presenting their claims independently. In further proceedings the Court of Appeal upheld Ian Kennedy J's decision to strike out actions against prescribers of the drugs on the ground that any benefit to the plaintiffs was very modest when compared with the cost of defending the claims: see *AB v John Wyeth and Brother Ltd (No 2)* [1994] 5 Med LR 149. Other cases include *Nash v Eli Lilly and Co* [1993] 4 All ER 383, CA (on limitation periods in the context of the anti-arthritic drug, Opren); and *Creutzfeld Jacob Disease Litigation v The Medical Research Council and the Secretary of State for Health* [1996] 7 Med LR 309 (extracted by Mildred in Miller, *Product Liability and Safety Encyclopaedia* (1997), Div III A, para [232]).

In spite of the ability of test cases and lead actions to provide practical solutions to complex problems, they may be less than completely satisfactory. As the Ontario Law Reform Commission noted in its Report on Class Actions (1982), Vol 1 pp 87–8:

First the test case procedure is not adequate where the claims are individually nonrecoverable. Since, by definition, claimants will not assert these claims, they cannot benefit from the bringing of a test case. Secondly, in the case of claims that are individually recoverable, the test case procedure suffers from a number of major drawbacks. For example, it may be very difficult to obtain the consent of all those who have commenced their own action that one of the many actions should be tried as a test case. The plaintiffs would have to come to an agreement regarding the particular action that should go forward. The choice of counsel to prosecute the test case may also give rise to disagreement among the plaintiffs. A more important drawback is the fact that the defendant may not agree to be bound by the result of the test case. In such a case, if the result of the test case is unfavourable to him, the defendant nevertheless may require the plaintiffs to proceed with their action individually, perhaps at great expense. Moreover, the trial of these claims will have been substantially delayed by the resolution of the test case, during which time the other actions will have been effectively frozen.

THE ELEMENTS OF REPRESENTATIVE OR CLASS ACTIONS

In *Davies v Eli Lilly & Co* [1987] 3 All ER 94, a case in which 'lead actions' had been agreed in some 1,500 claims arising out of the use of the drug Opren, Lord Donaldson, MR said (at p 96):

The concept of the 'class action' is as yet unknown to the English courts. In some jurisdictions, notably in the United States, where large numbers of plaintiffs are making related claims against the same defendants, there are special procedures laid down enabling all the claims to be disposed of in a single action. Clearly this is something which should be looked at by the appropriate authorities with a view to seeing whether it has anything to offer and, if so, introducing the necessary procedural rules. Meanwhile, the courts must be as flexible and adaptable as possible in the application of existing procedures with a view to reaching decisions quickly and economically.

Although the class action procedure is associated primarily with the United States of America, it has been discussed also in other jurisdictions, notably Australia, Canada and Scotland. The Australian Law Reform Commission has described the procedure as follows in its Discussion Paper No 11 (1979) p 4:

A class action is a legal procedure which enables the claims of a number of persons against the same defendant to be determined in the one action. In a class action one or more persons ('the plaintiff') may sue on his own behalf and on behalf of a large number of other persons ('the class') who have the same interest in the subject matter of the action as the plaintiff. The class members are not usually named as individual parties but are merely described. Although they usually do not take any active part in the litigation, they may nevertheless be bound by the result. It is, thus, a device for multi-party litigation where the interests of a number of parties can be combined in one suit. The procedure also enables one plaintiff to bring an action against a number of defendants.

In English law the procedural rule which approximates most closely to the class action is RSC Ord 15, r 12, which provides in part:

(1) Where numerous persons have the same interests in any proceedings, not being such proceedings as are mentioned in Rule 13, the proceedings may be begun, and, unless the Court otherwise orders, continued, by or against any one or more of them as representing all or as representing all except one or more of them.

. . .

(3) A judgment or order given in proceedings under this Rule shall be binding on all the persons as representing whom the plaintiffs sue or, as the case may be, the defendants are sued, but shall not be enforced against any person not a party to the proceedings except with the leave of the Court.
(4) An application for the grant of leave under paragraph (3) must be made by summons which must be served personally on the person against whom it is sought to enforce the judgment or order.
(5) Notwithstanding that a judgment or order to which any such application relates is binding on the person against whom the application is made, that person may dispute liability to have the judgment or order enforced against him on the ground that by reason of facts and matters particular to his case he is entitled to be exempted from such liability.

. . .

For many years it was believed that the representative action was not appropriate where the relief sought was damages. Indeed, there was a clear statement to this effect in *Markt & Co Ltd v Knight SS Co Ltd* [1910] 2 KB 1021, CA, where Fletcher Moulton LJ said that where the claim is for damages 'the machinery of the representative suit is wholly inapplicable'. However, this view has not been followed in more recent years: see e.g, *EMI Records Ltd v Riley* [1981] 2 All ER 838, [1981] 1 WLR 923; *Irish Shipping Ltd v Commercial Union Assurance Co plc* [1989] 3 All ER 853, [1990] 1 WLR 117, CA. This development is now reflected in *The Supreme Court Practice* (1997), Vol 1, para 15/12/2, which states: 'A representative action will lie to recover a debt or damages, even though the claim is made by numerous plaintiffs severally, or resisted by numerous defendants severally, even though each of them may be entitled to or liable for a different proportion of the total claim . . . '

In a subsequent section reference is made to some of Lord Woolf's proposals for dealing with the problems posed by multi-party actions. Initially, it is helpful to refer to developments in other jurisdictions.

A CANADIAN EXAMPLE

Naken v General Motors of Canada Ltd (1977) 92 DLR (3d) 100, Ontario Court of Appeal

The judgment of the Court was delivered by

Arnup JA. The single issue in this appeal is whether the action is properly constituted as a class action. Osler J, held that it was. Hughes J, granted leave to appeal under Rule 499(3)(b), stating that it appeared to him, in the words of the Rule, that there was good reason to doubt the correctness of the decision of Osler J, and the appeal involved matters of such importance that leave should be given.

On October 13, 1977, the Divisional Court allowed the appeal of the defendant, General Motors of Canada Limited, and struck out the statement of claim as disclosing no proper cause of action. (The action is no longer being pursued against the defendant Vauxhall Motors Limited.)

The style of cause describes the four plaintiffs as suing 'on behalf of themselves and suing on behalf of all other persons who have purchased new 1971 and 1972 Firenza motor vehicles'. Paragraph 1 of the statement of claim narrows the class by adding the qualification 'and who at the date of the writ had not sold or otherwise disposed of the vehicle'. (The writ was issued on July 13, 1973.)

The statement of claim reads, in part:

'4. The Defendants were at all material times manufacturers, assemblers and marketers of motor vehicles.

5. From in or about September 1970, until the date of the Writ in this action, the Defendants manufactured, assembled and marketed 1971 and 1972 Firenza motor vehicles in Ontario.

6. Each Plaintiff and each member of the class purchased new 1971 and 1972 Firenza motor vehicles in Ontario, manufactured, assembled and marketed by the Defendants.

7. Prior to or at the time each Plaintiff and each member of the class purchased a Firenza motor vehicle the Defendants warranted to all prospective purchasers that all Firenza motor vehicles manufactured, assembled or marketed by the Defendants, were or would be of merchantable quality, reasonably fit for use as a motor vehicle and were or would be 'durable', 'tough' and 'reliable'.

8. The warranty given to each Plaintiff and to each member of the class was breached in that an unusually large number of 1971 and 1972 Firenza motor vehicles were not of merchantable quality, were not reasonably fit for use as a motor vehicle, and were not 'durable', 'tough' and 'reliable'.

9. Because of this breach of warranty, the value of each and every 1971 and 1972 Firenza motor vehicle has depreciated in the re-sale marked.

10. As a consequence, the re-sale value of each Firenza motor vehicle is approximately $1,000 less than the re-sale value of a motor vehicle of comparable age, size and purchase price on the market.

The plaintiffs, therefore claim:—

(a) The sum of $1,000 for each Plaintiff and each member of the class;'

Particulars dated March 15, 1974, read, in part (the demand for particulars is not before us):

'The Plaintiffs submit the following Reply to the Defendant's General Motors of Canada Limited Demand for Particulars:

1.(a) 4,602 persons purchased new 1971 and new 1972 Firenza motor vehicles respectively in Ontario.

   (b) As of this date, the exact number who had otherwise sold or disposed of their vehicle at the date of the Writ is not known, however, upon Judgment being obtained each of the members of the class will be notified and will be entitled to recovery if they can demonstrate that they had not sold or otherwise disposed of their Firenza motor vehicles at the date of the Writ.

2.   The vehicles were purchased from third parties. The purchasers took delivery at different times, and in particular they took delivery of new 1971 Firenza motor vehicles from the date that they were first marketed and delivered and new 1972 Firenza vehicles from the date when they were first marketed and delivered.

3.   With respect to warranties: (1) merchantable quality, implied warranty; (2) reasonably fit for use as a motor vehicle, implied warranty; (3) 'durable', 'tough' and 'reliable'; written warranty published in newspaper ads on various dates and advertising materials distributed by the Defendant General Motors of Canada Limited.'

Paragraph 4 of these particulars then alleged 15 defects in 'the motor vehicle'.
Particulars dated March 12, 1975, read:

'The Plaintiffs submit the following reply to the Defendant's, General Motors of Canada Limited, Demand for Particulars:

The warranties referred to in paragraphs 7 and 8 of the Statement of Claim are contained in contracts made with the Defendants. The parties to the contract are General Motors of Canada Limited and each member of the class being persons who have purchased new 1971 and 1972 Firenza motor vehicles in Ontario. The date of the said contracts are the date of the purchase of the vehicles. The contracts were partly oral and partly written. The warranties referred to were expressly made in printed materials distributed by the Defendant, General Motors of Canada Limited, and contained in newspaper advertisements placed by the said Defendant in Ontario.'

I should observe that in the course of the argument before this Court, Mr Balaban (who led for the appellant plaintiffs) made a significant concession. He expressly abandoned any allegation of implied warranty, and stated that the plaintiffs would rely solely upon the warranties expressly made in printed material distributed by the defendant and in its printed advertisements. The effect of the concession was to eliminate from the case the implied warranties that the cars were of merchantable quality and reasonably fit for use as motor vehicles.

The Divisional Court discussed or referred to the various English and Canadian cases which have been cited and analyzed by counsel in each of the four Courts that have considered this case. The essential elements of the decision of the Divisional Court appear to have been these:
(1) It would not have been practical for the plaintiffs to establish that each of the 4,600-odd members of the class purchased his Firenza in reliance upon the advertised representation.
(2) There is no allegation of a common fund in which each member of the class has an interest pro rata.
(3) The action was not for damages to the class, as an entity distinct from its members, but rather was in reality the accumulation or lumping together of individual claims for losses personal to each purchaser.

Before considering these grounds, there are three comments I wish to make by way of background:
(1) These proceedings began as a defendant's motion under Rule 126. It has been recognized throughout this case that a statement of claim will be struck out under that Rule only in very clear cases. If the action could possibly succeed, the statement of claim should not be struck out.
(2) For the purposes of such a motion, the allegations of fact in the pleading must be assumed to be true, or as it is sometimes put, 'must be taken as capable of being proven' (*Shawn v Robertson et al* [1964] 2 OR 696 at 697, 46 DLR (2d) 363 at 364).
(3) In these days of mass merchandising of consumer goods, accompanied as it often is by widespread or national advertising, large numbers of persons are almost inevitably going to find

themselves in approximately the same situation if the article in question has a defect that turns up when the article is put to use. In many instances the pecuniary damages suffered by any one purchaser may be small, even if the article is useless. It is not practical for any one purchaser to sue a huge manufacturer for his individual damages, but the sum of the damages suffered by each individual purchaser may be very large indeed.

In such cases it would clearly be both convenient and in the public interest if some mechanism or procedure existed whereby the purchasers could sue as a class, with appropriate safeguards for defendants, who ought not to be subjected to expensive law suits by class action plaintiffs who cannot pay costs if they lose.

These views are not original with me. Much has already been written on these questions. They have engaged increasing attention in the last 20 years in the United States, particularly in California. The subject raises complicated questions of great difficulty in the areas of the delineation of the class, identity of the causes of action of the class members, discovery and production from plaintiffs, proof of the breach of contract or tort that caused loss to the class, assessment of damages and allocation of proceeds.

. . .

At the present time, the Court has no statutory guidelines nor relevant Rules (I capitalize the 'R' deliberately) except Rule 75. The question whether Rule 75, without more, can be used as the basis for consumer class actions in Ontario emerges as the central issue in this litigation. That Rule reads:

'75. Where there are numerous persons having the same interest, one or more may sue or be sued or may be authorized by the court to defend on behalf of, or for the benefit of, all.'

The English cases, decided on a very similar rule, which have been most frequently referred to in Ontario are *Duke of Bedford v Ellis* [1901] AC 1, and *Markt & Co Ltd v Knight SS Co Ltd* [1910] 2 KB 1021. The former came up to the House of Lords through the Chancery Division. The latter was a common law action. For a long time it was held in Ontario, following the judgment of Fletcher Moulton LJ, in the *Markt* case at 1040 that an action for damages could never be brought as a class action. Jessup JA, made it plain, however, in giving the judgment of this Court in *Farnham v Fingold* [1973] 2 OR 132 at 136, 33 DLR (3d) 156 at 160, that the statement of Fletcher Moulton LJ, so frequently relied upon had not been the judgment of the English Court of Appeal . . .

The statement of claim in this case has deliberately sought to avoid some of the stumbling blocks which have caused some other actions to fail. There is not, and in common sense there could not be, an allegation of a 'common fund', out of which all members of the class will be entitled to be paid some amount if the action succeeds. What is sought to be done by the statement of claim is to remove the objection that each plaintiff in the class really ought to be suing for his own particular damages. Paragraph 7 of the statement of claim, read with the particulars, is a plea that a warranty, contained in printed material distributed by the defendant General Motors of Canada and in newspaper advertisements placed by it in Ontario, was given to *all* prospective purchasers of Firenza motor vehicles. Paragraph 8 refers to the warranty 'given to each Plaintiff and to each member of the class'.

Further, it is alleged that each and every vehicle purchased by a member of the class depreciated in the resale market by 'approximately $1,000'. In the prayer for relief, $1,000 is claimed for each member of the class. Thus, it is argued, no individual assessment of damages is required.

Since it must be assumed, for the purposes of this appeal, that all allegations in the statement of claim are true, the plaintiffs have sought to avoid the difficulty of proving, at this stage, that a warranty was extended to every single purchaser. Clearly that has been alleged, but the concession made in argument that no implied warranties are relied upon, and the theory of the plaintiffs' case as put forward by their counsel demonstrate, on analysis, that the allegation cannot be taken as true.

The plaintiffs' theory is that each purchaser had a contract with General Motors of the type made famous in *Carlill v Carbolic Smoke Ball Co* [1893] 1 QB 256. General Motors (it is said) offered to all readers of its advertisement: 'If you purchase a Firenza from one of our dealers, we warrant that it is durable, tough and reliable.' It follows that only purchasers who saw the General Motors printed material or its published advertisement could have made a contract with General Motors, of which the warranty is a part. The plaintiffs' delineation of the class does not make this distinction or qualification.

Thus, there is not the necessary 'common interest' or identity of situation among the members of the class as presently defined in the pleadings, because the defined class includes purchasers who saw the printed materials or advertisements, and purchasers who did not. It cannot be said that 'if the plaintiffs win, everybody wins'.

. . .

As I stated earlier, the plaintiffs have skilfully attempted in their statement of claim and particulars to avoid the various obstacles that have stood in the way of other plaintiffs in reported cases. In my view they have not succeeded, in the light of their own delineation of the class on whose behalf they sue. I therefore agree with Griffiths J, that this is not a true case of damage to a class, as a class. As now put to us, it is a claim for damages by such purchasers as can show that they saw a General Motors advertisement or its printed material and in reliance upon it, bought a Firenza from a dealer. Only some, and not all, of the members of the class as presently pleaded succeed if these plaintiffs succeed.

. . .

However, our task at this juncture is not to lay down procedures governing the future progress of the action. It is simply to decide whether the action can properly be brought under Rule 75. I have found that the class as presently delineated by the plaintiffs is not a proper class under that Rule and the cases decided upon it. I have also indicated what the deficiency is. If that deficiency were corrected, the plaintiffs, in my view would have pleaded a good cause of action, properly brought as a class action.

In my view the interests of justice require that the plaintiffs should be given leave to amend their description of the class on whose behalf the action is brought, so as to conform with these reasons. It is more than five years since the action was commenced, but it is even longer since the 1971 and 1972 Firenzas were sold, and to dismiss the action (in effect) might well work an injustice to Firenza buyers on whose behalf it is brought.

In this respect my views are very similar to those expressed by Stark J in *Cobbold v Time Canada Ltd* (1976) 1 CPC 274, a class action brought on behalf of the Ontario residents with unexpired subscriptions to the Canadian edition of Time Magazine. Stark J refused to strike out the statement of claim, holding that the contracts between subscribers and the magazine publishers were identical except as to the length of term of the subscription, that the action was not improper because of the claim for damages, but that the class should be narrowed to exclude those subscribers who had accepted a refund or an alternative subscription term. He concluded (at 278):

'I am satisfied that, difficult as it may be to pursue to the end the roads the plaintiff has chosen, that it would be improper at this stage to foreclose his attempt. He has made out a prima facie case which requires an answer; and though changes may be needed in the style of cause and the statement of claim, I am not convinced that I should dismiss the action at this stage.'

I would, accordingly, dismiss the appeal, but reserving to the plaintiffs leave to deliver, within 30 days from the issue of our formal order, an amended statement of claim which would include such part of the particulars as remain relevant after the concession made in argument by counsel for the plaintiffs and thus would narrow the description of the class to include only those purchasers of 1971 and 1972 Firenzas who saw the printed materials or published advertisements of General Motors and, as a result, purchased a new Firenza from a dealer.

. . .

Appeal dismissed.

For an example of an action under the Ontario Class Proceedings Act 1992, see *Nantais v Telectronics Proprietary (Canada) Ltd* (1996) 129 DLR (4th) 110 (defective pacemaker leads).

SOME AMERICAN DEVELOPMENTS

If the procedural developments in English law have been both gradual and relatively uncontroversial, the same cannot be said of the United States of America which has seen the development of a veritable class action industry. However, there has perhaps been a tendency among English and Commonwealth commentators too readily to assume that the procedure provides an all-purpose remedy which can be called in aid whenever a group of consumers has some common complaint.

In reality, the procedure may be exceptionally complicated as is evident from the wording of the following provision.

Federal Rules of Civil Procedure for the United States District Courts

Rule 23. Class Actions

(a) **Prerequisites to a Class Action.** One or more members of a class may sue or be sued as representative parties on behalf of all only if (1) the class is so numerous that joinder of all members is impracticable, (2) there are questions of law or fact common to the class, (3) the claims or defenses of the representative parties are typical of the claims or defenses of the class, and (4) the representative parties will fairly and adequately protect the interests of the class.

(b) **Class Actions Maintainable.** An action may be maintained as a class action if the prerequisites of subdivision (a) are satisfied, and in addition:

(1) the prosecution of separate claims by or against individual members of the class would create a risk of
(A) inconsistent or varying adjudications with respect to individual members of the class which would establish incompatible standards of conduct for the party opposing the class, or
(B) adjudications with respect to individual members of the class which would as a practical matter be dispositive of the interests of the other members not parties to the adjudications or substantially impair or impede their ability to protect their interests; or

(2) the party opposing the class has acted or refused to act on grounds generally applicable to the class, thereby making appropriate final injunctive relief or corresponding declaratory relief with respect to the class as a whole; or

(3) the court finds that the questions of law or fact common to the members of the class predominate over any questions affecting only individual members, and that a class action is superior to other available methods for the fair and efficient adjudication of the controversy. The matters pertinent to the findings include: (A) the interest of members of the class in individually controlling the prosecution or defense of separate actions; (B) the extent and nature of any litigation concerning the controversy already commenced by or against members of the class; (C) the desirability or undesirability of concentrating the litigation of the claims in the particular forum; (D) the difficulties likely to be encountered in the management of a class action.

(c) Determination by Order Whether Class Action to be Maintained; Notice; Judgment; Actions Conducted Partially as Class Actions.

(1) As soon as practicable after the commencement of an action brought as a class action, the court shall determine by order whether it is to be so maintained. An order under this subdivision may be conditional, and may be altered or amended before the decision on the merits.

(2) In any class action maintained under subdivision (b)(3), the court shall direct to the members of the class the best notice practicable under the circumstances, including individual notice to all members who can be identified through reasonable effort. The notice shall advise each member that (A) the court will exclude the member from the class if the member so requests by a specified date; (B) the judgment, whether favorable or not, will include all members who do not request exclusion; and (C) any member who does not request exclusion may, if the member desires, enter an appearance through counsel.

(3) The judgment in an action maintained as a class action under subdivision (b)(1) or (b)(2), whether or not favorable to the class, shall include and describe those whom the court finds to be members of the class. The judgment in an action maintained as a class action under subdivision (b)(3), whether or not favorable to the class, shall include and specify or describe those to whom the notice provided in subdivision (c)(2) was directed, and who have not requested exclusion, and whom the court finds to be members of the class.

(4) When appropriate (A) an action may be brought or maintained as a class action with respect to particular issues, or (B) a class may be divided into subclasses and each subclass treated as a class, and the provisions of this rule shall then be construed and applied accordingly.

(d) Orders in Conduct of Actions. In the conduct of actions to which this rule applies, the court may make appropriate orders: (1) determining the course of proceedings or prescribing measures to prevent undue repetition or complication in the presentation of evidence or argument; (2) requiring, for the protection of the members of the class or otherwise for the fair conduct of the action, that notice be given in such manner as the court may direct to some or all of the members of any step in the action, or of the proposed extent of the judgment, or of the opportunity of members to signify whether they consider the representation fair and adequate, to intervene and present claims or defenses, or otherwise to come into the action; (3) imposing conditions on the representative parties or on intervenors; (4) requiring that the pleadings be amended to eliminate therefrom allegations as to representation of absent persons, and that the action proceed accordingly; (5) dealing with similar procedural matters. The orders may be combined with an order under Rule 16, and may be altered or amended as may be desirable from time to time.

(e) Dismissal or Compromise. A class action shall not be dismissed or compromised without the approval of the court, and notice of the proposed dismissal or compromise shall be given to all members of the class in such manner as the court directs.

Virtually every limitation and sub-clause of this detailed provision warrants the most careful scrutiny. The plaintiff must satisfy head (a) and one of the variants of head (b)—normally, in the case of a consumer class action, rule 23(b)(3). Even then, the requirements of notice of rule 23(c)(2) may be applied so stringently as effectively to preclude the class action from proceeding. The decision of the Supreme Court in *Eisen v Carlisle and Jacquelin* 417 US 156 (1974) provides a well-known example, the court holding that individual notice had to be given to over two million readily identifiable class members. The estimated cost was $225,000, as against the plaintiff investors' estimated loss of $70, and, in the words of Lumbard CJ in the court below, this 'put an end to this Frankenstein monster posing as a class action' (391 F 2d 555, 572, US Court of Appeals Second Circuit (1968)).

In other cases the 'best notice practicable' requirement has been satisfied in less demanding ways: see, eg, *Vancouver Womens' Health Collective Society v A H Robins Co Inc*, 820 F 2d 1359, US Court of Appeals Fourth Circuit, 1987 (notice by advertising sufficient in the case of foreign claimants in litigation involving the Dalkon contraceptive shield). Detailed comment on Rule 23 is contained in the *United States Code Annotated*, vol 28.

The following case gives some idea of the exceptional difficulties involved in managing the procedural aspects of mass tort litigation.

In Re Agent Orange Product Liability Litigation (MDL No 381), 818 F 2d 145, 1987, United States Court of Appeals, Second Circuit

The defendants were some nineteen or so chemical companies which had manufactured and supplied various herbicides including 'Agent Orange' for use by the military as defoliants in the Vietnam War. The herbicides which allegedly contained dioxin had, it was claimed, been manufactured to mandatory government specifications under the provisions of the Defense Production Act. This gave rise to the possibility of a government contract or 'Nuremberg' defence. The plaintiffs were Vietnam veterans who claimed to have been exposed to 'Agent Orange' when serving in Vietnam and to have suffered (or to be 'at risk' of suffering) physical injuries as a result. Such exposure was through direct spraying, being transported through sprayed areas, ingesting contaminated water or food and general transportation and handling. At one stage more than eight hundred plaintiffs were named and they purported to represent 2.4 million veterans who had served as combat soldiers in south-east Asia between 1962 and 1971, as well as most of the families or survivors of those veterans. Genetic injury to the children of Vietnam veterans was also alleged.

So far as the substance of the claims was concerned, there was considerable doubt as to whether the evidence would establish the capacity of Agent Orange to injure human beings. Even if it did, proof in any individual case would be extremely difficult. Matters were further complicated by the fact that an individual's exposure could not be traced to a particular defendant since the Agent

Orange produced by different manufacturers was mixed together in unlabelled barrels and, moreover, the dioxin content varied from one manufacturer to another. In addition to these difficulties, complex jurisdictional issues as to the basis of a federal claim and questions of sovereign or government immunity were raised. In the various initial proceedings Chief Judge Weinstein certified a Rule 23(b)(3) class, defined it, and set out the requirements for notice, both individual and through the news media. Some 2,440 class members opted out shortly before a settlement was reached and the defendants later sought and were granted summary judgment against them. The case was heard by the appellate court on a variety of issues, including the class certification and adequacy of notice and the position of those who had opted out.

Winter, Circuit Judge.

I. OVERVIEW AND SUMMARY OF RULINGS

By any measure, this is an extraordinary piece of litigation. It concerns the liability of several major chemical companies and the United States government for injuries to members of the United States, Australian, and New Zealand armed forces and their families. These injuries were allegedly suffered as a result of the servicepersons' exposure to the herbicide Agent Orange while in Vietnam.

. . .

The procedural aspects of this litigation are also extraordinary. Chief Judge Weinstein certified it as a class action at the behest of most of the plaintiffs and over the objections of all of the defendants. Certain issues, such as the damage suffered by each plaintiff, were not, of course, to be determined in the class action. Instead, they were to be left to individual trials if the outcome of the class action proceedings was favorable to the plaintiffs. Some plaintiffs opted out of the class action, but their cases remained in the Eastern District of New York as part of a multidistrict referral.

The class certification and settlement caused the number of claimants and the variety of ailments attributed to Agent Orange to climb dramatically. It also has caused disunity among the plaintiffs and increased the controversy surrounding this case. Correspondence to this court indicates that many of the original plaintiffs, most of whom joined the motions for class certification, were never advised that use of the class action device might lead to their being represented by counsel whom they did not select and who could settle the case without consulting them. In the midst of this litigation, original class counsel, Yannacone & Associates, asked to be relieved for financial reasons. Control of the class action soon passed to the PMC [Plaintiffs' Management Committee]. Six of the nine members of the PMC advanced money for expenses at a time when the plaintiffs' case, already weak on the law and the facts, was near collapse for lack of resources. This money was furnished under an agreement that provided that three times the amount advanced by each lawyer would be repaid from an eventual fee award. These payments would have priority, moreover, over payments for legal work done on the case.

The trial date set by Chief Judge Weinstein put the parties under great pressure, and just before the trial was to start, the defendants reached a $180 million settlement with the PMC. The size of the settlement seems extraordinary. However, given the serious nature of many of the various ailments and birth defects plaintiffs attributed to Agent Orange, the understandable sympathy a jury would have for the particular plaintiffs, and the large number of claimants, 240,000, the settlement was essentially a payment of nuisance value. Although the chances of the chemical companies' ultimately having to pay any damages may have been slim, they were exposed potentially to billions of dollars in damages if liability was established and millions in attorneys' fees merely to continue the litigation.

The district judge approved the settlement. It is clear that he viewed the plaintiffs' case as so weak as to be virtually baseless. Indeed, shortly after the settlement, he granted summary judgment against the plaintiffs who opted out of the class action on the grounds that they could not prove that a particular ailment was caused by Agent Orange and that their claims were barred by the military contractor defense.

In addition, Chief Judge Weinstein awarded counsel fees in an amount that was considerably smaller than had been requested by the attorneys involved. The size of the award was clearly influenced by his skepticism about whether the case should ever have been brought.

The final extraordinary aspect of this case is the scheme adopted by Chief Justice Weinstein to distribute the class settlement award. That scheme, which is described as 'compensation-based' rather than 'tort-based,' allows veterans who served in areas in which the herbicide was sprayed and who meet the Social Security Act's definition of disabled to collect benefits up to a ceiling of $12,000. Smaller payments are provided to the survivors of veterans who served in such areas. No proof of causation by Agent Orange is required, although benefits are available only for non-traumatic disability or death. The distribution scheme also provides for the funding of a foundation to undertake projects thought to be helpful to members of the class.

Many of the decisions of the district court were appealed, and we summarize our rulings here. In this opinion, we reject the various challenges to the certification of a class action. Although we share the prevalent skepticism about the usefulness of the class action device in mass tort litigation, we believe that its use was justified here in light of the centrality of the military contractor defense to the claims of all plaintiffs. We also approve the settlement in light of both the pervasive difficulties faced by plaintiffs in establishing liability and our conviction that the military contractor defense absolved the chemical companies of any liability. In a second opinion by this author, 818 F 2d 179, we affirm the distribution scheme's provision for disability and death benefits to veterans exposed to Agent Orange and their survivors. We reverse the scheme's establishment of a foundation; however, the district court may on remand fund and supervise particular projects it finds to be of benefit to the class. A third opinion by this author, 818 F 2d 187, affirms the grant of summary judgment against the opt-out plaintiffs based on the military contractor defense. On two grounds we hold that the chemical companies did not breach any duty to inform the government of Agent Orange's hazardous properties. First, at the times relevant here, the government had as much information about the potential hazards of dioxin as did the chemical companies. Second, the weight of present scientific evidence does not establish that Agent Orange caused injury to personnel in Vietnam. The chemical companies did not breach any duty to inform the government and are therefore not liable to the opt-outs.

In an opinion by Judge Van Graafeiland, 818 F 2d 194, we affirm the district court's dismissal of actions against the United States by veterans on the grounds that they are barred by the *Feres* doctrine and the discretionary function exception to the Federal Tort Claims Act. A second opinion by Judge Van Graafeiland, 818 F 2d 204, affirms the dismissal of an action against the United States by the chemical companies seeking contribution or indemnity for the $180 million they paid in settling with the plaintiff class. A third opinion, 818 F 2d 210, affirms the dismissal of civilian actions against the United States on discretionary function grounds and of similar actions against the chemical companies on statute of limitations and military contractor defense grounds. A final opinion by the same author, 818 F 2d 201, affirms the dismissal of the so-called 'direct' claims by families of veterans against the government on *Feres* and discretionary function grounds.

An opinion by Judge Miner, 818 F 2d 216, invalidates the PMC members' agreement to repay on an 'up front' basis treble the expenses that any of them advanced. We hold that this agreement creates a conflict of interest between the attorneys and the class by generating impermissible incentives to settle. A second opinion by Judge Miner, 818 F 2d 226, affirms the district court's award of counsel fees except with regard to the abrogation of one fee award.

The 'Agent Orange' litigation was unusual in that, contrary to the general belief, class actions are not normally regarded as an appropriate means of dealing with claims for personal injuries, at least within the federal courts. Certainly this was the view of the Federal Rules Advisory Committee in its note to rule 23 (see 39 FRD 69, 102 (1966)):

A 'mass accident' resulting in injuries to numerous persons is ordinarily not appropriate for a class action because of the likelihood that significant questions, not only of damages but of liability and defenses to liability, would be present, affecting the individuals in different ways. In these circumstances an action conducted nominally as a class action would degenerate in practice into multiple lawsuits separately tried.

The same reasoning seems equally applicable to individual disasters which share common characteristics. In a note Rosenberg has commented as follows (97 Harv LR 849, 908–9 (1984)):

Class Actions

. . .

Courts are often reluctant to certify class actions,[1] even in cases that fall within the conventional definition of public law litigation; when they do so, they frequently regard certification as but a grudging concession to pragmatism.[2] Their concern seems to be that the class action encourages the treatment of claims in a mass production fashion that does not sufficiently recognize differences among claimants.[3]

[1] See eg *In re Northern Dist of Cal 'Dalkon Shield' IUD Prods Liab Litig*, 693 F 2d 847 (9th Cir 1982), cert denied, 103 S Ct 817 (1983); *Re Federal Skywalk Cases* 680 F 2d 1175 (8th Cir), cert denied, 103 S Ct 342 (1982); *Ryan v Eli Lilly & Co* 84 FRD 230 (DSC 1979); *Yandle v PPG Indus* 65 FRD 566 (E D Tex 1974); *Rosenfield v A H Robbins Co* 63 AD 2d 11, 407 NYS 2d 196, appeal dismissed, 46 NY 2d 731, 385 NE 2d 1201, 413, NYS 2d 374 (1978); *Snyder v Hooker Chems & Plastics* 104 Misc 2d 735, 429 NYS 2d (Sup Ct 1980). But see *Payton v Abbott Labs* No 76–1514–S (D Mass Dec 6, 1983) (available Feb 1, 1984, on LEXIS, Genfed library, Dist file) (order decertifying class); *Re Federal Skywalk Cases* 97 FRD 365 (WD Mo 1982); *Re 'Agent Orange' Prod Liab Litig*, 506 F Supp 762 (EDNY 1980), modified. MDL No 381 (EDNY Dec 16, 1983) (certifying class generally under Fed R Civ P 23(b)(3), and on the question of punitive damages under Fed R Civ P 23(b)(1)(B)), writ of mandamus denied. No 83–3065 (2d Cir Jan 9, 1984); *Pruitt v Allied Chem Corp* 85 FRD 100 (ED Va 1980).
[2] See, eg *General Tel Co v Falcon* 457 US 147, 155 (1982); *Califano v Yamasaki*, 442 US 682, 700–01 (1979); *Hobbs v Northeast Airlines* 50 FRD 76, 79 (ED Pa 1970); 7A C. Wright & A Miller, Federal Practice and Procedure § 1783, at 115 (1972).
[3] 7A C. Wright & A Miller, *supra* n 2, § 1783, at 115.

A device similar to the class action is multi-district litigation under 28 USC § 1407. See Conway, 'The Consolidation of Multistate Litigation in State Courts', 96 Yale LJ 1099 (1987) and such cases as *Re Paris Air Crash*, 399 F Supp 732 (1975); *Re Air Crash Disaster at Washington DC*, 559 F Supp 333 (1983); *Re Air Disaster at Lockerbie, Scotland, on December 21, 1988*, 709 F Supp 231 (1989), affd

16 F 30 513; *Re Silicone Gel Breast Implants Products Liability Litigation*, 793 F Supp 1098 (1992). But here also, plaintiffs may run into strong opposition to consolidation and consequent defect: see *Re Asbestos Litigation*, 431 F Supp 906 (1977); *Re Rely Tampon Products Liability Litigation*, 533 F Supp 1346 (1982).

The Ontario Law Reform Commission Report on Class Actions contains helpful discussion of some developments in the United States. Having noted some of the limitations placed on class actions commenced in federal courts, it continues (Vol 1, pp 252–3):

Due, in part, to the jurisdictional restraints placed upon the commencement of consumer-oriented class actions in the federal courts, the state courts are becoming the more frequent forum in which these types of action are brought. That the focus is shifting to the state courts to make effective remedies available in relation to consumer claims is evidenced by the fact that an increasing number of states have adopted an expanded class action procedure modelled upon Federal Rule 23, which broadens the procedural basis in these states for the redress of consumer violations. Moreover, in terms of substantive remedies for consumers, many states have enacted consumer protection statutes designed to protect consumers and to provide remedies against unfair and deceptive trade practices. In addition, several of these consumer statutes include specific provision for class actions, usually modelled upon Federal Rule 23.

Notwithstanding the enactment in recent years of legislation designed to facilitate consumer class actions, there does not appear to have been a proliferation of such actions at the state level. The notable exception in this regard is California, where the Consumers Legal Remedies Act specifically provides a class action procedure to redress violations of that Act. In that jurisdiction, the opportunity for, and the utilization of, class actions in the consumer area has been increased significantly by a number of developments. First, judicial decisions with respect to the substantive law have facilitated, for example, proof of fraudulent misrepresentation in consumer class actions.[5] Secondly, decisions regarding the class mechanism itself, with respect to matters such as notice and novel methods of calculation and distribution of damages,[6] have facilitated the bringing of class actions. In other jurisdictions, however, at least in some areas of the law, consumer class actions have met with mixed success. This is particularly the case with respect to products liability class actions, in which damages are sought for injuries resulting from the use of a defective product.

[5] See *Vasquez v Superior Court of San Joaquin Cty* 4 Cal 3d 800, 484 P 2d 964 (SC 1971). In that case, instalment purchasers of frozen food and freezers alleged fraudulent misrepresentation on the part of the vendor. Reliance on the part of the plaintiff upon the fraudulent misrepresentation was argued by the defendant to be an element of the cause of action. The defendant asserted that, since each class member would have to prove that he or she actually relied on the misrepresentation in purchasing the goods, the matter could not proceed as a class action. However, the California Supreme Court held that, if it was found that material misrepresentations were made to class members, an inference could be drawn that the class had relied on such misrepresentations.

[6] See *Daar v Yellow Cab Co* 67 Cal 2d 695, 433 P 2d 732 (SC 1967).

As was noted in the above extract, some of the most interesting American developments have occurred in relation to the calculation and distribution of damages. This seems to have been especially true of cases in which the individual amounts involved may be relatively small. The Australian Law Reform Commission contains a helpful summary of some of the developments in its Discussion Paper (No 11) 'Access to the Courts—II Class Actions'. Having noted the traditional methods of assessment and the 'split trial' technique, the Discussion Paper continues (at para 45 et seq):

45. **Class-wide Assessment**: The split trial technique is useful only where
  • the size of the class is relatively manageable;
  • assessment will not be unduly protracted;
  • the identity of members of the class is known; or
  • records of either the plaintiff or the defendant are available.

However, it is quite impracticable in claims for mass economic injury where often none of these factors is present.
  • In the *Antibiotics Litigation*[1] commenced in 1969, more than 100 separate actions were filed, many of which were class actions brought by States on behalf of citizens, hospitals and other consumers within their boundaries. The action claimed treble damages for breach of anti-trust laws alleging price fixing by the defendants in relation to the sale of certain antibiotic drugs. Most of the actions were settled and a sum in excess of £160 million was distributed to members of the classes. Traditional methods were entirely unsuited to assessing damages. It was plainly impracticable, if not impossible, for each member of these enormous classes individually to prove a claim.

The courts in the United States have responded by developing methods of calculating damages by assessment on a class-wide basis which is then distributed to the members of the class. Modern techniques are applied. If the defendant's records are available, the use of appropriate mathematical formulae may establish the loss to the class as a whole. If records are not available, courts have used computers, surveys, sampling and polling techniques which are supported by expert evidence to compute the loss suffered by the class as a whole and the damages which should, therefore, be paid to the class as compensation for that loss. The use of these devices may seem peculiar to a traditional lawyer. But is it really so odd? In one of the cases in the *Antibiotics Litigation* it was observed:

'Most important management decisions in the business world in which these defendants operate are made through the intelligent application of statistical and computer techniques and these class members should be entitled to use the same techniques in proving the elements of their cause of action. The court is confident they can be successfully utilised in the courtroom and that their application will allow the consumers to protect their rights while freeing the court and the defendants of the spectre of unmanageability. In these circumstances the court cannot conclude that the defendants are constitutionally entitled to compel a parade of individual plaintiffs to establish damages. Assuming damages are later awarded on the basis of sales figures and that the total of individual claims then filed is less than the award, the court will consider what disposition to make of the residue.'[2]

Individual claims against the total fund are often processed by special masters or committees of counsel appointed by the court.

46. Use of the defendant's records may sometimes assist in identifying members of the class for the purpose of distributing damages. In the absence of such records, individual members of the class must come forward and prove their claims on the damages fund. The procedural steps involved are:
  • notice of the settlement;
  • submission of proof of claims;
  • verification of the claims; and
  • the actual distribution of damages.

Procedures for notice and verification of claims vary according to circumstances. It is not unusual when large sums are recovered for many of those who are entitled to claim to fail to do so. The surplus created is applied as directed by the court.

47. Fluid Recovery and Cy-près: Perhaps the most novel and controversial techniques for assessing and distributing damages which have been developed in the United States courts are fluid recovery and *cy-près* schemes. The *Yellow Cab Co Case*[3] illustrates the principles of both fluid recovery and *cy-près*.

- In violation of a city ordinance the Yellow Cab Co of California raised its fares by changing its meters. As a result many thousands of passengers were overcharged. The damage to each individual passenger was small. But the gain to the company and the damage to the taxi passengers as a group was substantial. One member of the class brought a class action on behalf of all Yellow Cab passengers in the period of the overcharge. The overcharge was incapable of individual assessment. It would be impossible to determine who had been passengers in Yellow Cabs; some passengers would not have been aware of the overcharge; some passengers aware of the overcharge either did not care or would not be able to calculate the amount of the overcharge in each individual journey or could not remember how often or when they used the defendant's taxi cabs. For the same reason distribution of damages to individuals would be entirely impracticable. The court approved the notion of fluid recovery in order to avoid denying recovery and permitting the defendant to retain the unlawful gain. The action was settled on the basis that the defendant would undercharge for a period estimated to cut out its unlawful gains.

The amount of the overcharge was calculated and the resulting fund was returned to the class by a scheme, called a '*cy-près* scheme', of reducing cab fares in future years below the authorised maximum. Damages were thereby recovered, managed and distributed on behalf of an entire class without proof of each individual claim and without the necessity for distribution.

48. Fluid recovery techniques could be applied where

- individual claims are too small or cannot be proved because of absence of records;
- individual members of the class cannot be identified; or
- individual members of the class are unlikely to claim.

Cy-près schemes could also assist where the costs of distributing damages could absorb the damages fund, where class members cannot be identified, or where class members fail to assert their individual claims and a surplus remains after distribution. The *Yellow Cab Case* is quite exceptional. Attempts to use fluid recovery techniques to assess damages have on subsequent occasions been denied in the United States.[4]

49. Dealing with the Surplus: Where a surplus remains unclaimed, the *cy-près* scheme will also permit an application of the fund to a charitable or otherwise beneficial public use, which is seen to be preferable to permitting a defendant to retain his unjust enrichment. In one of the cases in the *Antibiotics Litigation*, the States involved were required to submit plans to use funds for court-approved public health purposes so that the unclaimed portion of the settlement fund was applied 'for the benefit of consumers generally'.[5]

50. Are the New Techniques Desirable?: The techniques of proof of damage on a class-wide basis, fluid recovery and *cy-près* exhibit the capacity of the class action to be more than a procedural device to recover compensation for individual loss. By these procedures, class actions tend to assume the character of a consumer protection mechanism to deter unlawful conduct, force the wrongdoer to surrender unlawful profits and distribute those profits in a way to benefit class members. These techniques are defended as being

' . . . completely equitable, in as much as the amount of damage arrived at is likely to correspond to the total injury inflicted by the defendant or the extent of its unjust enrichment, regardless of how small or large the number of class members who came forward in the action. In addition, establishing a single comprehensive figure of a class award in one damage proceeding might best achieve a balance between affording plaintiffs relief and deterring future statutory violations in an action brought under one of the anti-trust or securities acts or some other public policy mandate'.[6]

51. Those critical of what they see as the abuses of class actions claim that such novel methods have altered the substantive law as to damages, have denied defendants the ability to examine each claim made against them, and are punitive in character. Fluid recovery and *cy-près*, it is said, benefit some but not all members of the class. The balance in the market place may be disturbed. Because it is required (for a time) to lower prices of goods or services to comply with a class action order, the defendant may enjoy a commercial advantage over its competitors. The damages fund in effect subsidises lower prices. Some consumers may benefit who were not the initial consumers who suffered loss. The proponents of class actions reply by asserting that certain legislation (particularly trade practices legislation) is designed to encourage private citizens to take their proper part in the enforcement of the law rather than rely on governments to do so for them. The premise of their response is that the defendant should not be permitted to retain illegal profits. To allow the defendant to insist upon proof of each claim individually will enable it, so it is said, to benefit from the cumbersome nature of legal proceedings and the lack of sophistication and indolence of the consumer, and will reward his foresight in wrongfully depriving the multitude of small amounts.

52. **The Options**: That these procedures—class-wide assessment of damages, fluid recovery and *cy-près*—result in an effective change in the substantive law relating to assessment of damages cannot be doubted. However, unless new techniques of assessing damages are adopted to supplement traditional methods the usefulness of the class action will be very limited. At the same time the interest of defendants in being able to test the claim against them must not be overlooked. Options available include

- to adhere to traditional methods, including the split trial. This will mean that class actions will be used on limited occasions only where claims are against a clearly established or readily computed common fund, where the class is small or where the claim can be very simply calculated;
- to permit class-wide assessment of damages only in addition to traditional methods but require the defendant to compensate only those who come forward within a certain time and prove their claim;
- to permit class-wide assessment as in the second alternative but require the defendant to pay the total amount of damages as assessed by the court. Damages will be paid to those who prove a claim. Any balance will be paid into a Class Actions Fund. The purpose of such a fund is noted in para 64;
- to permit fluid recovery and *cy-près* to be available in addition to class-wide assessment of damages with any surplus being paid into a Class Actions Fund. Some may argue that these techniques should be limited to class actions by governmental agencies.

Any procedure which requires a defendant to do more than pay damages to those who come forward with a claim is seen by some to have a punitive element. Because the purpose of the proceedings has moved beyond actual compensation of those who come forward to prove a personal claim, they urge that it may be more appropriate for the availability of these procedures to be restricted to government so that the primary objective of private class actions remains one of compensation and compensation alone. The issue is whether it is preferable for the enforcement of legislation to be left

- to private individuals who come forward—in the knowledge that they will usually be few, or
- to government agencies.

A further alternative might be to revise methods of assessing penalties in criminal prosecutions. Instead of maximum penalties being fixed by legislation, the penalty in appropriate cases could be fixed by reference to the total amount received by the defendant from the unlawful dealing. Claims by those who have suffered this loss could be made against the amount thereby recovered.[7]

---

[1] *Re Co-ordinated Pretrial Proceedings in Antibiotics Antitrust Actions* 333 F Supp 278 (1971). For an account of this litigation and subsequent settlement procedures see Wolfram, 'The

Antibiotics Class Actions', (1976) American Bar Foundation Research Journal 253; Lebedoff, 'Operation Money Back', (1975) 4 Class Action Reports 147.

[2] *Re Co-ordinated Pretrial Proceedings in Antibiotics Antitrust Actions* 333 F Supp 278 at 289 (1971).

[3] *Daar v Yellow Cab Co* 63 Ca R 724 (1967).

[4] See cases noted in Harvard Study 'Developments in the Law—Class Actions', 89 Harv LR 1318 at 1532–34.

[5] *West Virginia v Chas Pfizer Inc* 314 F Supp 710 (1970).

[6] Miller, 'Problems in Administering Judicial Relief in Class Actions under Federal Rule 23(b)(3)', 54 FRD 501, 509–510.

[7] Law Reform Commission of Canada, 'Criminal Responsibility for Group Actions' (1976), 39.

LORD WOOLF'S RECOMMENDATIONS FOR REFORM

In his Final Report on Access to Justice (July, 1996) Lord Woolf examined the problems surrounding multi-party actions in detail (see ch 17). His recommendations build on those of the Law Society's Civil Litigation Committee in its report, 'Group Actions Made Easier' (September, 1995). The basic requirement is that new procedures should achieve the following objectives (para 2):

(a) provide access to justice where large numbers of people have been affected by another's conduct, but individual loss is so small that it makes an individual action economically unviable;

(b) provide expeditious, effective and proportionate methods of resolving cases, where individual damages are large enough to justify individual action but where the number of claimants and the nature of the issues involved mean that the cases cannot be managed satisfactorily in accordance with normal procedure;

(c) achieve a balance between the normal rights of claimants and defendants, to pursue and defend cases individually, and the interests of a group of parties to litigate the action as a whole in an effective manner.

Lord Woolf's approach is based on the central role of a pro-active managing judge appointed to hear and control the case. After discussing certification of a multi-party situation (MPS), Lord Woolf continues:

36 At this early point the managing judge needs to be pro-active in addressing various key matters with the parties. Some of these will be decisions common to all complex litigation: identifying main and preliminary issues; drawing up a strategy for disclosure, for further investigative work and for the use of expert evidence; establishing a timetable. Others are specific to multi-party actions:

(a) definition of the group;

(b) considering the utility of sub-groups, lead cases or sampling;

(c) considering whether the MPS should be managed on an 'opt-out' basis;

(d) arrangements for giving notice of the action;

(e) establishing a filter by agreeing with the parties the diagnostic or other criteria to facilitate the identification of valid claims and the early elimination of weak or hopeless claims;

(f) determining the approach to costs.

He then discusses the crucial questions of 'opt-out' or 'opt-in' and notice as follows:

'Opt-out' or 'opt-in'

42. Typically multi-party rules in other jurisdictions adopt an 'opt-out' approach, in that a person's rights may be determined in a multi-party action without his or her express consent to or participation in the litigation (the approach is under rule 23 in the US, and similar rules in Ontario, British Columbia and Australia). Members of the group may, however, opt out—in other words, indicate that they wish to be excluded. If they opt out, a person is not able to benefit from any award of damages, although they may always bring a separate action. It has generally been considered that there would be difficulties in this jurisdiction in taking forward cases on an 'opt-out' basis because of the cost sharing rules, but the experience of 'opt-in' registers with cut-off dates has not been altogether positive or, indeed, helpful in resolving the allocation of costs, particularly since most multi-party actions are legally aided.

43. For personal injury claims, it has been argued that an 'opt-out' scheme is unfair to defendants because it does not enable them to know the size of the group and the number of claims and their nature. The Law Society's working party therefore recommended an 'opt-in' approach with the establishment of a register at the initial stage of certification; provisions for varying the criteria for joining the register, as the case developed; and provisions for establishing cut-off dates and for costs sharing. This is the preferred approach where there is a well defined or identifiable group of claimants.

44. There are, however, problems in establishing an 'opt-in' register too early in the life of a potential multi-party action where there is a large pool of unidentified claimants. Although the register may appear to give defendants an idea of the size of the group, experience has shown that early cut-off dates tend to result in a rush to register which encourages many weak or hopeless claims to be registered and inflates the pool of potential claimants. The bandwagon effect may raise unrealistic hopes of compensation from claimants. Adverse publicity may have a severe negative impact on the business of defendants at a stage when there has been insufficient investigative work to establish clear criteria for the claims or, in some cases, to establish any clear indication of causation.

45. In some circumstances defendants and the Legal Aid Board may well be aware that there are large numbers of people who might be affected by the product in question. In those circumstances the claim may be more manageable if the initial certification puts any further individual applications for legal aid on hold and provides for deemed inclusion of unidentified potential claimants on an 'opt-out' basis until definitive criteria can be established to provide for the effective filtering of potential claims before they are entered on the register. There is, however, a need for action to be taken in relation to the limitation period and this can only be effective if there are provisions to suspend or freeze the running of the limitation period on certification of the MPS, as in many other jurisdictions, so that further claimants whose claims were not being considered in detail at this stage were not disadvantaged. This will require primary legislation. In the absence of such legislation I have no doubt that courts will continue to exercise their discretion to admit latecomers since the existence of the MPS ensures that defendants are already aware of the potential claims against them.

46. The court should have powers to progress the MPS on either an 'opt-out' or an 'opt-in' basis, whichever is most appropriate to the particular circumstances and whichever contributes best to the overall disposition of the case. In some circumstances it will be appropriate to commence an MPS on an 'opt-out' basis and to establish an 'opt-in' register at a later stage.

Notice

47. If members of a group are to opt out, or to join the register, they must know about the multi-party action. Notice may also be necessary at various other times throughout the course of the proceedings, eg, determination of generic issues; on settlement. In reaching the decision on notice the court must have in mind the cost of such notice and its usefulness: in some cases notice may be so expensive as to be disproportionate to the costs and benefits of the litigation, or it may not serve a useful purpose.

48. In a multi-party action where there are many claims, each of which is small, there is little to recommend in a rule making notice to each potential claimant mandatory. The costs of identifying potential claimants, and preparing and sending the notice, will make the litigation as a whole uneconomic. In any event, where such claimants receive the notice and choose to opt out, they will receive nothing. Because with small claims it is uneconomic for them to litigate individually, they will almost invariably remain members of the group. In the United States, in small claims group actions, very few of the tens of thousands—in some cases millions—of potential claimants actually notified choose to opt out. Accordingly, courts must have the discretion to dispense with notice enabling parties to opt out having regard to factors such as the cost, the nature of the relief, the size of individual claims, the number of members of a group, the chances that members will wish to opt out and so on.

49. Once the claims become more substantial, however, individual notice is economically possible. It is difficult to set a figure and the matter must be left to judicial discretion, taking into account the factors I have already mentioned. Yet even if the court decides that notice must be given to members of a group, it should have a discretion as to how this is to be done—individual notification, advertising, media broadcast, notification to a sample group, or a combination of means, or different means for different members of the group. In each case the court must take into account the likely cost and benefit before deciding on the course of action.

50. The court should have a discretion to order by whom the advertising should be undertaken. The Law Society's working party recommended that the Law Society should provide further guidance to solicitors on advertisements placed in the early stages prior to the establishment of a group action. I welcome that. The Law Society also recommended that the timing and placement of subsequent advertisements should be approved by the court. There is also a need to approve the content of the advertisements and for the court to decide on the appropriate body who should place the advertisement—either the lead solicitor, the Law Society itself with its substantial media expertise, the Legal Aid Board or the court itself.

Lord Woolf concludes his discussion with the following summary:

Recommendations

My recommendations are as follows:

(1) Where proceedings will or may require collective treatment, parties or the Legal Aid Board should apply for a multi-party situation (MPS) to be established. This would suspend the operation of the Limitation Act. The court may also initiate an application. Within the MPS, part of the proceedings could be common to some or all of the claimants and other parts could be limited to individual claimants.

(2) Individual claimants would be able to join the MPS at the application stage and subsequently by entering their names on an initial register.

(3) The court should certify an MPS if it is satisfied that the group or groups will be sufficiently large and homogeneous, and that the cases within the MPS will be more viable if there is a collective approach than if they are handled individually.

(4) Lower value or local cases should be dealt with locally at appropriate courts by either a High Court or Circuit judge.

(5) A managing judge should be appointed at or as soon as possible following certification and should handle the action throughout.

(6) In appropriate cases additional support may be provided by the appointment of a deputy Master or deputy district judge from those practitioners who already have considerable experience of multi-party litigation.

(7) The court should have a residual power to approve the lead lawyer if a difficulty arises in appointing one.

(8) The court should usually aim to treat as a priority the determination of the generic issues while establishing economic methods of handling the individual cases.

(9) The court should have power to progress the MPS on an 'opt-out' or 'opt-in' basis, whichever contributes best to the effective and efficient disposition of the case.

(10) In reaching a decision on notice of the action to potential claimants, the court must take into account the cost of such notice and its usefulness.

(11) The court should be responsible for determining whether the action has merit and should proceed and the criteria which must be met by those wishing to join the action.

(12) The court should determine the arrangements for costs and cost sharing at the outset. The costs of action groups should be recoverable on taxation.

(13) The Lord Chancellor's Department and Legal Aid Board should consider the possibility of extending the upper limits of financial eligibility on the basis of increased contributions. In appropriate cases, with tight judicial management and control on costs it may be possible for assisted persons' liability to be assessed and fixed in advance.

(14) The possibility of a contingency legal aid fund should be reconsidered in the context of these proposals.

(15) The court has a duty to protect the interests of claimants, especially those unidentified or unborn.

(16) In appropriate cases the court should appoint a trustee.

(17) Multi-party settlements should be approved by the court especially where the defendant offers a lump sum settlement.

(18) The court should require an identified and finite group of claimants to have in place from the outset a constitution including provisions relating to acceptance of settlement.

NOTES

In para 58 of his discussion Lord Woolf comments: 'Other common law jurisdictions with a cost-shifting rule have not changed it when introducing special rules for multi-party actions. Multi-party actions are not so significantly different from ordinary litigation as to justify such a change.' However, modifications are considered to be appropriate: see recommendations (12)–(14), above. The Legal Aid Board has published a paper on 'Reforming the Legal Aid Board's Handling of Group Actions and Other High Cost Civil Cases' (June, 1997) and the Lord Chancellor's Department has issued a Consultation Paper 'Access to Justice: Multiparty Situations: Proposed New Procedures', 1997. The funding of group actions forms part of a wider debate on the future of civil legal aid and the extension of conditional fee agreements.

QUESTIONS

1. Do you favour an 'opt in' or 'opt out' procedure under a multi-party or class action system? Which procedure is adopted under rule 23 of the Federal Rules of Civil Procedure (above, pp 467–9) and what are the practical consequences of choosing one system, rather than the other? Is it satisfactory to leave the matter to the managing judge?

2. How would an English court deal with the situation which arose in (i) *Naken v General Motors of Canada Ltd* (above, pp 463–7) and (ii) *Daar v Yellow Cab*

Co (above, p 475) under (a) the present law and (b) Lord Woolf's proposals? Do you favour the approach adopted in the *Yellow Cab Co* case?
3. If an individual consumer forms part of a group which has relied on descriptions in a holiday brochure and is seeking to claim damages of around £1,000 are there any particular advantages in opting into (or not opting out of) a multi-party action?

CONSUMER ORGANISATIONS AND PUBLIC AGENCIES

INTRODUCTION

The above discussion is concerned mainly with collective redress through a representative or class action in situations in which a group of individual consumers has both sufficient incentive and the means to institute litigation. Frequently, however, an alternative approach will be needed. For example, we have noted that it is not uncommon for businesses to use, in standard form contracts, exemption clauses which are unenforceable in law by virtue of the Unfair Contract Terms Act 1977 or the Unfair Terms in Consumer Contracts Regulations 1994 and yet are remarkably effective in practice (see above, p 375 et seq). Where this happens adequate consumer protection may require that the use of such clauses be prevented, whether through the creation of criminal offences (for example under Part II of the Fair Trading Act 1973, below, p 538 et seq) or through injunctive relief. Public agencies or consumer organisations are likely to find a role here. Such control over exemption clauses constitutes a relatively modest extension of the powers to deal with persistent 'offenders' conferred on the Director General of Fair Trading by Part III of the Fair Trading Act 1973 (see p 547 et seq). Similarly, if more ambitiously, effective consumer redress may be advanced by allowing public agencies or consumer organisations to institute or take over proceedings on behalf of individual consumers or perhaps a group of consumers. There are precedents for this in some Commonwealth and American jurisdictions and on the continent of Europe.

The general nature of the developments envisaged by some commentators has been pointed to by Richard Tur in his article 'Litigation and the Consumer Interest: The Class Action and Beyond' (1982) 2 Journal of Legal Studies 135. Having referred to the position in France and Germany, Tur continues (at pp 162–3):

There are apparent virtues in combining the class action, increasingly characteristic of common law jurisdictions, and the role of groups developed in continental systems, most particularly in France. Two types of class actions would then be possible, first, the class action simpliciter or the 'internal plaintiff class action' in which one or several individuals take action on behalf of themselves and all other members of the class on the basis of a cause of action which he or they share with all other members; secondly, a type of group action which is taken on behalf of the consumer interest or the public interest by a group or association granted statutory standing to sue wherein, quite apart from injunctive or declarative relief and quite separate from damages in its own right for injury to the interest it fosters, damages on behalf of affected individuals may be sought and awarded. To distinguish this latter type of class action it may be called a 'public interest class action' or an 'external plaintiff class action'. Given the problems of management and initiative and the need to secure conformity between conduct and legal rules there would be a place for such external plaintiff class actions even where provision had been made in the legal system for the class action simpliciter. The external plaintiff class action would meet many of the difficulties of management and initiative and ensure that collective, knowledgeable, repeat playing defendants were met by collective, well-informed, experienced plaintiffs, to the betterment of the enforcement of the law. It would meet the point, as true today as when uttered 20 years ago that 'the rights which the law gives to the consumer too often go by default'.[1] And it meets in part, the observation that 'what is really needed in Britain is a procedure . . . whereby consumer protection agencies can take proceedings on behalf of consumers affected by a breach of the civil law'[2] albeit by substituting private, voluntary, extra-governmental groups for the regulatory agencies or governmental bodies originally contemplated by Ross Cranston.

Consequently, the first step beyond the class action suggested by a consideration of developments on the continent is the external plaintiff class action wherein consumer groups could take action on behalf of individual consumers and obtain damages on their behalf. This could meet the potential gap as regards initiative and management caused by the absence of any functional equivalent of the public interest lawyer and the contingent fee.

Continental jurisdictions have, in the main, rejected class actions and sought to stimulate litigation by relaxing the rules of standing both as relates to access to administrative courts and by way of statutory authorisation for some specified groups to facilitate action in defence of the collective interests fostered by these groups.

[1] Cmnd 1781, para 403 (1962).
[2] Cranston *Consumers and the Law* (1st edn) p 100.

THE UNITED KINGDOM

Certainly developments along these lines would not be without precedent in the United Kingdom. Professor Jolowicz noted in his article 'Protection of Diffuse, Fragmented and Collective Interests in Civil Litigation: English Law' (1983) 42 CLJ 222, 236–7:

The conferment on public authorities and governmental agencies of a power to take civil proceedings in the course of exercising their public functions is now commonplace. In certain circumstances, for example, the relevant Minister may petition the court for an order that a company be wound up if he considers 'that it is expedient in the public interest' that he should do so,[1] and in this way a civil remedy, developed for the protection of the private interests of persons such as the creditors of a company, is adopted for a public purpose. Similarly, the two Commissions concerned with the administration of the legislation against discrimination on account of race or sex are empowered not only to assist the victims of unlawful discrimination to take action before the court, but may in certain circumstances do so themselves in their own name.[2] Most strikingly, perhaps, an entirely new structure of civil litigation, with its own specialised court, has been created by the restrictive practices legislation whereby the Director of Fair Trading is put into the position of a plaintiff and placed under a duty to take proceedings in respect of 'registrable' restrictive trading agreement.[3]

[1] Companies Act 1967, s 35. See eg, *Re Lubin, Rosen and Associates Ltd* [1975] 1 WLR 122.
[2] The Race Relations Act 1976 is administered by the Commission for Racial Equality, and the Sex Discrimination Act 1975 by the Equal Opportunities Commission. Both Acts

emphasise the Commissions' duties to work towards the elimination of discrimination and to secure compliance with the law without recourse to the courts. The power of the Commissions to bring proceedings in their own name is, in general, exercisable only in cases of persistent unlawful discrimination or where the unlawful act does not cause damage to an individual who could, with the help if necessary of the Commission, bring an action himself.

[3] See now the Restrictive Practices Act 1976 and the Restrictive Practices Court Act 1976. Certain categories of agreement are, by the legislation, deemed to be contrary to the public interest unless the court is satisfied, on one or more specified grounds, that they should be approved. This creates a lis between the parties to the agreement, on the one hand, and the Director of Fair Trading on the other.

Since Professor Jolowicz wrote this wide-ranging article the powers of the Director General of Fair Trading have been extended beyond restrictive trading agreements. The Control of Misleading Advertisement Regulations 1988, SI 1988/915, reg 5, confers a power to seek an injunction to restrain the publication of a misleading advertisement (see below, p 530). Similarly, the Unfair Terms in Consumer Contracts Regulations 1994, SI 1994/3159, reg 8, confers a power to seek injunctive relief to prevent the continued use of a contract term which the Director considers is unfair (see above, p 334).

However, it is significant that these powers have been conferred by statute. In the absence of such provisions one must turn to the general law. In *Gouriet v Union of Post Office Workers* [1978] AC 435, [1977] 3 All ER 70, the House of Lords held that only the Attorney General could sue on behalf of the public to seek to prevent public wrongs and that declarations could be granted only to litigants whose own legal position was in issue. The position of the Attorney General in instituting civil proceedings in aid of the criminal law is considered further in *Attorney-General v Blake*, [1998] 1 All ER 833.

The rules of standing (see RSC Ord 53 and the Supreme Court Act 1981, s 31(3)) have been significantly relaxed, but only in relation to actions against public bodies: see, generally, Wade & Forsyth, *Administrative Law* (7th edn, 1994), p 708 et seq. If the Consumers' Association or the National Consumer Council were to seek an injunction against an advertiser or supplier of goods or services it seems that English law would not allow the action to proceed. No doubt, the position could be different in the unlikely event of such an organisation seeking judicial review of an (alleged) unwillingness of the Director General to exercise duties and powers which statute had imposed or conferred.

In the case of the power conferred by the Unfair Terms in Consumer Contract Regulations 1994 there is an additional complication in that the EC Directive on Unfair Terms in Consumer Contracts (93/13/EEC) provides:

Article 7

1 Member States shall ensure that, in the interests of consumers and of competitors, adequate and effective means exist to prevent the continued use of unfair terms in contracts concluded with consumers by sellers or suppliers.

2 The means referred to in paragraph 1 shall include provisions whereby persons or organizations, having a legitimate interest under national law in protecting consumers, may take action

according to the national law concerned before the courts or before competent administrative bodies for a decision as to whether contractual terms drawn up for general use are unfair, so that they can apply appropriate and effective means to prevent the continued use of such terms.

3 With due regard for national laws, the legal remedies referred to in paragraph 2 may be directed separately or jointly against a number of sellers or suppliers from the same economic sector or their associations which use or recommend the use of the same general contractual terms or similar terms.

Initially, the Department of Trade and Industry took the view that since there were no relevant administrative mechanisms, nor general provisions for representative actions, no implementing action was necessary in relation to art 7(2): see 'Implementation of the EC Directive on Unfair Terms in Consumer Contracts: A Consultative Document' (October 1993). This unsatisfactory view was modified in a further Consultation Document dated September 1994 which proposed (see p 23) that duties and powers should be conferred on the Director General of Fair Trading, although not on organisations which represented consumers generally. This proposal was carried through into reg 8 (see above, p 334). It has been argued that in confining entitlement to proceed to the Director General regulation 8 does not transpose article 7(2) correctly, although it should be noted that article 7(2) is itself linked firmly to 'persons or organisations, having a legitimate interest under national law in protecting consumers . . . ' The matter may be tested before the European Court of Justice: see *R v Secretary of State for Trade and Industry, ex p Consumers' Association* (Case C–82/96) (96/C 145/05). However, in a Press Release dated 6 June 1997 the Consumer Affairs Minister, Nigel Griffiths, MP, announced a change of policy to allow actions by consumer groups and the Lord Chancellor also indicated on 23 May 1997 that he intends to allow representative actions by such groups. Presumably, legislation will be needed to bring this about. It is envisaged that these initiatives will lead to the settlement of the above case. The Department of Trade and Industry has issued a consultation paper, 'Widening the Scope for Action under the Unfair Terms in Consumer Contracts Regulations 1994' (January 1998).

In a relatively recent development the European Commission has brought forward the following proposal which again envisages a role both for public bodies and consumer organisations. In its latest version as published in the Official Journal of the European Communities on 22 December 1997 (OJ C 389, p 51) it provides as follows:

COMMON POSITION (EC) NO 48/97

adopted by the Council on 30 October 1997 with a view to adopting Directive 97 . . . /EC of the European Parliament and of the Council of . . . on injunctions for the protection of consumers' interests

(97/C 389/04)

THE EUROPEAN PARLIAMENT AND THE COUNCIL OF THE EUROPEAN UNION,

Having regard to the Treaty establishing the European Community, and in particular Article 100a thereof,

Having regard to the proposal from the Commission,[1]
Having regard to the opinion of the Economic and Social Committee,[2]
Acting in accordance with the procedure laid down in Article 189b of the Treaty,[3]

(1) Whereas certain Directives, listed in the schedule annexed to this Directive, lay down rules with regard to the protection of consumers' interests;

(2) Whereas current mechanisms available both at national and at Community level for ensuring compliance with those Directives do not always allow infringements harmful to the collective interests of consumers to be terminated in good time; whereas collective interests mean interests which do not include the cumulation of interests of individuals who have been harmed by an infringement; whereas this is without prejudice to individual actions brought by individuals who have been harmed by an infringement;

(3) Whereas, as far as the purpose of bringing about the cessation of practices that are unlawful under the national provisions applicable is concerned, the effectiveness of national measures transposing the above Directives including protective measures that go beyond the level required by those Directives, provided they are compatible with the Treaty and allowed by those Directives, may be thwarted where those practices produce effects in a Member State other than that in which they originate;

(4) Whereas those difficulties can disrupt the smooth functioning of the internal market, their consequence being that it is sufficient to move the source of an unlawful practice to another country in order to place it out of reach of all forms of enforcement; whereas this constitutes a distortion of competition;

(5) Whereas those difficulties are likely to diminish consumer confidence in the internal market and may limit the scope for action by organizations representing the collective interests of consumers or independent public bodies responsible for protecting the collective interests of consumers, adversely affected by practices that infringe Community law;

(6) Whereas those practices often extend beyond the frontiers between the Member States; whereas there is an urgent need for some degree of approximation of national provisions designed to enjoin the cessation of the abovementioned unlawful practices irrespective of the country in which the unlawful practice has produced its effects; whereas, with regard to jurisdiction, this is without prejudice to the rules of private international law and the Conventions in force between Member States, while respecting the general obligations of the Member States deriving from the Treaty, in particular those related to the smooth functioning of the internal market;

(7) Whereas the objective of the action envisaged can only be attained by the Community; whereas it is therefore incumbent on the Community to act;

(8) Whereas the third paragraph of Article 3b of the Treaty makes it incumbent on the Community not to go beyond what is necessary to achieve the objectives of the Treaty; whereas, in accordance with that Article, the specific features of national legal systems must be taken into account to every extent possible by leaving Member States free to choose between different options having equivalent effect; whereas the courts or administrative authorities competent to rule on the proceedings referred to in Article 2 of this Directive should have the right to examine the effects of previous decisions;

(9) Whereas one option should consist in requiring one or more independent public bodies, specifically responsible for the protection of the collective interests of consumers, to exercise the rights of action set out in this Directive; whereas another option should provide for the exercise of those rights by organizations whose purpose is to protect the collective interests of consumers, in accordance with criteria laid down by national law;

(10) Whereas Member States should be able to choose between or combine these two options in designating at national level the bodies and/or organizations qualified for the purposes of this Directive;

(11) Whereas for the purposes of intra-Community infringements the principle of mutual recognition should apply to these bodies and/or organizations; whereas the Member

States should, at the request of their national entities, communicate to the Commission the name and purpose of their national entities which are qualified to bring an action in their own country according to the provisions of this Directive;

(12) Whereas it is the business of the Commission to ensure the publication of a list of these qualified entities in the *Official Journal of the European Communities*; whereas, until a statement to the contrary is published, a qualified entity is assumed to have legal capacity if its name is included in that list;

(13) Whereas Member States should be able to require that a prior consultation be undertaken by the party that intends to bring an action for an injunction, in order to give the defendant an opportunity to bring the contested infringement to an end; whereas Member States should be able to require that this prior consultation take place jointly with an independent public body designated by those Member States;

(14) Whereas, where the Member States have established that there should be prior consultation, a deadline of two weeks after the request for consultation is received should be set after which, should the cessation of the infringement not be achieved, the applicant shall be entitled to bring an action before the competent court or administrative authority without any further delay;

(15) Whereas it is appropriate that the Commission report on the functioning of this Directive and in particular on its scope and the operation of prior consultation;

(16) Whereas the application of this Directive should not prejudice the application of Community competition rules,

HAVE ADOPTED THIS DIRECTIVE:

Article 1

Scope

1. The purpose of this Directive is to approximate the laws, regulations and administrative provisions of the Member States relating to actions for an injunction referred to in Article 2 aimed at the protection of the collective interests of consumers included in the Directives listed in the Annex, with a view to ensuring the smooth functioning of the internal market.

2. For the purpose of this Directive, an infringement shall mean any act contrary to the Directives listed in the Annex as transposed into the internal legal order of the Member States which harms the collective interests referred to in paragraph 1.

Article 2

Actions for an injunction

1. Member States shall designate the courts or administrative authorities competent to rule on proceedings commenced by qualified entities within the meaning of Article 3 seeking:

(a) an order with all due expediency, where appropriate by way of summary procedure, requiring the cessation or prohibition of any infringement;

(b) where appropriate, measures such as the publication of the decision, in full or in part, in such form as deemed adequate and/or the publication of a corrective statement with a view to eliminating the continuing effects of the infringement;

(c) in so far as the legal system of the Member State concerned so permits, an order against the losing defendant for payments into the public purse or to any beneficiary designated in or under national legislation, in the event of failure to comply with the decision within a time limit specified by the courts or administrative authorities, of a fixed amount for each day's delay or any other amount provided for in national legislation, with a view to ensuring compliance with the decisions.

2. This Directive shall be without prejudice to the rules of private international law, with respect to the applicable law, thus leading normally to the application of either the law of the

Member State where the infringement originated or the law of the Member State where the infringement has its effects.

Article 3

Entities qualified to bring an action
For the purposes of this Directive, a 'qualified entity' means any body or organization which, being properly constituted according to the law of a Member State, has a legitimate interest in ensuring that the provisions referred to in Article 1 are complied with, in particular:
(a) one or more independent public bodies, specifically responsible for protecting the interests referred to in Article 1, in Member States in which such bodies exist; and/or
(b) organizations whose purpose is to protect the interests referred to in Article 1, in accordance with the criteria laid down by their national law.

Article 4

Intra-Community infringements
1. Each Member State shall take the measures necessary to ensure that, in the event of an infringement originating in that Member State, any qualified entity from another Member State where the interests protected by that qualified entity are affected by the infringement, may seize the court or administrative authority referred to in Article 2, on presentation of the list provided for in paragraph 3. The courts or administrative authorities shall accept this list as proof of the legal capacity of the qualified entity without prejudice to their right to examine whether the purpose of the qualified entity justifies its taking action in a specific case.
2. For the purposes of intra-Community infringements, and without prejudice to the rights granted to other entities under national legislation, the Member States shall, at the request of their qualified entities, communicate to the Commission that these entities are qualified to bring an action under Article 2. The Member States shall inform the Commission of the name and purpose of these qualified entities.
3. The Commission shall draw up a list of the qualified entities referred to in paragraph 2, with the specification of their purpose. This list shall be published in the *Official Journal of the European Communities*; changes to this list shall be published without delay, the updated list shall be published every six months.

Article 5

Prior consultation
1. Member States may introduce or maintain in force provisions whereby the party that intends to seek an injunction can only start this procedure after it has tried to achieve the cessation of the infringement in consultation with either the defendant or with both the defendant and a qualified entity, within the meaning of Article 3(a), of the Member State in which the injunction is sought. It shall be for the Member State to decide whether the party seeking the injunction must consult the qualified entity. If the cessation of the infringement is not achieved within two weeks after the request for consultation is received, the party concerned may bring an action for an injunction without any further delay.
2. The rules governing prior consultation adopted by Member States shall be notified to the Commission and shall be published in the *Official Journal of the European Communities*.

Article 6

Reports
1. Every three years and for the first time no later than five years after the entry into force of this Directive the Commission shall submit to the European Parliament and the Council a report on the application of this Directive.
2. In its first report the Commission shall examine in particular:

— the scope of this Directive in relation to the protection of the collective interests of persons exercising a commercial, industrial, craft or professional activity,
— the scope of this Directive as determined by the Directives listed in the Annex,
— whether the prior consultation in Article 5 has contributed to the effective protection of consumers.

Where appropriate, this report shall be accompanied by proposals with a view to amending this Directive.

Article 7

Provisions for wider action
This Directive shall not prevent Member States from adopting or maintaining in force provisions designed to grant qualified entities and any other person concerned more extensive rights to bring action at national level.

Article 8

Implementation
1. Member States shall bring into force the laws, regulations and administrative provisions necessary to comply with this Directive no later than 30 months after its entry into force. They shall immediately inform the Commission thereof.

When Member States adopt these measures they shall contain a reference to this Directive or shall be accompanied by such reference on the occasion of their official publication. The methods of making such reference shall be adopted by Member States.

2. Member States shall communicate to the Commission the provisions of national law which they adopt in the field covered by this Directive.

Article 9

Entry into force
This Directive shall enter into force on the 20th day following its publication in the *Official Journal of the European Communities*.

Article 10

Addressees
This Directive is addressed to the member States.

Done at . . .
For the European Parliament
The President
For the Council
The President

ANNEX

LIST OF DIRECTIVES COVERED BY ARTICLE 1*

(1) Council Directive 84/450/EEC of 10 September 1984 relating to the approximation of the laws, regulations and administrative provisions of the Member States concerning misleading advertising (OJ L 250, 19.9.1984, p 17).

(2) Council Directive 85/577/EEC of 20 December 1985 to protect the consumer in respect of contracts negotiated away from business premises (OJ L 372, 31.12.1985, p 31).

(3) Council Directive 87/102/EEC of 22 December 1986 for the approximation of the laws, regulations and administrative provisions of the Member States concerning consumer credit (OJ L 42, 12.2.1987, p 48), as last amended by Directive 97/ . . . /EC (OJ L . . .).

(4) Council Directive 89/552/EEC of 3 October 1989 on the coordination of certain provisions laid down by law, regulation or administrative action in Member States concerning the pursuit of television broadcasting activities: Articles 10 to 21 (OJ L 298, 17.10.1989, p 23 as amended by Directive 97/ . . . /EC (OJ L . . .)).

(5) Council Directive 90/314/EEC of 13 June 1990 on package travel, package holidays and package tours (OJ L 158, 23.6.1990, p 59).

(6) Council Directive 92/28/EEC of 31 March 1992 on the advertising of medicinal products for human use (OJ L 113, 30.4.1992, p 13).

(7) Council Directive 93/13/EEC of 5 April 1993 on unfair terms in consumer contracts (OJ L 95, 21.4.1993, p 29).

(8) Directive 94/47/EC of the European Parliament and of the Council of 26 October 1994 on the protection of purchasers in respect of certain aspects of contracts relating to the purchase of the right to use immovable properties on a timeshare basis (OJ L 280, 29.10.1994, p 83).

(9) Directive 97/7/EC of the European Parliament and of the Council of 20 May 1997 on the protection of consumers in respect of distance contracts (OJ L 144, 4.6.1997, p 19).

[1] OJ C 107, 13.4.1996, p 3 and OJ C 80, 13.3.1997, p 10.
[2] OJ C 30, 30.1.1997, p 112.
[3] Opinion of the European Parliament of 14 November 1996 (OJ C 362, 2.12.1996, p 236). Council common position of 30 October 1997 and Decision of the European Parliament of . . . (not yet published in the Official Journal).
[*] Directive Nos 1, 6, 7 and 9 contain specific provisions on injunctive actions

NOTES

1. An earlier recommendation of the Council of Europe had also sought to promote the role of consumer organisations: see Recommendation No R (81) 2 of the Committee of Ministers to the Member States on the Legal Protection of the Collective Interests of Consumers by Consumer Agencies (1981).

2. The Royal Commission on Legal Services (Cmnd 7648, 1979) (the Benson Commission) recommended that legal advice and assistance should be made available to groups which met certain criteria (see paras 12.62 and 12.63). However, the government response to the report did not accept that additional help should be provided: see Cmnd 9077, 1982, p 11.

SOME EXAMPLES FROM OTHER JURISDICTIONS

In contrast to English law there are examples in Commonwealth and continental jurisdictions of a somewhat broader approach allowing the intervention of public agencies and consumer organisations. In some instances this is linked specifically to the control of unfair contract terms, a point discussed in ch 7. Here our concern is with somewhat more general considerations.

An interesting Canadian example contains the following provisions for the bringing of actions by the Director of Trade Practices:

British Columbia Trade Practices Act 1996

Actions and proceedings

18 (1) In an action brought by the director, or any other person whether or not that person has a special, or any, interest under this Act or the regulations, or is affected by a consumer transaction, the court may grant either or both of the following:

(a) a declaration that an act or practice engaged in or about to be engaged in by a supplier in respect of a consumer transaction is a deceptive or unconscionable act or practice;

(b) an interim or permanent injunction restraining a supplier from engaging or attempting to engage in a deceptive or unconscionable act or practice in respect of a consumer transaction.

(2) If the court grants relief under subsection (1) it may make a further order requiring the supplier to advertise to the public in the media in a manner that will assure prompt and reasonable communication to consumers, and on terms or conditions the court considers reasonable and just, particulars of any judgment, declaration, order or injunction granted against the supplier under subsection (1)(a) or (b) or subsection (4).

(3) In an action under subsection (1), any person, including the director, may sue on the person's own behalf and, at the person's option, on behalf of consumers generally, or a designated class of consumers, in British Columbia.

(4) In an action for a permanent injunction under subsection (1)(b), the court may restore to any person who has an interest in it any money or property that may have been acquired because of a deceptive or unconscionable act or practice by the supplier.

(5) In an action brought by the director under subsection (1)(a) or (b), the court may award to the director costs, or a reasonable proportion of them, of the investigation of a supplier conducted under this Act.

(6) The director may apply, without notice to anyone, for an interim injunction under subsection (1)(b), and, if the court is satisfied that there are reasonable and probable grounds for believing there is an immediate threat to the interests of persons dealing with the supplier because of an alleged deceptive or unconscionable act or practice in respect of a consumer transaction, the court must grant an interim injunction on the terms and conditions it considers just.

(7) In an action brought under this section, or in an appeal from it, the plaintiff is not required to provide security for costs.

. . .

Substitute action of director

24 (1) The director may, on behalf of a consumer, commence or assume the conduct of proceedings, defend any proceedings brought against the consumer, with a view to enforcing or protecting the rights of the consumer respecting a contravention or suspected contravention of those rights or of any enactment or law relating to the protection of interests of consumers if the director is satisfied that

(a) the consumer has

(i) a cause of action

(ii) a defence to an action,

(iii) grounds for setting aside a default judgment, or

(iv) grounds for an appeal or to contest an appeal,

and

(b) it is in the public interest.

(2) The director must not commence, assume the conduct of or defend any proceedings under subsection (1) without first obtaining

(a) an irrevocable written consent of the consumer, and

(b) the written consent of the minister.

(3) The following rules apply to proceedings referred to in subsection (1):

(a) the director, on behalf of the consumer, has in all respects the same rights in and control over the proceedings, including the same right to settle an action or part of an action, as the consumer would have had in the conduct of those proceedings;

(b) the director may, without consulting or seeking the consent of the consumer, conduct the proceedings in the manner the director considers appropriate and proper;

(c) any money, excluding costs, recovered by the director belongs and must be paid to the consumer without deduction, and any amount, excluding costs, awarded against the consumer must be paid by and recoverable from the consumer;

(d) despite paragraph (c), in every case, any costs of the proceedings awarded by the court must be borne by, or paid to and retained by, the director.

(4) If

(a) a party to proceedings to which this section applies files a counterclaim, or

(b) the consumer on whose behalf the proceedings are being defended is entitled to file a counterclaim,

and that counterclaim is not related to

(c) the cause of action, and

(d) the interests of the consumer as a consumer

the court having jurisdiction in the proceedings must, on the application of the director, order

(e) that the counterclaim be heard separately, and

(f) that the consumer be made a party to the counterclaim in his or her own right.

(5) For the purposes of subsection (4), the court may make other orders or give directions that it considers just.

For discussion of the equivalent provisions in the earlier 1979 Act, see Belobaba, 'Unfair Trade Practices Legislation: Symbolism and Substance in Consumer Protection' (1977), 15 Osgood Hall LJ 327. See also below, p 566 where the British Columbia Act is discussed in relation to fair trading.

The following example is taken from an Australian Statute:

Consumer Affairs Act 1972 (Victoria)

PROCEEDINGS ON BEHALF OF CONSUMERS

9A. In this Part unless inconsistent with the context or subject-matter, 'consumer' does not include a body corporate.

9B. (1) Where—

(a) a consumer has made a complaint under this Act; and

(b) the Director is satisfied—

(i) that the consumer has a cause of action or a good defence to an action relating to a matter to which the complaint refers; and

(ii) that it is in the public interest to institute or defend proceedings on behalf of the consumer with a view to enforcing or protecting the rights of the consumer in relation to an infringement or suspected infringement by another person of those rights or of this Act or any other law relating to the interests of consumers—

the Director may, subject to this section, on behalf of and in the name of the consumer, institute proceedings against that other person or defend proceedings brought against the consumer.

(2) The director shall not under sub-section (1) institute or defend proceedings on behalf of a consumer unless—

(a) the amount claimed or involved in the proceedings does not exceed $10,000;

(b) the Minister has given his consent in writing subject to such conditions (if any) as he determines; and

   (c) the consumer has given his consent in writing and has not revoked that consent.

(3) A consumer may not except with the consent of the Director revoke a consent given for the purposes of sub-section (2).

9C. (1) Where, under section 9B, the Director institutes or defends proceedings on behalf of a consumer—

   (a) the Director may settle the proceedings either with or without obtaining judgment in the proceedings;

   (b) if a judgment is obtained in the proceedings in favour of the consumer, the Director may take such steps as are necessary to enforce the judgment;

   (c) an amount (other than an amount in respect of costs) recovered in the proceedings is payable to the consumer;

   (d) an amount in respect of costs recovered in the proceedings is payable to the Director;

   (e) the consumer is liable to pay an amount (not being an amount of costs) awarded against him in the proceedings; and

   (f) the Director is liable to pay the costs of or incidental to the proceedings that are payable by the consumer.

(2) Where, in proceedings instituted or defended under section 9B on behalf of a consumer—

   (a) a party to the proceedings files a counterclaim; or

   (b) the consumer is entitled to file a counterclaim—

and the counterclaim is not or would not be related to the proceedings and to the interests of the consumer as a consumer the Director may apply to the court hearing the proceedings for an order that the counterclaim be heard otherwise than in the course of those proceedings.

(3) The court may, where it makes an order under sub-section (2), make such ancillary or consequential provisions as it thinks just.

The above provisions have their counterparts in continental jurisdictions where the debates have followed very similar lines to those in the United Kingdom. This is hardly surprising since over the last two decades the protection of collective and diffuse interests—whether in relation to consumer affairs, the environment or other matters—has been a general preoccupation of Western legal systems.

The position in West Germany has been summarised by Professor Hein Kötz writing in the Civil Justice Quarterly (1982) 237, at p 247 et seq as follows:

The traditional standing rules are by no means costless. The price we pay for them is the emasculation of the policing function of private litigation and a corresponding extension of the areas in which wrongful conduct will remain unchallenged, not because there is an absence of rules defining illegal behaviour and imposing sanctions on the wrongdoer, but because there is an absence of plaintiffs prepared to invoke available judicial controls.

In principle it is of course the Government's task to implement public policy, particularly where that policy aims at protecting large segments of the public whose individual members are in a poor position to make use of existing procedures. However, setting up regulatory agencies to enforce the applicable law and thereby to safeguard the public interest is not always a satisfactory solution. Not only is the creation of such agencies an expensive and practically irreversible step. There is also evidence that governmental agencies tend to assume a bureaucratic outlook and to lose over the years the aggressiveness and flexibility necessary to cope with ingenious attempts to flout the policy of the law. Much has been written about what is called the 'capture' of regulatory agencies by the industries they are supposed to regulate. It has been contended that

'[r]egulatory bodies, like the people who comprise them, have a marked life cycle. In youth they are vigorous, aggressive, evangelistic, and even intolerant. Later they mellow, and in old age—

after a matter of ten or fifteen years—they become, with some exceptions, either an arm of the industry they are regulating or senile.'[1]

...

Professor Kötz then discusses a provision for reducing the cost of litigation in matters which affect the public interest, and continues:

The reduction machinery relieves the plaintiff from part of the financial risk connected with litigation, but it is of no assistance if the plaintiff is denied standing to sue. An important technique frequently used in Germany to stimulate private litigation in the public interest is to grant standing to certain groups or organisations to sue for injunctive relief in the civil court when it appears that actions brought by individuals are not a sufficiently effective means of protecting the public against illegal conduct. These grants are limited to certain fields of law, and are always based on specific statutory provisions.

The most prominent statutory authorisation for such group actions (*Verbandsklagen*) is found in the Law Against Unfair Competition.[2] Before 1965, the law conferred standing to sue only on the defendant's competitors and on trade associations. Nevertheless, the courts recognised that the policy of the law was not only to keep the competitive process free from unfair business practices, but also to secure protection for consumers at large. Because competitors and trade associations sometimes appeared to be rather slow in initiating litigation, an extension of standing to consumers' associations was made in 1965, allowing them also to seek injunctions restraining unfair business practices. This experiment has been fairly successful, perhaps not so much because of a very large number of actions brought, but principally because consumers' associations, now being able to wield the 'big stick' of a possible court action, are in a much better position to obtain 'voluntary' compliance from potential defendants. There is no doubt that consumers' associations are today making a valuable contribution to the enforcement of the policy of the Law Against Unfair Competition.

Standing to sue is granted to trade or consumers' associations by a number of other German statutes. The most recent example is section 13 of the Law on Standard Contract Terms[3] by which standing is conferred on consumers' associations to seek an injunction restraining the defendant from using or recommending standard contract terms found to be illegal under the law. If injunctive relief is granted the court order is registered in an official register kept by the Federal Cartel Office from which information is available to anybody against a nominal fee. Although the law has been in force for only three years many decisions have already been published in the legal periodicals. Most major industries and trade associations using or recommending standard terms for consumer contracts have meanwhile revised them in the light of the new law, and there is no doubt that this has occurred partly in order to escape the risk of being sued by consumers' associations.

It must be kept in mind, though, that the actions for which associations are granted a *locus standi* may only be brought for injunctive relief. Since associations are not allowed to sue for damages there exists in Germany no functional counterpart of the American class action. In recent years various proposals have been made in Germany trying to adapt the American class action to the German environment and, in some way, to provide consumers' associations with standing to sue for aggregated damages. A bill worked out by the Federal Ministry of Justice[4] and now before Parliament proposes an amendment of the Law Against Unfair Competition which would provide, first, that individual consumers shall have a claim for damages, if they bought goods relying on untrue statements of the seller, and, secondly, that these claims, after having been assigned individually to a consumers' association, can be enforced by it against the seller. If the action is successful the proceeds are to be distributed to the assignors who are not required to be members of the association. This bill has met with strong resistance by the industry, and it seems unlikely that it will be passed in the near future. . . .

[1] Galbraith *The Great Crash* (Boston, Houghton Mifflin, 1955) p 171.
[2] § 13 Absatz 1a of the . . . [Gesetz gegen den unlauteren Wettbewerb of June 7 1909, printed below]. See Grimes, 'Control of Advertising in the United States and Germany: VW Has a Better Idea,' 84 Harv LRev 1769 (1971) where it is argued that the German system of conferring standing to sue on associations should be adopted in the United States. A good description of the mode of operation of German consumers' associations in this field is given by von Falckenstein, *Die Bekämpfung unlauterer Geschäftspraktiken durch Verbraucherverbände* (Bundesanzieger Verlagsgesellschaft Köln 1977).
[3] *Gesetz zur Regelung des Rechts des Allgemeinen Geschäftsbedingungen* of December 9, 1976 (BCBI 1. 1 3317).
[4] See the draft of a Law for Amending the Law Against Unfair Competition of 29 September 1978, *Bundestags-Drucksache* 8/2145.

Section 13 of the Law on Standard Contract Terms to which Professor Kötz refers provides as follows:

Act Concerning the Regulation of the Law of Standard Contract Terms (1976) (AGB—Gesetz)

CHAPTER THREE—PROCEDURE

§ 13 Claims for Discontinuance and Retraction

(1) One who applies or recommends the application to legal transactions of stipulations in standard contract terms which are invalid under §§ 9 through 11 of this act may have a claim for discontinuance or retraction brought against him.

(2) Claims for discontinuance and for retraction may be brought only
  (1) by associations with legal capacity whose statutory duty it is to protect the interests of the consumer by giving information and advice, if these associations have as members other associations active in this sphere, or at least seventy-five natural persons;
  (2) by associations with legal capacity to advance commercial interests, or
  (3) by chambers of industry and commerce or chambers of artisans.

(3) The associations mentioned in paragraph 2 number 1 may not advance claims for discontinuance and retraction if the standard contract terms are applicable against a merchant and the contract belongs within the scope of his business or if the standard contract terms are recommended for application exclusively between merchants.

(4) Claims within paragraph 1 must be brought within two years commencing with the time when the claimant has acquired knowledge of the application or recommendation of invalid standard contract terms and, even without such knowledge, within four years commencing with the time of the application or recommendation.

Otto Sandrock in his article 'The Standard Terms Act 1976 of West Germany' (1978) 26 AJCL 551 (from which the above translation by Nina Galston is taken) comments (at p 567) in relation to this provision:

[The] number of authorised plaintiffs is still very restricted: the 'common man' has no right to drag an enterprise into court on the public charge of using unlawful standard contract terms. This privilege has been reserved for a small number of organizations which are considered experts in this field.

If the court deems the action well founded, the text of the order shall, according to § 17, set forth verbatim the standard contract terms objected to; state the kinds of legal transactions in which the standard contract terms may not be used because their use has been discontinued;

order discontinuing the application of standard contract terms similar in content; and finally, in the event of an order for retraction, order publication of the judgment in the same manner in which the recommendation was publicized.

Finally, § 20 sets up a scheme for registering claims and judgments. The court must inform the federal antitrust office (*Bundeskartellamt*) not only of all complaints introduced to prohibit the use of unlawful standard contract terms, but also of all judgments rendered thereon. Hence it will be easy to discover what proceedings have already been instituted on the unlawfulness of certain standard terms and what stage these proceedings have reached. Nor is there any need to introduce claims on clauses the use of which has already been declared unlawful. For § 21 extends the effect of *res judicata*: once the use of a certain clause by a proponent has been declared illegal, all of his customers are able to claim the protection granted by the earlier order of court.

Unlike the position in many other jurisdictions the French legal system does in principle make provision for the award of damages to consumer organisations suing in their own name. The background is outlined as follows in Fisch, 'European Analogues to the Class Action' (1979) 27 American Journal of Comparative Law 51, at 64–5:

A potentially more dramatic authorization was made in 1973 in the consumer field, as part of a law enacting, inter alia prohibitions against various forms of price discrimination and deceptive advertising. Art 46 of the rather vaguely titled 'Law for the Guidance of Commerce and the Crafts' (commonly known as the Loi Royer) reads in part as follows:

' . . . (D)uly registered associations whose explicit charter object is to defend the interests of consumers may, if they are approved for that purpose, bring private actions before any jurisdiction with respect to acts causing harm directly or indirectly to the collective interest of consumers.'[1]

An implementing decree contemplated by the provision requires a showing of longevity, activity and representativeness, along with certification by the Attorney General of the Court of Appeal for the district in which the organization has its seat;

[1] Law No 73–1193, 27 Dec. 1973, 'd'orientation du commerce et de l'artisanat,' art. 46 JCP 1974.III.41167. The courts had previously denied the action civile in cases of improper pricing and sales practices, as affecting only the public interest, see Bourat et Pinatel ¶ 1000 at pp 941–2.

As the above extract indicates, consumer organisations may institute proceedings only if they satisfy a number of criteria. Writing in *The Judicial and Quasi-Judicial Means of Consumer Protection* (EEC, 1976) (the Montpellier Symposium) Professor Jean Maury of the Montpellier Faculty of Law and Economics has summarised these as follows (footnotes omitted):

A. The Royer Law and the implementing Decree of 17 May laid down the *conditions* that have to be met by consumers' associations claiming authorization . . .

The first requirement is that the association must show that on the date on which it submits its application for approval it has been in existence for not less than one year from the date on which it was founded. The required period is therefore quite relative; it is not a question of restricting the civil action to groups which have already provided evidence over a long period that they are effective and representative. . . .

[It] is merely a question here of eliminating temporary groups set up, dare one say, ab irato, to deal with a particular offence and which would disappear as soon as their objective was achieved.

Secondly, the law specifies that an association must be able to show that it has a sufficient number of members. Here again, it is a matter of eliminating bodies which are not altogether serious or representative. The criterion fixed in the decree of 17 May varies enormously, however, depending on the number of people involved in the movement concerned. In the case of national associations it is very precise: only associations with not less than ten thousand individually paid up members on the date on which the application is submitted may claim approval. . . .

The requirement of ten thousand members is all the more exacting since there is an entirely different criterion for groups operating at regional or local level which is as flexible as the first is strict. Without going into greater detail the decree provides that the body 'shall show that it has a sufficient number of individually paid up members, having regard to the territory in which its activities are carried out'. Here, everything is left to the subjective assessment of the Government department responsible for examining the application for approval or the court or tribunal competent to deal with the appeal against a refusal. The apparent contradiction is even greater since in general it should be much easier, using subjective methods, to decide on the representative nature of national associations than on that of purely local bodies. It must be noted, however, that in practice it is quite easy to get round the law: national organizations unable to show a membership of ten thousand are generally represented at local level by groups which they need only ask to institute civil proceedings in criminal cases on their behalf. . . .

The final requirement relates to the *objective* of the association, which must have taken upon itself the duty of protecting consumers. This objective must be *genuine*. The approving authorities must carry out a thorough investigation into the type of activities carried on by the various applicants so as to exclude groups (generally local groups) which use consumer protection as a screen while pursuing purely commercial objectives. The Royer Law had already required that associations applying for approval should be independent of all types of business or employment.

Many national and local associations have been established of which the most influential is probably the Union Federale des Consommateurs (UFC). This association publishes *Que Choisir* which contains information similar to that in the Consumers' Association *Which?* Some of the actions which have been commenced have attracted widespread attention in the press, for example the cases of the Kléber-Colombes VI2 tyres (which allegedly burst at speed); talc Morhange (and the associated death of some thirty-six babies); the 'cocktails amaigrissants' (slimming claims) and the SEITA advertising campaign ('International News' cigarettes: 'emploi abusif et délictueux de l'anglais'—or passing off).

The Loi Royer does not preclude the payment of damages to a consumer organisation to vindicate the collective interest which it represents. Yet organisations cannot claim damages on behalf of individual consumers as such. In practice awards of damages were once confined to a nominal one franc. Although this is no longer so, the sums awarded to consumer organisations as a 'partie civile' may not bear any relation to the illicit profits gained by the organisation against which it is intervening. Indeed there is something all too familiar about the criticisms of French commentators when they complain about 'les amendes derisoires' and the difficulty of establishing a 'prejudice collectif'. A good example is provided by l'Affaire des vins Margnat where wine had been marketed as in one-litre bottles when in fact the contents were only 98 centilitres. Three consumer associations acting as partie civile were awarded damages of 20,000 francs each, yet the distributors' profits were almost 14 million francs. This and other French examples suggest that the solution to the problem of protecting the collective interests of consumers has proved as elusive in France as it is likely to be in the United Kingdom. There are no obvious solutions to the problem.

For further examples and discussion of the Loi Royer see *Le Monde* 30 October 1983 and *Le Bilan de l'Action Civile des Associations de Consommateurs depuis 1973* (Institut National de la Consommation, 1983).

QUESTIONS

In principle it cannot be right that the marketer of wine in the *Margnat* case (see above) should profit from his activity and at the consumer's expense. Yet it is very difficult to determine precisely how the matter should be tackled. Is it enough to ensure that the fine imposed in criminal proceedings is sufficiently high to remove the merchant's profit or should some attempt be made to recompense consumers whether individually or as a group? If so, consider the possible solution offered by the *Yellow Cab* case (above, p 475).

Is it possible to place a meaningful evaluation on the 'collective prejudice' suffered by an organisation representing a group of consumers? If consumer groups were to be accorded *locus standi* by statute what criteria should they be required to meet if they are entitled

    (i) to sue only for declarations and injunctions or

    (ii) to sue also for damages to be distributed to their members?

Do you agree with Professor Maury when he seems to assume (see above, p 495) that competent organisations must have a degree of permanence and that temporary groups will be set up *ab irato*? Would it be right to exclude an aircraft or drug disaster 'action group'?

CHAPTER 10

The consumer, codes of practice and advertising

INTRODUCTION

This chapter examines the role played by codes of practice in protecting consumers and enhancing the services provided to consumers. It involves an examination of codes promoted by various trade sectors and then consideration of the control of advertising, which is largely regulated by codes of practice and an injunction procedure supervised by the Director General of Fair Trading.

The main advantage of a self-regulating code is that it can be 'tailor made' to suit the problems most commonly met in any given industry. Consequently it can be more detailed and specific than is usually practicable even in subsidiary legislation and is inherently more flexible since parliamentary time is not needed to update it. Frequently, codes provide an arbitration or conciliation procedure with the aim of providing a quick and cheap method of settling a dispute. This aspect is noted above, at pp 423–5.

The disadvantages of such codes emanate from their essentially voluntary basis—they lack formal enforcement and are only binding on the members of the trade association in question. Often the very rogue operators that consumers complain about and that industry seeks to regulate are not members of the trade association and so are free to operate outside its ambit. Even if a trader is a member there is still controversy over the effectiveness of any sanction a trade association can enforce. Expulsion is the obvious course but may be thought to be too drastic a step. Alternatively it may not considered much of a punishment in the first place, as there is no requirement for a trader to be a member of a trade association to be able to trade. However, the adverse publicity involved in expulsion can certainly be unwelcome to the majority of traders. More general criticism attacks the modest nature of guarantees and wide variations in the codes themselves, some going little further than 'accepting' existing common law or statutory liability. If the code is endorsed by the Office of Fair Trading, however, it will be one with useful provisions which seek to deal with known problems.

Since 1973 the Office of Fair Trading has pursued a changing role in the creation and encouragement of codes of practice. The statutory source of the Director General of Fair Trading's obligations in relation to codes is to be found in the Fair Trading Act 1973, s 124(3), which provides as follows:

Without prejudice to the exercise of his powers under subsection (1) of this section, it shall be the duty of the Director to encourage relevant associations to prepare, and to disseminate to their members, codes of practice for guidance in safeguarding and promoting the interests of consumers in the United Kingdom.

(The cross-reference to subsection 1 relates to the powers of the Director to arrange for the publication of information and advice to United Kingdom consumers).

Although originating as something of a parliamentary afterthought, this duty grew into one of the Director's most important functions during the 1970s and early 1980s. The OFT originally undertook detailed negotiations over the wording of codes and codes were adopted covering many areas where consumer dissatisfaction had been recorded. Some twenty codes had been negotiated by early 1984. Since then OFT policy has been reviewed on several occasions, with often a less proactive approach being followed, this being reflected in the fact that currently 27 codes have OFT endorsement (although negotiations with interested bodies match the 1970s level). A major review of the OFT policy on codes has culminated in the publication of *Voluntary Codes of Practice A consultation paper*, (OFT, December 1996), which sought views on what the future approach to codes should be (see p 508).

In February 1998 *Raising Standards of Consumer Care, Progressing beyond codes of practice: A report by the Office of Fair Trading* was published by the Director General. It contains proposals to create a completely new regime for codes, with core standards for all traders together with sector-specific standards. The standards are proposed to be drawn up under the auspices of the British Standards Institution, with a new approval body created to supervise the scheme. There are also suggestions for a cross-sectoral logo and a directory of registered businesses. A redress scheme is proposed, possibly with an ombudsman. Consultations on the report will continue during 1998.

At the present time Guidelines introduced in 1991, (see below), are used when considering a code for endorsement. In addition, an element of independence in redress and disciplinary measures is now sought and reference is made to the Unfair Terms in Consumer Contracts Regulations 1994, (SI 1994/3159), see pp 332–6. The requirement, under section 6 of the Guidelines, to pick up judgments against members who go out of business has proved unrealistic and is generally waived.

Guidelines for Support of Individual Codes (OFT, 1991)

1. Under section 124(3) of the Fair Trading Act the Director General of Fair Trading has a duty 'to encourage relevant associations to prepare, and to disseminate to their members, codes of practice for guidance in safeguarding and promoting the interests of consumers in the United Kingdom'.
2. As part of this process, the Office has welcomed approaches from trade associations and others interested in introducing consumer codes and provides advice on what it would regard as 'best practice'. The attached guidelines set out a series of provisions which, at the present time, the Office believes to be best practice.

3. To further encourage the adoption of best practice, the Office is prepared to offer its support for codes which apply best practice as set out in the guidelines. This support will take the form of a foreword to the code signed by the Director General and welcoming the introduction of the code.

4. The code itself is the responsibility of the trade association which will ensure adequate provisions are made for monitoring, enforcement and publicity for the code. Where the Director General's name is associated with a code the Office may from time to time wish to consider complaints about the code and, if necessary, review its operation. The Director General will consider publicly withdrawing his support if he concludes that, eg the code is not adequately complied with or if recommended improvements are not adopted.

Guidelines on codes of practice

1. Organisational

The trade association should have a significant influence on the sector. In practice its membership would normally be a majority of firms in the sector but this would not preclude support for, eg a smaller trade association containing some of the more progressive elements in the industry and which was prepared to meet the other criteria. Nor would it rule out support for more than one code in a fragmented sector, though here it would be preferable if the various associations were to subscribe to a single code.

Compliance with the code must be mandatory on members of the association(s).

The trade associations must have the resources and disciplinary sanctions available to deal effectively with cases of non-compliance.

2. Preparation of the code

The trade association must be able to demonstrate that its members are prepared to observe its provisions.

Organisations representing consumers, enforcement bodies and advisory services must have been adequately consulted throughout the preparation of the code.

The Office's Competition Policy Division must be consulted when any application for support is received. Codes of practice containing standard terms and conditions to be adhered to by members of a trade association are usually of a kind which have to be provided to the office for registration under the Restrictive Trade Practices Act 1976. They must be provided to the Office within three months of being made or before they come into effect, whichever is earlier. The Office has a duty under the Act to consider whether such standard terms and conditions give rise to restrictions which could have a significant effect on competition. In encouraging a trade association to draw up a code of practice the Office will want to ensure that the restrictions in the code are insignificant. Broadly, the Office will wish to satisfy itself that the terms and conditions:

    are reasonably fair between the parties

    are not likely to mislead those who use them, and

    do not necessarily exclude variations to meet special circumstances.

3. Content of the code

The code must offer specific and worthwhile benefits beyond those which might be expected as a result of legal requirements and normal practice in the industry.

Without being unduly prescriptive or stringent, the code should require high standards within the particular business sector reflecting the legitimate expectations of reasonable consumers.

The code should normally include measures directed at the elimination or alleviation of consumer concerns and undesirable trade practices arising within the particular business sector.

As relevant, the code should address:

    marketing and advertising of goods and services;

quality of product and customer service;

terms and conditions of supply (including legibility, comprehensiveness and comprehensibility of written materials);

delivery dates;

guarantees and warranties;

protection of deposit or prepayments;

after-sale service, spare parts, etc.

Specific measures should be aimed at ensuring that consumers are supplied with adequate information about goods or services and the terms of supply (eg clear display of prices, estimates/quotations, detailed invoices, ready advice on technical aspects).

The code should require compliance with the British Code of Advertising Practice, the British Code of Sales Promotion Practice and other relevant codes of practice of similar standing.

Standards or requirements laid down by the code should be clear, precise and unambiguous and should be measurable whenever possible, eg specified time limits, applicability of British standards.

The code should include a requirement that members indicate compliance with the code—including use of identifying symbols, ready availability of copies of the code or publicity materials, etc.

The code should include a requirement that staff of complying organisations have access to a copy of the code and be aware of the code's requirements.

4. Complaints handling

Adequate machinery should be available, within the code, for dealing with complaints from consumers, to include:

(i) a requirement that members should have in place procedures for dealing with direct approaches from consumers and agree a specific time limit for responding to complaints;

(ii) a requirement that members should offer maximum co-operation with local consumer advisers or any other intermediary consulted by the consumer;

(iii) the availability of effective conciliation services directed at arranging an accommodation acceptable to both parties;

(iv) the availability of a low-cost, independent scheme of redress as an alternative to action in the courts. The scheme should be binding in that members of the trade associations should not be able to refuse to allow a complaint to go before the scheme if a customer so chooses and in that the member must accept a judgement made under the scheme. Any such scheme should be able to take into account possible breaches of the code where relevant to the complaint.

5. Monitoring and publicity

The operation of the code must be regularly monitored as follows:

(i) the trade association will publish annually a report on the operation of the code including in particular the numbers and type of complaints referred for conciliation and to the independent redress system. It would be preferable if the report were compiled by an independent person or body with powers to recommend actions to be taken under (iii) below. This information will be made available to the trade press;

(ii) copies of these reports and any publicity will be provided to the OFT;

(iii) the association will recommend and require its members to take action based on this information to improve their service to the customer; consumer satisfaction should be periodically assessed.

Copies of the code should be available without charge to customers, to members, to local consumer advisers and to others with a legitimate interest.

The trade association should publicise the code so that relevant members of the public are adequately aware of it.

6. Enforcement

Compliance with the code and procedures for handling of complaints should be mandatory on members of the trade association.

The code or articles of the trade association will establish procedure for handling of complaints of non-compliance by members with the code. The procedure will include time limits for dealing with these complaints.

The code or articles will also set out the penalties for non-compliance up to and including dismissal from the association.

Where it is appropriate to the industry the trade association will ensure that, in the event of any member defaulting on or being unable to comply with a judgment made by the courts or under the alternative redress scheme in favour of a consumer, eg through liquidation or withdrawing from trade association membership, mechanisms are in place to ensure the trade association meets the judgment against that member.

AN EXAMPLE OF A CODE

The following provides a good example of the ground covered by a code of practice which has been endorsed under the 1991 Guidelines.

Code of Practice for the Tyre and Fast Fit Trade

Introduction

The National Tyre Distributors Association (NTDA) was founded in 1933, it has 2,800 depots in membership and covers over 65% of the tyre and fast fit industry. This Code has been drawn up by the National Tyre Distributors Association to govern the conduct of members in relation to tyre and fast fit motor components and embodies principles which have been observed by the majority of the industry for many years.

The principles set out are not intended to interpret, qualify or supplement or supplant the law of the land. The NTDA regards it as a duty on their members that they accept the code in its entirety. The customers who feel dissatisfied with the treatment received from a member will be able to submit their grievance to the National Conciliation Service operated in conjunction with the NTDA. The customer also has a part to play in cooperating fully with the tyre and fast fit trade so that maximum benefit is gained from the purchase. In particular, by maintaining all tyres and fast fit motor components in accordance with the manufacturer's instruction and by observing the advice given by the member.

1. Replacement tyres and fast fit motor components

1.1. Members must bear in mind that in sales of goods to consumers they are responsible under the Sale and Supply of Goods Act 1994 that the goods are of satisfactory quality and fit for the purpose for which they are required. Statements, whether oral or in writing, containing any apparent conflict with this principle must be avoided.

1.2. Whenever goods are offered for sale a clear indication of cash price must be available to the customer. Each item of goods and service for supply should be shown net of VAT with a separate indication of the VAT charge or the inclusive price.

1.3. Terms must not be used in advertisements if they are likely to be misunderstood by the consumer or if they are not capable of exact definition. Members must be aware that under the Trade Descriptions Act it is an offence to make false claims in advertising. Members should be aware of the codes and standards set by the Advertising Standards Authority, the Independent Television Commission and the Radio Authority. These codes are self-regulatory, however the ASA has statutory back-up via the powers given to the Director General of Fair Trading under the Control of Misleading Advertisement Regulations (1988).

1.4. The member must not display any notices, or make any statements, which might mislead a consumer about his legal rights in relation to the purchase of faulty goods. Tyres and fast fit motor components removed will be made available for return to the customer and the customer will be told what arrangements are made with regard to the disposal of the tyres and fast fit motor components which are replaced ensuring that any disposal is undertaken under the environmental protection act requirements, unless the customer has agreed otherwise when sending back goods under the company's complaints procedure. If a charge is made for disposal consumers will be informed prior to invoicing.

2. Invoices

Invoices should give full details of the work carried out and the materials used. The amount and rate of VAT should be clearly indicated (see section 1.2 of this Code).

3. Customers' property

Members must exercise maximum care in protecting customers' property while it is in their custody and must not seek, by disclaimers, to avoid their legal liability for damage or loss. Members must carry adequate insurance to cover their legal liability and should strongly advise customers to remove any items of value not related to the car.

4. Advertising

4.1. Advertising by members must comply with the codes and standards set by the Advertising Standards Authority, the Independent Television Commission and the Radio Authority and with the requirements of the Trade Descriptions Act (see section 1.3 of this Code). In particular, references to credit facilities must conform to the appropriate legal requirements set at the time.

4.2. Advertisements must not contain any references to guarantees or warranties which would take away or diminish any rights of a customer nor should they be worded as to be understood by the consumer as doing so.

4.3. Claims and descriptions in advertisements should not be misleading.

5. Complaints handling

5.1. With a complaint which is not the subject of an insurance claim members must ensure, as appropriate, that effective and immediate action is taken with a view to achieving a just settlement of a complaint. To this end there will be, from the point of view of the customer, an easily identifiable and accessible arrangement for the reception and handling of complaints.

5.2. In addition, tyre and fast fit components' manufacturers must give every assistance to their dealers in handling complaints against product faults, or those in which the manufacturer is otherwise involved.

5.3. When complaints are raised through a third party, ie AA, RAC, Trading Standards Department or Citizens Advice Bureau, willing guidance must be given to that body and every attempt should be made to re-establish direct communication with the complaining customer and to reach a satisfactory settlement with him. Every effort will be made to settle any dispute within 6 months of the complaint or dispute being made. However, in the event of both parties opting for arbitration or conciliation, this time may need to be extended.

5.4. In the event that a complaint is not resolved, the member must make it clear to the customer that he has a right to refer it to the NTDA.

5.5. Manufacturers and dealers must give every assistance to the NTDA while it is investigating a complaint. The NTDA will establish liaison as necessary.

5.6. Where conciliation has failed to resolve a dispute the NTDA will cooperate in the operation of a low cost arbitration agreement which will be organized by the Chartered Institute of Arbitrators. The details of the arbitration arrangements will be given and customers must always be advised that they have the option of taking a claim to the courts. Customers must be told at the outset that they must choose between arbitration and going to court. If the consumer is unhappy with the result of arbitration they cannot then seek redress in the courts.

5.7. The award of the arbitrator is enforceable in law on all parties.

6. Monitoring

6.1. As subscribers to the Code of Practice, all members of the NTDA must make every effort to display the NTDA Customer Charter and, where appropriate provide customers with leaflets explaining their rights under the Code.

6.2. All members must maintain an analysis of justified complaints relating to any of the provisions of the Code of Practice and should take action on this information to improve their service to the customer.

6.3. The NTDA will analyze all complaints about the Code or matters referred to the Association for conciliation or arbitration. The results of such analyses will be published in the Annual Report of the NTDA and made available to the Director General of Fair Trading.

7. Customer protection

7.1. To conduct all transactions in accordance with all statutory and common law requirements.

7.2. To recognize that all customer complaints must be referred speedily to managerial level and to introduce and maintain an effective system to implement this principle.

7.3. To afford every customer the full facilities of the National Conciliation Service, and where appropriate, the arbitration facility.

7.4. To cooperate fully with the National Conciliation Service and arbitration panel whenever called upon to do so.

8. Towards the Association

8.1. To give public support to the NTDA and to participate regularly in their activities and deliberations by personal or delegated representation or correspondence.

8.2. Where appropriate to seek and heed advice from the NTDA in connection with the operation of our business.

8.3. To display publicly membership of the NTDA in such a manner as may be determined from time to time by the Association's Executive Council.

Conciliation Procedure for settling complaints

The vast majority of customers' transactions are handled expeditiously and satisfactorily. Most customer complaints can be rectified quickly and amicably at the time. However, a small minority are more complicated. The problem may have been caused by a misunderstanding or breakdown in communication between the parties concerned. The Conciliation Procedure therefore exists primarily to help resolve those disputes which cannot be quickly settled during the initial discussion between the two parties. The Association will also be available to Trading Standards Officers, Consumer Advice Centres, Citizen's Advice Bureaux, Motoring Organisations and other similarly recognized bodies to assist in securing resolution of complaints in which a member of the Association is involved.

1. **Object of the Conciliation Service** The object of the Conciliation Service shall be the settlement of any dispute or difference referred to the Association by a member of the public or a member of the Association.

2. **Application to Conciliation Service** All applications for the determination of any case shall be addressed to the NTDA at the address at section 7. A senior executive of the Association has full responsibility for the administration of the service.

3. **Scope of the Service**

3.1. Any complaint or dispute must be settled within 9 months of the completion of the work.

3.2. The service will be restricted to disputes affecting members of the Association.

4. **Conciliation Service Procedure**

4.1. When a request is received from a customer or a member of the Association, for conciliation a questionnaire (to be completed) will be provided. The complaint will then be referred, if necessary, to an independent panel appointed by the National Conciliation Service, who shall endeavour to achieve a settlement based on the facts at their disposal and any examination of the tyre and fast fit motor components as required. The report of the panel shall be issued to both parties and copied to the Association.

4.2. Any failure to achieve settlement as a result of the report of the panel can be referred for determination by an arbitrator appointed by the Independent Panel of Arbitrators through the National Conciliation Service, and assisted where necessary by any expert he may choose to have appointed. If requested by the customer, the member shall agree to go to arbitration.

5. **Cost of Service** The Association will undertake to pay all appropriate charges for investigation and examinations up to the process of arbitration.

6. **Membership Failure** Where a member has ceased trading and is unable to make any redress imposed upon him under the Conciliation Scheme, the NTDA will support the decision and take the necessary action.

7. **Where to Complain** The Conciliation Department, NTDA, Elsinore House, Buckingham Street, Aylesbury, Bucks HP20 2NQ.

Arbitration procedure

1. If it has not been possible to achieve a conciliation, the remaining facility that the Association can offer both parties is that of independent arbitration. Arbitration, under the auspices of the Association, offers to both parties an inexpensive means of resolving their dispute.

2. If the complainant elects to take the dispute to arbitration, both parties are obliged to follow the procedures of the scheme and to be bound by the Arbitrator's findings.

3. The complainant and the member will be required to sign the arbitration agreement. The arbitration proceedings will be governed by the Arbitration Acts of 1950/1979, in accordance with any amendments in force to these Acts at the time of signing the agreement, and the terms of the rules of the Independent Panel of Arbitrators.

4. A sole and independent Arbitrator will be appointed by the Independent Panel of Arbitrators through the National Conciliation Service. In all cases the Arbitrator may request the services of any expert he may choose to have appointed.

5. Neither the complainant nor the member has the right to appear or to be represented at the hearing unless the Arbitrator so decides. The parties shall enter submissions in writing in the form of points of claim and points of defence, together with all supporting documents the parties think relevant.

6. After considering all relevant evidence, reports and documents, the Arbitrator will make his award in writing to the Panel and copies will be provided to the Association and both parties. The Arbitrator's award, including his directions regarding costs, are legally binding and enforceable by law.

NTDA customer charter

The NTDA is the trade association for the fast fit and tyre industry in the UK.
The Association was founded in 1933 and has 2800 depots in membership covering over 65%
of the industry.
As a member of the NTDA we pledge the following to our customers:
  Fully itemized bills
  Fully trained personnel
  Safety guarantees
  Return of all replaced motor parts other than exchange units
  Environmentally safe disposal of tyres and fast fit motor components
  Commitment to the NTDA code of practice
  An effective complaints procedure administered by the NTDA
  Access to an independent arbitration facility
All members of staff have access to the Code of Practice and are fully aware of the procedures
should you have a complaint.

BENEFITS AND COSTS

The importance of such voluntary codes and the problems they present have been
recognised and discussed by successive Directors General. In 1975, in his Second
Report, the then Director, John Methven, wrote at pp 9–10:

I believe that proposals to change the law should be made only when absolutely necessary
because I have increasingly realised that extension of the law is no automatic panacea for consumer problems. It is all too easy to suggest measures for consumer protection which are either
impractical or prohibitively costly. It is no use hankering after wide criminal prohibitions which
are unenforceable; and if new laws are made there is still the problem of making sure that people
know about them and understand them.

. . .

Voluntary action
I have always considered that one of my most important functions is the duty to encourage voluntary codes of practice . . .
  Some of the draft codes which come into my Office for scrutiny are excellent, some provide
a basis for further work, and others need a good deal of effort before they merit consideration.
Codes, to be effective, must be carefully constructed and precise. General expressions of goodwill towards the customer, or declarations of good intent, are not nearly enough. Once a code
has been negotiated and publicised it cannot stop there. It must be kept up to date in the light
of changing expectations and events, and it must be monitored to see if it is working effectively.

. . .

  One criticism of codes has been that they are not subscribed to by those traders who most
need to raise their standards. I am aware of this difficulty, but if the majority of traders will regulate their activities by voluntary means, the problem of dealing with the rest becomes much
more manageable.

In his 1982 Report the Director (Gordon Borrie) referred more directly to some
of the disadvantages of these codes. He wrote (at p 11):

There are many other areas of trade, industry and the professions where self-regulation keeps standards high and provides for redress of complaints. The fairly recent inception within the insurance industry of schemes under which policy-holders can seek independent adjudication on disputes with their insurers is a good example of voluntary action to meet an obvious need. Self-regulation can bring its own problems when it includes restrictions on competition, such as those preventing members of a profession from publicising their services, but there is no doubt that self-regulation can provide a good or even better safeguard to the public than legal sanctions or, as with the advertising industry, be complementary to a measure of legal regulation that would need to be extended if self-regulation was absent.

Unfortunately, some measures of self-regulation may prove in practice to be less effective than was hoped. This Office has a statutory obligation to promote self-regulatory codes of practice to be promulgated by trade associations on behalf of their members for the benefit of consumers. Twenty such codes have been promoted covering a variety of industries. Generally, they have been useful—they have encouraged those large numbers of traders who are capable of trading fairly to raise their standards, to persuade them that the higher expectations of growing numbers of the public need to be met and that this can make good commercial sense. But self-regulatory codes have two principal weaknesses. First, they cannot be enforced against non-members—this may be felt to put member-firms, who are likely to be the more responsible traders, at a competitive disadvantage. Secondly, codes are difficult to enforce, even against members.

(See also Borrie, 'Laws and Codes for Consumers' [1980] JBL 315.)

Sir Bryan Carsberg, as Director, in the 1993 Report said (at pp 10–11):

Some problems of business practice can be dealt with effectively through the development of codes of practice by trade associations. Such a solution should always be explored. Doing so may help consumers by broadening the adoption of practices which may have developed through competition. This course of action may also provide helpful insights into the costs of regulation. But codes of practice are rarely sufficient solutions to the most difficult problems. The businesses which cause detriment to consumers may not belong to trade associations and, even if they do, the code of practice may not be enforceable in law. Furthermore trade associations may resist including provisions to deal with key issues such as compensation—and they cannot be compelled to do so.

Finally, the consultation paper issued by John Bridgeman, the current Director, states (in para 3.1):

Codes of practice have always been an area of difficulty for us, as evidenced by the number of times our policy has been reviewed. With a few notable exceptions, they do not appear to have been effective in reducing either malpractice or consumer dissatisfaction. Yet the speed and flexibility of the best self-regulation are highly attractive, and we have therefore continued to seek ways of bringing them to bear on a wider range of consumer problems.

A helpful statement of the benefits and costs of codes of practice is contained in the following extract:

'The Benefits and Costs of Voluntary Codes of Practice' by J F Pickering and D C Cousins (1982) (No 6) European Journal of Marketing 31, 35 (footnotes omitted)

The Impact on Consumers
From the point of view of consumer policy, the objective of a code of practice is to reduce consumer detriment which arises when consumers purchase goods or services which do not live up to their expectations prior to purchase and when they cannot obtain adequate redress to overcome their dissatisfactions and thereby to increase consumer welfare and total social welfare. While it is possible to describe theoretically the nature of such changes in consumer welfare and the influences upon it, it is much more difficult to provide an empirical measure to indicate even the direction of change, let alone the magnitude of any such change. Even if we could effectively measure the changes it may be extremely difficult to determine their causes.

. . .

In assessing the impact on consumers of codes of practice generally we have drawn extensively on reports produced by the Consumers' Association and the monitoring studies carried out by, and for, OFT. In addition, we have collected our own questionnaire and personal interview information from traders and their trade associations. While the significance of the impact varies from trade to trade, certain features are apparent that seem to have fairly general validity.

There are five major ways in which consumers appear to have benefited from the development of codes of practice. First, there has been some increase in awareness among consumers of their rights and of the protection that can be available to them. Such awareness is an important first step in taking action should problems and difficulties arise and is a key element in strengthening the position of customers in the interests of achieving a more effective balance between suppliers and purchasers in the market place. Secondly, codes have reiterated legal prohibitions on certain types of undesirable practice, eg exclusion clauses, the use of 'worth and value' claims, etc. While it appears that some traders still continue to adopt such practices, the incidence is now much reduced and the consumer is thereby better protected. Allied to this is a third area of improvement—namely the provision of better information to consumers. This improvement relates to both the quantity of information provided and also its quality in terms of the clarity and relevance of the information. Advertising is more accurate and informative, statements of prices are clearer and there is a wider use of informative labelling in a number of trades.

Fourthly, an improvement in the quality of products and/or services supplied has been apparent. Greater attention has been paid to overcoming the causes of product failure. Improved handling of after-sales servicing and repairs has been achieved in some trades. Some monitoring studies have indicated that when consumer complaints concerning a particular category of products or services are analysed according to whether the trader complained about was a participant in a code of practice or not, the share of such complaints accounted for by code participants often tends to be well below their share of the total trade and to be falling through time. This is encouraging evidence though it may well be that those who now participate in the code already had superior performance compared to non-participants even prior to the adoption of the code. Finally, and perhaps of greatest significance to consumers, has been evidence that, when problems have arisen, complaints handling procedures by companies have been improved, arbitration and conciliation services (often through the trade association) have been made more readily available and consequently it has become easier for the consumer to obtain redress.

Each of these developments appears to be an unambiguous benefit to consumers so long as there have not been other, undesirable, developments consequent upon these changes. The position in respect of these improvements is still by no means ideal since it is clear that many traders fail to attain the code's standards in all respects. It is also difficult to attempt to indicate the value of the improvements in consumer welfare, but they do certainly appear to be real and worth having.

The question then arises as to whether there have been any additional costs or disbenefits to consumers as a result of codes of practice. One problem is the failure of some traders to adhere fully to the code. As we have already noted, some still attempt to exclude part of their liability and others do not attain the minimum performance standards required by the code. While in one sense this indicates a failure to maximise the potential benefits of a code, it may also be a source of disbenefit to consumers where the effect of a code and its publicity has been to lead consumers to expect that all code participants will achieve the minimum standards specified in the code. Wilful failure by participants in a code to achieve the standards set is an example of 'free riding' and may impose costs upon both consumers and other traders. Associated with this is a difficulty that arises where traders are reluctant to agree to arbitration or where they do not encourage consumers to use the conciliation and arbitration procedures available. Again, this may be more a case of benefits not maximised if consumers remain unaware of the facilities for arbitration, but those who are aware of the possibilities in this respect will incur extra costs in making use of them. There is also some concern about difficulties that have been experienced in using the arbitration schemes, particularly where it was felt the arbitration was not impartial; there was a failure to give reasons for the arbitration decision; there was difficulty in obtaining adequate information about the procedures; and the time taken to deal with the matter was protracted.

Costs may be imposed upon consumers where the effects of the code are to rule out particular mixes of quality/service and price which consumers might still wish to purchase. It could be, for example, that by specifying minimum performance standards in relation to product servicing a code rules out slower but less expensive servicing arrangements. Clearly it is important that consumers should have adequate knowledge about the price/service/quality mix they are choosing in order to make an informed and effective choice. Also, it would be unfortunate if concern over particular performance standards led to the use of prescriptive standards which specify not only *what* standards should be achieved, but also *how* they are to be achieved. This would again restrict some aspects of consumer choice and possibly hinder innovation by traders. So far such restrictions on consumer choice do not appear to have been significant costs as a result of codes of practice, but it is important to try to ensure that such undesirable consequences do not occur.

A further potential cost to consumers is the possibility of higher prices. There may be two main causes for such an outcome: the effects of additional costs incurred by traders as a result of a code and the effects of a code in possibly reducing competition in a particular trade. As we shall observe in more detail in the next section, the introduction of a code of practice does cause traders to incur some extra costs. However, it appears that these costs are frequently small in total size and certainly as a proportion of turnover. While some traders reported that costs and prices had risen as a result of a code of practice, it seems unlikely that this is a general and significant consequence. Perhaps of rather greater long-term significance in this respect is the extent to which the introduction of a code of practice has increased the cohesiveness of the traders and enhanced the status and role of the relevant trade association. It was widely held that one of the consequences of the Restrictive Trade Practices legislation was that trade associations were generally weakened. It would be ironic if the competition-restricting scope of trade associations was to be increased now as a result of action encouraged and formally approved by OFT! At present the risks seem greater than the reality, but the implications ought not to be overlooked.

While not a direct cost, as such, to consumers, we should also note that it appears that the improvement in quality and service and complaint handling has not had much effect on those traders that do not participate in codes of practice. This is of some concern as, while there are important exceptions, it is often the case that non-participants have lower standards in these respects. The benefit to consumers may have been less than might otherwise have been the case. It is possible that non-participants have not been greatly affected because the markets concerned are not as competitive as some fondly believe or that non-participants in a code tend to serve distinct market segments from those operating the code. Alternatively it may be the case that the existence of a code is not a significant influence in consumer choice of traders to patronise. Certainly, traders believe that codes of practice have not affected consumer choice of outlets. It may be that consumers consider the benefits offered by a code to be insufficient to influence their conduct in this respect. Overall, however, we think it is probably because knowledge among consumers about codes of practice remains very low (and will do so until publicity is considerably increased) that non-participants have largely been unaffected by their existence. Again, this suggests that if it is held that codes of practice are beneficial to consumers the welfare gains could be further increased by appropriate action in the future.

On balance, our view of the net welfare effects of codes of practice on consumers is that there have been some worthwhile, if unmeasurable, gains. There is scope for further increases in the benefits to consumers if appropriate enforcement and publicity action is taken. There are actual and potential welfare losses that have to be set against these benefits. Effective monitoring and enforcement can help to reduce these losses and generally they do not appear to be substantial at the present time.

Thus we may conclude that consumers have, on balance, benefited and received an increase in net welfare as a result of the introduction of codes of practice. There is potential to increase these net benefits still further.

EVIDENTIAL STATUS OF CODES

Codes are not generally legally enforceable. However, provided a code of practice is sufficiently precise there is no objection in principle to its being given statutory form. This, as yet, is unusual in English law but one example is the Code of Practice for Traders on Price Indications which, by virtue of the Consumer Protection Act 1987, s 25, is given the force of law (see further ch 14). In other cases courts may be prepared to look at a code of practice as evidence of the better trade procedures followed in a sector of industry.

Two examples of this may be cited. In *Woodman v Photo Trade Processing Ltd* (1981) 7 May, unreported, Exeter County Court, reference was made to the Code of Practice for the Photographic Industry in assessing whether or not an exemption clause satisfied the reasonableness test under the Unfair Contract Terms Act 1977, s 11 (see ch 7 and above, p 343). In this case failure to follow the guidance given in the Code contributed to the clause being declared unreasonable. As a contrast, following the Motor Agents' Association Code of Practice in *Lewin v Rothersthorpe Road Garage Ltd* (1984) 148 JP 87, QBD, assisted in providing a due diligence defence under s 24 of the Trade Descriptions Act 1968 for a garage charged with a s 1 offence (false trade description of goods) caused by an employee (see ch 13). The company had adopted the code, instructed its salesmen in the operation of the code and had emphasised the importance of observing the code.

It is possible for failure to adhere to a particular provision of a code of practice by a member of the relevant trade association, who advertises such membership, to constitute an offence under s 14 of the Trade Descriptions Act 1968 (false statements as to services), as occurred in *Shropshire County Council v V G Vehicles (Telford) Ltd* (1981) 89 ITSA Monthly Review 91, Wrekin Magistrates Court. A fine of £200 was imposed on a garage claiming to subscribe to the Motor Agents' Association Code of Practice. This remains to be tested in the superior courts. (For a discussion of s 14 see below, p 642 et seq). The point is discussed by A J Street, 'Criminal Enforcement of Voluntary Codes of Practice' (1979) 87 ITSA Monthly Review 63.

TRADE ASSOCIATION SANCTIONS

The effectiveness of a code of practice depends at least in part on the willingness of the relevant trade association to impose sanctions where these prove to be necessary. Accordingly it is of interest to note that at least one code which is of major importance to consumers is backed by sanctions which have been applied in practice. The 1996 Annual Report of the Association of British Travel Agents shows that fines of £183,850 were levied on its members in a year.

ADVERTISING

INTRODUCTION

Advertising provides an important example of an area which is controlled largely through codes of practice. The following extract is helpful as indicating the structure of control (subsequent developments are noted in square brackets).

The Self-regulatory System of Advertising Control: Report of a Working Party, Department of Trade, 1980.

THE PRESENT STRUCTURE

11. Control of advertising in the United Kingdom currently takes two forms—statutory control and self-regulation—the one generally complementing the other. Some 80 separate statutes, orders and regulations are concerned with advertising to a greater or lesser extent. The main function of these provisions, insofar as they are concerned with the content of advertisements, is the negative one of restraining from publication limited categories of misleading or indecent advertisements. But many advertising practices do not lend themselves easily to precise definition and the voluntarily accepted codes of practice which underlie the self-regulatory arrangements are needed to complement and extend the legal constraints.

12. Codes of practice provide a positive approach to advertising control. They can reflect the spirit rather than the letter and can be readily reviewed and updated to take account of changing social conditions and public attitudes. They command a high degree of commitment from

the business community and encourage high standards of advertising to the benefit of consumer and advertiser.

13. This report is confined to the principal self-regulatory control in the UK—that administered by the Advertising Standards Authority in the print, cinema and poster media. The ASA was established in 1962. Since 1974 it has been financed by a surcharge of 0.1 per cent on the cost to the advertiser of advertisements (other than those appearing in the classified columns of the press). The funds generated by the surcharge are collected by the Advertising Standards Board of Finance (ASBOF), a body set up by the advertising business. The ASA is a company limited by guarantee and its directors are the Chairman and Council Members. The Chairman . . . is appointed by ASBOF which is obliged by its Articles of Association, before making any appointment, to consult in particular 'with the Department of Prices and Consumer Protection (or other equivalent Government Department) and with the Advertising Association'. The ASA Articles of Association provide that 'the Chairman shall not be engaged in the business of advertising' and shall be appointed only 'after consultation with the Members of the Council of the Authority'. Members of the Council, a majority of whom must also be independent, are appointed at the sole discretion of the Chairman who ensures that a balance is kept on the Council between the sexes, political persuasions, religious philosophies and social attitudes.

14. It is present policy to ensure that the proportion of independent or industry members remains at the maximum permissible level of 2 : 1 . . . The preponderance of independent members on the Council as a whole (9 out of 13), the mode of appointment of both ordinary Council Members and Chairman, the separation of the funding body (ASBOF) from both the Advertising Association and ASA (which therefore is not involved in soliciting contributions or chasing up reluctant contributors), together with the nature of the levy itself are, in total, designed to ensure that the supervisory element in the control arrangements is isolated from any possibility of pressure from the advertising business to support its interests against those of the general public.

15. The present arrangements provide for the Codes of Practice on which the control administered by the ASA is based to be drawn up by a committee of advertising interests, the Code of Advertising Practice Committee (CAP) [now called the Committee of Advertising Practice], in consultation with the ASA and trade and consumer interests. (There are two such Codes— the British Code of Advertising Practice (BCAP) and the British Code of Sales Promotion Practice [now called The British Codes of Advertising and Sales Promotion].) Joint approval is required for all changes in the Codes but the ASA is effectively the senior partner, having the right to override CAP decisions. Thus, as will be seen from paragraphs 13 and 14 . . . final decisions on the content of the Codes and on other applications in contested matters are ultimately in the hands of a body with a majority of independent members.

16. The Codes of Practice are enforced through action by the media. On the recommendation of the ASA, advertising space may be denied to or trading privileges withdrawn from those who contravene the Codes. The ASA also attaches importance to the deterrent value of adverse publicity resulting from its publication of regular reports on complaints in which details are given of offenders against the Codes.

In addition to the ASA, two further organisations involved with the control of advertising by means of codes of practice should be mentioned. First, there is the Independent Television Commission (ITC) which oversees the ITC Code of Advertising Standards and Practice, the ITC Rules on Advertising Breaks and the ITC Code of Programme Sponsorship, all concerning advertisements on independent television services regulated by the ITC. Second, the Radio Authority, with its Code of Advertising Standards and Practice and Programme Sponsorship, regulates independent radio services licensed by the Authority.

Statutory authority for the control of advertising by the ITC is derived from the Broadcasting Act 1990, s 9:

9(1) It shall be the duty of the Commission—
    (a) after the appropriate consultation, to draw up, and from time to time review, a code—
        (i) governing standards and practice in advertising and in the sponsoring of programmes, and
        (ii) prescribing the advertisements and methods of advertising or sponsorship to be prohibited in particular circumstances; and
    (b) to do all that they can to secure that the provisions of the code are observed in the provision of licensed services;

and the Commission may make different provision in the code for different kinds of licensed services.

A similar duty is created, under s 93 of the Broadcasting Act 1990, for the Radio Authority.

THE ADVERTISING CODES

The ASA, ITC and Radio Authority Codes of Practice all contain very similar measures and are all intended to be enforced according to the spirit of the code and not just by the letter of it. Full texts of all the codes can be found in *Butterworths Trading and Consumer Law*, Division 5.

ASA British Codes of Advertising and Sales Promotion (extracts)

INTRODUCTION

1.1. The Codes apply to:
    (a) advertisements in newspapers, magazines, brochures, leaflets, circulars, mailings, catalogues and other printed publications, facsimile transmissions, posters and aerial announcements
    (b) cinema and video commercials
    (c) advertisements in non-broadcast electronic media such as computer games
    (d) viewdata services
    (e) mailing lists except for business-to-business
    (f) sales promotions
    (g) advertisement promotions
    (h) advertisements and promotions covered by the Cigarette Code.
1.2. The Codes do not apply to:
    (a) broadcast commercials, which are the responsibility of the Independent Television Commission or the Radio Authority
    (b) the contents of premium rate telephone calls, which are the responsibility of the Independent Committee for the Supervision of Standards of Telephone Information Services
    (c) advertisements in foreign media
    (d) health-related claims in advertisements and promotions addressed only to the medical and allied professions
    (e) classified private advertisements

(f) statutory, public, police and other official notices

(g) works of art exhibited in public or private

(h) private correspondence

(i) oral communications, including telephone calls

(j) press releases and other public relations material

(k) the content of books and editorial communications

(l) regular competitions such as crosswords

(m) flyposting

(n) packages, wrappers, labels and tickets unless they advertise a sales promotion or are visible in an advertisement

(o) point of sale displays except for those covered by the Sales Promotion Code and the Cigarette Code.

1.3. The following definitions apply to the Codes:

(a) a *product* encompasses goods, services, ideas, causes or opportunities, prizes and gifts

(b) a *consumer* is anyone who is likely to see a given advertisement or promotion

(c) the *United Kingdom* rules cover the Isle of Man and the Channel Islands (except for the purposes of the Cigarette Code)

(d) a *claim* can be implied or direct, written, spoken or visual

(e) the Codes are divided into numbered *clauses.*

1.4. The following criteria apply to the Codes:

(a) the judgement of the ASA Council on interpretation of the Codes is final

(b) conformity is assessed according to the advertisement's probable impact when taken as a whole and in context. This will depend on the audience, the medium, the nature of the product and any additional material distributed at the same time to consumers

(c) the Codes are indivisible; advertisers must conform with all appropriate rules

(d) the Codes do not have the force of law and their interpretation will reflect their flexibility. The general law operates alongside the Codes; the Courts may also make rulings against matters covered by the Codes

(e) an indication of the statutory rules governing advertising and promotions is given in the Legislation section; professional advice should be taken if there is any doubt about their application

(f) no spoken or written communications with the ASA or CAP should be understood as containing legal advice

(g) the Codes are primarily concerned with advertisements and promotions and not with terms of business, products themselves or other contractual matter

(h) the rules make due allowance for public sensitivities but will not be used by the ASA to diminish freedom of speech

(i) the ASA may decide that it is not qualified to judge advertisements and promotions in languages other than English

(j) the ASA does not act as an arbitrator between conflicting ideologies.

ADVERTISING CODE

Principles

2.1. All advertisements should be legal, decent, honest and truthful.

2.2. All advertisements should be prepared with a sense of responsibility to consumers and to society.

2.3. All advertisements should respect the principles of fair competition generally accepted in business.

2.4. No advertisement should bring advertising into disrepute.

2.5. Advertisements must conform with the Codes. Primary responsibility for observing the Codes falls on advertisers. Others involved in preparing and publishing advertisements such as agencies, publishers and other service suppliers also accept an obligation to abide by the Codes.

2.6. Any unreasonable delay in responding to the ASA's enquiries may be considered a breach of the Codes.

2.7. The ASA will on request treat in confidence any private or secret material supplied unless the Courts or officials acting within their statutory powers compel its disclosure.

2.8. The Codes are applied in the spirit as well as in the letter.

Substantiation
3.1. Before submitting an advertisement for publication, advertisers must hold documentary evidence to prove all claims, whether direct or implied, that are capable of objective substantiation.

Relevant evidence should be sent without delay if requested by the ASA. The adequacy of evidence will be judged on whether it supports both the detailed claims and the overall impression created by the advertisement.

3.2. If there is a significant division of informed opinion about any claims made in an advertisement they should not be portrayed as universally agreed.

3.3. If the contents of non-fiction books, tapes, videos and the like have not been independently substantiated, advertisements should not exaggerate the value or practical usefulness of their contents.

3.4. Obvious untruths or exaggerations that are unlikely to mislead and incidental minor errors and unorthodox spellings are all allowed provided they do not affect the accuracy or perception of the advertisement in any material way.

Legality
4.1. Advertisers have primary responsibility for ensuring that their advertisements are legal. Advertisements should contain nothing that breaks the law or incites anyone to break it, and should omit nothing that the law requires.

Decency
5.1. Advertisements should contain nothing that is likely to cause serious or widespread offence. Particular care should be taken to avoid causing offence on the grounds of race, religion, sex, sexual orientation or disability. Compliance with the Codes will be judged on the context, medium, audience, product and prevailing standards of decency.

5.2. Advertisements may be distasteful without necessarily conflicting with 5.1 above. Advertisers are urged to consider public sensitivities before using potentially offensive material.

5.3. The fact that a particular product is offensive to some people is not sufficient grounds for objecting to an advertisement for it.

Honesty
6.1. Advertisers should not exploit the credulity, lack of knowledge or inexperience of consumers.

Truthfulness
7.1. No advertisement should mislead by inaccuracy, ambiguity, exaggeration, omission or otherwise.

Matters of opinion
8.1. Advertisers may give a view about any matter, including the qualities or desirability of their products, provided it is clear that they are expressing their own opinion rather than stating a fact. Assertions or comparisons that go beyond subjective opinions are subject to 3.1 above.

Fear and distress
9.1. No advertisement should cause fear or distress without good reason. Advertisers should not use shocking claims or images merely to attract attention.
9.2. Advertisers may use an appeal to fear to encourage prudent behaviour or to discourage dangerous or ill-advised actions; the fear likely to be aroused should not be disproportionate to the risk.

Safety
10.1. Advertisements should not show or encourage unsafe practices except in the context of promoting safety. Particular care should be taken with advertisements addressed to or depicting children and young people.
10.2. Consumers should not be encouraged to drink and drive. Advertisements, including those for breath testing devices, should not suggest that the effects of drinking alcohol can be masked and should include a prominent warning on the dangers of drinking and driving.

Violence and anti-social behaviour
11.1. Advertisements should contain nothing that condones or is likely to provoke violence or anti-social behaviour.

Political advertising
12.1. Any advertisement whose principal function is to influence opinion in favour of or against any political party or electoral candidate contesting a UK, European parliamentary or local government election, or any matter before the electorate for a referendum, is exempt from clauses 3.1, 7.1, 14.3, 19.2 and 20.1. All other rules in the Codes apply.
12.2. The identity and status of such advertisers should be clear. If their address or other contact details are not generally available they should be included in the advertisement.
12.3. There is a formal distinction between government policy and that of political parties. Advertisements by central or local government, or those concerning government policy as distinct from party policy, are subject to all the Codes' rules.

Protection of privacy
13.1. Advertisers are urged to obtain written permission in advance if they portray or refer to individuals or their identifiable possessions in any advertisement. Exceptions include most crowd scenes, portraying anyone who is the subject of the book or film being advertised and depicting property in general outdoor locations.
13.2. Advertisers who have not obtained prior permission from entertainers, politicians, sportsmen and others whose work gives them a high public profile should ensure that they are not portrayed in an offensive or adverse way. Advertisements should not claim or imply an endorsement where none exists.
13.3. Prior permission may not be needed when the advertisement contains nothing that is inconsistent with the position or views of the person featured. Advertisers should be aware that individuals who do not wish to be associated with the advertised product may have a legal claim.
13.4. References to anyone who is deceased should be handled with particular care to avoid causing offence or distress.
13.5. References to members of the Royal Family and the use of the Royal Arms and Emblems are not normally permitted; advertisers should consult the Lord Chamberlain's Office. References to Royal Warrants should be checked with the Royal Warrant Holders' Association.

Testimonials and endorsements
14.1. Advertisers should hold signed and dated proof, including a contact address, for any testimonial they use. Testimonials should be used only with the written permission of those giving them.
14.2. Testimonials should relate to the product being advertised.

14.3. Testimonials alone do not constitute substantiation and the opinions expressed in them must be supported, where necessary, with independent evidence of their accuracy. Any claims based on a testimonial must conform with the Codes.

14.4. Fictitious endorsements should not be presented as though they were genuine testimonials.

14.5. References to tests, trials, professional endorsements, research facilities and professional journals should be used only with the permission of those concerned. They should originate from within the European Union unless otherwise stated in the advertisement. Any establishment referred to should be under the direct supervision of an appropriately qualified professional.

Prices

15.1. Any stated price should be clear and should relate to the product advertised. Advertisers should ensure that prices match the products illustrated.

15.2. Unless addressed exclusively to the trade, prices quoted should include any VAT payable. It should be apparent immediately whether any prices quoted exclude other taxes, duties or compulsory charges and these should, wherever possible, be given in the advertisement.

15.3. If the price of one product is dependent on the purchase of another, the extent of any commitment by consumers should be made clear.

15.4. Price claims such as 'up to' and 'from' should not exaggerate the availability of benefits likely to be obtained by consumers.

Free offers

16.1. There is no objection to making a free offer conditional on the purchase of other items. Consumers' liability for any costs should be made clear in all material featuring the offer. An offer should only be described as free if consumers pay no more than:

    (a) the current public rates of postage
    (b) the actual cost of freight or delivery
    (c) the cost, including incidental expenses, of any travel involved if consumers collect the offer.

Advertisers should make no additional charges for packing and handling.

16.2. Advertisers must not attempt to recover their costs by reducing the quality or composition or by inflating the price of any product that must be purchased as a precondition of obtaining another product free.

Availability of products

17.1. Advertisers must make it clear if stocks are limited. Products must not be advertised unless advertisers can demonstrate that they have reasonable grounds for believing that they can satisfy demand. If a product becomes unavailable, advertisers will be required to show evidence of stock monitoring, communications with outlets and the swift withdrawal of advertisements whenever possible.

17.2. Products which cannot be supplied should not normally be advertised as a way of assessing potential demand.

17.3. Advertisers must not use the technique of switch selling, where their sales staff criticise the advertised product or suggest that it is not available and recommend the purchase of a more expensive alternative. They should not place obstacles in the way of purchasing the product or delivering it promptly.

Guarantees

18.1. The full terms of any guarantee should be available for consumers to inspect before they are committed to purchase. Any substantial limitations should be spelled out in the advertisement.

18.2. Advertisers should inform consumers about the nature and extent of any additional rights provided by the guarantee, over and above those given to them by law, and should make clear how to obtain redress.

18.3. 'Guarantee' when used simply as a figure of speech should not cause confusion about consumers' legal rights.

Comparisons

19.1. Comparisons can be explicit or implied and can relate to advertisers' own products or to those of their competitors; they are permitted in the interests of vigorous competition and public information.

19.2. Comparisons should be clear and fair. The elements of any comparison should not be selected in a way that gives the advertisers an artificial advantage.

Denigration

20.1. Advertisers should not unfairly attack or discredit other businesses or their products.

20.2. The only acceptable use of another business's broken or defaced products in advertisements is in the illustration of comparative tests, and the source, nature and results of these should be clear.

Exploitation of goodwill

21.1. Advertisers should not make unfair use of the goodwill attached to the trade mark, name, brand, or the advertising campaign of any other business.

Imitation

22.1. No advertisement should so closely resemble any other that it misleads or causes confusion.

Identifying advertisers and recognising advertisements

23.1. Advertisers, publishers and owners of other media should ensure that advertisements are designed and presented in such a way that they can be easily distinguished from editorial.

23.2. Features, announcements or promotions that are disseminated in exchange for a payment or other reciprocal arrangement should comply with the Codes if their content is controlled by the advertisers. They should also be clearly identified and distinguished from editorial (see clause 41).

23.3. Mail order and direct response advertisements and those for one day sales, homework schemes, business opportunities and the like should contain the name and address of the advertisers. Advertisements with a political content should clearly identify their source. Unless required by law, other advertisers are not obliged to identify themselves.

. . .

JUDICIAL SUPERVISION OF THE ENFORCEMENT BODIES

Actions seeking judicial review have been brought against the ASA and the Radio Authority. The following cases demonstrate the courts' approach to such regulatory bodies.

In *R v Advertising Standards Authority, ex p Insurance Services plc* (1989) 133 Sol Jo 1545, QBD, the court recognised that the ASA exercised a public law function which, if it did not exist would be exercised by the Office of Fair Trading, and was open to control by judicial review. The court quashed a decision by the ASA Council against an advertisement when it was proved that members of the ASA Secretariat had failed to pass all relevant information on to the Council.

The impact of ASA case reports was considered in the following case:

R v Advertising Standards Authority Ltd, ex p Vernons Organisation Ltd [1993] 2 All ER 202, Queen's Bench Division

The ASA had upheld a complaint made to it concerning an advertisement by Vernons Organisation which then sought leave for judicial review against the decision and a stay of the publication of the ASA's decision.

Laws LJ explained the position: The publication of the decision will, unless it is stayed by this court, take place in the shape of one of the authority's reports. It will be published on, I am told, 16 September of this year, and that publication will entail circulation of the case report to some 4,000 subscribers and it will be made available to members of the public who may ask for it. In the British Code of Advertising Practice one finds these words at para 21:

'Each advertisement, whether pin-pointed by this process or raised by means of complaint, is carefully scrutinised. Any requisite investigation is undertaken, and after the issues, when necessary, have been discussed by the ASA Council, appropriate action on any advertisement that contravenes the Code is put in hand. The outcome of concluded investigations is recorded each month in the Authority's "Case Report", which gives details of all complaints that have necessitated investigation, including the names of the advertisers and advertising agencies involved.'

At para 34 under a heading 'Case Reports' it is said:

'Copies are available on request of the reports of which are published at regular intervals by both ASA and CAP, and which give details of the complaints the two bodies have investigated. Reports identify those responsible for the advertisements involved, and why, and set out what action has been taken on those which contravene the Code.'

So one can see that what is enshrined in the code contemplates the publication of narrative case reports which, where appropriate, will contain criticism, perhaps detailed, of advertisers in relation to whom the authority has upheld complaints.

The applicants alleged that publication, as a concluded determination, of a decision which was subject to judicial review, would cause great damage to the reputation and standing of the company.

Laws LJ indicated: It seems to me that the case is, if anything, analogous to one where an administrative body has an adjudicative function and in the course of its duties publishes a ruling criticising some affected person and the ruling is later disturbed or reversed by an appropriate appellate process. There are many such instances and many of them involve the criticism of members of the public, corporate or natural.

I do not know of an instance in which a public body of that kind would fall to be restrained from carrying out what is no more nor less than its ordinary, but important, everyday duties simply upon the grounds that the intended publication contains material which is subject to legal challenge as being vitiated by some error of law. If the application for judicial review here is successful I cannot think but that there are ample means at the applicant's disposal to correct any adverse impression which what, ex hypothesi, would be an unlawful report may have given to the public. . . . I do not consider that the effects of that publication are damaging to the applicant in a manner which would be so irreparable, so past recall as to amount to a pressing ground, in the language of Strasbourg [a reference here to the European Convention on Human Rights], a pressing social need to restrain this public body from carrying out their functions in the ordinary way.

Application dismissed.

It was reported in *The Times*, 14 August 1997, that a company, Direct Line, had been successful in obtaining an injunction to prevent the issuing of a case report where the ASA had upheld a complaint against the company, pending a review of the decision.

The activities of the Radio Authority were scrutinised in:

R v Radio Authority, ex p Bull and another [1997] 2 All ER 561, Court of Appeal

Amnesty International (British Section) (AIBS) appealed against a Divisional Court decision ([1996] QB 169) refusing judicial review of decisions made by the Radio Authority concerning advertisements for commercial radio publicising the plight of people in Rwanda and Burundi. Under the Broadcasting Act 1990, s 92(2)(a)(i) advertisements for or on behalf of bodies whose objects were 'wholly or mainly of a political nature' are banned. The Radio Authority had come to the conclusion that AIBS was 'political' and had refused to broadcast the advertisements. In looking at the way the Radio Authority behaved in applying its Code of Practice and rejecting the case for judicial review, the following comments were made:

Lord Woolf MR: The authority is a regulatory body consisting of lay members which is intended to take a broad brush approach to its task. In the words of s 92(1) it was required to 'do all that they can to secure that the rules specified in subsection (2) are complied with'. This rather unusual statutory provision does not create an absolute obligation but instead places an obligation to do its best. . . . Because of its lay nature and the terms of s 92(1) the court should be prepared in this situation to allow the authority a margin of appreciation and only interfere with its decisions when there is a manifest breach of the principles applied on application for judicial review.

Brooke LJ: The task of a supervisory court in a case of this kind is not to concern itself with the merits of the decision of the decision-making body, unless that decision can be properly stigmatised as perverse or utterly irrational. If, as here, it is not suggested that the procedure has been unfair, the job of the court is simply to ensure that the law has been interpreted correctly, and that all material considerations have been taken into account. Like Lord Woolf MR, I can find no fault in the Radio Authority's interpretation of the law. It is, however, unclear to me, as it is to him, whether they did properly take into account every material consideration in reaching their decision in this case. But since they are a lay body charged with a difficult task on whom Parliament has imposed the unusual obligation of having 'to do all that they can to secure' the statutory objectives, I consider that it would be wrong for a court to interfere with the decision they made.

ASSESSMENT OF THE CONTROLS

The control of advertising was subject to considerable scrutiny in the 1980s, both within the United Kingdom and from a European perspective. The Department of Trade report, to which reference was made above, discussed issues of general importance and made recommendations for additional controls as the extracts below indicate.

The Self-regulatory System of Advertising Control: Report of a Working Party, Department of Trade, 1980

THE SCOPE OF THE WORKING PARTY'S DELIBERATIONS

17. The Working Party have concentrated on considering improvements in the machinery for dealing with misleading advertisements in the print, cinema and poster media. (They have not, however, concerned themselves with advertisements in any of these media for ethical medicines. These are subject to statutory control under the Medicines Act and to a Code of Practice which is administered by the Association of British Pharmaceutical Industry. Neither have they examined the separate controls exercised over mail order catalogues and certain other promotional techniques . . .) It follows that no attempt has been made to consider more general issues such as the role of advertising in the economy or any general effects upon culture and society which the totality of advertisements may have.

18. The Working Party recognised the existence of public interest and concern about issues of taste and morals in advertisements; and they noted that the British Code of Advertising Practice contained provisions for applying sanctions to advertisements that caused widespread or grave offence. They were informed by OFT that a very small proportion of advertisements surveyed (see paragraph 20) raised any apparent problems in this regard. They concluded unanimously that any attempt to impose further legal restraints in this area would raise difficult problems of legal policy and of definition; and that external control would inevitably raise the spectre of censorship. There was also the danger that any attempt to impose more stringent control in this area upon advertisements alone would cause resentment in the advertising business which considers that, in matters of public decency, the standards of advertisements are already substantially higher than those of much of the editorial content of newspapers and magazines (and of many of the feature films) in the context of which advertisements are seen.

THE WORKING PARTY'S OBJECTIVES

19. Legal and self-regulatory systems of control each have their particular strengths and weaknesses. In considering how the arrangements for advertising control which apply to the print, cinema and poster media could be improved in their application to misleading advertisements, the Working Party have been particularly concerned to ensure that any reinforcement of present self-regulatory controls should be approached in ways which will
   (a) permit the continuance of the flexibility inherent in codes of practice;
   (b) maintain the existing nexus of arrangements which comprise the self-regulatory control system;
   (c) foster the co-operation of the advertising industry on which the successful operation of the self-regulatory system will continue to depend.

REPORT BY THE DIRECTOR GENERAL OF FAIR TRADING

20. Relevant to the Working Party's task was the Report of the Director General of Fair Trading on the self-regulatory system which was published in November 1978. Although the report covered the whole field of advertising subject to the ASA control arrangements, it concentrated on the problem of misleading advertising. In general, the DGFT found that the strength of the self-regulatory system lay in the flexibility of operation of its Codes of Practice; in the fact that some advertisements could be vetted in advance; and in the willingness of those covered by the codes to obey their spirit without prompting. The principal deficiencies identified by the DGFT were the difficulty of dealing, by means of self-regulatory sanctions, with

those who operated entirely outside the ambit of the trade associations which sponsored and supported the Code of Advertising Practice and the absence from the self-regulatory system of a sanction which was both immediate and compelling in its effect.

21. The DGFT concluded that there was no need to create a wider framework of statutory advertising control but considered that some measure of legislative reinforcement of the self-regulatory system was necessary. He recommended that he should be given a power to apply to the High Court for an injunction in any case where he considered that an advertisement was likely to deceive, mislead or confuse with regard to any material fact. Other recommendations which he thought would make the practical operation of the ASA's system more effective included:

   (i)   reinforcement of the BCAP in relation to coverage of non-media advertising—ie point of sale material and sale brochures;

   (ii) some strengthening of the ASA Council;

   (iii) a revised complaints procedure with a strictly limited time period allowed for the substantiation of claims by the advertiser;

   (iv) the placing of greater emphasis on the monitoring and prevetting activities of the ASA;

   (v) action to increase public awareness of the place of the CAP Committee in the system of control and the need to publicise their findings;

   (vi) consideration to be given to additional sanctioning fines and corrective advertising.

ASSESSMENT OF THE DEFICIENCIES OF THE SELF-REGULATORY ARRANGEMENTS AND THE CASE FOR REINFORCEMENT

22. Against the background and findings of the DGFT's Report, the Working Party first considered possible weaknesses both in the coverage of the present arrangements, and in the effectiveness of the sanctions. They noted in particular that:

   (a) the self-regulatory arrangements do not embrace all forms of non-broadcast advertising;

   (b) in principle the ASA's sanctions can be applied effectively only in those cases where either the advertiser and/or the media subscribe to self-regulation;

   (c) self-regulation does not always permit the application of effective sanctions for dealing with those who are determined either to breach the Code or to defy a decision of the ASA: neither can immediate preventive action be taken against major misleading advertising abuses.

The Working Party agreed that this indicated that there was scope for improvement, though the AA did not think that the scale of the abuse identified by the DGFT . . . called for any statutory strengthening of the self-regulatory arrangements.

. . .

PRINCIPAL OPTIONS FOR STRENGTHENING THE SELF-REGULATORY ARRANGEMENTS

25. Four main options intended to meet the possible weaknesses in paragraph 22 were considered by the Working Party:

   (a) statutory recognition of Codes of Practice;

   (b) extension of the Trade Descriptions Act 1968;

   (c) the DGFT's Injunctive Proposal;

   (d) prohibition orders.

Statutory recognition of Codes of Practice

26. The possibility of giving the Codes of Practice the force of law was considered first. This would require their statutory recognition and therefore prior Ministerial approval. Such a system would thus no longer be genuinely self-regulatory. The main purpose of this approach would be to encourage compliance with the Codes by those who do not subscribe to the

existing voluntary arrangements. But if infringements of the Codes became an offence, the Codes would have to be so phrased that breaches could be seen sufficiently clearly to stand up to legal scrutiny. The text of the Codes would therefore become more legal and concentrate more on the letter than the spirit of control. Nor could the text of the Codes, if they became statutory regulations, be amended so readily and the flexibility of self-regulation would thus be reduced. This would be unfortunate. The Codes administered by the ASA are the most highly developed among a growing number of codes governing trade practices. Whether or not the notion of the statutory recognition of codes is accepted or rejected for other industries, the Working Party agreed that in the context of the control of the content of advertising, statutory recognition would be inappropriate. It would risk undermining what was commonly agreed to be an excellent example of self-regulation without substituting a mechanism which would more effectively protect the public interest.

27. An alternative form of statutory recognition would involve conferring upon the ASA Codes a status analogous to that of the Highway Code (that is the status of an officially recognised manual of good practice with persuasive authority in court proceedings). But this course would still require Ministerial approval of the Codes. It might also lead to conflict between the rulings of the courts and of the ASA on particular matters and would tend to undermine the authority of the ASA and the credibility of the self-regulatory arrangements. For these reasons the Working Party concluded that it should seek alternative measures.

Extension of the Trade Descriptions Act 1968

28. The second possibility considered by the Working Party was extension of the Trade Descriptions Act 1968 so that its provisions might more closely parallel those of the Codes and give them legal backing. The Working Party concluded that there were major objections to this course, namely that:

  (a) many of the provisions of the Code of Advertising Practice are framed in general terms, such as 'all advertisements should be legal, decent, honest and truthful' or 'all advertisements should be prepared with a sense of responsibility to the consumer'. Such general provisions would not be appropriate in the criminal law;

  (b) because many of the criminal courts are overburdened, prosecutions under the Act do not always receive high priority. In practice therefore there would be no certainty that proceedings under the Act would be sufficiently speedy to provide effective support for the existing self-regulatory arrangements.

The DGFT's injunctive proposal

29. The third possibility considered by the Working Party was based upon the DGFT's proposal to institute an injunctive procedure to restrain the publication of an advertisement. The proposal would require the prior creation by statute of a general duty which would be owed by the advertising industry at large not to publish an advertisement which was likely to deceive or mislead with regard to any material fact. The Director General would then be empowered to seek from the courts an order to prevent the publication of a particular advertisement when in his view publication would constitute a breach of the general duty. Failure to obey such an order would be a contempt of court and punishable as such, the penalty most commonly imposed being a fine.

. . .

33. . . . As a whole, the Working Party recognised the merit of a procedure which they believed would both sufficiently reinforce the self-regulatory arrangement of advertising control and meet the essential objectives of the EEC proposals. Accordingly they recommend to Ministers the adoption of the DGFT's proposals for an injunctive procedure.

. . .

[The injunctive procedure was introduced by the Control of Misleading Advertisements Regulations 1988 (SI 1988/915) in response to the European Directive on Misleading Advertising (84/450/EEC), see pp 528–32.]

Prohibition orders

35. The Working Party considered a fourth possibility which has much in common with their preferred solution—the injunctive procedure described above. This would also rest on the creation of the general duty described in paragraph 29. The DGFT would be empowered to issue an order prohibiting the publication of an advertisement where there was a breach of the general duty and where the likely detriment to the public was great compared with the likely loss and inconvenience to the advertiser. The sanction for any breach of the order would be a fine imposed by a court after application by the DGFT. The power would need to be accompanied by a right of appeal against decisions of the DGFT to make orders—either to the Secretary of State or to the courts.

36. The prohibition order procedure would allow an administrative authority (the DGFT) to take immediate action to control the content of advertisements subject to review by an appellate body, whereas the injunctive procedure rests on direct control by judicial decision on the DGFT's application. The practical effect of the issue of a prohibition order would, however, be the same as for a *successful* application for an injunction. The power in the hands of the DGFT to issue prohibition orders would undoubtedly be a speedy and effective remedy. It would be specially valuable in dealing with flagrant breaches of the general duty by small advertisers not subscribing to the ASA arrangements in localised campaigns where the overall damage to the public might not be regarded as sufficiently great to justify the seeking of an injunction. On the other hand, because an advertiser would invariably suffer damage at the time the publication of his advertisement was prevented, the procedure would be weighted against the advertiser unless an equally speedy appeals procedure could be provided. Moreover, the need to provide for the enforcement of the prohibition order would require the creation of a new criminal offence (although there are precedents for this in the Consumer Safety Act 1978 and in the Estate Agents Act 1979).

37. The Working Party noted that prohibition orders would, like the injunctive procedure, be a remedy of last resort to be used where the ordinary machinery of the ASA had been frustrated or was unlikely to be effective, or where a speedy remedy was needed. While it would be a more certain remedy, it would be more arbitrary and would move beyond reinforcing self-regulation towards a more direct control. This would be contrary to the objectives as set out in paragraph 19.

. . .

OTHER POSSIBLE IMPROVEMENTS

39. The Working Party also considered the following possible improvements to the existing control arrangements, referred to by the DGFT in his report.

Corrective advertising

40. The Working Party considered the case for introducing corrective advertising, that is a requirement on the advertiser to publish, at his own expense, corrections of false or misleading statements in his previously published advertisements.

41. In theory, corrective advertising seems an obvious, even attractive, sanction—fitting the punishment to the crime. But the development of corrective advertising in the United States (which probably has more experience of applying this form of remedy than any other country) has shown it to be difficult to apply in practice. The Federal Trade Commission has been successfully challenged on the grounds that it has not been able to show:

(a) that the consumer believed the false claim;
(b) that the false claim affected the consumer's purchasing decision; and

(c) that the consumer persisted in believing the false claim after the particular advertisement had been stopped.

42. United States experience suggests that it is difficult to estimate the overall damage to the consumer who has been exposed to false advertisements; but unless some reasonable estimate can be made, the financial penalty imposed on the advertiser could be disproportionately large. Moreover, our legal system and institutional arrangements differ greatly from the United States. The legal compulsions which it would be necessary to place on advertisers to publish corrections would not be consistent with and would be likely to destroy the self-regulatory arrangements in the United Kingdom. The Working Party were therefore not convinced of the case for introducing a statutory scheme of corrective advertising in the United Kingdom.

43. While the Working Party were not persuaded of the case for legally-imposed corrective advertising they agreed that substantial benefits would accrue if the self-regulatory arrangements were to extend ASA's present practices of publishing details of complaints which they have upheld in their monthly reports and of issuing *ad hoc* press releases dealing with particularly important cases. They believed that there was also scope for the ASA to develop the practice of securing corrective action including, where appropriate, corrective statements being made direct to individuals who had responded to misleading advertisements. They also considered that the ASA should intensify its efforts to persuade advertisers and advertising agencies to take advantage of the CAP Committee's willingness to advise on advertisements before publication, and that the Code should be reviewed with the intention of extending the use of disclosures and disclaimers in advertising messages in the interests of consumers. (Current examples of disclosures and disclaimers are the requirements to show in advertisements for toys and games if the cost of batteries is additional to the stated price, and to state in advertisements for slimming aids that these can only aid slimming as part of a caloric controlled diet.)

Fines

44. The DGFT suggested that consideration should be given to fining advertisers, agencies and publishers for persistent breaches of the Code or for any failure quickly to observe CAP Committee or ASA Council decisions. Some trade associations do indeed impose fines on their members as a measure to enforce codes of practice. The ASA, however, is not a trade association and could have no recourse to this form of penalty. The AA is a federation of trade associations and could not impose fines on these associations in respect of individual offenders. The imposition of fines would therefore have to be effected by the individual trade associations and this is a matter which they may wish to consider.

Redress for individual consumers

45. The Working Party considered the problem of redress for individual consumers who suffered economic loss because of misleading advertisements. Consumers can suffer loss, for which they cannot currently insist upon compensation, either if they spend time and money following up an advertisement which proves misleading, or if they buy a product relying on misleading information contained in an advertisement and the advertiser is not the retailer. (Many of the losses which individual consumers suffer as a result of misleading advertisements may not be large enough to justify the trouble and expense of legal proceedings; and in many other cases there may be no legal basis for any claim.) The Working Party agreed that in principle it was desirable, nonetheless, for consumers who suffer loss as a result of misleading advertisements to be compensated. The Working Party believed that the best way forward would be to explore the possibilities of setting up some conciliation and arbitration scheme run by advertisers. The ASA felt that it was not the appropriate body to manage such a scheme, since its role as arbiter of the content of advertisements might be prejudiced if it had to become involved in adjudicating upon individual consumer claims for redress. The AA representatives believed that this was a matter exclusively for advertisers rather than for the advertising business as a whole and, therefore, asked that it be referred to the Incorporated Society of British Advertisers (ISBA).

It was decided, therefore, that an exploration of this subject should be carried out outside the Working Party, and discussions are taking place, under the chairmanship of the Office of Fair Trading, between the Incorporated Society of British Advertisers, the Advertising Standards Authority and the National Consumer Council.

RECOMMENDATIONS

47. The Working Party recommend that:
   (i) The injunctive procedure proposed by the DGFT should be introduced and based on a new statutory duty not to publish an advertisement likely to deceive or mislead with regard to any material fact. They consider that such a measure should adequately reinforce the self-regulatory system of control and meet the essential objectives of the EEC proposals on the control of advertising (paragraph 33).
   (ii) The statutory duty referred to in (i) above should extend to advertising by Government (paragraph 34).
   (iii) The ASA should develop their procedures for publishing details of complaints which have been upheld, and for securing corrective action including, where appropriate, corrective statements being made to affected persons (paragraph 43).
   (iv) Advertising Trade Associations may wish to consider further the imposition of fines on their members to enforce codes of practice (paragraph 44).
   (v) The OFT should explore with the appropriate organisations the creation of a conciliation and arbitration scheme to secure redress for individual consumers (paragraph 45).

The Consumers' Association, in June 1997, issued a Policy Paper on the self-regulation of advertising. Its conclusions are as follows:

Self-regulation of Advertising Policy Paper, Consumers' Association, June 1997

Improvements needed
This paper has been concerned with the effectiveness of the ASA as a regulator. Our general conclusion is that there are problems with the enforcement of the BCASP. While it can be argued (and indeed has been by the ASA) that self-regulation is largely effective, the fact that the consumer benefits of advertising are to some degree ambiguous indicates a need to be absolutely sure that there are few breaches of the advertising codes.

   We conclude that the ASA's effectiveness is undermined by a combination of relatively weak sanctions, slow operation of the system, under-use of the stronger sanctions available and poor accessibility.

Recommendations
To improve this a number of changes are required:
Corrective advertising
One of the main problems when advertising has misled consumers is that even where a complaint has been upheld and the advert is not used again, the misleading impression may remain. Furthermore, arguably, consumers will not often be aware that they have been misled until it is brought to their attention. To overcome this problem, advertisers should be required to take remedial action. So for example, in the case of the Philip Morris advertising campaign [which sought to compare the risks of getting lung cancer from passive smoking with the risks of disease from apparently harmless activities such as drinking water in a misleading way] a similar scale campaign should have been carried out to inform consumers that in fact the evidence they had used to illustrate the relative risks of different activities was problematic and that their advertisements had been misleading.

In cases such as financial products, where consumers may have been persuaded to purchase products that will have a major impact on their financial well being, we would suggest that advertisers should be required to write to all such consumers to correct any misleading impressions.

Easier to complain

We would like to see the ASA accept complaints via all channels. It is particularly important in the case of the Internet that complainants can complain via e-mail. Complaints are the main way in which the ASA can gauge whether consumers are satisfied with advertising and a key to identifying breaches in the Codes. The Authority should also ensure that consumers are fully aware of how to contact it if they do wish to make a complaint.

Consumer representation

There should be strong consumer representation on both the BCAP and the ASA's council to ensure that the voice of the consumer is heard in the decision making process. The lack of real consumer input into its functioning might suggest to some observers that it is there to protect the industry rather than to promote the interests of consumers.

Greater transparency

Issues surrounding the transparency of the ASA decision-making process need also to be addressed. One reason for the ASA's slow response time is waiting for the advertiser to respond to the complainant's accusations; however, the complainant is not given a chance to address the advertiser's defence. While we recognise that commercial confidentiality may need to be respected in some cases, we would like to see a general rule that all information submitted by the advertiser is open to public scrutiny. Similarly, where the ASA has consulted experts, that advice should also be made public.

Powers to fine

Ultimately the ASA needs to be able to take effective retrospective action. The emphasis on specific advertising and the tendency to take no action once an advert has been withdrawn, means that there is little real disincentive for those companies which intend to wilfully mislead consumers or break the code in some other way. It is only through some form of punitive sanction that this will be prevented.

We would therefore like to see the ASA having the power to fine both persistent re-offenders, those who make major and wilful breaches of the code and those companies that cause consumers to suffer some form of direct harm (for example financial loss).

Monitoring

It is to be welcomed that the ASA carries out monitoring of its own effectiveness. We would like to see this extended to monitoring of how satisfied complainants are with the way in which complaints are handled and with the outcome of the complaint. However, while self-regulation continues to be the way in which print advertising is regulated we would like to see the OFT carry out ongoing monitoring of its overall effectiveness. This monitoring needs to be set against clear targets for variables in such areas as consumer awareness of the ASA, speed of complaints handling, compliance levels and satisfaction. The outcomes of such monitoring should be made fully public.

THE EEC DIMENSION

A draft Directive on misleading and unfair advertising was submitted to the Council of Ministers in 1978. Following discussions on it, the Council, to obtain agreement, removed the provisions relating to unfair and comparative advertising. A later draft on misleading advertising was eventually adopted in September 1984: Directive relating to the approximation of laws, regulations and administrative provisions of the Member States concerning misleading advertising (84/450/EEC). A further Directive 'concerning misleading advertising so as to include comparative advertising' was adopted on 6 October 1997 (OJ L 290 of 23.10.97, pp 18–23). Under it, comparative advertising, where explicit or implicit identification of competitors or their goods and services occurs, will be permitted if a number of conditions are met; for example, it must not mislead, denigrate or discredit trade marks, names etc., and where goods or services are compared they must meet the same needs or be intended for the same purpose.

Changes in UK law were required to implement the 1984 Directive. These were introduced, as of 20 June 1988, in the Control of Misleading Advertisements Regulations 1988 (SI 1988/915), which are reproduced, as amended. Further amendment will be necessary to implement the 1997 Directive.

Control of Misleading Advertisements Regulations 1988 (SI 1988/915)

1. Citation and commencement
These Regulations may be cited as the Control of Misleading Advertisements Regulations 1988 and shall come into force on 20th June 1988.

2. Interpretation
(1) In these Regulations—

'advertisement' means any form of representation which is made in connection with a trade, business, craft or profession in order to promote the supply or transfer of goods or services, immovable property, rights or obligations;

['the Commission' means the Independent Television Commission;]

'court', in relation to England and Wales and Northern Ireland, means the High Court, and, in relation to Scotland, the Court of Session;

'Director' means the Director General of Fair Trading;

['licensed service' means—

    (a) in relation to a complaint made to the Commission, a service in respect of which the Commission have granted a licence under Part I or II of the Broadcasting Act 1990; and

    (b) in relation to a complaint made to the Radio Authority, a service in respect of which the Radio Authority have granted a licence under Part III of that Act; and 'licensed local delivery service' means a service in respect of which the Commission have granted a licence under Part II of that Act;]

'publication' in relation to an advertisement means the dissemination of that advertisement whether to an individual person or a number of persons and whether orally or in writing or in any other way whatsoever, and 'publish' shall be construed accordingly.

['relevant body' means the Commission or the Radio Authority;

'on S4C' has the same meaning as in Part I of the Broadcasting Act 1990;

'the Welsh Authority' has the same meaning as in that Act.]

(2) For the purposes of these Regulations an advertisement is misleading if in any way, including its presentation, it deceives or is likely to deceive the persons to whom it is addressed or whom it reaches and if, by reason of its deceptive nature, it is likely to affect their economic behaviour or, for those reasons, injures or is likely to injure a competitor of the person whose interests the advertisement seeks to promote.

(3) In the application of these Regulations to Scotland for references to an injunction or an interlocutory injunction there shall be substituted references to an interdict or an interim interdict respectively.

3. Application

(1) These Regulations do not apply to—
  (a) the following advertisements issued or caused to be issued by or on behalf of an authorised person or appointed representative, that is to say—
    (i) investment advertisements; and
    (ii) any other advertisements in respect of investment business,
except where any such advertisements relate exclusively to any matter in relation to which the authorised person in question is an exempted person; and
  (b) advertisements of a description referred to in section 58(1)(d) of the Financial Services Act 1986.

(2) In this regulation 'appointed representative', 'authorised person', 'exempted person', 'investment advertisement' and 'investment business' have the same meanings as in the Financial Services Act 1986.

4. Complaints to the Director

(1) Subject to paragraphs (2) and (3) below, it shall be the duty of the Director to consider any complaint made to him that an advertisement is misleading, unless the complaint appears to the Director to be frivolous or vexatious.

(2) The Director shall not consider any complaint which these Regulations require or would require, leaving aside any question as to the frivolous or vexatious nature of the complaint, the [Commission, the Radio Authority or the Welsh Authority] to consider.

(3) Before considering any complaint under paragraph (1) above the Director may require the person making the complaint to satisfy him that
  (a) there have been invoked in relation to the same or substantially the same complaint about the advertisement in question such established means of dealing with such complaints as the Director may consider appropriate, having regard to all the circumstances of the particular case;
  (b) a reasonable opportunity has been allowed for those means to deal with the complaint in question; and
  (c) those means have not dealt with the complaint adequately.

(4) In exercising the powers conferred on him by these Regulations the Director shall have regard to—
  (a) all the interests involved and in particular the public interest; and
  (b) the desirability of encouraging the control, by self-regulatory bodies, of advertisements.

5. Applications to the Court by the Director

(1) If, having considered a complaint about an advertisement pursuant to regulation 4(1) above, he considers that the advertisement is misleading, the Director may, if he thinks it appropriate to do so, bring proceedings for an injunction (in which proceedings he may also apply for an interlocutory injunction) against any person appearing to him to be concerned or likely to be concerned with the publication of the advertisement.

(2) The Director shall give reasons for his decision to apply or not to apply, as the case may be, for an injunction in relation to any complaint which these Regulations require him to consider.

6. Functions of the Court

(1) The court on an application by the Director may grant an injunction on such terms as it may think fit but (except where it grants an interlocutory injunction) only if the court is satisfied that the advertisement to which the application relates is misleading. Before granting an injunction the court shall have regard to all the interests involved and in particular the public interest.

(2) An injunction may relate not only to a particular advertisement but to any advertisement in similar terms or likely to convey a similar impression.

(3) In considering an application for an injunction the court may, whether or not on the appli-

cation of any party to the proceedings, require any person appearing to the court to be responsible for the publication of the advertisement to which the application relates to furnish the court with evidence of the accuracy of any factual claim made in the advertisement. The court shall not make such a requirement unless it appears to the court to be appropriate in the circumstances of the particular case, having regard to the legitimate interests of the person who would be the subject of or affected by the requirement and of any other person concerned with the advertisement.

(4) If such evidence is not furnished to it following a requirement made by it under paragraph (3) above or if it considers such evidence inadequate, the court may decline to consider the factual claim mentioned in that paragraph accurate.

(5) The court shall not refuse to grant an injunction for lack of evidence that—

(a) the publication of the advertisement in question has given rise to loss or damage to any person; or

(b) the person responsible for the advertisement intended it to be misleading or failed to exercise proper care to prevent its being misleading.

(6) An injunction may prohibit the publication or the continued or further publication of an advertisement.

7. Powers of the Director to obtain and disclose information and disclosure of information generally

(1) For the purpose of facilitating the exercise by him of any functions conferred on him by these Regulations, the Director may, by notice in writing signed by him or on his behalf, require any person to furnish to him such information as may be specified or described in the notice or to produce to him any documents so specified or described.

(2) A notice under paragraph (1) above may—

(a) specify the way in which and the time within which it is to be complied with; and

(b) be varied or revoked by a subsequent notice.

(3) Nothing in this regulation compels the production or furnishing by any person of a document or of information which he would in an action in a court be entitled to refuse to produce or furnish on grounds of legal professional privilege or, in Scotland, on the grounds of confidentiality as between client and professional legal adviser.

(4) If a person makes default in complying with a notice under paragraph (1) above the court may, on the application of the Director, make such order as the court thinks fit for requiring the default to be made good, and any such order may provide that all the costs or expenses of and incidental to the application shall be borne by the person in default or by any officers of a company or other association who are responsible for its default.

(5) Subject to any provision to the contrary made by or under any enactment, where the Director considers it appropriate to do so for the purpose of controlling misleading advertisements, he may refer to any person any complaint (including any related documentation) about an advertisement or disclose to any person any information (whether or not obtained by means of the exercise of the power conferred by paragraph (1) above).

. . .

(7) Subject to paragraph (5) above, any person who knowingly discloses, otherwise than for the purposes of any legal proceedings or of a report of such proceedings or the investigation of any criminal offence, any information obtained by means of the exercise of the power conferred by paragraph (1) above without the consent either of the person to whom the information relates, or, if the information relates to a business, the consent of the person for the time being carrying on that business, shall be guilty of an offence and liable on summary conviction to imprisonment for a term not exceeding 3 months or to a fine not exceeding [level 5 on the standard scale] or to both.

(8) The Director may arrange for the dissemination in such form and manner as he considers appropriate of such information and advice concerning the operation of these Regulations as

may appear to him to be expedient to give to the public and to all persons likely to be affected by these Regulations.

[8. **Complaints to the Commission and the Radio Authority**
(1) Subject to paragraph (2) below, it shall be the duty of a relevant body to consider any complaint made to it that any advertisement included or proposed to be included in a licensed service is misleading, unless the complaint appears to the body to be frivolous or vexatious.

(2) The Commission shall not consider any complaint about an advertisement included or proposed to be included in a licensed local delivery service by the reception and immediate retransmission of broadcasts made by the British Broadcasting Corporation.

(3) A relevant body shall give reasons for its decisions.

(4) In exercising the powers conferred on it by these Regulations a relevant body shall have regard to all the interests involved and in particular the public interest.]

[9. **Control by the Commission and the Radio Authority of misleading advertisements**
(1) If, having considered a complaint about an advertisement pursuant to regulation 8(1) above, it considers that the advertisement is misleading, a relevant body may, if it thinks it appropriate to do so, exercise in relation to the advertisement the power conferred on it—

   (a) where the relevant body is the Commission, by section 9(6) of the Broadcasting Act 1990 (power of Commission to give directions about advertisements), or

   (b) where the relevant body is the Radio Authority, by section 93(6) of that Act (power of Radio Authority to give directions about advertisements).

(2) A relevant body may require any person appearing to it to be responsible for an advertisement which the body believes may be misleading to furnish it with evidence as to the accuracy of any factual claim made in the advertisement. In deciding whether or not to make such a requirement the body shall have regard to the legitimate interests of any person who would be the subject of or affected by the requirement.

(3) If such evidence is not furnished to it following a requirement made by it under paragraph (2) above or if it considers such evidence inadequate, a relevant body may consider the factual claim inaccurate.]

. . .

Regulations 10 and 11 provide similar protection by the Welsh Authority to that provided by the ITC for broadcasting on S4C.

It can be seen that the proposals for an injunctive power for the Director made in the DTI report of 1980 were introduced in these Regulations. A number of injunctions have been sought by the Director, the first one of which involving a slimming product:

Director General of Fair Trading v Tobyward Ltd [1989] 2 All ER 266, [1989] 1 WLR 517, Chancery Division

Hoffmann J There is before the court a motion by the Director General of Fair Trading for an interlocutory injunction to restrain the publication of misleading advertisements. The first respondent is a company which markets and has extensively advertised a product called 'SpeedSlim'. The product is sold in the form of tablets and is claimed to cause loss of weight. The second respondent is the sole director of the first respondent.

The Director General applies under reg 5 of the Control of Misleading Advertisements Regulations 1988, . . . The director has a duty under reg 4(1) to consider any complaints that advertisements are misleading. A duty expressed in such broad terms might impose on the director's office an unacceptable volume of work but it is qualified in two respects. First, he need not consider complaints which appear to be frivolous or vexatious; second, and much more important, he need not consider any complaint until the complainant has invoked what the regulations describe as 'such established means of dealing with such complaints as the Director may consider appropriate'.

The British advertising industry has a system of self-regulation which has been established under the auspices of its voluntary regulatory body, the Advertising Standards Authority (the ASA). There is a British Code of Advertising Practice which is administered by the code of advertising practice committee, and the committee and the ASA deal with complaints of breaches of the code. They are also willing to give guidance to advertisers on whether a proposed advertisement would be regarded as acceptable. So the proper working of the self-regulatory system is essential to the overall scheme of control, which contemplates that the director will deal only with exceptional cases in which for one reason or another self-regulation has proved inadequate.

If a complaint is referred to the director and he considers the advertisement to be misleading, he may apply to the court for an injunction. The regulations provide no other legal remedy. They do not make the publication of misleading advertisements unlawful. The only sanction is that, once an injunction has been made, the publication of an advertisement in breach of its terms will be a contempt of court and punishable as such. Under reg 6(1) the court may grant a final injunction only if it is satisfied that the advertisement in question is misleading, but this degree of persuasion is not required at the present interlocutory stage. In exercising this jurisdiction, the court must have 'regard to all the interests involved and in particular the public interest'.

Mr Justice Hoffmann explained how the ASA had received complaints about SpeedSlim advertisements which had been upheld as breaching the Code of Practice. Advice given by the ASA had been ignored and offending advertisements continued to be published. The matter had then been referred to the Director General. Six claims contained in the advertisements were alleged by the Director to be misleading. The court examined these and expert scientific evidence was detailed.

Hoffmann J continued: 'Misleading', as I have said, is defined in the regulations as involving two elements: first, that the advertisement deceives or is likely to deceive the persons to whom it is addressed and, second, that it is likely to affect their economic behaviour. In my judgment in this context there is little difficulty about applying the concept of deception. An advertisement must be likely to deceive the persons to whom it is addressed if it makes false claims on behalf of the product. It is true that many people read advertisements with a certain degree of scepticism. For the purposes of applying the regulations, however, it must be assumed that there may be people who will believe what the advertisers tell them, and in those circumstances the making of a false claim is likely to deceive. Having regard to the evidence of Professor Bender, which at present is the only scientific evidence before the court, there is in my judgment a strong prima facie case that these advertisements were likely to deceive in each of the six respects of which complaint is made. The other element, namely that the advertisement is likely to affect the economic behaviour of the persons to whom it is addressed, means in this context no more than that it must make it likely that they will buy the product. As that was no doubt the intention of the advertisement, it is reasonable to draw the inference that it would have such a result. I am therefore satisfied that the court has jurisdiction under reg 6 to make an injunction in this case.

The making of the injunction is, however, a matter of discretion, and I must consider whether in this case it would be appropriate to do so. There are two reasons why I think I should. First, the regulations contemplate that there will only be intervention by the director when the voluntary system has failed. It is in my judgment desirable and in accordance with the public interest to which I must have regard that the courts should support the principle of self-regulation. I think that advertisers would be more inclined to accept the rulings of their self-regulatory bodies if it were generally known that in cases in which their procedures had been exhausted and the advertiser was still publishing an advertisement which appeared to the court to be prima facie misleading an injunction would ordinarily be granted. The respondents did offer undertakings to the director which could not have been enforced by any legal process other than the making of an application such as this for an injunction. But they were in terms which the director thought to be inadequate. For example, the respondents were unwilling to give undertakings in respect of advertisements which the director thought to be misleading but which had already been booked into the magazines or newspapers, notwithstanding that it was known for some time that the director considered them to be objectionable. Then the respondents required qualifications to the wording of certain of the undertakings. For example, the undertaking not to claim that the use of the product can result in permanent weight loss was to be qualified by the words 'after cessation of the use of the product'. In my view the director was reasonable in objecting to that qualification, since the objectionable feature of the claim is the use of the word permanent in any circumstances. There are other qualifications with which it is not necessary for me to deal in detail, but I do not think that the terms of the undertakings which were offered were such as to make it inappropriate for the director to apply for an injunction today.

Second, in my view the interests of consumers require the protection of an injunction pending trial of the action. It does not seem to me that the respondents could complain of any legitimate interference with their business if they were restrained from making claims of the kind to which the director is here taking objection.

The judge went on to discuss the detailed wording of the injunction. When the action came to trial the High Court granted a permanent injunction on the same terms as the interlocutory injunction (OFT Press Release, No 30/89, 21 July 1989).

NOTES

1. In many instances, as was mentioned in the case above, the Director accepts an undertaking from the advertiser in lieu of seeking an injunction. There is no specific provision made for undertakings under these Regulations (cf. The Unfair Terms in Consumer Contracts Regulations 1994, reg 8(3), at p 334.)
2. The European Court of Justice, in *Procurer de la République v X*, Case C–373/90 [1992] ECR I–131, required it to be established that a *significant* number of consumers would be misled by an advertisement before it was judged to be in breach of the Misleading Advertising Directive.
3. For further materials discussing private law remedies in respect of misleading advertising, see above, pp 57–70.

QUESTIONS

1. The view is taken in some quarters that reliance on codes of practice to regulate the conduct of traders is misguided and ineffective, even where members of the trade association in question are concerned. Assuming that there is some merit in the view that a code of practice tends to be a cosmetic remedy for a more deep-seated problem, consider what alternative and practicable ways exist to improve the standard of the supply of goods and services to the consumer in a selected area.

2. The 1980 Board of Trade Working Party states (in para 11: see above, p 512) that there are some 80 separate statutes, orders and regulations concerned with advertising to a greater or lesser extent. Identify the main such statutes and subsidiary legislation in force at the present time.

CHAPTER 11

Aspects of the duty to trade fairly

INTRODUCTION

Although it is not strictly correct to say that the imposition of a statutory duty to trade fairly dates from the passing of the Fair Trading Act 1973, this Act is of such fundamental importance that it inevitably becomes the dominating feature in surveying the 'fair trading' scene in the United Kingdom.

Since the Fair Trading Bill, introduced into the House of Commons in November 1972, was not preceded by any sort of published enquiry, Green or White paper, a feature which attracted critical comment in debate (see 848 HC Official Report (5th series) col 469, 13 December 1972), it is difficult to trace the precise processes which led up to it. It seems probable that a draft Bill had been put in hand by the Civil Service, primarily within the Department of Trade and Industry, to improve the legislation on monopolies and mergers. This coincided with the appointment with Cabinet rank of a new and energetic Minister for Trade and Consumer Affairs, Sir Geoffrey Howe, within the giant Department of Trade and Industry.

Speaking to the Bill on its second reading, and explaining its objects, Sir Geoffrey Howe remarked that the Bill had two complementary purposes, firstly, the promotion of increased economic efficiency and secondly, protection of the consumer against unfair trading practices. He continued:

just as fair trading is good business, so consumer protection is in itself an integral part of the market economy. That is why competition policy needs to be considered, as it is in the Bill, as a whole. It is this integrated view of competition policy that leads to the first institutional innovation proposed in the Bill—the appointment of a Director General of Fair Trading . . . The Government have concluded that given the specialist and detailed nature of the work and the need for continuity in its performance, it would best be done by an independent official body.

(See 848 HC Official Report (5th series) col 454, 13 December 1972).

The Bill with a number of amendments (about 125 of approximately 4,000 proposed) became law on 25 July 1973.

This chapter covers aspects of Parts II and III of the Act and also includes consideration of whether there should be a general statutory duty to trade fairly, imposed in wider terms than under the 1973 Act.

DEALING WITH UNDESIRABLE CONSUMER TRADE PRACTICES

Part II of the Act was designed to provide machinery for carefully considered subsidiary legislation to prohibit, by means of criminal offences, consumer trade practices which were thought to be undesirable. (Part I makes provision for the appointment of a Director General of Fair Trading and his duties, and also for the establishment of an Advisory Committee to be called the Consumer Protection Advisory Committee). Part II then goes on to deal with the identification of undesirable consumer trade practices and, in appropriate cases, for recommendations to deal with these to be made and translated into subsidiary legislation.

THE METHOD OF CONTROL

The first and vital question is the definition of a 'consumer trade practice'. This is defined in s 13 of the Act as follows:

13. Meaning of 'consumer trade practice'
In this Act 'consumer trade practice' means any practice which is for the time being carried on in connection with the supply of goods (whether by way of sale or otherwise) to consumers or in connection with the supply of services for consumers and which relates—

  (a) to the terms or conditions (whether as to price or otherwise) on or subject to which goods or services are or are sought to be supplied, or
  (b) to the manner in which those terms or conditions are communicated to persons to whom goods are or are sought to be supplied or for whom services are or are sought to be supplied, or
  (c) to promotion (by advertising, labelling or marking of goods, canvassing or otherwise) of the supply of goods or of the supply of services, or
  (d) to methods of salesmanship employed in dealing with consumers, or
  (e) to the way in which goods are packed or otherwise got up for the purpose of being supplied, or
  (f) to methods of demanding or securing payment for goods or services supplied.

Section 14 deals with the method of referring such practices to the Advisory Committee. References may be made by the Secretary of State, any other Minister or the Director, subject to certain restrictions laid down in ss 15 and 16. The Advisory Committee is required to report to the person making the reference, the Secretary of State, and the Director, on whether or not the practice referred to them adversely affects the economic interests of consumers in the United Kingdom and may be assisted by the Director in investigating the reference.

Section 17 indicates a special procedure for references made to the Advisory Committee by the Director under s 14 which may result in a statutory instrument being created.

17. Reference to Advisory Committee proposing recommendations to Secretary of State to make an order

(1) This section applies to any reference made to the Advisory Committee by the Director under section 14 of this Act which includes proposals in accordance with the following provisions of this section.

(2) Where it appears to the Director that a consumer trade practice has the effect, or is likely to have the effect,—

    (a) of misleading consumers as to, or withholding from them adequate information as to, or an adequate record of, their rights and obligations under relevant consumer transactions, or

    (b) of otherwise misleading or confusing consumers with respect to any matter in connection with relevant consumer transactions, or

    (c) of subjecting consumers to undue pressure to enter into relevant consumer transactions, or

    (d) of causing the terms or conditions, on or subject to which consumers enter into relevant consumer transactions, to be so adverse to them as to be inequitable,

any reference made by the Director under section 14 of this Act with respect to that consumer trade practice may, if the Director thinks fit, include proposals for recommending to the Secretary of State that he should exercise his powers under the following provisions of this Part of this Act with respect to that consumer trade practice.

(3) A reference to which this section applies shall state which of the effects specified in subsection (2) of this section it appears to the Director that the consumer trade practice in question has or is likely to have.

(4) Where the Director makes a reference to which this section applies, he shall arrange for it to be published in full in the London, Edinburgh and Belfast Gazettes.

(5) In this Part of this Act 'relevant consumer transaction', in relation to a consumer trade practice, means any transaction to which a person is, or may be invited to become, a party in his capacity as a consumer in relation to that practice.

Having investigated the reference, the Advisory Committee must report to the Secretary of State, indicating whether or not the trade practice in question adversely affects the economic interests of consumers and, if so, whether it has or is likely to have one or more of the effects specified in s 17(2). If both these questions are answered in the affirmative, the Advisory Committee may either agree with the Director's proposals, agree with specified modifications or disagree and not suggest modifications.

Where the Advisory Committee has agreed with the Director's proposals, or agreed with modifications, the Secretary of State, by s 22, may, if he thinks fit, lay a draft statutory instrument before Parliament to give effect to the Director's proposals or the proposals as modified. The draft order must be approved by positive resolution before it comes into effect.

As a result of the references made by the Director, there have been four reports of the Advisory Committee. These are: 'Rights of Consumers, A Report on Practices Relating to the Purported Exclusion of Inalienable Rights of Consumers and Failure to Explain their Existence' (1974 HCP 6); 'Prepayment for Goods, A Report on Practices Relating to Prepayment in Mail Order Transactions and in Shops' (1976 HCP 285); 'Disguised Business Sales, A Report on the Practice of Seeking to Sell Goods without revealing that they are being Sold in the Course of a Business' (1976 HCP 355), and 'VAT-Exclusive Prices, A Report on Practices relating to Advertising, Displaying or otherwise Quoting VAT-Exclusive Prices or Charges' (1977 HCP 416).

Orders made under s 22 to date are as follows: The Mail Order Transactions (Information) Order 1976 (SI 1976/1812); the Consumer Transactions (Restrictions on Statements) Order 1976 (SI 1976/1813); the Consumer Transactions (Restrictions on Statements) (Amendment) Order 1978 (SI 1978/127); and the Business Advertisements (Disclosure) Order 1977 (SI 1977/1918).

Penalties for contravention of Orders so made are dealt with by s 23 as follows:

23. Penalties for contravention of order under s 22
Subject to the following provisions of this Part of this Act, any person who contravenes a prohibition imposed by an order under section 22 of this Act, or who does not comply with a requirement imposed by such an order which applies to him, shall be guilty of an offence and shall be liable—
  (a) on summary conviction, to a fine not exceeding £[5,000];
  (b) on conviction on indictment, to a fine or to imprisonment for a term not exceeding two years or both.

Offences under s 23 of the Act are subject to the defences specified in s 25. These follow the standard pattern of trading standards defences and provide for defences of mistake, reliance on information, act or default of another person, accident or some other cause beyond the defendant's control. Reasonable precautions and all due diligence must have been exercised. There is also a defence of innocent publication. These defences are considered elsewhere in this book. (See below, ch 15 at pp 709–25.)

In recent years no use has been made of the Advisory Committee and the Report on Non-Departmental Public Bodies (Cmnd 7797, January 1980) refers to its proposed abolition. This would, however, require primary legislation and 'the saving to public funds would be negligible'. Since 1983, members have not been re-appointed and where subsidiary legislation has been considered urgently necessary, as in the case of bargain offers, subsidiary legislation was made under s 4 of the Prices Act 1974. The preferred solution to many problems that have arisen is new primary legislation, for example the Consumer Protection Act 1987, Part III, the Timeshare Act 1992, and the Property Misdescriptions Act 1991.

THE BUSINESS ADVERTISEMENTS (DISCLOSURE) ORDER 1977

This Order provides a good example of the Part II procedure. The Order was made by the Secretary of State under powers contained in s 22 of the Fair Trading Act 1973. The Order followed a reference made by the Director under s 17 and the report of the Consumer Protection Advisory Committee which was laid before Parliament (HC 355 Session 1975/76).

The Director's dossier which accompanied his reference to the CPAC contained a summary of the practice and, in a Schedule, proposals for dealing with it.

Chapter I—summary

(1) The consumer trade practice covered by this reference is that of seeking to sell goods to consumers without revealing (whether deliberately or not) that the goods are being sold in the course of a business. We are primarily concerned with the use of classified advertisements in the local and national press although the reference also covers advertisements displayed in, for example, newsagents' or tobacconists' windows.

(2) A trader may advertise his goods clearly indicating (implicitly or explicitly) his business interest. He may, however, conceal that interest either unintentionally or deliberately: the reference deals with both forms of concealment. At the second stage of the practice, when the consumer has responded to the advertisement, the trader may immediately divulge the fact that he is selling goods in the course of business. Alternatively, he may leave the consumer with the mistaken impression that he is buying from a private individual. Such concealment at the second stage is usually deliberate and involves often quite elaborate techniques of deception.

(3) The consumer may suffer economic detriment during both the first and second stages of the practice. First, it may mislead him into making a response which he would not have made had he known the seller to be a trader. He may, as a result, suffer an economic loss—albeit small: the cost of a telephone call, or of travelling or the loss of working time. (Section 17(2)(b) of the Fair Trading Act, 1973 refers). At the second stage he may be misled into paying more for the goods than he might have done (indeed he may not even have completed the sale had he known he was dealing with a trader) (section 17(2)(b)). Having bought the goods, the consumer can suffer two other significant economic detriments if they turn out to be defective or misdescribed: either he or his adviser may be misled by the practice into believing that he enjoys only those rights which result from a contract with a private seller. These are weaker than consumers' rights against traders, eg there is no right to goods of merchantable quality and he may therefore forgo redress (this detriment is covered by section 17(2)(a)); and there may also be deception as to the availability of compensation (under the Powers of the Criminal Courts Act, 1973) resulting from a successful prosecution under the Trade Descriptions Act, 1968, because this latter Act does not apply to private sales (section 17(2)(b) of the Fair Trading Act is again relevant).

(4) We have considered, but rejected . . . relying solely on voluntary self-regulation of the practice by the media. Instead we propose that, where goods are being sold in the course of a business, advertisements should make this fact quite clear. To help advertisers to know where they stand, we propose that certain features of advertisements should be assumed to comply with this requirement. Such features are the inclusion of the words 'agent', 'dealer' or 'trader'; the inclusion of the seller's name when it is obviously a business or corporate name; or such size or format of the advertisement itself, which makes it unlikely to be taken as a private advertisement. We propose exemptions for advertisements displayed at or near the premises where the goods may be bought and those premises are clearly trade premises; for advertisements relating to a sale by auction or tender; and for advertisements classified as traders' advertisements in any publication which segregates traders' sales. We also propose a general exemption for advertisements for vegetable produce and certain other products commonly sold at the roadside.

. . .

Schedule—proposals

(1) That it should be unlawful for any person seeking to sell goods that are being sold in the course of a business to publish or cause to be published any advertisement indicating that the goods are for sale and likely to induce consumers to buy them unless the advertisement—

    (a) describes the seller by the word 'agent', 'dealer' or 'trader'; or

    (b) refers to the seller by a business name which cannot reasonably be taken to be the name of a private seller or, where the seller is a body corporate, by its corporate name; or

    (c) is by reason of its size or format unlikely to be taken as being other than a trader's advertisement; or

(d) otherwise makes it reasonably obvious that the goods are being sold in the course of a business.

(2) That there should be exempted from the requirements described in paragraph 1 advertisements,—

(a) displayed on or near premises where the goods may be bought provided the premises are obviously trade premises;

(b) relating only to sales by auction or tender;

(c) classified as traders' advertisements in publications in which the advertisements of trade and private sellers are classified separately;

(d) relating only to vegetable produce, eggs or dead animals, fish or birds gathered, produced, or taken by the seller.

The CPAC in its Report on the Practice of Seeking to Sell Goods without revealing that they are being Sold in the Course of a Business (May 1976) accepted the Director's proposals in the following terms:

The Proposals

19. The Director has recommended that an order should be made by the Secretary of State under section 22 of the Act to regulate the practice referred to us. The proposals are set out in the Schedule to the reference (page 2 of this report). The scope of any recommendations to be made by the Director in a reference of this kind is governed by section 19 of the Act which requires him to propose such provision as he may consider requisite for the purpose of preventing the continuance of the practice, or causing it to be modified, in so far as it may adversely affect the economic interests of consumers in the United Kingdom.

20. The Director's proposals deal with advertisements published by traders. They are intended to ensure that all such advertisements make it clear either expressly or by implication that the goods are being sold in the course of a business and not privately. The Director has specified four alternative requirements (paragraph 1 of the Schedule). In each case the aim is to ensure that the consumer will not be misled about the nature of the transaction. The Committee considered whether they should comment in detail on the specific requirements. However the Secretary of State under section 22 of the Act may make such provision as she considers appropriate for giving effect to them and we therefore do not consider it is necessary for us to embark on what would in effect amount to a drafting exercise. The proposals in paragraph 1 of the Schedule taken as a whole are acceptable to the Committee.

21. The Director has specified four exemptions from these requirements. Two of these (paragraph 2(a) and (c) of the Schedule) appear to be examples of advertisements which having regard to their location or context could not reasonably be said to mislead.

22. There is a specific exemption for advertisements relating only to sales by auction or tender (paragraph 2(b) of the Schedule). The Director has proposed this exemption because such sales are not 'consumer sales' under the Supply of Goods (Implied Terms) Act 1973. This means that the seller is entitled by law to sell on terms that exclude any responsibility for defects although it does not follow that he will necessarily do so.

23. The Committee have considered whether this exemption could be held to extend to goods offered for sale at a price 'o.n.o.' (meaning near or nearest offer). 'Or nearest offer' and related phrases are frequently to be found in classified advertisements and though we think it unlikely that goods advertised in this way could escape control by virtue of the exemption the possibility cannot be ruled out entirely. There is therefore a risk which we accept may be small that the exemption could lead to evasion from control. Since in our view no hardship would arise if sales by auction and tender were brought within the proposals we suggest that this exemption should be dropped.

24. The fourth exemption (paragraph 2(d) of the Schedule) concerns advertisements relating only to vegetable produce, eggs or dead animals, fish or birds gathered, produced, or taken by

the seller. We agree with the Director that such advertisements should be exempt, since there is no evidence of the character of the seller being important in transactions involving such goods. We understand that the term 'vegetable produce' includes flowers, fruit and vegetables.

25. The Director has explained that his proposals cover all sales in the course of a business, not simply sales of those goods which it is the seller's particular business to supply. We have noted that the professions are included in the definition of 'business' both in the Act and in the Supply of Goods (Implied Terms) Act 1973 and that the proposals cover a professional person selling assets used in his practice. For example a doctor wishing to sell his car which is being used wholly or partly in connection with his professional duties would have to make clear in any advertisement that the car was being sold in the course of a business. The Director considered the possibility of an exemption for advertisements of goods which it was not the seller's customary business to supply. However he concluded that this would create difficulties of definition and raise the possibility of evasion of control. We agree with the Director.

26. The representations we received strongly supported the Director's view that the practice referred was detrimental to consumers and should be controlled. Some representations we received questioned whether the Director's proposals could be effectively enforced. A few suggested alternative approaches to the control of the practice. However, we reached the conclusion that the Director's proposals would be a significant deterrent to those who might intentionally seek to mislead consumers, that they would be enforceable and that they should help to reduce the incidence of the practice.

27. The Committee therefore agree with the proposals set out at paragraph 1 of the Schedule to the reference and would agree with the proposals at paragraph 2 of the Schedule to the reference if they were modified in the manner specified in paragraph 23 of this report.

The Order was laid before Parliament in draft and was made on 21 November 1977. It states as follows:

Business Advertisements (Disclosure) Order 1977 (SI 1977/1918)

1(1) This Order may be cited as the Business Advertisements (Disclosure) Order 1977 and shall come into operation on 1st January 1978.

(2) The Interpretation Act 1889 shall apply for the interpretation of this Order as it applies for the interpretation of an Act of Parliament.

2(1) Subject to paragraphs (2) and (3) below, a person who is seeking to sell goods that are being sold in the course of a business shall not publish or cause to be published an advertisement—

(a) which indicates that the goods are for sale, and

(b) which is likely to induce consumers to buy the goods,

unless it is reasonably clear whether from the contents of the advertisement, its format or size, the place or manner of its publication or otherwise that the goods are to be sold in the course of a business.

(2) Paragraph (1) applies whether the person who is seeking to sell the goods is acting on his own behalf or that of another, and where he is acting as agent, whether he is acting in the course of a business carried on by him or not; but the reference in that paragraph to a business does not include any business carried on by the agent.

(3) Paragraph (1) above shall not apply in relation to advertisements—

(a) which are concerned only with sales by auction or competitive tender; or

(b) which are concerned only with the sale of flowers, fruit or vegetables, eggs or dead animals, fish or birds, gathered, produced or taken by the person seeking to sell the goods.

The following extract and case demonstrate the operation of the Order:

Butterworths Trading and Consumer Law, para 1[1320]

The order is aimed only at sales of goods to consumers, so if only business people are likely to buy the goods, the order would not seem to apply.

The business identity can be revealed in a number of ways. The name of the seller, indicated in the contents of an advertisement, could be sufficient: eg X & Co Ltd, X Co, X Enterprises etc. If a large advertisement appears in a paper, half a page for example, this size and format could be sufficient to indicate a business seller. Clearly, advertisements placed in 'Trade Sales' classified columns or trade journals, or marked '(trader)' or 'T', could also satisfy the regulations. The test is whether it is 'reasonably clear'—a question of fact for the court to decide.

Blakemore v Bellamy [1983] RTR 303, Queen's Bench Division

Webster J. This is a prosecutor's appeal by case stated by justices sitting at Croydon, who, on 12 November 1981, dismissed 18 informations preferred by the prosecutor against the defendant. Of those informations 16 alleged contraventions of section 23 of the Fair Trading Act 1973 and article 2(1) of the Business Advertisements (Disclosure) Order 1977, in that the defendant being a person seeking to sell goods, namely, a motor vehicle, in the course of business as a motor car dealer caused to be published advertisements indicating that the motor vehicle was for sale and was likely to induce consumers to buy the motor vehicle without making it reasonably clear that the motor vehicle was to be sold in the course of a business. The other two informations alleged contraventions of section 1(1)(a) of the Trade Descriptions Act 1968, one of them alleging that the defendant in the course of trade or business as a motor car dealer applied a false trade description as to the mileage of a motor vehicle, and the other alleging that in the course of trade or business as a motor car dealer he applied a false trade description as to the circumstances in which he had acquired the vehicle.

It is to be noted, therefore, that a material averment in each of the informations was that in publishing the relevant advertisement or in applying the relevant false trade description the defendant was acting in the course of business as a motor car dealer in 16 cases, or in the course of trade or business as a motor car dealer in the other two cases.

The justices dismissed all the informations because they were not satisfied that the defendant was acting in the course of a trade or business as a motor car dealer. They concluded that he was selling cars as a hobby.

Two questions, essentially, are asked by them in the case stated, each of which has been pursued in argument. The first is whether they misdirected themselves as to the meaning of the expressions 'business' or 'trade or business', and the second is whether, giving to those words their correct meaning, their finding was perverse; that is to say, one which no bench of justices could reasonably have reached. As that is one of the questions for us, it is perhaps more convenient to begin with the material evidence and then to advert to the justices' findings.

. . . So far as the material evidence is concerned, it amounted to this. Between April 1980 and 31 July 1981, the defendant had inserted a total of 21 advertisements in one or other of two newspapers relating to eight different motor cars; when interviewed by the trading standards officer, employed by the prosecutor, the defendant had stated that he was not a trader and that he did not keep a record of the cars he had sold, but that he was a car enthusiast and enjoyed cleaning them up purely as a hobby. His own evidence was that he had been a postman for over 12 years, usually on duty between 8.45 pm and 6 am. He was not a trader. He had been a car enthusiast since the age of 17. During 1979 he had sold two cars. Between April 1980 and January 1981 he sold a total of seven. He liked driving cars and frequently swapping them. He did not consider himself to be a dealer in motor cars. He repaired and worked on them himself. He usually bought the cars at auctions where he could get them cheap, and quite often he got a bargain. He bought them for his own use and he had driven all but three of them himself. On some of them he made a profit, on others a loss; overall he thought that he had probably broken even on the sale of them. He denied that he was a part-time trader. He claimed that he did not sell cars in order to make a profit, even though he did make a profit, as I have said, in some cases. He admitted that he claimed to have bought the cars for his own use and that he had not driven all of them. He admitted in cross-examination that he had not insured all of the cars and in any event that he had no garage and had to keep the cars on the road. He also admitted that he often had more than one car at a time and that sometimes he did some work on the cars before re-selling them and sometimes not.

On that evidence the justices found, first of all, not surprisingly, that the defendant was in full-time employment as a postman. They found that he had a great enthusiasm for motor cars and that at any one time he would usually own either one or two cars; that in 1979 he had two cars; and that between April 1980 and January 1981 he acquired and sold seven. They found that he did, on some sales, sustain a loss, on others break even and on three make a profit, but that overall he had made no significant profit. They found that there was no suggestion that any vehicles which he had sold were excessively priced or in any unsatisfactory condition. They made this finding:

'The defendant's repeated changes of motor cars were a hobby and did not constitute a trade or business as a motor car dealer. He was motivated by his enthusiastic interest in motor cars and not by commercial considerations. In particular his activities were not a professional practice, nor an undertaking carried out for gain or reward, nor an undertaking within the meaning of the Fair Trading Act 1973.'

In consequence, they decided that the prosecutor had not satisfied them that the defendant was acting in the course of a trade or business as a car dealer and they believed the defendant's evidence that his activities were merely a hobby and did not constitute a trade or business as a motor dealer. They therefore dismissed the informations.

Mr Jubb, on behalf of the prosecutor, first of all submits that a part-time activity can be a business. As to that there is no doubt. There is authority for that proposition in *Stevenson v Beverley Bentinck Ltd* [1976] RTR 543. Secondly he submits that the expression 'business' is wider than that of trade, and that is so.

Thirdly, Mr Jubb refers us to the definition of 'business' in section 137 (2) of the Fair Trading Act 1973 where, except in so far as the context otherwise requires in that Act:

' . . . "business" includes a professional practice and includes any other undertaking which is carried on for gain or reward or which is an undertaking in the course of which goods or services are supplied otherwise than free of charge.'

If that definition is to be incorporated into the two expressions which the justices had to apply to the facts of the case before them, then as Mr Jubb accepts, he would have to show that their finding that his activities did not constitute an undertaking was of itself a perverse finding.

As it seems to me, the effect of that definition is simply that, for the purpose of the Fair Trading Act 1973, a ' . . . "business" includes a professional practice and any other undertaking . . . ' It is not a definition which affects the meaning of the expressions 'business', or 'trade or business'. As it seems to me those expressions are to be given their ordinary meaning.

If that is so, the only submission left to Mr Jubb is that the justices misdirected themselves as to the ordinary meaning of those expressions. He submits that they did so, because, he suggests, their finding that the activity constituted a hobby and their conclusion that the defendant was not acting in the course of a trade or business is to be read as a direction for themselves that if he was carrying on a hobby, then for that reason there could have been no question of his carrying on a trade or business. In other words he submits that they directed themselves that a hobby on the one hand and a trade or business on the other are mutually exclusive, and he submits that that was a misdirection.

There is one authority which seems to me to bear on that submission namely, *Rolls v Miller* (1884) 27 Ch D 71. There on altogether different facts, to which I need not refer in detail, but they concerned a covenant in a lease where the same questions arose, namely, whether the activity in question did or did not constitute a business—Lindley LJ said, at p 88:

'When we look into the dictionaries as to the meaning of the word "business", I do not think they throw much light upon it. The word means almost anything which is an occupation, as distinguished from a pleasure—anything which is an occupation or duty which requires attention is a business—I do not think we can get much aid from the dictionary. We must look at the words in the ordinary sense . . . '

It seems to me that it is proper and right to treat for the present purposes the word 'pleasure' used in that case by Lindley LJ, as more or less synonymous with 'a hobby'. If it be the case—and I will assume for this purpose that it was the case—that the justices decided that the defendant was carrying on a hobby and that he therefore could not have been carrying on a trade or business, it does not seem to me that they misdirected themselves as to the ordinary meaning of the words 'trade or business'. Nor does it seem to me that the application of those words to the facts led to a conclusion which is in any sense perverse. In my view there was evidence which entitled them to find on the facts that the defendant was not carrying on a trade or business, albeit it might well have been the case that a different bench might have come to a different conclusion on the same facts. I would therefore dismiss this appeal.

Donaldson LJ. I agree. I only wish to add a word about one of these informations, namely, the eighteenth. In that case it was alleged that the defendant had applied a false trade description to a Vauxhall Cavalier motor vehicle by means of the following oral statement: 'The car has been left to me by my uncle who died. He had it from new'. The justices have found as a fact that the car had not been left to him by his uncle; still less had his uncle had it from new. The defendant had in fact acquired the car by purchasing it from Central Motor Auctions at Morden Road, Mitcham, on 26 November 1980; that is to say, within three weeks of the time when he was seeking to re-sell it.

He has been acquitted by the justices because, for the reasons which Webster J has been discussing in detail, they considered that he did not seek to sell it in the course of trade or business. But I should not like it to be thought that he committed no offence. A very obvious offence to which consideration might have been given with a view to prosecution was obtaining property by deception. I inquired why this had not been considered. I understood Mr Jubb for the prosecutor to say, which I can understand, that the local authority was concerned with trading standards and the possible prosecution of people for offences under the Fair Trading Act 1973 and other similar Acts and that it was not their function to consider prosecutions in general. As I have said, I can understand that; it is an administrative division, but it would, I think, be very unfortunate if they compartmentalised their activities to such an extent that, if they come across facts which appear to disclose a criminal offence of a type with which they do not deal, they were simply to shrug their shoulders and pass by on the other side. It is very important that where conduct as anti-social and potentially criminal as this comes to the notice of a trading standards authority, they should refer it to the police authority for consideration of the question whether it is appropriate to prosecute.

In saying that, I do not wish in any way to criticise the county borough of Croydon. I am merely drawing attention to the difficulties and possible dangers of an authority concerning itself solely with prosecuting over a narrow field without also taking steps to disseminate such information as it has of possible criminal activities to other authorities who may be concerned with other parts of the criminal law. But I entirely agree with everything Webster J has said.

Appeal dismissed with costs.

NOTE

For general discussion of the expression 'in the course of trade or business' see above, at pp 95–7, 356–60, and below, at pp 609–14. See also Harvey, 'Business or Pleasure', (1983) 127 Sol Jo 163, at 179, and Bragg, 'Horsetrader or Hobbyist—When is a Business Not a Business?' (1983) 91 ITSA MR 182. The decision in the above case is similar to that in *Smith v Lazarus* (1981) (unreported) 23 June, CA (Lexis transcript), above, at p 93, and may be contrasted with *Eiman v London Borough of Waltham Forest* (1982) 90 ITSA MR 204, QBD, referred to below, p 613 note 2.

CONTROLLING PERSISTENT OFFENDERS

Part III of the Fair Trading Act 1973 contains important provisions for dealing with the activities of persistent offenders. The key sections provide as follows:

PART III—ADDITIONAL FUNCTIONS OF DIRECTOR FOR PROTECTION OF CONSUMERS

34. Action by Director with respect to course of conduct detrimental to interests of consumers
(1) Where it appears to the Director that the person carrying on a business has in the course of that business persisted in a course of conduct which—
   (a) is detrimental to the interests of consumers in the United Kingdom, whether those interests are economic interests or interests in respect of health, safety or other matters, and
   (b) in accordance with the following provisions of this section is to be regarded as unfair to consumers,
the Director shall use his best endeavours, by communication with that person or otherwise, to obtain from him a satisfactory written assurance that he will refrain from continuing that course of conduct and from carrying on any similar course of conduct in the course of that business.
(2) For the purposes of subsection (1)(b) of this section a course of conduct shall be regarded as unfair to consumers if it consists of contraventions of one or more enactments which impose duties, prohibitions or restrictions enforceable by criminal proceedings, whether any such duty, prohibition or restriction is imposed in relation to consumers as such or not and whether the person carrying on the business has or has not been convicted of any offence in respect of any such contravention.
(3) A course of conduct on the part of the person carrying on a business shall also be regarded for those purposes as unfair to consumers if it consists of things done, or omitted to be done, in the course of that business in breach of contract or in breach of a duty (other than a contractual duty) owed to any person by virtue of any enactment or rule of law and enforceable by civil proceedings, whether (in any such case) civil proceedings in respect of the breach of contract or breach of duty have been brought or not.
(4) For the purpose of determining whether it appears to him that a person has persisted in such a course of conduct as is mentioned in subsection (1) of this section, the Director shall have regard to either or both of the following, that is to say—
   (a) complaints received by him, whether from consumers or from other persons;
   (b) any other information collected by or furnished to him, whether by virtue of this Act or otherwise.

35. Proceedings before Restrictive Practices Court

If, in the circumstances specified in subsection (1) of section 34 of this Act,—

   (a) the Director is unable to obtain from the person in question such an assurance as is mentioned in that subsection, or

   (b) that person has given such an assurance and it appears to the Director that he has failed to observe it,

the Director may bring proceedings against him before the Restrictive Practices Court.

37. Order of, or undertaking given to, Court in proceedings under s 35

(1) Where in any proceedings before the Restrictive Practices Court under section 35 of this Act—

   (a) the Court finds that the person against whom the proceedings are brought (in this section referred to as 'the respondent') has in the course of a business carried on by him persisted in such a course of conduct as is mentioned in section 34(1) of this Act, and

   (b) the respondent does not give an undertaking to the Court under subsection (3) of this section which is accepted by the Court, and

   (c) it appears to the Court that, unless an order is made against the respondent under this section, he is likely to continue that course of conduct or to carry on a similar course of conduct,

the Court may make an order against the respondent under this section.

(2) An order of the Court under this section shall (with such degree of particularity as appears to the Court to be sufficient for the purposes of the order) indicate the nature of the course of conduct to which the finding of the Court under subsection (1)(a) of this section relates, and shall direct the respondent—

   (a) to refrain from continuing that course of conduct, and

   (b) to refrain from carrying on any similar course of conduct in the course of his business.

(3) Where in any proceedings under section 35 of this Act the Court makes such a finding as is mentioned in subsection (1)(a) of this section, and the respondent offers to give to the Court an undertaking either—

   (a) to refrain as mentioned in paragraphs (a) and (b) of subsection (2) of this section, or

   (b) to take particular steps which, in the opinion of the court, would suffice to prevent a continuance of the course of conduct to which the complaint relates and to prevent the carrying on by the respondent of any similar course of conduct in the course of his business,

the Court may, if it thinks fit, accept that undertaking instead of making an order under this section.

NOTES

1. By s 41, the county court has a concurrent jurisdiction in certain cases and this is the jurisdiction which usually would be invoked. Part III also contains provisions to deal with the activities of persons who consent to or connive at courses of conduct detrimental to the interests of consumers (see ss 38 and 39 of the 1973 Act).

2. In 1989 the Office of Fair Trading issued a guidance booklet: 'Part III Assurances a new approach' to provide a clear statement of policy objectives and procedures to enable trading standards departments and the OFT to make better use of the assurance procedure.

3. The Annual Report of the Director General of Fair Trading and Press Releases issued by the Office of Fair Trading provide details of Part III proceedings and assurances. The following extracts are illustrative.

Annual Report of the Director General of Fair Trading 1996 p 29

Thirty assurances were given and one court order was made in 1996. . . . These cases related to a wide range of business practices followed by different types of trader.

. . .

Among cases where assurances were given were: two separate home-improvement firms, which gave assurances that they would carry out work as specified, within an agreed time and to a satisfactory standard, while not charging excessive amounts or failing to provide refunds; an independent servicing company; which—among other things—had made false statements about the services available, and had failed to comply with guarantee terms; and a property lettings company and its director, who gave assurances that they would refrain from failing to carry out a service with reasonable care and skill and from failing to transfer monies to clients.

The Director General took one case to the Court of Appeal in an attempt to overturn a decision made in the county court not to make an order in a case where the trader involved had failed to give any or any adequate redress when in breach of contract or any other duty owed to the consumer. Although the county court judge had agreed that the trader had persisted in always disputing claims for redress, he had decided that this was not an 'unfair course of conduct' as defined by the Act, as it did not constitute a failure to meet contractual or other obligations in civil or criminal law. The appeal was made on the basis that the judge had erred in law or had misconstrued the relevant provisions of the Act.

The Court of Appeal upheld the county court decision and dismissed the Director General's appeal. Because the failure to pay redress occurs only after there has been a breach of contract or some other duty, this judgment will not greatly affect the day-to-day work of the OFT. Nevertheless it does reinforce the OFT's long-held view that Part III of the Fair Trading Act provides an inadequate means to achieve the objective of countering traders who pursue unfair or improper business practices but whose behaviour, in itself, is not unlawful.

Office of Fair Trading Press Release No 59/96, 20 December 1996

BUSINESS ORDERED NOT TO SELL SICK DOGS

A court order was made yesterday against the partners in Pedigree Puppies, a Lancashire pet business which sold sick puppies, some of which died.

Richard Paul Baison and Peter John Chalmers Ogg also failed to supply promised pedigree certificates and Kennel Club papers, Southport County Court was told. Judge Urquhart made the order because Mr Baison and Mr Ogg would not give satisfactory assurances about their future behaviour to John Bridgeman, Director General of Fair Trading.

Lancashire Trading Standards Department received over a hundred complaints about Pedigree Puppies, of Windgate, Liverpool Road, Tarleton, Preston, between July 1994 and September 1995, the court was told.

The order, made under Part III of the Fair Trading Act, prohibits Mr Baison and Mr Ogg from continuing to sell sick dogs or dogs which do not have the pedigree claimed for them. The order binds them even if they go on to run another business.

Anyone who breaches a 'Part III' court order could be in contempt of court and risk a heavy fine or imprisonment.

Mr Bridgeman said today: 'It is contemptible to sell sick pets, particularly when many will be bought for children. This case shows that care should be taken in the choice of supplier by anyone planning to buy a pet as a Christmas present.'

Any evidence of a breach of the order by Mr Baison and Mr Ogg should be passed on to local Trading Standards Departments, who would also like to hear about similar conduct by other suppliers. Their address and telephone number can be found in the phone book.

NOTES

The Court ordered that:

the respondents [Mr Baison and Mr Ogg] do refrain from continuing the course of conduct hereinafter set out and from carrying on that or any similar course of conduct in the course of any business they carry on:

1. Committing breaches of contract with consumers by supplying goods
    (a) which do not correspond with the description by which they are sold as required by section 13 of the Sale of Goods Act 1979; or
    (b) which are not of satisfactory quality as required by section 14(2) of the Sale of Goods Act 1979 as amended; or
    (c) which are not fit for the purpose for which they have been bought as required by section 14(3) of that Act;
2. In contracts for the supply of dogs said to be pedigree dogs, committing breaches of contract by not supplying the pedigree certificate of the Kennel Club registration papers within the agreed time, or if no time has been agreed within a reasonable time, or at all;
3. Inducing customers to enter into contracts for the supply of goods by knowingly, recklessly, or negligently making false statements as to the nature and condition of those goods;
4. When in breach of contract with customers failing to give any or any adequate redress to those customers.

Mr Baison and Mr Ogg were ordered to pay the Director General's costs.

Office of Fair Trading Press Release No 49/96, 27 November 1996

SERVICE CONTRACT COMPANY GIVES ASSURANCES ON FUTURE BEHAVIOUR

National Homecare Ltd, one of the main independent servicing companies which deals with extended warranty contracts, and its directors have agreed to give written assurances to John Bridgeman, Director General of Fair Trading, about their future conduct.

As part of its service, the company has issued its customers with a Consumer Service Charter which laid down a series of standards which the company promised to meet in the course of its business. However, in numerous cases the company failed to meet its standards and also to honour compensation pledges.

Mr Bridgeman said:

'Details of 54 successful claims made against the company in the county courts were brought to my attention. These provided clear evidence of the company's unacceptable behaviour as they had acted persistently to the detriment of consumers.

The claims centred around making false statements as to the services being offered, failing to carry out work satisfactorily, failing to carry out work within the agreed time, a reasonable time or at all; failing to comply with guarantee terms, failing to provide refunds or offer redress to complainants.

I have asked for and accepted assurances from the company and its directors that these practices will cease. If the company fails to keep to these assurances, I have the power to make them enforceable through the courts.'

The assurances were given under the provisions of Part III of the Fair Trading Act 1973.

NOTES

1. The Director General of Fair Trading has obtained written assurances under Part III of the Fair Trading Act 1973 from National Homecare Ltd, a body corporate of Darlaston Road, Kings Hill, Wednesbury, West Midlands WS10 7TE and its directors Martin John Hovard, Peter Massey, Kevin Moat, Anthony James Tye, Jack Waldron, and Graham Young.

The full text of the Assurances given by the company on 30 September 1996 is as follows:

To refrain from continuing the following and from carrying on any similar course of conduct in the course of its business, namely:

1. Inducing consumers to enter into contracts for services by knowingly, recklessly or negligently making false statements as to the nature of those services;
2. In contracts for work:—
    (i) failing to provide services with reasonable care and skill as required by section 13 of the Supply of Goods and Services Act 1982;
    (ii) failing to carry out work within the agreed time or a reasonable time, as required by section 14 of the Supply of Goods and Services Act 1982, or at all;
    (iii) failing to comply with the terms of any contractual guarantee binding on National Homecare Ltd.
3. When in breach of contract, failing to provide any, or any adequate redress.
4. Committing offences under section 14(1)(a) of the Trade Descriptions Act 1968 by knowingly or recklessly making false statements as to the provision of services.

The directors gave similar assurances and also promised to refrain from:

carrying on any similar course of conduct in the course of any business which may at any time be carried on by me; and consenting to or conniving at the carrying on of any such course of conduct by any other body corporate in relation to which at any time when that course of conduct is carried on I am (or purport to act as) a director, manager, secretary or other similar officer or in which I have, at the time, a controlling interest.

NOTES

1. For details of the first contempt proceedings taken against a trader, a Mr Gilliam, see (1982) 90 ITSA MR 190; *Annual Report of the Director General of Fair Trading 1982* at p 53. As it was the first such case a further assurance was accepted by the court. Following breaches of this further assurance, a 14 day prison sentence was imposed: see (1983) 91 ITSA MR 202; *Annual Report of the Director General of Fair Trading 1983* at p 57.
2. The case of Saray Electronics (London) Ltd provides a good example of contempt proceedings against a company. In 1985 the company was fined £1,950 for contempt of court. When the company was again in contempt, in 1989, it was fined £50,000 and each of its two directors was fined £10,000 and given three months imprisonment, suspended for two years: see OFT Press Release No 26/89.
3. For a helpful comparison between Part III assurances and the complaints statistics received in the Office of Fair Trading see Hope, (1981) 89 ITSA MR 180.
4. In *R v Director General of Fair Trading, ex p F H Taylor & Co Ltd* [1981] ICR 292, importers of toys and electrical equipment, who had been convicted on

some 13 occasions for contravening safety regulations, challenged the entitlement of the Director to publicise assurances. In dismissing the application
Donaldson LJ commented (at pp 293–4):

> In 1973 Parliament established the office of Director General of Fair Trading. His duties
> include that of acting as a watchdog for consumers. As such he has been equipped both with
> a bark and a bite. . . . [In] cases in which such an assurance is given, it is the Director
> General's duty to monitor the future of the merchant or manufacturer concerned. He can-
> not do this effectively by means solely of his own staff. Accordingly, he has to ensure that
> others who are likely to learn of conduct which would constitute a breach of the assurance
> must be made aware that the assurance has been given and encouraged to report breaches
> to his office. The Director General needs no statutory authority to speak and write about
> his work and about the misdeeds of others with which he is concerned in his work. Both the
> Director General and his office have full freedom of speech, subject to the general law of
> defamation and to any special statutory restrictions.

As a result of this case and the guidance given by the court concerning publicity of assurances, the OFT adopted a more cautious approach and restricted its
publicity on new assurances given to including details in Annual Reports and
notifying Trading Standards Departments and other interested bodies. In
1989 there was a change of policy, detailed in the OFT booklet: 'Part III
Assurances, a new approach'. Assurances may be detailed in press releases and
advertised in local or, sometimes, national papers or magazines relevant to the
trader's business. After the introduction of the new publicity arrangements
there was some reduction in the number of assurances given, but the publicity
policy continues.

QUESTIONS

1. Is the de facto abolition of the Consumer Protection Advisory Committee and
   the consequential obsolescence of the Part II procedures in the 1973 Act a
   desirable slimming down of unnecessary bureaucracy, or does the present position leave a genuine gap? If the latter is so, how would you fill this gap?
2. Under Part III of the 1973 Act are there any special difficulties in applying the
   notion of 'persistent' misconduct in the case of companies which operate on a
   national, as opposed to local, basis?
3. Do you consider that the current powers of the Director under Part III of the
   1973 Act are (i) too extensive or (ii) too restricted or tightly circumscribed?
   (See further the text which follows.)

SHOULD THERE BE A GENERAL DUTY TO TRADE FAIRLY?

INTRODUCTION

Codes of practice designed to regulate sectors of industry on a voluntary and self-enforcing basis are comparatively widespread. Section 124(3) of the Fair Trading Act 1973 specifically states that it shall be the duty of the Director General to encourage relevant associations to prepare, and to disseminate to their members, codes of practice for guidance in safeguarding and promoting the interests of consumers.

However, these codes suffer from unavoidable defects. The best known and most damaging is that by no means all relevant traders are members of their trade association and amongst those that are not are likely to be found a high proportion of the rogue traders. (Codes are discussed in more detail in ch 10.)

ORIGINAL PROPOSALS

This problem was felt to be particularly acute in the home improvements sector and prompted the Director to propose a possible change of direction: the introduction of a general duty to trade fairly, in *Home Improvements—A Discussion Paper*, March 1982, OFT, and again in *Home improvements: a Report by the Director General of Fair Trading*, June 1983, OFT. In 1984, the Director wrote on the subject:

The Development of Consumer Law and Policy—Bold Spirits and Timorous Souls, by Sir Gordon Borrie, 36th Hamlyn Lectures, (London, 1984) pp 74–7

Ten years' experience of both Part III of the Fair Trading Act and codes of practice promoted under section 124 of the same Act suggests that these provisions could usefully be combined so that Part III could be applied (indirectly at least) to persistent breaches of codes as well as to persistent breaches of the civil and criminal law.

. . .

One possible way forward would be to create by statute a general duty to trade fairly in consumer transactions, a duty which would be enforceable only through detailed codes of practice prepared by the Office of Fair Trading for each sector of trade after consultation with relevant trade associations. Under Part III of the Fair Trading Act, persistent breaches of the new statutory duty (and indirectly, therefore, persistent breaches of the codes) could result in assurances or court orders and the codes would of course apply to all traders and not just those who belonged to relevant trade associations. The indications are that a legal development of these lines would find support among both consumer bodies and retailer organisations. Consumer bodies would welcome the wider scope and strengthened authority of codes of practice. Retailer organisations would also welcome the wider scope of the codes so that they covered traders who are outside the trade associations. The Motor Agents Association, for example, has many times stressed the unfairness involved in expecting its members to conform to higher standards of trading, such as providing customers with pre-sales information reports on used cars, when their non-member competitors are under no such obligation.

. . .

Under my proposals, what types of conduct should be treated as 'unfair' would be set out in codes of practice devised after consultation with relevant trade associations. It would be a matter for discussion whether such a code should receive the imprimatur of Parliament or the appropriate Minister before it became effective and whether, for example, breach of the code should be enforceable not only by the Director General of Fair Trading but also by any private individual who could show loss or damage arising from such breach.

The statutory imposition of a general duty to trade fairly would be a bold step and, by being directly linked to codes of practice in the preparation of which trade associations would have an important part to play, a novel dimension of democracy would be introduced because those directly affected would have a say (through their representative organisations) in the details of the rules that are to be applied to them.

To progress matters further in August 1986 the Office of Fair Trading issued *A general duty to trade fairly—A discussion paper* from which the following extracts are taken.

A General Duty to Trade Fairly—A Discussion Paper—Office of Fair Trading (London, 1986)

Chapter 5—Towards a General Duty to Trade Fairly
5.1. The Office considers . . . that the scale of consumer detriment is worryingly high in many areas. The analysis . . . lends weight to the view that current consumer law, despite its scope, has significant deficiencies, particularly in its application, and also that there are serious limitations to what can be achieved outside the formal legal framework by voluntary codes of practice. It is also evident . . . that a general duty is not a novel proposition in law. The questions which have next to be addressed are whether the situation could be significantly improved through the introduction of a statutory general duty to trade fairly and what form this might take . . .

The criminal and civil law
5.4. The criminal law has a well established role in relation to many aspects of trading standards and consumer protection . . . .. There is clearly room for debate over what practices are most appropriately controlled through the criminal law. It is common ground that in relation to certain acts such as fraud or dishonesty or those liable to cause people physical harm, criminal sanctions are essential. But as noted by Mr David Tench, the legal officer of the Consumers' Association, the creation of offences through the development of regulatory law, in consumer protection and in many other fields, has extended the use of the criminal law to include practices which are not in the public perception criminal in any real sense. [Tench, D, *Towards a Middle System of Law*, Consumers' Association, (London, 1981)] Similarly, one of the conclusions of a report by Justice is that 'only a minority of "criminal offences" involve any degree of moral turpitude in their commission.' [*Breaking the Rules*, a report by Justice, (London, 1980)]

5.5. There are drawbacks in extending criminal sanctions beyond those areas where there is general acceptance of the criminal nature of the behaviour being prescribed. Thus an American commentator notes 'Where the violation is not generally regarded as ethically reprehensible, either by the community at large or by the class of businessman, the private appeal to conscience is at its minimum and being convicted and fined may have little more impact than a bad selling season.' [Kadish, S H, 'Some observations on the use of criminal sanctions in enforcing economic regulations', University of Chicago Law Review, 30 (1963), No 3.]

5.6. There are a number of other difficulties associated with criminal legislation in this sphere. Such legislation is usually drafted very precisely in order to deal with particular malpractices which have been identified. This detailed and highly specific approach risks leaving some abuses unregulated. It may also deter both compliance and enforcement. The detailed regulations relating to price marking may be cited as a case in point.

5.7. The position of consumers may not be furthered by the use of criminal sanctions. Thus fining a trader may not help the consumer to obtain satisfactory redress even though there exists now the possibility of compensation orders being awarded to consumers in the criminal courts ... A criminal conviction, moreover, can stigmatise a trader to a greater degree than might generally be regarded as commensurate with the malpractice and can thus result in technical offences being the subject of lengthy appeals through the courts.

5.8. It has been argued during the Office's consultations that the position of consumers could be significantly improved if more determined use was made of the means of redress already open to them under the current civil law. The civil law, however, depends on the individual taking the initiative at his or her own expense and the great and understandable reluctance of consumers to pursue civil remedies acts as a major constraint on its effectiveness. In addition consumers may be deterred when seeking to enforce their existing civil rights against traders by, for instance, difficulties of establishing whether an agreement was reached, what its exact terms were and how they have been breached, and whether and by whose fault the consumer suffered damage. Consumers whose losses may be for sums that do not justify the cost and other drawbacks of litigation are commonly deterred in the face of these difficulties from seeking redress through the courts ...

Administrative sanctions
5.10. Controls in the form of administrative sanctions ... are not designed to enable the ordinary consumer to secure redress, and they have other limitations. The powers of the Director General under Part III of the Fair Trading Act to seek assurances from traders concerning their future conduct apply if the trader has persisted in a course of conduct detrimental to consumers' interests and there is evidence that the trader has breached civil or criminal law. The Director General can act only on the basis of proper evidence of persistence in a course of conduct. The procedure involves several stages and can inevitably be protracted. Thus while a miscreant trader may in the end be prevented from continuing the course of conduct which has damaged consumers the use of these powers has inherent limitations.

A general duty to trade fairly
5.11. In the light of the considerations already summarised in this chapter, the Office believes that an approach should be considered in which the existing body of statute and common law could be supplemented by the introduction into the law relating to consumer transactions of a broader concept of fair trading drawn up in such a manner as to increase the likelihood of satisfactory trading behaviour and improve consumers' opportunity of redress.

5.12. The Office has paid close attention to the trend ... to move away from highly detailed regulation in certain areas of law and to introduce general duties supplemented by regulations or codes indicating suitable positive standards. Notable examples are the general duties relating to health and safety at work, and the proposal to introduce a general safety requirement in relation to consumer goods. This development does not mean that less importance is attached to the use of the law in these areas. Rather there has been an increasing recognition that methods of control are needed which provide comprehensive coverage yet are sufficiently flexible to facilitate amendment in the light of developments in manufacturing and trading practices. It is evident that a general duty to trade fairly, supplemented by codes of practice, would not be as novel an innovation as it may first appear.

. . .

Form of a general duty to trade fairly

5.14. Without prejudice to the requirements of the existing general law, legislation would provide for the introduction in the United Kingdom of a general duty to trade fairly, which would be a broad statutory duty. It might alternatively be framed in terms such as a general prohibition on deceptive and misleading practices. Arguably this could be supplemented by specific prohibitions of particular unacceptable practices . . .

Codes of practice

5.16. The Office envisages that legislation would make provision for the general duty to be supported by codes of practice both vertical (by trading practice) and horizontal (by sector) setting out the trading practices which were regarded as acceptable (or unacceptable) in the sectors concerned. The Office proposes that such new-style codes should be introduced, taking account of discussions with the interests concerned, by the Director General of Fair Trading; it would seem appropriate for the codes to have the endorsement of the Secretary of State and be laid before Parliament . . .

5.20. The Office envisages approved codes containing a statement of general principles of fair trading pertinent to the sector but not being excessively detailed. Thus for example traders' obligations in respect of the provision of appropriate information, written estimates, spare parts, servicing or the features of extended warranties would be included in relevant sectors . . .

5.21. It should also be possible to facilitate the decriminalisation of particular areas of regulatory consumer protection legislation when a general duty and codes are in place by covering the same substantive points in codes. The Office does not see this as a weakening of consumer protection, but rather, given the proposed enforcement mechanism, it will enable the efficacy of the law to be improved to the benefit of consumers . . .

Implementation

5.23. There are various ways in which a general duty could be implemented. One option would be for the obligations under a general duty to trade fairly to apply only to the extent spelt out in approved codes of practice. Under this approach a general duty would in effect be introduced sector by sector. If no approved codes existed for a particular sector or trading practice, the ordinary law would prevail and the general duty would not apply. It would take time for codes to be introduced, and consequently consumers would have different rights, and traders different responsibilities in different sectors. On the other hand once approved codes were in place they would have statutory backing and would apply to all traders in the sector, not only to members of trade associations.

5.24. Alternatively it is arguable that a general duty might apply to all consumer transactions, whether or not approved codes were in place. With this approach codes would amplify the general duty as and when they are negotiated. The duty would be framed in general terms but might be accompanied by some basic definitions or illustrations of what is involved in unfair trading and, in the absence of codes specifically approved in this context, it would be for the courts over time to develop an interpretation of what is required and to define the relationship of the duty to existing law . . .

5.26. Under each of these approaches to a general duty, codes of practice, when approved, should be admissible in evidence in court proceedings concerning alleged breaches of the general duty. The plaintiff in any proceedings would be able to cite non-observance by the trader of the provisions of an approved code, while a trader would be able to provide evidence of his compliance with the code as a defence. It should remain open to a trader to adduce as a defence in proceedings evidence that he observed standards which, though not in conformity with the relevant approved code, afforded equivalent protection. Thus codes would have evidential rather than substantive significance and an important element of flexibility would be retained . . .

Enforcement
5.28. Local authority trading standards departments (and environmental health departments as appropriate) should be given a major role in enforcement. Without such a role for local enforcement agencies, which can act quickly on the basis of local information, a general duty would be unlikely to be effective in raising trading standards or improving redress. The Office proposes that in the event of a trading standards officer becoming aware, through complaint or otherwise, of instances of trading practices which he considers to be a breach of the relevant code, it would be open to the officer to make an informal approach asking the trader to comply with the code and, in a suitable case, ask the trader to give redress to aggrieved consumers. If the informal approach failed it would be open to the trading standards officer to serve the trader with a formal notice. This would set out the alleged breach of the code and invite the trader to propose a remedy which would include an undertaking to comply with the relevant code provisions and an offer to give suitable redress. If the trader complied with the formal notice, that would be the end of the matter. If, however, the trading standards officer were unable to obtain a satisfactory response, he could take action in the local county or sheriff court seeking a court order requiring the trader to comply with the relevant sections of the code and, where appropriate, to give suitable redress. If the trading standards officer's case were successful the court would grant a mandatory injunction or interdict ordering the trader to refrain from breach of the relevant sections of the code and would order redress to any consumers who had been injured by the breach of the code. Ultimately the sanctions for breach of the injunction would be a fine or imprisonment for contempt of court. In instances where financial compensation was not appropriate, an alternative sanction open to the court could be to declare the contract unenforceable. The above procedure could also be applied to breaches of the existing civil and criminal law.

5.29. In this way the trading standards officer would be enforcing the code and the general law in the public interest and also, in effect, pursuing a mass restitution suit on behalf of consumers . . . However in cases involving matters of general importance or difficult questions of law or fact it should be open to the Director General of Fair Trading to initiate cases instead of the local trading standards officer under paragraph 5.28 or to take over such cases at any stage of the procedure.

5.30. If there were persistent breaches of the general duty or the general law thus indicating a course of conduct, it might in addition be open to a trading standards department or the Director General to seek an injunction from the court to require the trader to cease the conduct . . .

5.33. Independently from the procedure outlined, individual consumers as well as the trader would of course have their normal rights to bring civil actions in the courts. This would take account of any obligations in contract, tort or delict as well as rights arising from the general duty to trade fairly under any approved relevant code. Should a consumer succeed in proving a breach of the general duty relevant to his contract he will have similar means of redress to those existing under the present law of contract: damages, declaration, injunctions or interdicts, specific performance and, possibly, the right to have goods repaired or replaced. In practice consumers are likely to be most interested in compensation or performance of their own contract.

RESPONSES

The proposals for a general duty to trade fairly generated a considerable response from consumer organisations, trade associations, trading standards departments and academics. For comments on the proposals see Harvey, 'Should there be a general duty to trade fairly?' (1984) 3 Trading Law 45; Thomas, 'A General Duty to Trade Fairly' (1985) 4 Trading Law 74; Circus, *Towards a general duty to trade fairly*, ITSA, (Southend-on Sea, 1988).

The Office of Fair Trading reported on the responses received and summarised them in the following extract:

Trading Malpractices, Office of Fair Trading (London, 1990)

3.16 . . . . Consumer and trading standards bodies almost unanimously supported the idea of a general provision in one form or another, although many had reservations about major areas of the proposals. Reactions from traders and trade associations were more mixed, being roughly equally divided between those supporting the approach in principle, and those against. Major representative bodies such as the Confederation of British Industry and the Institute of Directors expressed opposition. A number of those who broadly supported a general duty nevertheless favoured a restricted form under which it would apply only when supported by codes specifically approved for this purpose.

. . .

Table 5: Summary of the main arguments put forward in relation to a general duty

For	*Against*
Sufficient consumer detriment exists to warrant a general duty	A sufficient level of consumer detriment either does not, or has not yet been established to, exist
A general duty would fill serious gaps in the present consumer protection laws	Present consumer protection law is good enough
There are precedents for a general duty/such a radical approach would be justified	A general duty would reverse the present principles of law
Honest traders would have no particular difficulty in complying with a general duty	A general duty would create an unacceptable level of uncertainty for traders (and others) as to whether they were complying with its requirements
A general duty is the best way of tackling those consumer problems which are not presently adequately dealt with	If present consumer protection is not sufficient then specifically directed measures should be proposed or other means of protection than a general duty should be employed

Present forms of self-regulation are ineffective and/or would not be damaged by a general duty	Present forms of self-regulation are effective and would be undermined by a general duty
A general duty could be effectively enforced	Serious enforcement difficulties would be encountered
Resources required/cost implications are acceptable and justified by expected benefits	Resources required/cost implications make a general duty unacceptable or impractical

The conclusion reached by the Office of Fair Trading was that the 1986 proposals, in their original form, should not be pursued as they were, perhaps, overambitious in trying to both raise trading standards generally whilst at the same time improve the opportunity for consumer redress. Instead a different approach was adopted: that of modifying and expanding the assurance procedure under Part III of the Fair Trading Act 1973.

Trading Malpractices, Office of Fair Trading (London, 1990)

1.6. . . . My purpose now is to target harmful practices which distort the competitive market, but which appear to be largely immune from its disciplines. My proposals concentrate directly on tackling unlawful, deceptive or objectionable trading practices which have not been, or cannot be, controlled effectively by existing legislation. They recognise that it is necessary to aim at something of a moving target. Any new measure needs to be expressed in wide enough terms to act as a safety-net for current and future trading malpractices which harm consumers and reputable traders alike. At the same time it must provide sufficient certainty so as not to be a burden on the honest and reputable business and to ensure that it can be enforced where necessary without undue delay.

1.7. I believe that the proposals set out in this report meet these requirements and will command widespread support. I am proposing new legislation to regulate business practices which will enable the enforcement machinery to be purpose-built and integrated with the substantive provisions. There are thus two principal inter-linked strands:
— to streamline and strengthen the arrangements for dealing with businesses which repeatedly disregard the law;
— to extend the scope of these arrangements so that they can be used against business malpractices which are clearly objectionable, but which may not be currently unlawful.
I am proposing an administrative, rather than a criminal, measure. With the emphasis on improving future behaviour, I am convinced that—where the backing of legal sanctions is required—it is the civil courts, which are well used to injunctive-type proceedings, which should be involved. This has the further advantage of permitting the law to be cast in more general terms than would be normally acceptable for the creation of any new criminal offences.

1.8. The proposals, which take the form of a complete overhaul of Part III of the Fair Trading Act 1973, can be summarised as follows:
(i) In order to take action under the Fair Trading Act, the enforcement authority would need to show that the trader has carried on a course of conduct which is 'unfair' and detrimental to the interests of consumers in the United Kingdom.
(ii) As well as behaviour which involves breaches of existing legal requirements, the definition of 'unfair' in this context should be extended by adding two general provisions. The first would relate to 'deceptive or misleading' business practices, supported by a non-exhaustive list of illustrative acts or practices. The second—'unconscionable'

practices—is intended to deal with malpractices which would generally be regarded as indefensible or objectionable by virtue of their oppressive or exploitative nature. This would be backed by a set of factors or circumstances to be taken into account in individual cases.

(iii) The nature of the action should be re-cast as a more direct approach:

    (a) enforcement action would be initiated by issuing and serving a caution on a trader setting out the 'unfair' course of conduct alleged to have been carried on to the detriment of consumers' interests;

    (b) the caution would require the trader to discontinue (or not repeat) the course of conduct, or conduct of a similar type. At the discretion of the enforcement authority the caution may also include a requirement that the trader should take particular steps to modify his trading practices as may be specified;

    (c) it would be open to the trader to challenge the caution (whether it be the facts, the caution's legal validity or the remedy proposed) by application to the court;

    (d) the enforcement authority would apply to the court if the trader ignores the caution and has repeated or continued that (or a similar) course of conduct or if it believes that there is a risk of continuation or repetition;

    (e) in cases where it can be shown that there is likelihood of substantial detriment to the health, safety or economic interests of consumers, the enforcement authority would be entitled to make immediate application to the court, by-passing the caution procedure;

    (f) the court would have the power to:

      — revoke the caution;

      — accept undertakings from the trader; or

      — make an order to restrain continuation or repetition of the specified course of conduct, or conduct of a similar type;

    (g) breach of a court order would be punishable as a contempt of court, with the possibility of fines and/or imprisonment.

(iv) The ability to take action should be shared between the Director General Fair Trading and local trading standards authorities. There should be a dual power for both the Director General and local authorities to enforce the legislation as a whole, but no specific duties to take any steps. In cases of national or public importance—the identification of which will depend on circumstances of each case—the Director General would normally take action.

1.9. I am confident that the proposals put forward in this report would create an effective procedure for use against dishonest and cavalier traders whose conduct undermines all notions of fair trading. These proposals should hold no fears for the vast majority of traders who behave responsibly towards their customers. They will strengthen, not restrict, the ability of the competitive market to provide consumers with maximum choice of goods and services by striking the right balance between excessive uncertainty and excessive specificity. They will reinforce the advisory role of enforcement authorities, particularly by providing an alternative to prosecution or a sanction where otherwise none may exist. Where something more than advice is needed, the new arrangements will enable a positive and constructive approach to be taken to the task of cleaning up unacceptable business behaviour which has remained beyond the reach of current controls. At the same time, any traders involved would have ample opportunity to put their side of the case, with the courts having the final word.

1.10. Overall my view is that the proposed arrangements which build on the strengths of existing procedures, whilst eliminating the weaknesses, are necessary desirable and right for the modern market place of the 1990s.

. . .

5.17. The major innovation proposed by the OFT would be to widen the provisions which define an 'unfair' course of conduct. The existing definitions—limited to conduct which amounts to breaches of criminal or civil law obligations which are detrimental to consumers—should be extended by adding two general provisions, each of which would be supported by a 'shopping-list' of illustrative acts or practices.

(1) Deceptive or misleading practices

5.18. The first general provision would be cast in terms of business practices which are deceptive or misleading. This would be defined to include any oral, written or visual representation (including a failure to disclose) or any other conduct. The legislation would have to make clear reference to the effect, or likely effect, of the practice on the consumer(s) at whom it is directed, or whom it affects.

5.19. The general provision would be elaborated by a non-exhaustive list of acts or practices any of which, without limiting or prejudicing the generality of the main provision, would be treated as falling within it. The OFT proposes the following initial list of such acts or practices:

  (a) a representation that the subject of a consumer transaction has sponsorship, approval, performance characteristics, accessories, ingredients, quantities, components, uses or benefits that it does not have;

  (b) a representation that the supplier has a sponsorship, approval, status, affiliation or connection that he does not have;

  (c) a representation that the subject of a consumer transaction is of a particular standard, quality, grade, style or model that it is not;

  (d) a representation that the subject of a consumer transaction has been used to an extent that is different from the fact;

  (e) a representation that the subject of a consumer transaction is new or unused if it is not, or if it is deteriorated, altered, reconditioned or reclaimed;

  (f) a representation that the subject of a consumer transaction has a particular prior history or usage that it has not;

  (g) a representation that the subject of a consumer transaction is available for a reason that is different from the fact;

  (h) a representation that the subject of a consumer transaction has been made available in accordance with a previous representation if it has not;

  (i) a representation that the subject of a consumer transaction is available if the supplier has no intention of supplying or otherwise disposing of the subject as represented;

  (j) a representation that is such that a person could reasonably conclude that a price benefit or advantage exists, if it does not;

  (k) a representation that a service, part, replacement or repair is needed if it is not;

  (l) a representation that the purpose or intent of a solicitation of, or a communication with, a consumer by a supplier is for a purpose or intent different from the fact;

  (m) a representation that a consumer transaction involves or does not involve rights, remedies or obligations if the representation is deceptive or misleading;

  (n) a representation such that a consumer might reasonably conclude that the subject of a consumer transaction is available in greater quantities than are in fact available from the supplier, unless the limitation of availability represented by the supplier has been given reasonable prominence;

  (o) a representation as to the authority of a salesman, representative, employee or agent to negotiate the final terms of a consumer transaction if the representation is different from the fact;

  (p) where an estimate of the price of a consumer transaction is materially less than the price of the consumer transaction as subsequently determined or demanded by the supplier and the supplier has proceeded with his performance of the consumer transaction without the express consent of the consumer,—

(q) where the price of a unit of a consumer transaction is given in an advertisement, display or representation, the failure to give, in the same advertisement, display or representation, reasonable prominence to the total price of the consumer transaction; and the use, in an oral or written representation, of exaggeration, innuendo or ambiguity as to a material fact, or failure to state a material fact, if the representation is deceptive or misleading.

(2) Unconscionable practices

5.20. There should be little argument about the importance of controlling deception. There may be more controversy about whether action should also be available against non-deceptive practices which are seen as being in some other way unacceptable or objectionable. Should the law go further and deal with conduct which, while not necessarily misleading or deceptive, is nonetheless objectionable? Should action be taken, for example, in respect of conduct which takes advantage of consumers' lack of knowledge or lack of bargaining power, which inhibits their ability to choose freely or which is otherwise oppressive, exploitive or unscrupulous in its nature? In a nutshell, should the law tackle behaviour which, in all conscience, is unacceptable?

5.21. Appendix 3 summarises the limited progress which the courts have made towards developing any coherent doctrine of unconscionability. It is clear that, if the law is to regulate trade practices which involve undue exploitation—whether through disreputable behaviour or abuse of a dominant position—legislation must be enacted by Parliament. This has been the situation in most industrialised countries. Behind legislation of this nature lies the principle that the law should recognise certain basic ethical values of society—such as promoting honesty, openness and fair dealing and preventing exploitation. Such laws accept that the control of trading malpractices is not entirely a matter of correcting market defects but serves a wider purpose. This is especially the case where the trading practices in question have a particularly severe effect on the most disadvantaged consumers—the poorest, the over-indebted, the illiterate, the aged, racial and cultural minorities and so on.

5.22. The OFT's second general provision is therefore intended to deal with malpractices which would generally be regarded as indefensible or objectionable by virtue of their oppressive or exploitive nature. Again it is the effect, or likely effect, upon the 'target' consumer(s) which would count. This guards against the danger of excessive paternalism which is inherent in a proposal of this nature and recognises that there is no such thing as a unified, monolithic consumer interest. The diffuse nature of different types of consumers means that a purely 'market efficiency' approach to consumer protection and fair competition is insufficient. It is necessary to control practices which are regarded as exploiting particularly vulnerable groups, but to do so by reference to the actual or prospective impact on such people.

5.23 In considering the form of such a general control the OFT has again looked closely at overseas law and experience. It has also considered casting the provision in terms similar to those to be found in section 25(2)(d) of the Consumer Credit Act 1974. This section requires the Director General, in considering a person's fitness to hold a consumer credit licence, to take into account evidence tending to show that a person has engaged in business practices which appear to be ' . . . oppressive or otherwise unfair or improper (whether unlawful or not)'. A general prohibition cast in terms of practice which is 'oppressive, unfair or improper' would have the considerable advantage of the successful precedent established in the consumer credit sector. This sub-section has been very useful to the OFT and has added substantially to the effectiveness of the licensing system.

5.24. The disadvantage of words like 'unfair' or 'improper', however, is that they may be so wide and so subjective as to place excessive discretion in the hands of the enforcement authorities. What may be acceptable in the hands of a single Director General accountable to Parliament, and constantly in the public eye, might well prove to be unacceptable in the hands of numerous local enforcement bodies. Something which strikes the right balance, but is more tractable than 'unfairness' is therefore required.

5.25. The OFT believes that the narrower Canadian/Australian approach is to be preferred. This refers to 'unconscionable' conduct. In broad terms it can be said that unconscionable conduct will arise in a situation where a stronger party to a transaction knowingly takes wholly unfair advantage of that position to the detriment of the less powerful party. The provision would thus be aimed at conduct which grossly contravenes ordinary principles of fair dealing. The OFT's preference reflects a similar debate which took place when the Australian Trade Practices Act 1974 was amended so as to prohibit not just deceptive or misleading conduct, but also unconscionable conduct. 'Unconscionable', as opposed to merely 'unfair', conduct was deliberately chosen in an attempt to restrict the scope of judicial intervention against practices which might not previously have been unlawful. The Committee whose work led to the amendment in question thought that 'a general prohibition of 'unfair' conduct, as contained in the US Federal Trade Commission Act could, under Australian conditions, result in a considerable degree of uncertainty in commercial transactions'.

5.26. The OFT accordingly proposes that a course of conduct shall also be regarded as unfair to consumers for the purposes of this Act if it consists of any unconscionable acts, practices or conduct.

5.27. Although it is central that there should not—indeed cannot—be a definition of 'unconscionable' the OFT proposes, again mirroring the Canadian/Australian approach, that the reference to such conduct should be elaborated by taking into account a non-exhaustive list of factors or circumstances. This, again, would be expressed so as not to prejudice or limit the generality of the parent main provision. The OFT proposes the following initial list of factors or circumstances:

    (a) that the consumer was subjected to undue pressure to enter into the consumer transaction;

    (b) that the consumer was taken advantage of by his inability or incapacity reasonably to protect his own interest by reason of his physical or mental infirmity, ignorance, illiteracy, age or his inability to understand the character, nature or language of the consumer transaction, or any other matter related to it;

    (c) that, at the time the consumer transaction was entered into, there was no reasonable probability of full payment of the price by the consumer, and

    (d) that the terms and conditions on, or subject to, which the consumer transaction was entered by the consumer are so harsh or adverse to the consumer as to be inequitable.

Speaking in 1991, the Director, Sir Gordon Borrie, in the 15th Blackstone Lecture, 'Trading Malpractices and Legislative Policy' published in (1991) 107 LQR 559, stated (at pp 575–6):

To return to the need for a more comprehensive law to deal with trading malpractices generally rather than with the problems of particular market sectors, I have no doubt that a statutory prohibition of deceptive, misleading and unconscionable practices is needed, enforced by public officials using administrative and judicial enforcement powers . . . A legislative policy of this kind towards trading malpractices would free primary legislation from much of its clutter and detail but the businessman's yearning for certainty would be met by a range of regulatory instruments including secondary legislation, codes of practice, guidance and case law. Self-regulation would be complemented by enforcement through public officials.

NOTES

1. These proposals were made prior to the introduction of the Unfair Terms in Consumer Contracts Regulations 1994 (SI 1994/3159), discussed in ch 7, which concern 'unfair' terms.
2. As a follow-up to these proposals the Office of Fair Trading held a conference, noted in *Trading malpractices conference—issues paper*, Office of Fair Trading, 22 October 1991.
3. The Conservative Government's 1992 manifesto made a commitment to improve powers to deal with rogue traders and, following a general reappraisal, the next Director presented proposals to the President of the Board of Trade in November 1993. In response to these proposals the Department of Trade and Industry issued a consultation paper in December 1994 entitled *Reform of Part III of the Fair Trading Act 1973*. No action was taken before the change of Government in 1997.

CURRENT PROPOSALS

In September 1997 the current Director made further proposals to Mr Griffiths, the new Minister for Consumer and Corporate Affairs:

Office of Fair Trading Press Release No 39/97, 22 September 1997

. . .

Mr Bridgeman has made eight principal recommendations to Mr Griffiths:

1. Enforcers (the Office of Fair Trading and trading standards departments) should have the power to require a trader by order to discontinue (or not repeat) a course of conduct which satisfies the test that it is unfair.

2. Before issuing an order, enforcers should be required to inform the trader that they are minded to do so. The trader should then have (within a specified time) the right to require an immediate review of the intention to make the order by the superior officer of the enforcement officer initiating the action.

3. Once an order is made, there should be a specified period allowed for appeal to an independent judicial body. The order should come into effect after that period has elapsed without an appeal being made, or in the event of an appeal being made, when upheld by the judicial body.

4. If the enforcer has evidence that the trader is failing to comply with an order which had come into effect, it should have the power to apply to the judicial body for a sanction to be imposed against the trader. This sanction should be a fine, or a ban from carrying on a trade or trades as principal for a given period, as determined by the judicial body.

5. Failure to comply with an order of the judicial body imposing a ban or carrying on a trade or trades should be a criminal offence punishable by a fine or imprisonment. Prosecutions should be brought by the enforcer.

6. The proposed powers should be enforceable by trading standards authorities and the Director General.

7. A new basis has to be established to declare a practice unfair (even if it does not involve breaches of civil or criminal law) if it meets a statutory test of unfairness (eg gives rise to consumer detriment, exploits an imbalance in market power in the trader's favour to the disadvantage of the consumer and shows a lack of good faith).

8. The independent judicial body could be a local magistrates court or specially constituted 'Fair Trading Tribunal'. If a specialist tribunal is created, it might also consider appeals against adjudications under the functions of the Director General under the Consumer Credit Act 1974 and the Estate Agents Act 1979, which are currently heard by the Secretary of State.

Other recommendations
Mr Bridgeman also seeks the following additional powers for the Director General of Fair Trading and local authority trading standards departments:

(i) to be able to require a person, by order, to furnish specified information or documents (unless protected by legal professional privilege);
(ii) to be able freely to use for all enforcement purposes information made available;
(iii) to be able to issue an order to an accessory where the course of conduct has been carried on with the consent or connivance of the accessory or is attributable to his neglect.

Finally, the Director General proposes that 'controlling interest' and 'associate' should be redefined in the Fair Trading Act to achieve consistency with the Consumer Credit Act.

The OFT Report: *Selling Second-Hand Cars*, October 1997, repeats the recommendation of reform of Part III assurances in paras 2.19–2.29 as a means of dealing with problem car dealers.

QUESTIONS

1. What would be the advantages and disadvantages of pursuing the 1990 Office of Fair Trading proposals regarding Part III assurances? If adopted, would consumers receive appreciable benefits?
2. How do the 1997 proposals compare with the 1990 proposals in terms of the protection offered to consumers?
3. In view of the appreciable scaling down of proposed new measures from the original ideas of the mid 1980s, has the balance now swung too far in favour of business and away from the consumer?
4. Which of the representations in para 5.19, above, are covered by the Trade Descriptions Act 1968, or elsewhere?

SOME COMPARATIVE PROVISIONS

If English law were to adopt a broadly based provision controlling unfair trading practices a number of models would be available for possible adoption. These are comprehensively discussed in an important article from which the following extract is taken.

'Unfair Trade Practices Legislation: Symbolism and Substance in Consumer Protection' Belobaba (1977), 15 Osgoode Hall Law Journal 327, 345

2. THE PROHIBITED PRACTICES

An important feature of any comprehensive consumer trade practices enactment will be the statutory design of the prohibition provisions. The legislative draftsman has essentially three choices. He may choose to provide simply a general prohibition against all deceptive, misleading, or unconscionable conduct in consumer transactions. This is the approach taken in the *Federal Trade Commission Act*[1] which provides, inter alia, that 'unfair or deceptive acts or practices in commerce are declared unlawful'.[2] While this blanket prohibition is definitionally capable of protecting the consumer against all eventualities, its open-textured quality promotes needless uncertainty and excessive litigation.[3] A trade practices enactment that is fair to suppliers as well as consumers requires a greater degree of precision.

This concern for specificity may persuade the legislative draftsman to adopt the UK *Trade Descriptions Act*[4] approach, which provides an exhaustive listing of the specific practices that are proscribed by the legislation. Unlike the general prohibition technique, the exhaustive specification method cannot be criticized for lack of clarity. The problem here is one of inevitable under-inclusion. The listing of prohibited practices will invariably fall short of including every conceivable and innovative trade practice abuse.

'It is impossible to frame definitions which embrace all unfair practices. There is no limit to human inventiveness in this field. Even if all known unfair practices were specifically defined and prohibited, it would be at once necessary to begin all over again. If [a legislature] were to adopt this method of definition, it would undertake an endless task.'[5]

The third approach available to the draftsman is one that combines a general prohibition against unfair practices with a specific listing. This specific itemization of prohibited acts or practices does not limit the generality of the prohibition. This third approach seems to be the most appropriate for the effective regulation of consumer trade practices. The non-exhaustive, 'shopping list' coupled with a general prohibition provides an optimal combination of specificity and flexibility.

This third alternative was adopted by each of the provinces that have enacted consumer trade practice legislation. Noticeably influenced by the *Uniform Consumer Sales Practices Act*, . . . each of the four provincial enactments under consideration utilizes both the general prohibition and the 'shopping list' of unfair practices.

(a) The General Prohibition
The Ontario Act provides the clearest example of an open-textured general prohibition: '[n]o person shall engage in an unfair practice.'[6] Another provision proceeds to itemize those practices that are deemed to be unfair practices, one sub-part being devoted to 'false, misleading or deceptive consumer representations'[7] and the other to 'unconscionable consumer representations.'[8] The inter-relationship of the general proscription and the 'shopping list' of itemized prohibitions is somewhat more complex in the BC, Alberta, and Saskatchewan enactments. In the BC and Saskatchewan legislation there exists a 'double-barrelled' general prohibition, one provision providing an open-ended proscription of deceiving or misleading acts or practices,[9] and another provision providing similar generality with respect to 'unconscionable acts or practices.'[10] The only province that lacks an open-ended prohibition of unconscionable acts or practices is Alberta. The Alberta legislation does, however, prohibit any representation or conduct that has the effect 'or might reasonably have the effect' of deceiving or misleading any consumer.[11]

(b) The Deceptive Practices Shopping List
Why would a provincial legislative draftsman prefer to itemize illustrations of the acts or practices that are deemed to be deceptive or misleading under one heading and those that are suggested as unconscionable acts or practices under another? An ordinary consumer would not really care how the draftsman has characterised the unfair practice. His only concern would be effective redress. Indeed, one might be hard pressed to articulate any meaningful definitional distinction between the so-called 'deceptive or misleading acts or practices' and the 'unconscionable' ones. Lawyers have tended to explain this dichotomy by reference to the duality of

law and equity and the resulting division of responsibility for deception and unconscionability
. . . While a single listing of the deemed prohibitions may be more logical, the provincial enactments have retained the traditional distinction in drafting the 'shopping lists'.

Each of the provincial trade practices enactments has a fairly comprehensive listing of the
deceptive or misleading acts or practices that are deemed to be unfair practices: sixteen specifications in the BC Act, fourteen in the Ontario Act, and twenty-one in the Alberta and
Saskatchewan enactments.

[1] 15 USC, s 45(a) (1) (1970).
[2] Ibid.
[3] The FTC, however, has extensive rule-making powers which enable the agency to inject
some precision into the open-textured prohibitions.
[4] UK 1968, c 29.
[5] *Federal Trade Commission v The Sperry and Hutchinson Company* (1914), 405 US 233, per
White J at 240, quoting from HR Rep No 1142. 63d Cong 2d Sess 18–19.
[6] Ontario Act, s 3(1).
[7] Ibid, s 2(a).
[8] Ibid, s 2(b).
[9] BC Act, s 2(1); Saskatchewan Act, s 3(1).
[10] BC Act, s 3(3); Saskatchewan Act, s 4(1).
[11] Alberta Act, s 4(1)(d).

Broad provisions are also to be found in Australian legislation:

Trade Practices Act 1974 (Australia)

PART V—CONSUMER PROTECTION

Division I—Unfair Practices
52. (1) A corporation shall not, in trade or commerce, engage in conduct that is misleading or
deceptive or is likely to mislead or deceive.
(2) Nothing in the succeeding provisions of this Division shall be taken as limiting by implication the generality of sub-section (1).

NOTES

1. Sections 53 to 64 make provision for more specific practices including bait
   advertising (s 56), referral selling (s 57), coercion at place of residence (s 60)
   and pyramid selling (s 61).
2. For a detailed discussion of the operation of s 52 see Harland 'The Statutory
   Prohibition of Misleading or Deceptive Conduct in Australia and Its Impact
   on the Law of Contract' (1995) 111 LQR 100; Skapinker and Carter, 'Breach
   of Contract and Misleading or Deceptive Conduct in Australia' (1997) 113
   LQR 294.

CHAPTER 12

Aspects of the general criminal law relating to trading standards including consumer safety

GENERAL CRIMINAL LAW RELATING TO TRADING STANDARDS

INTRODUCTION

Control of fraudulent or dangerous practices by producers has been exercised by the criminal law of England and Wales over many centuries. It is, for instance, possible to trace the history of hallmarking legislation back to the 14th century. The motivation for this public control of trading practices was originally probably mixed. The consumer has not, until very recent times, had an effective voice as such in government. So although it would be an over-simplification to say that the consumer interest was traditionally never considered, it is probably justifiable to say that the main motivation for encouraging government to exercise control over the fraudulent trader came from competitors whose business was threatened.

So far as the consumer is concerned, the justification for the umbrella of criminal protection which is currently enjoyed is that it is not usually possible, simply by inspection of an article, to tell whether it is as described or, even if it is so, whether it is dangerous to consume or use. The classic illustrations of this point arise in the fields of hallmarking and the sale of food. In the case of hallmarking the fundamental need for protection arises because gold, silver and platinum are too soft to be of much practical use and normally need to be alloyed with other metals. This lowers the intrinsic value of the article, and it is therefore essential to establish by chemical analysis what proportion the precious metal content bears to the whole. In the case of food, the risk of toxicity arises either from deliberate adulteration by the manufacturer or seller or from the use of dangerous ingredients.

It must not be assumed that the consumer is necessarily without a civil remedy if injured, physically or financially, by purchasing an article where the sale or supply contravenes the criminal law. Civil compensation can be direct through a compensation order made by the court (see above, pp 429–33) or indirect. The indirect route will involve bringing a civil action in the County Court or the High Court either for breach of contract, or for a tort such as negligence which has incidentally been committed or, where appropriate, for breach of statutory duty. With regard to the tort of breach of statutory duty some statutes, notably the

Consumer Protection Act 1987 (below, p 586), give a specific civil right of action where a person is affected by certain contraventions of the Act or regulations made thereunder. In all cases, where a criminal conviction has previously been obtained, evidence of the conviction may be pleaded in a civil case to prove that the defendant committed the offence: see s 11 of the Civil Evidence Act 1968.

DE-CRIMINALISING REGULATORY OFFENCES

There has been increasing criticism over recent years of the volume of regulatory criminal offences and many of these lie in the area of trading standards. A glance at the six volume loose-leaf encyclopaedia entitled *Butterworths Law of Food and Drugs*, and at the numerous regulations made under the Food Safety Act 1990, the European Communities Act 1972 or allied statutes (and bearing in mind that most of these regulations impose criminal offences) emphasises graphically the extent of the problem. The objection to 'creating crimes like confetti' is well expressed by Lord Devlin in 'Morals and Quasi-Criminal Law and the Law of Tort' (Holdsworth Club Presidential Address, 17 March 1961) (quoted Borrie *The Development of Consumer Law and Policy—Bold Spirits and Timorous Souls*, p 55). Lord Devlin considered that the ordinary man still thinks of crime as conduct that is disgraceful or morally wrong. He adds:

But he cannot be expected to go on doing so for ever if the law jumbles morals and sanitary reg-ulations together and teaches him to have no more respect for the Ten Commandments than for the woodworking regulations. Meanwhile . . . it may cause him unnecessary distress if for some petty offence which he may not even himself have committed he is classed among crimi-nals and if in the machinery of the law he is processed as if he were one.

Approaching the matter from a different angle, Professor Atiyah has also warned that consumer protection can often be bought only at a cost which is passed on to those who purchase the goods or services in question: see 'Consumer Protection: Time to Take Stock' [1979] Liverpool Law Review, p 20.

David Tench in his book *Towards a Middle System of Law* (Consumers Association, 1981) proposed that regulatory offences should be no longer subject to criminal penalties but instead should be termed infringements or contraven-tions. These would attract civil penalties, a change which would supposedly remove from a person, found to have committed an infringement, the stigma of an infraction of the criminal law. (It is to be queried whether someone duly 'con-victed' of a 'penalty' and 'fined' a large sum of money will be too concerned whether the infraction is termed criminal or not). A similar idea was floated by Justice in its report entitled 'Breaking the Rules', the report estimating that there are over 7,000 offences within this category. One Director General of Fair Trading also gave cautious encouragement to it, albeit on a selective basis (see Borrie, *The Development of Consumer Law and Policy*, ch 3). Sir Gordon (now Lord) Borrie stated (op cit. p 58):

It is my own view that a wider *range* of powers than exist at present, to be exercised either directly by the local authority (subject to appeal to the courts) or exercised by application to the courts, eg for an order to stop illegal trading or to close down a shop, would be a useful addition to the enforcement armoury.

During the 1980s and 1990s the Conservative government was concerned to remove regulatory burdens from businesses and launched a Deregulation Initiative. The incoming Labour government has placed the emphasis on 'better' regulation, rather than 'deregulation'. The Chancellor of the Duchy of Lancaster, David Clark, announced, in July 1997, that the government would concentrate on 'ensuring that regulations are necessary, fair to all parties, properly costed, practical to enforce and straightforward to comply with.' A Better Regulation Task Force was established, in September 1997, and developments are awaited.

MENS REA

As is explained in some detail in ch 15 on statutory defences, the usual pattern of trading standards statutes is to create offences of strict liability subject only to statutory defences which will, typically, allow the defendant to plead reasonable precautions and due diligence. There are a few significant divergences from this pattern. For instance, s 14 of the Trade Descriptions Act 1968 (see below, p 642) relating to false or misleading statements as to services, etc requires a defendant to make a statement 'which he *knows* to be false' or '*recklessly* to make a statement which is false'. But the question may be asked—what is the position where a statute lays down an offence which involves no requirement of knowledge or recklessness, but does not either specifically directly or indirectly indicate that the offence is an absolute one? An example occurs in s 1(1) of the Hallmarking Act 1973, and the effect of this type of provision was considered in depth by the Divisional Court in the following case.

Chilvers v Rayner [1984] 1 All ER 843, [1984] 1 WLR 328, Queen's Bench Division

Robert Goff LJ. There is before the court an appeal by way of case stated from a decision of justices sitting at Guildford, under which they found the appellant guilty of an offence contrary to the Hallmarking Act 1973.

An information had been preferred against the appellant by the respondent, a trading standards officer, that he, in the course of trade as a dealer in jewellery and precious metals, supplied to Pia Theresia Hauselmann an unhallmarked article, namely an 18 carat Russian gold bangle, to which the description 'gold' was applied, contrary to s 1(1)(b) of the Hallmarking Act 1973. That charge was found to be proved and the appellant was fined £200 and ordered to pay a sum towards the prosecution costs. The case raises the question whether the offence created by s 1(1)(b) of the 1973 Act is an absolute offence.

The facts of the case, as found by the justices, are as follows. On 12 January 1982 Mrs Hauselmann purchased a Russian bangle from Orlando Jewellers, 1 Sydenham Road, Guildford, of which the appellant was the proprietor. The bangle was accurately described as 18 carat gold. It was offered at £671.77; that price was reduced by 40% as being part of a 'sale', and was further reduced to £383 in consideration of payment of £300 in cash and £63 by credit card. The appellant had purchased the bangle in 1979 from Celine Collection, with whom he had traded for some time, for £160. The bangle bore some markings, but was not hallmarked. The assay office to which the appellant sent items for hallmarking had not received this bangle to hallmark. On these facts, the justices concluded that the appellant had supplied an unhallmarked article to which the description 'gold' was applied.

Before the justices, the appellant contended that the prosecution had not established the essential ingredient of mens rea, whereupon the prosecution contended that the section did not require any proof of mental state on the part of the appellant. The justices formed the opinion that it was not necessary for the prosecution to prove mens rea and so found the case proved.

The question posed by the justices for the opinion of the court is:

'Whether the offence created by s 1(1)(b) of the Hallmarking Act 1973 is an absolute offence so that the prosecution does not have to prove mens rea.'

I turn next to the Hallmarking Act 1973. Section 1(1) provides as follows:

'Subject to the provisions of this Act, any person who, in the course of a trade or business—(a) applies to an unhallmarked article a description indicating that it is wholly or partly made of gold, silver or platinum, or (b) supplies, or offers to supply, an unhallmarked article to which such a description is applied, shall be guilty of an offence.'

By sub-s (2) it is provided that sub-s (1) shall not apply to a description which is permitted by Pt I of Sch 1 to the Act and, by sub-s (3) it is provided that sub-s (1) shall not apply to an article within Pt II of Sch 1. Part I of Sch 1 sets out a list of permissible descriptions, eg 'plated' or 'rolled' gold. Part II sets out a list of exempted articles, such as, for example, '1. An article which is intended for despatch to a destination outside the United Kingdom'.

It is striking that s 1(1) of the 1973 Act follows very closely the wording of s 1(1) of the Trade Descriptions Act 1968, to which indeed reference is made in other subsections of s 1 of the 1973 Act. Section 1(1) of the Trade Descriptions Act 1968 has been held to create an offence of absolute liability, subject to the statutory defences, in particular the defence set out in s 24 of the Act: see *Clode v Barnes* [1974] 1 All ER 1166, [1974] 1 WLR 544 and *Macnab v Alexanders of Greenock Ltd* 1971 SLT 121.

There is no equivalent of s 24 in the Hallmarking Act 1973. However, there are certain provisions of that Act creating other offences which expressly require knowledge on the part of the accused as an ingredient of the offence. Thus, s 4(4) provides that a person who knowingly makes a false statement in furnishing any information to an assay office, for the purposes of s 4(2) (ie for the purposes of showing the assay office to its satisfaction that the relevant article was made in the United Kingdom, with a view to its being hallmarked) shall be guilty of an offence.

Section 6, which is concerned with counterfeiting, creates a number of offences, each of which requires a specified intent on the part of the accused, or knowledge or belief by him, that the relevant object is counterfeit. It is of particular interest that s 6(1)(c) provides that any person who 'utters any counterfeit of a die or any article bearing a counterfeit of a mark . . . shall be guilty of an offence . . .' and that s 6(3) provides:

'For the purposes of subsection (1) . . . . a person utters any counterfeit die or article bearing a counterfeit of a mark if, knowing or believing the die or mark, as the case may be, to be a counterfeit, he supplies, offers to supply, or delivers the die or article.'

Here, the actus reus is very similar to that prohibited by s 1(1)(b). Yet here, unlike s 1(1)(b), knowledge or belief on the part of the accused that the die or mark is counterfeit is expressly made an ingredient of that offence.

Section 7(6) is also striking. It provides as follows:

'It shall be an offence for any person knowingly or any dealer to supply or offer to supply any article bearing any mark of the character of a hallmark and which under subsection (1) of this section may, if the article is in the possession of an assay office, be cancelled, obliterated or defaced, unless the article has been first submitted to an assay office to enable them at their discretion so to cancel, obliterate or deface that mark.'

In this subsection a distinction is therefore drawn between a dealer and other persons and whereas, in the case of other persons, knowledge on their part is an ingredient of the offence created by the subsection, no knowledge is required where the accused is 'a dealer'.

Having regard to these provisions of the Act, it came as no surprise that counsel for the appellant did not seek to argue that mens rea in the form of knowledge of the facts rendering the act an offence under s 1(1) was an ingredient of such an offence. Founding his argument on the speech of Lord Diplock in *Sweet v Parsley* [1969] 1 All ER 347 at 361–2, [1970] AC 132 at 163, he submitted that what had to be proved was the absence of belief, held honestly and on reasonable grounds, that the article was hallmarked. In his submission, it was not enough for the accused to escape conviction that he should have believed the article was hallmarked: he must have believed it to be so on reasonable grounds. So, he submitted, if there was absence of the relevant knowledge on the part of the accused, only if that absence of knowledge was attributable to his carelessness would he be convicted. . . .

In *Warner v Metropolitan Police Comr* [1968] 2 All ER 356 at 360, [1969] 2 AC 256 at 271–272 Lord Reid referred to the 'long line of cases in which it has been held with regard to less serious offences that absence of mens rea was no defence'. He continued:

'Typical examples are offences under public health, licensing and industrial legislation. If a person sets up as say a butcher, a publican, or a manufacturer and exposes unsound meat for sale, or sells drink to a drunk man or certain parts of his factory are unsafe, it is no defence that he could not by the exercise of reasonable care have known or discovered that the meat was unsound, or that the man was drunk or that his premises were unsafe. He must take the risk and when it is found that the statutory prohibition or requirement has been infringed he must pay the penalty. This may well seem unjust, but it is a comparatively minor injustice, and there is good reason for it as affording some protection to his customers or servants or to the public at large, Although this man might be able to show that he did his best, a more skilled or diligent man in his position might have done better, and when we are dealing with minor penalties which do not involve the disgrace of criminality it may be in the public interest to have a hard and fast rule. Strictly speaking there ought perhaps to be a defence that the defect was truly latent so that no one could have discovered it. But the law has not developed in that way, and one can see the difficulty if such a defence were allowed in a summary prosecution. These are only quasi-criminal offences and it does not really offend the ordinary man's sense of justice that moral guilt is not of the essence of the offences.'

Again, in *Sweet v Parsley* [1969] 1 All ER 347 at 362, [1970] AC 132 at 163, immediately after the very passage on which counsel for the appellant relied in support of his submission (where Lord Diplock set out the principle in *R v Tolson* (1889) 23 QBD 168, [1886–90] All ER Rep 26), Lord Diplock said:

'Where penal provisions are of general application to the conduct of ordinary citizens in the course of their everyday life the presumption is that the standard of care required of them in informing themselves of facts which would make their conduct unlawful, is that of the familiar common law duty of care. But where the subject matter of a statute is the regulation of a particular activity involving potential danger to public health, safety or morals, in which citizens have a choice whether they participate or not, the court may feel driven to infer an intention of Parliament to impose, by penal sanctions, a higher duty of care on those who choose to participate and to place on them an obligation to take whatever measures may be necessary to prevent the prohibited act, without regard to those considerations of cost or business practicability which play a part in the determination of what would be required of them in order to fulfil the ordinary common law duty of care. But such an inference is not lightly to be drawn, nor is there any room for it unless there is something that the person on whom the obligation is imposed can do directly or indirectly, by supervision or inspection, by improvement of his business methods or by exhorting those whom he may be expected to influence or control, which will promote observance of the obligation (see *Lim Chin Aik v R* [1963] 1 All ER 223 at 228, [1963] AC 160 at 174).'

In my judgment, the offence created by s 1(1) of the 1973 Act falls within the category of offences so described by Lord Reid and Lord Diplock. It is not a truly criminal offence, but an offence of a quasi-criminal character. True, an offence relating to hallmarking does not fall precisely within the description 'offences under public health, licensing and industrial legislation', or within the description 'involving danger to public health, safety or morals'. But I do not understand either Lord Reid or Lord Diplock to have been giving a complete list of the relevant offences, which must, in my judgment, having regard to the authorities, extend to include such matters as trade descriptions, although in such cases the absolute offence is of course subject to any statutory defences set out in the relevant Act of Parliament. Furthermore, in accordance with the passage in the advice of the Privy Council in *Lim Chin Aik v R*, referred to by Lord Diplock in *Sweet v Parsley*, it cannot be said that there is nothing which a person on whom the relevant obligations under the 1973 Act are imposed can do, in any of the manners indicated by Lord Diplock, which will promote the observance of the obligation.

For these reasons, I am satisfied that the offence under s 1(1) of the 1973 Act is, like the offence created by s 1(1) of the Trade Descriptions Act 1968, an absolute offence. I find myself in agreement with the opinion expressed by the justices in the case stated and I would answer the question posed for our decision in the affirmative and dismiss the appeal.

Forbes J. I agree.

Appeal dismissed.

QUESTIONS

Is the suggested distinction between offences categorised by the courts as 'truly criminal' and those as 'quasi-criminal' a real one? Is it, for instance, realistic to describe the conduct of a car dealer who deliberately winds back the odometer of a car which he then resells, as 'quasi-criminal' (since the prosecution is likely to be under the Trade Descriptions Act)? If not, how could Parliament more clearly demonstrate its intention with regard to criminal legislation to the courts? (See also *Wings Ltd v Ellis* [1984] 3 All ER 577 at 589, per Lord Scarman, below, p 664).

THE EXTENT OF PROTECTION UNDER THE CRIMINAL LAW

From data produced annually by the Office of Fair Trading it is clear that offences under the Weights and Measures Act 1985, the Trade Descriptions Act 1968 and the Food Safety Act 1990 give rise to the largest number of reported convictions. The position for 1996/97 is given in the table which follows:

Annual Report of the Director General of Fair Trading 1996, pp 77–82

Convictions in reported cases under consumer legislation

	No	Fines (£)
Consumer Credit Act 1974	60	52,250
Consumer Protection Act 1987		
Part II offences: safety	230	230,930
Part III offences: prices	147	274,549
Estate Agents Act 1979	—	—
Food Safety Act 1990		
Not of nature, substance or quality demanded	94	149,225
Unfit food	100	119,945
Labelling regulations and others	17	26,600
False or misleading description	59	37,510
Improvement notices	12	10,070
Food premises	6	950
Hygiene	98	153,660
Obstruction	2	150
Prohibition orders	1	—
Other offences	148	136,960
Fair Trading Act 1973		
Restrictions on Statements Order	30	17,225
Business Advertisements Disclosure Order	42	15,890
Hallmarking Act 1973	25	12,250
Package Travel Regulations	16	20,650
Property Misdescriptions Act 1991	22	32,450
Road Traffic Act 1972: unroadworthy vehicles	219	101,580
Trade Descriptions Act 1968		
False descriptions of goods (s 1)	1,134	919,446
False statements about services (s 14)	220	159,235
Weights and Measures Acts		
False or unjust equipment	14	3,800
Short weight or measure	53	13,302
Average weight and quantity offences	10	4,060
Packaged goods	24	27,770
Other offences	16	3,907
Other legislation enforced by Trading Standards and Environmental Health Departments . . .	1,544	1,009,779

An idea of the ambit of the main statutes imposing criminal liabilities in trading standards law can be gained from the study of the following Table.

The main criminal statutes affecting consumers

Subject Matter	Legislation
Inaccurate quantities	Weights and Measures Act 1985
Statement of and control of prices	Consumer Protection Act 1987; Mock Auctions Act 1961; Prices Acts 1974, 1975
Food quality and hygiene	Food Act 1984; Food Safety Act 1990
False descriptions	Trade Descriptions Act 1968, Trading Representations (Disabled Persons) Act 1958; Food Safety Act 1990; Property Misdescriptions Act 1991, Copyright, Designs and Patents Act 1988; Trade Marks Act 1994, Package Travel, Package Holidays and Package Tours Regulations 1994
Unsolicited goods and services	Unsolicited Goods and Services Acts 1971 and 1975
Consumer credit	Consumer Credit Act 1974
Consumer safety; Licensing; Labelling of dangerous products	Consumer Protection Act 1987; General Product Safety Regulations 1994; Animal Health Act 1981; Petroleum (Consolidation) Act 1928; Explosives Acts 1875 and 1923; Poisons Act 1972; Medicines Act 1968; Farm and Garden Chemicals Act 1967
Road safety	Road Traffic Act 1988
Insurance policy holders	Insurance Companies Act 1982; Policyholders Protection Act 1975; Financial Services Act 1986
Pressurised selling	Consumer Credit Act 1974, Timeshare Act 1992
Trading stamps	Trading Stamps Act 1964
Hallmarking of precious metal	Hallmarking Act 1973
Handling stolen goods/obtaining money by deception	Theft Act 1968 (ss 22,15)

ENFORCEMENT

The responsibility for the enforcement of trading standards offences very largely rests on the shoulders of local authorities. Local authorities generally act through their trading standards officers. Although in some quarters regarded as 'minor Town Hall officials', this is in fact far from the case. Trading standards officers are responsible for the enforcement of a forbidding mass of primary and subsidiary legislation, some of it of great technical complexity. They are normally graduates and are required to pass statutory examinations which test not only knowledge of law in depth but also materials technology, statistics, economics and other areas of knowledge germane to the enforcement of Trading Standards. Much of their work involves advising or warning traders, but if a prosecution is to be brought a trading standards officer is likely to take the necessary initiative. For an interesting discussion of attitudes and policies of Trading Standards Departments, see Cranston, *Regulating Business: Law and Consumer Agencies* (1979). See also *Smedleys Ltd v Breed* [1974] 2 All ER 21; *Wings Ltd v Ellis* [1984] 3 All ER 577, below, p 662.

In some cases, for instance weights and measures, the public is not permitted to bring a prosecution. Such a prosecution must be brought by or on behalf of a weights and measures authority or by a chief officer of police (Weights and Measures Act 1985, s 83). In other cases the public theoretically has a right of private prosecution (eg food and drugs, trade descriptions), but in practice it is usually more sensible for the consumer to make a report to his local Trading Standards Department and leave the expense of the prosecution to be handled by this arm of the local authority. In certain cases, eg most offences under the Trade Descriptions Act 1968 and offences under Regulations made under Part II of the Fair Trading Act 1973, the local weights and measures authority is under a duty to give to the Director General of Fair Trading notice of intended proceedings together with the summary of the facts on which the charges are to be founded. Proceedings must then be postponed until either 28 days have elapsed since the giving of that notice, or the Director has notified the authority that he has received the notice and the summary of the facts (Fair Trading Act 1973, s 130).

An example of the terms under which a statute makes its criminal enforcement the responsibility of a local authority is provided by the Fair Trading Act 1973. The extract which follows relates to enforcement of the Orders made under Part II of that Act, for example the Business Advertisements (Disclosure) Order 1977 (see p 543). Sections 27–32 are typical of the powers conferred on officers by legislation of this sort. The relevant sections run as follows:

Fair Trading Act 1973

ENFORCEMENT OF ORDERS

27. Enforcing authorities
(1) It shall be the duty of every local weights and measures authority to enforce within their area the provisions of any order made under section 22 of this Act; . . .
(2) Nothing in subsection (1) shall be taken as authorising a local weights and measures authority in Scotland to institute proceedings for an offence.

28. Power to make test purchases
A local weights and measures authority may make, or may authorise any of their officers to make on their behalf, such purchases of goods, and may authorise any of their officers to obtain such services, as may be expedient for the purpose of determining whether or not the provisions of any order made under section 22 of this Act are being complied with.

29. Power to enter premises and inspect and seize goods and documents

(1) A duly authorised officer of a local weights and measures authority, or a person duly authorised in writing by the Secretary of State, may at all reasonable hours, and on production, if required, of his credentials, exercise the following powers, that is to say—

    (a) he may, for the purpose of ascertaining whether any offence under section 23 of this Act has been committed, inspect any goods and enter any premises other than premises used only as a dwelling;

    (b) if he has reasonable cause to suspect that an offence under that section has been committed, he may, for the purpose of ascertaining whether it has been committed, require any person carrying on a business or employed in connection with a business to produce any books or documents relating to the business and may take copies of, or of any entry in, any such book or document;

    (c) if he has reasonable cause to believe that such an offence has been committed, he may seize and detain any goods for the purpose of ascertaining, by testing or otherwise, whether the offence has been committed;

    (d) he may seize and detain any goods or documents which he has reason to believe may be required as evidence in proceedings for such an offence;

    (e) he may, for the purpose of exercising his powers under this subsection seize goods, but only if and to the extent that it is reasonably necessary in order to secure that the provisions of an order made under section 22 of this Act are duly observed, require any person having authority to do so to break open any container or open any vending machine and, if that person does not comply with the requirement, he may do so himself.

(2) A person seizing any goods or documents in the exercise of his powers under this section shall inform the person from whom they are seized and, in the case of goods seized from a vending machine, the person whose name and address are stated on the machine as being the proprietor's or, if no name and address are so stated, the occupier of the premises on which the machine stands or to which it is affixed.

(3) If a justice of the peace, on sworn information in writing—

    (a) is satisfied that there is reasonable ground to believe either—

        (i) that any goods, books or documents which a person has power under this section to inspect are on any premises and that their inspection is likely to disclose evidence of the commission of an offence under section 23 of this Act, or

        (ii) that any offence under section 23 has been, is being or is about to be committed on any premises, and

    (b) is also satisfied either—

        (i) that admission to the premises has been or is likely to be refused and that notice of intention to apply for a warrant under this subsection has been given to the occupier, or

        (ii) that an application for admission, or the giving of such a notice, would defeat the object of the entry or that the premises are unoccupied or that the occupier is temporarily absent, and it might defeat the object of the entry to await his return,

the justice may by warrant under his hand, which shall continue in force for a period of one month, authorise any such officer or other person as is mentioned in subsection (1) of this section to enter the premises, if need be by force.

In the application of this subsection to Scotland, 'justice of the peace' shall be construed as including a sheriff and a magistrate.

(4) A person entering any premises by virtue of this section may take with him such other persons and such equipment as may appear to him necessary; and on leaving any premises which he has entered by virtue of a warrant under subsection (3) of this section he shall, if the premises are unoccupied or the occupier is temporarily absent, leave them as effectively secured against trespassers as he found them.

(5) Nothing in this section shall be taken to compel the production by a barrister, advocate or

solicitor of a document containing a privileged communication made by or to him in that capacity or to authorise the taking of possession of any such document which is in his possession.

30. Offences in connection with exercise of powers under s 29

(1) Subject to subsection (6) of this section, any person who—

    (a) wilfully obstructs any such officer or person as is mentioned in subsection (1) of section 29 of this Act acting in the exercise of any powers conferred on him by or under that section, or

    (b) wilfully fails to comply with any requirement properly made to him by such an officer or person under that section, or

    (c) without reasonable cause fails to give such an officer or person so acting any other assistance or information which he may reasonably require of him for the purpose of the performance of his functions under this Part of this Act,

shall be guilty of an offence.

(2) If any person, in giving any such information as is mentioned in subsection (1)(c) of this section, makes any statement which he knows to be false, he shall be guilty of an offence.

(3) If any person discloses to any other person—

    (a) any information with respect to any manufacturing process or trade secret obtained by him in premises which he has entered by virtue of section 29 of this Act, or

    (b) any information obtained by him under that section or by virtue of subsection (1) of this section,

he shall, unless the disclosure was made in the performance of his duty, be guilty of an offence.

(4) If any person who is neither a duly authorised officer of a weights and measures authority nor a person duly authorised in that behalf by the Secretary of State purports to act as such under section 29 of this Act or under this section, he shall be guilty of an offence.

(5) Any person guilty of an offence under subsection (1) of this section shall be liable on summary conviction to a fine not exceeding [level 3 on the standard scale], and any person guilty of an offence under subsection (2), subsection (3) or subsection (4) of this section shall be liable—

    (a) on summary conviction, to a fine not exceeding [the prescribed sum];

    (b) on conviction on indictment, to a fine or to imprisonment for a term not exceeding two years or to both.

(6) Nothing in this section shall be construed as requiring a person to answer any question or give any information if to do so might incriminate that person or (where that person is married) the husband or wife of that person.

31. Notice of test

Where any goods seized or purchased by a person in pursuance of this Part of this Act are submitted to a test, then—

    (a) if the goods were seized, he shall inform any such person as is mentioned in section 29 (2) of this Act of the result of the test;

    (b) if the goods were purchased and the test leads to the institution of proceedings for an offence under section 23 of this Act, he shall inform the person from whom the goods were purchased, or, in the case of goods sold through a vending machine, the person mentioned in relation to such goods in section 29(2) of this Act, of the result of the test;

and where, as a result of the test, proceedings for an offence under section 23 of this Act are instituted against any person, he shall allow that person to have the goods tested on his behalf if it is reasonably practicable to do so.

32. Compensation for loss in respect of goods seized under s 29

(1) Where in the exercise of his powers under section 29 of this Act a person seizes and detains any goods, and their owner suffers loss by reason of their being seized or by reason that the goods during the detention, are lost or damaged or deteriorate, unless the owner is convicted of

an offence under section 23 of this Act committed in relation to the goods, the appropriate
authority shall be liable to compensate him for the loss so suffered.
(2) Any disputed question as to the right to or the amount of any compensation payable under
this section shall be determined by arbitration and, in Scotland, by a single arbiter appointed,
failing agreement between the parties, by the sheriff.
(3) In this section 'the appropriate authority'—
    (a) in relation to goods seized by an officer of a local weights and measures authority, means
        that authority and
    (b) in any other case, means the Secretary of State.

INJUNCTIONS IN AID OF THE CRIMINAL LAW

An incidental side-effect of inflation is that the penalties imposed by the criminal
law do not always keep pace with the profits which may be derived from breaking
it. The question then arises as to whether it should be permissible to allow the
activity to be restrained in some other, more effective, way. The following case is
in point. (It is to be noted that the law on Sunday Trading has since been altered
by the Sunday Trading Act 1994.)

Stoke-on-Trent City Council v B & Q (Retail) Ltd [1984] 2 All ER 332, [1984] AC 754, House of Lords

Lord Templeman. My Lords, the appellants, B & Q (Retail) Ltd, challenge the right of the
respondents, Stoke-on-Trent City Council, to bring proceedings to restrain the appellants from
trading on Sundays from the appellants' shops in Stoke-on-Trent in breach of the Shops Act
1950.
    Section 47 of the 1950 Act provides that, save for certain authorised transactions, every shop
in England and Wales shall 'be closed for the service of customers on Sunday.' By s 71(1):

'It shall be the duty of every local authority to enforce within their district the provisions of this
Act . . . and for that purpose to institute and to carry on such proceedings in respect of contraventions of the said provisions . . . as may be necessary to secure observance thereof.'

    Section 71(2) directs every local authority to appoint inspectors for the purposes of the Act
and provides:

'. . . An inspector may, if so authorised by the local authority, institute and carry on any proceedings under this Act on behalf of the authority.'

    I agree with the observations of my noble and learned friend Lord Roskill concerning the
duty of the local authority under s 71 of the Act.
    The appellants' shops at Waterloo Road, Burslem and Leek Road, Hanley are within the dis-
trict of the council. The appellants' shops traded in prohibited articles on Sunday 11 April
1982, and after a warning from a council representative, again on 18 April. The appellants were
warned of legal proceedings on 19 April and traded in prohibited articles on 25 April.
    By s 59 of the 1950 Act the occupier of a shop which trades on Sundays in breach of the 1950
Act was made liable to a fine of £5 for a first offence and £20 in the case of a second or subsequent offence. By s 31 of the Criminal Justice Act 1972 the penalties were increased to £50 and
£200 respectively and those were the maximum penalties for offences up to 11 April 1983. By
ss 35 to 48 of the Criminal Justice Act 1982 from 11 April 1983 an occupier of a shop trading

in breach of the 1950 Act is liable to a maximum fine of £500 for any offence and the Home Secretary can by order, subject to a negative resolution by Parliament, increase the maximum penalty to an extent justified by any change in the value of money since July 1977.

In addition to initiating but not completing criminal proceedings which could have resulted in the imposition on the appellants of a fine of £50 for the first offence and £200 for every subsequent offence, the council on 5 May 1982 issued a writ in the Chancery Division of the High Court for an injunction to restrain the appellants from continuing to trade in breach of the 1950 Act. On 25 June 1982 Whitford J in those proceedings granted an interlocutory injunction restraining the appellants until trial of the action or further order from trading in breach of the 1950 Act. Against that order the appellants appealed unsuccessfully to the Court of Appeal (see [1983] 2 All ER 787, [1984] Ch 1) and now appeal to your Lordships' House.

. . .

. . . Where the local authority seeks an injunction, the court will consider whether the power was rightly exercised and whether in all the circumstances at the date the application for an injunction is considered by the court, the equitable and discretionary remedy of an injunction should be granted.

In the present case, when the council decided to institute proceedings and when Whitford J decided to grant an interlocutory injunction, the appellants had committed offences under the Shops Act 1950. The council invoked the assistance of the civil court in aid of the criminal law in order to ensure that the appellants did not commit further offences under the 1950 Act. The right to invoke the assistance of the civil court in aid of the criminal law is a comparatively modern development. Where Parliament imposes a penalty for an offence, Parliament must consider the penalty is adequate and Parliament can increase the penalty if it proves to be inadequate. It follows that a local authority should be reluctant to seek and the court should be reluctant to grant an injunction which if disobeyed may involve the infringer in sanctions far more onerous than the penalty imposed for the offence. In *Gouriet v Union of Post Office Workers* [1977] 3 All ER 70 at 83, [1978] AC 435 at 81 Lord Wilberforce said that the right to invoke the assistance of civil courts in aid of the criminal law is 'an exceptional power confined, in practice, to cases where an offence is frequently repeated in disregard of a, usually, inadequate penalty . . . or to cases of emergency . . . ' In my view there must certainly be something more than infringement before the assistance of civil proceedings can be invoked and accorded for the protection or promotion of the interests of the inhabitants of the area. In the present case the council were concerned with what appeared to be a proliferation of illegal Sunday trading. The council was by s 71 of the 1950 Act charged with the statutory duty of ensuring compliance with the 1950 Act. The council received letters from traders complaining of infringements of the Sunday trading legislation by other shops and intimating that the complainants would themselves feel obliged to open on Sundays in order to preserve their trade unless the 1950 Act was generally observed. The council could not treat some traders differently from others. The council wrote to warn infringing traders some of whom ceased to trade on Sundays as a result of the warnings. In one case where an ignored warning was followed by the issue of a writ the proceedings resulted in an undertaking to desist. In these circumstances there was ample justification for the council to take the view that it was expedient in the general interests of the inhabitants to take such steps as were necessary to ensure compliance by the appellants with the laws of Sunday trading.

It was said that the council should not have taken civil proceedings until criminal proceedings had failed to persuade the appellants to obey the law. As a general rule a local authority should try the effect of criminal proceedings before seeking the assistance of the civil courts. But the council were entitled to take the view that the appellants would not be deterred by a maximum fine which was substantially less than the profits which could be made from illegal Sunday trading. Delay while this was proved would have encouraged widespread breaches of the law by other traders, resentful of the continued activities of the appellants. The poor trader would be deterred by the threat of a fine; the rich trader would consider breaking the law each Sunday if illegal trading produced profit in excess of the maximum fine and costs. In *Stafford Borough Council v Elkenford Ltd* [1977] 2 All ER 519 at 528, [1977] 1 WLR 324 at 330 Bridge LJ said:

'We have been urged to say that the court will only exercise its discretion to restrain by injunction the commission of offences in breach of statutory prohibitions if the plaintiff authority has first shown that it has exhausted the possibility of restraining those breaches by the exercise of the statutory remedies. Ordinarily no doubt that is a very salutary approach to the question whether or not the court will grant an injunction in the exercise of its discretion, but it is not in my judgment an inflexible rule. The reason why it is ordinarily proper to ask whether the authority seeking the injunction has first exhausted the statutory remedies is because in the ordinary case it is only because those remedies have been invoked and have proved inadequate that one can draw the inference, which is the essential foundation for the exercise of the court's discretion to grant an injunction, that the offender is . . . "deliberately and flagrantly flouting the law".'

In the present case any doubt about the attitude of the appellants has been resolved by their attitude to the proceedings themselves. Whitford J concluded that the appellants were proceeding—

'on the basis that if an interlocutory injunction be not granted now they would be free to trade . . . they hope, if they are successful in staying the grant of an interlocutory injunction, that they are going to be able to continue to trade in defiance of the provisions of s 47 of the Shops Act 1950.'

Immediately on the opening of the appeal of the appellants to your Lordships' House, my noble and learned friend Lord Diplock inquired whether if the injunction were discharged the appellants intended to resume trading in defiance of the provisions of s 47 of the 1950 Act. No answer has been vouchsafed. Whitford J and the Court of Appeal took the view that on the law and the facts an injunction should issue and I would dismiss this appeal.

Lords Diplock, Fraser, Keith and **Roskill** agreed with **Lord Templeman.**

Appeal dismissed.

NOTE

For general discussion see Wade & Forsyth, *Administrative Law* (7th edn, 1994) pp 608–10.

QUESTION

Since the penalties for contempt on breach of an injunction under the Contempt of Court Act 1981 are markedly more severe than those for which Parliament made provision in the Shops Act 1950, is it desirable that these latter penalties should be effectively increased by the use of injunctions in aid of the criminal law?

CONSUMER SAFETY

A considerable number of statutes and regulations are concerned with consumer safety. Many relate to specific types of products, for example food and drugs, medicines, and poisons. Others are of more general application. The Consumer Protection Act 1987 provides the main general framework for protection, together with the General Product Safety Regulations 1994, SI 1994/2328, introduced in response to Council Directive 92/59/EEC on general product safety (OJ No L228, 11.8.92, p 24). There are several different criminal measures which can be used to ensure product safety, each of which will be considered.

SAFETY REGULATIONS

Sections 11 and 12 of the Consumer Protection Act 1987 (and their predecessors in the Consumer Protection Acts 1961–71, the Consumer Safety Act 1978, and the Consumer Safety (Amendment) Act 1986) are important for enabling the Secretary of State to make regulations imposing such safety standards as are, in his or her opinion, expedient to prevent or reduce the risk of death or personal injury from specified classes of goods. Initially this power was used only sparingly, but latterly there has been a considerable increase in the number of products covered.

Consumer Protection Act 1987

11. Safety regulations

(1) The Secretary of State may by regulations under this section ('safety regulations') make such provision as he considers appropriate . . . for the purpose of securing—

- (a) that goods to which this section applies are safe;
- (b) that goods to which this section applies which are unsafe, or would be unsafe in the hands of persons of a particular description, are not made available to persons generally or, as the case may be, to persons of that description, and
- (c) that appropriate information is, and inappropriate information is not, provided in relation to goods to which this section applies.

(2) Without prejudice to the generality of subsection (1) above, safety regulations may contain provision—

- (a) with respect to composition or contents, design, construction, finish or packing of goods to which this section applies, with respect to standards for such goods and with respect to other matters relating to such goods;
- (b) with respect to the giving, refusal, alteration or cancellation of approvals of such goods, of descriptions of such goods or of standards for such goods;
- (c) with respect to the conditions that may be attached to any approval given under the regulations;
- (d) for requiring such fees as may be determined by or under the regulations to be paid on the giving or alteration of any approval under the regulations and on the making of an application for such approval or alteration;
- (e) with respect to appeals against refusals, alterations and cancellations of approvals given under the regulations and against the conditions contained in such approvals;
- (f) for requiring goods to which this section applies to be approved under the regulations or to conform to the requirements of the regulations or to descriptions or standards specified in or approved by or under the regulations;

(g) with respect to the testing or inspection of goods to which this section applies (including provision for determining the standards to be applied in carrying out any test or inspection);

(h) with respect to the way of dealing with goods of which some or all do not satisfy a test required by or under the regulations or a standard connected with a procedure so required;

(i) for requiring a mark, warning or instruction or any other information relating to goods to be put on or to accompany the goods or to be used or provided in some other manner in relation to the goods, and for securing that inappropriate information is not given in relation to goods either by means of misleading marks or otherwise;

(j) for prohibiting persons from supplying, or from offering to supply, agreeing to supply, exposing for supply or possessing for supply, goods to which this section applies and component parts and raw materials for such goods;

(k) for requiring information to be given to any such person as may be determined by or under the regulations for the purpose of enabling that person to exercise any function conferred on him by the regulations.

(3) Without prejudice to the aforesaid, safety regulations may contain provision—

(a) for requiring persons on whom functions are conferred by or under section 27 below to have regard, in exercising their functions so far as relating to any provisions of safety regulations, to matters specified in a direction issued by the Secretary of State with respect to that provision;

(b) for securing that a person shall not be guilty of an offence under section 12 below unless it is shown that the goods in question do not conform to a particular standard;

(c) for securing that proceedings for such an offence are not brought in England and Wales except by or with the consent of the Secretary of State or the Director of Public Prosecutions;

(d) for securing that proceedings for such an offence are not brought in Northern Ireland except by or with the consent of the Secretary of State or the Director of Public Prosecutions for Northern Ireland;

(e) for enabling a magistrate's court in England and Wales or Northern Ireland to try an information or, in Northern Ireland, a complaint in respect of such an offence if the information was laid or the complaint made within twelve months from the time when the offence was committed;

(f) for enabling summary proceedings for such an offence to be brought in Scotland at any time within twelve months from the time when the offence was committed; and

(g) for determining the persons by whom, and the manner in which, anything required to be done by or under the regulations is to be done.

(4) Safety regulations shall not provide for any contravention of the regulations to be an offence.

(5) Where the Secretary of State proposes to make safety regulations it shall be his duty before he makes them—

(a) to consult such organisations as appear to him to be representative of interests substantially affected by the proposal;

(b) to consult such other persons as he considers appropriate; and

(c) in the case of proposed regulations relating to goods suitable for use at work to consult the Health and Safety Commission in relation to the application of the proposed regulations to Great Britain;

but the preceding provisions of this subsection shall not apply in the case of regulations which provide for the regulations to cease to have effect at the end of a period of not more than twelve months beginning with the day on which they come into force and which contain a statement that it appears to the Secretary of State that the need to protect the public requires that the regulations should be made without delay.

. . .

(7) This section applies to any goods other than—
- (a) growing crops and things comprised in land by virtue of being attached to it;
- (b) water, food, feeding stuff and fertilizer;
- (c) gas which is, is to be or has been supplied by a person authorised to supply it by or under [section 7A of the Gas Act 1986 (licensing of gas suppliers and gas shippers) or paragraph 5A of Schedule 2 to that Act (supply to very large customers an exception to prohibition on unlicensed activities) or under Article 8(1)(c) of the Gas (Northern Ireland) Order 1996];
- (d) controlled drugs and licensed medicinal products.

12. Offences against the safety regulations

(1) Where safety regulations prohibit a person from supplying or offering or agreeing to supply any goods or from exposing or possessing any goods for supply that person shall be guilty of an offence if he contravenes the prohibition.

(2) Where safety regulations require a person who makes or processes any goods in the course of carrying on a business—
- (a) to carry out a particular test or use a particular procedure in connection with the making or processing of the goods with a view to ascertaining whether the goods satisfy any requirements of such regulations; or
- (b) to deal or not to deal in a particular way with a quantity of the goods of which the whole or part does not satisfy such a test or does not satisfy standards connected with such a procedure,

that person shall be guilty of an offence if he does not comply with the requirement.

(3) If a person contravenes a provision of safety regulations which prohibits or requires the provision, by means of a mark or otherwise, of information of a particular kind in relation to goods, he shall be guilty of an offence.

(4) Where safety regulations require any person to give information to another for the purpose of enabling that other to exercise any function, that person shall be guilty of an offence if—
- (a) he fails without reasonable cause to comply with the requirement; or
- (b) in giving the information which is required of him—
  - (i) he makes any statement which he knows is false in a material particular; or
  - (ii) he recklessly makes any statement which is false in a material particular.

(5) A person guilty of an offence under this section shall be liable on summary conviction to imprisonment for a term not exceeding six months or to a fine not exceeding level 5 on the standard scale or to both.

NOTES

1. For a list of safety regulations made under this Act see Miller, *Product Liability and Safety Encyclopaedia*, Division IV.
2. By s 19(1) of the Act the word 'safe' 'means such that there is no risk, or no risk apart from one reduced to a minimum, that any of the following will (whether immediately or after a definite or indefinite period) cause the death of, or any personal injury to, any person whatsoever, that is to say – (a) the goods; (b) the keeping, use or consumption of the goods; (c) the assembly of any of the goods which are, or are to be supplied unassembled; (d) any emission or leakage from the goods or, as a result of the keeping, use or consumption of the goods, from anything else; or (e) reliance on the accuracy of any measurement, calculation or other reading made by or by means of the goods, and "safer" and "unsafe" shall be construed accordingly.'

3. The maximum fine which corresponds to 'level 5 on the standard scale' (see s 12(5) above) is currently £5,000, although this sum may be varied by statutory instrument to compensate for a change in the value of money.
4. Defences are available under s 39, for discussion of which see ch 15.
5. Section 41(1) enables an action for breach of statutory duty to be taken by persons affected by contraventions of safety regulations. It states 'An obligation imposed by safety regulations shall be a duty owed to any person who may be affected by a contravention of the obligation and, subject to any provision to the contrary in the regulations and to the defences and other incidents applying to actions for breach of statutory duty, a contravention of any such obligation shall be actionable accordingly.'
5. Two particular features of s 11(5) deserve mention. First, there is a requirement for the Minister to consult before making a safety regulation and second, in cases of urgency, it is possible to dispense with the consultation requirements and make regulations to last for no more than 12 months. These can then be replaced by permanent regulations, created following proper consultations, to take over from the temporary measure.

Litigation has arisen over the form which the consultation takes:

R v Secretary of State for Health, ex p United States Tobacco International Inc [1992] QB 353, [1992] 1 All ER 212, Queen's Bench Division

The applicants sought judicial review of the decision by a Minister to make the Oral Snuff (Safety) Regulations 1989 (SI 1989/2347) which prohibited the supply etc of oral snuff. The appellants (an American company) were the sole manufacturers of oral snuff in the United Kingdom, having set up their factory in Scotland with the aid of government grants in 1985. In 1986 the Committee on Carcinogenicity (COC) advised the government to ban oral snuff and on 28 February 1988 proposed regulations were announced. Representations from the applicants were invited but they were denied access to the reports upon which the decision to ban oral snuff was based. The court considered the question of fairness:

Taylor LJ. . . . [T]here are three reasons why consultation pursuant to s 11(5)(a) in the present case required a high degree of fairness and candour to be shown by the Secretary of State. First, the history. Although the applicants cannot successfully rely on the doctrine of legitimate expectation, the fact is that they were led up the garden path. The Secretary of State must have realised once the COC had recommended a ban in 1986 that if he accepted that advice, he would be executing a volte-face which would seriously affect the applicants. Secondly, although the regulations are of general application, they impinged almost exclusively on the applicants as the sole manufacturers and packagers of oral snuff in the United Kingdom. Thirdly, the effect of the regulations was likely to be catastrophic to the applicant's business in the United Kingdom, a business in which they had been encouraged by the government to invest substantial resources. It is well established that the claims of natural justice are particularly strong where a party is being deprived of a right previously enjoyed, especially if it involves loss of livelihood (see *McInnes v Onslow-Fane* [1978] 3 All ER 211, [1978] 1 WLR 1520 and *R v Barnsley Metropolitan BC, ex p Hook* [1976] 3 All ER 452, [1976] 1 WLR 1052).

For these reasons it was important that the Secretary of State, when he eventually decided to propose the regulations, should give the applicants a full opportunity to know and respond to the material and evaluations which led him to such a striking change of policy.

. . .

The Secretary of State's refusal to disclose, as he puts it, 'the text of the advice given in 1984, 1986 or on any other occasion by my own professional advisers' was adamant. He said that the applicants had been 'told the gist of it'. But all they were told was the conclusion, namely that a ban should be introduced, not the grounds for reaching it. The only reason advanced by counsel for the refusal of disclosure, other than the existence of an inflexible rule to that effect, was that the members of the COC might feel inhibited in expressing their views if they could be identified by those affected.

I find this unconvincing. The COC members are scientific experts of integrity and standing. Their function is to apply their expertise to the evaluation of scientific evidence, to reach conclusions and make recommendations. I cannot believe that they would be affected by the suggested inhibitions. Even if there were anything in the point, it could be overcome by suitable editing or blacking out of names. The Secretary of State did not even vouchsafe a summary of the committee's reasons – only the conclusions.

One cannot help feeling that the denial of the applicant's request was due to an inbuilt reluctance to give reasons or disclose advice lest it give opponents fuel for argument. One can understand and respect the need for ministers to preserve confidentiality as to the in-house advice they receive on administrative and political issues from their civil service staff. But, here, the advice was from a body of independent experts set up to advise the Secretary of State on scientific matters. I can see no ground in logic or reason for declining to show the applicants the text of the advice. In view of the total change of policy the regulations would bring about and its unique impact on the applicants, fairness demanded that they should be treated with candour. To conceal from them the scientific advice which directly led to the ban was, in my judgment, unfair and unlawful.

It may well be that, in the end, the decision reached by the Secretary of State may prove to be wise and in the public interest, but such a draconian step should not be taken unless procedural propriety has been observed and those most concerned have been treated fairly. Although the regulations were subject to annulment by negative resolution of the House of Commons and were not so annulled, Parliament would be concerned only with the objects of the regulations and would be unaware of any procedural impropriety. It is therefore to the courts, by way of judicial review, that recourse must be had to seek a remedy. In my judgment the applicants are entitled on this ground to an order of certiorari to quash the regulations.

Morland J gave judgment agreeing with Taylor LJ

Application allowed. Order of certiorari granted to quash the 1989 Regulations.

NOTE

Following a further period of consultation, the Tobacco for Oral Use (Safety) Regulations 1992, SI 992/3134 were introduced. These implement an EC Directive.

QUESTIONS

What advantages are there in making regulations under s 11? In what circumstances will the making of regulations not provide adequate protection for consumers from dangerous products? How might such situations be better dealt with?

PROHIBITION NOTICES AND NOTICES TO WARN

It is not always appropriate to make detailed regulations covering all products of a particular description or containing particular materials. Problems sometimes arise over particular manufacturers, importers or suppliers. On other occasions urgency may require that a particular hazard be dealt with or there may be a need to issue specific warnings. In these circumstances s 13 of the 1987 Act may prove helpful:

13. Prohibition notices and notices to warn
(1) The Secretary of State may—
  (a) serve on any person a notice ('a prohibition notice') prohibiting that person except with the consent of the Secretary of State, from supplying, or from offering to supply, agreeing to supply, exposing for supply or possessing for supply, any relevant goods which the Secretary of State considers unsafe and which are described in the notice;
  (b) serve on any person a notice ('a notice to warn') requiring that person at his own expense to publish, in a form and manner and on occasions specified in the notice, a warning about any relevant goods which the Secretary of State considers are unsafe, which that person supplies or has supplied and which are described in the notice.

. . .

(4) A person who contravenes a prohibition notice or a notice to warn shall be guilty of an offence and liable on summary conviction to imprisonment for a term not exceeding six months or to a fine not exceeding level 5 on the standard scale or to both.

. . .

(6) In this section 'relevant goods' means—
  (a) in relation to a prohibition notice, any goods to which section 11 above applies; and
  (b) in relation to a notice to warn, any goods to which that section applies or any growing crops or things comprised in land by virtue of being attached to it.

NOTES

1. To date there have been no notices to warn issued, but use has been made of prohibition notices.
2. An example of prohibition notices were those issued in December 1992 against fourteen suppliers of imitation jelly balls and similar products which created the potential danger of children sucking or swallowing them. The suppliers appealed against the notices, using the procedure laid down in Schedule 2, but the notices were confirmed.
3. Defences are available under s 39: see further ch 15.

Although s 13 of the 1987 Act empowers the Secretary of State to issue prohibition notices, and to require the publication of warnings, it does not contain provisions for the compulsory recall of goods which have been found to be unsafe. The possibility of introducing such a power was discussed in the following passages in the 1976 Green Paper.

Consumer Safety: A Consultative Document (Cmnd 6398) (1976)

Recall of unsafe goods

96. There is also at present no power to require those responsible for supplying dangerous goods:

   (i) to recall distributed, but unsold, stocks;
   (ii) to warn consumers of the hazard by publicity or any other means;
   (iii) where necessary, to make every effort to recall dangerous products already in the hands of the public.

There are two types of circumstance in which the imposition of such requirements might be necessary:

   (a) in respect of a particular manufacturer, importer or distributor who was in breach of a regulation or banning order or convicted of an offence against any general safety law of the kind discussed in paragraphs 80 to 84;
   (b) in respect of anyone who has supplied a product which fails to comply with a particular regulation (or banning order) made subsequently.

In the first case, a power to apply for a court order might be appropriate; in the second the Secretary of State might be empowered to lay down the requirements in the relevant regulation (or order). In either case it would seem reasonable to restrict the use of such powers to serious hazards only and possibly also to limit the period during which a trader remained liable to recall goods after he had supplied them.

97. Recovery of products in the hands of the public would pose problems as it is unlikely that, for most goods, there would be any record of the names and addresses of the purchasers. It would therefore seem necessary to designate some authority for the purpose of specifying the form and placing of the advertisements or other publicity which the trader must issue at his expense.

98. The manufacturer, importer or distributor concerned would face the prospect of liability not only for the cost of the publicity or recall operation itself but also for compensation or damages to the person to whom the goods have been supplied. This of course impinges on the wider question of liability discussed in paragraph 90. In the absence of any new legislation in the field of product liability, there might be particularly acute problems in the kind of case envisaged at (b) above, where no offence may have been committed and where there might therefore be more room for dispute over whether there was sufficient justification for imposing liability on someone in the supply chain and, if so, on whom.

To date no compulsory recall system has been initiated, and, as is indicated above, no actual use has been made of the 'notice to warn' provisions.

PROBLEM

Coffeetime has sold some ten thousand coffee pots through various retail outlets when it becomes apparent that all the pots are potentially dangerous because of a defect in the glue used to stick on their handles. On 1 June some three weeks after discovering the danger, Coffeetime has not taken any steps to alert the public and is continuing to supply further pots to retailers. On 3 June Adam is scalded when a handle comes away in his hand as he is pouring coffee. His friend, Bert, also owns a coffee pot which he has received as a gift from Adam and he decides that he cannot safely use it any further. Discuss what powers are available to the Secretary of State and whether any civil remedies are available to either Adam or Bert.

SUSPENSION NOTICES

To overcome the problem of potentially dangerous goods being supplied pending investigation and testing of the goods or prosecutions being brought, s 14 of the 1987 Act enables local authorities to suspend the supply of particular goods:

14. Suspension Notices

(1) Where an enforcement authority has reasonable grounds for suspecting that any safety provision has been contravened in relation to any goods, the authority may serve a notice (a 'suspension notice') prohibiting the person on whom it is served, for such period ending not more than six months after the date of the notice as is specified therein, from doing any of the following things without the consent of the authority, that is to say, supplying the goods, offering to supply them, agreeing to supply them or exposing them for supply.

(2) A suspension notice served by an enforcement authority in respect of any goods shall—
    (a) describe the goods in a manner sufficient to identify them;
    (b) set out the grounds on which the authority suspects that a safety provision has been contravened in relation to the goods; and
    (c) state that, and the manner in which, the person on whom the notice is served may appeal against the notice under section 15 below.

(3) A suspension notice served by an enforcement authority for the purpose of prohibiting a person for any period from doing the things mentioned in subsection (1) above in relation to any goods may also require that person to keep the authority informed of the whereabouts throughout that period of any of those goods in which he has an interest.

(4) Where a suspension notice has been served on any person in respect of any goods, no further such notice shall be served on that person in respect of the same goods unless—
    (a) proceedings against that person for an offence in respect of a contravention in relation to the goods of a safety provision (not being an offence under this section); or
    (b) proceedings for the forfeiture of the goods under section 16 or 17 below,
are pending at the end of the period specified in the first-mentioned notice.

. . .

(6) Any person who contravenes a suspension notice shall be guilty of an offence and liable on summary conviction to imprisonment for a term not exceeding six months or to a fine not exceeding level 5 on the standard scale or to both.

. . .

NOTES

1. 'Safety provisions' are defined in s 45(1) to mean 'the general safety requirement in section 10 . . . or any provision of safety regulations, a prohibition
   notice or a suspension notice'. In addition, by reg 11(b) of the General Product
   Safety Regulations 1994, the requirements of the 1994 Regulations are also
   'safety provisions'.
2. From April 1988–March 1993 1702 suspension notices were served.
3. Subsections (7) and (8) provide for compensation to be payable for any loss or
   damage caused to persons with an interest in the goods if no safety provision
   is contravened and there has been no neglect or default by that person.
4. An appeal procedure is laid down in s 15 and the court has ruled that this is
   the appropriate way to seek to overturn a suspension notice; the use of judicial
   review is not appropriate:

R v Birmingham City Council ex p Ferrero Ltd [1993] 1 All ER 530, Court of Appeal

Taylor LJ. Ferrero Ltd (Ferrero) make chocolate eggs called 'Kinder Surprise'. Each egg contains a plastic capsule containing in its turn a kit from which a small toy can be made. The object
is to enhance the attractiveness of the eggs to children. Ferrero have used a variety of different
toys in their eggs, many of which represent well-known cartoon characters. In October 1989 a
new toy, depicting the 'Pink Panther', was introduced. Tragically, a month later, on 5
November 1989, a little girl, just over three years old, swallowed one of the 'Pink Panther' feet
which had come loose from a toy. It lodged in her throat causing her death, from asphyxiation.
Three days later the appellants, Birmingham City Council, through their trading standards
office, issued a suspension notice under s 14 of the Consumer Protection Act 1987. The notice
prohibited Ferrero for a period of six months from that date from supplying 'Kinder Surprise'
eggs containing the 'Pink Panther' toy. Despite attempts by Ferrero to persuade them coupled
with offers of undertakings, the council declined to withdraw the notice.

Ferrero decided to apply for judicial review. They were granted leave, and the matter came
before Hutchinson J. On 7 March 1990 he granted to Ferrero an order of certiorari and quashed
both the decision of the council to issue the notice and their refusal to withdraw it. The council now appeal against those decisions.

Having explained the relevant statutory provisions, the grounds presented for judicial review and the views of the judge at first instance, Taylor LJ went on to consider whether judicial review or an appeal was the appropriate procedure to seek to
overturn the suspension notice. He cited judgments from *R v Epping and Harlow
General Comrs, ex p Goldstraw* [1983] 3 All ER 257 and *R v Chief Constable of the
Merseyside Police, ex p Calveley* [1986] 1 All ER 257, [1986] QB 424, and continued:

These are very strong dicta, both in this court and in the House of Lords as cited, emphasising
that where there is an alternative remedy and especially where Parliament has provided a statutory appeal procedure it is only exceptionally that judicial review should be granted. It is therefore necessary, where the exception is invoked, to look carefully at the suitability of the statutory
appeal in the context of the particular case. In the present context the statutory
provisions are all contained in Pt II of the 1987 Act, and are thus concerned with consumer

safety. Section 14 is clearly aimed at providing enforcement authorities with a means of swift, short-term action to prevent goods which have come to their notice from endangering the public. Section 14 is the only provision which enables action to be taken by a local authority against a trader, other than through the courts. The action does not require proof that the goods contravene a safety provision, but merely that the authority has reasonable grounds for suspecting they do. The notice is effective only for six months. It is intended to be an emergency holding operation. The suspension notice has to inform the recipient of his appeal rights (s 14(2)(c)), and the very next section, s 15, sets them out. They provide for application to a magistrates' court, which can set aside the notice only if satisfied that there has been no contravention of a safety provision. If the goods are not shown to be safe, the notice will remain in place. Conversely, if the goods are shown not to contravene the safety provision, the notice is set aside. Moreover, in that event, even if the enforcement authority had reasonable grounds for their suspicion, they are required to pay compensation to any person having an interest in the goods (s 14(7)).

As one would expect, therefore, the statutory emphasis is on the safety of the consumer. The provisions aim at withholding goods from the public if there is reasonable suspicion that they are unsafe. Unless they are then cleared of the danger, it is right that the suspension should remain, even if the process by which the enforcement authority reached its decision was flawed. It cannot be right that dangerous goods should continue to be marketed simply because of some procedural impropriety by the enforcement authority in the process of deciding to issue a suspension notice. Common sense dictates that the protection of the public must take precedence over fairness to the trader. So, if goods are in fact dangerous, it would be nothing to the point to show that, in deciding to issue a suspension notice, the local authority took into account an irrelevant matter or failed to take account of one which was relevant. Parliament has recognised this by making the sole issue, on a s 15 appeal, whether there has in fact been a contravention of the safety provision. Protection is given to the trader by providing for compensation if there has been no contravention.

An appeal under s 15 does not require leave, as judicial review does. It should therefore be capable of being brought on more quickly, which is an important consideration since the notice is only effective for six months. An appeal comes before justices, who can try, as a contested issue of fact on oral evidence, whether the goods are in contravention of a safety provision, whereas judicial review normally proceeds on affidavit evidence. A further appeal on the merits can be made by an aggrieved party to the Crown Court.

Accordingly, in the present case, there was available an appeal specifically provided by Parliament to enable a party aggrieved by a suspension notice to challenge it. The appeal was at least as expeditious, if not more so, than judicial review. It was more suited than judicial review to the resolution of issues of fact. The statutory scheme leant in favour of upholding the notice unless the goods were shown to be safe; but, should they turn out on appeal or otherwise to be safe, any aggrieved party was entitled to compensation.

Consideration was then given as to whether special circumstances existed here to justify judicial review. Taylor LJ ruled that the trial judge, in focusing on the reasonableness of the council's decision, its lack of consultation and refusal to accept an assurance, had erred in not considering what, in the context of the statutory provisions, was the real issue to be decided and whether the appeal procedure in s 15 was suitable to decide it. He rejected the suggestion that the council had a duty to consult, in particular as this could lead to delay. The appeal procedure provided the necessary safeguards for suppliers. The suggestion that the council ought to have accepted an undertaking was also rejected.

Russell LJ and Fox LJ agreed.

Appeal allowed. Leave to appeal to the House of Lords refused.

FORFEITURE

Section 16 enables enforcement authorities to apply to a court for an order of forfeiture of any goods which contravene safety provisions. If satisfied as regards the contravention, the court may order the forfeiture of the goods and destruction or disposal of them. There is an appeal procedure, with power to delay the operation of the forfeiture order pending an appeal. A similar procedure applies in Scotland under s 17. From April 1988 to March 1993, 299 forfeiture orders were made.

GENERAL SAFETY REQUIREMENT

A White Paper, 'The Safety of Goods' (Cmnd 9302 (1984)), examined the operation of the then current legislation: the Consumer Safety Act 1978, and developed the idea of introducing a general safety duty in relation to consumer goods:

The Safety of Goods, Department of Trade, Cmnd 9302, (1984)

A GENERAL SAFETY DUTY

33. The 1978 Act has effect only where specific requirements have been set in regulations, orders or notices. These cover only a limited number of categories and aspects of consumer goods. But dangers to safety and health can occur in almost any category of consumer product. There is no general statutory duty on suppliers to supply safe consumer goods as there is, for example, for articles and substances for use at work under Section 6 of the Health and Safety at Work etc Act 1974. The Consumers' Association has for many years advocated the introduction of such a duty.

34. The Government accepts that there is a case for widening the scope of the Act to place a general obligation on the suppliers of consumer goods to achieve an acceptable standard of safety where it is reasonable to expect them to anticipate and reduce risks arising from those goods. This would induce a greater sense of responsibility on the part of those suppliers who currently regard themselves as unaffected by the legislation (and who may not be adequately deterred by the common law duty of care). At the same time it would provide wider scope for swift remedial action by enforcement authorities in the case of newly identified dangerous products.

35. Local authority departments already deal informally with complaints about the safety of unregulated goods. They often seek to persuade suppliers to withdraw or modify such goods or draw cases to the attention of the Secretary of State for consideration of possible use of prohibition powers. The introduction of a general duty would enable them to take action on the basis of a legal obligation on suppliers.

Section 10 of the Consumer Protection Act 1987 introduced such a general safety duty:

10. The general safety requirement

(1) A person shall be guilty of an offence if he—
    (a) supplies any consumer goods which fail to comply with the general safety requirement;
    (b) offers or agrees to supply any such goods; or

(c) exposes or possesses any such goods for supply.

(2) For the purposes of this section consumer goods fail to comply with the general safety requirement if they are not reasonably safe having regard to all the circumstances, including—
(a) the manner in which, and purposes for which, the goods are being or would be marketed, the get-up of the goods, the use of any mark in relation to the goods and any instructions or warnings which are given with respect to the keeping, use or consumption of the goods;
(b) any standards of safety published by any person either for goods of a description which applies to the goods in question or for matters relating to goods of that description; and
(c) the existence of any means by which it would have been reasonable (taking into account the cost, likelihood and extent of any improvement) for the goods to have been made safer.

(3) For the purposes of this section consumer goods shall not be regarded as failing to comply with the general safety requirement in respect of—
(a) anything which is shown to be attributable to compliance with any requirement imposed by or under any enactment or with any Community obligation;
(b) any failure to do more in relation to any matter than is required by—
(i) any safety regulations imposing requirements with respect to that matter;
(ii) [repealed].
(iii) any provision of any enactment or subordinate legislation imposing such requirements with respect to that matter as are designated for the purposes of this subsection by any such regulations.

(4) In any proceedings against any person for an offence under this section in respect of any goods it shall be a defence for that person to show—
(a) that he reasonably believed that the goods would not be used or consumed in the United Kingdom; or
(b) that the following conditions are satisfied, that is to say—
(i) that he supplied the goods, offered or agreed to supply them or, as the case may be, exposed or possessed them for supply in the course of carrying on a retail business; and
(ii) that, at the time he supplied the goods or offered or agreed to supply them or exposed or possessed them for supply, he neither knew nor had reasonable grounds for believing that the goods failed to comply with the general safety requirement; or
(c) that the terms on which he supplied the goods or agreed or offered to supply them or, in the case of goods which he exposed or possessed for supply, the terms on which he intended to supply them—
(i) indicated that the goods were not supplied or to be supplied as new goods; and
(ii) provided for, or contemplated, the acquisition of an interest in the goods by the person supplied or to be supplied.

(5) For the purposes of subsection (4)(b) above goods are supplied in the course of carrying on a retail business; if—
(a) whether or not they are themselves acquired for a person's private use or consumption, they are supplied in the course of carrying on a business of making a supply of consumer goods available to persons who generally acquire them for private use or consumption; and
(b) the description of goods the supply of which is made available in the course of that business do not, to a significant extent, include manufactured or imported goods which have not previously been supplied in the United Kingdom.

(6) A person guilty of an offence under this section shall be liable on summary conviction to imprisonment for a term not exceeding six months or to a fine not exceeding level 5 on the standard scale or to both.

(7) In this section 'consumer goods' means any goods which are ordinarily intended for private use or consumption, not being—
  (a) growing crops or things comprised in land by virtue of being attached to it,
  (b) water, food, feeding stuff or fertiliser,
  (c) gas which is, is to be or has been supplied by a person authorised to supply it by or under [section 7A the Gas Act 1986 (licensing of gas suppliers and gas shippers) or paragraph 5A of Schedule 2 to that Act (supply to very large customers an exception to prohibition on unlicensed activities) or under Article 8(1)(c) of the Gas (Northern Ireland) Order 1996];
  (d) aircraft (other than hang-gliders) or motor vehicles;
  (e) controlled drugs or licensed medicinal products;
  (f) tobacco.

NOTES

1. It is interesting to compare the similar wording used in s 10(2)(a) and s 3(2)(a), the definition of a defective product for the purposes of Part I of the 1987 Act, see p 230.
2. Section 10 has been used extensively to enable the prosecution of suppliers of dangerous goods for which no specific safety regulations apply. From April 1988 to March 1993 699 cases were brought, with 498 convictions, 26 dismissals and 175 voluntary withdrawals.
3. In addition to the specific defences under sub-s (4), the general defences of s 39 apply, see further ch 15.
4. Under reg 5 of the General Product Safety Regulations 1994, s 10 is disapplied in all cases where the Regulations apply. The DTI indicated, in its *Guidance for Businesses, Consumers and Enforcement Authorities*, May 1995, para 8:

The Regulations largely replace section 10 . . . of the 1987 Act (regulation 5). However, section 10 will remain in being for use in certain, very limited circumstances. For example, section 10 will continue to apply to distributors (in this sense meaning persons other than the first placer on the market) of products which are subject to specific product directives where the UK implementing regulations only impose obligations on the person who first places the product on the market (for example, regulations implementing the personal Protective Equipment Directive).

General Product Safety Regulations 1994, SI 1994/2328

The Regulations came into force on 3 October 1994. Key provisions are as follows:

Interpretation
2. (1) In these Regulations:
      'the 1968 Act' means the Medicines Act 1968;
      'the 1987 Act' means the Consumer Protection Act 1987;

'the 1990 Act' means the Food Safety Act 1990;

'commercial activity' includes a business and a trade;

'consumer' means a consumer acting otherwise than in the course of a commercial activity;

'dangerous product' means any product other than a safe product;

'distributor' means any professional in the supply chain whose activity does not affect the safety properties of a product;

'enforcement authority' means the Secretary of State, any other Minister of the Crown in charge of a Government Department, any such department and any authority, council and other person on whom functions under these Regulations are imposed by or under regulation 11;

'general safety requirement' means the requirement in regulation 7;

'the GPS Directive' means Council Directive 92/59/EEC on general product safety;

'the 1991 Order' means the Foods Safety (Northern Ireland) Order 1991;

'producer' means

(a) the manufacturer of the product, when he is established in the Community, and includes any person presenting himself as the manufacturer by affixing to the product his name, trade mark or other distinctive mark, or the person who reconditions the product;

(b) when the manufacturer is not established in the Community—

(i) if the manufacturer does not have a representative established in the Community, the importer of the product;

(ii) in all other cases, the manufacturer's representative; and

(c) other professionals in the supply chain, insofar as their activities may affect the safety properties of a product placed on the market;

'product' means any product intended for consumers or likely to be used by consumers, supplied whether for consideration or not in the course of a commercial activity and whether new, used or reconditioned; provided, however, a product which is used exclusively in the context of a commercial activity even if it used for or by a consumer shall not be regarded as a product for the purposes of these Regulations provided always and for the avoidance of doubt this exception shall not extend to the supply of such a product to a consumer;

'safe product' means any product which, under normal or reasonably foreseeable conditions of use, including duration, does not present any risk or only the minimum risks compatible with the product's use, considered as acceptable and consistent with a high level of protection for the safety and health of persons, taking into account in particular—

(a) the characteristics of the product, including its composition, packaging, instructions for assembly and maintenance;

(b) the effect on other products, where it is reasonably foreseeable that it will be used with other products;

(c) the presentation of the product, the labelling, any instructions for its use and disposal and any other indication, or information provided by the producer; and

(d) the categories of consumers at serious risk when using the product, in particular children,

and the fact that higher levels of safety may be obtained or other products presenting a lesser degree of risk may be available shall not of itself cause the product to be considered other than a safe product.

. . .

Application and revocation

3. These Regulations do not apply to—

(a) second-hand products which are antiques;

(b) products supplied for repair or reconditioning before use, provided the supplier clearly informs the person to whom he supplies the product to that effect; or

(c) any product where there are specific provisions in rules of Community law governing all aspects of the safety of the product.

4. The requirements of these Regulations apply to a product where the product is the subject of provisions of Community law other than the GPS Directive insofar as those provisions do not make specific provision governing an aspect of the safety of the product.

. . .

General safety requirement

7. No producer shall place a product on the market unless the product is a safe product.

Requirement as to information

8. (1) Within the limits of his activity, a producer shall—

(a) provide consumers with the relevant information to enable them to assess the risks inherent in a product throughout the normal or reasonably foreseeable period of its use, where such risks are not immediately obvious without adequate warnings, and to take precautions against those risks; and

(b) adopt measures commensurate with the characteristics of the products which he supplies, to enable him to be informed of the risks which these products might present and to take appropriate action, including, if necessary, withdrawing the product in question from the market to avoid those risks.

(2) The measures referred to in sub-paragraph (b) of paragraph (1) above may include, whenever appropriate—

(i) marking of the products or product batches in such a way that they can be identified;

(ii) sample testing of marketed products;

(iii) investigating complaints; and

(iv) keeping distributors informed of such monitoring.

Requirements of distributors

9. A distributor shall act with due care in order to help ensure compliance with the requirements of regulation 7 above and, in particular, without limiting the generality of the foregoing—

(a) a distributor shall not supply products to any person which he knows, or should have presumed, on the basis of the information in his possession and as a professional, are dangerous products; and

(b) within the limits of his activities, a distributor shall participate in monitoring the safety of products placed on the market, in particular by passing on information on the product risks and co-operating in the action taken to avoid those risks.

Presumption of conformity and product assessment

10. (1) Where in relation to any product such product conforms to the specific rules of the law of the United Kingdom laying down the health and safety requirements which the product must satisfy in order to be marketed there shall be a presumption that, until the contrary is proved, the product is a safe product.

(2) Where no specific rules as are mentioned or referred to in paragraph (1) exist, the conformity of a product to the general safety requirement shall be assessed taking into account—

(i) voluntary national standards of the United Kingdom giving effect to a European standard; or

(ii) Community technical specifications; or

(iii) if there are no such voluntary national standards of the United Kingdom or Community technical specifications—

(aa) standards drawn up in the United Kingdom; or

(bb) the codes of good practice in respect of health and safety in the product sector concerned; or

(cc) the state of the art and technology
and the safety which consumers may reasonably expect.
. . .

Offences and preparatory acts

12. Any person who contravenes regulation 7 or 9(a) shall be guilty of an offence.

13. No producer or distributor shall—
   (a) offer or agree to place on the market any dangerous product or expose or possess any such product for placing on the market; or
   (b) offer or agree to supply any dangerous product or expose or possess any such product for supply,
and any person who contravenes the requirements of this regulation shall be guilty of an offence.

NOTES

1. Enforcement aspects are detailed in reg 11. Of particular note is the extension of s 13 of the 1987 Act (prohibition notices and notices to warn) to cover these Regulations and these Regulations are 'safety provisions' for the purposes of ss 14–18 of the 1987 Act (suspension notices, forfeiture and powers to obtain information).
2. The penalties for breach of regs 12 and 13 are 3 months' imprisonment, or a level 5 maximum fine or both (reg 17). For the purposes of these Regulations, ss 13(4) and 14(6) of the 1987 Act have a maximum period of imprisonment of 3, instead of 6 months. This is necessary because the Regulations are made under the European Communities Act 1972, for which the maximum period of imprisonment is 3 months.
3. The defences available are contained in reg 14 and are almost identical to those under s 39 of the 1987 Act, see further ch 15. In addition, the due diligence defences in reg 14 and s 39(1) of the 1987 Act may not be used by any person who has breached reg 9(b), see reg 14(5).
4. Appeal cases have not yet been reported on the 1994 Regulations but guidance on the likely effect of the Regulations can be found in the following: *The General Product Safety Regulations 1994, Guidance for Businesses, Consumers and Enforcement Authorities*, DTI, Consumer Safety Unit, May 1995; Cartwright, 'Product Safety and Consumer Protection' (1995) 58 MLR 222; Clarke, 'The General Product Safety Regulations 1994', (1995) 103 ITSA 2 MR 16; Howells, 'The General Duty to Market Safe Products in United Kingdom Law' [1994] LMCLQ 479; and Parry, 'Product Safety: European Style, An Appraisal' [1995] JBL 268.

QUESTION

During 1997 Oliver, the owner of a hardware shop, sold ladders manufactured by Climb-Easy Ltd to a number of customers, including one to Nathan. In December 1997, in another part of the country, Fred, a supplier of Climb-Easy ladders, was convicted of breaching reg 13 of the General Product Safety Regulations 1994. The ladders, because of their dangerous construction, were unstable and could topple over easily. Unaware of this, in January 1998 Oliver sold a ladder to Lewis and gave one to his sister, Melissa, as a present. In February 1998, Climb-Easy Ltd recalled all ladders from retailers. Further accidents occurred in March 1998 when ladders toppled over: Nathan was injured and a valuable vase, belonging to Lewis was broken.

What criminal offences have been committed? Consider also the civil liability arising here (see further chs 3 and 5).

INFORMATION GATHERING

In an attempt to ascertain the causes of accidents in and around the home the Consumer Safety Unit of the Department of Trade and Industry has, since 1976, operated the Home Accident Surveillance system. The purpose of the system is to collect data at Accident and Emergency Departments relating to patients requiring in-patient or out-patient treatment as the result of home accidents. Reports are published annually. The Institute of Trading Standards also operates a computer data base on hazardous products, HAZPROD, to facilitate the exchange of information.

Since 1984 the European Commission has co-ordinated information received from Member States to ensure that warnings about dangerous products are circulated within the Community. The Rapid Exchange System (RAPEX) allows information about steps taken at national level over products which pose a 'serious and immediate risk' (General Product Safety Directive, art 9) to be notified to the Commission, which then informs the other Member States, their responses being circulated. For further details see the General Product Safety Directive, arts 7–9 and the Annex. For discussion of RAPEX and EC consumer safety law generally, see Weatherill, *EC Consumer Law and Policy* (1997), ch 7.

CHAPTER 13

Trade descriptions: goods and services

INTRODUCTION

At least since the Merchandise Marks Act 1887 it has been recognised that a proper function of the statutory criminal law is to protect buyers of goods against false descriptions given in the course of trade. However, the Molony Committee found that the 1887 and succeeding Acts were defective in draftsmanship and enforced ineffectively. The Trade Descriptions Act 1968 was a result of the Molony Committee's recommendations. For details of the committee's criticisms and proposals see the Final Report of the Committee on Consumer Protection, Cmnd 1781 (1962) Part V at para 586 et seq.

As may be inferred from the number of convictions recorded in a year covered by the Director General of Fair Trading's Annual Report (see above, p 575) the 1968 Act attracts more reported cases on the interpretation of its apparently straightforward provisions than any comparable consumer statute.

The abundance of appellate decisions in this area is in part due to the relative affluence of a significant proportion of the defendants coupled with a reluctance by retailers who enjoy a national reputation for probity to have a conviction registered against them on what they regard as a technical point. However, a very large proportion of the defendants to charges concerning false trade descriptions relating to goods have been car sellers, and the incidence of fraud in this sector has more than once led the Director General to threaten either more stringent legislation or to use his powers to refuse consumer credit licences to persistent offenders, the latest recommendations being in *Selling Second-Hand Cars: a Report by the Office of Fair Trading*, October 1997.

This chapter and the one which follows concentrate on the key offences laid down by the 1968 Act: (i) applying a false trade description to any goods or supplying or offering to supply any goods to which a false trade description is applied (s 1); (ii) making a statement concerning the provision of services etc, knowing it to be false or being reckless in that regard (s 14); and (iii) giving misleading price indications (formerly in s 11 and now replaced by Part III of the Consumer Protection Act 1987).

The Act imposes strict liability with regard to false trade descriptions of goods. The offence (introduced in 1968) relating to services requires knowledge or recklessness. Thus, provided the defendant knows that a trade description has been applied (see *Cottee v Douglas Seaton (Used Cars) Ltd* [1972] 3 All ER 750, [1972] 1 WLR 1408 (below, p 615)) an offence under s 1 will have been committed unless the defendant can bring himself within one of the specified defences. This scheme is common to a number of trading standards offences (particularly weights and measures and food and drugs) and the defences available are discussed separately in this book: see ch 15.

Finally, before exploring the interpretation of the key offences mentioned above, the following points about the Act's operation should be borne in mind. First, the ambit of the 1968 Act extends to transactions between traders in addition to transactions between traders and the public. Second (and subject to a possible point involving s 23 of the Act, below, p 731), private persons are not subjected to criminal liability under this Act. However, such other statutory offences as obtaining property (including money) by deception contrary to s 15 of the Theft Act 1968 may have been committed in circumstances where the defendant, if operating in the course of a trade or business, would have contravened the Trade Descriptions Act 1968.

FALSE OR MISLEADING DESCRIPTIONS AS TO GOODS

The following are the principal provisions of the 1968 Act which are concerned with false or misleading descriptions as to goods:

Trade Descriptions Act 1968

PROHIBITION OF FALSE TRADE DESCRIPTIONS

1. Prohibition of false trade descriptions
(1) Any person who, in the course of a trade or business—
    (a) applies a false trade description to any goods; or
    (b) supplies or offers to supply any goods to which a false trade description is applied;
shall, subject to the provisions of this Act, be guilty of an offence.

(2) Sections 2 to 6 of this Act shall have effect for the purposes of this section and for the interpretation of expressions used in this section, wherever they occur in this Act.

2. Trade description
(1) A trade description is an indication, direct or indirect, and by whatever means given, of any of the following matters with respect to any goods or parts of goods, that is to say—
    (a) quantity, size or gauge;
    (b) method of manufacture, production, processing or reconditioning;
    (c) composition;
    (d) fitness for purpose, strength, performance, behaviour or accuracy;
    (e) any physical characteristics not included in the preceding paragraphs;
    (f) testing by any person and results thereof;
    (g) approval by any person or conformity with a type approved by any person;

(h) place or date of manufacture, production, processing or reconditioning;

(i) person by whom manufactured, produced, processed or reconditioned;

(j) other history, including previous ownership or use.

(2) The matters specified in subsection (1) of this section shall be taken—

    (a) in relation to any animal, to include sex, breed or cross, fertility and soundness;

    (b) in relation to any semen, to include the identity and characteristics of the animal from which it was taken and measure of dilution.

(3) In this section 'quantity' includes length, width, height, area, volume, capacity, weight and number.

(4) Notwithstanding anything in the preceding provisions of this section, the following shall be deemed not to be trade descriptions, that is to say, any description or mark applied in pursuance of—

    (a) [Repealed.]

    (b) section 2 of the Agricultural Produce (Grading and Marking) Act 1928 (as amended by the Agricultural Produce (Grading and Marking Amendment Act 1931) or any corresponding enactment of the Parliament of Northern Ireland;

    (c) the Plant Varieties and Seeds Act 1964;

    (d) the Agriculture and Horticulture Act 1964 [or any Community grading rules within the meaning of Part III of that Act];

    (e) the Seeds Act (Northern Ireland) 1965;

    (f) the Horticulture Act (Northern Ireland) 1966;

    (g) [the Consumer Protection Act 1987];

[any statement made in respect of, or mark applied to, any material in pursuance of Part IV of the Agriculture Act 1970, any name or expression to which a meaning has been assigned under section 70 of that Act when applied to any material in the circumstances specified in that section], any mark prescribed by a system of classification compiled under section 5 of the Agriculture Act 1967 [and any designation, mark or description applied in pursuance of a scheme brought into force under section 6(1) or an order made under section 25(1) of the Agriculture Act 1970.]

(5) (a) Notwithstanding anything in the preceding provisions of this section, where provision is made under the [Food Safety Act 1990, the Food Safety (Northern Ireland) Order 1991 or the Consumer Protection Act 1987] prohibiting the application of a description except to goods in the case of which the requirements specified in that provision are complied with, that description, when applied to such goods, shall be deemed not to be a trade description.

  [(b) where by virtue of any provision made under Part V of the Medicines Act 1968 (or made under any provisions of the said Part V as applied by an order made under section 104 or 105 of that Act) anything which, in accordance with this Act, constitutes the application of a trade description to goods is subject to any requirements or restrictions imposed by that provision, any particular description specified in that provision, when applied to goods in circumstances to which those requirements or restrictions are applicable, shall be deemed not to be a trade description.]

3. False trade description

(1) A false trade description is a trade description which is false to a material degree.

(2) A trade description which, though not false, is misleading, that is to say, likely to be taken for such an indication of any of the matters specified in section 2 of this Act as would be false to a material degree, shall be deemed to be a false trade description.

(3) Anything which, though not a trade description, is likely to be taken for an indication of any of those matters and, as such an indication, would be false to a material degree, shall be deemed to be a false trade description.

(4) A false indication, or anything likely to be taken as an indication which would be false, that any goods comply with a standard specified or recognised by any person or implied by the approval of any person shall be deemed to be a false trade description, if there is no such person or no standard so specified, recognised or implied.

4. Applying a trade description to goods

(1) A person applies a trade description to goods if he:
- (a) affixes or annexes it to or in any manner marks it on or incorporates it with:
  - (i) the goods themselves, or
  - (ii) anything in, on or with which the goods are supplied; or
- (b) places the goods in, on or with anything which the trade description has been affixed or annexed to, marked on or incorporated with, or places any such thing with the goods; or
- (c) uses the trade description in any manner likely to be taken as referring to the goods.

(2) An oral statement may amount to the use of a trade description.

(3) Where goods are supplied in pursuance of a request in which a trade description is used and the circumstances are such as to make it reasonable to infer that the goods are supplied as goods corresponding to that trade description, the person supplying the goods shall be deemed to have applied that trade description to the goods.

5. Trade descriptions used in advertisements

(1) The following provisions of this section shall have effect where in an advertisement a trade description is used in relation to any class of goods.

(2) The trade description shall be taken as referring to all goods of the class, whether or not in existence at the time the advertisement is published
- (a) for the purpose of determining whether an offence has been committed under paragraph (a) of section 1(1) of this Act; and
- (b) where goods of the class are supplied or offered to be supplied by a person publishing or displaying the advertisement, also for the purpose of determining whether an offence has been committed under paragraph (b) of the said section 1(1).

(3) In determining for the purposes of this section whether any goods are of a class to which a trade description used in an advertisement relates regard shall be had not only to the form and content of the advertisement but also to the time, place, manner and frequency of its publication and all other matters making it likely or unlikely that a person to whom the goods are supplied would think of the goods as belonging to the class in relation to which the trade description is used in the advertisement.

6. Offer to supply

A person exposing goods for supply or having goods in his possession for supply shall be deemed to offer to supply them.

Section 1 and the subsequent five sections which explain and expand it have received detailed attention from the courts. The following selected passages from a number of these decisions are designed to show how the courts have interpreted the key words and phrases in these sections.

'ANY PERSON'

'Any person' includes a corporation: see the Interpretation Act 1978, Sch I. In the common case where a trading standards offence has been committed by a company, provisions exist for making the company's directors and principal officers jointly liable and they, unlike the company, may be imprisoned—an important additional sanction. Section 20 of the Trade Descriptions Act is typical:

20. Offences by corporations
(1) Where an offence under this Act which has been committed by a body corporate is proved to have been committed with the consent and connivance of, or to be attributable to any neglect on the part of, any director, manager, secretary or other similar officer of the body corporate or any person who was purporting to act in any such capacity, he as well as the body corporate shall be guilty of that offence and shall be liable to be proceeded against and punished accordingly.

(2) In this section 'director', in relation to any body corporate established by or under an enactment for the purpose of carrying on under national ownership any industry or part of industry or undertaking, being a body corporate whose affairs are managed by the members thereof, means a member of that body corporate.

No doubt in most cases the person applying the false trade description to goods will be the seller or supplier of them. The following case raises the question whether the scope of the offence is thus limited or whether it is similarly applicable to buyers.

Fletcher v Budgen [1974] 2 All ER 1243, [1974] 1 WLR 1056, Queen's Bench Division

The facts are set out in the judgment of Lord Widgery CJ.

Lord Widgery CJ. This is an appeal by case stated by justices for the city of York in respect of their adjudication in the magistrates' court in York on 12 October 1973. Before them on that occasion were three informations preferred by the appellant prosecutor against the respondent. Each related to 9 December 1972. Each was concerned with a Fiat 500 motor car, which at that time the respondent was considering buying from its then owner. The respondent was engaged in the trade or business of a dealer in motor cars. When this Fiat was brought to him by its potential seller for him to consider its purchase, and he examined it in the course of his trade or business as a dealer in cars, he made three disparaging remarks about the car. First of all, he said there was no possibility of repairing it. Secondly, he said the repairs would not make the car safe, and, thirdly, summing up the whole situation, he said the only possible course of action with regard to the car would be for the car to be scrapped. The then owner of the car, a Mr Durkin, discouraged, and accepting that the car was good for scrap only, sold it to the respondent for £2.

To his astonishment no doubt he discovered very shortly afterwards that the car was being advertised for sale by the respondent at a price of £135. The justices found that the respondent had done repairs to the car to the value of about £56 and thus had managed to make the car sufficiently roadworthy for it to obtain its Ministry of Transport certificate. It was duly offered for sale, as I have said. The justices also found that the statements made by the respondent in regard to the car were false to his knowledge when he made the statements.

In other words, on its facts this is a very strong case. You have the non-trader who is selling the car; the motor trader who is buying it; an examination made by the potential buyer, jacking up the car and going underneath it; three extremely positive and unequivocal comments about the unsuitability of the car for any further use, and the ultimate result of the respondent having acquired the car for £2, being able apparently to sell it for a substantial profit.

Arising out of those facts there were, as I have said, three informations laid by the prosecutor against the respondent, alleging in each case that he had applied a false trade description to the car and thus committed an offence contrary to s 1 of the Trade Descriptions Act 1968.

His Lordship then summarised ss 1 to 4 of the Act and continued:

So at first blush one looks at the four sections and observes the wide ambit which they enjoy, and if when construing the statute, one looks at the words and sees what their natural meaning is, it seems that they cover this case.

But why? Because, according to s 1(1), the respondent was carrying on a trade or business, and it was in the course of his trade or business that he made the observations. Further, the trade description was applied to the goods because it was used in a manner likely to be taken as referring to the goods. That it was a false description is really beyond doubt, as I have already sought to demonstrate.

There is, therefore, on the face of it only one reason why the prosecution might be held unsuccessful in this case, and that would be on the fundamental proposition that, although the Act does not condescend in terms to say so, yet the scheme of ss 1 to 4 is restricted to false trade descriptions made by a seller of goods and cannot apply to a buyer of goods. If on a proper consideration of the Act it can be said with confidence that Parliament must have intended that it should not have been, so be it. If one cannot, on a consideration of the sections of the Act, conclude that buyers are necessarily excluded from its terms, then it would seem to me that a buyer is as much liable to be convicted as a seller under the terms of the sections to which I have referred.

Oddly enough, this is a point which has not arisen before. Perhaps the nearest to it is *Fletcher v Sledmore*.[1] That was a case with rather unusual facts in which the owner of a motor car had agreed to sell and, being a repairer of cars, had agreed to undertake certain repairs before the car was delivered to the buyer. The buyer was contemplating reselling it to sub-purchaser. He brought the sub-purchaser along to see the car in the state in which it was, partly dismantled for repair purposes, and the respondent, who was the original seller of the car, was present. On enquiry being made by the prospective sub-purchaser as to the quality of the car, the respondent volunteered the information that it was all right, it was a good little engine, and he had driven it himself.

That case raised a number of points not relevant in the instant case, but in the judgment of Eveleigh J there are some useful observations as to the scope of this Act, and I find them of assistance in the present problem. Having looked at the same sections to which I have already referred, he said:[2]

'Reading the words of the section, one sees no limitation which specifies the nature of the transaction in which the description of the goods is made. Counsel for the prosecutor has very properly drawn the court's attention to *Hall v Wickens Motors (Gloucester) Ltd*.[3] In that case the defendants, who were car dealers, sold a car, and some 40 days later received an oral complaint from the purchaser about the steering. The defendants replied "There is nothing wrong with the car". Examination of the car revealed in fact that it was defective. The defendants were charged with applying a false trade description to the car, namely, an oral statement that there was nothing wrong with it. They were convicted and appealed to quarter sessions, where the recorder accepted their submission that no offence had been committed under section 1(1)(a) of the Act of 1968.'

Then Eveleigh J goes on to deal with certain other aspects of that case, and he continued:[4]

'However, on the facts of this particular case it would not be right to say that the statement was unconnected with the supply or the sale of goods. There are no qualifications in section 1 as to the time when the representation is to be made. The only qualification there specifically to be seen is that it should be in the course of trade or business, in other words should be made as part of the business activities of the person charged. There is no reason to introduce any time qualification. The question then remains whether or not there is reason to introduce the qualification that the person charged should himself be a contracting party in the matters in which the representation is made. No such limitation appears in the section itself, and I see no reason why such a limitation should be implied.'

I cite that case because, as I have said, it indicates the attitude of this court towards suggestions made from time to time that the clear language of the statute should be restricted on some assumed basis that Parliament must have so intended.

A case in which a submission was made and upheld in this court is, however, *Wycombe Marsh Garages Ltd v Fowler*.[5] This was a case in which the owner of a car had taken the car to a garage to obtain a Ministry of Transport certificate. The accused in that case examined the car and came to the conclusion that the nearside tyres were defective to such a degree as to make it impossible to issue a certificate. He, therefore, refused the certificate, certifying that the tyres suffered from this particular defect. He was wrong. He was honestly wrong, but he was wrong, and eventually it was shown that the tyres suffered from no such defect.

Somewhat to the surprise of the members of the court sitting on that occasion, the authorities then proceeded to prosecute him with a criminal offence under s 1 of the 1968 Act. It was held that he had committed no such offence, and the value of the case, I think, is that it emphasises that the Act is only concerned with false trade descriptions applied to goods in association with a contract for the sale or supply of the goods. In other words, *Wycombe Marsh Garages Ltd v Fowler*[5] is valuable for the proposition that a person who merely makes an inspection of goods as a service to its owner, and who honestly certifies his findings, is not to be convicted of an offence under s 1 because although he may be said to have applied a trade description to the goods, he has not done so in a transaction associated with sale or supply of the goods.

There one has an example of this court imposing certain limitations on the wide words of the section, but in general we must take the Act as it stands. We must look at the language used and we must give it its natural consequences.

I confess to being surprised at the conclusion to which I have ultimately come because I confess that in considering this Act in the past I have subconsciously thought that it could only apply to false trade descriptions applied by the seller. I suppose that I had never before been required to think about the circumstances in which the public need to apply these restrictions to a buyer is every bit as much as is the public need to apply them to a seller. If one visualises the present case where the potential buyer of the goods is engaged in the trade or business of buying cars, and if one reminds oneself that this Act only applies to people who apply false trade descriptions in the course of a trade or business, then I think it becomes apparent that to allow the Act to operate according to its terms in the present case is not in any sense illogical and is not likely to run counter to any intention which Parliament may have had.

It seems to me that it is perfectly reasonable when the buyer is the expert and the seller may be the amateur, where the buyer makes an examination of the goods in his capacity as an expert and then proceeds to pronounce on the qualities or otherwise, that he should be as much liable to be restrained in his language as is a seller, who in the normal course of events is the man who knows all about the goods and who is to be restricted in any temptation to make false and misleading statements about them.

. . .

For those reasons I am persuaded that the justices were wrong, and I would allow the appeal and send the case back with a direction to continue the hearing in the light of this court's judgment.

Park J and **Forbes J** agreed.

Appeal allowed.

1 [1973] RTR 371.
2 [1973] RTR 371 at 375.
3 [1972] 3 All ER 759, [1972] 1 WLR 1418.
4 [1973] RTR 371 at 376.
5 [1972] 3 All ER 248, [1972] 1 WLR 1156.

The following comment on this case is contained in the 'Review of the Trade Descriptions Act 1968: A Report by the Director General of Fair Trading' (Cmnd 6628) (1976):

Statements by experts

107. . . . The case is to be contrasted with *Wycombe Marsh Garages Ltd v Fowler* [see above, p 607] in which it was held that a person who, in the course of his business, provides an expert service which involves reporting on the condition of goods commits no offence under section 1 if he makes a false statement about their condition. We first considered whether these two decisions are right in principle.

108. It seems to us that it would be entirely wrong if a trader called upon to make an independent assessment of goods committed an offence because, acting in good faith, he made an incorrect statement about them. To make a trader liable to conviction for an incorrect statement so made might well on balance tend to inhibit the communication of honest assessments rather than improve the quality of reports. We therefore endorse the principle established by the *Wycombe Marsh* Judgment.

109. On the other hand, we also think it right that a trader should be guilty of an offence if he deliberately asserts his expertise and then proceeds to make dishonest statements about goods offered to him with a view to purchasing them more cheaply. Such practices could be widespread. It was suggested to us for example, that some antique dealers made a deliberate practice of dishonestly misdescribing goods offered to them in the hope of persuading the seller to let them go cheaply. But it is to be noted that an offence under section 1 of the 1968 Act does not depend upon the establishment of dishonest intent; and we have reservations in this connection about the Judgment in the *Budgen* case . . .

PROBLEM

Gruniad has been having problems with his central heating boiler. He calls in a specialist, Chimes. Chimes examines the boiler and says, 'It is on its last legs. You need a new one'. The statement was made in good faith but was incorrect since the fault could have been cured by a cheap replacement part. Gruniad buys a new boiler from Chimes, trading in the old one in part exchange.

Consider Chimes' liability under the 1968 Act.

'IN THE COURSE OF A TRADE OR BUSINESS'

Section 1 requires the false trade description to have been applied etc 'in the course of a trade or business'. This phrase or phrases similar in intent are common to a number of civil and criminal statutes and there has been little overall consistency of approach in interpreting it. It is a common experience in the investigation of trading standards offences for the potential defendant to state that the sale in question was not in the course of a business. The following case considered the matter in relation to s 1 of the 1968 Act.

Davies v Sumner [1984] 1 WLR 405, Queen's Bench Division

Robert Goff LJ. There is before the court an appeal by way of case stated by the defendant, John Barry Davies, from an adjudication by the magistrates' court sitting at Flint. The case raises a question of construction of s 1(1) of the Trade Descriptions Act 1968.

It appears from the case that an information was laid charging the defendant that, in the course of trade or business, on 1 August 1981, at Bagillt in the County of Clwyd, he applied to certain goods, namely, a Ford motor car, a false trade description to the effect that the motor car had travelled 18,100 miles whereas the true mileage was in excess of 118,000 miles, contrary to s 1(1)(a) of the Trade Descriptions Act 1968.

The justices have set out in the case certain facts found by them. In substance, they are as follows. The defendant was, and still is, employed as a self-employed courier. He was engaged exclusively by the Harlech Television Co to transport films, video tapes and other items of that nature from Mold to Cardiff in South Wales, and on occasions from and to other places. For that purpose, the defendant had to provide his own car. The car which he provided was the Ford Capri car referred to in the information, registration no UDM 23OV. For his services, he was paid a fee for each journey and, in addition, a subsistence allowance. He was required to pay all the expenses involved, including the running costs of the vehicle. In respect of these expenses, the defendant claimed and was allowed tax relief as business expenses. Before the defendant bought this Ford Capri motor car for use in this work, he had rented a car. He bought the Ford Capri in June 1980. Such was the extent of his activities as a courier that between June 1980 and July 1981 he travelled over 100,000 miles. He then decided that the time had come to buy a new car to continue his business as a self-employed courier.

On 31 July 1981, the defendant went to the showrooms of a company, also called Davies, who were the Ford main dealers in Bagillt. He arranged to buy a new Ford, trading in the old Ford Capri, which had travelled 118,000 miles, in part-exchange. The defendant's car was examined by a salesman and the odometer showed only 18,100 miles. The reason for this was that the odometer was a five digital odometer so that, although the mileage had gone right round the clock, this did not appear on the odometer. The appearance of the vehicle was consistent with the vehicle having travelled 18,100 miles only. It was found that the salesman inquired about the mileage travelled, but nothing was said about any answers which may have been given to that inquiry. The new car was purchased for £8,270 and, receiving as he did £3,800 for his Capri motor car, the balance which the defendant had to pay to the garage was £4,470. Arrangements were made for the defendant to return to the garage on 1 August 1981 to pick up the new car. This he did, and at the same time he handed over his old car and signed a sales invoice to complete the transaction. It appears that the sales invoice included a declaration to the effect that the mileage of the old car was 18,100 miles. I think it right to record that we were told by Mr Waldron, on behalf of the defendant, that that figure was not in the original sales invoice but was added later. It is admitted by the defendant that he did not disclose the true mileage of the Ford Capri, and his contention is that he was never asked to do so.

On those facts, the justices convicted the defendant of the charge as stated, and imposed a fine of £120. He was ordered to pay costs, but no order as to compensation was made. The question stated for the opinion of the court is as follows:

'When a person who in the course of his occupation as a self-employed courier almost exclusively uses his car for the purpose of that occupation, disposes of that vehicle for another vehicle, is that a transaction in the course of "trade or business" for the purpose of section 1 of the Trade Descriptions Act 1968?'

Here the case against the defendant was that he did apply a false trade description to goods in the course of trade or business when, on the occasion of the trading in of his car, he did so with an odometer showing only 18,100 miles when the true mileage of the car was 118,100, and by signing a sales invoice stating that the mileage of the car was only 18,100.

The justices were referred to the decision of this court in *Havering London Borough Council v Stevenson* [1970] 1 WLR 1375. It seems that that authority influenced their decision to convict the defendant. In that case, the defendant carried on a car hire business. It was found that it was his usual practice to sell the motor cars he used in his business after about two years. He sold them at the prevailing trade price and paid the proceeds of the sales back into the business for the purchase of new vehicles. On one occasion, in accordance with that practice, he sold a motor car and falsely represented to the purchaser that the recorded mileage of the vehicle was less than the mileage which the vehicle had in fact travelled. On that basis, the case came before the justices on a charge under s 1(1)(b) of the Trade Descriptions Act 1968, but the charge was dismissed by them. The prosecutor then appealed, by way of case stated, to the Divisional Court. The court allowed the appeal. The reasons for that decision are to be found in the judgment of Lord Parker CJ who said, at p 1377:

'The defendant carried on a car hire business. I emphasise that it was a car hire business and not the business of a motor car vendor or dealer. He had a fleet of 24 cars, and made a regular practice of selling his hire cars after he had had them for about two years, when he chose to run his fleet down or when the condition of a particular vehicle warranted it. He never bought cars and sold them for a greater price. The defendant owned this Ford Corsair car and having used it in his car hire business, he put it up for sale in accordance with his usual practice. In November 1969, it was represented to Mr Carter, who bought the vehicle, that the motor car had a recorded mileage of 34,000 miles, and the speedometer recorded that mileage. In fact, as is found by the case, the mileage was over 50,000. Pausing there, for my part on those facts it seems to me that it was almost inevitable that this application of a false trade description was in the course of trade or business. It was not "for the purposes of trade or business" or even "by way of trade or business". Once it is found that a car hire business as part of its normal practice buys and disposes of cars, it seems to me almost inevitable that the sale of a car and the application of a trade description in the course of that sale was an integral part of the business carried on as a car hire firm.'

. . .

Before us, Mr Waldron for the defendant and Mr Scrivener for the prosecutor both accepted that the problem whether or not a sale, and therefore the application of a trade description in the course of that sale, arose in the course of a trade or business is to be solved by asking the question: did the sale form an integral part of the defendant's trade or business?

Mr Waldron submitted that in the present case the sale did not form an integral part of the defendant's business. He submitted that a distinction has to be drawn between cases such as *Havering London Borough Council v Stevenson* [1970] 1 WLR 1375 and the present case because, although in the present case the defendant used the car almost exclusively in the course of his business, it did not follow that, when he came to sell it, the sale formed an integral part of his business. In this connection, Mr Waldron gave a number of examples of cases where, he suggested, a sale did not form an integral part of a person's business. In particular, he gave the example of a country doctor who has two cars, using one car for his private affairs and the other car exclusively for visiting his patients in the course of his practice. I understand that the profession of a doctor does for present purposes constitute a trade or business. The time might come when he wanted to sell his second car in order to purchase a new one. Would that sale form an integral part of that doctor's trade or business? The answer, submitted Mr Waldron, is plainly not.

Mr Scrivener, on the other hand, submitted that if a person uses a car exclusively, almost exclusively or even substantially in the course of his trade or business, then any sale of that car would be a sale which formed an integral part of his business. He relied upon the fact that such a person would claim tax relief in respect of the use of his car and submitted that it would therefore be only right and proper that the sale should be considered as an integral part of his business.

I consider that Mr Scrivener's approach is not in accordance with the test laid down by Lord Parker CJ in *Stevenson's* case. On Lord Parker's test, we have to look at the nature of the business carried on by the person concerned; we have then to look at the transaction in question, and ask ourselves the question: Does that transaction form an integral part of that person's business? Where a car hire firm, which uses a number of cars in the course of its business, from time to time trades in cars in part-exchange for new ones, no doubt the transactions of disposing of old cars in part-exchange for new cars is an integral part of the car hire business. But if we turn to the example of the country doctor given by Mr Waldron, I do not think that the occasional trading in of a car used for his practice could properly be described as a sale which formed an integral part of his business. The mere fact that the doctor used his car for the purpose of his practice is not enough. Indeed, Mr Scrivener is really proposing an entirely new test. On his submission, the test would not be whether the sale formed an integral part of the person's business, but whether a particular asset used substantially during the course of his trade or business had been sold. In my opinion, that is a different test from that established by Lord Parker CJ.

I turn then to the question posed by the justices for the opinion of the court . . . [see above].

I would answer that question in the negative. It appears to me, on reading that question, that the justices applied the wrong test. They asked themselves not whether the disposal of the car was a transaction which formed an integral part of the defendant's business as a self-employed courier, but simply whether the car was almost exclusively used by the defendant for the purposes of his occupation as a self-employed courier. They therefore applied the test that has been urged upon us by Mr Scrivener and which I am not prepared to accept. I would therefore allow the appeal.

Forbes J. I agree. The justices, having had *Havering London Borough Council v Stevenson* [1970] 1 WLR 1375 drawn to their attention, have asked themselves the question, 'Was the use of the car an integral part of the business?' and not, 'Was the sale of the car an integral part of the business?' I agree with Robert Goff LJ that the question put to this court must be answered in the negative

Appeal allowed.

The prosecution's appeal to the House of Lords was dismissed for the following reasons given by Lord Keith and with which the other members of the House of Lords agreed ([1984] 3 All ER 831 at 834):

Any disposal of a chattel held for the purposes of a business may, in a certain sense, be said to have been in the course of that business, irrespective of whether the chattel was acquired with a view to resale or for consumption or as a capital asset. But in my opinion s 1(1) of the 1968

Act is not intended to cast such a wide net as this. The expression 'in the course of a trade or business' in the context of an Act having consumer protection as its primary purpose conveys the concept of some degree of regularity, and it is to be observed that the long title to the Act refers to 'misdescriptions of goods, services, accommodation and facilities provided in the course of trade'. Lord Parker CJ in the *Havering* case clearly considered that the expression was not used in the broadest sense. The reason why the transaction there in issue was caught was that in his view it was 'an integral part of the business carried on as a car-hire firm'. That would not cover the sporadic selling off of pieces of equipment which were no longer required for the purposes of a business. The vital feature of the *Havering* case appears to have been, in Lord Parker's view, that the respondent's business *as part of its normal practice* bought and disposed of cars. The need for some degree of regularity does not, however, involve that a one-off adventure in the nature of trade, carried through with a view to profit, would not fall within s 1(1) because such a transaction would itself constitute a trade.

In the present case it was sought to be inferred that the respondent, covering as he did such a large regular mileage, was likely to have occasion to sell his car at regular intervals, so that he too would have a normal practice of buying and disposing of cars. It is sufficient to say that such a normal practice had not yet been established at the time of the alleged offence. The respondent might well revert to hiring a car, as he had previously done. Further, the respondent's car was a piece of equipment he used for providing his courier service. It was not something he exploited as stock-in-trade, which is what the defendant was in substance doing with his cars in the *Havering* case. Where a person carries on the business of hiring out some description of goods to the public and has a practice of selling off those that are no longer in good enough condition, clearly the latter goods are offered or supplied in the course of his business within the meaning of s 1(1). But the occasional sale of some worn out piece of shop equipment would not fall within the enactment.

NOTES

1. There are several areas of the civil law of consumer protection where it is necessary to distinguish a 'business' transaction from a 'private' one. The conditions implied by s 14 of the Sale of Goods Act 1979 and similar provisions in related statutes, apply only if the seller sells 'in the course of a business'. Problems can arise both as to the meaning of 'in the course of' and 'a business': see above, pp 95–7. Also the protection against exemption clauses afforded to those who 'deal as consumer' as defined in s 12 of the Unfair Contract Terms Act 1977 differs from that provided for those in business, see above, pp 356–60. Of particular note is *R & B Customs Brokers Co Ltd v United Dominions Trust Ltd* [1988] 1 All ER 847, [1988] 1 WLR 321, CA, see above, pp 357–8, where the decision in *Davies v Sumner* was used to provide the relevant test for 'dealing as consumer' in a civil case.

2. Other areas of criminal law require the defendant to have acted 'in the course of a business' or to be conducting a business. For instance, firstly, under the Consumer Credit Act 1974, s 21, it is an offence to carry on a consumer credit business without a licence. Section 189(1) defines a consumer credit business as 'any business so far as it comprises or relates to the provision of credit under regulated consumer credit agreements'. (There is an exception for carrying out such transactions only occasionally: see s 189(2)). See further ch 6, especially pp 283–8. Secondly, the Consumer Transactions (Restrictions on

Statements) Order 1976 (as amended), which is discussed above, pp 384–7, applies only to persons who in the course of a business attempt to exclude consumers' inalienable rights under the Sale of Goods Act 1979. Thirdly, a similar phrase appears in the Unsolicited Goods and Services Act 1971, s 2, where it is an offence for a person without reasonable cause and in the course of any trade or business to make a demand for payment for what he knows are unsolicited goods. In *Eiman v London Borough of Waltham Forest* (1982) 90 ITSA Monthly Review 204, (QBD) the appellant had sent unsolicited copies of his privately published Urdu poetry to various London public libraries accompanied by a series of letters demanding payment. He argued that writing poetry was his hobby but the court upheld his conviction under s 2 since the letters were 'business' letters; it did not matter how small the activity was if it had a 'direct commercial involvement' (per Ormrod LJ). This decision of the Divisional Court contrasts oddly with its decision in *Blakemore v Bellamy* (above, p 544). The same expression is used in s 14 of the Trade Descriptions Act which is concerned with false statements as to services (see below, p 642) and finally a similar phrase occurs in s 20 of the Consumer Protection Act 1987 which covers statements as to prices (see below, pp 674–80).

3. In *Devlin v Hall* [1990] RTR 320, (QBD), a self-employed taxi proprietor was charged under s 1(1) of the 1968 Act concerning a false mileage recording on a former hire car he sold. As this was the first such sale, the court did not consider that it established a normal practice. A sufficient degree of regularity could not be established, nor was the transaction an integral part of the business. Both *Davies v Sumner* and the *R & B Customs Brokers* case were used to determine the issue.

4. In the *Havering London Borough* case referred to by Robert Goff LJ in *Davies v Sumner* above, there was no doubt that the defendant was operating a business. The only question was whether the supply of the car was 'in the course' of it. For other cases illustrating the application of the Act to secondary lines of business see, for example, *Southwark London Borough v Charlesworth* (1983) 147 JP 470, 2 TL 93 (QBD) (sale of electric fire by shoe repairer) and *Fletcher v Sledmore* [1973] RTR 371, referred to by Lord Widgery CJ in *Fletcher v Budgen*, above, p 606 (sale of car by panel beater). This latter case established also that the trade or business in the course of which the false trade description is applied need not involve a contractual relationship with the customer who is prejudiced by it. But the representation must have some connection with the supply of the goods in question. An assurance that there is 'nothing wrong with the car' given some forty days after its sale is not within s 1 of the Act: see *Wickens Motors (Gloucester) Ltd v Hall* [1972] 3 All ER 759, [1972] 1 WLR 1418, above, p 606. (For contrasting cases involving the supply of services, see *Breed v Cluett* [1970] 2 QB 459, [1970] 2 All ER 662 (QBD), below, p 645 and *R v Bevlectric* (1992) ITSA 12 MR 18, below, p 646.)

4. In yet other cases the issue will be whether the defendant's activity constitutes a 'trade or business' (the terms not being defined in the 1968 Act) or simply a pastime or hobby. For a case which perhaps goes to the limit in holding that

the defendant was not trading for the purposes of the Business (Advertisements) Disclosure Order 1977, see *Blakemore v Bellamy* [1983] RTR 303 above, pp 544–6 (postman selling second-hand motor vehicles). For a review of the total picture see Harvey, 'Business or Pleasure' (1983) 27 Sol Jo 163; Lawson, 'In the Course of a Trade or Business' (1984) 128 Sol Jo 24.

'APPLIES'

The offences created by s 1(1)(a) and (b) of the Act depend on the notion of 'applying' a false trade description to goods. Section 1(1)(a) covers a person who 'applies' such a description, for example by 'clocking' a car. Section 1(1)(b) covers a person who 'supplies' or 'offers to supply' (see below, p 620) goods to which such a description has been 'applied', as when an honest dealer is seeking to sell a car which someone else has clocked. Section 4 (above, p 604) explains what the process of 'applying' involves. The following cases illustrate some less obvious aspects of the verb.

Roberts v Severn Petroleum and Trading Co Ltd [1981] RTR 312, Queen's Bench Division

The facts are set out in the judgment of Donaldson LJ.

Donaldson LJ. In this case the prosecutor appeals against the decision of Shropshire Justices sitting at Wellington, Telford, who dismissed an information preferred by him against the defendants alleging an offence under the Trade Descriptions Act 1968.

What happened was this. A garage was run by a company called E R Thomas & Son, and in front of that garage there was the usual pole with a large 'Esso' sign. There was also a smaller 'Esso' sign over the garage itself. The petrol pumps there bore no indication of the manufacturer of the petrol. They simply indicated whether it was 2-star, 3-star or 4-star petrol.

The defendants were asked by Thomases to supply them with petrol in bulk, it being known to Thomases and of course to the defendants that the petrol would not be Esso petrol. The defendants arrived at the garage. The driver in fact saw the 'Esso' sign up and took instructions from his employers and thereafter he put the petrol into these tanks. What is said on behalf of the prosecutor is that that act of putting petrol into the tanks in a garage which displays signs which will convey to the public that the petrol sold from the garage is Esso petrol is an offence under s (1)(1)(a) of the Trade Descriptions Act 1968.

His Lordship referred to ss 1(1)(a), 2(1)(i), and 4(1)(b) and continued:

Mr Carlile on behalf of the prosecutor submits that the tanks of this garage were receptacles to which a trade description, namely, that the contents were the product of the Esso Petroleum Company, had been affixed.

He refers us to the decision of this court in *Stone v Burn* [1911] 1 KB 927 where a brewer placed Bass beer in bottles which were embossed with the name of another company and was held to be guilty of an offence under an earlier statute in much the same terms, notwithstanding that he put Bass labels on the bottles as well.

In the light of that decision it seems to me that the defendants were indeed committing an offence under the Trade Descriptions Act 1968 and should have been convicted. The justices in fact acquitted, and they ask in effect whether they were right to do so. I would answer the question in the negative.

Kilner Brown J. I agree.

Appeal allowed. On prosecutor withdrawing application, no order for case to be remitted to justices. Order for payment of prosecutor's costs of appeal out of central funds.

NOTES

For a case in which similar issues were raised see *Donnelly v Rowlands* [1971] 1 All ER 9, [1970] 1 WLR 1600, QBD. Here milk was placed by a private dairyman in bottles embossed with other dairies names. It was held that there was no false or misleading trade description as the name of the 'filling' dairy was clearly marked on the bottle tops. Consumers would understand that the name on the bottles merely indicated ownership of the bottles. For the associated tort of 'passing off' see *Salmon and Heuston on Torts* (21st edn, 1996) pp 382–5.

Cottee v Douglas Seaton (Used Cars) Ltd [1972] 3 All ER 750, [1972] 1 WLR 1408, Queen's Bench Division

The facts of this complex but important case are set out in some detail in the judgment of Lord Widgery CJ, below. However, it is crucial to note, as did his Lordship, that the information was preferred against the respondents under s 23 of the Act. They were not charged directly under s 1. Section 23 is discussed further in ch 15 below, pp 728–33. Here it is sufficient to say that in adopting this course the prosecution was probably taking on an unnecessary burden. If it is alleged that Dl (the honest dealer, Warry) committed an offence and that this was 'due to the act or default' of D2 (the respondents) D2 can be convicted usually under s 23 if, and only if, Dl would have been guilty (under s 1) if charged. So on the facts of this case the respondents' liability depended on Warry's being potentially liable also.

Lord Widgery CJ. This is an appeal by case stated by justices for the county of Somerset . . . on 16 December 1971. On that date they dismissed informations preferred by the appellant against the respondents, and to take one as being representative its terms were as follows, that between the 1 and 5 September 1970 inclusive, at Merriott in the county of Somerset, one Peter Leonard Warry, unlawfully in the course of a trade or business did offer to supply to one John Louis Shillabeer certain goods, namely a Ford Corsair motor car, to which a false trade description, namely an indication that the engine compartment bodywork of the motor car was in a sound condition, was applied by means of the use of plastic filler and paint to conceal rust corrosion and holes in the bodywork, contrary to s 1(1)(b) of the Trade Descriptions Act 1968. And further that the commission of the offence was due to the act or default of the respondents whereby the respondents were guilty of the offence by virtue of s 23 of the Trade Descriptions Act 1968.

The essential facts relating to this charge are as follows. For approximately two years prior to 28 May 1970 a Ford Corsair motor car, registration no 6505 NU, was in the ownership of a

Mr Meldrum. While the car was in his ownership Mr Meldrum had occasion to effect certain repairs to the bodywork of the vehicle inside the engine compartment. These repairs were called for partly as a result of an accident in which the vehicle had been involved, and partly by extensive rust damage to the bodywork. In making these repairs Mr Meldrum had used aluminium strip which he covered with plastic filler in certain areas and plastic filler alone in others. Having placed the plastic filler in position he rough filed it and painted it over with a grey zinc primer. The rest of the paintwork inside the engine compartment was off-white. Mr Meldrum made no effort to disguise the work he had done before he subsequently traded the car in to the respondents. It is important to emphasise this last-mentioned fact because any person of experience inspecting the car when Mr Meldrum sold it would have realised that some somewhat unconventional work of repair had been done by the insertion of this body filler into the structure of the car.

Following the acquisition of the Corsair by the respondents their manager inspected the car. He, of course, saw the plastic filler on the inside of the engine compartment, and knew that this particular car was prone to rust damage. He realised that the plastic filler was not disguised in any way. Because the car was in a generally poor condition and appearance the respondents' manager decided that it was not suitable for a retail sale by his company. He therefore offered it for sale to several local motor dealers in the used car trade, but all declined to buy it. In these circumstances the respondents' manager ordered that the car be removed to the repair shop of the respondents' parent company to have the bodywork at the relevant part repaired and tidied up as cheaply as possible. When the car was examined by the appropriate officer at the parent company's repair department he realised that to make a proper repair of this defective part of the engine compartment would be extremely expensive. Labour charges alone for renewing each panel would be about £30 and the cost to a retail customer would be between £60 and £70 per panel. He thought that this was more than the respondents could afford to spend on this car and therefore arranged that the engine compartment be steam cleaned and the rough plastic filler which Mr Meldrum had inserted be smoothed down. Thereafter the whole of the engine compartment was to be painted to blend with the manufacturer's original colours, and this would protect the metal of the compartment as well as covering up the plastic filler which Mr Meldrum had inserted. The car was then sold to Mr Warry, a motor dealer. He examined it carefully, he knew that cars of this type were liable to suffer rust damage at the point where Mr Meldrum's repairs had taken place, but he also observed that the engine compartment had been recently repainted and appeared to be in good condition, and he did not notice the repair work done by Mr Meldrum, it having now been covered by the repainting carried out by the respondents. Mr Warry bought the car on an 'as seen' basis. He would not have bought the car if the engine compartment had not looked sound. Mr Warry had the car resprayed. It was submitted to the Ministry of Transport for a certificate of roadworthiness which was granted. The Ministry of Transport examiner looked at the bodywork inside the engine compartment and did not observe Mr Meldrum's handiwork or any signs of rust damage. He accordingly passed the vehicle for use on the road and in due course it was sold to Mr Shillabeer. Mr Shillabeer drove the car for some 4,000 miles between September 1970 and March 1971 without particular incident, and nothing was done during that period about repairs to the engine body compartment. In March 1971, however, the car was again involved in a minor accident, and when work was done on it in consequence of that accident the defects to which I have referred came to light.

The issues in this case in the first instance amount to one which can be put shortly: if a motor trader carries out work of repair or restoration to a motor car, and the result of the work or restoration is that some feature of the car relating to its strength or performance is obscured and thus not readily visible to a prospective purchaser, does the trader on selling that car without disclosing the nature of the work and the defect which is obscured apply to the car a false trade description under s 1 of the Trade Descriptions Act 1968? It is of some importance to note that the sale relied on by the prosecution as being the sale to which the false trade description was applied was the sale by Mr Warry. It will be remembered that Mr Warry had not carried out the repairs which involved the insertion of the filler into the structure of the car, and, furthermore, that when he sold the car he was unaware that this work had been done. There is no specific finding on the fact but it is a reasonable inference that the justices were satisfied that Mr Warry neither knew of the nature of the repairs which had been done to the car nor was he in any sense negligent in failing to discover them. If the prosecution are right in this case it means that a seller can be guilty of this offence even though he is wholly unaware of the circumstances giving rise to his offence.

His Lordship then referred to ss 1(1), 2(1), 3, and 4(1) of the Act, above, and continued:

The appellant's argument accordingly is that the concealment of the structural weakness in this car was an 'indication' of the 'strength' of the vehicle (s 2) and false to a material degree (s 3). The resultant false trade description it is argued was incorporated with the car (s 4). Alternatively, if this did not amount to a trade description it was likely to be taken for such an indication and thus to be treated as a false trade description under s 3(3).

The statutory words are very wide, and it may be that they are capable of the meaning attached to them by the appellant, but the proposition is nevertheless a startling one. If the appellant is right the consequences will be serious for all engaged in the repair and restoration of antique furniture, china, and a variety of other goods whose skill is devoted to making repairs which cannot be detected thereafter. If goods so repaired are subsequently sold expressly as undamaged an offence is, no doubt, committed, but if the seller cannot simply keep silent, and must disclose the repair by virtue of the Act, the doctrine of caveat emptor will be deprived of much of its force.

The 1968 Act replaces the Merchandise Marks Acts 1887–1953 under which the applying of a false trade description to goods had been an offence since 1887, but counsel has not been able to draw our attention to any case in which the covering up of a defect in the goods themselves has been held to amount to such an offence. I do not think that the difference of language in the two Acts, such as it is, explains or justifies such an extension of criminal responsibility. It is, of course, important that motor vehicles should not be sold in an unroadworthy state but this is made an offence under s 68 of the Road Traffic Act 1960, and does not need to be covered by the Trade Descriptions Act 1968. The primary concern of the 1968 Act is not with the condition or quality of the goods themselves, but with the possibility that a buyer may be misled by a trade description which makes them look better than they really are. I accept that an alteration of the goods which causes them to tell a lie about themselves may be a false trade description for present purposes, but Mr Warry did not apply a false trade description to these goods since he did not himself cover up the defect in the car and, indeed, was unaware of the existence of the defect.

If the respondents had been directly charged in respect of their sale to Mr Warry it might have been open to the justices, in my opinion, to find that they were guilty of the offence, but the form of the charge employed required the prosecution to prove an offence by Mr Warry.

I cannot bring myself to accept that Parliament intended to make Mr Warry guilty of a criminal offence in the circumstances of this case, and the explanation may be that a supplier of goods does not commit an offence under s 1(1)(b) if he did not himself apply the false trade description to the goods and had no knowledge or means of knowledge that this had been done by another. If Mr Warry was not guilty of an offence the respondents in this case were not guilty either. I would dismiss the appeal.

Melford Stevenson J. I agree with the judgment which has just been delivered.

Milmo J. I agree that these appeals against the decisions of the justices must be dismissed. I have reached this conclusion with regret because I am satisfied that on the findings of fact the respondents have clearly committed an offence under s 1(1)(a) of the Trade Descriptions Act 1968 with which they were not charged but have not committed either of the offences under s 23 with which they were charged. The prosecution alleged that a Mr Warry, against whom no charge was preferred, had committed two offences under s 1(1)(b) of having in course of a trade or business (1) offered to supply, and (2) supplied, to a customer (Mr Shillabeer) certain goods, namely, a Ford Corsair motor car, to which a false trade description was applied and that the commission of those offences was due to the act or default of the respondents. The charges against the respondents fail unless the prosecution prove that Mr Warry committed one or other or both of these offences . . .

In this case, I have no doubt that in doing what they did to conceal the use which had been made of plastic filler in the engine compartment of the car, the respondents did something which was not only likely but obviously intended to be taken as an indication that the engine compartment was in a sound condition whereas it was far from it. In these circumstances having regard to the very wide language of s 3(3), they applied a false trade description to the car and therefore committed an offence under s 1(1)(a). Further, if Mr Warry committed an offence, it was entirely due to this act on the part of the respondents.

However, when Mr Warry sold the car he was unaware that any trade description of any sort was then applied to the car and there is no finding and no evidence that he was in any way at fault in failing to detect what had been done to it. Had he been aware that a trade description was attached to the car at the time he sold it, I am not prepared to say that lack of knowledge of its falsity would have afforded him a defence to a charge under s 1(1)(b) of the Act but I think that knowledge that, at the time of supply or offer to supply, a trade description is applied to the goods is an essential prerequisite of an offence being committed by the supplier under s 1(1)(b) of the Act.

I therefore find that the prosecution having failed to prove any offence on the part of Mr Warry, and the information having been laid under s 23 of the Act, the justices were right to dismiss the charges. I would therefore dismiss these appeals.

Appeals dismissed.

NOTES

1. A helpful analogy with Warry's position may be seen in *Warner v Metropolitan Police Comr* [1969] 2 AC 256, [1968] 2 All ER 356, HL (knowing that one possesses an object without knowing that the object is a dangerous drug).
2. It is difficult to reconcile the statements in the *Cottee* case with the wording of s 24(3) of the 1968 Act which enables a defendant (W) to avoid liability, when charged under s 1(1)(b) of the Act, if it can be shown that there was no knowledge that a false trade description had been applied to the goods, see ch 15 at p 725. The *Cottee* case appears to place the burden on the prosecutor to show knowledge of the existence of the description, whereas s 24(3) places the burden on the defendant to show excusable ignorance.
3. As to the position of the respondents, the case suggests that if they had been charged directly in respect of their sale to W it might have been open to the justices to convict. (Milmo J went further and was satisfied that they had clearly committed an offence under s 1(1)(a)). This means that it is at least strongly arguable that deceitfully disguising defects in goods, thus causing them to 'tell a lie' about themselves, amounts to applying a false trade description. For what may be a very fine distinction between disguising defects and

carrying out effective repairs compare *R v Ford Motor Co Ltd* [1974] 3 All ER 489, [1974] 1 WLR 1220, CA, below, p 625. This latter case is important also in illustrating the operation of 'applying' by virtue of s 4(3) of the Act.

4. In *R v A F Pears Ltd* (1982) 90 ITSA Monthly Review 142, the following facts arose. Pears had supplied to a chemist shop, a jar of Astral moisturising cream. The jar was marked as weighing 54 grammes and its contents (58.6 millilitres) were slightly in excess of this. A test purchase by a trading standards officer revealed that the jar was capable of holding 64.2 millilitres. However, the jar was double-skinned and had the inner container followed the external contours the capacity would have been 84.83 millilitres. On a charge under s 1(1)(b) the jury found the defendants guilty as charged. (For an unsuccessful prosecution in a not dissimilar case see (1984) 3 Tr Law, p 26).

QUESTIONS

1. No doubt some may find this and other examples of such packaging mislead-ing (whatever the commercial justification for it) even though the weight or volume is stated accurately. However, was a false trade description *applied*? (For a full definition of this word see above, p 604.)
2. In *Davies v Sumner* [1984] 3 All ER 831 at 832, above, p 609 et seq, Lord Keith said, 'There can be no doubt that the respondent, when he traded in his car, applied a false trade description to it . . .'. Do you agree?

In considering these and some of the following questions students of the crim-inal law may find a helpful analogy with a distinction which arises in the law of forgery. Professor Griew puts it as follows ([1970] Crim LR 548, 549): 'The dis-tinction, more shortly, is that between a thing which tells a lie about itself (the term "automendacious" might be coined by analogy with similar linguistic hybrids) and that which tells a lie about a matter extraneous to the document ("extramendacious").' For the present position see Smith and Hogan *Criminal Law* (8th edn, 1996), ch 17.

Consider the following cases in terms of potential liability under s 1 of the 1968 Act:

1. Dresden, a craftsman, repairs a valuable antique vase which has been sold to him with a broken handle. The repair is undetectable by the human eye but it is accepted that such a vase is significantly less valuable than one which has never been damaged. He sells it to a customer without disclosing its history.
2. The Bombsite garage has a second-hand car with a 'For Sale' sign standing on its forecourt. The car has a seriously defective engine and is not of satisfactory quality. Would it affect the position if Bombsite had used a special substance which would hide the defect for some fifty or so miles and the purchaser had (i) asked, (ii) not asked, to hear the engine before buying the car?
3. Chisel, an unknown but highly talented sculptor, creates a work in the dis-tinctive style of Rodin. Even the most knowledgeable private collector would

assume that the work is by Rodin but Chisel does not sign or otherwise describe it as such. He then puts the work on sale in his gallery.

Section 4(2) provides that an oral statement may amount to use of a trade description. On balance the Molony Committee was against bringing such oral misdescriptions within the Act: 'To make oral misdescriptions an offence would be to put a very powerful weapon in the hands of a disappointed shopper' (para 659). *Fletcher v Budgen* ([1974] 2 All ER 1243, [1974] 1 WLR 1056, discussed above, p 605) is one of many cases in which the offending misstatement was oral. No doubt because of anticipated difficulties of proof, a shorter time limit for prosecution was originally laid down by s 19(4) of the Act where an oral statement was involved. However, in England this provision has in effect been nullified by the general provision in s 127 of the Magistrates' Courts Act 1980 which now applies the time limits of three years from the commission of the offence or one year from its discovery by the prosecutor, whichever is the earlier, to all 'hybrid' offences (that is, those triable either summarily or on indictment). *Rees v Munday* [1974] 3 All ER 506, [1974] 1 WLR 1284, a leading case on time limits in relation to prosecutions is discussed in ch 15: see pp 734–6 especially.

'SUPPLIES OR OFFERS TO SUPPLY ANY GOODS TO WHICH A FALSE TRADE DESCRIPTION IS APPLIED'

Section 1(1)(b) catches those who passively supply goods bearing a false trade description without necessarily having applied it 'actively' (this being caught by s 1(1)(a)). Section 24(3) provides a special defence peculiar to this passive offence. The defendant may prove that he did not know, and could not with reasonable diligence have ascertained, that the goods did not conform to the description or that the description had been applied to the goods (see further below, p 725).

Section 6 of the Act provides that 'a person exposing goods for supply or having goods in his possession for supply shall be deemed to offer to supply them'. Obviously this is intended to avoid the distinction familiar in the law of contract between invitations to treat and offers for sale—both are caught. The following case provides a striking example of the breadth of the concept of offering to supply goods.

Stainthorpe v Bailey [1980] RTR 7, Queen's Bench Division

The defendant motor dealer advertised a van for sale knowing that the odometer incorrectly recorded a mileage of 36,000 miles, the true mileage being something over 97,000. Mr Fricker, an officer of the Trading Standards Department, visited the firm's premises and was re-directed to the home of the defendant. The van was parked outside the house. The officer asked, 'Is the van for sale?'; the defendant said, 'Yes, the keys are in it if you want to have a look round' and went to answer his telephone. When the defendant returned the officer had gone. The court was requested (inter alia) to consider whether the justices had been entitled to conclude as regards the third information that no offer to supply had been made, and thus no offence committed. Having decided that the defence under s 24 did not avail the defendant (his failure to check the mileage or to disclaim the odometer reading being fatal to the 'due diligence' defence), Michael Davies J continued:

In my view, on the facts as found by the justices, there can be no question whatsoever but that the defendant was exposing goods for supply and also indeed that he had the goods, namely, the motor van, in his possession for supply. That seems to me to be supported by the brief conversation he had with Mr Fricker and supported by the terms of the advertisement in the evening paper which quite plainly was offering for sale that very same vehicle.

I find the justices' reasons . . . namely, that

'the vehicle was not at the place of business and that there was nothing to indicate to members of the public that it was for sale and that there ought to have been an opportunity, before it could be said that there was such an offer, for the defendant to complete a preliminary conversation—presumably on the telephone—quite insufficient and wholly irrelevant to the matter which the justices had to decide. I find nothing in the case which justifies their finding that s 6 did not catch the facts here and in my judgment they were in error in that regard in respect of the third information . . . '

I would allow this appeal and return the matter to the justices with a direction to convict on all three informations.

Robert Goff J and **Lord Widgery** agreed.

Appeal allowed. Case remitted to the justices with a direction to convict on all three informations. Order for payment out of central funds of prosecutor's costs.

NOTE

The question of effective disclaiming false or doubtful odometer readings is dealt with under the separate head of 'disclaimers', below, p 633 et seq.

Where an order is placed for goods, specifying certain requirements, a later supply of goods which do not fulfil these requirements can amount to an offence. Section 4(3) assists in establishing that the description has been 'applied' to the goods. This is illustrated by *Shropshire County Council (David Walker) v Simon Dudley Ltd* (1997) Tr LR 69, QBD, where a council's order for a fire engine with specific modifications was not satisfied by an engine supplied without the modifications and offences under s 1(1)(b) arose.

A FALSE TRADE DESCRIPTION

Neither the word 'false' nor the phrase 'trade description' is fully understandable except in the context of ss 2 and 3 (above).

With regard to the meaning of 'false' an important qualification is introduced to take out of the criminal sphere over-enthusiastic, but not essentially inaccurate, descriptions of goods and other de minimis situations where otherwise the description might strictly be false. Section 3(1) states that the description must be 'false to a material degree'. However, the wording of the rest of that section clearly encompasses descriptions which, though not false, are misleading, or which, though not trade descriptions as defined, 'are likely to be taken' for an indication of any of the matters set out in s 2. If the description is false, it is no defence that the buyer was not deceived (though this may affect the penalty imposed): see *Chidwick v Beer* [1974] RTR 415.

Section 2 sets out a list of indications, direct or indirect, which if given with respect to goods will constitute a 'trade description'. (This is an improved version of what was formerly in s 3 of the Merchandise Marks Act 1887). Examples of the application of s 2 have already been given. For instance, in *Roberts v Severn Petroleum and Trading Co Ltd* ([1981] RTR 312, above, p 614) the offending trade description applied to petrol by the Esso sign was an indication of the 'person by whom manufactured, produced, processed or reconditioned . . . '; and in the *Douglas Seaton* case ([1972] 3 All ER 750, above, p 615) there was an indication of 'strength'. 'Composition' under s 2(1)(c) has been held to cover the component parts of a package of goods as well as the materials of which a product is comprised: see *British Gas Corpn v Lubbock* [1974] 1 All ER 188, [1974] 1 WLR 37 (hand-held battery torch with cooker) and *Denard v Smith and Dixons Ltd* (1990) 155 JP 253 (computer software with a computer).

In some respects this list is very wide. For example, the reference in s 2(1)(d) to 'fitness for purpose' may be thought to make most breaches of s 14(3) of the Sale of Goods Act 1979 (see above, p 80) criminal offences. In *Shropshire County Council (David Walker) v Simon Dudley Ltd* (1997) Tr LR 69, QBD, express contractual requirements were not complied with (see above). Concern was expressed, by Phillips LJ, at p 82, that

> 'offences under the Act will be committed on many occasions where a breach occurs of a contract for the sale of goods . . . I do no think that this is a satisfactory state of affairs, but it may be justified by the need to attempt to ensure fair trading in a very wide variety of circumstances. The consequence is, however, that technical offences will be committed in circumstances where a civil law claim is the only remedy that the facts of the case require. Trading standards officers must exercise discretion when deciding whether or not a particular case warrants the intervention of the criminal law.'

Yet there are also significant omissions. In discussing the point in the 'Review of the Trade Descriptions Act 1968' (Cmnd 6628 (1976)), the Director General of Fair Trading noted that there were doubts about such matters as 'indications of the identity of a supplier or distributor and the standing, commercial importance or capabilities of a manufacturer . . . of goods' (para 127), and 'indications of the contents of books, films, recordings etc including their authorship' (para 128). Turning to a more general problem the report continues:

Review of the Trade Descriptions Act 1968, Cmnd 6628 (1976)

Availability of goods

130. Indications in advertisements and elsewhere that goods are available from stock may cause a prospective buyer to go to some trouble to visit the trader in question; and if the indication is untrue the former person suffers the loss of time and money. At its worst an indication that goods are available when they are not is a feature of bait advertising and switch-selling. In some cases in the past prosecutions have been taken under section 14 on the basis that the availability of goods is a 'facility', but in our view this seems to stretch the meaning of the word too far. Our preliminary conclusion was, therefore, that false or misleading indications of the availability of goods should be made a specific offence under the Act . . .

131. The proposed new offence was welcomed by the National Consumer Council and many of those concerned with enforcement as a substantial new weapon to deter bait-advertising and switch-selling and practices which characterise some, but not all, 'one day' sales held in hired halls. However it was clear from comments from the trade that our proposals could also have serious repercussions on the activities of reputable traders and could cause cash-flow problems forcing them to acquire stock before seeking to advertise and to hold it until the advertisement is published. In the case of advertisements in some publications this 'lead time' runs into months . . .

132. On reconsideration, therefore, we have concluded that the abuse with which we sought to deal is too small to justify the introduction of a measure which would clearly present great difficulties for the vast majority of traders who do not seek to deceive and for those concerned with the day-to-day administration of the Act. Problems of this kind arise mainly in connection with 'one-day' sales and mail order trading, and these are areas of trading where Part II of the Fair Trading Act might be invoked to provide any control needed by statutory order. **We make no recommendation therefore on indications of availability so far as the 1968 Act is concerned.**

NOTE

For Part II of the Fair Trading Act, see above, p 538 et seq. In some jurisdictions the problems noted in the above extract are dealt with more directly. For example the Australian Trade Practices Act 1974, s 56 provides in part as follows:

Bait advertising

(1) A corporation shall not, in trade or commerce, advertise for supply at a specified price, goods or services if there are reasonable grounds, of which the corporation is aware or ought reasonably to be aware, for believing that the corporation will not be able to offer for supply those goods or services at that price for a period that is, and in quantities that are, reasonable having regard to the nature of the market in which the corporation carries on business and the nature of the advertisement.

It is not every false description which leads to an offence under the 1968 Act. If the description does not fall under the finite list contained in s 2(1) no offence under the Act can arise. This can be seen in the following case:

Cadbury Ltd v Halliday [1975] 2 All ER 226, Queen's Bench Division

Chocolate bars produced by the appellants had printed on their wrappers the words 'extra value' as tax changes had allowed more chocolate to be supplied for the same price. Although these labels were discontinued after five months, shops were unaware of this and bars of differing weights were displayed, in some cases a higher price being charged for lighter bars, marked 'extra value', than for unmarked heavier bars. It was alleged that this constituted an offence under s 1(1)(b).

Ashworth J, having referred the ten paragraphs (a)–(j) in s 2(1) stated: The important point which emerges from a study of the ten paragraphs is that they are all matters in respect of which truth or falsity can be established as a matter of fact . . .

In my view the word 'value' introduces a quite different concept on which opinions may well differ. To say that an article is valuable is, of course, to apply a description to it, but in my view such description is not a trade description within the meaning of s 2. In this case the alleged trade description consists of the words 'extra value' and the additional 'extra' only increases the difficulty: inevitably one asks 'extra of what'? It might involve comparison with other similar articles previously on sale, and no doubt there are other possibilities. Counsel for the respondent contended that the words denoted extra weight, but while that is probably the explanation why the wrappers were originally introduced I am not persuaded that this is the only or indeed the obvious meaning of the two words. . . . I am of the opinion that the respondent failed to establish what is an essential element in proceedings against the appellant, namely, that a false trade description was applied to the goods, and accordingly I would allow this appeal.

Lord Widgery CJ and Michael Davies J both agreed.

Appeal allowed. Convictions quashed.

This situation could now be covered as a pricing offence by s 20 of the Consumer Protection Act 1987, see ch 14.

QUESTIONS

Having regard to the wording of s 2(1) (above, p 602) is a trade description confined to an indication of the 'physical characteristics' of goods or their 'history'? Is a false indication that spare parts are readily available a 'trade description'?

PROBLEM

Ada aged 80 lives alone in a large Victorian house with many fine antiques. Trader, an antique dealer, knocks on her door and is invited in. He examines a fine Queen Anne table and says, 'A fine table that. Worth a good £200. I'll give you £250 for it.' Ada who has no idea of present-day values agrees to sell the table to Trader at that price. As Trader well knows the table is worth over £2,000.

Consider Trader's liability under the 1968 Act.

There follows a selection of cases on two areas of motor vehicle sales which cause particular trouble. These are cases of cars and other vehicles which are described wrongly as being 'new' or in 'excellent' or 'beautiful' condition and of cars etc which are 'clocked'.

'NEW' AND 'BEAUTIFUL' CARS

It is trite law that *simplex commendatio non obligat*—a mere commendation is not a warranty. Nor is the exaggeration endemic in the second-hand car trade necessarily a description 'false to a material degree' under s 3(1). But calling a vehicle 'new' when it is not, or calling a vehicle which is significantly defective in 'excellent condition throughout' *(Chidwick v Beer* [1974] RTR 415), in 'really exceptional condition throughout' *(Furniss v Scholes* [1974] RTR 133), in 'showroom condition throughout' *(Hawkins v Smith* [1978] Crim LR 578), or in 'excellent condition' *(R v Nash* [1990] RTR 343) have all been held to involve the application of a false trade description.

The meaning of 'new' in relation to a car was discussed in the following case:

R v Ford Motor Co Ltd [1974] 3 All ER 489, [19741 1 WLR 1220, Court of Appeal

Ford Motor Company (Fords) were charged (count 1) under s 1 of the 1968 Act with supplying to Parkway Garage a Ford Cortina car with a false trade description (that the car was new) applied to it. The second count was that Parkway Garage had supplied to a Mr Rogers the same Ford Cortina car with the same false trade description applied, in contravention of s 1, and that this was due to the act or default of Fords, contrary to s 23 of the 1968 Act. Bridge J gave the judgment of the court:

Bridge J . . . The facts can be quite shortly stated. The Ford Cortina motor car referred to in both counts of the indictment was manufactured by Fords in April 1971. It was then sent, presumably by transporter, to Liverpool where it was intended to be exported in satisfaction of an order from a customer in Malta, but in due course that order was cancelled and the Cortina was then transferred to a compound at Speke. Whilst in the compound, and in the care, it is to be inferred, of Fords' forwarding agents, the Cortina was damaged by a collision with a trailer. It is unnecessary for purposes of this judgment to go at length into the detail of the damage that was caused. Sufficient indication of its extent, which was to some extent in controversy, can be given by stating that the trade cost of the repairs effected was of the order of £50. It was in fact repaired at the expense of the insurers to Fords' forwarding agents. Later the car was delivered to Parkway . . . On 1 December 1971 the Mr Rogers referred to in the second count of the indictment came to Parkway, wanting to buy a new Ford Cortina . . . Mr Rogers was taken to see the car and he bought it.

The documentation as between Fords and Parkway which was in evidence relating to this transaction, although quite voluminous, nowhere shows the word 'new' being in terms applied directly to describe this vehicle, although it is correct to observe that the expression 'new vehicle' occurs in a warranty which was furnished with the motor car, albeit in a context which in the judgment of this court does not show that phrase being used as an express trade description of the vehicle. The documents passing, however, between Parkway and Mr Rogers include an invoice which in terms describes the vehicle sold to Mr Rogers as one new Ford Cortina 1600 GT four door saloon as per makers' specifications.

The trial of this matter before the Crown Court occupied five days, and much of that time was taken up by submissions made on behalf of Fords at the close of the evidence for the prosecution that there was no case for Fords to answer on the basis that there was no evidence that

Fords had applied the trade description 'new' to the vehicle in question, or alternatively that, if they had, there was no evidence that the vehicle was not new. The trial judge, with whom this court feels the greatest sympathy, for he was unquestionably faced with difficult problems, with evident hesitation overruled the submissions made to him on behalf of Fords and left the matter to the jury, who in due course convicted Fords on both counts. Fords now apply to this court for leave to appeal against their conviction, the submissions before us being essentially first to the effect that there was no evidence proper to be left to the jury either that the trade description 'new' had been applied to the vehicle, or that, if applied, it had been false; secondly on the broad ground that the trial judge in leaving the issues to the jury misdirected them on certain essential matters.

Before considering the argument in further detail, it will be convenient to refer to the relevant sections of this not altogether straightforward statute. . . .

His Lordship then referred to ss 1(1), 2(1), 3(1), 4(3) and s 23 of the Act, above, pp 602–4 and below, p 728 and continued:

The first question which we have to determine is whether on the true construction of the relevant provisions of ss 2 and 4 there was any evidence on which the jury could be invited to find that when the car subsequently sold to Mr Rogers was supplied by Fords to Parkway, the trade description 'new' was applied to it. Counsel's argument for the Crown on this part of the case has ranged widely over the evidence relating to the course of dealing between Fords and Parkway, which he submits shows it to have been well understood by the parties on this occasion that a new car was to be supplied. The argument seems to us at times necessarily to involve the proposition, although this was disclaimed by counsel, that whenever there is an implied term of a contract of sale relating to a matter falling within one of the paragraphs from (a) to (j) of s 2(1), there must be a corresponding application of a trade description to the goods supplied under that contract. This seems to us to go much too far; it would be very startling if, for instance, the effect of the 1968 Act were to make a criminal of every seller of goods by description who delivers goods in breach of the condition of merchantable quality which is implied by s 14(2) of the Sale of Goods Act 1893.

But a very much narrower and more concentrated version of the argument can be founded not on the course of dealing between the parties, or the evidence as to what they understood or expected, but on the terms of a single document which was in evidence in the case . . .

Considering in detail the terms of that pro forma order which the evidence shows to have been used by Parkway to order the Cortina in question from Fords, although we have not the original document before us, we have come to the conclusion that this document does indicate that the vehicle ordered is contemplated as being a vehicle which will come either from manufacturers' stock at the factory or off the production line. If the words appeared at the top 'please supply the following new vehicles' it would in our judgment in substance add nothing to what the language of the document by necessary implication already shows. Accordingly we have reached the conclusion that in the terms of the statute this was a request made by Parkway to Fords which gave an indirect indication that the trade description 'new' was applied to the vehicle which Parkway requested Fords to deliver, and that being so the second part of s 4(3) was in our judgment similarly satisfied by the evidence, that is to say the circumstances were such as to make it reasonable to infer that the goods supplied pursuant to that request were supplied as goods corresponding to that trade description, and it follows therefore that Fords as the person supplying the goods in accordance with s 4(3) are deemed to have applied that trade description to the goods.

It is necessary next to turn to the trial judge's summing-up to see how this issue was left to the jury. The trial judge, if he did not withdraw from the jury entirely the argument of counsel for the Crown that the course of dealing – 'the new procedure', as it was described in argument—afforded a sufficient basis to say that Fords had applied to this car the trade description 'new', he at all events treated that submission so critically that it is difficult to think the jury thereafter paid much attention to it.

He went on, however, to say:

'Whatever you may think about that you must consider all the evidence and the documents and the whole of the surrounding circumstances, because all the documents and evidence are before you. But I suggest that this much is true and is the law. If work is done to a car to make it look new when it is not that can be a trade description.'

Then he repeated that sentence as one to which great importance was to be attached. Later on further down the same page he said:

'So if combining what I have been saying together, if work were done on a car to make it look new when it was in fact not new and if that could be a trade description, and if that trade description was so used, used in a manner likely to be taken by Parkway as referring to this car, then it would be applied to the car.'

It is apparent that the principle that the trial judge had in mind in giving the jury those directions was a principle which no doubt he thought was derived from the judgments of the Divisional Court in *Cottee v Douglas Seaton (Used Cars) Ltd*.[1] That was a trade description case concerned with a car which having sustained serious damage by rust to parts of the body work which had been extensively eaten away, had been 'repaired' by the application of plastic filler and subsequently had been painted over so that the fact that the rust damage had been replaced by plastic filler could not be detected by a straightforward examination in such a way as to give the vehicle the appearance in the relevant parts of still comprising sound metal. In giving the leading judgment Lord Widgery CJ said:[2]

'I accept that an alteration of the goods which causes them to tell a lie themselves may be a false trade description for present purposes . . . '

Counsel for Fords submits, and we think rightly, that a clear distinction is to be drawn between 'repairs' undertaken to an article which are of such a nature as to have the effect of concealing a significant defect without removing it on the one hand, and repairs simpliciter on the other which are properly and effectively carried out and which have the effect of restoring the article repaired to a sound and satisfactory condition. We accept counsel's submission that repairs which fall into the second class of those two categories should not properly be regarded as of themselves giving such an indication as to the character of the goods repaired as to amount to a false trade description.

No doubt it was just the danger of such an argument being advanced which Lord Widgery CJ had in mind in an earlier passage in the judgment from which a citation has just been made, when he observed in respect to one aspect of the appellant prosecutor's argument in *Cottee's* case:[3]

'If the appellant is right the consequences will be serious for all engaged in the repair and restoration of antique furniture, china, and a variety of other goods whose skill is devoted to making repairs which cannot be detected thereafter. If goods so repaired are subsequently sold expressly as undamaged an offence is, no doubt, committed, but if the seller cannot simply keep silent, and must disclose the repair by virtue of the Act the doctrine of caveat emptor will be deprived of much of its force.'

We conclude that in the circumstances of this case to seek to derive, as the trial judge's direction to the jury seemed to do, a false trade description applied to this vehicle as being new exclusively from the circumstance that it had been effectively repaired after being damaged, would open just the floodgate of which Lord Widgery CJ in the passage cited was apprehensive, and which in our judgment should be kept firmly shut. Accordingly we reach the conclusion that the trial judge left the issue to the jury 'was there here a false trade description applied to this vehicle to the effect that it was new' on the wrong basis.

The question then arises whether that misdirection must be fatal to the convictions. The answer is in our judgment: not necessarily so. If the jury could and should properly have concluded from the . . . order that the trade description 'new' was applied to this Cortina by Fords before it was supplied to Parkway, then provided always that appropriate directions were given to the jury as to the tests they should apply in considering the question whether the vehicle was properly described as new, it would not in our judgment matter that the trial judge had derived, and invited the jury to derive, the trade description from a incorrect source.

It is necessary, therefore, to turn to see how the question was dealt with, what does 'a new vehicle' mean, what is involved in describing a motor car as 'new'. The trial judge deals with that matter in this way. He first refers the jury to the de minimis principle very properly; aptly enough he says 'We lawyers put it in Latin but it can equally be stated in plain English that the law takes no account of trifles'. He then sets out five tests which had been suggested by counsel for the Crown in argument as tests which a motor car must satisfy if it is to conform to the description 'new': first it must not have been sold retail before; secondly it must be a current model; thirdly it must not have had extensive use—each of those criteria are elaborated in the summing-up. Then one comes to the vital passage:

'There were two other things which [counsel for the Crown] said must also be satisfied before you can say that the manufactured article is new. He said it should be in mint condition as produced at the factory and later at the end of his case he added a fifth. He said it should not have been repaired by any third party.'

The trial judge leaves those criteria to the jury virtually without comment, save only what he added when he said:

'One other thing on this question of "new" I offer for your consideration is this. A good deal of the defence case has been devoted to showing that the car was in excellent condition when it reached Mr Rogers and that the damage had been made good. If we say about something that it is as good as new, are not we really say it is not new? If, having bought something that was not new you show it to a friend and say "It is as good as new" are you not saying "It is not new but it is as good as new."'

The effect of the summing-up, particularly in the light of that last comment when added to counsel for the Crown's fifth criterion of what qualities a new car must exhibit must have been in our judgment to leave in the jury's mind that any significant damage—meaning thereby any damage in excess of minimal damage—sustained by a new car after it leaves the factory must have the result of rendering it no longer new irrespective of how well repairs may have been done.

. . .

But the heart of this case really turns on the fifth criterion, the suggestion that a car ceases to be new as soon as it sustains any significant damage and irrespective of the quality of the repairs. This is a test which we do not find it possible to accept. It seems to us that in this respect the questions to be asked when a car has sustained damage which has thereafter been repaired, both events having occurred away from the manufacturer's premises, are first: what is the extent and nature of the damage? and second: what is the quality of the repairs which have been effected? If the damage which a new car after leaving the factory has sustained is, although perhaps extensive, either superficial in character or limited to certain defined parts of the vehicle which can be simply replaced by new parts, then provided that such damage is in practical terms perfectly repaired so that it can in truth be said after repairs have been effected that the vehicle is as good as new, in our judgment it would not be a false trade description to describe such a vehicle as new.

An example suggested in the course of argument was of the engine of a new car sustaining serious damage, for instance for lack of oil on its journey from the factory to the dealer's premises. If the dealer removed the defective engine and replaced it with a brand new engine from the factory, we can see no reason in common sense why the resulting vehicle should not still be described as a new car. So also if superficial damage to part of the body were sustained, but is perfectly repaired either by panel beating followed by respraying, or by replacement of individual panels with new panels; if a perfect result can be achieved, why, one may ask rhetorically, should the car no longer qualify to be described as new? Of course, the question whether the repairs which have been undertaken in any particular case have attained the necessary degree of perfection to entitle the car to be described as new must be a matter of fact and degree to be decided by the tribunal of fact before whom the question arises. On the other hand we certainly accept that a point must be reached when damage, particularly accident damage, is so serious in its nature and extent that the car is no longer capable of being repaired in such a way as to qualify for the description 'new'. It is unnecessary and perhaps undesirable to try to define the point at which that degree of damage is reached, but an example which readily springs to mind is damage which involves distortion of the vehicle frame or chassis. For these reasons we have come to the conclusion that the question whether or not this yellow Ford Cortina sold by Parkway to Mr Rogers was falsely or truly described as a new car was not left to the jury with appropriate directions . . .

Application granted; appeal allowed; convictions quashed. Leave to appeal to the House of Lords refused.

¹ [1972] 3 All ER 750, [1972] 1 WLR 1408 (see above, p 615).
² [1972] 3 All ER at 757, [1972] 1 WLR at 1416.
³ [1972] 3 All ER at 757, [19721 1 WLR at 1415.

NOTES

1. Compare *R v Ford Motor Co Ltd* (above) with *Routledge v Ansa Motors (Chester-le-Street) Ltd* [1980] RTR 1 where a van manufactured in 1972, converted into a caravanette, and first registered on 1 August 1975 was described on a sales invoice as 'one used 1975 Ford Escort Siesta'. The justices accepted a submission of no case to answer. On appeal the Divisional Court held that the justices should have considered whether it was likely that on reading these words an average customer would believe that 1975 was the date of manufacture. If so, they should then have considered whether the date was 'false to a material degree'.

2. In *R v Anderson* (1988) 152 JP 373, CA, the appellant car dealer had registered new cars in its name to meet import quotas imposed on the producer, Nissan. The cars were subsequently sold to customers as 'new' cars. Convictions were upheld as, although the cars were in mint condition, 'new' could be taken to mean that there had been no previous registered keepers of the vehicles.

QUESTIONS

On the application of s 4(3) consider the following case:

Alice enters Shaver's Egg Shop and says, 'I would like a dozen new laid eggs please'. Shaver sells her a dozen eggs from a tray. They are not 'new laid' but are edible and of good quality. Has Shaver committed an offence contrary to s 1 of the 1968 Act? Is there liability under s 13 of the Sale of Goods Act 1979 (above, pp 80 and 87–95)?

'CLOCKED' CARS

The Director General of Fair Trading, in *The Purchase of Used Cars, A consultation paper from the OFT*, September 1996, stated that figures published by the Independent Mileage Verification Association showed that, in the first 8 months of 1994, 8.1 per cent of cars with more than four owners had been 'clocked' and this figure went up to 13.67 per cent for the same period in 1995. The Institute of Trading Standards Administration estimates the cost to the consumer of unscrupulous car dealers is around £100 million a year. The Director has used his powers under Part III of the Fair Trading Act 1973 to deal with 'persistent offenders' (see above, p 547), but feels these are inadequate, see *Selling Second-Hand Cars, A report by the OFT*, October 1997, paras 2.19–2.29 and above, p 565. He also exercises his powers to withhold, suspend or revoke the consumer credit licences of 30–40 dealers a year when dealers are convicted of trade descriptions offences. (Under the 1981 version of the Motor Code of Practice members must verify odometer readings or warn customers that this has not been done).

Altered mileages are 'descriptions' within s 2(1)(i)–(j) above, being a false indication of the history, previous ownership or use of the vehicle. The following case is of general interest and importance.

Holloway v Cross [1981] 1 All ER 1012, Queen's Bench Division

Donaldson LJ. This is another of the odometer cases. Mr Holloway, who is a motor trader, appeals by case stated against his conviction by the magistrates for Kent sitting at Chatham on 16 August 1978.

The charges were the usual charges under ss 1(1)(a) and (1)(b) of the Trade Descriptions Act 1968 of applying a false trade description to any goods in the course of trade or business and supplying or offering to supply goods to which a false trade description is applied.

The facts were these. The appellant had bought a Triumph motor car which had been first registered in 1973. The mileage was, in fact, in excess of 70,000. When he bought it the odometer reading was slightly over 700 miles. The purchaser saw the car and asked what its correct mileage was. He was told by the appellant, as was the fact, that he did not know. However, the appellant also said that he would make inquiries. Apparently it was necessary to do some minor repairs on the car and the purchaser came back, with a view to buying the car, on 1 October 1977. He and the appellant co-operated in completing a document known as a 'used car invoice'.

The appellant asked the purchaser what was the purchaser's estimation of the car's mileage but, perhaps not surprisingly, the purchaser was unable or declined to make any suggestions initially. The appellant then asked the purchaser if he thought that a figure of 45,000 sounded correct. This was accepted by the purchaser on the basis, no doubt, that it sounded correct, and the invoice was completed by the appellant to read 'Recorded mileage indicator reading is 716 estimated 45,000'.

The magistrates found that the purchaser would not have bought the car if he had known its true mileage was 73,000. They found that the figure of 45,000 miles was an average figure for a vehicle of this make, age and appearance, and that the method of calculating mileage, that is to say on the basis of make, age and appearance, is not always accurate or reliable. The magistrates went on to find that on the same occasion, when delivery was being taken and this invoice was being made up, the appellant gave the purchaser a warranty document issued by an insurance company, which applied to cars under six years of age, which of course this car was, but only if they had covered less than 60,000 miles.

They found that the appellant, in putting forward the estimate of 45,000 miles, used his knowledge of the motor trade and the general condition of the car and the information given in Glass's Guide. On that evidence, the magistrates came to the conclusion that the description 'estimated 45,000 miles' did not come within s 2 of the Trade Descriptions Act 1968 and so was not a trade description as such. Therefore, so far as s 2 was concerned, there could have been no application of a false trade description.

However, they held that it was within the extension to the concept of a false trade description, which is provided by s 3(3). Let me therefore refer briefly to those two sections. Section 2(1) provides:

'A trade description is an indication, direct or indirect, and by whatever means given, of any of the following matters with respect to any goods or parts of goods, that is to say . . . (j) other history including previous ownership or use.'

What was said below, and has extensively been repeated here, is that inasmuch as this statement was a mere statement of the appellant's opinion, it could not come within s 2.

Section 3(3), however, reads as follows:

'Anything which, though not a trade description, is likely to be taken for an indication of any of those matters and, as such an indication, would be false to a material degree, shall be deemed to be a false trade description.'

The magistrates accepted that what was said and done was not an application of a trade description in the strict sense of the words but as being within the extended meaning provided by s 3(3) . . . The question which is left for the opinion of this court is:

'Whether the appellant's opinion, based on the condition and general appearance of the car, concurred in by the purchaser that it had travelled some 45,000 miles, expressed in the invoice as "estimated 45,000 miles" in the absence of any evidence or suggestion by the prosecution that the said estimate was not made bona fide, amounted in law to a false trade description.'

Counsel for the appellant, who has argued this appeal with conspicuous moderation and clarity, submits that this 'estimated 45,000' was neither a trade description within s 2 nor within the extension of s 3(3). His argument is really very simple. What it amounts to is this. The purchaser was interested to find out, since the matter was in doubt, what was the information of the appellant as to the mileage of the car. Taking the facts as a whole, the purchaser knew perfectly well that the appellant did not know what the mileage was. All he wanted was an expert opinion. He got an expert opinion, and it was a bona fide expert opinion. That, he says, is the end of the matter. He adds for good measure that it is entirely irrelevant that there was an insurance company in the background or that the warranty document was given. He says that the charge relates solely to the application of the words 'estimated 45,000 miles'.

In my judgment that is an undue simplification. If it is a valid argument in relation to s 2(1) and that the words, taken in the circumstances in which they were used, do not fall within s 2(1), which, I may say, is somewhat debatable, bearing in mind that s 2(1) relates to an indication 'direct or indirect', it seems to me almost clear beyond argument that if this was not a trade description it was likely to be taken by the purchaser as an indication of the history of the vehicle and, of course, if so taken was false to a material degree. There cannot have been any point in asking the opinion of the seller as to the mileage which seems to have been done, except with a view to obtaining an indication of what the mileage was in fact. Once I have said that, I have, I think really said everything that need be said. That was the conclusion of the magistrates. In my judgment they were entitled to reach that conclusion. I would personally have been slightly surprised if they had reached any other conclusion. I would, therefore, answer the question of law by saying that the words complained of did amount, in law, to a false trade description within the meaning of s 3(3).

Hodgson J. I agree. I would only add this. Speaking personally, I am far from satisfied that the prosecution were right to concede that this expression of opinion was not an indirect indication of previous use directly within s 2. Had that been the way the prosecution had put the case, and had the magistrates come to a decision on s 2, then I would go this far with counsel for the appellant: that many of the findings of fact would have been quite irrelevant because s 1 creates an offence of strict liability which can only be got out of by a special defence set out under s 24. But, once the prosecution were going on s 3(3), it was then necessary for the magistrates to decide whether what was said was likely to be taken for an indication, and in deciding that I think they were right to take into account the matters, or at least many of the matters, on which they made findings of fact.

Appeal dismissed.

QUESTIONS

The above case is but one of many involving 'clocked' cars. Others are noted in the section on disclaimers which follows. Undoubtedly many defendants in such cases are wholly unmeritorious. However, is it desirable that criminal offences should be based on bona fide estimates or expressions of opinion, especially when such an opinion has been requested by the person prejudiced?

　　What advice would you give to an honest car dealer who is requested to give such an estimate?

PROBLEM

Collector enters the Provincial Art Boutique where he sees a painting of Salisbury Cathedral which is signed 'J. Constable'. He asks the owner, Poussin, 'Is this the original painting by Constable?' Poussin replies, 'Attribution of such works of art is a matter on which judgment may differ. However the overwhelming opinion, which I share, is that it is indeed the original painting'. This is an entirely accurate statement of the expert opinion of the time. Three months later it is revealed that the painting is a modern copy by Greating.

　　Subject to the availability of a possible defence under s 24 of the Act, below, p 710 et seq, has Poussin committed an offence under the 1968 Act? Is he civilly liable for a breach of contract (see further Sale of Goods Act 1979, s 13 and

Harlingdon & Leinster Enterprises v Christopher Hull Fine Art Ltd [1991] 1 QB 564, [1991] 1 All ER 737, CA, above, pp 87–95 and 88–90 especially) or misrepresentation? (see above, pp 22–5).

NOTE

For the problems caused by misattributed or mislabelled musical instruments (a fertile source of trouble in practice) see Harvey and Shapreau, *Violin Fraud, Deception, Forgery and Law Suits in England and America*, 2nd edn, (OUP, 1997) chs 3 and 5.

DISCLAIMERS

The nature of the practice

Since the passing of the Act a widespread practice has grown up whereby a trader may seek to avoid the application of a trade description by disclaiming that description in such a way that the potential purchaser should not be affected by it. The practice is especially prevalent in the case of 'clocked' cars but, as the following extracts illustrate, problems may arise in other areas also:

Review of the Trade Descriptions Act 1968: A Report by the Director General of Fair Trading (Cmnd 6628 (1976))

DISCLAIMING AND VARYING DESCRIPTIONS

The need for disclaimers

146. Section 1 of the 1968 Act makes both the application of false trade descriptions to goods and the supply of goods to which a false trade description is applied, offences. In some circumstances, however, section 1 may occasion problems for a trader who wishes to comply with the law for he may come into possession of goods to which a description has already been applied by someone else and which he knows to be false or the accuracy of which he doubts. While, if the description is a printed label, it may be an easy matter to erase it, this solution is not so readily available where, for example, the goods are of metal and the description is engraved or stamped on the goods.

147. A trader may also find himself facing difficulties where he himself applies a description to goods to be supplied at some future date, for example, in a catalogue or advertisement, and he subsequently realises that the description does not match the goods he proposes to supply. Again, there may be a simple solution in that the trader can (and should) seek to supply some other goods that do conform with the description; but one can conceive of circumstances where this is not a practical proposition, for example where the article is an antique and the prospects of finding a similar article which matches the description are remote.

. . .

150. It did not seem to us that there should be any derogation of the responsibility of the trader for the description of his goods as at present imposed, and it was in this light that we examined how far traders should be allowed to disclaim responsibility for trade descriptions by saying in effect to prospective customers 'take no notice of this description'. This is by no means a

simple issue to decide for disclaimers may take a number of different forms. The Institute of Trading Standards Administration classified them into five categories, namely:

   (a) those relating to specific goods and associated with the original description in such a way as to nullify or amend it, for example, 'X brand shirts – seconds' or 'the odometer reading is *not* a true indication of the miles covered by this vehicle';

   (b) those expressed in general terms which in fact amend but are not directly associated with particular descriptions, for example, 'all sizes quoted are approximate';

   (c) those which, although directly associated with a specific description, are of a general 'non-guarantee' nature which affects the image conveyed only to the extent of introducing an element of doubt, for example, 'the colour may not exactly correspond to that illustrated above', or 'this mileage is not guaranteed';

   (d) those of a general 'non-guarantee' nature which are not directly associated with any particular description and which affect the image conveyed (to the extent that they are seen) only by introducing an element of doubt, for example 'the colour of goods may vary slightly from the illustration in this catalogue'; and

   (e) implied disclaimers, for example, where transactions take place between two traders on terms which, by custom, are known to include a disclaimer of some kind.

Moreover different situations might arise according to whether goods are new or are second-hand. We would observe that this classification indicates that there is a very fine line between disclaiming a description and applying a qualified description or disassociating goods from a description for example by using such words as 'the colour of the goods is roughly that indicated in the illustration' . . .

Should the use of disclaimers be regulated?

151. A number of people told us that they thought that disclaimers should either be banned or their use closely controlled by new legislation. Anything less was regarded by these bodies as creating a loophole which would be exploited to the full by unscrupulous traders. The National Consumer Council and a number of enforcement authorities all of which particularly favoured a ban on disclaimers in respect of self-applied descriptions said that, while it would be bad enough if a trader could escape his obligations under section 24 by saying that he could not guarantee the accuracy of a trade description, it would be intolerable if it was possible for a trader to apply a false trade description and then avoid all liability by saying that it might not be correct.

152. Trade organisations, on the other hand, argued that it would be impossible to conduct normal business if the use of disclaimers was prohibited. In their view it was also necessary to permit the continued use of disclaimers in respect of new goods. The most commonly cited reason—and one quoted by the Multiple Shops Federation, the Mail Order Traders' Association, the Association of British Travel Agents, among other trade bodies—was the fact that catalogues and other printed material had to be prepared long before they were actually needed, and that however much care was taken subsequently the goods or services actually supplied might differ in detail. Moreover, much printed material was designed for long life and it would be impracticable to withdraw or reprint catalogues etc whenever changes were made to specifications. Sometimes it was even known in advance that changes in descriptions were possible, for example, in the case of motor vehicles, computers and other sophisticated equipment where there was continuous process of development and where it was to everyone's advantage that technological improvements should be incorporated as soon as possible even though this meant that the goods supplied differed from the original description.

. . .

159. There is a clear risk in permitting the use of disclaimers. We have already endorsed the proposition that whenever it is reasonable to do so, traders should be expected to check descrip-

tions already applied to goods when the goods are received. If the use of general disclaimers were lawful, traders might cease to make such checks and simply seek to repudiate all responsibilities for the accuracy of descriptions. Dishonest traders might be tempted to apply false descriptions and then protect themselves by disclaimers in the hope that the disclaimer would not entirely negative the impact of the description on prospective customers.

160. However, if disclaimers were to be completely prohibited, the problems we have touched upon in paragraphs 146–148 above would be virtually insuperable, particularly in relation to second-hand goods where the accuracy of descriptions on, for example, antiques often cannot be checked and where the obliteration of the description by defacement might spoil the goods. There is also the special problem of odometers on used cars. Returns from local authorities indicate that tampering with these to understate the true mileage is the most prevalent offence dealt with by enforcement authorities.

161. In considering whether disclaimers should be permitted, we have borne in mind the scope of the statutory defences described above. These suggest to us that it is only sensible that an honest trader coming into possession of goods bearing a trade description whose truth he doubts should be entitled to avoid conviction by negating the description in appropriate cases. We must conclude therefore than an absolute ban on disclaimers is not warranted.

. . .

166. . . .[W]e continue to see an attraction in leaving the matter to be regulated by case law. To lay down a series of statutory rules might be to provoke dishonest traders to try to circumvent them, and there may be considerable difficulties in formulating legislation covering every eventuality in an appropriate manner. We adhere therefore to our preliminary view that no amendment of the Act to regulate disclaimers is necessary.

QUESTIONS

As para 150 of the above Review notes, 'there is a very fine line between disclaiming a description and applying a qualifying description . . . ' Do such expressions as 'the colour of goods may vary slightly from the illustration in this catalogue' and 'all sizes quoted are approximate' constitute (i) disclaimers or (ii) qualified descriptions? Are they exemption clauses for the purposes of (or otherwise controlled by) the Unfair Contract Terms Act 1977, above, p 325 (see pp 350–55, especially); or are they potentially 'unfair terms' for the purposes of the Unfair Terms in Consumer Contracts Regulations 1994, above, pp 332–6?

The most recent consideration of disclaimers occurs in *Selling Second-Hand Cars, A Report by the Office of Fair Trading*, October 1997, where the Director General, in para 2.31, recommends that consideration should be given to changing the law to make disclaimers ineffective where reasonable checks on the mileage have not been made. An alternative approach would be to use a reformed Part III of the Fair Trading Act 1973, see further pp 564–5.

Judicial guidance

One of the most comprehensive discussions of the position regarding disclaimers occurs in the following case:

R v Southwood [1987] 3 All ER 556, [1987] 1 WLR 1361, Court of Appeal

The appellant, a second-hand car dealer, was convicted on ten counts under s 1(1)(a) of the 1968 Act for selling cars with reduced odometer readings. It was alleged that he was responsible for these alterations. In one case the mileage had been reduced from 50,887 miles to zero, had then been driven for some time, and a mileage of 2,890 was displayed. On invoices a disclaimer was printed, stickers were placed across the face of the speedometer (but not usually obscuring the odometer reading) indicating 'We do not guarantee the accuracy of the recorded mileage. To the best of our knowledge and belief, however, the reading is incorrect.' Notices in the sales office also indicated that all mileages were incorrect. Having explained the facts and quoted ss 1, 4, 23 and 24 of the Act, Lord Lane CJ continued:

Lord Lane CJ. Section 1 of the Act is clearly intended to impose strict liability on the applier of the false trade description (under s 1(1)(a)) and the supplier of the article (under s 1(1)(b)): see *McNab v Alexanders of Greenock Ltd* 1971 SLT 121 and *Taylor v Smith* [1974] RTR 190. . . .

An odometer reading is at least capable of being a trade description: see *R v Hammertons Cars Ltd* [1976] 3 All ER 758 at 761, [1976] 1 WLR 1243 at 1245, where Lawton LJ said:

'In our judgment, a reading on a mileometer on a motor car is an indication of the use which it has had. It follows that it is a trade description and if the reading is false . . . it is capable of being a false trade description.'

It would seem to follow logically that if a dealer falsifies the mileage reading on a car which is offered for sale, he applies a false trade description to goods in the course of a trade, and so commits an offence under s 1(1)(a). He would have no escape under the provisions of s 24. It seems somewhat illogical to allow him to use a so-called 'disclaimer' to avoid conviction. The 'disclaimer', assuming it to be in the terms of those in the instant case, would be saying: 'This is a false trade description. I assert that it is a false trade description, and because I assert that it is a false trade description it ceases to be a false trade description applied to goods, and consequently I am not guilty of a contravention of s 1(1)(a).' The assertion does not cause the description to be any less false than it was originally, nor does it cause the description to cease to be applied to the car. It seems that on the strict wording of the Act, therefore, the so-called 'disclaimer' provides no defence to a person charged under s 1(1)(a).

Before reaching any conclusion on this aspect however, it is necessary to examine the considerable body of authority which exists on the concept of the 'disclaimer'. Most of the decisions emanate from the Divisional Court, and most of them are cases on s 1(1)(b) . . .

Norman v Bennett [1974] 3 All ER 351, [1974] 1 WLR 1229 was [a] Divisional Court case involving a charge under s 1(1)(b). The following passage appears in the judgment of Lord Widgery ([1974] 3 All ER 351 at 353–354, [1974] 1 WLR 1229 at 1232:

'This case raises, I think for the first time, a need for the court to think a little more deeply about the extent to which a false trade description can be disclaimed, so as to prevent the supplier of the goods from committing a criminal offence. Earlier authorities have recognised the possibility of such a disclaimer but have not gone in any detail into the circumstances in which that can be done. I think that where a false trade description is attached to goods, its effect can be neutralised by an express disclaimer or contradiction of the message contained in the trade description. To be effective any such disclaimer must be as bold, precise and compelling as the trade description itself and must be as effectively brought to the notice of any person to whom the goods may be supplied. In other words, the disclaimer must equal the trade description in the extent to which it is likely to get home to anyone interested in receiving the goods. To be effective as a defence to a charge under s 1(1)(b) of the 1968 Act any such disclaimer must be made before the goods are supplied'

The next decision in point of time is *R v Hammertons Cars Ltd* [1976] 3 All ER 758, [1976] 1 WLR 1243. The first matter which the Court of Appeal then decided, as already explained, was that the reading on a car's odometer was a trade description. The court also turned to consider the question of whether a 'disclaimer' can be an effective protection to a person charged under s 1(1)(b), as the appellant in that case had been.

The judgment of Lawton LJ contains the following passage ([1976] 3 All ER 758 at 762, [1976] 1 WLR 1243 at 1248):

'Each case must depend on its own facts; but in most cases of the kind now before the court a mileometer reading is on the motor car for the prospective purchaser to see and to take into consideration when deciding whether to buy. If dealers do not want prospective purchasers to take any notice of mileometer readings they must take positive and effective steps to ensure that the customer understands that the mileometer reading is meaningless. Whether any such steps were taken, and if they were whether they were effective, is always a matter for assessment by the justices in the case of summary proceedings and by the jury when there is a trial on indictment. We should expect both justices and juries to find that a casual remark in the course of oral negotiations or "small print" in a contractual document were not effective.'

Later Lawton LJ, when dealing with the appeal against sentence, said ([1976] 3 All ER 758 at 764–765, [1976] 1 WLR 1243 at 1250–1251):

'The Trade Descriptions Act 1968 was intended by Parliament to provide protection for the public against unscrupulous and irresponsible traders. Section 1(1)(a) deals with those who are proved to have been actively unscrupulous, as for example by turning back mileometers; and s 1(1)(b) with those who did not take the trouble to check as best they can that mileometer readings are genuine.'

Although we agree respectfully that it is usually the case that s 1(1)(a) will be dealing with the dishonest trader and s 1(1)(b) with the careless trader, nevertheless that will not always be the case.

K Lill Holdings Ltd v White [1979] RTR 120 was another Divisional Court decision involving s 1(1)(b). The defendants bought a second-hand car with the odometer reading 59,000 miles. They altered the reading to 'zero' and, having made what were described as full disclaimers, they sold the car a month or two later to S. S resold the car to J, a dealer, who in his turn sold the car the M with a false trade description applied, in that the odometer by then recorded 5,000. The defendants were convicted of contravening s 23 of the 1968 Act on the basis that J in the course of trade had supplied to M a car to which a false trade description had been applied by means of the odometer contrary to s 1 of the Act and that the commission of the offence was due to the defendants' act or default. It was held that the defendants' action in returning the instrument to 'zero' did not justify the contention that the commission of the offence by J on the sale to M was due to the defendants' act or default because they ceased to be responsible before that sale took place.

The decision is clearly not strictly in point so far as the present case is concerned, but a passage in the judgment of Lord Widgery CJ, is perhaps relevant. He said (at 123):

'Whilst it is no business of ours to recommend or otherwise approve practices of the trade, I feel bound to say that I can see a good deal of merit in this method of winding back the odometer, because it does seem to me that, for the time being at all events, it puts the problem of a false odometer out of the reckoning because no one will be misled by such a record. However, that is what they did for better or worse. They also placed a disclaimer inside the cab of the motor car. That, of course, is something which has been laid down in this court as being a method of escaping responsibility for this kind of trouble. To make matters as good as possible, they also had a notice up in their office disclaiming the accuracy of the mileages displayed on their cars. They seem to have done practically everything which this court has ever recommended that dealers in motor cars should do in order to avoid this kind of problem.'

Corfield v Starr [1981] RTR 380, another Divisional Court decision, was a case where the defendant had been charged with offences under both s 1(1)(a) and s 1(1)(b). He had bought for resale a second-hand motor car whose true mileage was some 55,000 miles. He replaced the odometer with one which displayed a mileage of about 35,000 miles and attached a notice to the dashboard which read 'With deep regret due to the Customer's Protection Act we can no longer verify that the mileage shown on this vehicle is correct.' The defendant then sold the motor car. He was charged with applying a false trade description and also with supplying a car to which a false trade description had been applied. The justices came to the conclusion that the notice was as 'bold, precise and compelling' as the trade description, and that it acted as a disclaimer. They acquitted the defendant. The Divisional Court held that the so-called disclaimer was inadequate and the justices had been wrong. Bingham J (at 384), obiter, doubted whether there was any distinction to be drawn on this aspect of the matter between s 1(1)(a) and s 1(1)(b) of the Act. Donaldson LJ (at 384) took the view that some 'disclaimers' could themselves amount to a false trade description, and suggested that in appropriate cases the terms of the 'disclaimer' itself might be used as the basis of an allegation that there had been a false trade description.

Finally we come to the decision on which the recorder in the present case based his directions to the jury . That is *Newman v Hackney London BC* [1982] RTR 296, another Divisional Court case. The defendant company in the course of their business as dealers bought a second-hand motor car on which the odometer reading was some 46,000 miles. They altered the odometer to read 21,000 miles and attached a sticker to the instrument disclaiming, but not obscuring, the recorded mileage. They offered the vehicle for sale and it was bought. They were charged with contravening s 1(1)(a) of the 1968 Act, in that they had applied a false trade description to the car by altering the odometer reading. They were convicted and appealed to the Crown Court, raising the defence that no offence had been committed because the sticker neutralised the reading and amounted to an effective disclaimer. The Crown Court took the view that the doctrine of disclaimers was not applicable to an offence under s 1(1)(a), and dismissed the appeal. The Crown Court hearing took place before the publication of the decision in *Corfield v Starr*. The Crown Court judge, in a judgment which was clearly approved by the Divisional Court, having cited a passage from the judgment of Lawton LJ in *R v Hammertons Cars Ltd*, said:

'It is clear from that case that the Court of Appeal sees those who offend against s 1(1)(a) in a rather different light from those who breach section 1(1)(b). The former are unscrupulous and the latter irresponsible. In *Waltham Forest London Borough Council v TG Wheatley (Central Garage) Ltd* [1978] RTR 157 Lord Widgery CJ, sitting in the Divisional Court, dealt with the creation of the disclaimer notice in these cases. He said (at 162): "The disclaimer notice is the creation of the courts. It is not dealt with in the Act at all, and it has been developed in order to recognise the obvious justice of enabling a person to explain the falsity of a speedometer reading by saying, 'I am not suggesting that this is guaranteed. I disclaim any responsibility for it. You must not rely on it."'. When a motor trader is the innocent purchaser of a motor vehicle to which a false trade description has been applied by a previous owner, by winding back the odometer, one can see the justice of providing enabling machinery to permit the motor trader to pass the vehicle on in the same condition without being caught up in the history of the vehicle of which he has no knowledge. There is something objectionable in convicting a man for an offence of which he has no prior knowledge and in which he has not knowingly participated. But can the same considerations be applied to the person who actually applied the false trade description—in the words of Lawton LJ . . . the person who has been "actively unscrupulous" by turning back the mileometer? Does the justice of the matter require that such a person be enabled to disclaim his own deliberate fraud in order to avoid conviction for what would otherwise be a criminal offence committed quite deliberately? We think not.'

(See [1982] RTR 296 at 300–301.)

In the course of approving that judgment, Ormrod LJ in the Divisional Court said (at 302–303):

'The distinction which the Crown drew was the distinction between applying and supplying. [Counsel for the defendant] submits that there is no valid distinction between those two offences for this present purpose and that the disclaimer doctrine should apply equally to those who apply a false trade description. In my judgment, there is a world of difference between the two offences. It is perfectly true that the application of a false trade description must, in some way, be related to a sale or prospective sale but, looking at the Act itself, I am disposed to take the view that the offence is committed when the false trade description is applied to the vehicle or goods and that it is at the time when the odometer reading is altered to read a meaningful figure like 21,000 miles. In that light, a disclaimer has no application at all. . . .'

By the time that judgment was delivered, the decision in *Corfield v Starr* had been published.

Counsel for the appellants contends that there is no proper distinction to be drawn, so far as this matter is concerned, between s 1(1)(a) and s 1(1)(b). That being so, runs the argument, the judgment of the Court of appeal in *R v Hammertons Cars Ltd*, although it referred only to s 1(1)(b), constrains this court to hold that a proper disclaimer is effective to absolve a defendant from liability under both s 1(1)(b) and s 1(1)(a). He derives assistance, he submits, from the dictum of Bingham J in *Corfield v Starr*, which was not applied in *Newman v Hackney London BC*.

We disagree. The decision in *R v Hammertons Cars Ltd* is certainly binding on us so far as s 1(1)(b) is concerned. It is not open to us, in the light of that decision, to hold that a disclaimer has no effect when the defendant is charged with supplying a motor vehicle with a false trade description. We take the view, however, that there is a proper distinction to be drawn between the two subsections.

Apart from the reasons advanced by the Crown Court judge and also by the Divisional Court in *Newman v Hackney London BC*, there is the following consideration. Section 24(3) protects the defendant charged under s 1(1)(1)(b) who did not know about any misdescription and could not have discovered it by the exercise of reasonable diligence. It does not cater for the defendant who has exercised diligence and as a result of that diligence has discovered that the odometer displays a false reading. There must be some method whereby he can protect himself. He should not be in a worse position than the man who is protected by s 24(3).

The answer seems to lie in s 24(1)(b). That section must mean that it is a defence to show that the defendant took all reasonable precautions and exercised all due diligence to avoid (or, one must add, to attempt to avoid) the commission of an offence under the Act. Thus the defendant who by making enquiries discovers the falsity of a reading would no doubt be able to protect himself by frankly disclosing the result of his enquiries in such a way that any purchaser would be in the same state of knowledge as the dealer himself.

Turning from s 1(1)(b) to s 1(1)(a), could the same considerations apply to the dealer who has actually falsified the instrument? It seems to us to be absurd to suggest that the actual falsifier could, by any stretch of the imagination, be said to have taken all reasonable precautions to attempt to avoid the commission of an offence merely by issuing a disclaimer, however expressed. By his initial actions in falsifying the instrument he has disqualified himself from asserting that he has taken any precautions, let alone all reasonable precautions.

We have not found this an easy matter to decide, but we have come to the conclusion that the judgment of the Divisional Court in *Newman v Hackney London BC* was correct and that there is a distinction so far as 'disclaimers' are concerned between the two subsections, and that it is not open to a person charged under s 1(1)(a) to rely on any disclaimer.

The direction of the recorder on this aspect of the case was accordingly correct.

. . .

There remains the question to which we adverted at the outset, namely whether the person who 'clocks' the odometer reading to zero is in any better position than he who reduces the reading to an intermediate figure. The argument seems to be that if the reading is reduced to an absurdly low figure, no one will be misled.

Apart from the difficulty which it would present to the jury or justices of deciding what is a sufficiently low figure, the fact that no one was misled, or was likely to be misled, is an irrelevant consideration. It seems to us that the person who 'zeroes' the instrument is applying a false trade description just as much as the man who reduces the reading to, say 15,000 miles. If someone buys a car with a false reading already registered on the instrument the falsity of which comes to his knowledge, his protection against a charge under s 1(1)(b) will then be a suitable and candid intimation to the customer of the falsity, thereby bringing himself within s 24(1). Our view is that clocking is not a proper method of attempting to avoid liability.

This appeal against conviction is dismissed.

Appeal against conviction dismissed. Appeal against sentence allowed and sentence varied.

NOTES

1. In considering disclaimers, it is important to note the words of Widgery LCJ in *Waltham Forest London Borough Council v TG Wheatley (Central Garage) Ltd* [1978] RTR 157, at 162, above, p 638, where he indicated that the disclaimer doctrine is a creation of the courts to protect 'innocent' sellers.

2. The guidance supplied by Widgery LCJ in *Norman v Bennett* [1974] 3 All ER 351, [1974] 1 WLR 1229, as quoted above, p 636, is of crucial importance. The disclaimer, to be effective, 'must be as bold, precise and compelling as the trade description itself and must be as effectively brought to the notice of any person to whom the goods may be supplied'.

3. The *Southwood* case drew a clear distinction between s 1(1)(a) and s 1(1)(b) charges in relation to disclaimers, ruling out their use under the former subsection and permitting them under the latter. Two cases show the contrasting effects of this. In *Kent County Council v Price* (1994) 158 LG Rev 78, QBD, a market trader, selling clothing, was able to rely on cards stating 'brand copy' to avoid liability, under s 1(1)(b), for displaying branded T-shirts which were not authentic. In contrast, the harshness of the position under s 1(1)(a) can be seen in *Southend BC v White* (1992) 156 JP 463, QBD, where a car was vandalised whilst in the hands of a car dealer and had to have a replacement odometer fitted. Its mileage, originally 98,000 miles, now read as 45,000, the car was priced as one of 98,000 miles, and it was marked 'not warranted'. It was sold to a dealer who would understand that the mileage was incorrect. Nevertheless, Nolan LJ stated: 'neither the respondent's disclaimer of the accuracy of the odometer nor the purchaser's knowledge of its inaccuracy could prevent the description from being false or constitute a defence against the charge under s 1(1)(a). Various suggestions were made by the court as to

how the dealer might have acted to prevent an offence arising, for example by a notice declaring the true situation or by raising s 24

4. An interesting development occurred in a s 1(1)(a) case in *R v Carl Bull* (1996) 160 JP 241, CA. A car was sold with an incorrect mileage recording which was written in a box on the invoice. After the mileage figure there was an asterix which was explained by the following words: 'Trade Descriptions Act 1968. We have been unable to confirm the mileage recorded on this odometer and therefore it must be considered as incorrect.' It was not suggested that the garage had altered the mileage itself. The court decided that the prosecution had failed to establish that at the time the trade description was 'applied', ie was written on the invoice, it was 'false'. The qualification of the recording was already present as it was being written and this could be distinguished from the *Newman* case where the deliberate alteration of the mileage was the 'applying' and no disclaimer or qualification was present at that moment in time. The court was anxious not to suggest that this case be seen a pointer to avoiding the strict liability of the Act. In the words of Waterhouse J:

> '[In] considering a case of this kind, if there is a statement to the effect that the mileage is considered to be incorrect, the decision may ultimately turn on the positioning of that statement in relation to the quoted odometer reading and other relevant circumstances. The essential point here is that the statement about the incorrectness appeared immediately after the number and was highlighted by an asterix so that it is unarguable that the qualification was not part of the trade description.'

5. In some cases there was confusion between the use of a disclaimer, which in effect, 'rubbed out' the false trade description, and the s 24(1) defence (discussed further in ch 15). It was suggested that to be successful in establishing 'all reasonable steps and all due diligence' under s 24(1)(b) an effective disclaimer had to be present. The position has been clarified in *London Borough of Ealing v Taylor* (1995) 159 JP 460, where it was confirmed that an effective disclaimer was not a pre-requisite for a s 24(1) defence, although often a disclaimer would be present.

6. The practice of disclaiming motor odometer readings by turning them back to zero before sale of a used motor (thereby rendering any future reading false), although initially approved by the Divisional Court in *K Lill Holdings Ltd v White* [1979] RTR 120, above, p 637, was condemned in *Southwood*. Although some merit may be seen in the argument that no-one would be deceived by a recording of zero, it is the fact that the car becomes a 'rolling-lie' which makes the practice objectionable.

7. The *K Lill* case also provides an example of the 'passing-over' effect of s 23 which enables an actual or potential defendant who blames a third party for the offence to bring that party before the court. For another such case, see *Cottee v Douglas Seaton (Used Cars) Ltd* [1972] 3 All ER 750, [1972] 1 WLR 1408, above, p 615 and for more general discussion of s 23 see below, pp 728–33.

PROBLEM

Rentaford runs a car-hire business. The odometer cable of a hire car becomes disconnected during use when the car has done 30,000 miles in a year. Twelve months later Rentaford has the cable re-connected. The car is then sold by auction to a dealer, Shark. The odometer reads 30,000 but the true mileage is about 60,000. Shark puts the car up for sale on his garage forecourt with a notice on the odometer reading 'Mileage NOT Guaranteed'.

Discuss the position of Rentaford and Shark under the 1968 Act. Would it affect the position of Rentaford or Shark if the odometer had gone all the way round the clock so that the true mileage was 130,000 rather than the 30,000 indicated? (Cf *Davies v Sumner* [1984] 1 WLR 405, affd. [1984] 1 WLR 1301, HL, above, p 609.)

QUESTIONS

Is Donaldson LJ correct in suggesting, in *Corfield v Starr* (above, p 638) that a disclaimer might constitute a false trade description? Which part, if any, of s 2 above would it fall within?

NOTES

For helpful discussion of this area see Bragg, *Trade Descriptions* (Oxford, 1991), and 'More Mileage in Disclaimers' (1982) 2 LS 172; Lawson, 'On disclaiming liability for a false mileometer' (1987) 84 LS Gaz 2760, and Holgate, 'Clocking, Disclaimers, Offences and Defences and the Trade Descriptions Act 1968' (1993) JPN 294. See also the Office of Fair Trading Report: *Selling Second-Hand Cars: a report by the Office of Fair Trading* (October 1997) which contains discussion of the various ways in which the clocking of cars may be prevented.

FALSE STATEMENTS AS TO SERVICES, ACCOMMODATION AND FACILITIES

INTRODUCTION

The following provision is concerned with false statements as to services:

Trade Descriptions Act 1968

14. False or misleading statements as to services etc
(1) It shall be an offence for any person in the course of any trade or business—
   (a) to make a statement which he knows to be false; or

(b) recklessly to make a statement which is false;

as to any of the following matters, that is to say,—

    (i) the provision in the course of any trade or business of any services, accommodation or facilities;

    (ii) the nature of any services, accommodation or facilities provided in the course of any trade or business;

    (iii) the time at which, manner in which or persons by whom any services, accommodation or facilities are so provided;

    (iv) the examination, approval or evaluation by any person of any services, accommodation or facilities so provided; or

    (v) the location or amenities of any accommodation so provided.

(2) For the purposes of this section—

    (a) anything (whether or not a statement as to any of the matters specified in the preceding subsection) likely to be taken for such a statement as to any of those matters as would be false shall be deemed to be a false statement as to that matter; and

    (b) a statement made regardless of whether it is true or false shall be deemed to be made recklessly, whether or not the person making it had reasons for believing that it might be false.

(3) In relation to any services consisting of or including the application of any treatment or process or the carrying out of any repair, the matters specified in subsection (1) of this section shall be taken to include the effect of the treatment, process or repair.

(4) In this section 'false' means false to a material degree and 'services' does not include anything done under a contract of service.

'ANY PERSON'

For a reference to this expression see above, pp 605–8.

'IN THE COURSE OF ANY TRADE OR BUSINESS'

This expression has been considered in some detail in relation to false statements concerning goods, above, pp 609–14. A further aspect of general importance arose in the following case.

R v Breeze [1973] 2 All ER 1141, [1973] 1 WLR 994, Court of Appeal

The appellant had listed his name under the title 'Architects' in the Yellow Pages telephone directory and had placed the letters 'ARIBA' after his name. Further he had assured a person who was seeking the services of a qualified architect that he was such a person. In reality he had passed only his intermediate examination

Lord Widgery CJ held that s 14(1)(a)(i) extended to false statements as to the qualifications of a person rendering a service (see also below, p 653) and continued:

However, it has been argued that s 14 has no application to professions, but only to businesses. It has therefore been submitted that the activity in this case should not be regarded as being in

644   Trade descriptions

the course of a trade or business, because it is in the course, so the argument goes, of a profession, and therefore not struck at by s 14 at all.

The first answer to that submission, and the one on which we would wish to rely, is that it does not lie in the mouth of this appellant to say that he is conducting an activity of a professional character when he lacks the professional qualifications necessary for the carrying on of that profession. We are quite unable to see how, given that the appellant's activity is of a commercial and business character, he can escape from the obligation under the section by saying that his work was really professional when at the same time he lacked the professional qualification necessary. That in itself in our judgment is enough to dispose of the argument that this case is concerned with profession and not business, and we do not, therefore, find it necessary today finally to decide whether s 14 has application to genuine professional men or not. All we would say is that we do not wish anything which is said in the course of this judgment to suggest that professional men are not within the ambit of s 14.

Accordingly, it seems to us that this conviction was properly entered as a matter of law, and that the appeal against conviction must be dismissed . . .

Appeal against conviction dismissed. Appeal against sentence allowed and fine varied.

NOTE

The issue of whether or not professionals are included within the phrase 'in the course of a trade or business' was considered in *D C E Roberts v Desmond Joseph Leonard and Mark Alexander Bryan* (1995) 14 Tr LR 536. In this case it was questioned whether offences under s 1 of the Act could apply to veterinary surgeons. Having referred to *R v Breeze*, Simon Brown LJ stated: 'For my part, however, I have not the least doubt that the term "trade or business" in the 1968 Act is apt to include professionals too. The *Concise Oxford Dictionary* definition of "business" includes: "Habitual occupation, profession, trade." I can see no reason to exclude professional men from the scope of this legislation.'

MAKING A STATEMENT

In many cases it will be a simple matter to pinpoint precisely when a statement is 'made' and moreover to conclude that a given person either has or has not 'made' it. However, this may not be true of statements which are published to the general public, as in the case of holiday brochures and advertising, and there are additional difficulties where the defendant is a body corporate. These matters are discussed in *Wings Ltd v Ellis* [1984] 3 All ER 577, [1984] 3 WLR 965, below at pp 662–9 and pp 715–6. See also *Coupe v Guyett* [1973] 2 All ER 1058, [1973] 1 WLR 669, below, p 729.

A FALSE STATEMENT

Liability under s 14 depends on the prosecution establishing that the relevant statement was 'false'. This may seem to be both obvious and straightforward but in fact the area is one of great complexity. The same is true of the related requirement of mens rea, that is knowledge or recklessness as to the falsity of the statement. The cases which follow illustrate a number of points:

Breed v Cluett [1970] 2 All ER 662, [1970] 2 QB 459, Queen's Bench Division

It was alleged that on or about 23 April 1969 the respondent builder recklessly and falsely stated to the purchaser of a bungalow that it was 'covered by the National House-Builders Registration Council ten-year guarantee'. Contracts for the sale of the bungalow had been exchanged on 3 April whereupon the purchaser had an equitable interest in the bungalow.

Lord Parker CJ stated the facts and described the informations as set out in the case stated, and continued:

. . .

Here the allegation is that the respondent recklessly made a statement as to the provision in the course of any trade or business of a service. The justice dismissed the information on the ground that, the contracts having been exchanged on 3rd April, there was a binding obligation. Whatever happened and whatever representations or statements were made thereafter, there was a binding contract which the vendor and purchaser had to complete, and accordingly the statement made on 23rd April could not be an inducement to enter into or to complete a contract.

In my judgment, to approach the matter in that way is to give too narrow a construction to s 14 of the Act. The statements there referred to are not, as it seems to me, confined to statements inducing the entering into of a contract. There may well be statements made after a contract is completed, a contract for repairs to my motor car, a contract for repair to my roof, stating the effect of what has been done by way of repair which may constitute an offence if made recklessly, even though the contract has been completed and the payment has been made . . .

Cooke J and **Bridge J** agreed.

Appeal allowed. Case remitted with direction to convict the respondent.

NOTE

For a contrasting case where the charge was under s 1 of the Act and the post-contractual statement concerned the condition of goods see *Wickens Motors (Gloucester) Ltd v Hall* [1972] 3 All ER 759, [1972] 1 WLR 1418 and above, pp 606 and 613.

PROBLEM

On 1 April Shark sells to Ada a car which has defective brakes. On the very same day Bert brings his car in to Shark to have the brakes serviced. The work is not done but Bert is charged for it. On 1 May both Ada and Bert return to complain and Shark says, 'Both of your brakes were in perfect condition when they left me.'

Consider Shark's liability under the 1968 Act.

As Lord Parker CJ's examples in *Breed v Cluett* illustrate the requirement that the statement be false may be satisfied where it relates to the past, for example, 'I have treated your attic with a preservative against dry-rot'. This is confirmed in *R v Bevelectric Ltd* (1992) 100 ITSA 12 MR 18, CA, where false statements were made that broken washing machines had needed replacement motors. By implication this suggested that a genuine assessment had been made as to the extent of any necessary repair, which was untrue. Such statements were held to be within s 14. Similarly where a statement relates to the present, for example, 'This spray I am using in your attic is a preservative against dry-rot'. Much more difficult (and yet of fundamental importance) is the distinction between statements of fact and unfulfilled promises which is drawn in the following case:

R v Sunair Holidays Ltd [1973] 2 All ER 1233, [1973] 1 WLR 1105, Court of Appeal

MacKenna J read the following judgment of the court at the invitation of Stephenson LJ. Sunair Holidays Ltd, the appellants in this case, are a company selling package tours abroad. In the autumn of 1969 they published a brochure, 'Sunair Summer 1970' containing particulars of hotels in Spain, Italy and other countries in which they offered accommodation for the summer season of 1970. One of these was the Hotel Cadi at Calella on the east coast of Spain. Mr Bateman got a copy of Sunair's brochure from a travel agency in Romford some time after Christmas 1969, read it, chose the Hotel Cadi, and on 7 January 1970 bought tickets from Sunair for a Whitsun holiday at that hotel for himself and his family beginning on 27 May 1970. When they got to Calella in May they were dissatisfied with the hotel, and on their return to England Mr Bateman complained to the authorities who started criminal proceedings against Sunair. The proceedings were by way of an indictment containing six counts. Each count charged Sunair with making a false statement about the Hotel Cadi in the 1970 brochure contrary to s 14(1)(b) of the Trade Descriptions Act 1968. In each case the statement was said to have been made on 7 January 1970, the date when Mr Bateman bought the tickets.

We shall quote the particulars of the six allegedly false statements, using in each case the words of the indictment:

Count 1 ' . . . that the Hotel Cadi, Calella, had a swimming pool, whereas there was no swimming pool at the said hotel.'
Count 2 ' . . . that there were push chairs for hire at the Hotel Cadi, Calella, whereas no push chairs were available.'
Count 3 ' . . .that the Hotel Cadi, Calella, had its own night club, whereas there was no such night club at the said Hotel.'
Count 4 '. . . that cots were available at the Hotel Cadi, Calella, whereas no cots were available.'
Count 5 ' . . . that there was dancing every night in the discotheque of the Hotel Cadi, Calella, whereas there was no discotheque at the said Hotel.'
Count 6 ' . . . that the Hotel Cadi, Calella, provided good food with English dishes available as well as special meals for children, whereas no English dishes or special meals for children were available.'

The case was tried at the Woodford Crown Court in October 1972 before his Honour Judge Mason QC and a jury. The judge held that there was no case for Sunair to answer on count 4, that relating to the cots. He left the other five to the jury, who convicted on counts 1, 2 and 6, those relating to the swimming pool, the push chairs and the food, and acquitted on counts 3 and 5, those relating to the night club and the discotheque. Sunair appeal against their convictions and against the fines imposed on them by the judge.

His Lordship then quoted s 14(1) and (2)(b) of the Act (see above, pp 642–3) and continued:

The two questions raised by this appeal can now be stated: (1) whether s 14, as the appellants now contend, is limited to representations of facts, past or present, or whether it includes assurances about the future, and, if the appellants' contention is right; (2) whether the jury's verdict on counts 1, 2 and 6, or any one of them, can be upheld. Before we consider these two questions we shall quote those parts of the brochure which relate to the Hotel Cadi, and state a few of the facts about the hotel.

'Hotel Cadi, Calella. A new, very comfortable hotel in the centre of Calella and only about 20 yards from the beach. Luxurious lounge, with local decor, looks out on the sea. Well-stocked bar, *Swimming pool*. Modern restaurant: the food is good, with English dishes also available—as well as special meals for children. The friendly, informal Hotel Cadi also has its own night club; there is dancing every night in the discotheque. Lift to all floors. All bedrooms have a private w.c. and bath, and terrace. Cots also available. Push chairs for hire. Laundry service.'

The words 'swimming pool' were underlined in red. On the same page of the brochure particulars were given of the prices, including air travel, of a holiday at this hotel during a season beginning on 7 March and ending on 6 October, lower prices at the beginning and end of the season and higher in the middle.

The hotel had been open during the summer of 1969, though apparently it had not been used that year by the appellants. It then had a room used as a discotheque and a night club, but no swimming pool. The owners of the hotel planned to improve it during the winter of 1969–1970. The upper floors at the rear of the hotel were to be rebuilt and a swimming pool was to be constructed on the roof. The room used for the discotheque and night club was to be enlarged. The hotel closed down for the winter and did not re-open until April or May 1970. In the meantime the builders went to work, but not as quickly or as efficiently as had been hoped. When the Batemans were at the hotel, the principal meals consisted of soup, chops, steaks or chicken, always served with chips, and ice-cream and mousses and the like for a pudding. The main dish is said to have been cooked in the Spanish style, presumably in oil. Children could have their meals an hour earlier than the adults, but there were no special dishes provided for them. By 27 May, the date when the Batemans arrived, the swimming pool had been built, but because of cracks or leaks it could not be filled with water. The discovery of these cracks and leaks and making them good took time, and this work was still being done while the Batemans were at the hotel. The larger room for the discotheque and the night club had not been finished, though the artistes who were to perform at the night club were at the hotel. Push chairs were not available at the hotel itself, though they could be hired from a shop in a neighbouring street.

The appellants had made their contract with the owner of the hotel in April 1969. Under this the owners were to reserve accommodation for 130 of the appellants' customers at prices payable by the appellants and fixed by the contract. The appellants knew of the owners' intention to build a swimming pool. Because of the delay in the completion of the building work the appellants did not send any of their customers to the hotel until 27 May when the Batemans and others arrived.

So much for the facts. We come now to the construction of s 14. The section deals with 'statements' of which it can be said that they were, at the time when they were made, 'false'. That may be the case with a statement of fact, whether past or present. A statement that a fact exists now, or that it existed in the past, is either true or false at the time when the statement is made. But that is not the case with a promise or a prediction about the future. A prediction may come true or it may not. A promise to do something in the future may be kept or it may be broken. But neither the prediction nor the promise can be said to have been true or false at the time when it was made. We conclude that s 14 does not deal with forecasts or promises as such. We put in the qualifying words 'as such' for this reason. A promise or forecast may contain by implication a statement of present fact. The person who makes the promise may be implying that his present intention is to keep it or that he has at present the power to perform it. The person who makes the forecast may be implying that he now believes that his prediction will come true or that he has the means of bringing it to pass. Such implied statements of present intention, means or belief, when they are made, may well be within s 14 and therefore punishable if they were false and were made knowingly or recklessly. But if they are punishable, the offence is not the breaking of a promise or the failure to make a prediction come true. It is the making of a false statement of an existing fact, somebody's present state of mind or present means.

. . .

This section has been considered by the Divisional Court in several cases, of which we shall cite three.

His Lordship then referred to *Sunair Holidays Ltd v Dodd* [1970] 2 All ER 410, [1970] 1 WLR 1037, where the Divisional Court had held that a statement in a holiday brochure 'all twin-bedded rooms with . . . terrace' was accurate when made in as much as the appellants had contracted with the hotel for the provision of such rooms for their clients. Hence no offence had been committed even though in the result the hotel management provided a room without a terrace. He continued:

The second case is *Bambury v Hounslow London Borough Council* [1971] RTR 1. Bambury was the director of a company selling motor cars. A customer saw a Ford Cortina at the company's premises on which the word 'guaranteed' appeared. He negotiated for the purchase of the car with Bambury, who told him that the word 'guaranteed' meant that if anything went wrong with the car during the next three months the company would put it right, and that this guarantee would be recorded in a book. The customer bought the car, receiving an invoice which contained a printed condition excluding the company's liability for faults. The car developed several faults, including one in the clutch. The company made good some of them, but pretended that there was nothing wrong with the clutch which eventually was repaired by another garage at a cost to the customer of £17. Bambury was charged with having recklessly made a statement which was false—

'as to the provision in the course of trade or business of a facility, namely, a guarantee to effect repairs to the car for three months from the date of purchase.'

The justices convicted, finding—

'that the defendant's statement as to provision of the guarantee was false and made recklessly by him either well knowing that it would not be or without caring whether or not it would be honoured.'

The conviction was upheld for the following reasons given by Lord Parker CJ, [1971] RTR at 6.

'In my judgment the justices here came to a conclusion to which they were fully entitled to come . . . The fact that the contractual obligations were not complied with is consistent with one or other of two matters: one, a failure to perform their contractual obligations which they had entered into; or secondly, the fact that there never was an entering into of any contractual obligations at all. The justices . . . found that the original statement that they were entering into contractual obligations was a false one. They might have come to a different conclusion, but in my judgment there was clearly evidence . . . that the original statement was false.'

Lord Parker CJ was distinguishing between a statement by Bambury that his company were undertaking an obligation to repair the car, which would be true or false at the time when the statement was made, and the undertaking itself, if one were given. Bambury would be liable under s 14 if the first alternative was the right one, and if the statement was untrue. That would be because he had made a false statement about an existing fact, namely his company's undertaking of an obligation. But he would not be liable on the second alternative, even if the company thereafter failed to perform the undertaking.

Beckett v Cohen [1973] 1 All ER 120, [1972] 1 WLR 1593 is the third case. There a builder had promised that he would build a garage within ten days and that it would be similar to an existing garage. He did not finish the garage in time, and the one he built was in some respects different from the existing garage. In respect of his failure to complete in time, he was charged with having made a statement, 'which was false as to the time at which a service, namely the building of a garage, would be provided.' In respect of the differences between the two garages, he was charged with having made a statement which was 'false as to the manner in which such a service would be provided'. The justices upheld the builder's submission that s 14(1)—

'only covered false statements as to services which had already been provided or were currently being provided, whereas the informations referred to a service which "would be provided" and therefore fell outside the scope of s 14(1) of the Act'.

The prosecutor's appeal was dismissed. This is what Lord Widgery CJ said ([1973] 1 All ER at 121,122; [1972] 1 WLR at 1596):

'. . . This section matches earlier provisions in the Act dealing with the sale of goods. The purpose of the earlier sections is to prevent persons when selling goods from attaching a false description to the goods, and in the same way s 14 is concerned, as I see it, when services are performed under a contract, to make it an offence if the person providing the services recklessly makes a false statement as to what he has done. The section specifically refers to the reckless making of a statement which is false. That means that if at the end of the contract a person giving the service recklessly makes a false statement as to what he has done, the matter may well fall within s 14, but if before the contract has been worked out, the person who provides the service makes a promise as to what he will do, and that promise does not relate to an existing fact, nobody can say at the date when that statement is made that it is either true or false. In my judgment Parliament never intended or contemplated for a moment that the Act should be used in this way, to make a criminal offence out of what is really a breach of warranty.'

We accept the distinction drawn in this passage between statements of fact, past or present, and promises about the future, and agree with the view that s 14 deals with the first but not the second. A statement about the quality of a service already provided is a statement of past fact and is covered by the section. A statement of existing fact may also be covered, as, for example, if a hotel advertises that its services currently provided include the provision of afternoon tea; if that service is not being provided at the time when the statement is made an offence may be committed. A statement about existing facts would not cease to be within the section because the person making it warranted that it was true and that the facts would continue to exist in the future. In that limited sense the section can apply to warranties. But it does not apply to promises about the future unless, as we said earlier, the promise can be construed as an implied statement of a present intention or the like, in which case it may be that it is caught by s 14, as it would be by s 15 of the Theft Act 1968, which includes in its definition of deception false statements of present intentions.

In answer to the first question stated above, we hold that s 14 is limited to statements of fact, past or present, and does not include assurances about the future.

It remains to consider the second question whether, on this reading of the section, the jury's verdict on counts 1, 2 and 6 or any of them can be upheld.

In the court below the prosecution contended that the words 'swimming pool' in the appellants' 1970 brochure meant that a swimming pool had already been built and was in existence on the date in January 1970, when Mr Bateman made his bookings. They seem to have contended in the alternative that the words meant that a swimming pool would be in existence on 7 March 1970 which was the earliest date given in the brochure for bookings at the Hotel Cadi. They contended that in either case the statement was false. The appellants contended that the words related only to the future and meant that a swimming pool would be in existence on 27 May 1970, when Mr Bateman's bookings took effect. Both parties seem to have agreed that the words about push chairs, English dishes and special meals for children, related to the future in the case of this hotel which was not open in January 1970, when the statements about these matters were made. Neither party contended that if any of the statements related only to the future they were not caught by s 14. *Beckett v Cohen* [1973] 1 All ER 120, [1972] 1 WLR 1593, had not yet been decided, and the point which it established about the meaning of the section had apparently not occurred to counsel on either side or to the judge himself. The appellants' case was that the words about the pool, the chairs and the food all related to the future, and that the assurances on those matters were substantially fulfilled.

Other points of construction were raised by the appellants at the trial. What was meant by 'English dishes also available'? What was the meaning of 'special meals for children'? Did this mean special dishes or only special meal times? What was meant by 'Push chairs for hire'? Did this mean that there would be chairs for hire at the hotel itself, or would it be enough that there were chairs for hire in a neighbouring shop? Somebody had to construe the brochure to answer these questions of construction and the question whether the words about the swimming pool related to the present or the future. Both parties were agreed in the court below and before us that it was for the jury to construe the document as it would be in proceedings for libel. This was the view taken in the earlier case of *R v Clarksons Holidays Ltd* (1972) 57 Cr App Rep 38, and tacitly approved by this court to which the case was brought on appeal. Following this precedent we shall assume that this is the right course, observing only that if it is right statements in books on evidence which treat libel proceedings as the only exception to a rule that the construction of documents is for the judge may need to be revised: see *Cross on Evidence*[1] and the article on Evidence in Halsbury's Laws of England.[2]

Treating the question of construction as one for the jury, the judge directed them as follows:

'You must ask first: "What do these statements mean?", beginning, as I suggest you should, by asking yourself whether when [the appellants] made those statements they were representing to the people who read the brochure that the physical facilities, if I can so describe them, of the Hotel Cadi existed, as the prosecution suggest they were, on the date when Mr Bateman booked his holiday, namely, 7 January 1970; or were they representing that those facilities would exist on what was said to be the earliest possible booking date, 7 March 1970? . . . Or, third, [were the appellants] representing that those physical facilities would exist . . . when Mr Bateman arrived at the hotel, namely, 27 May? Those are the three possibilities.'

[1] 3rd edn (1969) pp 50, 51.
[2] 3rd edn, vol. 15, p 276, para 503.

His Lordship then referred to the possible distinctions (notably between the swimming pool, and the food and push-chairs) on which the judge had elaborated to assist the jury in selecting the appropriate date and continued:

What further direction ought the judge to have given the jury? If our reading of s 14 is right he should have told them, in the case of the swimming pool, that if they construed the words as relating to the future, which was the appellants' contention, they should acquit them on count 1, and that in any event, they should acquit them on counts 2 and 6 which both sides agreed related to the future. He did not do so, because this point had not been taken by the appellants. Instead he went on to direct the jury that having chosen the date to which any of these statements related, they should then consider whether it was true at that date, and if it were not and they found that it had been recklessly made they could convict the appellants. This was wrong.

Counsel for the Crown in this court, asked, what did the appellants lose by the judge's failure to give the right direction on count 1? The answer is clear. They lost their chance of an acquittal on this count, which would have been their right if the jury construed the words about the swimming pool as relating to the future, as they may have done. We cannot uphold the conviction on this count, not knowing whether the jury construed the words as relating to 7 January, or whether they construed them as relating to 27 May and convicted the appellants only because they found that the swimming pool had not been completed by that date.

Counsel for the Crown appeared to argue that even if s 14 were limited to statements of existing facts, the convictions on the three counts should still be upheld on the ground that the brochure impliedly represented that satisfactory arrangements had already been made by the appellants for the provision of these facilities or services in the future, and that such arrangements had not, in fact, been made on 7 January. This was not how the charges were framed in the indictment. It is not how the case was fought in the court below. It is not how the case was summed up by the judge. It is impossible to uphold these convictions on this or any other ground, and they must be quashed.

Appeal allowed: convictions quashed.

NOTES

1. The reasoning of MacKenna J was approved in *British Airways Board v Taylor* [1976] 1 All ER 65, [1976] 1 WLR 13, HL, a case which arose out of the appellant's policy of overbooking flights to counteract the effect of 'no-shows'.

   Lord Wilberforce said (at pp 68, 17): My Lords, the distinction in law between a promise as to future action, which may be broken or kept, and a statement as to existing fact, which may be true or false, is clear enough. There may be inherent in a promise an implied statement as to a fact, and where this is really the case, the court can attach appropriate consequences to any falsity in, or recklessness in the making of, that statement. Everyone is familiar with the proposition that a statement of intention may itself be a statement of fact and so capable of being true or false. But this proposition should not be used as a general solvent to transform the one type of assurance with another: the distinction is a real one and requires to be respected particularly where the effect of treating an assurance as a statement is to attract criminal consequences, as in the present case. As Lord Widgery CJ said in *Beckett v Cohen*[1] it was never intended that the 1968 Act should be used so as to make a criminal statement out of what is really a breach of warranty.

   [1] [1973] 1 All ER 120 at 122, [1972] 1 WLR 1593 at 1596, 1597.

   On the facts of the case the House of Lords held that the justices had been entitled to find that the statement 'I have pleasure in confirming the following

reservations for you:—London/Bermuda Flight BA 679—Economy Class—
29 August Dep 1525 hours Arr 1750 hours' was a false statement within s 14(1)
of the Act.

2. It is evident from the above cases that there is a very fine distinction between
(i) a false statement of fact which may give rise both to civil liability and liability under s 14 of the 1968 Act and (ii) a simple promise as to the future
which may give rise to civil liability for breach of warranty only.

3. Presumably the potential falsity of a statement may be affected also by an
appropriately worded disclaimer. Commenting on this point the 'Review of the
Trade Descriptions Act' (Cmnd 6628 (1976)) said:

Disclaiming and varying descriptions
148. At present few, if any, problems of this type occur in connection with statements about
services for a number of reasons. First, it is not an offence under the 1968 Act to supply a
service which does not correspond with a description applied to it. Secondly, one cannot
physically mark a description upon a service. Thirdly, inadvertent misstatements do not
give rise to an offence under section 14 which is concerned only with false statements made
deliberately or recklessly.

No doubt this is true generally of blatant disclaimers, but there is ample scope
for suitably qualified statements as to the nature etc of the services provided
(cf para 150 of the above report, above, p 633).

4. Lord Wilberforce noted in the *British Airways* case that s 14(2)(a) of the Act concentrates attention on the probable reaction of the consumer addressee of the
statement, this being determined as a matter of fact. See also *Cowburn v Focus
Television Rentals Ltd* (1983) 2 Tr L 89, 92, where Forbes J is reported as saying: 'So long as a reasonable person might interpret a statement in a way which
would make it false, then, owing to s 14(2)(a), as a statement "likely to be taken
for such a statement", it becomes false . . . ' However, the reasonable person
must still understand the statement as referring to one of the matters listed in s
14(1)(b)(i)–(v), above, p 643, and it is not in terms sufficient if he concludes that
the statement is *misleading* as opposed to false.

QUESTIONS

1. In a passage in the *Sunair Holidays* case which was cited with approval by Lord
Edmund-Davies in the *British Airways* case, Mackenna J states that a person
who makes a promise which he does not intend to keep makes a false statement
of an existing fact, namely as to his 'present state of mind or present means'
(see above, p 648). Undoubtedly this is so, but is a false statement as to one's
intentions a statement as to a matter listed in s 14(1)(b)(i)–(v) (see above, p 643
and below)?

2. Consider the following cases in terms of potential liability under s 14 of the
1968 Act:
   (i) Alexi calls in Furnace, a central heating specialist, and tells him that she
   needs a new boiler and that it must be installed by Christmas. Furnace

says, 'I can make no promises but I shall make every effort to ensure that my brother Rex, who has his own company, does it well before then'. Rex is given the work and does not complete it on time. Furnace admits that he had never intended to persuade Rex to do so since he knew that he was already heavily over-committed.

(ii) Ada wishes to have solar heating installed in her home. Loge, a salesman of such systems, tells her, 'In my estimate you will save at least 50 per cent on your heating bill'. Loge knew that this was highly optimistic and in the result Ada's saving was only 10 per cent.

THE PROVISION ETC OF ANY SERVICES, ACCOMMODATION OR FACILITIES

Many of the most important cases falling within s 14 of the Act involve the holiday trade and 'services, accommodation or facilities' provided in relation to it. However, the section goes well beyond this so that it covers, for example, such services as home improvements, car repairs, dry-cleaning, film processing and the like. Some assistance as to the scope of the words the 'provision' and 'nature' of any 'services, accommodation or facilities' is provided by the following cases:

R v Breeze [1973] 2 All ER 1141, [1973] 1 WLR 994, Court of Appeal

The facts of this case involving a person who described himself falsely as a qualified architect are noted above, p 643 where another aspect of the case is discussed. Having stated the facts Lord Widgery CJ continued:

Lord Widgery CJ. . . . In this case the prosecution relied on s 14(1)(a)(i), that is to say, they said that by calling himself an architect when he was not, he in the course of a trade or business made a false statement as to the provision in the course of any trade or business of any service. It seems to this court that the first question logically for consideration, and perhaps the most difficult and fundamental question, is whether if a man carrying on a trade or business in the provision of services falsely gives himself a personal qualification which he does not possess, the giving of that personal qualification can fairly be said to come within the words which I have read of s 14(1)(a)(i), namely whether the giving himself of that qualification is a false statement as to the provision of any services.

It has been argued forcefully by counsel for the appellant, to whom the court is indebted for his argument, that the phrase which I have just read, that which refers to the provision of any services, is a phrase concerned with the nature of the services performed, not with the identity or qualifications of the person who performs them. In other words, he says that given that the appellant was doing the work of an architect, the fact that he falsely described himself as an architect does not amount to a false statement as to the provision of the services.

The court has given careful consideration to this matter, because it clearly is one of considerable importance, and it has come to the conclusion that there is no reason for saying that a man carrying on business whose business is the provision of services does not commit an offence under s 14(1)(a)(i) if he adopts to himself a personal qualification which he does not enjoy.

For example, and one quotes it only as an example, suppose that a motor mechanic sets up in business to repair motor cars, and suppose that he announces to his prospective customers that he did a five year apprenticeship with Rolls-Royce when that is not the fact. We think that in a case of that kind it could perfectly properly be said that the man in question, in the course of a trade or business, had made a statement which he knew to be false and that it was a statement as to the provision of services which he offered, because it goes without saying, that a qualified man is likely, in general, to do a better job than an unqualified man, and the fact that a man has qualifications, such as an architect or an apprentice with five years' experience with Rolls-Royce, is the sort of factor which goes to the likely quality of the service which he will perform, and is, we think, without any straining of language, properly to be taken to be within the term that the statement is made as to the provisions of services, to quote the actual statutory words.

There is no doubt in our judgment in this case that the appellant was carrying on what on the face of it was a business. He was carrying on a continuous activity with a view to gain and profit by drawing plans for people who wanted them. There is no doubt he made this false statement in the course of that activity, and for the reasons which I have already given, we think it comes within the terms of s 14(1)(a)(i).

. . .

Accordingly, it seems to us that this conviction was properly entered as a matter of law, and that the appeal against conviction must be dismissed.

Appeal against conviction dismissed. Appeal against sentence allowed and fine varied.

It seems that sometimes prosecuting authorities have sought to extend the scope of s 14 beyond what might be thought to be its natural boundaries. However, as the following case illustrates, the courts have not been over receptive to these attempts.

Newell and Taylor v Hicks (1984) 148 JP 308, Queen's Bench Division

The appellants were Renault sales managers and they had placed advertisements in newspapers. One such advertisement read:

'A video cassette recorder absolutely free with every X registration Renault. All you have to do is place a firm order at Renault Wolverhampton from July 6th.'

The Justices found that this statement was false in as much as the trade-in allowance made on customers' old vehicles was reduced when they wished to take advantage of the offer. They convicted the defendants who had been charged under s 14 of the Act and they now appealed to the Divisional Court.

Robert Goff LJ, having stated the facts of the case, continued: Under each of the informations with which these two appellants were charged, it was alleged that a certain statement was false as to 'services or facilities provided in the course of the said trade or business namely as to the provision of free video cassette recorders, contrary to s 14(1)(b) of the Trade Descriptions Act.' There is no dispute, of course, that what was done was in the course of a trade or business. That, therefore, leaves for consideration the question whether what was done constituted a statement as to the provision of a service or, alternatively, a statement as to the provision of a facility.

Mr Underhill's [who appeared for the appellants] first submission was that in no case did it do so, because the statements contained in the various advertisements or circulars related to the supply of a certain item of goods, namely, a video cassette recorder, which did not constitute the provision of a service or the provision of a facility within s 14(1) of the Act.

Mr Underhill submitted that, in this Act, a distinction is drawn in various sections between supply of goods on the one hand and the provision of services on the other. An example is to be found in s 13 of the Act, which is headed: 'False representations as to supply of goods or services.' There are indeed other sections in the Act where a distinction is drawn between the supply of goods on the one hand and the provision of services on the other. Mr Underhill further submitted that, in any event, if the words 'services and facilities' are given their ordinary natural meaning, that meaning would not embrace, apart from exceptional cases, the supply of goods.

In this connection he prayed in aid a decision of this court in *Westminster City Council v Ray Alan (Manshops) Ltd* [1982] 1 All ER 771, [1982] 1 WLR 383. That case was also concerned with a prosecution under s 14(1) of the Trade Descriptions Act 1968. There it was alleged that a false statement was made as to the nature of a facility provided in the course of a trade or business by displaying a sign outside a shop, bearing the words: 'Closing Down Sale', when in fact the shop was not closing down and the accused persons continued to trade. It was held by the stipendiary magistrate, and again by this court, that that did not constitute a contravention of s 14(1) of the Act, for the reason that the statement was not as to the provision of a facility. Ormrod LJ, who delivered the principal judgment in the case had this to say about the word 'facility' in the Act (at p 773):

'Counsel for the respondents had contended that a closing down sale in relation to a shop selling goods is not properly described as a "facility" or "the provision of a facility". She contended that a "facility" must be something ancillary to the sale. But leaving that point aside, the real point is that other sections of the Act deal with the sale of goods,'

and I pause there to say that I think Ormrod LJ must have been referring there to the supply of goods,

'whereas s 14 is primarily concerned with misleading statements as to the provision of services, accommodation or facilities. I think counsel's argument can be summarised by saying that the word "facilities" in s 14 should be construed ejusdem generis with the preceding words "services" and "accommodation".

When one looks at s 14(1) one sees that the three nouns are grouped together in all but one of the various sub-heads under that section, namely the phrase "services, accommodation or facilities" is repeated over and over again.

I have come to the conclusion that that submission is right, that the word "facilities" where it occurs in s 14 should be construed in relation to the two words preceding it, "services [and] accommodation".

Perhaps one can illustrate the difference in this way. Hotels or businesses of all kinds provide services, meaning that they do something for the customer. Others provide facilities in the sense that various things are made available to customers to use if they are so minded in a more passive sense than the activities implied in the word "services".

In those circumstances I think the magistrate arrived at the right conclusion when he said that he was not satisfied that to advertise a closing down sale was to make any representation relating to a facility and accordingly I think he was right to reach that conclusion. The word is obviously of very wide meaning, and we have to be careful of it because it has become more and more popular in commercial circles. Almost anything can be described as a "facility" and accordingly, as this is a penal statute, we have to construe it strictly. For those reasons, as to the first information, I would hold that the magistrate was right.'

I would respectfully agree with and adopt what Ormrod LJ there said, that the word 'facility' is a word which is subject to a very wide use in commercial circles and, possibly, in ordinary speech as applying to almost anything that can be made available commercially. Even the sale of goods has been described, in some instances, as a facility. I also agree with Ormrod LJ, as we are here concerned with a criminal statute, it would be wrong to stretch the meaning of the word facility in this way.

Mr Underhill submitted that, in considering the words 'services' and 'facilities' in this context, we should regard the typical meaning of the word 'services' in this Act to be doing something for somebody. I agree with that. I would not attempt, any more than Mr Underhill did in his submission, to offer a definition of 'services'. But, generally speaking, it is correct that 'services' in this context should be regarded as doing something for somebody; that is, so to speak, the core of the meaning of that word. Typical examples of services given in the course of argument were a laundry, or dry cleaning, or repairing a car.

On the other hand, a 'facility', Mr Underhill submitted in the course of argument, is providing somebody with the 'wherewithal' to do something for himself.

Again, broadly speaking, I agree. Some typical examples of facilities which were given in the course of argument were providing the facility of a car park so that a person, to use Mr Underhill's expression, is provided with the wherewithal to park his car; or the facility of a swimming pool, so that a person is given the facility to go and swim. There may also be less simple examples than these. It appears that, for example, the provision of credit may fall within either the word 'service' or the word 'facility'. However, we do not have to decide that particular point on this occasion, although I myself incline to the opinion that it falls within the expression 'service'.

Furthermore, I for my part am satisfied that, apart from exceptional circumstances, to which I shall refer in a moment, the supply of goods does not fall within the words 'services' or 'facilities'. I am fortified in my view of the natural meaning of the words 'services' and 'facilities' by the fact that in the Act itself we can see, in the earlier sections, a contradistinction drawn between supply of goods on the one hand and the provision of services on the other.

I have said that there may be exceptional circumstances, although the point does not really arise in this case. I simply draw attention to the possibility that the word 'services', for example, may, in certain circumstances, embrace and include the supply of goods. To give examples posed in the course of argument, when a car is serviced very often oil is provided, for example for an oil change; or when laundry services are rendered, sometimes stiffeners are placed in the collars of shirts. It may be that, in those circumstances, the service may embrace and include the supply of goods. The point does not have to be decided for the purposes of the present case, but I draw attention to it as a point which arose in the course of argument. In the present case, we are concerned with persons who, concerned to promote the sale of motor cars, caused statements to be published about the cars, to the effect that if a certain car was bought within a certain period a free video cassette recorder would be provided with the car. So the main contracts of this case were not contracts for services; they were plainly contracts for the supply of goods. So, we are not here concerned with the exceptional type of case to which I have just indicated.

In this case, we are concerned with the question whether the offer of a free video cassette recorder constituted a statement as to the provision of a service or the provision of a facility. Having regard to the understanding of the words 'service' and 'facility' which I have already expressed in this judgment, I am satisfied that we are here concerned with statements as to the supply of an item of goods (albeit free, and not by way of sale), and that such statements did not constitute statements as to the provision of a service, or as to the provision of a facility. I, for my part, therefore accept Mr Underhill's first submission.

I turn then to his second submission. The complaint against his clients was that they made statements that a video cassette recorder would be supplied free with certain cars. The complaint was directed towards the word 'free'. The magistrates regarded the statement as false because they considered that the video cassette recorders would not be free. In those circumstances, submitted Mr Underhill, the allegation was that the statements were false as to the price of the goods referred to, in that it was stated that no charge would be made for the relevant goods.

Mr Underhill then turned to s 14(1) of the Act. He submitted that the price for services or accommodation or facilities is not dealt with in that subsection. He pointed out that sub-s (i) of 14(1) is directed towards statements as to the provision of services, accommodation or facilities; that (ii) is concerned with statements as to their nature; that (iii) is directed towards statements as to the time at which, the manner in which or the persons by whom they are provided; that (iv) is concerned with the examination, approval or evaluation by any person of them; and that (v) is concerned with location or amenities of accommodation. It follows, therefore, that there are five specified matters. It also follows, submitted Mr Underhill—and with this I agree—that since there are five specified matters, it is impossible, as a matter of construction, to read the word 'provision' in s 14(1)(i) as referring to anything other than the fact of providing, because if it were to be read widely as to embrace, for example, the terms upon which the services, accommodation or facilities were being provided, including their prices, the effect would be to render the words of (i) so wide as to render (ii), (iii), (iv) and (v) surplusage. The ordinary presumption against surplusage must militate very strongly against any submission which is founded upon such a broad meaning of the word 'provision'.

It seems to me, therefore, to be plain that, as a matter of construction, the word 'provision' can only be read as being concerned with the fact of providing services, accommodation or facilities and not as relating to the terms upon which they are provided. That being so, it appears that nowhere in s 14 is there specified, as one of the relevant matters, the price at which the services, accommodation or facilities are provided. Therefore, nowhere does the section strike, so to speak, at a statement that certain services, accommodation or facilities are being provided free, when in fact they are going to be charged for; nor at a statement that certain services, accommodation or facilities are being provided at price X, when in fact they are being provided at a higher price, Y. It may well be that there is a lacuna in this section. If so, I draw attention to the omission. But our duty is to construe the section as it stands, and I for my part am satisfied that the matter of price is not covered by s 14(1) of the Act. It follows, therefore, that I accept Mr Underhill's second submission also. . .

Mann J. I agree. I would wish to add this. I share my Lord's surprise that s 14 does not comprehend statements as to price in relation to services, accommodation and facilities. Plainly it does not. The omission is, in my judgment, surprising.

Appeals allowed.

NOTES

1. In *Dixons Ltd v Roberts* (1984) 148 JP 513 the Divisional Court held that the statement, 'refund the difference if you buy Dixon's Deal products cheaper locally at time of purchase and call within seven days' was not capable of giving rise to liability under s 14 of the Act. Forbes J is reported as saying it was 'impossible to accept that the offer of a refund of part of the price of goods can be taken as an offer to provide services'.

2. The decision in the *Ray Alan* case attracted some criticism (see, eg, Stevenson (1982) 42 MLR 710, 712). Certainly a straightforward distinction between ss 1–6 (goods) and 14 (services) does not seem tenable. For example it has been held to be an offence under s 14 to state falsely that goods are available 'on approval' or 'carriage free' (see *MFI Warehouses Ltd v Nattrass* [1973] 1 All ER 762, [1973] 1 WLR 307, below) or for a promotional offer to state 'Hire 20

feature films absolutely free when you rent a video recorder' when postage and packing are charged *(Cowburn v Focus Television Rentals Ltd* (1983) 2 Tr L 89).

3. *Newell and Taylor v Hicks* was distinguished in *Ashley v London Borough of Sutton* (1995) 159 JP 631, QBD. The appellant was convicted of 10 offences under s 14(1)(b) regarding a 90-day money-back guarantee on a book detailing a betting strategy. The guarantee was not fulfilled. The court decided that it was a 'strategy' which was being provided and hence this was a service and not goods. Further the representation regarding the refund was not a representation as to price, but was a statement about the nature of the provision of services; therefore s 14 was applicable.

4. Many of the above situations, prosecuted under s 14, arose either because the false statement was wrongly identified as concerning a service or facility instead of goods, or because the pricing of services or facilities was not covered by the original s 11. Section 14 sometimes offered the only possible chance of a conviction for an objectionable practice. The expanded coverage of s 20 of the Consumer Protection Act 1987, the clear inclusion of services and facilities under s 22, and the broad meaning of 'misleading' under s 21 now mean that a pricing offence will be available: see further ch 14.

QUESTION

Is it potentially an offence against s 14 for a brochure to state falsely that an hotel has 'First Class Shopping Facilities Incorporated' where (i) there are no such facilities, (ii) there are facilities but they are distinctly third-rate?

PROBLEM

The following advertisements appear in a brochure published on 1 May 1997 advertising the attractions of Senta on Sea: (i) 'XY Supermarket: Late Night Shopping until 8.00 every evening from March–September'; (ii) 'Smart Marina: Berths available for yachts up to 20 metres'. In fact the XY Supermarket always closes at 6.00 pm and the marina cannot take yachts of more than 16 metres. Discuss the advertiser's potential liability under s 14 of the 1968 Act.

'Accommodation' in s 14 refers to holiday accommodation and does not include descriptions applied to houses, land etc, which are advertised for sale or rent. Such matters also do not fall under 'goods' and s 1. No protection was given for any misdescriptions by estate agents until the introduction of the Property Misdescriptions Act 1991. This Act makes it a strict liability offence, for those in the course of an estate agency business, or a property development business, to give a false or misleading statement about any matter prescribed under the current order: the Property Misdescriptions (Specified Matters) Order 1992 (SI 1992/2834). The Order applies to 33 aspects of describing properties, from address, location, and room sizes to planning permissions, easements, and maintenance charges. For the position as regards the pricing of property, see ch 14 at p 681.

KNOWLEDGE OR RECKLESSNESS

Section 14 is unusual in requiring 'mens rea'. It also follows that the defences provided for in s 24 (all reasonable precautions taken and all diligence shown) will have only a limited application: see *Coupe v Guyett* [1973] 2 All ER 1058, [1973] 1 WLR 669, below, p 729, but cf *Wings Ltd v Ellis* [1984] 3 All ER 577, [1984] 3 WLR 965, below, pp 662–9 and 715–6. The following is the leading case most directly in point as to the meaning of the word 'reckless' for the purposes of s 14(1)(b).

MFI Warehouses Ltd v Nattrass [1973] 1 All ER 762, [1973] 1 WLR 307, Queen's Bench Division

The facts are set out in the judgment of Lord Widgery CJ:

Lord Widgery CJ. This is an appeal by case stated by justices . . . in respect of their adjudication as a magistrates' court sitting at Chester on 27 March 1972. On that date the justices convicted the appellants of two offences contrary to s 14(1) of the Trade Descriptions Act 1968 . . .

The circumstances of the case were these. For some time the appellants had been selling by mail order a wooden door which is described as a louvre door because it had slats in it through which air could pass for purposes of ventilation. The terms on which these doors were advertised and sold was that they could be had on 14 days' approval without prepayment and that 25p carriage should be charged on each door. After a while the appellants marketed a set of sliding door gear designed to be used with the louvre doors, the purpose of which was to enable these doors to be assembled in such a way as to make a sliding partition. The intention of the appellants was that these sliding door sets should be sold only with a set of louvre doors and not separately. Their intention when the door gear was sold with the doors was that no extra carriage charge should be made in respect of the inclusion of the sliding door gear, and that the same period of approval should be available for the door gear as was for the doors. The advertisement complained of referred to the door gear as being 'carriage free' which was intended by the appellants to indicate that no additional carriage charge would result if the door gear was ordered with the doors. Furthermore, the advertisement in referring to 14 days' free approval did not distinguish between an order for doors and door gear respectively, it not having been in the minds of the appellants that the gear should be sold separately in any instance.

The purchaser referred to in this case read the advertisement as meaning that the sliding door gear could be bought separately. One may say at once that he was not to be blamed for reaching that conclusion because it was one which might well have been reached by an intelligent reader of the advertisement itself. Accordingly he placed an order for door gear and was surprised to find that he was expected to pay carriage on the door gear notwithstanding the reference to 'carriage free' in the advertisement, whereas in the other case the purchaser was surprised to find that he could not obtain the door gear on 14 days' free approval but was required to make payment before despatch.

The explanation of this is that the clerk who dealt with the order treated it as one which did not entitle the buyer to the facilities of free approval or free carriage because it was an order for the gear in isolation and not coupled with an order for doors. The justices found that if the clerk in question had referred the matter to the appellants' chairman the latter would then have appreciated that the advertisement was ambiguous and would have instructed the clerk to honour the terms of the advertisement. In fact the matter was not referred to the appellants' chairman and the purchaser raised complaint, which resulted in the bringing of these charges.

Lord Widgery quoted s 14 of the 1968 Act and continued:

The justices found that the advertisement constituted a false statement made by the appellants in the course of their trade or business in regard to the provision of facilities within the meaning of s 14(1). The only remaining question, therefore, was whether that statement had been made 'recklessly' within the meaning of the section. The only further finding which goes to the thought given by the appellants to the correctness or otherwise of their advertisement is to be found in para 2(j) of the stated case which states:

'that the [appellants] by their Chairman studied the said advertisement for 5 or 10 minutes or thereabouts prior to approving it but did not think through sufficiently the implications thereof and did not appreciate that it in fact offered the said folding door gear as an item which could be separately purchased on the terms stated.'

Argument in the court below, as in this court, centred on the meaning of the word 'reckless'. For the appellants it was argued that 'reckless' here had its familiar common law meaning derived from *Derry v Peek*,[1] that is to say, that 'recklessness' implies a total irresponsibility and a total lack of consideration whether the statement was false or true. It was argued that on this construction a statement could not be made recklessly unless the conduct of the maker was on the threshold of fraud or he had shown himself ready to run a risk with the truth. Such conduct, it was said, could not be found against the appellants on the facts which the justices had accepted and, in particular, having regard to the consideration given to the advertisement by the appellants' chairman.

For the respondent it was contended that the word 'reckless' in the present context had a wider meaning than that in *Derry v Peek*.[1] It was contended that if the draftsman had intended the word 'reckless' to have its normal common law meaning, he would not have thought it necessary to include a specific definition clause in the section. Furthermore, when the definition clause was examined again it was to be observed that it referred to a statement made 'regardless of whether it is true or false'. It was contended that the normal meaning of 'regardless' is 'without having regard to'. It was accordingly contended that this Act placed on sellers a duty to give active consideration to whether their advertisements were true or false, and that unless the advertisement had been examined with this end in view it was open to the prosecution to contend that the advertisement was issued without regard to whether it was true or false. Attention was also directed to the final phrase in s 14(2)(b) namely, 'whether or not the person making it had reasons for believing that it might be false'. It is argued that this phrase shows the intention of the legislature to require sellers to examine their advertisements for falsity even though it is not shown that they had any independent reason for suspecting that the advertisement was false.

The only reference to this question in authority on this particular section is to be found in Lord Parker CJ's judgment in *Sunair Holidays Ltd v Dodd*[2]. There, after reading the section, Lord Parker CJ observed:[2]

'In other words this by statute is importing the common law definition of "recklessly" as laid down in *Derry v Peek*[1] and adopted ever since.'

It does not appear that this dictum was essential to the decision in the case with which Lord Parker CJ was concerned and there is no reason to suppose that there had been argument on it.

For these reasons I would be disinclined to accept Lord Parker CJ's word as being the final pro-nouncement on this question, and think that it behoves this court to look into the matter again. I am supported in this view by a comment made by Roskill LJ in giving the judgment of the court in *R v Clarksons Holidays Ltd*;[3] it was not necessary for him to express any final view on the point but he indicated his impression that Lord Parker CJ's observation[2] would not be accepted if the matter were fully argued. That the word 'reckless' may have more than one meaning in law is apparent from a consideration of the judgment of Salmon J in *R v Mackinnon*[4]; and the judgment of Donovan J in *R v Bates*.[5] I am inclined to think that it was the fact that the word 'reckless' has more than one meaning which prompted the draftsman to give a special definition of that word in the Act with which we are presently concerned, and I think, therefore, that we should approach the problem of construction by having regard to that definition rather than to preconceived notions of what the word 'reckless' should mean. I have much sympathy with the view of Salmon J[4] that where a criminal offence is being created and an element of the offence is 'recklessness', one should hesitate before accepting the view that anything less than '*Derry v Peek*[1] recklessness' will do. On the other hand, it is quite clear that this Act is designed for the protection of customers and it does not seem to me to be unrea-sonable to suppose that in creating such additional protection for customers Parliament was minded to place on the advertiser a positive obligation to have regard to whether his advertise-ment was true or false.

I have accordingly come to the conclusion that 'recklessly' in the context of the 1968 Act does not involve dishonesty. Accordingly it is not necessary to prove that the statement was made with that degree of irresponsibility which is implied in the phrase 'careless whether it be true or false'. I think it suffices for present purposes if the prosecution can show that the advertiser did not have regard to the truth or falsity of his advertisement even though it cannot be shown that he was deliberately closing his eyes to the truth, or that he had any kind of dishonest mind. If I had taken the contrary view I would have held that the facts found in this case would not support the conviction. On the opinion which I have just expressed, however, I think that the justices were entitled to convict in this case, and that the explanation of their decision is that they considered that the appellants' chairman did not have regard to the falsity or otherwise of what was written on his behalf. Accordingly, I would dismiss the appeal.

Ashworth J and **Willis J** agreed.

Appeal dismissed.

[1] (1889) 14 App Cas 337, [1886–90] All ER Rep 1.
[2] [1970] 2 All ER 410 at 411, [1970] 1 WLR 1037 at 1040.
[3] [1972] Crim LR 653.
[4] [1958] 3 All ER 657 at 658, [1959] 1 QB 150 at 152.
[5] [1952] 2 All ER 842.

NOTE

For a general discussion of recklessness in the criminal law, see Smith and Hogan *Criminal Law* (8th edn, 1996), pp 90–115.

QUESTIONS

1. Suppose that the defendant trader does have regard to the truth or falsity of the statement and concludes, quite unreasonably and wrongly, that it is true. Is this to be deemed 'reckless' within s 14(2)(b) of the 1968 Act?

2. Is the trader who gives no thought at all to the truth or falsity of the statement
   (i) more or (ii) less blameworthy than the trader in question 1 above?

The following decision of the House of Lords is of considerable interest both to
the scope and interpretation of s 14 of the 1968 Act and to the question of corporate criminal liability. Only the former aspect of the case is considered in this
chapter, corporate liability being discussed in ch 15 below, at pp 715–6.

Wings Ltd v Ellis [1984] 3 All ER 577, [1984] 3 WLR 965, House of Lords

The Divisional Court had certified the following question as being of general public importance:

'Whether a Defendant may properly be convicted of an offence under s 14(1)(a) of the Trade
Descriptions Act 1968 where he had no knowledge of the falsity of the Statement at the time
of its publication but knew of the falsity at the time when the statement was read by the complainant.'

The facts appear in the speech of Lord Templeman.

Lord Templeman. My Lords, this appeal raises a short question of construction of certain
provisions of the Trade Descriptions Act 1968. Section 14, so far as material, provides:

'(1) It shall be an offence for any person in the course of any trade or businesses (a) to make a
statement which he knows to be false . . . as to any of the following matters, that is to say . . .
(ii) the nature of any . . . accommodation . . . provided in the course of any trade or business.
(4) In this section "false" means false to a material degree . . .'

The respondent, Wings Ltd, was convicted by magistrates of an offence under s 14, that conviction was quashed by the Divisional Court and the prosecutor appeals to your Lordships'
House.

In the course of its business as a tour operator, the respondent distributed to travel agents a
brochure giving details of accommodation provided for the respondent's customers. Shortly
after the brochure was distributed, the respondent discovered that the brochure contained a
statement which was false to a material degree, namely that the accommodation provided at the
Seashells Hotel in Sri Lanka was furnished with air-conditioning.

On 13 January 1982 Mr Wade, having read the brochure, booked, through a travel agent, a
Wings holiday at the Seashells Hotel for three weeks beginning on 3 March 1982. The travel
agent telephoned the respondent's sales agent to make a provisional booking and Mr Wade then
signed the booking form which was included in the brochure acknowledging, inter alia, that he
had read and agreed to certain conditions contained in the brochure. Mr Wade was not
informed by the travel agent or subsequently by the respondent that air-conditioning was not
provided at the Seashells Hotel and only made that disagreeable discovery for himself when he
reached the hotel. The prosecutor alleged that the respondent had committed an offence under
s 14 by making to Mr Wade a relevant statement which was false to a material degree and which
the respondents knew to be false.

The respondent argued that on the true construction of s 14 it only made one statement, ie
when it circulated the brochure; at that date it did not know the statement was false and therefore it never committed an offence. But the statement was repeated to Mr Wade by the uncorrected description of the accommodation at the Seashells Hotel contained in the brochure
furnished by the respondent to Mr Wade in the course of the negotiations which were finalised

by the respondent's acceptance of Mr Wade's booking. The 1968 Act was intended to ensure that the brochure was accurate and that Mr Wade was not misled. The brochure was inaccurate, the respondent knew that it was inaccurate and Mr Wade was misled. The ingredients for an offence under s 14 were compounded. To hold otherwise would be to emasculate s 14 and to place a premium on carelessness by the respondents which, as will appear, is the subject of express provisions contained in s 24 of the Act.

The respondent never intended to make a false statement to Mr Wade. The respondent had instructed its employee sales agent to inform the travel agent that, contrary to the brochure, the accommodation at the Seashells Hotel was not furnished with air-conditioning but with overhead fans. If all had gone according to plan, the respondent would not have committed an offence. The sales agent would have told the travel agent. In turn the travel agent would have told Mr Wade and the statement made by the respondent to Mr Wade would have been the statement in the brochure as orally corrected. In the events which happened, however, the respondent committed an offence under s 14 but without intending to do so. The 1968 Act makes provision for this possibility in s 24 . . .

Having quoted s 24(1) and (2), see p 710, Lord Templeman continued:

The respondent did not attempt to put forward a defence under s 24. In order to succeed in any such defence the respondent would first have been obliged to explain the introduction of a false statement into the brochure. There was a vague suggestion that this was a typographical error. The magistrates were not asked to decide and had no evidence on which to decide whether the respondents 'took all reasonable precautions and exercised all due diligence' in the employment and supervision of the blundering typist and the blundering proof reader. Moreover, it was certainly not clear that the respondent 'took all reasonable precautions and exercised all due diligence to avoid the commission' of an offence under s 14 after it discovered that the brochure contained a false statement. By relying on an oral correction being made by the sales agent and transmitted by the travel agent, the respondent accepted the risk of committing an offence under s 14. The respondent exposed Mr Wade to the serious risk that he would not be made aware of the correction and the added risk that he would not be able to prove that he had not been made aware of the correction. It may or may not have been practicable to send out correction slips to travel agents. In any event, if the respondent, on receiving the booking form signed by Mr Wade, had written to Mr Wade, if necessary through the travel agent, confirming the oral correction which ought to have been conveyed to Mr Wade and explaining that since the publication of the brochure the respondent had discovered that the Seashells Hotel was equipped with overhead fans but not with air-conditioning, then Mr Wade could have withdrawn the booking or accepted the correction and the respondent would not have committed an offence. In the course of argument before your Lordships, counsel for the respondent, on instructions, demurred to the suggestion that written confirmation of an intended oral correction was necessary to avoid the commission of an offence and advanced the explanation, illuminating and disturbing, that the brochure contained a large number of errors. But the 1968 Act is infringed and only infringed by statements which are false to a material degree and are known to be false and it is no comfort to Mr Wade to learn that other customers of the respondent might have been deceived by other false statements. It is impossible to determine whether a defence under s 24 would have succeeded because the respondent, no doubt for good commercial reasons, did not rely on any such defence. It was not open to the Divisional Court to invent a different defence, and to make its own dubious finding and to quash the conviction by asserting that when the respondent discovered that the statement in the brochure was false 'it immediately did all that could reasonably be expected in order to neutralise the error once it had been made'.

By creating a new criminal offence under s 14 Parliament indicated that the civil remedies for breach of contract and criminal sanctions for fraud are insufficient to protect the public against false statements in mass advertisements. It is necessary that the falsity should be known but by s 24 Parliament has indicated that good intentions and mistake do not by themselves constitute a defence. The accused must plead and prove the circumstances specified in s 24 before a defence of mistake can succeed. The 1968 Act, being clear, must be enforced.

My noble and learned friend Lord Scarman has courteously considered the complicated arguments advanced on behalf of the respondent and accepted in part by the Divisional Court. This case is another example of the importance of concentrating on the language and objects of an Act of Parliament; this case is another illustration of the desirability of the simple approach.

I would allow the appeal and answer the certified question in the affirmative.

Lord Scarman stated that 'the basic issue between the parties is whether on its proper construction s 14(1)(a) of the 1968 Act creates an offence of strict, or more accurately semi-strict, liability or is one requiring the existence of full mens rea'. Having analysed the facts as stated in Lord Templeman's speech and referred to the issue of corporate liability (see below, pp 715–6) he went on to discuss the 'proper construction of s 14(1)(b)' as follows:

Lord Scarman: My Lords, the subject matter and structure of the 1968 Act make plain that the Act belongs to that class of legislation which prohibits acts which 'are not criminal in any real sense, but are acts which in the public interest are prohibited under a penalty', as Wright J put it in *Sherras v De Rutzen* [1895] 1 QB 918 at 922, [1895–9] All ER Rep 1167 at 1169. In construing the offence-creating sections of the 1968 Act it will, therefore, be necessary to bear in mind that it may well have been the intention of the legislature 'in order to guard against the happening of the forbidden thing, to impose a liability upon a principal even though he does not know of, and is not a party to, the forbidden act done by his servant': see *Mousell Bros Ltd v London and North Western Rly Co* [1917] 2 KB 836 at 844, [1916–17] All ER Rep 1101 at 1105 per Viscount Reading CJ.

While, however, the subject matter of the 1968 Act is such that the presumption recognised by Lord Reid in *Sweet v Parsley* [1969] 1 All ER 347 at 349, [1970] AC 132 at 148 as applicable to truly criminal statutes, 'that Parliament did not intend to make criminals of persons who were in no way blameworthy in what they did', is not applicable to this Act, it does not necessarily follow that merely because an offence-creating section in the Act is silent as to mens rea its silence must be construed as excluding mens rea. As Lord Reid said, in the absence of a clear indication than an offence is intended to be an absolute offence one must examine all relevant circumstances in order to establish the intention of Parliament (see [1969] 1 All ER 347 at 350, [1970] AC 132 at 149).

What the relevant circumstances are may now be said to have been settled in a line of cases of which the greatest is *Sweet v Parsley* and the most recent is a decision of the Privy Council in a Hong Kong appeal, *Gammon (Hong Kong) Ltd v A-G of Hong Kong* [1984] 2 All ER 503, [1984] 3 WLR 437. At the end of the day the question whether an offence created by statute requires mens rea, guilty knowledge or intention, in whole, in part, or not at all, turns on the subject matter, the language and the structure of the Act studied as a whole, on the language of the particular statutory provision under consideration construed in the light of the legislative purpose embodied in the Act, and on 'whether strict liability in respect of all or any of the essential ingredients of the offence would promote the object of the provision': see *Gammon (Hong Kong) Ltd v A-G of Hong Kong* [1984] 2 All ER 503 at 507, [1984] 3 WLR 437 at 444–445 and *Sweet v Parsley* [1969] 1 All ER 347 at 362, [1970] AC 132 at 163 per Lord Diplock.

In the light of the foregoing it is now necessary to determine the proper construction to be put on the words of s 14(1)(a). The necessary ingredients of the offence as formulated in the subsection are that (1) a person in the course of a trade or business (2) makes a statement (3) which he knows to be false (4) as to the provision in the course of trade or business of any services, accommodation or facilities. The respondent submits that the essence of the offence is knowingly making a false statement. The appellant submits that it suffices to prove that the statement was made on a person's behalf in the course of his business and that its content was false to the knowledge of the person carrying on the business.

My Lords, I accept the appellant's construction as correct. First, it advances the legislative purpose embodied in the Act, in that it strikes directly against the false statement irrespective of the reason for, or explanation of, its falsity. It involves, of course, construing the offence as one of strict liability to the extent that the offence can be committed unknowingly, ie without knowledge of the act of statement; but this is consistent with the social purpose of a statute in the class to which this Act belongs. And the strictness of the offence does no injustice: the accused, if he has acted innocently, can invoke and prove one of the statutory defences. Second, the appellant's submission has the advantage of following the literal and natural meaning of the words used. The subsection says not that it is an offence knowingly to make the statement but that it is an offence to make the statement.

The respondent's counsel, however, in support of his submission made a number of telling points. None of them is, in my judgment, strong enough to overcome the difficulties in his way. First, he relied on the general principles governing the interpretation of the provisions of a criminal statute. They are, however, for the reasons already developed, not applicable to this statute. Second, he submitted that he who makes a statement must as a matter of common sense know that he is making it. This is not so, however, when one is dealing, as in this statute, with statements made in the course of a trade or business. It would stultify the statute if this submission were to be upheld. Third, he contrasted the wording of para (a) with para (b). Paragraph (b) provides that it is an offence 'recklessly' to make the false statement. The inference arises, therefore, that the offence under para (a) requires proof of a deliberate false statement. This, with respect, I believe to be his best point, but it cannot prevail against all the indications to which I have referred in favour of the interpretation put on para (a) by the appellant.

But this is not the end of the respondent's case. There remains the question: did the respondent make any statement at all as to the air-conditioning of the hotel bedroom on 13 January when Mr Wade read it? The respondent's submission was that such a statement was made only once, on publication of the brochure in May 1981. The importance of the question is not only that the prosecution pinned its case to 13 January 1982 but that in May 1981 the company did not know the statement was false whereas in January 1982 it did know it was false.

This submission was not open to the respondent company before the magistrates or in the Divisional Court. The Court of Appeal had decided in *R v Thomson Holidays Ltd* [1974] 1 All ER 823, [1974] QB 592 that a new statement is made on every occasion that an interested member of the public reads it in a brochure published by a company engaged in attracting his custom. The court considered that communication is the essence of statement. My Lords, I think *R v Thomson Holidays Ltd* was correctly decided, even though I do not accept the totality of the court's reasoning. A statement can consist of a communication to another; and in the context of this Act and the circumstances of this class of business I have no hesitation in accepting the court's view that communication by an uncorrected brochure of false information to someone who is being invited to do business in reliance on the brochure is 'to make a statement' within s 14(1)(a). But there can be statements which are not communicated to others. It was unnecessary for the Court of Appeal to hold that communication was of the essence, and to that extent only I think the court erred.

The respondent's case that it only made one statement, ie on publication of the brochure, is as fallacious in its way as is the view of the Court of Appeal that without communication there is no statement. I have no doubt that a statement as to the air-conditioning in the hotel was made when the brochure was published. But further statements to the same effect were made whenever persons did business with the respondent on the strength of the uncorrected brochure, which so far from being withdrawn continued to be the basis on which the respondent was inviting business. There is no injustice in this being the effect of the statute. If the respondent believed that there was no default on its part when the false description was communicated to Mr Wade, it should have admitted that the offence was committed and called evidence to establish a s 23 or s 24 defence. Instead, the respondent chose to argue that no offence had been committed at all, an argument which for the reasons I have given, I believe to be unsustainable.

Accordingly, I hold that the respondent company did make a statement as to the air-conditioning to Mr Wade on 13 January 1982. This conclusion renders it unnecessary to deal with the ingenious, if far-fetched, analogy which the respondent sought to draw between this case and your Lordships' analysis of a 'result crime' in the arson case of *R v Miller* [1983] 1 All ER 978, [1983] 2 AC 161, and which found favour with the Divisional Court. I will say only that to construe the words 'to make a statement which he knows to be false' in the context of this Act as being capable of covering a physical act of statement completed or perfected at a later date by a damaging result when it is read appears to me to be an unhelpful and over-elaborate approach to the interpretation of an Act intended to protect the public by provisions which the public can understand without a lawyer at their elbow. Making a statement consists of the act of statement. If it has consequences, so be it: the consequences are not the statement.

For these reasons I would make answer to the certified point of law as follows. A statement which was false was made by the respondent company in the course of its business when it was read by Mr Wade, an interested member of the public doing business with the respondent company on the basis of the statement. The offence was committed on that occasion because the respondent company then knew that it was false to state that the hotel accommodation was air-conditioned. The fact that the respondent was unaware of the falsity of the statement when it was published as part of the brochure in May 1981 is irrelevant. If the respondent believed it was innocent of fault, it was open to it to prove lack of fault. It did not do so.

Like my noble and learned friend Lord Brandon (whose speech in draft I have had the opportunity of reading), I cannot think, though I understand the genuine difficulties which faced the respondent, that it was improper to prosecute in this case.

I would allow the appeal.

Lord Keith of Kinkel and Lord Brandon of Oakfield delivered concurring speeches, Lord Brandon neatly pin-pointing a central issue thus:

Lord Brandon: In the present case, I regard the false statement about air-conditioning contained in the respondent's brochures as having been a continuing false statement, that is to say a false statement which continued to be made so long as such brochures remained in circulation without effective correction. I should regard a statement made in an advertisement exhibited on a street hoarding in the same way.

Being of the opinion that the certified question is ineptly expressed, I would amend it to read as follows: whether a defendant may properly be convicted of an offence under s 14(1)(a) of the Trade Descriptions Act 1968 where he has made a continuing false statement, which he did not know was false when he first made it, but which, having come to know of its falsity at some later time, he has thereafter continued to make. Having amended the certified question in that way, I should answer it with a simple Yes.

I understand, however, that the rest of your Lordships are of the opinion that the certified question can be answered satisfactorily as it stands. On that footing, I agree with the answer to such question proposed by my noble and learned friend Lord Scarman.

I would only add that, in my opinion, there was nothing unreasonable, let alone improper, in the bringing of a prosecution against the respondent in this case.

Lord Hailsham concurred 'without qualification with the result' as expressed by Lord Scarman 'but arrived at the conclusion by a slightly different route and with feelings of somewhat greater sympathy with the respondent'. He dealt, in particular, with the making of the statement, knowledge of its falsity and the prosecution policy as follows:

Lord Hailsham: The Divisional Court held (as it clearly was right to do if it were in point) that it was bound by the decision of the Court of Appeal, Criminal Division, in *R v Thomson Holidays Ltd* [1974] 1 All ER 823, [1974] QB 592. That decision is not binding on your Lordships' House, but it is relevant to consider how it was used by the Divisional Court (see [1984] 1 All ER 1046 at 1050, [1984] 1 WLR 731 at 737). *R v Thomson Holidays Ltd* itself arose from an attempt by the travel company to plead autrefois convict in respect of an indictment under s 14(1)(b)(ii) of the 1968 Act. The company had already pleaded guilty to a breach of this section in respect of the same brochure in the previous year, but the new indictment was based on further complaints by two customers who had subsequently and separately booked holidays as the result of their reading of it. The Court of Appeal (in my opinion correctly) held that the two further readings by the two new complainants constituted two new 'statements' for the purposes of s 14 and therefore disclosed two new offences. But in the instant case the Divisional Court made use of the authority to establish the general proposition, taken, with respect, out of context from the judgment of Lawton LJ in R *v Thomson Holidays Ltd* [1974] 1 All ER 823 at 828, [1974] QB 592 at 597, that 'a statement is made when it is communicated to someone'. With respect, this needs further analysis. When, in the course of a trade or business, a brochure containing a false statement is issued in large numbers through a chain of distribution involving several stages, and intended to be read and used at all or some of the stages, it does not follow that it is only 'made' at its ultimate destination. It may be 'made' when it is posted in bulk, when the information is passed on by telephone or in smaller batches by post, and when it is read by the ultimate recipient, provided that at each stage what happens is in accordance with the original intention of the issuing house. The respondent made a valiant attempt to induce your Lordships to declare that *R v Thomson Holidays Ltd* was wrongly decided. In my view the attempt fails. It does not follow from this that a prosecution policy of excessive zeal involving repeated attempts to convict a firm in respect of each separate communication of an individual copy of a brochure ought to meet with anything but reprobation from the courts. That must depend on the circumstances.
. . .

It will be apparent from what I have already said that I have no difficulty at all in deciding that the statement was made at the time Mr Wade read the brochure, ie on 13 January 1982. The statement may also have been made at various other stages in the chain of distribution and was certainly made to other recipients. What renders the charge particularly objectionable to the respondent is that, at the time when Mr Wade read the statement, the respondent quite honestly believed that it would only be read by a member of the public in a corrected and therefore accurate form. The respondent had used its best endeavours to correct the statement and it genuinely thought that these had succeeded. It had succeeded down the chain as far as Sandra Leathers and, if her 's 9 statement' is correct, one stage further down the line than this. I am not sure, in view of the drafting of the case, that I am entitled to go this far, since the finding in the case does not proceed beyond the delphic sentence: 'Mr Wade was never informed of the lack of air conditioning either by the travel agent or by [the respondent], although the travel agent *might well have known*' (my emphasis). I will, however, assume in the respondent's favour, and I think it is probably the case, that no other finding than that the correction had reached the travel agent was open to the magistrates. But it did not reach Mr Wade, and there is an unambiguous finding to this effect. The statement was made both when it was issued and when it reached Mr Wade. It was in the form originally intended by the respondent. It had followed the chain of distribution intended by the respondent, and, when it reached its destination, it was false in a material particular. If this case had been a civil claim by Mr Wade in contract, there would have been no possible answer to it, and my own opinion, for what it is worth, is that a claim in the civil courts resulting in an adequate award of damages for inconvenience and a return of his money to Mr Wade might well have been a way of disposing of this matter far preferable to what has in fact occurred, since Mr Wade would have received damages adequate to recoup his estimated loss and something in addition to compensate for him for his disappointment: see *Jarvis v Swans Tours Ltd* [1973] 1 All ER 71, [1973] QB 233 and *Jackson v Horizon Holidays Ltd* [1975] 3 All ER 92, [1975] 1 WLR 1468. Without intending in any way to express a concluded view, it may well have been that if the respondent had made a prompt and generous offer of compensation when the error was first brought to its attention it would have saved itself a good deal of trouble and anxiety.

Fortunately or unfortunately the criminal law has been invoked. There would have been no possible harm in this if the charge had been simply of an absolute offence although, had the case been heard after 31 January 1983 when s 67(1)(b) of the Powers of Criminal Courts Act 1983 came into effect (see the Criminal Justice Act 1982 (Commencement No 1) Order 1982, SI 1982/1857), I would have hoped that a compensation order would have been made in whole or in part in preference to a fine. Many of the offences created by the 1968 Act, for example those created by ss 1, 11, 12 and 13, to which I need not refer in detail, come clearly within the ordinary definition of an absolute offence. But offences under s 14 emphatically are not like these. Offences under s 14 require as an essential ingredient of the offence knowledge by the maker of the statement that it was false (s 14(1)(a)) or recklessness in the making of it (s 14(1)(b)). Any ordinary person reading the section would think that this ingredient was an almost classic statement that to be found guilty of this offence the maker of the statement must be fraudulent in the traditional sense, and anyone reading an account of the conviction after reading the section would think that the offender had been convicted of fraudulent conduct. I can fully understand the sense of outrage felt by the owners of a decent business who in my view were not, on the facts of the case, at all dishonest, and acted throughout in good faith, when they found themselves not only convicted of such an offence but fined £500, which is by no means a negligible penalty, on each of the two summonses on which they were charged.

. . .

Having said all this, I am bound to say that I am not at all happy about the position to which I have felt constrained to come, and, without criticising the authorities who mounted the present proceedings and persisted in the present successful appeal, I would say that there is room for caution by prosecuting authorities in mounting proceedings against innocent defendants. In the case of an absolute offence, the late Viscount Dilhorne had some very salutary remarks as to the considerations which prosecuting organisations ought to bear in mind before instituting proceedings in consumer cases (see *Smedleys Ltd v Breed* [1974] 2 All ER 21 at 32–33, [1974] AC 839 at 855–857) and I consider that they should be even more careful in cases which ordinary people would read as containing an implication of fraud, but where the offender was of excellent reputation and had acted honestly. Whatever else the 1968 Act was meant for it was intended to supplement and not to substitute the ordinary law of contract, and was not designed to bring on respectable traders who had acted honestly the reputation of having been guilty of fraudulent conduct of which in fact they were innocent.

But for these reasons and with these reservations I would allow the appeal. I would answer the certified question in the affirmative but with a qualification by saying, 'Yes, unless the defendant has raised a successful defence under s 24 of the 1968 Act and provided that the reading by the complainant was part of the chain of consequences intended and authorised by the defendant prior to its receipt by the complainant.'

Appeal allowed.

NOTES

1. For a useful discussion of the *Wings* case see Stephenson 'Unknowingly Making a Knowingly False Statement' (1985) 135 NLJ 160.
2. For a further reference to the *Thomson Holidays* case in the context of compensation orders see above, p 432. For further discussion of s 24, see below pp 709–25. For references to the discretion to prosecute see *Smedleys Ltd v Breed* [1974] AC 839, [1974] 2 All ER 21, HL.

QUESTIONS

In the light of *Wings,* (a) to what extent is it still true to say that mens rea is a necessary ingredient of s 14, and (b) is it possible to deduce why the respondent, 'no doubt for good commercial reasons' (per Lord Templeman) chose not to rely on the defence provided by s 24?

PROBLEMS

1. Annabelle wishes to have her dress cleaned for her Graduation Ball. She takes it to Kleaneasy whose window display has long advertised, 'Try our 24 Hour Service'. What is the position under s 14 of the Act, if (i) Kleaneasy tells her, 'Sorry dear, we had to give that up weeks ago. I must take the sticker down'; (ii) Kleaneasy accepts the dress for a '24 Hour Service' knowing he is so overcommitted that it is most unlikely that he will complete the work and then by a stroke of good fortune does so; (iii) Kleaneasy accepts the dress and his system which is usually very efficient breaks down so that the dress is uncleaned for the Ball?

2. The Blue Sky Travel Company publishes a holiday brochure in January 1997, advertising a 'package-holiday' based on the Hotel Carmen in the Dominican Republic. The holiday season runs from March to September and this is the first season in which the recently build hotel will be open to guests. In its brochure Blue Sky states that: (i) the hotel is 200 yards from the nearest beach; (ii) the hotel provides English style cooking; (iii) each room has a balcony with an uninterrupted view over the sea; (iv) there is a private swimming pool and (v) disco dancing every night. An artist's impression of the swimming pool with appropriately bronzed bodies features prominently in the brochure which contains the following statements in its booking conditions: 'Not all advertised facilities may be available during your holiday. Swimming pools may have to be closed for maintenance and other activities cancelled for lack of support. The Dominican Republic is a developing tourist centre and building operations may sometimes affect your enjoyment and the view from your hotel . . . '

On 1 February 1997 Maxwell reads the brochure and books a two-week holiday for himself and his family to begin on 15 April. When the Maxwells arrive at the hotel they have the following complaints: (i) although the hotel is 200 yards from the beach 'as the crow flies' there is a railway line in between and in practice a one-mile walk: the management of Blue Sky is aware of this fact; (ii) the food is cooked in a distinctly 'Caribbean' style; (iii) their room has a balcony but the view over the sea is largely cut off by two enormous cranes which were erected on 15 March 1997 for use in building another hotel. The management of Blue Star was informed of this development on 20 March but did not tell its clients until their arrival at the hotel; (iv) the swimming pool, although under construction in January, has still not been completed; (v) disco dancing has been cancelled owing to lack of support.

Discuss Blue Star's liability under s 14 of the 1968 Act.

PROPOSALS FOR REFORM

The following are some proposals for reforming s 14 of the Act:

Review of the Trade Descriptions Act 1968: a Report by the Director General of Fair Trading (Cmnd 6628, October 1976)

49. Our conclusions at this stage may be summarised as follows:
   (i) the consumer does not readily distinguish between statements made in relation to goods and statements made in relation to services; he is as easily misled by one as the other and his loss may be as great in one case as the other;
   (ii) so far as possible the sanctions against the false statements should be the same in both cases;
   (iii) a relaxation of section 1 would not be justified; harmonisation should, therefore, be effected by bringing offences in relation to services as far as possible into line with offences in relation to goods.

. . .

106. Our further recommendations in regard to section 14 (ie additional to those already set out in paragraph 49) may be summarised as follows:
   (i) it should be made an offence to supply any services, accommodation or facilities to which a description has been applied and which do not correspond with that description except that a person shall not be guilty of this offence if, before he provides any services etc, he takes reasonable steps to inform the intended recipient that this is so but that he will be providing services, etc which differ in certain respects;
   (ii) the provisions of sections 4 and 5 of the Act should apply *mutatis mutandis* to this offence;
   (iii) it should continue to be an offence to make false statements about the past or present supply of services etc;
   (iv) it should continue to be an offence to make false statements in respect of the future supply of any services, accommodation or facilities but only in the following circumstances;
      (a) where the falsity of the statement can be demonstrated at the time it is made, irrespective of whether the services etc are provided; or
      (b) where the statement involves holding out or undertaking that services etc will be supplied and the person making the statement can be shown to have no intention of supplying them, or no reasonable expectation that they can be supplied by him or any other person either at all or in the form that has been described;

(v) the offences at (i), (iii) and (iv)(a) should be absolute, subject only to the section 24 defences.

NOTE

No action has been taken to implement these proposals. For discussion of reform proposals stimulated by a Department of Trade and Industry review of the Act in the early 1990s see two articles by Cartwright: 'The Future of the Trade Descriptions Act' (1991) 141 NLJ 888, and 'Reforming the Trade Descriptions Act 1968', 3 Consumer Policy Review 34.

CHAPTER 14

False price claims

INTRODUCTION

Pricing controls were first introduced in s 11 of the Trade Descriptions Act 1968 to deal with false and misleading indications of the price of goods. No protection was offered as regards pricing of services, accommodation and facilities, although sometimes pricing issues were dealt with under s 14 of the 1968 Act: see *MFI Warehouses Ltd v Nattrass* [1973] 1 All ER 762, [1973] 1 WLR 307, QBD, discussed at p 659. It became apparent that there was a need for more extensive control over price indications, in particular 'bargain offers' which led to the introduction of the Price Marking (Bargain Offers) Order 1979, SI 1979/364. Despite subsequent amendments, this Order proved unsatisfactory and, in places, unenforceable. In 1984 an Inter-Departmental Working Party reviewed the legislation on false and misleading price information and made recommendations for complete reform of the area.

Review of Legislation on False and Misleading Price Information: Report of the Inter-Departmental Working Party—Summary of Conclusions

Conclusions

. . .

(9) There should be a general legislative prohibition on traders providing consumers with false or misleading information about prices. (Paragraphs 5.2–5.8).

(10) Such a general legislative prohibition on its own would lead to severe practical difficulties. In the absence of detailed supplementary provisions the trade and the enforcement authorities would be unsure as to which practices the courts would hold to be misleading. Given the wide variety and ingenuity of marketing methods it would be many years and a large number of prosecutions before a satisfactory body of case law could be built up. (Paragraphs 5.9–5.10).

(11) A combination of a rather general piece of primary legislation and very detailed provisions in secondary legislation is what exists at present (in the shape of Section 11 of the Trade Descriptions Act 1968 and the Price Marking (Bargain Offers) Order 1979). This has been found wanting in many respects and the resultant criticisms are the origin of this review. (Paragraphs 1.12–1.16). An examination of the reasons for this suggests to us that a different means of providing detailed material to support a general prohibition of false or misleading price information needs to be found. (Paragraphs 5.11–5.13).

(12) We consider a statutory code of practice containing practical guidance would be the best means of providing much of the necessary detailed support for a general prohibition on false or misleading price information. During the last ten years a number of Acts have contained provisions for such a statutory code which is not legally binding—so that failure to observe any provision of the code does not itself render a person liable to any proceedings—but which is given a status which enables it to be admissible in evidence. Thus the courts can have regard to compliance or non-compliance with it in any relevant cases which come before them and it provides both traders and enforcement authorities with guidance on the day-to-day matters they need to deal with on the subject in question. We consider that these precedents would be useful ones to follow. (Paragraphs 5.18–5.20, 5.22–5.26 and 5.28).

(13) It is a matter for further consideration how many of the detailed provisions should go in the primary or subordinate legislation and how many in such a code. (Paragraph 5.21).

(14) Such a code should be drawn up by the Secretary of State with the advice of the Director General of Fair Trading, and in consultation with representative bodies of the trade, representative bodies of the enforcement authorities and consumer organisations. (Paragraphs 5.20 and 5.28) . . .

(25) The legislation in this area should apply not only to price indications for goods but also to those for services (including commission charges), facilities and accommodation. Hiring, hire purchase transactions, leasing, and rental should also be covered. In principle we consider that land and buildings on it should also be covered. (Paragraphs 4.13–4.16).

As a result of these proposals, Part III of the Consumer Protection Act 1987 introduced a new regime for the control of misleading price indications from 1 March 1989; the Price Marking (Bargain Offers) Order 1979 and s 11 of the Trade Descriptions Act 1968 being repealed as of that date.

PART III CONSUMER PROTECTION ACT 1987

20. Offence of giving misleading indication

(1) Subject to the following provisions of this Part, a person shall be guilty of an offence if, in the course of any business of his, he gives (by any means whatever) to any consumers an indication which is misleading as to the price at which any goods, services, accommodation or facilities are available, (whether generally or from particular persons).

(2) Subject as aforesaid, a person shall be guilty of an offence if—

    (a) in the course of any business of his, he has given an indication to any consumers which, after it was given, has become misleading as mentioned in subsection (1) above; and

    (b) some or all of those consumers might reasonably be expected to rely on the indication at a time after it has become misleading; and

    (c) he fails to take such steps as are reasonable to prevent those consumers from relying on the indication.

(3) For the purposes of this section it shall be immaterial—

    (a) whether the person who gives or gave the indication is or was acting on his own behalf or on behalf of another;

    (b) whether or not that person is the person, or included among the persons, from whom the goods, services, accommodation or facilities are available; and

    (c) whether the indication is or has become misleading in relation to all the consumers to whom it is or it was given or only in relation to some of them.

(4) A person guilty of an offence under subsection (1) or (2) above shall be liable—

    (a) on conviction on indictment, to a fine;

    (b) on summary conviction, to a fine not exceeding the statutory maximum.

(5) No prosecution for an offence under subsection (1) or (2) above shall be brought after whichever is the earlier of the following, that is to say—

(a) the end of the period of three years beginning with the day on which the offence was committed; and

(b) the end of the period of one year beginning with the day on which the person bringing the prosecution discovered that the offence had been committed.

(6) In this Part—

'consumer—

(a) in relation to any goods, means any person who might wish to be supplied with the goods for his own private use or consumption;

(b) in relation to any services or facilities, means any person who might wish to be provided with the services or facilities otherwise than for the purposes of any business of his; and

(c) in relation to any accommodation, means any person who might wish to occupy the accommodation otherwise than for the purposes of any business of his;

'price', in relation to any goods, services, accommodation or facilities, means:

(a) the aggregate of the sums required to be paid by a consumer for or otherwise in respect of the supply of the goods or the provision of the services, accommodation or facilities; or

(b) except in section 21 below, any method which will be or has been applied for the purpose of determining that aggregate.

A number of appeals have arisen concerning the operation of Part III and some pre-Act cases, decided under s 11 of the 1968 Act, may still be applicable. There follows a discussion of the key aspects of s 20, its related sections, and the statutory code of practice introduced in accordance with the recommendations of the 1984 Review (see above).

IN THE COURSE OF ANY BUSINESS OF HIS

The wording of s 20 demonstrates a change from other consumer protection statutes in that it prevents the prosecution of employees. This matter came before the House of Lords as an early issue for resolution:

Warwickshire County Council v Johnson [1993] AC 583, [1993] 1 All ER 299, House of Lords

Lord Roskill. My Lords, on 24 November 1989 Warwickshire County Council (the respondents) as the prosecuting authority laid an information against the appellant in respect of an offence allegedly committed against s 20(1) of the Consumer Protection Act 1987 on 29 May 1989. The appellant was on that date the manager of the Stratford-upon-Avon branch of Dixons Stores Group Ltd (Dixons). The wording of the information is of some importance and I set it out in full, emphasising the most crucial words:

'Neil Kirk Johnson gave, *in the course of a business of his*, to Graham Rodney Thomas an indication by means of a notice stating "We will beat any TV HiFi and Video price by £20 on the spot" which was misleading as to the price at which a JCV remote control television was offered in that the price was not £20 less that the price at which it was offered by another person in Stratford-upon-Avon contrary to Section 20(1) of the Consumer Protection Act 1987.'

The essential facts are not in dispute. The appellant with the authority of Dixons had placed outside the shop a notice in the terms set out in the information. On 29 May while the notice was still displayed Mr Thomas saw a TV set of the particular kind in question offered for sale elsewhere in Stratford-upon-Avon at a price of £159.95. Mr Thomas then went to Dixons and was told that Dixons had an identical set in stock. Mr Thomas thereupon took the appellant to see the set on sale elsewhere for £159.95. But when Mr Thomas sought to purchase the set at Dixons for £139.95 the appellant refused to sell it, apparently asserting that he was within his rights in refusing to sell the set at the reduced price. Mr Thomas reported the matter to the respondents' trading standards department. Later, when he was interviewed by an officer of that department, the appellant frankly agreed that he had been wrong but said he had acted in the heat of the moment when he was under pressure. These proceedings then followed.

The information came before the justices at Stratford-upon-Avon on 27 April 1990. They dismissed the information. They reached the conclusion that the notice was not misleading but they also held that the appellant 'was . . . acting in the course of a business of his'. The respondents understandably applied to the justices for a case to be stated. After considerable delay the case was signed on 23 November 1990. The appeal came on for hearing in the Divisional Court on 2 April 1992. That court (Stuart-Smith LJ and Popplewell J) allowed the appeal for the reasons given in the judgment of Popplewell J (see 156 JP 577). They held that the notice was misleading because the appellant refused to honour the terms of the notice in that he refused to 'beat any TV HiFi or Video price by £20 on the spot'. They also held, contrary to the appellant's submission on the second issue, that in failing to honour the notice the appellant was acting 'in the course of any business of his', interpreting that phrase as meaning 'in the course of his business, trade or profession'. The Divisional Court dealt with the question of sentence by granting the appellant an absolute discharge upon payment by him of the costs of the appeal to the Divisional Court.

The appellant invited the Divisional Court to certify two points of law of general importance. The Divisional Court certified these two questions:

'1. Whether for the purposes of section 20(1) of the Consumer Protection Act 1987 a statement, which in itself is not misleading on the face of it, can be rendered misleading by virtue of the fact that, even in the absence of evidence to show a general practice or intention to dishonour the offer contained therein, on one occasion the person making the statement declined to enter into a contract within the terms of the statement.

2. Whether for the purposes of section 20(2)(a) of the Consumer Protection Act 1987 an employed branch manager who fails to comply with a price indication so that the same is to be regarded as misleading does so "in the course of any business of his".'

In addition to the two items so certified the appellant in his printed case raised a third issue not raised—it could not be so raised—in the Divisional Court. Before the hearing of this appeal, your Lordships' House had heard the further submissions in *Pepper (Inspector of Taxes) v Hart* [1993] 1 All ER 42, [1992] 3 WLR 1032 but had not at that time given judgment. The appellant invited your Lordships in seeking to resolve the second issue to look at what was said in your Lordships' House on 12 March 1987 (485 HL Official Report (5th Series) col 1140 ff) by the minister concerned, Lord Beaverbrook, at the report stage of the then Consumer Protection Bill when replying to an amendment moved by Lord Morton of Shuna. Lord Morton was supported on this occasion by Lord Denning. It was said that, if your Lordships when considering the second issue found the language of s 20(1) and (2)(a) ambiguous, the ambiguity should be resolved in favour of the appellant by reason of what was then said by the minister as to the clear intention of these subsections.

My Lords, your Lordships' House has now given judgment in *Pepper (Inspector of Taxes) v Hart*. It has thus become proper in the strictly limited circumstances defined by Lord Browne-Wilkinson in his speech, with which the majority of their Lordships who heard that appeal agreed, to have regard to what was said in Parliament in the course of the passage of the Bill. I should mention for the sake of completeness that your Lordships were assured that when the Bill was passed through the later stages in your Lordships' House and also when it reached another place there was no further reference at any stage to this issue. But before considering this matter further I shall first consider the two questions of construction.

As to the first question, it was strenuously argued that because the notice was not mislead-ing on its face it could not subsequently become misleading by a refusal to honour its terms. It was said that it never ceased to be a genuine offer. Overcharging could not of itself convert that notice, itself not misleading, into a notice which was misleading. Counsel for the appellant frankly admitted that Mr Thomas was misled. I ask: by what was Mr Thomas misled? There can only be one answer. Mr Thomas was misled by the notice. I find myself in complete agree-ment with the reasoning of the Divisional Court on this issue (156 JP 577 at 580):

'The notice is a continuing offer and whether it is misleading or not can only be tested by somebody taking up the offer. It was misleading because [the appellant] did not in accordance with the terms of the notice beat any TV, hi-fi, video price by £20 on the spot.'

To hold otherwise would be seriously to restrict the efficacy of this part of the consumer pro-tection legislation. Seemingly innocent notices could be put up and then when such notices were followed by a refusal to honour them by a person acting in the course of his business no offence would be committed. I would therefore answer the first question certified Yes.

The second certified question is more difficult. At first sight the answer given by the Divisional Court has the appeal of simplicity and common sense. The appellant's business was to manage Dixons branch at Stratford-upon-Avon. His refusal arose in the course of that business. Hence he is guilty of the offence charged. It does not matter that he had no business of his own.

The Divisional Court was referred to a number of cases, some in the last century, all deci-sions upon the construction of other statutes and upon very different facts. The second certi-fied question must be answered by referring to this statute (the Consumer Protection Act 1987) and to what can be deduced from its language in the various relevant sections. For ease of ref-erence I shall set out the relevant parts of those sections to which your Lordships were referred:

Lord Roskill quoted from ss 20, 39, 40(1), and 45(1) and then continued:

During the argument it was suggested that some support for the respondents' construction of s 20(1) might be found in s 40(1). It was suggested that the words 'in the course of any busi-ness of his' might be read not as referring to the immediately preceding words 'some other per-son' but to the earlier phrase, namely the person who has committed 'an offence to which section 39 above applies'. But there are a number of difficulties in the way of this suggested con-struction. First it involves construing these words otherwise than in the order in which they appear in the subsection. Secondly, the somewhat opaque drafting of s 40(1) involves the incor-poration via s 39(5) of the language of s 20(1) into the opening words of the subsection. This involves treating the phrase 'in the course of any business of his' as also appearing in the open-ing words of s 40(1). This seems to me to make it impossible to relate those same words when they appear later in the subsection as applying to the 'person' mentioned in the opening words. Thirdly and apart from these difficulties, as my noble and learned friend Lord Ackner pointed out during the argument, the appellant was charged with an offence against s 20(1) and not with an offence against s 40(1).

The obscurity of this language has puzzled commentators, to whom it has seemed odd that when a misleading notice or advertisement is published the person responsible for refusing to honour the advertisement, if an employee and not the owner of the business in question, is not guilty of an offence against s 20(1). In commenting upon the decision of the Divisional Court in the present case Professor J C Smith wrote in discussing the phrase 'any business of his' ([1992] Crim LR 644 at 644–647):

'The inconvenience of holding that the offence can be committed only by the owner of the business is obvious but what did the draftsman mean by this emphatic and inelegant phrase if he did not mean any business belonging to the defendant? Perhaps the answer to the difficulty is to be found in section 40(1) [he then set out the text of s 40(1) and continued:] There is an ambiguity here. Does "any business of his" refer to a business of "any person" or of "some other person"? If the latter, we are no farther forward; but, if the former, there is no difficulty about convicting the employee. This assumes that the employer is guilty of the offence as well—ie that the offence is one imposing strict liability and vicarious liability.'

Professor Smith thus highlights the problem of construction but does not resolve it. I have already indicated the impossibility of construing these words out of their natural order and the effect of the incorporation of s 20(1) into s 40(1).

Counsel also drew attention to the commentary in O'Keefe *Law Relating to Trade Descriptions* Div 2, para 3081. After setting out the differences between the position under s 23 of the Trade Descriptions Act 1968 and this legislation, the author suggests that the latter legislation is more restrictive than the former and continues:

'The main difference between the Trade Descriptions Act 1968, s 23 and the 1987 Act, s 40(1) is that the latter contains a pre-requisite to any prosecution. This is that the commission of the [misleading price offence under s 20(1)] offence must have been committed by the other person "in the course of any business of his". Section 45 defines "business" as including "a trade or profession . . . " It is therefore submitted that an employee whose act or default results in the commission by his or her employer of an offence contemplated by s 39 *cannot* be prosecuted as the actual offender under s 40(1), though this proposition remains to be tested by a court of record. If this is a correct interpretation of s 40(1) it is quite a startling conclusion compared with the previous practice under the now repealed price offences contained in the 1968 Act.' (O'Keefe's emphasis.)

It clearly appeared strange to these learned commentators, as indeed it appeared to some of your Lordships during the argument, that the person actually responsible for what happened, as the appellant clearly was, should be immune from conviction. But study of these various sections and the changes between the Trade Descriptions Act 1968 and this legislation has led me to conclude that the words 'in the course of any business of his' must mean any business of which the defendant is either the owner or in which he has a controlling interest. Not without some reluctance I find myself unable to share the view taken by the Divisional Court. I would therefore answer the second certified question No.

I have, in respectful agreement with Professor Smith, criticised the drafting of these sections and I share his particular criticism of the drafting of s 40(1). As already stated it is now, within the limitations already mentioned, permissible to have regard to statements by a minister in Parliament in order to ascertain the true intention of ambiguous legislation the interpretation of which has become a matter of controversy.

As already stated at the report stage of the Bill which became the Consumer Protection Act 1987, Lord Morton of Shuna moved an amendment to cl 20(1) of the Bill, as it then was, to delete the words 'of his'. He said (485 HL Official Report (5th series) col 1140):

'The words "of his" appear to be quite unnecessary and unnecessarily restrictive. What is to be the position of somebody who is giving a misleading price indication in the course of his employer's business, possibly unauthorised by his employer? Is that employee who is acting against instructions to be safe from prosecution? That is the way it reads. There does not appear to be a necessity for the words "of his". The sense would remain if it is just "in the course of any business", which would restrict the subsection to a business use, so to speak, but allow the prosecution of somebody who might say, Well, it was not my business. I was acting for somebody else when I gave the misleading price.'

Lord Denning added: 'The words "of his" are not only unnecessary but misleading.'

In reply the minister, Lord Beaverbrook, said (cols 1142–1143):

'On the main point of this amendment as set out by the noble Lord, Lord Morton, it is a general principle of law that employers are largely responsible for the actions of their employees. I believe that it is especially right that this principle should apply in the case of misleading price indications. Policy on price indications in an individual store is rarely in the hands of individual employees, but it is more often a matter of centrally determined company policy. It is for the employer to ensure that his procedures and staff training are adequate and appropriate to prevent misleading price indications being given to consumers. I therefore think it is right so to draft the Bill that proceedings are directed against employers—that is the corporate body standing behind the misleading price indication—rather than individual employees. Accordingly we have included the words "of his" in the Bill to ensure that individual employees will not be prosecuted. It is of course for employers to institute systems and staff training to ensure that their employees do not give misleading price indications. If, in spite of all these precautions, a rogue employee nevertheless gives a misleading price indication, then the defence of due diligence, as set out in Clause 39, is likely to be available to his employer. But I have to say that I see little point in prosecuting individual employees in these circumstances.'

At the end of the short debate the minister said (col 1143):

' . . . I think that we would like to look at this again carefully to see whether something has been missed and whether it can be looked at further.'

Lord Morton of Shuna then withdrew his amendment. As already stated the matter was never raised again.

In my view the answers given by the minister are consistent with the construction I have felt obliged to put upon this legislation. Although the minister said that the government would look into the matter again there are no further references to this issue at any later stage of the progress of the Bill through Parliament. The adoption of the contrary construction would be to reach a conclusion contrary to the plain intention of Parliament simply because the draftsman has used language which on one view has failed to give effect to that intention. On the second certified question I must therefore respectfully differ from the Divisional Court. I would answer No. It follows that the appeal must be allowed and the conviction set aside. . . .

Lords Griffiths, Emslie, Ackner and **Lowry** agreed.

Appeal allowed.

NOTES

1. For discussion of the meaning of 'misleading', see s 21 below and the notes thereon.
2. This decision was the first case, following *Pepper (Inspector of Taxes) v Hart* [1993] 1 All ER 42, [1992] 3 WLR 1032, where reference was made to the Parliamentary debates on a Bill to aid construing the meaning of the words in the Act.
3. For a further reference to s 40(1) see ch 15, p 733.
4. The effect of this decision is to prevent employees (and private individuals) being prosecuted for pricing offences under the Act. If a company successfully raises a s 39 defence (see ch 15, at pp 710–11) naming an employee as the person whose act or default has caused an offence to occur, no further criminal

proceedings may be brought, cf *Nattrass v Timpson Shoes* [1973] Crim LR 197, under the former s 11 of the Trade Descriptions Act 1968.

QUESTION

As the manager of Dixons realised that he had been wrong to refuse to sell the television at the reduced price, how can it be said that the notice detailing the price reduction scheme was a 'misleading indication'? (See further, *All ER Annual Review 1993*, pp 86–87.)

'In the course of a business' was further discussed in *Denard v Burton Retail Ltd* (1997) *The Times*, 19 November, QBD. Here, within some of Burton's shops, another company, Baird, operated concessions. Price labels, marked 'Burton', were attached to goods owned by Baird, by Baird's employees, but payments were made at the Burton's till and Burton's receipts were issued. Although Burton had no means of checking the price labels and erroneous labels were attached by Baird's employees, Burton was held liable under s 20 for offences committed in the course of Burton's business (Baird having already pleaded guilty to the offences). The court, on analysing the relationship between Burton and Baird, decided that it was Burton's business that was involved.

GOODS, SERVICES, FACILITIES, AND ACCOMMODATION

The 1987 Act has considerably widened the scope of pricing offences beyond goods to include services, facilities, and accommodation, which were omitted from the pricing provisions of the 1968 Act. There are definitions of each of these terms:

Goods

Section 45(1) indicates that 'goods': 'includes substances, growing crops and things comprised in land by virtue of being attached to it and any ship, aircraft or vehicle'. 'Substance' is further defined as meaning 'any natural or artificial substance, whether in solid, liquid or gaseous form or in the form of a vapour, and includes substances that are comprised in or mixed with other goods'. The pricing of domestic gas supplies is, therefore, covered here, whilst electricity falls under the definition of services and facilities.

Services and facilities

22 Application to provision of services and facilities
(1) Subject to the following provisions of this section, references in this Part to services or facilities are references to any services or facilities whatever including, in particular:
  (a) the provision of credit or of banking or insurance services and the provision of facilities incidental to the provision of such services;

(b) the purchase or sale of foreign currency;
(c) the supply of electricity;
(d) the provision of a place, other than on a highway, for the parking of a motor vehicle;
(e) the making of arrangements for a person to put or keep a caravan on any land other than arrangements by virtue of which that person may occupy the caravan as his only or main residence.

(2) References in this Part to services shall not include references to services provided to an employer under a contract of employment.

(3) References in this Part to services or facilities shall not include references to services or facilities which are provided by an authorised person or appointed representative in the course of the carrying on of an investment business.

(4) In relation to a service consisting in the purchase or sale of foreign currency, references in this Part to the method by which the price of the service is determined shall include references to the rate of exchange.

(5) In this section:

'appointed representative', 'authorised person' and 'investment business' have the same meanings as in the Financial Services Act 1986;

'caravan' has the same meaning as in the Caravan Sites and Control of Development Act 1960;

'contract of employment' and 'employer' have the same meanings as in [the Employment Protection Act 1996];

'credit' has the same meaning as in the Consumer Credit Act 1974.

NOTE

There is some overlap between the 1987 Act and other statutes, for example the advertising of the price of credit is, in addition, regulated by the Consumer Credit Act 1974, see further ch 6, at pp 298–9.

Accommodation

23 Application to provision of accommodation etc.

(1) Subject to subsection (2) below, references in this Part to accommodation or facilities being available shall not include references to accommodation or facilities being available to be provided by means of the creation or disposal of an interest in land except where—

(a) the person who is to create or dispose of the interest will do so in the course of any business of his; and
(b) the interest to be created or disposed of is a relevant interest in a new dwelling and is to be created or disposed of for the purpose of enabling that dwelling to be occupied as a residence, or one of the residences, of the person acquiring the interest.

(2) Subsection (1) above shall not prevent the application of any provision of this Part in relation to—

(a) the supply of any goods as part of the same transaction as any creation or disposal of an interest in land; or
(b) the provision of any services or facilities for the purposes of, or in connection with, any transaction for the creation or disposal of such an interest.

(3) In this section—

'new dwelling' means any building or part of a building in Great Britain which—

(a) has been constructed or adapted to be occupied as a residence, and

(b) has not previously been so occupied or has been so occupied only with other premises or as more than one residence,

and includes any yard, garden, out-houses or appurtenances which belong to that building or part or are to be enjoyed with it;

'relevant interest'—

    (a) in relation to a new dwelling in England and Wales, means the freehold estate in the dwelling or a leasehold interest in the dwelling for a term of years absolute of more than twenty-one years, not being a term of which twenty-one years or less remains unexpired;

    (b) in relation to a new dwelling in Scotland, means the *dominium utile* of land comprising the dwelling, or a leasehold interest in the dwelling where twenty-one years or more remains unexpired.

NOTES

1. The 1987 Act extended controls over pricing to cover houses in a limited way. The requirements of being a new dwelling for use as a home and the restriction of the control to those who created or disposed of the interest in the course of business, means that the usual advertising of 'second-hand' property by estate agents is not regulated by the 1987 Act.

2. Gaps in the protection offered by the 1987 Act have since been filled by the Property Misdescriptions Act 1991. Under the Property Misdescriptions (Specified Matters) Order 1992, SI 1992/2834, Sch, para 16, the price and previous price of property (other than that covered by s 23 of the 1987 Act) are prescribed matters under s 1 of the 1991 Act, with associated criminal liability for false statements. Both 'second-hand' and commercial property can give rise to offences.

3. An example of a pricing offence concerning a house was reported in *The Times*, 16 January 1991, when it was claimed that a house had been reduced from £194,950 to £164,950. The highest price asked had been £185,000 for two weeks only. The estate agent was fined £800.

'TO ANY CONSUMERS'

The 1987 Act is more limited than earlier provisions as only price indications *given to consumers* are protected. This means that where a false price indication is given at a 'trade only' warehouse, between two businesses, between a local authority and a business, etc, no offence can arise.

It has been questioned whether misleading price indications discovered by trading standards officers in the course of their inspections of businesses fall under the terms of s 20. In *Toys 'R' Us v Gloucestershire County Council* (1994) 13 Tr Law 276, (1994) 158 JP 338, QBD, discussed further below, it was held that they did. If a shop is visited during opening hours, any ticket prices seen are those seen by customers also; it did not matter that the officer did not wish to be supplied with the goods.

QUESTIONS

What arguments can be put forward in favour of limiting the protection of Part III to consumers only? Is it the case that all traders can be considered capable of 'looking after themselves'?

A PRICE INDICATION

'Price' is defined in s 20(6) as the 'the aggregate of the sums required to be paid by a consumer'. A problem arises where shelf markings or price tickets on goods do not coincide with prices obtained from scanning bar codes. In such circumstances an offence will not always arise. The situation is discussed in the following case.

Toys 'R' Us v Gloucestershire County Council (1994) 13 Tr Law 276, (1994) 158 JP 338, Queen's Bench Division

Kennedy LJ. This is an appeal by way of case stated from a decision of the justices for the petty sessional division of Gloucester who, on December 4, 1992, at Whitminster, found the appellants guilty of 34 offences contrary to s 20(1) of the Consumer Protection Act 1987.

Having quoted parts of ss 20(1) and 21(1)(a) Kennedy LJ continued:

The allegation in each of the informations was that the appellants on four dates in 1991 at their toy supermarket in Gloucester had given to consumers by means of a price sticker an indication of price which was misleading as to the price at which the goods were available. On the first date, July 30, 1991, one offence was alleged; on the second date, August 2, 1991, one offence was alleged; on the third date, August 9, 1991, 13 offences were alleged; and on the fourth date, December 20, 1991, 19 offences were alleged.

The facts were not in dispute and as found by the magistrates can be summarised as follows. On July 30, 1991 a Mr Parker's two sons selected each a pair of swimming goggles with price stickers. When the first son went to the till and the cashier caused the price to be displayed by means of the bar code, the price displayed was higher than that on the sticker. Mr Parker pointed out the discrepancy to the cashier, who then voided the till and manually entered and charged the lower price. For the second son the cashier entered the transaction manually in accordance with the sticker and charged the price on the ticket. Two offences were alleged. The appellants pleaded guilty to the first son, so this appeal concerns only the second son.

On August 2, 1991, because of Mr Parker's complaint, a trading standards officer went to the store to make a test purchase. Again swimming goggles were selected priced £2.99. At the till the bar code generated a display price of £3.49, but the cashier noticed the discrepancy, voided the transaction and manually entered and charged £2.99.

On August 9, 1991, there was a repeat performance of what happened on August 2. The enforcement officer, Mr Willis, then entered the store and with the co-operation of the staff carried out a price check. Items were selected from the display area and scanned at a till set aside for the purpose and set to training mode. If the price displayed was higher than the one indicated on the item, it was seized. No purchase was made. The exercise was allegedly in conformity with s 29 of the Act. Twelve specimen items were seized, that amounted to 13. There were therefore 13 charges arising out of that day's activities.

On December 20, 1991 two test purchases were made when higher prices were displayed at the till and charged than were displayed on the items. The appellants pleaded guilty to charges arising out of those two transactions.

A further price check was then carried out identical to that performed on August 13, 1991. Many discrepancies were revealed and 19 specimen charges were preferred.

Arguments before the magistrates

Before the magistrates and before us the prosecution case has been quite simple. It is that the price at which the goods were available was the price generated on the visual display known as "the Price Look Up or P.L.U." at the till. The price on the ticket attached to the goods being lower, the offences were proved.

The defence case was and is that the ticket price was the price at which the goods were available because that was the price the appellants intended to charge even though on some occasions a higher price was asked because a cashier failed to notice or had drawn to his or her attention the fact that the ticket price was lower than the price on the P.L.U.

The appellants also contended that if, on any occasion, an offence was committed it was an offence contrary to s 20(2) of the Act and not an offence contrary to s 20(1). They further contended that a trading standards officer when making a test purchase is not a consumer as defined by s 20(6), so any charges based on such a purchase should fail. Finally the appellants submitted both to the magistrates and to us that the price check procedure adopted by the trading standards officer on August 9, 1991 and again on December 20, 1991 was *ultra vires*, going beyond the powers given to investigating officers in s 29 of the Act.

I turn now to consider each of the defence submissions in turn.

The main submission

It is unfortunate that having regard to the nature of the appellants' primary submission the magistrates have not made any express findings of fact about the policy and practice of the appellants when there was a discrepancy between the ticket price on an item and the price displayed on the P.L.U., but as the evidence, all of which was adduced by the prosecution, was not disputed and as nothing turned on the credibility of witnesses, counsel agreed that we could look at the material before the magistrates to make good that lacuna. The relevant evidence is to be found in two interviews which Mr Willis, the trading standards enforcement officer, had with Mr Muzika, the finance director and an administrator of the appellants. The first interview was on September 27, 1991, after the price check on August 9, 1991 and the second interview was on February 4, 1992, following the price check on December 20, 1991. In summary Mr Muzika said that the P.L.U. price would come from the appellants' current price list, and would be the price the appellants intended to charge but that cashiers were required to check tickets, and if the ticket showed a lower price that was the price to be charged. When discrepancies were known to exist in relation to a particular line of goods (there being 18,000 lines in all) the P.L.U would not display a price but would be set to read "enter price", which would ensure that the attention of the cashier was directed to the ticket. Of course errors occurred but, in Mr Muzika's words during the first interview:

'The fall back in case of error is that the cashier as part of procedure is required to check the price label on every item with that displayed by the till and override any discrepancy arising to the customer's advantage.'

At the second interview Mr Muzika reiterated the appellants' position. He was asked:

'Q. Is it company policy for till operators to check the price tickets after scanning the bar code?
A. Yes.
Q. Can you explain why this was not done on December 20, 1991 when Mr Gardiner purchased the items ie Barbie Clothing Boutique and Battleship Blow-Up.
A. No. She did not follow procedure.'

There was no evidence to the contrary nor was Mr Muzika's credibility impugned, so I am satisfied that the magistrates, if they had directed their minds to the issue, would have found that the appellants did require cashiers to check price tickets, and if they found a price lower than the price displayed on the P.L.U. to charge the lower price. Life being what it is, it is not surprising that cashiers did not always check as they should have done.

With that addition to the findings of fact I return to s 20(1). In my judgment Mr Treacy is right in his submission that the relevant time is the time at which the indication as to price is given, that is to say in the context of this case when the item was on the shelf with the ticket attached to it. That is clear from the words of the section, and also from the decision of this Court in *Doble v David Grieg Ltd.* [1972] 1 WLR 703, a case decided under similar but not identical provisions to be found in s 11(2) of the Trade Descriptions Act 1968.

So the next question is in the words of s 20(1)—was the price ticket misleading as to the price at which the goods were available. The magistrates in the case stated unfortunately deserted the wording of the statute although its wording is in no way obscure, and it may be that they fell into error. They said at p 8 of the case stated:

'As the prices displayed were lower than the correct prices and were only applicable if the discrepancy was noticed, which would have necessitated the till being voided and the lower price being entered manually, we determined that the prices were misleading, as defined by s 21(1)(a) and (b).'

The statute does not require ascertainment of 'the correct price'. All it requires is ascertainment of the price at which the goods were available, bearing in mind that price is defined in s 20(6) as the sums 'required to be paid by a consumer'. Mr Matheson submits that as it was the policy and practice of the appellants to charge the price on the ticket, that was the price at which the goods were available. If a customer had asked a passing store manager 'What sum will I be required to pay for this article?', the reply would have been the price on the ticket, and if the store manager knew that there had been a price increase he might have added 'Make sure the cashier does not charge you the new price'. In my judgment Mr Matheson's general submission is unanswerable and it can be tested by reference to a shopkeeper who owns and runs his own small supermarket. He may choose not to relabel all the tins on his shelves when having had a fresh delivery he decides to put up the price, so some tins on the shelf have the old price and some have the new price. He sets the price list which feeds the P.L.U. to the new price, but he is careful. Whenever a customer tenders at the till a tin bearing the old price he charges the old price. Even Mr Treacy was not inclined to submit that the tins bearing the old price were not available at that price for the purposes of s 20(1). Does it make any difference that in the present case we are concerned not with a one-man shop but with a large supermarket? In principle the answer must be no, but Mr Treacy submits that because cashiers make errors the price ticket is not really the price at which the goods are available, it is only the price at which they are available on a conditional basis, the condition being that either the cashier or the customer notices the discrepancy. The condition could, of course, be put the other way round, namely that the goods are available at the ticket price unless the cashier or customer fails to notice the discrepancy, which brings me back to s 20 and s 21. As Mr Treacy pointed out this Act was intended to protect consumers, so when considering what the customer is required to pay the Court will not be bound by the attitude of the management, but because in this case the management policy, apparently operated in practice subject to errors, was to charge the ticket price, it seems to me that the magistrates should have started from the standpoint that an offence under s 20(1) could only be established if it could be shown that despite the policy in reality goods were not available at the ticket price. In other words, that cashiers and customers did not notice discrepancies and correct them or cause them to be corrected. If that is what the evidence showed it would, in my judgment, be open to the Court to find that even when the goods were on the shelf the goods were not in fact available at the ticket price, and the price shown on the ticket was misleading because it was less than in fact it was. So what happens in practice is important, as suggested by the Code of Practice issued by the Secretary of State, para 2.1.1 in Part II of which is cited in the case stated. It reads:

'The Consumer Protection Act makes it an offence to indicate a price for goods or services which is lower than the one that actually applies, for example showing one price in an advertisement, window display, shelf marking or on the item itself, and then charging a higher price at the point of sale or checkout.'

Effect on the charges

If I am right as to the law it necessarily follows that the appellants should not have been convicted of any of the 34 offences which they contested, because it will be recalled that:

(1) on July 30 1991 the cashier entered the price manually in accordance with the ticket and the customer paid that price;

(2) on August 2, 1991 the same occurred, the cashier having noticed that the ticket price was less than the P.L.U. price.

(3) for the first transaction of August 9, 1991 the pattern was followed as on August 2, 1991. The remaining 12 summonses relating to August 9, 1991 related to items collected during the price check. They were not presented to cashiers in the normal course of business and, having regard to the appellants' policy and practice, there was nothing to show that they were not available at the ticket price, albeit they each generated a higher price on the P.L.U.

(4) the same can be said about all 19 specimen charges arising out of what occurred on December 20, 1991.

Was Section 20(2) the more appropriate section?

That means that I can deal in less detail with Mr Matheson's remaining submissions.

I do not accept that s 20(2) has any application to the facts of this case. Mr Matheson submitted that it might be said that the ticket price became misleading when the P.L.U. showed a different price. But in my judgment s 20(2), as Mr Treacy submitted, is intended to deal with a quite different situation—the advertisement or shelf barker which ceases to be accurate because of some event which takes place after it was displayed. For example if an advertisement claims that the vendor's price is less than that of a competitor, who then reduces his price.

. . .

Accordingly I would allow the appeal and remit the matters to the justices with a direction to acquit.

Mr Justice Scott Baker. I agree.

NOTE

The effect of the decision to examine the policy of the shop in this instance, and to consider what price the shop intended to charge before deciding whether a misleading price indication had been given, makes the prosecution's task more difficult. Here it was not enough to check the prices displayed on the computer to establish the offence. It would be an offence only if it could be shown that, despite the company policy of intending to charge the ticket price, in practice the higher, computer price would be charged.

An important restriction on the operation of s 11 of the Trade Descriptions Act 1968 is likely to apply also with respect to s 20 of the 1987 Act. Where a price has been agreed under a contract, but delivery of the goods is delayed until a later date, an attempt to increase the contract price, on presentation of the invoice at or after delivery, is considered as a matter of contract law only and will not give rise to a criminal offence. Two cases under the 1968 Act illustrate this principle. In *Miller v Pickering Bull & Co Ltd* [1981] 3 All ER 265, QBD, a contract was made to supply a local authority with fruit and vegetables according to a specified formula. When items were delivered, the delivery notes indicated prices higher than the contract prices. Subsequently, in *Simmons v Emmett* [1982] Tr Law Rep 189, QBD, buttonholes were ordered for a wedding at specified prices but higher prices were charged on delivery. In both instances the courts decided that there was no criminal liability as there were no false price indications given; the agreed contract prices were binding. It is suggested that a similar result would occur under s 20, the 'price' being the contract price and no misleading price indication being given prior to the making of the contract.

'MISLEADING'

It is only 'misleading' price indications which constitute offences. Section 21 provides a definition of 'misleading' indications.

21. Meaning of 'misleading'

(1) For the purposes of s 20 above an indication given to any consumers is misleading as to a price if what is conveyed by the indication, or what those consumers might reasonably be expected to infer from the indication or any omission from it, includes any of the following, that is to say—

(a) that the price is less than in fact it is;

(b) that the applicability of the price does not depend on facts or circumstances on which its applicability does in fact depend;

(c) that the price covers matters in respect of which an additional charge is in fact made;

(d) that a person who in fact has no such expectation—

    (i) expects the price to be increased or reduced (whether or not at a particular time or by a particular amount); or

    (ii) expects the price, or the price as increased or reduced, to be maintained (whether or not for a particular period); or

(e) that the facts or circumstances by reference to which the consumers might reasonably be expected to judge the validity of any relevant comparison made or implied by the indication are not what in fact they are.

(2) For the purposes of section 20 above, an indication given to any consumers is misleading as to a method of determining a price if what is conveyed by the indication, or what those consumers might reasonably be expected to infer from the indication or any omission from it, includes any of the following, that is to say—

(a) that the method is not what in fact it is;

(b) that the applicability of the method does not depend on facts or circumstances on which its applicability does in fact depend;

(c) that the method takes into account matters in respect of which an additional charge will in fact be made,

(d) that a person who in fact has no such expectation—

    (i) expects the method to be altered (whether or not at a particular time or in a particular respect); or

    (ii) expects the method, or that method as altered, to remain unaltered (whether or not for a particular period); or

  (e) that the facts or circumstances by reference to which the consumers might reasonably be expected to judge the validity of any relevant comparison made or implied by the indication are not what in fact they are.

(3) For the purposes of subsections (1)(e) and (2)(e) above a comparison is a relevant comparison in relation to a price or method of determining a price if it is made between that price or that method, or any price which has been or may be determined by that method, and—

  (a) any price or value which is stated or implied to be, to have been or to be likely to be attributed or attributable to the goods, services, accommodation or facilities in question or to any other goods, services, accommodation or facilities; or

  (b) any method, or other method, which is stated or implied to be, to have been or to be likely to be applied or applicable for the determination of the price or value of the goods, services, accommodation or facilities in question or of the price or value of any other goods, services, accommodation or facilities.

NOTES

Subsection (1) is concerned with prices which are misleading, whereas subsection (2) applies to misleading methods of calculating prices, where, for example, a formula is used such as meat being advertised at £5 per kilo, but in making the calculations £6 per kilo is used. Although when a price indication is read it may not appear to be misleading, if, when it is tested by a customer, the trader does not comply with the indication, an offence can arise: see *Warwickshire County Council v Johnson* [1993] AC 583, [1993] 1 All ER 299, House of Lords, above, pp 675–9.

It is not necessary for evidence to be produced that any particular person has been misled by a price indication for there to be an offence: see *MFI Furniture Centres Ltd v Hibbert* (1996) 160 JP 178, QBD, and *A G Stanley Ltd (t/ a Fads) v Surrey County Council Trading Standards Office* (1995) 103 ITSA 7 MR 26, QBD, below, p 689.

Each of the five examples of misleading indications will now be considered. It is to be noted that there is over-lap between the paragraphs and some indications may fall under two or more paragraphs.

(a) the price is less than in fact it is

This is perhaps the most common form of misleading price indication. It covers situations where there is more than one price ticket on the goods and the higher one is charged, where the price on the shelf-edge is less than the price charged at the till, or where a wrong, lower price, ticket is on the goods, etc. For an example of this see *Toys 'Я' Us v Gloucestershire County Council* (1994) 13 Tr Law 276, (1994) 158 JP 338, QBD, above, pp 683–6.

(b) that the applicability of the price does not depend on facts or circumstances on which its applicability does in fact depend

This covers situations where there are undisclosed restrictions on an offer which mean in certain circumstances a higher price will be charged. Two cases on the Trade Descriptions Act 1968 provide useful examples. In *Read Bros. Cycles*

(Leyton) Ltd v Waltham Forest London BC [1978] RTR 397, QBD, a motorcycle was advertised as 'list price £580, our price £540' but when a purchaser wished to buy it by trading-in his old motorcycle, he was charged £580 with a trade-in allowance of £90, thereby increasing the price by £40. In *Clive Sweeting v Northern Upholstery Ltd* (1983) Tr Law Rep 5, QBD, a three piece suite was advertised at £699 but it transpired that the suite was only available at this price in a beige colour, other colours costing £739. The restriction of the advertised price to a particular coloured suite was not made clear in the advertising. In both instances there was an offence. See now the Code of Practice, para 1.4 in particular, below, p 698.

(c) that the price covers matters in respect of which an additional charge is in fact made
A typical example of this would be a customer buying do-it-yourself items from a builders' merchants and being informed at the till that VAT is payable on top of the ticket price on the goods. The pre 1987 Act case of *Richards v Westminster Motors Ltd* [1976] RTR 88, QBD, where a car was advertised at £1,395 but at the time of purchase VAT was added making the selling price £1,534.50, illustrates this situation. See the Code of Practice, para 2.2 at pp 700–1, for further examples where problems may arise.

(d) expected price increases, reductions or maintenance
Shops, in their advertising, often suggest there is a need to purchase goods immediately to avoid some future price increase, for example after a Budget or at the end of a sale event. In many instances there are, in fact, no plans to alter the advertised price. The case of *A G Stanley Ltd (t/a Fads) v Surrey County Council Trading Standards Office* (1995) 103 ITSA 7 MR 26, QBD, below, appears to fall under s 21(1)(d) as well as s 21(1)(e).

(e) the facts or circumstances by reference to which consumers might reasonably be expected to judge the validity of any relevant comparison made or implied by the indication are not what in fact they are
This rather complicated provision covers situations where consumers, reading an advertisement, gain an incorrect impression of what is being offered or of the comparison being suggested by the advertisement. An example would be if a price comparison was made with a 'recommended price' which the consumer would presume was a genuine manufacturers' recommended price, but, in fact, there is no such 'recommended price'. Similarly, a conviction was upheald in *Mirror Group Newspapers v Northants County Council* [1997] Crim LR 883, when *The People* advertised 'a £50 watch for just £4.99' and goods were not available on the open market for the purposes of comparison. The following is a case illustrating the operation of s 21(1)(e):

A G Stanley Ltd (t/a Fads) v Surrey County Council Trading Standards Office (1995) 103 ITSA 7 MR 26, Queen's Bench Division

Mr Justice Scott Baker. . . . . The appellants were convicted of two offences under section 20 of the Consumer Protection Act 1987 for giving misleading indications as to price in respect of an occasional table that was for sale.

The facts can be shortly stated . . . On 2 April 1992, the occasional table was priced at £7.99. On 14 October 1992 the price of the table was reduced to £4.99 in a 'Style and Value' promotion. There was a point of sale notice on or near the tables . . . which records 'Style and Value, Occasional Table, Chipboard, save £3, now £4.99' (in large figures), 'was £7.99'. The tables continued to be available at this price until 12 March 1993.

In the meantime, on 10 November 1992, the tables were advertised in the press in what was described as a 13-day event which must end on Tuesday, 24 November. The advertisement . . . is headed: 'FADS SUPER SAVERS 13 DAY EVENT MUST END TUES 24TH NOV', and then refers to a number of different items that were on sale, one of which was the table. The advertisement with regard to that runs as follows. In the top right-hand side there is a picture of the table covered with a tablecloth, which was also in the sale, and then the body of the advertisement reads: 'OCCASIONAL TABLE was £7.99, NOW ONLY £4.99.'

10 November was the date of the first offence, and this advertisement forms the basis of it. On 12 November, or thereabouts the 13-day event commenced. On 24 November, or thereabouts, the 13-day event ended, but contrary to what the advertisement had said, the table continued to be priced at £4.99 and remained in the 'Style and Value' promotion that it had previously been in before the 13-day event. On 27 November Mr Muddell bought one of these tables for the advertised price of £4.99.

On 15 December the 'Style and Value' promotion ended, but the table continued to be priced and available for sale at £4.99. On 21 December the Christmas sale began. The table was still priced at £4.99, but there was now a slightly different point of sale notice . . . It is now headed: 'SALE ROUND OCCASIONAL TABLE, NOW £4.99 WAS £7.99.' On 30 December Mr Muddell went to the store, saw the point of sale notice, to which I have just referred, and bought three more of these tables, each at the advertised price of £4.99. It is that purchase that gives rise to the second of the two offences.

Finally to complete the chronological story, on 12 March 1993 the price of the table was increased to £7.99.

Mr Justice Scott Baker referred to the charges under s 20 of the Consumer Protection Act 1987, s 21(1)(e), s 25 regarding the effect of the Code of Practice, and the existence of a Code. The relevant parts of the Code were identified as paras 1.2.2 and 1.2.3 (see below, p 697). He continued:

The appellants argue that the company complied with the code. Up until the 10 November advertisement, it is argued the previous price was £7.99. The tables were on sale at that price between 2 April 1992 and 13 October 1992. The words '*last* price' in (a) of paragraph 1.2.2 means not the last price in time, but the last numerically different price from that at which the item was on sale at the material date. The '*last* price' argues Mr Howard, for the appellants, at which the product was available to consumers, was £7.99. It was available at that price for a period substantially in excess of 28 consecutive days during the previous six months, and therefore, by definition, the code was complied with. This argument, in my judgment, overlooks the fact that the product was available to customers between 13 October and the start of the 13-day event, to which I have referred, at £4.99, in other words, during the period that it was being offered in the 'Style and Value' promotion.

When one turns to look at . . . the advertisement in the newspaper, the advertisement states clearly 'Was £7.99 save £3'. The clear indication, in my judgment, from that advertisement is that the price was £7.99 immediately before the commencement of the Super Savers 13-day event, and the statement: 'Must end Tue 24 Nov' conveyed the message that there was every likelihood that the price would revert to £7.99 at or about that date.

The appellants argue that they complied with the literal meaning of paragraph 1.2.2. But I do not think this is correct because it involves construing 'previous price' as meaning the identical price ie £4.99 and treating as the critical factor the slightly different circumstances in which the table was offered for sale ie the Style and Value promotion rather than the 13-day event. What is critical for the customer is the price not the label attached for the particular promotion.

Turning to the 30 December, the appellants' argument here is that the point of sale notice clearly shows that the previous price was £7.99. It is further argued, although in my judgment it is not material to the issues, that Mr Muddell was not misled when he bought the three tables, because he had bought one earlier at the same price on 27 December. Again, it is argued that the last price of £7.99, at which the product was available to customers, had been available for 28 days or more, and that the six months provision was complied with. It is also argued that the code was complied with as at 30 December.

For the respondents, the point is taken in the same way, that in reality the position was that immediately before the sale the table was on offer at £4.99, and that therefore there was a breach of the code. In each instance, in my judgment, both the advertisement and the point of sale notice contained the very clear message that immediately prior to the event with which each document was concerned, the table had been on sale at a higher price. In fact it had not.

Mr Scholz, for the respondents, argues the appeal in this way. He says that underlying the whole of this case, and cases like it, is the legislation about misleading price indications. The purpose of the code, which is brought in under powers given by the Act, is to ensure that price comparisons are meaningful. He says that when one looks at paragraph 1.2.2 of the code, essentially one is working back from the date of the current offer. What the code is designed to allow for is the retailer making a comparison with a price that he has charged at some point in the last six months, for a period in excess of 28 consecutive days. However, he goes on that the article cannot have been sold at a different price between that earlier time and the time of the current offer.

He draws attention to the fact that there are not infrequently situations where goods are on offer at a particular price for a period of weeks or months, and then taken off the market altogether before being put back on the market at a lower price, and that paragraph 1.2.2 has to be interpreted to cater for this situation He draws particular comfort from the last sentence of paragraph 1.2.2 that 'the product must not have been offered at a different price between that 28 day period and the day when the reduced price is first offered'. He argues, and I agree with him about this, that that sentence throws some light on the meaning of '*last* price' in paragraph 1.2.2(a).

The appellants' argument rests on the contention that the '*last* price' in paragraph 1.2.2(a) must mean the last different price, and not the last price in time. If it does mean the last different price, there are considerable difficulties in construing 'different' in the last sentence in paragraph 1.2.2.

Mr Scholz also gains comfort from the use of the word 'reduced' in paragraph 1.2.c. He goes on, that in determining whether paragraph 1.2.2 of the code was complied with, it is necessary to ask a number of questions:

'(i) What was 'the last price at which the product was available to consumers in the previous 6 months'?'

He submits, and I accept this submission, that the words used in the code bear their ordinary meaning and that the six months period referred to is the six months period prior to the date indicated by the price comparison.

'(ii) Was the product available to consumers "at that price [ie, the previous price] for at least 28 consecutive days in the previous 6 months"?'

The previous price of £7.99 so satisfies this requirement.

'(iii) Had the product been offered at a different price [ie, at a price different to the "previous price"] between that 28 day period [ie, the period during which the "previous price" applied] and the day when the reduced price is first offered?'

He submits that 'the day' being referred to is the start date specified in the indication, the indication being the newspaper advertisement and/or the point of sale material, making the price comparison, as was on the facts of this case, the 12 November and 21 December 1991.

I accept these points by Mr Scholz. When one asks these questions, it seems to me clear that there has in this case been a breach of the code.

Paragraph 1.2.3 continues:

'If the previous price in a comparison does not meet one or more of the conditions set out in paragraph 1.2.2 above:

  (a) the comparison should be fair and meaningful; and
  (b) give a clear and positive explanation of the period for which and the circumstances in which the higher price applied."

In my judgment, far from being fair and meaningful in this case, the comparison was misleading . . .

There is one further point taken by Mr Howard, for the appellants, and it is this. He contends that if the Code of Practice is ambiguous, that this being a code made under a criminal statute, any ambiguity should be resolved in favour of the appellants. For my part, I think that the meaning of the code is clear, and I do not accept that there is any ambiguity. In my judgment the code has to be construed in the context of the legislation under which it is made and, when it is so construed, I find no difficulty in my conclusion as to what it means.

For these reasons I would dismiss this appeal.

Lord Justice Rose agreed.

Appeal dismissed.

NOTES

1. Although this was argued under s 21(1)(e), the court did suggest that it might also fall under s 21(1)(d), above.
2. For the Code of Practice, see below, pp 694–703.
3. Mention is made of a '28 day in the previous six months' provision of the Code. This rule existed under s 11 of the Trade Descriptions Act 1968, in the form of a rebuttable presumption that the goods had been offered at the higher price for 28 days in the preceding six months. For a case on the interpretation of the 1968 Act, see *House of Holland Ltd v London Borough of Brent* [1971] 2 QB 304, [1971] 2 All ER 296, QBD.
4. An example where a prosecution was unsuccessfully brought under s 14 of the 1968 Act was *Westminster City Council v Ray Alan (Manshops) Ltd* [1982] 1 All ER 771, [1982] 1 WLR 383, QBD, mentioned above, p 655. Here a shop advertised a closing down sale for 18 months without the shop closing. This would now be likely to fall under s 21(1)(e) and could give rise to an offence.

PROBLEM

Hotrod is the manager of a garage and motor accessories shop, owned and operated by Zero Petroleum plc. Complaints have been made to the Loamshire Trading Standards Department about a number of transactions entered into on the premises.

(i) Speedy complained that he was required to pay a 3p per litre surcharge when he purchased 4 litres of petrol for his lawnmower. There was a small notice in the shop, by the till, stating that it was company policy to impose a surcharge on buyers of petrol who purchased less than 5 litres.

(ii) Banger went to buy a sponge, attracted by a notice in the Loamchester Echo a few weeks previously stating 'all screen-wash accessories half-price'. Hotrod explained that the offer had expired, and charged him the full price for the sponge.

(iii) Crank required four new tyres for his car. He saw a poster outside the garage, put up by Hotrod, claiming that the tyre prices at the garage were the lowest in Loamshire. Crank was charged £250 for four new tyres; he has since discovered that similar tyres were available at another outlet in the county for £50 each.

(iv) At the garage car-wash there is a sign saying 'Carwash for Old-Age Pensioners—£1—weekdays only'. Gaffer, an old-age pensioner, took his car through the carwash on Easter Monday and was required to pay £1.50, the full price, as the attendant explained that the offer did not apply on Bank Holidays.

Advise Loamshire Trading Standards Department on criminal liability.

SECTION 20(1)

The offence under s 20(1) requires the following elements to be present: (i) a person, (ii) in the course of any business of his, (iii) giving an indication, (iv) to any consumers, (v) which is misleading (vi) as to the price at which any goods, services, facilities or accommodation are available, (vii) generally or from a particular person. If all these are established by the prosecution an offence will arise, subject to the defence provisions of s 24, (see pp 706–7), and s 39(1), (see pp 710–1).

SECTION 20(2)

This is a separate offence and concerns the situation where a correct price indication is given initially then something happens to require an increase in the price, thereby making the original indication incorrect. It is necessary that paragraphs (a), (b), and (c) are all established by the prosecution before the offence arises. Thus it must be shown that: (i) a person, (ii) in the course of any business of his, (iii) gave an indication, (iv) to any consumers, (v) which has become misleading, (vi) at least some of the consumers can reasonably be expected still to rely on the, now incorrect, indication (eg the indication was given in a monthly magazine which is still current), and (vii) the defendant has failed to take all reasonable steps to prevent those consumers from still relying on the indication (eg by putting up correcting notices).

This offence is most likely to arise where brochures, catalogues, etc, are printed with a long life expectancy, for example, for mail order and holidays and where prices may be subject to change because of tax rate changes, surcharges, changing fuel charges etc. Part 3 of the Code of Practice, see below, pp 702–3, deals with this offence specifically and businesses can be expected to go to considerable lengths to ensure that consumers are notified of price alterations.

Section 20(2) is not subject to the general 'due diligence' defence of s 39(1), see p 710, as one element of the offence itself is the failure to take reasonable steps. It is, however, subject to the defence provisions of s 24(1), (2), and (3), see below, pp 706–7.

CODE OF PRACTICE

Provision is made, in s 25, for the approval of codes of practice to assist in the interpretation of s 20 and to encourage desirable practices in giving price indications.

25. Code of Practice

(1) The Secretary of State may, after consulting the Director General of Fair Trading and such other persons as the Secretary of State considers it appropriate to consult, by order approve any code of practice issued (whether by the Secretary of State or another person) for the purpose of—

    (a) giving practical guidance with respect to any of the requirements of section 20 above; and

    (b) promoting what appear to the Secretary of State to be desirable practices as to the circumstances and manner in which any person gives an indication as to the price at which any goods, services, accommodation or facilities are available or indicates any other matter in respect of which any such indication may be misleading.

(2) A contravention of a code of practice approved under this section shall not of itself give rise to any criminal or civil liability, but in any proceedings against any person for an offence under section 20(1) or (2) above—

    (a) any contravention by that person of such a code may be relied on in relation to any matter for the purpose of establishing that that person committed the offence or of negativing any defence; and

    (b) compliance by that person with such a code may be relied on in relation to any matter for the purpose of showing that the commission of the offence by that person has not been established or that that person has a defence.

(3) Where the Secretary of State approves a code of practice under this section he may, after such consultation as is mentioned in subsection (1) above, at any time by order—

    (a) approve any modification of the code; or

    (b) withdraw his approval;

and any reference in subsection (2) above to a code of practice approved under this section shall be construed accordingly.

(4) The power to make an order under this section shall be exercisable by statutory instrument subject to annulment in pursuance of a resolution of either House of Parliament.

NOTES

1. It is clear that breach of any provision in a code made under s 25 does not, in itself, create a criminal offence. It may be used to help establish an offence or to negative a defence. Likewise, compliance with code provisions may assist in establishing a defence or in negativing an offence. A s 25 code is therefore similar to the Highway Code in its operation.
2. To date one code has been approved under s 25: the Code of Practice for Traders on Price Indications, which was made by the Consumer Protection (Code of Practice for Traders on Price Indications) Approval Order 1988, SI 1988/2078. It came into force on 1 March 1989.

The Code of Practice for Traders on Price Indications

Introduction

The Consumer Protection Act

1. The Consumer Protection Act 1987 makes it a criminal offence to give consumers a misleading price indication about goods, services, accommodation (including the sale of new homes) or facilities, It applies however you give the price indication—whether in a TV or press advertisement, in a catalogue or leaflet, on notices, price tickets or shelf-edge marking in stores, or if you give it orally, for example on the telephone. The term 'price indication' includes price comparisons as well as indications of a single price.

2. This code of practice is approved under section 25 of the Act which gives the Secretary of State power to approve codes of practice to give practical guidance to traders. It is addressed to traders and sets out what is good practice to follow in giving price indications in a wide range of different circumstances, so as to avoid giving misleading price indications. But the Act does not require you to do as this code tells you. You may still give price indications which do not accord with this code, provided they are not misleading. 'Misleading' is defined in section 21 of the Act. The definition covers indications about any conditions attached to a price, about what you expect to happen to a price in future and what you say in price comparisons, as well as indications about the actual price the consumer will have to pay. It also applies in the same way to any indications you give about the way in which a price will be calculated.

3. **Price comparisons**. If you want to make price comparisons, you should do so only if you can show that they are accurate and valid. Indications which give only the price of the product are unlikely to be misleading if they are accurate and cover the total charge you will make. Comparisons with prices which you can show have been or are being charged for the same or similar goods, services, accommodation or facilities and have applied for a reasonable period are also unlikely to be misleading. Guidance on these matters is contained in this code.

4. **Enforcement**. Enforcement of the Consumer Protection Act 1987 is the responsibility of officers of the local weights and measures authority (in Northern Ireland, the Department of Economic Development)—usually called Trading Standards Officers. If a Trading Standards Officer has reasonable grounds to suspect that you have given a misleading price indication, the Act gives the Officer power to require you to produce any records relating to your business and to seize and detain goods or records which the Officer has reasonable grounds for believing may be required as evidence in court proceedings.

5. It may only be practicable for Trading Standards Officers to obtain from you the information necessary to carry out their duties under the Act. In these circumstances the Officer may seek information and assistance about both the claim and the supporting evidence from you. Be prepared to cooperate with Trading Standards Officers and respond to reasonable requests for information and assistance. The Act makes it an offence to obstruct a Trading Standards Officer intentionally or to fail (without good cause) to give any assistance or information the Officer may reasonably require to carry out duties under the Act.

6. Court proceedings. If you are taken to court for giving a misleading price indication, the court can take into account whether or not you have followed the code. If you have done as the code advises, that will not be an absolute defence but it will tend to show that you have not committed an offence. Similarly if you have done something the code advises against doing it may tend to show that the price indication was misleading. If you do something which is not covered by the code, your price indication will need to be judged only against the terms of the general offence. The Act provides for a defence of due diligence, that is, that you have taken all reasonable steps to avoid committing the offence of giving a misleading price indication, but failure to follow the code of practice may make it difficult to show this.

7. Regulations. The Act also provides power to make regulations about price indications and you should ensure that your price indications comply with any such regulations. There are none at present. [There are now three.]

8. Other legislation. This code deals only with the requirements of Part III of the Consumer Protection Act 1987. In some sectors there will be other relevant legislation. For example, price indications about credit terms must comply with the Consumer Credit Act 1974 and the regulations made under it as well as with the Consumer Protection Act 1987.

Definitions

In this code:

Accommodation includes hotel and other holiday accommodation and new homes for sale freehold or on a lease of over 21 years but does not include rented homes.

Consumer means anyone who might want the goods, services, accommodation or facilities, other than for business use.

Price means both the total amount the consumer will have to pay to get the goods, services, accommodation or facilities and any method which has been or will be used to calculate that amount.

Price comparison means any indication given to consumers that the price at which something is offered to consumers is less than or equal to some other price.

Product means goods, services, accommodation and facilities (but not credit facilities, except where otherwise specified).

Service and Facilities means any services or facilities whatever (including credit, banking and insurance services, purchase or sale of foreign currency, supply of electricity, off-street car parking and caravan sites) *except* those provided by a person who is an authorised person or appointed representative under the Financial Services Act 1986 in the course of an investment business, services provided by an employee to his employer and facilities for a caravan which is the occupier's main or only home.

Shop means any shop, store, stall or other place (including a vehicle or the consumer's home) at which goods, services, accommodation or facilities are offered to consumers.

Trader means anyone (retailers, manufacturers, agents, service providers and others) who is acting in the course of a business.

Part 1: Price comparisons

1.1. Price comparisons generally

1.1.1. Always make the meaning of price indications clear. Do not leave consumers to guess whether or not a price comparison is being made. If no price comparison is intended, do not use words or phrases which, in their normal, everyday use and in the context in which they are used, are likely to give your customers the impression that a price comparison is being made.

1.1.2. Price comparisons should always state the higher price as well as the price you intend to charge for the product (goods, services, accommodation or facilities). Do not make statements like 'sales price £5' or 'reduced to £39' without quoting the higher price to which they refer.

1.1.3. It should be clear what sort of price the higher price is. For example, comparisons with something described by words like 'regular price', 'usual price' or 'normal price' should say whose regular, usual or normal price it is (eg 'our normal price'). Descriptions like 'reduced from' and crossed out higher prices should be used only if they refer to your own previous price. Words should not be used in price indications other than with their normal everyday meanings.

1.1.4. Do not use initials or abbreviations to describe the higher price in a comparison, except for the initials 'RRP' to describe a recommended retail price or the abbreviation 'man. rec. price' to describe a manufacturer's recommended price (see paragraph 1.6.2 below).

1.1.5. Follow the part of the code (sections 1.2 to 1.6 as appropriate) which applies to the type of comparison you intend to make.

1.2. Comparisons with the trader's own previous price

1.2.1. General. In any comparison between your present selling price and another price at which you have in the past offered the product, you should state the previous price as well as the new lower price.

1.2.2. In any comparison with your own previous price:

(a) the previous price should be the *last* price at which the product was available to consumers in the previous 6 months;

(b) the product should have been available to consumers at that price for at least 28 consecutive days in the previous 6 months; and

(c) the previous price should have applied (as above) for that period at the *same* shop where the reduced price is now being offered.

The 28 days at (b) above may include bank holidays, Sundays or other days of religious observance when the shop was closed; and up to 4 days when, for reasons beyond your control, the product was not available for supply. The product must not have been offered at a different price between that 28 day period and the day when the reduced price is first offered.

1.2.3. If the previous price in a comparison does not meet one or more of the conditions set out in paragraph 1.2.2 above:

(i) the comparison should be fair and meaningful; and

(ii) give a clear and positive explanation of the period for which and the circumstances in which that higher price applied.

For example 'these goods were on sale here at the higher price from 1 February to 26 February' or 'these goods were on sale at the higher price in 10 of our 95 stores only'. Display the explanation clearly, and as prominently as the price indication. You should *not* use general disclaimers saying for example that the higher prices used in comparisons have not necessarily applied for 28 consecutive days.

1.2.4. Food, drink and perishable goods. For any food and drink, you need not give a positive explanation if the previous price in a comparison has not applied for 28 consecutive days, *provided* it was the last price at which the goods were on sale in the previous 6 months and applied in the same shop where the reduced price is now being offered. This also applies to non-food perishables, if they have a shelf-life of less than 6 weeks.

1.2.5. Catalogue and Mail order traders. Where products are sold only through a catalogue, advertisement or leaflet, any comparison with a previous price should be with the price in your own last catalogue, advertisement or leaflet. If you sell the same products both in shops and through catalogues etc, the previous price should be the last price at which you offered the product. You should also follow the guidance in paragraphs 1.2.2(a) and (b). If your price comparison does not meet these conditions, you should follow the guidance in paragraph 1.2.3.

1.2.6. Making a series of reductions. If you advertise a price reduction and then want to reduce the price further during the same sale or special offer period, the intervening price (or prices) need not have applied for 28 days. In these circumstances unless you use a positive explanation (paragraph 1.2.3):

the highest price in the series must have applied for 28 consecutive days in the last 6 months at the same shop: and

you must show the highest price, the intervening price(s) and the current selling price (eg '£40, £20, £10, £5').

1.3. Introductory offers, after-sale or after-promotion prices

1.3.1. Introductory Offers. Do not call a promotion an introductory offer unless you intend to continue to offer the product for sale after the offer period is over and to do so at a higher price.

1.3.2. Do not allow an offer to run on so long that it becomes misleading to describe it as an introductory or other special offer. What is a reasonable period will depend on the circumstances (but, depending on the shelf-life of the product, it is likely to be a matter of weeks, not months). An offer is unlikely to be misleading if you state the date the offer will end and keep to it. If you then extend the offer period, make it clear that you have done so.

1.3.3. Quoting a future price If you indicate an after-sale or after-promotion price, do so only if you are certain that, subject only to circumstances beyond your control, you will continue to offer identical products at that price for at least 28 days in the 3 months after the end of the offer period or after the offer stocks run out.

1.3.4. If you decide to quote a future price, write what you mean in full. Do not use initials to describe it (eg 'ASP', 'APP'). The description should be clearly and prominently displayed, with the price indication.

1.4. Comparisons with price related to different circumstances

1.4.1. This section covers comparisons with prices:

(a) for different quantities (eg '15p each, 4 for 50p');
(b) for goods in a different condition (eg 'seconds £20, when perfect £30');
(c) for a different availability (eg 'price £50, price when ordered specially £60');
(d) for goods in a totally different state (eg 'price in kit form £50, price ready assembled £70'); or
(e) for special groups of people (eg 'senior citizens' price £2.50, others £5').

1.4.2. General. Do not make such comparisons unless the product is available in the different quantity, conditions etc at the price you quote. Make clear to consumers the different circumstances which apply and show them prominently with the price indication. Do not use initials (eg 'RAP' for 'ready-assembled price') to describe the different circumstances, but write what you mean in full.

1.4.3. 'When perfect' comparisons. If you do not have the perfect goods on sale in the same shop:

(a) follow section 1.2 if the "when perfect" price is your own previous price for the goods;
(b) follow section 1.5 if the "when perfect" price is another trader's price; or
(c) follow section 1.6 if the "when perfect" price is one recommended by the manufacturer or supplier.

1.4.4. Goods in a different state. Only make comparisons with goods in a totally different state if:
  (a) a reasonable proportion (say a third (by quantity)) of your stock of those goods is readily available for sale to consumers in that different state (for example, ready assembled) at the quoted price and from the shop where the price comparison is made; or
  (b) another trader is offering those goods in that state at the quoted price and you follow section 1.5 below.
1.4.5. Prices for special groups of people If you want to compare different prices which you charge to different groups of people (eg one price for existing customers and another for new customers, or one price for people who are members of a named organisation (other than the trader) and another for those who are not), do not use words like "our normal" or "our regular" to describe the higher price, unless it applies to at least half your customers.

1.5. Comparisons with another trader's prices
1.5.1. Only compare your prices with another trader's price if—
  (a) you know that his price which you quote is accurate and up-to-date;
  (b) you give the name of the other trader clearly and prominently, with the price comparison;
  (c) you identify the shop where the other trader's price applies, if that other trader is a retailer; and
  (d) the other trader's price which you quote applies to the same products—or to substantially similar products and you state any differences clearly.
1.5.2. Do not make statements like 'if you can buy this product elsewhere for less, we will refund the difference' about your 'own brand' products which other traders do not stock, unless your offer will also apply to other traders' equivalent goods. If there are any conditions attached to the offer (eg it only applies to goods on sale in the same town) you should show them clearly and prominently, with the statement.

1.6. Comparisons with 'Recommended Retail Prices' or similar
1.6.1. General. This Section covers comparisons with recommended retail prices, manufacturers' recommended prices, suggested retail prices, suppliers' suggested retail prices and similar descriptions. It also covers prices given to co-operative and voluntary group organisations by their wholesalers or headquarters organisations.
1.6.2. Do not use initials or abbreviations to describe the higher price in a comparison *unless*:
  (a) you use the initials 'RRP' to describe a recommended retail price; or
  (b) you use the abbreviation 'man. rec. price' to describe a manufacturer's recommended price.
Write all other descriptions out in full and show them clearly and prominently with the price indication.
1.6.3. Do not use a recommended price in a comparison unless:
  (a) it has been recommended to you by the manufacturer or supplier as a price at which the product might be sold to consumers;
  (b) you deal with that manufacturer or supplier on normal commercial terms. (This will generally be the case for members of co-operative or voluntary group organisations in relation to their wholesalers or headquarters organisations); and
  (c) the price is not significantly higher than prices at which the product is generally sold at the time you first make that comparison.

1.7. Pre-printed prices
1.7.1. Make sure you pass on to consumers any reduction stated on the manufacturer's packaging (eg 'flash packs' such as '10p off RRP').
1.7.2. You are making a price comparison if goods have a clearly visible price already printed on the packaging which is higher than the price you will charge for them. Such pre-printed

prices are, in effect, recommended prices (except for retailers' own label goods) and you should follow paragraphs 1.6.1 to 1.6.4. You need not state that the price is a recommended price.

1.8. References to value or worth
1.8.1. Do not compare your prices with an amount described only as 'worth' or 'value'.
1.8.2. Do not present general advertising slogans which refer to 'value' or 'worth' in a way which is likely to be seen by consumers as a price comparison.

1.9. Sales or special events
1.9.1. If you have bought in items specially for a sale, and you make this clear, you should not quote a higher price when indicating that they are special purchases. Otherwise, your price indications for individual items in the sale which are reduced should comply with section 1.1 of the code and which ever of sections 1.2 to 1.6 applies to the type of comparison you are making.
1.9.2. If you just have a general notice saying, for example, that all products are at 'half marked price', the marked price on the individual items should be your own previous price and you should follow section 1.2 of the code.
1.9.3. Do not use general notices saying, eg 'up to 50% off' unless the maximum reduction quoted applies to at least 10% (by quantity) of the range of products on offer.

1.10. Free offers
1.10.1. Make clear to consumers, at the time of the offer for sale, exactly what they will have to buy to get the 'free offer'.
1.10.2. If you give any indication of the monetary value of the 'free offer', and that sum is not your own present price for the product, follow whichever of sections 1.2 to 1.6 covers the type of price it is.
1.10.3. If there are any conditions attached to the 'free offer', give at least the main points of those conditions with the price indication and make clear to consumers where, before they are committed to buy, they can get full details of the conditions.
1.10.4. Do not claim that an offer is free if:
  (a) you have imposed additional charges that you would not normally make;
  (b) you have inflated the price of any product the consumer must buy or the incidental charges (for example, postage) the consumer must pay to get the 'free offer'; or
  (c) you will reduce the price to consumers who do not take it up.

Part 2: Actual price to consumer

2.1. Indicating two different prices
2.1.1. The Consumer Protection Act makes it an offence to indicate a price for goods or services which is lower than the one that actually applies, for example, showing one price in an advertisement, window display, shelf marking or on the item itself, and then charging a higher price at the point of sale or checkout.

2.2. Incomplete information and non-optional extras
2.2.1. Make clear in your price indications the full price consumers will have to pay for the product. Some examples of how to do so in particular circumstances are set out below.
2.2.2. Limited availability of product. Where the price you are quoting for products only applies to a limited number of, say, orders, sizes or colours, you should make this clear in your price indication (eg 'available in other colours or sizes at additional cost').
2.2.3. Prices relating to differing forms of products. If the price you are quoting for particular products does not apply to the products in the form they are displayed or advertised, say so clearly in your price indication. For example, advertisements for self assembly furniture and the like should make it clear that the price refers to a kit of parts.
2.2.4. Postage, packing and delivery charges. If you sell by mail order, make clear any additional charges for postage, packing or delivery on the order form or similar document, so

that consumers are fully aware of them before being committed to buying. Where you cannot determine these charges in advance, show clearly on the order form how they will be calculated (eg 'Post Office rates apply'), or the place in the catalogue etc where the information is given.
2.2.5. If you sell goods from a shop and offer a delivery service for certain items, make it clear whether there are any separate delivery charges (eg for delivery outside a particular area) and what those charges are, before the consumer is committed to buying.

Value Added Tax
2.2.6(i) Price indications to consumers. All price indications you give to private consumers, by whatever means, should include VAT.
2.2.7(ii) Price indications to business customers. Prices may be indicated exclusive of VAT in shops where or advertisements from which most of your business is with business customers. If you also carry out business with private consumers at those shops or from those advertisements you should make clear that the prices exclude VAT and:
  (i) display VAT-inclusive prices with equal prominence, or
  (ii) display prominent statements that on top of the quoted price customers will also have to pay VAT at 15% (or the current rate).
2.2.8(iii) Professional fees. Where you indicate a price (including estimates) for a professional fee, make clear what it covers. The price should generally include VAT. In cases where the fee is based on an as-yet-unknown sum of money (for example, the sale price of a house), either:
  (i) quote a fee which includes VAT; or
  (ii) make it clear that in addition to your fee the consumer would have to pay VAT at the current rate (eg 'fee of 1% of purchase price, plus VAT at 15%').
Make sure that whichever method you choose is used for both estimates and final bills.
2.2.9(iv) Building work. In estimates for building work, either include VAT in the price indication or indicate with equal prominence the amount or rate of VAT payable in addition to your basic figure. If you give a separate amount for VAT, make it clear that if any provisional sums in estimates vary then the amount of VAT payable would also vary.
2.2.10. Service, cover and minimum charge in hotels, restaurants and similar establishments. If your customers in hotels, restaurants or similar places must pay a non-optional extra charge, eg a 'service charge':
  (i) incorporate the charge within fully inclusive prices wherever practicable; and
  (ii) display the fact clearly on any price list or priced menu, whether displayed inside or outside (eg by using statements like 'all prices include service').
Do not include suggested optional sums, whether for service or any other item, in the bill presented to the customer.
2.2.11. It will not be practical to include some non-optional extra charges in a quoted price; for instance, if you make a flat charge per person or per table in a restaurant (often referred to as a 'cover charge') or a minimum charge. In such cases the charge should be shown as prominently as other prices on any list or menu, whether displayed inside or outside.
2.2.12. Holiday and travel prices. If you offer a variety of prices to give consumers a choice, (for example, paying more or less for a holiday depending on the time of year or the standard of accommodation), make clear in your brochure—or any other price indication—what the basic price is and what it covers. Give details of any optional additional charges and what those charges cover, or of the place where this information can be found, clearly and close to the basic price.
2.2.13. Any non-optional extra charges which are for fixed amounts should be included in the basic price and not shown as additions, unless they are only payable by some consumers. In that case you should specify, near to the details of the basic price, either what the amounts are and the circumstances in which they are payable, or where in the brochure etc the information is given.

2.2.14. Details of non-optional extra charges which may vary, (such as holiday insurance) or of where in the brochure etc the information is given should be made clear to consumers near to the basic price.

2.2.15. If you reserve the right to increase prices after consumers have made their booking, state this clearly with all indications of prices, and include prominently in your brochure full information on the circumstances in which a surcharge is payable.

2.2.16. Ticket prices. If you sell tickets, whether for sporting events, cinema, theatre etc and your prices are higher than the regular price that would be charged to the public at the box office, ie higher than the 'face value', you should make clear in any price indication what the 'face value' of the ticket is.

2.2.17. Call-out charges. If you make a minimum call-out charge or other flat-rate charge (for example, for plumbing, gas or electrical appliance repairs etc carried out in consumers' homes), ensure that the consumer is made aware of the charge and whether the actual price may be higher (eg if work takes longer than a specific time) before being committed to using your services.

2.2.18. Credit facilities. Price indications about consumer credit should comply with the relevant requirements of regulations under the Consumer Credit Act 1974 governing the form and content of advertisements.

2.2.19. Insurance. Where actual premium rates for a particular consumer or the availability of insurance cover depend on an individual assessment, this should be made clear when any indication of the premium or the method of determining it is given to consumers.

Part 3: Price indications which become misleading after they have been given

3.1. General

3.1.1. The Consumer Protection Act makes it an offence to give a price indication which, although correct at the time, becomes misleading after you have given it, if:

    (i) consumers could reasonably be expected still to be relying on it; and

    (ii) you do not take reasonable steps to prevent them doing so.

Clearly it will not be necessary or even possible in many instances to inform all those who may have been given the misleading price indication. However, you should always make sure consumers are given the correct information before they are committed to buying a product and be prepared to cancel any transaction which a consumer has entered into on the basis of a price indication which has become misleading.

3.1.2. Do not give price indications which you know or intend will only apply for a limited period, without making this fact clear in the advertisement or price indication.

3.1.3. The following paragraphs set out what you should do in some particular circumstances.

3.2. Newspaper and magazine advertisements

3.2.1. If the advertisement does not say otherwise, the price indication should apply for a reasonable period (as a general guide, at least 7 days or until the next issue of the newspaper or magazine in which the advertisement was published, whichever is longer). If the price indication becomes misleading within this period make sure consumers are given the correct information before they are committed to buying the product.

3.3. Mail order advertisements, catalogues and leaflets

3.3.1. Paragraph 3.2.1 above also applies to the time for which price indications in mail order advertisements and in regularly published catalogues or brochures should apply. If a price indication becomes misleading within this period, make the correct price indication clear to anyone who orders the product to which it relates. Do so before the consumer is committed to buying the product and, wherever practicable, before the goods are sent to the consumer.

3.4. Selling through agents

3.4.1. Holiday brochures and travel agents Surcharges are covered in paragraph 2.2.15. If a price indication becomes misleading for any other reason, tour operators who sell direct to consumers should follow paragraph 3.3.1 above; and tour operators who sell through travel agents should follow paragraphs 3.4.2 and 3.4.3 below.

3.4.2. If a price indication becomes misleading while your brochure is still current, make this clear to the travel agents to whom you distributed the brochure.

Be prepared to cancel any holiday bookings consumers have made on the basis of a misleading price indication.

3.4.3. In the circumstances set out in paragraph 3.4.2, travel agents should ensure that the correct price indication is made clear to consumers before they make a booking.

3.4.4. Insurance and independent intermediaries. Insurers who sell their products through agents or independent intermediaries should take all reasonable steps to ensure that all such agents who are known to hold information on the insurer's premium rates and terms of the cover provided are told clearly of any changes in those rates or terms.

3.4.5. Agents, independent intermediaries and providers of quotation systems should ensure that they act on changes notified to them by an insurer.

3.5. Changes in the rate of value added tax

3.5.1. If your price indications become misleading because of a change in the general rate of VAT, or other taxes paid at point of sale, make the correct price indication clear to any consumers who order products. Do so before the consumer is committed to buying the product and, wherever practicable, before the goods are sent to the consumer.

Part 4: Sale of new homes

4.1. A 'new home' is any building, or part of a building to be used only as private dwelling which is either:

   (i) a newly-built house or flat, or

   (ii) a newly-converted existing building which has not previously been used in that form as a private home.

4.2. The Consumer Protection Act and this code apply to new homes which are either for sale freehold or covered by a long lease, ie with more than 21 years to run. In this context the term 'trader' covers not only a business vendor, such as a developer, but also an estate agent acting on behalf of such a vendor.

4.3. You should follow the relevant provision of Part 1 of the code if:

   (i) you want to make a comparison between the price at which you offer new homes for sale and any other price;

   (ii) you offer an inclusive price for new homes which also covers such items as furnishings, domestic appliances and insurance and you compare their value with, for example, High Street prices for similar items.

4.4. Part 2 of the code gives details of the provisions you should follow if:

   (i) the new houses you are selling, or any goods or services which apply to them, are only available in limited numbers or range;

   (ii) the sale price you give does not apply to the houses as displayed; or

   (iii) there are additional non-optional charges payable.

NOTES

1. An advisory committee was set up by the Department of Trade and Industry to monitor the Code of Practice, but its recommendations for improvement and reform, which included greater use of legally backed regulations, were rejected by the then Government in 1992.

2. It is to be noted that some matters, for example concerning 'value' and 'worth' claims, were previously prohibited under the Price Marking (Bargain Offers) Order 1979, SI 1979/364, but are now only contained in the code, see para 1.8. Failure to follow the code provisions on this matter no longer constitutes a criminal offence, but may be evidence to assist in proving an offence.

In *MGN Ltd v Ritters* (1997) 16 Tr Law R 427, QBD, watches described as 'worth £50' were advertised, in a newspaper promotion, for £4.99. A few of the watches were available in the shops some weeks later from £19.95 to £49.95, some were priced at less that £4.95 and no evidence was produced that any had actually been sold. The court decided that the seller had normally to show that the item was already available on the open market at the higher price to justify the price comparison. The conviction of the newspaper publishers was upheld.

3. For discussion of paras 1.2.2 and 1.2.3 see *A G Stanley Ltd (t/a Fads) v Surrey County Council Trading Standards Office* (1995) 103 ITSA 7 MR 26, QBD, above, pp 690–92.

QUESTIONS

Is it preferable to have detailed rules regarding pricing, with all provisions contained in the legislation or does a general prohibition, with a code of practice as guidance, provide better protection for consumers? Are there any aspects of the Code which seem inadequate? Are there any pricing practices which you have come across which are not referred to in the Code? Should some matters, currently contained in the Code, be outlawed by regulations (see below)?

PROBLEM

Soft Interiors Ltd, a firm selling carpets and soft furnishings, wish to advertise a Spring Sale. They want, wherever possible, to indicate a price comparison and to make items as attractive as possible to purchasers, but are concerned not to infringe the criminal law.

Explain the legal constraints which are applicable and indicate how they may advertise discontinued lines, seconds and damaged items, remnants, and reductions on normal stock of carpets and soft furnishings.

REGULATIONS

To be able to deal with specific problem areas and new developments in price indications, an order-making power has been given to the Secretary of State under s 26 of the 1987 Act:

26. Power to make regulations

The Secretary of State may, after consulting the Director General of Fair Trading and such other persons as the Secretary of State considers it appropriate to consult, by regulations make provision—
- (a) for the purpose of regulating the circumstances and manner in which any person—
  - (i) gives any indication as to the price at which any goods, services, accommodation or facilities will be or are available or have been supplied or provided; or
  - (ii) indicates any other matter in respect of which any such indication may be misleading;
- (b) for the purpose of facilitating the enforcement of the provisions of section 20 above or of any regulations made under this section.

(2) The Secretary of State shall not make regulations by virtue of subsection (1)(a) above except in relation to—
- (a) indications given by persons in the course of business; and
- (b) such indications given otherwise than in the course of business as—
  - (i) are given by or on behalf of persons by whom accommodation is provided to others by means of leases or licences; and
  - (ii) relate to goods, services or facilities supplied or provided to those others in connection with the provision of the accommodation.

(3) Without prejudice to the generality of subsection (1) above, regulations under this section may—
- (a) prohibit an indication as to a price from referring to such matters as may be prescribed by the regulations;
- (b) require an indication as to a price or other matter to be accompanied or supplemented by such explanation or such additional information as may be prescribed by the regulations;
- (c) require information or explanations with respect to a price or other matter to be given to an officer of an enforcement authority and to authorise such an officer to require such information or explanations to be given;
- (d) require any information or explanation provided for the purposes of any regulations made by virtue of paragraph (b) or (c) above to be accurate;
- (e) prohibit the inclusion in indications as to a price or other matter of statements that the indications are not to be relied upon;
- (f) provide that expressions used in any indication as to a price or other matter shall be construed in a particular way for the purposes of this Part;
- (g) provide that a contravention of any provision of the regulations shall constitute a criminal offence punishable—
  - (i) on conviction on indictment, by a fine;
  - (ii) on summary conviction, by a fine not exceeding the statutory maximum;
- (h) apply any provision of this Act which relates to a criminal offence to an offence created by virtue of paragraph (g) above.

(4) The power to make regulations under this section shall be exercisable by statutory instrument subject to annulment in pursuance of a resolution of either House of Parliament and shall include power—
- (a) to make different provision for different cases; and
- (b) to make such supplemental, consequential and transitional provision as the Secretary of State considers appropriate.

(5) In this section 'lease' includes a sub-lease and an agreement for a lease and a statutory tenancy (within the meaning of the Landlord and Tenant Act 1985 or the Rent (Scotland) Act 1984).

To date three such regulations have been made. First, are the Price Indications (Methods of Payment) Regulations 1991 (SI 1991/199) which concern situations where different prices are charged, depending upon the method of payments selected, for example, if an additional charge is made for paying by credit card. The Regulations state how and where information is to be displayed regarding any differential pricing.

Second, are the Price Indications (Bureaux de Change) (No 2) Regulations 1992 (SI 1992/737) which, as their name suggests, concern how and where prices are to be displayed at bureaux de change, to make clear what exchange rates operate, what fees or commissions are charged, any differences for travellers cheques or currency etc, and to require receipts to be given, including specified details of the transactions.

Finally, there are the Price Indications (Resale of Tickets) Regulations 1994 (SI 1994/3248). These affect the re-sale of tickets for places of entertainment, including theatres, exhibitions, sporting events etc. Consumers have to be informed of the face value of the ticket, the location of any seat or space, where relevant, and any features of the seat or space which could adversely affect the use or enjoyment of it which are known to, or could be expected to be known by, the person giving the price indication. This does not prevent tickets being re-sold at inflated prices, but does enable consumers to make informed decisions regarding the worth of such tickets prior to purchase.

DEFENCES

Although defences are dealt with in detail in ch 15,(see especially s 39 of the 1987 Act, at pp 710–11, which is of particular relevance to s 20(1) offences) brief mention will be made here of s 24 of the 1987 Act. This contains four specific defences in relation to s 20 offences.

First, under sub-s (1) there is a defence, where regulations permit price indications in a particular form, that the defendant has followed the regulations:

24(1) In any proceedings against a person for an offence under subsection (1) or (2) of section 20 above in respect of any indication it shall be a defence for that person to show that his acts or omissions were authorised for the purposes of this subsection by regulations made under section 26 below.

It will be rare that such a defence will arise as there are currently only three such regulations and it would be unlikely that, by following the requirements of the regulations, a misleading price indication would arise.

The second defence is where price indications are given in books, newspapers, etc, as part of the editorial material and not as advertisements, for example in an interview with an author about a newly published book, the wrong price is announced.

24(2) In proceedings against a person for an offence under subsection (1) or (2) of section 20 above in respect of an indication published in a book, newspaper, magazine, film or radio or television broadcast or in a programme included in a cable programme service, it shall be a defence for that person to show that the indication was not contained in an advertisement.

The third defence is that of innocent publication of a misleading price indication by a person who is in the business of publishing advertisements. It is similar to s 25 of the Trade Descriptions Act 1968, see p 726.

The final defence is concerned with situations where manufacturers issue recommended prices for the supply of their goods by retailers, but where a retailer charges more than the recommended price, thereby making the manufacturer's list misleading. In such a case the manufacturer may have a defence.

24(4) In any proceedings against a person for an offence under subsection (1) of section 20 above in respect of any indication, it shall be a defence for that person to show that—

   (a) the indication did not relate to the availability from him of any goods, services, accommodation or facilities,

   (b) a price had been recommended to every person from whom the goods, services, accommodation or facilities were indicated as being available;

   (c) the indication related to that price and was misleading as to that price only by reason of a failure by any person to follow the recommendation; and

   (d) it was reasonable for the person who gave the indication to assume that the recommendation was for the most part being followed.

It is to be noted that this only applies to s 20(1) offences and that all the requirements must be satisfied before the defence can operate. It is suggested that in such cases not only will the manufacturer have a defence under s 24(4) but also the retailer will not commit an offence as the retailer has not given a misleading price indication. An example under the 1968 Act, *Feiner v Barnes* (1973) 71 LGR 477, still seems applicable.

QUESTION

Given the considerable flexibility permitted by the Code of Practice, is it necessary to have such extensive defence provisions for pricing offences?

CHAPTER 15

General statutory defences in consumer protection legislation

INTRODUCTION

Trading standards offences usually involve strict liability—that is liability without mens rea (see above, pp 571–4). Nevertheless, the accused should have a defence where prevailing notions of justice suggest that it would be wholly unfair to fasten the discredit of a criminal conviction on a trader who is morally innocent. Defence sections in modern consumer protection statutes take a number of different forms. Statutes passed from the 1980s onwards tend to have a fairly standard single limb defence requiring due diligence and the taking of all reasonable steps, whereas earlier statutes favoured a two limb test requiring proof of a particular circumstance coupled with due diligence and reasonable precautions. In some cases, for example under s 11(2) of the Video Recordings Act 1984, a nonstandard defence section is provided.

In all defences there is a reversal of the burden of proof, with the defendant required to satisfy the court on the balance of probabilities. The measures required by the court to be taken to satisfy defence requirements may vary depending upon the nature of the offence involved, see Parry, 'Judicial approaches to due diligence' [1995] Crim LR 695.

This chapter will examine the most common forms of defence, some specific defences, and will also consider related issues: the bypass provisions and time limits

DUE DILIGENCE DEFENCE

INTRODUCTION

As mentioned above, there are two versions of this defence which have given rise to much reported litigation. The two-limb version is common to many statutes including the Trade Descriptions Act 1968, the Fair Trading Act 1973, and the Consumer Credit Act 1974. The position under the Trade Descriptions Act 1968 will be taken as the primary example. The single-limb version is well-illustrated by the Consumer Protection Act 1987, s 39.

Section 24 of the 1968 Act provides:

24. Defence of mistake, accident, etc.

(1) In any proceedings for an offence under this Act it shall, subject to subsection (2) of this section, be a defence for the person charged to prove—

(a) that the commission of the offence was due to a mistake or to reliance on information supplied to him or to the act or default of another person, an accident or some other cause beyond his control; and

(b) that he took all reasonable precautions and exercised all due diligence to avoid the commission of such an offence by himself or any person under his control.

(2) If in any case the defence provided by the last foregoing subsection involves the allegation that the commission of the offence was due to the act or default of another person or to reliance on information supplied by another person, the person charged shall not, without leave of the court, be entitled to rely on that defence unless, within a period ending seven clear days before the hearing, he has served on the prosecutor a notice in writing giving such information identifying or assisting in the identification of that other person as was then in his possession.

NOTES

1. Subsection (1) details the defence provisions, whilst sub-s (2) is a procedural requirement, involving the defendant giving, normally, seven days' notice to the prosecution as to the identification of the other person when 'act or default of another' or 'reliance on information' is raised under sub-s (1).

2. It is applicable to all offences under the 1968 Act: *Wings Ltd v Ellis* [1984] 3 All ER 577, [1984] 3 WLR 965, above, p 662.

3. In effect the section demands a proven absence of mens rea and of negligence on the part of the person seeking to rely on it and thus it will have only a limited relevance where the offence charged is under s 14: see *Coupe v Guyett* [1973] 2 All ER 1058, [1973] 1 WLR 669, below, p 729 and cf *Wings Ltd v Ellis* [1984] 3 All ER 577, [1984] 3 WLR 965, above p 662.

The more modern, single-limb version of the defence can be found in the Consumer Protection Act 1987, s 39:

39. Defence of due diligence

(1) Subject to the following provisions of this section, in proceedings against any person for an offence to which this section applies it shall be a defence for that person to show that he took all reasonable steps and exercised all due diligence to avoid committing the offence.

(2) Where in any proceedings against any person for such an offence the defence provided by subsection (1) above involves an allegation that the commission of the offence was due:

(a) to the act or default of another; or

(b) to reliance on information given by another;

that person shall not, without the leave of the court, be entitled to rely on the defence unless, not less than seven clear days before the hearing of the proceedings, he has served a notice under subsection (3) below on the person bringing the proceedings.

(3) A notice under this subsection shall give such information identifying or assisting in the identification of the person who committed the act or default or gave the information as is in the possession of the person serving the notice at the time he serves it.

(4) It is hereby declared that a person shall not be entitled to rely on the defence provided by subsection (1) above by reason of his reliance on information supplied by another, unless he shows that it was reasonable in all the circumstances for him to have relied on the information, having regard in particular:

    (a) to the steps which he took, and those which might reasonably have been taken, for the purpose of verifying the information; and

    (b) to whether he had any reason to disbelieve the information.

NOTES

1. In comparison with the 1968 Act, sub-s (1) provides a more simplified defence, with similar, but more explicit, procedural requirements in sub-ss (2) and (3).
2. It applies to offences under ss 10, 12(1), (2), and (3), 13(4), 14(6) (safety offences, see further ch. 12, pp 582–95) and 20(1) (pricing, see further ch 14).
3. A more rigorous 'reliance on information' procedure is included, see below, p 718.

These defences have been subject to considerable judicial interpretation and the main points are best considered individually.

ACT OR DEFAULT OF ANOTHER PERSON

To satisfy this provision the accused is required to show that another person was responsible for the offence in question—there is no requirement that the 'other' person be brought before the court. The words 'another person' have caused difficulty where the defendant is a company and the offence arises out of the act or default of one of its servants. The crucial point is whether the servant alleged for the purposes of TDA 1968, s 24(1)(a), of the defence to be 'another person' is really the alter ego of the company. *Beckett v Kingston Bros (Butchers) Ltd* [1970] 1 QB 606, [1970] 1 All ER 715 is a case in point. In the leading case on corporate criminal liability the issue arose in a slightly different way when it became necessary to determine precisely who is the 'he' who must exercise all reasonable precautions etc for the purposes of s 24(1)(b).

Tesco Supermarkets Ltd v Nattrass [1972] AC 153, [1971] 2 All ER 127, House of Lords

The appellant company owned a large number of supermarket stores and set up a reasonable and efficient system of instruction and inspection for ensuring that their employees complied with the requirements of the Trade Descriptions Act 1968. The shop had displayed a 'flash' offer on a poster relating to money off the usual price of washing powder, but they had run out of the specially marked reduced packets and consequently a customer failed to get a packet at the reduced price. The shop manager—a Mr Clement—had failed to supervise the actions of an assistant who had put out on display the only remaining packets marked at the full price. The company was charged under s 11(2) of the Trade Descriptions Act 1968, and appealed against conviction to the House of Lords.

Lord Reid. . . . The relevant facts as found by the justices were that on the previous evening a shop assistant, Miss Rogers, whose duty it was to put out fresh stock found that there were no more of the specially marked packs in stock. There were a number of packs marked with the ordinary price so she put them out. She ought to have told the shop manager, Mr Clement, about this but she failed to do so. Mr Clement was responsible for seeing that the proper packs were on sale, but he failed to see to this although he marked his daily return 'All special offers OK'. The justices found that if he had known about this he would either have removed the poster advertising the reduced price or given instructions that only 2s 11d was to be charged for the packs marked 3s 11d. Section 24(2) requires notice to be given to the prosecutor if the accused is blaming another person and such notice was duly given naming Mr Clement.

In order to avoid conviction the appellants had to prove facts sufficient to satisfy both parts of s 24(1) of the 1968 Act. The justices held that they—

'had exercised all due diligence in devising a proper system for the operation of the said store and by securing so far as was reasonably practicable that it was fully implemented and thus had fulfilled the requirements of section 24(1)(b).'

But they convicted the appellants because in their view the requirements of s 24(1)(a) had not been fulfilled; they held that Mr Clement was not 'another person' within the meaning of that provision. The Divisional Court ([1970] 3 All ER 357, [1971] 1 QB 133) held that the justices were wrong in holding that Mr Clement was not 'another person'. The respondent did not challenge this finding of the Divisional Court so I need say no more about it than that I think that on this matter the Divisional Court was plainly right. But that court sustained the conviction on the ground that the justices had applied the wrong test in deciding that the requirements of s 24(1)(b) had been fulfilled. In effect that court held that the words 'he took all reasonable precautions . . .' do not mean what they say; 'he' does not mean the accused, it means the accused and all his servants who were acting in a managerial or supervisory category. I think that earlier authorities virtually compelled the Divisional Court to reach this strange construction. So the real question in this appeal is whether these earlier authorities were rightly decided. But before examining those earlier cases I think it necessary to make some general observations.

. . .

In my judgment the main object of these provisions [sc. such as s 24] must have been to distinguish between those who are in some degree blameworthy and those who are not, and to enable the latter to escape from conviction if they can show that they were in no way to blame. I find it almost impossible to suppose that Parliament or any reasonable body of men would as a matter of policy think it right to make employers criminally liable for the acts of some of their servants but not for those of others and I find it incredible that a draftsman, aware of that intention, would fail to insert any words to express it. But in several cases the courts, for reasons which it is not easy to discover, have given a restricted meaning to such provisions. It has been held that such provisions afford a defence if the master proves that the servant at fault was the person who himself did the prohibited act, but that they afford no defence if the servant at fault was one who failed in his duty of supervision to see that his subordinates did not commit the prohibited act. Why Parliament should be thought to have intended this distinction or how as a matter of construction these provisions can reasonably be held to have that meaning is not apparent.

In some of these cases the employer charged with the offence was a limited company. But in others the employer was an individual and still it was held that he, though personally blameless, could not rely on these provisions if the fault which led to the commission of the offence was the fault of a servant in failing to carry out his duty to instruct or supervise his subordinates. Where a limited company is the employer difficult questions do arise in a wide variety of circumstances in deciding which of its officers or servants is to be identified with the company so that his guilt is the guilt of the company.

I must start by considering the nature of the personality which by a fiction the law attributes to a corporation. A living person has a mind which can have knowledge or intention or be negligent and he has hands to carry out his intentions. A corporation has none of these; it must act through living persons, though not always one or the same person. Then the person who acts is not speaking or acting for the company. He is acting as the company and his mind which directs his acts is the mind of the company. There is no question of the company being vicariously liable. He is not acting as a servant, representative, agent or delegate. He is an embodiment of the company or, one could say, he hears and speaks through the persona of the company, within his appropriate sphere, and his mind is the mind of the company. If it is a guilty mind then that guilt is the guilt of the company. It must be a question of law whether, once the facts have been ascertained, a person in doing particular things is to be regarded as the company or merely as the company's servant or agent. In that case any liability of the company can only be a statutory or vicarious liability.

. . .

Normally the board of directors, the managing director and perhaps other superior officers of a company carry out the functions of management and speak and act as the company. Their subordinates do not. They carry out orders from above and it can make no difference that they are given some measure of discretion. But the board of directors may delegate some part of their functions of management giving to their delegate full discretion to act independently of instructions from them. I see no difficulty in holding that they have thereby put such a delegate in their place so that within the scope of the delegation he can act as the company. It may not always be easy to draw the line but there are cases in which the line must be drawn . . .

In some cases the phrase alter ego has been used. I think it is misleading. When dealing with a company the word alter is I think misleading. The person who speaks and acts as the company is not alter. He is identified with the company. And when dealing with an individual no other individual can be his alter ego. The other individual can be a servant, agent, delegate or representative but I know of neither principle nor authority which warrants the confusion (in the literal or original sense) of two separate individuals.

The earliest cases dealing with this matter which were cited were *R C Hammett Ltd v Crabb, R C Hammett Ltd and Beldam* (1931) 145 LT 638, [1931] All ER Rep 70, and *R C Hammett Ltd v London County Council* (1933) 97 JP 105. In both the servant of the accused company had infringed the provisions of s 5(2) of the Sale of Food (Weights and Measures) Act 1926. Section 12(5) exempted the employer from penalty if he charged another person as the actual offender and could prove:

' . . . to the satisfaction of the court that he had used due diligence to enforce the execution of this Act, and that the said other person had committed the offence in question without his consent, connivance or wilful default . . . '

In the earlier case the offence was committed by the shop manager personally and he knew that he was committing an offence. A conviction was quashed on the ground that the magistrate had treated the question whether the employer had used due diligence as one of law, that it was really one of fact and that there was no evidence on which the magistrate could reach his decision. In the second case the offence was committed by a subordinate; the shop manager had warned him but had not exercised due diligence to see that his instructions were obeyed. Again the justices convicted on the ground that the owners were responsible for lack of due diligence in their manager. This time the conviction was upheld by the same court. It was argued for the respondents that the employer is responsible for the acts or omissions of all persons above the actual offender. It seems to me obvious that this is a matter of law depending on the proper construction of the statutory provision. But Lord Hewart CJ, did not so regard it. He said that there was evidence on which quarter sessions could arrive at their opinion and that they were entitled to come to the conclusion that the appellants were responsible for the manager's lack of due diligence.

I find these cases most unsatisfactory. There is no explanation of how it could be a question of fact whether the provisions of s 12(5) meant that what the employer had to prove was that he personally had used due diligence, or that he also had to prove that some or all of his servants had also done so. But the court did not deal with that. Nevertheless because the only difference between the two cases appears to have been that in the first the shop manager was himself the offender whereas in the second the fault was lack of supervision, these cases have been thought to afford authority for the proposition that an employer has a defence if the only fault was in the actual offender but not if there was fault of any of his servants superior to the actual offender. I can find no warrant for that proposition in the terms of s 12(5). Both parts of the provision—that the employer had used due diligence and that the offence had been committed without his consent, connivance or wilful default—appear to me plainly to refer to the employer personally and to no one else.

I agree with the view of the Lord Justice-General (Lord Cooper) in a case dealing with the same Act *Dumfries and Maxwelltown Co-operative Society v Williamson* 1950 JC 76 at 80 that:

'The underlying idea manifestly is that there should not be vicarious responsibility for an infringement of the Act committed without the consent or connivance of an employer . . .'

. . .

What good purpose could be served by making an employer criminally responsible for the misdeeds of some of his servants but not for those of others? It is sometimes argued—it was argued in the present case—that making an employer criminally responsible, even when he had done all that he could to prevent an offence, affords some additional protection to the public because this will induce him to do more. But if he has done all he can how can he do more? I think that what lies behind this argument is a suspicion that justices too readily accept evidence that an employer has done all he can to prevent offences. But if justices were to accept as sufficient a paper scheme and perfunctory efforts to enforce it they would not be doing their duty—that would not be 'due diligence' on the part of the employer. Then it is said that this would involve discrimination in favour of a large employer like the appellants against a small shopkeeper. But that is not so. Mr Clement was the 'opposite number' of the small shopkeeper and he was liable to prosecution in this case. The purpose of this Act must have been to penalise those at fault, not those who were in no way to blame.

The Divisional Court, [1970] 3 All ER 357, [1971] 1 QB 133, decided this case on a theory of delegation. In that they were following some earlier authorities. But they gave far too wide a meaning to delegation. I have said that a board of directors can delegate part of their functions of management so as to make their delegate an embodiment of the company within the sphere of the delegation. But here the board never delegated any part of their functions. They set up a chain of command through regional and district supervisors, but they remained in control. The shop managers had to obey their general directions and also to take orders from their superiors. The acts or omissions of shop managers were not acts of the company itself.

In my judgment the appellants established the statutory defence. I would therefore allow this appeal.

Lord Pearson stated on the issue of who is 'another person': . . . Section 24 requires a dividing line to be drawn between the master and any other person. The defendant cannot disclaim liability for an act or omission of his ego or his alter ego. In the case of an individual defendant, his ego is simply himself, but he may have an alter ego. For instance, if he has only one shop and he appoints a manager of that shop with full discretion to manage it as he thinks fit, the manager is doing what the employer would normally do and may be held to be the employer's alter ego. But if the defendant has hundreds of shops, he could not be expected personally to manage each one of them and the manager of one of his shops cannot in the absence of exceptional circumstances be considered his alter ego. In the case of a company, the ego is located in several persons, eg those mentioned in s 20 of the Act or other persons in a similar position of direction or general management. A company may have an alter ego, if those persons who are or have its ego delegate to some other person the control and management, with full discretionary powers, of some section of the company's business. In the case of a company, it may be difficult, and in most cases for practical purposes unnecessary, to draw the distinction between its ego and alter ego, but theoretically there is that distinction.

Lord Morris, Viscount Dilhorne, and **Lord Diplock** agreed that the appeal should be allowed.

Appeal allowed.

A similar issue arose, albeit in a slightly different context, in *Wings Ltd v Ellis* [1984] 1 All ER 1046, [1984] 1 WLR 772, DC; revsd [1985] AC 272, [1984] 3 All ER 577, HL, above, p 662, where the charge was one of recklessly making a false statement concerning the provision of services contrary to s 14(1)(b) of the 1968 Act.

Mann J, delivering the judgment of the Divisional Court, said: The appellant is a limited company and it is established that, where the commission of an offence under the 1968 Act requires a specific intent, then a corporate defendant is not guilty unless the requisite intent was a state of mind of one or more of those natural persons who constitute the directing mind and will of the company. Lord Widgery CJ described such persons as 'the ruling officers' in *Coupe v Guyett* [1973] 2 All ER 1058 at 1063, [1973] 1 WLR 669 at 675 . . .

Although the descriptions vary, the concept is clear. A company cannot be guilty of an offence unless the specified state of mind was a state of mind of a person who is or forms part of the directing mind and will of the company. As to the personal liability of such persons, see s 20 of the 1968 Act.

Was there evidence on which a reasonable bench of justices, properly instructed, could be sure that there was recklessness by such a person in the present case?

'Recklessness' means failing to have regard to the truth or falsity of the statement (see *MFI Warehouses Ltd v Nattrass* [1973] 1 All ER 762 at 768, [1973] 1 WLR 307 at 313). We can find nothing in the evidence which suggests that a person ruling the company was privy to the selection of the photograph. In particular, we reject the respondent's suggestion that Michael Stephen-Jones, who approved the photograph and who variously called himself a 'long haul development manager' and 'the contracts manager', could be inferred to be a member of the relevant class. The most that could be said for the respondent is that the members of this class, although establishing a system, failed to establish a system which would have prevented the mistake which occurred. That failure cannot, in our judgment, constitute 'recklessness'. There may be cases where the system is such that he who establishes it could not be said to be having regard to the truth or falsity of what emerged from it, but that is not this case.

For the reasons which we have given, the appeal in regard to the conviction under s 14(1)(b) must be allowed and the conviction quashed.

Although the prosecution appealed to the House of Lords only on the charge requiring proof of knowledge under s 14(1)(a) of the Act, the arguments in terms of the requirements for corporate liability were essentially the same. The approach of Mann J received no support in the House of Lords.

Lord Scarman said: The 1968 Act, of course, to be of any value at all in modern conditions has to cover trades and businesses conducted on a large scale by individual proprietors, by firms and by bodies corporate. The day-to-day business activities of large enterprises, whatever their legal structure, are necessarily conducted by their employees, and particularly by their sales staff. It follows that many of the acts prohibited by the Act will be the acts of employees done in the course of the trade or business and without the knowledge at the time of those who direct the business. It will become clear that the Act does cover such acts when one comes to consider the terms of the two statutory defences to which I have already referred. The Act also makes specific provision consistent with this view of its operation in respect of businesses carried on by bodies corporate. Section 20 provides that, where an offence has been committed by a body corporate and was committed with the consent or is attributable to the neglect of a director or other officer of the company, he '*as well as the body corporate*' is guilty of the offence.

Both Lord Scarman and Lord Hailsham LC (see ibid pp 286–7, 582) were clear that the 1968 Act extended to such cases. For further discussion of the position in the case of an unincorporated employer see *Coupe v Guyett* [1973] 2 All ER 1058, [1973] 1 WLR 669, below, p 729.

The refusal by the court in the *Tesco* case to hold the company responsible for the acts of its employees gave rise to disquiet in some quarters. However, it should be noted that it has been held, regarding s 24(1), that the defendant must prove not only that the offence was due to the act or default of another but that he had done all that could reasonably be expected by way of inquiry and investigation to identify the other person. The point arose in *McGuire v Sittingbourne Co-operative Society* [1976] Crim LR 268. In defence to a charge under s 11(2) the defendants served notices on the prosecutor pursuant to s 24(2) alleging that the offences were due to the act or default of the managers or other persons whom the defendants could not identify. In a letter amplifying the notices they named all the assistants in the shop at the relevant time. The justices held that they had established the defence. The prosecution appealed on case stated to the Queen's Bench Division. The appeal was allowed, the Court holding that the onus was on the defendants to establish, on the balance of probabilities, that they had done all that could reasonably be expected of them in the way of inquiry and investigation as to who was responsible for the default.

Lord Widgery added:

Unless some little care is taken in regard to these matters, we may find the administration of this Act sliding down to the sort of slip-shod level at which all a defendant has to do is say in general terms that the default must have been due to something in the shop, one of the girls or some expression like that, and thereby satisfy the onus cast upon him.

The more specific wording of s 39(3) of the 1987 Act enacts this in statutory form.

The Director General of Fair Trading's Review of the Trade Descriptions Act

(Cmnd 6628 (1976)),in commenting on the *Tesco* decision, suggests (at para 54) that it may be:

responsible for the emergence of a misleading picture of the extent to which the Act is being contravened, particularly in relation to corporate retailing. It appears that some companies trading on a national scale are willing to shoulder the blame for all offences originating within their organisation, whatever the circumstances which led to their commission. Others, however, seek to avoid conviction for offences by pointing to the precautions they have taken and blaming the member of the staff responsible for the particular offence. The enquiries mentioned above have shown that, with few exceptions, local authorities are unwilling to prosecute employees, such as shop managers, in cases where the trader has argued that an offence has arisen from the employee's act or default.

Yet, swayed by Lord Reid's reasoning in the *Tesco* case, the report concluded:

63. . . . .
(i) the imposition of vicarious liability for offences arising from the act or default of employees would not be justified;
(ii) consideration should be given to adding words to the existing statutory defence to ensure that a trader is not provided with a defence by reference to the act or default of a person under his control unless he can show that the method of trading he adopts, and which led to the offence, does not involve a high inherent risk that offences will be committed through the act or default of employees, having regard to their skill, training and the complexity of the system.

The *Tesco* decision is not without its difficulties as is evident from the following extract from Sir Gordon Borrie's Hamlyn Lectures, *The Development of Consumer Law and Policy* (1984), at pp 52–3.

Justifying the result of the *Tesco* decision, Lord Reid said this:[1]

'It is sometimes argued—it was argued in the present case—that making an employer criminally responsible, even when he has done all that he could to prevent an offence, affords some additional protection to the public because this will induce him to do more. But if he has done all he can how can he do more?'

Lord Reid's point seems to be logically impeccable. Yet it may be all too easy for the employer to *appear* to have done all he can, to point to systems and precautions and the training of staff. And the mere suggestion of such a defence being raised may induce Trading Standards Departments not to proceed for the simple reason that in practice the defence is difficult to counteract. Very soon after the *Tesco* decision, the Law Commission expressed its support of the principle that companies should be criminally liable in the regulatory field, and specifically liable to prosecution under the Trade Descriptions Act:[2]

'The main objective of criminal law is the prevention of crime and it is argued that the publicity attendant upon the prosecution of companies has a strong deterrent effect. The prosecution of a company for the commission of an offence symbolises the failure of control by the company, and it is socially desirable to have the company's name before the public. We think that it is probably true that the publicity given a corporation . . . is valuable in the field of regulatory offences the purpose of which is often to ensure adherence to proper standards, for example in respect of foodstuffs, drugs and other articles of consumption. This publicity achieves its effect in the main through reports in the local press, so having a maximum impact upon consumers. . . '

[1] [1972] AC 153, 174; [1971] 2 All ER 127, 135.
[2] *Criminal Liability of Corporations*, Law Commission Working Paper No. 44 (1972), para 48.
  See also the view of Professor Glanville Williams: 'That a company should not be liable for

an offence of negligence committed by its branch manager, who after all represents the company in the particular locality, is a considerable defect in the law . . . What is evidently needed is a statutory redefinition of the officers whose acts and mental states implicate the company.' (Glanville Williams *Textbook of Criminal Law* (2nd edn, 1983) p 973).

It is to be noted that the wording of ss 20(1) and 40(1) of the 1987 Act (see above, p 674 and below, p 733, respectively) remove any question of prosecutions being taken against employees for the purposes of pricing offences under the 1987 Act.

MISTAKE

It was held in *Birkenhead and District Co-operative Society Ltd v Roberts* [1970] 3 All ER 391, [1970] 1 WLR 1497, where the alleged offence arose out of the mislabelling by the defendant's servant of a joint of beef, that a 'mistake' by any person other than the one charged would be the defence of 'act or default of another person' and that seven days' notice would have had to be given in accordance with the requirements of s 24(2). In the words of Fisher J 'the word "mistake" means mistake by the person charged, and not a mistake by any other person.'

RELIANCE ON INFORMATION SUPPLIED TO HIM

As with act or default of another, it is necessary, under s 24(2) of the 1968 Act, and s 39(2) of the 1987 Act, to give notice to the prosecutor of an intention to raise this defence. For s 24(1), although the statute is silent on the point, it is generally considered that the information must be provided by a reliable source for the defence to be maintained. In *Barker v Hargreaves* [1981] RTR 197, (see further, below, p 725) the defendant was not able to claim reliance on an MOT test certificate to show the condition of the vehicle—the certificate clearly stating that it should not be relied upon as evidence of the mechanical condition of the vehicle.

The 1987 Act requirements are more stringent as, under s 39(4), the defendant has to establish reasonable reliance in the light of what he did and could have done to verify the information and also whether he had any reason to disbelieve the information.

ACCIDENT, OR CAUSE BEYOND ACCUSED'S CONTROL

To establish these defences it is necessary to prove something which is unexpected, beyond control, and which normal diligence and precaution would not uncover. The defence has been discussed in the Divisional Court in the context of s 26 of the Weights and Measures Act 1963. The following leading case is in point.

Bibby-Cheshire v Golden Wonder Ltd [1972] 3 All ER 738, [1972] 1 WLR 1487, Queen's Bench Division

A crisp packet marked '15 drams' was found on purchase to weigh only 9 drams. The defendants pleaded as a cause beyond their control that a normally accurate and reliable machine had for no anticipated reason proved not to be so. It was further said that the machine was set to produce overweight bags—17.5 drams which most packets did weigh—and that there was no machine accurate enough never to produce underweight bags. The justices held that the manufacturer had satisfied s 26(1)(a) and the prosecution now appealed to the Divisional Court.

Melford Stevenson J having stated the facts of the case continued: The defence made available to the respondents charges them with proving (a) that the commission of the offence was due to a mistake or to an accident or some other cause beyond his control; there is here no suggestion of a mistake, no suggestion of an accident, and we have to consider the words: 'some other cause beyond his control'. It is established here that there was in use a machine, whatever may be said of it, which was of a kind which would not be expected in the ordinary course of its functioning to go wrong beyond the very slight figures of error that I have indicated, and evidence also accepted that it was the best machine available at the time when this offence was committed. For myself, those considerations on the findings of fact expressed in the case seem to me to bring this case within the words 'some other cause beyond his control', but that is not enough; one has to continue:

' . . . and that he took all reasonable precautions and exercised all due diligence to avoid the commission of such an offence in respect of those goods by himself or any person under his control.'

The matters that I have already recited, . . . appear to me to satisfy the phrase: 'exercise all due diligence to avoid the commission of such an offence'. The justices who heard the detailed evidence on which their findings are based, plainly came to that conclusion, and in my view they were justified in reaching that conclusion. It is true they do not in express terms exclude the possibility of a cause beyond the respondents' control, but I think that does arise by clear implication from the paragraph of the case where they express their opinion, and from the question as framed by them.

I think that they were justified in finding that the burden of establishing this offence had been discharged by the respondents, and that they were right in dismissing this information.

Milmo J agreed.

Widgery LCJ. In these cases of machines producing quantities of goods less than they are expected to produce I think it is open to the accused under the Weights and Measures Act 1963 to plead as a cause beyond his control the fact that a machine normally accurate and reliable, has on occasion for no anticipated reason proved to be inaccurate or unreliable.

Appeal dismissed.

In other cases it has been held that a retail baker has no 'control' over a wholesale baker who supplies him with loaves: see *McIntyre & Son v Laird* 1943 JC 96; *Trickers (Confectioners) Ltd v Barnes* [1955] 1 All ER 803, [1955] 1 WLR 372. Also an unusual breakdown or unlikely defect in machinery may be a bona fide accident beyond control, see *Wolfinder v Oliver* (1932) 147 LT 80. See also *Marshall v Herbert* [1963] Crim LR 506 for a defence in which the unexpected illness of an employee was held to be a cause beyond the defendant's control (the defence, however, failing on diligence).

There appear to be no reported cases on what the nature of a 'mistake' or 'accident' amounts to under the 1968 Act. It will be noted that the *Bibby-Cheshire* case (above) specifically rejected any suggestion of any mistake or accident. The decision depended on the meaning of 'some other cause beyond his control'. It is thought that the paucity of authority on the meaning of 'mistake' or 'accident' is not so much because of the unlikelihood of such things occurring; it is rather because of the great difficulty for the defendant in establishing the second line of defence—ie that the mistake or accident occurred despite taking all reasonable precautions and exercising all due diligence. The two limbs of the defence in this respect are almost inherently contradictory.

REASONABLE PRECAUTIONS/STEPS AND ALL DUE DILIGENCE

Under the two-limb defences, if an individual blames, for example, his supplier he must prove additionally that he satisfied the requirements under s 24(1)(b)—that is, that he took all reasonable precautions *and* exercised all due diligence, the conditions being cumulative, not alternative. In the case of the s 39(1) defence, the core of the defence is the reasonable steps and due diligence requirement.

Many cases have been before the courts on these requirements and two underlying principles are discernible:

(a) the person charged must at least have done something—to sit back and do nothing is not sufficient;

(b) the question of what are reasonable precautions/steps must be decided on the facts of each individual case.

Section 24(1)(b) was considered in *Tesco Supermarkets Ltd v Nattrass* [1972] AC 153, [1971] 2 All ER 127, above, p 711. Lord Diplock's speech contains the following helpful analysis:

Lord Diplock: What amounts to the taking of all reasonable precautions and the exercise of all due diligence by a principal in order to satisfy the requirements of s 24(1)(b) of the Act depends on all the circumstances of the business carried on by the principal. It is a question of fact for the justices in summary proceedings or for the jury in proceedings on indictment. However large the business, the principal cannot avoid a personal responsibility for laying down the system for avoiding the commission of offences by his servants. It is he alone who is party to their contracts of employment through which this can be done. But in a large business, such as that conducted by the appellants in the instant appeal, it may be quite impracticable for the principal personally to undertake the detailed supervision of the work of inferior servants. It may be reasonable for him to allocate these supervisory duties to some superior servants or hierarchy of supervisory grades of superior servants, under their respective contracts of employment with him. If the principal has taken all reasonable precautions in the selection and training of servants to perform supervisory duties and has laid down an effective system of supervision and used due diligence to see that it is observed, he is entitled to rely on a default by a superior servant in his supervisory duties as a defence under s 24(1) as well as, or instead of, on an act or default of an inferior servant who has no supervisory duties under his contract of employment.

This passage was quoted with approval and followed by the Divisional Court in *Nattrass v Timpson Shops Ltd* [1973] Crim LR 197.

Sherratt v Geralds The American Jewellers Ltd (1970) 114 Sol Jo 147, Queen's Bench Division

The defendants were charged with supplying a wristwatch marked 'divers watch' and 'waterproof' to which false trade descriptions were applied contrary to s 1(1)(b) of the Trade Descriptions Act 1968. After being immersed in water for one hour the watch stopped and filled with water. The defendants had not carried out any tests but relied on the wholesalers' reputation and their experience that the watches had previously not caused any trouble. The magistrate found that the defendants had taken all reasonable precautions and exercised all due diligence within s 24(1)(b) of the Act. The prosecution appealed.

Lord Parker CJ is reported as having made the following observations: [The] defences in s 24(1)(a) and (b) had to be proved on the balance of probabilities; the burden being on the defendants. Clearly they had taken no precautions, relying on previous dealings with the wholesalers. To succeed, they had to show that if no precautions were taken, there were none reasonably to be taken. Whatever 'all due diligence' might mean, there was clearly an obligation to take any reasonable precautions that could be taken. The watch was designed to withstand pressures of five atmospheres at the front, but no one had suggested that it was necessary to dive 170 ft as a reasonable precaution. The elementary precaution of dipping the watch in a bowl of water would have prevented the offence. While there was evidence that the defendants had discharged the burden of proof under para (a), there was no evidence on which it could be said they had brought themselves within para (b). The case should go back with a direction to convict. The magistrate might feel that there were mitigating circumstances obliging him not to impose a very severe penalty.

Ashworth and Talbot JJ agreed.

Appeal allowed.

The above principles were upheld in *Garrett v Boots Chemists Ltd* (16 July 1980, unreported). The respondents were charged with having on sale pencils which breached the Pencils and Graphic Instruments (Safety) Regulations 1974 by having a higher lead and/or chromium content than permitted. The facts were not in dispute but the defendants pleaded that they had taken all reasonable precautions—they had previously informed their supplier about the new regulations and made it a condition in their order of supply that pencils conformed to the standards. The magistrates found that the defendants had taken all reasonable precautions and to take random samples was not necessary. The prosecution appealed to the Divisional Court.

Lord Lane CJ allowed the appeal and after commenting on the facts of *Sherratt v Geralds The American Jewellers Ltd* stated: 'All reasonable precautions' are strong words. It has been suggested by Mr Scrivener, on behalf of the appellant, that one obvious and reasonable precaution which could have been taken in the present case was to take random samples of the various batches of pencils which arrived at the premises of Messrs Boots the Chemists Limited.

Of course I scarcely need say that every case will vary in its facts; what might be reasonable for a large retailer might not be reasonable for the village shop. But here, dealing with a concern the size of Boots, it seems to me that one of the obvious precautions to be taken was random sample, whether statistically controlled or not. One does not know whether the random sample would have in fact produced detection of the errant pencils. It might have, it might not have. But to say that it was not a precaution which should reasonably have been taken does not seem to me to accord with good sense.

Whatever the circumstances may be so far as other retailers are concerned, on the facts of this case it seems to me that no Bench of Magistrates, properly instructed in the law, could properly have come to the conclusion that Messrs Boots the Chemists had discharged the burden here which lay upon them.

Accordingly the case was remitted to the justices with a direction to convict.

Subsequent cases concerning safety offences demonstrate clearly a tightening of requirements to satisfy due diligence defences in relation to sampling. The following three cases are useful examples.

Rotherham Metropolitan Borough Council v Raysun (UK) Ltd (1988) 8 Tr Law 6, Queen's Bench Division

Imported wax crayons were sold in breach of both the Trade Descriptions Act 1968, s 1(1)(b), and the Consumer Safety (Amendment) Act 1986, s 12(6). The defence sections in question were s 24(1) of the TDA 1968 and s 12(2) of the 1986 Act (which was worded in very similar terms to s 39(1) of the 1987 Act). The defendants relied to some extent on sampling done in Hong Kong, which had been inadequately supervised. In addition, some sampling occurred in the United Kingdom.

Woolf LJ, having commented on earlier decisions, including the *Garrett* case, stated: With regard to the sampling which took place in this country, the selection of one packet of crayons in respect of an importation of a batch of 10,000 dozen crayons, as counsel for the appellants points out, is a very modest sample indeed. By itself, in my view, certainly in relation to offences of this sort, it does not indicate the taking of the standard of care required by the relevant statutory provisions. I recognise that, if the sampling had been supported by evidence that indicated that the standard throughout a large consignment such as 10,000 dozen packets could be expected to be the same, then it is conceivable that to choose one sample in relation to such a large batch might suffice. But, in the absence of any supporting evidence of that sort, in the absence of any evidence indicating why the respondents had selected only one packet of crayons out of a batch of 10,000 dozen crayons, this does not appear to me to be the sort of proportion which would comply with the standards laid down in the relevant statutory provisions.

Hutchinson J agreed and the case was remitted to the magistrates with a direction to convict.

A greater level of sampling was established in the next case, but this still did not satisfy the court. The onus was placed on the defendant to establish what was a reasonable level of sampling and that this had been complied with.

P & M Supplies (Essex) Ltd v Devon County Council [1991] Crim L R 832, (1991) 99 ITSA 10 MR 20, Queen's Bench Division

Offences arose under s 12(1) of the Consumer Protection Act 1987 (see above, p 585) and a s 39(1) defence was raised by the appellants. Testing took place on various soft toys, regarding the attachment of their eyes, which the magistrates summarised as follows:

'Of the 14 leg variety a total of 22,744 toys were imported and out of that total only 114 toys (0.5%) (228 eyes) were tested . . . Of the 24 leg variety a total of 11,592 toys were imported and out of that total only 150 toys (1.29%) (300 eyes) were tested . . . Of the 6 leg variety a total of 42,624 toys were imported . . . and out of that total only 114 toys (0.26%) (228 eyes) were tested . . . Therefore out of a total of 76,960 toys imported only 378 (0.49%) were randomly sampled by the appellants and only 18 toys were sent to the public analyst.'

Nolan LJ, having examined the facts and the magistrates' decision to convict, continued: Mr Reynolds submitted that the appellant had produced evidence of a reasonable system, devised in consultation with the local Trading Standards Department, being carried out by the company. No evidence has been called by the respondent in rebuttal of that evidence put forward by the appellant. The decision, he submitted, as one could infer from the findings of the Justices, following the contentions of the respondent, was evidently based on the inadequacy of the number of tests carried out. But in the absence of any bench-mark as to what did constitute a reasonable number of tests, any reasonable Bench of magistrates, submitted Mr Reynolds, should, and would, have acquitted the appellant in this case.

He pointed to the difficulties encountered by the appellant in carrying on his business in the light of the decision of the Justices. If the number of tests carried out by him was insufficient then how much greater a number should he carry out in the future. He told us that the company had been prosecuted for a similar offence before a Birmingham Bench and had been acquitted. It was undesirable, he said, that there should be this disparity in decisions of different Benches of Justices in different parts of the country.

Mr Scrivener, leading counsel for the respondent, submitted that the Justices had to make a decision on the evidence put before them. It was for the appellant to establish, first, by independent statistical evidence or otherwise, that his testing system was adequate to the type of goods and the number of goods involved. Secondly, it had to be established that the testing system was in practice carried out scrupulously.

The findings of the Justices show they were not satisfied on either ground. Accordingly, submitted Mr Scrivener, there could be no question here of there being a failure on the part of the Justices to arrive at a reasonable decision. On the facts found by them they were fully entitled, if not bound, to decide as they did. Had the decision of the Justices clearly rested on the number of tests alone, I would be left in doubt as to whether they had approached the matter correctly. It seems to me that it is not practicable to decide that a given number of tests is inadequate without having a clear idea of what an adequate number of tests would be.

This case illustrates the need for Benches of magistrates to be given help about these matters, preferably in the form of independent statistical evidence as to what should be done by a reasonable trader in these circumstances to avoid the sort of danger which the regulations are intended to prevent. We were told that some such evidence had been produced, by the prosecution as it happened before the Birmingham Bench.

At the end of the day I am bound to conclude that the absence of such evidence in the present case is something which must be laid at the door of the defence. The burden of proof was on them; they failed to discharge it . . .

Watkins LJ. I agree. As to whether a defendant in such circumstances, as were presented to the Justices in this case, had taken reasonable steps and exercised all due diligence is a matter which can only be resolved by Justices as a matter of fact. That had been decided in a number of cases where this kind of legislation has been in point. The Justices here had a difficult task seeing, as my Lord has said, that they were given no assistance upon the kind of standard which either ought to be adopted or is in fact adopted by traders such as the defendants. Whether that evidence could have come from the trade itself or from British Standard Institution literature, I feel quite unable in the light of what we know to say; but true it is that where defendants have to discharge such a burden, as is implicit in the terms of s 39(1), they simply cannot rely upon the prosecution producing evidence in rebuttal to repair omissions in evidence, which it was plainly their duty to put before the court if they are to have any hope whatsoever of establishing that they had in fact taken all reasonable steps and exercised all due diligence in testing material which in this case had come from abroad . . .

Appeal dismissed.

The final example discussing both the amount of sampling undertaken and the quality of the testing applied is:

London Borough of Sutton v David Halsall PLC (1995) 103 ITSA 1 MR 30, Queen's Bench Division

Magistrates had accepted a due diligence defence regarding the sale of flammable Halloween capes in breach of safety regulations. Evidence of testing by the respondent showed that of a shipment of 4,608 capes, 5 were tested by the in-house safety officer. The magistrates indicated that this was an appropriate sample as established by British Standards. However, the test method used did not comply with British Standards. Further, larger, batches of capes were received with a similar sampling procedure used.

Kennedy LJ, having referred to the *Garrett* case stated: What needs to be done will depend upon the facts in each case, but the authorities . . . show that an importer such as the respondent company in the present case, may be able to satisfy the burden of proof if, for example, the importer buys from an established manufacturer who he has reason to trust, who is aware of his requirements, and in particular the safety requirements laid down by English law, and if the importer then subjects the goods to sampling. The sampling should however itself be properly organised random sampling, with a sufficient number of samples being properly tested to indicate compliance with the specifications.

On the facts the respondents failed to show that from each consignment an appropriate sample was tested and, as the tests did not meet British standards, the tests conducted were inadequate. The case was remitted to the justices with a direction to convict.

NOTES

1. For further discussion of defences see Weatherill 'Unsafe Goods: Protecting the Consumer and Protecting the Diligent Trader' [1990] JBL 36; Parry

'Judicial Approaches to Due Diligence' [1995] Crim LR 695; and Cotter 'Due Diligence: the Disappearing Defence' (1992) 142 NLJ 133 and 170.

2. It is apparent from examining the authorities that the most stringent due diligence requirements arise in safety cases, with less demanding standards required in some trade descriptions cases and in most pricing cases.

SPECIFIC DEFENCES

There are many examples where legislation provides specific defences for certain categories of offences to mitigate the rigour of strict liability. Some examples are discussed below.

TRADE DESCRIPTIONS ACT 1968, s 24(3)

This section, although similar to the s 24(1) defence, discussed above, is limited to a specific offence:

Section 24(3)
In any proceedings for an offence under this Act of supplying or offering to supply goods to which a false trade description is applied it shall be a defence for the person charged to prove that he did not know, and could not with reasonable diligence have ascertained, that the goods did not conform to the description or that the description had been applied to the goods.

This is, in effect, a defence of innocent supply of goods. It only applies to offences under s 1(1)(b) of the 1968 Act (see above, p 620). The difference between s 24(3) and s 24(1) (see p 710) is that s 24(3) requires only that the exercise of 'reasonable diligence' would not have shown up the offence. The point is well illustrated by the following case.

Barker v Hargreaves [1981] RTR 197, Queen's Bench Division

A second-hand car dealer advertised a car as being 'in good condition' throughout. The car was badly corroded, but this was partly hidden by undersealing and a battery. The Divisional Court upheld the justices' conviction under s 1(1)(b) of the Trade Descriptions Act 1968.

Donaldson LJ having summarised the facts of the case remarked: There is a very clear distinction between the two subsections. Under subsection (1) it is necessary for the defendant to prove that he took all reasonable precautions and exercised all due diligence to avoid the commission of 'such an offence', that is to say, an offence under the Act. Subsection (3), on the other hand, is directed to the particular offence and it says that it is a defence to prove that he did not know of the facts constituting the particular offence and could not with reasonable diligence have ascertained that the goods did not conform to the description, again pointing to the particular complaint . . .

The Crown Court found that the defendant had no system for ascertaining the condition of the vehicles being sold. He relied solely on MOT tests. Accordingly, I am quite clear that he cannot rely on section 24(1).

When it comes to section 24(3) it is a different defence because it relates to the specific defects which were found in the vehicle and form the basis of the charge. Those are the corrosion defects. But, unlike under section 24(1), where he can rely on information received from other people, when it comes to section 24(3) it is no answer that he was misled by others. What he has to do is to show that it was a latent defect, that is to say, a defect which could not with reasonable diligence have been ascertained.

It was decided in *Denard v Abbas* [1987] Crim LR 424, QBD, that an objective test is to be applied when determining what the defendant could have ascertained. Here a market trader, illiterate in English, was prosecuted for selling 'pirate' tapes. He was judged in his position as a trader, not as someone with the same personal attributes regarding intelligence, command of English etc, and the defence failed. This does not appear to accord strictly with the wording of the section.

INNOCENT PUBLICATION

A quite common defence, that of 'innocent' publication of advertisements, can be found in, inter alia, s 25 of the Trade Descriptions Act 1968, s 24(3) of the Fair Trading Act 1973, and Sch 3, para 5 to the Hallmarking Act 1973.

Trade Descriptions Act 1968, s 25

In proceedings for an offence under this Act committed by the publication of an advertisement it shall be a defence for the person charged to prove that he is a person whose business it is to publish or arrange for the publication of advertisements and that he received the advertisement for publication in the ordinary course of business and did not know and had no reason to suspect that its publication would amount to an offence under this Act.

VIDEO RECORDINGS

Section 11 of the Video Recordings Act 1984 and its interpretation provides an interesting contrast to the approach taken under s 24(1) of the Trade Descriptions Act 1968. The relevant offence and defences are both contained in s 11:

11 Supplying video recording of classified work in breach of classification
(1) Where a classification certificate issued in respect of a video work states that no video recording containing that work is to be supplied to any person who has not attained the age specified in the certificate, a person who supplies or offers to supply a video recording containing that work to a person who has not attained the age so specified is guilty of an offence unless the supply is, or would if it took place be, an exempted supply.

(2) It is a defence to a charge of committing an offence under this section to prove—
    (a) that the accused neither knew nor had reasonable grounds to believe that the classification certificate contained the statement concerned,

(b) that the accused neither knew nor had reasonable grounds to believe that the person concerned had not attained that age, or

(c) that the accused believed on reasonable grounds that the supply was, or would if it took place be, an exempted supply by virtue of section 3(4) or (5) of this Act.

. . .

The leading authority on this section is *Tesco Stores Ltd v Brent London Borough Council* [1993] 1 WLR 1037, [1993] 2 All ER 718, QBD. A video with an '18' classification was sold to a 14-year old boy, by a cashier, which led to a conviction against Tesco under s 11(1) of the 1984 Act. The boy was clearly under 18. Tesco appealed against the conviction.

Staughton LJ indicated: The main and almost the only question on this appeal is thus whether s 11(2)(b) of the 1984 Act is concerned with the knowledge and information of the employee who supplies the video film or only with the knowledge and information of those who represent the directing mind and will of Tesco Stores Ltd.

Having discussed the case of *Tesco Supermarkets Ltd v Nattrass* [1972] AC 153, [1971] 2 All ER 127, HL, see p 711–15, he continued:

The present case in concerned with a different statute, the Video Recordings Act 1984. The offence section here is s 11(1). Mr Stephenson for Tesco Stores Ltd concedes that this section too provides for an offence which may be committed vicariously by an employee acting in the course of his employment. The question then is whether s 11(2), the defence section, is concerned with the knowledge and information of the company, where it is a company that is the accused, by those who manage its affairs, or whether it looks at the knowledge and information of the employee who actually supplies the video film.

In my judgment s 11(2) of the 1984 Act is different both in language and content from s 24 of the 1968 Act. I see no reason why it should necessarily have the same meaning as that laid down in *Tesco Supermarkets v Nattrass*. The language here draws no distinction between the accused and those under his control. The content is concerned with knowledge and information, not due diligence. It is, as I have already suggested, absurd to suppose that those who manage a vast company would have any knowledge or any information as to the age of a casual purchaser of a video film. It is the employee that sells the film at the check-out point who will have knowledge or reasonable grounds for belief. It is her knowledge or reasonable grounds that are relevant. Were it otherwise, the statute would be wholly ineffective in the case of a large company, unless by the merest chance a youthful purchaser were known to the board of directors. Yet Parliament contemplated that a company might commit the offence (see s 16 of the 1984 Act).

By contrast the single-handed shopkeeper would be less readily able to rely on the defence section, although he would fare better if he had an assistant serving at the counter while he was at the back of the shop. I cannot believe that Parliament intended the large company to be acquitted but the single-handed shopkeeper convicted.

The court concluded that s 11(2) referred to the knowledge and information of the employee through whom the company supplies the goods. Given the knowledge of the assistant, the conviction was upheld.

'BYPASSING' PROVISIONS

The provisions to be discussed here can be found in s 23 of the Trade Descriptions Act 1968, s 20 of the Food Safety Act 1990, s 32 of the Weights and Measures Act 1985, s 24 of the Fair Trading Act 1973, and (in a modified version, see below, p 733) s 40(1) of the Consumer Protection Act 1987. They allow the prosecution of a person other than the person apparently committing the offence where 'the commission by any person of an offence' is alleged to be due to the act or default of that other person. Under s 23 of the 1968 Act that other person may be charged and convicted whether or not the person actually committing the offence is prosecuted. Therefore strictly speaking the sections are not defence provisions, but are provided to streamline what could otherwise be a cumbersome process.

Section 23 of the Trade Descriptions Act 1968 provides as follows:

23. Offences due to fault of another person
Where the commission by any person of an offence under this Act is due to the act or default of some other person that other person shall be guilty of the offence, and a person may be charged with and convicted of the offence by virtue of this section whether or not proceedings are taken against the first-mentioned person.

For examples of the procedure in use see *Cottee v Douglas Seaton (Used Cars) Ltd* [1972] 3 All ER 750, [1972] 1 WLR 1408, above, p 615 and *R v Ford Motor Co Ltd* [1974] 3 All ER 489, [1974] 1 WLR 1220, above, p 625. The following is a typical example of a charge bringing in s 23.

AB on the—day of—in the course of a business of selling musical instruments supplied to CD a violin to which a false trade description, namely that the violin was the work of Stradivarius and made in 1720, was applied, contrary to s 1(1) of the Trade Descriptions Act 1968. And the commission of the offence was due to the Act of EF of—, whereby the said EF is guilty of an offence by virtue of s 23 of the Trade Descriptions Act 1968.

Two main points to consider are firstly the procedural difficulties involved in the phrase 'commission by any person of an offence . . .' and secondly the requirement of showing direct causal connection between the offence by the first person and the act or default of the second.

'. . . COMMISSION BY ANY OTHER PERSON OF AN OFFENCE'

The immediate difficult question, since s 24 of the Trade Descriptions Act 1968 prescribes a defence where an offence occurred due to the 'act or default of another', is what scope is left for s 23? A basic prerequisite of s 23 is that an offence must have been committed (see *Cottee v Douglas Seaton (Used Cars) Ltd*, above, p 615) which is something s 24 apparently denies. This problem was discussed in the following case.

Coupe v Guyett [1973] 2 All ER 1058, [1973] 1 WLR 669, Queen's Bench Division

The defendant, a car repair workshop manager, was employed by the owner, Miss Shaw, who was registered in the Business Names Register as the sole proprietor but took no active part in the business. In an invoice of the business the defendant recklessly made a false statement as to repairs carried out on a car. Charges were preferred against the owner under s 14(1)(b) of the Trade Descriptions Act and against the defendant under s 23. The justices hearing the charges together acquitted the owner on the grounds that she had neither made nor authorised, nor even been aware of the making of, the false statement and in any event had a valid defence under s 24. They acquitted the defendant on the ground that since the owner was acquitted a s 23 conviction was not open to them. The prosecution now appealed to the Divisional Court.

Lord Widgery CJ, having stated the facts of the case continued: At first sight there appears to be something of a conflict between ss 23 and 24, because s 23 contemplates that the person first referred to therein shall have committed an offence by reason of the act or default of another. When one moves on to s 24, it becomes apparent that someone who has otherwise committed an offence but has done it through the act or default of another has a special statutory defence. Accordingly it is difficult at first sight to see how the two sections can be fitted together. But the conflict has been resolved, and one can seek guidance on it in the speech of Lord Diplock in *Tesco Supermarkets Ltd v Nattrass* [1971] 2 All ER 127 at 152,153; [1972] AC 153 at 195–197. The solution of the conflict is this, that when a person first named in s 23 has no defence to the charge except the statutory defence under s 24, he or she can properly still be regarded as having committed the offence for the purpose of s 23. On the other hand, in my judgment, if the person first referred to in s 23 has a defence on the merits, as it were, and without reference to s 24, then it is not possible to operate s 23 so as to render guilty the person whose act or default gave rise to the matter in complaint.

With that for background, one must now attempt to see what the justices made of the position of Miss Shaw. The prosecution were clearly saying that Miss Shaw and the respondent were guilty, subject of course to Miss Shaw's defence under s 24 but not otherwise. The justices took a different view. Their actual words were:

'We dismissed the summons against Miss Shaw on the grounds that although she was the registered owner of Advance Autos, she personally neither made nor authorised nor was she even aware of the making of the false statement and that in any event she had a valid defence under section 24 of the Act.'

If the justices had taken the view that Miss Shaw was to be acquitted solely because of the statutory defence, then for the reasons I have already given it would have been open to them to convict the respondent. If on the other hand they were right in saying that Miss Shaw was entitled to be acquitted on other grounds, then they would not be in a position to convict the respondent under the terms of s 23. Accordingly counsel for the appellant has been faced with the somewhat uphill task of trying to satisfy us that the justices were wrong in law when they concluded that Miss Shaw should be acquitted on grounds other than the grounds of the statutory defence. If he can do that, then of course the conviction of the respondent must follow; if he cannot, then the acquittal of the respondent was in my judgment right.

In order to allege that Miss Shaw was guilty of the offence and was able only to rely on her defence under s 24, counsel for the appellant has to urge and establish that not only the statement made by the respondent, the falsity of which gave rise to the proceedings, but also the mental state of the respondent must be attributed to Miss Shaw. I think, without deciding it, that in these circumstances it may well be right to say that the statement can properly be attributed to Miss Shaw, because after all, it was her business, and the statement was made on behalf of the business. So far as that point is concerned I could be easily persuaded that the making of the statement simpliciter could be attributed to Miss Shaw, the principal.

But that is not enough unless one can also attribute to her the state of mind alleged, namely that the statement was made recklessly. As I understand it, as a general proposition of the criminal law a principal is not to be made immediately liable, in an offence involving mens rea, merely because his servant or agent had the necessary mental intent. As a question of general principle I would have thought it wrong to allow the mental state of the respondent to be attributed to Miss Shaw so as to complete the offence so far as she is concerned.

Counsel for the appellant has ranged widely over the rest of the Act and has referred us, as I have said, to Lord Diplock's speech in the *Tesco* case, [1971] 2 All ER at 150–159, [1971] AC at 193–203, to show that generally speaking the scheme of this Act is to make the employer liable in the first instance, subject to his possible defence under s 24, and that that should be so in cases of strict liability is not I think surprising. It is the case that most, if not all, of the other offences under this Act are offences of strict obligation; and it seems to me consistent with principle in those cases that the employer should be the person primarily responsible when an infringement occurs.

But s 14 of the Act is peculiar in many ways. It deals with services, and deals with services for the first time, because they were not dealt with in the Merchandise Marks Acts 1887 to 1953 and also contains the specific mental element of knowledge of falsity or recklessness to which I have already referred. For my part I do not think it would be consistent with principle or required by the terms of this Act, looked at as a whole, that the mental element attributed properly to the respondent should be also attributed to Miss Shaw in the circumstances of this case.

I recognise that the situation may appear at all events to be somewhat different where the employer in a case of this kind is a limited company, because again it is established in principle that the actions and the state of mind of the ruling officers of a company may be attributed to the company. Accordingly, somewhat different considerations may apply in those circumstances. Here we have no question of a company, we have two individuals, and I think the result should be as I have stated.

This may mean, of course, that the defence under s 24 will rarely, if ever, be appropriate to a charge under s 14. I say that because, if I am right, in order to establish the charge under s 14 you have to show knowing falsity or recklessness, which themselves are inconsistent with the statutory defence. But be that as it may, I think in this case the justices were entirely justified in saying that Miss Shaw was to be acquitted on the general grounds as opposed to the statutory defence, and once they reached that conclusion it was inevitable, having regard to the form of the charge, that they should acquit the respondent as well. For those reasons I would dismiss the appeal.

Ashworth J and **Bridge J** agreed.

Appeal dismissed.

Section 24(1)(a) would be clearer on this point if it referred to 'the commission of the alleged offence'.

QUESTIONS

Is the decision in this case consistent with the approach of the House of Lords in *Wings Ltd v Ellis* [1984] 3 All ER 577, [1984] 3 WLR 965, above, pp 662–9 ?

Would it make any difference if someone in Miss Shaw's position had (i) been running a 'large scale' business, or (ii) set up a limited liability company?

PROBLEM

Art is the sole proprietor of a second-hand car business but he does not play an active part in it, leaving matters to his foreman, Bert. Bert assures a prospective purchaser of a car that it is 'a grand little runner. I would stake my life on it.' Art neither authorises the statement nor even knows that it has been made. In fact the car is unroadworthy. Discuss the liability of Art and Bert under the 1968 Act.

PRIVATE INDIVIDUALS

A further question is whether a third party due to whose act or default an offence has been committed may be prosecuted by virtue of s 23 when he is a private individual. This has been resolved in the following case.

Olgeirsson v Kitching [1986] 1 All ER 746, [1986] 1 WLR 304, Queen's Bench Division

A private seller of a vehicle with a recorded mileage of 30,000 miles knew that it had had a replacement odometer fitted and that its true mileage was about 74,000 miles. When selling the car to a garage, the owner indicated that the true mileage was about 38,000 miles. On appeal against conviction under s 23, McNeill J gave the judgment of the court.

McNeill J. The appellant contended before the justices that s 23 of the 1968 Act had no application in this case because the appellant was not a person acting in the course of a trade or business when the vehicle was sold by him to John Roe. The respondent contended that the words in s 23 had to be given their ordinary meaning and as such could apply to any person whether acting in the course of a trade or business or not. The justices accepted the respondent's contention and convicted the appellant, fining him £100 and ordering him to pay costs.

The question for the opinion of this court is:

'Were we right to conclude that the appellant in his capacity of a private individual and not acting in the course of any trade or business was guilty of an offence contrary to section 23 of the Trade Descriptions Act 1968.'

Counsel for the appellant makes the same submission to this court, namely that s 23 has no application because the appellant was not a person acting in the course of a trade or business when he sold the vehicle. The contention could be summarised in this way, that the section should be read so as to include after the words 'some other person' some such words as 'who is engaged in or connected with the trade or business of selling motor cars.' I do not attempt to phrase that more elegantly because the more detailed the phraseology becomes the more confusing and complicated it becomes, but essentially what was said by counsel on the appellant's behalf was that this section only applies to those who, if they were concerned with s 1 of the Act were dealing in the course of a trade or business.

He then quoted s 1 of the 1968 Act and continued:

Counsel for the appellant accepts that s 23 is not so limited in terms but submits that on a proper construction of s 23 it is and the words there should be so read. He poses the question rhetorically: can a private individual, not acting in the course of a trade or business, be guilty under s 23? He contends that Parliament must have intended the construction for which he argues because this is a statute which is designed to protect the citizen from the trader and Parliament, he said, could not have intended that a private individual should be guilty of an offence under this Act if the private individual was in no way connected with the trade or business, in this case the motor business.

Speaking for myself, I do not think that that is a necessary implication. I do not see why it should have been intended by Parliament that that result should follow dealing with, what has been called, the third party or bypass provisions of the 1968 Act, including s 23.

Counsel also contended that if the section reads without the words which he says should be included a private citizen could be liable for an act or default whether or not reckless or careless. That is an argument that might have had merit in other cases. It has none in this, where the justices found that what the present appellant did was done with full knowledge that what he was doing was false. Counsel also contended that if you have a chain transaction in which a motor car passes from private individual to private individual to motor trader and so on it may be that the fortuitous interposition of a motor trader might make a private individual further back in the chain liable under this section. The question which of course arises in consideration of that last submission is essentially one of causation. If it is found that a private individual was the cause of, to use the words of the statute, 'the first-mentioned person's' offence or, in the words of the statute, if the offence was 'due to the act or default of some other person', it does not seem to me that if the act or default is established there is anything unusual or contrary to the public interest in saying that such a person may be private rather than in trade. Quite apart from that, a private individual might in the circumstances have such protection as is given by the provisions of the statute limiting the time within which proceedings may be brought.

Having considered further arguments for and against applying s 23 to private individuals, McNeill J ruled in favour of it applying.

Mustill LJ. I agree.

Appeal dismissed.

NOTES

1. The bypass provision under s 23 may be used against employees as well a private individuals, see for example *Nattrass v Timpson Shoes Ltd* [1973] Crim LR 197.

2. There is also always the possibility of an individual committing an offence under another statute, for example obtaining property by deception contrary to s 15 of the Theft Act 1968. Also on appropriate facts, at common law a private individual could be charged as a secondary party aiding and abetting another's commission of an offence against the Trade Descriptions Act itself. However, mens rea would then have to be proved even though the principal offender might be subject to strict liability under s 1 of the Act: see generally Smith and Hogan *Criminal Law* (8th edn, 1996) pp 141–2.

3. For a case under the former Food and Drugs Act 1955 in which an individual employee of a third party was held guilty under s 113(1) even though he was

in no way involved in the sale of food: see *Meah v Roberts* [1978] 1 All ER 97, [1977] 1 WLR 1187 (QBD) (leaving of caustic soda during cleaning of lager dispenser in restaurant, the soda being sold thereafter mistakenly as lemonade).

In s 40(1) of the Consumer Protection Act 1987, Parliament chose to make it clear that, not only may employees not be prosecuted by means of the bypass provision, but also private individuals could not be prosecuted either.

40. Liability of persons other than the principal offender
(1) Where the commission by any person of an offence to which section 39 above applies is due to an act or default committed by some other person in the course of any business of his, the other person shall be guilty of the offence and may be proceeded against and punished by virtue of this subsection whether or not proceedings are taken against the first-mentioned person.

For discussion of 'in the course of any business of his' see *Warwickshire County Council v Johnson* [1993] AC 583, [1993] 1 All ER 299, HL, above, pp 675–9.

ACT OR DEFAULT: DIRECT CAUSAL CONNECTION

The bypass provision cannot be used where there are two separate offences or possible offences not causally connected. So much is implicit in the words 'due to the act or default'. So in *Tarleton Engineering Co Ltd v Nattrass* [1973] 3 All ER 699, [1973] 1 WLR 1261 it was held that the justices had adopted the wrong approach in holding that the commission of an offence by auctioneers in selling a 'clocked car' was due to the act or default of the defendants who had entered it in the auction. This case was followed in *Taylor v Smith* [1974] RTR 190. See also *K Lill Holdings Ltd (trading as Stratford Motor Co) v White* [1979] RTR 120, above, p 637.

TIME LIMITS

The prosecution of trading standards offences is subject to provisions as to time limits. These must be observed, and if the limits are in any case exceeded, it raises, upon the appearance of the defendant, a defect which is incurable and cannot be waived notwithstanding that the defendant raises no objection (*Dixon v Wells* (1890) 25 QBD 249).

In summary proceedings, s 127 of the Magistrates' Courts Act 1980 imposes a general time limit on laying informations within six months from the time when the offence was committed. However, taking the Trade Descriptions Act 1968 as an example, all except one offence under the Act are triable either way, that is either summarily or on indictment. The current position is that, pursuant to s 19, no prosecution for an offence under the 1968 Act can be commenced after the expiration of three years from the commission of the offence or one year from its discovery by the prosecutor, whichever is the earlier. (The only summary offence in the Act (obstructing an officer under s 29) is subject to a special time limit of 12 months from the commission of the offence (s 19(2)).

Originally, if the offence was committed by the making of an oral statement there was yet a third time limit—namely the 'normal' one for summary offences of six months from the commission of the offence. This point should be borne in mind when reading the case printed below. It should also be noted that although s 19(4) which contains this six months stipulation has not been formally repealed, it has ceased to have effect; the time limit of three years now applies to such offences, since they are triable on indictment or summarily, that is 'either way'.

The significance of time limits for present purposes is that it is necessary to identify the precise moment when the offence was committed in order to assess whether the time limit has been exceeded. For instance, if a vehicle is falsely described by advertisements in a journal and is subsequently purchased by a buyer visiting the premises on which the vehicle stands, when is the false trade description 'applied' for the purposes of s 1 of the Act? This was one of the points which came before the Divisional Court in the following case.

Rees v Munday [1974] 3 All ER 506, [1974] 1 WLR 1284, Queen's Bench Division

Two informations were laid concerning false trade descriptions applied to a Bedford goods vehicle. The magistrates convicted on both charges. Lord Widgery CJ gave the judgment of the court.

Lord Widgery CJ. . . . The dates are important. On 29 October 1971 the appellant advertised in a motor trade journal, Commercial Motor, that he had for sale a Bedford goods vehicle, which was 'in first class condition throughout'. In the same advertisement was the reference to it being of '12 yd' capacity. A potential buyer interested in buying such a vehicle visited the appellant at his premises in Surrey on 30 October 1971. A bargain was struck there and then, that is to say in the course of the interview, a contract for sale was made, but the vehicle was kept on the appellant's premises a short while, partly because something had to be done to it, and partly because it was desired to keep it there until the purchaser's cheque had been cleared. In fact, the vehicle was delivered to the purchaser in Somerset by a servant of the appellant on 2 November 1971. The informations in this case were both laid on 1 November 1972 and the matters that concern this court are unhappily related to whether the informations were preferred in time.

Special rules apply to cases in magistrates' courts under the Trade Descriptions Act 1968 and they are to be found in s 19 of the Act itself. Section 19(2) provides:

'Notwithstanding anything in section 104 of the Magistrates' Courts Act 1952, [now section 127(1) of the Magistrates' Courts Act 1980], a magistrates' court may try an information for an offence under this Act if the information was laid at any time within twelve months from the commission of the offence.'

I take that provision first of all because it is from there that the appellant's first point arises. The limitation, I remind myself, is 12 months from the commission of the offence. The offence is the supply of the goods to which the false trade description is applied. One gets that from s 1(1)(b) of the 1968 Act, and that indeed is the provision under which these charges were laid.

So in deciding whether the information was or was not laid within the appropriate 12 months' period, it is the date of supply from which the 12 months begins to run.

As will be observed, the information is laid on 1 November 1972, within the 12 month period if the date of supply is the date when the vehicle was driven down to Somerset because that was 2 November 1971; a close-run thing perhaps, but just in time if delivery is the date when supply occurs and, therefore, the date of the commission of the offence. If, as the appellant argues, the vehicle was supplied on 30 October when the contract for sale was struck, then, of course, the informations were too late by one day. On this point the sole question for us to consider is whether this vehicle was supplied within the meaning of the 1968 Act at the date when the contract for sale was made or at the date when it was physically delivered.

For my part I think that the proper construction of this Act requires supply to be treated here as the date of delivery. I can see that there are arguments which might be advanced for applying the Sale of Goods Act 1893 [now 1979] to this situation and saying that an article is supplied when the property passes by virtue of that Act. But I think for my own part that that would be an unnecessary and undesirable complication to attach to this already somewhat difficult Act, and I think that the proper meaning of supply in this context is the delivery of the goods as delivered by the seller, or notification that they are available for delivery if they are to be collected by the buyer. On that basis the goods were supplied on 2 November 1971, the offence was committed on that date, the information came along on 1 November 1972, just in time, and there is nothing in the appellant's first point.

The second point, still concerned with the time of the laying of the information, arises out of s 19(4), which says:

'Subsections (2) and (3) of this section do not apply where— . . . (b) the offence was one of supplying goods to which a false trade description is applied, and the trade description was applied by an oral statement . . . '

So that if one brings oneself within sub-s (4)(b) the period is no longer 12 months but only six months, and quite clearly on any view of the matter the informations were laid more than six months after the commission of the offence in this case. Thus this is a wholly alternative and separate point taken by the appellant and it requires consideration of how the false trade description was applied, because if it was applied by an oral statement, then under s 19(4) it would seem that the appropriate limitation period is six months.

To consider the circumstances in which a false trade description is applied one goes back to s 4(1), again reading the words that are relevant only:

'A person applies a trade description to goods if he . . . (c) uses the trade description in any manner likely to be taken as referring to the goods.'

The contest here is between counsel for the respondent, who says that the trade description was applied when the advertisement was published and therefore was a written trade description, and the contention of counsel for the appellant, who says until the buyer arrived at the seller's yard and had the vehicle pointed out to him, no trade description had been applied to that vehicle. Accordingly he says that the situation is apt to be described by the words in s 19(4) that here the trade description was applied by an oral statement.

Just go back for a moment again to the facts found because there are one or two facts which I think are of assistance on this second point: the first is not only did the appellant publish the advertisement in Commercial Motor, as I have already described, but he had only one lorry answering that description on his premises at the relevant date. When the would-be buyer, a Mr Ridler, came up from Dulverton and visited the appellant's premises on 30 October, the appellant stated that the specific lorry, the number of which is given, was the lorry referred to in the advertisement. Mr Ridler looked at other lorries before agreeing to buy the Bedford.

Counsel for the appellant argues that it would be to ignore reality to suppose that all that happened when the buyer arrived at the seller's yard was that the seller simply said: 'There it is; take it or leave it.' No doubt certain other niceties of discussion took place. But one cannot get away from the fact, I think, that when the advertisement was published there was only one lorry of that description in the seller's possession, and I think that the description was applied to that lorry when the advertisement itself was published. I think that is an example of the trade description being used in a manner likely to be taken as referring to the goods because if there was only one lorry of that description, that fact would indicate to anybody that the trade description applied to that one vehicle. If that is right, if the trade description was applied by the written advertisement, of course there is no room for arguing that it was subsequently applied by an oral statement, and counsel for the appellant's second submission goes as well.

I do not find the second point quite as easy as the first, but on the whole my conclusion on the facts of this case is that the trade description was not applied orally within the meaning of s 19(4) and that accordingly the special period of limitation of six months does not apply in this case. That means that both informations, as the justices found, were in time, the convictions were right and the appeal should be dismissed.

Melford Stevenson J and **Talbot J** agreed.

Appeal dismissed.

QUESTION

Should the conclusion on the first point have been different if the relevant offence had been one of 'selling', rather than supplying?

Index